GLOBAL INSIGHTS

PEOPLE AND CULTURES

Farah • Flickema • Hantula • Johnson
Karls • Resnick • Thuermer

GLENCOE

Macmillan/McGraw-Hill

New York, New York   Columbus, Ohio   Mission Hills, California   Peoria, Illinois

Mounir A. Farah, Ph.D., is Department Chair of Social Studies in the Monroe, Connecticut, public schools and an adjunct lecturer of Social Science at Western Connecticut State University. He has taught history at New York University and has lectured at many nationwide teachers' conferences and workshops. Past president of the Connecticut Council for Social Studies and a member of the Middle East Institute, the Middle East Studies Association, and the International Activities Committee of the National Council for the Social Studies, Dr. Farah has been a contributing writer to several works and has authored numerous articles and reviews. He is coauthor of Glencoe's *The Human Experience.*

Thomas O. Flickema, Ph.D., is Executive Vice President at Northern State University in Aberdeen, South Dakota. Formerly Dean of the Graduate School at the University of Nebraska at Kearney, and Chairman of the History Department and Director of Latin American Studies at California State University, Fullerton, he has authored several articles on historical research and written reviews for *The Hispanic-American Historical Review* and *The Americas.*

James Neil Hantula, Ph.D., is an Associate Professor in the Department of Teaching at the University of Northern Iowa, where he is Chair of the Social Studies Department, and a co-ordinator of the Geographic Alliance of Iowa. He teaches at the Malcolm Price Laboratory School and is an active member of the National Council for Geographic Education, Geography Special Interest Group (SIG) of the National Council for the Social Studies, the American Historical Association, the Organization of American Historians, the National Education Association, and Phi Delta Kappa.

Ellen C.K. Johnson, Ph.D., is Associate Professor of Anthropology and Education at the College of Du Page in Glen Ellyn, Illinois. She has taught social studies at the University High School in Urbana, Illinois as well as in the Urbana public schools. She participated in a women and development study in India, has done South Asia outreach work, and was a high school international studies coordinator. She belongs to the Committee on Teaching about Asia of the Association for Asian Studies and participates in education committees and task forces of the American Anthropological Association.

Andrea Berens Karls, Ph.D., is an educator and coauthor of Glencoe's *The Human Experience.* Educated at Wellesley College and Harvard University, she has taught at both the elementary and secondary levels. Ms. Karls was formerly Program Associate at Global Perspectives in Education, Inc., where she edited and wrote curriculum materials and worked with teachers. She is a member of the National Council for the Social Studies and the American Historical Association.

Abraham Resnick, Ph.D., is a retired Professor of Education at Jersey City State College, New Jersey, and for many years was Director of The Instructional Materials Center at the Rutgers University Graduate School of Education. The author of several text and trade books for children, he has conducted educational field research as the guest of the Bulgarian, Romanian, Soviet, and Japanese governments.

Katherine Thuermer, Ph.D., served as a curriculum specialist in African Studies at Michigan State University, where she coordinated the community and school outreach program. A graduate of Yale University, she has lived and worked in Ghana, Mali, Madagascar, and Tanzania, as a Peace Corps Volunteer, in public health with Catholic Relief Services, and with Operation Crossroads Africa. She is currently the Director of Communications for Population Services International based in Washington, D.C.

Send all inquiries to:
GLENCOE DIVISION
Macmillan McGraw-Hill
936 Eastwind Drive
Westerville, OH 43081-3374

ISBN 0-02-822689-5 (Student Edition)
ISBN 0-02-822690-9 (Teacher's Edition)
Printed in the United States of America

2 3 4 5 6 7 8 9 10 -RRD-W- 99 98 97 96 95 94 93

Consultants

GENERAL CONTENT CONSULTANT

Theodore M. Black, Sr.
Chancellor Emeritus
New York State Board of Regents

MULTICULTURAL CONSULTANT

Sheilah Clarke-Ekong, Ph.D.
Department of Anthropology
University of Missouri
St. Louis, Missouri

GEOGRAPHY CONSULTANT

Sarah W. Bednarz, Ph.D.
Lecturer
Department of Geography
Texas A & M University
College Station, Texas

RELIGION CONSULTANT

John L. Esposito, Ph.D.
Loyola Professor of Middle
  East Studies and Professor
  of Religious Studies
College of the Holy Cross
Worcester, Massachusetts

AFRICA

Florence Agbonyitor, Ph.D.
Dean of Academic Administration
Southeastern University
Washington, D.C.

CHINA

Samuel C. Chu, Ph.D.
Professor of History and
  Departmental Vice Chair
Ohio State University
Columbus Ohio

JAPAN

Kenji Kenneth Oshiro, Ph.D.
Professor of Geography and
  Departmental Chair
Wright State University
Dayton, Ohio

INDIA

Shuby Dewan
Instructor
College of Du Page
Glen Ellyn, Illinois

LATIN AMERICA

Jesus Mendez, Ph.D.
Associate Professor of History
Barry University
Miami Shores, Florida

MIDDLE EAST

Jerry Green, Ph.D.
Director
Middle East Studies Center
University of Arizona
Tucson, Arizona

Yvonne Haddad, Ph.D.
Professor of Islamic History
University of Massachusetts
Amherst, Massachusetts

Joseph R. Rosenbloom, Ph.D.
Professor of Classics
Washington University
St. Louis, Missouri

Sayyid M. Syeed, Ph.D.
Director
International Institute of Islamic
  Thought
Herndon, Virginia

COMMONWEALTH OF INDEPENDENT STATES

Mary F. Zirin
Independent Researcher-
  Translator
Altadena, California

EUROPE

Patrice Berger, Ph.D.
Associate Professor of History
  and Departmental Chair
University of Nebraska
Lincoln, Nebraska

James P. Krokar, Ph.D.
Associate Professor of History
De Paul University
Chicago, Illinois

Teacher Reviewers

Dale Backlund
Social Studies Teacher
Columbia River High School
Vancouver, Washington

Susan Cobb
Social Studies Teacher
Fredonia Senior High School
Fredonia, New York

Robert E. Edison
History Instructor
Pearl C. Anderson Learning Center
Dallas, Texas

William Fetsko, Ph.D.
Humanities Coordinator
Liverpool Central School District
Liverpool, New York

Jessie B. Gladden
Social Studies Supervisor
Baltimore City Public Schools
Baltimore, Maryland

Maxene Kupperman-Guiñals
Teacher of English & Humanities
Richard R. Green High School of
  Teaching
New York City, New York

Joshua H. Leopold
Geography/Social Studies Instructor
Laura F. Osborn Senior High School
Detroit, Michigan

Nicholas Maraventano
Social Studies Teacher
Jericho High School
Jericho, New York

Debra Mitchell
Director, Center for International
  Studies
Dr. Phillips High School
Orlando, Florida

Sarah Quinlin-Sheridan
Social Studies Teacher
Abington Heights High School
Clarks Summit, Pennsylvania

Barbara Schubert
English-Language Arts/History-
  Social Sciences Coordinator
Santa Clara County Office of Education
San Jose, California

The intent of Global Insights is to provide global knowledge and understanding by having the peoples of eight different geographical regions speak for themselves about the elements that have shaped their lives and made them the way they are today. The text is divided into eight units—Africa, China, Japan, India, Latin America, the Middle East, the Commonwealth of Independent States, and Europe.

Unit Openers and Reviews

Each unit opens with a descriptive photograph, a brief rationale, a unit table of contents, and an **"At A Glance" chart that provides a statistical overview of the region.** Each unit concludes with a two-page Unit Review that includes a brief summary of unit content; **review and critical thinking questions; a practicing skills activity**; a **Developing a Global Viewpoint activity**, which enables the reader to develop a personal viewpoint on a particular global issue; and **a one-page feature** called **"Cultural Connections"** that shows how the particular region studied in the unit influenced or was influenced by another region.

Chapter Organization

Each unit is divided into six or seven chapters, beginning with a chapter on geography and the environment and then covering such topics as history, religion, the arts, and daily life. Each chapter opens with a theme-related photograph, **a chapter outline** that includes key terms and chapter objectives, a primary or secondary source that sets the tone for the chapter themes, and a brief narrative that leads into or reinforces that theme.

Primary and Secondary Source Readings

Throughout the chapter, author narrative is interwoven with primary and secondary source readings. To promote ease of reading and comprehension, the chapter is divided into sections and subsections, the headings of which serve as a content outline. In addition, vocabulary terms appear in boldface type and are defined where they first appear.

Section and Chapter Reviews

Following each major section is a series of **recall and critical thinking questions.** Concluding each chapter is a Chapter Review that consists of a summary of key points, a vocabulary activity, and **comprehensive questions related to critical thinking and analyzing key global studies concepts and geographic themes.** The Chapter Review concludes with a one-page **Building Skills** activity that teaches and provides practice in **critical thinking, social studies,** and **study and writing skills.**

Special Features

Supplementing the basic chapter and unit content are four kinds of special features—**Focus on People, Case Study, Global Focus,** and **Global Images**. The Focus on People features consist of one-page profiles of key individuals or groups. The Case Studies, also one page in length, focus one particular issue integral to the development of the culture under study. The Global Focus, which varies in length (either one or two pages), serve to put the chapter topic or theme into perspective. The Global Images feature provides a photo collage of the arts of a particular culture.

Visual Aids

Throughout *Global Insights,* there is a wide variety of photographs and full-color illustrations, maps, charts, graphs, and diagrams designed to support, reinforce, and supplement the written word. The text concludes with an appendix that contains additional elements designed to broaden the reader's horizons even further. These include a full-color atlas; a glossary that provides pronunciations for and definitions of all terms that are boldfaced in the text and a comprehensive, cross-referenced index; and a listing of suggested resources for both teachers and students.

CONTENTS

CONTENTS

CONTENTS

CONTENTS

CONTENTS

CONTENTS

CONTENTS

CONTENTS

CONTENTS

Features

CONTENTS

Skills

Maps

CONTENTS

Charts and Diagrams

Concepts

Today as never before, the world's diverse cultures affect each other in many different ways. The purpose of Global Studies is to develop our understanding of the lands and cultures that share the world with us. We are given insights into the lives of peoples that are different from—and, at the same time, very similar to—our own. Global Studies also encompasses broad concepts that provide an understanding of the world and the factors affecting its development.

Global Insights introduces fifteen key global concepts or themes. Each chapter highlights and develops several of these concepts.

INTERDEPENDENCE focuses on how the decisions and actions of one group or nation have an impact on other groups or nations.

CULTURE deals with all of the ideas, customs, and objects that people have developed for living in social groups.

SCARCITY discusses the impact of the environment and human decision-making on the availability of natural resources, goods, and services.

EMPATHY focuses on how people of one culture relate to those of another—sometimes in experiencing a similar environment or sharing a common experience.

CHANGE includes environmental, political, social, religious, and economic transformations that influence people and their daily lives.

ENVIRONMENT emphasizes the diversity of the global environment and the ways in which people affect it or are affected by it.

DIVERSITY focuses on the variety of the world's peoples and cultures, contrasted with the desire for uniformity or commonality and the relative lack of variance in some societies.

IDENTITY discusses how people define themselves and their place/purpose in the world and how they are defined and regarded by others.

TECHNOLOGY includes the combination of skills and tools that make economic activity possible in any given society.

POWER concerns the ways in which individuals, groups, or nations exert their influence upon others.

POLITICAL SYSTEMS relates to the way people organize their political affairs in the form of customs, procedures, and institutions.

HUMAN RIGHTS discusses the efforts of individuals, groups, and governments that have promoted (or hindered) human rights.

CHOICE involves situations in which people have to make choices between different alternatives.

JUSTICE focuses on the role of law in securing equal treatment for citizens.

CITIZENSHIP concerns the ties that bind people to the political unit(s) in which they live.

GEOGRAPHIC THEMES

Geography—the study of the earth and how people use its resources—is an integral part of Global Studies. It is the responsibility of geography to supply answers about where a place is, what it is like, how the people live there, how people from different places interact with one another, and how one place on earth is like others on earth. The geography of a region not only includes its physical landscape, natural resources, and climate but also the people who have settled there and their distinctive way of life. The civilizations of the world's peoples—the countless elements that make up their cultures—is notably influenced by the interplay of geographic features. Geographers use themes to help organize their study of geography into purposeful patterns. Organizing information by themes helps make sense of the vast amount of information we have learned about the many distinctive places that make up our world.

Location

A place's position on the earth's surface—its location—constitutes one of the five themes of geography. Location can be either absolute (one particular spot of ground) or relative (position as compared to some other place). *Location* answers the question "Where is that?"

This map of London was drawn by hand around 1574.

Modern map making uses photography as a tool. A Landsat satellite provided data for this image of England.

1

Place

A place's physical and human characteristics tell what is special about it and what makes it different from all others. Landforms, climate, and culture combine to make up the particular flavor of a particular place. *Place* answers the question "What is that place like?"

Life in South Asia is dominated by the area's many rivers. Here boats travel the Ganges River.

Timbuktu, in Mali, West Africa, is at the southern edge of the Sahara. The mud brick buildings and nomads' tents give the city and its surroundings a strong sense of place.

Human/Environment Interaction

The theme of human-environmental relations describes how people use, affect, and are affected by their surroundings. Through such interaction, people change the environment in which they live. *Relationships within places* answers the question "How do people there live?"

In the Netherlands, people have created a series of dikes and canals to control the water, which otherwise would flood the low land.

The people of Japan make efficient use of the small amount of land that is available for farming in their mountainous island nation; they still have to rely on imports for most of their food needs.

Movement

People interacting across the globe is a mark of interdependence, the need humans have to utilize skills and resources from around the earth. People travel, communicate, and trade goods, ideas, and information. *Movement* answers the question "How do the people in this place interact with peoples in other places?"

Today, satellites transmit information almost instantly from one place to another, making earth a "global village."

Region

Region is the ultimate theme of geography. Regions—how areas form and change—display unity through their characteristics, some physical, some human. The study of regions allows geographers to answer the question "How is this place like other places on the earth?"

These herders in the Central Asian republic of Kyrgyzstan tend their flocks of sheep in a region that is characterized by semi-arid land and a harsh climate.

The ruins of the ancient city of Machu Picchu atop a mountain in the Peruvian Andes of South America are evidence of the ability of the Inca to adapt to their environment.

3

Africa

The continent of Africa has a long and rich historical tradition. For centuries, however, Europeans knew very little about this vast continent or its peoples. Eventually, Africa's wealth of natural resources captured the interest of European powers. The result was a period of Western domination, brought to an end in many cases only after years of resistance and struggle. Today, Africa is made up of more than 50 independent nations. Each has its own ethnic, religious, linguistic, and cultural traditions, and each is working to develop and achieve a better standard of living for its peoples.

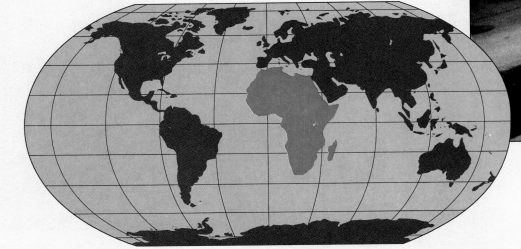

AT A GLANCE

LAND AREA: 11,314,780 sq. mi. (29,305,265 sq. km.)

LAND RESOURCES:
cropland: 6.4%
pasture: 31.1%
forest/woodland: 24.0%
other land: 38.5%

WILDERNESS AREA: 27%

MAJOR MOUNTAIN RANGES: Ahaggar, Atlas, Drakensberg, Mitumba, Ruwenzori, Tibesti

MAJOR RIVERS: Limpopo, Niger, Nile, Orange, Zaire, Zambezi

MAJOR LAKES: Chad, Malawi, Tanganyika, Victoria

POPULATION: (1992 est.) 598,300,000

POPULATION UNDER 15/OVER 65: 45%/3%

LIFE EXPECTANCY: 53 yrs.

POPULATION PROJECTION: 1,437,000,000 (by 2025)

POPULATION DENSITY: 59/sq. mi. (23/sq. km.)

URBAN POPULATION: 30%

LARGEST CITIES: (millions)
Kinshasa, Zaire (3.0)
Casablanca, Morocco (2.1)
Algiers, Algeria (1.7)
Abidjan, Côte d'Ivoire (1.5)

CHAPTER OUTLINE

People and Places to Know

Cape of Good Hope, Madagascar, Mount Kilimanjaro, Great Rift Valley, Zambezi River, Niger River, Nile River, Zaire River, Wangari Maathai, the Efe, Sahara, Sahel, Nairobi, Lagos, Dakar

Key Terms to Define

rain forest, savanna, subsistence farming, cash crop

Objectives to Learn

1. **Describe** Africa's varied geography and climate.
2. **Explain** how people have adapted to Africa's geography and climate.
3. **Summarize** the impact of urbanization on present-day African cultures.

East African savanna

Adapting to the Environment

> ... In a hoarse voice Muti . . . began singing the song of Africa, and not one Muti sang but a hundred Mutis, ten thousand Mutis, and they all sang the song that was Africa.
>
> And as they sang there was a deep calm.
>
> *And this is what they sang.*
>
> *Nkosi Sikele' Afrika . . .*
>
> which means God Bless Africa. God bless the sun-scorched Karoo (the Great Karoo plateau) and the green of the Valley of a Thousand Hills. God bless the mountain streams that chatter impudently when they are high in the hills and are young, but roll lazily from side to side like old women in the Great Plains. And the dry pans which twist their tortured bosoms to the hot skies. And the mighty waters that hurl themselves against her shores and mockingly retreat only to come again with a new energy as if to engulf the mielies [corn] and the land and the villages and the towns, even great Africa itself. God bless the cataracts that taunt the solemn rocks and the African sky that spits blood in the evening. And the timeless hills where the shy roebuck rears its tragic eyes and the dassie [rabbit] sips in silent pools. And the blue krantzes [cliffs] where man has still to breathe. God bless this Africa of heat and cold, and laughter and tears, and deep joy and bitter sorrow. God bless this Africa of blue skies and brown veld [grass-land], and black and white and love and hatred, and friend and enemy.
> God bless this Africa, this Africa which is part of us. God protect this Africa. God have mercy upon Africa.
>
> *And still they sang.*
>
> *Maluphakonyisw' Upshondo Lwayo. . . .*

*A*frica is many things to many people. To the people who fought for independence, it is a continent demanding its rightful voice in world affairs. To the peanut farmer of Mali and the businesswoman of Zimbabwe, it is home. To them and others like them, the "deep joy" of knowing the history of their people, of sharing communal life and family values, is balanced by the "bitter sorrow" of hard times. Africa finds its population growing faster than its ability to feed itself. To the black people of the Republic of South Africa, Africa is proof that the struggle to attain justice will not stop until the entire continent is free. To Richard Rive, the black South African who wrote the opening words of this chapter, it is the land that defines "great Africa itself."

Source: Richard Rive. "African Song" in *Black African Voices.* Scott Foresman & Co., 1970, p. 300.

S E C T I O N   1

The African Continent

Lying astride the equator, the enormous landmass of Africa, situated in both the northern and southern hemispheres, stretches over 11,300,000 square miles (29.3 million square kilometers). If one were to fly from the northernmost point in Tunisia to the Cape of Good Hope in South Africa, the distance would be the same as traveling from New York to San Francisco—and back.

The continent, which accounts for 20 percent of the world's land area and is home to 12.5 percent of its population, is made up of 54 nations. Included are several island states, the largest of which is Madagascar. The borders of the countries were marked out by Europeans during Africa's colonial period.

EXAMINING PHOTOGRAPHS *Victoria Falls, located on the Zambezi River, measure 343 feet (105 meters) in height. What two African nations are divided by the Zambezi River?*

Because the borders were chosen without regard to the unity of the different peoples living in the area, today each country is home to a variety of ethnic groups, languages, religions, and customs.

Most of Africa consists of a large, rolling plateau that ranges from 500 to 4500 feet (152.4 to 1371.6 meters) above sea level. A narrow coastal belt encircles the continent. There are few inlets, large bays, gulfs, or natural harbors. The mountains that do exist are relatively small, having been worn away by hundreds of millions of years of erosion. The tallest peak still standing is Mount Kilimanjaro in Tanzania. It is 19,340 feet (5803.2 meters) high. Breaking the monotony of the plateau is the Great Rift Valley—a long, narrow break in the earth's surface that runs for over 3000 miles (4800 kilometers) through the eastern highlands of Ethiopia and Kenya.

The variety of vegetation and the extreme physical features of the African landscape—scorching deserts, lush rain forests, and even snowcapped mountains on the equator—can be linked to the climate. Of vital importance is the amount and distribution of rainfall a region receives each year. In fact, Africa's major climatic zones can be roughly identified by the amount of rainfall each region receives.

The area that receives the most rainfall is the **rain forest**, or a heavily wooded area found in warm, humid regions mostly near the equator. In Africa, the rain forest is a large zone that stretches across equatorial Africa from the Atlantic to the Great Rift Valley. To the north and south of this zone lies the less watered **savanna**, or grasslands. Further north and south of the savanna are the semiarid lands and the deserts. Finally, at the northernmost part and southernmost tip of the continent, the people enjoy a Mediterranean-type climate.

Africa also has extensive river systems. The rivers have played an important role in the continent's history and development. The Zambezi River, in southern Africa, divides the nations of Zambia and Zimbabwe. The Niger, in West Africa, helps water the parched, semiarid Sahel that stretches from Mauritania to the edge of the Sudan. The Nile, which flows from Uganda and Ethiopia into Egypt, creates fertile farmland along its banks for thousands of miles. It is the longest river in the world.

The Zaire River, once known as the Congo, is Africa's second longest river. Below, one writer talks about the river, and the land through which it winds:

> The river rises in southeastern central Africa. . . . This is flat, open country, a highland savanna thinly covered in scrub and twisted thorn trees, solitary silver baobabs and yellow elephant grass, and spotted with those giant sandcastle-like structures that the driver ants build. . . .
>
> This was once a land of great herds of wild game . . . but it is no longer. For this plateau . . . lies in the continent's copper belt and contains astonishingly rich deposits of malachite ore. The Baluba and Balunda . . . of this region mined and smelted it, using the giant ant hills for their ovens, as long ago as the fourteenth century. . . . But in the twentieth century the European colonizers of the plateau . . . scarred the savanna into an ugly moonscape with their huge open-pit mines and killed or drove off the magnificent herds. . . .
>
> Plumes of dust, whipped off the charred and cracked earth by sudden gusts of hot wind, blow hard against you in the dry season, tearing at your eyes and choking in your mouth. And, in the rainy season, ferocious thunderstorms lash across this ruined highland plain, flooding its lakes and rivers and turning huge tracts of it into swamp. . . .
>
> The river's descent from the highland savanna to the rain forests occurs over a distance of some 500 miles (800 kilometers). . . . The descent is perceptible main-

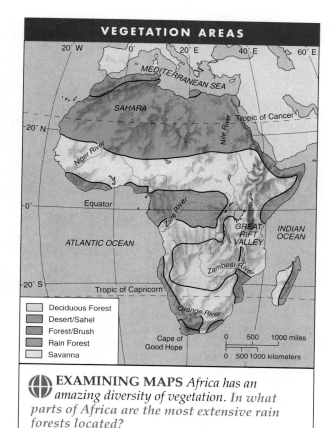

VEGETATION AREAS

Deciduous Forest
Desert/Sahel
Forest/Brush
Rain Forest
Savanna

EXAMINING MAPS *Africa has an amazing diversity of vegetation.* **In what parts of Africa are the most extensive rain forests located?**

ly by the steadily increasing richness of the vegetation. The grass becomes thicker, stands of acacia trees form into shady woods, in which weaverbirds nest in great chattering flocks. . . .

But at Kongolo the river suddenly funnels into the Portes d'Enfer, the Gates of Hell, a startling gorge in the floor of the savanna . . . where the waters boil up alarmingly and turn into impassable rapids. . . .

It is seemingly endless. . . . The river, fed by dozens of tributaries, has widened now . . . and, rolling ever northward, has taken on the glinting, greasy-gray color of the heavy, lowering sky. . . .

The villages along the river now belong mostly to the Lokele. . . . They are famous for their "talking" drums, which one hears day and night sending messages of boats' progress downriver, so that at every

EXAMINING PHOTOGRAPHS
Shown here, in Zambia, is one of many river markets in central and southeastern Africa. Canoes and barges transport goods and small businesses, bringing buyers and sellers together. Why do floating markets prosper in Africa?

village we pass the Lokele are expecting us and come out in their canoes loaded with goods to trade. . . .

This trade is the chief occupation and entertainment of the journey. The lower decks and cargo barges turn into thriving market places, floating bazaars. Stalls are set up to barter or sell manufactured goods, barbers go into business, laundries materialize, butchers prepare the animals and fish brought aboard, restaurants serve meals from open fires, beer parlors spring into existence complete with brassy music from transistor radios. . . .

But one morning you wake up and go on deck and you discover that . . . there are high, rugged yellow limestone hills rearing up on both banks. These are the Crystal Mountains. . . .

From Matadi to Banana, the river . . . steadily widens . . . and once again we find sizable islands standing in its stream. Its banks are heavily forested, now mainly with palm trees and mangroves and . . . giant water ferns.

Two sandy peninsulas, some 15 miles (24 kilometers) apart and arcing out into the Atlantic form the . . . mouth. The river . . . rushes to it and through it and then well beyond it. . . . And we can see the

river's waters, in their unrelenting flow, staining the ocean's surface for scores of miles offshore with the mud and vegetation carried down on the long journey from the savanna highlands.

SECTION 1 REVIEW

CHECKING FOR UNDERSTANDING
1. **Define** rain forest, savanna.
2. **List** some of Africa's major rivers.

CRITICAL THINKING
3. **Drawing Conclusions** How have Africa's rivers aided human contacts?

SECTION 2

Working the Land

Some people think of the African continent as a tropical paradise. But geography and climate have long made it a challenge to human settlement. Many parts suffer from

Source: From THE RIVER CONGO by Peter Forbath. Copyright © 1977 by Peter Forbath. Reprinted by permission of Harper Collins Publishers and Martin Secker Warburg Limited.

Africa

ENVIRONMENTAL AWARENESS

In recent years, people all over the world have become more aware of their environment and the need to preserve and protect it. In Africa, sensitivity to the environment has long been important. Below is a description of recent efforts to reforest the land in Kenya:

We started with seven trees in a small park in Nairobi," says Wangari Maathai, who founded Kenya's Green Belt Movement. Since that planting in 1977, the poor, rural women who make up the movement have grown ten million trees. Yet two years ago, the movement was declared "subversive" and kicked out of its government-owned office. . . .

Where the Green Belt Movement has taken root, "you just see trees everywhere," Maathai says. In a village near Nairobi, a woman started a community nursery and now sells fruit that she grows on her land. An elementary-school campus was transformed from a bald patch of dirt to a shady grove where each child "adopts" a tree.

At first, the government supported the fighters. . . . But two years ago, the Green Belters protested the government's plan for a sixty-story building in Uhuru Park, downtown Nairobi's biggest patch of green. Foreign investors withdrew when they saw opposition to the tower. Angry officials then kicked the Green Belt Movement out of its Nairobi office, and asked women working in the nurseries, "Are you trying to overthrow the Kenyan government?"

The movement's forty-member staff now works in Maathai's three-bedroom house, and lately Maathai has been rallying rural women who dropped out after the harassment began. Telling people "You can have power, you can lead yourself" has always been a Green Belt goal. As long as arrogant leaders rule unchecked in Africa, Maathai says, "it is not surprising that we should have these civil wars, these instabilities, which eventually express themselves in . . . the misery of famine, the misery of starving children, and the misery of refugees."

To see that Africa doesn't have to be that way, visit a small Nairobi park, where two of the movement's first seven trees still grow. "I quite often visit those trees and find people walking under them," Maathai says. "Traders sit under the trees and sell their wares. . . . Little do they know. . . .

DRAWING CONCLUSIONS

1. How have Kenyan women improved the environment in their country?
2. In what other ways do you think their movement has been successful?

Source: Ted Kleine. "A Tree Grows in Nairobi," in *Mother Jones*, September/October 1991, p. 41.

poor soils and little rain. Other areas, however, have fertile soil and even rainfall. Yet those with dense vegetation attract parasites that prevent the raising of livestock. Also, rivers often have waterfalls that reduce their navigability.

Despite the obstacles, many Africans have adapted to, or changed, their environment to meet their needs. Agriculture employs more workers than any other economic activity. Africa leads the world in the production of cacao, cassava, cloves, and sweet potatoes. It is also a major producer of coffee, bananas, cotton, peanuts, rubber, tea, and sugar.

About 60 percent of Africa's cultivated land is used for **subsistence farming**—that is, for growing food crops for a farmer's own use. An increasing number of African farmers, however, are producing **cash crops**, produce grown mainly for export. This shift from subsistence farming to cash crops is causing difficulties. Farmers who grow only cash crops cannot rely on a steady income because of constantly changing prices on the global market. In addition, food shortages occur in some areas because a decreasing number of farmers are growing food crops.

In addition to farming, Africans are engaged in herding, fishing, mining, and manufacturing. In central and southern Africa, miners work the largest concentration of minerals in the world.

LIVING IN THE RAIN FOREST

The third largest rain forest in the world is found in Central Africa. Like those of Central America, South America, and Southeast Asia, it is made up of three layers of vegetation—a ground cover of plants and ferns, a dense layer of trees and climbers, and a canopy of giant broad-leaved evergreen trees, some as high as 150 feet (45.7 meters).

As in other climatic zones in Africa, the rain forest, even with its dense vegetation, supports agriculture. In some parts of the rain forest, small communities of farmers cultivate such root crops as cassava and sweet potatoes. As one scholar explains, theirs is a difficult task because they "are not

EXAMINING PHOTOGRAPHS
Women do three-fourths of Africa's agricultural work. Only a small amount of government spending, however, goes to programs for rural women. What kinds of farming are done in Africa?

content to take what the forest offers them, but they change it. . . . For them the forest is . . . the enemy force against which they struggle to wrest and keep the earth in the clearings."

Below, an anthropologist who lived in the Ituri forest of Zaire talks about the forest and the Efe people who live in it:

The Efe had placed their wet-season camp at the top of a gentle rise, so the site could drain in a heavy rain. They cleared an oval area about 50 feet at its widest, leaving only . . . hardwoods towering overhead.

Around the periphery stood nine huts, each with a small doorway facing in toward the center. The Efe had built by driving saplings into the soft ground, bending them, and weaving in branches to form a domed latticework, then shingling it with mongongo leaves. . . .

. . . The Ituri [forest] contains Africa's richest abundance of forest mammals. The Efe pursue more than 45 different animals for meat, which supplies half their protein. Meat also is prized by (neighboring) Lese villagers, and the Efe trade it for garden produce and goods such as pots, pans, knives, and ax blades. . . .

Part of the Efe's success in exploiting the forest stems from their mobile lifestyle. If they could not move from one place to another unencumbered by possessions, they would soon deplete the resources within easy walking distance of their settlement and have to turn to sedentary agriculture or starve. . . .

In keeping their way of life more or less intact even as forces of modernization advance, the Efe show a remarkable, even puzzling resilience. But whether they can control their own destiny is sadly in doubt. Since the Efe's subsistence and social structure are dependent upon the ability to forage and hunt freely over large areas of forest, their fate is inextricably tied to the future of the forest itself.

Pressure on the forest comes in many forms, but the most devastating is the ever growing number of Africans seeking free land on which to cultivate crops. The area available to the Efe and other African foragers shrinks daily. Some already live as impoverished horticulturalists or work as poorly paid laborers on coffee plantations.

Unless areas of forest are set aside, it seems inevitable that the way of life currently practiced by the Efe will cease to exist. Then one of the world's unique cultures, a culture from which we can learn so much about ourselves, will be lost forever.

FARMING THE SAVANNA

Savanna covers more than one-third of the African continent and is home to many farmers and herders. Below, a Senegalese writer relates how the seasons can shape the life of a savanna farmer:

According to Oumar's calculations, the rainy season would be coming in a matter of days. A few puffs of wind, laden with heat, were all that stirred in the air. The clouds had stopped moving. The young man continued his long walks across the savanna. . . . Now days and weeks mattered little. Only the seasons ordered his existence.

The rainy season began. Nature seemed painted on a deep green canvas with a sea-blue sky.

The rain fell unremittingly, persistently. Even as she drank it in, the earth, spewing up water, flooded the rich fields where water birds flocked down. . . .

In the bush, hunting was becoming difficult; the animals had abandoned the streams, now that they found pasture and water everywhere. . . .

Source: Robert C. Bailey, "The Efe Archers of the African Rain Forest," in *National Geographic*, November, 1989, pp. 670, 678, 685, 686.

The strongest animals of the forest . . . could no longer easily track down their prey, and at nightfall began to approach the villages where the herds were kept. The hyena took a terrible toll there and some of the large beasts were able to carry off oxen or cattle from inside the enclosures.

Little by little the landscape changed color; from deep green it became grayish. The clouds piled up and remained motionless for long periods. Nights became long for the peasants. Knots of birds emigrated toward the east. While awaiting the harvest, people devoted themselves to their favorite games, and the merchants restocked their cloth. . . .

The life of the farmer is not always restful: he sows, he weeds, he struggles, then he waits for the harvest. But when he feels the joy of seeing his work completed, his field ripening before his eyes, the fine sprigs standing up, . . . a man forgets that he is tired; he wishes he had given even more of this strength, and his heart fills with pride and joy. Yes, life, this life of labor, is a good one.

"Oh my land, my beautiful people!" sang Oumar as he trod this ground.

He walked alone through the fields, dreaming who knows what? He stopped in front of a ground-nut plant to straighten its leaves, freed a fly caught by a spider, avoided stepping on a beetle; a little further on he separated two millet stems, propped up a heavy corn stalk. . . .

He had constructed an immense granary, propped up on stilts to avoid the moisture. With very simple tools he had widened the stream; the *fayats*, big boats that could carry ten or twelve people, were moored side by side. Wild vines wound all through the palm-grove. The wide leaves of the water lilies covered the sleepy surface of the water.

The harvest was at hand.

Following in the wake of the hot season, the clouds were returning. The clear blue sky and the gray green earth foretold renewal; the trees and all the greenery seemed freshly painted once again.

The end of the bad season drew the farmers away from their distractions, and the festivities ended. Holiday clothes were returned to the bottom of the wooden trunks. People had spent all they had and had gone into debt during the inactive period. Nothing was left in the granaries

EXAMINING PHOTOGRAPHS
Many wild animals in Africa feed on fruits, leaves, and other vegetation of their habitats. Here, an elephant is eating bark from a tree in Kenya. Why do animals compete with people for savanna land in Africa?

and everyone hoped for a good crop—if God willed it.

Oumar had sold half of his crop; he hoped to sell the rest at a high price to the large companies. He resumed his work, enlarging his fields, increasing the number of his rice-paddies, and even taking up growing cassava. He had become severe and hard like all those who work the earth and live off it.

The savanna also supports a large wildlife population. To prevent the many different species of wildlife from becoming extinct, a number of African governments have established national game parks, particularly in countries in eastern and southern Africa. This has led many people to associate these areas chiefly with wildlife even though domestic farm herds greatly outnumber the wildlife population.

In recent years, the competition for savanna land between humans and animals has become critical in some smaller nations. In Rwanda, for example, farmers have had to encroach on forest highlands which traditionally were the home of the now rare mountain gorillas. The demands for pastureland and firewood also have taken their toll. This had led many African countries to pass laws to help protect the natural environment and to prevent rural areas from becoming unproductive wastelands.

THE NEED FOR RAIN

Much of Africa north of the equator receives very little rainfall. In this area is the world's largest tropical desert—the Sahara. It stretches over 3.2 million square miles (8.3 million square kilometers). A great many years ago, the desert was a fertile region that supported a thriving civilization. Today, most of it is uninhabitable. Some nomads,

Source: Sembene Ousmane. *O Pays, Mon Beau Peuple* as cited in *Palaver: Modern African Writings* by Wilfred Cartey, E.P. Dutton, Inc., 1970, pp. 116–118.

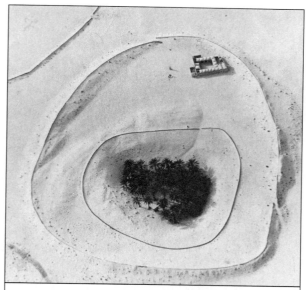

EXAMINING PHOTOGRAPHS *Pictured here is an oasis in Algeria. Saharan oases are watered by underground streams and by rains blown from nearby mountains.* Why are oases important to the Tuareg?

such as the Tuareg, however, continue to live there as they have for centuries. Camel caravans, long used for transportation, are being replaced by trucks.

On the southern border of the Sahara is the Sahel, which in Arabic means "coastal land." Between 1968 and 1974, a drought in the Sahel destroyed livestock and caused many West Africans to starve.

In the 1980's and early 1990's, many African countries felt the destructive effects of little or no rain. In the East African nations of Ethiopia and Somalia, famine caused by drought and worsened by civil war has led to mass starvation. Below, an American journalist visiting Africa describes what he observed in Ethiopia:

The Ogaden region, the badlands of Ethiopia, is a vast triangular stretch of parched scrubland bordering Somalia. In the best of times, it gives grudgingly of itself to more than 1 million inhabitants, mostly nomads, pastoralists and small-time farmers. . . .

This time, civil wars in Ethiopia and Somalia have combined with a severe three-year drought to produce hunger and deprivation that most relief specialists say is more severe in Ogaden than during the catastrophic 1984-85 famine. Although rains came this spring, they were light and lasted less than a month. Already the scattered grasslands that nomads depend on are yellowing.

Conservative estimates indicate that well over 1,000 have died . . . because of the drought, especially during the tortuous and dangerous trek from Somalia, and in the camps where the hungry have gathered. . . .

Workers of the U.N. High Commissioner for Refugees started operations . . . , flying in huge transport planes packed with grain. The Somali war struck just as that group had been planning to repatriate [return home] most of the Ethiopian refugees with a year's supply of food, livestock, and other goods.

"We were ready to come home after such a long time away," said Mohammed Abdullah Sahel, 45, through an interpreter. "But their [repatriation] program failed, out belongings were looted and we were again left with nothing."

Sahel is luckier than some. He managed to salvage prized metal tools with which he fashions crude grinding stones for grain. But although it takes up to two days to hew the stones, they sell for just 2.50 birr ($1.25) apiece in town. That is hardly enough to feed his wife and seven children; on one recent day the family had a pot of soup prepared from goat's hooves and grain scavenged in town. . . .

Relief officials can only deal now with pulling the refugees back from the brink of further catastrophe. But concern is mounting over how to resettle hundreds of thousands of displaced people. . . .

"Sure I would like to go back to my no-madic life. It is my nature," said 30-year-old Hali Musa Hadai, whose family lost all 40 goats and two camels in the drought. "But my babies were dying, so I had to come here and stop moving around. What else could I do?"

SECTION 2 REVIEW

CHECKING FOR UNDERSTANDING
1. **Define** subsistence farming, cash crop.
2. **State** why the change of seasons is important on the savanna.

CRITICAL THINKING
3. **Determining Cause and Effect** Explain the cause of drought and its effect on areas of Africa.

SECTION 3

Urbanization

African history is rich with evidence of ancient cities that once were great centers of learning and of trade. Later, during the colonial periods, cities were created to serve the economic needs of the European powers. In southern Africa, for example, a tax was imposed on Africans that had to be paid in cash. This forced many Africans to leave the countryside and seek jobs in the cities so that they could pay the tax. Today, although nearly three-fourths of the population remains rural, Africa is the fastest urbanizing continent in the world. The bright lights of Nairobi (Kenya), Lagos (Nigeria), and Dakar (Senegal) are attracting so many people that experts predict that the population of many African cities will double every 10 years. In the following reading, a Kenyan author shows the mixed emotions a move to the city can evoke:

Source: Jennifer Parmelee. "Famine Visits Again in Anguished Ogaden" in *The Washington Post,* June 25, 1991, pp. A1, A14.

EXAMINING PHOTOGRAPHS *Since the 1960's many African cities have become increasingly crowded as people move from the rural areas. Shown is Ibadan, Nigeria's second largest city, an example of rapid urbanization. How has the growth of cities affected African agriculture?*

It was a dark night. Njoroge and Kamau stood on the "hill.". . .

"Do you see those distant lights?"

"Yes."

"That's Nairobi isn't it?" Njoroge's voice trembled slightly.

"Yes," Kamau answered dreamily.

Njoroge peered through the darkness and looked beyond. Far away a multitude of lights could be seen. Above the host of lights was the grey haze of the sky. Njoroge let his eyes dwell on the scene. Nairobi, the big city, was a place of mystery that had at last called away his brothers from the family circle. The attraction of this strange city that was near and yet far weakened him. He sighed. He could not yet understand why his brothers had just decided to go. Like that.

"Do you think that they've found jobs?"

"Kori said that jobs there are plenty."

"I see."

"It is a big city. . . ."

"Yes-it-is-a-big-city."

"Mr. Howlands often goes there."

"And Jacobo too. . . . Do you think they'll forget home?"

"I'm sure they won't. None can forget home."

"Why couldn't they work here?"

"Do you think they didn't want to? You know this place. Even there where they go, they will learn that mere salary without a piece of land to cultivate is nothing. Look at Howlands. He is not employed by anybody. Yet he is very rich and happy. It's because he has land."

Cities in Africa today have the same problems as cities elsewhere—overcrowding, crime, and pollution. In addition, as more people move to the city in search of better opportunities, fewer remain in the rural areas to grow food for the urban population.

SECTION 3 REVIEW

CHECKING FOR UNDERSTANDING

1. **Explain** the reasons why many Africans today have left the countryside for the cities.

CRITICAL THINKING

2. **Identifying Assumptions** With what does Kamamu equate wealth and happiness?

Source: Ngugi wa Thiong'o. *Weep Not, Child.* Heinemann Educational Books Ltd., pp. 40–41.

Global Concerns

HUNGER

"Eating is the right of everybody."
—Swahili proverb

Many African nations have been experiencing a severe food crisis. There are many reasons for this, including drought and a fall in the price of African export products. The main reason, however, is that the production of food cannot keep up with the needs of the growing population.

FOCUSING ON THE ISSUE In the excerpt that follows the focus is on the West African nation of Niger. After reading the excerpt and studying the maps that follow it, write a short paper on the food crisis in Africa. Include information about the status and the causes of the crisis as well as possible solutions for it.

. . . Wearing a conical hat and mirror sunglasses to deflect the sun's glare, Amadou Oumarou shows a group of visitors the sum of his labours in a wilderness of sand just outside the capital (Niamey). They consist of a few rows of dry millet, some shrivelled wisps of sorghum, a few emaciated goats and a houseful of hungry children. "There is too little rain, too little manure, and my animals eat what little crop I have," says Mr. Oumarou.

His lament is a common one throughout much of Sudano-Sahelian Africa, where rainfall averages have fallen in the last 30 years to record lows, causing a string of droughts that have sent food production and agricultural exports plummeting.

In common with most farmers, Mr. Oumarou blames lack of rain. . . . Meanwhile, the country's population has doubled to 7.5 million. It is not clear why Sahelian Africa is drying up, or whether "normal" patterns of rainfall will ever return. Some climate experts believe drought may be linked to increasing deforestation and global warming, and

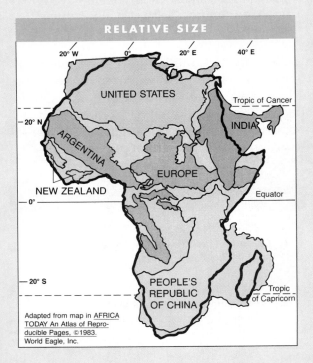

RELATIVE SIZE

Adapted from map in AFRICA TODAY An Atlas of Reproducible Pages, ©1983. World Eagle, Inc.

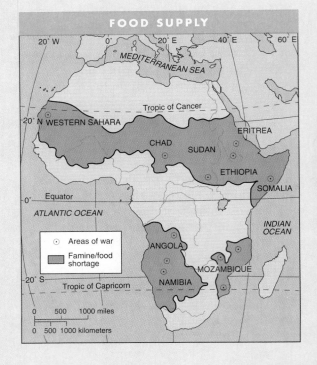

FOOD SUPPLY

⊙ Areas of war

Famine/food shortage

therefore, possibly permanent, while others see it as a cyclical phenomenon. . . .

. . . Development experts advocate making the best of existing conditions to maximize food production. "The region's population is increasing by three percent per year," says Charles Renard, a Belgian agronomist at . . . the International Crops Research Institute for the Semi-Arid Tropics (ICRISAT) in Niamey. "Yet food production is increasing only one percent.". . .

In experiments conducted in Burkina Faso, Mali, and Niger, ICRISAT has shown that with a few modest changes in farm practices, soil fertility can be dramatically improved to produce higher yields. "By adding phosphorus alone to the soil, local varieties farmed traditionally have achieved a threefold increase in yields," says Mr. Renard. By rotating grains with nitrogen-fixing legumes such as cowpeas and chickpeas and adding phosphorus, farmers . . . achieved even better results. . . .

Source: Reprinted with pemission from *World Development*, Emma Robson, "Sahelian Africa Awaits its 'Green Revolution'" November, 1991, Pergamon Press Ltd."

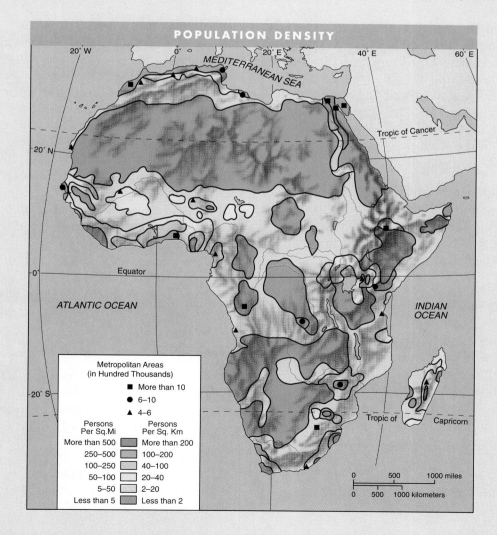

POPULATION DENSITY

Metropolitan Areas
(in Hundred Thousands)

■ More than 10
● 6–10
▲ 4–6

Persons Per Sq.Mi	Persons Per Sq. Km
More than 500	More than 200
250–500	100–200
100–250	40–100
50–100	20–40
5–50	2–20
Less than 5	Less than 2

Chapter 1 Review

SUMMARY

The continent of Africa, made up of 54 nations, has many ethnic groups, languages, religions, and customs. It also has a variety of physical features and vegetation, each of which is affected by the amount and distribution of rainfall.

Agriculture employs more workers than any other activity. Both rain forest and savanna support farming. A recurrence of drought in the semiarid Sahel and other parts of Africa, caused by the lack of seasonal rains, has had a destructive effect on agriculture, livestock, and people.

Africa is the fastest urbanizing continent in the world. This rapid growth in cities has led to overcrowding, slums, inadequate sanitation, crime, and pollution.

USING VOCABULARY

Write a paragraph describing the African environment and the economic activities of Africans using the following terms:

rain forest   **subsistence farming**
savanna   **cash crop**

REVIEWING FACTS

1. **Describe** the location of Africa.
2. **State** how many independent nations comprise Africa today.
3. **Cite** some of the major climatic regions of the African continent.
4. **List** some of the major rivers of Africa.
5. **Explain** why Africa's rivers are important to the continent's development.
6. **State** why the change of seasons is important in the savanna areas of Africa.
7. **Discuss** the kinds of problems herders in the Sahel and farmers in the fain forest have to overcome.

8. **State** how geography and climate influence the lifestyles of Africans.
9. **Indicate** why many young Africans left the countryside during the period of rule by European colonial powers.
10. **Discuss** what problems have arisen as a result of Africans moving from rural areas to urban centers.

CRITICAL THINKING

1. **Identifying Alternatives** Africa's cities have grown tremendously in recent years. If you were an African, would you live in the city and risk not finding a job, or would you stay in the countryside and farm your own plot of land? Explain your answer.
2. **Predicting Consequences** Explain what impact there is on a region when its people migrate in large numbers from the countryside to cities.
3. **Making Comparisons** Compare the lifestyle of Africans in the rain forest with that of Africans in the savanna.
4. **Synthesizing Information** Like other parts of the world, Africa has many environmental problems. What steps have Africans taken to protect their environment?

ANALYZING CONCEPTS

1. **Change** How have Africans reacted to increasing urbanization?
2. **Scarcity** What effect have changing climatic conditions had on Africa's food supply?

GEOGRAPHIC THEMES

1. **Place** Describe the savanna.
2. **Region** How has the Sahara changed over the centuries?

Understanding a Map Key

In studying global cultures, maps are important sources of information. They can show geographic features, economic resources, and even the distribution of human-made resources such as wealth and education.

To make the best use of maps, you have to know how to read them. Mapmakers use various symbols such as colors, lines, and other shapes and pictures to represent information. To unlock the meaning of these symbols, use the *key*, also called the *legend*, which usually appears at the bottom or top of the map. In addition to explaining map symbols, the legend often includes a *scale*. The scale shows the relationship between the unit of measure on the map and a unit of measure, such as inches or centimeters.

The following steps will help you understand a map key or legend:

- Read the map title to identify the general topic of the map.
- Study all symbols in the map key and find examples of each one on the map.
- Check the scale.

EXAMPLE

Look at the map at the top of the page. Notice that the map title

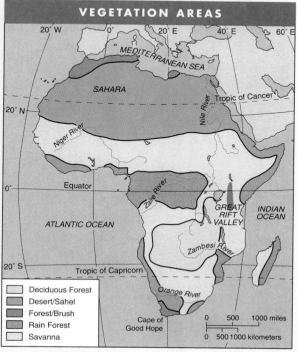

VEGETATION AREAS

MEDITERRANEAN SEA
SAHARA
Tropic of Cancer
Niger River
Nile River
Equator
Zaire River
GREAT RIFT VALLEY
INDIAN OCEAN
ATLANTIC OCEAN
Zambesi River
Tropic of Capricorn
Orange River
Cape of Good Hope

Key:
- Deciduous Forest
- Desert/Sahel
- Forest/Brush
- Rain Forest
- Savanna

0   500   1000 miles
0 500 1000 kilometers

is "Vegetation Areas"; this indicates that the map shows the various vegetation areas of Africa. Then study the key or legend at the bottom of the map. The key uses different colors to show the five kinds of vegetation. What are the vegetation areas? *(deciduous forest, desert/Sahel, forest/brush, rain forest, savanna)* Notice that savanna lands are represented by the color yellow. What kind of vegetation is shown by the color brown? *(desert/Sahel)* What color represents rain forests? *(dark green)* What kind of vegetation is located on the southwestern tip of Africa? *(forest/brush)* By examining the map key in this way, you can unlock a great deal of information.

Next measure the scale of distance. The scale is under three-quarters of an inch [1.9 centimeters]. That distance represents 1200 miles [1,931 kilometers] on the map. Therefore, an inch [2.54 centimeters] would represent about 1600 miles [2,575 kilometers]. Now measure Africa's length from its most northern to its most southern tip, and multiply that number of inches [centimeters] by 1600 miles [2,575 kilometers]. How big is Africa from north to south? *(over 4800 miles, 7,724 kilometers)*

PRACTICE

Study the map on page 19 and then answer the questions below.

1. What is the main topic of this map?
2. What do the colors on the map represent?
3. What color is used to show areas with 40–100 people per square kilometer?
4. What is the population density of the yellow areas?
5. What do the black triangles represent?
6. What symbol is used to show metropolitan areas of over 1 million people?
7. Are most of Africa's densely populated areas along the coast or inland?

CHAPTER OUTLINE

1 Early African Societies

2 From Imperialism to Nationalism

People and Places to Know
Egypt, Ghana, Great Zimbabwe, Axum, Mali, Timbuktu, Songhai, Swahili, Sofala, Kilwa, Mombasa, Liberia, Patrice Lumumba, Kwame Nkrumah

Key Terms to Define
oral tradition, Islamic empire, mosque, imperialism, nationalism

Objectives to Learn
1. **Identify** and describe several early African societies.
2. **Compare** European and African views of imperialism and relate how nationalism came about in Africa.

West African in traditional clothing

African Heritage

"—Centuries before the discovery of the "new world," Africa had thriving cities that were centers of trade and technology.

—As early as the 14th century Africa had centers of learning at Timbuktu and Jenne that drew scholars and theologians from throughout the Muslim world.

—During the Middle Ages, when justice throughout much of the world was determined by the sword, great kingdoms in Africa had courts of law.

—When the Normans invaded a little-known island called England in 1066 A.D., they could muster an army of only 15,000 soldiers. In the same year, the West African state of Ghana could put 200,000 warriors in the field.

—When the Arabs invaded Europe in the 8th century A.D.., they were able to push all the way through Spain into France. When they invaded North Africa, they were stopped in their tracks.

—When most Europeans were still pagans, in the 4th century A.D., the ancient kingdom of Ethiopia (then called Aksum) was a center of Christianity and could claim to be the oldest Christian empire in the world; its stone churches, built in the 12th century, are among the wonders of the world."

The above comments may surprise many Westerners, who over the years have come to believe that Africa was "discovered" by Europeans, that before the Europeans penetrated Africa it was a desolate continent inhabited by fantastic and mythical creatures. But the truth of the matter is that the African continent is the home of humankind's earliest known ancestors. Recently discovered fossils show that humans lived in its eastern and southern savannas 4 million years ago.

Over the past 25 years or so, many new sources of information have become available about the African continent, especially about the daily life of the people and the rise of great states. Written accounts left by early Arab and African travelers and scholars have been given careful attention. Language studies, satellite photography, and archaeology are supplying new data. In addition, historians are beginning to recognize the value of African **oral traditions**, the legends and history of a society passed by word of mouth from one generation to the next. From all these sources, a picture of Africa as a continent with a rich and diverse past and heritage has emerged.

Source: From THROUGH AFRICAN EYES; VOLUME 1, THE PAST, THE ROAD TO INDEPENDENCE, by Leon E. Clark. Copyright © 1988, 1991 by Leon E. Clark.

Early African Societies

The earliest African societies were bands of people who hunted game and gathered wild plants. Several thousand years ago, the development of agriculture changed their way of life. As the knowledge of agriculture spread, small villages began to grow up on the African continent.

Within these agricultural communities were people who specialized in crafts. Iron-smiths, for example, made tools that they traded for items produced by neighboring societies. This trade took place not only within Africa but with nations across the sea. In parts of Africa, it was trade that led to the development of large states and empires.

One of the earliest African states was ancient Egypt, which grew up along the Nile River. Other early northeast African states were Kush and Meroë (MEHR·oh·EE), which were early centers of iron working. Another was Ghana. The first West African state to gain control of the gold-salt trade established by North African Arab merchants, it dominated West Africa for nearly 1000 years. Still another was Monomotapa in southeastern Africa. It traded with the Asian empires of the East. The ancient Monomotapan city of Great Zimbabwe, Africa's largest city during the 1400's AD, has gained worldwide recognition for its architecture.

Great Zimbabwe, however, was not the only major city, state, or empire of early Africa. Equally important were Axum, Mali, Timbuktu, Sofala, Kilwa, and Mombasa.

AXUM

Axum's importance was due to its strategic location on the trade route between Asia and the Mediterranean world. Through Adulis, Axum's main port on the Red Sea, were exported gold, ivory, rhinoceros horn, tortoise shell, and spices. Below, a Greek traveler visiting the king of Axum in 525 AD describes how the Axumites obtained gold, a process that later was called "the silent gold trade:"

The King . . . every other year . . . sends thither [to Sasu] special agents to bargain for the gold, and these are accompanied by many other traders—upwards, say, of five hundred—bound on the same errand as themselves. They take along with them to the mining district oxen, lumps of salt, and iron, and when they reach its neighbourhood they make a halt at a certain

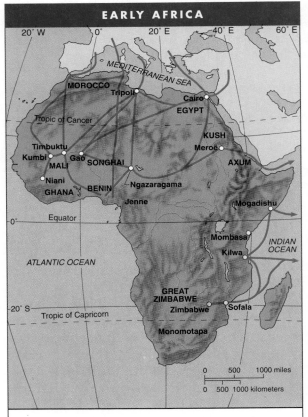

EARLY AFRICA

20° W   0°   20° E   40° E   60° E

MEDITERRANEAN SEA
MOROCCO
Tripoli
Cairo
EGYPT
Tropic of Cancer
KUSH
Meroë
Timbuktu
Kumbi   Gao
MALI   SONGHAI
AXUM
Niani   BENIN   Ngazaragama
GHANA
Jenne
Mogadishu
Equator
Mombasa
Kilwa   INDIAN OCEAN
ATLANTIC OCEAN
GREAT ZIMBABWE
Zimbabwe   Sofala
20° S   Tropic of Capricorn
Monomotapa

0   500   1000 miles
0   500   1000 kilometers

EXAMINING MAPS *Before the modern era, trade routes crossed northern Africa and extended from the continent's east coast to distant Asian ports.* **What geographic features might have aided Africans in the transport of goods?**

EXAMINING PHOTOGRAPHS *Only ruins remain of Great Zimbabwe, once the largest city in Monomotapa, an ancient African state. Noted for its architecture, Great Zimbabwe was built of slabs of granite fitted without mortar.* **How did improved agriculture contribute to the development of early African societies?**

spot and form an encampment, which they fence round with a great hedge of thorns. Within this they live, and having slaughtered the oxen, cut them in pieces, and lay the pieces on the top of the thorns, along with the lumps of salt and the iron. Then come the natives bringing gold in nuggets like peas . . . and lay one or two more of these upon what pleases them—the pieces of flesh or the salt or the iron, and then they retire to some distance off. Then the owner of the meat approaches, and if he is satisfied he takes the gold away, and upon seeing this its owner comes and takes the flesh or the salt or the iron. If, however, he is not satisfied, he leaves the gold, when the native seeing that he has not taken it, comes and either puts down more gold, or takes up what he had laid down, and goes away. Such is the mode in which business is transacted with the people of that country, because their language is different and interpreters are hardly to be found. The time they stay in that country is five days more or less. . . .

Source: J.W. McCrindle (tr. & ed.). *The Christian Topography of Cosmas, an Egyptian Monk.* Bedford Press, 1897, pp. 52-53.

MALI

In the 1200's, one of the most powerful empires of Africa was Mali in West Africa. Under the rule of Mansa Musa, it became an **Islamic empire,** a nation-state whose official religion is Islam. Beautiful **mosques**, Muslim houses of worship, were built in the important towns. Before long, Mali became known as a great center of learning, and scholars came from many lands to live and study in its large commercial centers. Below, Ibn Battuta (IHB·uhn ba·TOO·tah), a North African scholar who set out in the 1300's to visit all the Muslim nations of the world, gives his view of Mali and its people:

When I decided to make the journey to Mállí [Mali], . . . I hired a guide . . . and set out with three of my companions. . . .

We . . . came to the river of Sansara, which is about ten miles (16 kilometers) from Mállí. It is their custom that no persons except those who have attained permission are allowed to enter the city. I had already written to the white [North African] community [there] requesting them to

EXAMINING PHOTOGRAPHS *In many areas of West Africa today, traditional leaders, such as the one shown here, still carry on the ceremonies and customs of the early West African kingdoms. Although having no power in the national governments of modern Africa, these leaders often handle local affairs and provide a colorful link to the past. How were rulers regarded by their subjects in early West African kingdoms such as Mali?*

hire a house for me, so when I arrived at this river, I crossed by the ferry without interference. Thus I reached the city of Málí, the capital of the king of the blacks. . . .

I was at Málí during the two festivals of the sacrifice and the fast-breaking. On these days the sultan takes his seat . . . after the midafternoon prayer. The armour-bearers bring in magnificent arms—quivers of gold and silver, swords ornamented with gold and with golden scabbards, gold and silver lances, and crystal maces. At his head stand four amirs [princes] driving off the flies. . . . The commanders, qádí, and preacher sit in their usual places. . . . A chair is placed for Dugha [the interpreter] to sit on. He plays on an instrument made of reeds . . . and chants a poem in praise of the sultan. . . .

The [blacks] possess some admirable qualities. They are seldom unjust, and have a greater [hatred] of injustice than any other people. Their sultan shows no mercy to anyone who is guilty of the least act of it. There is complete security in their country. Neither traveller nor inhabitant in it has anything to fear from rob-

bers or men of violence. They do not [take] the property of any white man who dies in their country. . . . On the contrary, they give it into the charge of some trustworthy person among the whites, until the rightful heir takes possession of it. They are careful to observe the hours of prayer, and assiduous in attending them in congregations, and in bringing their children to them. On Fridays, if a man does not go early to the mosque, he cannot find a corner to pray in, on account of the crowd. . . .

Another of their good qualities is their habit of wearing clean white garments on Fridays. . . . Yet another is their zeal for learning the [Quran].

TIMBUKTU

In 1468, another empire, the Songhai (SAWNG·hy), took over the Malian city of Timbuktu. Under the rule of the Songhai, Timbuktu thrived. In the following excerpt,

Ibn Battuta: Travels in Asia and Africa, 1325–1354, H.A.R. Gibb (tr.). Routledge & Kegan Paul PLC, 1929, pp. 321–322, 323, 328–330.

EXAMINING ART
Abraham Cresques was the first European to draw a map of North Africa. His map, drawn in 1375, is shown here. At lower right of the map is a sketch of Mansa Musa, a wealthy and powerful Muslim leader of Mali. How did Islam affect life in Mali?

Leo Africanus, a North African scholar and traveler, describes Timbuktu and its people as he saw them in the 1500's:

There is a most stately temple to be seen, the walls whereof are made of stone and lime; and a princely palace. . . . Here are many shops of artisans, and merchants, and especially of such as weave linen and cotton cloth. And hither do the Barbary [North African] merchants bring cloth of Europe. All the women of this region except maid-servants go with their faces covered, and sell all necessary food. The inhabitants, and especially strangers there residing, are exceeding rich, insomuch, that the king married both his daughters unto two rich merchants. Here are many wells, containing most sweet water; and so often as the river Niger overflows, they convey the water thereof by certain channels into the town. Corn, cattle, milk, and butter this region yields in great abundance: but salt is very scarce here. . . . The rich king has many plates and scepters of gold, some of which weigh 1300 pounds

[585 kilograms]: and he keeps a magnificent and well furnished court.

. . . Whosoever will speak unto this king must first fall down before his feet, and then taking up earth must sprinkle it upon his own head and shoulders: which custom is ordinarily observed by them that never saluted the king before, or come as ambassadors from other princes. He has always three thousand horsemen, and a great number of footmen that shoot poisoned arrows, attending upon him. They have often skirmishes with those that refuse to pay tribute, and so many as they take, they sell unto the merchants of Timbuktu. . . . Here are great store of doctors, judges, priests, and other learned men that are bountifully maintained at the king's cost and charges. And hither are brought diverse manuscripts or written books out of Barbary, which are sold for more money than any other merchandise. The coin of Timbuktu is of gold without any stamp or inscription. . . .

Source: Adapted from *The Historie and Description of Africa* by Leo Africanus. John Pory (tr.) and Dr. Robert Brown (ed.). Hakluyt Society, Vol. III, 1896, pp. 824–825.

SOFALA, KILWA, AND MOMBASA

Between the 1100's and 1300's, African peoples who came to be known as the Swahili (swah·HEE·lee) built cities along Africa's east coast that traded extensively with the Middle East, India, and China. Each city was independent with its own ruler. Below, a Portuguese sailor who went to Africa in the early 1500's tells what he observed in three of the cities—Sofala, Kilwa, and Mombasa:

The Moors [Swahili] of Sofala kept these ware [goods brought by traders from other kingdoms] and sold them afterwards to the heathen of the Kingdom of Benametapa, who came thither laden with gold which they gave in exchange for the said cloths without weighing it. These Moors collect also great store of ivory which they find hard by Sofala, and this also they sell in the [Indian] kingdom of Cambay. . . . These Moors are black, and some of them tawny; some of them speak Arabic, but the more part use the language of their country. They clothe themselves from the waist down with cotton and silk cloths, and other cloths they wear over their shoulders like capes, and turbans on their heads. Some of them wear small caps dyed in grain . . . and other woolen clothes in many tints. . . .

In this same Sofala now of late they make great store of cotton and weave it, and from it they make much white cloth, and as they know not how to dye it, . . . they take the Cambay cloths, blue or otherwise colored, and unravel them and make them up again, so that it becomes a new thing. With this thread and their own white they make much colored cloth, and from it they gain much gold. . . .

Going along the coast . . . , there is an island . . . called Kilwa, in which is a Moorish town with many fair houses of stones and mortar, with many windows after our fashion, very well arranged in streets, with many flat roofs. The doors are of wood, well carved. . . . Around it are streams and orchards and fruit-gardens with many channels of sweet water. It has a Moorish king over it. From this place they trade with Sofala, whence they bring back gold. . . .

Further on, an advance along the coast towards India, there is an isle . . . on which is a town called Mombasa. It is a very fair place, with lofty stone and mortar houses well aligned in streets after the fashion of Kilwa. . . . It has its own king, himself a Moor. The men are in color either tawny, black or white and also their women go very bravely attired with many fine garments of silk and gold in abundance. This is a place of great traffic, and has a good harbor, in which are always moored craft of many kinds. . . .

This Mombasa is a land very full of food. Here are found many very fine sheep . . . , cows and other cattle in great plenty, and many fowls. . . . There is much millet and rice, sweet and bitter oranges, lemons, pomegranates, Indian figs, vegetables . . . , and much sweet water. The men thereof are oftentimes at war but seldom at peace with those of the mainland, and they carry on trade with them, bringing thence great store of honey, wax and ivory.

SECTION 1 REVIEW

CHECKING FOR UNDERSTANDING
1. **Define** Islamic empire, mosque.
2. **Detail** the features of Axum, Mali, Timbuktu, and the Swahili cities.

CRITICAL THINKING
3. **Synthesizing Information** What factors were most important in the development of early Africa?

Source: From *The Book of Duarte Barbosa*, Mansel Longworth Dames (tr.), as cited in *The African Past: Chronicles from Antiquity to Modern Times.* Reprinted by permission of Curtis Brown, Ltd. Copyright © 1964 by Basil Davidson.

History

THE ATLANTIC SLAVE TRADE

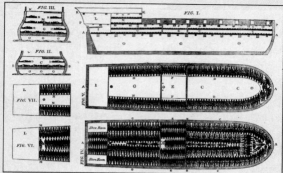

Out of the Portuguese explorations in the 1400's grew an evil that came to be known as the Atlantic slave trade. Over the next 4 centuries, Europeans transported millions of Africans across the Atlantic Ocean to work in the Americas. This forced removal caused tremendous suffering and hardship. In 1756, an 11-year-old Ibo from Nigeria named Olaudah Equiano was captured and sold into slavery. Below, he tells his story:

. . . One day, when . . . only I and my dear sister were left to mind the house, two men and a woman got over our walls, and in a moment seized us both, and . . . they stopped our mouths and ran off with us into the nearest wood. Here they tied our hands and continued to carry us as far as they could. . . . [The] only comfort we had was in being in one another's arms . . . and bathing each other with our tears. . . . The next day . . . my sister and I were separated while we lay clasped in each other's arms. . . . She was torn from me and immediately carried away. . . .

. . . I continued to travel, sometimes by land, sometimes by water, through different countries and various nations, till at the end of six or seven months . . . I arrived at the sea coast.

The first object which saluted my eyes when I arrived . . . was the sea, and a slave ship . . . waiting for its cargo. These filled me with astonishment, which was converted into terror. . . . I no longer doubted of my fate; and quite overpowered with horror and anguish, I fell motionless on the deck and fainted. When I recovered a little I found some black people around me. . . .

I was put down under the decks, and there . . . with the loathsomeness of the stench and crying together, I became so sick and low that I was not able to eat. . . . [On] my refusing to eat, one [white man] held me fast by the hands and laid me across I think the windlass, and tied my feet while the other flogged me se-

verely. . . . I inquired . . . what was to be done with us; they gave me to understand we were to be carried to these white people's country to work for them. . . . At last, when the ship we were in had got in all her cargo, they made ready [to sail] . . . , and we were all put under deck. . . .

The closeness of the place and the heat of the climate, added to the number in the ship . . . almost suffocated us. This produced copious perspiration, so that the air soon became unfit for respiration . . . , and brought on a sickness among the slaves. . . . The shrieks of the women and the groans of the dying rendered the whole a scene of horror. . . . In this manner we continued to undergo more hardships than I can now relate, hardships which are inseparable from this accursed trade.

DRAWING CONCLUSIONS

1. What was the Atlantic slave trade?
2. How would you have reacted had you been Olaudah Equiano?

Source: The Interesting Narrative of the Life of Olaudah Equiano, or Gustavus Vassa the African, Written by Himself. Abridged and edited by Paul Edwards as *Equiano's Travels.* Heinemann Educational Books, Ltd., 1967, pp. 16, 24, 25–30.

SECTION 2

From Imperialism to Nationalism

For many years, European colonies in Africa were limited to the coastline of the continent. Beginning in the late 1800's, however, Europeans found in the interior of Africa vast lands and huge amounts of raw materials.

By setting up colonies, the Europeans could supply raw materials to their factories at home and provide new markets for their products. **Imperialism**—the policy of establishing colonies and building empires—could be very important to their economic and political goals.

By 1914, Britain, France, Germany, Portugal, Spain, and Italy had partitioned, or divided, nearly all of Africa among themselves. Only Liberia, which had been founded by freed slaves from the United States, and Ethiopia, remained solely under African control.

THE EUROPEANS

During the colonial era, the Europeans made many attempts to justify imperialism. Most Europeans would have agreed with the views expressed below by a British colonial officer:

> Let it be admitted at the outset that European brains, capital, and energy have not, and never will be, expended in developing the resources of Africa from motives of pure philanthropy; that Europe is in Africa for the mutual benefit of her own industrial classes, and of the native races in their progress to a higher plane. . . .
>
> By railways and roads, by reclamation of swamps and deserts, and by a system of fair trade and competition, we have added to the prosperity and wealth of these lands, and checked famine and disease. . . . We are endeavoring to teach the native races to conduct their own affairs with justice and humanity, and to educate them alike in letters and in industry. . . .
>
> . . . British methods have not perhaps in all cases produced ideal results, but I am profoundly convinced that there can be no question but that British rule has promoted the happiness and welfare of the primitive races. . . . If there is unrest, and a desire for independence, . . . it is because we have taught the value of liberty and freedom. . . . Their very discontent is a measure of their progress.

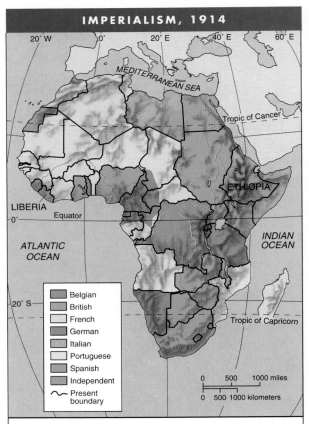

IMPERIALISM, 1914

Belgian
British
French
German
Italian
Portuguese
Spanish
Independent
Present boundary

EXAMINING MAPS *The "Scramble for Africa," the rush by European powers to claim African territory, began during the 1880's. By 1914, only two lands remained completely free of European rule.* **What were these two lands?**

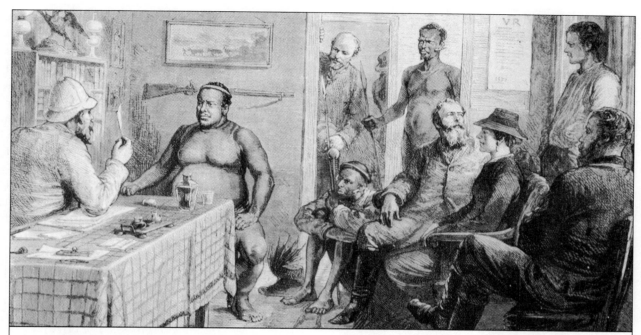

EXAMINING ART *This print shows negotiations between an African leader and a British soldier regarding colonial rule. European nations forced their laws on colonized African states.* *What European nations colonized Africa?*

We hold these countries because it is the genius of our race to colonise, to trade, and to govern.

THE AFRICANS

Most Africans, however, did not share this view. Below, Patrice Lumumba, a Congolese independence-fighter, recalls what it was like to live under Belgian rule:

We have known the back-breaking work exacted from us in exchange for salaries which permitted us neither to eat enough to satisfy our hunger, nor to dress and lodge ourselves decently, nor to raise our children. . . .

We have known the mockery, the insults, the blows submitted to morning, noon and night because we were "negres

Source: Sir F.D. Lugard. *The Dual Mandate in British Tropical Africa.* William Blackwood & Sons, Ltd., 1929, pp. 617–619.

[black]." Who will forget that to a Negro one used the familiar term of address; not, certainly, as to a friend, but because the more dignified forms were reserved for Whites alone?

We have known that our lands were despoiled in the name of supposedly legal texts, which in reality recognized only the right of the stronger.

We have known the law was never the same, whether dealing with a White or a Negro; that it was accommodating for the one, cruel and inhuman to the other.

We have known the atrocious suffering of those who were imprisoned for political opinion or religious beliefs: exiles in their own country. . . .

We have known that in the cities there were magnificent houses for the Whites and crumbling hovels for the Negroes, that a Negro was not admitted to movie theaters or restaurants, that he was not allowed to enter so-called "European"

EXAMINING PHOTOGRAPHS *The closely spaced houses in this Ghanaian town are made of mud walls and have metal roofs. How does this typical town housing compare to the housing shown in the photo to the right?*

stores, that when the Negro traveled, it was on the lowest level of a boat, at the feet of the White man in his deluxe cabin.

And, finally, who will forget the hangings or the firing squads where so many . . . perished, or the cells into which were brutally thrown those who escaped the soldiers' bullets—the soldiers whom the colonialists made the instruments of their domination?

From all this, my brothers, have we deeply suffered.

In many parts of Africa, Africans fiercely resisted colonial rule. An example is Zaire, which King Leopold of Belgium established as his own personal colony in the late 1800's. He called the colony the Congo Free State. The

Source: Patrice Lumumba. "The Independence of the Congo" in *Africa Speaks.* James Duffy and Robert A. Manner (eds.). D. Van Nostrand Company, Inc., 1961, pp. 90–91.

Congolese were forced to work for the colony, and many died of disease. Resistance was met with torture or death. By 1907, world opinion forced the Belgian government to seize the colony from Leopold. During the first 24 years of colonial rule in the Congo, nearly 1.5 million Congolese—nearly one-half of the population—died.

Although all African efforts did not meet with success, the Africans did not give up. Between the outbreak of World War I in 1914 and the start of World War II in 1939, the seeds of **nationalism,** a people's demand for

EXAMINING PHOTOGRAPHS *This stately home in Zimbabwe reflects the privileged lifestyle enjoyed by whites during colonial rule in some African countries. What were some characteristics of colonial rule in Zaire?*

EXAMINING PHOTOGRAPHS *Led by Kwame Nkrumah, the Gold Coast was the first British African colony to gain independence. It became Ghana. How did colonial education aid African nationalists?*

independence, grew. A generation of young educated Africans, determined to see their countries free from colonial rule, headed nationalist movements.

Most nationalists agreed with Kwame Nkrumah (KWAH·may ehn·KROO·muh), who later became the first president of Ghana, when he declared: "We want to be able to govern ourselves in this country of ours without outside interference, and we are going to see that it is done!" Below, another nationalist leader, Nnamdi Azikiwe (en·nahm·dee ah·zee·KAY·way) of Nigeria, challenges British colonizers to explain why African soldiers should fight for the British for freedom and democracy when there was none for them at home:

It is very significant that in the last two world wars, African peoples were inveigled into participating in the destruction of their fellow human beings on the ground that . . . the world should be made safe for democracy—a political theory which seems to be an exclusive property of the good peoples of Europe and America, whose rulers appear to find war a profitable mission and enterprise. . . .

Today, in Nigeria, thousands of ex-servicemen are unemployed; they are disillusioned and frustrated, while some of them have been maimed for life. . . . In spite of their war efforts, the people of Nigeria . . . have been denied political freedom, economic security, and social emancipation. Our national identity has been stifled to serve the selfish purposes of alien rule. We are denied elementary human rights. We are sentenced to political servitude, and we are committed to economic serfdom. Only those who accept slavery as their destiny would continue to live under such humiliating conditions without asserting their right to life and the pursuit of freedom. . . .

SECTION 2 REVIEW

CHECKING FOR UNDERSTANDING
1. **Define** imperialism, nationalism.
2. **Discuss** reasons for the European colonization of Africa.

CRITICAL THINKING
3. **Recognizing Ideologies** On what principles were African demands for independence based?

Source: Nnamdi Azikiwe. *A Selection from the Speeches of Nnamdi Azikiwe.* Cambridge University Press, 1961, pp. 61–63.

OPPOSING VIEWS OF COLONIALISM

European colonial rule in Africa lasted a relatively short time—in most areas, from the 1870's to the 1960's. It brought, however, major changes to Africa and sparked strong opinions among Africans and Europeans.

The White Man killed my father,
My father was proud.
The White Man seduced my mother,
My mother was beautiful.
The White Man burnt my brother beneath the noonday sun.
My brother was strong.
His hands red with black blood
The White Man turned to me;
And in the Conqueror's voice said,
"Boy! a chair, a napkin, a drink."[2]

FOCUSING ON THE ISSUE The quotes that follow present different views of the European role in Africa. Based on the statements made in the quotes, answer the following:
1. How did Europeans perceive their role in Africa?
2. How did Africans perceive the European role in Africa?
3. Put yourself first in the place of an African and then of a European, and explain why you might have objected to or been in favor of European colonialism.

What use is missionary teaching? The white men can read and write, but it doesn't make them good.

When the whites came to our country, we had the land and they had the Bible; now we have the Bible and they have the land.

I contend that we are the first race in the world and that the more of the world we inhabit the better it is for the human race. I contend that every acre added to our territory provides for the birth of more of the English race, who otherwise would not be brought into existence. . . . I believe it to be my duty to God, my Queen and my Country to paint the whole map of Africa red. . . . That is my creed, my dream and my mission.[1]

---

[1] *Source:* Cecil Rhodes as quoted in *A Plague of Europeans* by David Killingray. Penguin Books, Ltd., 1973, p. 84.

I got into a rickshaw, locally called a go-cart. It was pulled in front by two government negroes and pushed behind by another pair, all neatly attired in white jackets and knee breeches, and crimson cummerbunds yards long, bound round their middles. Now it is an ingrained characteristic of the uneducated negro, that he cannot keep on a neat and complete garment of any kind. It does not matter what that garment may be; so long as it is whole, off it comes.[3]

---

[2] *Source:* David Diop. "Martyr" as cited in *An Anthology of West African Verse.* Olumbe Bassir (ed. & tr.). Ibadan University Press, 1957, p. 53.

[3] *Source:* Mary Kingsley. *Travels in West Africa.* Virago Press, 1897, p. 31.

... my object is to open up traffic along the banks of the Zambesi, and also to preach the Gospel. The natives of Central Africa are very desirous of trading, but their only traffic is at present in slaves . . . : it is therefore most desirable to encourage the former principle, and thus open the way for the consumption of free productions, and the introduction of Christianity and commerce. By encouraging the native propensity for trade, the advantages that might be derived in a commercial point of view are [great]; nor should we lose sight of the [many] blessings it is in our power to bestow upon the unenlightened African, by giving him the light of Christianity. Those two pioneers of civilization—Christianity and commerce—should ever be inseparable.[4]

In an evening in the bush I always wore a long evening dress to keep up my morale but also one had to wear mosquito boots; there were mosquitoes and sand-flies everywhere and the long dress was a great help.

... [The] Development Officer would come along and have dinner with me—he in a dinner suit and I in an evening dress—and we would walk along the bush path talking and everyone gathered to see us. . . . I think they wondered why we got all dressed up and covered ourselves when it was so frightfully hot. In an evening I would often play my . . . records. . . . All the village would come. We'd sit round and we would have these records on and then always there was a drummer with his drum and he would start drumming. . . . And it was absolutely beautiful, . . . and I can't tell you how friendly they were. And although I was often on my own I was safer there than I would have ever been anywhere in England today.[5]

We have been engaged in drawing lines upon maps where no white man's foot ever trod; we have been giving away mountains and rivers and lakes to each other, only hindered by the small impediment that we never knew exactly where the mountains and rivers and lakes were.

I look back with deep gratitude to my early years, which I spent at Lubwa, a mission station of the Church of Scotland in the Northern Province of Northern Rhodesia [Zambia]. My father was an evangelist. . . . My mother . . . is a woman of deep spiritual understanding, and what I know of the Christian faith I learned from her. I think I can say in all honesty that the one thing which influenced me more than any other in the first years of my life was the deep Christian faith of my parents, and the fact that I was living in a community on the Mission Station which was based on love, friendship and kindness. I think it is important to emphasize this point because it was a spiritual and psychological shock to me when I left my home and the Mission Station and found myself facing the hard realities of society in Northern Rhodesia.[6]

[4] Source: David Livingstone. Lecture at Cambridge University in 1857 as quoted in Africa by Phyllis M. Martin and Patrick O'Meara. Indiana University Press, 1977, p. 126.

[5] Source: Catherine Dinnick-Parr as quoted in Tales From the Dark Continent by Charles Allen, Andre Deutsch, 1979, pp. 155–156.

[6] Source: From THROUGH AFRICAN EYES; VOLUME 1, THE PAST, THE ROAD TO INDEPENDENCE, by Leon E. Clark. Copyright © 1988, 1991 by Leon E. Clark.

Chapter 2 Review

SUMMARY

Early African societies based on agriculture developed into large states and empires. From the 1200's to 1400's, a series of powerful empires, such as the Mali and Songhai, ruled in West Africa and became important centers of trade, learning, and Islamic culture. Meanwhile, in East Africa, the Swahili built coastal city-states that developed trade with Asia.

After a period of exploration, Europeans during the 1800's found in Africa vast lands for settlement and huge amounts of raw materials. By 1914, the European powers had divided nearly all of the continent among themselves. In many parts of Africa, however, Africans fiercely resisted colonization. Between 1914 and 1939, nationalism spread as young educated Africans worked to free their countries from colonial rule.

USING VOCABULARY

Use these vocabulary words in a paragraph about the major forces that have shaped African history.

oral tradition   imperialism
Islamic empire   nationalism
mosque

REVIEWING FACTS

1. **Identify** the economic activity that brought prosperity to Kush and Meroë.
2. **Name** the ancient Monomotapan city that has gained worldwide recognition for its architecture.
3. **Describe** life in Mali at the height of its power.
4. **List** the areas that traded extensively with the Swahili coastal cities.

5. **Identify** the "Scramble for Africa" that occurred during the late 1800's.
6. **Explain** the factors that caused the European colonization of Africa.
7. **Indicate** how some Europeans justified colonial rule in Africa.
8. **Discuss** how many Africans reacted to European colonization.
9. **State** the goal of African nationalist movements.

CRITICAL THINKING

1. **Demonstrating Reasoned Judgment** Many historians say that African history has long been presented in a distorted manner. Why do you think this was the case?
2. **Analyzing Information** What role do you think trade played in African societies?
3. **Predicting Consequences** How do you think Africa would be different if the Europeans had never colonized it? How do you think Europe would be different?
4. **Identifying Central Issues** If you were African, would you have become a nationalist? Explain.

ANALYZING CONCEPTS

1. **Technology** How did technology aid the rise of early African civilizations?
2. **Political Systems** What factors were responsible for the rise of nationalism in Africa?

GEOGRAPHIC THEMES

1. **Movement** How did contact between Africa and other parts of the world influence the development of early African empires?
2. **Location** How did Axum's location affect the development of its economy?

Building Skills
SOCIAL STUDIES

Comparing Historical Maps

A political map contains information about the political and social organization of a region. On political maps, land is organized into empires, nations, states or provinces, cities, townships, or counties. Political boundaries, however, are human-made and often change. By studying maps of the same area at different points in history, you can learn a great deal about how the region has changed over time.

Use the following steps to compare historical maps:
- Study two maps that show the same area at different times.
- Identify the date, political boundaries, and place names shown on each map.
- Determine what aspects of the two maps are the same and what aspects are different.
- Summarize how the area has changed over this period of time.

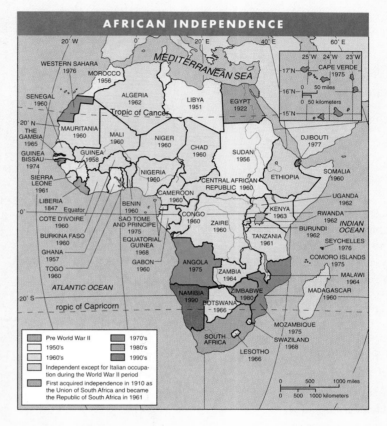

AFRICAN INDEPENDENCE

Legend:
- Pre World War II
- 1950's
- 1960's
- 1970's
- 1980's
- 1990's
- Independent except for Italian occupation during the World War II period
- First acquired independence in 1910 as the Union of South Africa and became the Republic of South Africa in 1961

EXAMPLE

Look at the maps of Africa on pages 24 and 30 of your text. The first map is titled "Early Africa." What is the second one called? *(Imperialism, 1914)* By examining both maps, you can compare how Africa looked before and after colonization by European nations. On the map of early Africa, there are no clear boundaries between the African territories named on the map. On the other map, the European colonies are shown by areas of different colors. For example, British colonies are brown.

What color is used to show Portuguese colonies? *(yellow)* French colonies? *(light green)* There are few similarities between the two maps. The names of early African territories have completely disappeared on the second map. How did Africa change during this period? *(Europeans divided the land into distinct areas controlled by their governments.)*

PRACTICE

Compare the map of colonial Africa on page 30 with the map of modern Africa shown above. Then answer the questions that follow.

1. How are boundaries between European colonies shown on the 1914 map?
2. How are boundaries between African nations shown on the map of Africa today?
3. How do you think European imperialism in Africa affected the use of language and communication among Africans?
4. Using these maps, summarize the political changes in Africa between 1914 and today.

People and Places to Know
Gulf of Guinea, the Hausa, the Fulani, the Ibo, the Yoruba, the Nok, Kano, Katsina, Zaria, Lagos, Benin Empire, Yakubu Gowon, Biafra, Ibadan, Wole Soyinka, Flora Nwapa

Key Terms to Define
compound, urban migration

Objectives to Learn
1. **Identify** the major characteristics and traits of the Nigerian people.
2. **Recognize** historic obstacles to national unity in Nigeria.
3. **Describe** rural and urban ways of life in Nigeria.

Nigerian man dressed for a festival

Nigeria

"The last time I visited Nigeria . . . , a night storm felled a large tree across a road in my home village. The following morning, a cluster of people formed beside the tree—men and women on . . . some early morning errand, children on their way to school. Some of the people were dressed to travel a distance. Others were in ragged house or work clothes, and their faces were streaked with sleep.

The scene made me shimmer with nostalgia. I was forty years old and had been away from the village for more than twenty, but I could recall countless such scenes from my childhood. . . .

Many things had changed since I had been a child in this village, but many things had also stayed the same. In composition and age, in manners and speech, in clothes' style and interpersonal relationships, the crowd was eternal. A few things had been updated, but all of the old archetypes were there. Something, though, had changed in a radical way—the cohesion and collective spirit of the people. Had this been thirty years before, the elders on the scene would have declared that all personal and private work in the village had to cease, until the obstruction was removed from the road. . . .

However, no elder spoke up on this occasion. . . . The unspoken consensus seemed to be that the obstructed road was now a government road, and not the village's responsibility. . . .

When I left home two weeks later, the tree was still there. . . .

Back in the United States, I have been continually saddened by this episode. . . . I realise that my home village is quickly becoming "mass". Family compounds, which used to contain more than twenty grown men and twice as many wives, are now disbanding into one-man compounds. . . . The tom-tom no longer sounds for Community Work Day, a day of the week set aside for such things as cleaning the village paths, repairing the market stalls, and doing whatever needed to be done on the premises of the local primary school. . . ."

These observations by a Nigerian who teaches in the United States reflect the reaction of many Nigerians who return home after having spent a long time overseas.

Nigeria, which is located along West Africa's Gulf of Guinea, makes up about 3 percent of Africa's landmass. With close to 120 million people—about 18 percent of the population of Africa—it is the continent's most populous state. Nigeria's rich history, traditionally strong economy, and the determination of its people made it a leader on the continent.

Source: T. Obinkaram Echewa. *West Africa*, April 30, 1984, pp. 928–929.

SECTION 1

The People

Nigeria's population is as diverse as it is large. More than 250 different peoples, or ethnic groups, live in Nigeria. The Hausa kola-nut trader, the Fulani cattle herder, the Benin chief, and the Abuja potter all call themselves Nigerians. The four largest groups, however, are the Hausa and the Fulani in the north of the country, the Ibo in the southeast, and the Yoruba in the southwest.

Even though Nigeria has sought to forge a national identity over the years, ethnic identity still remains important. Today's Nigerians are proud of who they are and where their origins lie. As one specialist noted, "ethnicity . . . remains strong because it is a means of identifying people, of categorizing strangers, of obtaining favors, and of acquiring help in times of insecurity."

The diversity of the people is reflected in many ways—from ways of earning a living to art to language to customs to tradition to choice of religion. Although Islam and Christianity are the major religions, other religious beliefs also thrive, often combined with Christian ones. Some of the more traditional religions are characterized by the worship of gods and spirits that represent the natural elements and which followers believe protect them from destructive forces.

Christianity and Islam have led to a move away from many of the traditional ways. Christianity is especially strong among the Ibos. Christian churches are a familiar sight in many parts of the country, especially in Iboland, south of the Benue River and east of the Niger River. Yorubas, on the other hand, tend to belong to independent African churches or to be strong followers of the Muslim religion. The Hausas and the Fulanis also tend to be Muslim.

Much of Nigeria's power lies in the determination, talent, and versatility of its people. Below, an African American educator who visited Nigeria relates her experiences with and impressions of that talent and versatility:

I have for many years dreamed of visiting the land of my forefathers. . . . I have always felt a need, a yearning to

EXAMINING PHOTOGRAPHS
For centuries, the Fulani of northern Nigeria have been nomadic cattle herders, moving their livestock between seasons of the wet/dry savanna grazing areas. Because the Fulani measure wealth in terms of how many cattle they own, even the many who have become settled village farmers tend to keep large herds. What other large ethnic group lives in northern Nigeria?

come "full circle," and touch base with my "other part." Visiting Africa afforded me the opportunity to see, feel, live and experience—first hand—the culture, the land, and the people who are the [offspring] of "The Motherland," the cradle of all mankind. In retrospect, my Nigerian experience was the most enlightening of my life; I came to know a warm, creative, spirit-filled people who love and live life.

Everywhere we travelled, we were greeted with the words, "You are welcome" spoken with heartfelt sincerity. As guests in many homes, businesses, educational, and political institutions, we met Nigerians of all walks of life who were delighted to share their country with us.

I was astounded at the courtesy, the national pride, and the genuine respect for life and people all so pervasive throughout the society.

I marvelled at the strength of the family unit and its many successful undertakings—religious, moral, and academic teaching; security for the aged; training grounds in marriage and parenthood for the youth.

I envied the enthusiasm for learning displayed by teachers and students alike. I applauded the high priority given education by the government.

I delighted in the artistic nature of the people most evident in the beautiful wares displayed in the open markets. What many Nigerians can do with a piece of leather, or some beads, or seeds, or a piece of cloth in a dye pit, or a weaving loom, or with butterfly wings . . . is phenomenal. Their ability to maximize usage of their environment with little waste is praiseworthy.

I respected the fervor with which the Nigerians adhered to their commitments. The deep sense of loyalty to religion, to family, to country, to self, is in all aspects of the society.

My impressions of Nigeria? It is a land growing, developing, inhabited by a vibrant people who have customs, tradi-

EXAMINING PHOTOGRAPHS *The Yoruba are well-known for their artistry in wood. Here, a young woodcarver creates a scene from daily life. What is another source of inspiration for Nigerian artists?*

tions, and values that they live and teach daily. It is an artistic culture. It is a land of many hues of skin color, many languages, and many lifestyles, all of which seem to respond to a common throbbing pulse.

SECTION 1 REVIEW

CHECKING FOR UNDERSTANDING
1. **Identify** the four major ethnic groups of Nigeria and the part of the country in which each is most prevalent.
2. **Indicate** what religions are practiced in Nigeria.

CRITICAL THINKING
3. **Making Generalizations** What two generalizations might you make about the Nigerian people based on the impressions of the African American educator who visited Nigeria?

Source: June Grundy. "Some Thoughts on Nigeria" in "Nigeria," Department of Curriculum and Instruction, University of Kentucky, 1981.

EXAMINING PHOTOGRAPHS *Nigeria has more than 250 different ethnic groups. These groups differ from each other in language and in some of their customs, traditions, and dress. The photo above shows people from the four largest groups (from left to right): the Hausa, the Yoruba, the Ibo, and the Fulani. How did these ethnic groups shape the development of Nigeria's early history?*

SECTION 2
Historical Perspective

The Nok culture of central Nigeria was one of Africa's earliest civilizations. Over 2000 years ago, it mastered the use of iron. Today's Nigerians are proud of the Nok and of the other early societies that gave them their rich history and heritage. That history is taught in school and celebrated through religious festivals, poetry, drama, dance, music, art, and storytelling. Many customs and religious traditions practiced today can be traced to the societies and states that flourished in Nigeria hundreds and even thousands of years ago.

THE EARLY YEARS

Around 1000 AD, the powerful Hausa states of Kano, Katsina, and Zaria arose in the northern part of Nigeria and established long-distance trading ties with various lands in the Mediterranean world. The Hausa states remained powerful until the nineteenth century, when they were defeated by the Fulani in a series of devastating wars. As a result of the Fulani military victory, most of northern Nigeria became part of a vast Islamic empire.

In the early 1600's, the Yoruba settled the present-day city of Lagos. It became the southernmost outpost of the Benin Empire. During the era of the slave trade, human cargo was shipped from the Lagos port to Brazil, the Caribbean, and North America.

It was also in the 1600's that European explorers, sailing the inland areas along Nigeria's major rivers, discovered many products valuable for trade. Shortly after, traders and missionaries began to arrive. By the mid-1800's, with the seizure of Lagos, the British began their takeover of the country. In 1914, they declared all of Nigeria a British colony.

Nigerians resisted British rule of their country for decades. Finally, on October 1, 1960, Nigeria gained its independence.

CIVIL WAR

For a time after independence, there was peace. But before long, tension began to grow among various groups. The northern region, which had the largest population, controlled the federal government. Fearful that the northerners would ignore their needs and concerns, Ibo military leaders seized control in January 1966. Anti-Ibo rioting broke out in the north, leading to the death of many Ibos. In July, northern army officers staged a coup and set up a military government headed by General Yakubu Gowon. In an attempt to avoid domination of the federal government by any one ethnic group, Gowon's government divided the country into 12 states.

This reform, however, came too late. In May 1967, Ibo leader Lt. General E.O. Ojukwu took over the Eastern Region and

EXAMINING PHOTOGRAPHS *Nigerian police in colonial uniforms observe the 1960 Independence Day celebrations. Each state has its own chief police officer. Why was Nigeria divided into 12 states?*

EXAMINING PHOTOGRAPHS *This terracotta (clay) head, produced by the Nok, is among the oldest known examples of African sculpture. Besides clay, what other natural material did the Nok master?*

EXAMINING PHOTOGRAPHS *Although Nigerian forces were strengthened with British, Soviet, French, and Spanish arms, these Ibo soldiers fought courageously for Biafra's independence. What last-minute action did the Nigerian government take in an attempt to avert civil war?*

declared it the independent Republic of Biafra. The result was full-scale civil war, which lasted for 30 months. General Gowon's federal forces crushed Biafra's movement for secession, or withdrawal from a national union. Thus, Nigeria's territorial unity was preserved.

One of the many Nigerians caught in the war was the novelist Elechi Amadi. Separated from his family for two years, he spent much of the war in prison. Below, in an excerpt from his diary, Amadi talks about his efforts to be reunited with his family:

❚ rushed to Igwuruta, from where the bulk of refugees seemed to be streaming in. A fantastic sight greeted me. Sprawled in the school compound and all around were over ten thousand refugees. . . .

I moved through the seething sea of humanity, trying to trace my family. . . . At every step someone hugged me, weeping with joy.

'They said you were dead. . . . '

'Well, I am alive. Please, where is my family?'

'Your mother is on the way, a few miles back, maybe. I saw her.'

'And my wife?'

'I didn't see her. They say she is at Ata. I doubt if she has started moving.'

'And my father?'

'At Mbaise.'

I rushed away in search of my mother. I picked her up at Umuechen—a dirty, emaciated and utterly miserable woman, mourning for her only child. She could not hug me at first because my uncle and other relations carried me shoulder high, weeping like children. . . .

. . . Our search led us to Owerri. There was a large refugee camp there. . . . Many of my relations were there, and hell broke loose when they saw me. . . . I tried to peer around to look for my wife and children. I could not, so great was the crush on me. In the end I actually cried out:

'Where is my wife?'

'She has just left for Port Harcourt,' someone said.

'My children?' I gasped again.

'They are clinging to you.'

I looked down. Two of my children were clinging to my feet. . . . I was afraid to ask for the rest, but one by one I fished them out. I took them to the car along with other relations, and stuffed them with food. I arrived at Port Harcourt late in the evening. I rushed into the house, and my mother heaved a sigh of relief. . . .

Then [my wife] Dorah came rushing at me. We wept.

I picked up my father the next day just four miles [6.4 kilometers] from home. Clad in a tattered ancient black overcoat, and with a white beard, he was pushing his bicycle along. . . . He did not weep as he hugged me, but I knew he felt more than everybody else.

SECTION 2 REVIEW

CHECKING FOR UNDERSTANDING

1. **Discuss** how modern Nigerians regard the societies and states that flourished in Nigeria in the distant past.
2. **Summarize** Nigerian history from around 1000 AD to 1960.

CRITICAL THINKING

3. **Determining Cause and Effect** What led to civil war in Nigeria? What impact did the war have?

Source: Elechi Amadi. Sunset in Biafra: A Civil War Diary. Heinemann Educational Books Ltd., 1973, pp. 181–184.

SECTION 3

Nigeria Today

In the 1970's, the discovery of oil in Nigeria led to an economic boom. Until this time, Nigeria had been largely agricultural. During the boom, however, many farmers moved to the cities in search of jobs. As a result, agriculture production fell so greatly that, for the first time, Nigeria had to import food.

EXAMINING PHOTOGRAPHS *Workers on this oil rig at Port Harcourt drill a well to tap the country's clean-burning, low-sulphur oil. How did the oil boom of the 1970's affect Nigeria's ability to feed its people?*

Then, in the 1980's, there was a glut, or oversupply, in the world's oil market, which caused oil prices to fall. Nigeria, meanwhile, had come to depend on oil revenue, or income. The loss of much of that income, coupled with high government spending, wage increases, and greater transportation costs, led to economic problems.

In 1983, Nigeria's civilian government was overthrown by Major-General Muhammadu Buhari (moo·hahm·MAH·doo boo·HAH·ree). Promising to correct the sluggish economy, he focused on diversifying, or varying, the economy. Making Nigeria self-sufficient once again in agriculture was a major goal.

In 1985, Buhari's government was overthrown by the Nigerian army, and Ibrahim Babangida (ee·brah·HEEM bah·bahn·GHE·dah) was made president. Like Buhari, his goal was to improve the economy. To this end, he slashed the value of the country's currency and imposed tough economic reforms. These steps led food production to rise, non-oil exports to increase, and Nigerian exports to be more attractive in other countries. At the same time, however, they impacted the life of many Nigerians by making the price of food and imports soar.

Babangida also promised a return to a democratic, civilian government in late 1992. In December 1991, a major step toward this end was taken when elections were held for state governors and legislators.

In early 1992, growing political and social instability threatened to derail the movement toward democracy. Riots erupted in Lagos over fuel shortages and soaring prices. In the northern part of the country, a land dispute led to clashes between Christian and Muslim groups. The economic and religious disturbances aroused widespread fears that Nigeria's military leaders would find excuses to delay handing power over to a civilian government. In response to the demonstrations, the government arrested two opposition leaders who had accused the government of corruption and mismanagement of the economy.

WAYS OF LIFE

Over three-fourths of the Nigerian people live in rural towns and villages. Most of these people make their homes in enclosed **compounds**, or homesteads, in mud, wood, or cement houses with garden plots and yards. The majority of them earn their living raising such crops as cotton, cocoa, yams, cassava, sorghum, corn, rice, peanuts, rubber, palm oils, and palm kernels. Some engage in fishing, herding, small-scale industry, and craft production. The food and manufactured goods they produce are sold locally or transported to larger markets in the cities. As one author explains, although many Nigerians end up leaving their village or town of birth, they do not forget their roots:

EXAMINING PHOTOGRAPHS *Sun-dried bricks and thatch are used in the construction of the houses and storage buildings of this compound in northern Nigeria.* What percent of the Nigerian population live in rural towns and villages today?

Attachment to one's home village is striking in Nigerians of all groups. Everyone knows where he or his parents came from. Even if he seldom goes there, it is where he belongs; he has title to land there and can farm if he wants. . . . He usually knows where everyone else from his village has gone and very many areas have associations of local sons and daughters who keep in touch wherever they may be.

The home town or village matters most where marriage is concerned. Most Nigerians marry someone not only from the same ethnic group, but from a nearby area. . . .

Attachment to the home village means attachment to tradition, including traditional authority.

In recent years, however, many Nigerians have left their rural homes to find work and a better standard of living in the cities. The three largest cities are Lagos, Kano, and Ibadan. While all three have modern architecture and many modern conveniences, each has a different flavor. Kano, for example, lies at the edge of the Sahara and is the capital of Kano state. Built in the 1500's, it once was the point of departure for the great trade caravans that crossed West Africa. The chief commercial city of northern Nigeria, Kano really is two cities in one. The old walled town reflects the Muslim culture and the age-old traditions of the Hausa. Outside the wall lies the new, modern sector where most non-Hausa dwellers make their home.

Ibadan, on the other hand, is in the western state of Oyo. Today the second largest city in Nigeria, it was built in the late 1700's or early 1800's by the Yoruba. A trading and industrial center, Ibadan has one of the largest open-air markets in Africa. Like many Yoruba towns, it thrives as an agricultural market city. A fair number of the people who live in the city work nearby farms.

Source: John Harris. "The Peoples of Nigeria" in *New African Survey,* August 1983, p. 63.

Then there is Lagos, which lies along the coast. The largest city of Nigeria and the most populous in Africa, Lagos is one of the fastest growing cities in the world. It is also the chief port of Nigeria, has the greatest concentration of industry in the country, and is a major commercial hub.

Of all the cities, Lagos has probably suffered the most from **urban migration**, the flow of people to the cities. From 1960 until recently, Lagos served as the national capital. But, as conditions in the city worsened, the government acted on an earlier decision to build a new capital at Abuja in central Nigeria. An official press release explaining the decision said that Lagos was a place of "perennial traffic jams, intolerable congestion, chaotic sanitary situation, inadequate social amenities, an alarming crime rate." In the following article, a visiting journalist offers his opinion:

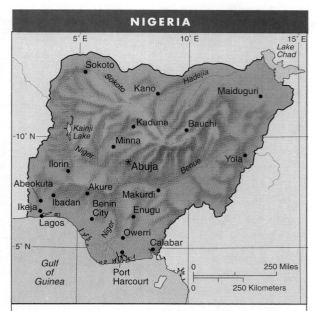

EXAMINING MAPS *Nigeria, with its diversity of ethnic groups, gained independence from Britain in 1960. Today, Nigeria has a federal form of government. The national capital is the newly built city of Abuja. Where is Abuja located?*

There is . . . just a word of advice: When traveling in this mad, beautiful, thrilling, wholly exasperating country, it is probably wise to gird for the unexpected.

A hand-painted sign nailed to the rear of a gasoline truck barreling along a street in this city of 2 million the other night perhaps said it best: "Nigeria: God's Case, No Appeal."

It is a country with daunting social problems and shocking economic extremes but incredible wealth in people, language, and culture. Go to the north, to the ancient city of Kano, and you are transported to a time of sultans and mosques where men in flowing gowns stop in their tracks five times a day to wash their feet and pray.

While Kano reflects deep cultural history, Lagos . . . is modern through and through—big cars, garish billboards, noise, eye-stinging smog and high-rise edifices slicing the sky. While many northerners value a fine sense of manners and grace, most people in Lagos . . . don't suffer fools. In fact, they don't like them. . . .

Lagos is . . . big, hot . . . and a pure hellhole to move about or work in. It is also a place of astonishing contrast and incongruity. State-of-the-art highway overpasses, for instance, tower over ancient fishing villages set on the edge of fetid lagoons.

And like New York, or any other big American city for that matter, crime flourishes here. With the economy in crisis and inflation soaring, more and more Nigerians are turning to international drug smuggling to make ends meet. . . .

EXAMINING PHOTOGRAPHS *Tununbu Square appears to be a relatively peaceful island in the midst of hectic downtown Lagos, whose busy port handles more cargo than all other West African ports put together. Why have many rural Nigerians moved to Lagos and other cities in recent years?*

EXAMINING PHOTOGRAPHS *These children are among the nearly 5 million who are benefiting from the Nigerian government's free elementary school education program, which was begun in 1975. How do Nigerians feel about the education of their youth?*

Meantime, armed robbery has become a growth industry here. A couple of months ago, Oderinde and a French passenger in his cab were robbed at gunpoint by four holdup men on the expressway. . . .

Since then, Oderinde said, he avoids driving at night. And he does not stop for red lights anymore, either. Few Lagos drivers do.

If Chicago is a city of big shoulders, and Paris is the city of light, then this is surely the city of no rules. . . .

What makes all this endurable, of course, is the people. People in Lagos are exceptional—bold, defiant, argumentative, inventive, rude, proud. They talk, they scream, they embrace friends and strangers alike, they express their minds. They are a bright contrast to . . . Africans in some other countries where years of political repression have taken a spiritual toll. As Pini Jayson, editor of a political news monthly here, says: "We are the heartbeat of Africa."

NIGERIAN YOUTH

Nigerians believe that the future of their country depends on the young people, that "our children are our wealth." For this reason, the government has made education a top priority. To further stress concern for the young, it also has initiated the National Youth Service Corps, which requires educated young Nigerian men and women to spend a year

Source: Neil Henry. "No Appeal in the City of No Rules" in *The Washington Post*, December 11, 1989, p. A24, © 1989 *The Washington Post.* Reprinted with permission.

EXAMINING PHOTOGRAPHS *These young workers are developing a tree nursery as part of a government program to reforest land damaged by soil erosion. Why has the Nigerian government made education of youth a top priority?*

doing community service. The reasons are explained in the excerpt below from the Corps handbook:

The objectives of the National Youth Service Corps Scheme are . . .

(a) to inculcate discipline in our youths by instilling in them a tradition of industry at work, and, of patriotic and loyal service to the nation. . . ;

(b) to raise the moral tone of our youths by giving them the opportunity to learn about higher ideals of national achievement and social and cultural improvement;

(c) to develop in our youths attitudes of mind, acquired through shared experience and suitable training, which will make them more amenable to mobilisation in the national interest;

(d) to develop common ties among our youths and promote national unity by ensuring that:

(i) as far as possible, youths are assigned to jobs in states other than their states of origin;

(ii) each group, assigned to work together, is as representative of the country as possible;

(iii) the youths are exposed to the modes of living of the people in different parts of the country with a view to removing prejudices, eliminating ignorance and confirming at first hand the many similarities among Nigerians of all ethnic groups.

(e) to encourage members of the Corps to seek, at the end of their Corps service, career employment all over the country, thus promoting the free movement of labour;

(f) to induce employers . . . to employ more readily qualified Nigerians irrespective of their states of origin; and

(g) to enable our youths to acquire the spirit of self-reliance.

SECTION 3 REVIEW

CHECKING FOR UNDERSTANDING

1. **Define** compound, urban migration.
2. **Discuss** the impact of oil on the Nigerian economy.

CRITICAL THINKING

3. **Making Generalizations** Make two generalizations about the government of Nigeria during the 1980's.
4. **Synthesizing Information** Identify the major problems confronting Lagos.

Source: National Youth Service Corps. Decree No. 24, *National Youth Service Handbook, 1986.* Directorate Headquarters, Lagos, pp. 3–4.

Africa

WOLE SOYINKA AND FLORA NWAPA

Over the past decades, a number of Nigerian writers have gained international recognition. Among these are Wole Soyinka (WOH·lay soy·IHN·kuh) and Flora Nwapa (FLOH·ruh ehn·WAH·pah).

Wole Soyinka is a university professor who in 1986 became the first African to win the Nobel Prize for literature. Educated in Nigeria and England, Soyinka is one of a small number of Nigerians who have written for English-speaking audiences.

Soyinka's first play, *The Inventors*, was performed in 1957. Within a few years, Soyinka founded several theater companies, which he used to build up a new kind of

Nigerian drama that was written in English but incorporated the words, music, dance, and pantomime of traditional African festivals.

In 1967, Soyinka published his first major collection of poems. That same year, he began a two-year prison term in Nigeria for writings sympathetic to secessionist Biafra. In 1969 and 1970 respectively, a play and a major collection of verse appeared about his ordeal. Also released in 1970 was Soyinka's first novel—*The Interpreters*, considered by many the first truly modern African novel.

Many of Soyinka's works reflect his concern with the tension between the old and the new in modern Africa. A strong believer in literary dialogue between cultures, he also is an outspoken advocate of human rights.

Flora Nwapa is an Ibo teacher and administrator who in 1966 became the first Nigerian woman to have a novel published. Titled *Efuru*, it was but the first of many works by Nwapa to be published. In 1977, after having achieved considerable success as a writer, Nwapa set up her own publishing firm—Tana Press. Her goal was to publish well-illustrated books for children about Nigerian life, books that incorporated folklore and fantasy. By 1984, Nwapa had published 12 stories, 7 of which she had written herself.

Nwapa believes that most women feel a need to work outside the home and to be financially independent. In her books, she often writes about women who are independent and who take charge of their own lives. Married and the mother of three children herself, she also focuses on the problems women face in marriage and with children.

TAKING ANOTHER LOOK

1. Who are Wole Soyinka and Flora Nwapa?
2. What do you think are some of their major achievements?

Chapter 3 Review

SUMMARY

Nigeria is Africa's most populous nation and is home to more than 250 different ethnic groups. There is diversity in religion as well, including Islam, Christianity, and traditional religions.

A British colony for many decades, Nigeria became independent in 1960. That same decade, it suffered a violent civil war. In the 1970's, the discovery of oil resulted in an economic boom that led the nation to depend on oil reserves. The falling off of those reserves led to economic and political problems.

Although most Nigerians still live in rural areas, urban migration has increased in recent years. This, as well as other changes, has severely affected the quality of life in major urban areas.

USING VOCABULARY

Imagine that you are a Nigerian diplomat. Use the two terms below in a speech to foreign visitors about the diversity of your nation.

compound   urban migration

REVIEWING FACTS

1. **Explain** why ethnic identity is important to many Nigerians.
2. **Discuss** how the Hausa of early Nigeria were affected by the Fulani.
3. **Specify** how long Nigeria was under British rule and the year in which it gained independence.
4. **Tell** where the majority of Nigerians live and how they make their living.
5. **List** the agricultural products grown by Nigerian farmers.

6. **Explain** why the Nigerian capital was moved from Lagos to Abuja.
7. **List** the main objectives of the National Youth Service Corps.

CRITICAL THINKING

1. **Synthesizing Information** What are some characteristics that might be used to describe the Nigerian people?
2. **Predicting Consequences** In what ways might Nigeria be different today if the Fulani had not defeated the Hausa in the 1800's?
3. **Drawing Conclusions** Why do many Nigerians who leave their villages or towns of birth not forget their roots?
4. **Making Comparisons** What are the three largest cities of modern Nigeria? In what ways are they the same? In what ways are they different?

ANALYZING CONCEPTS

1. **Diversity** Some experts believe that the forces that bind a nation together include a common language, a shared history, and a core region with which to identify. Based on this, do you think it is realistic to expect Nigerians to form a national identity? Explain.
2. **Change** The oil boom of the 1970's brought many changes to Nigeria. Do you think the changes were beneficial? Give reasons for your answer.

GEOGRAPHIC THEMES

1. **Location** Describe Nigeria in terms of its absolute and relative locations.
2. **Movement** Discuss some of the ways in which urban migration has impacted Nigeria.

Building Skills

CRITICAL THINKING

Analyzing Information

In studying different cultures, you must learn to analyze many kinds of written information. Social science information can be divided into two major types—primary sources and secondary sources. *Primary sources* are documents that were recorded by eyewitnesses to an event, such as letters, diaries, government documents, speeches, photographs, and news articles. *Secondary sources* are documents created after an event occurred. Secondary sources often combine information from many sources. For example, this textbook is a secondary source.

Primary and secondary sources offer different kinds of information. Secondary sources usually offer a broader view of events, while primary sources often give details of how individuals experienced events. Here are some steps to follow in analyzing information from primary and secondary sources:

- Determine whether a document is a primary or secondary source.
- Identify who created it and when.
- Examine the document and try to answer these questions: Who is it about? What is it about? When did it happen? Where did it happen? Why did it happen?

EXAMPLE

Reread Section 2 under the heading "Civil War" on pages 43–45. The first three paragraphs describe the civil war in Nigeria from 1967 to 1970. Because the author was not present at these events, this section is a secondary source.

Now look at the excerpt on pages 44–45. Is this a primary or secondary source? Why? *(primary; because the author experienced the events described)* Find the author's name, Elechi Amadi, in a footnote following the passage. What was the full title of Amadi's book? *(Sunset in Biafra: A Civil War Diary)* When was it published? *(1973)* In this passage, Amadi describes his efforts to locate his family during the war. What had happened to Amadi's family? *(They were scattered in many different areas.)* How did Amadi's family react when they saw him? *(overjoyed)*

PRACTICE

Read the excerpt enclosed in the box below. It was written by Uthman dan Fodio, an eighteenth-century Fulani who helped to lead a rebellion against the Hausa government. Then answer the following questions.

1. Is this a primary or secondary source?
2. Who was the author of this document?
3. Do you think the author is Muslim? Why or why not?
4. What policies of the Hausa government are named by the author?
5. Do you think the author approves or disapproves of the Hausa government? Why?

> *One of the ways of their [Hausa] government is to compel the people to serve in their armies, even though they are Muslims . . . and whosoever does not go, they impose upon him a money payment. . . . One of the ways of their government . . . is that if you have an adversary . . . and he . . . gives them some money, then your word will not be accepted by them, . . . unless you give them more than your adversary gave. One of the ways of their government is to shut the door in the face of the needy. One of the ways of their government is their forbidding to the worshippers of God part of that which is legal for them, such as the veiling of women, . . . and turbans for men. . . .*

Source: Writings of Uthman dan Fodio in *The African Past: Chronicles from Antiquity to Modern Times*, p. 324. Reprinted by permission of Curtis Brown, Ltd. Copyright © 1964 by Basil Davidson.

CHAPTER OUTLINE

1 Early Years

2 Apartheid

3 A Future in Question

People and Places to Know
the San, the Khoikhoi, Nelson Mandela, Cape of Good Hope, Boers, the Transvaal, African National Congress, Sharpeville, Soweto, *Inkatha*, Desmond Tutu, Frederik W. de Klerk

Key Terms to Define
apartheid, pass law, reserve, homeland, township

Objectives to Learn

1. **Summarize** the history of South Africa.
2. **Define** *apartheid* and assess its effect on South Africa.
3. **Discuss** the current political, economic, and social situation in South Africa.

Schoolchildren in Johannesburg, South Africa

South Africa

" We, the people of South Africa, declare for all our country and the world to know:
—that South Africa belongs to all who live in it, black and white, and that no government can justly claim authority unless it is based on the will of all the people; . . .
—that our country will never be prosperous or free until all our people live in brotherhood, enjoying equal rights and opportunities; . . .
The people shall govern!
Every man and woman shall have the right to vote for and to stand as a candidate for all bodies which make laws; . . .
The rights of the people shall be the same, regardless of race, colour or sex; . . .
All national groups shall have equal rights! . . .
All people shall have equal right to use their own languages, and to develop their own folk culture and customs; . . .
The people shall share in the country's wealth! . . .
The land shall be shared among those who work it! . . .
Freedom of movement shall be guaranteed to all who work on the land;
All shall have the right to occupy land wherever they choose; . . . All shall be equal before the law!
No one shall be imprisoned, deported or restricted without a fair trial; . . .
All shall enjoy equal human rights! . . .
There shall be work and security! . . . "

The above declaration is part of the "Freedom Charter" adopted unanimously at a "Congress of the People" in 1955. The close to 3000 delegates from all over South Africa who attended the Congress were protesting the official policy of **apartheid**, or "separate development" of the races. The white South African government, however, responded by calling the charter a treasonable document and arresting 156 of the people involved in its creation.

Source: "The Freedom Charter of South Africa." The United Nations Centre against Apartheid, 1979, pp. 3–7.

Under apartheid, South Africa's white minority ruled the non-white majority. Apartheid remained government policy for more than 40 years.

In 1991, following several years of government reforms designed to dismantle apartheid, South African president Frederik W. de Klerk announced, "Now everybody is free of [apartheid]. Now it belongs to history." However, much remains to be done. Many agree with the reporter who said that South Africa "still has a long way to go before apartheid will truly belong to history."

SECTION 1

Early Years

The original inhabitants of South Africa lived in the region as early as 6000 BC. One of the earliest groups, the San (SAHN), lived in small communities, hunting game and using the skins and furs for clothing. Another group, the Khoikhoi (KOY·KOY), were nomadic herders who kept large flocks of sheep and herds of cattle. Later, Bantu-speaking people from other parts of Africa, skilled in making iron farm tools and weapons, began moving into the area.

Nelson Mandela, South Africa's foremost black leader, describes what life was like before the Europeans came:

Then our people lived peacefully, under the democratic rule of their kings . . . ,

EXAMINING ART *Khoikhoi homes of bent saplings and woven grass mats were waterproof, easily transportable, and often arranged in a circle. Why did the Khoikhoi resist the Dutch settlers?*

and moved freely and confidently up and down the country. . . . Then the country was ours, in our own name and right. We occupied the land, the forests, the rivers; we extracted the mineral wealth beneath the soil and all the riches of this beautiful country. We set up and operated our own Government, we controlled our own armies and we organized our own trade and commerce. . . . The names of Dingane and Bambata, among the Zulus, . . . and others in the north, were mentioned as the pride and glory of the entire African nation.[1]

THE EUROPEANS

In 1652, the Dutch East India Company established a supply base at the Cape of Good Hope. Before long, European settlers began arriving and setting up businesses and farms, and the supply base became a thriving settlement known as Cape Colony.

At first, the San and the Khoikhoi were willing to trade with the settlers, who called themselves Afrikaners or Boers. But when the settlers began to demand more animals than the Africans were willing to part with and to take over Khoikhoi grazing land, the Africans rebelled. As the leader of the original Dutch expedition noted in his diary:

(The Khoikhoi) strongly insisted that we had been appropriating more and more of their land, which had been theirs all these centuries, and on which they had been accustomed to let their cattle graze, etc. They asked if they would be allowed to do such a thing supposing they went to Holland and they added: It would be of little consequence if you people stayed here at the fort, but you come right into the interior and select the best land for yourselves.[2]

---

[1] *Source:* Nelson Mandela. *No Easy Walk to Freedom.* Heinemann Educational Books Ltd., 1965, p. 147.

[2] *Source:* Jan Van Riebeek, as cited in *Apartheid, The Facts.* Mayibuye Centre, University of the Western Cape, 1983, p. 9.

EXAMINING PHOTOGRAPHS *In this late 1800's photo from the Transvaal, white prospectors and African workers are shown outside a mine dug into the 62-mile (100-kilometer) long, gold-bearing rock formation known as the Witwatersrand. The Witwatersrand gold fields remain the world's richest today. What resource first attracted white prospectors to the Transvaal?*

The Africans were no match for the settlers' guns. They were forced to earn their living as laborers for the Boers or to leave the area entirely.

Then, in 1806, the Dutch lost control of Cape Colony to the British. The Boers, who wanted to preserve their religion, culture, and way of life, resented the British and the changes they made. Much of the Boer way of life depended on slave labor. When the British abolished slavery, many Boers were financially ruined.

In 1836, to rid themselves of British rule and preserve their Afrikaner culture, thousands of Boers headed northeast into the interior of the country. On their journey, known as the Great Trek, they met with strong resistance from several African peoples who resented their trying to take over African land. In some cases, the competition for land turned into war. Although some African groups, like the Xhosa (KOH·suh) and the Zulu, fought fiercely, by the mid-1850's, the Boers were able to establish two independent republics—the Transvaal and the Orange Free State.

DIAMONDS, GOLD, AND WAR

In 1879, diamonds were discovered in the northeast in the Transvaal, and Africans were recruited to work in the diamond fields. Life in the fields was hard. Below, a European describes conditions at the time:

Hardly a more dreary existence can be imagined than that of the early days. . . . Not a single substantial dwelling afforded shelter from the burning sun: men lived under canvas, and the owner of an iron or wooden shanty was looked upon as a lord. . . . The dust and the flies, and worse, pervaded everywhere; they sat down with you to meals and escorted you to bed. The want of good food and pure water brought on disease, and many a poor fellow . . . succumbed to the fever. . . . Today [1875] all this is changed. . . . Kaffir [insulting name for Africans] labour is mainly employed in all the less responsible operations of the mines: in drilling holes for the dynamite cartridges, in picking and breaking up the ground in the claims and *trucking* it away. . . . For every three truckloads of ground daily hauled

EXAMINING ART *This 1901 illustration depicts a Boer surprise attack on British supply wagons during the Anglo-Boer War. The Boers used daring raids such as this because the British forces outnumbered them by some 500,000 to 88,000. Not until late in the war did the British gain the upper hand.* What was the result of the Anglo-Boer War?

out of the mine there is on an average one Kaffir labourer employed, and to every five Kaffirs there is one white overseer or artizan.

In 1886, gold was discovered in the same region. Suddenly, the territory became a valuable prize, and thousands of British colonists rushed in to stake their claims. The discoveries led to increased hostilities between the Boers, who ruled two territories, and the British, who also controlled two territories. In 1899, the hostility erupted into the Anglo-Boer War, which placed various African groups between the warring whites as both sides demanded aid and cooperation. The war, which lasted until 1902, resulted in the loss of many British, African, and Boer lives.

The British won the war, and in 1910 they combined the two Afrikaner republics and their two colonies into the Union of South Africa, a self-governing country within the British Empire.

Source: Theodore Reunert, "Diamond Mining at the Cape," as cited in *Colonial Rule in Africa.* Bruce Fetter (ed.). The University of Wisconsin Press, 1979, pp. 62–64.

SECTION 1 REVIEW

CHECKING FOR UNDERSTANDING
1. **Discuss** what life was like for Africans before the Europeans arrived.
2. **Explain** the reasons for the Great Trek.

CRITICAL THINKING
3. **Determining Cause and Effect** What effect did the discovery of gold and diamonds have on South Africa?

SECTION 2

Apartheid

Many Afrikaners believed in the superiority of the white race. A new South African constitution adopted in 1910 supported that belief. As a result, conditions for non-whites—especially blacks—worsened.

In 1912, in an effort to better their condition, blacks established the African National Congress (ANC). Under the slogan "We are one people," it worked to unite Africans around the country. But, despite the ANC's

Africa

THE WHITES OF SOUTH AFRICA

The white community of South Africa is divided into two main groups—Afrikaners and English-speakers. Although the two groups have worked together to consolidate their control over the country, feelings between them often are strained. As can be seen in the comments below—the first by an Afrikaner and the second by an English-speaker—their differences are deep-rooted in history:

One of the events that most affected our lives was the Anglo-Boer War. . . . My dad and twenty-two pals started a little army up in the north and pinned down ten thousand British troops. . . . My dad and his men knew the country . . . , and they knew the farmers who lived in the area. The farmers were all on their side. Their fathers and grandfathers had trekked—many of them had died on the trek—and now they were not about to give up what their fathers and grandfathers had died for. My dad and his pals were finally captured. . . . My dad spent the last six months of the war in a British jail. When he was about to be released, the commanding officer said, 'Let's forgive and forget, Mr. van der Merwe.' *My dad looked at him for a long time and finally said, 'Forgive, I can. Christ taught us to forgive. Forget, I can't. It's history.' And that's what he told us, his three sons.*

When my eldest brother went off to varsity [college], my dad told him, 'You grew up in an Afrikaans area. You have learned to hate the English, but they are here to stay. My job was to shoot them. Your job is to live with them.'[1]

I lived in the eastern Transvaal for five years before I married Duncan. It was the loneliest time in my life, but I got to know the Afrikaans mentality. They talk about the trek and the 1900 war and the Zulu Wars and the suffering of the Afrikaans people as though no one else has ever suffered.

I was a young girl then, living alone, and not once . . . was I invited to an Afrikaans home. I was the outsider, the enemy, I suppose. They have never forgiven us for winning the Boer War, and I don't think they ever will. It runs in their blood. You can't understand them without understanding the war. It has given them an inferiority complex. They don't like us. They blame us for their problems. They don't consider us true South Africans. They say we always call England home. That makes me mad. . . .

. . . I have a strong feeling for England, but I have never been there and I do not consider England my home. I am a South African, and my children are South African. I love my country.[2]

[1] *Source:* Hennie, from WAITING: THE WHITES OF SOUTH AFRICA by Vincent Crapanzano. Copyright © 1985 by Vincent Crapanzano. Reprinted by permission of Random House, Inc.

[2] *Source:* Carol Reid, from WAITING: THE WHITES OF SOUTH AFRICA by Vincent Crapanzano. Copyright © 1985 by Vincent Crapanzano. Reprinted by permission of Random House, Inc.

DRAWING CONCLUSIONS

1. What two groups make up South Africa's white community?
2. What lasting effect has the Boer War had on white South Africans?

efforts, laws continued to be passed that were designed to separate the races and restrict the activities of non-whites.

In 1948, the Afrikaner Nationalist Party won control of the government. During the election campaign, its leader, D. F. Malan, had promised that if he won, he would preserve a "pure white race." In his victory speech, he proclaimed, "Today, South Africa belongs to us once more, for the first time since Union. May God grant that it will always remain so."

After the election, apartheid became official government policy, and the population was divided into four racial categories—Africans, Whites, Coloreds (those of mixed European and African descent), and Asians. Under apartheid, most whites enjoyed a high standard of living, while most non-whites suffered from poverty and discrimination.

POLICY AND PRACTICES

Apartheid proved to be particularly harsh on blacks. They could not vote or participate in the political processes of their own nation. They could not travel freely. Until 1986, under a series of **pass laws** dating back to the early 1900's, all blacks over the age of 15 had to carry passbooks that indicated such information as place and date of birth, race category, and place of employment.

The pass laws also restricted where black South Africans could work and live. Living restrictions came into being in 1913 with the Native Land Act. It prevented Africans from buying or owning land outside small areas known as **reserves**. Thirty-seven years later, the Groups Area Act was passed. It divided 13.7 percent of South Africa's land into 10 **homelands**, or *bantustans*, for the black population. The rest of South Africa was reserved for whites. Asians and Coloreds were allowed to live in segregated areas within

"white" South Africa. Blacks already living in urban areas were removed to locations outside the cities, known today as **townships**. The townships were supposed to be stopping places for Africans until they were moved to the homelands. But, by the 1990's, they were home to almost 14 million black South Africans.

The government's goal was to have each homeland become an independent nation. Beginning in 1976, it declared four of them independent states under the leadership of selected black chiefs. Although no country in

EXAMINING PHOTOGRAPHS
The man being carried off in a truck is one of about 3.5 million black South Africans forcibly relocated by the government between 1960 and 1985. What law established the homelands?

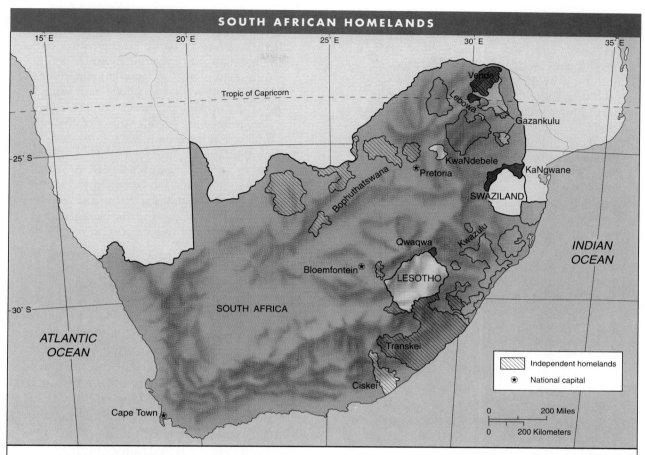

SOUTH AFRICAN HOMELANDS

15° E   20° E   25° E   30° E   35° E

Tropic of Capricorn

Venda
Lebowa
Gazankulu
25° S
KwaNdebele
Pretoria ✱
KaNgwane
Bophuthatswana
SWAZILAND
INDIAN
OCEAN
Qwaqwa
Kwazulu
Bloemfontein ✱
LESOTHO
30° S
SOUTH AFRICA
ATLANTIC
OCEAN
Transkei

Independent homelands
✱ National capital

Ciskei

Cape Town ✱

0   200 Miles
0   200 Kilometers

🌐 **EXAMINING MAPS** *The South African government set up the homelands along ethnic lines: Transkei—mostly Xhosa speaking; Bophuthatswana—mostly Tswana speaking; Venda—mostly Venda speaking; Ciskei—mostly Xhosa speaking; Lebowa—mostly North Sotho; Gazankulu—mostly Shangaan; Kwa Ndebele—mostly Ndebele; Ka Ngwane—mostly Swazi; Qwaqwa—mostly South Sotho; Kwa Zulu—mostly Zulu.* Why were the homelands established?

the world recognized their independence, the Africans living in them lost their South African citizenship. This caused serious repercussions in the African community.

Africans living in homelands have had to overcome many problems. For example, although black workers are the backbone of the economy, most economic activity takes place in white areas. This forces those who live in the homelands to become migrant laborers. This, in turn, creates a problem for the families they leave behind. As follows, a woman who lives in the Lebowa homeland,

about 300 miles (480 kilometers) from Johannesburg, comments:

We were brought here by my husband Obed. He works in town, in Johannesburg. He only sends me 40 rand [South African money] because where he works he doesn't get enough money. . . . Then I go to the store. I buy a big bag of mealie meal [corn meal] for 15 rand and I buy three bags of coal. I buy sugar and soap and that's the end of that money. If the children get sick then I go outside to borrow money from neighbours. Here there's no work, we just sit around.

It's very bad here, nothing grows. It doesn't rain. When you have planted nothing grows. We don't know what to do. I don't like it here but I stay because I don't know where to go. Here there is no food. . . .

[Obed] only comes once a year. . . . When he comes everybody's so happy. The children run to meet him at the bus-stop. Some of them cry and when he asks why they are crying they say it is with joy. They never know when he is coming. We wish that we can just stay with him, if the white people wouldn't refuse me, staying with him for about three months to be able to talk and plan things and discuss everything together.

RESISTANCE

Black African resistance to white encroachment on African land and infringement of African rights has existed since Europeans first settled on the Cape. Although the strategies have changed over the years, the goal—basic rights for all—has not. Below, an African explains the reason his people have been discontent:

The white oppressors have stolen our land. They have destroyed our families. They have taken for themselves the best that there is in our rich country and have left us the worst. They have the fruits and the riches. We have the backbreaking toil and the poverty.

We burrow into the belly of the earth to dig out gold, diamonds, coal, uranium. The white oppressors and foreign investors grab all this wealth. It is used for their enrichment and to buy arms to suppress and kill us.

In the factories, on the farms, on the railways, wherever you go, the hard, dirty, dangerous, badly paid jobs are ours. The best jobs are for whites only.

In our own land we have to carry passes; we are restricted and banished while the white oppressors move about freely.

Our homes are hovels; those of the whites are luxury mansions, flats, and farmsteads.

There are not enough schools for our children; the standard of education is low, and we have to pay for it. But the government uses our taxes and the wealth we create to provide free education for white children.

SHARPEVILLE The struggle over land and political rights has led to social unrest and violence. In 1960, blacks in the township of Sharpeville demonstrated against the pass laws. The demonstration, which resulted in the death of 69 blacks, led the government to pass harsher laws, jail people without trial, and outlaw such anti-apartheid organizations as the ANC. These actions convinced many blacks that their goals could not be achieved peacefully or nonviolently.

The following year, the ANC, which had gone underground, formed a military wing called *Umkhonto We Sizwe*, "Spear of the Nation." Led by activist lawyer Nelson Mandela, it swore to oppose the government by violent means. Following his arrest, Mandela explained why *Umkhonto* had been formed:

How many more Sharpevilles would there be in the history of our country? And how many more Sharpevilles could the country stand without violence and terror becoming the order of the day? And what would happen to our people when that stage was reached? In the long run

Source: From AFRICAN CONTEMPORARY RECORD, ANNUAL SURVEY AND DOCUMENTS: 1968–1969, Colin Legunn and John Drysdale (New York: Holmes & Meier Publishers, Inc. 1969, pg. 721) Copyright © 1969 by Africa Publishing Corporation. Reprinted by permission of the publisher.

Source: We Make Freedom: Women in South Africa, Beata Lipman and Pandora, an imprint of Harper Collins Publishers Limited.

we felt certain we must succeed, but at what cost to ourselves and the rest of the country? And if this happened, how could Black and White ever live together again in peace and harmony? These were the problems that faced us, and these were our decisions.

Experience convinced us that rebellion would offer the Government limitless opportunities [to] . . . slaughter . . . our people. But it was precisely because the soil of South Africa is already drenched with the blood of innocent Africans that we felt it our duty to make preparations . . . to use force in order to defend ourselves against force. If war were inevitable, we wanted the fight to be conducted on terms most favourable to our people. The fight which held out prospects best for us and the least risk of life to both sides was guerrilla warfare.

SOWETO In 1976, thousands of students in the township of Soweto peacefully protested a new regulation that made Afrikaans the language of instruction in school. When the unarmed students were fired upon by the police, hundreds were killed. This led to more protests, which left hundreds more dead and forced many young Africans into exile. Below, an African woman describes the effect the situation had on her family:

In 1976 I had three children in high school in Soweto: two were doing their final year. . . . The boy was very active—politically active; the girl in a smaller way. . . . We, as parents, got no sleep—the police came at eight, or at ten, at twelve or even at three in the morning: all this just to look for him. . . .

They would ransack the house every time, looking for him: they'd look under the bed, even in the fridge. Everyone would be woken—it was terrible. So many children were arrested but mine never

Source: Nelson Mandela. *No Easy Walk to Freedom.* Heinemann Educational Books Ltd., 1965, pp. 173–174.

EXAMINING PHOTOGRAPHS *The 1976 Soweto uprising led to clashes between blacks and the police that lasted more than a year. What action started the uprising?*

were. The boy was being sought, but . . . he disappeared completely. We only realised when I was called to the police station to be questioned: . . . —they wanted to know if I had relatives in . . . Zimbabwe or other places. When I said I didn't have any they said that as soon as I heard from him I must come and let them know. . . .

Eventually I heard from a friend that they'd gone: it took over six months before we knew where they were. We were relieved that they had gone—if they'd stayed around we might have buried them a long time ago. . . .

It's heartbreaking to lose your children. Each time you dish up, you find that you're missing two plates on the table. . . . I'm only hoping that one day, somehow, somewhere, I'll be able to see [them].

A little over a year later, global attention again focused on South Africa. After anti-apartheid organizations had been banned in the 1960's, South African blacks had formed new organizations. Known as the

Source: We Make Freedom: Women in South Africa, Beata Lipman and Pandora, an imprint of Harper Collins Publishers Limited.

EXAMINING PHOTOGRAPHS *During the 1980's funeral processions often became mass demonstrations against apartheid.* **What happened in black townships during the 1980's?**

Black Consciousness Movement, they emphasized the pride and cultural heritage of the African people. In 1977, Steve Biko, a movement leader, was detained and held in solitary confinement. When his death from beatings by the police went unpunished, the outraged global community condemned the South African government. It responded by banning 2 newspapers and 18 Black Consciousness organizations.

CHECKING FOR UNDERSTANDING
1. **Define** pass law, reserve, homeland, township.
2. **Relate** what happened as a result of events in Sharpeville and Soweto.

CRITICAL THINKING
3. **Determining Cause and Effect** Discuss how apartheid became official government policy in South Africa and the ways in which it affected non-whites.

SECTION 3

A Future in Question

The 1980's was for South Africans a time of violent change, marked by a mixture of reform, revolt, repression, and resistance. As anti-apartheid sentiment grew, so did demonstrations, protests, and police response. In the black townships, unrest—and violence—accelerated. Many black South Africans found themselves in different camps politically. Some supported the beliefs and methods of the African National Congress (ANC). Others backed those of *Inkatha,* a predominantly Zulu movement headed by Chief Mangosuthu Buthelezi (mahn·gah· SOO·thoo Boo·teh·lay·zee), chief minister of the Kwa Zulu homeland.

In 1984, the leader of the Anglican Church in South Africa, Archbishop Desmond M. Tutu, won the Nobel Peace Prize for his efforts to bring about nonviolent change. In 1986, he called on the nations of the West to impose sanctions on South Africa. The United States responded by banning South African imports and loans and investments in South Africa. The South African government also responded. Bowing to the pressure, it ended the pass laws and offered blacks an advisory role in government.

Other reforms also came about during the 1980's. No longer could people be removed to the homelands by force. No longer was it against the law for people of different races to marry. Some black trade unions were legalized, and some blacks were allowed to own their own homes, have their families live with them, and change jobs. Asians and Coloreds were allowed limited representation in the government.

During this period, not all South African whites supported apartheid. Some agreed with the following view expressed by an Afrikaner farmer:

God put us all on this earth to live to-gether, . . . and that means we'll have to learn to do it or perish. 'Apartheid' is an evil because it sets men against men, builds barriers where there were none and gets in the way of natural processes of change and growth that, prior to 1948, were well on their way to creating a new kind of society in this country. Now I don't delude myself that I have to love the black man or the Colored. Liking him will do. Because if I want respect for my-self and my own kind then I must give it to others. It's that simple. During the Sec-ond World War, . . . I learned . . . that men of all kinds can live and be together, regardless, and like each other. Death taught us a lot about valuing life and its variety, you see, so to come home from a war like that to find hate and separation preached in my own country disgusted me. And to see a country as gifted as this turned into a fortress of race sickens me. No—it's wrong, this business of 'apartheid.' Wrong because it's unnatural. And unless we take down within the next few years the whole ugly structure it has taken thirty years to build up, it will de-stroy everything we have managed to cre-ate here and with it, South Africa.

Source: Barbara Villet. *Blood River.* Everest House/Dodd, Mead & Company, Inc., 1982, pp. 56–57.

In 1989, Frederik W. de Klerk became pres-ident of South Africa. Announcing that "apartheid must go" and that "discrimina-tion must be eliminated," he lifted the long-standing ban on the ANC and other black opposition groups, released Nelson Mandela from prison, and repealed the law that re-quired segregation in public places.

Early in 1991, de Klerk announced plans to end all apartheid racial separation laws and proposed a "multiparty conference" to con-sider a new constitution. By the end of the year, South Africans no longer were required to register as white, black, Asian, or colored;

citizens of all races were told they could live in any area of the country they chose to; and blacks were allowed to own land anywhere in South Africa. Hospitals were opened to all races, and segregation was outlawed in some state schools. In addition, an agree-ment aimed at ending fighting among the various black organizations was signed by the South African government and the ANC, *Inkatha,* and 20 smaller black groups.

Some whites, however, still favor varying degrees of apartheid. One of the ways they have managed to keep it alive is discussed in the newspaper article that follows:

White town councils across the Transvaal and Orange Free State are recoiling in hor-ror at the demise of the Separate Ameni-ties Act, which not only removes racial discrimination at public facilities but also makes it an offense to bar anyone on the grounds of race. Searching for new ways of keeping blacks at bay, most have in-voked 1939 legislation that permits them to charge non-residents for use of their facilities.

If you are black, it will cost you $190 to borrow a book from the library in the rural Transvaal town of Bethal. Should a black person want to take a dip in the public pool in Sasolburg, it will also cost him or her $190. The charge officially cov-ers the cost of a season ticket, but the price is prohibitive, and designed to be so.

Vanderbijl Park, also in the Transvaal, is typical of many towns resisting integra-tion. Its largely blue-collar population of 75,000 joined the pro-apartheid Conserva-tive Party when government reforms began. The "Whites Only" signs may be gone, but residents still want segregation.

"We certainly expect a number of whites to be unhappy at having to share any facilities," said Petrie Lauw, the town clerk. One of those is Elna Kourie. She was adamant that her children were going

nowhere near a swimming pool used by blacks. "AIDS," she said. "Those blacks have AIDS, and they'll give it to everyone else. It'll get into the pool. And if they don't have AIDS, they'll just use the place as a bath." Her attitude is common among Vanderbijl Park's whites, which explains why even members of the reform-minded National Party contributed to a unanimous council vote in favor of limiting access to the pool.

There are at least 20 councils taking such measures and many more considering them. Some councils are threatening to close facilities rather than share them if the residents-only rules are overturned by the courts.

High expectations for peaceful change were further crushed by the outbreak of violence between rival political groups within the black townships. Many black South Africans blamed the de Klerk government for stirring up the troubles and called for an immediate end to white rule in South Africa. Tensions were also heightened when police and defense forces in the homeland of Ciskei

opened fire on thousands of peaceful demonstrators, killing 28.

De Klerk's government denied involvement in stirring up unrest, but it began to yield to pressure and announced an overhaul of police forces. This cleared the way for the appointment of the first black police generals in South African history. Meanwhile, the violence hindered peace talks on South Africa's political future between the government and the ANC. Observers, however, believed that despite setbacks both sides were committed to the negotiating process.

Source: From "Keeping Blacks Out," excerpted from "Indian Express" New Delhi in *World Press Review*, April 1991, page 22.

SECTION 3 REVIEW

CHECKING FOR UNDERSTANDING
1. **Name** the two major black political groups in South Africa.
2. **List** the reforms made by the South African government in the 1980's and 1990's.

CRITICAL THINKING
3. **Analyzing Information** A political commentator once said that South Africa was a country where you "hoped on Monday but despaired on Tuesday." Explain how this statement applies to South Africa during the 1980's and 1990's.

Government

THE END OF APARTHEID

Eighty-six percent of South Africa's voters turned out for the March 17, 1992, whites-only referendum on ending apartheid. The following comments reflect some of South Africans' views regarding the referendum and its outcome.

FOCUSING ON THE ISSUE Based on the information in the chapter and the views expressed in the comments, write a short paper explaining why you agree or disagree with the following statement made by Harry Schwartz, the South African ambassador to the United States, soon after the referendum: "The message is that white South Africa is prepared to move toward democracy."

I voted "Yes." It's the only thing to do for the future of this country. My (black) workmates don't have the vote and I must vote for them.

Construction worker
Chris Bakker, Johannesburg

We were brought up believing whites and blacks should live apart, and that's probably the way we'll die.

C.P. Katzen, Johannesburg

I am so glad. I was afraid the apartheid people would win and there would have been war. Now we can all be brothers and sisters.

Mary Mbuza, Cape Town

The moves taken by whites have been such that confidence is being created. We have a beautiful country and people are starting to take off their masks and we are starting to see the true colors. People are saying we can for once trust a white.

Playwright Gibson Kente,
Soweto

A lot of people are apprehensive about the future, but they thought a yes vote was a better bet than returning to the past. Professor of Political Science David Welsh, University of Cape Town[1]

I will be voting to break with racism; to break the link—

hopefully once and for all—between skin color and economic privilege. In so doing I will also be liberating myself from racial guilt.

Corporation executive
Bobby Godsell,
Johannesburg[2]

I don't have that much hope for this. We haven't got our freedom yet.

Daniel Khumalo, Soweto

It still showed that we still don't have a right to vote, and the white people are still the people who will decide whether to make a democratic country or not. But now we can see that whites are serious about sharing power. And we can see that the majority of whites who we thought were our enemies are now on our side.

Law student Mandla
Ndlazi, Soweto[3]

[2] *Source:* The Embassy of South Africa. *South Africa Update.* Number 2, 1992.

[1] *Source:* "Voters flock to the polls in S. Africa" in *The Columbus Dispatch,* March 18, 1992, p. 1A.

[3] *Source:* Christopher S. Wren. "Many in Soweto Begin To Trust Whites More" in *The New York Times,* Sunday, March 22, 1992, p. 8.

Chapter 4 Review

SUMMARY

African societies flourished in South Africa during ancient times. In the 1600's, European settlers—Afrikaners or Boers—arrived. Soon they were in competition for land with Africans. Then, in the late 1800's, the discovery of diamonds attracted many British colonists. A war between the British and the Boers led to the founding of the Union of South Africa in 1910.

Many Afrikaners believed in the superiority of the white race. When their party won the national election in 1948, it made apartheid official. Under apartheid, which proved especially harsh on Africans, all non-whites were deprived of civil rights. Although demonstrations, pressure from other nations, and economic necessity finally led the South African government to begin dismantling apartheid, many issues are unresolved.

USING VOCABULARY

Imagine that you are a black South African teenager. Use the terms below in a letter you are writing to a cousin in the United States.

apartheid   pass law
reserve   township
homeland

REVIEWING FACTS

1. **Discuss** how the Africans reacted to the coming of Europeans.
2. **Arrange** in chronological order major events in South Africa from 1652 to 1948.
3. **Indicate** when *Umkhonto We Sizwe* was formed, who formed it, and why it was formed.
4. **State** how the African National Congress was established.

5. **Discuss** some of the restrictions apartheid placed on black South Africans, and how blacks reacted to these restrictions.
6. **Tell** what led to the Black Consciousness Movement and what it emphasized.

CRITICAL THINKING

1. **Recognizing Ideologies** What Afrikaner belief resulted in apartheid?
2. **Analyzing Information** An African chief once referred to homelands as "the white man's garbage can." Give reasons why you do or do not think this is a fair appraisal.
3. **Demonstrating Reasoned Judgment** For many, the Freedom Charter was a major political event in the history of South Africa. Give reasons why you agree or disagree with this view.
4. **Predicting Consequences** Nelson Mandela once stated that "there will never be peace in this country until the principle of majority rule is accepted." How might majority rule impact the whites of South Africa?

ANALYZING CONCEPTS

1. **Environment** Explain how discovery of gold and diamonds changed South Africa's history.
2. **Human Rights** According to one white South African author, "apartheid itself cannot be equated with injustice—it rests on too sound a basis for that." Present an argument to support or to refute this.

GEOGRAPHIC THEMES

1. **Movement** How did the establishment of homelands affect many black workers?
2. **Region** What official government policy made South Africa unique among the nations of Africa during modern times?

Drawing Conclusions

Imagine yourself in this situation: On returning home from school, you discover that a favorite cassette tape is missing. One month ago, when a similar incident occurred, you discovered that your brother had borrowed a tape without asking permission. You draw the conclusion that your brother has done so again.

Drawing conclusions is the process of using facts and your own knowledge, experience, and insight to form judgments about events. It allows you to understand ideas that are not stated directly. However, beware of drawing the *wrong* conclusion. To avoid this, find additional information to prove or disprove your conclusion.

Use the following steps in drawing conclusions:

- Review the facts that are stated directly.
- Use your own knowledge, experience, and insight to form conclusions about these facts.
- Find information that proves or disproves your conclusions.

EXAMPLE

We can apply these steps to the example of the missing cassette tape. The fact or evidence was that your tape was missing. You also knew that your brother has previously borrowed tapes without asking. So, you decided that he had probably borrowed this one too. To prove or disprove your conclusion, you could look for the tape in your brother's room, or ask your brother if he borrowed it. If neither of these supports your conclusion, you must draw another one. Perhaps you have lost the tape or loaned it to someone and forgotten about it.

PRACTICE

Read the following passage by Ellen Khuzwayo, a black social worker from Gazankulu, South Africa. Then answer these questions.

1. What medical problems existed when Ellen Khuzwayo arrived in Gazankulu?
2. What were the problems with the local water supply?
3. What conclusion can you draw about the causes of medical problems in Gazankulu?
4. Upon what evidence did you base this conclusion?
5. Do you think Ellen Khuzwayo helped the women of Gazankulu solve some of their problems? Why or why not?
6. How could you test the accuracy of this conclusion?
7. What conclusion can you draw about how Ellen Khuzwayo's work changed the community of Gazankulu?

> *I got there* [Gazankulu] *in the drought season.* Two of every three children were stricken with kwashiorkor [disease caused by malnutrition]. *There was gastroenteritis* [disease of the stomach and intestines] . . . *I didn't know where to start . . . I plunged in, talking nutrition to people who had no food. They were lost, but so was I at first. . . . I got there and I said, "Look ladies, maybe we should start by growing vegetables . . . here are seeds. . . ."* They said, 'There's no water'—*they were drawing water from a dam a mile to half-a-mile* [1.6 to .8 kilometers] *away. . . . This was not clean water and yet they used this water for drinking too . . . , the goats were a menace to whatever they were going to grow. We had to sit down and devise a means—we said, 'Look, we can get some bush and use it as a fence.' Very few responded at first . . . we put our seeds in and, strangely enough, the crops came up . . . it was like a miracle during that time . . . then we talked about powdered milk. . . . We clubbed together as women and went on bulk buying and we got milk through these clubs; . . . .*

Source: We Make Freedom: Women in South Africa, Beata Lipman and Pandora, an imprint of Harper Collins Publishers Limited.

6 9

CHAPTER OUTLINE

People and Places to Know
the Swahili, Jomo Kenyatta, Kenya African Union, the Kikuyu, Central Province, Nairobi, Daniel T. arap Moi, KANU, Great Rift Valley, the Maasai

Key Terms to Define
uhuru, harambee, lingua franca

Objectives to Learn

1. **Describe** the effect of foreign influences in Kenya's history and development.
2. **Recognize** the importance of the land to the Kenyan people.
3. **Explain** the challenges Kenya faces in adapting to change.

Kenyan landscape

Kenya

> "Where did the land go? . . ."
>
> I am old now, but I too have asked that question in waking and sleeping. I've said "What happened, O Murungu [African god], to the land which you gave to us? Where, O Creator, went our promised land?" At times, I've wanted to cry or harm my body to drive away the curse that removed us from the ancestral lands. I ask, "Have you left your children naked, O Murungu?"
>
> I'll tell you. There was a big drought sent to the land by evil ones who must have been jealous of the prosperity of the children of the Great One. . . . The sun burnt freely. Plague came to the land. Cattle died and people shrank in size. Then came the white man as had long been prophesied by Mugo wa Kibiro, that Gikuyu seer of old. He came from the country of ridges far away from here. Mugo had told the people of the coming of the white man. . . . So the white man came and took the land. But at first, not the whole of it.
>
> Then came the war. It was the first big war. . . . All of us were taken by force. We made roads and cleared the forest to make it possible for the warring white man to move more quickly. The war ended. We were all tired. We came home worn out but very ready for whatever the British might give us as a reward. But, more than this, we wanted to go back to the soil and court it to yield, to create, not to destroy. But ng'o! The land was gone.
>
> My father and many others had been moved from our ancestral lands.

*I*n the above excerpt from the work of a Kenyan author, an elderly man laments the loss of African land and asks the god Murungu why this has happened. His question is the same one asked by Kenyans for many years. Land has been an important issue for the 42 black ethnic groups that make up nearly 99 percent of the nation's population. This is especially true for the Kikuyu (ky·KOO·yoo), the majority ethnic group.

The East African nation of Kenya has had a long and rich history. After a relatively short

Source: Ngugi wa Thiong'o. Weep Not, Child. Heinemann, 1964, p. 25.

period of British colonial rule, it finally emerged as an independent nation in 1963. Since that time, Kenya has prospered economically and has raised the standard of living of the people.

The path, however, has not always been smooth. Although Kenya ranks among the most prosperous and well-educated countries in Africa, it is not without problems. Still, says one observer, "there is an impressive *uhuru* (oo·HOO·roo) or independent spirit among the people" and "an astonishing *harambee* (har·ahm·bay) or pulling together spirit."

SECTION 1

Foreign Rule to Independence

By the 1000's AD, foreign influence was being felt in East Africa as Arab traders introduced their religion of Islam and its customs to the Bantu-speaking people along the coast. In time, some of them married Africans. Eventually a new people and culture known as Swahili (swah·HEE·lee) emerged. Their language, a mixture of Bantu and Arabic, became a *lingua franca*, or common language, that was used for trade up and down the coast. It also was used in the Swahili cities that flourished until the 1300's.

The next group of foreigners to show interest in the coastal areas was the Portuguese, who wanted a port of call on the way to India. By 1507, they had taken the coastal cities, wrested the gold trade from the Swahili, and established supply posts. By the late 1600's, however, their power had declined. They were defeated by Arabs, who kept control of the coast for close to 200 years.

The Arabs, the Swahili, and the Portuguese all had confined their control to the coastal areas. In 1895, however, the British penetrated the interior. Within two years, they had control of most of present-day Kenya. Believing there was great wealth in Uganda, which they also controlled, they set out immediately to build a railway from there to the coast. Much of the work on the railway was done by laborers recruited from India, and after it was completed, 7000 of them stayed in Kenya. The railway headquarters was established in a few tents about halfway between the port city of Mombasa and Lake Victoria. In later years, because of its location, Nairobi came to be known as "the place of cold waters."

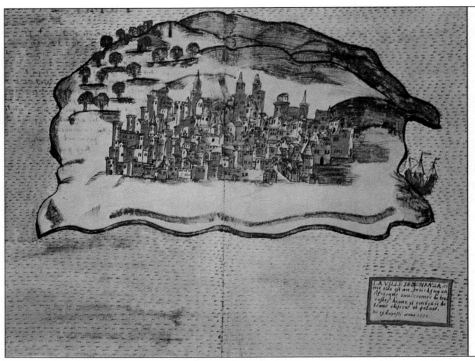

EXAMINING ART
After the Portuguese seized the Swahili island-city of Mombasa, they built the fortified town pictured in this early French drawing. Mombasa became the central base from which the Portuguese controlled the coastal Indian Ocean trade. **Who defeated the Portuguese?**

The British soon realized that not enough goods were coming out of Uganda to make the railway profitable. So they recruited British settlers to raise coffee and tea for export and to turn Kenya into a "white man's country." The settlers were attracted to the highlands by the temperate climate, which was much like that of their European homeland. For years to come, the millions of acres that they staked out for their plantations were known as the "White Highlands."

The settlers used African labor to work their plantations. Most Africans had no choice but to work for the British. The British government had levied a tax on them. Since they were not allowed to compete with the plantation owners by growing cash crops, they had to work the plantations in order to earn the money to pay the tax.

EARLY NATIONALIST MOVEMENT

By the 1920's, the Europeans not only controlled the government but owned the best farmland as well. The Africans, meanwhile, grew more dissatisfied. Finally, in 1929, a young Kikuyu leader named Jomo Kenyatta (JOH·moh ken·YAH·tuh) went to Great Britain to argue on behalf of the Africans.

Kenyatta remained in England off and on until 1946, when he returned home to assume the leadership of the Kenya African Union (KAU), a political party that had been formed two years earlier. One of the KAU's chief goals was to gain Africans access to their original land in the highlands. Below, an African whose family's lands had been taken over by the British, remembers the first KAU rally he attended:

It was July 26, 1952 sand I sat in the Nyeri Showgrounds packed in with a crowd of over 30,000 people. The Kenya African Union was holding a rally and it was presided over by Jomo Kenyatta. He talked first of LAND. In the Kikuyu country, nearly half of the people are landless and have an earnest desire to acquire land so that they can have something to live on. Kenyatta pointed out that there was a lot of land lying idly in the country and only the wild game enjoy that, while Africans are starving of hunger. The White Highland, he went on, together with the forest reserves which were under the Government control, were taken from the Africans unjustly. . . .

. . . He asked the crowd to show by hands that they wanted more land. Each person raised both his hands. And when he asked those who did not want land to show their hands, nobody raised. . . .

The other point that Jomo Kenyatta stressed . . . was African FREEDOM. He raised the KAU flag to symbolize African Government. He said Kenya must be freed from colonial exploitation. Africans must be given freedom of speech, freedom of movement, freedom of worship and freedom of press. Explaining this to the people, he said that with the exception of freedom of worship, the other freedoms are severely limited with respect to the Africans. . . .

I was struck by . . . [the KAU's flag's] red colour in the middle of black and green, which signified blood. . . .

When Kenyatta returned on the platform for the third time . . . he explained the flag. He said, 'Black is to show that this is for black people. Red is to show that the blood of an African is the same colour as the blood of a European, and green is to show that when we were given this country by God it was green, fertile and good but now you see the green is below the red and is suppressed.'. . . Special Branch [government] agents were at the meeting . . . so Kenyatta couldn't speak his mind directly. What he said must mean that our fertile lands (green) could only be regained by the blood (red) of the African (black). That was it! The

black was separated from the green by red: the African could only get to his land through blood.

RESISTANCE AND REVOLT

As more and more African farmers lost their land, a group of Kikuyu decided to take action. They formed a secret movement, which the Europeans called Mau Mau. The movement's chief goal was to gain back the ancestral lands of the Kikuyu. The movement also sought greater unity among Kenya's Africans and demanded new government policies to improve the welfare of Africans. Those who wanted to join the movement and fight for freedom had to take an oath, or pledge, like the one that follows:

If I reveal our secrets, let this oath turn against me;

Source: Donald Barnett and Karari Njama. *Mau Mau From Within: Autobiography and Analysis of Kenya's Peasant Revolution.* Monthly Review Press, 1966, pp. 73–75. Copyright © 1966 by Donald Barnett and Karari Njama. Reprinted by permission of Monthly Review Foundation.

If I spy falsely, let this oath against me; . . .

If I leave any comrade in danger, let this oath turn against me;

If I kill a leader to gain promotion or a higher post, let this oath turn against me;

If I surrender before we have gained our Independence, let this oath turn against me;

If I see a weapon of the enemy and fear to take it, let this oath turn against me;

If I hand over my gun or our books to the enemy, let this oath turn against me;

If I kill a fellow soldier out of enmity, let this oath turn against me;

If I betray our country or our nationalists, let this oath turn against me.

Source: Waruhiu Itote (General China). *Mau Mau General.* East African Publishing House, 1967, pp. 275–276.

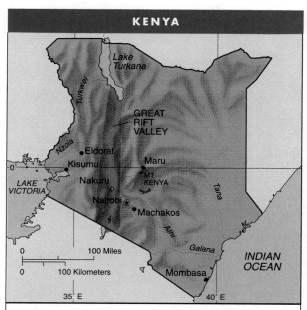

KENYA

EXAMINING MAPS *Kenya consists of three distinct geographic regions: a tropical coastal strip on the Indian Ocean, dry inland plains, and fertile highlands.* In which geographic region is Nairobi, Kenya's capital, located?

EXAMINING PHOTOGRAPHS *The Parliament Building (with clock tower), Kenyatta Conference Center, and Hilton Hotel are identifiable landmarks of downtown Nairobi.* Why was Nairobi first settled?

In 1953, the British declared a state of emergency and placed almost 80,000 Africans in detention camps. Kenyatta was accused of leading the movement and was jailed. African resistance continued until 1956, when the colonial government yielded and began the process toward Kenyan self-government. In 1963, after free elections, Kenya became an independent nation under the leadership of Jomo Kenyatta.

SECTION 1 REVIEW

CHECKING FOR UNDERSTANDING
1. **Define** *lingua franca.*
2. **Discuss** why British settlers came to Kenya and how their coming affected the Africans.

CRITICAL THINKING
3. **Expressing Problems Clearly** What problems did Jomo Kenyatta and the KAU want to solve?

SECTION 2
The Way of Life

Today, the Kenyan population is made up of people of many different heritages and backgrounds. The largest ethnic group is the Kikuyu, followed by the Luhya, the Kamba, the Luo, and the Kalenjin. More than one-half the people are Christians. About 40 percent practice traditional religions.

THE CITIES

Kenya has a number of major cities. The largest and most important is Nairobi, the nation's capital since 1905. With the following words, a visitor gives her impressions of this city whose diversity mirrors that of Kenya itself:

EXAMINING PHOTOGRAPHS *These giant "tusks" form arches over the main thoroughfare of modern Mombasa, Kenya's second largest city and East Africa's main port. Many tourists from around the world are attracted each year to the city's resort hotels and white sand and coral beaches.* What is Kenya's largest city?

Nairobi: full of vitality, international, intercultural, interreligious, interracial. . . . A city where an American Indian from Oklahoma meets Asian Indians at church; where one meets a couple of Asian extraction (who formerly lived in Uganda and are now living in Canada) at the home of a man from Goa and a woman from the Seychelles; where Protestants and Catholics share in a worship service with an Egyptian Coptic priest as speaker; where a Chinese professor from Taiwan, but recently moved from Australia, is found teaching at the University of Nairobi; where the landscape is silhouetted by Protestant church spires, Anglican, Catholic or Legio Maria cathedrals, Moslem mosques, Hindu or Sikh temples.

Take a look at the skyline of downtown Nairobi: round-tepee roofed Kenyatta Conference Center; the luxurious modern Hilton Hotel in the round; elegant history-filled Norfolk Hotel . . . ; the University of Nairobi; Parliament Building; Maridadi Fabrics Center; Mathare Valley with its thin paper huts; the Indian dukas and curio shops of Biashara Street; the country bus station. . . .

The fantastic flora: flame trees, blue jacaranda; many varieties of hibiscus; the violet/blue/white yesterday, today and tomorrow shrub; the yellow cassias and coral flames; beautiful paper-like bougainvillea at all seasons; hoop pines and she oaks (look like weeping willows); orchids and passion flowers.

The weather: near perfect. It is warm and sunny in the middle of the day with generally cool nights. There are rains in November–December and March–June with sufficient in between to keep lawns lush and blossoms blooming.

The green groceries: shelves lined with pineapples, papayas, bananas, coconuts, mangoes, limes, tomatoes, avocados, plums (in December), rhubarb and green vegetables.

This is Nairobi—city of the sun, city of flowers, plus a national museum, a national park with wild animals five minutes away from the business section, Leakey Institute, the Bomas depicting traditional life styles and dances. . . .

Source: Lucile Peak Wardin. "Kenya Kaleidoscope" in *The Bridge,* (Fall, 1980), p. 14.

THE COUNTRYSIDE

Although Kenyan cities have grown in recent years, about four-fifths of the people still live in rural areas and make their livings from raising crops or livestock. Prime farmland, however, is very scarce. Most of it lies in the southwestern highlands, which straddle the Great Rift Valley. Below, a tea-picker on a small farm in Kaptel in Kenya's Nandi District talks about his life and the role tea plays in the Kenyan economy:

Most of Kenya's tea is grown in twelve districts, stretching from Kitale to Meru. There is also a tea belt running about 160 kilometers (100 miles) along the eastern slope of the Aberdares, from Limuru to Nyeri. The big plantations are found to the east of the Rift Valley and on the western slopes of the Mau Escarpment.

A lot of tea is grown around Kericho. That's where the large plantation companies are located. . . . The tea estates

EXAMINING PHOTOGRAPHS *Tea-pickers often work part-time, spending most of the year raising crops for their own families. Tea is Kenya's most important cash crop after coffee. Where is Kenya's best farmland located?*

(plantations) around the town are delightful to see: vast fields of shiny-leaved, green bushes growing in neat rows.

Tea-picking goes on throughout the year. It's amusing to see the rows of tea-pickers on the estates with their bright-yellow, plastic aprons. They carry baskets on their backs. We pick "two-and-a-bud." That's two leaves of the tender shoot of a tea plant. I get paid 150 shillings a month, about a third of what I could get working as a laborer in the town.

The tea-growing areas lie at an altitude of between 1,800 and 2,400 meters (6 to 8,000 feet). Kericho, known as "the most fertile tea area in the world," has an ideal climate for tea growing. It gets plenty of rain for most of the year. . . .

There are about 138,000 small-sized tea "farms" in Kenya, each averaging less than a hectare (2.5 acres). Together they grow 36 percent of Kenya's tea. In all, they cover 53,586 hectares (133,965 acres), producing about 146,000 tons of green tea leaf, or about 33,000 tons of ready-made tea. . . .

Kenya has many tea factories. . . . A factory . . . is supplied by about 3,400 growers. The factories are about 11 kilometers (7 miles) apart. Leaf-collecting centers are located between them. Tea farmers don't have to carry their crop for more than two kilometers (1.5 miles).

S E C T I O N   2   R E V I E W

CHECKING FOR UNDERSTANDING
1. **Point out** some of the major characteristics of Nairobi.
2. **Indicate** where most of the people of Kenya live and how they make their livings.

CRITICAL THINKING
3. **Drawing Conclusions** Why is tea important to the economy of Kenya?

Source: Zulf M. Khalfan and Mohamed Amin. "Kenya is famous for its good tea" in *We Live in Kenya,* The Bookwright Press, 1984, pp. 26–27.

Patterns of Change

Since independence, Kenya has changed a great deal. With that change has come many problems, including rising unemployment, high rates of population growth, and government abuses of human rights.

GOVERNMENT

Kenya is a republic, which in 1982 became a one-party state. At its head since 1978 has been Daniel T. arap Moi (uh·RAP moy). For many years, Kenya was viewed as one of the freer countries of Africa. In 1990, the government, however, was criticized for corruption, human rights violations, and its refusal to allow political dissent. In December 1991, president Moi bowed to the growing pressure for reform. Below, a journalist describes what happened:

In the expensive, modern Kasarani Arena in the Moi Sports Complex where he spoke, there was an air of resignation about the president as he bowed to rapidly escalating domestic and international pressures for democratic reforms. . . .

"The power stems from the people," Moi told the party delegates in the arena.

The truth of these words was evident, for this time it is not the power of Moi's party that has carried the day. As in the other African countries making reforms, it is the power of his critics demanding an end to detention of political opponents, an end to the ban on publications criticizing the government, an end to torture by the police, and an end to the ban on opposition political parties. . . .

There was quick reaction to Moi's grudging acceptance of a multiparty system.

"I think everyone's quite happy about it. They've been looking forward to this," says Peninnah Wohjoro, a secretary in Nairobi.

"That's what should have been done two or three years ago," says Joseph Odero Jowi, a supporter of the Forum for Restoration of Democracy (FORD), one of Kenya's opposition groups whose leaders are likely to form a new party. "As long as we have just one party, there will be no other to chase them around and make them accountable," says Mr. Jowi.

Henry Maina Thairu, a retired primary school director and now owner of a small shop in rural, central Kenya, hopes the reforms will not only bring accountability but help Kenya's poor.

"The people we have in the government have proved themselves to be—may I use the proper word—robbers," Mr. Thairu says. "People are suffering in very many ways. They can't afford school fees. And they are naked; they only have a tattered shirt, or one very dirty pair of trousers. [Some] don't even have shoes."

But not everyone was happy with the change. A Nairobi taxi driver, who was reluctant to give his name, said he agrees with Moi that multiparty politics will bring multi-ethnic conflicts, with tribes forming competing parties.

And at the sports arena, party delegate Abdul Rahman Bafadhil gave an impassioned and much-applauded speech stressing the need to continue under the Kenya African National Union (KANU) Kenya's sole party since 1982.

Outside the arena, Mr. Bafadhil said Kenya's many tribes cannot hold together under multiparty politics. He blamed former colonial powers for drawing international boundaries that divided Africa's people.

He blamed the hunger in Africa on the West's urging African nations to grow cash crops to earn hard currency in order to buy Western products.

"We don't eat coffee," he said.

Source: Robert M. Press. "Kenya's Moi Bows to Calls for Multiparty Elections." Reprinted by permission from *THE CHRISTIAN SCIENCE MONITOR* © 1991. The Christian Science Publishing Society. All rights reserved.

EXAMINING PHOTOGRAPHS *In 1991, President Daniel T. arap Moi legalized multiparty politics in Kenya. What later events threatened to halt Kenya's move toward democracy?*

By mid-1992, opposition political parties had formed in response to President Moi's legalization of multiparty politics. The parties received support from key officials in the Kenyan government. They quit public office after accusing President Moi of corruption.

Meanwhile, ethnic clashes erupted in Kenya's rural western provinces. They claimed as many as 2000 lives and left about 50,000 people homeless. The conflict was described as the worst of its kind since Kenya won independence in 1963. It was considered unusual for Kenya, which normally enjoyed political and ethnic stability.

The unrest pitted members of the smaller Kalenjin ethnic group against those of the Kikuyu, the Luo, and the Luyha, the three largest ethnic groups. The opposition parties accused Moi of starting the violence in order to discredit the country's move toward democracy. In response, Moi banned all political meetings, declaring "there will be no politics and no public meetings until law and order is restored."

LEARNING TO ADAPT

For some Kenyans, the changes that have taken place have been hard to accept. One such group is the Maasai, pastoralists of the southern Kenyan plains and the Great Rift Valley. Most like their traditional way of life and do not want to change it. For years, they have resisted government efforts to make them into farmers. One Maasai elder explained the reason for their opposition with these words: "Before, it was a sin for us to cultivate the land; it was bad to show God that you had turned the land upside down." Below, a journalist doing research in East Africa tells the story of a Maasai named James Morinte:

Five years ago, when he was a Maasai *moran* [warrior], James Morinte and his six fellow [*morani*] set off to fight the lion. They'd sung songs together around their fire the night before, working up their bravery. . . . Now they trotted together, single file through the forested glades of Kenya's Isuria Escarpment which rises above the Maasai Mara Game Reserve. Their spears gleamed sharply in the morning sun, and their red robes looked bright against the forest green. They followed the track of the lion until he tired. Then, . . . he turned to face them.

"We made a circle around the lion and when he leaped at me, I dropped to my knee and held my shield, like so, above my head," said Morinte, demonstrating as he walked along the escarpment heading toward his brother's *manyatta* (home). "I kept my spear upright and plunged it into

EXAMINING PHOTOGRAPHS *The modern watch and traditional jewelry of this Kenyan point up the mix of new and old in much of Africa today. What are some changes taking place among the Maasai?*

his heart. And so I became 'the one who killed the lion.'"

For the Maasai, . . . there is no greater honor. Morinte's action signified all that a *moran* should be: strong and brave while under attack, the coolheaded defender of cattle and village. Yet the need for such bravery, and for the warriors at all, is becoming less and less apparent as the Kenyan government—as well as educated Maasai leaders—moves to encourage the . . . (Maasai) to set aside their spears and wandering ways. . . .

. . . when European explorers first came to East Africa, they found the Maasai occupying . . . some 12 percent of the land. . . . [They] had a social system centered on a privileged class of young warriors, the morani. These young men defended the [group] from wild animals and added to its wealth by raiding other [peoples] for their cattle. (Maasai legends assert that after creating the world, God gave them "all the cattle upon Earth," so that cattle seen in the possession of other [groups] were presumed to be either stolen or lost.) They were the dominant [group] of East Africa, proud and certain of their ways. But by the time of Kenyan independence . . . , the Maasai had been, in the words of Ole Hassan Kamwaro, the Narok County Council Chairman, "left far behind."

"Today, however, we are on the run," he said. "We are retaining some traditions, like the respect for our elders. But other things are changing. For example, the morani will disappear. We don't want our young men to go about roaming, stealing cows, wasting their time. Instead, they should go to school. . . ."

. . . At his grandmother's insistence, Morinte went to school and learned English, and now, rather than tend his cattle, he works as a tour guide . . . in the Mara. Although he has given up many of his Maasai ways, and wears cut-off Levis and a digital watch, Morinte retains an intimacy with the land and animals. He knows how to follow the faint tracks of a dik-dik,

EXAMINING PHOTOGRAPHS *As more land goes into agricultural production, and animals on the Maasai Mara Game Reserve increase their numbers and spill over the reserve's boundaries, it is becoming more difficult for Maasai like these to find adequate grazing land for their cattle. Of what importance are cattle to the Maasai?*

find the scat of a leopard and use the trees and shrubs that provide the Maasai with everything from toothbrushes to poisons. He clearly likes being out among the animals, both wild and domestic, and stops to carefully examine his brother's flocks of goats and sheep. Even though he earns a daily wage from his work as a guide, Morinte's real wealth—these flocks and his cattle—are sequestered here on the Isuria escarpment.

"You cannot be a Maasai unless you have cattle," he explained. . . .

From the bushes, two small Maasai boys appeared. They were smiling . . . , and carried long switches for tending their flocks. Morinte greeted them. . . .

"This is how I spent my childhood," he said with a shy smile. "We spent our days with the herds, running here and there, watching out for lions. If we saw a lion, then we ran home to tell our fathers, so the morani could hunt it. But these boys, I

think, will not be *morani*. They will . . . learn the traditions. But they will not hunt the lion."

SECTION 3 REVIEW

CHECKING FOR UNDERSTANDING

1. **Explain** why President Moi agreed in 1991 to make reforms.
2. **State** what the government of Kenya wants the Maasai to do and why many Maasai are opposed.

CRITICAL THINKING

3. **Predicting Consequences** How do you think President Moi's actions will affect Kenya's political future?

Source: Virginia Morell. "Maasai!" in *International Wildlife Magazine,* May-June 1985.

History

THE KIKUYU AND THE EUROPEANS

When the Europeans first came to Kenya, the Kikuyu believed they would soon tire of Africa and return home. So they welcomed them and gave them the right to build on African land. After a while, however, it became evident that the Europeans were there to stay.

FOCUSING ON THE ISSUE The following Kikuyu tale shows how the Kikuyu viewed their relationship with Europeans. Read the tale and then write an essay explaining how the Kikuyu and the Europeans related to each other. Conclude with a discussion of how the Kikuyu thought they could solve the problems of the Europeans and why they felt justified in doing so.

. . . Once upon a time an elephant made a friendship with a man. One day a heavy thunderstorm broke out, the elephant went to his friend . . . and said . . . : "My dear good man, will you please let me put my trunk inside your hut to keep it out of this torrential rain?" The man . . . replied: "My dear good elephant, my hut is very small, but there is room for your trunk and myself. Please put your trunk in gently." The elephant thanked his friend, saying: "You have done me a good deed and one day I shall return your kindness.". . . As soon as the elephant put his trunk inside the hut, slowly he pushed his head inside, and finally flung the man out in the rain, and then lay down comfortably inside his friend's hut, saying: "My dear good friend, your skin is harder than mine, and as there is not enough room for both of us, you can afford to remain in the rain while I am protecting my delicate skin from the hailstorm."

The man . . . started to grumble; the animals in the nearby forest heard the noise and came to see what was the matter. All stood around listening to the heated argument between the man and his friend the elephant. In this turmoil the lion came along roaring, and said in a loud voice: "Don't you all know that I am the King of the Jungle! How dare anyone disturb the peace of my kingdom?" On hearing this the elephant . . . replied in a soothing voice, and said: "My lord, there is no disturbance of the peace in your kingdom. I have only been having a little discussion with my

friend here as to the possession of this little hut. . . ." The lion, who wanted to have "peace and tranquillity" in his kingdom, replied in a noble voice, saying: "I command my ministers to appoint a Commission of Enquiry to go thoroughly into this matter and report accordingly." He then turned to the man and said: "You have done well by establishing friendship with my people, especially with the elephant who is one of my honorable ministers of state. Do not grumble any more, your hut is not lost to you. Wait until the sitting of my Imperial Commission, and there you will be given plenty of opportunity to state your case." . . .

The elephant got busy with other ministers to appoint the Commission of Enquiry. The following elders of the jungle were appointed . . . : (1) Mr.

Rhinoceros; (2) Mr. Buffalo; (3) Mr. Alligator; (4) The Rt. Hon. Mr. Fox to act as chairman, and (5) Mr. Leopard to act as Secretary to the Commission. . . .

The Commission sat to take the evidence. The Rt. Hon. Mr. Elephant was first called. He came along with a superior air . . . , and in an authoritative voice said: "Gentlemen of the Jungle, there is no need for me to waste your valuable time in relating a story which I am sure you all know. I have always regarded it as my duty to protect the interests of my friends. . . .

He invited me to save his hut from being blown away by a hurricane. As the hurricane had gained access owing to the unoccupied space in the hut, I considered it necessary, in my friend's own interests, to turn the undeveloped space to a more economic use by sitting in it myself. . . ."

After hearing the Rt. Hon. Mr. Elephant's conclusive evidence, the Commission called Mr. Hyena and other elders of the jungle, who all supported what Mr. Elephant had said. They then called the man, who began to give his own account of the dispute. But the Commission cut him short, saying: "My good man, please confine yourself to relevant issues. We have already heard the circumstances from various unbiased sources; all we wish you to tell us is whether the undeveloped space in your hut was occupied by anyone else before Mr. Elephant assumed his position?" The man began to say: "No, but—" But at this point the Commission declared that they had heard sufficient evidence from both sides and retired to consider their decision. After enjoying a delicious meal at the expense of the Rt. Hon. Mr. Elephant, they reached their verdict, called the man, and declared as follows: "In our opinion this dispute has arisen through a regrettable misunderstanding due to the backwardness of your ideas. We consider that Mr. Elephant has fulfilled his sacred duty of protecting your interests. As it is clearly for your good that the space should be put to its most economic use, and as you yourself have not yet reached the stage of expansion which would enable you to fill it, we consider it necessary to arrange a compromise to suit both parties. Mr. Elephant shall continue his occupation of your hut, but we give you permission to look for a site where you can build another hut more suited to your needs, and we will see that you are well protected."

The man, having no alternative, and fearing that his refusal might expose him to the teeth and claws of members of the Commission, did as they suggested. But no sooner had he built another hut than Mr. Rhinoceros charged in . . . and ordered the man to [leave]. A Royal Commission was again appointed to look into the matter, and the same finding was given. This procedure was repeated until Mr. Buffalo, Mr. Leopard, Mr. Hyena, and the rest were all accommodated with new huts. Then the man decided that he must adopt an effective method of protection, since Commissions of Enquiry did not seem to be any use to him. . . .

Early one morning, when the huts already occupied by the jungle lords were all beginning to decay and fall to pieces, he went out and built a bigger and better hut a little distance away. No sooner had Mr. Rhinoceros seen it than he came rushing in, only to find that Mr. Elephant was already inside, sound asleep. Mr. Leopard next came in at the window, Mr. Lion, Mr. Fox, and Mr. Buffalo entered the doors, while Mr. Hyena howled for a place in the shade and Mr. Alligator basked on the roof. Presently they all began disputing about their rights of penetration . . . and while they were all embroiled together the man set the hut on fire and burnt it to the ground, jungle lords and all. Then he went home saying: "Peace is costly, but it's worth the expense," and lived happily ever after.

Source: Jomo Kenyatta. *Facing Mt. Kenya: The Tribal Life of the Gikuyu.* Harcourt Brace & Co., 1965, pp. 47–51.

Chapter 5 Review

SUMMARY

Kenya had a rich history long before the 1000's AD, when Arab traders first introduced Islam to East Africa. After the Arabs came the Portuguese and then the British, whose goal was to turn Kenya into a "white man's country." By the 1920's, Europeans controlled Kenya's government.

In 1963, after many years of resistance to colonial rule, Kenya became independent. Today Kenya is a republic that is home to a diverse population. Of the many different ethnic groups that make up the population, the largest is the Kikuyu.

In recent years, Kenyan cities have grown in size and importance. Still, about four-fifths of the people live in rural areas and make their living raising livestock or crops. While some groups have resisted change, others have called for more. In 1991, the government bowed to the pressure and promised to institute political and economic reforms, including adoption of a multiparty system.

USING VOCABULARY

Imagine you are a Kenyan. Write a poem of 10 lines or less titled *My Kenya*. Use the following terms in the poem.

uhuru   *lingua franca*
harambee

REVIEWING FACTS

1. **Name** the first foreigners to influence the people of Kenya.
2. **Specify** how British control differed from that of the Arabs, the Swahili, and the Portuguese.
3. **Identify** the goal of the Kenya African Union (KAU). The Mau Mau movement.
4. **Indicate** the year Kenya gained its independence and the name of its first president as an independent nation.
5. **Name** the five largest ethnic groups in Kenya today.
6. **Indicate** where Kenya's most productive farmland is located.
7. **State** why President arap Moi was opposed to adopting multiparty politics in Kenya.

CRITICAL THINKING

1. **Making Comparisons** What did the Kenya African Union (KAU) and the Mau Mau have in common? In what ways did they differ?
2. **Drawing Conclusions** Why did the colonial government single out the Kikuyu for "punishment" in the 1950's?
3. **Predicting Consequences** Experts estimate that if the Kenyan population continues to grow at present growth rates, that population will double in 17 years. In what ways might this affect Kenyans?

ANALYZING CONCEPTS

1. **Culture** In what ways did early Arab traders influence the East Africans?
2. **Change** What are some of the ways in which Kenya has changed over the past 50 years or so?

GEOGRAPHIC THEMES

1. **Place** Why are the highlands important to the economy of Kenya?
2. **Human-environment Interaction** According to a Maasai elder, "Before, . . . it was bad to show God that you had turned the land upside down." What effect has this belief about their relationship with the environment had on the Maasai?

Identifying Assumptions

Imagine that a candidate for your school's student government made the following speech: "Students should be allowed to vote on school regulations. Only if students have a greater say about these rules can we improve school morale and reduce discipline problems." This statement contains several *assumptions*—ideas that speakers or writers believe the audience already shares. The candidate has assumed that school morale and discipline are important problems, and that student participation in rule-making will improve these problems.

Assumptions often appear in persuasive writing, such as editorials and speeches, in which writers are trying to convince others to share their opinions. Because assumptions are believed to be true, usually no facts are offered to support them. Sometimes speakers and writers base complex arguments on incorrect or false assumptions. Therefore, it is important to identify assumptions and check their accuracy against facts before accepting a speaker's opinions.

Because many assumptions are not stated directly, identifying them can be difficult. Here are some steps to follow in identifying assumptions:

- Read or listen to the material carefully.
- Identify the speaker's point of view.
- Identify stated and unstated assumptions underlying the speaker's views.

> "People have high expectations of an MP. They see us as providers; people who should help to supply them with their basic needs—jobs, food, good health and shelter. I believe in motivating people to help themselves. They must not expect the government to provide them with everything on a plate. I'm encouraging the government to set up more Harambee projects. Harambee is Kenya's motto. It means 'pulling together' or 'self-help.'"

- Find facts which can verify the accuracy of these assumptions.

EXAMPLE

Read the boxed excerpt written by Phoebe Asiyo, a Member of Parliament (MP) in Kenya. In this excerpt, the writer expresses the opinion that government should motivate people to help themselves. Two assumptions underlie this opinion. First, the writer states that people expect "the government to provide them with everything on a plate." Second, Phoebe Asiyo makes an unstated assumption that motivating people to help themselves will be more effective. No facts are given to support either assumption. To check the accuracy of the first assumption, you must find evidence that people have asked for and expect direct aid from the government. To check the second assumption, find information on the effectiveness of *harambee* programs in providing for people's basic needs.

PRACTICE

Reread the discussion of Jomo Kenyatta's speech on pages 73–74. Then answer these questions:

1. What was the purpose of Kenyatta's speech?
2. What assumptions does Kenyatta make about the relationship between land and hunger in Kenya?
3. How could you check the accuracy of this assumption?
4. What other assumptions does Kenyatta make about land?
5. What evidence does Kenyatta give to support these assumptions?
6. In the third paragraph, what assumptions does Kenyatta make about African freedom?
7. What facts are needed to check the accuracy of these assumptions?
8. In the last paragraph, what does the writer assume about the meaning of the KAU flag?

Source: Zulf M. Khalfan and Mohamed Amin. "246 babies die out of every 1,000 born" in *We Live in Kenya.* The Bookwright Press, 1984, pp. 6–7. Reprinted with permission of Franklin Watts, Inc., New York.

CHAPTER OUTLINE

1 Music

2 Oral Literature

3 Visual Arts

4 Masks

5 Films

People and Places to Know
mbaqanga, adire cloth, Souleymane Cissé

Key Terms to Define
polyrhythm, talking drums, tonal, proverb

Objectives to Learn

1. **Identify** and describe the principal art forms of African society.
2. **Examine** how the arts are integrated into daily life in many parts of Africa.
3. **Recognize** the influence of African arts on other cultures.

Decorative water cups, Morocco

The Arts in Daily Life

"December, dry and beautiful, the season of the rice harvest, always found me at Tindican, for this was the occasion of a splendid and joyful festival, to which I was always invited, and I would impatiently wait for my young uncle to come for me. The festival had no set date, since it awaited the ripening of the rice, and this, in turn, depended on the good will of the weather. . . .

On the day of the harvest, the head of each family went at dawn to cut the first swath in his field. As soon as the first fruits had been gathered, the tom-tom [drum] signaled that the harvest had begun. This was the custom; . . .

Once the signal had been given, the reapers set out. With them, I marched along to the rhythm of the tom-tom. The young men threw their sickles into the air and caught them as they fell. They shouted simply for the pleasure of shouting, and danced as they followed the tom-tom players. . . . [It] would have been impossible for me to have torn myself away from their spirited music, from their sickles flashing in the rising sun, from the sweetness of the air and the crescendo of the tom-toms. . . .

When they had reached the first field, the men lined up at the edge . . . , their sickles ready. My uncle Lansana or some other farmer . . . then would signal that the work was to begin. Immediately, the black torsos would bend over the great golden field, and the sickles begin to cut. Now it was not only the morning breeze which made the field tremble, but also the men working. . . .

"Sing with us," my uncle would command.

The tom-tom, which had followed as we advanced into the field, kept time with our voices. We sang as a chorus, now very high-pitched with great bursts of song, and then very low, so low we could scarcely be heard. Our fatigue vanished, and the heat became less oppressive. . . .

. . . They sang and they reaped. Singing in chorus, they reaped, voices and gestures in harmony. They were together!—united by the same task, the same song. It was as if the same soul bound them."

*I*n the above excerpt, a writer from Guinea remembers the rice harvests of his youth. The image he recalls is a mixed one in which the heat, men, and music are blended into one. It is hard to separate the music from the rest of the image. This often is true in Africa. There, the arts are interwoven with many aspects of everyday life. Music, drama, dance, poetry, sculpture, storytelling, and other art forms are a common denominator of life and very much a part of the African heritage.

Source: Excerpts from THE DARK CHILD by Camara Laye, translated by James Kirkup and Ernest Jones. Copyright © 1954, renewal copyright © 1982 by Camara Laye. Reprinted by permission of Hill & Wang, a division of Farrar, Straus & Giroux, Inc.

Music

In Africa, music is a major art form. It accompanies other art forms and is a vital part of many religious ceremonies. In villages, where many activities are performed by groups, music often provides the motivation and rhythm for various tasks.

MUSICAL INSTRUMENTS

African music is known for its **polyrhythm**, or use of two or more rhythm patterns at once. For example, while one instrument or singer is using a pattern of three beats, another may be using a pattern of five. Then there is the drum music of West Africa, which often uses overlapping polyrhythms.

There is a great variety of African musical instruments. In the words of a Ghanaian scholar, "Almost anything that resonates [vibrates] can be pressed into musical service in Africa. The inventory of musical instruments is breathtaking." Some instruments, like the drums, gourd xylophone, and thumb piano, are found throughout the continent. Instruments such as drums, horns, bells, xylophones, and whistles traditionally have been used to send special signals or messages.

Of special interest are the **talking drums** of West Africa. They are unique because they imitate speech. This is possible because many African languages are **tonal**. This

EXAMINING PHOTOGRAPHS *The women pounding grain to a steady rhythm and the man dancing to the beat of a drum provide two examples of the use of music in African life. For what type of rhythm pattern is African music known?*

means that different words are made by raising or lowering the pitch of one's voice while pronouncing the same syllable. The word *tsó* for example, when spoken at a high pitch, means "stand." But, when spoken at a lower pitch, *tsó* means "cut." By using different types of drums and special techniques of playing, the drummer can produce the various tones of the language and, thus, understandable words and sentences.

In the past, the talking drums were used to relay messages about warfare, call people together, report special events, praise gods and royalty, and communicate with the supernatural world. Although today they still are used at royal ceremonies, they generally are used more in musical performances than for communication.

PROTEST SONGS

In Africa, as elsewhere, music is more than just the sound of instruments. It also is the sound of the human voice raised in song. Through song, emotions can be expressed and people can be inspired and united. This has been the case in many African nations during their struggles for independence. In these nations, protest songs have played a vital role. In the words of the president of Zimbabwe, "The *Chimurenga* [war of liberation] songs helped to instill grim determination among all actors in the revolutionary process." He went on to explain that whenever the freedom fighters "lost hope, were starving, wounded or subjected to surprise attacks by the enemy, they did not give in. Instead, they turned to the revolutionary songs to refurbish their spirits." Below is an excerpt from one of their songs:

Let the precious blood of our heroes flow
   like the raging Falls.
My mind cannot rest,
I am constantly thinking about the

Welfare of the masses.
Our precious blood is being spilled
For the people's freedom.
The liberation of the masses
Will flow from the sacrifices we are
   making.
Freedom will crown our efforts in the
   struggle for Zimbabwe. . . .

Our determination to free the
Motherland, has brought us face to
   face with death.
In the mountains.
In the raging waters of flooded rivers.
But together, with the comradeship
Cemented by mutual love,
We come to each other's rescue in the
   hour of need,
And together overcome the problem.
. . . .

If death should come today,
I would accept it with every part of my
   body;
I shall have satisfied myself that
I've fulfilled my solemn undertaking to
   die for Zimbabwe.
My body will have performed my duty to
   my nation,
The duty which is mine this side of the
   grave.
My body will have performed my duty to
   my nation,
The duty which is mine this side of the
   grave.

SECTION 1 REVIEW

CHECKING FOR UNDERSTANDING
1. **Define** polyrhythm, talking drums, tonal.
2. **Indicate** some of the functions performed by music in Africa.

CRITICAL THINKING
3. **Evaluating Information** What role do you think protest songs have played in modern Africa?

Source: "All the Peoples of Africa," in *Songs that Won the Liberation War* by Alec J.C. Pongweni, The College Press, 1982, pp. 62–63.

FOCUS ON PEOPLE

Africa

SOUTH AFRICAN MUSICIANS

In the past few decades, Africa's cities have produced a number of musicians who combine traditional African dance rhythms and modern "pop" music. One of the most outstanding of these groups is Mahlathini and the Mahotella Queens from South Africa. The excerpt below describes their music and its global impact:

People in the audience couldn't keep their feet still as the veteran South African musicians played and sang the lilting, infectious music called mbaqanga. *It was the musical style Paul Simon introduced to the United States with his groundbreaking cross-cultural album "Graceland" in 1986.*

Since then, music has been pouring out of South Africa, to the delight of both musicians from that country and thousands of new fans around the world. Mahlathini and the Mahotella Queens, who have been playing for more than 30 years in their own country, never dreamed of success outside South Africa. Yet now they're becoming international stars. . . .

Before an Earth Day performance . . . , I chatted with members of the group . . . : lead singer Simon Nkabinde (whose stage name is Mahlathini); Hilda Tloubatla, one of the Mahotella Queens; and West Nkosi, saxophonist for the Makgona Tsohle Band, the combo that backs the group.

The Queens perform in colorful dress, with Mahlathini decked out in traditional Zulu costume, complete with leopard-skin vest. They sing in Zulu, with a few words of English thrown in, and their songs are about the ups and downs of daily life—more personal than political.

Stylistically, the music is rooted in tradition, but it bears the marks of pop technology— the synthesizer, computer, and "dance mix." They're very much aware of the need to reach audiences without losing the African roots that have ex- erted such a strong influence on pop music around the world. . . .

Nkosi regards music as the leading edge in the movement toward freedom in his own country: "Music has got no language. It has got no color. In our country . . . we have not been privileged in a lot of things. But we had our freedom in music. That's the only place where we had our freedom—that's all.". . .

"So we decided to make this type of music, which is called mbaqanga. *This music managed to get all these groups together to share their views and their enjoyment and their crises. It became very, very popular for every black population that lived in South Africa, and even the neighboring countries. . . ."*

TAKING ANOTHER LOOK

1. Who are Mahlathini and the Mahotella Queens?
2. What do you think their art form reveals about South Africa and its people?

Source: Amy Duncan. "Zulu Roots, Pop Sounds" in *The Christian Science Monitor,* May 10, 1990, p. 11. Reprinted by permission from THE CHRISTIAN SCIENCE MONITOR © 1990 The Christian Science Publishing Society. All rights reserved.

EXAMINING PHOTOGRAPHS
A village elder tells traditional stories to a group of boys in Côte d'Ivoire village. The children are encouraged to memorize these stories, which are often creation myths about the beginnings of their people. What is oral literature?

SECTION 2

Oral Literature

Another African art form is oral literature, which has been passed down from generation to generation. Often used in religious ceremonies and recited to music, oral literature records the past and teaches traditions and values. Myths, legends, histories, stories, fables, poems, riddles, songs all are forms of oral literature. So are **proverbs**, short sayings that express a well-known truth or fact. Proverbs are especially common throughout Africa. Almost every African group has its own proverbs that take in nearly every situation and point of view. Below are some examples:

Swahili (East Africa):
"A bad brother is far better than no brother." (Blood is thicker than water.)

"A loud drum will soon split. (Loud promises are hollow.)

Yoruba (West Africa):
"He fled from the sword and hid in the scabbard." (Out of the frying pan into the fire.)

"Mouth not keeping to mouth, and lip not keeping to lip, bring trouble to the jaws." (Talk is silver, silence is gold.)

"One who does not understand the yellow palm-bird says the yellow palm-bird is noisy." (Men are prone to despise what they do not understand.)[1]

Hausa (West Africa):
"Even The Niger {River} has an island." (The mightiest things do not have it all their own way.)

"God made beautiful the silk cotton tree, the rubber tree must cease being angry." (Quarrel not with what God ordains.)

"If music changes so does the dance." (One must move with the times.)[2]

Source: "Politics in Swahili Proverbs" by Albert Scheven in *Curriculum Materials for Teachers 1983.* African Studies Program, University of Illinois, pp. 212–214, 216, 218.

[1] *Source:* "Yoruba Proverbs" in *The Horizon History of Africa,* Volume I. American Heritage Publishing Company, Inc., 1971, p. 207.

[2] *Source:* "Hausa Proverbs" in *The Horizon History of Africa,* Volume I. American Heritage Publishing Company, Inc., 1971, p. 248.

The Arts of Africa

Since ancient times, Africans have developed a variety of arts, especially sculpted figures, masks, decorated cloth, jewelry, baskets, and pottery. They also have excelled in various forms of music.

? What African art forms have influenced the arts in other parts of the world?

BASKET WEAVING
Woman weaving a traditional African basket.

JEWELRY
West African beaded bracelets.

MASK
Golden pendant mask made by the Baule of the Côte d'Ivoire.

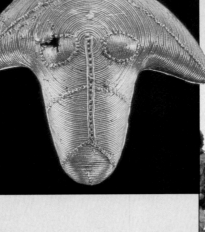

CLOTH DECORATING
Anti-bird Ghost spirit figure, drawn in ink by Nigerian artist Taiwo Olanyi.

MUSIC
Contemporary African band performing popular music.

Zulu (Southern Africa):
"He cries with one eye." (He pretends to be sorry when he is not.)
"The sheep has killed an elephant." (The impossible has happened.)

SECTION 2 REVIEW

CHECKING FOR UNDERSTANDING
1. **Define** proverb.
2. **State** what is considered to be oral literature.

CRITICAL THINKING
3. **Demonstrating Reasoned Judgment** Of what value is oral literature?

SECTION 3

Visual Arts

A third important African art form is visual arts. From ancient times to the present, Africans have used visual arts in many different forms and materials from bronze statues to elephant-hair bracelets. The elaborately carved staff of a chief, the colorful paintings splashed on the side of a bus, and the elegantly designed gold necklace all are visual arts created over the centuries by Africans and enjoyed today by people the world over.

Today, there are thousands of artists in the towns and cities of Africa fashioning pots, carving wooden masks, designing buildings, sculpting statues, and weaving and dyeing cloth. Although these works of African art are being sought by collectors around the world, for most Africans they are everyday articles. An example is *Adire* cloth, an indigo-blue printed fabric traditionally produced by the Yoruba of Nigeria. In the following, a writer describes the work of two young

Nigerian women who create modern versions of this traditional cloth:

The achievement of two female artists from Oshogbo, Senabu and Kikelemo . . . is unique and exciting. . . .

Senabu and Kikelemo were both trained in the production of *adire eleko* cloth, a starch-resistant technique . . . patterned on only one side of the cloth. A paste is made of cassava (a tropical plant), water and various local chemicals, which is applied in streaks onto a plain white cloth. After dying with one or two colors, the parts treated with the cassava 'gum' emerge darker than the other areas, and with a different texture.

EXAMINING ART *In Nigeria, cloth dyeing is an art form often used by women.* Adire *cloth, shown here, is made in set patterns by a cloth-dyeing expert.* What African ethnic group produces Adire *cloth?*

Source: "Zulu Wisdom" in *The Horizon History of Africa*, Volume II, American Heritage Publishing Company, Inc., 1971, p. 428.

Where the two women depart from tradition is that they create strong integrated pictorial images like paintings, exclusive to one length of cloth. These can be hung as tapestries, because each is a 'picture' on its own, with a focal point. Even when their cloths are made up into caftan-styled dresses, each length is a unique piece. Although they employ many of the same design motifs as the *Adire Eleko*, such as animals, certain symbols, kings and queens, their imagery also goes far beyond the stylised, formal, almost abstract effect of the *Adire*. The Oshogbo womens' cloths tell a story, often with stunning emotional impact. . . .

Senabu creates scenes and tells stories on her cloths; . . . the cloths give one the feeling of a lively but ordered world. . . . Her complex cloths incorporate many different elements, which build up to a total picture of Yoruba life. . . . [Her work] is free, energetic, rhythmic and sensual. . . . [She uses] trees as a foil for her figures. Her real and mythical animals are particularly beautiful. . . .

Senabu's use of colour is more experimental than that of Kikelemo. Both use the traditional blue-black indigo a great deal, and the classic *Adire* method in which the finished design is re-dipped in indigo to turn the blue and white to a softer, richer monochrome [painting done in different shades of one color]. Both women also use sharp greens, blue-greens and rich ochre.

Though Kikelemo too sometimes departs from the indigo, when she does, it is with a great bold statement of colour—brilliant deep red or a massive purple. Her images are much heavier, more sculptural. . . .

The overwhelming impact of Kikelemo's work is carried by wide sweeping lines and bulky forms. Her mask-like figures have considerable depth. Though she is working on a flat surface, her images are sculptural in concept. . . . This is the territory of imposing gods and menacing animals. . . . Within her god's mask-like face,

she will often leave areas of pure colour, but the heavy bodies of the animals are usually filled in with surging pattern. . . .

Both women . . . successfully combine the stimulus of contemporary Oshogbo life with the richness of an ancient feminine craft.

SECTION 3 REVIEW

CHECKING FOR UNDERSTANDING
1. **Discuss** how Africans tend to view most visual arts.

CRITICAL THINKING
2. **Making Comparisons** What makes the cloths of Senabu and Kikelemo different from most traditional *Adire* cloths?

SECTION 4

Masks

Still another African art form is the mask, which generally is carved out of wood and worn with a ceremonial costume that covers the entire body. Although masks are used in a variety of ways, they generally are associated with religious ceremonies or rituals.

In some religious ceremonies, masks symbolize the respect a community has for its ancestors. The carving of the masks and the performing of dances while wearing them symbolize the link between the living and the dead. Those who wear the masks and perform the songs and dances are acting not as themselves but as spirits. In this role, they show people what their ancestors wish for them. On the next page, two journalists who visited a Côte d'Ivoire (koht dee·VWAHR) village describe what they saw:

Source: "Daughters of Oshogbo" by Chandana Juliet Highet in *New African,* October 1984, pp. 50–51.

After dinner a small figure covered with grasses ran into the compound, surrounded by chanting children. "The apprentice masks are bidding you welcome," Albert informed us. "They are in training to be important masks some day."

Ivoirians [people of Côte d'Ivoire] refuse to acknowledge the human behind the mask, so one never says "masked man," or "masked figure," only "mask." Masks are integral to peasant life—divine, visible links to the ancestors, serving different social roles. There are comedians, dancers, singers, storytellers who amuse and beguile. There are warrior masks who keep order and punish offenders of tribal law. There are masks of wisdom, whose powers are called upon only rarely.

Aubine and I were invited to a great feast day for masks by Dao Bonnot, mask chief at Bangolo in Wè country. "We have chosen our century man," he informed us. "He is the oldest man in the region. We will now give him a wonderful funeral while he is alive."

He added that after this supreme recognition, the century man must live out the remainder of his days as a nonentity, inside his compound. "The mask of masks, Nanh-Sohou, who was never born and is as old as the earth, will watch over him till he dies."

We were warned not to talk directly to masks, or approach too close. We listened as the village chief intoned the mask call.

"We have offered 3 cows, 20 sheep, 20 roosters, and 10 hens. The masks are satisfied!"

Then we heard a jingling noise. Through the winding alleys between [houses] moved a procession of perhaps 200 dancing men and women, surrounding numerous fearsome masks. Each mask walked slowly, pompously. At the end of the line stood an all-white, lion-faced mask, taller than the others, who would take a step only every 15 seconds or so. At each step, his white-costumed [attendants kneeled], rang little bells, and cried out praise to the mask.

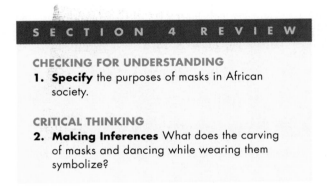

SECTION 4 REVIEW

CHECKING FOR UNDERSTANDING

1. **Specify** the purposes of masks in African society.

CRITICAL THINKING

2. **Making Inferences** What does the carving of masks and dancing while wearing them symbolize?

SECTION 5

Films

Over the past few decades, African films have grown into an important and popular art form. The films are welcomed in the continent because, unlike many imported films, they portray the real problems and lifestyles of African people. Below, a prominent Malian filmmaker named Souleymane Cissé, tells how he became interested in films and what he sees as the future of African films:

During my infancy I was always fascinated by cinema. I went as often as possible to the movies, without really realizing at the time that I could make a career out of the profession. When I was 18 years old I started gradually to become conscious of my affinity to the movie industry. At that time I was a member of a Malian youth group and I became a film projectionist. It was only in 1961 when I received a three-month scholarship to study this profession in the Soviet Union that I became fully cognisant of my love for the Seventh Art. . . .

I started [my cinema career] by realising current affairs films for the Ministry of Information and doing short documentaries on Malian subjects. I managed to complete some small feature films which attracted the attention of film critics abroad. This gave me the opportunity to push forward. I was able to finish a full-length feature film entitled *Den Muso* (The Young Girl). . . . For the first time the film attempted to show daily life in contemporary Mali. A broad public of all ages went to see the film. Then I realised that it was possible to move into . . . films of fiction. . . .

Source: Michael and Aubine Kirtley. "The Ivory Coast-African Success Story" in *National Geographic*, July, 1982, p. 123.

EXAMINING PHOTOGRAPHS *Malian filmmaker Souleymane Cissé has won recognition throughout the world for his contributions to the film industry. Where was Cissé trained in filmmaking?*

EXAMINING PHOTOGRAPHS *This is a scene from one of Souleymane Cissé's most successful films,* Finyé (The Wind), *which is about a young man and woman who fall in love during a student rebellion in an African city.* Finyé *was presented at the 1986 New York and Cannes film festivals, where it received high marks from critics.* What obstacles confront African filmmakers?

For me cinema is an art which is meant to have an impact on life, and it is in this precise framework that I produced *Baara* [a film about the condition of workers in urban areas]. After independence, Mali . . . opened up factories and started large construction schemes requiring a plentiful labor force. I said to myself that now that this working class is being formed it should also learn to organise itself in defence of its interests. Since the working class in . . . Africa has little in common with working classes in developed countries, I had to pinpoint an original angle for the film. That is why *Baara* takes at the beginning a young porter as its principal protagonist [hero]. He is a young man from the rural area who drifts into town in search of work. . . . The film also focuses on an executive, the type of person who in independent Africa has become rich because of his relations in the state apparatus instead of by the fruit of his labour. . . .

I would say . . . that African cinema is not properly understood by African leaders. When this finally does occur, and I hope it will be in the near future, it will be an important step forward. In addition, African businessmen have no notion of the possibilities of African cinema. . . . Much depends on the will of African film makers. Our films are also poorly distributed in Africa and elsewhere around the world. A film which is not properly distributed cannot be profitable. This is a situation which must be overcome, though these problems do not mean that one should be pessimistic about the future of African cinema.

SECTION 5 REVIEW

CHECKING FOR UNDERSTANDING

1. **State** what Cissé thinks is the role of films in the world today.

CRITICAL THINKING

2. **Analyzing Information** Why do you think African-made films are popular in Africa?

Source: Howard Schissel. "People's film-maker" in *West Africa,* May 7, 1984, pp. 973–974.

Cultural Values

THE TRUE VALUE OF ART

In recent years, African art has been taken out of the continent by non-African collectors. This worries many Africans, who point to the fact that, for many collectors, the value of the art is a material one, which is not so for Africans. This contrast is highlighted in the following account.

FOCUSING ON THE ISSUE
Read the account and answer these questions. Then explain in your own words the point of the account.

1. How does the American businessman perceive the value of the Dogon doors?
2. How does the Dogon chief perceive the value of the Dogon doors?
3. What is meant by the phrase, "the secret of abundance is of a nonmaterial nature"?
4. Do you agree with Ibrahima's assertion that the main problem with Westerners is that they turn everything into money? Explain.

One of the most beautiful lessons [Ibrahima] and my African friends have taught me . . . is that the greatest abundance, that which lights the clearest flame of joy in one's heart, is of a nonmaterial nature. I'll never forget a discussion I had on this theme with Ibrahima, his son Ali, and Thelonius, a black American anthropologist, . . . in Kinkiliba, Ibrahima's village. Thelo-

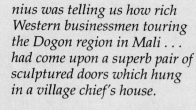

nius was telling us how rich Western businessmen touring the Dogon region in Mali . . . had come upon a superb pair of sculptured doors which hung in a village chief's house.

"He immediately asked the chief, through an interpreter . . . if he could buy them," said Thelonius, who at that time was living in the Dogon village.

At first the chief was indignant. "Why do you want my doors?" he asked. "Don't you have a door on your house?" Thelonius had inwardly chuckled: he knew the businessman had a large mansion with full-time day and night guards, burglar alarms and watch-dogs. "I am just asking you if you'll sell me your doors," the man repeated, "for 50,000 Malian francs." And he waved 105,000Fr bills in the chief's face. The chief was visibly taken back: that was at least a year's income for him. He hesitated. These "toubabs" (white men) were hard to comprehend. But he had not paid his taxes because the harvest had been very poor . . . "75,000." The industrialist added five more notes to the wad.

"It was the most obscene thing I had ever seen in my life," Thelonius added. "This foreigner with 2 cameras at his belt and an embarrassed interpreter, adding bill upon bill until the chief said, 'Come into my hut,' because the whole village was by then assembled."

He gave in at 150,000Fr, that is, at $300, a small, dry crumb for the businessman. The next day a Land Rover came from the capital—300 miles [480 kilometers] away—to fetch the century-old doors while gaping villagers watched. So their doors were as precious as that? Their doors were really money?

Today, in the businessman's home country, these doors are insured for $15,000. Today also, in the Dogon country, you will not find any more original carved doors. These century-old symbols—literally priceless, for how do you fix a price on beauty, on memories, on symbols?—have been turned into money. They are no longer valued as expressions of beauty or of culture. They have become things. We Westerners have turned thoughts into things to be possessed. . . .

"That's the main problem with you Westerners," Ibrahima interjected, "you turn everything into money. Everything you touch. It's as if you had big paintbrushes and went round the world painting large DM, $, Fr or [pound] signs onto everything you see. . . ."

Ali said slyly, smiling, "'Time is money' you say. But doesn't that sum up the spiritual misery of a civilization? Real time is the occasion, renewed day after day, to start living. Time is a pair of cupped hands that you lift up towards heaven that they may be filled with beauty and joy, friends and parents, love and gentleness, courage and trust, children of your hopes, dreams of holiness and adventure. Real living destroys time, and hence the pursuit of money and the belief that money can buy joy. . . ."

It must be true that real abundance is not material, for everything beautiful I have ever seen, every courageous act I've ever witnessed, every gesture of love I've ever admired, every friend I've cherished, I carry around with me, every day, every hour, not as memories of the past or hopes of the future, but as examples and realities to be enjoyed and treasured now.

Sometimes I think I am the richest person on earth.

Source: Pierre Pradervand. "The richest person on earth" in *The Christian Science Monitor*, May 11, 1977, p. 28.

Chapter 6 Review

SUMMARY

In Africa, the arts are interwoven with many aspects of daily life. African music, known for its polyrhythm, ranges from traditional talking drums to modern protest songs. Oral literature, passed down from generation to generation and recited to music, records the past and teaches traditions and values.

Africans have used the visual arts in many forms and materials from ancient times to the present. For most of them, works of art are everyday materials that have been used for generations for practical and religious purposes. Masks, although used in a variety of ways, are generally associated with religious rituals.

Over the past few decades, films have become a popular African art form because they portray the concerns of modern Africa.

USING VOCABULARY

Write sentences about African arts using these vocabulary words.

polyrhythm   tonal
talking drums proverbs

REVIEWING FACTS

1. **Identify** the major characteristics of African music.
2. **List** the kinds of musical instruments used in Africa.
3. **Discuss** what makes talking drums unique and what they have been used for.
4. **Summarize** the role of songs and singing in modern Africa.
5. **List** the various types of oral literature produced by Africans.
6. **Explain** how Africans have used oral literature throughout their history.
7. **Name** some of the African art forms that are considered visual arts.
8. **Discuss** how Africans regard many of the items that are considered works of art by collectors around the world.
9. **State** how Africans make and wear masks.
10. **Indicate** the themes that are portrayed in African films today.
11. **State** how filmmakers, like Souleymane Cissé, regard the future of African films.

CRITICAL THINKING

1. **Making Comparisons** Songs have been important to independence and liberation movements in Africa. Do you think this is unique to Africa? Why or why not?
2. **Predicting Consequences** If there were no oral literature, the lives of many Africans would be different. Why and in what ways?
3. **Demonstrating Reasoned Judgment** An African musician recently said about artists, "It is important that they care about what surrounds them, and about what is around them because they are influential." Do you agree or disagree with this statement? Explain.

ANALYZING CONCEPTS

1. **Culture** How would you explain the statement, "In Africa, art is not separate from life"?
2. **Identify** Identify some of the social roles that African masks can represent.

GEOGRAPHIC THEMES

1. **Human-Environment Interaction** How do Africans use music in their daily lives?
2. **Movement** What African art forms do you think have aided in the spread of ideas from one place to another in Africa?

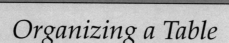
Organizing a Table

To simplify the task of learning, information can be organized into groups of related facts and ideas. One way to organize information is to arrange it in a chart called a *table*. A table presents written or numerical information in columns and rows. It enables you to remember and compare information more easily.

Follow the steps below to organize information in a table:

- Decide what information must be organized.
- Identify several major categories of ideas or facts about

the topic and write these as column headings across the top of a piece of paper.

- Find information that fits into each category and write these facts or ideas under the appropriate column heading.

EXAMPLE

The chart shown below organizes facts about African art forms. Notice that the first column heading identifies the different kinds of art. The next three columns present information about art forms.

The information in the columns reveals similarities and differences between oral literature and visual arts. For example, both oral literature and visual arts record the past and have either practical or religious purposes. Visual arts, however, are also practiced for beauty's sake. What are some similarities and differences in the characteristics of oral literature and visual arts? (*Oral literature appeals to sense of hearing while visual arts appeal to sense of sight. Both use traditional methods.*)

Characteristics, Uses, and Examples of African Art Forms			
ART FORMS	**CHARACTERISTICS**	**USES**	**EXAMPLES**
oral literature	recited, sometimes to music; passed from generation to generation; found in nearly every African group	record past; teach values and traditions; praise deities and royalty	myths, legends, praise songs, and proverbs
visual arts	practical as well as decorative; appeal to the sense of sight; made by traditional methods; use traditional as well as modern symbols	for beauty's sake; show rank or office; record the past and keep traditions; in daily tasks and for religious and other purposes	sculpture, clothing, jewelry, carvings, pottery, cookware, tapestries, utensils, tools

PRACTICE

Reread the sections on Africa's music (pages 88–89), masks (pages 94–96), and films (pages 96–97). After you have finished reading, organize this information into a table and then answer the following questions.

1. What major categories of ideas or facts did you identify about the topics in your reading?
2. What general title did you select for your chart?
3. What column headings did you include in your chart?
4. Did you find any similarities among these art forms? If so, name two.
5. Did you find any differences among these art forms? If so, name two.

CHAPTER OUTLINE

1 The Need to Develop

2 Facing the Challenges

People and Places to Know

the Horn of Africa, the Sahel, Organization of African Unity

Objectives to Learn

1. **Identify** the challenges to development that many African nations face today.

2. **Describe** the steps that African nations are taking to meet their development goals.

A Classroom in Kenya

Challenges to Development

> " . . . there is more to modern Africa than a vast, flat plain of failure. A learning curve can be discerned. Governments have finally started to sift sense out of nonsense. . . . Many African leaders have stopped blaming their problems on the legacy of colonialism. . . . Smothering state control is being lifted from the marketplace. Farmers in many reforming countries are being paid a decent price to grow food, and they have responded . . . with record crops. These tentative efforts have won the attention of rich countries, and Africa's share of world development aid has nearly doubled in recent years.
>
> For the first time in the post-independent era, the continent is no longer a chessboard in a global Cold War. The Russians are no longer coming. Africa is not a region that the United States can win or lose to communism. . . .
>
> More fundamentally, Africa's learning curve is etched into the everyday lives of human beings caught up in the fitful process of shifting from one set of rules to another. Hundreds of millions of Africans are lurching between an unworkable Western present and a collapsing African past. Their loyalties are stretched between predatory governments and disintegrating tribes. . . . At its heart the great experiment in modernity that continues to rattle Africa goes on inside individuals, as they sort out new connections with their families, their tribes, and their countries.
>
> Though continuously battered, African values endure. They are the primary reason why . . . the continent is not a hopeless or even a sad place. It is a land where the bonds of family keep old people from feeling useless and guarantee that no child is an orphan, where religion is more about joy than guilt, where when you ask a man for directions he will get in your car and ride with you to your destination. . . . "

The journalist who wrote these words acknowledges that Africa is faced with many major problems. At the same time, however, he believes that "Africa's problems, as pervasive and ghastly as they seem, are not the final scorecard on a doomed continent."

While Africans are aware of the problems, they do not agree on the origins or the solutions. Colonialism, local power struggles, un-

just and corrupt regimes, foreign "experts," dependence on the West—all have been named as the cause of the problems. One Nigerian economist believes that "the problem lies with the major agents of development. Each of them propagates an idea of development corresponding to its interests and images of the world." While all Africans do not agree with this, they do agree that the problems must be resolved and development intensified.

Source: Blaine Harden. *AFRICA Dispatches from a Fragile Continent.* W. W. Norton & Company, 1990, pp. 16–20.

SECTION 1

The Need to Develop

In African nations, as in other nations of the world, the basic aim of development is to improve the quality of life. Nations often pursue this goal by developing their natural resources, industrializing, and modernizing agriculture. For many African nations, however, this has proved to be a difficult task.

Much of the difficulty stems from the colo-nial period. For example, the present-day boundaries of most African nations are the same as those set up by the colonial powers. Because little consideration was given to eth-nic groups at the time, today most African nations are made up of various ethnic groups that may not speak the same lan-guage or may be former rivals. In addition, many ethnic groups are divided among sev-eral nations. Such conditions make it very hard to create the sense of national identity that is needed for a nation's people to work together toward common development goals.

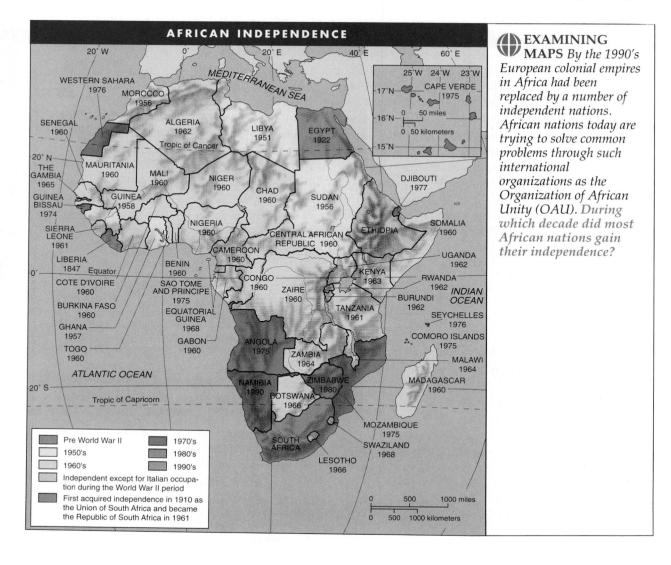

AFRICAN INDEPENDENCE

WESTERN SAHARA 1976
MOROCCO 1956
SENEGAL 1960
ALGERIA 1962
Tropic of Cancer
LIBYA 1951
EGYPT 1922
CAPE VERDE 1975
THE GAMBIA 1965
MAURITANIA 1960
MALI 1960
NIGER 1960
CHAD 1960
SUDAN 1956
DJIBOUTI 1977
GUINEA BISSAU 1974
GUINEA 1958
NIGERIA 1960
SOMALIA 1960
SIERRA LEONE 1961
CENTRAL AFRICAN REPUBLIC 1960
ETHIOPIA
CAMEROON 1960
UGANDA 1962
LIBERIA 1847
BENIN 1960
Equator
CONGO 1960
KENYA 1963
RWANDA 1962
COTE D'IVOIRE 1960
SAO TOME AND PRINCIPE 1975
ZAIRE 1960
BURUNDI 1962
INDIAN OCEAN
BURKINA FASO 1960
EQUATORIAL GUINEA 1968
TANZANIA 1961
SEYCHELLES 1976
GHANA 1957
GABON 1960
ANGOLA 1975
COMORO ISLANDS 1975
TOGO 1960
ZAMBIA 1964
MALAWI 1964
ATLANTIC OCEAN
NAMIBIA 1990
ZIMBABWE 1980
MADAGASCAR 1960
BOTSWANA 1966
Tropic of Capricorn
MOZAMBIQUE 1975
SOUTH AFRICA
SWAZILAND 1968
LESOTHO 1966

Pre World War II
1950's
1960's
1970's
1980's
1990's
Independent except for Italian occupa-tion during the World War II period
First acquired independence in 1910 as the Union of South Africa and became the Republic of South Africa in 1961

0   500   1000 miles
0   500   1000 kilometers

EXAMINING MAPS *By the 1990's European colonial empires in Africa had been replaced by a number of independent nations. African nations today are trying to solve common problems through such international organizations as the Organization of African Unity (OAU).* During which decade did most African nations gain their independence?

EXAMINING PHOTOGRAPHS *Cattle and goats (above, left) forage in a field littered with abandoned engine parts. Participating in a development project, a farmer (above, right) tries out a new planting technique. What was the economic goal of the newly independent African nations?*

A DECLINING ECONOMY

Following independence and throughout the 1970's and 1980's, the new African governments worked to develop their economies. Their goal was to export enough manufactured goods, minerals, and cash crops to earn the income needed. While some of the nations tried to do this on their own, several looked to such international agencies as the World Bank for funding and technical assistance.

Some progress was made during this period, but the degree of development hoped for did not come about. One reason was that there was not enough money, spare parts, or trained people to operate and maintain the new systems. Another was that production gains made by some farmers were canceled out by the high rate of population growth.

Another was that not enough research was done before a project was put into effect. The project discussed in the following article, undertaken in Botswana, is just one of many that did not meet expectations:

Here huge tracts have been cleared; the heavy "black cotton" soil has been planted with sorghum, maize, and sunflowers. Towering over the trees, three colossal concrete silos were visible from miles away. Each was stocked with enough sorghum to fill 74,000 sacks of 150 pounds apiece.

This was Mpandamatenga, a project consisting of some fifty 2,200-acre leasehold farms launched four years ago—the government's biggest effort to increase food production and amass reserves against future droughts. As Ben Mathe, a retired senior official at the Bank of Botswana, and Mavis Thale, the wife of a Gaborone executive, told me on the Tlale farm, the scheme has not gone well.

"We didn't know what we were getting into," Mavis said, gazing out over flatland stretching for miles in every direction. "We've been invaded by elephants, eland, and sables, by locusts and *podile* beetles, which suck the sorghum dry."

Rats and mice attack the fields at night. "They come by the millions and dig out newly planted seed," Ben said. "There is no drainage. Rain collects where it falls. You need big tractors to work this soil, at least four of them per farm. A lot of us bought the wrong equipment. It broke down. . . ." He gestured to a distant junkyard of rusting machinery. "We got financing from the National Development Bank, but they won't loan us more until we pay back what we owe. To get the big machines, we had to mortgage another farm down south and our home in Gaborone. And every grain of this year's harvest will go to the NDB!" He sighed. "Four of us have sold out already."

I tried to offer solace: "It's carved on the soul of every farmer that next year will be better." Ben smiled. "That's what keeps us going."

Unfavorable global conditions also had a part in the disappointing rate of development. The oil shortage during the 1970's, for example, forced many African countries to use their limited export earnings to buy high-priced oil from other countries. During the 1980's, the worldwide decline in economic activity caused the prices of the goods that Africa exported to fall. Then the over-abundance of oil caused oil prices to drop. The result was that the value of the products Africa exported did not increase in relation to the goods it imported.

By the 1990's, these conditions had combined with others, such as political unrest, to bring Africa to a state of economic crisis. At the same time low prices for their goods in the global marketplace caused their earnings to be greatly reduced, many African nations found themselves forced to borrow more money to buy food to feed their growing populations. Their debt kept increasing, and governments found that they could not pay back money borrowed from international banking agencies.

In 1991, African ministers at a session of the Economic Commission for Africa (ECA) and at the Conference of Ministers tackled the economic challenges of the 1990's. Noting that for the twelfth year in a row the standard of living of the average African had fallen, they made several proposals. One was that the international community support a form of debt cancellation. Another was a new "international agenda for cooperation" to provide Africa with the resources needed for economic reform.

DROUGHT AND FAMINE

The drought and famine sweeping Africa today is not new to most Africans. Over the last 30 years, all but 5 nations south of the Sahara have suffered severe food shortages. At least 22 nations in the region continue to suffer the long-term effects of the drought of the 1980's, called one of the worst droughts of the century.

Absence of rainfall is only one cause of drought and famine in Africa. Other factors contribute as well—intensive agricultural use, overgrazing, ill-advised development programs, population pressures, civil war, and repressive governments. Below, a journalist discusses the magnitude of the problem:

Throughout Africa, 20 million people were assessed as "at risk" at the start of 1991 by the United Nations Food and Agriculture Organisation (FAO) following two years of bad harvests in many countries, with the latest estimates of 5.1 million tons of food aid required and hundreds of millions of dollars for transport to deliver it. . . .

Source: Arthur Zich. "Botswana: The Adopted Land" in *National Geographic,* Vol. 178, No. 6, December 1990, pp. 94-96.

EXAMINING PHOTOGRAPHS *As in other parts of the world, forests in many parts of Africa are being destroyed at an alarming rate because of the collection of firewood, the expansion of agricultural fields, soil erosion, and drought. Here, forestry agents in Burkina Faso examine tree saplings that will later be planted to combat this loss of forests. What other factors besides the loss of forests have made the African drought worse?*

Those comparing today's drought with that of 1984-1985 go beyond tonnages. Reports from the Geneva-based League of Red Cross and Red Crescent Societies emphasize the vulnerability of millions of Africans: deeper national economic crises, bigger debts, eroded welfare structures, increased populations, degraded environments, renewed conflict and refugee flows, and the poor grain and livestock reserves of farmers and herdspeople who had not recovered from the last disaster when the latest crisis arrived.

Appeals for victims of Liberia's civil war have joined calls for help for 4 million threatened in Mozambique and Angola . . . , but it is in the Horn and Sahel where fears are greatest. . . .

Political and military factors are hampering food deliveries in Sudan, Ethiopia, and Somalia. Increasing numbers of displaced people and refugees are fleeing fighting in all three countries. In the Sahel, two years of patchy rains have left Chad, Niger, Burkina Faso, Mali, and Mauritania struggling to secure enough food aid to keep hunger from becoming starvation. . . .

Up to 10 million people are at risk in Sudan. . . . Camps of the displaced have formed . . . in the west since a severe harvest failure last year . . . , while thousands are trekking into Omdurman to join many who never left after the last famine. In the east, worst hit are again Beja people of the Red Sea hills, whose old and young have begun to beg. . . .

Across the Sahel, no country has escaped the impact of the drought. . . . Population movements have begun as one response to food shortages. . . .

From the Red Sea to the Atlantic, failed rains this year could be the final factor deciding the fate of millions of poor farmers and nomads. Often far beyond aid supply lines, they face a simple choice: death—or survival in impoverishment, losing lands and herds, migrating into grim urban slums to await the next crisis. Even if rains come, disrupting deliveries during the hungriest time of the year, many will have already eaten or traded seeds and livestock; others are abandoning their fields in despair.

Source: Nick Cater. "The Forgotten Famine" in *Africa Report,* May-June 1991, pp. 60–62. Copyright © 1991 by the African-American Institute. Reprinted by permission of *Africa Report.*

POPULATION GROWTH

Although Africa is enormous, there are vast areas of desert and rain forest. The amount of land available for farming and herding, therefore, is not that great. Over the past few decades, Africa's population has begun to catch up with the available land. Farm plots are smaller, which makes it harder for farmers to produce enough to feed their families and to raise export crops.

The 2.9 percent yearly population growth rate of Africa is currently the highest of any continent in the world. According to some experts, if the population continues to grow at this rate, it will double in 23 years. Some African countries have tried to resolve the problem by encouraging family planning, the use of methods to control and space the number of births. One of those countries is Kenya. In the following magazine article, a

journalist discusses why Kenyan leaders felt they needed a population program:

Marriage is almost universal in Kenya. Most women marry early. . . . The average age for first marriage today is under twenty. Only three percent of married women prove infertile. And the other 97 percent have lots of children. In the late 1970s the average Kenya wife could be expected to produce eight children. Immunization and better medical care meant more and more of those children survived infancy and childhood.

For most Kenyans, this all seemed like good news. Kenyans want children. They are the focus of life. . . .

But if children are a source of joy, population is not. Half the population is under the age of fifteen. Since only a small minority will ever inherit land, the best hope for the rest is education. And the cost of education, housing, and medical care transfers wealth from parents to children. It also takes up wealth that might be invested in businesses that provide jobs. Even with schooling, many will remain unemployed. The returns promised in old age grow smaller and smaller. And life is harder for the young. . . . There is fear that by the year 2000 Kenya will be unable to support its population. Says one Kenya demographer, "There are dismal prospects for the future."

Such apprehension is not new to Kenya, which was the first subSaharan African nation to adopt a population policy. . . .

In practice, Kenya's population program consists chiefly of telling people their options and providing contraceptive technology for those who want it. . . . "People in Kenya aren't yet ready to be told how many children they can have," says Wangari Maathai, coordinator of the Kenya Green Belt Movement.

Nevertheless, population growth seems to be slowing. A recent study found that the number of children a mother might expect to have in her lifetime had

EXAMINING PHOTOGRAPHS *This West African billboard is an attempt to convince more Africans of the need for family planning. Why is family planning important to the future of Africa?*

dropped from 7.7 in 1984 to 6.7 in 1989. It found that women are getting married later and that between 1977 and 1989 the percentage of women using contraceptive methods . . . rose from 7 to 27. Perhaps more surprising, almost half the currently married women said in the survey that they did not want to have any more children, and 26 percent said they wanted more but not within two years.

EXAMINING PHOTOGRAPHS *Some of the leaders and officials of the 50 member nations of the OAU are shown arriving for a meeting in Kenya.* What is the purpose of the OAU?

SECTION 1 REVIEW

CHECKING FOR UNDERSTANDING
1. **List** reasons why the rate of African development has been disappointing.
2. **Identify** factors that have contributed to drought and famine in Africa.

CRITICAL THINKING
3. **Identifying Alternatives** Suggest two solutions to population growth in Africa. Discuss advantages and disadvantages of each.

SECTION 2
Facing the Challenges

Some African nations are joining together to try to solve their problems. This is being done not only on a nation-by-nation basis but also through regional and continent-wide cooperation. One of the foremost cooperative agencies is the Organization of African Unity (OAU), founded in 1963. It promotes economic cooperation among members, tries to settle political disputes, and strongly supports African liberation movements.

In 1980, OAU leaders drew up a blueprint for economic revival of Africa that called for self-sufficiency in food production and in-

Source: Peter Steinhart. "Beyond Pills and Condoms" in *Audubon,* January 1991, pp. 22, 24.

dustrial development by the year 2000, the construction and expansion of transcontinental highways and railroads, the increase of intra-African trade, and the creation and strengthening of regional economic organizations. In 1985, the OAU reaffirmed and modified its plan. But, at the same time, members admitted that Africa was near "economic collapse."

Today, most African leaders agree that a big part of the crisis in Africa is centered around development planning. They do not believe that more new programs are the answer. Instead, they must find better ways to implement the programs already in place. The international community, they say, has to contribute to sustain African growth and development. But the major burden must be assumed by the Africans themselves. One African leader put it this way: "There is no other way out. African countries must come together as an integrated force to promote their own destiny."

CASE STUDY

Africa

WOMEN AND DEVELOPMENT

Women in Africa share a common desire for a better life. As the article below states, some progress has been made but, much remains to be done:

The lot of African women is not only unfair, it also costs Africa money. With vast underemployment, Africa needs to encourage small businesses. In much of western Africa women dominate commerce. But in other parts of the continent banks will not lend to women. Most of Africa's farmers are women. But their efforts to improve yields are often thwarted. . . . The World Bank is so concerned at this wasted potential that a third of its African loans include special mention of how they should help women.

Yet in some ways women's lot continues to get harder. As the towns grow, men drift away from the land, abandoning their traditional share of farm work. As schools multiply, women also get less help from children. The ecological disasters creeping across Africa add to women's workloads. . . . In deforested parts of Zimbabwe, women spend a fifth of their time collecting wood for cooking and brewing.

Too much of the help that Africa's farmers need misses them because it is not aimed at women. Most of the continent's agricultural advisers are men, who feel uncomfortable advising other men's wives. Incentives to farmers are often misconceived as when Kenya sought to encourage tea-growers by paying an annual bonus to the (male) owners of the land, rather than to the wives who did the work.

Outsiders trying to help Africa's villages naturally ask village authorities what sort of help they need. The authorities are men. Ask a Kenyan chief what his people want, and he is likely to request water for the cattle, since men traditionally do the herding. The women, who do three-quarters of Kenya's farming, might prefer a village store, to save a long walk to the town. . . .

Reformers try to help women with changes to the law, but old attitudes die hard. . . . Modern law has limited reach

in Africa, whose customary codes . . . still govern the way many . . . people live.

Swazi women before consulting a doctor or buying land are often made to produce written permission from their husbands. . . . Custom often prevails even where social change has made it absurd. A widow may find all her belongings snatched away by her dead husband's brother. That made some sense when brother and widow lived in the same village, and the widow became the brother's responsibility. . . .

Most widows are ignorant of the laws that protect them. A better deal for women thus depends on education, and that in turn depends on lower birth rates. Africa's girls and boys attend primary school with comparable diligence; but later on far more girls drop out than boys. Their mothers called them home to look after their younger brothers and sisters' or the teacher sends them home because they themselves are pregnant.

DRAWING CONCLUSIONS

1. Why have African women not benefited from development?
2. Why is it important for women to be more involved?

Source: "Women's value, men's worth" in *The Economist,* November 10, 1990, p. 54. © 1990 The Economist Newspaper Ltd. Reprinted with permission.

LITERACY CHART

EXAMINING ART *According to 1990 UNESCO figures, some 168 million Africans aged 15 years and over are illiterate. More than 100 million are women. Even though the figures do not take into account those literate in languages other than a nation's official language, the number of Africans who cannot read or write remains staggering. This Senegalese literacy chart, on which appear words in the Mandingo language, helps promote literacy by tying together the learning of reading and writing with a person's cultural, economic, technical, and political environment.* What impact has Africa's economic problems had on education?

	C	C	c	c	cakka				o	o		xooda
	e	e	e	e	kande			P	P	P		tepu
	g	g	g	tiga			┌	┌	r	r		fúníír
	J	J	J	j	jambangine		W	W	w	w		ewela
	∏	∏	n	n	siine			Y	Y	y	y		yoot

EDUCATION

During the colonial period, most Africans were denied access to education. In the 1960's, the newly independent African nations made education a priority. Their goals were universal, free, compulsory elementary education; secondary education for 30 percent of those completing primary school; and university education for 20 percent of those completing secondary school.

During the next several decades, much progress was made. But, in more recent years, because of Africa's economic crisis, education budgets have suffered drastic cuts. There have been other problems as well, including a lack of qualified teachers and the inaccessibility of schools for many young people in rural areas. Even more serious has been the decline in the quality of schooling. The number of students repeating a grade or dropping out completely has been on the rise.

African leaders, however, recognize that with 65 percent of the African population under age 25, education must be a priority. In 1990, when children from Soweto welcomed him home from prison, South African leader Nelson Mandela issued what the reporter who wrote the following excerpt calls "a heartfelt plea:"

"Tomorrow is school," [Mandela] said. "We—your parents, your brothers, your sisters—love you, and we want you to lead this country. But you cannot carry out that responsibility if you have not got the weapons, the weapons of education. . . ."

About two hours later, . . . Mandela emerged again with his wife . . . to thank the children for their greetings and urge them to devote themselves to their schoolwork "in spite of the difficult circumstances under which you have to study."

"That is the best way of welcoming me back," he said. "Some people think the

ANC has been saying to our children: freedom before education. But that's not true. We have always said our children should go back to school."

AIDS

One of the major challenges confronting Africans is AIDS, a fatal disease caused by a virus that attacks the body's immune system. It is an epidemic that is sweeping the entire continent. In the early 1990's, it was estimated that close to 7 million Africans were already infected with the virus.

Governments throughout Africa have initiated programs to educate their people about the disease and to combat and control its spread. The Kenyan government is an example. It has identified AIDS as the nation's number one health challenge and has taken the lead in educating its citizens about the disease and its prevention. The following newspaper article discusses some of the methods being used to reach Kenyans:

EXAMINING PHOTOGRAPHS *Health officials state that education is the key to halting the spread of AIDS epidemic. How many Africans are believed to be infected with the virus?*

The Kenyan AIDS media campaign features radio programs translated into eight languages. Lessons aimed at teens spotlight popular musicians. Programs for adults feature medical experts who answer questions submitted on postcards by listeners. Each day, local papers carry news, features and letters to the editor about AIDS and AIDS prevention, all orchestrated by the Kenyan government.

Traditional health workers . . . are enlisted in the effort. It is possible to go into the homes of Kenyan "medicine men" and find government AIDS education posters alongside shelves lined with healing gourds and bags of ground roots.

. . . The government together with a sizable number of . . . international and national nonprofit agencies has embarked on

. . . doing health education the most effective way—one person at a time.

Near the foothills of Mount Kilimanjaro, health workers on motorcycles fan out across the hillsides telling mothers to bring their children to the Presbyterian church. The main sanctuary is two trees and a semicircle of branches. Under their leaves a health educator . . . leads a group of women through a question-and-answer period about AIDS.

In Korogocho, one of Nairobi's largest slums, local residents hired and trained by World Vision, a U.S. relief agency, move through the marketplace of narrow alleys. They visit women selling vegetables from open air stalls, local teachers out shopping and truck drivers in town for the day from upcountry farms. In small groups, the health workers provide details on how HIV is transmitted and share news of local residents felled by the disease. . . .

Source: Scott Kraft. "Get Education to Lead Nation, Mandela Tells Pupils," *Los Angeles Times,* February 14, 1990, p. A8. Copyright 1990, *Los Angeles Times.* Reprinted by permission.

In a small cinder-block apartment house in the center of the district, the AIDS education office has posted a chart that lists the number of personal AIDS-prevention discussions for that month—measured in the thousands. . . .

Kenyan health officials believe that the very poor are among the easiest to educate. As Joseph Mwongela, a Kenyan health education officer explains, "The impoverished have an asset that makes health education possible—time. They will come to a meeting. They will listen to a 30-minute radio program."

The majority of Kenyans, however, are the working poor. . . . To reach this group, the Kenyan government is trying to institute AIDS education programs in the workplace and women's clubs in major urban centers.

SELF-RELIANCE

For many Africans, the key to a more prosperous future lies in self-reliance and economic cooperation. Africans working on their own or in partnership with development organizations have built irrigation systems, increased family food production, and raised health standards and education levels. Below, a journalist discusses what Africans have accomplished in Sudan:

Lowku Kery looks down and takes the hand of a naked child. Immediately surrounding him, there are dozens of other hands—small and thin—seeking the same attention. These children . . . eagerly follow Mr. Kery as he shows a visitor around the Panyanyang refugee camp along the Sobaat River. . . .

The scene at Panyanyang is one of wretched squalor. There is no sanitation and no shelter, save the foot-high tents some children have erected out of shreds of cloth as protection against the incessant rain. . . .

Source: Steve Rabin. "Kenya: AIDS as if It Mattered." *The Washington Post,* November 17, 1991, p. C5.

The scene at Panyanyang is one we in industrialized countries have witnessed all too often on television newsclips. . . .

What we normally don't get a chance to see is . . . the self-reliance and initiative on the part of those affected while international relief agencies scurry to reach the scene.

Take Kery, a schoolteacher who fled the civil war in Sudan two years ago to take refuge at Itang camp in Ethiopia. There, with donated supplies, residents established schools, health centers, and their own form of government. He was director of one of Itang's schools until the school was bombed. . . . Kery then led some 3,500 children on a 10-day trek across the border back to Sudan. Now he directs this children's camp—supervising the supervision of meager supplies, overseeing the provision of scant health care, and organizing the children into patrols searching for edible plants.

Or take the workforce of Sudanese men, down the river from the children's camp, who rebuilt an airstrip by hand out of bricks they pulled from bombed-out buildings. They are now digging a drainage ditch so the rains don't wash out the supply planes' landing strip. About 100 yards away, these men have marked out the spot where a much larger plane has managed to drop 141 tons of food.

SECTION 2 REVIEW

CHECKING FOR UNDERSTANDING

1. **Indicate** who must assume the major burden for African development.
2. **Discuss** what the Kenyan government is doing to combat AIDS.

CRITICAL THINKING

3. **Demonstrating Reasoned Judgment** Do you think education should be a priority in Africa? Give reasons.

Source: Annie Foster. "Behind the Tragic Images of Africa" in *The Christian Science Monitor,* July 12, 1991, p. 19.

GLOBAL FOCUS

Multicultural View

UNITY THROUGH A COMMON LANGUAGE

For there to be development and progress in African nations, there must be unity among the people. Most African governments recognize that a single common language would greatly reduce misunderstanding and help to unite their people. But choosing a language that would be acceptable to everyone is not an easy task. Within the borders of each nation, hundreds of languages may be spoken, and across the continent, there are more than 1500 separate languages.

Some Africans have suggested that Swahili, also known as Kiswahili, be adopted as the common language for the entire continent. About 50 million people in the world can effectively communicate in Kiswahili today. In the newspaper interview that follows, a young Ghanaian student studying Kiswahili at the University of Dar es Salaam in Dar es Salaam, Tanzania explains why he thinks more African countries should make Kiswahili their official national language.

FOCUSING ON THE ISSUE Read the interview, and study the map that accompanies it. Then defend or refute the following statements:

1. Africa should have a common language.
2. Kiswahili is an ideal choice for a single common language for Africa.
3. A foreign language would be a better choice than Kiswahili for a single common language for Africa.
4. Most people in Africa will be receptive to a national language.

. . . Kiswahili is the most widely spoken language in the eastern part of Africa. For the people of western Africa, learning and knowing Kiswahili, therefore, brings them closer to their brothers in eastern Africa. . . .

I think you will also agree that Kiswahili is on the way of becoming one of the major world languages. A knowledge of two or three such languages puts one at an advantage. Wherever he goes, he can communicate with less problems. It is like having an international currency in one's pocket. . . .

. . . Some African countries have adopted French and English as their official national languages. Of course, if the French and the British had not come and colonized, such a strange thing as having French as a "national language" of an

African state would be unheard of.

Declaring a foreign language a "national language" when less than 10 per cent of the population are conversant with that language is nothing but the height of absurdity. It is only a handful [of] educated elite who use such an alien "national language."

What makes matters complicated is the fact that however committed you are in trying to spread and popularize such languages to the masses, it becomes very difficult for the majority to grasp them. There is no relationship at all between these alien languages and the vernaculars [local languages].

If, on the other hand, a language like Kiswahili is introduced in Ghana or in Nigeria and efforts are made to popularize it, after a few years you are likely to have more people capable of speaking at least broken Kiswahili as compared to those capable of speaking English. . . .

To most Africans, Kiswahili is easier to learn compared to alien languages. This is explained by the fact that it is predominantly a Bantu language, and therefore has a close relationship with other Bantu languages. My experience is that even before I grasped the ABC's of Kiswahili, I could not be lost completely when listening to people conversing in the language. You at least get a

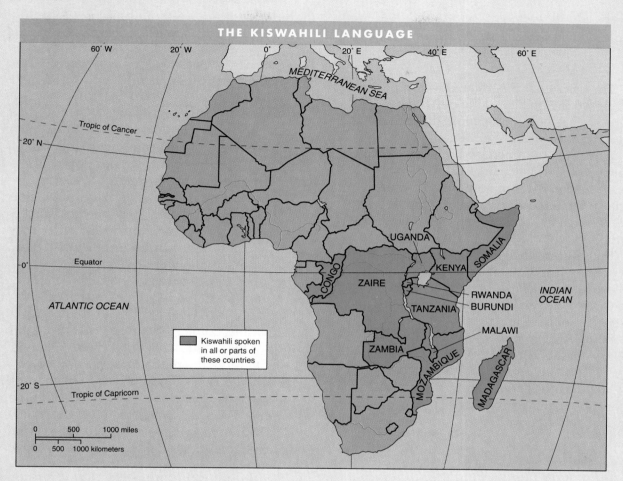

THE KISWAHILI LANGUAGE

MEDITERRANEAN SEA

Tropic of Cancer

20° N

Equator

UGANDA

SOMALIA

KENYA

CONGO

ZAIRE

RWANDA
BURUNDI

INDIAN
OCEAN

ATLANTIC OCEAN

TANZANIA

MALAWI

Kiswahili spoken
in all or parts of
these countries

ZAMBIA

MOZAMBIQUE

MADAGASCAR

20° S

Tropic of Capricorn

0   500   1000 miles

0   500   1000 kilometers

vague idea of what the speakers are talking about. . . .

With a completely alien language like English, things are different. You have to go through a rigorous study in order to be conversant with the basics of it. . . .

Another advantage of Kiswahili is that it is likely to be acceptable among different [ethnic groups]. In Africa there are [ethnic group] rivalries. . . . Given such a situation, picking one of the vernaculars and de-claring it a national language will not only be scratching a healing wound, but the exercise will also fail. Some people will not accept the proposal, even if they have no strong reasons for their refusal. . . .

Fortunately, a good number of people in most of the African countries look at Kiswahili as a neutral African language. They are ready to adopt it as a national language without the feeling that a certain [ethnic group] has been favoured and honoured.

Frankly, African states—consisting of different ethnic groups (most of them are)—will have no choice but to adopt Kiswahili, if at all they are determined to settle the national language question once and for all. People capable of seeing decades ahead have no doubt about this.

Source: Henry Muhanika. "Kiswahili is spreading" in the *Tanzanian Sunday News,* March 30, 1980, p. 5.

Chapter 7 Review

SUMMARY

The basic aim of African development is to improve the quality of life of Africans. This process has been made more difficult by decisions made during the colonial period.

African governments have been working since independence to develop their economies, and some progress has been made. For a variety of reasons, the degree of development hoped for has not always been attained.

In its efforts to develop, Africa is faced with a great many challenges. Included among these are financial debt, famine, population growth, inadequate education budgets, and an AIDS epidemic.

Some African nations are joining together to try and solve their problems and promote development. Most Africans believe that while the international community has to contribute, the key to a more prosperous future is self-reliance.

REVIEWING FACTS

1. **State** the basic aim of development in African nations.
2. **Explain** how global conditions in recent decades have affected the economies of many African nations.
3. **Discuss** the relationship between population growth and agricultural production in Africa today.
4. **Explain** why many African nations are deeply in debt.
5. **List** the education goals targeted in the 1960's by newly independent African nations.
6. **Give examples** of some of the problems from which African education suffers.

7. **Specify** what many Africans consider the key to a prosperous future.

CRITICAL THINKING

1. **Analyzing Information** Do you think the statement, "The future stems from the past," relates to African development? Give examples to support your answer.
2. **Drawing Conclusions** The state of the global economy has had a great influence on economic development in Africa. What does this indicate to you about the interdependence of nations?
3. **Expressing Problems Clearly** Huge amounts of aid have been provided to African areas hit hard by drought and famine. Some Africans say that this aid is not the solution to the problem. What do you think the problem is? Do you agree that aid is not the solution? Explain.
4. **Demonstrating Reasoned Judgment** In the late 1980's, Africa's total debt was equal to the annual value of all its products. What does this suggest about Africa's ability to ease its economic crisis?

ANALYZING CONCEPTS

1. **Scarcity** In what ways might drought or a severe food shortage in one African nation severely impact neighboring nations?
2. **Interdependence** Do you agree with the view that for Africans self-reliance and economic cooperation are the key to development and to a more prosperous future? Give reasons to support your answer.

GEOGRAPHIC THEMES

Regions Why have decisions made during the colonial period made African development more difficult?

Writing a Topic Sentence

The object of most written material is to inform the reader about someone or something. Generally, the material is divided into paragraphs. A paragraph is a group of sentences that develops a single main idea, or principal focus. It contains at least one sentence that presents the main idea. Usually, the main idea of a paragraph is stated in a *topic sentence*. The other sentences explain or give detail or description about the main idea.

While most topic sentences appear at the beginning of the paragraph, they sometimes appear at the end, or even in the middle. Some paragraphs have no topic sentence and the main idea is not stated directly. However, writing a good topic sentence for each paragraph will make what you write clearer and more precise.

The following steps will help you in writing topic sentences:

- Read the paragraph carefully, and determine the general focus or subject.
- Read the paragraph again, sentence by sentence. For each, ask yourself what would happen if that sentence were not in the paragraph. Would the rest of the sentences tie together and make sense? If the answer to the question is no, you probably have identified the sentence that contains the main idea. In that case, identify the idea.
- Check the remaining sentences to determine if they support the idea put forth in the sentence you have just chosen. Do they describe, explain, or give details about the main idea?
- Write the main idea as a topic sentence.

EXAMPLE

Read the following paragraph about Africa:

In African nations, as in other nations of the world, the basic aim of development is to improve the quality of life. Nations often pursue this goal by developing their natural resources, industrializing, and modernizing agriculture. For most African nations, this has proved to be a difficult task.

All the sentences in this paragraph discuss a single main idea—economic development in Africa. The first sentence explains the purpose of development. The second sentence discusses how this goal is achieved. This sentence, however, makes sense only because it refers to the first sentence. Similarly, the third sentence states that the task is difficult in Africa. The second and third sentences give details about the main idea—economic development in Africa. The first sentence is the topic sentence because it most clearly expresses the main idea.

PRACTICE

Read the following paragraphs. Then write the topic sentence for each one. Topic sentences may or may not appear in the paragraphs.

1. For many Africans, the key to a more prosperous future lies in self-reliance and economic co-operation. Africans working on their own or in partnership with development organizations have built irrigation systems, increased food production, and raised health standards and education levels.

2. The government of Tanzania has promised to equip buildings that villagers construct themselves. In this way, it hopes to encourage its people to lead the way in their own development. Government officials recognize that central authorities and international aid organizations cannot do for people what they must do for themselves.

3. One of the major challenges confronting Africans is AIDS, a fatal disease caused by a virus that attacks the body's immune system. It is an epidemic that is sweeping the entire continent. In the early 1990's, it was estimated that close to 7 million Africans were already infected with the virus.

4. Fatima first began to help the women deliver their babies at the age of eleven. There was another midwife in the village, with whom she worked as an assistant. Neither of them ever had any formal education at a nurses' college, or any other kind of professional medical training, but they had skilled hands and success with most of the deliveries.

African Arts and Europe

The arts of Africa have been admired by Europeans since the early days of European imperialism. In the 1500's, the Portuguese were greatly impressed with the detailed bronze work and delicate ivory carving from West Africa. Later, other Europeans came to Africa and returned to their homelands with beautiful wood carvings from West Africa and finely woven and embroidered cloth from Central Africa. Explorers brought back these works of art as momentoes of their journeys. Missionaries displayed African artifacts to show the lifestyles of the cultures they sought to convert to Christianity. By the early 1800's, collectors and museums through-out Europe had ransacked Africa for the continent's art.

In the early decades of this century, enthusiasm for African art had spread to Europe's painters and sculptors. At this time, a group of innovative artists became fascinated by traditional African sculpture. The strong, geometric forms of African masks and carved wooden figures appealed to these artists who were searching for a new style. The idea that a painting or sculpture should exactly resemble its subject and conform to traditional European ideals of beauty seemed outdated. Artists were looking for an approach that would reflect the twentieth century. The simplicity and symbolic quality of African sculpture answered this need.

The encounter with African art directly influenced the works of such European artists as Georges Braque, Henri Matisse, and Maurice de Vlaminck. The influence of African arts on European artists is most obvious in the work of Spanish artist Pablo Picasso. African sculpture liberated him from old attitudes about painting. Picasso's

painting is known for its geometric figures with mask-like faces.

The impact of African arts is far-reaching. The continent's art forms continue to have a powerful impact on Western art. They also have opened the way for the appreciation of the art of other cultures.

Making the Connection

1. How did traditional African arts influence European artists?

2. Why do you think European artists regard African art as a suitable form of artistic expression for the twentieth century?

Unit 1 Review

SUMMARY

Africa, which stretches across the Equator and spans nearly 60 lines of latitude, has a broad and varied landscape. In this environment, the peoples of Africa have developed a rich historical tradition. During ancient times, powerful kingdoms and territories thrived in parts of Africa. Major change came with Europe's discovery of the continent. By the early 1900's, Europeans had colonized most of Africa.

In time, many Africans came to resent European rule. Their resistance finally resulted in independence for most African nations. Since independence, African governments have worked to develop their economies and better the lives of their people.

REVIEWING THE MAIN IDEAS

1. **Indicate** why Westerners should have a different picture of Africa today than they did in the past.
2. **Discuss** how physical environment and history have influenced African life.
3. **Compare** the European and African views of imperialism in Africa.
4. **State** why African nations have made education a priority.
5. **List** the major challenges with which Africa is confronted currently.

CRITICAL THINKING

1. **Making Comparisons** In what ways are Nigeria, South Africa, and Kenya the same? In what ways are they different?
2. **Demonstrating Reasoned Judgment** In the view of the Assistant Secretary-General of the UN Center for Social Development and Humanitarian Affairs, "The role of women in the future of Africa is important because women constitute one of the most valuable and dependable resources which Africa cannot afford to waste." Give reasons why you agree or disagree with this statement.
3. **Predicting Consequences** Some experts have predicted that as many as 50 million Africans could die of AIDS by the year 2000. What are some of the ways in which this might impact African development?

PRACTICING SKILLS

Read the two statements below, the first made by an Indian journalist and the second by an African academic. Then, for each, identify any assumptions made, draw a conclusion about Africa or Africans, and find information in the unit that proves or disproves your conclusion.

Development is about choices—giving the rural poor the opportunity to choose between taking assistance from the government and being left alone.

I think many Africans understand now that we can't keep blaming colonialism for all our problems. The large part of the blame ought to rest on our shoulders.

DEVELOPING A GLOBAL VIEWPOINT

One of the major problems facing Africa is its high rate of population growth. What other parts of the world suffer from a high rate of population growth? How has this affected their development and the quality of life of their citizens? What have some of them done to control population growth? Do you agree with the stand taken by the United States at a 1984 conference in Mexico City that there is no need for international programs in family planning? Explain.

China

China, the world's oldest living civilization, probably always has been the most populous nation on earth. In addition to its long history and large population, it always has had a rich and varied culture. While in the past the Chinese preferred to develop their land and their culture with little foreign influence, in recent years they have opened the door to other nations and other peoples. China is modernizing, industrializing, and becoming an important part of the world community. For these reasons, it is of value to see the Chinese as they see themselves and to understand how they have reached the point where they are today.

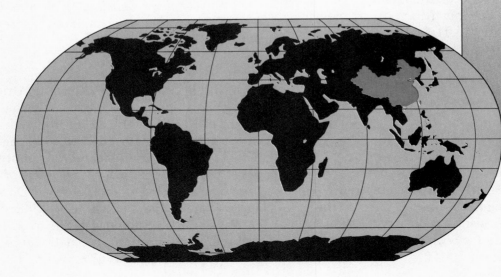

AT A GLANCE

LAND AREA: 3,696,032 sq. mi. (9,572,678 sq. km.)

LAND RESOURCES:
cropland: 10.4%
pasture: 34.2%
forest/woodland: 13.6%
other land: 41.8%

WILDERNESS AREA: 22%

MAJOR MOUNTAIN RANGES:
Altai, Tianshan, Qilian Kunlun, Karakorum, Tanggula, Heng-duan, Gangdise, Himalayas

MAJOR RIVERS: Huai, Huang He, Liao, Xi Jiang, Xun Jiang, Yangtze, Zhu Jiang

POPULATION: (1992 est.) 1,165,800,000

POPULATION UNDER 15/OVER 65: 28%/6%

LIFE EXPECTANCY: 69 yrs.

POPULATION PROJECTION: 1,590,800,000 (by 2025)

POPULATION DENSITY: 309/sq. mi. (119/sq. km.)

URBAN POPULATION: 26%

LARGEST CITIES: (millions)
Shanghai (7.1)
Beijing (6.0)
Tianjin (4.9)
Shenyang (3.8)

People and Places to Know
the Huang He, Dongbei, the Takla Makan, the Gobi, the Manchurian Plain, the North China Plain, Beijing, Shanghai, Yangtze River, Zhu Jiang

Key Terms to Define
yang and yin, ethnic group, steppe, loess, population density

Objectives to Learn
1. **Specify** China's physical features and their role in its development.
2. **Compare** royal and commercial cities of traditional China.
3. **Describe** traditional Chinese feelings for the countryside.

Chinese river scene

The Land Under Heaven

> In far-off times the Universe . . . was an enormous egg. One day the egg split open; its upper half became the sky, its lower half the earth, and from it emerged P'an Ku [Pan Gu], [the first] man. Every day he grew ten feet [3.05 meters] taller, the sky ten feet [3.05 meters] higher, the earth ten feet [3.05 meters] thicker. After eighteen thousand years P'an Ku [Pan Gu] died. His head split and became the sun and moon, while his blood filled the rivers and seas. His hair became the forests and meadows, his perspiration the rain, his breath the wind, his voice the thunder—and his fleas our ancestors.

This legend of Pan Gu was developed by the early Chinese to explain the origins of China. The huge egg symbolized **yang and yin,** the major forces of life. From the union of yang and yin, Pan Gu was born.

Belief in yang and yin was important to the people who lived in the Land Under Heaven, the term the early Chinese used to describe the territory on which they built their settlements. The Land Under Heaven was centered at first in the valley of the Huang He, or Yellow River, of East Asia. Here, the first Chinese settlements developed more than 4000 years ago. In time, the people of the valley expanded their control into neighboring areas and formed the land of China.

In spite of their conquests, the Huang He people, who became known as Chinese, were mostly cut off from other civilizations, largely because of such geographic factors as seas, mountains, and rain forests. This lack of outside contacts, however, aided in the formation of a common culture throughout China.

These early Chinese felt deeply about the land, and their way of life was rooted in the natural environment. They viewed Heaven and Earth as one and believed that each influenced the other through the activity of yang and yin.

The workings of nature were observed carefully. Astrologers and recordkeepers studied and noted the movement of stars and planets as well as any natural occurrences. They held that such happenings were portents, or hints of future changes. These changes might include a military victory, a new government, or bad economic times.

It also was believed that human behavior had an effect on nature. If human actions, especially those of the ruler, were in harmony with nature, the portents would be favorable. But if human actions upset the balance of nature, such natural and human disasters as floods and political chaos would follow. Thus, the early Chinese made every effort to live in accord with their surroundings.

Source: Michael Sullivan. *The Arts of China*. University of California Press, 1977, p. 13.

123

Variety of the Land

Today China has a total area of almost 3.7 million square miles (9.57 million square kilometers). It is the second largest nation in Asia and the third largest in the world. Few nations have as diverse a natural environment. This can be seen below as a Chinese author describes a railway journey from Guangzhou in southern China to the capital, Beijing (Bay Jing), in northern China:

The first part of [Chu Pin's] journey took him northward through his own province of [Guangdong]. . . .The province was separated from central China by high mountain ranges. . . .

. . . [Chu Pin's] train took him across the mountain range and plunged into the valley of Hunan. Everything changed: the climate, the language, the people's dress, and the flora—the fruit trees and flowers.

. . . [Guangdong] was subtropical, with palm trees, pomelos (a kind of grapefruit), and Chu Pin's favorite fruit, the leechee.

. . . Hunan was the rice bowl of China. As the train hurtled past the mountainous region he saw tall bamboo forests, vast green hillsides with luxuriant vegetation, and [waterfalls] and winding torrents. Everywhere he saw terraced rice fields. . . .

Most impressive was the number of streams and canals, for this was the basin of the [Dongting] Lake, the biggest lake in China. . . . The lake was just south of the great Yangtze River. . . . The land was flat and level, and the great river bent and curved in its meanderings. . . .

. . . Chu Pin took the train right through [Henan]. He was in North China now. . . .

. . . Chu Pin noticed that the Northern Chinese were taller in stature than the Southern Chinese. They also seemed poorer, for instead of the brick houses of South China, he saw principally mud houses.

The water buffalo of the South had disappeared, and the beasts of burden now were mules, donkeys, and horses. Instead of the rice paddies covered by water, he saw wheat fields standing in dry land, and instead of sugar cane, he saw corn.

CHECKING FOR UNDERSTANDING
1. **Describe** the environment of China, noting any differences among the regions of the country.

CRITICAL THINKING
2. **Evaluating Information** How might China's physical size affect its role in world affairs today?

Mountains

Mountains cover one-third of China. Of the 14 highest mountain peaks in the world, 9 are in China or on its borders. The highest mountain ranges are concentrated in the west. They include the Altai, Tianshan, Qilian, Kunlun, Karakorum, Tanggula, Hengduan, Gangdise, and Himalayas. Below, a Chinese explorer describes his travels in China's mountainous west:

Driving northwest from Kangding, we climbed steeply among breathtaking snow-clad mountains that seemed to continue forever. . . . We set out amid pines and birches, which gradually gave way to junipers and rhododendrons. Below 4,000

Source: Lin Yutang. *The Chinese Way of Life*. World Book, Inc., 1959, pp. 10–15. Reprinted by permission of Taiyi Lin Lai and Hsiang Ju Lin.

meters (13,000 feet) above sea level the trees ended and there were only low shrubs, grasses, and a profusion of blue and yellow poppies. . . .

On July 6, near Nam Co, Zhang [one of the author's companions] came down with mountain sickness. . . . We rushed Zhang to the nearest hospital. . . .

There we learned . . . that mountain sickness, caused by insufficient oxygen, is common among drivers along the Lhasa-Golmud road. When their trucks are stuck at such high elevation, the drivers strain themselves in freeing the vehicles, at the same time suffering from the hostile weather that can aggravate mountain sickness or cause pneumonia or both. . . .

But miraculously Zhang began to recover, and within days he was well enough to travel. . . .

On the road once more we continued north, climbing higher and higher until we arrived at Tanggula Pass—at 5,300 meters (17,388 feet) the highest point we were to reach during our expedition. . . . From here we had 600 kilometers [360 miles] to go before we reached Golmud, only 3,200 meters [10,560 feet] above sea level. Slowly, then, we descended from the roof of the world to what were merely the eaves.

In the eastern part of China, mountains are generally lower than in the western area, and there are many highland regions. Northeastern China, also known as Dongbei (Manchuria), is partly composed of mountains that are heavily forested. In addition, it has numerous highlands. In southeastern and south central China, the 3000-to-4000-foot (914-to-1219-meter) peaks are favorite tourist spots because of their lush vegetation, wide variety of animal life, and the many ancient temples and monasteries studding their slopes.

Source: Wong How-Man. "People of China's Far Provinces." *National Geographic*, Vol. 165, No. 3, March 1984, pp. 291–293, 294, 300.

EXAMINING PHOTOGRAPHS *The Great Wall of China, begun in the third century BC, was built to protect China from invaders from the north. What type of protection from invaders does the environment provide?*

SECTION 2 REVIEW

CHECKING FOR UNDERSTANDING
1. **State** how much of China is mountainous.
2. **List** the highest mountain ranges in China.
3. **Describe** how the Chinese regarded their mountains in the past.

CRITICAL THINKING
4. **Making Generalizations** What do you think are the drawbacks and the benefits of living or traveling in a mountainous environment?

SECTION 3

Desert, Steppe, and Plain

China has desert areas, as well as mountains, in the northwest. North of the Kunlun Mountains is one of the world's largest and driest deserts—the Takla Makan. Farther north along China's border with Mongolia is the Gobi. Both the Takla Makan and the Gobi are rich in mineral resources, but few people live in either place.

South and east of the deserts is the **steppe**, or generally treeless grasslands. The nomadic herders known as Mongolians who live in the steppe use it as grazing land for their sheep and ponies. Since the area gets relatively little rainfall, there is little agriculture. Below, a writer describes the life of two young people and their families who live on the steppe:

Sugula's and Drol's families belong to the same work team. Each family is in charge of a thousand sheep. When the pasturage in one area is exhausted, Sugula's and Drol's families move on to new grazing grounds. Because they have to roam about so much, they live in tents which are called yurts. The tents are shaped like great mushrooms. . . . When-

ever the pasturage in one area is exhausted, Sugula and Drol help their families pack their belongings in carts. They take down the yurt felts. . . . Then they take apart the framework of the yurts and strap the individual pieces of wood to the sides of the carts. . . . With the herders on horseback driving the flocks, and the older people and the children taking turns guiding the plodding oxen or getting a ride on the carts, they set off for greener pastures. . . .

[Sugula's] grandparents live in a three-room brick and stone house in the headquarters town. . . .

Most of the other people who live in the little town belong to a work team that builds sheds, pens, and kunluns. A kunlun is an enclosure protected by low walls to keep the cattle out. The grass in the kunluns is cut periodically and stored away in the sheds. It will be used to tide the livestock over the leanest winter months.

Then there are snows and blinding blizzards, and the bucket-shaped stoves in the

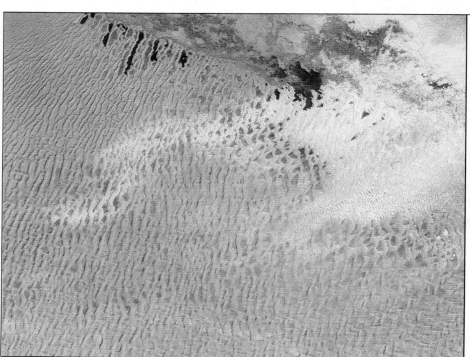

EXAMINING PHOTOGRAPHS *This photograph of the dunes of the Takla Makan was taken from a National Aeronautics and Space Administration (NASA) satellite with a special camera. Many of the dunes are curved, and some extend up to 20 miles (32 kilometers). In the upper right portion of the photo, part of the desert shown is covered by snow. What other deserts are there in China?*

EXAMINING PHOTOGRAPHS *Most nomadic herders on the steppe of China live in yurts like the one pictured here. These portable dwellings can house entire families and protect the occupants from harsh weather. Warmth generally is provided by bucket-shaped stoves. Why do nomads find this type of housing convenient?*

yurts glow red with burning chips of dried cattle dung. The chips . . . serve for fuel here, as wood is so scarce. Meals are hearty, consisting of steamed millet and noodles and hard cheese and great hunks of . . . barbecued mutton. All is washed down with strong tea and fiery drafts of liquor. . . . This food fuels the herders, who must wander far and wide searching for scant pasturage for their gaunt flocks, and who must mount long night watches against the ravenous wolves whose howling floats over the stepplands. . . .

But in this land not all is harsh. Winter gives way to the green loveliness of spring, spangled with flowers, melodic with the song of the lark. It is a time of plenty. . . .

South of the steppe are the plains of northern China. In the far northeast is the Manchurian Plain. In the south of the Plain,

where there is an opening to the sea, are some of China's best harbors. Farther inland, the Plain has fertile soil and large deposits of coal and iron. These deposits have made the Manchurian Plain the leading industrial area of China.

South of the Manchurian Plain lies the wide North China Plain, the western part of which is covered with **loess** (loos). This fertile, yellow soil carried by the wind from the Gobi makes the Plain a rich farming area. It also is an industrial area, with most industries centered around the large cities of Beijing, Tianjin, Shanghai, Nanjing, and Hangzhou.

SECTION 4

Rivers

China is a land of many rivers. Most of the major rivers begin in the mountainous west and run through China's north, central, and southern regions. Of the northern rivers, the Huang He (Yellow River) is the longest. It flows slightly less than 3000 miles (4800 kilometers) before emptying into the sea. Because it often floods over a large area and causes great destruction, it has been called "China's Sorrow."

In central China, the longest river is the Yangtze (Chang Jiang). It is almost 4000 miles (6400 kilometers) long—the third longest river in the world. Its valley has rich agricultural land and numerous industrial centers. Most of the industry is concentrated around the large cities of Shanghai, Wuhan, and Changsha. Below, a passenger on a boat trip describes a journey on the Yangtze:

Mottled hills appeared in the mist on both sides of the river, and here, just above Chang Shou, the river narrowed to about seventy-five feet [22.9 meters]. The ship slowed to negotiate this rocky bottleneck and gave me time to study the hills. . . .

. . . .Every inch of these hills was farmland. . . . On the steepest slopes were terraces of vegetables. How was it possible to water the gardens on these cliff-faces? I . . . saw a man climbing up the hillside, carrying two buckets on a yoke. He tipped them into a ditch and . . . started down the hill. No one is idle on the Yangtze. In the loneliest bends of the river are solitary men breaking rocks and smashing them into gravel. . . .

One day I was standing at the ship's rail. . . . We saw some trackers . . . pulling a junk [Chinese boat]. The men skipped from rock to rock, they climbed, they hauled the lines attached to the junk, and they struggled along the steep rocky tow-path. They were barefoot. . . .

The junks and these trackers will be on the river for some time to come. Stare for five minutes at any point on the Yangtze and you will see a junk sailing upstream with its ragged, ribbed sail; or being towed by yelling, tethered men. . . . There are many new-fangled ships and boats on the river, but I should say that the Yangtze is a river of junks and sampans [Chinese boats], fuelled by human sweat. . . .

In the days that followed we passed through the gorges. . . . The gorges are wonderful, and it is almost impossible to exaggerate their splendour; but the river is long and complicated, and much greater than its gorges. . . .

[As] soon as we left [Bai De] the mountains rose—enormous limestone cliffs on each side of the river. There is no shore: the sheer cliffs plunge straight into the water. . . . Looking ahead through the gorges you see no exit, only the end of what looks like a blind canyon. . . .

. . . It is not only the height of the gorges, but the narrowness of the river . . . which makes it swift. . . . The scale gives it this look of strongness, and fills it with an atmosphere of ominous splendour. . . .

EXAMINING PHOTOGRAPHS *The Yangtze, the longest river in Asia, has served as a major trade route for centuries. Gorges, like the ones above, often make the Yangtze impossible to navigate. Through what part of China does the Yangtze River flow?*

Next to the Yangtze in volume of flow is the Zhu Jiang (Pearl River). In many ways, it is one of the most important rivers in the country. In its humid valley are produced about 50 percent of China's grain, 20 percent of its jute, and such other products as rubber, oil palm, coffee, and sisal hemp. About 95 percent of the valley is hills and mountains which contain many valuable minerals.

The rivers of China, however, also have a destructive side. Over the centuries, the Chinese often have faced the destruction of their land by floods, which they blamed on the "wild rivers." Chinese tradition states that around 3000 BC a man named Yu was the first to tame the rivers. Three days after Yu got married, he left his new bride to help people cope with the flooding. He labored for 13 years without returning home. Finally, his efforts were successful. Nine rivers were dredged, and the flooding was stopped.

Yu also had the people build embankments and dikes along the Huna He River. Centuries later, another official directed the building of the Dujiangyan irrigation system on the Min River in central China. The system, which has been adapted and modernized over the years, is still in use as one of China's largest water control projects.

SECTION 4 REVIEW

CHECKING FOR UNDERSTANDING
1. **List** the major rivers of China.
2. **Explain** what Yu contributed to the development of China.

CRITICAL THINKING
3. **Evaluating Information** Which river do you think is the most important to China's economic well-being? Explain.

China

NORTH, SOUTH, EAST, WEST, AND CENTER

The Chinese who lived in the Land Under Heaven developed their land and led their lives in accordance with a set of structured beliefs. For them, certain forces were sacred and were related to the general pattern of human existence.

One force was cardinal directions. There were five of these—north, south, east, west, and center. Each was associated with a season of the year. North represented winter, and south represented summer. East symbolized spring, and west symbolized fall. Center represented all seasons. Each direction and season, in turn, was related to and described in terms of another force—color. North was black, and south was red. East was green, and west was white. Center was yellow, the color of the soil of the valley where Chinese civilization began.

Each cardinal direction, season, and color also was symbolized by and related to an

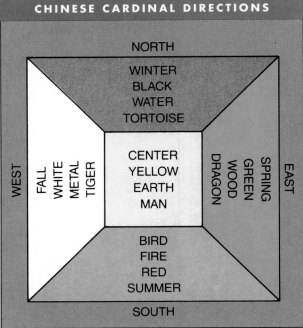

CHINESE CARDINAL DIRECTIONS

NORTH
WINTER
BLACK
WATER
TORTOISE

WEST — FALL WHITE METAL TIGER

CENTER
YELLOW
EARTH
MAN

EAST — SPRING GREEN WOOD DRAGON

BIRD
FIRE
RED
SUMMER

SOUTH

"activity," or element. There were five activities—water, fire, wood, metal, and soil. Each was related to the other, and each was a power in the world. Water was associated with north and fire with south. Wood symbolized east, and metal symbolized west. Earth represented center. Tradition stated that "[The nature of] Water is to moisten and descend; of Fire, to flame and ascend; of Wood, to be crooked and straighten; of Metal, to yield and to be modified; of Soil, to provide for sowing and reaping."

Five sacred animals were still another force. Each animal was related to a cardinal direction. The tortoise symbolized

north and the bird south; the dragon was east and the tiger west. At the center were humans.

Belief in these forces and in their relationship one to the other was so strong that the Chinese built their royal cities in accordance with them. Each city was laid out in the form of a square. In the center was the palace. To the north was the marketplace, while to the south was the sacred place. The emperor entered the city by the south gate and faced south to receive officials and conduct public business. The temples where most religious services were held were located near the south central gate. Thus, the Chinese showed that the forces had to be taken into account.

DRAWING CONCLUSIONS

1. What were the five cardinal directions? With what forces was each associated?
2. How did the various forces in which the Chinese believed affect the way in which the people lived?

SECTION 5

Cities and Villages

Experts believe that for a long time China has had more people than any other country in the world. Today, more than 1 billion people—about one-fifth of the world's population—live in China. Most of these people live under crowded conditions. About 95 percent live on only 45 percent of the available land. While the mountainous west has few people, the eastern part of China has a high **population density**, or number of people per square mile or square kilometer. It is in this area that the major cities and farming areas of the country are located.

CITIES

In old China, there were two different kinds of cities. One was the royal, or political, city. This was where the capital and the home of the ruler were found. The other was the commercial city. This was the home of merchants, skilled workers, and businesses. Each type of city prompted emotional responses by the people who lived there.

A royal city was laid out in a square grid. At the center was the palace, to the north the marketplace, and to the south the sacred place. The ruler entered the city through the south, while officials entered through the east and west gates. Each side of the city was associated with a season—the north with winter, the south with summer, the east with spring, and the west with fall. An observer describes Chang-an, a major royal city during the early Middle Ages:

EXAMINING PHOTOGRAPHS *Early Chinese commercial cities bustled with activities as merchants, skilled workers, and artisans carried out their daily business tasks. What other type of city existed in traditional China?*

EXAMINING PHOTOGRAPHS *This photograph of Beijing was taken from a National Aeronautics and Space Administration (NASA) satellite. In the far right center of the photo, the wall of the old city can be seen.* *What could one find inside the walls of a royal city?*

The city wall enclosed an area of some 30 square miles [78 square kilometers], divided by a grid of broad avenues. . . . Nearly one million people lived within the walled compound. . . . Walls . . . were [everywhere]. Gates and doors closed at sunset and opened at sunrise. Private life of the well-to-do was private indeed. Rooms opened to interior courts and gardens. Beauty was hidden from the public eye which, from the lanes and streets, could see only blank walls. . . .

. . . The great avenues, though carefully maintained, were quiet. Footpaths, drainage ditches, and fruit trees lined the principal carriageways. . . . These avenues . . . were not so much passageways that linked the people in different sections of the city as open spaces that kept the people apart. If the daytime traffic on these avenues was small, it became nonexistent after dark. With the closing of the gates life withdrew into the intimacy of the houses.

In contrast to the quiet order of a royal city was the loosely planned commercial, or trading, city. Here the incentive was profit and enjoyment of life. Not content with life in a royal city, the ruler at times moved the capital to a commercial city. One ruler, for example, moved the capital to the city of Hangzhou. Below, an observer gives his account of that major commercial city:

The walls of [Hangzhou] were irregular in shape. It had thirteen unevenly spaced gates. . . . The principal pig market . . .

Source: Yi-Fu Tuan. *Topophilia: A Study of Environmental Perception, Attitudes, and Values*. George Allen & Unwin Ltd., 1974, pp. 176–177.

China

YANG AND YIN

The divided circle in the photograph to the right is the symbol of yang and yin. The eight trigrams, or figures of three, that surround it are the *ba gua* said to hold the key to knowledge. Many centuries ago, Chinese philosophers identified yang and yin as the major forces, or energy modes, in life. The Chinese believed that the two forces were within every natural object and that the activity of one or the other controlled the universe. The two were constantly interacting. In a process that never ended, they produced each other, influenced each other, and destroyed each other. Thus, any single object could show the characteristics of yang at one moment and the characteristics of yin at another moment.

Yang was the positive force and was masculine in character. It was active, warm, dry, bright, and aggressive. The sun and Heaven were considered yang. So was fire, the south side of a hill, and the north bank of a river. Horses were yang because they rose front-end first. The *shen*, or good spirits, were yang. Men, too, were predominantly yang. They were celestial and of great worth.

Yin was the opposite force and was feminine in character. It was dark, cool, wet, mysterious, secret, and submissive. Shadows and Earth were yin. So was the north side of a hill and the south bank of a river. Camels were yin because they rose hind-end first. The *gui*, or evil spirits, were yin. Women, too, were predominantly yin. They were earthy and of no great worth.

As legend goes, either yang or yin controlled the seasons and life. To achieve the perfect life, the correct balance had to be maintained between the forces of yang and yin. Care had to be taken not to upset the delicate harmony of the two forces. If it were upset, the result could be a change in the natural order of things. Too much yang in a person's actions, for example, might cause drought, famine, and fire. Too much yin, on the other hand, might bring out-of-season rains and floods. Life for the Chinese, then, was a striving to achieve harmony with nature and not upset the balance of yang and yin.

DRAWING CONCLUSIONS

1. What were the features of yang? Of yin?
2. In what ways do you think belief in yang and yin reflected the Chinese feeling for land and nature?

EXAMINING PHOTOGRAPHS *In China's Gansu province, farmers grow an herb called "rape-seed." They often carry their crop to market in horse- and donkey-drawn carts. What is life like in the Chinese countryside?*

occupied the city's center. . . . [The avenues] teemed with pedestrians, horse-riders, people in sedan chairs and in passenger carts. Besides roads the city was served by canals, with their heavy traffic of barges loaded with rice, boats weighed down with coal, bricks, tiles, and sacks of salt. More than one hundred bridges spanned the canal system within the city walls, and where these were humpbacked and joined busy arteries they caused traffic to congest. . . . [The streets] were lined with shops and dwellings that opened to the traffic. . . . The [lack] of land forced the buildings to go up to three to five stories. Commercial activity permeated the city and its suburbs. . . . The principal pig market was not far from the main artery. Several hundred beasts were butchered every day in slaughterhouses that opened soon after midnight and closed at dawn. . . . City life in . . . [Hangzhou] continued . . . late into the night.

Today in China, many people continue to live in commercial and political cities.

Source: Yi-Fu Tuan. *Topophilia Environmental Perception, Attitudes, and Values.* George Allen & Unwin, Ltd., 1974, pp. 22–25.

The cities themselves, however, have changed in a great many ways. The largest city in China is Shanghai, with more than 7 million people. The capital city of Beijing is home to about 6 million people. In these and in other cities, the old is mixed with the new.

COUNTRYSIDE

While the cities of China remain important, more people today live in the countryside. About 74 percent of China's 1 billion people live in rural villages where most of the houses are built tightly against each other and there are few backyards or gardens. Many Chinese share a special feeling for the countryside. In the past, even those officials who had to live in the city escaped whenever possible to the countryside. "All I ask," said one second-century city dweller, "is good lands and a spacious home, with hills behind and a flowing stream in front, ringed with ponds or pools, set about with bamboos and trees, a vegetable garden to the south, an orchard to the north."

Eighteen centuries later, many Chinese still feel the same about rural life. Below, a 23-year-old Chinese city dweller tells about his "escape" to the countryside outside of Beijing for a holiday weekend:

Once again I feel the autumn wind, gentle but warmer, as I walk along the road. . . . A beautiful road. . . . It is margined with poplar trees and curves off the main road amid far rice fields.

I hear the jingle of harness bells! I turn around and see a cart pulled by three horses coming my way. As it draws closer, I can hear the carter's humming. I summon up my courage. "Hey, Grandpa, can you give me a lift?"

"Hop on." I try to thank him but he doesn't seem much encouraged with words. He sings away. . . .

We approach the village. . . . He points out where I can do some fishing.

It is a typical north China village. Very tall trees. Low houses. They are separated by dwarf mud walls, grey, about a hundred. The main street is a mud path casually winding in this maze. At each of the numerous turns awaits a surprise: a giant of an ox grazing sullenly, a few idling chickens cackling at the sight of me, a dog recoiling then following me, at times a pig swaggering and grunting in my way.

It is hard but I find the village store. It sells books, tobacco and cigarettes, clothes, farm tools, fresh meat and food. I don't know what kind of store to call it. . . . On the counter I find steamed buns filled with vegetables and fried fish, rather crudely prepared but a banquet for a starving man.

With my stomach full, I stroll outside the village toward a pond. My dream of fishing consists of shady trees, a windless day and green water with a lot of weeds.

A boy of about 16 is standing at the pond looking as if he's at the end of his patience. . . . I offer conversation by asking about himself. He is a native of the village, attending high school and helping his parents with the housework and farming. . . .

The boy seems to enjoy my company. We talk and fish. . . . Judging by the light, it is about two o'clock now, and all we have caught are three small ones. Another half hour goes by. . . . "Is there an empty house somewhere?" I ask him. He thinks of the chicken farm. . . .

I am prepared for the enormous hospitality of the country people, but even so the warm welcome of the head of the production team [of the chicken farm] surprises me. . . . When I introduce myself . . . , the man, in his forties . . . looks astonished. He drags me down to a seat and prepares me a cup of tea. . . .

Soon the wife comes in with her sickle and straw hat. She has been cutting rice all day long, but when she sees her husband talking with me, she starts cooking. . . .

Her parents, having a different schedule, are already finished and are watching a TV program. The food is delicious. The wife has cut fresh leeks from their private plot and done them up with eggs from their own hens. There is a big fried carp deep in sauce. . . .

In the night I sleep soundly. No street lamps, no city noise. The faint whistle of a distant train seems to emphasize the depth of darkness. It is a night one searches for all one's life. . . .

SECTION 5 REVIEW

CHECKING FOR UNDERSTANDING

1. **Describe** the kinds of cities that existed in old China.
2. **State** where most of China's people live today.

CRITICAL THINKING

3. **Making Generalizations** How do most Chinese people regard the countryside? Why do you think they hold these beliefs?

Source: Xu Xaoping. "Getting Away From the City" in *China Reconstructs*, Vol. 23, No. 2, February 1984. China Books & Periodicals Inc., pp. 66–67.

GLOBAL FOCUS

Geography

LAND, CLIMATE, AND PEOPLE

FOCUSING ON THE ISSUE
Based on the information in the four maps that follow and in the chapter, present an argument to defend these statements:

Few nations have as diverse a natural environment as China.

Climates in China are as varied as those of the continental United States.

The pressure on the land to produce is great.

Most Chinese live under crowded conditions.

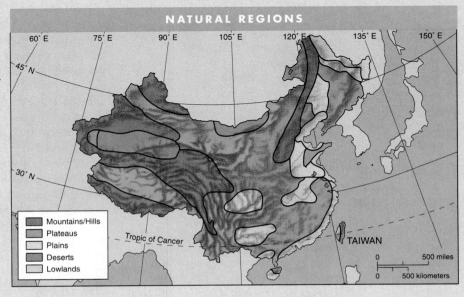

NATURAL REGIONS

60° E 75° E 90° E 105° E 120° E 135° E 150° E
45° N
30° N

Tropic of Cancer

TAIWAN

- Mountains/Hills
- Plateaus
- Plains
- Deserts
- Lowlands

0   500 miles
0   500 kilometers

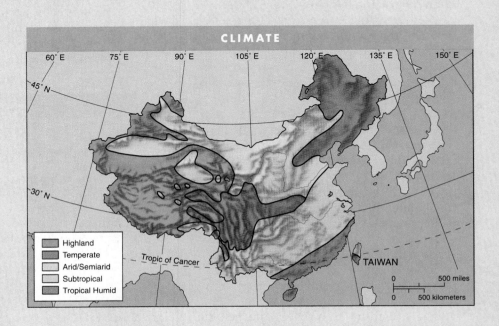

CLIMATE

60° E 75° E 90° E 105° E 120° E 135° E 150° E
45° N
30° N

Tropic of Cancer

TAIWAN

- Highland
- Temperate
- Arid/Semiarid
- Subtropical
- Tropical Humid

0   500 miles
0   500 kilometers

LAND USE

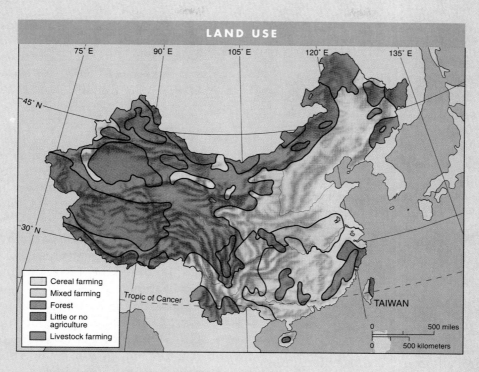

75° E   90° E   105° E   120° E   135° E

45° N

30° N

Cereal farming
Mixed farming
Forest
Little or no
agriculture
Livestock farming

Tropic of Cancer

TAIWAN

0   500 miles
0   500 kilometers

POPULATION DENSITY

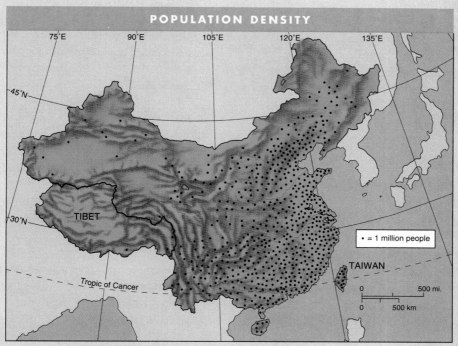

75°E   90°E   105°E   120°E   135°E

45°N

30°N

TIBET

• = 1 million people

TAIWAN

Tropic of Cancer

0   500 mi.
0   500 km

Chapter 8 Review

SUMMARY

China, the Land Under Heaven, began in the valley of the Huang He about 4000 years ago. The people of China felt deeply about the land and formed a way of life rooted in the natural environment. They believed that natural happenings and human actions influenced each other.

Today China is the second largest nation in Asia and the third largest in the world. Few nations have as diverse a natural environment—lofty mountains, long and twisted rivers, fertile river basins and plains, parched deserts, and treeless steppe.

Most of the people of this populous nation live in the eastern half of the country, where the major cities and farming areas are.

Although cities have played an important role as political and commercial centers, most of the population live in rural areas.

USING VOCABULARY

Imagine that you are traveling in early China. Using the terms below in sentences, explain the sights and the challenges of your journey.

yang and yin   loess
steppe   population density

REVIEWING FACTS

1. **Describe** the different kinds of environments in China.
2. **Compare** life in China's western region with life in China's eastern region.
3. **Explain** the relationship between the Chinese way of life and the environment.
4. **Discuss** how the early Chinese explained the origins of China.
5. **Specify** the location of the earliest Chinese settlements.
6. **State** the location of China's desert areas and the kinds of resources found in them.
7. **Explain** why the Zhu Jiang is an important river.

CRITICAL THINKING

1. **Predicting Consequences** The Chinese believed that human behavior has an effect on nature and can upset its balance. How do you think this affected Chinese behavior?
2. **Analyzing Information** Explain how China's physical features have both aided and hindered the development of Chinese civilization.
3. **Demonstrating Reasoned Judgment** The early Chinese held the concept of two totally different types of cities—political and commercial. Do you think this concept is practical today? Explain.
4. **Determining Cause and Effect** Explain how the distribution of China's population has affected the development of the natural environment. Give examples to support your answer.

ANALYZING CONCEPTS

1. **Environment** How did the environment help the Chinese develop a unique civilization that had a strong sense of its own identity?
2. **Culture** What did the Chinese believe they had to do to achieve the perfect life?

GEOGRAPHIC THEMES

1. **Human-Environment Interaction** What advantages and disadvantages do China's river valleys have for human settlement?
2. **Place** Why is most of Chinese industry located in the eastern part of the country?

Outlining

Outlining is an excellent way to organize ideas and facts in a clear, logical order. In an outline, related ideas and facts are grouped together. This enables you to understand and remember information more easily.

Outlines begin with broad ideas, followed by more specific facts. Information is grouped into three categories: main ideas; subtopics, or parts of main ideas; and supporting details. Use the following steps to outline material:

- Identify the general topic of the outline and write the topic in the form of a question.
- Write the main ideas that answer the general topic question. Label these with Roman numerals.
- Write subtopics under each main idea. Label these with capital letters.
- Write supporting details for each subtopic. Label these with Arabic numerals and lower-case letters.

EXAMPLE

Suppose you want to prepare for a test on Chapter 8 by outlining the material. Turn the chapter title into a question, such as "What is the land of China like?" Use each section heading as a main idea in the outline. The beginning of your outline would look like this:

How might you describe the land of China?

I. The variety of the land
II. Mountains
III. Desert, steppe, and plain
IV. Rivers
V. Cities and villages

Read the material in each section to find subtopics and supporting details for each main idea. For example, an outline of Main Idea III might look like this:

III. Desert, steppe, and plain
  A. China's deserts
    1. Takla Makan
      a. north of the Kunlun Mountains
      b. one of the world's biggest deserts
    2. Gobi
      a. on Mongolian border
      b. windswept and nearly treeless
  B. China's steppe
    1. treeless grasslands
    2. inhabited by nomadic herders
  C. Plains regions
    1.
    2.

What supporting details could be added to subtopic C? (*The Manchurian Plain is a leading industrial area; the North China Plain is a rich farming area.*)

PRACTICE

On a separate sheet of paper, copy the following outline for Main Idea V. Then fill in the missing subtopics and details.

V. Cities and Villages
  A. China's population
    1. China has over 1 billion people.
    2.
  B. China's cities
    1. Royal cities
      a. location of the capital and the ruler
      b.
    2.
      a. loosely planned commercial centers
      b.
  C.
    1. 75% of China's people live in rural villages
    2.

CHAPTER OUTLINE

People and Places to Know

the Xia, the Qin, the Han, the Grand Canal, the Mongols, Genghis Khan, Kublai Khan, the Manchus, the Qing, Cixi

Key Terms to Define

mandate, dynasty, ideology, bureaucrat, barbarian, *kowtow*

Objectives to Learn

1. **Describe** the dynastic system of government in traditional China.
2. **Explain** the effects its view of the outside world had on China.
3. **Identify** factors that led to the downfall of China's dynastic system.

Summer Palace in Beijing

The Mandate of Heaven

> [The ceremony] was held at dawn, and I had to get out of my bed at two A.M.—how willingly you can imagine. For most of the long ride to the temple I felt very sorry for myself. Gradually, however, the impressiveness of the situation and the magnificence of my surroundings took me out of myself. The sky was a deep, luminous blue that was quite unbelievable. The temples and the pine trees had indeed passed before my eyes on other occasions, but my senses were so sharpened by the dawn that I now realized that I had never before really seen, much less appreciated them. After many years I can still see the details of that ceremony much more clearly than I see the room about me. And I now understand why the Chinese held court at dawn. If it had been my business to deliberate upon affairs of states, I would have done a far better job of it that morning than I could ever do over a luncheon table, or drowsing in midafternoon.

In these words, a Westerner described a visit to the court of the ruler of China. To the Westerner, dawn seemed an odd time to begin a day of government business. In traditional China, however, the official day began at dawn. The time of day and the journey to the temple impressed visitors with the ruler's authority.

The Chinese regarded their ruler as the Son of Heaven. According to tradition, the Son of Heaven governed on the basis of a principle known as the Mandate of Heaven. If he were just, the Son received a **mandate**, or right to rule, from Heaven, the supreme ruler. If he did not govern properly, he lost the mandate, and someone else became the Son of Heaven.

For a great many years, China was governed by a series of **dynasties**, or ruling

Source: H.G. Creel. *Chinese Thought from Confucius to Mao Tse-tung.* The University of Chicago, 1953, p. 261.

families. Each dynasty consisted of a line of rulers from the same family. Twenty-four dynasties ruled China before the dynastic system came to an end in 1912.

Until 1912, Chinese history was divided into periods based on the reigns of the dynasties. During each period, dynastic government was the same whether the times were good or bad, and one ruler was followed by another from the same family. The central government usually was strong, and there was unity throughout the country. To justify its authority, each dynasty promoted an **ideology**, or political philosophy.

Sometimes, rulers faced threats of internal rebellion and foreign invasion. When these challenges became overwhelming, they often led to the collapse of the dynasty and to the onset of chaos. To establish order and reunite the country, a new dynasty would emerge.

SECTION 1

Dynastic Government

The first dynasty was the Xia (SYAH). Although the origins of the Xia are shrouded in legend, scholars today believe that the dynasty began about 4000 years ago. It was followed by the Shang, which, in turn, was followed by the Zhou (JOH). Below, a modern historian notes what happened when the Shang was replaced by the Zhou:

The Duke of [Zhou] tirelessly lectured the conquered Shang peoples about the Mandate of Heaven. He told them that [Zhou] leaders had no selfish wish to glorify themselves by attacking Shang. He said that they had no choice in the matter once Heaven commanded them to punish Shang. He advised the newly conquered peoples to abide by Heaven's decision. He pointed out to them firmly that he was prepared to make them do so if need be. The Duke of [Zhou] understood the double-edged [meaning] of the new doctrine. [Zhou] could not retain its rule unless its kings ruled in such fashion as to remain in Heaven's good graces. To do that they must rule fairly and kindly. Thenceforth no Chinese ruler was above challenge. Any challenger proved the point of his claim merely by succeeding. The doctrine of the Mandate of Heaven was solidly established before many decades had passed. It remained thereafter the cornerstone of all Chinese political theory.

In 221 BC the Zhou were replaced by the Qin. The Qin was the first dynasty to unite China under one ruler. Its first—and only—ruler, Zheng, named himself Shi Huangdi (Shur Hwang Dee), or First Emperor. A strong ruler, Shi Huangdi acted cruelly to-

ward his subjects and tried to end freedom of thought. In time, his policies led to a civil war. His dynasty was overthrown, and a new dynasty called the Han came to power.

The Han dynasty expanded China's borders and set up a national capital at Changan. One of its greatest accomplishments was the establishment of a stable government. The government was made up of four main parts—a single ruler, government officials, a system of laws, and an official ideology.

The single ruler was the emperor. He made laws, took charge of the government, and interpreted the ideology. When he wanted to change a law, he had only to issue a new order. Below, a concerned guest discusses the attitude toward the law with a Chinese official:

You are supposed to be dispenser of justice for the Son of Heaven, and yet you pay no attention to the statute books, but simply decide cases in any way that will accord with the wishes of the ruler. Do you really think that is the way a law official should be?

[The official replied:] And where, may I ask, did the statute books come from in the first place? . . . Whatever the earlier rulers thought was right they wrote down in the books and made into statutes, and whatever the later rulers thought was right they duly classified as ordinances. Anything that suits the present age is right. Why bother with the laws of former times?

An emperor who ruled for many years was considered a good ruler. Many Chinese believed that "the people are like grass, the ruler like the wind. As the wind blows, so the grass inclines." Others said that "when a prince's conduct is correct, his government is effective without issuing orders. If his per-

Source: Charles O. Hucker. *China's Imperial Past.* Stanford University Press, 1975, p. 55.

Source: Ping-ti-Ho (tr). *China in Crisis Vol. I. China's Heritage and the Communist Political System.* University of Chicago, 1968, pp. 18, 19.

MAJOR CHINESE DYNASTIES

EXAMINING CHARTS *From earliest recorded times to the beginning of the twentieth century, China was ruled by a series of dynasties.* Under which dynasty was China united for the first time under one ruler?

XIA Dynasty 1994–1523 BC

SHANG Dynasty 1523–1028 BC

ZHOU Dynasty 1028–256 BC

QIN Dynasty 221–206 BC

HAN Dynasty 206 BC–220 AD

SIX Dynasties 220–581

SUI Dynasty 581–618

TANG Dynasty 618–907

FIVE Dynasties 907–960

SONG Dynasty 960–1280

YUAN Dynasty 1280–1368

MING Dynasty 1368–1644

QING Dynasty 1644–1912

sonal conduct is not correct, he may issue orders but they will not be followed."

The emperor was aided by many **bureaucrats,** or government officials, who were appointed to office on the basis of examinations that tested their knowledge of Chinese literature, philosophy, and affairs of state. Some bureaucrats reported directly to the emperor. To make sure that no official became too powerful, the emperor did not allow officials to stay in one place for long or serve in their home provinces. Sometimes he gave an official several jobs to do at the same time so that the official could not master any one. At other times, he gave one job to several different officials.

The bureaucrats were organized into six ministries—civil service, revenue, ceremonies, war, punishments, and public works. Each province also had its own network of officials. A post office handled official correspondence, and business was passed up through the ranks to the emperor for his decision. There were nine ranks of officials. Each rank wore special clothes and caps with a different color badge.

The law was enforced with heavy penalties, but its effects were softened by the more humane officials. These officials were devoted followers of the philosopher Kongzi (KONG·DZUH), or Confucius. Known as Confucians, they did not often challenge a

EXAMINING PHOTOGRAPHS *The Forbidden City, which served as the emperor's residence, was located within the Imperial City. A screen of nine dragons, one of which is pictured here, protected the entrance to the royal palace.* Why did the emperor live in a special place?

law when it had to do with a peasant. But when it had to do with a noble or other members of the upper class, they might work to have the law changed or abolished. Some emperors did not like the changes made by the Confucians and tried to keep them out of government. One Han emperor, upon hearing a plea to make the law more humane by allowing more Confucians in government, said:

> The . . . dynasty has its own laws and institutes, which embody and blend the principles of realistic statecraft as well as those of ancient sage-kings. How could I rely entirely on moral instruction which [is alleged to have] guided the government of the [Zhou] dynasty? Moreover, the ordinary Confucians seldom understand the needs of changing times. They love to praise the ancient and to decry [condemn] the present, thus making people confused about ideals and realities and incapable of knowing what to abide by. How could the Confucians be entrusted with the vital responsibilities of the state?

Source: Ping-ti-Ho (tr.) *China in Crisis Vol. I. China's Heritage and the Communist Political System.* University of Chicago, 1968, pp. 12–13.

SECTION 1 REVIEW

CHECKING FOR UNDERSTANDING
1. **Define** bureaucrat.
2. **Identify** the major contributions of the Qin and Han dynasties.
3. **Describe** the powers of Chinese emperors.

CRITICAL THINKING
4. **Analyzing Information** Were the Qin and the Han effective rulers? Explain.

SECTION 2
Dynastic Change

When the Han dynasty ended about 220 AD, China entered a period of disorder. It lasted until the late 500's. From then until the early 1200's, a series of strong dynasties—the Sui, the Tang, and the Song—ruled China and restored its greatness as a world civilization.

One of the most noted rulers during this period of dynastic power was Wendi, the founder of the Sui (SWAY) dynasty. To display his power, Wendi began many projects. One was the new city of Changan. Another was a canal connecting Hangzhou near the lower Yangtze to Lo-yang in the north, and eventually, Beijing. Later, this system of canals and rivers was called the Grand Canal. It became an important route for shipping products between north and south China and for sending troops to guard China's northern frontier.

About 1200, China entered another period of dynastic decline and became prey to invaders from the north. The most successful of these invaders were the Mongols, a group of peoples from the steppe region of what is now Outer Mongolia. The Mongols, led by Genghis Khan, conquered an empire that stretched across Asia, from Korea to eastern Europe in the north, and from south China to Asia Minor in the south.

Genghis Khan's grandson, Kublai Khan, founded the Yuan dynasty in China. Although he adopted aspects of Chinese culture and government, he did not allow the Chinese to take part in the government. Under Kublai Khan, China became known for its splendor and culture. Below, Marco Polo, a western merchant and traveler, describes the rules followed when Kublai Khan held court:

When his Majesty holds a grand and public court, those who attend it are seated in the following order. The table of the sovereign is placed on an elevation, and he takes his seat on the northern side, with his face turned towards the south; and next to him, on his left hand, sits the Empress. On his right hand are placed . . . persons connected with him by blood. . . . The other princes and the nobility have their places at still lower tables; and the same rules are observed with respect to the females, the wives of the . . . relatives of the Great Khan being seated on the left hand, at tables in like manner

gradually lower; then follow the wives of the nobility and military officers: so that all are seated according to their respective ranks and dignities, in the places assigned to them, and to which they are entitled. . . .

Officers of rank are . . . appointed, whose duty it is to see that all strangers who happen to arrive . . . and are unacquainted with the etiquette of the court are suitably accommodated with places. . . . At each door of the grand hall, or of whatever part the Great Khan happens to be in, stand two officers . . ., one on each side, with staves in their hands, for the purpose of preventing persons from touching the threshold with their feet, and obliging them to step beyond it. . . . But, as strangers may be unacquainted with the prohibition, officers are appointed to introduce and warn them. This precaution is used because touching the threshold is regarded as a bad omen. . . . The numerous persons who attend at the sideboard of his Majesty, and who serve him with [food] and drink are all obliged to cover their noses and mouths with handsome veils or cloths of worked silk, in order that his [food] or his wine may not be affected by their breath. . . . When the [meal] is finished, and the tables have been removed, persons of various descriptions enter the hall, and amongst these a troop of comedians and performers on different instruments. Also tumblers and jugglers, who exhibit their skill in the presence of the Great Khan. . .

Mongol rule in China began to decline during the 1300's. The Chinese resented Mongol controls and wanted their own dynasty. After a series of rebellions finally drove out the Mongols, a peasant rebel leader named Zhu Yuanzhang (JOO YOO·AHN·JAHNG) became emperor. Zhu reunited the country and established a

Source: *The Travels of Marco Polo.* From Book II, Chapter 13. The Marsden Translation revised and edited, Horace Liveright, Inc., 1933. Copyright renewed 1955 by Manuel Komroff.

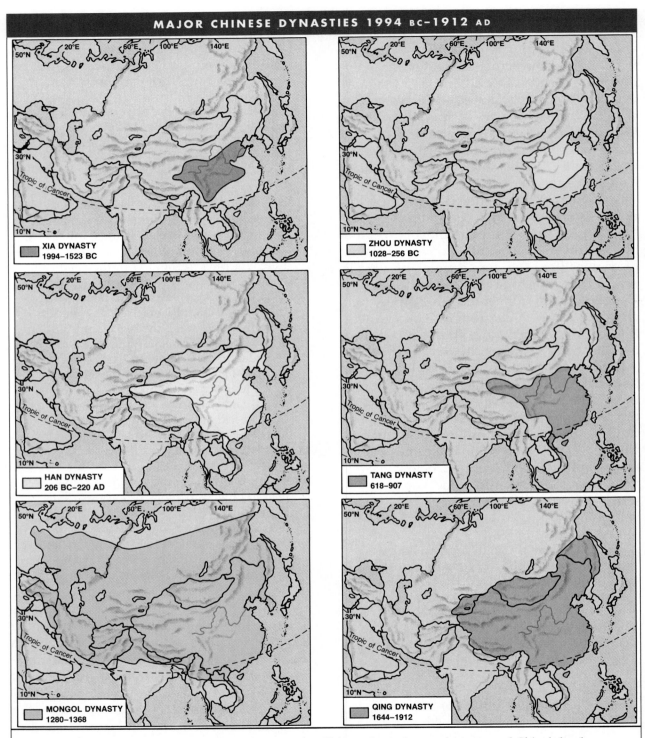

MAJOR CHINESE DYNASTIES 1994 BC–1912 AD

XIA DYNASTY
1994–1523 BC

ZHOU DYNASTY
1028–256 BC

HAN DYNASTY
206 BC–220 AD

TANG DYNASTY
618–907

MONGOL DYNASTY
1280–1368

QING DYNASTY
1644–1912

EXAMINING MAPS *Throughout the centuries, Chinese dynasties sought to expand China's borders. Under which dynasty did China reach its greatest territorial extent?*

capital at Nanjing in southern China. There, he founded the Ming dynasty.

Early Ming rulers introduced government reforms and promoted economic prosperity. But, in time, a series of weak emperors came to the throne, and by the 1600's, the Ming dynasty was near collapse. In 1644, invaders from the north known as Manchus captured China, overthrew the Ming ruler, and established a new dynasty called the Qing (Ching). Like the Mongols, the Qing were foreigners who borrowed aspects of Chinese culture but kept themselves apart from the Chinese.

SECTION 2 REVIEW

CHECKING FOR UNDERSTANDING
1. **Identify** Genghis Khan, Kublai Khan.
2. **State** how Wendi showed his power.
3. **Describe** the attitude of the Mongols toward the Chinese.

CRITICAL THINKING
4. **Making Comparisons** What did the Qing have in common with the Mongols?

SECTION 3

China and the Outside World

Under Qing rule, the Chinese maintained their traditional belief that China was the "Middle Kingdom," the center of the world. In spite of contacts with foreigners through trade, the Chinese did not borrow new ideas and practices. They believed that their culture was superior to all others and wanted to protect their civilization from foreign influences. To the Chinese, foreigners were **barbarians,** or uncivilized people.

The Chinese viewed the world in terms of five zones of culture. At the center was the emperor. Next to him, in the first zone, was the royal family. In the second zone were lords who paid tribute to the emperor. In the third were the people who lived on the borders of China. In the fourth were friendly barbarians. In the fifth zone were the barbarians who viewed China as a strange land.

To show respect and that they recognized the superiority of the Chinese, visiting barbarians were expected to bow down before the emperor, present gifts, and perform certain ceremonies.

The cash value of the gifts was not important, but the gift-giving ceremony was. Ambassadors to the Chinese court were expected to perform the *kowtow*. Upon command of a lowly usher, the ambassador would kneel three times before the ruler and touch his head to the ground three times.

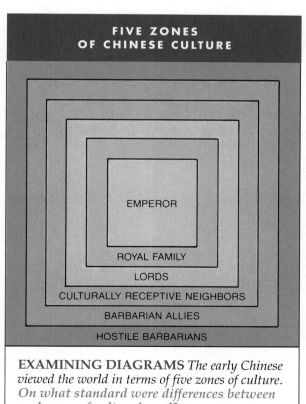

FIVE ZONES OF CHINESE CULTURE

EMPEROR
ROYAL FAMILY
LORDS
CULTURALLY RECEPTIVE NEIGHBORS
BARBARIAN ALLIES
HOSTILE BARBARIANS

EXAMINING DIAGRAMS *The early Chinese viewed the world in terms of five zones of culture. On what standard were differences between each zone of culture based?*

China

KANG XI

Kang Xi (Kong See) ruled China from 1662 to 1722. A gifted ruler, he was interested in the arts, literature, and science. In an order given in 1722, he talked about his role as emperor. Part of what he said is noted below:

All the Ancients used to say that the emperor should concern himself with general principles, but need not deal with the smaller details. I find that I cannot agree with this. Careless handling of one item might bring harm to the whole world, a moment's carelessness damage all future generations. Failure to attend to details will end up endangering your greater virtues. So I always attend carefully to the details. . . .

When I had been twenty years on the throne I didn't dare [think] that I might reign thirty. After thirty years I didn't dare [think] that I might reign forty. Now I have reigned fifty-seven years. The ["Five Classics"] says of the five joys:

The first is long life;
The second is riches;
The third is soundness of body and serenity of mind;
The fourth is love of virtue;
The fifth is an end crowning the life.
The "end crowning the life" is

placed last because it is so hard to attain. I am now approaching seventy, and my sons, grandsons, and great-grandsons number over one hundred and fifty. The country is more or less at peace and the world is at peace. Even if we haven't improved all manners and customs, and made all the people prosperous and contented, yet I have worked with unceasing diligence and intense watchfulness, never resting, never idle. So for decades I have exhausted all my strength, day after day. . . .

I am now close to seventy, and have been over fifty years on the throne—this is all due to the quiet protection of Heaven and earth and the ancestral spirits; it was not my meager virtue that did it. Since I began reading in my childhood, I have managed to get a rough

understanding of the constant historical principles. Every emperor and ruler has been subject to the Mandate of Heaven. Those fated to enjoy old age cannot prevent themselves from enjoying that old age; those fated to enjoy a time of Great Peace cannot prevent themselves from enjoying that Great Peace.

Over 4,350 years have passed from the first . . . Emperor to the present, and over 300 emperors are listed as having reigned. . . . In the 1,960 years from the first year of [Zheng] . . . to the present, there have been 211 people who have been named emperor and have taken era names. What man am I, that among all those who have reigned long . . . , it should be I who have reigned the longest?

TAKING ANOTHER LOOK

1. How does Kang Xi view the Mandate of Heaven?
2. Judging from Kang Xi's description, do you think he had the Mandate of Heaven?

Source: From EMPEROR OF CHINA by Jonathan D. Spence. Copyright © 1974 by Jonathan D. Spence. Reprinted by permission of Alfred A. Knopf Inc.

EXAMINING ART
This seventeenth-century scroll painting depicts a royal family, which represents the highest level of culture in traditional Chinese thought. What activities do you see in the painting that would support this belief?

CHINA AND GREAT BRITAIN

During ancient and medieval times, most barbarians were willing to go along with such Chinese customs as the *kowtow*. During later times, however, ambassadors from some Western countries refused to do so. When the British representative visited in 1793, he agreed to kneel only on one knee rather than perform the full *kowtow*.

The Western countries, who wanted a part in the China trade, forced themselves on the Chinese. They got special treatment for themselves and became unwelcomed partners in China's trade with the world. They also backed missionaries who were trying to convert the Chinese to western ways. A Chinese emperor explained how he felt about this in the following letter to King George III of Great Britain:

Let us consider the teachings of Christianity which are upheld in your kingdom. They are merely the teachings which have been fostered until now by the different countries of Europe. The Sacred Emperors and Illustrious Rulers of the Celestial Empire [China] have, ever since the creation of the world, handed down their own teachings from time to time. The earth's millions have a standing guide provided for them to follow and would not seek to be led astray by outlandish doctrines.

The Europeans who have accepted service in Our capital city live within the Palace grounds and are not allowed to establish relations with Our subjects. They are forbidden to preach their faith. The distinction between Chinese and barbarian is thus strictly maintained. The wish of your envoys that barbarians be allowed to preach their faith as they wish is even more impossible to grant than anything else.

Finally, the emperor gave the following warning:

We now set forth once more Our meaning for your instruction, O King. We trust that you will share Our views and forever be obedient. You will thereby continue to enjoy your due share of the blessings of peace.

Source: E.H. Parker (tr.). "The Emperor of China to King George the Third," in *Nineteenth Century*, Vol. XL, No. 233, July 1896, pp. 48–53.

After Our clear pronouncement, you, O King, should be careful not to heed the misguided words of your subjects. . . . Do not allow your barbarian merchants to send their ships to forbidden places in search of trade. Know that the laws of the Celestial Empire are very strict and that the civil and military officers in charge of each place will do their duty faithfully and will not allow your ships to proceed there. They will at once drive them away and out to sea so that the barbarian merchants of your kingdom will have gone to all their trouble in vain.

Do not say that you were not warned! Tremble and obey! Do not ignore our commands!

CHINA AND THE UNITED STATES

The United States tended to follow the leadership of Great Britain in regard to China. When American traders first came to China in the 1780's, they accepted the dominance of Great Britain. While some criticized the British attitude, most found the British companies useful for trade.

In the 1840's, the United States took its first official step toward making a treaty with China. The American president sent the following letter to the Chinese emperor:

I, John Tyler, President of the United States of America, . . . send you this letter of Peace and Friendship, signed by my own hand.

I hope your health is good. China is a Great Empire, extending over a great part of the World. The Chinese are numerous. . . . The rising Sun looks upon . . . rivers and mountains equally large, in the United States. Our Territories . . . are divided from your Dominions . . . by the Sea. . . .

Now, my words are, that the Governments of two such Great Countries,

should . . . respect each other, and act wisely. . . .

The Chinese love to trade with our People. . . . Let the people trade . . . make a Treaty with [the representative of the president] . . . so that nothing may happen to disturb the Peace, between China and America. . . .

And so may your health be good, and may Peace reign.

The American ambassador brought President Tyler's letter to China. The Chinese emperor gave the following answer to the president:

The Great Emperor presents his regards to the President and trusts He is well.

I the Emperor having looked up and received the manifest Will of Heaven, hold the reins of Government over . . . the [Middle Kingdom], regarding all within & beyond the border seas as one and the same Family.

Early in the Spring the Ambassador of Your Honorable Nation . . . arrived from afar. . . .

Moreover, [my representative] took [your] Letter and presented it for My Inspection, and Your sincerity and friendship being in the highest degree real, . . . my pleasure and delight were exceedingly profound.

All, and every thing, they had settled regarding the [treaty]. . . .

. . . I trust the President . . . to be extremely well satisfied and delighted.

THE CHINESE RESPONSE

Soon, the United States shared the same status as Great Britain. Unlike China, both had gone through an industrial revolution. With their new technology, they developed strong military forces. Taking advantage of

Source: E. H. Parker (tr.). "The Emperor of China to King George the Third," in *Nineteenth Century*, Vol. XL, No. 233, July 1896, pp. 48–53.

Source: Hunter Miller (ed.). *Treaties and Other International Acts of the United States of America*, Vol. IV, Government Printing Office, pp. 660–661.

EXAMINING PHOTOGRAPHS
During the 1800's, Chinese emperors had many visits from western ambassadors who came to get trading privileges for their countries. Each ambassador wanted to make sure no other country got more in the way of trading concessions. Which Western powers were among the first to send ambassadors to China?

China's technological weakness, the Western countries increased their power and areas of influence in China.

Many Westerners, however, did not understand the Chinese way of life and looked down on the Chinese. As Western power grew over the years, more and more Chinese began to resent the foreigners and their role in China. In the 1900's, a Chinese leader asked:

In the world today, what position do we occupy? Compared to the other peoples of the world we have the greatest population and our civilization is four thousand years old; we should therefore be advancing in the front rank with the nations of Europe and America. . . . Today we are the poorest and weakest nation in the world, and occupy the lowest position in international affairs. Other men are the carving knife and serving dish; we are the fish and the meat. . . . As a consequence China is being transformed everywhere into a colony of the foreign powers.

Source: Sun Yatsen as quoted in *Modern China: The Story of a Revolution* by Orville Schell and Joseph Esherick. Alfred A. Knopf, Inc., 1972, p. 48.

SECTION 3 REVIEW

CHECKING FOR UNDERSTANDING
1. **Define** barbarian, *kowtow*.
2. **Explain** how the Chinese emperor regarded Western influence in China.

CRITICAL THINKING
3. **Identifying Central Issues** What did Americans hope to gain in China?

SECTION 4

The End of Dynastic Rule

During the late 1800's, famine and rebellions weakened China. Below, an opponent of the Qing dynasty describes the hardships experienced in western China and the effect on the peasants there:

There was no rain, and only a light flurry of snow that winter, so the winter crops were poor. The next spring rains failed.

. . . In the hot summer months that followed, the grain bins of the Ting [a powerful landowning family] remained full from previous harvests, but the peasants began to starve. . . .

In the second summer of the drought the people lost all faith in the Rain God, and haggard members of the ancient Ko Lao Hui, or Elder Brother secret society, began whispering in the villages. Peasants arose from their beds at night to mutter against the merciless skies and the blank moon.

One early summer day . . ., someone lifted his head and cried out: "Listen!"

Old Three heard a strange sound. . . . [The] strange sound grew louder, coming from the north where a cloud of dust was rising along the Big Road.

From the dust cloud there soon emerged a mass of human skeletons, the men armed with every kind of weapon, footbound women carrying babies on their backs, and naked children. . . . . . . The avalanche of starving people poured down the Big Road, hundreds of them eddying into the Zhu courtyard, saying: "Come and eat off the big houses!" . . .

Blessed rain fell during the late summer and autumn that year and the famine ended. By then many landowning peasants had sold everything and sunk into the ranks of tenants. Tenants had become coolies or soldiers or labourers on the landed estates. And all were in debt to moneylenders.

In addition to famine and uprisings, the Qing lost territory to Japan and the Western nations. Many Chinese came to believe that if China were to meet the "foreign threat," it had to acquire the technology of the West. Conservative supporters of the Qing did not agree and continued to oppose reforms.

In 1908 Empress Cixi (Tsuh·See), an opponent of reform, died. Her death further weakened China. In 1911 a widespread uprising forced Cixi's successor, the young emperor PuYi, to give up his throne. In the following year, China became a republic.

EXAMINING PHOTOGRAPHS *Empress Cixi, pictured below, was one of the most powerful women in Chinese history. Known also as the Dowager Empress, she ruled during the late 1800's. What did Cixi oppose?*

SECTION 4 REVIEW

CHECKING FOR UNDERSTANDING
1. **Indicate** China's form of government after the 1911 uprising.

CRITICAL THINKING
2. **Determining Cause and Effect** What factors weakened the Qing dynasty and led to its downfall?

Source: From THE GREAT ROAD: THE LIFE AND TIMES OF CHU TEH by Agnes Smedley. Copyright © 1956 by The Estate of Agnes Smedley. Reprinted by permission of Monthly Review Foundation.

History

CHINA AND THE WEST

As can be seen on this map showing the spheres of influence in China, in the 1800's, Western nations were making their influence felt in China. At the same time, some Chinese emigrated to the United States.

To many Chinese, the Westerners were barbarians with little culture or learning. To many Westerners, the Chinese were the barbarians. Each believed the other was prejudiced against them. Each was right. Two examples of this prejudice can be seen in the excerpts that follow. The first excerpt describes regulations imposed on British merchants and their families living and working in China in the 1800's. The second excerpt is a report on incidents involving Chinese working in mining regions in the United States in the 1800's.

FOCUSING ON THE ISSUE Read the excerpts, study the map, and answer these questions:
1. What Western nations had gained a foothold in China?
2. Why do you think the Chinese imposed strict rules on the British in Guangzhou?
3. How do you think the Chinese in China felt about

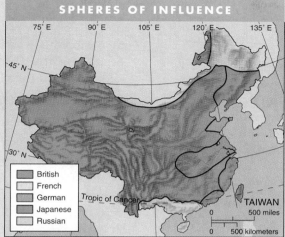

SPHERES OF INFLUENCE

75° E   90° E   105° E   120° E   135° E
45° N
30° N

British
French
German
Japanese
Russian

Tropic of Cancer

TAIWAN

0   500 miles
0   500 kilometers

what happened to the Chinese in California?
4. Based on the information in the chapter, what led to much of the prejudice of the Chinese? Of the Westerner? Explain.

. . . **N**o foreign devil could stay in Canton [Guangzhou] the year round, or any time except the season, from September to March, when tea and raw silk were brought down to the coast for sale. For the rest of the year the merchants must withdraw to Macao, which the Portuguese occupied not quite independently of Chinese supervision . . . in the Canton factory [the foreigner] was practically in prison. He could not stray outside the factory [trading post] limits, though on three days of the year, . . . he might visit one of the islands nearby. But even there he must

not [mix] with the [Chinese]. Foreign devils could not keep arms, nor must their warships enter the Pearl [Zhu Jiang] River. Wives and families must not ever visit the factories. No women at all were permitted.[1]

At least as early as 1852, widespread agitation and harassment of the Chinese was occurring in the mining regions of [California]. By 1862, the California Legislature's Joint Select Committee on the Chinese population was itself reporting that

"Your committee were furnished with a list of eighty-eight Chinamen, who are known to have been murdered by Collectors of the Foreign Miner's License Tax—sworn officers of the law. But two of the murderers have been convicted and hanged. Generally, they have been allowed to escape with the slightest punishment."

"The above number of Chinese who have been robbed and murdered comprise, probably, a very small proportion of those who have been murdered. . . ."[2]

[1] Source: Emily Hahn. *China Only Yesterday 1850-1950*. Brandt & Brandt, 1963, pp. 13–14.

[2] Source: Lowell K.Y. Chun-Hoon. "Teaching the Asian-American Experience," in *Teaching Ethnic Studies*, pp. 128–129. Copyright © 1974 National Council for the Social Studies. Reprinted by permission.

Chapter 9 Review

SUMMARY

Chinese rulers claimed that their authority came from the Mandate of Heaven. According to tradition, a ruler lost the mandate and fell from power as a result of governing unjustly. In fact, a ruler governed until defeated by opponents, who then formed a new government.

Until 1912 China was governed by a series of dynasties. Under each dynasty the government consisted of the emperor, bureaucrats, a system of laws, and a political ideology.

The Chinese believed that their country was the "Middle Kingdom" and that they were superior to all other cultures. In the 1700's and 1800's, Western countries forced the Chinese to trade with them and tried to convert the Chinese to western ways. This caused resentment among the Chinese.

After a national uprising in 1911, the dynastic system came to an end. A year later, China was proclaimed a republic.

USING VOCABULARY

Explain why each of these terms is used in a chapter about government in traditional China.

mandate   bureaucrat
dynasty   barbarian
ideology   *kowtow*

REVIEWING FACTS

1. **Explain** how laws were determined under dynastic government.
2. **Discuss** how the government of China was established under Han rulers.
3. **Explain** how Chinese emperors kept bureaucrats from becoming too powerful.
4. **Name** the foreign dynasty that ruled China from the 1200's to the 1300's.

5. **State** who established the Qing dynasty.
6. **Discuss** how the Chinese viewed themselves and the rest of the world.
7. **Summarize** the Chinese attitude toward Western traders and missionaries.

CRITICAL THINKING

1. **Identifying Central Issues** What is meant by the statement, "For both the ruled and the ruler, the Mandate of Heaven was a two-edged sword for stability and change"?
2. **Evaluating Information** What were the strengths of the dynastic system in China? What were the weaknesses? Do you think China could have been governed better under another system of government? Give examples to support your answers.
3. **Making Comparisons** What basic cultural differences separated China and the West?
4. **Recognizing Bias** What factors promoted the Chinese attitude of superiority? Did Westerners hold a similar attitude about their own culture? Explain.

ANALYZING CONCEPTS

1. **Power** What limits were placed on the powers of emperors and bureaucrats? Were they effective? Explain.
2. **Change** How was the outcome of the national uprising in 1911 different from earlier political upheavals in China?

GEOGRAPHIC THEMES

1. **Human-Environment Interaction** How did Chinese emperors transform China's environment?
2. **Location** How did China's location south of the steppe affect its development?

Determining Cause and Effect

Events in the world occur not at random but because something makes them happen. One event produces another event. The first event or person that makes something happen is a *cause*. The result is an *effect*. The link between cause and effect is called a *cause-and-effect relationship*. Cause-and-effect relationships explain *why* things happen. The diagram below illustrates a simple cause-and-effect relationship.

The ruler does not rule properly.
(*cause*)

↓

The ruler loses the right to govern.
(*effect*)

Reality, however, is seldom described so simply. Often, one event produces several effects. For example, a fire in a business district may cause businesses to lose money, employees to lose income, traffic to be disrupted, and so on. Similarly, several different events may combine to produce an effect. A forest fire could be caused by dry weather, high winds, and a careless camper dropping a lit cigarette in a pile of leaves. Also, an effect, in turn, can become the cause of another event. In the example of the forest fire, the fire is an effect. However, it then causes other effects, such as loss of property, loss of lives, and so on.

Use the following steps to determine cause-and-effect relationships among events:

- Ask yourself why particular events happen.
- Identify the outcomes of events.
- Statements often contain "clue words" that will alert you to cause and effect. Look for cause-effect "clue words" such as *led to, brought about, produced, because, as a result of, so that, thus, outcome, as a consequence, resulted in, gave rise to,* and *therefore.*
- At times, there are no "clue words." In their place, however, may be the word "and" or a comma.

EXAMPLE

Read this statement: *In time, Shu Huanodi's harsh policies led to civil war.* In this sentence, the "clue words," *led to,* indicate a cause-and-effect relationship. Shu Huanodi's harsh policies are the *cause;* the civil war is the *effect.*

Read this statement: *Many westerners did not understand the Chinese way of life and looked down on the Chinese.* Notice that this sentence contains no clue words. To identify the cause-effect relationship, ask yourself whether one event explains why the other event occurred. Because westerners did not understand the Chinese way of life (cause), they looked down on the Chinese (effect).

Remember that causes and effects may not appear in the same sentence, or even in the same paragraphs. Sometimes, many sentences are needed to explain connections between causes and effects.

PRACTICE

A. Identify causes and effects in the two statements below. Remember, there may be more than one cause and effect in each statement.

1. When rulers faced threats of internal rebellion and foreign invasion, these events often led to the collapse of the dynasty and the onset of chaos.
2. To make sure that no official became too powerful, the emperor did not allow officials to stay in one place for long or serve in their home provinces.
3. Some emperors did not like the changes in law made by Confucian officials and tried to keep them out of government.
4. The Chinese resented Mongol controls and wanted their own dynasty. In the 1300's, a series of rebellions drove out the Mongols.

B. Find two more cause-and-effect relationships in this chapter. For each one, identify causes and effects.

People and Places to Know
Silk Road, Yen Shu, Tao Chi

Key Terms to Define
gentry, compound, civil service, acupuncture, calligraphy

Objectives to Learn
1. **Describe** the class structure of traditional China and discuss the roles of each social group.
2. **Understand** China's civil service system.
3. **Identify** the role of women in traditional China.
4. **Examine** the arts of traditional China.

The Chinese emperor and his court

The Few and the Many

> The ancients who wished to be [greatly] virtuous throughout the kingdom, first ordered well their own states. Wishing to order well their states, they first regulated their families. Wishing to regulate their families, they first cultivated their persons. Wishing to cultivate their persons, they first [made right] their hearts. Wishing to [make right] their hearts, they first sought to be sincere in their thoughts. Wishing to be sincere in their thoughts, they first extended to the utmost their knowledge. Such extension of knowledge lay in the investigation of things.
>
> Things being investigated, knowledge became complete. Their knowledge being complete, their thoughts were sincere. Their thoughts being sincere, their hearts were then [made right]. Their hearts being [made right], their persons were cultivated. Their persons being cultivated, their families were regulated. Their families being regulated, their states were rightly governed. Their states being rightly governed, the whole kingdom was made tranquil and happy.

*I*n traditional China, students carefully studied teachings such as the one above. These teachings illustrated a "chain of reasoning" argument. Students had a program of study that included the memorization and analysis of books known as the Confucian classics, the writing of essays, and the appreciation and writing of poetry. Many years of study were necessary to complete the program, and a large number of students never reached their goals.

The few students who did reach their goals became members of the upper class and served as China's rulers and leaders. As members of the upper class, they valued close family ties and followed set rules of behavior in human relationships. They considered themselves superior to those of the lower classes.

The lifestyles of the upper class were supported by the hard work of the lower classes. Expected to respect and obey those of the upper class, the members of the lower classes received little reward for their efforts. Despite this, they endured and, during the twentieth century, emerged as China's leaders.

Women formed their own distinct group in traditional Chinese society. Whether members of the upper class or the lower classes, as females they were considered inferior to males. Not until the twentieth century were they able to change their status and increase their influence.

Source: Reprinted by permission of the publishers from THE UNITED STATES AND CHINA, Fourth Edition, by John King Fairbank, Cambridge, Mass.: Harvard University Press, Copyright © 1979, 1983 by the President and Fellows of Harvard College. © 1976 by John King Fairbank.

SECTION 1
The Upper Class

The upper class of traditional China consisted for the most part of three distinct categories of people. One was the **gentry**, wealthy landowning families. Another was government officials. The third was the scholars. It was not unusual for an individual to belong to all three categories.

THE GENTRY

Most members of the gentry owned vast rural estates. Most often, however, they lived in large, high-walled urban **compounds**, enclosed yards with many buildings, in homes with tiled roofs, courtyards, and gardens.

The gentry played an important role in local affairs. They rented their land, loaned money, collected taxes, served as judges, and led the militia. The ladder of success was easier for their sons to climb than for the sons of other social groups. In the words of one Chinese historian:

> The gentry of old China were a special group. They had political, economic, and social privileges and powers and led a special way of life. The gentry stood above the large mass. They dominated the life of Chinese communities. They provided the rules of society and of man's relation to man. During the later years [of the dynastic period], the gentry's position and qualifications became formalized. A ring of formal privileges relieved them from physical labor and gave them prestige and a special position in relation to the government.

Source: Chang Chung-li. *The Chinese Gentry*. University of Washington Press, 1955, p. xiii. (Adaptation)

GOVERNMENT OFFICIALS

Until the twentieth century, China's government officials came from the ranks of the gentry. In early times, they controlled China's central government, holding most government posts and making government appointments on the basis of family ties.

This changed, however, when the Han emperors created a **civil service**, a bureaucracy in which officials were hired on the basis of examinations rather than on birth. The examinations tested candidates on their knowledge of Chinese literature and philosophies. To pass them, it was necessary to write with style as well as understanding.

During ancient and medieval times, members of the lower classes were not allowed to take the examinations. In time, however, this changed. "In education," said members of the upper class, "there is no difference between social classes." Despite this, the upper class still had the advantage—they had the wealth that was needed to help their sons study for the examinations.

EXAMINING PHOTOGRAPHS *Built by the Mongol, Ming, and Qing dynasties, enclosed compounds, such as the one shown here, can still be seen in Beijing.* How did these homes reflect the status of the gentry?

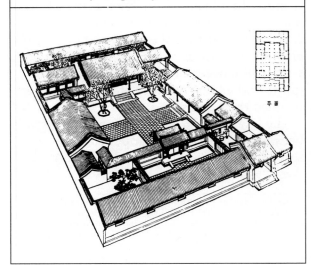

EXAMINING PHOTOGRAPHS *This copper engraving shows a government official of traditional China with his family. They enjoyed the good life and prestige of the upper class. Who held most government posts before the Han dynasty?*

There were four levels of examinations—local, provincial, imperial, and those given by the emperor. Passing a local examination meant that a person could go on to take the more difficult provincial test, which most often required three days of writing during a week. The one in twenty who passed this test could then take the imperial test, which was given every third year in the capital city. The one in two hundred who passed the imperial examination was allowed to take the test given by the emperor. No one failed this test. It served only to rank the order of excellence of the officials.

With each level of examination a scholar passed, he gained higher status and new privileges. Below, a Chinese author discusses the prestige accorded government officials and the reaction of the Chinese to the examination system:

The official's status is exalted, his name distinguished, his power great, and his prestige incomparable. . . . In ancient times the commoners were divided into four major . . . orders, namely, scholars, peasants, artisans [skilled laborers], and merchants, each engaging in its own occupation and each performing its own function. . . . Since the introduction of the examination system . . . scholars have forsaken their studies, peasants their ploughs, artisans their crafts, and merchants their trades; all have turned their attention to but one thing—government office. This is because the official has all the combined advantages of the four without requiring their necessary toil. . . .

SCHOLARS

Those who passed all four levels of the civil service examinations became known as scholars. Generally, there were more scholars than there were government jobs.

In later years, in an effort to earn more income, the government began to sell jobs. The result of this was more jobs for the wealthy and fewer for the scholars. Some scholars became teachers for very little pay and "plowed with the writing brush." Few were able to climb the ladder of success. An exception was the scholar Tang Gui, whose story is told below:

T'ang Kuei [Tang Gui] was born in a poor family. His father, being an invalid, could not earn a living. T'ang Kuei never wanted to be anything but a scholar, al-

Source: Ping-ti Ho (tr.). *The Ladder of Success in Imperial China.* Columbia University Press, 1962, p. 46. Reprinted by permission.

China

THE WANG CLAN

The Wang clan, one of the most successful families of traditional China, was rich and well-known. Below, a Chinese author explains how and why it attained such success:

The Wang clan has for generations risen to fame. This success is due to its strict family instruction. At times of family gatherings, such as weddings and funerals, new years and festivals, or ancestral worship, each member of the family must wear clothes proper to his status before the ceremony is held. Those who have attained official ranks are splendid in official hats and sashes. Those who have failed the tests are doomed to wear short commoners' jackets. This sharp contrast in status makes the slow ones ashamed. Therefore, the father instructs his son, the wife urges her husband that everyone must study hard and make good in examinations and officialdom. This is why the Wang clan has produced so many holders of higher degrees and officials and has become a clan of national renown.

Then the Wang clan began to lose prestige. Soon it became poor and forgotten. Some neighbors gave the following reasons for this:

World affairs constantly change. Nowadays people often think that in view of their present prosperity they should have nothing to worry about for the rest of their lives. In truth many of them sink in almost no time. Almost always, human fortunes are bound to change.

The ancestor's wealth and honor were first obtained by serious studies. The descendants, being used to a life of ease, looked down upon studies. If a family acquired its fortune through hard work and saving, its descendants, with a fortune at their disposal, in most cases forget about industry and

thrift. This is the basic reason the clan declined.

Generation after generation, each son got an equal share of inheritance. Each generation was larger than the one before it. Each share of the inheritance became smaller and smaller.

Wang VI was by nature extravagant. He built a huge home to house all of his females, and when his children went out they were followed by tons of servants. His jewels, curios, ancient bronzes, porcelains, and paintings were without price. At a New Year's Eve feast he always hung up a lantern made of pearls. All wine cups were very old and made of jade. When he returned home, his sedan chair was first placed in front of the middle gate. . . .

TAKING ANOTHER LOOK

1. Why did the Wang clan remain rich and famous for so many years?
2. How do you think the Wang clan could have avoided its fall?

Source: Ping-ti Ho (tr.). *The Ladder of Success in Imperial China.* Columbia University Press, 1962, p. 130. Reprinted by permission.

though the family had not produced any degree holder. In the last half of the fifteenth century, essays by successful candidates were not yet compiled and printed for sale. T'ang Kuei saw the chance of making a living by selecting and editing them for sale. In order to support his parents, younger brothers, and sisters, he sometimes went to neighboring counties to sell his collections of winning test essays. . . .

When he was sixteen, he passed the local examination. He was therefore hired by a local family as a teacher. After placing first in the reviewing tests that followed, he become better known. His salary was increased. Not until then could he provide proper food and basic necessities for his parents and pay for his brothers' and sisters' weddings.

SECTION 1 REVIEW

Checking for Understanding
1. **Define** gentry, compound, civil service.
2. **Identify** the upper classes of traditional China.

CRITICAL THINKING
3. **Analyzing Information** Why were few scholars able to climb the ladder of success?

SECTION 2
The Lower Classes

Like the upper class, the lower classes consisted of several different groups of people. The largest group was the peasants, who made up 80 percent of the population. They lived in the country and provided the food that China needed to survive. Then there were the scientists, merchants, and soldiers.

Source: Ping-ti Ho (tr.). *The Ladder of Success in Imperial China.* Columbia University Press, 1962, p. 269, 270 (Adaptation). Reprinted by permission.

Despite the many contributions they made to China, they were considered third-class citizens.

PEASANTS

Peasant life styles varied in traditional China. Common to most peasants, however, were values passed down from one generation to another. Also common were small families of four to six persons.

Peasant homes usually were made of brown sun-dried brick, bamboo, or stones and had stone or earth floors and paper windows. The land a peasant owned was divided among the sons of the family. As a result, the amount of land for any one family was small.

The peasants' survival depended on the harvest. In most cases, good harvests yielded enough to meet the basic needs of their families. Bad harvests brought debts

EXAMINING PHOTOGRAPHS *In traditional China, peasants spent the greater part of their lives doing back-breaking work to grow rice, the main crop. How did peasants spend the income they earned from their harvests?*

and famine. Because of these conditions, peasant rebellions against the local gentry and government were not uncommon. In most cases, however, the rebellions failed, and conditions did not change.

To survive in bad times, peasants could rent or sell their land or leave their village. Some often ended up selling one of their children to work as a servant under terms much like those stated in the contract below:

> Contract agreed on the third day of the 11th moon of the year. . . . The monumental-stonemason Chao Seng-tzu, because . . . he is short of commodities and cannot procure them by any other means, sells today, with the option of re-purchase, his own son Chiu-tzu to his re-lation . . . the lord Li Ch'ien-ting. The sale price has been fixed at 200 bushels of corn and 200 bushels of millet. Once the sale has been concluded, there will neither be anything paid for the hire of the man, nor interest paid on the commodities. If it should happen that the man sold . . . should fall ill and die, his elder brother will be held responsible for repaying the part of the goods [corresponding to the period of hire which had not been com-pleted.] If Chiu-tzu should steal anything of . . . value from a third person, . . . it is Chiu-tzu himself [and not his employer] from whom reparation will be demanded. . . . The earliest time-limit for the repur-chase of Chiu-tzu has been fixed at the sixth year. It is only when this amount of time has elapsed that his relations are au-thorized to repurchase him.

Another option open to the peasant in need was to obtain a loan. Interest rates, however, were very high. An interest charge of 20 percent per month for a cash loan or 50 percent for grain at harvest time was not

Source: Jacques Gernet. *Daily Life in China in the 13th Century.* Reprinted by permission of Georges Borchardt Inc. English translation copyright © 1962 by George & Allen Unwin, Ltd. Copyright © 1959 by Libnarie Hachette.

unusual. Loan contracts like the medieval one that follows were common:

> On the first day of the third moon of the year . . ., Fan Huai-t'ung and his brothers, whose family is in need of a little cloth, have borrowed from the monk Li a piece of white silk 38 feet [11.6 meters] long and two feet and half an inch [0.61 meters, 1.25 centimeters] wide. In the autumn, they will pay as interest 40 bushels of corn and millet. As regards the capital, they will repay it [in the form of a piece of silk of the same quality and size] before the end of the second moon of the follow-ing year. If they do not repay it, interest equivalent to that paid at the time of the loan . . . shall be paid monthly. The two parties having agreed to this loan in pres-ence of each other shall not act in any way contrary to their agreement.

SCIENTISTS

Chinese scientists gave the world paper and printing, chemical explosives, the me-chanical clock, the compass, canal locks, the crossbow, the kite, cast iron, watertight com-partments, and certain drugs. They also con-tributed a system of measures, irrigation techniques, flood control devices, canals, and military defenses. It was their skill that was responsible for the Grand Canal, the Great Wall, and the superiority of Chinese ships and sails.

The scientists also accomplished much in the field of medicine. Chinese doctors, for example, developed **acupuncture,** a method of treating pain by piercing the skin at vital points with needles. They were vaccinating people for smallpox 700 years before the Eu-ropeans began to do so. They also showed that stomachaches, fevers, colds, malaria, and other ailments could be eased or cured by using ginseng and other roots. Another

Ibid., p. 103.

EXAMINING ART *A water clock rotated the instruments of this eleventh-century Chinese astronomical observatory so they would be in time with the motion of the stars.* *Why did early Chinese scientists and inventors receive so little recognition?*

example of early scientific advances in medicine is the operation described below, which was performed in the third century AD:

Finding that the arm . . . had been pierced to the bone by a poison arrow, the sensible doctor told his adult patient precisely what he was about to do to him: "In a private room I shall erect a post with a ring attached. I shall ask you, sir, to insert your arm in the ring, and I shall bind it firmly to the post. Then I shall cover your head with a quilt so that you cannot see, and with a scalpel I shall open up the flesh right down to the bone. Then I shall scrape away the poison. This done, I shall dress the wound with a certain preparation, sew it up with thread, and there will be no further trouble."

The tough old veteran in fact played a game of chess while the surgeon performed his operation, a young boy holding a basin under the arm. "Although your wound is cured," the doctor admonished him later, "you must be careful of your health, and especially avoid all excitement for a hundred days. . . ."

Although the scientists made these and other significant contributions and seldom used their skills for profit or to gain power, they were given little recognition by the upper class. Because China had so many workers, there was little incentive to invent anything to save labor, and the government was not very interested in the invention of technology with wide application.

MERCHANTS

Merchants received even less attention than scientists in traditional China. Since they did not work with their minds like scholars or with their hands like laborers, the

Source: Excerpts from THE CHINESE LOOKING GLASS by Dennis Bloodworth. Copyright © 1966, 1967 by Dennis Bloodworth. Reprinted by permission of Farrar, Straus & Giroux, Inc.

EXAMINING ART *Peasants in traditional China relied on knickknack peddlers to supply articles that they could not make themselves. Why were wealthy merchants feared by the upper class?*

upper class placed them at the bottom of society. As one Chinese historian noted:

The law despises merchants, but the merchants have become rich and noble; it esteems the farmers, but the farmers have become poor and humble. What is esteemed by the people is despised by the ruler; what is scorned by officials is honored by the law.

Many merchants were among the richest people in China. It was this wealth that members of the upper class feared because they knew that it could be used to destroy them. To limit the merchants, the government forbade them to deal in certain goods, such as salt and iron.

Others, however, often had a different view. A peasant father thought himself lucky

Source: Ch'u T'ung-tsu. *Han Shu* in *Han Social Structure.* University of Washington Press, 1973, p. 111.

if he married a daughter to a rich merchant. Some merchants were generous to the poor. According to one visitor, in bad weather merchants would "find out which families are the worst off, take note of their distress, and when night falls, push through the cracks in their doors some scraps of gold or silver, or else cash coins or notes."

The merchants helped China's economic development by exchanging products both inside and outside of China. They opened trade routes between China and the rest of the world. Along the Silk Road between China and Europe, they exchanged Chinese silk, lacquerware, and porcelain for ivory and glass. During medieval times, they sparked a "commercial revolution" in China that encouraged new technology and ideas.

SOLDIERS

Like scientists and merchants, soldiers were largely neglected in traditional China—except during times of crisis. Many Chinese believed that "good iron is not used to make a nail or a good man to make a soldier." In general, soldiers were thought to be needed rather than respected. The one exception to this was generals.

Although seldom praised, soldiers were important to China's survival. They secured the borders and kept peace within those borders. This included protecting the people from the attacks of outlaws, rebels, and invading barbarians. During medieval times, the soldiers expanded China's borders to Afghanistan and Korea.

According to an ancient Chinese army manual, the highest skill of the soldier was to "subdue the enemy without fighting." Soldiers were to make people obey without resorting to physical violence. Violence was to be used to keep the peace only after all else had failed. War tactics were based on "tricks." According to one Chinese strategist:

All warfare is based on deception.
Therefore, when capable pretend incapacity; when active, inactivity.
When near, make it appear that you are far away; when far away, that you are near.
Offer the enemy a bait to lure him; pretend disorder and strike him.

SECTION 3

Women

In traditional China, women of all classes were considered inferior to men. The Chinese view of a woman's ideal role is evident in the following sayings:

A woman from a wealthy family dresses simply so that she can match the level of her poorer husband.
A woman's place is in the kitchen. The affairs of government do not concern her.

Women were expected to yield to, rather than exercise, authority. In the following excerpt, an author of traditional China offers advice to Chinese women:

Source: Adapted from THE ART OF WAR by Sun Tzu, translated by Samuel B. Griffith. Copyright © 1963 by Oxford University Press. Used by permission.

EXAMINING ART *The use of long stirrups, shown in this Tang pottery figure, gave a steadier ride at a full gallop, making the cavalry a superior force.* ***How did Chinese soldiers try to make people obey?***

Let a woman modestly yield to others; let her respect others; let her put others first, herself last. Should she do something good, let her not mention it; should she do something bad, let her not deny it. Let her bear disgrace; let her even endure when others speak or do evil to her. Always let her seem to tremble and fear.

In the husband and wife relationship, the husband was the authority. The wife had little income and few property rights. If she did not bear a son, her husband might bring another wife into the family. There were many restrictions on women outside the home as well. They could not be

Source: Nancy Lee Swan. *Pan Chao: Foremost Woman Scholar of China.* 1932. 1968 Reprint by Russell and Russell Publishers, p. 32.

government officials or soldiers. Despite this ban, however, some women did manage to become powerful in government. Some, such as the Empress Wu, ruled in their own right. Others, such as Empress Cixi, served as temporary rulers who acted on behalf of a young or sickly ruler.

SECTION 3 REVIEW

CHECKING FOR UNDERSTANDING

1. **Explain** how women were regarded in traditional China.

CRITICAL THINKING

2. **Making Comparisons** Compare the roles of traditional Chinese women with those of modern American women.

SECTION 4

The Arts

In traditional China, the upper class had the time, education, and wealth to pursue an interest in the arts. Even though many of the lower classes did not, they still managed to enjoy some of the many artistic forms and styles. Chinese art included bronze vases; bowls and plates; carved jade jewelry and religious objects; glazed pottery and stone sculptures; painting and lacquerware; rubbings of tombstones; woodcuts; ceramics; and decorative arts. There also was dance, opera, architecture, and writing and painting with a brush.

Although art was enjoyed for art's sake, it usually was enjoyed most for its attempts to achieve spiritual meaning. Elements of nature, such as flowers, birds, and animals, appeared often. Each carried symbolic meanings. The plum blossom, for example, stood for courage, hope, and purity. Geese were a symbol of happy married life. The tiger represented energy, strength, and cunning.

One of the most important symbols was the dragon. While to a foreigner the dragon seemed to be an interesting fantasy, to some Chinese it was a symbol for an emperor, a sign of the zodiac, or a hero in a folktale.

WRITING WITH A BRUSH

In traditional China, writing was an important art form that a young man "on the way up" had to learn. This was a difficult process because the Chinese writing system is based on a system of "pictures," or symbols called characters, rather than on an alphabet. When the characters were written with a brush and ink, they became an art known as **calligraphy**, which allowed the "painter," or calligrapher, to express ideas and reveal inner feelings. Calligraphy was a valued activity that contributed to such other areas of Chinese culture as painting, drama, and literature. Chinese poets, in particular, aimed to recreate mood and atmosphere in their works. Many of their poems described brief moments of intense feelings such as those expressed in the poem below by Yen Shu, who lived about 1000 AD:

Among green willows and fragrant grass
  along the road of post stations
Youth discards you and slips away
In the tower the fifth watch bell
  shatters what's left of dreams
Beneath the blossoms, the sorrow of part-
  ing and March rain
More bitter to love than not—
One inch unravels to a thousand, ten
  thousand threads
Somewhere is an edge of heaven, an end
  of earth
But to longing, there is no end.

Source: Yen Shu. "Mu lan Hua" from *Tz'u Poetry* in *Asia*, July/August, 1983. Julie Landau (tr.), p. 42.

The Arts of China

The Chinese began producing works of art as early as the 5000's BC. Since that time, their work has included scroll paintings, pottery, jade carvings, and lacquerware (varnished items).

? What group in traditional China devoted the most attention to the arts?

JADE MASTERPIECE
Emperor's seal/ stamp with carvings

SCULPTURE
Gold-leafed female lion at the Forbidden City, Beijing

LACQUERWARE
Varnished dish showing Chinese dragon

ARCHITECTURE
Elaborately decorated roof of the Imperial Palace, Beijing

POTTERY
Porcelain vase with lotus design

CHINESE OPERA
Chinese actress performing traditional role

PAINTING WITH A BRUSH

Chinese artists who painted with a brush also were inspired by nature. Their works expressed feelings and were not meant to be lifelike.

By the 900's AD artists used landscape painting to capture the special quality of the environment. When people were portrayed, it was only as part of a scene. The scene itself was more an arrangement of mountains and water than a view of the land. Often, vertical calligraphy was part of the painting. Thus, to appreciate fully most landscapes, the viewer needed some knowledge of calligraphy and Chinese life.

One of the most famous painters was Tao Chi, who lived from 1641 to 1720. His painting, "Waterfall on Mount Lu," is a hanging scroll. On one side of the painting is a poem by Li Bo, part of which appears below.

SECTION 4 REVIEW

CHECKING FOR UNDERSTANDING
1. **Define** calligraphy.
2. **List** several art forms that developed in traditional China.

CRITICAL THINKING
3. **Synthesizing Information** What major themes inspired traditional Chinese artists?

I am the madman of the Ch'u country
Who sang a mad song disputing
    Confucius.
. . . Holding in my hand a staff of green
    jade,
I have crossed, since morning at the
    Yellow Crane Terrace,
All five Holy Mountains, without a
    thought of distance,
According to the one constant habit of my
    life.
. . . Lu Mountain stands beside the South-
    ern Dipper
In clouds reaching silken like a
    nine-panelled screen,
With its shadow in a crystal lake
    deepening the green water.
The Golden Gate opens into two
    mountain-ranges.
A silver stream is handing down to three
    stone bridges
Within sight of the mighty Tripod Falls.
Ledges of cliff and winding trails lead to
    blue sky
And a flush of cloud in the morning sun,
Whence no flight of birds could be blown
    into Wu.

Source: The Jade Mountain: A Chinese Anthology translated by Witler Bynner from the texts of Kiang Kang-Hu. Copyright 1929 and renewed 1957 by Alfred A. Knopf Inc. Reprinted by permission of Alfred A. Knopf, Inc.

Cultural Values

CHINESE WISDOM

A major type of Chinese literature is the folktale, which was used to pass values from one generation to another. Chinese leaders use the following folktale in their speeches.

FOCUSING ON THE ISSUE Read the tale, and answer these questions:

1. What would you say is the most important value held by the foolish old man? The wise old man?
2. What do you think is the point or moral of the tale? Might peasants of traditional China recognize the moral? Explain.
3. Why might rulers in old China have wanted their

people to know this folktale? Why might modern Chinese leaders want their people to know it?

Many years ago there was an old man who lived in Northern China. People called him the Foolish Old Man of North Mountain. His house faced south and beyond his doorway stood the two great peaks, Tai-hung and Wangwu, which blocked his view.

So one day he called his sons together and told them he wanted to get rid of the mountains. They each took a shovel and with great determination, they began to dig up the mountains.

A Wise Old Man saw them busily digging away and he laughed at them. "How silly of you to do this," he told

them. "It's impossible for you few to dig up these two high mountains."

The Foolish Old Man replied, "When I die, my sons will carry on; when they die, there will be my grandsons, and then their sons and grandsons, and so on until the job is done.

"High as they are, the mountains cannot grow any higher and with every bit we dig, they will be that much lower. You see, we will clear them away."

So, having answered the Wise Old Man, the Foolish Old Man and his sons went on digging.

Source: Marie-Louise Gebhardt. *The Foolish Old Man Who Moved Mountains.* Friendship Press, 1969, pp. 100–101.

Chapter 10 Review

SUMMARY

In traditional China, the upper class—gentry, government officials, and scholars—set the rules of behavior for the lower classes—peasants, scientists, merchants, and soldiers. Although ignored or looked down upon by the upper class, each of the lower classes made significant contributions both to China and to the world.

Women formed their own distinct group in traditional Chinese society. They were considered inferior to men and were expected to yield to male authority.

Government officials were chosen on the basis of civil service examinations. There were four levels of examinations—local, provincial, imperial, and those given by the emperor.

The arts of traditional China were diverse and included writing and painting with a brush. Nature was a common source of inspiration for most Chinese artists.

USING VOCABULARY

Use each of the following words in a paragraph about the different classes of people in traditional China.

gentry	acupuncture
compound	calligraphy
civil service	

REVIEWING FACTS

1. **State** the role of the gentry in traditional Chinese society.
2. **Explain** how a person became a government official in traditional China.
3. **List** the contributions of scientists, merchants, and soldiers to China's development.

4. **Describe** the restrictions placed on women in traditional China.
5. **Describe** the Chinese writing system and how it was used as an art form.

CRITICAL THINKING

1. **Evaluating Information** In traditional China, members of the upper class said, "In education there is no difference between social classes." Based on the information in the chapter, do you think the upper class really believed this? Give examples to support your answer.
2. **Predicting Consequences** Third-class citizens were looked down upon in traditional China despite their many accomplishments. In what ways do you think Chinese society and China might have been different if there had been no scientists, merchants, or soldiers? If they had been more honored members of society?

ANALYZING CONCEPTS

1. **Identity** What was the role of women in traditional Chinese society?
2. **Technology** Why were Chinese inventions not applied to the development of the country's economy?
3. **Culture** What goods were exchanged by Chinese and foreign merchants along the Silk Road?

GEOGRAPHIC THEMES

1. **Movement** How did Chinese merchants open contact between China and foreign areas?
2. **Human-Environment Interaction** Why were harvests important to China's peasants?

Reading a Diagram

Suppose you buy a new bicycle and discover that you must assemble the parts before you can ride it. A *diagram*, or a drawing that shows how the parts fit together, would make this job much easier. Diagrams can also illustrate how things work. Most diagrams include text that labels the parts or explains relationships between them.

Here are some steps to follow in reading a diagram:

- Read the title or caption of the diagram to find out what it represents.
- Read all labels on the diagram.
- Read the legend and identify symbols and colors used in the diagram.
- Look for numbers indicating a sequence of steps, or arrows showing the direction of movement.

EXAMPLE

Chinese sailors used sailing techniques and navigational inventions to explore the continents of Asia and Africa 2000 years before Europeans adopted these practices. The rudder, which allowed sailors to steer without using oars, was used in China by the first century AD. Examine the diagram of a Chinese rudder shown below and note the different parts.

The diagram shows that the tiller is attached to the rudder. This allows a person on deck to steer the boat by pushing the tiller right or left.

The rudder can also be hoisted out of shallow water to prevent damage. What part shown on the diagram controls this movement? *(rudder hoisting windlass)*

PRACTICE

One of China's most important inventions was the iron plow. Used by the Chinese as early as the 500's BC, the plow was not used in Europe until the 1700's AD—2000 years later! Study the diagram of a Chinese plow with its different parts, and then answer the following questions:

1. What connects the handle to the whippletree?
2. How do the plowshare and moldboard work together?
3. To what is the plowshare attached?
4. What is the purpose of the whippletree?
5. Which parts do you think were made of iron?
6. Why would the plow be more efficient than a pitchfork or shovel?

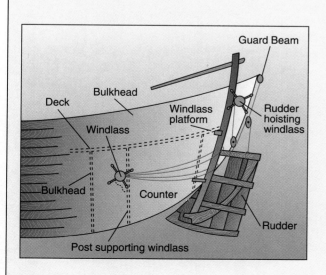

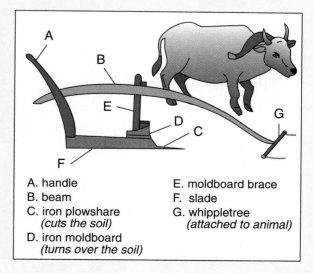

A. handle
B. beam
C. iron plowshare *(cuts the soil)*
D. iron moldboard *(turns over the soil)*
E. moldboard brace
F. slade
G. whippletree *(attached to animal)*

People and Places to Know
Lao-zi, Kong-fu-zi, Mencius, Mo-zi, Buddhists, Muslims, Franciscans, Jesuits, Protestants

Key Terms to Define
ethics, sage, filial piety, divination, classics

Objectives to Learn

1. **Identify** traditional Chinese religious practices and beliefs.

2. **Summarize** the teachings of ancient China's major thinkers.

3. **Describe** the impact on China of Buddhism, Islam, and Christianity.

Temple of Heaven in Beijing

The Chinese Heritage

Source: Arthur Waley (ed.). *The Analects of Confucius.* George Allen & Unwin Ltd., 1938, pp. 102–103.

"
1. The Master said, It is Goodness that gives to a neighbourhood its beauty. One who is free to choose, yet does not prefer to dwell among the Good—how can he be accorded the name of wise?

2. The Master said, Without Goodness a man
   Cannot for long endure adversity,
   Cannot for long enjoy prosperity.
   The Good Man rests content with Goodness; he that is merely wise pursues Goodness in the belief that it pays to do so.

3,4. Of the adage Only a Good Man knows how to like people, knows how to dislike them, the Master said, He whose heart is in the smallest degree set upon Goodness will dislike no one.

5. Wealth and rank are what every man desires; but if they can only be retained to the detriment of the Way he professes, he must relinquish them. Poverty and obscurity are what every man detests; but if they can only be avoided to the detriment of the Way he professes, he must accept them. The gentleman who ever parts company with Goodness does not fulfil that name. Never for a moment does a gentleman quit the way of Goodness. He is never so [worried] but that he [clings] to this; never so tottering but that he [clings] to this. "

"The Master" who spoke these thoughts was Confucius, whom many consider China's greatest philosopher. He was one of a number of important thinkers in traditional China. Despite the differences in their teachings, all were more concerned about life in this world than in the supernatural and devoted themselves to **ethics**, or the study of moral principles. Ethics, they believed, provided a key to understanding the workings of nature. If humans adapted to nature rather than try to change it, a harmonious balance would be achieved in human affairs.

These thinkers shaped China's beliefs and values for centuries. They passed on to the Chinese a high regard for education and the use of knowledge to guide conduct. Over time, this heritage of thought and practice underwent important changes. The wisdom of such **sages**, or wise teachers, as Confucius became mixed with earlier religious beliefs; foreign religions entered the country and gained Chinese converts. From this diversity of belief, the Chinese developed a unique pattern of faith and practice that has continued into modern times.

SECTION 1

Traditional Chinese Beliefs

In traditional China, the people believed that many gods, goddesses, and spirits ruled the universe. To gain the approval of these deities and to ward off evil, they offered sacrifices of animals and grain. In the spring and fall, Chinese emperors performed sacrifices to the two chief deities—the gods of the Heaven and the Earth. They did this to insure the fertility of the soil and a plentiful harvest.

Another characteristic of traditional Chinese religion was **filial piety**, or reverence for parents and ancestors. Children were expected to take care of their elderly relatives, to obey them, and to bury them properly after death. Departed ancestors and their deeds were to be remembered, and sacrifices were to be offered to them. It was believed that such prayers and sacrifices joined together the worlds of the living and the dead.

The Chinese also held that, because of their contact with the gods, goddesses, and spirits, dead relatives were able to help living family members. Any Chinese who forgot to honor their ancestors were viewed with extreme disfavor. An old belief held that neglected ancestors wandered about as "homeless ghosts," punishing those family members who had abandoned them.

Because of the importance of ancestors, each Chinese home had a small altar. There, the names and deeds of deceased family members were remembered, and small sacrifices of wine and rice were offered. In the 1800's, a Western scholar described in this way the altar of one wealthy Chinese family and the ceremony its members performed:

> At the back of the room, standing against the wall and taking up almost the whole length of it, a long table of varnished wood forms the altar. On this altar are stands holding small lacquered tablets, chronologically arranged, on which the names of the ancestors are inscribed. Hanging at the very top of the wall is the sign of the deity; and in front of the tablets are lights and incense burners. Lastly, at some distance from the altar, there is a common square table with chairs round it, and in the middle of the table a register with books on each side of it.
>
> Everybody has put on his best clothes and is waiting. The father and mother . . . enter, followed by two acolytes [worship assistants], and take their places in front

EXAMINING ART *This painting shows a family giving thanks before the family shrine for the harvest. What did the Chinese believe happened to family members who forgot to honor their ancestors?*

of the altar. They address a short invocation [appeal] to Heaven, and those present chant the ancestral hymn. . . . A variety of things are offered: . . . a pigeon or a chicken, fruits, wine and grain, either rice or wheat, whichever is grown in the district. Or wine alone, with rice or wheat, may be offered. The two acolytes go to fetch these offerings, the wife takes them from their hands and gives them to her husband, who lifts them above his head, his wife standing beside him, and places them on the altar in sign of thanksgiving. The father then reads the names of the ancestors inscribed on the tablets, and recalling them more particularly to the memory of the family, he speaks in their name. . . . The corn and wine that he has just consecrated [dedicated] to them, which are a symbol of the efforts made and the progress realized, he now returns, on behalf of the ancestors, to those present, in token of their [unbreakable] union. Lastly, the officiator [leader] exhorts the family to meditate on the meaning of this true communion, on the engagements that it implies, which all present swear to carry out and then, after a last prayer, a meal is served, in which the consecrated offerings are included.

In addition to reverence for ancestors, the Chinese believed in **divination**, or the foretelling of the future. It was used to decide the place for a building, the time for religious services, or the outcome of a battle. To determine the future, fortune-tellers used such techniques as studying lines in stalks of grain or analyzing cracks on bones and shells. They also practiced the reading of such signs in nature as the flow of water or the surface of the landscape. In time, most of the principles and techniques of divination were recorded in a book called *Yi Jing,* or the *Book of Changes.*

Source: G. E. Simon. *La Cite' Chinoise* in *China* by L. A. Lyall, Charles Scribner's Sons, 1934, pp. 28–30.

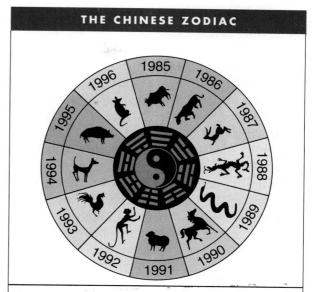

THE CHINESE ZODIAC

EXAMINING CHARTS *The zodiac, a band of stars believed to influence people's lives, is used in astrology. The Chinese zodiac, shown here, has a different animal sign for each of its 12 parts. What does each of these signs represent?*

SECTION 1 REVIEW

CHECKING FOR UNDERSTANDING
1. **Define** filial piety, divination.

CRITICAL THINKING
2. **Determining Cause and Effect** How might Chinese religious beliefs have influenced traditional Chinese society?

SECTION 2

Daoism

Between 700 BC and 300 BC, China went through a period of political turmoil. During this time, the first great Chinese thinkers appeared, each with his own answer to China's problems. Among the earliest of these thinkers were the teachers of a philosophy known as Daoism, which means the "Way of

Nature." Although scholars know very little about the origins of Daoism, they believe that in its earliest form, it was a philosophy of nature that stressed humanity's need to adapt to its natural surroundings.

The founder of Daoism supposedly was named Lao-zi, or "the Master." According to one tradition, he began his career as a record keeper in the court of the emperor. But he came to dislike the corruption of court life and finally retired from his post to seek peace of mind in nature. While wandering throughout the country, Lao-zi may have written some of Daoism's principal book, the *Dao De Jing*, or *The Way and Its Power*. The *Dao De Jing* became one of the **classics**, or major and lasting works, of Chinese literature. Its themes are the need for human simplicity and closeness to nature.

TEACHINGS

The early Daoists taught that the universe was united by *Dao*, a mysterious force which determined the destiny of all things and could not be changed. Therefore, if they were not in harmony with *Dao*, all human ambition and achievement were in vain.

The Daoists held that people should reject society, live simply in harmony with nature, and reflect on the meaning of *Dao*. The Daoists also believed that people who truly seek *Dao* should let events take their natural course and not interfere. The Daoist poem below illustrates this teaching:

Nature does not have to insist,
Can blow for only half a morning,
Rain for only half a day,
And what are these winds and these rains but natural?
If nature does not have to insist,
Why should man?

Source: Witter Bynner. *The Way of Life.* John Day Co., 1944, p. 38 (XXIII).

Although Daoist teachings focused chiefly on the individual, they also included views on society and government. The Daoists strongly opposed the existence of a large powerful government with a bureaucracy and many laws. Their vision of an ideal society was carefully explained in the following manner in the *Dao De Jing:*

Let there be a small country with a few inhabitants. Though there be labor-saving [devices], the people would not use them. Let the people mind death and not migrate far. Though there be boats and carriages, there would be no occasion to ride in them. Though there be armor and weapons, there would be no occasion to display them.

Let people revert to the practice of rope-knotting [instead of writing], and be contented with their food, pleased with their clothing, satisfied with their houses, and happy with their customs. Though there be a neighboring country in sight, and the people hear each other's cocks crowing and dogs barking, they would grow old and die without having anything to do with each other.

RELIGION

As a philosophy little concerned about gods, rituals, and the afterlife, early Daoism appealed only to the educated few. It had little to offer the uneducated masses. But by the 100's AD Daoism had undergone a major change. Without denying its original beliefs, it gradually became a religion complete with deities, priests, temples, and sacrifices.

The change from a philosophy to a religion was encouraged by Daoism's stress on the importance of life. The Daoists had always taught that a person who faithfully followed *Dao* would enjoy a long life. To carry this

Source: Tao Te Ching in *Sources of Chinese Tradition,* compiled by William Theodore de Bary, Wing-tsit Chan, and Burton Watson. Columbia University Press, 1960, pp. 63–64.

belief further, scholars and priests sought ways to master the body and prolong life indefinitely.

The Daoist religion won wide appeal among the masses and became one of the major faiths of China. Its chief support came from the peasants, who lived and worked close to the soil. At the same time, Daoist philosophy influenced poets and artists who sought inspiration in natural beauty.

S E C T I O N   2   R E V I E W

CHECKING FOR UNDERSTANDING
1. **Define** classics.

CRITICAL THINKING
2. **Identifying Central Issues** What were the basic principles of Daoism?

S E C T I O N   3

Confucianism

In spite of Daoism's widespread popularity, the most important ethical philosophy of traditional China was Confucianism. It was based on the teachings of Kong-fu-zi, better known to Westerners as Confucius.

The teachings of Confucius respected the traditional wisdom and beliefs of the Chinese and were intended to be a guide to conduct, not a religion. Confucius himself showed little interest in the deities and seemed to approve of religious rituals chiefly as a means of uniting the people. In time, however, his philosophy, Confucianism, became a religion, and Confucian ethical values became the foundation of traditional Chinese society and government.

EXAMINING ART *This rubbing of a stone engraving shows Confucius as a court official. The verse on the right refers to his achievements and virtue. What were Confucius's teachings intended to be?*

CONFUCIUS

Confucius was born in 551 BC to a noble family that had lost its wealth during the Zhou dynasty. Because his parents died when he was young, he had to make his own way in the world. A talented student, he developed an interest in the workings of society and searched for the factors that contributed to good government.

After Confucius completed his studies, he entered government service. He also served as a teacher and attracted a great number of students. In his teachings, Confucius revealed his concern about the poor condition of the Chinese government. He pointed out to his students that government existed for the well-being of the people, not for the enrichment of the rulers. He urged China's leaders to put aside military conquests and to work for the good of the country. He also criticized the appointment of government officials on the basis of family ties rather than ability. He believed that only well-educated officials should serve in the government.

Confucius's views gained him many enemies, and he was forced to resign his government post. During the final years of his life, he spent his time teaching and studying Chinese literary classics. After his death in 479 BC his followers worked to carry out his political and social aims.

EXAMINING PHOTOGRAPHS *Beihai Park in Beijing, its gardens often compared to a three-dimensional landscape painting, was a retreat for scholar-officials.* Who was known as the "Supreme Sage"?

TEACHINGS

Confucius's followers recorded his teachings in a work known as the *Analects.* The work, which later became one of the Chinese classics, stressed several themes. One was described by the word *li,* the outward practice of doing the right thing. Confucius taught that society functions smoothly when it follows *li.* People know their place in society and act for its welfare rather than for their own selfish interests. Another theme was *ren,* or the inner attitude of being humane, loving, and good. According to the *Analects,* Confucius explained the meaning of *ren* to his students in the following way:

When Fan Ch'ih asked about *jen* [ren], the Master said: "Love people."
  When Yen Yüan asked about *jen,* the Master said: "If you can control your selfish desires and subject them to the rules of propriety [being proper] and if you can do this for a single day, it is the beginning of *jen* for the entire world. *Jen* is self-sufficient and comes from your inner self; it requires no outside help." Yen Yügan asked for more details. The Master said: "Don't see the improper; don't hear the improper; don't talk about the improper; and don't act improperly."
  When Chung Kung [Zhong Gong] asked about *jen,* the Master said: "When you meet a person outside of your house, greet him as if he were a great noble. If, as a government official, you have to impose . . . duties on the people, you should approach your task with the same seriousness that you would use in performing a religious ritual. Don't do to others what you yourself do not desire."

Confucius believed than *ren* and *li* should determine all human relationships. In his view, there were five important relationships

Source: Reprinted with permission of Macmillan Publishing Company from THE AGELESS CHINESE: A HISTORY, Third Edition, by Dun J. Li. Copyright © 1978, 1971, 1965 Charles Scribner's Sons.

—ruler and ruled, father and son, husband and wife, older brother and younger brother, and friend and friend. In defining these relationships, he laid stress on the importance of rank. Rulers, for example, were above the ruled, men were superior to women, and the older was ahead of the younger. Only friends enjoyed a position of social equality, but they were expected to treat each other with respect and courtesy. Each person in an inferior position owed respect and obedience to those above him or her. On the other hand, those in a superior position were expected to care for and set a good example for those below them. If the "proper" conduct were carried out in each of the five relationships, the requirements of *ren* and *li* would be fulfilled and a just society would result.

Confucius also taught that for the people to act morally, a good government was necessary. He felt that poor government with tyrannical rulers influenced people to do wrong, while conscientious rulers encouraged them to do good.

CONFUCIAN SCHOLARS

After Confucius's teachings became more widely known, he was given the title of "Supreme Sage," and some of his ideas were taken up by other scholars. One of these scholars was Mencius (372 BC—289 BC). Mencius, who was born and raised near Confucius's home province and was a student of Confucius's grandson, came to be known as the "Second Sage." In time, his teachings were recorded in the book *Mencius.* Below, in a conversation recorded in *Mencius,* a critic and Mencius discuss human nature:

"**H**uman nature is like water current," said [the critic]. "If it is led to the east, it flows eastward; if it is led to the west, it flows westward. Like water which can be led to either of the two directions, human nature is neither good nor bad. It depends

EXAMINING ART *In this painting, a servant prepares ink as two scholars appear to be contemplating the composition of a poem. With what did Mencius compare human nature? Why?*

upon the direction towards which it is led."

[Mencius said,] "The goodness of human nature is like water's natural inclination to move downward. As water is inevitably moving downward, there is no man in the world who is not good. If you beat water hard, it jumps up and can rise higher than your forehead. . . . But, is this the nature of water? It acts contrary to its nature because it is given no other choice. If a man does bad things, he, like water, has been forced to do them and has not been given a better choice. His wrongdoing has nothing to do with his inherent nature which is good."

Another follower of Confucius was Zhu Xi (1130 AD—1200 AD), who combined the teachings of Confucius and others into the

"Four Books." For the next 700 years, the "Four Books" were studied and memorized. They became the basis of the civil service examinations, which were given until 1905.

Confucianism, regarded as a philosophy by scholars, gradually became a religion for the masses. By 500 AD shrines and temples had been built to Confucius, and many Chinese came to look on him as a god.

SECTION 4

Other Faiths and Viewpoints

Although Confucianism emerged as the dominant influence in Chinese life, it was not without rivals or critics. An important critic was Mo-zi, who lived from 480 BC to 400 BC. Mo-zi shunned the Confucian evolution to learning and the arts and urged people to follow more practical pursuits. He also criticized the Confucian emphasis on social rank and duties. Instead, he called for an end to the privileges of the wealthy and the creation of a new society in which all people would be loved and treated equally. Mo-zi presents his view of the ideal society:

What is it like when righteousness is the standard of conduct? The great will not attack the small, the strong will not plunder the weak, the many will not oppress the few, the cunning will not deceive the simple, the noble will not disdain the humble, the rich will not mock the poor, and the young will not encroach upon the old. And the states in the empire will not harm each other with water, fire, poison, and weapons. Such a regime will be auspicious to Heaven above, to the spirits in the middle sphere, and to the people below. Being auspicious to these three, it is beneficial to all.

BUDDHISM

One rival to Confucianism was the foreign religion of Buddhism, which merchants from India brought to China during the first century AD. The first Chinese converts to Buddhism came from the upper class, who were attracted by the religion's complex philosophy and elaborate ceremonies. Later, it spread among the lower class, who hoped for release from their poverty in Buddhist afterlife.

By the 300's AD, Buddhist beliefs were seen in Chinese religious practices, literature, scholarship, art, and architecture. At the same time, traditional Chinese beliefs and ways influenced the teachings and practices of Buddhism in China. For most Chinese, Buddhism, Daoism, and Confucianism complemented each other, and they combined the practices of all three.

ISLAM

Another foreign religion that influenced China was Islam, which began in the Middle East during the 600's AD. It was first brought to China a century later by traders. These Muslims, or followers of Islam, lived in their own settlements apart from the Chinese.

Then, in the 1200's, when the Mongols invaded China, they brought with them

Source: Mo Tzu in *Sources of Chinese Tradition,* compiled by William Theodore De Bary, Wing-tsit Chan, and Burton Watson. Columbia University Press, 1960, p. 49.

many Muslim soldiers who settled in China and married Chinese women. For the first time, Islam spread to the general population. The largest number of converts, however, was among the non-Chinese minorities in the western part of the country. This area remains a stronghold of Islam today.

CHRISTIANITY

Christianity was less successful than Islam in establishing a foothold in China. The first Christian missionaries from western Europe were Franciscans, a group of Roman Catholic clergy, who reached China during the Mongol period.

Later, during the 1500's, another Roman Catholic group called Jesuits headed a more successful missionary effort. Jesuit priests shared their skills in mathematics with Chinese scholars and won the respect of the Chinese by adopting Chinese dress and customs. As a result, in 1692, the Chinese emperor allowed Chinese converts to Christianity to practice their faith freely. The Catholic pope in Rome, however, blocked the Jesuit effort to adapt Christianity to Chinese ways. The Chinese emperor viewed this as foreign interference in Chinese affairs and banned the practice of Christianity in China.

In the 1800's, under pressure from the Western powers, the Chinese allowed Christian missionaries to enter China once again. Many of the new missionaries were Protestants from North America and Europe. With the backing of their governments, they preached Christianity and built schools, hospitals, and universities. Many Chinese, however, viewed Christianity as a foreign religion linked to Western efforts to dominate China. As a result, attacks against missionaries and Chinese Christians were common.

Although only a small minority of Chinese accepted Christianity, those who did had a

EXAMINING PHOTOGRAPHS *Jesuit priests were admired more for their knowledge of science than for their religion by the Chinese, who accepted them as scholars from abroad. Why did a Chinese emperor ban Christianity?*

noticeable impact on China. A number of Chinese Christians accepted Western ways and supported efforts to modernize their country.

SECTION 4 REVIEW

CHECKING FOR UNDERSTANDING
1. **List** the foreign religions that gained a foothold in China.
2. **Explain** how the foreign religions influenced China and the Chinese.

CRITICAL THINKING
3. **Making Comparisons** Compare the teachings of Mo-zi with those of Confucius. Which do you think had the most impact on China?

Religion

CONFUCIANISM, DAOISM, AND BUDDHISM

For hundreds of years, Confucianism has been one of the world's major religions. Like other religions, it has provided guidelines for its followers. **FOCUSING ON THE ISSUE** Listed below are guidelines for Confucianism and some other religions as well. After reading the guidelines and studying the chart, answer the following questions:

1. How are the Confucian guidelines the same as the others? Different? Based on the information in the chapter and in the chart, how do you think a follower of Confucius would respond to each guideline? Explain.

2. Using your knowledge of Confucianism and other world religions, how is Confucianism similar to other faiths? How is it different? What effect do you think Confucianism and other religions have had on the development of China?

First put yourself in order, then be sure you act justly and sincerely towards others. Then you will find happiness.
   —The *Analects* of Confucius

Perform right action, for action is superior to inaction.
—The *Bhagavad-Gita* of India

The world is a divine vessel:
It cannot be shaped;
Nor can it be insisted upon.
He who shapes it damages it;
He who insists upon it loses it.
Therefore the sage does not
   shape it, so he does not
   damage it;
He does not insist upon it,
so he does not lose it.
         —The *Dao De Jing*

Devoutly trust the law of love;
Do not denounce the creed of others.
Devoutly promote the sense of equality;

Do not arouse discriminatory feelings.
Devoutly awaken the sense of compassion;
Do not forget the sufferings of others.
Devoutly cultivate a [friendly manner]; . . .
   —*Ippen Shonin Goroku* of Japan

Decay is (found) in all . . . things.
Work out your salvation with diligence.
      —*Dialogues of the Buddha*

. . . what is good; and what does the Lord require of (you), but to do justly, and to love mercy, and to walk humbly with (your) God.
         —The *Bible* (Micah)

Love your enemies, bless them that curse you, do good to them that hate you, and pray for them which despitefully use you, and persecute you, that

you may be children of your Father . . . in heaven.
         —The *Bible* (Matthew)

Those who believe and do deeds of righteousness, and perform the prayer, and pay the alms— their wage awaits them with their Lord, and no fear shall be on them, neither shall they sorrow.
         —The *Quran* (Sura II)

Be kind to parents, and the near kinsman,
and to orphans and to the needy,
and to the neighbor who is of kin,
and to the neighbor who is a stranger,
and to the companion at your side,
and to the traveller, and to that your
right hand owns.
         —The *Quran* (Sura IV)

CHARACTERISTICS OF THE MAJOR PHILOSOPHIES/RELIGIONS OF CHINA

PHILOSOPHIES/ RELIGIONS	DAOISM	CONFUCIANISM	BUDDHISM
ORIGIN	Based upon the teachings of Lao-zi, "The Master."	Based upon the teachings of Confucius.	Imported from India and based upon the teachings of Siddhartha Gautama (the Buddha).
MAJOR BELIEFS	Civilization is corrupt and humanity has a need for simplicity and closeness to nature. The origin of creation and its force is the Dao (The Way). The Way can be found by reinterpreting ancient traditions of nature worship and divination. A life lived according to the Dao is a healthy human life.	The moral understanding "What you do not wish for yourself, do not do to others," is at the foundation of social institutions. Everyday life is the arena of religion. All human relationships should be determined by *li, ren,* and the Five Relationships. In a well-disciplined society ceremonies, duties, and public service are emphasized daily.	Life is suffering. Suffering is caused by desire for things to be as they are not. Suffering, however, has an end. The means to the end are the Middle Way of moderation and the Eightfold Path—Right Views, Right Intentions, Right Speech, Right Action, Right Occupation, Right Effort, Right Concentration, and Right Meditation.
CHARACTERISTIC	Adherents vary in beliefs. Some seek immortality through the arts of magic, breath control, and alchemy; offers an alternative to Confucianism.	Confucian ethical values became the foundation of Chinese society and government.	Has split into several branches, virtually extinct in India by the 12th century AD, although influential in China and Japan.

Chapter 11 Review

SUMMARY

Traditional Chinese thinkers, devoted to ethics, shaped China's beliefs and values, encouraging education and promoting knowledge as a guide to conduct.

Daoism stressed humanity's need to adapt to nature. Its emphasis on the importance of life encouraged its change from a philosophy of the upper class to a religion of the lower classes.

The most important ethical philosophy of traditional China was Confucianism, which was based on the teachings of Confucius. Confucian ethical values became the foundation of Chinese society and government.

Several foreign religions also influenced the Chinese. These included Buddhism, which came from India; Islam, which came from the Middle East; and Christianity, which came from Europe and North America. All were an influence on China and the Chinese.

USING VOCABULARY

Using the following terms, write a paragraph describing traditional Chinese beliefs and values.

ethics   divination
sage   classics
filial piety

REVIEWING FACTS

1. **Discuss** the role of Chinese emperors in traditional Chinese religion.
2. **Describe** the methods the Chinese used to predict the future.
3. **Explain** how Daoism changed over the centuries.
4. **Name** Daoism's principal book that became one of the classics of Chinese literature.
5. **Discuss** the importance of the "Four Books" of Confucianism.
6. **Identify** the Confucian concepts of *li* and *ren*.
7. **Compare** the impact of Buddhism and Islam on Chinese life.

CRITICAL THINKING

1. **Predicting** Traditional Chinese thinkers encouraged a high regard for education. In what ways do you think China would be different if education had not been a priority?
2. **Demonstrating Reasoned Judgment** Which beliefs of Confucianism and Daoism do you think are valuable today? Give reasons for your answers.
3. **Evaluating Information** A critic of Mencius stated that "Like water which can be led to either of the two directions (east or west), human nature is neither good nor bad. It depends upon the direction towards which it is led." Do you agree with him? Use examples to support your argument.
4. **Predicting Consequences** What negative outcomes might result for a society with the view of women held by Confucianism?

ANALYZING CONCEPTS

1. **Culture** How did the Chinese honor their deities and ancestors?
2. **Diversity** In what ways can traditional China be considered a diverse society?

GEOGRAPHIC THEMES

1. **Location** How did China's location favor the spread of Buddhism within its borders?
2. **Movement** What impact did Western Christian missionaries have on the Chinese?

Hypothesizing

Suppose that you arrive in school one morning and find that you are the only one there! Naturally, you would begin to search for explanations for this unusual situation. Perhaps your watch shows the incorrect time and you are very early. Perhaps you forgot that the class was supposed to meet at a different place that day. Each possible explanation is called a *hypothesis.*

Once you have formed some hypotheses, you must figure out which one is correct. To do so, gather as many facts as possible about each hypothesis. For example, to check the accuracy of your watch, you could look at other clocks in the school. If your watch is correct, then you must determine whether the class is meeting in another location. How could you test this hypothesis? *(ask someone in the office, check other possible locations in the building, ask other students or teachers if they know where the class is meeting)*

Forming and testing hypotheses is important in studying any subject. When you encounter unfamiliar events or trends, hypothesize explanations for them and then try to figure out which hypothesis is correct. The following steps will help you in this process:

- Identify the event, trend, or condition you want to explain.
- List facts that may relate to causes for this event, trend, or condition.
- Based on these facts, state possible hypotheses for the event, trend, or condition.
- Gather information that can prove or disprove each hypothesis.

EXAMPLE

Chapter 11 states: "The largest number of converts to Islam in China was among the non-Chinese minorities in the western part of the country, which remains a stronghold of Islam." Suppose you want to understand why Islam is strongest among non-Chinese minorities in western China. First, identify information that might help explain this condition. For example, you know that western China is geographically isolated from the rest of the country. Also, you know that Islam spread most extensively in China during the Mongol invasion. The Chinese, however, resented Mongol rule.

So what explanations or hypotheses can be based on this information?

1. Because Islam was associated with unpopular Mongol invaders, many Chinese were not attracted to it.
2. Because the western part of the country is closer geographically and culturally to the Islamic Middle East than to China, Islam is strongest there.

To test each hypothesis, you may want to find more information about relations between Chinese and Mongols, the effects of geographic isolation of western China, and the cultural connections between non-Chinese minorities in western China and the Middle East.

PRACTICE

Read the statement below and answer the questions that follow it:

Between 700 BC and 300 BC, . . . the first great Chinese thinkers appeared, each with his own answer to China's problems.

1. What event, trend, or condition do I want to explain?
2. What facts do I have that may relate to causes for this event, trend, or condition?
3. What one or two hypotheses might explain this event, trend, or condition?
4. What information would help me test each hypothesis?

People and Places to Know
Hong Kong, Korea, Taiwan, the Boxers, Sun Yat-sen, Guomindang, Chiang Kai-shek, Mao Zedong, Zhou Enlai

Key Terms to Define
opium, unequal treaty, extraterritoriality, provisional, dictatorship, warlord, collective, commune

Objectives to Learn
1. **Summarize** circumstances that led to the Chinese Revolution.
2. **Identify** the goals of the Chinese Revolution.
3. **Describe** changes that followed formation of the People's Republic of China.

Communist Parade in Shanghai

The Chinese Revolution

> " We hail from all corners of the country and have joined together for a common revolutionary objective. And we need the vast majority of the people with us on the road to this objective. . . . In times of difficulty we must not lose sight of our achievements, must see the bright future and must pluck up our courage. The Chinese people are suffering; it is our duty to save them and we must exert ourselves in struggle. Wherever there is struggle there is sacrifice, and death is a common occurrence. But we have the interests of the people and the sufferings of the great majority at heart, and when we die for the people it is a worthy death. Nevertheless, we should do our best to avoid unnecessary sacrifices. Our cadres must show concern for every soldier, and all people in the revolutionary ranks must care for each other, must love and help each other.
>
> From now on, when anyone in our ranks who has done some useful work dies, be he soldier or cook, we should have a funeral ceremony and a memorial meeting in his honour. This should become the rule. And it should be introduced among the people as well. When someone dies in a village, let a memorial meeting be held. In this way we express our mourning for the dead and unite all the people. "

The above speech was given by Mao Zedong (MOW DZU DOONG), China's major twentieth-century revolutionary leader. Mao's achievements were the high point of a long period of revolution in China that began about 1840 and lasted well into the 1970's. The Chinese Revolution went through several phases of development. It began with peasant rebellions against the corrupt Qing dynasty and foreign powers. Later, it spread to the small and Western-educated middle class, which wanted a democratic republic and an end to foreign controls.

In 1911, the ruling dynasty was overthrown and a republic established. This, however,

did not bring to an end mounting dissatisfaction among students, workers, and peasants. Leadership of the revolution then passed from the middle class to Communist intellectuals, or thinkers, and their allies in the poorer classes.

In 1949, after two decades of upheaval, the Communists, led by Mao Zedong, established the People's Republic of China. Mao remained the major leader of the People's Republic until his death in 1976. While in power, he taught his people that the Chinese Revolution was a continuing struggle against old ways. After Mao's death, his teachings came under criticism from new leaders who wanted to modernize China's society by less revolutionary means.

Source: Mao Zedong. "Serve the People" in *Selected Works of Mao Tse-tung.* Vol. III, Foreign Language Press, 1967, pp. 177–178.

SECTION 1

Beginnings

The roots of the Chinese Revolution date back to the 1800's. At the time, China was in decline, beset by famine, drought, and violence. The ruling Qing emperors lacked the vision and leadership skills of earlier Chinese rulers, and many government officials opposed reforms. Even those officials who favored change did not want to give up the traditional system completely.

CHINA AND FOREIGN POWERS

During the 1800's, China became involved in a series of humiliating wars with the technologically stronger Western countries whose governments used force to open China for trade. Great Britain, the most powerful Western nation, sold the Chinese **opium,** an addictive drug made from poppies. When, in 1839, the Chinese government tried to stop its sale, the British made war on China.

The Opium Wars, which occurred during the 1840's and 1850's, resulted in the first of many **unequal treaties** between China and the West. These treaties treated China as an inferior nation and opened it to further Western influence. The 1842 Treaty of Nanking (Nanjing), for example, made China pay money and surrender Hong Kong to the British. It also forced the Chinese government to grant **extraterritoriality** to British merchants in China. This meant that they no longer were under the control of Chinese law. Following Britain's lead, other Western nations soon began to demand and receive similar or even greater privileges.

China's greatest setback, however, came not from the West but from Japan, its Asian neighbor. Unlike China, Japan had modernized its society and by the 1890's was challenging China's dominance in East Asia. In 1894, the two rivals went to war over Korea. When China lost the war, it was forced to recognize Korea's independence. It also had to give the island of Taiwan and the Pescadores Islands to Japan. In addition, Japan gained even more trading privileges than the trading privileges won by the Western nations.

EXAMINING ART
When British merchants turned to smuggling, the Chinese cracked down and began to rigorously enforce their trade ban on opium, leading to the breakout of the Opium Wars. A fierce naval battle fought at Cheunpu in 1841 is depicted in this painting. What was China forced to do under terms of the treaty that ended the wars?

PEASANT REBELLIONS

While China was battling foreign powers, it faced problems within its own borders. From 1850 to 1900, a wave of peasant rebellions swept through China.

THE TAIPING REBELLION The longest and most violent was the Taiping Rebellion, which lasted from 1851 to 1864. It began in southern China and spread throughout the country. The Taiping rebels developed an ideology that combined Christianity and traditional Chinese beliefs. They sought to overthrow the Qing dynasty and create a new society based on equality and shared property. In 1853, they stated their goals in the following declaration:

The distribution of land is made according to the size of the family, irrespective of sex, with only the number of persons taken into account. The larger the number, the more land they shall receive; the smaller the number, the less land they shall receive. . . . All lands under Heaven shall be farmed jointly by the people under Heaven. If the production of food is too small in one place, then move to another where it is more abundant. All lands under Heaven shall be accessible in time of abundance or famine. If there is a famine in one area move the surplus from an area where there is abundance to that area, in order to feed the starving. In this way the people under Heaven shall all enjoy the great happiness given by the Heavenly Father, Supreme Lord and August God. Land shall be farmed by all; rice, eaten by all; clothes, worn by all; money, spent by all. There shall be no inequality; and no person shall be without food or fuel. . . .

Everywhere in the empire mulberry trees shall be planted beneath the walls. All women shall raise silkworms, spin cloth and sew dresses. Every family in the empire shall have five hens and two sows, without exception. . . . For under Heaven all belongs to the great family of the Heavenly Father, Supreme Lord and August God. In the empire none shall have any private property, and everything belongs to God, so that God may dispose of it. In the great family of Heaven, every place is equal, and everyone has plenty. . . .

The Taiping Rebellion almost toppled the Qing dynasty, but divisions among the rebel leaders weakened rebel efforts. With the backing of the gentry and the Western powers, the dynasty organized effective armies that eventually defeated the rebels.

THE BOXER UPRISING In 1900, another uprising broke out. It was led by a secret society called the Society of Righteous and Harmonious Fists. Known in English as the Boxers, its members believed that their country's problems could be solved if foreigners and their "evil influences" were expelled from China. The Boxers were violently anti-Christian and killed Western missionaries and thousands of Chinese who had converted to Christianity. The Qing dynasty secretly supported the Boxers and refused to take measures against them. Eventually, military forces from eight foreign nations defeated them, forcing China to pay $333 million and make more concessions.

Following the Boxer Uprising, the Qing dynasty set out to reform Chinese society. It promised to adopt a democratic constitution and introduce a Western-style educational system and army. But these efforts came too late. In 1905, the middle class and students began to turn to revolution. At first, the Qing managed to put down the revolts. But, in October 1911, the revolutionaries received the backing of the army. By the end of the year, all of China had renounced the rule of the Qing, forcing the emperor to give up the throne.

Source: "The Land System of the Heavenly Dynasty" in *Chinese Sources for the Taiping Rebellion, 1850–1864.* J. C. Cheng. Oxford University Press, 1963, pp. 39–40.

EXAMINING PHOTOGRAPHS *In this photo taken in 1912, Sun Yat-sen is shown presiding over China's first parliament. The details of parliamentary procedure were considered important to Sun, who described them in his Plan for National Reconstruction. This plan, together with the "Three Principles," summarize Sun's key political doctrines.* How did Sun propose to improve China's industry?

SECTION 1 REVIEW

CHECKING FOR UNDERSTANDING
1. **Define** opium, unequal treaty, extraterritoriality.
2. **Explain** why the Taiping Rebellion failed.

CRITICAL THINKING
3. **Determining Cause and Effect** What led China into wars with Great Britain and Japan? What was the result of the wars?

SECTION 2

A Divided China

In 1911, China became a republic with Dr. Sun Yat-sen as **provisional**, or temporary, president. Although officially a democracy, China lacked national unity. Also, most Chinese were illiterate peasants who had no experience in self-government. As goals for the new republic, Sun announced "Three Principles of the People"—Nationalism, Democracy, and Livelihood—which he described as follows:

[**N**ationalism]. . . . For the most part . . . the people of China can be spoken of as completely . . . Chinese. With common customs and habits, we are completely of one race. . . . But the Chinese people have only family and clan solidarity; they do not have national spirit. Therefore even though we have . . . people gathered together in one China, in reality they are just a heap of loose sand. . . .
[Democracy]. . . . For it is our plan that the political power of the reconstructed state will be divided into two parts. One is the power over government; that great power will be placed entirely in the hands of the people. . . . The other power is the governing power; that great power will be placed in the hands of the government. . . .
[Livelihood]. . . . Our first method consists in solving the land question. . . . The plan which we are following is simple and easy—equalization of landownership. . .

[Our second method consists of solving the industrial problem. To promote industry], we must build means of communication, railroads and waterways, on a large scale . . . we must open up mines . . . we must hasten to develop manufacturing.

Sun, however, did not have the power to achieve his goals. Failing to get the full support of the army, he stepped aside in favor of General Yuan Shih-k'ai. Yuan cared little for Sun's "Three Principles" and set up a **dictatorship,** or one-person rule, with the backing of army officers. Meanwhile, Sun's supporters had formed a political party known as the Guomindang (KWOH·MIN·TANG), and most went into exile.

CIVIL WAR

When Yuan died in 1916, the national government had no real power, and political turmoil swept China. Local military leaders known as **warlords** fought each other for control of the provinces. Sun and his Guomindang followers established a base of power in Guangzhou in southern China. Their aim was to reunite China under one republican, democratic government.

Sun realized that he needed a strong army to defeat the warlords. To achieve this goal, he sought help from the West but was refused. Sun then turned to the Soviet Union, which agreed to give him aid. With the help of Soviet advisers, a Guomindang army was organized in 1924. Sun appointed a young military officer named Chiang Kai-shek to head the new army.

Like Sun, Chiang was influenced by Western ways. He married Soong Meiling, the American-educated daughter of a Chinese businessperson. Chiang, however, gave less support to the democratic values that had inspired Sun. When Sun died in 1925, Chiang became the new leader of the Guomindang. In 1928, he won a major victory against the warlords.

Source: Sun Yat-sen in *Sources of Chinese Tradition.* William Theodore de Bary (ed.). Columbia University Press, 1960, pp. 768–769, 772–773, 776, 778.

CHINESE COMMUNISM

In his efforts to gain control of China, Chiang had to deal with a rival political organization—the Chinese Communist party. Organized in 1921, the party appealed to students, intellectuals, and urban workers unhappy with the failure of the 1911 revolutionaries to meet the needs of the lower classes and to remove foreign influences.

The Communists wanted to carry the revolution forward. They planned to introduce radical social changes that would remove influences of the past, end reliance on foreign powers, and transform China into a modern industrialized nation. They were ordered by the world communist movement to join the Guomindang, form their own army, and support Chiang in his struggle against the warlords.

Soon, however, the Communists and the Guomindang began a struggle for power. In 1927, fearing a communist takeover, Chiang directed a campaign against urban Communists. More than 3000 Communists were killed during this campaign. The communist leaders who survived fled to the hills of southern China, where they set up communist local governments.

In 1928, Chiang eliminated the last of the warlords and was elected president of the republic. After a decade of violence, most of China seemed to be united under Chiang's government.

SECTION 2 REVIEW

CHECKING FOR UNDERSTANDING
1. **Define** provisional, dictatorship, warlord.
2. **Identify** Sun Yat-sen, Guomindang, Chiang Kai-shek.
3. **List** the problems faced by China's new republican government.

CRITICAL THINKING
4. **Recognizing Ideologies** What were the goals of the Communists? Why do you think they joined the Guomindang?

THE CHINESE REVOLUTION

EXAMINING TIME LINES *The events of the Chinese Revolution have spanned nearly two centuries. What have been its major objectives?*

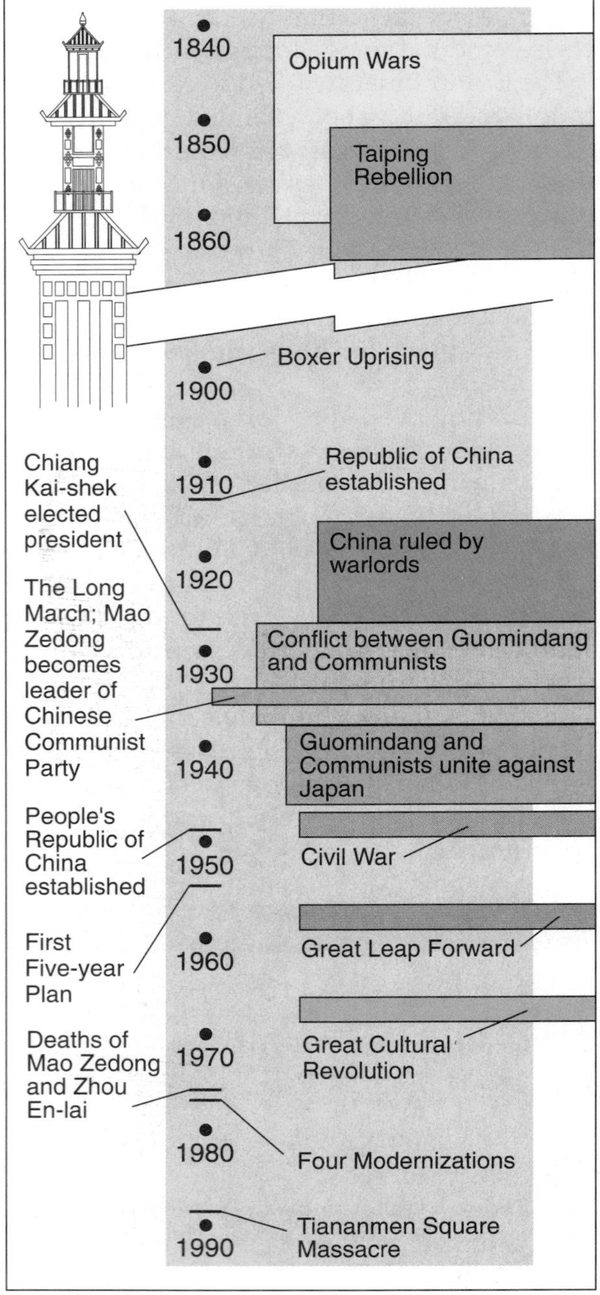

- 1840 — Opium Wars
- 1850 — Taiping Rebellion
- 1860
- Boxer Uprising — 1900
- Chiang Kai-shek elected president
- 1910 — Republic of China established
- The Long March; Mao Zedong becomes leader of Chinese Communist Party
- 1920 — China ruled by warlords
- 1930 — Conflict between Guomindang and Communists
- 1940 — Guomindang and Communists unite against Japan
- People's Republic of China established
- 1950 — Civil War
- First Five-year Plan
- 1960 — Great Leap Forward
- Deaths of Mao Zedong and Zhou En-lai
- 1970 — Great Cultural Revolution
- 1980 — Four Modernizations
- 1990 — Tiananmen Square Massacre

Guomindang, Communists, and the Japanese

Once in power, Chiang worked to strengthen his government and control the spread of communism. He relied largely on force, abandoning the democratic principles of the early Guomindang. Under his leadership, China gradually became a dictatorship, and such social reforms as equality for women and land reform for poor peasants were neglected.

Instead, Chiang stressed social discipline through a return to Confucian values. This won him the support of the rural gentry and the Western-educated middle class, both of which were against any social reforms that would endanger their privileges. At the same time, Chiang worked to promote industrial growth, sponsoring the building of roads, railroads, waterways, and ports.

Meanwhile, in their rural retreats, the Communists rebuilt their leadership and army. One of their most influential members was Mao Zedong, a former librarian and writer. Under his direction, the Communists gained widespread support in rural areas. Mao declared that peasants, not urban workers, would lead a future Communist revolution in China.

THE LONG MARCH

Before Mao's ideas were accepted by the party, the Communists faced a series of military attacks from Chiang's forces. To escape the Guomindang armies, 90,000 Communists, including Mao Zedong, retreated from southern China and headed to northwestern China. Their retreat, which later became known

CASE STUDY

China

WOMEN AND THE REVOLUTION

One of the goals of the Communists was to improve the status of women. Deng Yingchao, the wife of Zhou Enlai, explains below the role women played in the May Fourth Movement, the opening event of the revolution:

I was a sixteen-year old student . . . when the May Fourth Movement began in 1919. . . . On May 4, . . . the students in Peking [Beijing] staged a massive demonstration. . . . [Shortly afterwards] such organizations as . . . the Association of Patriotic Women . . . came into existence. Most members . . . were actually women students. . . . Simple and uncomplicated we relied heavily on our selfless patriotism for our strength. . . .

We . . . stressed the importance of propaganda work. Many oratorical teams were organized, and I was elected captain of speakers for the Association. . . . My duty was to provide speakers in different areas on a regular basis.

At the beginning we, as female students, did not enjoy the same freedom of movement as our male counterparts, insofar as our speaking tours were concerned. According to the feudal custom of China, women were not supposed to make speeches in the street; we, therefore, had to do our work indoors. We gave speeches in such places as libraries and participated in scheduled debates, all inside a hall or room. . . .

In the wake of the May Fourth Movement came the feminist movement which was in fact one of its democratic extensions. Among the demands we raised at that time were sexual equality, abolition of arranged marriage, social activities open to women, freedom of romantic love and marriage, universities open to women students, and employment of women in government institutions. The first

step we took toward sexual equality was to merge the associations of male and female students . . . to form a new organization which students of both sexes could join. . . .

As pioneers in the feminist movement who had had the rare opportunity to work side by side with men, we female students in the merged association were conscious of the example we had to set so that no man in the future could deny women the opportunity to work on the ground of alleged incompetence. In short, we worked doubly hard. . . . Each department . . . was always headed by two chairpersons, one male and one female, and the female chairperson had as much authority as her male counterpart. The merger was such a success that the students in Peking [Beijing] decided to follow our example.

DRAWING CONCLUSIONS

1. How did the revolution affect women?
2. Do you think most women would have supported Deng Yingchao? Explain.

Source: Dun J. Li. "My Experience with the May Fourth Movement" reprinted with permission of Charles Scribner's Sons, an imprint of Macmillan Publishing Company from MODERN CHINA: FROM MANDARIN TO COMMISSAR by Dun J. Li. Copyright © 1978 Dun J. Li.

as the Long March, took about two years and covered nearly 6000 miles (9600 kilometers). Below, a Communist soldier who took part in the march describes what happened:

Our forces were confronted with desperate odds. The enemy gave us no rest. We had some kind of skirmish at least once a week. . . . At night we dared not sleep in towns or villages for fear of surprise attack. We had to make our beds in the forests of the mountains. For nearly two years I never undressed at night, but slept with even my shoes on. So did most of our men. . . .

We never had enough to eat. Had it not been for the help of the people we would have starved. . . . The farmers gladly shared with us what rice they had. . . . The farmers hated the thought of the landlords returning and to them our defeat meant the return of the landlord system. . . .

We lost all contact with the outside. We were like wild men, living and fighting by instinct. Many of our best commanders were killed, or died of disease. We had no medicines and no hospitals. Our ammunition ran very low. Many of our guns became useless. . . .

At times we retired into the uninhabited forests. We learned the trails . . . foot by foot. We knew every corner of the mountains. We learned to fast with nothing to eat for four or five days. And yet we became strong and agile as savages.

Although only a few thousand Communists survived, the march proved that the Communists were strong enough to successfully resist Chiang. As a result, support for the Communists increased, and Mao Zedong emerged as the major leader of the party.

WAR WITH JAPAN

While the Guomindang and the Communists were fighting each other, the Japanese expanded into China. In 1931, the Japanese occupied Manchuria. Six years later, they extended their invasion into the rest of China. In spite of their differences, Mao and Chiang allied against the Japanese. The Chinese Communists fought against the Japanese in the north, while the Guomindang led resistance in the south. Chiang's troops were no match for the Japanese. In the end, the Guomindang retreated to the interior, leaving the Japanese in control of eastern China.

During World War II, China helped the Western nations in the Pacific War. In return, the Western nations ended the last of the "unequal treaties." The United States, in particular, sent aid to Chiang's forces. The cost of the war, however, imposed hardships on the Chinese people and weakened support for the Guomindang government. In addition, the growth of corruption among Chiang's advisers heightened public distrust of Chiang.

THE LONG MARCH 1934–35

— Route of the Long March

EXAMINING MAPS *In the Long March, 90,000 Chinese Communists traveled more than 6000 miles (9600 kilometers). From whom were they escaping?*

Source: Han Ying, as related in *The Battle for Asia* by Edgar Snow. Random House, 1941, pp. 131–132.

EXAMINING PHOTOGRAPHS *On the Long March, the Communists suffered heavy losses from daily bombings by Chiang Kai-shek's air force. Though he was seriously ill with a fever, Mao Zedong (center) led the Communist retreat. He and his followers were plagued by heavy rains and flooded rivers on the first half of their journey. Many did not survive the 18 mountain crossings and the bitter cold. What happened as a result of the Long March?*

COMMUNIST ADVANCE

As discontent grew, the Chinese Communists increased their influence. After gaining control of large areas of northern China, they made radical changes. They divided the property of landlords among the peasants, introduced medicine and education, and raised the status of women. All of these changes further weakened the Guomindang's hold over the people.

After the defeat of Japan by the Allies in 1945, the Communists and the Guomindang once again faced each other. In order to avoid a civil war, the United States tried to bring the two groups together. The Communists, however, accused the United States of backing the Guomindang while pretending to take no sides. Although the United States insisted that its aid to Chiang was not intended for use in a civil war, Chiang believed that the aid would help him win back China.

In the civil war that followed, Chiang was defeated. He took his followers to the island of Taiwan, where he continued the Republic of China. The Communists, meanwhile, ruled mainland China, where, in 1949, they formed the People's Republic of China.

SECTION 3 REVIEW

CHECKING FOR UNDERSTANDING
1. **Describe** how Chiang governed China during the 1930's and 1940's.
2. **State** the significance of the Long March.

CRITICAL THINKING
3. **Determining Cause and Effect** How did World War II impact China?

SECTION 4

The People's Republic

The government of the People's Republic of China was influenced by three dominant groups—the Communist party, the bureaucrats, and the army. The party made policy. The bureaucrats carried it out, and the army enforced it. Almost all the leaders in the military and the bureaucracy held high positions in the party. Mao Zedong served as chairman, while Zhou Enlai, a noted revolutionary leader, served as prime minister.

Upon taking power, the Communists enjoyed wide support in China. Those Chinese who opposed the new government were either sent to labor camps or executed. Labor unions, youth groups, and women's associations assisted the party in furthering public support for its policies. In addition, the government strengthened support for communism by introducing long-awaited reforms. Public sanitation and health were greatly improved. Education was stressed and illiteracy reduced. Women were given full equality with men.

ECONOMIC POLICIES AND FOREIGN AFFAIRS

The communist government worked to transform China from a technologically backward nation into a modern industrial-agricultural state. To develop rural areas, it completed the seizure of land from landlords and redistributed it among the peasants. In time, however, the peasants were required to combine their plots into agricultural **collectives**, or units in which the land is jointly owned. With Soviet aid, industrial production increased, and in 1953, the first Five-Year Plan for economic growth got underway. The plan stressed such heavy industry as coal, iron, and steel production. It also brought commerce, banking, and industry under government control.

In 1958, a more ambitious economic plan known as the Great Leap Forward was launched. Under it, collectives were merged into larger government-controlled units called **communes.** In industrial production, human labor, rather than complex technology, was stressed. Factory workers were forced to work long hours to meet goals.

Within two years, it became clear that the Great Leap Forward was in trouble. Food shortages, industrial mismanagement, and peasant resistance to communes brought the program to a halt. Even so, China did make significant economic gains under communist rule. By the mid-1960's, it was ranked among the ten leading industrial nations in the world.

At the same time China was developing its economy, it also sought to increase its influence overseas, especially among the newly independent states of Asia and Africa. By the late 1950's, however, its ties to the Soviet Union began to weaken. The two nations soon became involved in a bitter feud over their mutual borders and over the interpretation of communist ideology. In 1960, the Soviets withdrew their economic support from China, forcing the Chinese to forge ahead on their own as a military power. Four years later, the Chinese exploded their first atomic bomb.

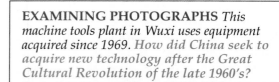

EXAMINING PHOTOGRAPHS *This machine tools plant in Wuxi uses equipment acquired since 1969. How did China seek to acquire new technology after the Great Cultural Revolution of the late 1960's?*

GREAT CULTURAL REVOLUTION

The failure of the Great Leap Forward and the Chinese-Soviet split led to a deep division within the Chinese Communist party. Moderates, headed by Deng Xiaoping (DUHNG SYOW-PING), wanted practical reforms. Radicals, led by Mao and his wife Jiang Qing, insisted on strict obedience to revolutionary principles. To end the influence of the moderates, Mao began a movement known as the Great Cultural Revolution. Moderates, accused of betraying communism, were removed from office, while students loyal to Mao formed groups called Red Guards. Below, a Chinese journalist sympathetic to Mao and the Red Guards comments on activities in Beijing:

During the past week and more Red Guards have scored victory after victory as they pressed home their attack against the decadent [corrupt] customs and habits of the exploiting classes. Beating drums and singing revolutionary songs, . . . Red Guards are out in the streets doing propaganda work, holding aloft big portraits of Chairman Mao, extracts from Chairman Mao's works, and great banners with the words: "We are the critics of the old world; we are the builders of the new world." They have held street meetings, put up big character posters, and distributed leaflets in their attack against all the old ideas and habits of the exploiting classes. As a result of the proposals of the Red Guards and with the support of the revolutionary masses, shop signs which spread odious feudal and bourgeois ideas have been removed, and the names of many streets, lanes, parks, buildings, and schools tainted with feudalism, capitalism, or revisionism [moderate communism] or which had no revolutionary significance have been replaced by revolutionary names.

Source: "Red Guards Destroy the Old and Establish the New," *Peking Review*, September 2, 1966, in *Changing China*. J. Mason Gentzler (ed.). 1977, p. 351. Praeger Publishers, an imprint of Greenwood Publishing Group, Inc., Westport, CT.

The Great Cultural Revolution was a time of disorder and confusion throughout China. Schools closed, factory production dropped, and violence erupted. Finally, in 1968, Mao and Zhou Enlai called on the army to restore order. Although in the next few years Chinese political and social life quieted, the conflict between moderates and radicals within the Communist party continued.

TOWARD CHANGE

By 1969, China had entered a more moderate period. To offset the growing feud with the Soviets and to acquire the technology to build their economy, Chinese leaders sought to improve relations with Western nations. In 1972, United States President Richard Nixon visited China. At the end of his visit, Nixon and his Chinese hosts pledged to work toward improving relations between their countries.

On January 8, 1976, Zhou Enlai died. Many observers expected continued political success for the moderates. But, Mao, too, was dying, and the radicals gained influence in the government. When, on September 9, Mao died, an era of Chinese history came to an end. Although China's future was uncertain, friends and enemies alike recognized Mao as the most influential Chinese leader of the century.

SECTION 4 REVIEW

CHECKING FOR UNDERSTANDING
1. **Define** collective, commune.
2. **Identify** Zhou Enlai, Five-Year Plan, Great Leap Forward, Great Cultural Revolution, Red Guards.
3. **Explain** why the Chinese sought to improve relations with Western nations.

CRITICAL THINKING
4. **Identifying Central Issues** What issue divided moderates and radicals during the last years of Mao's rule in China?

History

CONFLICTING VIEWS OF MAO ZEDONG

FOCUSING ON THE ISSUE Below are contrasting views on the death of Mao Zedong. One expresses the opinion of the Communists, who rule mainland China. The other expresses the opinion of the Guomindang, or Nationalist, government of Taiwan. Read each viewpoint; then answer these questions:

1. What is the Chinese Communist view of Mao Zedong's life and career? What is the Guomindang's view?
2. Which viewpoint do you accept? Explain. How do you feel history will judge Mao Zedong?

At 12:10 AM, September 9, 1976, Comrade [Mao Zedong], the esteemed and beloved leader of our party, armed forces, and nation, the great teacher of international [workers], and the champion of all the oppressed people and nations, passed [away], despite all meticulous medical care after he had fallen ill.

Chairman [Mao Zedong] was the founder and long-time leader of the Chinese Communist Party, the Chinese People's Liberation Army, and the People's Republic of China. He led our party, our armed forces, and all the Chinese people in waging a successful struggle against imperialism, feudalism, and bureaucratic capitalism. This great victory has not only liberated the Chinese people and improved the situation in the East but also raised new hope for all the oppressed peo-

ple and nations in the world that wish to be free.

The death of Chairman [Mao Zedong] is a great loss to our party, our armed forces, and all the people in the nation. It is a great loss to the international [workers] and all the revolutionary people in the world. The grief over his death is bound to be immensely felt by all the revolutionaries both at home and abroad.

The Central Committee of the Chinese Communist Party calls upon the Party, the armed forces, and all the people in the nation to transform their grief into strength. It calls upon them to carry on the cause left behind by our great leader and teacher Chairman [Mao Zedong].[1]

[Mao Zedong], the bandit chieftain of the CCP [Chinese Communist Party], finally died early yesterday morning.

A brutal, treacherous psychopath, [Mao Zedong] embodied the worst in human nature. His career was a career of [unending] betrayal of his nation and immea-

---

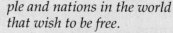

[1] *Source:* Dun J. Li. "Peoples Daily" reprinted with permission of Charles Scribner's Sons, an imprint of Macmillan Publishing Company from MODERN CHINA: FROM MANDARIN TO COMMISSAR by Dun J. Li. Copyright 1978 Dun J. Li.

198

surable harm to his own people. His crime was a crystallization of all the crimes committed by the most wanton traitors and bandits. He was in fact the number one tyrant in history, unprecedented both here and abroad.

After the CCP's illegal occupation of the Chinese mainland in 1949, [Mao Zedong], by invoking the excuse of a "proletarian [working class] dictatorship," conducted a systematic campaign of murdering the Chinese people. According to evidence provided by a variety of sources, the people whom he had murdered numbered no less than 60 million between 1949 and 1976. During his whole career that covered a period of fifty years, the number of people who had died because of his rebellion and violence came close to 100 million. No one, not even Hitler and Stalin, could match him in bloodthirstiness.

To maintain his tyrannical rule, he did not hesitate to declare as his enemy the five-thousand-year-old civilization of China and all the noble values that formed part of this civilization. He opposed heavenly reason as well as the humanity of man. What was objectively right became wrong to him, and vice versa. . . . Now that he is dead, it is most natural that all of us shall rejoice.

The death of [Mao Zedong] marks not only the end of the darkest period in Chinese history but also the beginning of a new era when the Republic of China will rise to restore the mainland and to save all the people therein.

Source: Dun J. Li. "Central Daily News" reprinted with permission of Charles Scribner's Sons, an imprint of Macmillan Publishing Company from MODERN CHINA: FROM MANDARIN TO COMMISSAR by Dun J. Li. Copyright © 1978 Dun J. Li.

Chapter 12 Review

SUMMARY

The Chinese Revolution began in the 1800's as a wave of uprisings against corrupt rulers and Western interference. After the fall of the monarchy in 1911, China became a republic under the Guomindang party.

The Communist party continued the Chinese Revolution and came into conflict with the Guomindang. The Communists defeated Guomindang forces, driving Chiang's government to the island of Taiwan. In 1949, mainland China became the Communist-ruled People's Republic of China. The Communist government worked to transform China into a modern industrial-agricultural state.

USING VOCABULARY

Use the following terms in writing a short essay about the Chinese Revolution.

opium	dictatorship
unequal treaty	warlord
extraterritoriality	collective
provisional	commune

REVIEWING FACTS

1. **Summarize** the goals of the Boxers and the outcome of their uprising.
2. **Discuss** Sun Yat-sen's "Three Principles" and the reason why he initiated them.
3. **State** how Chiang Kai-shek became president of the republic.
4. **Summarize** the events that brought the Communists to power in China.
5. **List** the three groups that influenced the government of the People's Republic of China.

6. **Explain** the purpose of the Cultural Revolution and its impact on Chinese society.

CRITICAL THINKING

1. **Identifying Alternatives** If you were a Chinese living in China at the time of the Boxer Uprising, would you have been sympathetic to the Boxers? Why or why not? Would you have joined the Boxers? Why or why not?
2. **Recognizing Ideologies** Do you think Sun Yat-sen's "Three Principles of the People" were realistic goals at the time? Explain. Do you think they would be realistic today? Explain.
3. **Analyzing Information** Mao Zedong taught the Chinese people that the Chinese Revolution was a continuing struggle against old ways. What do you think he meant by the "old ways"?
4. **Determining Cause and Effect** Explain why there were "two Chinas" after 1949.

ANALYZING CONCEPTS

1. **Choice** Why do you think Mao Zedong undertook the Long March? What other choices did he have?
2. **Change** What changes occurred in China's relations with the West and with the Soviet Union between 1949 and the mid-1970's?

GEOGRAPHIC THEMES

1. **Movement** Discuss the relationship between foreign influence and revolution in China.
2. **Location** Where was the Guomindang government located during World War II? Why did it choose this location?

Reading a Time Line

A *time line* is a visual way to show the order of events within a time period. Time lines can represent different time spans. The two time lines shown below are exactly the same length. The first one shows a time span of 1000 years (1000 to 2000 AD); however, the second represents only 10 years (1990 to 2000 AD).

```
AD |___|___|___|___|___|
  1000 1200 1400 1600 1800 2000
```

```
AD |___|___|___|___|___|
  1990 1992 1994 1996 1998 2000
```

On the first time line, the spaces between the dates represent periods of 200 years each. What periods are represented by the spaces on the second time line? *(two years)* Some time lines have a break, showing a gap in the time span. Often, the section on one side of the gap is divided into different spaces than the section on the other side.

Here are some steps to follow in reading a time line:
- Determine the total time span represented. Notice whether dates given are BC or AD.
- Identify the time periods represented in the spaces on the time line.
- Notice breaks in the time line and changes in spacing before or after breaks.
- Study the order in which events occurred.

EXAMPLE

The time line at the bottom of the page illustrates the history of China's dynasties during a certain segment of time. It begins at 1000 BC and ends at 1600 AD. What is the total time span covered in the time line? *(2600 years)* What periods do the spaces in the time line represent? *(500 years)* Where does the break occur? *(between 220 and 600 AD)* Also notice that the most important Chinese dynasties are represented by bars on one side of the time line,

while important events are shown on the other side. During which dynasty was Confucius born? *(Zhou)* Notice the order of the events. Was the oldest book printed before or after gunpowder was invented? *(after)* By studying time lines in this way, you can get a clear picture of what happened and when it happened.

PRACTICE

Use the time line on page 192 to answer the questions that are given below:

1. What time span does the time line cover?
2. What periods are represented by the intervals on the time line?
3. Where does the break on the time line occur?
4. How are single events shown? How are longer, more complex events shown?
5. Which event occurred first—the Boxer Uprising or the Taiping Rebellion?

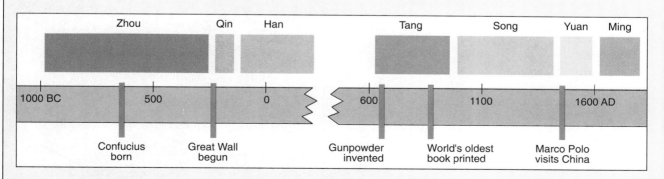

| Zhou | Qin | Han | | Tang | Song | Yuan | Ming |

1000 BC ——— 500 ——— 0 ⟩⟨ 600 ——— 1100 ——— 1600 AD

Confucius born — Great Wall begun — Gunpowder invented — World's oldest book printed — Marco Polo visits China

People and Places to Know
Deng Xiaoping, Tiananmen Square, Han Chinese, Tibet, Dalai Lama, Hainan

Key Terms to Define
entrepreneur, lama, special economic zone

Objectives to Learn

1. **Identify** causes of growing unrest after the death of Mao Zedong.

2. **Describe** unrest in China and the government's crackdown on it.

3. **Explain** the status of China's ethnic minorities.

4. **Summarize** recent economic reforms in China.

Protests in Beijing's Tiananmen Square, June 1989

China After Mao

"On the night of June 2 we were walking down the street when we heard: "The troops have entered Beijing! Tiananmen Square has been surrounded!" Immediately, people began barricading the route with trash carts and bicycle carts. We encountered a bus without a license plate at the Xinjiekou intersection. The bus was filled with young crew cuts. They were supposed to be in disguise, but it was obvious that they were soldiers. Some were plainly apprehensive. We began shouting at them, "You soldiers don't even have the guts to wear your uniforms or show military plates!"

People were . . . pleased with themselves for having stopped the bus. The bus tried to make a U-turn to leave, but a young man pushed his bicycle cart in front of it and shouted at the top of his lungs, "Students! Block the other side!" But the driver skillfully swerved around the bicycle cart. I asked myself, "Should I stand in front of it and block it?" We all hesitated for a moment, and then the bus was gone. The young man said angrily, "You college boys are all cowards! How can you fight for democracy?"

The next morning, Changan Avenue was packed with people. Several army buses were stopped on the road with their tires slashed. Inside them, people had found bayonets, machine guns, ammunition, and bags of butcher knives. These were displayed on top of the bus.

The soldiers rolled up the windows and we could see them sweating inside. A young man punched at one of the windows with his fist. "Open the window!". . . . "Open up! The last time you guys came, we gave you food and water. Nobody's going to feed you this time! You know those four people on hunger strike in the square? You're going to join them!". . . . "

*I*n the above excerpt, a Chinese student vividly describes reactions to the crackdown on pro-democracy demonstrators in Beijing's Tiananmen Square on June 4, 1989. This violent event was a dramatic turning point in modern Chinese history. It ended an era of reforms that had begun after the death of Mao Zedong in 1976 and ushered in a period of repression.

Before the Tiananmen Square massacre,

Source: Hou Tianming in *Children of the Dragon.* Human Rights in China, Inc., Collier Books, 1990, pp. 125–126.

hopes for change had been high in China. Mao's successors had borrowed capitalist practices from the West to strengthen the economy. Benefiting from these economic reforms, many Chinese demanded political changes that would give the people a voice in government.

Unwilling to yield any of its absolute power, the communist leadership responded to these appeals with force and bloodshed. Because of the Tiananmen tragedy, China's political future appears very uncertain as the country approaches the twenty-first century.

Economic Reforms

During the late 1970's and 1980's, China went through a period of profound economic and social change. Following Mao's death in 1976, the power struggle between moderates and radicals increased within the Chinese Communist party. The moderates favored practical economic and social reforms. The radicals wanted to return to the policies of the Cultural Revolution. Led by Deng Xiaoping (DUHNG SYOW·PING), the moderates eventually won control of the government.

Under Deng, the Communist party remained in firm control of political affairs. In making economic policy, however, Deng indicated that he was willing to learn from the capitalist West if it could contribute to China's well-being. In 1978, the Chinese Communist party announced a plan to modernize China by the year 2000. Known as the Four Modernizations, it stressed the need for major improvements in agriculture, industry, science and technology, and the military. During the next two decades, the Chinese hoped to increase national productivity and make their standard of living equal to that of the industrialized West.

In a speech given to Chinese Communist leaders in 1982, Deng discussed his firm belief that the reforms would strengthen the Communist system.

EXAMINING PHOTOGRAPHS *Although a dedicated revolutionary as a young man, Deng Xiaoping supported moderate policies when he emerged as the major leader of China in the 1970's.* **What was Deng's attitude to the West?**

> Economic construction is . . . the basis for the solution of our external and internal problems. For a long time to come, at least for 18 years till the end of the century, we must devote every effort to the following four tasks: to restructure the administration and the economy and make our cadre [Communist party worker] ranks more revolutionary, younger, better educated and more competent professionally; to build a socialist civilization that is culturally and ideologically advanced; to combat economic and other crimes that undermine socialism; and to rectify the Party's style of work and consolidate its organization. . . . These will be the most important guarantees that we shall keep to the socialist road and concentrate our efforts on modernization.

Source: Deng Xiaoping. "Opening Speech at the Twelfth National Congress of the Communist Party of China," September 1, 1982, as quoted in *Fundamental Issues in Present-Day China.* Beijing: Foreign Language Press, p. 4.

The first goal of the reform program was to revive agriculture, which had been neglected in favor of such heavy industry as coal and steel production. To boost food production, the government decided to appeal to the peasants' desire for profits and greater personal freedom. It set up the rural "responsibility system," in which land was still owned by the communes, but families farmed individual plots. Each family signed a contract stating how much of a crop had to be turned over to the commune. Families kept or sold any surplus they produced. The new system helped to increase farm output as well as the income of peasant farmers.

Deng and his supporters introduced the responsibility system in industry, too. Although the government still controlled major industries, factory managers could now decide to produce many goods on the basis of supply and demand rather than by government decree. After taxes, any profits a factory earned could be used to pay workers or to buy modern equipment.

Deng also wanted to open China to the rest of the world. He favored close cooperation with the West to bring money and businesses into China. For the first time since the 1949 revolution, Western businesspeople and tourists were encouraged to visit the country. With foreign help, the Chinese government built new hotels, resorts, and conference centers.

EXAMINING PHOTOGRAPHS *Chinese agriculture flourished as a result of the agricultural reforms introduced in the late 1970's. What is the responsibility system?*

CHECKING FOR UNDERSTANDING
1. **Describe** the Four Modernizations and their purposes.

CRITICAL THINKING
2. **Recognizing Ideologies** What aspects of the economic reforms do you think reflected communist thinking? Capitalist thinking?

SECTION 2

Growing Discontent

During the early 1980's, the economic reforms benefited many Chinese citizens. Agricultural and industrial production steadily rose, and the average annual income for peasants and workers doubled. Japanese, American, and European financiers and industrialists invested in China, developed its industry, and tapped its natural wealth. In the country's cities and villages, a number of ambitious Chinese **entrepreneurs,** or people

who risk their resources for potential profit, set up their own small businesses. Many Chinese entrepreneurs opened restaurants, repair shops, and clothing stores. With greater economic opportunities, many Chinese could afford consumer goods, such as radios and televisions, that were once luxuries beyond their reach.

Along with these successes, the reforms had brought their share of problems by the end of the decade. In many cases, the new capitalist ideas and practices clashed with traditional communist values. Some Chinese benefited from the reforms more than others. Those who did not benefit blamed the reforms for creating differences in wealth and undermining the communist emphasis on social equality. Others pointed to the rise in unemployment and the increase in crime because of the government's loosening of controls. In the following excerpt, a young Chinese-Canadian educator describes the mood in Beijing, where he taught during the late 1980's:

The last quarter of 1988 saw dramatic change in attitude of the general public. Inflation had reached two digits. People realized that things they desired were slipping further and further beyond their reach. . . .

Bureaucratic corruption became a way of life. Nearly every day there [were] stories of official wrongdoing involving bribery, embezzlement, extortion, and wasted resources. . . .

The economy was slipping into chaos. While Zhao Ziyang, the reformist secretary general of the Communist party trumpeted the virtues of continued opening to the West and deepening reforms, the hard-liner Premier Li Peng advocated slowing down the economy. The contradictions became sharper all the time. . . . Huge projects were abandoned and left to rot. This included many grandiose joint-venture hotels which were in various stages of construction. But it also included badly needed housing for a rapidly growing population.

Crime became more frequent and violent. . . . A kind of desperation crept into
the life of Beijing. . . .

. . . The lack of facilities for the care of
the aged has pushed [students] into the
laps of the next generation. Parents look
upon children as insurance against the
day when they can no longer earn their
keep. Thus they bind their children to
themselves by refusing to let them grow
up. For many young people, going to college was the first time they were away
from their parents. The experience was
traumatic at first, because they had never
fended for themselves before. But once
they got used to it, a whole new world
opened up to them. In the colleges, along
with foreign technology the young have
acquired rock and roll, tight jeans, brightly colored T-shirts, punk hair styles, night-
clubs, Rambo, Sydney Sheldon novels,
and break dancing. Some have been in-
duced to think for themselves. Tantalized
by half-understood Western philosophies,
youth seethed with discontent.

Source: **Michael David Kwan.** *Broken Portraits: Personal Encounters
with Chinese Students.* China Books and Periodicals, Inc., 1990,
pp. xi–xiv.

SECTION 2 REVIEW

CHECKING FOR UNDERSTANDING
1. **Define** entrepreneur.
2. **State** the successes of the economic reforms
that were introduced by Deng Xiaoping and
the moderates in the Chinese government.
3. **Explain** why many Chinese became
discontented with the state of government,
society, and the economy during the late
1980's.

CRITICAL THINKING
4. **Determining Cause and Effect** How do you
think divisions within the Chinese Communist
party leadership about social and economic
reforms affected public attitudes?

SECTION 3
The Crackdown

During the late 1980's, many Chinese also
expressed concern about the lack of political
freedom in China. As a result of Deng's reforms, some of them had studied overseas,
where they had gained firsthand experience
of democratic ways. Chinese writers, artists,
teachers, and students especially wanted the
Communist government to respect human
rights and to guarantee freedom of speech
and freedom of the press. As the fear of government repression lessened, they also demanded an end to political corruption and
the creation of a new political system that
would allow the people a voice in government.

During April and May of 1989, hundreds
of thousands of students filled Tiananmen
Square in Beijing calling for democracy.
They were joined by doctors, factory work-
ers, journalists, and teachers, many of them
Communist party members.

In the excerpt below, a sculptor describes
how the students built a statue known as
"the Goddess of Democracy" to symbolize
their hopes and dreams:

Nothing excites a sculptor as much as
seeing a work of her own creation take
shape. But although I was watching the
creation of a sculpture that I had had no
part in making, I nevertheless felt the
same excitement. It was the "Goddess of
Democracy" statue that stood for five
days in Tiananmen Square. . . .

. . . The site on the square where the
statue was to be erected had been carefully chosen. . . . The statue was to be set up
just across Changan Avenue [from the
portrait of Mao Zedong at the main entrance of the Forbidden City]. . . . [It] was
made so that once assembled it could

not be taken apart again but would have to be destroyed at once.

. . . By noon on May 30, it was ready for the unveiling ceremony, for which many people had waited all night. . . .

. . . The ceremony was very simple and moving. A statement had been prepared about the meaning of the statue and was read by a woman, probably a student at the Broadcasting Academy, who had a good Mandarin accent. "We have made this statue," the statement said, "as a memorial to democracy and to express our respect for the hunger-strikers, for the students who stayed in the square so many days, and for all others involved in the movement." Two Beijing residents, a woman and a man, had been chosen at random from the crowd and invited . . . to pull the strings that would "unveil" the sculpture. When the cloths fell, the crowd burst into cheers, there were shouts of "Long live democracy!" and other slogans, and some began to sing the "Internationale" [a socialist anthem]. . . .

That night there were strong winds and rain. We rushed to the square in the morning to see if the statue had been damaged. But it had endured this first serious test without harm. We took this as a good omen.

For a few days, it looked as if the demonstrators might prevail, that the government might offer some of the political reforms they demanded. The hardliners in the leadership, however, had increased their power with Deng Xiaoping's support. In the early hours of June 4, soldiers opened fire on the people. In scenes millions of people around the world witnessed on television, the hope for democratic reform in China was shattered as the Chinese government chose to use force and shed blood. Throughout the country, those who supported political change were shot, imprisoned, tortured, or silenced.

EXAMINING PHOTOGRAPHS *Chinese students who were demanding democratic reforms erected a "Goddess of Democracy" in Beijing's Tiananmen Square. What was the outcome of the students' protests?*

SECTION 3 REVIEW

CHECKING FOR UNDERSTANDING

1. **List** the groups who demonstrated in Tiananmen Square.
2. **Explain** why the students erected the "Goddess of Democracy."

CRITICAL THINKING

3. **Expressing Problems Clearly** Why do you think China's leaders promoted economic, but not political, reforms?

Source: Cao Xinyuan in *Children of the Dragon.* Human Rights in China, Inc., Collier Books, 1990, pp. 116–122.

SECTION 4

Ethnic Rights

Since the Tiananmen Square massacre, China's Communist leaders have acted to stem growing unrest among China's many ethnic groups. Of every 100 people in China, 93 are Han Chinese; the remainder are peoples from at least 55 other groups, including Kazakhs, Mongols, Uigurs, and Tibetans. Most of these peoples inhabit about half of China's land area, but tend to live in remote or border regions. Because many of them inhabit remote areas, some have retained many of their traditional languages and ways of life. Others, however, speak dialects of Chinese and live much like the Han Chinese.

One of China's most important ethnic groups is the Tibetans, who live on a high, wind-swept plateau in central Asia surrounded by some of the world's tallest mountain ranges. Their remote country, known as Tibet, was once an independent Buddhist kingdom ruled by **lamas,** or Tibetan monks. The most important of the lamas, whose title was the Dalai (High) Lama, lived in a large palace in Lhasa, Tibet's capital and largest city.

In 1950, Communist Chinese armies invaded Tibet and made it part of the People's Republic of China. Chinese leaders placed restrictions on the practice of Buddhism and tried to force the Tibetans to become Chinese. In 1959, the Tibetans staged an unsuccessful rebellion, and the ruling Dalai Lama fled abroad. From exile, the Dalai Lama has led a nonviolent campaign to free his homeland, receiving the 1989 Nobel Peace Prize for his efforts.

From the 1960's to the 1980's, massive immigration of Han Chinese threatened to make the Tibetans a minority in their own land. In the late 1980's, many Tibetans

EXAMINING PHOTOGRAPHS *The people of Tibet continue to practice their traditional Buddhist faith in spite of restrictions by Communist Chinese authorities.* **What Tibetan religious leader has supported freedom for his homeland?**

staged demonstrations against Chinese rule and demanded protection of their human rights. Chinese soldiers sent into Tibet by the government put down the demonstrations and enforced an uneasy peace. With their mission accomplished, many of the troops were withdrawn in 1990. Below, an American journalist traveling in Tibet describes life in Lhasa since their departure:

 . . . caught a pedicab to the Barkhor, the market around the Jokhang Temple, which has been the focal point of independence demonstrations. As it happened, that day, June 8th, was a religious festival marking the birth, death, and enlightenment of the

CASE STUDY

HONG KONG: AN UNCERTAIN FUTURE

China

On the southern coast of China is Hong Kong, one of Asia's busiest ports. Most of Hong Kong's people are Chinese, but the territory has been under British rule since the 1800's. In 1997, Great Britain will finally return Hong Kong to China. The excerpt below describes the mood of Hong Kong's people as they await the coming of Chinese rule.

As 1997 approaches, the miracle of Hong Kong is called into question. Will the communist dinosaur swallow this capitalist jewel? While officials in Beijing have promised that Hong Kong's social and economic system will "remain unchanged for 50 years," that assurance is not widely trusted in the colony.

Martin Lee, Hong Kong's most prominent liberal, is worried, "The date of 1997 is looked upon as doomsday," he said. "The Chinese are more concerned with control than with prosperity. They don't seem to care whether the goose will continue to lay golden eggs. They just want to control the goose. . . ."

Round-faced, cheerful Lok

Chi Ming, who sells men's clothes in a department store, is 23. He expressed the present-mindedness and fatalism of many Hong Kongers of his generation. . . .

Lok Chi Ming expects that the communists will clamp down on the colony's free-wheeling night life and ever popular Canto-rock music. . . . His favorite disco is called Nineteen 97—the choice of name perhaps expressing Hong Kong's clear-eyed enjoyment of today in full realization that tomorrow is a question mark. "Some people are scared of 1997," Lok said. "I'm not—nothing can stop it. I don't have the money to leave, so what can I do about it?" . . .

In 1989 and 1990 the human drain from Hong Kong increased dramatically, with more than 100,000 citizens leaving to live elsewhere. . . . There will be more, judging from the look of things. . . .

Meanwhile, . . . practical Hong Kong gets on with life. Buildings rise and fall, children in uniform go dutifully to school, old ladies buy fresh vegetables at neighborhood food stands, huge audiences watch Cantonese movies full of romance and martial arts, people flock to Buddhist temples on festival days to placate gods and ghosts with paper money, food, and wine. . . .

Another half million Hong Kong people may well have left by 1997, but most ordinary folk will still be here, and they will accommodate. . . .

DRAWING CONCLUSIONS

1. How is Hong Kong responding to the coming of Chinese rule?
2. What impact do you think Chinese rule will have on Hong Kong?

Source: Ross Terrill. "Hong Kong—Countdown to 1997" in *National Geographic,* February, 1991, pp. 108, 116–118, 125, 128.

Buddha, and Lucy [the tour guide] had said that foreigners would not be safe near the temple. Yet I was made to feel not only safe but welcome in the crowd of thousands of Tibetans, many of whom had come in from the countryside to donate either currency or pictures of the Dalai Lama, which are highly valued, to monks and beggars encircling the Jokhang. A few of those I encountered saluted me by saying "Dalai" and giving a thumbs-up salute, and two men . . . flashed at me from under their shirts medallions displaying symbols . . . in the shape of an eagle-like bird [a national symbol], but most of the Tibetans I saw greeted me apolitically . . . possibly because I was seen as a harbinger [forerunner] of a return of tourists after the lifting of martial law. . . .

For the most part, my impression of Lhasa was of two communities, roughly divided by Hongshan, the hill on which the Potala Palace [home of the Dalai Lama] stands. What both Chinese and Tibetans call the "red city" is in the west, and it includes factories, government offices, the Army base, a medical school, a television transmitter, compounds for Chinese cadres, and the Holiday Inn. Most Lhasans live in the "white city," to the east, many of them in alleys around the Jokhang. In addition to the geographical separation, Lhasa's Tibetan and Han communities coexist in what are in effect, separate time zones: The Chinese live by Beijing time, and feel that the Tibetans are lazy, because they rise at least two hours later, according to their own sun time. The Lhasans' sun time, however, gives them evening hours relatively free of the Chinese presence, and the city now boasts such attractions as video parlors, a dance hall, a cinema, cafés, and several pool halls.

Another facet of Tibetan life . . . is a hunger for education. It was not money that small children begged from me but my pen. In their publications the Chinese frequently claim that before 1951 the only Tibetans to receive schooling were boys who left their families (not always voluntarily) to become monks. Now the region is said to support sixty-seven secondary and elementary schools and twenty-four hundred and fifty-three primary schools, where classes of both boys and girls are taught in both Tibetan and Mandarin, but, even by China's count, more than half of Tibet's children still do not attend school, and the most promising of those who do are sent far from their families to continue their education in eighteen schools that have been established in Chinese cities.

. . . There is, however, a small university in Lhasa, and at Drepung Monastery, . . . west of the city, I encountered a group of five of its students. . . . Drepung is one of the few sites on the Lhasa tourist itinerary where, even under the eye of a Han [Chinese] guide, it is possible to mingle with Tibetans. Formally, . . . passes carried by authorized tour guides are required for admission, but the checkpoint is more than a mile (1.9 kilometers) away, at a highway turnoff, and is easily bypassed by Tibetan pilgrims on muleback or on foot. The People's Armed Policemen see them coming and going through the hills, but take no action. "In Tibet," the Chinese say, "the sky is high and the emperor is far away."

SECTION 4 REVIEW

CHECKING FOR UNDERSTANDING

1. **Define** lama.
2. **Describe** the peoples who make up China's population.
3. **Discuss** the relationship between Han Chinese and Tibetans.

CRITICAL THINKING

4. **Analyzing Information** Why do you think the Chinese government has sent Tibetan students to study in Chinese cities?

Source: Fred C. Shapiro. "Report from China." Reprinted by permission; © Fred C. Shapiro. Originally in The New Yorker.

SECTION 5
Search for Prosperity

The Chinese government's crackdown on political opposition has slowed the pace of economic reforms at home and has damaged China's prestige abroad. Fearing instability, some foreign investors have backed away from business ventures in China. Others, however, have continued to support business activity in the country.

One economic success story has been the **special economic zones** established by the Chinese government along China's south and southeast coasts. In these zones, private enterprises set up by foreign businesses are allowed to thrive with little government interference. The introduction of outside capital and advanced technology since the late 1970's has brought economic prosperity and a certain measure of freedom to the zones.

Below, a journalist describes business activities in Hainan, China's newest province and largest special economic zone:

[Hainan] has so far stressed a . . . growth plan including infrastructure projects [highways, railroads, etc.], construction, and processing that would tap tropical crops like rubber, coconut, oil palm, and sugar. The plan also calls for self-sufficiency in grain. Some 80 percent of Hainan's 6.4 million people still make a living from agriculture. But even mainstream politicians are willing to depart from central government policies to speed the island's development. . . .

. . . Industry on the island is to expand at more than 20 percent a year. Hainan also plans more daring economic reforms than the rest of the country, encouraging widespread private enterprise and freeing prices.

Already, the free market determines the prices of some 90 percent of goods sold on the island, with coal, fertilizer, and rice some of the few exceptions. . . .

Politically, Hainan leaders have resisted the conservative backlash by Marxist ideologues and continue to promote a policy of "small government, large society."

"The best government is the smallest one," says Liao, a former Beijing scholar and an admirer of Thomas Jefferson. Liao drafted the island's political reform plan.

Upon becoming a province in 1988, Hainan scaled down its government organs to 27, half the national average. Nevertheless, Hainan was dealt a serious blow when hard-liners ousted [Governor] Liang Xiang on corruption charges in 1989. He is said to be still living in Haikou [the capital of Hainan] as investigations into alleged graft continue.

This spirit of enterprise and independence also is seen in coastal areas that are not part of the special economic zones. These areas include coastal cities that have reestablished closer trading ties with Japan, Southeast Asia, and North America. As the following excerpt explains, people in coastal cities, such as Shanghai, pursue their own quests for success, often ignoring or downplaying hardline government policies:

Beijing may harp on ideology and strut with cultural pride, but practical-minded Shanghai is back to making money and welcoming foreign visitors in the process.

"We know how to do things in Shanghai," said Han, a 30 year-old who earns 500 yuan [$107] a month driving a taxi through his city's tangled streets. "We are more civilized," he added proudly, explaining why there was no Shanghai massacre in 1989. On China's National Day, October 1, 1990, the nation's largest and most Western-looking city was a festival of consumerism as shoppers licked ice

Source: Anne Scott Tyson. "Chinese Island Seeks Fast Growth." Reprinted by permission from THE CHRISTIAN SCIENCE MONITOR © 1991 The Christian Science Publishing Society. All rights reserved.

cream cones in crammed Nanjing Road, grabbed at silks in department stores, and presented sticky moon cakes as gifts at parties. Prompted by former mayor Zhu Rongji—named a deputy prime minister in April 1991 and one of the few widely admired politicians in China—this port city of 13 million has taken the lead in trying to put June 4 behind the nation.

In a northern industrial suburb, I found the entrepreneurial spirit very alive at the Harmony Café, where Ji Wenhua employs five people. He opened his business, about the size of an American living room, in 1981 as a breakfast shop and gradually expanded it. Now 35, he maneuvers his way through a jungle of per capita tax, security tax, business tax, sanitation tax, and commercial tax and still manages to clear about 3,000 yuan [$639] a month. Ji had previously worked in a factory and felt his wage there was too low. The "iron rice bowl" system, which guarantees employment but kills initiative, became too stifling, so he decided to risk striking out on his own.

Like many independent-minded Chinese of his generation, Ji concluded that the freedom that comes from making money is the best prize life can offer. For young businessmen like Ji life goes on, essentially unchanged by the events of May and June 1989.

SECTION 5 REVIEW

CHECKING FOR UNDERSTANDING

1. **Define** special economic zone.
2. **Explain** how Han and Ji reflect the outlook of many people in Shanghai and China's other coastal cities.

CRITICAL THINKING

3. **Demonstrating Reasoned Judgment** Indicate how China's economy has been affected by the Communist government's political crackdown on opponents.

Source: Ross Terrill. "China's Youth Wait for Tomorrow" in *National Geographic,* July, 1991, p. 131.

Global Concerns

POPULATION GROWTH

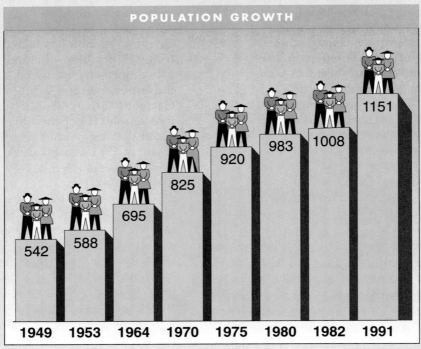

POPULATION GROWTH

1949	1953	1964	1970	1975	1980	1982	1991
542	588	695	825	920	983	1008	1151

With more than 1 billion people, China today faces the problem of overpopulation, or having more people than an area has resources to support. This enormous population growth has been due in part to a high birth rate during most of this century. According to population experts, if the average Chinese family continues to have as many as three children, in a century China's population could be as great as that of the world today—5.5 billion. This will lead to a shortage of jobs, food, housing, and social services.

To slow population growth, Chinese leaders have been try-ing to convince couples to have only one child. They hope to get 80 percent of the newlyweds in the cities and 50 percent of those in rural areas to agree. To win acceptance of this "one family-one child" policy, the government uses a system of rewards and punishments. Couples who promise to have only one child are given monthly cash bonuses, free medical care, and special benefits in education, housing, and jobs. Those who break their promise must face fines and reduction in pay and loss of benefits.

Although the policy has gained widespread support, it is difficult to tell what its long-term results will be. Many experts claim that the goal of limiting the population to 1.2 billion by the end of the century is not realistic. They explain that the high cost of the benefits offered to one-child families is an obstacle as is the Chinese regard for large families and preference for sons.

The government insists that it has to push for its plan in spite of obstacles. Otherwise, it claims, living standards will not improve and the drive toward modernization will fail.

FOCUSING ON THE ISSUE Study the graphs in this Global

Focus on China's population. Then, based on the graphs and the other information on these two pages, answer these questions:

1. What was China's population in 1949? In 1975? By how much did the population increase from 1975 to 1991?

2. How large will the population of China be in the year 2070 if China's families were to average one child? Two children? Three children?

3. Why does the Chinese government want to control population growth in China? With what means is it trying to achieve this goal?

4. Do you agree or disagree with the government's population policy? Explain your answer. Do you think that such a policy could work in your country? Why or why not?

5. What other methods do you think the Chinese government could take to reduce the population growth of China?

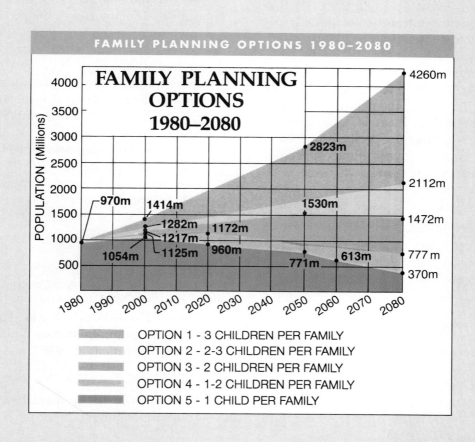

FAMILY PLANNING OPTIONS 1980–2080

FAMILY PLANNING OPTIONS 1980–2080

POPULATION (Millions)

970m 1414m 1282m 1217m 1125m 1054m 1172m 960m 1530m 771m 613m 2823m 4260m 2112m 1472m 777 m 370m

1980 1990 2000 2010 2020 2030 2040 2050 2060 2070 2080

OPTION 1 - 3 CHILDREN PER FAMILY
OPTION 2 - 2-3 CHILDREN PER FAMILY
OPTION 3 - 2 CHILDREN PER FAMILY
OPTION 4 - 1-2 CHILDREN PER FAMILY
OPTION 5 - 1 CHILD PER FAMILY

Chapter 13 Review

SUMMARY

In the late 1970's, the Chinese government began economic reforms to modernize China by the year 2000. While maintaining a socialist economy, the government borrowed capitalist practices from the West and gave Chinese peasants and workers incentives to increase productivity.

By the late 1980's, the economic reforms had brought prosperity, but democratic ways were still opposed by the government. In the spring of 1989, the Communist leadership responded with force against a growing pro-democracy movement. It also crushed stirrings for freedom among the Tibetans.

The Chinese government's crackdown on political dissent slowed the pace of economic reform at home and damaged China's prestige abroad. Economic prosperity, however, continued in many areas of China, especially in the special economic zones.

USING VOCABULARY

Use each vocabulary word in a sentence about recent economic or political developments in China.

    entrepreneur   special economic zone lama

REVIEWING FACTS

1. **Give reasons** for the struggle between moderates and radicals in the Chinese Communist party during the 1970's.
2. **Summarize** the changes in China's relations with the outside world from the mid-1970's to the early 1990's.
3. **Examine** the role of Chinese students in the democracy movement of the late 1980's.

4. **Describe** the impact of religion on Tibet's desire for freedom.
5. **Discuss** why China's Communist leaders agreed to establish special economic zones in China's coastal areas.

CRITICAL THINKING

1. **Determining Cause and Effect** In the mid-1970's, Chinese leaders introduced economic reforms and opened China to the West. What effect do you think their actions had on the rise of the pro-democracy movement in the late 1980's?
2. **Making Comparisons** Modernization is the main goal of China, yet it means something quite different in the countryside than in the city. What do you see as the main differences? What would you do to bridge the gap?
3. **Predicting Consequences** Since the Tiananmen Square massacre, China's Communist leadership has suppressed political reform movements in China. Do you think their hard-line policy will succeed? Explain.

ANALYZING CONCEPTS

1. **Interdependence** In what ways have China and the West influenced each other since the mid-1970's?
2. **Human Rights** What specific demands did the Beijing demonstrators make to the Chinese government in 1989?

GEOGRAPHIC THEMES

1. **Regions** How do the special economic zones link China to other parts of the world?
2. **Location** Where is Tibet located? How do you think its location has affected its influence in world affairs?

Making Generalizations

If you say to a friend, "My dad is a great cook," you are making a *generalization*, or a general statement, about your father. If you add that your father has a diploma from a cooking school in Paris and is a chef for a famous restaurant, you have provided evidence to support your generalization.

In many fields of study, it often is necessary to use assorted facts and bits of information about specific situations to create a larger picture of past or present events. For example, archaeologists who find pieces of pottery and remnants of tools from ancient cultures use these artifacts to create theories of how people lived thousands of years ago.

Although authors sometimes provide both generalizations and supporting details, in many cases only the details are given and you must make the generalizations on your own. When making generalizations, be sure that the supporting statements are directly related to the topic. If not, your generalization may be incorrect.

Here are some steps to follow in making generalizations:

- Gather facts, examples, or statements related to your topic.
- Identify similarities or patterns among these facts.
- Use these similarities or patterns to form generalizations about the topic.
- Test your generalizations against other facts and examples.

EXAMPLE

Read the following statements:

1. Mao Zedong's successors began an ambitious plan to modernize China's economy without following Mao's strict revolutionary course.
2. Mao Zedong's successors borrowed capitalist ideas and practices from the West to strengthen the Chinese economy.
3. Since the death of Mao Zedong, Chinese workers and peasants have been given greater incentives to work harder and produce more.

To form a generalization based on these statements, first look for similarities among them. All three statements discuss economic changes in China after Mao Zedong's death, especially the loosening of communist ideology and the adoption of some capitalist methods. Therefore, a logical generalization is: *Since the death of Mao Zedong, China has adopted some capitalist practices to improve its economy.*

PRACTICE

Write a generalization based on each group of statements below.

A. 1. Since the late 1970's, agricultural production has risen steadily in China.
   2. Since the late 1970's, the average annual income for Chinese peasants has increased.
   3. Many Chinese peasants can now afford consumer goods that were once considered luxuries.
B. 1. The Chinese government has built new hotels and resorts to encourage foreign business and tourism.
   2. In the 1980's, a number of foreign specialists were working in China.
   3. In the 1980's and early 1990's, many Chinese students were studying at foreign universities.
C. 1. Chinese women have more difficulty fulfilling their career aspirations than men because women are also responsible for housework and childrearing.
   2. Arranged marriages are still common practices in parts of China.
   3. About 70 percent of the people in China who cannot read and write are women.

CHAPTER OUTLINE

People and Places to Know
the Politburo, Dong Kena, Cobra, Young Pioneers

Key Terms to Define
totalitarian, cadre

Objectives to Learn
1. **Evaluate** the role the Communist party plays in Chinese life.
2. **Detail** changes that have taken place in rural and urban lifestyles in China.
3. **Describe** the status of women and young people in China today.

The port city of Guangzhou

Daily Life in Modern China

> Nowhere is the wholesale destruction of China's past . . . so graphically evident than in the face of the country's cities, and of Beijing in particular. There is a story told . . . that when Mao and his comrades stood atop Tiananmen proclaiming the establishment of the People's Republic, the Chairman turned to Liang Sicheng, China's greatest urban planner . . . , and, waving his hand over the panorama of graceful yellow tile roofs, emerald-green tree tops and magnificent city walls, said that he wished to see "chimneys all over Beijing." He got his wish. . . .
>
> After four decades of Communist rule, Beijing has changed. The brute forces of political upheaval, social need, explosive industrialization—all have conspired to pave over the old Beijing of temples, walls, gardens, and neighborhoods with a metropolis forested by monotonous ashen cement apartment towers, smoke-stacked factories, and leaden government buildings. Only in recent years, fueled by a realization that the city's visible heritage has all but vanished, have any gestures been made to save and rebuild. . . .

This description of Beijing provides an insight into life in a modern Chinese city. Since the communist revolution in 1949, the Chinese have seen many changes in their daily lives. As a result of the Communist drive for modernization, the country has become more industrialized, the cities have grown in size and population, and the standard of living is better. At the same time, the people have had to endure the destruction of significant aspects of their pre-communist heritage. They also have had to deal with a series of rapid shifts in government policy.

In spite of the benefits and problems brought by constant change and modernization, certain elements of the Chinese past remain. The Chinese continue to hold to their traditional arts and festivals and to maintain a high regard for family life and education. These traditions have helped bolster Chinese morale during recent trying periods. They have also given the Chinese a strong sense of identity.

Because of the upheavals of the past few decades, it is difficult to say what the future holds for China. Throughout their long history, the Chinese have faced many political, social, and economic uncertainties. Yet they have managed to meet each crisis with self-confidence and to make significant contributions to world civilization. Many experts believe that, whatever lies ahead, the Chinese will continue to make a powerful impact on global affairs.

Source: Edward A. Gargan. *China's Fate: A People's Turbulent Struggle with Reform and Repression 1980–1990*. Doubleday, 1990, pp. 61, 63.

SECTION 1

The Communist Party

The Chinese Communist party has a dominant role in the lives of the people. Its 48 million members, however, make up only 4 percent of China's population. In theory, the party's most powerful institution is the National Party Congress, whose 2700 representatives meet periodically. The Congress elects the Central Committee that oversees party activities between meetings. In practice, however, party policies are set by the Politburo, a group of about 25 top party officials within the Central Committee. The Politburo also exercises strict control over government.

In its methods of operation, the Chinese Communist party is **totalitarian.** That is, its control extends beyond politics to almost all major areas of life. Its most direct impact is at the local level. Government and party committees run the provinces, counties, and townships. **Cadres,** personnel who serve on the committees, are responsible for solving many of the practical, everyday problems of the people. Economic reforms and political upheavals, however, are profoundly changing the way the Chinese Communist party operates in

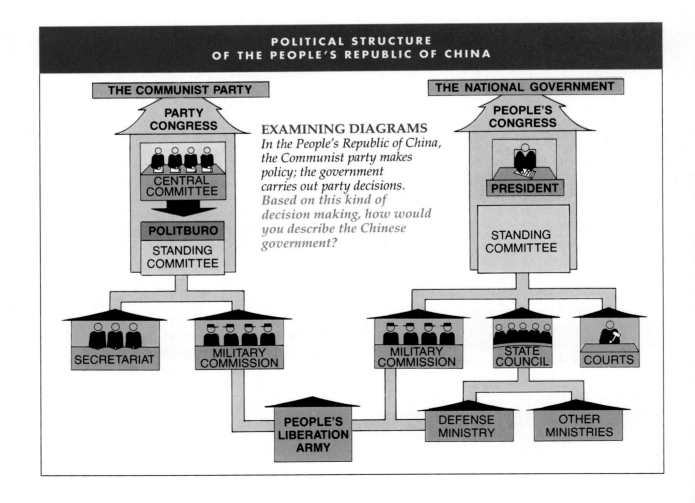

POLITICAL STRUCTURE OF THE PEOPLE'S REPUBLIC OF CHINA

THE COMMUNIST PARTY

PARTY CONGRESS

CENTRAL COMMITTEE

POLITBURO

STANDING COMMITTEE

SECRETARIAT

MILITARY COMMISSION

THE NATIONAL GOVERNMENT

PEOPLE'S CONGRESS

PRESIDENT

STANDING COMMITTEE

MILITARY COMMISSION

STATE COUNCIL

COURTS

PEOPLE'S LIBERATION ARMY

DEFENSE MINISTRY

OTHER MINISTRIES

EXAMINING DIAGRAMS
In the People's Republic of China, the Communist party makes policy; the government carries out party decisions. Based on this kind of decision making, how would you describe the Chinese government?

many areas of China. The following excerpt discusses the role of a party official in one small Chinese village:

In the midst of Zouping [district] is a village of 1,100 where Wu Baohua . . . has been Communist Party secretary for 25 years. Wu is soft-spoken and polite, but his face expresses a sanguine [peaceful] dignity without a trace of self-importance. . . .

Unlike Guangdong, where Deng's injunction to "seek truth from facts" has led provincial officials to cite "unique local conditions" as a way of drifting as far from Communism as Beijing can tolerate, Wu's village represents the opposite tendency. In many ways it is still a collectivist town. The village employs doctors and covers all medical costs—a practice no longer common in China, where many must pay for health care out of their own pockets. Land is privately owned, but much of its cultivation is accomplished by group effort.

The neighborhood committees that exist almost everywhere in China—watchdog groups that keep an eye on everyone and everything—are unnecessary in Wu's village. In tone and in fact, he controls almost every aspect of village life—and the villagers have prospered thanks to his wisdom. . . .

When this summer's drought threatened to devastate the village's wheat and vegetable crops, Wu proposed that water from the Yellow [Huang He] River—unused previously because it was so muddy—be tapped immediately. Within 36 hours, 4,000 Chinese, including Wu, were digging a new irrigation ditch two miles long. The entire job was completed in twelve hours.

On the wall of one of the newest buildings in Wu's village is a saying widely heard during the Cultural Revolution two decades ago: PREPARE FOR WAR, PREPARE FOR NATURAL DISASTERS, SERVE THE PEOPLE. Wu makes no apologies. "Of course I know the slogan's

origins," he says. "But there is nothing wrong with these words. We should use more of what Mao taught. His themes were self-reliance and sacrifice. I say to our leaders, more of that and less riding around in fancy cars. . . ."

SECTION 1 REVIEW

CHECKING FOR UNDERSTANDING

1. **Define** totalitarian, cadre.
2. **Discuss** how the Chinese Communist party is organized.
3. **Explain** what responsibilities are carried out by cadres.

CRITICAL THINKING

4. **Drawing Conclusions** How do you think recent upheavals have affected the way the Communist party operates in China today?

SECTION 2

In the Countryside and the City

Most Chinese live in rural areas and work as farmers. Although many of the farmers still rely on human and animal labor, economic reforms have enabled them to buy farm machinery and consumer goods. As a result of increased production and income, Chinese peasants in some areas now live as well—or even better than—urban residents. Lee Shaywing, a middle-income farmer who was interviewed by an American writer below, is an example:

I told Shaywing I was interested in how village life in China had changed in the last ten years. "The biggest change in my

Source: Howard G. Chua-Eoan. "A Day in the Life of China" in *Time*, October 2, 1989, p. 75. Copyright 1989 The Time Inc. Magazine Company. Reprinted by permission.

EXAMINING PHOTOGRAPHS *On the outskirts of Luda, a city in northeastern China, 26 peasant families have built themselves new houses, thanks to an increase in their incomes. One of these houses, shown here, contains six rooms, a kitchen, three storerooms, and has indoor plumbing. Why do some Chinese peasants in rural areas now live as well or better than some urban residents?*

life has been in recent years, since about 1981," he replied, tipping his chair back on two legs against the wall of his house. Between 1981 and 1982, [the village of] Lolam's land, which until then had been consolidated into a commune and farmed by the villagers collectively, was distributed to each household to use as they wished. . . .

"Since the policy [of communes] was relaxed," Shaywing went on, "we can do more and earn more. Look at me. We've got 1.2 mou [about half an acre] of land now. . . . I've got more pigs and more chickens. In 1981, I was given my own land. About three years ago, they readjusted the land and I got more because my son got married and his wife lives here. Of course I'd like to get some more land now. . . . A principal source of Shaywing's income, though, is not his farming but his investment in a plastics factory. . . . Shaywing scrimped, sold some pigs, borrowed from relatives, and invested one thousand yuan [about $213] in the . . . factory, more a workshop actually than anything else. "Every year I get about a thousand yuan in income," he boasted.

Source: Edward A. Gargan. *China's Fate.* Doubleday, 1990, pp. 105–106.

The cities of China have changed as much as the rural areas in the past few decades. Before 1949 most urban residents were poor and lived in dirty, overcrowded conditions. Today China's cities, especially in coastal areas, are centers of the country's industry and commerce. Although the cities are still crowded, life is very different. Streets are kept clean of dirt and trash. Most people are better fed and clothed. The economic reforms, however, have increased the gap between lower- and upper-income groups. This is illustrated below as a Chinese journalist describes the lives of Li Yutian, a department store administrator, and Jin Wenjiang, a constructor worker, in the city of Tianjin:

Li Yutian . . . lives with his wife, Zhang Qi, and their nine-year-old son in a new flat with a floor space of 35 sq. m. [42 sq. yds.] The couple . . . work at the Tianjin Department Store. Zhang is a section boss and Li is also an administrator. . . .

Zhang . . . keeps monthly records of the family's income and expenses. Her records show that in May 1990 the couple's income was 419.7 yuan [about $90], while their expenses were 353.79 yuan [about $76]. The family . . . belongs to the upper-medium income group.

They have purchased a color TV, furniture, tape recorder, cameras, refrigerator and carpet . . . The main daily expense is food; the refrigerator is always full, but quickly empties. . . .

According to Zhang, since most young couples have only one child, the parents will give the child whatever it wants. . . . To enrich their child's educational environment, the Lis bought a piano in 1987 and recently Li's parents gave him 1,000 yuan [$213] to buy a Chinese-made pupil computer. . . .

It was difficult to reach Jin Wenjiang's house among the group of poor one-story houses. The simply built house belongs to Jin's family. Its walls feel damp whenever it rains. Since Jin would have to pay for renovations, the family puts up with the situation. The municipal government has registered families with less than 2.5 sq. m. [about 3 sq. yds.] living space per person in order to provide new houses for them. Since Jin's son and daughter were out of the city for schooling, his family did not qualify. Now his son has returned and his daughter will be back next year, so housing will be a severe problem. . . .

Jin. . . . working in the construction company, has a monthly income of 160 yuan [$35]. His wife is jobless, but she tries to help support the family. In summer she sells popsicles and earns nearly 100 yuan [$22] a month. The son . . . works in a machine factory as an apprentice for a monthly income of over 70 yuan [$15]. Now the average monthly income per family member is 62 yuan [$14], nearly double what it was in 1985, but it still falls within the low-income category. Since 1985, the family has bought an electric fan, washing machine and some other appliances. Next summer the daughter will graduate and the family may be able to improve its current conditions.

Source: Li Jianguo and Cheng Diaodui. "How are Tianjin Families Doing?" in *China Today,* October, 1990, pp. 17, 19.

SECTION 2 REVIEW

CHECKING FOR UNDERSTANDING

1. **Describe** how life has changed for many Chinese peasants since 1949.
2. **Specify** how life in China's cities has changed since 1949.

CRITICAL THINKING

3. **Evaluating Information** What area of Chinese life do you think has experienced the most change in the past few decades? Explain.

SECTION 3

Women

Women have gained many benefits from recent changes in Chinese society. Today, more than 40 million work in a variety of occupations, many in industrial trades. The number who hold top-level positions, however, is still very low. Even those in top positions face many challenges because they are women. Below, Dong Kena, one of China's leading women film directors, comments on how she blends her professional and personal lives:

At home I'm a wife, daughter-in-law, mother, daughter, and grandmother all in one, but usually I concern myself only with important family matters and never let trivia influence my work. My husband is a great help to me both with housework and my career. In the forty years of our marriage we've never had a serious quarrel with one another and never had any emotional crises, which is quite rare among artistic couples like us. . . . My husband's criticisms and suggestions are essential for every film I make. Sometimes, when I was outside Beijing with my cast, he would send his comments on the film by post.

EXAMINING PHOTOGRAPHS *In recent years, Chinese women in greater numbers have been employed in factories and laboratories. Today, women represent more than 36 percent of the work force.* *What positions still remain largely closed to Chinese women?*

I have a basic tenet for my career: to serve the majority of the audience and never pander to low taste. A second principle is never to stop once you have started until you reach success. . . .

It's much harder to be a female director than a male one. Any bit of success comes from hard striving, but you should not be too proud of yourself even if you've accomplished something, because film is a comprehensive art that needs the cooperation of many departments. . . .

Many women, especially young women, are becoming bolder in demanding equal rights with men. The following excerpt discusses the efforts of an all-female rock group to find acceptance in the male-dominated music industry:

Source: Bao Wenqing. "Three Award-Winning Women Film Directors" in *China Today*, March 1990, pp. 24–25.

All Yu Jin has to do is switch on her keyboard, lean into a few notes, and she has defied etiquette in China with enough daring to make Madonna seem like Mary Poppins. . . .

Yu and other members of Cobra, China's first all-woman rock-and-roll band, break plenty of iron-clad proprieties simply by tearing into a few roaring bars of classic Rolling Stones.

Cobra is arguably the freest and boldest force for feminism in a country where the state-controlled "women's movement" is as restrained and predictable as a garden club meeting.

"The traditional concept for what women in China should do is to give birth to children and cook," says Wang Xiaofing, Cobra's drummer.

"Chinese people traditionally don't think women can achieve anything, but I think we can achieve a lot," she says, sweeping her palm through a head of spikey black hair tinted brown at the tips.

Even members of all-male rock groups belittle Cobra because of the gender of its members. Although many of China's male musicians trumpet a defiant message, they ironically fail to appreciate Cobra's own feminist [attack on established beliefs].

"A lot of men who play rock-and-roll despise us and say there's no way we'll play well," according to Yu. "But after hearing us, many of them have changed their minds and accepted us," she says. . . .

SECTION 3 REVIEW

CHECKING FOR UNDERSTANDING
1. **Describe** the role of women in China today.

CRITICAL THINKING
2. **Determining Cause and Effect** What factors do you think have helped advance women's equality in China?

Source: James L. Tyson. "Making Music, Making Waves" in THE CHRISTIAN SCIENCE MONITOR, September 11, 1991, p. 14. Reprinted by permission from THE CHRISTIAN SCIENCE MONITOR © 1991 The Christian Science Publishing Society. All rights reserved.

EXAMINING PHOTOGRAPHS *These Chinese schoolchildren are attending an art class in Shanghai. Since 1949, the Communist government has strongly promoted educational advances. At what age do children begin school in China?*

SECTION 4

Young People

In China young people are regarded as "the wealth of the country," and since 1949, the government has made strides in education. Today children begin elementary school about the age of 6 or 7. Five years later, they take an exam to go to high school, where they are separated into groups based on a particular field of study.

After graduation from high school, most young people start work in a factory, farm, or shop. A few, however, go on to university studies. To enter a university, a candidate must pass a difficult examination. Competition is fierce because there are more people who want to enroll than there are places.

Although Chinese students work hard at their studies, they still find time to participate in activities outside of school. Many young people are involved in youth organi-

zations. The Young Pioneers is a children's organization to which about 50 percent of China's youngsters belong. Its purpose is to train children to be good citizens. To this end, it sponsors many community service projects. The Communist Youth League, on the other hand, is an honor organization for high school students. To become a member, a student must be at least 15 years of age and have an excellent academic and political record. The League prepares a limited number of select candidates for membership in the Communist party.

Chinese young people enjoy such sports as ping pong, basketball, soccer, and gymnastics. In recent years, Chinese athletes have been talented competitors in international sporting events. Before the 1992 Olympics, a Chinese journalist describes the career of Li Jing, one of China's newest gymnastic stars:

Li's success is as much attributable to determination as to natural talent. Over

EXAMINING PHOTOGRAPHS
Gymnastic champion Li Jing concentrates as he circles the pommel horse at the 1992 Olympic Games in Barcelona, Spain. Li won two silver medals at the Olympics. Besides gymnastics, what other sports activities are enjoyed by Chinese young people?

the last 15 years, he has developed a formidable training program. This includes running 30 kilometers [19 miles] every three days to develop muscular strength and stretching his legs with . . . weights fixed to his feet in order to correct a slight bone distortion beneath his knees. Every movement in every one of his routines has been repeated thousands of times, so that even the most technically difficult feats, such as the "Arabian forward roll"—a stretched jump with an 180-degree turn in the middle followed by a somersault—can be carried out faultlessly.

Last winter, I went to watch Li Jing in training. When he finally managed to find a few moments in between a set of exercises aimed at ironing out a few hitches in one of his floor routines, he described the challenges that stood before him over the next two years: "We're facing the World Gymnastic Championships . . . and the . . . Olympic Games—as a gymnast, these two have got to be the ultimate life-time challenge. Only by going all out until

these two are over can I hope to win honor for our socialist homeland."

Huang Yubin, [one of] Li's coaches . . ., believes Li has got what it takes to compete at the highest level: "His movements are always harmonious and graceful. He bears all hardship uncomplainingly and has an immense will to win. Over the last few years, his mental approach has matured and he's one of the most conscientious trainers I've ever known."

SECTION 4 REVIEW

CHECKING FOR UNDERSTANDING

1. **State** the educational opportunities that are open to Chinese young people.

CRITICAL THINKING

2. **Making Comparisons** How do you think the lives of Chinese youth compare with those of youth in your country?

Source: Xie Enhua. "China's New Gymnastics Star," in *China Pictorial,* March, 1991, p. 20.

China

THE OTHER CHINA

Since 1949, there have been two Chinas. In that year, the Communists won mainland China and set up the People's Republic. The Guomindang fled to the island of Taiwan, 100 miles [160 kilometers] off China's southeast coast. The official name of the Guomindang government in Taiwan is the Republic of China.

Taiwan's climate is subtropical with hot summers, mild winters, and a great deal of rainfall. Shaped like a tobacco leaf, the island is about 250 miles [400 kilometers] long and 60 to 90 miles [96 to 144 kilometers] wide, three-fourths of which is steep, forested mountains. On the western third of the island, where most of the people live, the land is suitable for farming. With more than 20 million people, Taiwan is one of the most densely populated islands in the world.

About 17 million of the people of Taiwan are Taiwan Chinese whose ancestors came to Taiwan from the mainland around 1600. Another 3 million are mainland immigrants who fled to Taiwan in 1949. In addition to these two groups, about 100,000 Malay-speaking groups live in the mountains. While the Taiwanese control business, the mainlanders dominate the government. Although this led to much tension in the past, as a new generation replaces the old, the conflict has eased. More Taiwanese are entering the government, and the "mainlanders" are adopting Taiwanese ways.

After 1949, both the Communists and the Guomindang considered Taiwan a part of China. Each claimed to be the legal government of all of China. However, in recent years, the Guomindang leadership in Taiwan has edged away from its old dream of retaking the Chinese mainland. It has also relaxed its strict political hold on Taiwan, allowing opposition parties to organize and to compete in elections. Individuals in Taiwan enjoy more personal freedom than those living on the mainland.

Taiwan's move toward full democracy has been aided by a booming economy, which experts have called one of Asia's "economic miracles." Along with South Korea, Hong Kong, and Singapore, Taiwan is considered a "little tiger" of international economics. Taiwan now exports a variety of goods ranging from food to textiles and electronic equipment. As a result of rapid economic growth, Taiwan has one of Asia's highest standards of living. Many Taiwanese are confident that their strong economy will ensure the continued survival of the Republic of China.

DRAWING CONCLUSIONS

1. What is meant by the term *the other China*?
2. If you were Chinese, how would you react to the statement that China is "one country with two systems"? Why would you react this way?

Geography

THE TWO CHINAS

FOCUSING ON THE ISSUE Facts about the "two Chinas" —the People's Republic of China and the Republic of China— are noted in the charts below. Which facts do you consider

PEOPLE'S REPUBLIC OF CHINA

Land Area: 9.57 million square kilometers (3.7 million square miles)
Population: 1.1 billion (74% rural)
Major Cities:

Shanghai (7.3)	Beijing (5.6)	Tianjin (4.5)
Shenyang (3.5)	Wuhan (3.2)	Guangzhou (2.9)
Chongqing (2.2)	Harbin (2.4)	Nanjing (2.1)
Xi'an (1.9)	Dalian (1.7)	Changchun (1.6)
Chengdu (1.6)	Taiyuan (1.4)	Qingdao (1.4)
Jinan (1.3)	Lanzhou (1.2)	Fushun (1.2)

TV Stations: 5363 (government)
TV Receivers: 623 (government)
Radio Receivers: 126 million
Gross National Product: $413 billion
Per Capita Gross National Product: $360

*1990 Estimates

REPUBLIC OF CHINA

Land Area: 35,979 square kilometers (13,892 square miles)
Population: 20.2 million (29% rural)
Major Cities:
Taipei (2.7)   Kao-hsiung (1.4)
TV Stations: 38 (private and commercial)
Radio Stations: 61 (private, commercial, and government)
TV Receivers: 6.7 million
Radio Receivers: 13.6 million
Gross National Product: $150.8 billion
Per Capita Gross National Product: $7510

*1990 Estimates

most important as shapers of development? As barriers to development? Explain.

Both the People's Republic of China and the Republic of China have constitutions. Below are several articles of each. After reading the articles, describe two ways in which the communist government is constitutionally different from the Guomindang government. Based on what you have read in this chapter, do you think each constitution gives a true picture of how government operates in each China? Give examples to support your answers.

Based on the information in the charts, the articles of the constitutions, and the chapter, what similarities can you find between the two Chinas? What do you view as the most striking differences? In each case, explain your answer.

PEOPLE'S REPUBLIC OF CHINA

Article 1. *The People's Republic of China is a socialist state under the people's democratic dictatorship led by the working class and based on the alliance of workers and peasants. The socialist system is the basic system. . . .*

Article 2. *All power in the People's Republic of China belongs to the people. The organs through which the people exercise state power are the National People's Congress and the local people's congresses at various levels. . . .*

Article 3. *The state organs of the People's Republic of China apply the principle of democratic centralism.*

The National People's Congress, and the local people's congresses at different levels, are instituted through democratic election.

Source: Keesing's Contemporary Archives: Record of World Events, Volume XXIX, No. 2, February 1983, Longman, p. 31954.

REPUBLIC OF CHINA

Article 1
The Republic of China, founded on the Three Principles of the People [Nationalism, Democracy, Livelihood], shall be a democratic republic of the people, to be governed by the people and for the people.

Article 2
The sovereignty of the Republic of China shall reside in the whole body of citizens.

Article 25
The National Assembly shall, in accordance with the provisions of this constitution, exercise political powers on behalf of the whole body of citizens.

Source: From REPUBLIC OF CHINA YEARBOOK, 1991–1992, Kwang Hwa Publishing Company, 1991. Pages 571, 572. Reprinted by permission.

Chapter 14 Review

SUMMARY

Since the communist drive for modernization, China has become more industrialized, its cities have grown, and the standard of living has improved for many Chinese.

The Chinese Communist party has a dominant role in national life and is totalitarian in the way it functions. Government and powerful party committees run the provinces, counties, and townships, while cadres are responsible for political matters and solving everyday problems.

Although most Chinese live in rural areas and work as farmers, China's cities, especially in coastal areas, are the country's centers of industry and commerce.

Young people are regarded as "the wealth of the country," and since 1949, the government has made great strides in advancing their education. Most of them find time, however, to participate in a variety of activities outside school.

USING VOCABULARY

Use the following terms in writing a short essay about the role of the Communist party in China today.

totalitarian   cadre

REVIEWING FACTS

1. **List** the most powerful institutions within the Chinese Communist party and their functions.
2. **Cite** the problems that China's peasants and workers face in spite of recent economic improvements.
3. **Describe** the educational system in China today.

4. **Discuss** the benefits gained by women as a result of recent changes in China's society and economy.

CRITICAL THINKING

1. **Recognizing Ideologies** China is often described as a totalitarian society. What are the characteristics of such a society? Do totalitarian societies exist elsewhere in the world today? Explain.
2. **Analyzing Trends** The drive for modernization has opened more opportunities for women in the Chinese economy. Do you think that the women presented in the chapter excerpts are typical of working women in China today? Why or why not?
3. **Making Comparisons** Is there any group or groups in your country equivalent to the Chinese cadres? What are they? In your view, how do their responsibilities compare with those of the cadres?
4. **Synthesizing Information** In traditional China, officials in the imperial government were selected on the basis of examinations. Do examinations serve the same purpose in China today? Explain.

ANALYZING CONCEPTS

1. **Citizenship** Name the youth organizations that exist in China today and describe the purpose of each. How are they similar to and how do they differ from youth organizations in your country?
2. **Culture** What sports activities are popular among young people in China?

GEOGRAPHIC THEMES

1. **Location** Where is Taiwan located in relation to the Chinese mainland?
2. **Place** Why is housing in great demand in China's cities?

Interpreting Primary Sources

Primary sources are accounts of events by people who witnessed or experienced them. They include diaries, autobiographies, journals, eyewitness news reports, letters, photographs, and oral interviews. For example, if you witness a fire or live through a great storm and then write about your experiences, you have created a primary source about that event.

Primary sources can bring events to life and reveal their emotional impact on people. Suppose you find two news stories about an earthquake in western China. One gives statistics on deaths and injuries; the other is a victim's account of searching the rubble to find remains of her home and children. The second story, a primary source, will enable you to feel the human loss more keenly. However, because primary sources reflect the views of individuals, they often miss the "big picture."

In interpreting primary sources, notice how the author's emotions and opinions have colored the account of an event. A student demonstrator in Tiananmen Square might give a very different account of the protests than would a soldier or government official. In addition, determine *when* the source was written. If many years have passed since the event occurred, the writer may have forgotten or confused some details.

To interpret primary sources, use the following steps:
- Identify the author of the document.

- Identify when and where the document was written.
- Identify the main topic of the document.
- Separate facts from emotions and opinions.
- Determine what kind of information the document provides and what is missing.

EXAMPLE

Reread the excerpt by the woman film director Dong Kena on pages 223–224. The main topic is the way she has combined family and career. Look at the footnote below the excerpt. When was this article published? *(March 1990)* Notice that this writer is generally quite positive about combining work and home life. What opinions does she give about relations with her husband? *(helpful, never have serious quarrels, relies on his criticisms)* Do you think all these statements are true? Why or why not? *(Answers will vary. Some students may accept them; others may wonder if she was glossing over problems.)*

PRACTICE

Read the account given by a female student leader who supported democracy in China. Answer the questions that follow.

I am Chai Ling. I am the chief commander of the Tiananmen Square Command Post. At 4 p.m. of June 8, I made this tape recording. . . . I think I am the most quali-

fied person to comment on the events of June 4. . . .

At 9 p.m., all the students in Tiananmen Square stood up . . . and took an oath: 'I will defend Tiananmen Square with my young life. My head may be chopped off, my blood may be shed, but the people's square cannot be abandoned. With our young life, we are willing to fight till the last minute'. . . .

After 10:30 p.m., . . . the students slowly walked out of their tents, quietly sat there, waiting for the slaughterers' knives. We were conducting a war between love and hatred, not a battle of weapons. . . . What we were waiting for was sacrifice. . . .

1. Is the account a primary source? Why or why not?
2. Is Chai Ling "the most qualified person to comment" on this event? Why or why not?
3. How much time passed between the event and the creation of the account? How does this affect its reliability?
4. What is the main topic of this document?
5. What information does the account give about the mood and beliefs of the students?
6. What emotional terms are used to describe the students' opponents?

Source: Yi Mu and Mark V. Thompson. *Crisis at Tiananmen: Reform and Reality in Modern China.* China Books and Periodicals, 1989, pp. 265–267.

The Confucian Influence on Japan

China gave many spiritual and intellectual gifts to neighboring lands, especially to the island nation of Japan. Among these was Confucianism, which spread to Japan in the late 500's AD. Confucian values and attitudes so appealed to the Japanese that by the 1600's they influenced almost every aspect of Japanese society.

The Japanese first came in contact with Confucianism in the late 500's when their rulers adopted Chinese political ideas based on its philosophy. The Confucian emphasis on strong centralized government helped Japanese rulers strengthen their power. Later, Confucian concern for obedience to authority led to the division of Japanese society into a ranked order of social groups, each with distinct roles and responsibilities.

Over the centuries, an understanding of Confucianism as a moral philosophy gradually developed in Japan. Schools were opened that taught Confucianism to ordinary people. By the 1600's, Confucianism was recognized as the way to a just and harmonious society. It served as a code of conduct that guided nearly all of Japanese behavior. The emphasis on proper conduct in personal relationships and the belief that society could be changed through education and hard work were among the important Confucian principles that shaped Japan.

Today, Confucianism continues to influence the Japanese. One of the clearest examples can be seen in the importance the Japanese attach to status in relationships. Nearly all relationships are arranged according to rank; those between persons of unequal status, which is usually based on age, are governed by strict etiquette.

The Confucian influence can also be seen in the workplace. Corporations are organized by rank according to age and education. It is uncommon for a worker to be promoted over an older one—even if the individual's skills are superior. Also, a company's employees share a deep sense of group identity. The ideal Japanese worker is a good team player who cooperates rather than competes. An individual who stands out among the group threatens to disrupt the group's harmonious functioning and jeopardizes everyone's welfare. Ultimately, the Japanese believe that what benefits the group also is in the best interests of the individual.

Making the Connection

1. What are some of the Confucian beliefs that influence Japan today?

2. How do you think Confucian values affect innovation in Japan's business and technology?

Unit 2 Review

SUMMARY

China is the world's oldest living civilization. Because of geographic isolation, early Chinese society developed with little outside influence. Governed by dynastic rulers and scholar-bureaucrats, most Chinese at this time were poor peasants who suffered many injustices. Among the values upheld in traditional China were loyalty to family, devotion to learning, and reverence for nature.

In the early 1900's, foreign influences and peasant discontent led to the overthrow of the last dynasty and the proclamation of a republic. Unable to solve China's many problems, the Guomindang government was replaced by a communist system in 1949. Guomindang leaders fled to the island of Taiwan, where they continued their rule.

On the mainland, the Communists have worked to create a modern urban-industrial state. Recent economic reforms have increased the standard of living, but the communist leadership has opposed political reforms.

REVIEWING THE MAIN IDEAS

1. **Explain** how the major physical features of China influenced the Chinese attitude toward the natural environment.
2. **Discuss** some of the similarities and differences between the attitudes the Chinese traditionally held about themselves and the outside world and the attitudes they hold today.
3. **List** the social groups of traditional China and those of China today.
4. **Examine** the ways family life and the role of women have changed in China over the centuries. What factors were responsible for these changes?

CRITICAL THINKING

1. **Analyzing Ideologies** Early Chinese rulers based their right to rule on the Mandate of Heaven. How do China's current Communist leaders justify their hold on power?
2. **Making Comparisons** Confucianism and Daoism had a profound influence on Chinese society before the political and social revolutions of the twentieth century. How do the beliefs and values of both of these philosophies compare with those of modern Chinese communism?
3. **Making Decisions** British-ruled Hong Kong is expected to become part of China in 1997. If you were a Hong Kong citizen, would you approve of this transfer? Why or why not? Would you remain in Hong Kong or emigrate to another part of the world? Why or why not?

PRACTICING SKILLS

Analyzing Primary and Secondary Sources Which of the following is the most accurate source of information about the personality of Mao Zedong? Explain.
a. diary of a Red Guard written during the Cultural Revolution
b. memoirs of a party official who was on the Long March

DEVELOPING A GLOBAL VIEWPOINT

In the 1980's hopes for democratic reform soared in China, but were crushed in the Tiananmen Square massacre. What other parts of the world saw a surge of support for democracy during the past decade? How successful were these efforts? Do you think democracy will triumph in China in the near future? Explain.

Japan

In 1945, Japan was a nation devastated and defeated by a world war. Today, it is the leading economic power in Asia. The economic success of the Japanese, along with other aspects of Japanese culture, have been shaped in a special way by geography and history. Throughout the centuries, the Japanese have been skillful in borrowing from other peoples while still keeping their own traditions and national identity. Today, they are trying to reach their national goals while maintaining close ties with the United States. They also are assuming a more active role in world affairs, especially in promoting economic growth in Asia.

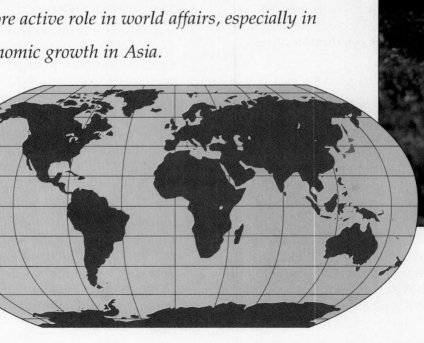

CHAPTERS

AT A GLANCE

LAND AREA: 145,870 sq. mi. (377,801 sq. km.)

LAND RESOURCES:
cropland: 12.4%
pasture: 1.2%
forest/woodland: 66.7%
other land: 19.2%

WILDERNESS AREA: 0%

MAJOR MOUNTAIN RANGES:
Japan Alps, Kanto, Kyushu, Mikuni, Shikoku

MAJOR BODIES OF WATER:
Biwa Lake, East China Sea, Inland Sea, Korea Strait, Osaka Bay, Pacific Ocean, Philippine Sea, Sea of Japan, Shinano River, Tokyo Bay

POPULATION: (1992 est.) 124,400,000

POPULATION UNDER 15/OVER 65:
18%/13%

LIFE EXPECTANCY: 79 yrs.

POPULATION PROJECTION:
124,100,000 (by 2025)

POPULATION DENSITY:
854/sq. mi. (330/sq. km.)

URBAN POPULATION: 77%

LARGEST CITIES: (millions)
Tokyo (8.6)
Osaka/Kobe/Kyoto (3.1)
Yokohama (3.0)
Nagoya (2.1)

CHAPTER OUTLINE

People and Places to Know
Hokkaido, Honshu, Shikoku, Kyushu, Mount Fuji, Japan Alps, Japan Current, Oyashio Current, Inland Sea, Shiretoko Peninsula, Tokyo, Yokohama, Osaka, Nagoya

Key Terms to Define
myth, archipelago, monsoon, typhoon, bonsai, *tsunami*

Objectives to Learn

1. **Summarize** early views of Japan and its people.
2. **Analyze** the importance of mountains, sea, and plains to Japanese culture.
3. **Compare** urban and rural life in Japan.

Mount Fuji

236

The Great Island Country

" Long centuries ago, when the world was a shadowy mist, the Islands of Japan were born of the sea. Among the many gods inhabiting this misty abode were Izanagi and Izanami. One day, while they were standing on the Floating Bridge of Heaven, talking with each other, Izanagi said: "I wonder what is down below us?" This aroused Izanami's curiosity, and they began to think how they might find out. Taking the Jewel-Spear of Heaven, Izanagi lowered it into the air and swung it around in an effort to strike something, for he could not see through the dense mist. Suddenly the spear touched the ocean. When Izanagi raised it, salty water dripping from it was dried by the wind, becoming hard, and forming an island in the middle of the sea.

"Let us go down and live on the island," said Izanagi. And so they descended from the Floating Bridge of Heaven to live on the island. Soon they had created the Great-Eight-Island-Land and given birth to three noble children: the Sun Goddess and her brothers the Moon God and the Storm God. The Sun Goddess, whose name was Amaterasu-Omi-Kami, also had a family. Her [great-great-great] grandson Jimmu became the first Emperor (Tenno or Mikado) of Japan. "

This **myth,** or traditional story, about the origin of Japan comes from an eighth-century Japanese work called the *Kojiki,* or *Records of Ancient Matters.* In this and such other early works as the *Nihongi,* or *Chronicles of Japan,* were some of the first descriptions of Japan and its environment. The descriptions referred to a land of mountainous islands surrounded by an ever-present ocean. The land had numerous clear streams and was favored with a temperate climate.

Today, the Japanese **archipelago,** or chain of islands, is about 145,000 square miles (376,000 square kilometers) in area. It forms a curve off the coast of East Asia. There are four main islands—Hokkaido, Honshu, Shikoku, and Kyushu—and thousands of smaller ones. Honshu is the largest and most populated island and is a leading cultural center of Japan.

Awe of the environment has been a major characteristic of the Japanese way of life. In early times, the sun, mountains, and the sea were especially important to the people of Japan. Standing on the summit of a mountain, they experienced the glow of the sun as it rose from the Pacific Ocean. They expressed their love of the land in poetry, in prose, and in painting—a tradition still carried on by the Japanese today.

Source: Morton Wesley Huber. *Vanishing Japan.* Morton Wesley Huber with permission of AMPHOTO, 1965.

SECTION 1

The Beginning

The first mention of Japan in written history was in a dynastic history of China compiled about 297 AD. The Chinese did not think that the people of the land they called Wa were especially important, except for trade and occasional military threat. In their history, the Chinese wrote the following about their "barbarian" neighbors:

The people of Wa . . . dwell in the middle of the ocean on the mountainous islands southeast of . . . Tai-fang. . . . Today, thirty of their communities maintain [communication] with us through envoys and scribes. . . .

The land of Wa is warm and mild. In winter as in summer the people live on raw vegetables and go about barefooted. They have (or live in) houses; father and mother, elder and younger, sleep separately. They smear their bodies with pink and scarlet. . . . They serve food on bamboo and wooden trays, helping themselves with their fingers. . . .

. . . In their meetings and in their deportment, there is no distinction between father and son or between men and women. . . . There are class distinctions among the people, and some men are vassals of others. Taxes are collected. There are granaries as well as markets in each province, where necessaries are exchanged under the supervision of the Wa officials.

The people of Wa did not agree fully with the Chinese view. They felt they were equal—and perhaps even superior—to the Chinese. Despite the strong Chinese influence on their lives, the people of Wa continued to develop their own way of life. They displayed an unusual ability to adapt other ways of life to their particular environment.

EXAMINING PHOTOGRAPHS *Hokkaido and Akan Lake, shown here, reflect the ancient description of Japan as a land of mountainous islands. What special ability did the early Japanese display?*

SECTION 1 REVIEW

CHECKING FOR UNDERSTANDING
1. **State** how the Chinese felt about the people of Wa.

CRITICAL THINKING
2. **Analyzing Information** What were several features of life in Wa?

SECTION 2

Mountains

One important aspect of Japan's environment is mountains. Almost 70 percent of the landscape is covered by rugged mountain ranges and steep hills. The mountains,

Source: Sources of Japanese Tradition, Ryusaku Tsunoda, William Theodore de Bary, and Donald Keene (eds.), 1958, © Columbia University Press, New York. Reprinted by permission from the publisher.

EXAMINING PHOTOGRAPHS *On their way to the summit of Mount Fuji, summer hikers climb along a steep trail over loose lava ash. Located on Honshu, about 60 miles (97 kilometers) west of Tokyo, Fuji, which rises to 12,388 feet (3776 meters), is Japan's highest mountain and one of the world's most perfect volcanic cones. Why is Fuji considered an inactive volcano?*

which are divided by rocky gorges and narrow valleys, have thick forests on their lower slopes. Flowing through them are swift, shallow rivers and thundering waterfalls.

The Japanese archipelago itself is the upper part of a great mountain range rising 20,000 to 30,000 feet (6000 to 9000 meters) from the floor of the Pacific Ocean. The archipelago lies on the Pacific's "rim of fire," where the earth's crust is not stable and is shifting constantly. As a result, earthquakes and volcanic eruptions are common.

Of the more than 190 volcanoes in Japan, one of the most famous is Mount Fuji. Most Japanese consider Fuji a sacred symbol of their country. Since Fuji has not erupted since 1707, it is considered an inactive volcano. Every July and August, some 300,000 Japanese climb to the top of Fuji.

Mountain climbing is popular throughout Japan and is undertaken in all seasons. Many climb the Japan Alps, which include all of the country's highest peaks except Mount Fuji. Below, visitors describe their initial impressions of a climb they made in September:

A typhoon had passed over the Japan Alps the day before, and its boisterous afterwinds jostled and taunted us as we climbed the flank of Tateyama (9892 feet) [2967.6 meters]. Thick clouds boiled around our booted feet. A sheet of cold rain streamed over the ridge, twisting and flapping like laundry pinned to a line.

With gruff impatience . . . , the wind picked up our guide, a . . . young fellow named Hidehiko Noguchi, and blew him against a large rock. The same gust filled my rain jacket like a sail and knocked me down. . . .

Invigorated by the stinging rain and buffeted by the gale, we pushed on and arrived at the crest of the ridge. Suddenly the clouds were parted by fingers of sunlight. Beyond the ridge lay the silvery Sea of Japan. In every other direction the jagged peaks of the Japan Alps soared as high as 10,000 feet [3048 meters]: Yari— "spear," Tsurugi—"sword," Yatsu—"eight peaks."

In early September some of these summits were already dusted with snow. . . . [all] were touched by the tantalizing mystery of mountains we had yet to climb. In the weeks ahead, we would stand on many of these summits. For now, though, we were content with what we had found on our very first climb—the serenity and beauty of a unique region of Japan, a place so little known to the outside world that we would encounter . . . Japanese who had never before met a foreigner. . . .

Why "Alps"? In Tokyo, before we set out for the mountains, Dr. Yasuo Sasa, president of the Japanese Alpine Club, explained how these mountains, which are so bound up with the Japanese spirit, happen to bear such an un-Japanese name.

"We Japanese always revered our high mountains and made pilgrimages to them," said Dr. Sasa, "but it had never occurred to our ancestors to climb them for sport. Then, in the latter part of the 19th century, English climbers saw them for the first time. The meadows and crags, the wildflowers and highland animals of our mountains reminded them of the European Alps—and so they got their name. . . ."

On almost every high summit, pilgrims have built a shrine. Here, it is traditional to leave a five-yen coin, called a *goen,* a word that also means "bond" or "close relationship" and implies that he who leaves the offering will remember the place and be remembered by it—and, with luck, return.

At the summit of Tateyama's Oyama peak, on a shaft of rock not much larger at the tip than a dining-room table, stands a famous shrine. Thousands of small flat stones form the pavement of its tiny courtyard; on each pebble, a pilgrim has written, with ink and brush, his name and the date on which he visited the summit.

SECTION 2 REVIEW

CHECKING FOR UNDERSTANDING
1. **Discuss** how the Japanese regard Mount Fuji.

CRITICAL THINKING
2. **Identifying Central Issues** Why do you think mountainous areas are an important aspect of the environment of Japan?

Source: Charles McCarry, "The Japan Alps" in *National Geographic,* August, 1984, pp. 240, 242.

SECTION 3
The Sea

Just as important to the Japanese as the mountains is the sea. The sea plays a vital role in Japan's climate, which ranges from warm subtropical in the southernmost islands to cool in the north. Northern Japan is influenced by the very cold Oyashio Current and southern Japan by the warm, dark-blue Japan Current. Hokkaido has a continental climate with warm summers and cold winters. Northern Honshu, on the other hand, is more temperate. Southern Honshu and the other two major islands have a subtropical climate. **Monsoons,** or seasonal winds, blowing across the seas also influence the climate of Japan. They bring rain in summer and, in the north, snow in winter. Each year, **typhoons,** severe tropical hurricanes, strike the country.

The sea is important to the Japanese for business and commerce as well as for its effect on the climate. Because Japan has limited natural resources, the people must depend on sea trade. They import most of their raw materials for manufacturing and then send the finished goods to other countries. The Japanese also rely on the sea for food. Japan has one of the largest fishing fleets in the world, contributing about 15 percent of the world's catch.

No part of Japan is more than 70 miles (112 kilometers) from a seacoast. The Pacific Ocean lies to the east and south of Japan. The Sea of Japan washes the western coast .

The Japanese coastline, which totals more than 17,000 miles (27,200 kilometers), is rough, craggy, and highly irregular. All along it are capes, headlands, peninsulas, islands, and bays. Many of the bays offer good harbors and ports, through which pass the country's vital sea trade.

EXAMINING PHOTOGRAPHS *Off the northernmost tip of Hokkaido lies Rebun Island, whose terrain is typical of much of the rugged natural beauty of coastal Japan. This photo, taken in spring, shows the island's steep grassy hills, which rise above narrow plains and scenic bays. What is the greatest distance one would need to travel in Japan to reach a seacoast?*

One of the most famous seacoast areas is in southern Japan along the Inland Sea, which separates Honshu and Shikoku. Below, a passenger on a boat describes the calm and gentle appearance of the thousands of small islands which dot the Inland Sea:

A typical island of the Inland Sea, as you pass in the boat, consists of: a village clustered on the beach, one road along the shore, others—alleys—running back to the hills then stopping, sometimes a wide road going over the mountains to the other side, sometimes a sea road continuing around the island. Then, in the middle, as seen from the water, near the shore a temple in a grove, often the only grove on the island, or a stone torii, a shady walk, a shrine in the shade. Near it the largest building, the general store; on either side of it black houses, roofs of cemented gray tile—black and white, salt and pepper. Then the yellow or green iron-roofed ticket-house and, much farther away, a red torii for the fishermen, for the goddess. And then—on a spit—the graveyard, the gravestones high, rectangular, like teeth. Then seaweed racks, an

overturned boat or two, and the island slides down and back into the sea it came from.

In direct contrast to the islands of the Inland Sea is the wild, untamed, and unspoiled coastal area in the northern part of Hokkaido. Below, a voyager gives her impressions of Hokkaido's Shiretoko Peninsula:

The early boat left at 5:30 AM, just as a catch of flounder was being unloaded at the fishermen's cooperative. The sun soon warmed the damp air and the scent of resin from the thickly forested hills and mountains beyond came drifting out to sea where it mingled with the smell of the tide. . . .

. . . Nakamura [the guide] pointed to the shore, where strips of level ground at the water line afforded space for a few scattered huts. The huts, he told me, are used by fishermen . . . in the short summer season when the harvest of giant kelp, *konbu*, is on. *Konbu* is a sort of sea vegetable with thick, wide leaves—dark green in its natural state, but almost black

Source: Donald Richie. *The Inland Sea.* Weatherhill, 1971, p. 134.

and stiff as leather when it is dried and cut into sheets. It is an important ingredient in many Japanese recipes and is a basic element in soup stock.

I marveled at the vegetation. The hills were bright with . . . flowering plants. To think that this rugged horn-shaped peninsula—surrounded by ice floes all winter—could burst into such bloom come spring! . . .

Nakamura was looking forward to the coming season: "A few more months, and we'll be out there at the huts. We work all day, everybody together, gathering and drying—we dry it here, even though the sun isn't too hot, and the air isn't too dry—and at night everybody drinks by lantern light. At other times of the year, there's not a soul around that place.". . .

Finally, the cliffs of the northwest coast loomed into sight, rising to heights of two hundred meters [660 feet] and extending unbroken for ten-kilometer [6 miles] stretches, relenting only occasionally. . . . These cliffs, with their black and white horizontal stripes, are a striking phenomenon: molten lava spread in sills through fossil-rich, sedimentary rock while the mass was still submerged; then volcanic activity beneath the ocean floor pushed the whole out of the sea, creating these massive cliffs.

Volcanic activity was not, however, the only force involved in the creation of these cliffs. The wind and sea have shaved them into fantastic shapes. . . . The Ainu, as well as the Japanese, have given names to some: Penguin-no-hana (Penguin's Nose), Shishi-iwa (Lion Rock), Tako-iwa (Octopus Rock). . . . It is a sea-bird's paradise. . . . Narrow rivers, whose sources are in the mountains sixteen hundred meters (5280 feet) up above, fall in cascades of white over the dark cliffs. In winter they freeze solid. Foliage tops the cliffs, and beyond them rise the Shiretoko range.

Source: From *NATIONAL PARKS OF JAPAN* by Dorothy Britton and Mary Sutherland. Published by Kodansha International, Ltd. Copyright © 1981. Reprinted by permission. All rights reserved.

SECTION 3 REVIEW

CHECKING FOR UNDERSTANDING
1. **Define** monsoon, typhoon.

CRITICAL THINKING
2. **Making Generalizations** Why do you think the sea is important to the Japanese?

SECTION 4

The Plains

Narrowly squeezed between the seacoast and the base of the mountains are the plains areas of Japan. Although they make up only one-eighth of the total land area, most of the 124 million Japanese live on them.

The plains have profoundly shaped Japanese culture. Living in such small crowded areas has led the Japanese to develop an elaborate system of etiquette, or manners, to make human relationships easier to manage. The influence also can be seen in other areas. Japanese gardeners, for example, have become known for their skill in reproducing nature on a small scale. They often arrange miniature gardens and grow **bonsai**, or dwarfed trees. In the passage that follows, the meaning that bonsai holds for the Japanese is described:

Through bonsai, the city dweller, who daily sees concrete and steel, can have a bit of greenery to himself. Though enclosed by four walls, he can escape in his imagination into a natural world that exists in his little trees. For a few minutes, walls can be made to vanish, an inch-high mound of moss can become a green meadow, a small rock a mountainside, a few seedlings an entire forest. This is the magic of bonsai.

Source: Sunset Editorial Staff. *Bonsai: Culture and Care of Miniature Trees.* Lane Books, 1971, pp. 5–6.

Japan

EARTHQUAKES IN JAPAN

Among the most striking of Japan's natural phenomena are earthquakes. The archipelago has about 1500 a year. In most cases, they are minor and cause little damage. But every few years, severe earthquakes occur, causing loss of life and property. Great waves called *tsunami*, set off by vibrations of the earth, are particularly destructive, creating much damage along Japan's Pacific coast.

One of the worst earthquakes occurred in 1923 in the Tokyo area. Whole villages were buried, many city buildings were destroyed, and close to 100,000 people died. Midori Yamanouchi, a survivor, tells what it was like:

I was a girl living on the outskirts of Tokyo. . . . My best friend and I had just learned to sew new-style Western dresses for our dolls instead of old-style Japanese kimonos, and I had gone to her house to show her a doll's hat I had just made.

Suddenly her garden fence fell over. Then the dishes in the kitchen crashed to the floor, and the grandfather clock tipped over onto the floor right next to where we were sitting. We ran outside, and as the shaking stopped a little, I started home.

All around, the bamboo was trembling and rustling. I was afraid. Bamboo is supposed to be a safe place during an earthquake because its roots twine together so tight that the earth can't split open beneath you and the trees can't fall on you. But it was shaking so much I wasn't sure. When I got to our house, I found all the neighbors in our backyard because we had the best bamboo grove anywhere around. Everybody stayed right there from noon, when the earthquake began, until almost midnight.

All afternoon we watched black smoke billow up from the city, and when night came we saw the sky glow red. Someone said that a new volcano had erupted in downtown Tokyo, but later we learned that the smoke and red glow came from fires. People were cooking lunch when the earthquake started, and they ran outside without thinking to turn off the gas or put out the charcoal. Kitchens caught fire, and from them, whole houses. Soon the city was flaming. Waterpipes broke so the firemen couldn't do much.

My mother carried our brazier outside the house and started cooking rice enough to last for days and days. She said that it would be a long time before everything would be normal again, and she was right. Twelve relatives came to live with us because their homes were ruined, and the whole neighborhood used our well for a week. It was the deepest one around, and everyone was afraid that water from shallow wells might be unsafe to drink until we could clean up the debris. . . .

DRAWING CONCLUSIONS

1. What impact have earthquakes had on Japan?
2. Do you think you would react as calmly as Midori did? What would you do?

Source: Hermann Schreiber. "The Tremor Next Time," in *Geo,* July 1981, Vol. 3, Knapp Communications Corporation, pp. 127–29.

The plains areas are important for other reasons as well. The country's major industries, most of its important cities, and its best farmland are on the plains. For this reason, the plains support not only a great number of people but also a wide variety of lifestyles.

URBAN LIFE

Seventy-seven percent of Japanese live in urban areas that in appearance closely resemble similar areas in Western cities. The difference is that in Japan the past remains very much a part of urban life. Along the narrow side streets of most cities are small shops that sell such traditional items as straw mats and elaborately dressed Japanese dolls. Parks, gardens, and religious shrines also are found close to the modern districts.

Since World War II, Japanese cities have grown tremendously because of the large numbers of people who have migrated from rural to urban areas. As a result, like cities in many other parts of the world, cities in Japan are faced with such problems as overcrowding, housing shortages, and pollution. At the same time, however, the crime rate in Japanese cities is lower than that of many cities in the United States. Although there are poor neighborhoods, there are few slums.

More than one-third of the urban population live in four metropolitan areas located on the plains of Honshu—Tokyo, Yokohama, Osaka, and Nagoya. The largest of these is the capital city of Tokyo, which is made up of a number of districts, cities, localities, and villages. Below, a journalist discusses modern-day Tokyo:

Over the past century, Japan has developed Tokyo into a huge metropolis out of the design to create a centralized society," says Hisatake Togo, managing director of the Tokyo Institute for Municipal Research.

By concentrating much of the nation's industry, finance, culture, higher educa-tion, trade, science, media, and political authority in one city, Japan has not only been able to catch up with the West, but Tokyo is now poised to become the global manager of new "knowledge-based" industries, guiding new technologies and world finance.

"Tokyo has already become a post-industrial society," says Kiyoji Murata, a Chuo University economics professor.

With its cozy triangle of business, bureaucrats, and politicians, Tokyo serves as the mother of all Japanese industry. About two-thirds of Japan's "information" workers and its big corporate headquarters are located in the city.

Tokyo is home to 34 percent of the nation's university students, 40 percent of its bank loans, and 93 percent of its research institutes. With only 3.6 percent of the nation's land, Tokyo commands 20 percent of Japan's gross national product.

Its city budget exceeds China's, even though the population of Tokyo proper is only 11.85 million. One quarter of Japan's 123 million people live within 35 miles of the emperor's palace.

"Such concentration has done much for Japan," says Akio Maekawa, the city's deputy planner. "But we are afraid that it might start to weaken our country. Tokyo is too big in the economy and is creating big gaps in income."

Since 1980, government has made various efforts to disperse business from central Tokyo and into seven urban "subcenters" and eight satellite cities.

But these efforts have only acted like "a cup saucer," says Dr. Togo, drawing in more business and helping to boost land prices to the highest in the world. Building one mile of road in Tokyo costs about $300 million, with 94 percent of that going just to buy land.

Polls show most Tokyoites are satisfied with their city life—until the topics of housing and transport are raised. . . .

On paper, Tokyoites have the highest

Crowded with tall office buildings, busy streets, and freeways, Tokyo is one of the largest cities in the world. In addition to its reputation as a world leader in business and industry, Tokyo is also recognized for its art galleries, museums, concert halls, and other cultural attractions. What are some major characteristics of life in Tokyo?

average yearly incomes in the world . . . , but have mediocre living standards, according to the government. As one example, 12 percent of homes in the city are not connected to sewer lines. And the city will run out of garbage dump sites in 1995. Its electricity and water capacities are often stretched.

Despite Tokyo's reputation as an urban paradise because of its safety, cleanliness, and efficiency, the maladies of a rich nation's megalopolis are all too real to the people living in it.

Skyrocketing housing costs have pushed people to live farther and farther away. Condominiums cost 10 times an average annual salary, according to the Urban Development Association.

"It's pretty well impossible for young people to get married and buy a house in Tokyo," says Michiro Okuda, a sociologist at Rikkyo University.

Average commuting time has risen to 45 minutes each way, compared to 25 minutes in Osaka. Many workers commute several hours a day, sapping their productivity, family life, and in the crush of human bodies, their humanity.

An estimated 20,000 commuters take the bullet train every day, traveling hundreds of miles at high speed and great expense. Trains and subways carry twice the planned capacity. . . .

The demographic shape of Tokyo resembles a doughnut as high property prices have pushed more residents to the outskirts, drying up inner neighborhoods in what is called a "decentralized concentration." By day, the downtown population is 2.5 million, but at night it drops to one-eighth of that.

Many city politicians worry that they have lost more than one-quarter of their voters. Last March, Japan's oldest primary school had to close its doors in the city because it had only 57 pupils. . . .

Source: Clayton Jones. "Tokyo: 'World's First Technopolis'" in *The Christian Science Monitor,* November 20, 1991, p. 10. Reprinted by permission from THE CHRISTIAN SCIENCE MONITOR © 1991 The Christian Science Publishing Society. All rights reserved.

EXAMINING PHOTOGRAPHS *In Japan, most tea is grown in Shizuoka and Uji, outside the city of Kyoto. Tea-drinking, introduced to Japan from China in the 1100's AD, has become an important Japanese tradition. Besides tea, what other important crops are grown in the Japanese countryside?*

RURAL LIFE

For hundreds of years, Japan was largely a rural society. But today only about 23 percent of the Japanese people live in the countryside. Most are farmers and their families who grow rice, wheat, fruit, vegetables, tobacco, and tea. Most own their own land and, because of the use of chemical fertilizers and advanced agricultural methods, produce high crop yields.

Although generally these rural dwellers earn less than city dwellers, their standard of living has improved in recent years. Most have a small house, a color-television set, and modern kitchen appliances. Many have cars. Below, rural life is described by an American journalist who traveled through the countryside with a Japanese friend from the city:

The train chugged upcountry, passing through hot-spring villages. . . . The railroad paralleled the Himekawa, a river that seemed to flow granite, so stony and gray it was. . . .

At last the incline leveled to a high flatness split by the Azusa River and surrounded by the mountains called the roof of Japan. Even at this elevation, rice fields lay in all directions. . . .

At Misato, a farm village . . . , we left the railroad and headed west up into the foothills, where we took a room at a mountain inn. . . . We were the last to sit down at the long tables already laid with the meal. . . .

We drank Kirin beer, but the farmers . . . drank sake [Japanese liquor made from fermented rice] from bottles the size of a short boy. They drew the corks with their teeth and looked down the slopes onto their fields with satisfaction. But they speculated, too, about weather and the harvest. Bound tightly around their temples were *hachimaki,* small towels to absorb sweat and aid concentration. . . .

From our room, Tadashi and I watched dusk come down the valley to conceal smoke from burning rice straw of last year and only then to reveal the orange fires. . . .

All night long the birds struck their calls against the dark. Toward dawn the cuckoos got into it with their ceaseless two notes, then a rooster, and finally the chirping small ones. . . .

Michisada-san was waiting in the big hot communal bath, and we soaked together with a grower of mulberry leaves and watched through a somewhat steamy window the fertile plain. . . .

Instead of the road, Tadashi and I followed the shortcut under the big pines into the valley orchards and vineyards. The rocky soil was fertile once it got water, so, although too far above the river here for paddyfields, it produced fruit, melons, and chestnuts through a computer-controlled sprinkler system. Down the dusty road until we reached a farmhouse. Tadashi knew the son and his bride.

The Misawa family had lived in Nagano, which means long field, for a thousand years, most of the time as rice growers. After the war, . . . Daimaru Misawa bought land inexpensively on the dry slope. He cleared mountain pine and, with other villagers, put in a cooperative irrigation system. In the '50s he built a home, then a larger one ten years ago. His 4.4-acre [1.8-hectare] farm is about twice the average acreage here, and his grapes, apples, peaches and melons have done well. The eldest son, Isamu, has just installed a new, promising method for improving grape production with vinyl tents. . . .

To welcome us, the women, Michiko and Fuyuko, served barley tea, buns stuffed with pigweed, pickles, garden strawberries, and grape juice from the vineyards. . . .

The family returned to stripping fruit. From a branch carrying six olive-size young peaches, the women plucked all but the largest so that it might grow to its maximum. This attention to each fruit gave them a good living.

Tadashi and I hiked down lanes lined with mugwort [an herb] smelling like sage, through a bamboo thicket, into a blossoming locust grove, on past rice fields and small houses. The oldest houses had thatched roofs caked with moss, while the newer had synthetic tiles and solar panels. "Japan," Tadashi said, "is always a mixture."

By each home was a garden of leeks, bottle gourds, eggplants, cucumbers, cabbages, tomatoes. Along the lanes ran yew hedges and irrigation troughs rushing a swift, cold water, which sometimes carried clover blossoms that children had tossed in a mile away. Shadows from the wings of circling black kites [birds] sent pigs squealing, and wind from a dark mountain storm set scarecrows to flapping.

Often out of a paddyfield, muddy prints from bare feet walked bodiless up the road to the next plot. . . . Occasionally, unexpected, dark rice-field birds rose screeching into the air. . . .

Walking, I began to notice carved stones along the lanes. Dozens of them there were: at crossroads, above fields, at boundaries. Although each white granite rock was unique, every one showed two relief figures cut into a naturally smoothed stone about three feet [.91 meters] high. "*Dosojin*," Tadashi said. "Shinto roadside god. . . ."

On the route back to the farm, Tadashi and I came to a crossroads *Dosojin* carved with compass directions. Most potently of all Japanese symbols, these wayside stones reveal how life is a journey wherein the traveler sees that it is the earth itself on which paths cross and from which journeys proceed toward union with otherness. "*Dosojin* shows us the way," Tadashi said.

SECTION 4 REVIEW

CHECKING FOR UNDERSTANDING

1. **Define** bonsai, *tsunami*.
2. **List** the cities in which one-third of Japan's population live.

CRITICAL THINKING

3. **Making Comparisons** How do urban and rural life in Japan compare?

Geography

THE PHYSICAL AND HUMAN GEOGRAPHY OF JAPAN

FOCUSING ON THE ISSUE Based on the information in the four maps, decide whether each of the following statements about Japan is true or false. Give reasons for your choices.

1. The island of Hokkaido has a subtropical climate.
2. Japan's largest cities are on Kyushu.
3. Japan consists of four major islands.
4. Japan has few natural resources.
5. The greatest number of Japanese live on the island of Honshu.
6. The Japan Current brings cold moist air to Japan.
7. Most of Japan is covered by mountains.
8. Japan's closest neighbor on the Asian mainland is China.
9. Japan receives little rain in the late summer and early fall.
10. Shikoku is the largest of all the Japanese islands.

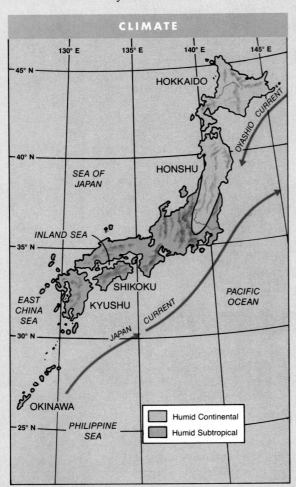

CLIMATE

SEA OF JAPAN

HOKKAIDO

OYASHIO CURRENT

HONSHU

INLAND SEA

SHIKOKU

EAST CHINA SEA

KYUSHU

JAPAN CURRENT

PACIFIC OCEAN

OKINAWA

PHILIPPINE SEA

Humid Continental
Humid Subtropical

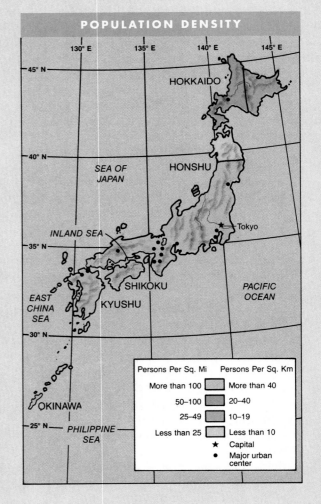

POPULATION DENSITY

SEA OF JAPAN

HOKKAIDO

HONSHU

INLAND SEA

Tokyo

SHIKOKU

EAST CHINA SEA

KYUSHU

PACIFIC OCEAN

OKINAWA

PHILIPPINE SEA

Persons Per Sq. Mi	Persons Per Sq. Km
More than 100	More than 40
50–100	20–40
25–49	10–19
Less than 25	Less than 10
★ Capital	
● Major urban center	

Name	Percent of Labor Force in Agriculture	Rural/Urban Population	Area in Square Miles	Population/Natural Increase
Japan	11	24/76	143,749	122,200,000 (0.6%)
China	74	71/29	3,705,390	1,062,000,000 (1.3%)
Taiwan	20	33/67	12,456	19,600,000 (1.2%)

Based on the information in the chart, write a paragraph comparing Japan with China and Taiwan.

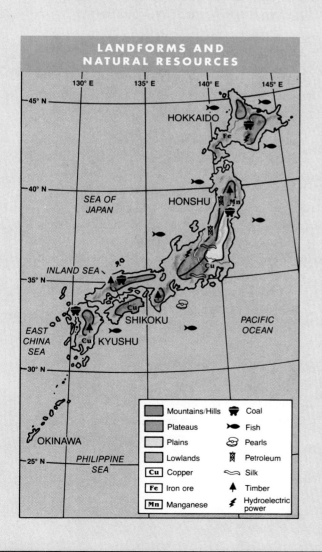

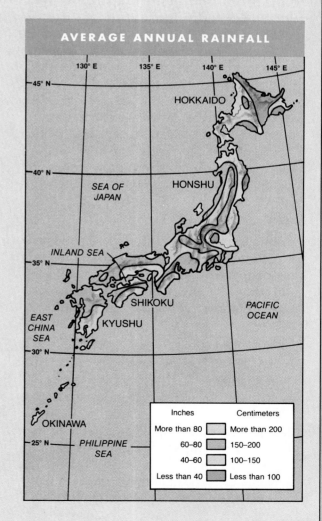

Chapter 15 Review

SUMMARY

The Japanese archipelago, off the coast of East Asia, is made up of four major islands and thousands of smaller ones. A long, irregular seacoast has given the Japanese a close relationship with the sea, on which they depend for food and trade.

Nearly 70 percent of Japan's landscape is covered by mountains. Because of its location on the Pacific "rim of fire," Japan often has earthquakes and volcanic eruptions. Between the seacoast and the mountains lie the plains areas, where most Japanese live and where the major industries, most important cities, and best farmland are found.

About 77 percent of the Japanese people live in urban areas. Japanese urban life is modern but has close ties to the past. About 23 percent of the Japanese live in rural areas. Most are farm families who own their own land and are very productive.

USING VOCABULARY

Using the following terms, write a paragraph describing Japan's environment and its impact on the Japanese.

myth	monsoon	bonsai
archipelago	typhoon	*tsunami*

REVIEWING FACTS

1. **List** the four major islands of the Japanese archipelago.
2. **State** the characteristics of Japan's mountainous areas.
3. **Explain** how the Japan Alps get their name.
4. **Discuss** the impact of ocean currents on Japan's climate.
5. **Name** the type of climate found in the southern part of the island of Honshu.

6. **Explain** why the Japanese economy is so dependent on sea trade.
7. **Specify** how the plains areas have shaped Japanese life and culture.
8. **Explain** how Japanese farms are organized.
9. **Name** the four metropolitan areas located on the plains of Honshu.
10. **State** how Japanese cities often differ from those in Western countries.

CRITICAL THINKING

1. **Identifying Alternatives** In what ways do you think Japan's geographical location has been both an advantage and a disadvantage?
2. **Making Comparisons** How do traditional Japanese attitudes toward nature differ from the traditional attitudes of the West? Which viewpoint do you prefer? Why?
3. **Drawing Conclusions** Despite their ruggedness, how might Japan's mountains benefit the national economy?
4. **Identifying Central Issues** In the final reading of the chapter, Tadashi states, "Japan is always a mixture." How does this describe both urban and rural life in modern Japan?

ANALYZING CONCEPTS

1. **Environment** What are the major characteristics of the coastline of Japan?
2. **Scarcity** How has scarcity of usable land affected Japan's population distribution?

GEOGRAPHIC THEMES

Region Why is Japan considered a part of the Pacific area's "rim of fire"?

Reading a Climate Map

Climate is the overall pattern of weather in a given region. It is defined by two main factors: *temperature* (hot or cold) and *precipitation* (wet or dry). Combinations of these factors produce many kinds of climates. Below is a list of seven major types of climates:

1. *Tropical rain forest*—hot and wet all year
2. *Tropical desert*—hot and dry
3. *Steppe*—semiarid, can be hot or cold
4. *Subtropical*—hot summers, mild winters, can be dry or humid
5. *Continental*—warm summers, cold winters, can be dry or humid
6. *Subarctic*—cold winters, cool summers
7. *Polar*—cold and dry all year

What causes one place to have a different climate than another? Several factors create climatic variations. The temperature of a region is largely determined by latitude. Regions nearer to the Equator will be warmer than those nearer to the Poles. However, not all regions at the same latitude have identical climates. The climate of coastal areas is strongly affected by ocean currents. These regions may be warmed by tropical currents or cooled by polar currents. Elevation also affects temperature and moisture. Higher elevations are cooler than lower ones.

Climate maps illustrate differences in precipitation, temperature, or both. Here are steps to follow in reading a climate map:
- Read the title to identify the climatic factors shown on the map.
- Read all the text and labels on the map.
- Study the legend to identify the specific meaning of the symbols on the map.
- Use the symbols in the legend to interpret the information on the map.

EXAMPLE

Look at the climate map of Japan on page 248. Read all the labels and study the map key. Notice that the major islands of Japan are labeled as well as the bodies of water surrounding them. What two ocean currents appear on the map? *(Japan Current, Oyashio Current)* Notice that Japan stretches from 46°N to 26°N. How do you think that might affect its climate? *(Northern sections may be cooler than southern sections.)* The map key shows two kinds of climate—humid continental and humid subtropical. Why do you think all of Japan has a humid climate? *(It is surrounded by water.)* Which islands have a continental climate? *(Hokkaido and part of Honshu)* What factors produce the cooler climate in northern Japan? *(cold ocean current from the north, farther from Equator)*

PRACTICE

Study the map "Average Annual Rainfall" on page 249 and answer the questions below:

1. What do the colors in the map key represent?
2. What color is used to show annual rainfall amounts of 150–200 centimeters?
3. What does the color brown represent?
4. Does it rain more on Shikoku or Hokkaido?
5. How much rain usually falls on Okinawa?
6. Which is the driest island?
7. How much rain falls on Kyushu each year?
8. Which island has the greatest variation in rainfall amounts? Explain why.

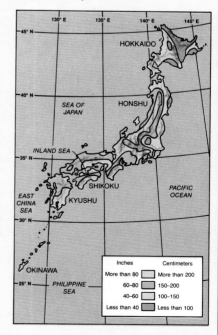

Inches	Centimeters
More than 80	More than 200
60–80	150–200
40–60	100–150
Less than 40	Less than 100

**People and Places
to Know**
Shōtoku Taishi, Kotoku,
the Fujiwaras, Minamoto
Yoritomo, Tokugawa
Ieyasu, Matthew Perry

Key Terms to Define
clan, *shogun,* shogunate,
bakufu, daimyo, samurai

Objectives to Learn

1. **Specify** Chinese
   influences on early
   Japan.
2. **Trace** the political and
   social development of
   early Japan.
3. **Summarize** traditional
   Japan's relations with
   the West.

*Model of Samurai
warrior in full
regalia*

Traditional Japan

> After living in Japan for a while, Izanagi and Izanami returned to heaven. There they created many other gods and goddesses, including a sun-goddess called Amaterasu and a storm-god called Susanowo.
>
> Amaterasu was a gentle, lovely goddess. She gave life to everything around her. But Susanowo was wild and fierce. He stormed around causing trouble.
>
> One day Susanowo visited Amaterasu. He behaved so badly that she hid in a cave. The other gods and goddesses had to play a trick with a mirror to get her back out.
>
> Another day Susanowo killed an eight-headed dragon who was about to eat a young girl. In the dragon's tail he found a sword. Susanowo gave the sword to Amaterasu to make up for his bad behavior. Then he married the girl he had saved.
>
> Susanowo and his wife had many children. But none of them was good enough to rule Japan. So Amaterasu sent her grandson, Ninigi, to rule. She gave him three [items] to take with him. One was the mirror that had brought her from the cave. The second was jewel[s] from inside the cave. And the third was [a] sword from the dragon's tail.
>
> "Use these to rule Japan," said Amaterasu. "You and your descendants will rule forever."
>
> Ninigi married and had three sons. One of them, Hoori, married the daughter of the sea-god. They had one son, who married and had four children. And one of those children was Jimmu Tenno, the great-great-great-grandson of the sun goddess and the first human emperor of Japan.

This legend describes what the people of traditional Japan, Japan before 1868, believed about the beginnings of the Japanese monarchy. Like most legends, it has its basis in fact. For example, although the origins of the three items described in the legend are unknown, the items known as the Regalia probably did exist. A replica of the mirror is housed in a palace shrine. Replicas of the sword and the jewels are in the Imperial

Source: Carol Greene. *Enchantment of the World.* Children's Press, 1983, pp. 51–52.

Palace in Tokyo. The Regalia symbolize Japan's imperial family, one of the oldest royal families in the world.

Historians trace the origins of Japanese royalty to the 500's AD, a period when history began to be recorded in Japan. At that time, the country was controlled by warring **clans**, or groups based on family ties and headed by a chief. Before long, the Yamato clan emerged as the most powerful and extended its rule over most of the country. Its leaders later became emperors of Japan.

An Emerging Civilization

The Japanese monarchy helped unite the country. At the same time, its military exploits helped bring the Japanese into contact with other peoples on the Asian mainland. One of these peoples was the Chinese, who had the most advanced civilization in East Asia at the time. The Japanese soon developed close ties with the Chinese. In time, they modeled their society on the Chinese way of life. They also borrowed the Chinese system of writing and accepted the Buddhist religion brought by Chinese missionaries.

SHŌTOKU'S CONSTITUTION

About 587 AD, Empress Suiko and her adviser, Prince Shōtoku, encouraged the Japanese to accept Chinese political ideas. They believed that by adopting the Chinese system of imperial rule they could increase the power of the dynasty. In order to do so, the Confucian values of orderly society and obedience to authority were especially stressed.

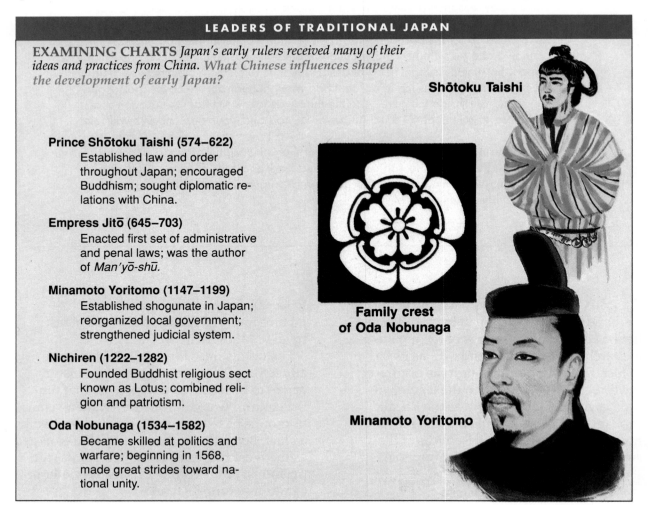

LEADERS OF TRADITIONAL JAPAN

EXAMINING CHARTS *Japan's early rulers received many of their ideas and practices from China. What Chinese influences shaped the development of early Japan?*

Prince Shōtoku Taishi (574–622)
Established law and order throughout Japan; encouraged Buddhism; sought diplomatic relations with China.

Empress Jitō (645–703)
Enacted first set of administrative and penal laws; was the author of *Man'yō-shū*.

Minamoto Yoritomo (1147–1199)
Established shogunate in Japan; reorganized local government; strengthened judicial system.

Nichiren (1222–1282)
Founded Buddhist religious sect known as Lotus; combined religion and patriotism.

Oda Nobunaga (1534–1582)
Became skilled at politics and warfare; beginning in 1568, made great strides toward national unity.

Shōtoku Taishi

Family crest of Oda Nobunaga

Minamoto Yoritomo

This can be seen below in an excerpt from Shōtoku's constitution:

Harmony is to be valued, and an avoidance of . . . opposition to be honored. All men are influenced by [self-interest], and there are few who are intelligent. Hence there are some who disobey their lords and fathers, or who maintain feuds with the neighboring villages. But when those above are harmonious and those below are friendly, and there is [agreement] in the discussion of business, right views of things spontaneously gain acceptance. Then what is there which cannot be accomplished? . . .

. . . When you receive the imperial commands, fail not . . . to obey them. The lord is Heaven, the vassal is Earth. Heaven overspreads, and Earth upbears. When this is so, the four seasons follow their due course, and the powers of Nature obtain their [fulfillment]. If the Earth attempted to overspread, Heaven would simply fall in ruin. Therefore is it that when the lord speaks, the vassal listens; when the superior acts, the inferior yields. . . .

. . . The ministers and [civil servants] should make [proper] behavior their leading principle, for the leading principle of the government of the people consists in [proper] behavior. If the superiors do not behave [properly], the inferiors are disorderly: if the inferiors are wanting in proper behavior, there must necessarily be offenses. Therefore it is that when lord and vassal behave . . . [properly], the distinctions of rank are not confused; when the people behave . . . [properly], the government of the commonwealth [works properly].

TAIKA REFORMS

Almost 50 years later, another Japanese emperor, Kotoku, and his advisers began the

Source: Sources of Japanese Tradition. Ryusaku Tsunoda, William Theodore de Bary, and Donald Keene (eds.), 1958, © Columbia University Press, New York. Reprinted by permission of the publishers.

Taika, or "Great Change," reforms that introduced the Japanese to more features of the Chinese style of government. These included proclaiming the emperor ruler and landlord of all Japan, establishing a bureaucracy to carry out government duties, and putting into effect a central system of taxation and a land distribution program. The reforms divided the country into provinces, districts, and villages whose government was run by officials who reported to the emperor.

In 710, to provide a setting for the government, a capital city called Nara was built. With its broad streets and rows of wooden homes, palaces, and Buddhist temples, it soon became the political and religious center of Japan. The construction of Nara symbolized Japan's emergence as an important Asian civilization.

SECTION 1 REVIEW

CHECKING FOR UNDERSTANDING

1. **Indicate** the features of the Chinese style of government that the *Taika* reforms brought to Japan.

CRITICAL THINKING

2. **Identifying Central Issues** What effect do you think the *Taika* reforms had on the position of the emperor?

SECTION 2

The Heian Period

In the 790's, a new capital was built. Called Heian, later it was renamed Kyoto. This marked the beginning of Japan's Heian period, which lasted until the late 1100's. During this period, a powerful noble family named Fujiwara gained power over the emperor and his court.

EXAMINING ART *In this scene of court life in early Japan, three warriors, known as* samurai, *are eating main dishes of rice while a woman prepares to serve them a rice liquor known as* sake. *The robes worn by* samurai *were characterized by V-shaped necklines and signified the* samurai *position in society. By what was court life symbolized during the Heian period?*

Because the emperor and court officials had little political authority, they used their time to develop court ceremonies and to support the arts. Before long, court life was symbolized by elegance, manners, and love of natural beauty. Court officials and their wives wrote poems, stories, diaries, and essays. The selection below from a young woman's diary reveals the importance of the romantic and the artistic to members of the court:

On a very dark night . . . when sweet-voiced reciters were to read Sutras [Buddhist scriptures] throughout the night, another lady and I went out towards the entrance door of the audience room to listen to it, and after talking fell asleep, listening, leaning, . . . when I noticed a gentleman had come to be received in audience by the Princess. . . .

He spoke gently and quietly. . . . 'Who is the other lady?' he asked of my friend. He said nothing rude or amorous like other men, but talked delicately of the sad, sweet things of the world, and many a phrase of his with a strange power enticed me into conversation. He wondered that there should have been in the court one who was a stranger to him, and did not seem inclined to go away soon.

There was no starlight, and a gentle shower fell in the darkness; how lovely was its sound on the leaves! 'The more deeply beautiful is the night,' he said; 'the full moonlight would be too dazzling.' Discoursing about the beauties of spring and autumn he continued: 'Although every hour has its charm, pretty is the spring haze; then the sky being tranquil and overcast, the face of the moon is not too bright; it seems to be floating on a distant river. At such a time the calm spring melody of the lute is exquisite.

'In autumn, on the other hand, the moon is very bright; though there are mists trailing over the horizon we can see things as clearly as if they were at hand. The sound of wind, the voices of insects, all sweet things seem to melt together. . . .

'But the winter sky frozen all over magnificently cold! The snow covering the earth and its light mingling with the moonshine! Then the notes of the *hichiriki* [a pipe made of seven reeds] vibrate on the air and we forget spring and autumn.' And he asked us, 'Which captivates your fancy? On which stays your mind?'

My companion answered in favor of autumn and I, not being willing to imitate her, said:

Pale green night and flowers all melting into one in the soft haze—Everywhere the moon, glimmering in the spring night. So I replied. And he, after repeating my poem to himself over and over, said: 'Then you give up autumn? After this, as long as I live, such a spring night shall be for me a memento of your personality.'

Source: The Daughter of Takasue. *The Sarashina Diary* in *Anthology of Japanese Literature*. Donald Keene. George Allen & Unwin (Publishers) Ltd., 1968, pp. 151–152.

SECTION 2 REVIEW

CHECKING FOR UNDERSTANDING
1. **Identify** the actual rulers of Japan during the Heian period.

CRITICAL THINKING
2. **Making Generalizations** What were the major concerns of the emperor's court during the Heian period?

SECTION 3

The Shoguns

The rule of the Fujiwaras, who were opposed by several great clans, came to an end in 1185. A dispute had developed between two of the most powerful clans—the Taira and the Minamoto. These families fought for control of the imperial court at Kyoto. Minamoto Yoritomo, the leading member of the Minamoto family, gained support from warriors in the provinces, and in 1185, he and his forces fought and defeated the Taira in the naval battle of Dannoura. Below, a thirteenth-century Japanese writer gives his account of the event:

The forces of the Genji [Minamoto] went on increasing, while those of the Heike [Taira] grew less. The Genji had some three thousand ships, and the Heike one thousand, among which were some of Chinese build. . . .

Both sides set their faces against each other and fought grimly without a thought for their lives, neither giving an inch. But as the Heike had on their side an emperor endowed with . . . the Three Sacred Treasures of the Realm, things went hard with the Genji and their hearts were beginning to fail them, when suddenly something that they at first took for a cloud but soon made out to be a white banner floating in the breeze came drifting over the two fleets from the upper air, and finally settled on the stern of one of the Genji ships, hanging on by the rope.

When he saw this, Yoshitsune [Yoritomo's brother], regarding it as a sign from the [war god], removed his helmet and after washing his hands did [homage]; his

EXAMINING ART *Minamoto Yoritomo founded the line of feudal lords who ruled Japan for 700 years. Here, he is dressed in the* sokutai *costume, worn only by high officials.* **Who did Yoritomo defeat in 1185?**

EXAMINING ART *The lives of many peasants improved under Tokugawa rule. Using fertilizers and new farm tools, peasants doubled the amount of rice planted and reduced by 20 percent the labor needed to harvest it.* Why did the *Tokugawa* shoguns divide the people into rigid classes?

men all followed his example. . . .

As things had come to this pass, Shige-yoshi, who for three years had been a loyal supporter of the Heike, made up his mind that all was lost, and suddenly for-sook his allegiance and deserted to the enemy. . . .

. . . Later on the men of Shikoku and Kyushu all left the Heike in a body and went over to the Genji. Those who had so far been their faithful retainers now turned their bows against their lords and drew their swords against their own mas-ters. On one shore the heavy seas beat on the cliff so as to forbid any landing, while on the other stood the [crowded] ranks of the enemy waiting with leveled arrows to receive them. And so on this day the struggle for supremacy between the Genji and the Heike was at last decided.

THE KAMAKURA SHOGUNATE

After Yoritomo defeated the Taira, he pledged loyalty to the emperor. In return, the emperor awarded Yoritomo the title of *shogun,* or commander-in-chief. Yoritomo became the real ruler of Japan. He and his warriors left the court at Kyoto and settled

Source: "The Fight at Dan no ura" from *The Tale of the Heike* in *Anthology of Japanese Literature to the Nineteenth Century.* Donald Keene. George Allen & Unwin (Publishers) Ltd., 1968, pp. 173–176.

in the small seaside town of Kamakura. There, they set up a **shogunate,** or military government, which the Japanese called *bakufu,* or "tent government," after the shel-ters in which military officers lived. Yorito-mo's soldiers took control of government tasks, ran country estates, and replaced the nobles as supporters of the arts.

THE TOKUGAWA SHOGUNATE

Yoritomo died in 1199. After his death, fighting among his heirs weakened the shogunate, and by the 1300's, Japan was di-vided among rival nobles. Finally, in 1600, a general named Tokugawa Ieyasu (toh·kuh·GAWH·ah ee·YAH·soo) won an important victory and united all of Japan. He had the emperor name him *shogun* and took mea-sures to ensure that power stayed in the Tokugawa family. The center of Tokugawa rule was the village of Edo, which later be-came known as Tokyo.

To maintain social stability and to limit ri-vals, the Tokugawa *shoguns* imposed a rigid social structure. The people were divided into four classes—warriors, artisans, mer-chants, and peasants. All class positions were hereditary, passed from one family member to the next, and members of one

Japan

TOKUGAWA IEYASU

Known for his strong personality, Tokugawa Ieyasu rose to fame as a soldier and eventually conquered all of Japan. His success brought the country the longest period of peace and prosperity in its history as he and his family controlled the office of *shogun* until 1868. The following official Japanese account describes Ieyasu's personality and habits and tells why he achieved such success:

Having lived from boyhood to manhood in military encampments, and having suffered hardship after hardship in countless battles, large and small, His Lordship had little time to read or study. Although he had conquered the country on horseback, being a man of [natural] intelligence and wisdom, he fully appreciated the impossibility of governing the country on horseback. According to his judgment there could be no other way to govern the country than by a constant and deep faith in the sages and the scholars, and as a human being interested in the welfare of his fellow human beings, he patronized scholarship from the very beginning of his rule. Thus, he soon gained a reputation as a great [enthusiast] of letters and as one with a taste for elegant prose and poetry. On one occasion, Shimazu Yoshihisa, whose Buddhist name was Ryuhaku, took the trouble to arrange a poetry composition party in Ieyasu's honor, only to learn that His Lordship did not care at all for such a vain pastime. He listened again and again to discourses on [such Chinese classics as] the Four Books . . . and the History of the Former Han Dynasty. . . .

. . . He also extolled the spirit of personal sacrifice and the utterances and deeds of loyalty to the state of such [great Chinese statesmen] as T'ai Kung-wang, Chang Liang, Han Hsin, Wei Cheng, and Fang Hsuanling. And among the warriors of our country he constantly asked for discourses on the General of the Right of Kamakura (Minamoto Yoritomo). Whatever the subject, he was interested, not in the turn of a phrase or in literary embellishments, but only in discovering the key to government— how to govern oneself, the people, and the country.

TAKING ANOTHER LOOK

1. Who was Tokugawa Ieyasu? In what skills did he excel?
2. In what ways did Ieyasu embody ideals of traditional Japan?

Source: Sources of Japanese Tradition. Ryusaku Tsunado, William Theodore de Bary, and Donald Keene (eds.), 1958, © Columbia University Press, New York. Reprinted by permission of the publishers.

class were not allowed to perform tasks that belonged to another class. Below, a Japanese writer of the time recounts Ieyasu's views on the role and tasks of each class:

Once, Lord Tōshō [Ieyasu] conversed with Honda, Governor Sado, on the subject of the emperor, the shogun, and the farmer. "Whether there is order or chaos in the nation depends on the virtues and vices of these three. The emperor, with compassion in his heart for the needs of the people, must not be remiss in the performance of his duties—from the early morning worship of the New Year to the monthly functions of the court. Secondly, the shogun must not forget the possibility of war in peacetime, and must maintain his discipline. He should be able to maintain order in the country; he should bear in mind the security of the sovereign; and he must strive to dispel the anxieties of the people. One who cultivates the way of the warrior only in times of crisis is like a rat who bites his captor in the throes of being captured. The man may die from the effects of the poisonous bite, but to generate courage on the spur of the moment is not the way of a warrior. To assume the way of the warrior upon the outbreak of war is like a rat biting his captor. Although this is better than fleeing from the scene, the true master of the way of the warrior is one who maintains his martial discipline even in time of peace. Thirdly, the farmer's toil is proverbial—from the first grain to a hundred acts of labor. He selects the seed from last fall's crop, and undergoes various hardships and anxieties through the heat of summer until the seed grows finally to a rice plant. It is harvested and husked and then offered to the land steward. The rice then becomes sustenance for the multitudes. Truly, the hundred acts of toil from last fall to this fall are like so many tears of blood. Thus, it is a wise man who, while partaking of his meal, appreciates the hundred acts of toil of the people. Fourthly, the artisan's

occupation is to make and prepare wares and utensils for the use of others. Fifthly, the merchant facilitates the exchange of goods so that the people can cover their nakedness and keep their bodies warm. As the people produce clothing, food and housing, which are called the "three treasures," they deserve our every sympathy."

THE WAY OF THE WARRIOR

During the period of the shogunates, political power was held by various ranks of warriors. Directly under the emperor and the *shogun* were lords known as *daimyo* (DY·mee·oh), who built castles and controlled vast rural estates. To protect their lands and the peasants who farmed the lands for them, the *daimyo* secured the services of warrior-retainers. These warriors were called *samurai*. As the following account shows, even if one was born a *samurai*, one had to endure a great deal of training and adhere to a strict set of rules:

[Suzuki] Taro was born a samurai. . . . His father had been a samurai. His sons would be samurai. It was far better to be born a samurai than to be born a farmer or a merchant. Only about one person in twenty was a samurai, and only samurai could bear swords or hold administrative office. . . .

From the age of fifteen on, Taro carried two swords: a long sword and a short one. To carry these instruments of death at all times made Taro deeply aware of his mission in life, the mission of all samurai: to serve his lord bravely and loyally, and to set an example for others. Should any situation arise in which dishonor seemed likely, Taro would use the short sword to end his own life, displaying in his ritual suicide his selflessness and devotion to his lord.

Source: Sources of Japanese Tradition. Ryusaku Tsunoda, William Theodore de Bary, and Donald Keene (eds.), 1958, © Columbia University Press, New York. Reprinted by permission of the publishers.

EXAMINING ART *This high-ranking* samurai *is being attended by other* samurai, *one of whom is holding his bow and helmet.* Samurai *followed a strict code of honor known as* bushido. *What was a* samurai's *mission?*

To grow up as a samurai meant learning the military arts, so Taro spent many hours wrestling and fencing and riding and studying archery. But Japan had enjoyed . . . peace, and in peacetime one needed other skills as well. So Taro studied reading and writing and, as he grew older, began to read the Chinese classics. . . .

Taro's training was strict, for becoming a worthy samurai was not an easy task. At the age of six Taro began to memorize the Chinese classics. . . .

Taro met his teacher all during the year. Fall and spring were no problem, but the heat of the summer sometimes made him so weak he thought he would faint. The winter cold brought a different kind of suffering. His clothing was not heavy, and the room was unheated. Using a fire simply to warm himself Taro knew was the way of a weakling. When his hands became too cold to hold his writing brush, his teacher would say, "Dip them in that bucket of water." The water in the bucket was ice-cold. When his bare feet became numb, his teacher would say, "Go run around in the snow. . . ."

Samurai were supposed to be above such matters as money and commerce. Ideally, a samurai never handled money. But Taro . . . had no servants, and so he often wound up going to the market himself. To hide his embarrassment, he usually went out after dark. Taro's family and almost all the other samurai families lived near the castle of the lord. . . .

Taro had never ventured more than five miles [8 kilometers] away from home. From the top of the hill near his house he could see the ocean, but he had never been in a boat. Nor was it likely that he would travel at all until he was eighteen or twenty. Then his lord might well order him to Edo to serve there as a guard.

SECTION 3 REVIEW

CHECKING FOR UNDERSTANDING
1. **Define** shogun, shogunate, *bakufu, daimyo, samurai.*
2. **Explain** how Minamoto Yoritomo became ruler of Japan.

CRITICAL THINKING
3. **Analyzing Information** Into what classes were the Japanese divided? What was the role of each?

SECTION 4
Contact With the West

Because of their isolated island location, the Japanese felt safe from foreign powers. Then, during the 1500's, the first Europeans—Portuguese and Spanish traders and missionaries—reached Japan's shores. Be-

Source: The Past: The Road from Isolation, Volume I of Through Japanese Eyes. Richard H. Minear (ed.). Praeger Publishers, 1974, pp. 42, 43, 46, 48.

fore long, they had gained great influence. By 1614, about 300,000 Japanese had accepted Christianity.

Fearing that European ways were a threat to their power, Tokugawa rulers forbade the practice of Christianity and ended Japanese contacts with the European world. All western Europeans except the Dutch were barred from Japan. Because the Dutch were interested only in trade and not in conquest or conversion, the Japanese were less worried about their influence and allowed them to remain at one isolated port. Through them, however, a small amount of information about the West continued to flow into Japan.

ECONOMIC AND SOCIAL CHANGE

Isolation from the West did not stop the development of Japanese society and Japan's economy. During the 1700's and 1800's, internal trade increased. Merchants grew wealthy and became an important social group. Towns began to play a dominant role in Japanese life. At the same time, ambitious *daimyo* introduced more efficient farming methods on their estates and increased their rice yields. Soon, in the new urban areas, the Tokugawas' rigid social order began to break down, and class divisions blurred.

Gradually, the ban on foreign contacts relaxed, and some Japanese began to read Western books and study Western ideas. But, most Japanese still did not want foreigners in their country. Below, a prominent Japanese scholar of the early 1800's explains why Westerners were not necessary or welcome:

Our Divine Land is where the sun rises and where the [primary] energy originates. The heirs of the Great Sun have occupied the Imperial Throne from generation to generation without change from time immemorial. Japan's position at the

EXAMINING ART *In this seventeenth-century Japanese painting, European missionaries and Japanese converts stroll in front of roadside shops selling wild animal skins, cloth, and other decorative objects. The priests at the left are Jesuits. Those in brown robes are Franciscans. In the scene at the top, Christian samurai participate in a Catholic Mass. Some Christianized samurai helped build ties between European traders and Japanese merchants. Why was Christianity banned in Japan?*

EXAMINING ART *Japan's brisk internal trade during the 1700's and 1800's is reflected in this busy street scene at the Edo bridge, the end point for all highways leading into the city. How were the social classes affected by the increase in trade during this period?*

[summit] of the earth makes it the standard for the nations of the world. Indeed, it casts its light over the world, and the distance which the resplendent imperial influence reaches knows no limit. Today, the alien barbarians of the West, the lowly organs of the legs and feet of the world, are dashing about across the seas, trampling other countries underfoot, and daring, with their squinting eyes and limping feet, to override the noble nations. What manner of arrogance is this! . . .

Let, therefore, our rule extend to the length and breadth of the land, and let our people excel in manners and customs. Let the high as well as the low uphold righteousness [duty]; let the people prosper, and let military defense be adequate.

If we proceed accordingly and without committing blunders, we shall fare well however forceful may be the invasion of a powerful enemy. But should the situation be otherwise, and should we indulge in leisure and pleasure, then we are placing our reliance where there is no reliance at all. . . .

PERRY'S MISSION

In 1853, the government of the United States decided to force Japan to end its isolation. It sent Commodore Matthew Perry to

Source: New Proposals by Aizawa Seishisai in *Sources of Japanese Tradition*. Ryusaku Tsunoda, William Theodore de Bary, and Donald Keene (eds.), 1958, © Columbia University Press, New York. Reprinted by permission of the publishers.

EXAMINING ART
When Matthew Perry's American vessels steamed into the Japanese harbor at Edo Bay on July 8, 1853, the goal was to reopen Japan to trade after 214 years of isolation. Seven months later, his goal was achieved as the Tokugawa leaders signed a treaty granting the United States trading rights at two Japanese ports. Of what significance to Japan was the re-opening of trade with the West?

Japan to demand that the Japanese government grant trading privileges to the United States. Below, a Japanese describes Perry's vessels as they steamed into Edo harbor:

Some things I still remember. One morning there was a great hubbub. When I asked what it was all about, I was told that in the offing there were ships on fire. I ran to the top of the mountain to get a good look. There was a crowd of people there, all stirred up and making guesses about the burning ships on the horizon. Then those ships came nearer and nearer, until the shape of them showed us they were not Japanese ships but foreign ones, and we found that what we had taken for a [fire] on the sea was really the black smoke rising out of their smokestacks. When we came down, there was excitement all over town. . . .

"What a joke, the steaming teapot fixed by America—Just four cups [ships], and we cannot sleep at night!"

Perry told the Japanese that if they did not agree to a treaty within a year, there would be war. The *shogun*, realizing that Japan's defenses could not withstand the superior military power of the United States, eventually bowed to Perry's demand. By 1858, Japan had signed treaties not only with the United States, but with a number of other Western nations as well. This finally opened Japan to the rest of the world. At the same time, it marked the end to traditional Japan.

SECTION 4 REVIEW

CHECKING FOR UNDERSTANDING

1. **Discuss** the reason for Commodore Perry's mission to Japan. What was the mission's outcome?

CRITICAL THINKING

2. **Recognizing Bias** How did the Japanese regard Westerners? How do you think Westerners regarded Japan and its people? What might account for the attitudes of both groups?

Source: Japanese eyewitness in *Black Ship Scroll.* Oliver Statler. Charles E. Tuttle Company, Inc. of Tokyo, Japan, 1963, pp. 8–9.

CASE STUDY

Japan

THE JAPAN EXPEDITION

Commodore Matthew Perry was sent to Japan to open that country for trade. Many Americans, however, thought that Perry's mission should have other goals as well. They agreed with the views expressed below in a March 17, 1852 editorial in the *New York Daily Tribune*:

It seems we are to send a fleet to Japan, and to enter the Capital City at all hazards. The interests of American trade require that commercial communication be opened with that recluse region, and a numerous array of armed vessels will proceed to state that fact to the Japanese Government, and to open the gates of its ports. It is a fair suspicion in the premises that the greatness of America is better understood at Washington than at Jeddo [Edo], and that the Japanese will be unable immediately to discern the great advantage of trading with a nation which makes the overture from the cannon's mouth. It may be also presumed that they will decline to accede to such propositions so made, until they have learned, as they *infallibly will learn, by much bombarding and battering, that we are determined to give them the benefits of commercial communication with us.*

In this state of things, going thus into pagan realms, it behooves us not to lose the opportunity of laboring for the spiritual benefit of the benighted [unenlightened] Japanese. Let not these misguided men, fighting for their own, perish without benefit of clergy. Why should we not combine instruction with mercantile benefit, and while we get from the Japanese such articles as we wish, leave some of our morality in exchange? We might be the gainers in that bargain. To this end, and to impart a moral luster to the expedition, we *suggest that some of the many chaplains in the United States now unemployed, be dispatched to Japan with the fleet, and while the ships lie before Jeddo [Edo], bombarding the city, and stray boatsfull of obstinate Japanese are captured and brought on board our ships, the reverend gentlemen might exert all their genius in the conversion of such natives. . . .*

We should, indeed, be truly sorry to see the American government engaged in any undertaking of this magnitude to which it would be unwilling to give the [improving] aspect of a [care] for the moral welfare of the people concerned.

DRAWING CONCLUSIONS

1. What purpose did the writer have in mind when he wrote this editorial? Did he think the expedition was a good idea?
2. What does the editorial reveal about American attitudes at the time toward Japan?

Source: "The Japan Expedition." Editorial in the *New York Daily Tribune*, Vol. XI, No. 3, 405, March 17, 1852, p. 4.

Chapter 16 Review

SUMMARY

Under a monarchy, the Japanese modeled their government on Chinese principles, borrowed the Chinese system of writing, and accepted the religion of Buddhism from Chinese missionaries. Beginning in the 790's, the political authority of the emperor declined; and by the 1600's, all of Japan was united under the rule of military officials known as *shoguns.*

During the 1600's, after a century of European contacts, Tokugawa *shoguns* barred most western Europeans from Japan. Despite isolationism, Japan's society and economy developed steadily. In time, the social order imposed by the Tokugawa rulers broke down, and the ban on foreign contacts was relaxed.

In 1853, the United States government sent a fleet headed by Commodore Matthew Perry to Japan to demand trading privileges. On threat of war, the Japanese opened their country to the rest of the world.

USING VOCABULARY

Use each vocabulary word in a sentence about the relationship of government and the military in early Japan.

clan	shogunate	*daimyo*
shogun	*bakufu*	*samurai*

REVIEWING FACTS

1. **Name** the principle that was stressed in the Shōtoku constitution.
2. **Explain** what the construction of Nara symbolized.
3. **Name** the emperor under whose rule the *Taika* reforms were introduced.
4. **Characterize** the Heian period of Japan's history.

5. **Discuss** the form of government established in Japan by Minamoto Yoritomo.
6. **Explain** how Tokugawa *shoguns* maintained social stability.
7. **State** what the village of Edo was later called.

CRITICAL THINKING

1. **Evaluating Information** How would you explain the following statement? *In many ways, the history of traditional Japan is a story of the influence of other cultures.*
2. **Checking Consistency** Do you agree with the statement that Japan has been ruled continuously by an emperor since 660 BC? Explain.
3. **Demonstrating Reasoned Judgment** The Tokugawas divided the Japanese into four classes. To which class would you have liked to belong? Why?
4. **Synthesizing Information** Do you think it was wise of the Japanese to isolate themselves from foreign contact? Explain. Would it be possible for a nation to do so today? Explain.

ANALYZING CONCEPTS

1. **Identity** How did the lifestyle of the Heian court compare with that of the *samurai*?
2. **Change** In what ways did Japan's society and economy change during the 1700's and 1800's?

GEOGRAPHIC THEMES

1. **Movement** What ideas and practices did the Japanese borrow from other civilizations?
2. **Human-Environment Interaction** On what did Japan's noble and warrior classes rely for their wealth?

Writing a Paragraph

Most effective prose writing is organized into *paragraphs,* or groups of sentences that express a single main idea. Well-organized paragraphs enable readers to understand the writer's ideas more easily.

Most effective paragraphs share four characteristics. First, each paragraph expresses one main idea, which is usually—but not always—stated in a topic sentence. Second, all other sentences in the paragraph support or explain the main idea. Third, the sentences are arranged in a logical order. Finally, sentences and thoughts are linked by transitional words and phrases, such as *first, next, finally, also, because, however, in order to,* and *therefore.* Transitional words clarify relationships between ideas, making it easier to follow the writer's thoughts.

Here are some steps to follow in writing effective paragraphs:

- State the main idea of the paragraph as a topic sentence.
- Choose details that support or explain the main idea.
- Arrange the topic sentence and details in a logical sequence.
- Link the sentences with transitional words.

EXAMPLE

Read the first paragraph under the heading, "Economic and Social Change" on page 262. The main idea of this paragraph is stated in a topic sentence at the beginning: "Isolation from the West did not stop the development of Japanese society and Japan's economy." What details develop the main idea? *(Internal trade increased; merchants gained wealth and power; towns grew; agricultural production increased; social and class divisions loosened.)* Notice that the order of the sentences reflects the cause-and-effect relationships between these events. Increased trade caused merchants to become wealthier; this caused towns to grow, and so on. What transitional words connect these ideas? *(during the 1700's and 1800's, at the same time, soon)*

There are, however, many ways to organize paragraphs. Read the first paragraph under the heading, "The Kamakura Shogunate," on page 258. In this paragraph, the main idea is in the *third* sentence: "Yoritomo became the real ruler of Japan." Now read the first paragraph under the heading, "The Tokugawa Shogunate," on the same page. The ideas in this paragraph are arranged, not by causal relationships, but in chronological order. The first sentence gives the date of Yoritomo's death—1199. What dates are given in the second and third sentences? *(1300's, 1600)*

PRACTICE

A. The sentences below discuss the effects of Japan's isolation on its national character. After reading the sentences, arrange them into a paragraph with a topic sentence, supporting details, and transitional words as needed.

1. The Japanese seem to view the rest of the world, even the Koreans or Chinese, as "others."
2. The isolation of Japan has had many important by-products.
3. Throughout history, the Japanese have shown almost a mania for distinguishing between "foreign" borrowings and elements regarded as "native" Japanese.
4. It has produced a strong sense of Japanese self-identity and an unusual degree of cultural unity.

B. Choose a main idea that is related to the material in Chapter 16. Write a paragraph about this main idea, using a topic sentence, supporting details, and transitional words as needed.

**People and Places
to Know**
Mutsuhito, the Meiji,
Korea, Manchuria,
Hideki Tojo, Hiroshima,
Nagasaki, Douglas A.
MacArthur

Key Terms to Define
diet, *zaibatsu*, militarism,
civilian

Objectives to Learn
1. **Describe** Japan under
   the Meiji.
2. **Summarize** the factors
   that involved Japan in
   war in the Pacific.
3. **Relate** the changes the
   end of World War II
   brought to Japan.

*Downtown Tokyo
at night*

Modern Japan

It is a winter's evening in Tokyo. In a four-roomed house . . . a family sits after supper enjoying the glow from an electric foot-warmer . . . sunk in the centre of the floor. Over the shallow square pit that contains the heater is a low table. . . . Round the table, sitting on cushions on the floor with their stockinged feet hanging into the pit . . . sit . . . old Mrs. Saito, her son, her daughter-in-law, and favourite grandchild. . . .

In the Saito household there is a reflection of the tensions that afflict Japanese families today—. . . opposition of half-discredited tradition and [tradition-shattering] experiment. Saito Mamoru [the grandson] and his sister . . . are products of the [post-World War II] American Occupation, Japan's fourth and latest cultural invasion. . . .

Near the Shinto God-shelf, a small shrine on the wall . . ., there is a miniature Buddhist temple, a reminder of the first cultural invasion . . ., that of Buddhism from China in the sixth century A.D. In the cramped little kitchen there are the remains of a sponge-cake . . . introduced to Japan by the Portuguese in the sixteenth century, together with Christianity. . . . This second cultural invasion . . . was not substantial. . . .

The third invasion, also from the West, began in the middle of the nineteenth century. . . . It lasted with varying degrees of intensity until the outbreak of the Pacific War [World War II]. Its manifestations in the Saito house are too numerous to be listed; they include . . . every article of Western use in the home—from the strip lighting to the shoes . . . standing in the front porch, from the coathangers in the cupboard to the boy's bicycle pump near the kitchen door. The family now [has] a flush lavatory, refrigerator, washing machine, and fly screens on the windows. . . .

. . . [Mingled] with these adaptations and borrowings from abroad are the traditional [items] of Japanese life: the straw *tatami* matting covering the floor; . . . the rice container with its flat wooden server . . .; Mrs. Saito's set of ceremonial tea utensils; the *kakemono,* the hanging scroll, in the recess of the main room; the *sake* (rice wine) bottles and cups; the teapot in the kitchen. . . . Most of them, it is true, derive from China or from Chinese influence. But they have become uniquely and traditionally Japanese.

This description of a modern Japanese household reveals a characteristic of Japan—the ability to absorb foreign influences and at the same time keep its own traditions.

Source: From A HISTORY OF MODERN JAPAN, by Richard Storry (Pelican Books, 1960), copyright © Richard Storry, 1960, 1961, 1968. Reprinted by permission of Penguin Books Ltd.

Yet, it cannot be denied that during the past 100 years, the West has had a great impact on Japan. In the late 1800's, Japan adopted Western technology and became a leading industrial nation. Later, in World War II, it became one of the first Asian nations to use Western weapons against the West.

SECTION 1

A New Era

Japan's opening to the West in the mid-1800's stimulated the country's modernization. In 1867 and 1868, reform-minded leaders reestablished imperial rule in the name of the young emperor, Mutsuhito. His rule, which lasted from 1868 to 1912, was called *Meiji* (may·jee), or "enlightened rule." Although Mutsuhito became the symbol of a new era in Japanese history, the real power was held by the *samurai* who had overthrown the Tokugawa shogunate.

MODERNIZATION

Mutsuhito believed Japan had to modernize. He summed up his beliefs in this poem:

> May our country,
> Taking what is good,
> And rejecting what is bad,
> Be not inferior
> To any other.

Under Mutsuhito's leadership, the Meiji set out to make Japan a modern nation capable of competing with the West. The official capital was moved from Kyoto to Edo, which was renamed Tokyo. A constitution was adopted that set up a new government in which the emperor ruled with the help of a prime minister, cabinet, and **diet,** or legislature. The military ranks of *daimyo* and *samurai* were put to an end and replaced by a modern army and navy. All Japanese were declared equal under the law.

Meiji leaders also encouraged industrialization. To this end, they established a system of universal education designed to produce patriotic, highly skilled citizens and sent people abroad to study and borrow Western ideas and methods. In addition, they revised the tax system to raise money for investment, founded a modern banking system, and supported the building of a postal and telegraph network, railroads, factories, and ports. Government-backed **zaibatsu** (zy·BAHT·soo), large family-owned businesses, soon controlled most of Japan's economy. By the early 1900's, Japanese could look back with pride on what their nation had accomplished. Fifty years later, a Japanese writer summed it up as follows:

> By comparing the Japan of fifty years ago with the Japan of today, it will be seen that the nation has gained considerably in the extent of territory, as well as in population, which now numbers nearly fifty million. The government has become con-

EXAMINING ART
Western fashions became very popular among well-to-do Japanese during the late Meiji period, bringing about an early home industry in making Western-style dresses. As a result, sewing machines became an important early import. How did Meiji leaders encourage industrialization?

EXAMINING MAPS
The Russo-Japanese War began in 1904, when Japan attacked Russian forces at Port Arthur in Manchuria. Later, the Japanese navy nearly destroyed a Russian fleet in the Tsushima Straits. The Japanese military also won significant land victories at Liaoyan and Mukden. The conflict, however, exhausted both nations; and in 1905, the Treaty of Portsmouth ended fighting. What were Japan's gains in the Russo-Japanese War?

RUSSO-JAPANESE WAR 1904–1905

stitutional not only in name, but in fact, and national education has attained to a high degree of excellence. In commerce and industry, the nation has made rapid strides. The nation's general progress, during the short space of half a century, has been so sudden and swift that it presents a spectacle rare in the history of the world. This leap forward is the result of the stimulus which the country received on coming into contact with the civilization of Europe and America, and may well, in its broad sense, be regarded as a benefit conferred by foreign contacts. It was foreign contacts that brought to life the national consciousness of our people, and it is foreign contacts that have enabled Japan to stand as a world power. We possess today a powerful army and navy, but it was after western models that we laid their foundations. We established a draft in keeping with the principle "all our sons are soldiers." We promoted military education, and encouraged the manufacture of arms and the art of ship building. We have reorganized the systems of central and local administration, and effected reforms in the educational system. All this is nothing but the result

of adopting the superior features of western institutions.

MILITARY SUCCESS

Upon becoming a modern nation, Japan sought the respect of the Western powers. In the 1890's and early 1900's, the Japanese began to compete with the nations of the West in establishing overseas empires. Because the Japanese needed more natural resources for their economy and more room for their growing population, they wanted to expand into east Asia and the Pacific Ocean area. As a result, in 1894, they went to war with China for control of Korea. China was defeated easily the following year.

After their victory over China, the Japanese faced growing rivalry with Russia for control of Korea and Manchuria. Finally, in 1904, they declared war on the Russians. Although they won important battles on land and on sea, the fighting exhausted not

Source: Fifty Years of New Japan, Vol. II by Okuma Sigenobu in *Sources of Japanese Tradition*, Ryusaku Tsunoda, William Theodore de Bary, and Donald Keene (eds.). 1958 © Columbia University Press, New York. Reprinted by permission of the publishers.

only them, but the Russians as well. Within a year, a treaty ended the Russo-Japanese War. Under its terms, Japan won recognition of its hold on Korea. For the first time in the modern era, an Asian nation had triumphed over a major European one.

Japan's triumph gained it a great deal of prestige as a world military power. At the same time, its military success developed in the Japanese people strong feelings of nationalism. When World War I erupted, the Japanese saw in it the opportunity to further expand their empire and joined the fight against the Germans. After the Germans were defeated, Japan gained a number of islands in the Pacific. Japan's chief interest, however, was in a greater role in China. Of prime concern was the Chinese province of Manchuria, which the Japanese felt they had to dominate for China's sake as well as their own. A prominent Japanese military leader explained the Japanese view in the following way:

Manchuria is for the Japanese the only region for expansion. Manchuria is Japan's life-line. Thus, we must secure for our people the guarantee that they can settle there and pursue their occupations in peace. If this problem cannot be disposed of by diplomatic means, then we have no other alternative but to resort to arms. . . . The head of the Ministry of Foreign Affairs should go to China when the opportunity presents itself . . . and frankly divulge Japan's true aims and explain Japan's position. . . . I am sure that this would be a step toward [easing] ill-feeling between the two countries.

. . . Now, are not Japan and China the only true states in Asia? Is it not true that other than these two countries there is no other which can control all of Asia? In short, we must attempt the solution of our myriad problems on the premise of "Asia for the Asians." However, Japan is an island country. She is a small, narrow island country which cannot hope to support within its island confines any further increase in population. Thus, she has no alternative but to expand into Manchuria or elsewhere. That is, as Asians the Japanese must of necessity live in Asia. China may object to the Japanese setting foot in Manchuria, but had not Japan fought and repelled Russia from Manchuria, even Peking might not be Chinese territory today. Thus, while the expansion of Japan into Manchuria may be a move for her own betterment and that of her people, it would also be a necessary move for the self-protection of Asians and for the co-existence and co-prosperity of China and Japan.

SECTION 1 REVIEW

CHECKING FOR UNDERSTANDING
1. **Define** diet, *zaibatsu*.
2. **Discuss** the goal of the Meiji leaders in late nineteenth-century Japan. What did they do to accomplish this objective?

CRITICAL THINKING
3. **Determining Cause and Effect** Why did the Japanese try to expand overseas? What was the result of their efforts?

SECTION 2

Drift to War

Although Japan became a world power during World War I, the Japanese still were faced with both foreign and domestic problems. Japan was a member of the League of Nations, a new world organization set up after the war. Japanese interest in the League, however, was slight because the League devoted much of its attention to

Source: San-kō Iretsu by Takahashi in Sources of Japanese Tradition, Ryusaku Tsunoda, William Theodore de Bary, and Donald Keene (eds.). 1958 © Columbia University Press, New York. Reprinted by permission of the publishers.

problems of the West. But when the League spoke out against Japan's interest in China, the Japanese turned against it. Eventually, they withdrew completely from the League.

Another source of tension was the restrictions the United States placed on Japanese immigration in 1924. In response, the Japanese staged demonstrations and refused to buy American goods. Japanese bitterness increased even more when Western pressure forced Japan to reduce its claims on China and accept Western interests there.

While the Japanese were trying to sort out their foreign problems, they were faced with growing social and economic problems at home. Of major concern was the large growth in population. With emigration cut off to such places as the United States, something had to be done at home to help cope. In the hope that new factories and markets would provide work for large numbers of people, renewed emphasis was placed on manufacturing and foreign trade. This led thousands of Japanese to leave the countryside to find jobs in the towns and cities.

Although working and living conditions often were miserable in the urban areas, those who lived there tended to fare better than those who lived in rural areas. Below, a Japanese writer remembers and comments on life in Tokyo during the 1920's:

I doubt that in those years . . . there was anyone even among the most ardent supporters of Tokyo who thought it a grand metropolis. The newspapers were unanimous in denouncing the chaotic transportation and the inadequate roads of "our Tokyo." I believe it was the *Advertiser* which in an editorial [protested] against the gracelessness of the city. Our politicians are always talking about big things, social policy and labor problems and the like, it said, but these are not what politics should be about. Politicians should be thinking rather of mud, and of laying

streets through which an automobile can pass in safety on a rainy day. I remember the editorial because I was so completely in agreement. . . . Twice on my way from Asakusa Bridge to Kaminari Gate I was jolted so violently from the cushion that my nose hit the roof of the cab. . . . And so, people will say, it might have been better to take a streetcar. That too could be a desperate struggle. . . . With brisk activity in the financial world, all manner of enterprises sprang up, and there was a rush from the provinces upon the big cities. Tokyo did not have time to accommodate the frantic increase in numbers and the swelling of the suburbs. . . . For the general populace there was no means of transport but the streetcar. Car after car

EXAMINING PHOTOGRAPHS *Japanese women and men make their way down a busy sidewalk in this early 1920's photo of Tokyo's fashionable Ginza district. What was Tokyo like in the 1920's?*

EXAMINING PHOTOGRAPHS *In this photo, taken in the 1930's, Emperor Hirohito reviews the Japanese army. Although Hirohito, who became Japan's 124th emperor in 1926, officially headed the armed forces and the government, he had little real power. Late in 1941, the militarists gained complete control of the government under a new prime minister, General Hideki Tojo. **Who held the real power in Japan in the 1930's?***

would come by full and leave people waiting at stops. At rush hour the press was murderous. Hungry and tired, the office worker and the laborer, in a hurry to get home, would push their way aboard a car already hopelessly full, each one for himself, paying no attention to the attempts of the conductor to keep order. . . . The crowds, a black mountain outside a streetcar, would push and shove and shout, and we could but silently lament the turmoil and how it brought out the worst in people. . . . They put up with it because they were Japanese, I heard it said, but if a European or American city were subjected to such things for even a day there would be rioting.

By the 1930's, Japan's leaders had become frustrated both with the difficulties at home and those abroad. As a result, they abandoned democratic reform at home and cooperation with the West. At the time, political power was largely in the hands of military and urban industrialists. Although the emperor, Hirohito, was a constitutional monarch, he could not control the military.

Finally, those who supported **militarism,** or a war-like policy, removed the **civilian,** or non-military, politicians and took over control of the government. Western cultural influences were limited, and a return to such traditional Japanese values as physical courage and strict obedience to authority were encouraged. The country's military forces were strengthened, and preparations were made for an attack on the Asian mainland.

Source: From *LOW CITY, HIGH CITY* by Edward G. Seidensticker. Copyright © 1983 by Edward Seidensticker. Reprinted by permission of Alfred A. Knopf.

SECTION 2 REVIEW

CHECKING FOR UNDERSTANDING
1. **Define** militarism, civilian.
2. **Specify** the changes the new military leadership made in Japan's policies.

CRITICAL THINKING
3. **Analyzing Information** What problems did Japan face during the 1920's and 1930's?

SECTION 3

Expansion

Japan's primary target in Asia was China, which had been weakened by civil war. In 1931, Japanese forces took control of Manchuria. Six years later, they invaded the eastern part of China, forcing the Chinese government to retreat to the interior of the country.

Two years later, World War II broke out in Europe. While the Europeans were busy with the war, the Japanese turned their attention to Southeast Asia which, at the time, was largely controlled by the Europeans. The Japanese needed oil, rubber, and other mineral resources, and Southeast Asia was rich in all of these. The Japanese government announced its plans to create a "Greater East Asia Co-prosperity Sphere" that united all of East and Southeast Asia under Japanese rule. At the same time, it strengthened its ties to Germany and Italy.

WAR IN THE PACIFIC

Japan's expansion in Asia created tensions with the United States, which cut off all exports to Japan. While negotiations between the two powers dragged on, the Japanese government prepared for war. On December 7, 1941, Japanese bombers attacked the large United States military base at Pearl Harbor in Hawaii. The bombing, which took the Americans by surprise, led to the Pacific War between Japan and the United States. Below, a Japanese woman tells how the war affected her family:

My elder brother was sixteen when the Pacific War started, and Father was very keen that he should join the navy. Right from the day the war broke out, he kept going on at my brother to take the exam for the naval cadets' school. Father, you see, had been turned down for military service in peacetime because he was too short, and I think that had perhaps given him some sort of complex about it. But in fact my brother didn't really seem enthusiastic about the war. In the end, it was decided that his whole class at Middle School should apply to become naval cadets. At that time it was still voluntary in theory, but as all his friends were going to apply, my brother more or less had to try as well. In any case, he failed because his eyesight wasn't up to standard, and later he went off to a pharmacy college . . . , so he never did get [drafted].

But still my father used to go on complaining: 'Isn't anybody in this house going to go and serve their country?' At that time, towards the end of my second year at Girls' School, I'd become friendly with a girl called Okada. . . . Anyway, in the winter of Second Year Okada and I made a vow that we would go every morning to the Kōshū Shrine to pray for victory. It was very, very cold at that time of year, but I would get up early and eat breakfast, and then I would walk up to the shrine through the frost and mist, and meet Okada-san there, and after we'd prayed we would go to school together.

From those early morning meetings we developed another idea. We decided that, by the time we finished school, it might already be too late to offer ourselves for service to our country, so instead we would leave school right away and volunteer for the nursing corps. We told our teacher about the plan, and he must have been quite impressed by our determination, because I remember that he got in touch with a man from the local newspaper, who came and took our photographs and wrote a little article about us, how patriotic we were and so on. For me, I wanted to do it, partly out of patriotism, but partly because, since girls couldn't be [drafted], it seemed like the only way for us to take a main role in the great drama that was taking place. . . .

It's funny, although I knew that being a front-line nurse was very dangerous, I never thought about the danger or the possibility of dying when I went to volunteer. When you are fighting for your country I suppose you don't think about death.

The Japanese won extensive victories in Southeast Asia and in the Pacific. By 1942, they ruled an empire that stretched from the Aleutian Islands near Alaska south to the Solomon Islands in the western Pacific, and from Wake Island west to Burma. That same year, however, they suffered their first major defeats to the United States, and over the next three years, they were gradually driven from islands they had taken earlier.

THE BOMB AND SURRENDER

By the end of 1944, Japan was being bombed by American planes. But, in spite of the American advance, the Japanese refused to surrender. As a result, the United States decided to end the war by using a new secret weapon—the atomic bomb, a bomb whose destructive force is caused by the splitting of atoms of a heavy chemical element. On August 6, 1945, the Americans dropped the first atomic bomb on the city of Hiroshima. Several days later, they dropped a second and larger one on the city of Nagasaki. The Japanese—and the rest of the world—were horrified by the results. Hundreds of thousands of Japanese were killed, many more were maimed, and parts of the cities were reduced to rubble. Below, author John Toland relates the experiences of some Japanese caught by the bombing:

Hiroshima was serene and so was the sky above it as the people continued on their daily routine. Those who noticed the three parachutes imagined that the plane had been hit and that the crew was bailing out. . . .

Source: Tsutsumi Ayako in *Shōwa: An Inside History of Hirohito's Japan.* Tessa Morris-Suzuki. The Athlone Press Limited, 1984, pp. 145–146.

Several hundred yards north of Aioi Bridge . . . , Private Shigeru Shimoyama, a recent draftee, looked up and idly peered through his thick glasses at one of the drifting chutes. . . . He had been in Hiroshima four days and was already "bored to death." He wished he were back in Tokyo making school notebooks. All at once a pinkish light burst in the sky like a cosmic flash bulb.

Clocks all over Hiroshima were fixed forever at 8:15.

The bomb exploded 660 yards [594 meters] from the ground into a fireball almost 110 yards [99 meters] in diameter. Those directly below heard nothing, nor could they later agree what color the *pika* (lightning) flash was—blue, pink, reddish, dark-brown, yellow or purple.

The heat emanating from the fireball lasted a fraction of a second but was so intense . . . that it melted the surface of granite within a thousand yards [900 meters] of the hypocenter, or ground zero—directly under the burst. Roof tiles softened and changed in color from black to olive or brown. All over the center of the city numerous silhouettes were imprinted on walls. On Yorozuyo Bridge ten people left permanent outlines of themselves on the railing and the tar-paved surface. . . .

Private Shimoyama was 550 yards [495 meters] north of ground zero. He was not directly exposed to the *pika* flash or his life would have been puffed out, but the blast hurled him into the vast barnlike warehouse, driving him into the collapsing roof beam where five long nails in his back held him suspended several feet off the ground. His glasses were still intact. . . .

A thousand yards [900 meters] on the other side of the hypocenter, Mrs. Yasuko Nukushina was trapped in the ruins of the family *sake* store. Her first thought was of her four-year-old daughter, Ikuko, who was playing outside somewhere. Unaccountably, she heard Ikuko's voice beside her: "I'm afraid, Mama." She told the child they were buried and would die

EXAMINING PHOTOGRAPHS
In this photo taken at Hiroshima a few hours after the atomic bomb was dropped, victims wait to receive first aid from medical personnel, who themselves were burned and injured. Today, thousands of people gather at Hiroshima's Peace Memorial Park each year to mark the anniversary of the bombing. Why did the United States drop atomic bombs on Japan?

there. Her own words made her claw desperately at the wreckage. She was a slight woman, . . . but in her frenzy she broke free into the yard. All around was devastation. . . . People drifted by expressionless and silent like sleepwalkers in tattered, smoldering clothing. . . . She watched mesmerized until someone touched her. Grasping Ikuko's hand, she joined the procession. . . .

Half a dozen blocks south, fifteen-year-old Michiko Yamaoka had just left home for work at the telephone office. She remembered "a magnesium flash," then a faraway voice calling "Michiko!" Her mother. "I'm here," she answered but didn't know where that was. She couldn't see—she must be blind! She heard her mother shout, "My daughter is buried under there!" Another voice, a man's, advised the mother to escape the flames sweeping down the street. . . . She was going to die. Then came a shaft of light as concrete blocks were pushed aside by soldiers. Her mother was bleeding profusely, one arm skewered by a piece of wood. She ordered Michiko to escape. She herself was staying to rescue two relatives under the ruins of their house.

Michiko moved through a nightmare world—past charred bodies—a crying baby sealed behind the twisted iron bars of a collapsed reinforced-concrete building. She saw someone she knew and called out.

"Who are you?" the other girl asked.

"Michiko."

The friend stared at her. "Your nose and eyebrows are gone!"

Michiko felt her face. It was so swollen that her nose seemed to have disappeared. . . .

Dr. Fumio Shigeto, head of internal medicine at the hospital, never reached his office that morning. On his way to work, he was waiting for a trolley at the end of a long line which bent around the corner of the Hiroshima railway station, 2000 yards [1800 meters] east of the hypocenter. The flash seemed to turn a group of girls ahead of him white, almost invisible. . . . As he dropped to the sidewalk, covering eyes and ears, a heavy slate slammed into his back. Whirls of smoke blotted out the sun. In the darkness he groped blindly to reach shelter. . . .

A breeze from the east gradually cleared the area . . . , revealing an incredible scene: the buildings in front of the station

EXAMINING PHOTOGRAPHS *On September 2, 1945, aboard the United States* battleship Missouri *in Tokyo Bay, the Japanese formally surrendered. Shown signing for Japan is General Yoshijiro Umezu. Standing at the microphone is General Douglas MacArthur, who signed for the United States and its allies, some of whose leaders are standing behind MacArthur. How was Japan's system of government altered after the war?*

were collapsed, flattened; half-naked and smoldering bodies covered the ground. Of the people at the trolley stop he alone, the last one in line, was unhurt. . . .

Dr. Shigeto started for the hospital but was stopped by an impenetrable wall of advancing flames. He turned and ran for open space. . . .

A nurse approached him. . . . She begged him to help another doctor and his wife lying on the ground. His first thought was: What if this mob of desperate people discovers I am a physician? He couldn't help them all. "Please treat my wife first," said the injured doctor. . . . Shigeto gave the woman a . . . shot. . . . He rearranged the bandages the nurse had applied and then turned to the other wounded, treating them until he ran out of medicine and supplies. There was nothing else he could do. He fled toward the hills.

The bombings made Japanese leaders realize that the war was lost and that they had to surrender. One Japanese soldier described

---

Source: From *THE RISING SUN* by John Toland. Copyright © 1970 by John Toland. Reprinted by permission of Random House Inc.

his reaction to the emperor's announcement of surrender as follows:

At noon we assembled in the nearest convenient place, which happened to be the village hall of the little village . . . where we had been training. We stood to attention in front of the radio, all in our formal uniforms, with swords at our belts. Unfortunately, the radio in the village hall was very bad, and it was hard to hear what the emperor was saying. Afterwards, we began to argue about what it meant. . . .

In the end, we decided to send someone back to the base to find out what it meant. The hall . . . had a big matted room on the first floor . . . , so while we were waiting for him to come back we all went up there and sat on the *tatami* [straw matting]. Then he returned, and told us that the government had accepted the [demand for complete surrender], and that we were all to behave calmly and sensibly. . . .

It was very hot. We all sat collapsed on the *tatami* in our formal uniforms. None of us said anything. I kept thinking: 'What have we been doing for the last year and a half? Every day we've been facing death. So many people have died. What was it all for?'

I felt full of regret and bitterness, but at the same time I also thought: 'Perhaps I am going to survive. Perhaps this thing they call peace is going to come. . . .'

The next day, several things happened almost at once. First, an officer arrived . . . and gave us a speech. He said: 'The broadcast which you heard yesterday was a fake. . . . His Majesty's true wish is that we should fight on to the very last soldier.' When we heard that, most of us felt that it must be true. After all, it fitted in with everything that we had been taught for four years. . . .

But then, soon after, a man from the Imperial Headquarters arrived and gave us another speech, saying that the broadcast was true. The Emperor, he said, was concerned with the fate of future generations.

AFTER 1945

After the war ended, an American army of occupation under General Douglas A. MacArthur governed Japan. Under MacArthur's rule, Japan was given a democratic constitution that ended the power of the military and guaranteed the basic freedoms of the Japanese people. Emperor Hirohito kept his throne but renounced his claim to divine authority. After Hirohito's death in 1989, his son Akihito became emperor.

In postwar Japan, local government was strengthened. The army and navy were disbanded, and Japan renounced the right to use force in its foreign policy. Women were granted certain rights, including the right to vote. The educational system was reformed along American lines. Economic reforms also were introduced. The large *zaibatsu* were reduced in size, and labor unions were

encouraged. Farmers were given the opportunity to own their own land.

In September 1951, the American occupation came to an end as the Japanese signed a peace treaty with most of the nations they had fought against in the war. Not too long afterward, tensions that had risen between the communist and the Western nations brought Japan and the United States into an alliance. A security treaty was signed that allowed the United States to have military bases and troops in Japan. With the American military in Japan, the Japanese government saw little need to spend much on defense. As a result, during the two decades after the Pacific War, the government was able to help rebuild the country's industries.

The Japanese studied modern Western technology and became skilled and well-trained. They invested heavily in new factories and developed foreign trade, exporting finished goods in return for energy resources and other raw materials.

Today, Japan has one of the highest rates of economic growth of all industrialized nations. The most developed nation in Asia, it has one of the highest standards of living in the world. As a result of this economic success, Japan is now playing a larger role in world affairs. During the Persian Gulf War in 1991, Japan gave financial help to nations affected by the conflict. It did not, however, send troops, because of its constitution's ban on all warfare except for defense.

SECTION 3 REVIEW

CHECKING FOR UNDERSTANDING

1. **Chronicle** the events that led to Japan's surrender in 1945.
2. **Indicate** how the American occupation changed Japan.

CRITICAL THINKING

3. **Identifying Central Issues** Why do many people believe that Japan should have more say in world affairs?

Source: Saito Mutsuo in *Shōwa: An Inside History of Hirohito's Japan.* Tessa Morris-Suzuki. The Athlone Press Limited, 1984, pp. 186–187.

Multicultural View

CHANGE AND MODERNIZATION IN JAPAN

FOCUSING ON THE ISSUE In the 100 or so years following the arrival of American warships in Edo Bay, the Japanese experienced change in all areas of life. The time line on these pages notes some of the events that took place during those years. Study the time line and the information in the chapter. Then, in writing, defend or refute the following statement: *The men of Meiji and the West carried out a revolution in Japanese life.* Cite specific examples to support your argument. Conclude by speculating how Japan might be different today if it had remained closed to the West.

1860	1870	1880	1890	1900	1910

1867
The use of Western clothing is authorized throughout the army and navy

1872
The first telegraph opens

The first railway line opens

The first private bank opens

Light industry develops

Compulsory education is instituted

1889
The first constitution is created

1890
The first political parties are formed and the first general election for a House of Representatives is held

The first skyscraper with the first elevator - dots the Tokyo skyline

1904
Heavy industry develops

1910
Korea is annexed

1920	1930	1940	1950	1960

1925
The government gives all Japanese males the right to vote

Radio broadcasting starts

1946
The emperor renounces all claims to divinity

Land reform policy is instituted

1947
A new democratic constitution goes into effect - women given the right to vote for the first time

1954
Sony becomes the first Japanese company to produce transistors

Chapter 17 Review

SUMMARY

In the late 1800's, Meiji reformers began to transform Japan into a modern nation. By the early 1900's, Japan had emerged as the dominant power in East Asia.

After World War I, social and economic problems led the Japanese to abandon democratic reform and cooperation with the West. In the 1930's, Japan's military expanded into Asia, creating tensions with the United States. The Japanese attack on Pearl Harbor in 1941 opened the Pacific conflict in World War II—a struggle that ended in 1945 after the United States dropped atomic bombs on the Japanese cities of Hiroshima and Nagasaki.

Following the Japanese surrender, the United States military occupied Japan and introduced a democratic constitution. Today Japan is one of the world's most developed nations, with a high rate of economic growth and a high standard of living.

USING VOCABULARY

Use the following vocabulary words in a statement about political changes in Japan during the past century.

diet   militarism
zaibatsu   civilian

REVIEWING FACTS

1. **Name** the group that held real power in Japan during the Meiji period.
2. **Explain** why the Japanese were bitter toward the West after World War I.
3. **Discuss** how Japan's population growth contributed to the country's social problems during the 1920's.
4. **Examine** the reasons the Japanese gave for territorial expansion in China.
5. **State** how the Pacific War ended in 1945.
6. **Summarize** political and social changes in Japan after 1945.

CRITICAL THINKING

1. **Evaluating Information** In writing about Japan, an author once said, "Probably no people change so quickly on the surface and so slowly beneath as the Japanese." How would you interpret this statement? Give examples to support your interpretation.
2. **Synthesizing Information** Imagine you are an unemployed worker in Japan in the 1930's. Would you support the military's policies? Why or why not?
3. **Predicting Consequences** What do you think might have happened if the United States had not dropped atomic bombs on Japan to end World War II?
4. **Making Generalizations** What characteristics in Japan's national character aided the Japanese in recovering from the effects of defeat in World War II?

ANALYZING CONCEPTS

1. **Technology** What steps did Meiji reformers take to modernize Japan?
2. **Political System** What changes have promoted Japanese prosperity since World War II?

GEOGRAPHIC THEMES

1. **Movement** The West has had a great impact on Japan. What impact has Japan had on the West?
2. **Place** What factors made East Asia an attractive area for Japanese expansion?

Writing an Essay

An *essay* is a short composition that expresses the author's viewpoint on a single subject. Essays can be written on any subject, and they can inform, persuade, or entertain.

A well-written essay has three basic parts: the introduction, the body, and the conclusion. The *introduction* is composed of one or more paragraphs that should stimulate the reader's interest and state the general subject of the essay and the author's viewpoint.

The *body* of the essay consists of paragraphs that develop the subject and viewpoint stated in the introduction. Each paragraph should present an argument in favor of the author's viewpoint and should give evidence—facts and examples—supporting the argument.

Finally, the essay ends with a *conclusion* which restates and supports the author's opinion. Transition words and phrases are used to link one paragraph to the next.

Follow these steps in writing an essay:

- Research facts and opinions about your topic. Then decide what your position is.
- Write the essay, including an introduction, arguments, evidence, and a conclusion, arranging them in a logical order.
- Add transitions to connect the paragraphs.
- Revise the essay until it clearly expresses your viewpoint on the topic.

EXAMPLE

Read the short essay below:

[1] Within a period of 50 years, Japan has made more progress than any other nation in the history of the world. However, Japan's progress was not accomplished alone. In fact, Japan owes a great deal to the West.

[2] Indeed, Japan's advances have been remarkable. Less than 150 years ago, it was a feudal agricultural country. Now it is one of the most powerful nations on earth. Not only have commerce and industry grown rapidly, but Japan has a constitutional government and an excellent educational system.

[3] This progress is due mostly to Japan's contact with the West. This contact brought to life a national consciousness which enabled Japan to become a world power. In addition, because the West has supported Japan's post-World War II defense, Japan has been able to use Western technology to develop a highly productive consumer economy.

[4] However, Japan adopted more than Western technology. In fact, many of the institutions of which Japan is most proud were modeled after those of the West— the powerful army and navy, the draft, military education, the reformed educational system.

[5] All this progress came about because Japan adopted the best features of Western civilization.

Paragraph 1 is the introduction to the essay. It states the general subject: Japan's progress in the last 50 years. What viewpoint does the author have about Japanese progress? *(Much of it is due to the West.)* Paragraphs 2, 3, and 4 make up the body of the essay. Paragraph 2 argues that Japan's progress has been remarkable. What evidence is given to support this? *(rapid change from feudal to industrial economy, constitutional government, excellent education, rapid growth)* How do Paragraphs 3 and 4 support the author's viewpoint? *(explain how the West contributed to Japan's progress)* Notice the first sentence in Paragraph 4; this sentence connects the ideas in the previous paragraph to those in the next. What is the function of Paragraph 5 in this essay? *(conclusion; sums up the author's view)*

PRACTICE

Use the guidelines above to write an essay expressing your viewpoint on the United States decision to use the atomic bomb on Japan to end World War II. You may want to research this topic more fully before writing your essay.

CHAPTER OUTLINE

1 Religion

2 Festivals and Celebrations

3 The Written and Spoken Word

4 Crafts and Other Arts

People and Places to Know
Shinto, Buddhism, Zen, Akihito, Murasaki Shikibu, Yasunari Kawabata, Ennosuke

Key Terms to Define
kimono, kami, sect, *kanji, kana, haiku, Noh* play, *kabuki, origami, ikebana, cha-no-yu*

Objectives to Learn

1. **Compare** Shinto and Buddhist beliefs and their influences on Japan.
2. **Describe** Japanese celebrations and festivals.
3. **Discuss** Japanese literature and drama.
4. **Recognize** Japanese art and values it expresses.

Japanese children's festival

284

Religion and the Arts

" I once felt sadness at the impermanence and constant change of all worldly things. . . . But I finally realized that there is not really anything sad in it at all. Impermanence is, rather, a manifestation of life itself. A flower [always] in bloom would be [empty] of beauty. The knowledge of the shortness of a flower's life, of its fate to soon wither and die, is what makes a flower beautiful. . . .

Encounters with natural landscapes must always be considered once-and-forever affairs. Nature is alive, and constantly changing. The same is true of human beings. We are destined to follow an eternal cycle of growth and decline, life and death. Nature and human beings are forever linked to this cycle. . . .

I was weak both in body and spirit as a child. I grew up in Kobe, but during my middle school years I spent time in the home of a certain acquaintance near the sea on Awaji Island, close to Kobe. Day after day I would stand facing the sea, my back to the mountains, staring out over the waters. It was during these days that I first sensed the tremendous forces around and within my own existence. Nature, the origin of all life, gave me my initial artistic inspiration. . . .

I scrutinize the wonders of nature, and record these impressions on canvas. The reason I observe things so closely is not to analyze natural phenomena as such, but rather to understand the life therein in clear, accurate terms, without a trace of exaggeration. "

These words, spoken by Kaii Higashiyama, one of the foremost painters of modern Japan, reflect the Japanese appreciation of beauty—both in nature and in the ordinary events of daily life. Over the centuries, the Japanese have developed a variety of beliefs, customs, and art forms to express their delight in plain and simple things.

This trait is one of the many aspects of traditional Japanese culture still very much alive in Japan in spite of modernization. Some of

Source: Kaii Higashiyama, as cited in *The Dawns of Tradition*. Nissan Motor Co., Ltd., 1983, pp. 82–83.

these traditions have been passed on to the West, especially in architecture, literature and film, crafts, and artistic design. At the same time, however, the Japanese have added to their heritage cultural forms of the West. Among these are Western entertainment and Western-style clothing. In Japan, for example, it is not unusual to see a person dressed in the traditional garment known as a *kimono* walking along talking with another person wearing American-style jeans. Almost nowhere else on earth have the cultures of East and West blended so thoroughly.

Religion

Japanese culture has been strongly influenced by religion. The Japanese have never held to belief in a single, all-powerful deity beyond time and space. Instead, they looked to the world around them for the meaning of life and, in the beauty of the earth's changing seasons and forms, found a pattern that also applied to human life.

Today, many of Japan's population claim to be followers of Shinto. Most Japanese, however, are Buddhists. Because the teachings of Shinto and Buddhism support each other, many Japanese belong to both religions at the same time.

SHINTO

Early in their history, the Japanese developed a set of religious beliefs and practices that later came to be known as Shinto, or "the way of the gods." At the heart of Shinto is the concept of **kami,** or "divine spirit." Below, a young Japanese student offers his interpretation of the traditional meaning of *kami:*

I do not yet understand the meaning of the term *kami*. Speaking in general, however, it may be said that *kami* signifies, in the first place, the deities of heaven and earth that appear in the ancient records and also the spirits of the shrines where they are worshipped.

It is hardly necessary to say that it includes human beings. It also includes such objects as birds, beasts, trees, plants, seas, mountains, and so forth. In ancient usage, anything whatsoever which was outside the ordinary, which possessed superior power, or which was awe-inspiring was called *kami*. Eminence here does not refer merely to the superiority of nobility, goodness, or [praiseworthy] deeds. Evil and mysterious things, if they are extraordinary and dreadful, are called *kami*. It is needless to say that among human beings who are called *kami* the successive generations of sacred emperors are all included. The fact that emperors are also called "distant *kami*" is because, from the standpoint of common people, they are far-separated, majestic, and worthy of reverence. In a lesser degree we find, in the present as well as in ancient times, human beings who are *kami*. Although they may not be accepted throughout the whole country, yet in each province, each village, and each family there are human beings who are *kami*, each one according to his own

EXAMINING PHOTOGRAPHS *In Tokyo, statues like this one of white, grinning foxes with bushy tails are found in front of shrines devoted to Inari, the popular Shinto rice god.* What are the basic beliefs of Shinto?

MAJOR RELIGIONS OF JAPAN

	RELIGIONS	MAJOR BELIEFS
EXAMINING CHARTS *Shinto and Buddhism have been Japan's leading religions since ancient times. What contributions have these religions made to Japan?*	SHINTO 	*Kami*, or "divine spirits," can be found in nature and in the processes of creativity, disease, and healing. Shinto emphasizes sacred space and sacred time. Practices vary in local communities and shrines. Rituals often honor ancestors and forces of nature.
	BUDDHISM 	Existence is a continuing cycle of death and rebirth. The chief obstacle to inner peace lies in one's desires. People can gain *nirvana*, a state of peace and happiness, by ridding themselves of attachments to worldly things. The means to this end include the Middle Way of moderation, wherein one practices restraint and follows the teachings of the Buddha.

proper position. The *kami* of the divine age were for the most part human beings of that time and, because the people of that time were all *kami*, it is called the Age of the Gods *(kami)*.

In 1947, a new democratic constitution ended the ties between Shinto and the government and granted freedom of religion to all Japanese. Despite this, many Japanese today value Shinto as an expression of their cultural heritage. The practice of Shinto rituals have contributed to such Japanese characteristics as reverence for nature, love of simplicity, and concern for cleanliness and good manners.

Source: Motoori Norinaga, as quoted by D.C. Holton in *The National Faith of Japan*. Routledge & Kegan Paul PLC, 1938, pp. 23–24.

BUDDHISM

Japanese culture also has been shaped by Buddhism. After Buddhism arrived from China in the 500's AD, it won converts first among the nobles and then among the common people. Buddhists taught about the impermanence of life and the need to seek inner peace.

Eventually, Japanese Buddhism developed into a number of **sects**, or smaller religious groups, many of which linked religion and patriotism and stressed reverence for nature. Some of the sects were introduced to Japan from outside the country, while others were founded in Japan as a response to social conditions. One important sect was Zen, which was brought from China in the 1100's. Especially popular among warriors, it taught that the way in which one could achieve inner peace was through bodily discipline and meditation.

Throughout Japanese history, Buddhism sparked cultural awakenings. It had a great influence on the arts. Many artists and writers in traditional Japan were monks who set up libraries of Buddhist writings. In addition, the government built Buddhist temples and shrines that held bronze, wooden, and lacquer, or varnished, statues of Buddha as well as religious paintings and other works of art.

Today, most Japanese use Buddhist rituals in funerals and memorial rites for the dead.

Like Shinto, Buddhism is used to affirm family ties and to provide continuity with the past. Below, a young Buddhist priest discusses his religion and his role as a priest:

Let me explain in plain language the difference between Buddhism and Christianity. Christ is an absolute being, but the Buddha, who is the equivalent of Christ, is not thought of as divine. He is more of a teacher who taught how people should live harmoniously together, and in this way become closer to God. . . . My job is to teach the ways of Buddha. . . .

I was born a priest's son and went to a Buddhist university to learn about my religion. After graduation, a student who wishes to become a priest must go

EXAMINING PHOTOGRAPHS *This large bronze statue of the Buddha Amitabha in Kamakura, Japan, dates from the thirteenth century. Through time, the original Buddha has become many Buddhas, each with its own special qualities and followers. What are the basic beliefs of Japanese Buddhism?*

through special training before he is allowed to administer a temple. To begin with, he must receive the Buddhist commandments from his master; in my case, my father. Then he must go through a hard period of self-denial, getting up at 4 A.M. every day to learn the duties of being a priest.

The severest training takes place in deepest winter. The young priests shut themselves in the temple for a hundred days, and through a vigorous program of physical self-denial, deepen their understanding of Buddha's ways. Rising at 3 A.M. and not retiring until midnight, they pour cold water on themselves every three hours, seven times a day, to purify their body, and then sit formally reading the *sutras* [lines from the scriptures]. Food is served twice a day, but it is only soft, watery rice. The idea of these trials is to conquer the desires of the body, such as hunger, sleeplessness and pain. I had to endure all this training before attaining my present position as one of the priests administering this temple in Tokyo.

My daily routine begins with the morning service in the temple. . . . I may conduct several services for the dead during the day. I also have a pastoral role to play—giving advice to runaways and those with domestic problems. I have even been made a godfather to an abandoned baby! The day ends with the evening service and the solemn chanting of the *sutras*.

SECTION 1 REVIEW

CHECKING FOR UNDERSTANDING
1. **Define** *kami*, sect.
2. **Specify** the attitudes the Japanese hold toward religion and nature.

CRITICAL THINKING
3. **Synthesizing Information** Discuss the characteristics of Shinto and Buddhism.

Source: Kazuhide Kawamata. "All over the world religious beliefs are in danger" in *We Live in Japan*. The Bookwright Press, 1984, pp. 30–31.

SECTION 2
Festivals and Celebrations

The religions of Japan have encouraged the celebration of many festivals, most of which celebrate the seasons, commemorate family occasions, or honor gods or the spirits of the dead. One of the most popular festivals celebrates the New Year. The celebration begins on January 1 and lasts for three days. During this time, the people dress in their most elaborate *kimonos*, visit friends and relatives, and exchange gifts.

Some festivals are celebrated only in certain regions of Japan. Below, a Japanese journalist discusses the spring and fall festivals held in Takayama, a small city in the mountains of central Japan:

The Spring Festival, which has lasted for 740 years, takes place in the area of Hie Shrine, while the Autumn Festival is held near Sakurayama Hachiman Shrine. . . . Highlight of the festivals is a gala procession of special floats, which accompanies two ancient dance performances and marionette shows.

Between intervals of the procession, some people dance "Tokeigaku," a unique folk dance of the Hida region, in which young men dance and beat gongs, dressed in white costumes decorated with dragon and feather designs. Ancient *gagaku* music and the reverberations of the *tokei* [cockfighting] gongs stir up the festival mood to a high pitch. Young men formerly performed this dance at the festivals, but from seven years ago the roles were handed over to children. . . .

All the parents enthusiastically desire to have their children included in this group. . . . Everyone is filled with happy anticipation as the festival day approaches.

On the other hand, "Urayasu no Mai" is a solemn dedicatory dance performed by girls in the shrine compound. On the day of the performance, they appear colorfully dressed in their finest clothes. . . .

Finally comes the soul of the festivals: a fabulous procession, led by the Tokeigaku and Shishi-Mai [Lion Dance] dancers and local residents in ancient ceremonial dress, of three- and four-tier lantern-bedecked floats. These splendid "Ships of the Night" are decorated with elaborate carvings and metal trim, and reach heights of seven meters [23.1 feet].

There are 23 of these . . . floats . . . some featuring open, roofless tops on which are placed huge drums to pound out a rhythm for the handlers. Each of the floats has received official designation as an important cultural property of national folklore so as to be preserved for posterity.

The preservation of this aspect of the festivals is the responsibility of 18 *yataigumi* (float groups). Each group includes a number of households, from eight for the smallest float to 269 for the largest. . . .

Most of the floats were built or reconstructed some 100 years ago, and are today stored in special buildings where they are protected from extreme changes in temperature or humidity. . . . Each required several years at least to complete, and the attachment of the people of Takayama to these floats is total. They are the key to and major attraction of the twin festivals of Takayama, but more importantly represent the dedication and skills of the traditional Hida craftsman—thus providing a vital link with the heritage of centuries past.

Quite different were the 1990 celebrations to mark the crowning of the nation's 125th emperor. More than 2000 Japanese watched the formal seating on the Chrysanthemum Throne of emperor Hirohito's son Akihito. Several days later a Shinto ceremony called the *Daijosai* was held, also to enthrone the new emperor. As a private event of the imperial family, it was carried out in secrecy. The emperor began the *Daijosai* with a bath of "purification." Then he offered newly harvested rice to the Shinto gods.

Source: "Takayama Festival" in *Japan Pictorial*, Vol. 4, No. 2, 1981, pp. 5, 7.

While some Japanese were in favor of both ceremonies, others were not because government funds were used to pay for them. Still others believed that only the official ceremony should have been held because the postwar Constitution provided that previous imperial law no longer would be followed.

SECTION 2 REVIEW

CHECKING FOR UNDERSTANDING
1. **State** what many of the Japanese festivals celebrate.

CRITICAL THINKING
2. **Making Comparisons** In what ways are New Year celebrations in Japan and in the United States similar? Different?

SECTION 3
The Written and Spoken Word

Another link with the heritage of centuries past is the Japanese language, which is distinctly different from other Asian languages. Although the people of early Japan borrowed the Chinese system of writing, the Japanese language has little in common with the Chinese one. The Chinese characters, or picture words, used in written Japanese are known as *kanji*. Although they are still in use today, they are used with symbols called *kana*, which express different sounds rather than entire words. Special forms of *kana* are used in writing. Both *kanji* and *kana* are used in everyday language. It is estimated that in order to read a Japanese newspaper one must know at least 1800 *kanji*.

LITERATURE AND FILM

The Japanese have a rich literary heritage. Two of the oldest surviving Japanese works, probably written in the 700's AD, are legendary accounts found in the *Kojiki* and the *Man'yoshu*, a large collection of poems. The first great prose literature was written around the year 1000 by women of the emperor's court at Heian. One of these women, Lady Murasaki Shikibu, wrote *The Tale of Genji*, which describes the romances and adventures of a Japanese prince. Some literary experts believe the work to be the world's first novel.

In addition to novels, the Japanese developed special forms of poetry. One popular type is *haiku*, which developed in the 1600's. Consisting of three lines and 17 syllables, it usually expresses a mood or feeling. The most noted writer of *haiku* was the seventeenth-century poet Bashō Matsuo. Below are two of his more famous *haiku*:

The summer grasses—
Of brave soldiers' dreams
The aftermath.

Such stillness—
The cries of the cicadas
Sink into the rocks.

Literature from Europe and North America began to enter Japan after its opening to the West in the 1800's. Many Western books were translated into Japanese, and by the 1900's, Japanese writers were blending Western themes with their own. In 1968, Yasunari Kawabata, best known for his works titled *Snow Country* and *1,000 Cranes*, became the first Japanese literary figure to receive the Nobel Prize for Literature.

Many literary themes have been used in Japanese motion pictures. Today, Japan has one of the largest and most productive film industries in the world. Such Japanese film directors as Akira Kurosawa have earned worldwide praise for their work. Many of the films, Kurosawa's *The Seven Samurai* for one, deal with the warriors of the past.

DRAMA

The Japanese also are known for their traditional forms of drama, one of the oldest of which is the **Noh play.** Created during the 1300's, *Noh* plays developed out of religious dances and were used to teach Buddhist ideas. Later, they were based on early Japanese history and legends. There was little plot. The emphasis, instead, was on human emotions and, very often, tragedy. Many *Noh* plays are still performed today. The actors, who wear masks and elaborate costumes, dance, gesture, and chant poetry on a bare stage. They are accompanied by a chorus.

Another form of traditional Japanese drama still performed today is the **kabuki** play. Originating in the 1500's to entertain the common people, *kabuki* was more popular than *Noh* because it was easier to follow and understand. Most *kabuki* themes centered on Japanese history or such domestic events as romances or family quarrels.

Today, as in the past, all roles in *kabuki* drama are played by men who wear heavy, elaborate costumes and mask their faces with thick makeup. Such feelings as joy, anger, and sadness are portrayed in exaggerated form. In recent years, some of the most famous *kabuki* actors have been honored as notable performers. One of the current leading performers is Ennosuke, who is discussed below by a Japanese journalist:

He is at once direct and retiring, with a small boy's bashful charm. The rigors of a kabuki actor's life have honed him into a single-minded missionary. He is completely dedicated to his art. He does not appear on modern drama stages, in television, films, or commercials. He is unmarried. He has cheerfully admitted that he has no hobbies. "Kabuki is my interest,"

EXAMINING PHOTOGRAPHS *As seen in this photo, traditional* Noh *actors wear exquisite, embroidered kimonos and wooden masks. Because the masks express little emotion, actors must convey the emotions of their characters through gestures rather than facial expressions. What is emphasized in* Noh *plays?*

EXAMINING PHOTOGRAPHS *Lavish costumes and colorful stage sets characterize* kabuki *theater, which has been popular in Japan for centuries. Here, two actors perform a scene in a recent* kabuki *production.* *Who plays all the roles in* kabuki?

he has said. "I love my job. I'm very lucky." He writes, designs, directs, produces and performs kabuki with that perfectionism only known to one whose art truly is his life.

Zealousness runs in his family. His greatgrandfather, the first Ennosuke, rose from the lowest rank of bit players to establish that branch of the far-flung Ichikawa acting family known by the guild name "Omodaka-ya." After him his son En'ō marched in the vanguard of the sweep toward modern theater in Japan, and forged the *shin-buyō*, "New Dance," revolution in kabuki. En'ō raised and trained his grandson, and the stamp of his eccentric genius was already on the boy when he took the name Ennosuke III in 1963 just weeks before the old man's death. . . .

Ennosuke's life in the theater has perhaps been more rigorous than most. Finding himself head of the Omodaka-ya at barely 24, he [renounced] the usual course . . . of sheltering beneath the wing of an older higher-ranking actor, and struck out on his own. The going was tough. . . . The many directions in which he now, at 45, is able to stretch himself, are the harvest of this hard apprenticeship thoroughly learning his trade. . . . But with modernity came the severance of kabuki's roots as a . . . theater of the people, and the waning of the influence upon it of single personalities like those of the earlier geniuses. . . .

It is precisely Ennosuke's mission to put kabuki back in touch with its roots as a popular theater. His own visionary addition is the idea that today, in the 20th—

EXAMINING PHOTOGRAPHS *The Japanese have developed landscape gardening into a highly developed art form. Public buildings, hotels, and private residences in Japan all have beautiful gardens that reproduce nature on a small scale. The Japanese especially love flowers, which they arrange in various styles for the interiors of their homes and for the altars of temples and shrines. What are some features of Japanese gardens?*

and 21st—Century, the people to whom kabuki belongs comprise the entire world community. Ennosuke's mission is to make kabuki understandable to everyone and loved by all.

SECTION 3 REVIEW

CHECKING FOR UNDERSTANDING
1. **Define** *kanji, kana, haiku, Noh* play, *kabuki.*
2. **Distinguish** between the *Kojiki* and the *Man'yoshu* and *The Tale of Genji.*

CRITICAL THINKING
3. **Making Comparisons** In what ways are the *Noh* play and *kabuki* similar? In what ways are they different?

Source: "Ennosuke's Kabuki: A Very Personal Theater" in *Japan Pictorial,* Vol. 8, No. 1, 1985, p. 9.

SECTION 4
Crafts and Other Arts

The written and spoken word are not the only forms of artistic expression used by the Japanese. They also have developed a variety of crafts and other arts that express their artistic values. One of these is a form of landscape gardening in which nature is copied on a small scale. Japanese gardeners have made an art of building gardens complete with artificial hills and ponds surrounded by trees and flowering shrubs. Some of the gardens, with their carefully placed rocks, raked sand, and a few plants, are centers of meditation and reflect the simplicity of Zen Buddhism.

Other Japanese arts of long standing include ceramics, ivory carving, lacquer ware, silk weaving, embroidery, enameling, and *origami*, the art of folding paper into decorative objects, *ikebana*, flower arranging, and *cha-no-yu*, the tea ceremony. Zen Buddhists regarded the art of flower arranging as a natural expression of their religion. Even warriors practiced it to help them achieve composure. The tea ceremony developed during the 1400's and 1500's, when Japanese men would meet in a small house in a secluded garden to drink tea and discuss a work of art. In the passage that follows, a Japanese woman discusses flower arranging and the tea ceremony:

I have always liked flowers, and I first began to practice *Kado* [*ikebana*] while I was still at school. . . . *Kado* is the art of increasing the natural beauty of flowers by shaping and arranging them according to set rules.

Sado [*cha-no-yu*] is the ceremony of drinking tea. It has more difficult rules of movement than *Kado*. In fact to learn how to eat the cake served with the tea properly can take three months of practice, and it takes a year to learn to drink tea correctly. Moreover, to learn all the movements of the ceremony thoroughly—making the tea with a bamboo implement called a *chasen* and serving your guests correctly with tea and cake—takes at least several years.

Both Sado and Kado have a long history which stretches back at least six centuries. The reason why I took up both these

EXAMINING PHOTOGRAPHS *These Japanese women, dressed in formal* kimonos, *instruct an audience in the proper ritual of the tea ceremony, once the exclusive privilege of the elite of Japanese society. What are some of the things one must learn to become accomplished at Sado?*

EXAMINING PHOTOGRAPHS *An ikebana, or Kado, artist stands beside a flower arrangement he has entered in one of the many ikebana shows held in Japan each year. When selecting the best ikebana, judges consider many things, including the quality and attractiveness of the vase and the way the arrangement is displayed. What does the ikebana artist try to accomplish?*

arts is because both of them share the same principle—the respect for beauty. Art should not be separate from ordinary life —it is part of it. This is why I enjoy teaching these accomplishments to my pupils.

I worked as a secretary for six years before I became a teacher, and the manners and tact I learned in this job have served me well. Etiquette is very important in *Sado* and *Kado*, so I train my pupils very strictly. I see *Kado* as a hobby, really. It brings great pleasure to gaze at beautiful flowers, and to touch them with your hands. *Sado*, on the other hand, is really part of everyday life. It has its ordinary actions, such as putting on the kettle and cleaning up the tea room, but it also emphasizes the beauty of movement—this is why I spend so much time teaching the correct way to bow or to hold the tea bowl. And of course, my pupils have to practice over and over again before they can make tea correctly. It is not easy. But gradually, after much repetition, they begin to understand the right attitude needed for this ancient ceremony. Good tea utensils are also important for *Sado*. . . .

In the old days it was compulsory for all Japanese to become accomplished at *Kado* and *Sado*. Times may have changed, but people are still eager to learn. I teach fifteen pupils of all ages. We always finish with a pleasant chat after relaxing our minds with tea and flowers. Many things come and go in this chaotic world, but as long as we still treasure tranquillity of mind, *Sado* and *Kado* will live on among the Japanese.

SECTION 4 REVIEW

CHECKING FOR UNDERSTANDING
1. **Define** origami, ikebana, cha-no-yu.
2. **Identify** some crafts and arts the Japanese have developed to express their artistic values.

CRITICAL THINKING
3. **Drawing Conclusions** Why are flower arranging and the tea ceremony important to the Japanese?

Source: Kazuhide Kawamata. "It takes a year to learn to drink tea correctly" in *We Live in Japan.* The Bookwright Press, 1984, pp. 16–17.

The Arts of Japan

For many centuries, the arts of Japan were influenced by China. The Japanese, however, gradually developed their own unique styles. Since the late 1800's, Western influences have appeared in the arts of Japan.

? **What types of drama have developed in Japan?**

PAINTING
Scroll painting of samurai warrior.

DRAMA
Mask used in Noh *play.*

CLOTHING
Ceremonial silk robe.

ARCHERY
Archer performing ancient technique.

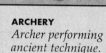

PORCELAIN
Vase based on nature themes.

Chapter 18 Review

SUMMARY

The two major religions of Japan—Shinto and Buddhism—both affirm family ties and provide continuity with the past. Shinto, the oldest of the two religions, contributed to many Japanese characteristics, including reverence for nature and love of simplicity. Buddhism, which came from China and sparked cultural awakenings in Japan, stresses reverence for nature and the need for inner peace. Both religions have encouraged the celebration of many festivals.

Another link with the past is the Japanese language. The written word is important to the Japanese, who have a rich literary heritage dating back to the 700's AD.

The Japanese also have a rich theatrical and artistic heritage. Two traditional forms of drama, the *Noh* play and the *kabuki*, are still performed today. Many traditional arts and crafts also continue to thrive today.

USING VOCABULARY

Use each of the following terms in a sentence.

kimono	*kanji*	*Noh* **play**	*ikebana*
kami	*kana*	*kabuki*	*cha-no-yu*
sect	*haiku*	*origami*	

REVIEWING FACTS

1. **Name** the two major religions of Japan.
2. **Give examples** of the ways in which Buddhism influenced the arts of Japan.
3. **Explain** what the *Daijosai* is and why it was carried out in secrecy.
4. **State** how *Noh* plays developed.
5. **Describe** how religion has influenced Japanese gardening.

CRITICAL THINKING

1. **Analyzing Information** "That, I was assured, remains the spirit of Japan—love of color and love of nature—cherry blossoms or a mountain in the bright morning—almost a definition, a trademark picture of Japan." Based on the information in this chapter, do you think this is a valid generalization about Japan? Explain your answer.
2. **Drawing Conclusions** In what ways have Japan and the Japanese been influenced by religion? Give examples to support your answer.
3. **Demonstrating Reasoned Judgment** Explain why you agree or disagree with this statement: "For the Japanese, the perpetuation of tradition is a way of preserving their identity in a world of ceaseless change moving towards uniformity of life style and of thought."
4. **Synthesizing Information** In what ways have the Chinese influenced the Japanese?

ANALYZING CONCEPTS

1. **Culture** How important is tradition in Japan? Give examples.
2. **Environment** How do the Japanese view nature and the environment?

GEOGRAPHIC THEMES

1. **Human-Environment Interaction** How have the Japanese altered their physical environment to express their artistic values?
2. **Region** What do Japanese beliefs, customs, and art forms reflect?

Making Inferences

Suppose that your elderly grandfather walks to the corner store every day to buy groceries. Today, however, it is snowing, and the streets are icy. From these facts, you *infer* that your grandfather will not go out today and won't have any groceries. Therefore, you call him up and offer to go to the store for him.

In this situation, your grandfather did not tell you his plans directly. But you made an inference based on available information about your grandfather's physical condition, the weather, and the condition of the streets. In other words, you formed a conclusion based on the facts on hand.

People make inferences every day, often without even realizing it. Inferences can be narrow and involve specific people, places, and events, as in the example above. They also can be broad statements about how general principles operate. For example, you might read an article about life in one Japanese village and make inferences about all Japanese village life. To avoid making incorrect inferences, however, always base your inferences on facts and logic and try to find evidence that proves or disproves them.

The following steps will help you make inferences:

- List all the stated facts and ideas.
- List all other information that is relevant to the situation or subject.
- Summarize this information.
- Decide what inferences can be made based on the information.

EXAMPLE

Read the following paragraph about the Japanese artist Hokusai:

Hokusai adopted the style of other Japanese printmakers. At the same time, however, he incorporated his own ideas into his works. He developed his own unique kind of illustrations and became the first Japanese printmaker to focus on landscapes. Other artists of his time and his class kept the names their parents gave them and lived out their lives in the places where they were born. Hokusai changed his name more than 30 times and moved more than 90 times.

What inferences can be made about Hokusai from the information given here and in other parts of the chapter? First, list the facts presented: Hokusai used traditional Japanese printmaking styles, but adapted them to fit his own artistic vision; also, rather than staying with his family and community, he changed both his name and residence many times. Next, think about other information related to this subject. In traditional Japan, the arts were supposed to be passed down with little change from one generation of artists to the next. Family values and loyalty were very important. Putting all this information together, what inference can you draw about Hokusai? (*He was unusual, not bound by tradition.*)

PRACTICE

Reread the passage on pages 295–296 in which a Japanese woman describes flower arranging and the tea ceremony. Then answer the questions below:

1. How is *Kado* different from Western flower arranging? Upon what do you base this inference?
2. What facts are given about the skills involved in performing *Sado*?
3. What do you think is "the right attitude" for performing *Sado*? Upon what do you base this inference?
4. How do *Sado* and *Kado* develop "tranquillity of mind"? Upon what do you base this inference?

**People and Places
to Know**
go-between, Naoe
Wakita, *juku*

Objectives to Learn
1. **Describe** Japanese
   marriage customs and
   practices.
2. **Compare** Japanese
   family life before and
   after 1945.
3. **Examine** the role and
   status of Japanese
   women.
4. **Characterize** the lives
   of young people in
   Japan.

Tokyo rush hour

Japanese Society

"As soon as Kotaro Nohmura, an executive director of Taiyo Kogyo, an Osaka tent manufacturer, arrives home from work at nearly midnight, he looks in on his four children. They are asleep, just as they were when he left for work at 7:30 that morning. . . .

. . . Six days a week, Nohmura gets up at 7 and eats a Western-style breakfast. . . . Then he is out the door and into a Toyota . . ., which he drives 40 minutes to his company's head office in . . . Osaka. . . .

Nohmura spends most of his mornings at his desk in a cubbyhole office. He likes his small space, saying, "I can get almost everything I need without having to stand up every time." There he writes reports and discusses new tent designs with engineers. The executive almost never goes to business lunches. . . . He spends the afternoon making the rounds of local customers and inspecting tents being constructed. Then he calls it a day at about 5:30.

But Nohmura's work is far from finished. On a typical recent evening he first went to a meeting of the Osaka Jaycees. . . .

After the Jaycees' session, Nohmura went on to his evening's business entertainment. He escorted a favored client and one of the client's associates to an elegant restaurant . . . where . . . they dined on a twelve-course meal. . . .

When Nohmura returned home, his wife greeted him at the door. Then over a quiet cup of green tea, the couple talked about the coming Sunday, when the whole family would be going out to the beach for a picnic. Sunday will constitute Nohmura's one day off."

Nohmura's busy schedule reflects some of the changes that have taken place in Japan during this century. Changes such as this one have had a great impact on family life. In traditional Japan, the family was the center of national life. Each family member had to follow certain rules of conduct, and all forms of individual expression were discouraged. Grandparents and older aunts and uncles were respected and cared for by the younger family members. The father or the eldest male was the head of the family, supervised its activities, and commanded complete obedience from his wife and children.

In recent years, much has changed. Family ties remain strong, but each family member is allowed more freedoms. Young people often are influenced more by friends than by family. The male's power over family affairs has declined. Since the male now spends more time at work than at home, the wife and mother often becomes the center of the family. For many older Japanese, these changes have been hard to accept.

Source: "A Hard Day's Night" in *Time*, August 1, 1983, p. 42
Copyright 1983 Time Warner, Inc.

Marriage

In traditional Japan, parents arranged their children's marriages. Even today, many Japanese marriages are informally arranged, mostly through family and friends, but also through counseling and computer-dating services. Also, many young people are remaining single or are choosing their own marriage partners. The average age of the bride and groom also has changed. Close to two-thirds of the men and one-third of the women do not marry before the age of 30. In addition, the honeymoon, a custom which did not come into being until after World War II, has become very popular.

Regardless of who makes the marriage plans, in Japan a wedding is an important event. As a Japanese journalist explains below, today most weddings are lavish, costly, and a blend of the old and the new:

Weddings in Japan still follow many of the traditions and customs which have been around for centuries, although newer customs are being added. One of the oldest is the formal engagement ceremony, in which a person selected as a "go-between" is dispatched by the parents of the groom-to-be to deliver certain lucky gifts to the household of the betrothed young lady. Packages of dried fish [signifying long life and happiness], kegs of *sake* [rice wine] and other such tokens were sent in days of old. Today, the groom-to-be's family merely writes the names of the gifts on a piece of fine, ceremonial paper.

Cash money also changes hands during the go-between's official call. By custom, the amount should be equivalent to about three months' salary of the groom-to-be. . . . But then, . . . the betrothed girl's family sends the go-between back to the groom-to-be's house to return some of the money. . . .

EXAMINING PHOTOGRAPHS *A Japanese bride in traditional dress and her groom in Western-style dress pose for a photograph at a Shinto shrine in Kyoto.* What is the go-between's role today?

The old custom of long engagements is still in fashion. . . . How long? In a poll of 1981 newlyweds, the "period of contact before marriage" lasted about a year for some 30 percent, while 57 percent were wed within two years. Go-betweens also continue to play a big role . . . as they have since as long ago as the early 8th century. When a couple decides to "tie the knot," and if all the parents approve, an official go-between is appointed to make the final arrangements. The groom-to-be usually selects a senior employee or executive of his company to do the job. . . .

And still another one of the older customs is picking the most [favorable] date possible for the ceremony itself, and astrology of the ancient Asian kind has a lot to do with these undertakings. Sundays and holidays in the spring and fall months, when the weather is best, are the most popular. . . . The best day of all is called *taian,* and some believe that marriages . . . on this day are assured of success, happiness and prosperity. . . .

. . . Expenditures [for the wedding] . . . are made without regret. . . . In gross figures, $8.3 billion is spent each year on wedding ceremonies and receptions. . . .

Who pays? By custom, the bride and groom themselves bear about half the costs . . . , while the remainder comes from their parents. . . . This investment naturally strengthens the bond between the two parental households; in view of this, the more elaborate and expensive the wedding, the better it demonstrates the parents' love for their children, and the more effectively it shows neighbors the power and unity of the families. . . .

Money saved on the ceremonies is usually spent . . . on the relatively new custom of the honeymoon. . . .

The honeymoon over, fewer than 12 out of 100 couples return to the groom's (or bride's) former home. Instead, the typical couple moves into a brand-new home, packed full of new furniture, appliances, and clothing. The majority (about 60 percent) of new couples rent their own apartments or houses. . . .

In the old days, a couple was fortunate to begin a marriage with nothing but a few basic possessions—kitchen utensils, bedding and so on. Today, the "basics" include refrigerator, a washing machine, an electric rice-cooker and a color TV. Some young people even list an air-conditioner, a video-tape recorder, an electronic oven and other such goods as "necessities." As a result, yet another "custom" is being added to the wedding scene—starting out on a new life happily in debt to the "buy-now, pay-later" credit merchants.

Source: "The Romantic World of Weddings" in *Japan Pictorial*, Vol. 7, No. 4, 1984, p. 9.

SECTION 1 REVIEW

Checking for Understanding
1. **Give examples** of ways in which marriage has changed in Japan in modern times.

CRITICAL THINKING
2. **Making Generalizations** Based on the information in the section, make two generalizations about marriage in Japan.

SECTION 2

Family Life

Before 1945, many Japanese lived in large family groups with grandparents, parents, and children all in one house. Today, many Japanese live in smaller family groups that consist of only parents and children. Some families, however, have tried to maintain family ties associated with the past. They try, for example, to look after their parents in old age and often set aside a separate area of their homes for them. Below, a Japanese housewife discusses her daily life and the blend of old and new in her household:

I am a housewife living in Saitama, which is a northern suburb of Tokyo. The Saitama area is quite flat and used to be an agricultural area producing mainly rice, but today it has been transformed into suburbs. . . .

My family have been farmers for generations and our house is still surrounded by some rice fields and farmland—though there are more houses than before. My husband is 32 years old and we have three daughters—the eldest one is 7. We live with my parents and grandmother. These days the size of Japanese families has become smaller and smaller, the average size being about four. My family, which consists of eight from four generations, is big by Japanese standards.

My husband works in a bank. I worked in the same bank when I left high school. After a few years I met my husband. . . . As I have one younger sister but no brothers, my parents adopted him as their heir when we got married.

My house is an old two-story building which was built more than a hundred years ago. It has three traditional Japanese rooms, two Western-style rooms and one kitchen. By Japanese standards the house is big, but . . . there is not much storage space. . . . In Japan, most families have their own house. The quality of houses has been drastically improved recently, and they can no longer be described as "rabbit hutches" as they were in the past. Nevertheless, they are still not as big on average as European or American houses.

I usually get up at six o'clock and prepare breakfast. Washing, cleaning and shopping are my main chores, which I do after my family leaves for work. In the afternoon, I take my daughters to piano, calligraphy or swimming lessons by car. I start preparing dinner at about half-past six. Each generation likes different sorts of food, so it is difficult for me to satisfy the whole family. For example, my daughters like hamburgers, curry, and corn soup; my husband likes *tempura* (fried fish and vegetables) and meat; and my parents like traditional Japanese stew. After dinner, I wash the dishes and send the children to bed around nine o'clock. After they go to bed I can finally relax watching TV and chatting with my husband and parents. It is not until about half-past eleven that I go to sleep.

One of the things Japanese people are very concerned about is their health. That is partly because the cost of our health care has sharply increased, but a more significant reason may be that the quality of everyday food has got worse, and that they lack physical exercise. I did not bother doing physical exercise, because I thought I was too busy with the housework. However, I realized I needed more exercise so I joined a volleyball club organized by housewives in my town.

Apart from health, what worries me most is our family's living expenses. Although my husband's salary rises regularly, our family's financial situation is deteriorating, because inflation is higher than pay raises. Therefore, housewives like me have to be thrifty. . . .

EXAMINING PHOTOGRAPHS *This Japanese family, equipped with a tennis racket and bat, is enjoying an outing at a local city park. Picnics and outings such as this one are popular forms of entertainment for many city dwellers. What do some Japanese wives and mothers do during a typical weekday?*

Our desire in the future is to get our house rebuilt and to give our three daughters a university education.

Source: Kazuhide Kawamata. "The Japanese are very concerned about their health" in *We Live in Japan*. The Bookwright Press, 1984, pp. 36-37.

SECTION 2 REVIEW

CHECKING FOR UNDERSTANDING
1. **State** one way in which family groups have changed in Japan since 1945.
2. **Point out** ways in which some Japanese households reflect a blend of old and new.

CRITICAL THINKING
3. **Drawing Conclusions** What are some typical concerns of a modern Japanese family?

SECTION 3

Women

In traditional Japan, the status of women was lower than that of men. Men led, and women were expected to obey. After World War II, however, Japanese women officially were given equal rights with men in all fields. Today, although most Japanese women still are concerned about a home and family, many are taking jobs outside the home.

Although Japanese women actively participate in political and social life, traditional ideas remain strong. While in the home, many women now tend to manage the finances and make important decisions, but they rarely disagree with their husbands in public.

The situation is much the same in the job market. Although more than half of the medical technicians, teachers, and entertainers in Japan are women, only one-fourth of major Japanese corporations have women in middle-management or higher. When it comes to pay, job security, or promotions, women are significantly worse off than men in almost any type of job. In fact, the annual income of the average working woman amounts to only half of that of a man. In the magazine article that follows, two journalists discuss the role of Japanese women in the work world:

One aspect of the Japanese corporate culture that has proven more resistant to change is the almost complete exclusion of women from the business world. In all, there are about 25 million working women in the country, about 40 per cent of the labor force. But many of those women hold part-time jobs in the retail industry or work for large corporations as "office ladies"—serving tea, answering the phone and greeting male visitors at the elevator. Most leave their jobs when they get married, either because they prefer to remain at home and raise children or because their bosses pressure them to resign. "Normally, women are given very few responsibilities," said Hirosi Hashimoto, 27, a Toyota spokesman in Tokyo. "That's why companies encourage them to leave after only a few years—if they stayed any longer, they would start to complain."

Another impediment for women who aspire to careers in business is the long-standing tradition in Japan of after-hours socializing. Indeed, Japanese businessmen usually consider it essential to develop personal relationships with potential partners and customers by entertaining them lavishly in expensive bars and private clubs that cater specifically to men. Those establishments typically employ dozens of attractive young women . . . to sit and flirt with the customers and pour their drinks; the bill for an evening can easily exceed $150 a person. Not surprisingly, female business associates are usually unwelcome on such outings—even though important decisions can be made in the course of an evening.

Despite the obstacles they face, a relatively small number of women do manage to scale the corporate ladder and enter the select ranks of professionals and managers. But the achievement often requires substantial personal sacrifice. A 1989 labor ministry survey of women who reached the level of section head or above in a large company found that 60 per cent were not married and 72 per cent had never changed jobs. In addition, women interviewed for the survey used, on average, only a quarter of their annual paid vacation days.

Naoe Wakita, 54, is one of those success stories. Since 1988, she has been president of Dentsu Eye Inc., a Tokyo-based marketing firm that specializes in advertisements aimed at women. Wakita says that Japan's 1986 Equal Employment Opportunity Law has helped to increase the number of jobs open to women—but she adds that the progress to date has been painfully slow. "Unfortunately, most women are still not prepared for managerial roles," she said. "From the moment they are born, they are taught how to be subservient to men. And most men know only how to be in charge of women."

A subsidiary of Japan's giant Dentsu Inc. advertising agency, Dentsu Eye has tried to minimize the potential for friction between the sexes by hiring mainly women: only six of its 43 employees are men. But that creates new problems, Wakita says, because about half of her female employees quit as soon as they get married. "It's hard on the company," she added, "But the truth is that many women do not want to work like men—they prefer to sit at home by the window or have fun. It's changing, but only very slowly."

EXAMINING PHOTOGRAPHS *At a Mazda auto plant in Hiroshima, a female member of the management team confers with plant employees. Compared to men, how are Japanese women faring in their careers?*

SECTION 3 REVIEW

CHECKING FOR UNDERSTANDING
1. **Describe** the role played traditionally by Japanese women.
2. **Give reasons** why most Japanese working women leave their jobs after they marry.

CRITICAL THINKING
3. **Making Inferences** Based on the information in this section, what might you infer about the status of Japanese women? Explain.

SECTION 4

Young People

The Japanese youth of today enjoy greater freedoms than those of earlier generations. One thing that has not changed, however, is the emphasis on education. The school year runs 240 days, from April through March of

Source: Ross Laver and Masako Shimizu. "Will The Steam Run Out?" in *Maclean's*, November 18, 1991, pp. 53–54.

Japan

A MATTER OF CONCERN

One of the major issues currently facing the Japanese government is the low birthrate. All through the 1980's, the birthrate in Japan declined. As evidenced in the article below, by 1990 the government was openly expressing its concern:

A couple of years ago, university professor Naohiro Ogawa was rushed to a big Tokyo hospital. Despite his emergency, doctors told him that no beds were available—unless he was willing to be placed in the maternity ward.

"They told me only about 10 babies are born there every month," says Mr. Ogawa. . . .

That male patients now inhabit a once all-female domain is just one result of a rapid decline in Japan's birthrate. Last year, the rate hit a low of 10.1 per 1,000 persons. This is a drop from 34.5 right after World War II and the lowest rate among such advanced countries as the United States, . . . Germany, and Sweden.

While much debate has focused on how a shortage of offspring is rapidly turning Japan into the world's most aged society, little has been said about whether the birthrate should—or can—be

increased. But in a sign of new concern, Prime Minister Toshiki Kaifu said in a March 2 policy speech, "We must make an effort to positively support the desire of young people to have children—the future of Japan depends upon it."

One reason for the high-level concern is that government health officials predicted in 1986 that the birth rate would go up. But it didn't.

Last year, the number of births fell to 1.24 million, down 71,000 over the previous year. The fertility rate, or the average number of children a woman bears in a lifetime, declined to 1.66 in 1988, far lower than the 2.1 needed to keep a stable population. . . .

Researchers say the major causes for the decline are delayed marriages and the rising costs of child-rearing. They say parental pressure to marry and have children has declined, contributing to a steady rise in the average age of marriage. . . .

Increasingly, working women are either becoming attached to their careers or simply enjoy the financial independence that allows them overseas travel or other leisure activities. Many young women fear that marriage will deprive them of their lifestyle. . . .

For men, marriage is often delayed because Japan's corporate culture demands long working hours that leave little time for social life. . . .

Japan's poor housing conditions are dissuading many young people from marriage, experts also point out. . . . The drop of national fertility rate since 1985 . . . "coincides with the time when land prices started to soar. . . ."

Economists warn that Japan should start preparing for an unavoidable slowdown of the economy.

The second postwar baby boom generation, now entering university age, could be Japan's last big consuming and producing cohort.

DRAWING CONCLUSIONS

1. Why has Japan's birthrate been so low?
2. Why might a continuing decline in the birthrate result in an economic slow down?

Source: Keiko Kambara. "Japan's Birthrate Hits Low" in The Christian Science Monitor, March 20, 1990, p. 4. Reprinted by permission from THE CHRISTIAN SCIENCE MONITOR © 1990 The Christian Science Publishing Society. All rights reserved.

the following year, with a summer vacation break. Children start their education at age 6. At 15, they may leave school for work. Most, however, continue their studies at the high school level until they are 18, and then about one-third go on to university.

EXAMINATIONS

To get into high school and university, Japanese students must pass difficult examinations. Because the number of openings are limited, students compete fiercely to do well in the exams and to get into the best schools. Although Japanese schools have produced a highly skilled work force, many Japanese feel that the fierce competition that exists has had bad effects on many Japanese youths. Below, a Japanese author discusses this problem:

Japan's system of education has been reduced to a contest to pass examinations rather than a means by which students are intellectually nourished. Failure at school will influence any child's future so most parents are obsessed with sending their children to "better" schools.

Japan is full of cram schools called "juku" where children are given extra training in how to cope successfully with tests. The juku method is based entirely on memory drills and has nothing to do with understanding a subject. Some of the juku students are as young as three or four years old, and they spend at a minimum of two hours a day in order to qualify for acceptance in kindergarten.

Roughly 180,000 juku are in service for five million pupils, aged 7 to 15. This means that at least 30 percent of all children in the compulsory grades from elementary school through junior high school attend extra classes after school. . . .

. . . Private schools tend to offer more freedom than the public schools which are run by . . . the Ministry of Education. There are also striking differences between public and private schools because of methods of selecting teachers and textbooks. In public schools, both are rigidly controlled by the government.

Many private schools take children from kindergarten through high school and in a few cases even through university levels.

EXAMINING PHOTOGRAPHS *These Tokyo public high school students attend class 5 ½ days a week and study such subjects as the Japanese language, math, science, social studies, art, music, and physical education. They are also offered job training. Today, nearly one-third of all upper secondary students attend private schools.* Why do many Japanese parents send their children to juku?

EXAMINING PHOTOGRAPHS *Like other teenagers in different parts of the world, these Japanese teenage boys are spending part of the afternoon reading their favorite magazines and comics. What do many Japanese youth do for entertainment?*

Once accepted, therefore, a student does not have to strive desperately to succeed in examinations since he can move on to the next grade with teachers' recommendations.

Obviously, many parents consider the expensive tuition, entrance fees and huge donations involved in private education all worthwhile. . . .

Some parents, however, strongly support public education. Masanori Iwashita, for instance, sends both of his daughters to public elementary schools near their home in Chofu City. In the public schools, Iwashita says, "children learn automatically that there are very different kinds of people in society; consequently they cope with each situation. Private school is expensive and walled-off and detached from the reality of life."

Whether they are in public or private schools, most students are faced with entrance examinations to universities so every day in high school is spent concentrating on entrance examinations. Once accepted, students can relax since they are virtually assured of passing.

This is only a temporary refuge, however, because soon the students are employed by companies with strict schedules which will continue for the rest of their lives.

SOCIAL LIFE

Despite the emphasis on education, life is not all work for Japanese youth, who enjoy rock music, modern fashions, motor bikes, television and movies, and comic books. Many young people are members of youth clubs, which meet after school. At these meetings, club members can pursue their personal interests and hobbies. Sports, such as baseball and judo, also are popular. Below, a young Japanese explains how and why he became interested in judo and how it has influenced his life:

I was born in Kumamoto district of Kyūshū. . . . In traditional Japanese folklore, people from this part of the country have been called *mokkasu*, which means stubborn or hard to please. I'm afraid this is right in my case. From an early age I was unyielding, stubborn and extremely

Source: Yoshiko Sakuri. "Fear of failing crucial exams fills Japan's 'cram schools' with students" in *World Paper*, January 1984, p. 13.

EXAMINING PHOTOGRAPHS *A black-belted judo master teaches a young boy one of the methods of throwing an opponent.* How are the martial arts different from modern sports?

rough. I was big even as a child at kindergarten. . . . Unfortunately my size and muscular power caused some problems in the playground. Sometimes fights would get out of hand, and, without intending it, I would hurt others. . . . So when I was 9, my mother decided to send me to the local judo school where I could let off steam.

Judo, like karate and kendo [a Japanese form of fencing], is one of the Japanese martial arts. The big difference between these activities and modern sports is that in the martial arts, the spiritual side is very important. In judo we improve our skills by repeatedly practicing attacking or defending movements, and the aim is not only to increase our physical strength, but our spiritual strength as well. This is the way that the martial arts have been used to train body and soul for centuries. . . .

For someone like me who loved to be active, judo was most suitable. I started to practice enthusiastically and after only four months I won the Kumamoto Judo Tournament. . . . In a few years I became the best in Japan for my age and people started calling me "Monster Child." At about this time I moved to the Kanagawa district near Tokyo in search of the best school to develop my judo. I also enrolled in Tokai University to continue my studies. In my second year here I won the All Japan Judo Tournament. Then in my fourth year all my dreams came true and I won the World Championship title. Since then I have held the All Japan title for six consecutive years, and the World title twice.

It's now fifteen years since I first started judo. It's difficult to continue anything so long, and especially difficult when it is something as demanding as judo. Although practice is important, it is not good enough just to put in a lot of hours. What counts is the amount of mental and physical concentration you put into your practice in a set period of time. It is not possible to win with muscle power alone. To bring one's strength into play one must have physical and spiritual power. This is the fascination and charm of judo. . . .

My day begins at 6:30 A.M. and I am hard at work by 7 o'clock. I take a break mid-morning to do my research work at the university and continue my judo practice at 4:30 P.M. for a further three hours. Altogether I suppose I average about five or six hours' practice a day.

SECTION 4 REVIEW

CHECKING FOR UNDERSTANDING

1. **Explain** why some Japanese prefer private schools to public schools.
2. **Name** some of the leisure activities enjoyed by Japanese youth.

CRITICAL THINKING

3. **Demonstrating Reasoned Judgment** The Japanese believe that if you are not achieving, you have not tried hard enough. Explain why you agree or disagree.

Source: Kazuhide Kawamata. "Judo develops the mind and body together" in *We Live in Japan*. The Bookwright Press, 1984, pp. 26–27.

Cultural Values

CHANGING LIFESTYLES

FOCUSING ON THE ISSUE Each of the photographs below illustrates a major lifestyle change that has taken place in Japan in recent years. For each, identify the change and discuss its impact on Japan and on the Japanese.

Chapter 19 Review

SUMMARY

Traditionally, the family was the center of national life in Japan, and each family member was expected to follow certain rules of conduct. In modern Japan, family ties still remain strong, but family members are allowed more freedom and individual expression.

No longer are all marriages formally arranged by parents. Many young people choose their own mates, and most brides and grooms are older than in the past. Families are smaller as well, and fewer generations live together under one roof. Women are better educated and make important family decisions. Although traditional ideas of the woman's role remain strong, many Japanese women work outside the home—at least until they marry.

Japanese youth enjoy greater freedoms than did the Japanese youth of earlier generations. Even so, education is still emphasized. A place in junior high school, senior high school, and university depends on the outcome of examinations. The fierce competition this has fostered and the extreme stress this has placed on students is a cause of concern for many Japanese. Despite the academic demands placed on them, however, many Japanese youth find time to enjoy a variety of leisure-time activities.

REVIEWING FACTS

1. **List** six changes that have taken place in Japanese society during this century.
2. **Identify** traditional marriage customs still being practiced in Japan.
3. **Specify** what the primary concern of most Japanese women is.
4. **Explain** why Japanese students are so competitive.

CRITICAL THINKING

1. **Demonstrating Reasoned Judgment** Do you think the following statement is true? "Even though in today's Japan the roles of individual family members have changed from those of the past, Japan is still basically a male-dominated society." Explain your answer, and give examples to support it.
2. **Drawing Conclusions** For several years now, Japan has been faced with a huge labor shortage. Do you think this might impact attitudes toward women in the workplace? Explain.
3. **Predicting Consequences** Young people in Japan today often are influenced more by friends than by family members. What effect might this have in the future on the traditional Japanese concept of family?
4. **Identifying Alternatives** Some Japanese feel that the fierce competition among Japanese students has had a bad effect on many Japanese youths. Suggest two alternatives to the examinations that create the competition and point out the advantages and disadvantages of each.

ANALYZING CONCEPTS

1. **Identity** How has the role of women changed in Japan in recent decades?
2. **Choice** In what ways does modern Japanese society reflect a blend of the old and the new?

GEOGRAPHIC THEMES

Movement In what ways has modern Japanese society been influenced by the West?

Analyzing Trends

Almost any current magazine or newspaper probably contains an article about trends, or general movements in a certain direction or changes of direction. There are trends in all aspects of society—weather, housing, fashion, education, business, and politics. For example, if many school districts start to increase the length of the school day, or the number of days in the school year, this step is evidence of an educational trend toward more schooling.

By analyzing trends, we can identify patterns of change within society. Trends also provide a basis for making forecasts about the future, which are essential to decision making. For example, if the school year becomes longer, taxpayers must provide more funding to pay for it. Also, individuals may decide that it is not a good time to open a summer camp because fewer students could attend.

Sometimes it is hard to tell whether a trend is just a short-lived fad or evidence of a more permanent change. In the 1930's, for example, American women began wearing pants. What started as a fad has now become an accepted part of modern American culture. Despite our best attempts, often the only way to find out whether a trend will continue is to wait and see.

Use the following steps to analyze trends:

- Read material or study statistics that describe changes within a society.
- Identify changes and particularly patterns of change.
- Ask: What will happen if the current patterns continue in the future?
- Ask: What factors could change the current patterns of development?

EXAMPLE

Read the passage below, describing changes in the relations of Japanese couples:

Before the middle of this century, it was customary for a Japanese wife to follow a pace behind her husband on the street, carrying children or packages or whatever had to be carried. Over the years, the wife began to gain equal status with her husband. Today, husband and wife walk side by side; and the children and packages are often carried by the husband. The wife drives the family car as much as the husband. In the past, a husband would refuse to help with the housework; increasing numbers now do a number of household tasks.

First, notice that the writer compares traditional and modern aspects of relations between Japanese husbands and wives. What are some of the changes? (*Wives no longer walk behind husbands carrying packages; they drive cars; husbands help with housework.*) What is the pattern of these changes? (*Husbands treat wives with more respect and equality.*) If these trends continue, what might Japanese marriages of the future be like? (*They will be more like partnerships between equals.*)

PRACTICE

Read the passage and then answer the questions below:

In traditional Japan the family was the center of national life. Younger family members respected and cared for grandparents, aunts, and uncles. The father or eldest male was the center of the family. He expected and received obedience from his wife and children.

Today, family ties are still strong, but individual family members have more freedom. Younger family members are influenced more by their friends than by the family. Because the male spends most of his time at work rather than at home, the wife often becomes the center of the family.

1. What trends are identified in this passage?
2. What evidence is given about family life in modern Japan in the above passage for these trends?
3. What might happen in the future in Japan if these trends continue?
4. What future developments could change the current direction of Japanese family life and practices?

CHAPTER OUTLINE

1 Work—A Way of Life

2 Recreation

**People and Places
to Know**
keiretsu, Nippon Hōsō
Kyōkai (NHK)

Key Terms to Define
service industry,
*shinjinrui, karoshi,
pachinko, kyudo, kendo,
sumo, yokozuna*

Objectives to Learn
1. **Examine** the Japanese
   attitude toward work
   and how it has
   influenced Japan.
2. **Identify** popular forms
   of recreation in Japan.

*Japanese workers
processing seafood*

Work and Leisure

"   Some two miles [3.2 kilometers] north of the glittering lights of Tokyo's Ginza district is a lesser-known commercial enclave that, in its way, is every bit as dazzling. Called Akihabara, it is a booming bazaar that spills over 20 blocks and is probably the world's most fiercely competitive market for electrical goods. In hundreds of sprawling stores and cubbyhole shops [decorated] with brightly colored banners proclaiming bargains, customers can buy almost any type of vacuum cleaner or video-cassette recorder, refrigerator or radio, humidifier or home computer. Familiar brands such as Sony and Sharp are surrounded by scores of less familiar names: Nakamichi, Denon and Oki. At one store can be found 205 varieties of stereo headphones, 100 different color television sets and 75 kinds of record turntables. While some stores are relatively sedate, others flash lights, blast out rock music and station salesmen on the sidewalk to [pitch for] patrons. . . .

     The bedlam at Akihabara goes a long way toward explaining why Japan has conquered consumer electronics markets around the world. For Japanese companies, competition begins at home. To survive and prosper, they must turn out products with exceptionally low prices, outstanding quality, and innovative features. If Japanese firms can outpace their local rivals, foreign competitors often prove to be pushovers. Says a top Japanese electronics executive: "Our target is not some other country; our target is ourselves." "

A hundred years ago, Japan was an isolated land untouched by the Industrial Revolution that was sweeping Europe. Today, Japan is one of the world's leaders in trade and is considered by many the most technologically advanced nation in the world.

The Japanese have a highly skilled labor force that values hard work, group loyalty, and innovation. In the drive for markets and profits, the Japanese have been willing to learn from other countries and to improve on what they have learned. The result of this is

Source: Charles P. Alexander. "Fighting It Out" in *Time,* August 1, 1983, p. 38. Copyright 1983 Time Warner, Inc.

a strong economy known throughout the world for its efficiency, high growth rates, and low unemployment. Many other industrial nations now look to Japan as a model for the improvement of their own economies.

Japan's economic success, however, has not been achieved without some loss. The fast pace of industrialization has made daily life more stressful. Rapid change has undermined many traditional practices, and public services have been neglected. Even so, most experts believe that many of these problems can be solved and that the strengths of the economy far outweigh the weaknesses.

SECTION 1
Work—A Way of Life

Japan's economic success has been aided in great part by the business skills of leading companies. While workers in smaller industries often receive low wages and few benefits, those in the larger ones generally receive good wages and employment for life. These firms take pride in quality and invest in worker training programs and computerized automation. To ensure excellence, they promote good working relationships between managers and workers.

THE WORK ETHIC

In return for what they offer workers, the larger Japanese companies demand total loyalty. The acceptance of personal sacrifice for the greater good of the company is expected. The life style and attitudes of Susumu Sato, discussed in the magazine article that follows, are typical of most Japanese of his generation:

Susumu Sato has spent 21 years working for Mitsubishi Heavy Industries Ltd., one of Japan's leading makers of industrial machinery. Now a senior manager in the power-plant engineering department, he earns $88,000 a year and is entitled to 20 days annual vacation. But Sato merely smiles when asked how he likes to spend his four weeks of holidays. "I suppose I could go away for a month with my family," the 42-year-old engineer said between mouthfuls of sushi in his compact, two-bedroom house in a quiet Nagasaki suburb. "But actually, I never take more than five or six days off a year, including sick days. If I took more, my co-workers and customers would start to ask questions about my attitude." A workaholic by Western standards, Sato is a product of the famed Japanese work ethic. . . .

. . . Workers like Sato, technically skilled, dedicated to his job and willing to make major sacrifices in his private life for the good of his company, are among Japan's most valuable assets. . . .

Like most Japanese, Sato has been under pressure to succeed since childhood.

EXAMINING PHOTOGRAPHS
Crowded desks and busy workers attest to the Japanese ethic of hard work, dedication, and loyalty to one's company. What do large Japanese companies do to ensure excellence?

EXAMINING PHOTOGRAPHS *It is not unusual in Japan for large companies to provide their employees such extra benefits as dormitories and housing, child-care, discount stores, and recreational facilities. In this photo, factory workers play a form of table tennis over a low net on an outdoor court provided by the factory owners. What are the* keiretsu?

. . . [At] 17, Sato entered the four-year mechanical engineering program at Tokyo University. . . . Founded in 1877, . . . the university is so revered that the select few who attend it are said to have been awarded a "passport to heaven."

After graduation, Sato received job offers from several of the country's largest manufacturers. He chose to work for Mitsubishi Heavy Industries on the advice of his eldest brother, who several years earlier had joined the staff of Mitsubishi Bank. The two companies are among hundreds of interdependent firms that comprise one of Japan's six giant *keiretsu*—powerful business groupings that figure prominently in almost every facet of the country's economy. . . .

From the moment he joined the company, Sato says, he assumed that he would work for Mitsubishi throughout his career. . . . Since salaries of most large Japanese companies tend to be based on an employee's number of years of service rather than on individual merit, there is rarely much of a financial incentive . . . to switch jobs.

But the prospect of lifetime job security was only one attraction. . . . In Japan, an individual's identity and social ranking are closely tied to his employer. As a result, when people introduce themselves they normally give their company's name and their surname only, rather than their first and last names. . . . Explained Ryozo Yanagiuchi, a senior executive at Osaka-based Matsushita Electric Industrial Co. Ltd.: " . . . The guiding principle is that the company is more important than the individual."

Sato and his wife, Mayui . . . have three children: two sons, 11 and 9, and a daughter, 6. . . . But although he works only a few kilometres from home, Sato rarely sees his children during the week. By 7:45 a.m., he leaves in his four-door Mitsubishi Gallant—he says he would prefer a Toyota or Nissan, but only Mitsubishi vehicles are allowed in the company parking lot—for the five-minute drive to the office. Often, he does not return home until 9 or 10 p.m., after the children are asleep. "Sometimes I joke that I am a single parent between Monday and Friday," Mayumi Sato said wryly. "I can't even make plans for the weekend because I never know when my husband is going to have to work."

On the job, Sato has few of the comforts that North American managers of his rank and experience take for granted. His days

Japan

SERVICE INDUSTRIES

Japan's prosperity in recent years has encouraged the growth of service industries, industries designed to meet consumer needs. These include fast-food chains and amusement parks. Below, a journalist comments on this trend:

The Japanese first tasted American fast food—Howard Johnson's and Kentucky Fried Chicken—at the 1970 World Exposition in Ōsaka. At the time, their income per capita [per person] was $1,702. . . . By 1980, that number was $7,672, or close to the $10,094 of the United States, and American-style fast food franchises, as well as amusement parks, supermarkets, and other service businesses, had sprouted from Kyūshū to Hokkaidō.

Indeed, McDonald's (with more than 450 Japanese outlets), Kentucky Fried Chicken (430), and other U.S. fast-food eateries probably owe little of their success to their cuisine; the more than 1,500 take-out sushi [raw fish] outlets run by one Japanese company attest to the superior appeal of native dishes. Both Japanese and American chains, however, have profited from the growth in disposable income and from the fact that 40 percent of all married women now work at least part-time.

Meanwhile, a new breed of "office ladies"—young, single working women living with their parents—has entered the consumer ranks, and the slow spread of the five-day work week has allowed more time for excursions and amusements.

The markets thus created or expanded were made to order for the formula . . . devised by U.S. service companies. One example is Tokyo Disneyland, which opened in April, 1983. While it did not invest in the project, Walt Disney Productions provided the local developer with 300 volumes detailing everything from costume design to crowd control. The result: a 114-acre [45.6 hectares] park identical to its counterparts in California and Florida. In 1983, some 10.4 million Japanese strolled with Mickey and Minnie, rode on the Mark Twain Riverboat, or listened to Slue Foot Sue sing. . . .

Until recently, notes Tokyo economist Kusaka Kimindo . . . , "Japanese companies, bound by a reliance on 'serious' industries, neglected to develop amusements." Now they make and market Windsurfers, hang gliders, and other "fun" items—for home and, of course, export. . . .

The Japanese are also taking service technology . . . further. Some five million vending units sell everything from shoes to mixed drinks. And at a suburban Tokyo supermarket, robots unload trucks and restock aisles. In Japan . . . , leisure and prosperity are now the mothers of commercial invention.

DRAWING CONCLUSIONS

1. Why have service industries grown in recent years in Japan?
2. What is the meaning of the statement, ". . . leisure and prosperity are now the mothers of commercial invention"?

Source: James Gibney. "Consumption as Culture." From THE WILSON QUARTERLY, Summer 1985. Copyright 1985 by the Woodrow Wilson International Center for Scholars.

are spent in a large rectangular office crammed with long rows of identical grey desks. . . . There are no carpets, no partitions and no secluded spaces for employees who want privacy. To save time, he eats lunch at his desk—a Japanese-style boxed meal . . . his wife prepares for him each morning.

As a result of working in . . . close proximity, Sato says he and his co-workers know almost every aspect of one another's private lives. . . . The closeness extends beyond the office: on weekends, Sato and his colleagues frequently work out together at the company-run health club and attend games played by the company-sponsored semiprofessional baseball team. In the event of injuries at work or play, employees receive free treatment at a fully equipped, company-owned hospital. . . .

Although he is clearly proud of his country's tradition of self-sacrifice, Sato complains that many younger Japanese—the so-called *shinjinrui*, or new human race—have little appetite for hard work. "In every aspect of our society, we are becoming more Americanized," he said sadly. "Perhaps 10 or 20 years from now, Japanese businessmen will avoid long hours and demand 20 or 30 days of vacation a year. I'm worried about the future."

THE *SHINJINRUI*

Many younger Japanese do not have the same attitudes about work as their elders. Known as *shinjinrui*—new human race—they are not willing to conform to the values of the majority. As they see it, no one should suffer *karoshi*, death from overwork. The young Japanese discussed in the article that follows is an example:

In a country in which few qualities are more important than loyalty to an employer, Motohiro Baba refuses to play by

the rules. At 28, the brash Nagasaki native has already changed jobs twice. After graduating from Tokyo's University of Agriculture and Technology, Baba went to work for a computer company affiliated with the powerful and renown Mitsui industrial group. As a "Mitsui man," Baba was almost assured of lifetime employment, annual salary increases and slow but steady progress up the corporate ladder. But instead of celebrating his good fortune, Baba quickly became dissatisfied. "I was bored stiff working at a big firm like Mitsui," he recalled. "In a Japanese company, teamwork is more important than individuality. That's good if everyone shares the same goal, but if your approach is different, things become very hard. I found it stressful because I had to keep my opinions to myself." Two years after joining Mitsui, Baba did the unforgivable. Seeking more responsibility and the possibility of foreign travel, he resigned from the Mitsui firm and joined the Tokyo branch of a French-owned chemical company.

When that firm encountered financial difficulties in 1989, Baba switched to the marketing department of Cargill North Asia Ltd., a subsidiary of the Minneapolis-based food industry giant Cargill Inc. "I like my work because of the independence," said Baba, whose current duties include trying to increase U.S. beef exports to Japan. "At most Japanese companies, I would not be given the green light to work on my own sales strategies. . . . "

Fulfilling his ambition to travel, Baba recently spent six months in Kansas on a company-sponsored training program. He also visited Calgary for several days to learn about the beef industry there. He says that he returned to Tokyo more disillusioned than ever about the traditional Japanese approach to work and life. "Older Japanese say that Japan is a wonderful country, but that's because they are comparing today's conditions to the way things were when Japan was destroyed

---

Source: Ross Laver and Masako Shimizu. "The Company Man" in *Maclean's*, November 18, 1991, pp. 55–57.

EXAMINING PHOTOGRAPHS
Golf is a popular form of recreation in Japan, and the country has over a thousand golf courses and driving ranges. This three-decker driving range enables large numbers of Japanese golfers to practice their shots. What other kinds of Western sports are enjoyed in Japan?

during the war," said Baba, whose father was a kamikaze pilot awaiting his turn to fly when the Second World War ended. "But I represent the new generation. Personally, I'm fed up with Tokyo—the housing standards are deplorable and most people don't even know how to relax. . . . "

Baba says that for now, he intends to concentrate on his career and has no plans to get married. . . . But if and when he does marry, he said that his family will be his top priority. "I do not believe that a married man should work long hours and neglect his family like most Japanese men do," he said.

SECTION 1 REVIEW

CHECKING FOR UNDERSTANDING
1. **Define** *shinjinrui, karoshi.*
2. **Explain** why workers are among Japan's most valuable assets.
3. **Account** for the view of some older Japanese that the *shinjinrui* have "little appetite for hard work."

CRITICAL THINKING
4. **Recognizing Ideologies** What is the guiding principle of most major Japanese companies?

Source: Ross Laver and Suvendrini Kakuchi. "Turning Away From Teamwork" in *Maclean's*, November 18, 1991, p. 51.

SECTION 2

Recreation

Japanese life does not consist entirely of work. For most Japanese, Sunday is the free day of the week—the day they do most of their shopping, take strolls, and, when the weather is good, admire flowers and visit shrines. On Sundays—and any other days they have the time—the Japanese also watch television, read, attend the theater, and enjoy a variety of games and sports. One game especially enjoyed in cities is *pachinko*, a pinball game that first appeared in Japan after World War II.

The main leisure activity of most Japanese, however, is sports—all kinds of sports, from fishing and hunting to mountain climbing and the martial arts. There are traditional sports, such as *kyudo,* archery; *kendo*, a form of fencing using bamboo swords; *sumo*, a form of wrestling; and judo. There are Western sports, such as volleyball, tennis, baseball, and golf. Golf, for example, was not introduced to Japan until the beginning of this century. Today there are more than 1200

Huge sumo *wrestlers parade around the ring before an exhibition.* Sumo *tournaments attract large, enthusiastic crowds, and many matches are shown on television. What are the origins of* sumo *wrestling?*

golf courses in Japan and almost as many golf driving ranges. Some are even found on the roofs of buildings.

SUMO WRESTLING

Sumo wrestling did not become a professional sport until the 1700's. But it began long before as a Shinto religious ritual intended to amuse the gods. As the article that follows points out, even today *sumo* wrestlers spend only about 20 to 60 seconds of a match actually wrestling and about four minutes performing traditional Shinto rites—bowing to each other, clapping their hands to attract the gods, stamping their feet to drive out evil, and sprinkling salt to purify the wrestling ring:

> **S***umo* wrestlers can hardly be described as typically Japanese in appearance. For they are men of unusual size. . . . These giants are to be distinguished from their compatriots in another way. Their long hair is arranged in the old pre-Meiji manner bound up in a top-knot; and it is unusual to see them wearing anything but Japanese dress. During bouts in the ring they wear only highly elaborate loincloths. . . .

A typical *sumo* bout is over almost before it has begun. It is exceptional for a fight to last more than a few seconds, since a contestant wins, either if he forces his opponent beyond the circular ring, bordered with straw padding, or if he makes him touch the ground with any part of his body (except the soles of his feet). Before a fight starts there is much preliminary display by the two wrestlers. They scatter salt on the ring as an act of purification. They get down on their haunches and face each other, their clenched fists on the sand of the ring. But they will not spring at each other until both feel ready for the fray. They will rise again, walk back with measured tread, pick up salt and scatter it; and then, once again, down they get in the posture of preparedness. But even now they do not open the bout. They rise to their feet and repeat what they did before. When at last they hurl themselves at each other the impact is immense; and so is the enthusiasm of the spectators, breaking out in a roar.

A *sumo* wrestler has to have more than great weight. He also must possess great strength, balance, speed, and mental

Source: Richard Storry. *Japan.* David White, 1969, pp. 119–120.

discipline. His training begins as soon as he finishes junior high school. He lives in a dormitory-gymnasium called a stable. As an apprentice, he not only has to learn to fight but also has to clean the training grounds, cook and serve food, and act as a servant to senior wrestlers. To "bulk up" to the average weight—200 to 350 pounds (90 to 160 kilograms), he consumes enormous amounts of rice and *chankonabe*, "wrestler's stew," which he washes down with beer and *sake*, an alcoholic beverage made from fermented rice.

Sumo matches are televised, and every year 15-day-long tournaments are held in Tokyo and other big cities. The wrestlers are idolized by their fans. Grand champions—*yokozuna*—are national heroes. The wrestler's careers, however, are brief; they must retire at age 30.

BASEBALL

In Japan, the baseball season runs from April to October, and every autumn there is a World Series. There are hundreds of non-professional teams and a large number of professional ones. Most large cities have their own team. Tokyo, for example, is home to the Yomiuri Giants, while Osaka has its Hanshin Tigers. As a Japanese journalist explains in the following article, baseball is popular with Japanese of all ages:

Few would argue that the sport most watched by the average Japanese is baseball. At the professional level, the sport consists of two six-team leagues, which battle through 130-game seasons lasting nearly seven months. In terms of sheer popular interest, the nod goes to the national high school tournaments, held each spring and summer. Each and every game is broadcast from start to finish on both television and radio, with no commercial breaks. Seven sports newspapers published in Tokyo focus their coverage on baseball. And, for those who find the lure of the diamond too great to resist, there are many varieties of sandlot baseball (known literally as "grass baseball" in Japanese) to indulge in.

EXAMINING PHOTOGRAPHS
A state-of-the-art electronic scoreboard keeps fans informed during a baseball game in one of Tokyo's large stadiums. How long does the baseball season run in Japan?

EXAMINING PHOTOGRAPHS
These young players belong to one of Japan's many youth baseball teams. What sports are now challenging sandlot baseball's popularity?

The popularity of sandlot ball may be glimpsed by visiting a local park or river bed any Sunday. From dawn to dusk, teams come and go, playing their games and moving along. There are children's teams with mothers in tow, teams of balding, overweight middle-aged office workers, and lately, many more women's teams.

The craze is no longer limited to weekends. The popularity of "morning baseball" is now on the rise, with teams assembling long before office hours to play. When the games are over, all players depart, naturally, for their respective jobs. . . .

It is difficult to calculate the active sandlot baseball population, because many of the games are played by pickup teams who gather for a single afternoon's enjoyment. The Leisure Development Center estimates the total at around 12.5 million players—about ten percent of the population. And with almost all male adults having some experience with the sport, the potential roster is certainly much greater. . . .

Although seldom given the attention it deserves, a major factor behind the popularity of baseball among the masses in Japan is a [locally made] ball, invented

over six decades ago. The standard baseball has remained basically the same ever since the sport was introduced in Japan in 1872—a cork core, wrapped tightly with leather or horsehide. . . . Whether thrown or batted, such a ball presents a genuine physical threat to anyone untrained in the finer points of the game.

This problem was solved in 1919, when a Japanese developed a hollow rubber "soft-type" baseball. Differing from the larger "softball" pitched underhanded, this ball is the same size as its standard counterpart, and may be gripped and pitched in normal overhand fashion. Even the hardest contact with the body will cause little more than a colorful bruise. The safety of this ball has helped popularize baseball among the masses, as it gives every sandlotter the satisfaction of playing the same basic game as the pros on TV.

Yet, sandlot ball is not without its drawbacks. The greatest is the shortage of fields. Playing time in full-fledged professional stadiums is expensive, and must be booked months in advance. Use of fields managed by local authorities is almost always determined by lottery. The rising population density in urban areas often

EXAMINING PHOTOGRAPHS
Since World War II, television has become a popular pastime in Japan, especially among children and young people. These Japanese youngsters are watching a popular cartoon show. Japan is noted for its high-quality animated film features, many of which have won international awards. How much time does the average Japanese family spend each day watching television?

forces team managers to search out sand-lots (real ones) or river beds as game sites.

Over the past few years, the rise in tennis, skiing, golf and other leisure-oriented sports has caused many younger people to lose interest in baseball. But the appeal of the grass diamond is deep-rooted, and is more than capable of weathering this and other challenges.

Yet boyhood dreams be as they may, probably the greatest secret behind the popularity of sandlot ball is that it is played primarily for fun. Why, almost all team managers announce to their teams before the game: "All right, get out there and fight. But don't anybody get hurt."

TELEVISION

Another popular pastime among the Japanese is watching television. In fact,

the Japanese lead the world in the number of hours spent in front of the television set. The average Japanese family spends 8 hours and 15 minutes a day watching television. In the excerpt below from a magazine article, a journalist comments on the Japanese passion for television:

In few countries does television exert as much influence as it does in Japan. As Tokyo critic Satō Kuwashi puts it, "Most Japanese worship TV with blind devotion. . . ."

. . . So enamored are the Japanese of the medium that, when polled recently on which one of five items—newspapers, TV, telephones, automobiles, and refrigerators —they would keep if they could have only *one,* 31 percent . . . answered "television."

NHK [Nippon Hōsō Kyōkai, or Japan Broadcasting Corporation] spokesman Yoshinari Mayumi asserts that television

EXAMINING PHOTOGRAPHS

In suburban Tokyo, many middle-class residents live in modern homes like this one with a television and radio (in the corner) and such furnishings as floor-to-ceiling drapes, dining table and chairs, and carpeting. What kinds of television programs do Japanese viewers enjoy?

"fulfills a collective Japanese urge—to be all of a group together, watching TV." Indeed, Japan's "group" mentality has encouraged the medium's rapid growth. In 1959, six years after broadcasting began, networks advertised the marriage of crown Prince Akihito with the slogan "Let's all watch the Prince's marriage on TV." Japanese bought four million sets that year. . . .

During the 1970's, color TVs, cars, and "coolers" (air conditioners) made up the "three Cs"—a trinity of appliances, possession of which signified membership in the middle class. Today, 98 percent of all Japanese households have color sets. . . .

Most Japanese TV sets stay tuned to one of the two channels operated by NHK, a nonprofit network created by the government 32 years ago. . . .

On NHK's Channel One in Tokyo, viewers get a steady diet of news (38 percent of broadcast time), soap operas, sports, variety shows (23 percent), and "cultural" programs (16 percent) such as concerts, local folk festivals, and a recent 30-minute documentary on ancient Chinese caravan routes. Channel Three serves educational fare: high school science courses, music instruction, English, Russian, and Chinese lessons, and the finer points of *Go*, a Japanese game akin to checkers.

Even the NHK programs that fall in the "entertainment" category take pains to promote national values. One of the more successful Japanese soap operas was NHK's "Oshin," the rags-to-riches story of a waif who became a supermarket magnate. From 1983 to 1984, the series ran for a total of 297 episodes. . . .

Japan's five commercial networks . . . are far less [educational]. Their most popular offerings are homegrown variety specials hosted by comedians and musicians. . . . U.S. imports fill 15 to 20 percent of airtime, but programs such as "Dallas" and "Kojak" seem relatively tame. . . . Japanese prefer their own samurai dramas, soap operas, and detective stories. . . . They also enjoy . . . sports programs.

SECTION 2 REVIEW

CHECKING FOR UNDERSTANDING

1. **Define** *pachinko, kyudo, kendo, sumo, yokozuna.*
2. **Describe** the Shinto rites that are a part of modern-day *sumo* wrestling.
3. **Explain** why baseball is so popular in Japan.

CRITICAL THINKING

4. **Analyzing Information** How has television affected modern Japanese society?

Source: James Gibney. "The Japanese and TV: Blind Devotion." From *THE WILSON QUARTERLY,* Summer 1985. Copyright 1985 by the Woodrow Wilson International Center for Scholars.

Chapter 20 Review

SUMMARY

Modern Japan is a world leader in technology and trade . Much of Japan's economic success is due to the business skills of Japanese companies and to the dedication of Japanese workers.

In Japan, the work ethic is very strong. Companies offer employees a wide variety of benefits, including lifetime employment. In return, employees are expected to make major sacrifices in their private lives for the good of the company. Today, however, many of the younger generation do not agree with the philosophy that the company is more important than the individual. The *shinjinrui* want a more leisurely lifestyle and greater freedom to express their own ideas.

Even those Japanese who work long hours have some leisure time. During their leisure time, the Japanese enjoy a variety of activities, games, and sports.

USING VOCABULARY

Consider each of the terms below as a caption for a photograph. Describe the photograph that you would use for each.

karoshi	*sumo*	*yokozuna*
kendo	*shinjinrui*	
pachinko	*kyudo*	

REVIEWING FACTS

1. **Speculate** about what factors have helped make the economy of Japan strong.
2. **List** benefits offered by Japanese companies.
3. **Discuss** how many Japanese companies ensure quality in their products.
4. **Discuss** the relationship in Japan between an employer and an individual's identity and social ranking.

5. **Explain** how attitudes regarding work and lifestyles are changing among some Japanese young people.
6. **Give examples** of leisure activities enjoyed by the Japanese.

CRITICAL THINKING

1. **Drawing Conclusions** Most Japanese work long hours most days of the week. What effect might this have on their family lives? On their regard for and practice of traditional Japanese values and beliefs?
2. **Recognizing Bias** When speaking about the Japanese lifestyle and work ethic, Motohiro Baba indicates his bias. Is his bias negative or positive? Give examples to support your answer.
3. **Making Comparisons** According to Japan Broadcasting Corporation spokesperson Yoshinari Mayumi, the Japanese have a passion for television because it "fulfills a collective Japanese urge—to be all of a group together, watching TV." Do you think this is the case in your country? Explain.

ANALYZING CONCEPTS

1. **Change** What effect has a prosperous economy had on Japan and on the Japanese?
2. **Culture** How is uniformity implied in the Japanese work ethic?
3. **Empathy** To what do the *shinjinrui* attribute the older generation's approach to work and life?

GEOGRAPHIC THEMES

Movement Some Japanese feel that Japanese society is becoming too Americanized. What are some examples of Western influence in Japan?

Taking Notes

Experts agree that one of the best ways to remember something is to write it down. *Taking notes*—writing down information in an orderly and brief form—not only helps you remember. It also makes your task easier. Have you ever taken notes on material in library books only to discover that you could not understand your notes later. Good notes can help you remember material presented by teachers in class, study for a test, and prepare to write research reports.

But whatever their purpose, good notes share several characteristics: the material should be paraphrased, or written in your own words; ideas should be expressed in short phrases and abbreviations instead of complete sentences; notes should be readable and include main ideas and supporting facts.

There are several ways to take notes. When taking notes on material presented in class, write the key points and important facts and figures in a notebook. Copy words, statements, or diagrams drawn on the chalkboard. Ask the teacher to repeat important points you have missed or do not understand. When studying textbook material for a test, organize your notes into an outline (see Chapter 8 skill).

When preparing a research report, take notes on cards. Notecards help you organize information from many sources and should include the title, author, and page number of the source.

Next, list the main idea and supporting statements of each paragraph that is related to your research topic. Once you have completed your research, put together all the cards that discuss the same main idea.

Use the following steps in taking good notes:

- Identify the purpose of your notes and use a method appropriate to that purpose.
- Write main ideas and supporting details.
- Paraphrase, write clearly and neatly, and use abbreviations and phrases.
- For a research report, include the title, author, and page numbers of each source on notecards. Then, gather the notecards from various sources that discuss the same main idea.

EXAMPLE

Suppose you are writing a research report on the topic, "The Japanese and Work." First, identify main idea questions about this topic, such as "What are Japanese attitudes toward work?" "How do these attitudes differ from American attitudes?" and "How do Japanese work values affect Japan's economy?" Now find material about each main-idea question.

Using this text as a source, read the material on page 316 and prepare a notecard like the one below:

Title: *Global Insights*
Authors: *James Hantula, et al.*
Page No: *316*
Main Idea: *Japan's economic success is due partly to attitudes of big business and workers.*
1. *lg companies offer gd wages, security, emphasize quality*
2. *companies promote tmwk*
3. *wkrs loyal to co, willing to mk sacrifices*

The card contains information about the source including the page number on which the information appears. This helps you find it again if necessary. Which main idea does the information on the card address? (*How do Japanese work values affect their economic success?*) Notice the abbreviations. What do "lg", "gd", "co", and "tmwk" stand for? (*large, good, company, teamwork*) When using abbreviations, make sure you can understand them later.

PRACTICE

Suppose you are writing a research report about the recent growth of service industries in Japan. Write 3 main-idea questions about this topic. Then use page 318 as a source and prepare 3 to 5 note-cards based upon this material.

Main Idea Questions:
1.
2.
3.

Made in Japan

In the decades since World War II, Japan has focused its attention on refining imported technology and developing new technology of its own. This, along with aggressive marketing, has given the Japanese a worldwide reputation for high-quality, state-of-the-art products. Today the Japanese sell their goods from markets in Cairo, Egypt, to car lots in Topeka, Kansas. In addition, names like Sony, Hitachi, Nikon, and Toyota are recognized by almost everyone.

The spread of Japanese technology has changed the way people live and think about the world. In the deserts of Saudi Arabia, for example, people who only 20 years ago depended on camels for transportation now drive Japanese pickup trucks. Televisions, transistor radios, and VCRs imported from Japan connect once isolated peoples in countries such as the Philippines, India, and Brazil to the larger world. This has increased the flow of ideas between nations and furthered change in everything from governments to the kind of music that is popular in a country. Along with this, it has brought people all over the world closer together and given them a sense of global community.

Japanese technology has also affected the way people do business. Office equipment manufactured by the Japanese, such as copiers, computers that perform sophisticated graphics, and fac-

simile machines with telephones, have revolutionized the work place. In the United States, as well as in other countries, they save time, reduce costs, and give employees the flexibility of working from their homes. The laptop computer, introduced by the Japanese in the mid-1980's, even allows computer users to take their work with them when they travel.

Japanese technology has influenced the world in another important way, too. The popularity of Japanese automobiles and electronics has increased competition between Japan and other industri-

al countries that export similar goods. In the United States, for example, there is concern that the country may fall behind the Japanese who are investing large sums of money for technological research and development. Recent Japanese breakthroughs in a number of areas from space robots to voice-activated computers have many business leaders and policymakers believing that the Japanese may soon be the world's leaders in high technology. One American business analyst has described the Japanese as the "new Americans."

Making the Connection

1. How has Japanese technology affected the world today?

2. What are some of the ways in which Japanese technology has affected your life?

Unit 3 Review

SUMMARY

Japan's island location off the coast of East Asia has given its people a sense of identity and protection. The sea, however, did not prevent outside influence, especially from China and the West. The Japanese borrowed heavily from other cultures and made new ideas and practices uniquely their own.

Traditional Japan—Japan before 1868—was ruled by warriors under the symbolic authority of an emperor. In the late 1860's, with the coming of Meiji rule, Japan underwent a period of reform and modernization. In time, Japan became a major world power. Events that took place after World War I led the Japanese to turn toward militarism. Following defeat in World War II, Japan became a democracy and began to rebuild its economy. Today Japan is recognized as a great economic power.

REVIEWING THE MAIN IDEAS

1. **Discuss** the ways in which Japan and the Japanese people have been shaped by geography and environment.
2. **Identify** the arts in which the Japanese have excelled, and tell how those arts reflect the values of the people.
3. **Indicate** how life in modern Japan reflects the culture of both the East and the West. Give examples to support your answer.
4. **Examine** the ways family life and the role of women have changed in Japan in modern times. What factors have contributed to these changes?

CRITICAL THINKING

1. **Making Comparisons** Compare Japan of the 1990's with Japan of the 1930's.
2. **Synthesizing Information** From a religious and cultural standpoint, how do the Japanese view life? In what way is their view similar to and different from that of your culture?
3. **Evaluating Information** What do you think this statement means? Do you agree or disagree with the statement? Explain. "The productivity of the Japanese economy has been so high because of the delicate sense of balance inherent in the Japanese people."

PRACTICING SKILLS

Making Inferences Read the statements about the Japanese and about Japanese entrepreneur Den Fujita. What inference might be made about Fujita? Write a paragraph explaining why you believe your inference is correct.

1. The Japanese believe that Japan should be a nation of small shopkeepers.
2. Fujita has brought fries to people who were said to prefer rice.
3. Fujita is a "master importer" in a nation geared to the export trade.
4. The Japanese are urged to sacrifice for the common good.

DEVELOPING A GLOBAL VIEWPOINT

Japan is a leader in world trade. It has been exporting increasingly more goods to the rest of the world since World War II. But, at the same time, it limits the amount of foreign goods that it allows into the country and places large taxes on many of those that are allowed. What effect might this have on the sale in Japan of imported goods? What do you think is the reaction of other nations to this practice? If you were the leader of another nation, would you trade with Japan? Explain.

India

India and several other countries make up the area known today as South Asia. Because of their location in the Indian Ocean and the size of their populations, the countries of South Asia are of major importance. India is the largest and most populous of these nations. Its ancient civilization has given birth to two great religions—Hinduism and Buddhism. Its ideal of nonviolence has been adopted in many areas of the world. Above all, India is a place of contrasts—of new and old, of unity and diversity. It is unique in that it has produced a democratic nation-state out of one of the most diverse populations in the world.

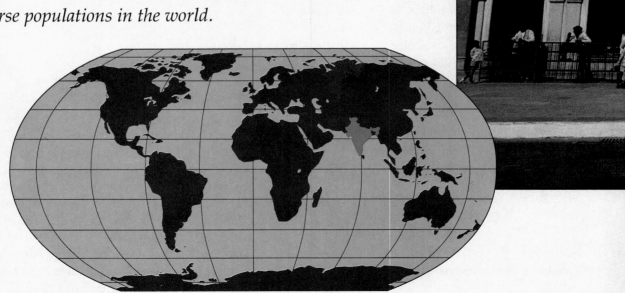

AT A GLANCE

LAND AREA: 1,269,346 sq. mi. (3,287,590 sq. km.)

LAND RESOURCES:
cropland: 57.0%
pasture: 4.0%
forest/woodland: 22.5%
other land: 16.6%

WILDERNESS AREA: 0%

MAJOR MOUNTAIN RANGES: Eastern Ghats, Hindu Kush, Himalayas, Karakorum, Patkai, Vindhya, Western Ghats

MAJOR RIVERS: Brahmaputra, Ganges, Godavari, Krishna, Mahanadi, Tapti

POPULATION: (1992 est.) 882,600,000

POPULATION UNDER 15/OVER 65: 36%/4%

LIFE EXPECTANCY: 57 yrs.

POPULATION PROJECTION: 1,383,100,000 (by 2025)

POPULATION DENSITY: 701/sq. mi. (271/sq. km.)

URBAN POPULATION: 26%

LARGEST CITIES: (millions)
Bombay (8.2)
Delhi/New Delhi (5.2)
Calcutta (3.3)
Madras (3.3)

CHAPTER OUTLINE

People and Places to Know
Arabian Sea, Bay of Bengal, the Himalayas, Khyber Pass, Indo-Gangetic Plains, Indus River, the Punjab, Thar Desert, Brahmaputra River, Ganges River, Deccan Plateau

Key Terms to Define
subcontinent, peninsula, alluvial soil, cremate, orographic lifting, legend

Objectives to Learn
1. **Locate** and describe the major environmental regions of South Asia.
2. **Recognize** the importance of water in South Asia.
3. **Discuss** how South Asia's physical geography affects the lives of its people.

Himalayan village

Land and Water

> " Mother, I bow to thee!
> Rich with thy hurrying streams,
> Bright with thy orchard gleams,
> Cool with thy winds of delight,
> Dark fields waving, Mother of might,
> Mother free.
>
> . . . .
>
> Thou art wisdom, thou art law,
> Thou our heart, our soul, our breath,
> Thou the love divine, the awe
> in our hearts that conquers death.
> Thine the strength that nerves the arm,
> Thine the beauty, thine the charm.
> Every image made divine
> In our temples is but thine. "

These are the words of the national song of India. India, along with Pakistan, Nepal, Bhutan, Bangladesh, and Sri Lanka, make up the diverse area known as South Asia. Some geographers also view Afghanistan, the Maldives, and Myanmar as part of the area. South Asia is a **subcontinent,** a very large landmass smaller than a continent. It extends southward from the Himalayas to Cape Comorin and Sri Lanka, a distance of about 2000 miles (3200 kilometers). Its **peninsula,** a piece of land nearly triangular in shape and surrounded on two sides by water, juts into the Indian Ocean, which it divides into the Bay of

Bengal and the Arabian Sea.

About one-fifth of the world's population lives in South Asia. Of this, almost 76 percent live in India, which is by far the largest country of the subcontinent. India, which takes up about three-fourths of South Asia's total area, is the seventh largest country in the world in area. Until 1947, most of South Asia was largely one unit and shared a common history.

In the past, many of today's national boundaries did not exist. So, people, ideas, and rulers moved freely across South Asia. Even today, many aspects of people's lifestyles are similar throughout the subcontinent. One problem many people face, for example, is how to conserve, use, and control rain and river water.

Source: "Vande Mataram." Sri Aurobindo (tr.). Sri Aurobindo Birth Centenary Library, Vol. 8, pp. 309–310.

SECTION 1

The Himalayas

The Himalayas, which means "house of snow," are one of the three major environmental regions of South Asia. Rather than being a single mountain range, they are three parallel ranges. Separated by canyons and valleys, they extend for more than 1500 miles (2500 kilometers) in an east-west arc across the northern part of South Asia. With the Karakorum and Hindu Kush mountains,

EXAMINING PHOTOGRAPHS *Below shale and sandstone cliffs, a roadway winds through the narrow Khyber Pass, which connects northern Pakistan with Afghanistan.* Why is the pass historically important?

they form a 100-to-200-mile (160-to-320-kilometer)-thick barrier between South Asia and the rest of the continent.

The southernmost range, which rises abruptly from the plains, is the Siwalik. Next is the Himachal, a range that boasts high, rugged mountains. North of the Himachal are the Great Himalayas, which have the highest peaks in the world. One is Mount Everest, which is 29,028 feet (8848 meters) high. In the west, the Himalayas merge into a lofty plateau known as the Pamir Knot. In the east, they extend southward and form the Naga Hills.

The slopes of the Himalayas are steep with few level strips of land. Many glaciers and rushing rivers are found in the mountains. The soil is poor, and because so many forests have been cut, there is concern about erosion. There are only a few passes through the mountains. One of these is the Khyber Pass in the Hindu Kush Mountains, which stretch across Pakistan. Through the Khyber Pass came great migrations of people and invading armies that in the past pushed their way into the river valleys of northern India.

Most of the people who make their home in the Himalayas live in small valleys and pockets scattered throughout the mountains. Because of the cold and the isolation, life is hard. But there also are several large valleys known for their beauty, such as the Central Valley in Nepal and the Vale of Kashmir. Three relatively large kingdoms can be found in the mountains. They are Nepal, Bhutan, and Sikkim, which is now a part of India. Other small kingdoms also existed. One of these was Zanskar, which was founded in 930 AD. Below, a European traveler in the Himalayas gives his impression of the area of this ancient kingdom as it is today:

[My] climb was amply rewarded by the incredible view. I had risen to over one thousand feet [304.8 meters] above the valley and I could now see a new horizon of snow-covered peaks: they formed the tormented sea of the Great Himalayan Chain, in the heart of whose folds I was now standing. Looking at the flat valley beneath me, set in a gargantuan upheaval of tormented ranges, I saw Zanskar for the first time for what it truly was: the lost valley of all dreams. . . . In the setting sun I could see the two rivers glitter where they met, before disappearing to the north down a valley flanked by red, green, and black peaks. There was no natural exit to this little corner of paradise which lay in the heart of the world's most inhospitable mountains. . . .

Near the monastery an old man directed me a little further up the mountain where stood three great stones a little over six feet [1.82 meters] tall. . . . They represented three standing Buddhas. . . . Having searched in vain for inscriptions I photographed the stellae [carved stone pillars] and then set off to Lobsang's house.

On the way I passed a group of women busily weeding a field of barley, on the edge of which two long strips of newly dyed woollen cloth were laid out to dry. . . . With their permission I took photographs of them against the staggering background of the fierce Matterhorn-like peaks that rose on the other side of the valley. Then, leaving the girls singing away I walked up a parched, grassless slope and followed a little irrigation ditch that led me to Lobsang's . . . home. . . .

The setting itself is enchanting: a lone house high upon the barren slopes of a great mountain covered with snow and ice. Small and rectangular with a flat roof, fuzzy with great mounds of brushwood, the house overlooked all of Zanskar, moreover it stood surprisingly in an oasis of green fields enclosed by a stone wall. Fast-flowing rivulets ran through the fields, bubbling a constant tune, as beside the house they formed a natural fountain.

Facing south the house had three small, shuttered windows, which turned a blind eye to a sea of summits above the green carpet of the valley beneath, patched with grey and dotted with toy-like villages. In the sunset the peaks glistened with gold while a wind descended the mountain and brought the freezing breath of glaciers. Chattering with the cold, Lobsang directed me to enter his house by a ladder of twisted pieces of wood that led up to the roof.

SECTION 1 REVIEW

CHECKING FOR UNDERSTANDING

1. **State** the major physical characteristics of the Himalayas.

CRITICAL THINKING

2. **Drawing Conclusions** What factors make life difficult in the Himalayas?

SECTION 2

The Indo-Gangetic Plains

A second major environmental region of South Asia is the Indo-Gangetic Plains, a huge crescent-shaped area at the foot of the Himalayas. The plains stretch from the Arabian Sea in the west to the Bay of Bengal in the east. There are very few trees on the plains, and the soil in most places is rich and fertile. Often it is **alluvial soil,** soil laid down by the rivers when they flood. One traveler reacted to the plains in this way:

Almost as impressive as the Himalayas, the Indo-Gangetic plains have a majesty of their own. Unfolding in seemingly endless flatness and monotony, they stretch on and on for over 1,500 miles [2400 kilometers] from west to east, dotted with village after village of tight clusters of box-like

Source: From *ZANSKAR* by Michael Peissel. Copyright © 1979 by Michael Peissel. Used by permission of the publisher, Dutton, an imprint of New American Library, a division of Penguin Books USA Inc.

EXAMINING PHOTOGRAPHS *Thousands of Hindus gather to bathe in the sacred waters of the Ganges River in the belief that the waters will make them pure. What part does the Ganges play in Hindu funeral rituals?*

mud huts with mud or thatched roofs (or sometimes roofs of handmade tiles). Between the villages lies the same patchwork quilt of tiny fields separated from one another by low mud banks in irregular . . . patterns. Along the few roads, bullock carts move with a primeval slowness that itself seems to enlarge the mighty plains. The traveler crossing the plains by car (or even by plane) almost begins to believe that there is no world but this.

Through the plains run three important rivers. All three begin in the Himalayas. All three supply water for irrigation. In the west is the Indus, which is made up of the waters of five tributaries in the Punjab, a region of Pakistan and northwestern India. This area is very rich agriculturally and sometimes is called "the breadbasket of South Asia." Although wheat is the staple crop, vegetables, some cotton, and pulses, or beans, also are grown in this area. Along the lower part of

Source: Beatrice Pitney Lamb. *India—A World in Transition*. Holt, Rinehart & Winston, 1975, p. 10.

the river's course, however, some of the soil is salty and no longer good for agriculture.

To the east and west of the Indus, the plains are very dry. At the India-Pakistan border is the Thar Desert with its sand dunes, gray-brown and desert soils, and scant scattered vegetation. The desert is about 500 miles (800 kilometers) long and 275 miles (440 kilometers) wide. At its eastern edge, in the states of Rajasthan and Gujarat, it is a little less arid, and some varieties of grain called millet can be grown.

The second river, found in the northeast, is the Brahmaputra. It has its source on the Plateau of Tibet and flows through Assam and into Bangladesh. There, not far from the Bay of Bengal, it joins with the Ganges River. A great many people live in the large delta area of the two rivers, even though the land, much of it in Bangladesh, is generally flat and can flood easily.

The third river, the Ganges, is fed by tributaries flowing out of the mountains in the north. It runs through semi-arid country there and then through the rich agricultural area of the Indian state of Uttar Pradesh. Finally, it emerges into the marshy delta area of West Bengal and Bangladesh. Some of the most fertile soil in India is found along the route of the Ganges. Here wheat, rice, jute, sugar cane, pulses, vegetables, and spices are grown. Rice, grown especially along the southeastern part of the river, accounts for 40 percent of the food produced in India. Wheat accounts for another 25 percent.

The Ganges is a very special river for those of the Hindu faith. They believe that it is sacred and can cleanse their souls and make them pure. Many Hindus make pilgrimages to the river just to bathe in its holy waters. In addition, after the body of a deceased person has been **cremated,** or burned, on a funeral pyre, the ashes are thrown into the river. In the following excerpt, a visitor to the Ganges describes a pilgrimage:

Before them was the river. Across it came the yellow dawn, the first dapples of sunlight now at the middle of the river. As one they raised their hands on high and recited the salute to the sun. Then slowly, just as hundreds of others along the bank were doing, they walked down the steps and into the river. With cupped hands they bent and brought the water above their heads, pouring down over their faces. Then each in his own way performed the ritual of washing, watching the priest ahead in the water. When the gestures were finished they stood and watched in awe as the dawn sunshine splashed over them, blessing and warming and greeting them as it had never, quite, done before. Some went out of the water and sat on the steps watching strangers. Others repeated the ritual in the name of someone at home. . . . After a time two . . . boats . . . pulled in to the shore where they stood. Ashin explained that these boats would take them the length of the city. . . .

Up and down and across the ghats [platforms on the bank of the river] moved the crowds. . . . At first it took a moment to realize that the ghat which the villagers had just left was now full of strangers. As the boats swung from the bank and pulled further away the villagers strained to see a group of priests descending a flight of steps in procession. Each carried a furled umbrella, each held his skirts above the damp of the steps, and each walked solemnly directly into the water, the pile of umbrellas mimicking the firewood on the next ghat. This was the central burning ghat where those who died in the city were burned, and their ashes given to the holy river. Already three small family groups were waiting beside their draped corpses. A priest sat near each. Someone was struggling to light the first fire, a body was moved forward. The flames caught and jumped.

Source: From *THIRD-CLASS TICKET*, by Heather Wood. Copyright © 1980 by Heather Wood. Published by Penguin Books. Reprinted by permission of the author.

SECTION 3

The Peninsula

South of the plains is the Peninsula, the third major environmental region of South Asia. Much of the mineral wealth of India is found in the northeastern part of the Peninsula. The Peninsula begins with rows of hills and low mountains that stretch from east to west. Called the Vindhya Hills, they act as the dividing line between North India and South India. The mountains are very old and greatly weathered.

South of the Vindhya Hills is rolling country, broken occasionally by groups of hills. This is the Deccan Plateau, which is shaped like a triangle pointed south. The plateau takes up the southern two-thirds of India and makes up most of the peninsula. It is bordered on the west and the east by low mountain ranges called the Western Ghats and the Eastern Ghats. Because the Western Ghats are much higher than the Eastern Ghats, the plateau slopes downward from west to east and most of the rivers crossing it flow eastward. The Ghats are fringed by narrow coastal plains which are very fertile and heavily populated. Some of India's largest cities are found in this area. Between the Ghats, however, are some very dry areas that are not very productive and have sparse population.

The soils and rainfall patterns of the Peninsula support a variety of crops as well as grazing land for animals. Below, an observer describes the relationship of people and environment in Kerala, a small Indian state located on the tropical, southwest corner of the Peninsula:

I knew . . . that [Kerala] was a place like no other in India. Coconut palms throw cool shadows over quiet backwater canals. Fishermen in wide conical hats glide by in jet black canoes. A peasant up to his knees in a flooded rice field hitches a water buffalo to his plow. It looks, for all the world,

EXAMINING PHOTOGRAPHS *Shaded by a thatched roof, these Indian women pound grain into flour, a common practice in many villages of the Peninsula.* *What do the soil and rainfall patterns of the Peninsula support?*

like India's corner of paradise. . . .

A stroll beneath the palm trees, however, reveals that paradise has gotten crowded. Roads overflow with humanity. Overloaded buses, listing like boats ready to capsize, swerve around groups of schoolgirls. Trucks honk at bicyclists. Motorized rickshas graze old men pulling oxcarts. Young herders swat at cattle to keep them out of traffic.

With more than 29 million people, Kerala is one of the most crowded rural spots on earth. Stretching 580 kilometers (360 miles) along the Malabar Coast, it squeezes a population larger than California's into a tenth of the space. Most of the people live along the coast, laced by 41 rivers and more than a thousand canals.

This morning I'm standing beside one of those canals in the town of Kottayam, waiting for a ferry to Alleppey. . . .

It's going to be another scorcher. At 7:30 the thermometer reads 33°C (92°F). A drought has tormented the region for months. For the second year in a row the September monsoon rains have failed, and drinking water has all but vanished. Village women leave jugs along the road each morning in hope that a government water truck will come by to fill them. . . .

When the ferry arrives, about 40 people get on. . . .

Now the ferry chugs past hundreds of ducks; their down blankets the water like petals of flowers. The boat's engine, which has no cover, is making a racket. But through the din I hear a gentle voice singing. It belongs to a grizzled-faced old man sitting near the back of the boat, who rocks back and forth as he sings.

The canal serves many functions. In it, one fellow bathes; another brushes his teeth with his finger; a woman throws back her long black hair after having washed it; a girl lifts a jug of water onto her shoulder.

The landscape now opens onto an endless expanse of rice fields, which are separated from the canal by dikes. At one stop some rice threshers come aboard. I talk

EXAMINING PHOTOGRAPHS
Villagers often use one section of the village compound as a central work and meeting area, where they also visit with friends and share news about the village and the outside world. How does the environment affect life in the Indian state of Kerala?

with an old woman named Pennamma. "I can't remember how long I've worked in the fields," she says, covering an embarrassed smile with her hands. "All my life, I guess." . . .

We leave the canal, start across Vembanad Lake and approach Alleppey. Most of the passengers are napping. I hear the gentle singing again behind me. . . .

SECTION 3 REVIEW

CHECKING FOR UNDERSTANDING
1. **Describe** the types of terrain that make up the Peninsula.

CRITICAL THINKING
2. **Making Generalizations** What advantages and disadvantages does the environment bring to the people of Kerala?

SECTION 4
Water—the Key to Life

Although the land has a very special meaning for most South Asians, water is considered even more crucial. Water is holy; it purifies. Water also enables crops to grow

Source: Peter Miller. "India's Unpredictable Kerala," in *National Geographic*, May 1988, pp. 596–597, 601, 605.

and limits what can be grown where.

In South Asia, water is distributed unevenly, both geographically and seasonally. The most rain falls in the Western Ghats, the hills of Assam and nearby areas, and the lands in the southern foothills of the Himalayas. The heavy rainfall in these areas is due chiefly to **orographic lifting.** Moisture-filled clouds reach the mountains and are forced upward, where the cooler and thinner air causes them to drop their moisture. Because the Himalayas are so high, they keep the cold continental winter winds north of the Indian subcontinent and keep the moisture from the southerly winds on the southern side of the mountains.

Although most of South Asia has 3 different seasons in a year, almost 80 percent of its rainfall comes during 1 season alone. The winter, which lasts from October through February, is cool, clear, and relatively dry. The summer, which runs from March to mid-June, is hot and dry. Then, in mid-June, the rainy season sets in.

During the rainy season, seasonal winds called monsoons spread across the continent to water the parched land. One Indian writer describes what happens:

[The] people have lost all hope. They are disillusioned, dejected, thirsty and

EXAMINING PHOTOGRAPHS *Monsoons bring most of the rainfall on which Indian life depends, but too much rain can have serious consequences. Here, a man wades through floodwaters to reach his flood-damaged home in West Bengal.* *When does most of the rainfall come to South Asia?*

sweating. . . . A hot petrified silence prevails. Then comes the shrill, strange call of a bird. Isn't there a gentle breeze blowing? And hasn't it a damp smell? And wasn't the rumble which drowned the bird's cry the sound of thunder? The people hurry to the roofs to see. The same ebony wall is coming up from the east. A flock of herons fly across. There is a flash of lightning which outshines the daylight. The wind fills the black sails of the clouds and they billow out across the sun. A profound shadow falls on the earth. There is another clap of thunder. Big drops of rain fall and dry up in the dust. A fragrant smell rises from the earth. Another flash of lightning and another crack of thunder like the roar of a hungry tiger. It has come! Sheets of water, wave after wave. The people lift their faces to the clouds and let the abundance of water cover them. . . .

But after a few days the flush of enthusiasm is gone. The earth becomes a big stretch of swamp and mud. Wells and lakes fill up and burst their bounds. In towns, gutters get clogged and streets become muddy streams. In villages, mud walls of huts melt in the water and thatched roofs sag and descend on the inmates. Rivers, which keep rising steadily from the time the summer's heat starts melting the snows, suddenly turn to floods as the monsoon spends itself upon the mountains. All this happens in late August or early September. Then the season of the rains gives way to autumn.

Source: From *TRAIN TO PAKISTAN (MANO MAJRA)* by Kushwant Singh. Copyright © 1956 by Grove Press, Inc. Used by permission of Grove Press, Inc.

India

"MOTHER EARTH"

Much of South Asia is agricultural, and a large number of people work the land. Below, an Indian farmer explains how he feels about the land and why:

Bhadre Gowda, the husband of Thayee, was ploughing a millet field, up and down, up and down, turning the soil to catch the next torrent of rain: the bullocks pulled and he pushed as the wooden plough shuddered through the ground. We watched from a bank, and when he stopped for a rest he came and sat beside us. The sun was hot on our backs.

He was a handsome man with the fine features of his sister Bhadramma—the same straight nose, the same delicate eyebrows over bright kind eyes, the same wide mouth expressive of thought and feeling.

'Yes, we worship the land,' he said. 'It's our life. It's beautiful. It's always beautiful. But the most beautiful is when it's green, when the crops are large and fruitful. Then it's like a woman. How much more beautiful it is when she wears her jewels, does her hair, wears fine clothes. And when she takes them off, how empty we feel.

'Yes, when we cut the crops we feel empty. But then we know we'll be starting to plant again, controlling the land, making it bear fruit. And then we feel happy. We feel satisfied in working the land where we grow our life.'

He unwound the small torn scarf from his head and wiped the sweat from his face: his chin was black with stubble, his skin dry and dark from the constant exposure to sun. He looked poor, almost beggarly, with a shirt ripped at the shoulder, and most of the buttons missing.

'You see, we feel the land, just as we feel the rain. We don't see it, splashing down on the paths; we feel it cold on our backs. And the sun—we don't see it, a beautiful sunset as you say. We feel it in the morning when it's cool, when it gives us light to work by; we feel it when it burns our backs and

we want the shade of the tree; we feel it in the late afternoon softened by a breeze; and then when it goes down and takes away our light, we feel we've done a full day's work. Then we can sleep in peace.'

He sat quietly, his forehead puckered, his eyes half-closed, and his body began to sway.

"We have great affection and trust for Mother Earth. When we're alive, it's she who gives us rice, gives us food. It's she who takes us in when we're dead. If we don't work the land how will we get food? If we trust her she'll always give. See, this year there was no rain. But now it's come, now we can live and prosper. We should trust her. We should trust her more than our own mother. . . . "

He closed his eyes; his body was silent now.

DRAWING CONCLUSIONS

1. How does Bhadre Gowda feel about the land and the elements?
2. How do you think attitudes about the land affect the way South Asians farm?

Source: Sarah Hobson. *Family Web: A Story of India.* Academy Chicago, 1982, pp. 208–209.

Farmers depend heavily on the summer monsoons. If they come in time and bring enough rain, the farmers will have the water they need to make their crops grow. There also will be water to fill storage tanks or basins and canals that have developed over time. During the dry season, this water will be used to irrigate crops. If, however, the monsoons come too late or do not bring enough rain, the crops—and the farmers— will suffer.

The rain also supplies the rivers with water. Too much rain at once, however, causes the rivers to flood. Some rivers, such as the Indus, Ganges, and Brahmaputra, also receive water from melting snow and so have water all year long. Some of the rivers of the Peninsula, however, dwindle to a trickle in the dry season. Farmers in this area must catch and store rainwater in basins and tanks.

The water in the rivers is used for many different purposes, from transport to irrigation to hydroelectric power. Sometimes, however, the purposes conflict. An example of this is the Bhakra-Nangal, one of the largest of India's water projects. It is supposed to generate electricity as well as store water for irrigation. But when there is a shortage of water, it means less electricity to run pumps to get water out of wells.

Water, then, is very important in South Asia. A **legend,** or popular story handed down from earlier times, tells how the Hindu god Shiva sent Ganga, the river maid, down from the high Himalayas to help the people:

Far away in the Himalaya Mountains in the north of India, the great god Shiva slept. And as he slept, the winds blew and the snow fell and the ice settled on his face and head. But Shiva was weary and continued to sleep as the sun blazed down on the plains and valleys of Hindustan [the Indian subcontinent] and cruelly burned . . . grass and trees. For, at that time, there were no rivers to water the land. The people cried out in their anguish for water but the god, unmoved, slept.

In the mountains there lived a great king called Himavat with his fair wife, Mena, and their lovely little daughter, Ganga. . . .

From time to time, King Himavat would go down into the plains of India, and whenever he returned from a journey, his heart was heavy and his face sad.

"What ails you?" asked Mena, and Ganga clambered upon her father's knee and said, "What is it, father?"

The king said, "The land suffers for want of water; the crops shrivel and die; the cattle waste; men and women go thirsty to give water to their children. But Shiva sleeps and seems not to care. . . ."

Then Ganga said, "Can no one do anything about this?" The king raised his heavy eyes and looked upon his child.

"Yes, Ganga," he replied, "there is help but it is hard to win. If a girl pure as ice and white as snow would leave her home and go down and dwell forever in the sultry plains, then from her life freely given, would flow life for the perishing people and her name would be sacred and beloved by all in Hindustan."

Ganga, though, was just a young girl and didn't want to leave her beautiful ice cavern. . . .

Then, one day, Himavat came in with a baby, dying in his arms. The soft skin was blistered; the little lips were black and parched; the mouth was open; the eyes, fixed and glassy. Himavat laid the child on Ganga's lap.

"It is dying of thirst," he said.

Ganga bent over the little face and, as she did so, a drop of water fell from her hair on the parched lips. In an instant the flush of life returned to it. The baby opened his eyes and gurgled with joy.

Ganga sprang to her feet.

"Father," she cried, "Mother, I will go if I can save children."

And as she spoke she went to the . . . ice cavern where she had dwelt in innocent but selfish joy, and there the miracle happened. The beautiful little girl with golden bright hair and white hands vanished and, in her place, a stream of pure soft water . . . danced on the golden bright sands and the water, as it ran, whispered, "I am Ganga, Ganga, and I go to bless the thirsty plains and to bring water to dying children."

And wherever Ganga turned flowers sprang up to welcome her; stately trees bowed over her waters; fainting cattle grew strong; children played upon her banks; strong men bathed in her torrents and women washed themselves in her pools. Ganga, the Maid, had become Ganga, the Mother, the river of life and joy.

And this is why Ganga has become the symbol of life to Hindustan, and the Ganges the river of life. This is why men think that the Ganga, as she flows, murmurs, "To give oneself for others is duty; to spread happiness around one for others is joy." And this is why the Hindu, dying far from the sacred river, prays that his ashes may be thrown into the Ganga's red-brown depths, so that dying, he may return to the source of life.

SECTION 4 REVIEW

CHECKING FOR UNDERSTANDING
1. **Define** orographic lifting, legend.
2. **Explain** why farmers depend heavily on the monsoons.

CRITICAL THINKING
3. **Making Generalizations** How is water "the key to life" in South Asia?

Source: "Ganga the River Maid—and Other Indian Legends" in *Intercom*, June 1978, Center for Global Perspectives in Education, Inc., p. 8. Reprinted by permission of The American Forum.

GLOBAL
FOCUS

Geography

THE ENVIRON-MENT AND ECONOMIC PATTERNS OF SOUTH ASIA

FOCUSING ON THE ISSUE Based on information in the four maps that follow, defend or present arguments to refute this statement: *In South Asia, land, water, and survival are linked. Without one, there cannot be the other.*

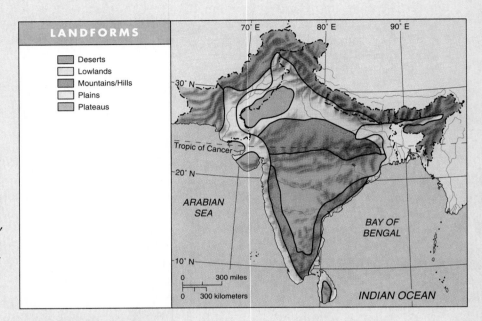

LANDFORMS	
	Deserts
	Lowlands
	Mountains/Hills
	Plains
	Plateaus

70° E   80° E   90° E

30° N

Tropic of Cancer

20° N

ARABIAN
SEA

BAY OF
BENGAL

10° N

0   300 miles

0   300 kilometers

INDIAN OCEAN

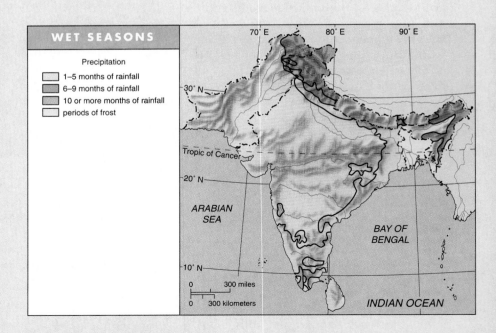

WET SEASONS	
Precipitation	
	1–5 months of rainfall
	6–9 months of rainfall
	10 or more months of rainfall
	periods of frost

70° E   80° E   90° E

30° N

Tropic of Cancer

20° N

ARABIAN
SEA

BAY OF
BENGAL

10° N

0   300 miles

0   300 kilometers

INDIAN OCEAN

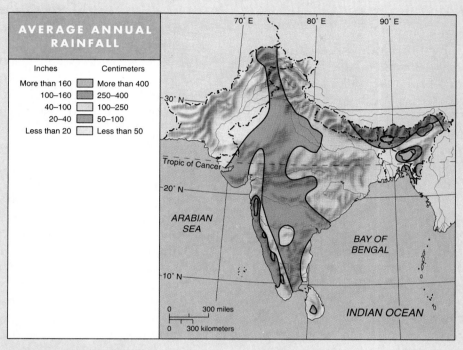

AVERAGE ANNUAL RAINFALL

Inches	Centimeters
More than 160	More than 400
100–160	250–400
40–100	100–250
20–40	50–100
Less than 20	Less than 50

70° E
80° E
90° E
30° N
Tropic of Cancer
20° N
ARABIAN SEA
BAY OF BENGAL
10° N
INDIAN OCEAN

0   300 miles
0   300 kilometers

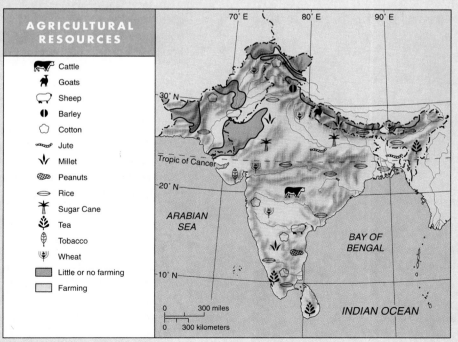

AGRICULTURAL RESOURCES

- Cattle
- Goats
- Sheep
- Barley
- Cotton
- Jute
- Millet
- Peanuts
- Rice
- Sugar Cane
- Tea
- Tobacco
- Wheat
- Little or no farming
- Farming

70° E
80° E
90° E
30° N
Tropic of Cancer
20° N
ARABIAN SEA
BAY OF BENGAL
10° N
INDIAN OCEAN

0   300 miles
0   300 kilometers

Chapter 21 Review

SUMMARY

The subcontinent of South Asia includes the nations of India, Pakistan, Nepal, Bhutan, Bangladesh, and Sri Lanka. India takes up about three quarters of South Asia's total area.

South Asia has three major environmental areas—the Himalayas, the Indo-Gangetic Plains, and the Peninsula. The cold and isolation of the Himalayas—a mountain barrier between South Asia and the rest of the continent—make life difficult for the people who live there. The rivers of the Indo-Gangetic Plains supply water for irrigation of the area's fertile soil, which provides a variety of crops. The Peninsula has mountains and coastal plains, but most of it consists of the Deccan Plateau.

Water is a resource highly valued by South Asians. Farmers depend on the rainy season and monsoons to bring them enough rain to water their crops and to store for use during the dry season.

USING VOCABULARY

Use the following vocabulary words to write a paragraph describing South Asia's three major environmental areas.

subcontinent	cremate
peninsula	orographic lifting
alluvial soil	legend

REVIEWING FACTS

1. **Name** the route used by migrants and invaders in the past to enter northern India.
2. **List** the crops grown in the Indo-Gangetic Plains.
3. **Describe** the delta region where the Ganges and Brahmaputra rivers join.
4. **State** where much of the mineral wealth of India is found.
5. **Explain** why the Western Ghats, the hills of Assam, and the southern foothills of the Himalayas get the most rainfall.
6. **Discuss** the kinds of seasons found in South Asia.

CRITICAL THINKING

1. **Analyzing Information** More than one-half of the population of India live on the Indo-Gangetic Plains. Why do you think this is?
2. **Making Comparisons** Compare life in the Himalayas with life in the Indo-Gangetic Plains. In which area would you prefer to live? Explain.
3. **Predicting Consequences** Why do rainfall patterns in South Asia make catching and controlling water so important?
4. **Expressing Problems Clearly** Explain the following statement: "The monsoons dominate economic life in many areas of South Asia. They mean life and death to the people of the region."

ANALYZING CONCEPTS

1. **Diversity** What physical features characterize South Asia as a region of the world and distinguish it from other world regions?
2. **Environment** How are the major rivers of South Asia used by the people of this region?

GEOGRAPHIC CONCEPTS

1. **Region** How is the Punjab area of India like the midwestern area of the United States?
2. **Location** Where are the Indo-Gangetic Plains located?

Interpreting a Special-Purpose Map

As you learned earlier, different types of maps provide different kinds of information. You have already studied some of the most common types of maps—political, physical, and climate.

Another type of map, one that shows information about a specialized subject, is the *special-purpose*, or *thematic*, map. A special-purpose map can cover almost any subject—economic, political, social, cultural, and almost anything that can be expressed geographically. It can also be a map that shows the distribution of economic resources, languages, religions, wealth, ethnic groups, and election results.

To get the most information from special-purpose maps, you must study all the symbols, labels, and colors used on the map. The following steps will help you interpret special-purpose maps:

- Read the map title to determine the subject and purpose of the map.
- Read all the labels on the map to identify the geographic region and other information listed on the map.
- Identify each symbol and color shown in the map key.
- Locate the symbols and colors on the map.
- Form hypotheses and generalizations based on the map information.

EXAMPLE

Look at the map of India's agri-cultural resources on page 345. This map gives economic information about India. In the map key, each agricultural resource is indicated by a symbol. What do the colors on the map represent? *(farming and non-farming areas)* By finding the colored areas on the map, it is apparent that most of India's land is used for agriculture. Now locate the various resource symbols on the map. Notice that cattle are raised primarily in central India. Where is tea grown? *(eastern and southern India)* What is the most widely-grown crop in India? *(rice)* Which resources are least plentiful in India? *(barley, goats, peanuts, tobacco)* How can you tell? *(Each resource was shown in only one place on the map.)*

PRACTICE

Study the special-purpose map shown above and answer the following questions:

1. What is the subject of this map?
2. What do the colors on the map represent?

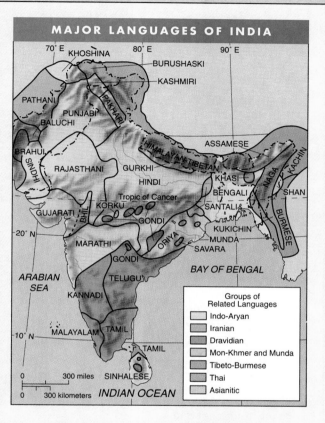

MAJOR LANGUAGES OF INDIA

Groups of Related Languages
- Indo-Aryan
- Iranian
- Dravidian
- Mon-Khmer and Munda
- Tibeto-Burmese
- Thai
- Asianitic

3. What do the labels on the map represent?
4. Naga, Kachin, and Burmese are all examples of which group of languages?
5. In which part of India are Iranian languages spoken?
6. What group of languages is most commonly spoken in southern India?
7. What is the most widely-spoken group of languages in India?
8. Why do you think India has so many different languages?

CHAPTER OUTLINE

1 Marriage

2 Family Life

3 Indian Women

4 Village Life

5 City Life

People and Places to Know
Delhi/New Delhi, Ahmadabad, Bombay, Madras, Calcutta

Key Terms to Define
dowry, nuclear family, extended family, joint family, *purdah*, *panchayat*

Objectives to Learn

1. **Relate** traditional and modern marriage customs in India.

2. **Analyze** the advantages and disadvantages of Indian family structures.

3. **Explain** the changing status of Indian women.

4. **Describe** city and village life in India.

Indian flower seller

The Indian People

"   Listen, friend, for I will talk too long. It is close to my heart. What gives people hope? It is good harvests? Is it the weddings? Is it a feast? No, these are the pleasures which pass. We hope because we have children and we see again all things new in their eyes. You say that cannot be so for all, since all do not have children, and all who have are not happy? Yes? Is it so? Listen, again. For a nation, for a land of many people, children are the times to come, the lives we have not yet led, the houses not yet built, the pictures not yet made. All that gives us hope, gives us reason to struggle through the illnesses and the loneliness and the years of drought. Why? I shall tell you. Because we are taught by all we know of the past that what each can do becomes greater if his chances become greater. We think we do not know what comes in the future, but we think it will not be the same as the past. There will be other chances and other problems. The fate is not written twice in the same way, you of the villages say. Out of each that is different . . . comes something new which gives another hope. . . .

The power of India lies in the cities, and mostly I think it is wicked. But what endures all powers? The village. . . . That is the memory which India must hope to hold and withstand whatever the powers do. . . .

. . . The village changes whenever there is a new family begun or an old one dies. It is what is kept and how the change is made which you record and which I call the remembering. . . .

. . . As long as there is remembering there is home. "

India is home to about 880 million people. Of all the nations in the world, only China has a larger population. Indian society is diverse. This diversity is regional, ethnic, cultural, linguistic, religious, and educational. It also is rural/urban and class based. So what is true for one Indian or group of Indians is not necessarily true for another. Children and home, however, are important to all Indians. Through them, the past is carried into the future.

Today India is changing. Some traditional beliefs remain important to many of the Indian people. Other traditional beliefs are undergoing change. Change can be seen in the social system, in attitudes about marriage, about the family, and about the role of women. It can be seen in the villages, where about three-fourths of India's people live, and in the cities, which comprise the third largest urban population in the world.

Source: From *THIRD CLASS TICKET* by Heather Wood. Copyright © 1980 by Heather Wood. Published by Penguin Books. Reprinted by permission of the author.

Marriage

For Indians, marriage is a process that takes place through time. Traditionally, marriages were arranged by the families or friends of the prospective bride and groom and were the special task of a girl's father or brother. Most brides were very young by Western standards and were expected to stay at home, away from men outside the family. A Hindu bride had to have a **dowry**—money or property that a woman brings to her husband at marriage. The dowry was intended to secure good treatment for the girl in her husband's family, give her a portion of the wealth of her family, and start the young couple in life.

In recent years, changes have taken place both in marriage arrangements and in

EXAMINING PHOTOGRAPHS *This couple is being married in a Hindu ceremony in the north-central Indian city of Jhansi. Traditionally, why did Hindu brides have a dowry?*

household life. Below, a housewife from Yamunanager talks about some of them:

It's thirty-eight years since I got married and became a housewife. Mine was a traditional, arranged marriage. In those days, what one calls "love" marriages were almost unheard of. Nobody dared to marry against their parents' wishes or marry out of their caste [social group].

Times are changing slowly and most young people I meet nowadays want to marry somebody of their own choice. But by and large parents still put up terrific opposition if their children want to marry someone they've met and fallen in love with on their own.

We allowed our sons complete freedom to marry whomever they chose. My sons didn't demand any dowry. . . . And their wedding ceremonies were simple.

Hindu weddings are generally very pompous affairs. People tend to treat a wedding as a chance to show off their wealth. The whole house is decked out in multicolored lights. There's a band playing songs from the movies over loudspeakers, and a fireworks display often is thrown in. And the amount of food and sweets and drinks and the number of relatives and guests! . . .

Since my children are abroad, there's not much to do at home. . . . A woman comes to do the cleaning and washing twice a day. I think we're fortunate to have even this part-time help. In the past, it was easy to hire servants. Now it's becoming more and more difficult to find them. Soon, I think we'll have to do all the housework ourselves. Most households in India don't have gadgets like dishwashers and washing machines or electric stoves.

Gas stoves too, you'll find only in big towns and cities. Most families manage to cook on *chullahs* (charcoal fires) or coal fires or kerosene stoves. For our laundry, we have to depend upon the local *dhobi* (washerman).

You
may never meet,
but he could be
the man
in your life.

He is an engineer. Twenty-six.
Shy. Wants to marry.
And he's somewhere out there.
All it would take is something to
bring you together.

Thousands of couples have been
brought together by The Times of
India. People meant for each other.
People who could live happily ever
after. Let The Times of India do
it for you—put an ad in the
Matrimonial Columns of The Times
of India.

You
don't know her,
but she could be
the girl
in your life.

She's a graduate. Attractive,
with a horoscope to match!
And she'd say yes if you asked
her to marry you.
All it would take is something
to bring you together.

Thousands of couples have been
brought together by The Times of
India. People meant for each other.
People who could live happily ever
after. Let The Times of India do
it for you—put an ad in the
Matrimonial Columns of The Times
of India.

EXAMINING PHOTOGRAPHS *These photographs were taken from an advertisement in the matrimonial section of* The Times of India, *which encourages men and women to advertise for their own marriage partners. How do Indian men view arranged marriages?*

Unless we have guests, I have plenty of spare time. So I help my husband in the shop with his filing and typing. . . .

Sitting in the shop and watching customers, I often point out to my husband how customs have changed. . . .

But change comes so slowly in India. People say, "What has to happen will happen. . . . "

In 1978, a law was passed setting a minimum marriage age for Indians of the Hindu religion, the major religion of India. Males must be 21 or older and females, 18 or older. The dowry also has been outlawed. But it still remains an important part of many Indian marriages. Today, the bride and groom are likely to have met before the wedding, particularly if they are from the educated middle and upper classes. Even if they cannot select their spouses, they can veto the man or woman who has been chosen for them.

Source: Veenu Sandal. *We Live in India.* The Bookwright Press, 1984, pp. 32–33.

It is not uncommon today, especially in the cities, for parents to advertise in a newspaper for matches for their children. Advertisements such as the ones below, from *The Times of India*, are typical:

ALLIANCE INVITED FOR SINDHI GIRL BEAUTIFUL, FAIR, TALL, SLIM, HOMELY [GOOD HOMEMAKER], INTELLIGENT, PRESENTABLE, WORKING, . . . 45 KG [99 LB]. LIBRA ZODIAC. BELONGING TO RESPECTABLE BUSINESS FAMILY. ONLY WELL-SETTLED HANDSOME BOYS WITH SOBER HABITS OF MATCHING AGE FROM RESPECTABLE FAMILY. . . .

For an Oswal Swetamber girl from highly respectable and cultured family, 20 ½ years, 45 kg [99 lb], 156 cms [5 ft. 2 ½ in.], slim, fair, beautiful, sweet natured, active, well versed in household work besides artistic talents, intelligent, convent educated, first class B.S.C. from Rajasthan University, presently residing abroad with parents

—required a suitable vegetarian, non-smoking, smart, educated, Oswal match from any profession/business. Parents and girl shall be in India during September 1984 to finalise match.[1]

Opinions are mixed about marriage customs today. Some Indians see no reason for change. Below, a 28-year-old explains why he approves of arranged marriages:

The mechanics of how you select your wife is of no importance. It would make no difference if you plucked her off a tree. It is the life that comes afterwards. That counts. For example, do you make your own trousers? Why do you go to a tailor without losing face? For obvious reasons. The tailor knows his business whereas if you made your own, it would sit ill on you, that is all. Let someone who knows you deeply and knows the meaning of marriage with some experience in it select a woman for you. She won't kill you I think. On the other hand if you don't believe in anyone because you can't or if no one has earned your faith, choose one yourself. I would, if I believed in no one. . . . I have faith, belief, trust and things, in a lot of people. . . . So I don't have to go about frantically falling in love.[2]

Other Indians, however, feel that arranged marriages should be a thing of the past. The bachelor who placed the following advertisement in *The Times of India* makes his belief clear:

A jovial and cheerful but a very lonely young journalist (33) is searching for a real perfect soulmate with true love philosophy view matrimony invites direct

correspondence from emotional sentimental, softnatured, understanding and really good looking girl willing to share my happiness and sorrows, riches and rags, ideals and aspirations. Dowry loathed and severely condemned. No arranged marriages please!

[1]*Source*: The Times of India, No. 193, Vol. CXLVII, Sunday, August 5, 1984, pp. 3, 4.

[2]*Source*: Anees Jung. "A Bride from the Blues" in *They Live in India: Vignettes of Contemporary Indian Lives. Vol. III—The Urban Scene*. The Educational Resources Center, The State Educational Department of New Delhi, p. 17.

SECTION 1 REVIEW

CHECKING FOR UNDERSTANDING
1. **Define** dowry.
2. **Discuss** ways in which marriage customs have changed in India in recent years.

CRITICAL THINKING
3. **Drawing Conclusions** Based on the newspaper ads, what characteristics seem to be desired in a marriage partner?

SECTION 2
Family Life

Indian families generally are very close, and social life often revolves around family activities. Relatives try to live near and help one another. Those who live in the city go back to visit village relatives. Rural relatives who go to the city to work or go to school often live with their relatives there.

In India, there is a traditional family cycle through time that includes **nuclear families**—a set of parents and their children and **extended families**—parents, children, and other relatives. For many Indians, the traditional family pattern is the **joint family,** which consists of a husband and wife; the sons and the sons' wives and children; and unmarried daughters. Sometimes it includes other relatives, such as an aunt or cousin. Married daughters live with the families of their husbands. Their children are considered part of the husband's family.

Source: The Times of India, No. 193, Vol. CXLVII, Sunday, August 5, 1984, p. 2.

EXAMINING PHOTOGRAPHS *A joint family, such as this one in Madras, India, shares home and income and cares for the welfare of all its members. Such a family often consists of several generations of family members.* **Why do some Indians prefer living in a joint family?**

The joint family is still strong in India today, although it is more common among the wealthy than the poor. Some Indians prefer this arrangement for several reasons. One is that many members of high status families are bound together by tradition or because, by staying together, they all can live better. Another has to do with interdependence. Members of a joint family rely on one another and often work together. Merchants, for example, may prefer a joint family because family members can pool ideas, labor, money, and risk. Farmers may prefer it because there are more people to work the land. In the interview below, a young woman tells why she prefers the joint family:

Q*uestion:* You obviously live in a modern family and have had education. Two years of college, I think you said. As you consider marriage, would you rather live in a traditional joint family or be alone with your husband?

Radha: Oh, the joint family, absolutely. I would never consider anything else.

Question: Why? You would have so much less freedom, so much less opportunity to know your husband and enjoy doing things with him.

Radha: I would be too lonely without the other women, without all the uncles, aunties, and children. Also I would have to do all the housework. . . .

Question: Then, what of your relationship with your husband? Isn't this important to you?

Radha (hesitantly): What is a husband? He goes to work, he sees his friends. He would never discuss things with me, would never take me to the cinema. We would go to visit relatives, but that is all.

Question: Then, what of your relationship with your children? You would have them all to yourself in a separate family.

Radha: It would be too much! I have seen my friend almost crazy because of her children. They haven't other children to play with, aunties to go to, and they are always crying and fighting.

Question: But little children do grow up. Can you think of them as going to school and having school friends?

Radha: That would happen, of course. But mostly I can only think that I would want my son to care for me when I am old. That can only happen in a joint family.

Source: Margaret Cormack and Kiki Skagen (eds.) *Voices From India.* Praeger Publishers, 1972, pp. 243–244.

Joint families, however, are not without problems. Pooling earnings can lead to jealousy and bickering. Family members may want to spend their money as they choose and live independently. Some couples have no children. Relatives do not always get along.

When the father of a joint family dies, the property is divided among the sons. One son takes over and cares for his mother as part of an extended family. The other sons, with their wives and children, set up separate or nuclear households. Although by law widows are allowed to remarry, many—especially older ones—do not.

In an Indian family household, the oldest able male is considered the head. He has the authority to make family decisions, market crops, organize household labor for heavier agricultural tasks, and deal with strangers. The oldest able female is in charge of domestic affairs. Generally the mother of the sons or the wife of the eldest brother, she supervises the food, health care, raising of children, and cleaning. Young wives hold the lowest place in the household, especially before they have sons. Their mothers-in-law maintain control and may be quite strict with them. In a joint family, men and women tend to have very separate daily activities.

Children are greatly loved. Although small children generally are pampered and indulged, in poorer families those five years old or older may be expected to help with household labor and the care of younger brothers and sisters. In a joint family, children always have someone to play with them or to comfort and feed them. But while they learn to get along with many different people living close together, at times, they become very dependent on others.

SECTION 2 REVIEW

CHECKING FOR UNDERSTANDING
1. **Define** nuclear family, extended family, joint family.
2. **Describe** the roles of the oldest able male and female in an Indian family.

CRITICAL THINKING
3. **Synthesizing Information** What are the advantages and disadvantages of joint family living?

EXAMINING PHOTOGRAPHS *man is poling his dugout boat across the smooth waters of Dal Lake, nestled in the mountains near Srinagar in northernmost India. He and other local men earn a portion of their family income by ferrying food and other goods to the many houseboats that line the lakeshore each summer. What is the typical role of the oldest male in an Indian household?*

EXAMINING PHOTOGRAPHS *One of an Indian woman's major household responsibilities is to prepare meals for the family. This woman, cooking on a gas stove and dressed in a colorful traditional garment called a* sari, *is making* chapatis—*flat, round whole wheat flour breads. These are usually served with a soup containing* dal—*beans—with vegetable curries and rice. Together,* chapatis *and* dal *make a complete protein.* How do modern Indian women view traditional customs?

SECTION 3

Indian Women

Indian women have a pivotal role in families and households, especially if they are the mothers of sons. Indian men have a great respect for their wives as the mothers of their children. In Indian tradition and belief, women have always been represented as both strong and weak. They are the goddess *Shakti*, the power and energy of the world. Below, a Bengali widower explains the traditional Hindu ideal of a woman's role:

My wife passed away with most of her wishes fulfilled as a Hindu woman. She saw her daughters married and well-established in life. Her only son had a good college career, and she had selected his bride, and her son got his special training in America, and was in a good post. . . . She was quite happy and proud of her position in life, with a husband and a son upon whom she doted and on whom she could also rely. . . . The Sanskrit [classical language of India] adage says that the wife is the Home, and the ideal wife has been characterized . . . as the Mistress of the House, Adviser and Manager of Affairs, Trusted Friend as well as beloved Pupil in the Fine Arts. . . . My wife, born to the tradition [of joint-family living], accepted it as a matter of course and she went on for any amount of sacrifice. . . . She was very much in love with life, and yet she often [showed] in her behavior a strange detachment and objectivity which we frequently see in our Indian womanhood.

In the past, many Indian women covered their faces and were secluded from strangers. This practice—*purdah*—originated as an attempt to protect them from the gaze of invaders. Today, although many women in

Source: Suniti Kumar Chatterji. *In Memorium Kamala Devi, 1900–1964: A Husband's Offering of Love and Respect,* as quoted in *Bengali Women* by Manisha Roy. The University of Chicago Press, 1975, pp. 128–129.

villages and other remote areas still practice *purdah*, most educated women of the middle and upper classes do not. The Indian constitution grants women equal rights with men. They can vote, inherit property, and divorce. The social and cultural framework of Indian society, however, has sometimes prevented them from exercising all their rights.

Indian feminists, who view *purdah* and other customs that limit women and put them under the control of men as restrictive and demeaning, have been working since 1975 to publicize the situations and concerns of Indian women. Women of the upper and middle classes especially are pressing to uplift the status of women in Indian society.

SECTION 3 REVIEW

CHECKING FOR UNDERSTANDING
1. **Define** *purdah*.
2. **Discuss** the rights of women in India today.

CRITICAL THINKING
3. **Making Generalizations** What two generalizations might be made about the traditional role of women in Indian society?

SECTION 4
Village Life

Lifestyles tend to differ throughout India. One of the chief reasons for this has to do with whether a person lives in a village or in the city. There are more than 575,000 villages in India. In the state of Bengal, villages are nearly continuous. Some are clusters of houses with fields lying all around. Others may consist of scattered homesteads.

Although most villages are self-sufficient, they are not isolated. Landlords and members of the *panchayat*, the local body of elders elected to office, link villages with the wider society. Village development workers and school teachers bring information to improve living and farming. Villagers often market crops in towns and cities and travel to other villages and towns. Some also make pilgrimages to temples or holy places. In addition, many city dwellers have village roots and return often to check on their property or to visit relatives.

Many villagers have contact with the outside world via radio or television. Radios have been a feature of village life for several years. Television sets are relatively new. Today, more than 9000 Indian villages have government-purchased television sets, through which the government tries to promote educational programming.

In most villages are brick homes owned by the wealthy and mud houses that belong to the poor. Homes vary in size according to the wealth of their owners, but all have areas for sitting, sleeping, and cooking. Most villages have such public facilities as a community center and clinic, a school, and temples. There also are wells, shade trees, water tanks, and a grazing area for animals.

The main occupation of most villagers is farming. Sometimes a few wealthy landlords own much of the land and hire others to work the fields. Men, women, and children all may work in the fields. Women play a major role in processing agricultural products. They also prepare much of what is grown for eating or for selling in the market.

Villagers not engaged in farming may produce such items as pots or furniture or provide such services as washing clothes or cleaning drains. Many of the items produced in the village are used by the villagers themselves or by those in nearby villages.

Change is coming slowly to many of the villages. Below, an American author of a book about India discusses some changes:

"How," I asked Mihil Lal Shukla [the village priest] . . . "has the village of Chirora [in Uttar Pradesh] changed since your boyhood?" . . .

Shukla rocked on the balls of his feet, scratched his skinny chin and lapsed into silence. He couldn't think of anything. . . .

"What about the dirt road I came in on?" I coached him.

True, said Shukla, that's pretty new. Someone in the crowd of goggling onlookers in the dusty village square volunteered that the road was 15, maybe 16 years old; new enough by Chirora's standards.

What if someone got sick in the old days? Well, said Shukla, they had to carry him out to the main road, and the nearest doctor in those days might be five or six miles [8 or 9.6 kilometers] away. Now the

EXAMINING PHOTOGRAPHS *At this "sweetwater," or drinking water, well in a village in western India, women and girls fill jars in which they carry water to their homes. The jars they balance on their heads, sometimes as many as three at once, are made by a local potter. Clay pots are preferred over tin ones because they keep the water cooler longer. Besides wells, what other public facilities are found in most Indian villages?*

doctor is two or three miles [3.2 or 4.8 kilometers] away.

What happened during the rainy season? "We were completely cut off," said Shukla. And if someone got sick then? As often as not they died.

That afternoon . . . I walked through the fields with Indrapal Singh, . . . a "young-blood"—a forward-thinking, model farmer. Indrapal used high-yielding seeds, fertilizer, herbicide. . . .

"Why don't you buy a tractor?" I asked. The Government, which considers the modernization of farming crucial, makes interest-free loans for farm equipment.

Indrapal pondered for a moment. "Why should I go into debt?" he answered. "I have enough to eat and drink, to provide for my family. . . ."

Chirora looked like most of the other north Indian villages I had seen. Narrow mud alleys snaked among mud houses, leaving the village awash in muck after the rain; cows and bullocks wandered glassyeyed across . . . courtyards; temples displayed . . . clay idols. . . . We want change, I would be told by old Brahmins [members of the highest Hindu caste] and young farmers alike. But, of course, it will never come, they would add, even though I could see that it had. . . .

When I first arrived in Chirora, I was taken by a group of friendly . . . farmers on a tour of the fields. We wound between tiny plots of a half-acre or less, each with its microenvironment of crops. . . .

We wandered past two shirtless, slender men who were watering a raised field by rhythmically dipping a bucket in an irrigation ditch and depositing the water in another ditch 12 inches [30 centimeters] above. We fetched up at the pump-operated tube well that was supposed to be irrigating the fields, but which received power only between 9 P.M. and 4 A.M. . . . "Power supply," said a well-dressed farmer as we stood around the idle pump, "is *bilkul* bogus"—absolutely bogus.

The speaker . . . turned out to be the owner of the machinery he was cursing. His name was Natwar Singh. . . . Natwar . . . owned 35 *bighas*, or 17 ½ acres [7 hectares]—a very big farm by local standards. . . .

Natwar . . . had graduated from college and taken a degree in law. Sometimes Natwar talked of finding some clients and doing the work for which he was trained, but he couldn't take his professional ambitions very seriously. "You see," he said . . . , "I am my father's only son. I have to stay in the village. What else can I do?" . . .

On my initial tour of the village, I was surprised to see that perhaps half of the houses were built of brick. . . . But one of the village's neighborhoods . . . was a sea of crumbling mud huts topped by piles of thatch. . . . Here, it turned out, was Chirora's third and lowest caste group, the Untouchables, known in India as Harijans. . . .

Only a few of the families owned enough land to make a living; the rest got by haphazardly. Most of them worked as *mazdoors*, or day laborers. . . .

Wrapped in a sense of defeat, the Harijans were excluded from the life of the village.

SECTION 4 REVIEW

CHECKING FOR UNDERSTANDING
1. **Define** panchayat.
2. **Explain** why Indian villages are not totally isolated.
3. **Cite** the ways in which Indian villagers earn their livings.

CRITICAL THINKING
4. **Making Inferences** After reading about the village of Chirora, what might a foreigner infer about the role of tradition in village life and about the reactions of some villagers to the changes taking place in their village?

Source: James Traub. "A Village in India: Reluctant Progress" in *The New York Times Magazine,* September 9, 1984, pp. 106, 129–130, 132–133. Copyright © 1984 by *The New York Times.* Reprinted by permission.

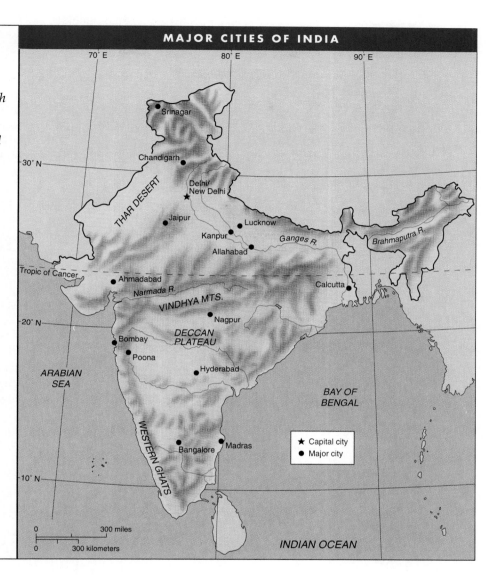

MAJOR CITIES OF INDIA

EXAMINING MAPS *India's cities are centers of trade, industry, government, and education. Some, such as Jaipur and Bangalore, were founded by Indian princes before the colonial period; others, such as Bombay and Calcutta, were built by India's British colonial rulers. Because India today is largely a rural nation, many city dwellers still maintain close ties with their ancestral villages.* **What major cities are located on or near the Ganges River?**

City Life

Millions of Indians, most of them seeking jobs and a better life, have left their villages and are swelling India's cities. In 1881, only 9 percent of the Indian population lived in cities. By 1989, the number had risen to 28 percent. Today, at least 12 cities—Calcutta,

Bombay, Delhi/New Delhi, Madras, Bangalore, Hyderabad, Ahmadabad, Kanpur, Puna, Nagpur, Lucknow, and Jaipur—are home to more than 1 million people.

Different cities are important for different reasons. Some, such as Varanasi and Allahabad, are important for religious reasons. Others, such as Delhi/New Delhi, serve important functions as political centers. Still others are industrial centers like Ahmadabad or commerce and shipping centers like Bombay, Madras, and Calcutta.

India

THE OLD AND THE NEW

Many Indians are content with a lifestyle that blends the old and the new. Manubhai, the young stockbroker presented below, is one of those people:

Manubhai works in a square, run-down building on a narrow, noisy street of Bombay's business district. . . . A row of small rooms, offices of shareholders and stockbrokers, line the passage to the main building. Manubhai conducts his business in one of these rooms.

A short, stocky man with thick round spectacles and a round happy face, he sits behind a desk with two telephones. A radio blares out figures. Portraits of gods with marigolds threaded around their frames, hang behind him and beside him. . . . "I like my business" Manubhai confided to me in the din. "But my knowledge of the market is not fine, just good. As I am an honest and moral man I am able to earn enough and lead a good life." And these earnings go to share a good life with seventeen other members of his family, six adults and 11 children!

"I joined the stock business in 1952 . . . " said Manubhai. "And I joined the business right after my matriculation," added his older brother. . . . "My father was sick at that time and my brother needed an extra hand" continued Manubhai. "We both had it easy compared to our father. . . . He had struggled for many years in several little businesses . . . before he got a job in a brokerage house and moved to Bombay. After ten years he . . . had started his own stock business. One was able to live well with very little in those days. . . . What my father spent in a year, I spend in a day now. . . .

Today Manubhai lives in a large apartment in a well-to-do suburb of Bombay, owns a car, eats better and lives better. "My children have a better life than I did as a child. They eat more nourishing food, go to better schools, and know much more about cars and movies than I ever did. They are also more intelligent, ask more questions and argue. Perhaps they see many more things, are open to wider influences and all in all, have better living conditions than I and my brother did," said Manubhai.

Manubhai is aware of this, and he is not averse to his children growing up in a world radically different from his. But he continues to keep his own world intact. His world is built around a joint family and the puja [worship] room. "A joint family has tremendous advantages in business and day to day life. My brother and I are excellent business partners and have never had any differences. . . . Living in a joint family I can afford to take a month off. . . . My brother simply takes care of my business and his wife takes care of my children," said Manubhai while the rest grinned approval.

DRAWING CONCLUSIONS

1. In what kind of environment does Manubhai live?
2. Do you think Manubhai is representative of many Indians today? Explain your answer.

Source: Anees Jung. *They Live in India: Vignettes of Contemporary Indian Lives. Vol. III—The Urban Scene.* The Educational Resources Center, The State Educational Department of New Delhi, pp. 7–9.

Most of the cities have temples and mosques, bazaars and shopping areas, commercial areas, and an "old city" area that was the core of town life before the city grew and expanded. Within the city, people with similar backgrounds and wealth tend to live in the same districts. Lifestyles are very much related to wealth. Nowhere is the contrast greater than in Calcutta. It has elegant boulevards, air-conditioned restaurants, and palatial homes for the wealthy. But it also has some of the most crowded slums in the world, with more than 100,000 people occupying each square kilometer. Several hundred thousand of the poorest of the poor literally live and die on the streets.

Severe overcrowding has affected other cities as well. Bombay, for example, is India's busiest seaport and its commercial and major international business center. It is also a major film hub. More films are produced here each year than in Hollywood. Bombay is home to many wealthy Indian business people, industrialists, and movie stars. At the same time, however, severe overcrowding has taken its toll. Nearly one million people live in flimsy shelters without proper sanitation. In the words of one Indian, "the millions of hopefuls who stream into the city strain its ability to cope to the breaking point." In the article that follows, an Indian journalist discusses the problem:

EXAMINING PHOTOGRAPHS *Calcutta, India's third largest city, has some of the most crowded living and working conditions in the world. Traffic jams occur often in the downtown area of the city. What contrasts exist in Calcutta?*

Author V.S. Naipaul once observed that in Bombay you can always find some form of life lower than whatever miserable state you have observed. Today, slum life in Bombay no longer constitutes low life; you are expected to specify what kind of slum, what kind of pavement. . . . There are slums where dwellers switch on technicolour lights and have ceiling fans, there are others where residents open a refrigerator and offer you a cold drink, there are slums where the only space where women can bathe are two stone slabs . . . screened by tatters of jute and rags. And there are slums where there is nothing—no water or power and virtually no shelter. . . .

In Goregaon East, there is one such slum where recent squatters . . . have made their home in empty plots in a down-at-heel industrial estate. A few scrawny chickens grovel in the filth of the cramped huts; a woman is making rotis [bread] on a fire lit by wood shavings. Her husband, she says, is away at work: he collects cow-dung from stables and sells it as fuel in better-off slums. They came to Bombay two years ago to escape starvation. "If there was food in the village, why would we have come here?

There is nothing here. . . . "

. . . In another pocket of shanties across the road, . . . a man called Pandhari Tekhade, who arrived in Bombay in the late 1960's . . . , says he still earns his wage in the city doing odd jobs. . . . "Of course," he agrees, life is worse than in the village. But what is happiness? Happiness is being able to at least eat. . . . "

Life in other slums compares better. . . . Ovadipada is an example. . . . It resembles a self-sufficient little township, its boundaries provided with a pan shop, a grocery store and even a kiosk selling cold drinks. Inside, the lanes are clean with cement drains, electricity fixtures outside doors and nameplates. A room fifteen feet square [1.35 square meters] here can cost Rs 30.000 [$2565].

N.V. Poojari . . . lives in one such room. When he moved to Ovadipada he bought the place for Rs 11.000 [$940.50]: since then, he has constructed a kitchen at the back, put in a tiled floor, "bought" three electricity connections and his young son now has a proper school desk complete with a table fan. Poojari earns Rs 1,100 [$94.05] a month, but much of it is spent paying off the slum landlord who de-

EXAMINING PHOTOGRAPHS
Modern high-rise apartment and office buildings line Bombay's famous Marine Drive. Bombay is India's largest city with a population of over 8 million. Located on an island off the western coast of India, Bombay has been one of the country's major ports since the mid-1700's. **What other activities support Bombay's economy?**

EXAMINING PHOTOGRAPHS *Like cities in other parts of the world, India's cities show striking contrasts between wealth and poverty. In Bombay, luxury apartments rise within walking distance of slum shelters made of scraps of wood, cloth, and metal. What is one of Bombay's major challenges?*

mands a price for every facility. "You pay Rs 30 [$2.57] a month for living here, another Rs 30 [$2.57] for every electricity point in the room, Rs 20 [$1.71] a month for water. . . . Other residents of Ovadipada complain bitterly. . . . Says one: "You have to pay for every wall, there are different owners for each. If a room has four walls, you have to sometimes end up paying rent to three different owners."

. . . Life for that vast segment of the city population loosely known as the middle class can be as competitive and harrowing especially when they are being driven out to live in the slums. . . . In the thick of the industrial estates of Malad, shanty towns have sprouted on the hilly tracts deep in the hinterland. At the end of a long track with stones sharp as knives, across a dirty stream, and high along a ridge in the hill is . . . Waishet Pada. Living conditions are slightly better than the earlier slums. . . . But the astonishing fact about this slum is that all its 300-odd inhabitants formerly lived in Parel: most of them were textile workers who were slowly forced to move out because of their growing families.

Ramibai is one such immigrant . . . who looks old beyond his 28 years. He was pushed out of his family's one room . . . because the room couldn't accommodate the size of the growing family any more.

"This place seemed ideal for me," he says of his perch on the hillside. "It was clean, uncrowded and cheap." He explains that the slum that has materialised there since he moved in was originally a forest encroachment. "But we've managed everything in six years, a water connection, power connection, everything. . . . For Ramibai there is no alternative to living in Bombay. His job, family and future are here. Like millions of others for whom survival has become a daily battle, Ramibai somehow always manages to find a way of making things work.

SECTION 5 REVIEW

CHECKING FOR UNDERSTANDING
1. **Specify** why many Indian cities have grown greatly in population in recent decades.
2. **Identify** India's largest cities.

CRITICAL THINKING
3. **Formulating Questions** If you were asked to write a report on the lifestyles of the poor in the cities of India, what three questions might you ask that have not been answered by the information provided in this section?

Source: "Low Life: A Daily Battle" in *India Today*, November 15, 1983, pp. 58–59.

Chapter 22 Review

SUMMARY

The Indian population is both numerous and diverse. Some of the diversity is the result of changes that have been taking place in Indian society in recent years. Some Indians continue to hold traditional beliefs and practice traditional customs. Others, however, are adopting new attitudes, especially about the social system and the conduct of daily life.

Traditionally, marriages were arranged by the family or friends, and a dowry was expected. The joint family was the most common family pattern. More recently, many young men and women select their own mates, and fewer households consist of joint families.

Diversity and change are also evident in rural and urban life. Although the majority of the Indian people still live in rural villages, millions have migrated to the cities.

USING VOCABULARY

Explain why each of the following terms might be used in a magazine article about the lifestyles of the Indian people.

dowry	joint family
nuclear family	*purdah*
extended family	*panchayat*

REVIEWING FACTS

1. **Summarize** the attitudes of Indians today about traditional marriage customs.
2. **State** the purpose of a dowry.
3. **Tell** what happens when the father of a joint family dies.
4. **Name** the family member who is considered the head of an Indian household.
5. **Explain** how Indian women have been represented in Indian tradition and belief.

6. **Describe** a "typical" village in India.

CRITICAL THINKING

1. **Predicting Consequences** About 80 percent of the female population of India is illiterate. One of the things Indian women of the upper and middle class emphasize is the importance of education for women. What effect might the improved education of women have on Indian society?
2. **Demonstrating Reasoned Judgment** Most villages of India are undergoing changes. What factors do you think have led to change in village life and practices?
3. **Drawing Conclusions** In what ways might overcrowding affect the cities of India?
4. **Making Comparisons** What major factors do rural life and city life in India have in common? What is different about urban and rural living in India?

ANALYZING CONCEPTS

1. **Identity** How do the Indian people view marriage, the family, and the roles of men and women?
2. **Diversity** In what ways is Indian society diverse?
3. **Change** What are some major changes that have taken place in India in recent years?

GEOGRAPHIC THEMES

1. **Movement** What explanation can you offer for the migration of millions of Indians from the countryside to the cities?
2. **Place** Although about one-half of India's land can be farmed, most Indian farmers have small farms. What do you think might account for this?

Determining Relevance

Suppose you want to find a video store in your neighborhood that rents VCRs. To locate the store, you would check the local telephone directory. Instead of reading the whole book, however, you would look for the *relevant* information, or information related to your concern. By reading the column marked "Video Recording Equipment—Sales and Rentals," you can find a video store near your home that rents VCRs.

In researching any kind of information, whether it concerns renting VCRs or doing a term paper, you can become lost in the details you find. To avoid this, you must learn to *determine the relevance* of each piece of information. This means you select only information that is directly related to your research topic.

Information can be related to a topic in several ways. It can define or explain the topic. It can illustrate or serve as an example. Finally, it can describe a cause or consequence of the topic. Determining relevance enables you to find information that helps to answer your research question.

Follow these steps in determining relevance:

- State your research topic or question.
- Find information on this topic or question.
- For each piece of information that you find, ask: does this define, explain, illustrate, or describe a cause or consequence of this topic?
- Eliminate all information that is not relevant.

EXAMPLE

Read the following paragraph:

[1] *Carol is 16 years old, so she is now old enough to get a learner's permit to drive.* **[2]** *She is tall, has blonde hair, plays basketball, and gets good grades in school.* **[3]** *Carol really likes to work on car engines with her older brother.* **[4]** *With a learner's permit, Carol can drive only with a licensed driver in the car.* **[5]** *Her friend Tanya also has a learner's permit.* **[6]** *Tanya's parents allow her to drive the family car as long as one of her friends who has a driver's license accompanies her.* **[7]** *Tanya's family and Carol's family both own year-old Chevrolets.* **[8]** *Carol's parents do not care what Tanya is or is not allowed to do.* **[9]** *They insist that Carol cannot drive their family car unless one of them accompanies her.*

Suppose we want to find information relevant to this topic: Carol's learner's permit. Sentence 1 is relevant because it explains why Carol can get a learner's permit. Sentences 2 and 3 are irrelevant; they give facts about Carol's appearance and interests, but not about her learner's permit. Is Sentence 4 relevant? Why or why not? *(yes, explains what learner's permit allows Carol to do)* The next two sentences are irrelevant, because they discuss Tanya's learner's permit, not Carol's. Which of the remaining sentences are relevant? Why? *(Sentence 7 is not relevant because it is about the cars, not the learner's permit; sentences 8 and 9 are relevant because they describe Carol's parents' rules regarding her learner's permit.)*

PRACTICE

Decide whether each statement below is relevant or not relevant to the topic "Living in Bombay." For each relevant statement, explain how it is related to the topic. For each statement that is not relevant, explain why you think it is unrelated.

1. Many Indians are unhappy about living in the countryside.
2. Some areas of Bombay have no water or power and provide too little shelter for their many inhabitants.
3. Bombay is a commercial and international business center and the hub of India's film industry.
4. There are different levels of living conditions in Bombay.
5. Many poor people in Bombay are able to work, but they are paid too little to afford decent housing.
6. In parts of Calcutta, more than 100,000 people occupy each square kilometer of territory.

CHAPTER OUTLINE

People and Places to Know
Hindus, Varanasi, Brahmins, Kshatriyas, Vaisyas, Sudras, Muslims, Sikhs, Buddhists, Jains, Christians, Parsis

Key Terms to Define
reincarnation, *karma*, *dharma*, *gurus*, yoga, *sadhus*, *varnas*, *jatis*, untouchables

Objectives to Learn
1. **Describe** the major beliefs and practices of Hinduism.
2. **Analyze** the caste system and how it affects India's people.
3. **Identify** and characterize other important religions in India.

Image of Buddha in a monastery of northern India

Religions of India

> " Heart of mine, awake in this holy place of pilgrimage,
> In this land of India on the shore of vast humanity.
> Here do I stand with arms outstretched to salute man divine,
> And sing his praise in many a gladsome paean [hymn of praise].
> These hills that are rapt [enclosed] in deep meditation,
> These plains that clasp their rosaries [prayer beads] of rivers,
> Here you will find earth that is ever-sacred;
> In this land of India, on the shore of vast humanity. . . .
>
> Come O Aryans, come non-Aryans, Hindu, Mussalman [Muslim]
> come,
> Come ye Parsees, come O Christians, come ye one and all,
> Come Brahmins, let you be hallowed by holding all by hand.
> Come ye all who are shunned, wipe out the dishonour,
> Come to the crowning of the Mother, fill the sacred bowl
> With water that is sanctified [made holy] by the touch of all
> In this land of India, on the shore of vast Humanity. "

The above poem is the work of an early twentieth-century Indian poet named Rabindranath Tagore (ruh·BEEN·druh·NAHT tuh·GAWR). In the poem, Tagore expresses love for his land and longs for the unity of its people. At the same time, he recognizes an important fact—India is a land of amazing diversity.

The people of India belong to a variety of ethnic groups that together speak 14 major languages and more than 844 minor languages and dialects. India also is a land of many religions. This diversity of ethnic group, language, and belief is the result of many centuries of foreign invasion. With each group of invaders came new ideas and practices that often blended with existing ones.

Although modern India has no official religion and religious freedom is guaranteed by law, religion continues to play an important role in daily life. Religious teachings and rules often influence whom one marries and chooses for friends. They also can affect where and at what a person works as well as what he or she eats or wears.

Source: Rabindranath Tagore. "The Song of India" in *Aspects of Indian Culture*. Mahendra Kulasrestha (ed.). Vishveshvaranand V.R. Institute, 1961.

SECTION 1

Hinduism

The major religion of India is Hinduism, with more than 700 million followers known as Hindus. Hindus make up 83 percent of the population and have played a leading role in the development of Indian civilization. Their religion, which is one of the world's oldest, developed gradually over centuries rather than being founded on the teachings of one person or one sacred text.

Hinduism is based on a number of different beliefs and practices. One is the worship of many gods and goddesses. The three most important gods are Brahma, the creator of the universe; Vishnu, its preserver; and Shiva, its destroyer. A number of goddesses, who represent the creative or energetic aspects of life, also are revered. They include Lakshmi, goddess of good fortune, wealth,

and prosperity; and Parvati, wife of Shiva, and Mother of the universe, and goddess of life and death.

Hindu thinkers view all of life as sacred and stress the unity of all life. They believe that all living things—gods, goddesses, humans, and animals—have souls that are part of one eternal spirit called Brahman, the world soul. Many Hindus practice nonviolence toward living creatures. They try not to harm animals and do not eat meat.

Closely related to this belief is the concept of **reincarnation,** the belief that a soul continues through a series of lives on the way to union with the eternal spirit. Hindus believe that in each life the soul takes on the form of a human or some other life form. The sum of a person's past lives, which is carried into new lives, is the person's *karma.* People are born who they are because of *karma.* The way in which a person lives in a particular life is determined by how well he or she carried out his or her *dharma*, or special moral

---

EXAMINING ART *Below left, bedecked in flowers and precious jewels, are the god Vishnu, preserver of the universe, and his wife Lakshmi (also, below right), goddess of wealth and prosperity. The elephant-headed figure (below center) is Ganesa, or Ganapati, god of wisdom and good fortune. Also called the "Remover of Obstacles," Ganesa is prayed to at the start of any undertaking.* **Why do many Hindus practice nonviolence toward living creatures?**

duty, in past lives. For example, a person who is a street sweeper today may have been, in an earlier existence, a priest who disobeyed his *dharma*. The sweeper, however, by being good and faithful to his *dharma* today may be born a priest in the next life. The goal is to be reborn at higher and higher levels until union is achieved with the eternal spirit.

Hindus are aided in their spiritual search by **gurus**, or teachers, whom they revere. To discipline both mind and body, some Hindus practice a form of physical exercise and worship known as **yoga**. There also are a number of sacred writings that explain how one should conduct his or her life. One of the most important of these is quoted below. Known as the *Bhagavad Gita* (BUHG·uh·vuhd GEE·tah), or *Song of the Soul*, it was written about 500 BC:

In the bonds of works I am free, because in them I am free from desires. The man who can see this truth, in his work he finds his freedom. . . .

He whose undertakings are free from anxious desire and fanciful thought, whose work is made pure in the fire of wisdom: he is called wise by those who see. In whatever work he does such a man in truth has peace: he expects nothing, he relies on nothing, and ever has fullness of joy.

He has no vain hopes, he is the master of his soul, he surrenders all he has, only his body works: he is free from sin. He is glad with whatever God [the eternal spirit] gives him, and he has risen beyond the two contraries here below; he is without jealousy, and in success or in failure he is one: his works bind him not.

He has attained liberation: he is free from all bonds, his mind has found peace in wisdom, and his work is a holy sacrifice. The work of such a man is pure.

Greater is thine own work, even if this be humble, than the work of another, even if this be great. When a man does the work God gives him, no sin can touch this man.

And a man should not abandon his work, even if he cannot achieve it in full perfection; because in all work there may be imperfection, even as in all fire there is smoke.

PRACTICES

For most Indians, Hinduism is a way of life. The basis of Indian society, law, literature, art, and philosophy, it influences daily life through a number of religious practices. For example, Hindus follow daily rituals of devotion, washing, and prayer. They also follow strict dietary rules. When they die, their bodies are cremated, and the ashes are scattered over such sacred rivers as the Ganges.

Another Hindu practice is the honoring of deities at public temples. In these temples, which are found all over India, are carved statues of deities, people, and events from Indian religious stories. Worshippers view the statues, pray, and make offerings of food and flowers. Through these actions of devotion, Hindus believe they are bringing holiness into their lives. The temples are administered by priests, who also perform religious rituals. Priests are expected to be familiar with ancient texts and to know Sanskrit, the ancient language of India. Below, a Hindu priest talks about his duties:

My day at the temple begins at half-past four in the morning and ends at eight o'clock every night. It's a long day, but I don't mind one bit, as I devote all the time to the service of God.

Source: From THE BHAGAVAD GITA translated by Juan Mascaró (Penguin Classics, 1962), copyright © 1962 Juan Mascaró. Reprinted by permission of Penguin Books Ltd.

EXAMINING PHOTOGRAPHS *One of the practices of the Hindu religion is to bathe in the waters of a sacred river. For this reason, each year millions of Hindus will flock to the Ganges River. One of the holiest sites of the Ganges is upriver from Varanasi at Allahabad, where the Ganges and Yamuna rivers come together. It is here that the Kumbh* Mela *is held. In addition to ritual bathing, what are some other Hindu religious practices?*

Which God, you ask? Well, we Hindus have 330 million deities. . . .

It's part of my duty as a priest to offer prayer to the idols, to bathe them with milk and honey, and to dress them. Then, every day, other temple priests and I have to organize the distribution of free food. Our temple feeds about thirty or forty poor people every day. The temple gets its money from donations.

Only a Brahman [high-born person] can become a priest in a temple. He must be learned in the ancient Sanskrit texts known as *Vedas*. He must also know how to conduct weddings, birth and death ceremonies and so on. . . .

There are so many holy cities and places. They're usually on the banks of rivers or up on the snowy mountains. Cities like Hardwar, Rishikesh and Varanasi are on the riverside. Pilgrimage centers like Badrinath, Kedarnath and Amarnath are high up in the mountains. Half the year the pilgrims can't get to them because of the snow.

But I must tell you about the Kumbh *Mela*, which is held every twelve years and is the world's greatest religious fair.

At Kumbh, millions and millions of Hindus gather from all over India to take a bath in the holy Ganges.

With so much going on, life remains busy and full for me. I can't tell you how happy and fortunate I feel serving God and the people.

Even though there are priests and regular services in temples, Hindu worship is an individual matter. While some *sadhus* (SAH doos), or "holy men," are attached to temples, others wander on their own all over India. Devout Hindus give them food as a good deed. Also, Hindu worship is centered more in the home than in the temple. Every Hindu's home has a spot set aside for worship and meditation, or the silencing of thoughts to gain enlightenment. Apart from special acts of worship, Hindus regard ordinary tasks as sacred. They believe that each action, if performed well, will bring a person closer to perfection and union with the eternal spirit.

Source: "We Hindu people have thousands of gods" in *We Live in India*. Veenu Sandal. The Bookwright Press, 1984, pp. 20–21.

India

A HINDU HOLY CITY

For Hindus, the fact that the ancient Indian city of Varanasi (vuh·rah·nuh·SEE), also known as Benares, is a rail and trade center is secondary to the fact that it is a holy city. Each year, more than 1 million Hindus make pilgrimages to Varanasi to pay homage at one of the city's temples and to bathe in the sacred Ganges River. But, as indicated in the article below, some Indians see the city in a different light:

Varanasi symbolizes the energy of ancient Hindu learning and art. Situated on the confluence [meeting point] of the Ganges and the Varana River (from which it gets its most common name), Varanasi is one of the few cities in the world that still lives by its ancient traditions—which date from the 6th century BC.

Today, the former Maharajah [princely ruler] of Benares continues to hold a mythical grip on the . . . city. . . .

"Benares is not a city but a state of mind," he tells me, . . . "If you have reached this . . . city you cannot go anywhere else; you cannot be reborn.

When the river washes away the good and the evil, there is no rebirth. Once you know this you can abandon yourself to the freedom of who you are."

"Every Benaresi knows this and indulges in it. You can listen to music all night and wake up early to see the sun rise, have a cold bath in the river and watch it flow, ever changing and yet the same. You rise to see the sun and return to see it set, and you tell yourself that like the sun man too must go. But while he lives in this city he lives fully. . . .

But for one merchant family that has made a fortune from the selling of the legendary saris of Benares, there is another side to the holy city.

Varanasi is decaying, the river is polluted, and the people are decrepit, says the family patriarch. . . . It is a city where trucks honk all night, where streets are filled with nothing but shops whose keepers haggle and sell at all hours, where women buy so many saris, and men do nothing. . . .

The women of this household, dressed in nylon saris . . . sit in wicker chairs on the verandah. . . .

What does the city mean to them?

"Nothing," they say. . . .

Do they bathe in the holy river? "No. We take the children to swim when we go for picnics in the summer on the other—the cleaner—side of the ghats."

"We want the city to become modern," says the eldest daughter-in-law. . . .

As I say goodbye I ask the family patriarch if he ever leaves Benares. "I am an old man and I don't want to go anywhere lest I die in another place and miss out on my 'moksha' [liberation]," he said with a laugh.

DRAWING CONCLUSIONS

1. What kind of city is Varanasi?
2. What does the city reveal about the relationship between tradition and modern life in India today?

Source: Anees Jung. "The Holy Ganges" in The Christian Science Monitor. June 28, 1985, pp. 18–19.

CELEBRATIONS AND PILGRIMAGES

Hindus celebrate many holidays. One of the most important is Diwali, which marks the arrival of winter and symbolizes the victory of good over evil. Celebrated in both cities and villages, in some areas it is called the Festival of Lights because during the celebrations homes and businesses are aglow with electric lights, candles, and oil lamps.

Another important holiday is Holi. Its purpose is to purify the fields so they will yield good crops. Celebrated in the spring, Holi is regarded as a "fun" festival. On the eve of Holi, bonfires are lit to symbolize ridding the earth of the evils of the past year. The next day, people roam the streets, throwing colored water on each other and painting each other's foreheads. People dye their hair and clothes various shades of red and purple, and children play practical jokes.

Many Hindus consider it their religious duty to make pilgrimages, or sacred journeys, to shrines. One of the many pilgrimages takes place at Puri. There, large crowds gather each year to watch an image of the god Juggernaut travel to its summer temple. Below, a visitor to India describes a Puri pilgrimage in which he took part:

Outside the temple, in the town and on the roads leading to it, there was excitement in the air. There was an increasing noise made by a surging orchestra of creaking, tinkling rickshaws and pilgrims' sandals slip-slapping on the road. Many people peeled away from the main body of marchers and crossed the hot sand dunes to the sea. . . . There were several hundred dunking themselves under the supervision of fishermen. . . .

It would be impossible to say how many were in Puri that day. People talked of a million or more. I guessed there were at least several hundred thousand who had been gathering since long before dawn. . . . People crammed every window, balcony, rooftop, ledge, tree and hoarding [wooden fence], and I paid a few rupees to get onto a roof packed with squirming bodies. There was a strong smell of sweat and camphor and sandlewood. It was . . .

EXAMINING PHOTOGRAPHS *These buildings and images of deities reflected in the river are brightly lit in celebration of Diwali, the Festival of Lights. One of the purposes of Diwali is to honor the goddess Lakshmi.* **What is the purpose of the Hindu holiday Holi?**

hot and humid. . . . Down in the street cows and bullocks ran amok and people shouted and scattered. . . .

Excitement grew through the afternoon. More pilgrims pressed in, their foreheads daubed with paint. Men jigged incessantly to the beat of drums. . . . Hundreds of women had cut off their hair and brought their shining tresses in offering. There was a constant cracking and spluttering as people smashed coconuts on the ground and anointed themselves with the milk, falling to their knees in prayer.

All eyes were on three monstrous vehicles standing abreast. . . . These are great chariots as large as houses, [topped] by decorated pavilions in which . . . three gods ride to their summer house. The largest is Juggernaut's. . . . It has a red dome and the whole . . . structure is 45 feet [13.5 meters] high. . . .

At about five o'clock long thick ropes were attached to the chariots and men rushed forward to grab them. By tradition, 4,200 men pull each wagon, but there seemed to be more of them than that. . . .

At last, the chariots began to tremble and move. The din was terrific. . . . The platforms shuddered and the ground shook. . . . This was no half-hearted carnival, but a [display] of India's religious energy, an event of great power whose participants were singleminded in their devotion and enthusiasm. . . . The people surged forward and tossed rice, marigolds and coconut shards at the wagons, and scooped up brown dust where the wheels had passed and rubbed it onto their heads. The eyes of men and women were wide and shiny with adoration, tears blobbed their dusty faces. The chariots moved a few yards at a time and then paused while the draggers drew breath. By nightfall they were halfway and the progress stopped while the weary haulers slept. The journey resumed next morning. This time I watched from the street. I have an indelible memory of the towering monsters advancing and people running from

EXAMINING ART *In this painting, a Kshatriya receives guests at his court. Traditionally, the Kshatriya made up the military class of Hindu India. In what sacred writing are the* **varnas** *described?*

the grinding wheels, under which, years ago, some of the devoted used to hurl themselves in sacrifice and to achieve an ultimate bliss.

THE CASTE SYSTEM

Hindus have traditionally been divided into four categories known as *varnas.* These categories are Brahmins, or priests; Kshatriyas (kuh·SHA·tree·yuhz), or warriors; Vaisyas, or farmers and merchants; and Sudras, or servants. Together, they make up the caste system of India. The *Bhagavad Gita* describes each of the *varnas* as follows:

Source: Trevor Fishlock. *Gandhi's Children.* Universe Books, New York, 1983.

The works of Brahmins, Kshatriyas, Vaisyas and Sudras are different, in harmony with the . . . powers of their born nature.

The works of a Brahmin are peace; self-harmony, austerity and purity; loving-forgiveness and righteousness; vision and wisdom and faith.

These are the works of a Kshatriya; a heroic mind, inner fire, constancy, resourcefulness, courage in battle, generosity and noble leadership.

Trade, agriculture and the rearing of cattle is the work of a Vaisya. And the work of the Sudra is service.

JATI The caste groupings to which most Hindus relate and within which they live are called *jatis*. In each area, *jatis* are ranked in order from high to low. Each *jati* is linked to a specific occupation and has its own rules for diet, marriage, and other social practices. A person's social standing often depends on his or her *jati*. Each person is born into his or her *jati* and cannot change *jatis*.

Hinduism and the caste system have been closely tied together. Often, fulfilling one's *dharma* has meant performing one's *jati* obligations. Because strict Hindu social rules require that those of a higher *jati* avoid contact with those of a lower one, members of a *jati* generally do not mix socially with or marry someone of a different *jati*.

In recent years, the caste system has been challenged. The government, for one, has tried to put an end to the system, whose restrictions it views as barriers to modernizing the country. Government officials claim that because of the system, the poor have had little opportunity to improve their lives. Caste has also been challenged by the recent spread of education and the growth of modern urban industrial life, which have led Hindus of different *jatis* to mix freely in public places. As a result, some Hindus now marry outside their *jatis*.

The caste system, however, is an old tradition that yields only slowly to change, and few Hindus are willing to see it end completely. They view it as an important part of Hinduism that links religious belief and social behavior. They point out that *jatis* perform practical functions by passing craft skills from one generation to another and providing social and educational benefits to their members.

UNTOUCHABLES At least 25 percent of India's population are Sudras, the lowest ranked of all the *varnas*. Some of these Sudras work at the dirtiest jobs, such as handling dead animals or sweeping streets. These people came to be known as **untouchables.** Because they work with dirt, death, or blood, they have been viewed as impure by other Hindus.

The position of untouchables in Indian society has improved a good deal in the last 30 or so years. Since India's constitution outlaws discrimination against them, many untouchables have entered government service. Some have acquired land. Even so, a large number of Hindus still cling to the old traditions that keep some of the untouchables in an inferior status. Below, an Indian journalist discusses the life of some women who are sweepers in private homes:

The work is very tiring. It involves climbing flights of stairs, carrying garbage on the head for long distances, and working in a bent posture for hours together. Maternity leave is unknown. Most women continue to work almost to the day of childbirth, and they have to provide substitutes for the days they are absent. Their salaries for these days go to the substitutes.

Source: From *THE BHAGAVAD GITA* translated by Juan Mascaró (Penguin Classics, 1962), copyright © 1962 Juan Mascaró. Reprinted by permission of Penguin Books Ltd.

EXAMINING PHOTOGRAPHS *This Hindu priest is reading from the* Rig-Veda, *the oldest sacred text of Hinduism.* To what varna do Hindu priests belong?

. . . Bimla [a 26-year-old sweeper] says: Most of my employers address me as Jamadarni (sweeperess). There is no personal relationship with them. I clean the latrine, throw away garbage, sweep the stairs and driveways. I am not supposed to sweep the other rooms, though sometimes when the servant is absent, I am asked to stand in. I get very tired, carrying dustbins and bending over the stairs fifteen times a day."

The older women are more resigned to facing such humiliation but some of the younger ones seethe with indignation, like Kamla, who has been working since the age of 11, and is now a mother of four: "Who says there is no untouchability? Even after all these years, I am not allowed to go anywhere near the kitchen. I work for Baniyas who are very fussy. There is one relative of theirs—she says she is a school teacher—she lifts up her sari if she has to pass me. When she does that, I feel like throwing acid on her face. Don't we have hearts and bodies just like you?

Source: Malavika Karlekar. "The 'Unclean' Who Keep the City Clean" in *Manushi*, July-August, 1979, p. 52.

SECTION 2

Islam

After Hinduism, the most important religion of India is Islam. With about 96 million Muslims, or followers of Islam, India is ranked as the fourth largest Muslim nation in the world. Preached in the 600's AD by an Arabian religious leader named Muhammad, Islam spread from the Arabian Peninsula to North Africa and eventually to India. Today, some Indian Muslims are descendants of a variety of Islamic peoples who invaded and settled India from the eighth to the thirteenth centuries. Others are former Hindus who have converted to Islam as a result of Muslim missionary efforts.

Muslims believe in one all-powerful God whose teachings are recorded in a holy book called the Quran (Koran). They have opposed the traditional caste system and religious images on the grounds that all human beings are equal and that God is a spiritual being beyond all forms. Although they eat meat, Muslims do not eat pork, which they regard as unclean.

Although Muslims have played an important role in Indian government, economy, society, and culture for centuries, they have often been in conflict with the Hindus. In modern India, however they officially enjoy equal rights with Hindus. Many live in the cities and are actively involved in all levels of government and industry. Others, however, remain in the villages and follow a more traditional lifestyle. Below, a visitor describes the lifestyle of a Muslim family she met in an Indian village:

Rehana bibi is 30 years old and lives in the Muslim community of Rustampura. She was educated in an elementary school not far from her present home. At 16, she married a local villager named Kolokhan bhai Garashia. They share a house with Kolokhan bhai's elder brother and his family.

Rehana bibi and Kolokhan bhai have

EXAMINING PHOTOGRAPHS *This Muslim woman runs a store similar to the one in Rustampura, described on this page. What is the status of Muslims in India today?*

three children—two sons and a daughter. They want their sons to be educated so they will have better job opportunities. Their daughter, however, probably will leave school when she becomes a teenager, marry, and assume the role of a housewife. Until she marries, she can help Rehana bibi and Kolokhan bhai in the small shop they rent and run across the street from their home. There, they sell a variety of goods, including vegetables, powders, seeds . . . and soap.

Rehana bibi and Kolokhan bhai are devout Muslims. Every Thursday, Kolokhan bhai spends the entire day at the Darga, a local shrine where pilgrims gather to pray and to receive advice from a "holy man." Rehana bibi stays in the shop and reads her prayer book until there are customers to be served. . . .

In keeping with the beliefs of Islam, Rehana bibi and Kolokhan bhai are very generous. They believe that charity and generosity to others is a form of service to Allah [God]. Kolokhan bhai knows what poverty is and that the poor need to have their basic needs met, so he often gives offerings to beggars. He is reluctant, however, to receive financial help from his wealthier in-laws or even from his own brother. He and Rehana bibi usually try to make ends meet through their own efforts. Hopeful about a brighter future, they have made plans to expand both their house and their shop.

SECTION 2 REVIEW

CHECKING FOR UNDERSTANDING

1. **Describe** the origins of Islam and how the religion spread to India.

CRITICAL THINKING

2. **Identifying Assumptions** Why do you think Indian Muslims oppose the caste system and religious images?

Source: Sumita Shukla. "Case Study of Rehana bibi Garashia" in *Households and Families in Rustampura Village* by Ellen C.K. Johnson and Sumita Shukla, pp. 8–9, 11, 12–13.

SECTION 3
Other Religions

In addition to Hinduism and Islam, India also has a number of other religions. One of these is Sikhism. Founded in the 1500's by a teacher named Guru Nanak, it rejects the caste system and combines the Muslim belief in one God with the Hindu belief in reincarnation. Most of its 17 million followers, known as Sikhs, live in the Indian state of Punjab. The rest live in India's major cities. While most Sikhs are business people or farmers, Sikhs generally are known for their military skills. Many of them serve as one of the largest and best-trained groups in the Indian army.

Another religion of India is Buddhism, which emerged in India during the 500's BC. Its founder, the Indian prince Siddhartha Gautama, wanted to reform Hinduism. Known as Buddha, or "Enlightened One," he disregarded the caste system and taught that anyone could reach spiritual perfection. He knew that suffering was a fact of life. But he taught that it could be overcome by renouncing desires and by finding peace of mind through meditation and good deeds.

In spite of Hindu opposition, Buddhism spread throughout India and later became influential in Southeast and East Asia. Today, although only about 6 million Indians—1 percent of the population—are Buddhists, Buddhism has given to India a rich heritage of art, architecture, and literature.

A third minority religion is Jainism. Like Buddhism, it arose in the 500's BC as a protest against the caste system. Its founder, a *guru* named Mahavira, gave up his wealthy way of life to travel throughout the country to spread his message. Today, Jainism has over 3 million followers in India. Known as Jains, they emphasize nonviolence and have extended the Hindu ban on killing

EXAMINING PHOTOGRAPHS *A Sikh worshipper meditates in front of the Golden Temple at Amritsar in northwestern India, center of the Sikh faith.* ***What Hindu and Muslim beliefs have been combined in Sikhism?***

to include all living things, even insects. Traditionally they have refused to farm for fear of plowing under living things and have devoted themselves to trade and business instead. Today, many are wealthy and have high positions in the Indian economy.

A fourth minority religion in India is Christianity, with about 18 million followers. Most Christians live in the south, where tradition states that an apostle of Jesus named Thomas founded churches in the first century AD. When the Portuguese reached India in the 1500's, they won converts to Catholicism. Two hundred years later, the British brought the first Protestant missionaries to India. Both the Catholic and Protestant missionaries built hospitals and schools and won converts among the untouchables.

EXAMINING PHOTOGRAPHS *Buddhist monks play long brass horns and such other instruments as drums, bells, and cymbals to open sacred festivals. How do Buddhists believe the suffering of life can be ended?*

Still another religion in India is that of the Parsis, a people who came to India from Persia between 700 and 900 AD. Today, many Parsis live in Bombay and are leaders in industry and in the professions. Their beliefs are based on the teachings of Zoroaster, a Persian religious leader who lived around 1000 BC and who saw the world as a battleground between the forces of good and evil. The religion of the Parsis is called Zoroastrianism. In the following excerpt, an American writer discusses the Parsis in Bombay:

This community of about 80,000—the largest concentration of Parsis in the world—has [had] an influence in Bombay far out of proportion to its numbers. Though . . . businessmen from other groups have now broken the Parsis' near monopoly on wealth in this wealthiest of Indian cities, three Parsi names still stand out: Tata (hotels, steel mills, trucks, chemicals), Wadia (textile mills), and Godrej (typewriters and electric refrigerators among a host of other products).

Philanthropy [the rich aiding the poor] and civic responsibility have been Parsi touchstones for generations. I saw those three names repeatedly as donors to hospitals, schools, Bombay's sparkling new National Centre for the Performing Arts, and the Tata Institute of Fundamental Research. S.P. Godrej, the . . . head of the Godrej organization, sketched a typically Parsi philosophy as he showed me around his company's spacious garden township at Vikhroli, on the edge of Bombay.

"Our workers come to us with only their hands," Mr. Godrej said, as his arm swept a horizon of factories, housing blocks, schools, and—above all, that commodity so rare elsewhere in Bombay—space. "Our job is to give them skills. Today three-quarters of the Godrej working force of 12,000 live here. Their children go to school here. Our idea is to transform the so-called working classes into middle classes."

Source: John Scofield. "Bombay, the Other India" in *National Geographic*, July 1981, pp. 122–123.

SECTION 3 REVIEW

CHECKING FOR UNDERSTANDING
1. **List** some other religions of India besides Hinduism and Islam and the approximate time period each appeared in India.

CRITICAL THINKING
2. **Predicting Consequences** What impact do you think each minority religion has had on Indian culture?

Religion

DIVERSITY AND DISSENSION

In 1947, more than 200,000 Indians lost their lives as a result of clashes between Hindus and Muslims. India has solved many of its problems since then, and many Indians of different religions live side by side in peace. But, as the map on this page shows, tensions among the nation's diverse religious and ethnic groups continue to create conflict that erupts into violence.

Conflict between Hindus and Muslims is responsible for much of the unrest.

Even more violent, however, is the conflict between Hindus and Sikhs. Sikh separatists in the state of Punjab have been fighting since 1982 to make the state an independent nation. They argue that the nation denies them cultural freedom and the full wealth of their land.

FOCUSING ON THE ISSUE Read the following comments by Sikhs and Hindus, and answer these questions:
1. What do you think may be some causes of Hindu-Sikh tensions?
2. Do you think the Indian government could take

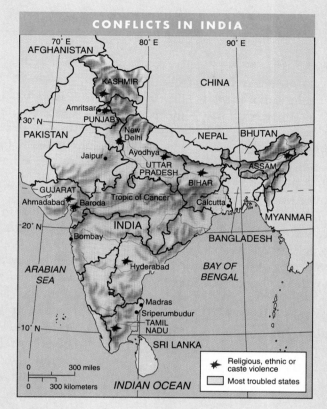

CONFLICTS IN INDIA

★ Religious, ethnic or caste violence

▢ Most troubled states

0   300 miles
0   300 kilometers

steps to reduce the tension between Hindus and Sikhs? Explain. What steps, if any, do you think the government should take?

"It's the politicians who have created conflict between Hindus and Sikhs. They are after one thing, and that is power. It's people like us who suffer."
—Sikh truck driver

"The Government must accept our identity as Sikhs. You must understand that Sikhs don't want to merge into the Hindu mainstream. We must protect our religion."
—Sikh businessman

"I was uprooted once and made a refugee. I won't let it happen again. And I won't leave because the Sikhs want to set up an independent state here. This is my home and I will fight and die here."
—Hindu textile merchant

"You see this finger. You see the finger-nail here. And you see the skin around it. Now the Sikhs are the finger-nail and Hindus are the skin around. How can you separate the finger from the finger-nail?"
—elderly Sikh

"What's wrong if Sikhs want a separate personal law? What's wrong if Sikhs don't want Hindu immigrants to vote in Punjab? Really, the whole thing is rather silly. It's like a younger brother asking an older brother for a chocolate or toffee. And the older one is making such a fuss."
—Sikh housewife

Source: Sunil Sethi. *India Today*, September 30, 1983, pp. 98–103.

Chapter 23 Review

SUMMARY

Modern India guarantees religious freedom by law. The major religion of India is Hinduism. Stressing the unity of all life, Hindus practice special acts of worship but also regard ordinary tasks as sacred.

Hindus traditionally have been divided into four *varnas* and thousands of *jatis*. In recent years, the government has challenged the inequalities of the caste system.

After Hinduism, the second religion of India in numbers is Islam. Muslims believe in one God and oppose the caste system. Over the centuries, they have played an important role in India.

Among India's other religions are Sikhism, Buddhism, Jainism, Christianity, and Zoroastrianism. Followers of each of these faiths have contributed to the cultural and economic development of India.

USING VOCABULARY

Each of the following terms pertains to Hinduism, the major religion of India. Use these terms to explain some of the basic beliefs and practices of Hinduism.

reincarnation	*gurus*	*varnas*
karma	**yoga**	*jatis*
dharma	*sadhus*	**untouchables**

REVIEWING FACTS

1. **Name** the four main *varnas*. What is the role of each?
2. **Summarize** attitudes towards the untouchables in India today.
3. **Discuss** the status of Muslims in modern India.
4. **Discuss** the teachings of Buddha. Which Hindu beliefs and practices did he accept?

Which did he reject?
5. **Explain** the relationship of Sikhism to Hinduism and Islam.
6. **Describe** the basic beliefs of the Jains and their impact on Indian life.
7. **Name** the founder of the religion of the Parsis. What was his basic viewpoint?

CRITICAL THINKING

1. **Recognizing Ideologies** Do you think the statement that Hinduism is more than a religion is an accurate one? Explain.
2. **Expressing Problems Clearly** Based on what you know about Hinduism, do you think the caste system can be ended in India? Explain.
3. **Making Comparisons** What do Islam and the other religions of India have in common with Hinduism? In what ways are they different from Hinduism?
4. **Synthesizing Information** In recent years a number of untouchables have converted from Hinduism to Buddhism. Explain the special appeal that Buddhism might have for untouchables.

ANALYZING CONCEPTS

1. **Diversity** What role does religious diversity play in modern India? Do you think it helps or hinders development? Give examples to support your answers.
2. **Empathy** What is the *varna* system? Has it benefited all Indians? Explain.

GEOGRAPHIC THEMES

1. **Movement** How did invasions and migrations affect the religious development of India?
2. **Place** What kinds of places symbolize to Hindus the sacredness of all life?

Building Skills

CRITICAL THINKING

Checking Consistency

Societies develop rules of conduct and laws that are based on shared values or principles. For example, in our society most people believe that murder and theft are wrong, so our laws punish people who commit those acts. If an individual's or a society's actions agree with its principles, we say that actions and principles are *consistent*. If they do not agree, we say that actions and principles are *inconsistent*.

Checking the consistency of actions with principles enables you to determine how deeply particular principles are valued. For example, suppose your friend says that he or she hates people who cheat on tests, but you discover this friend looking over your shoulder on the next exam. Obviously, your friend does not value this principle very deeply. On a larger scale, our society criticizes violence and says that conflict should be resolved peacefully. Yet violent movies and television shows are very popular and bring in huge profits. This indicates that our nonviolent principles do not really affect our behavior. The following steps will help you check the consistency of actions and principles:

- Identify the principle that the group or individual holds.

- Analyze the actions of the group or individual.

- Determine whether the actions agree or disagree with the stated principles.

EXAMPLE

Read this excerpt taken from your text on page 377.

Jains . . . emphasize nonviolence and have extended the Hindu ban on killing to include all living things, even insects. Traditionally they have refused to farm for fear of plowing under living things and have devoted themselves to trade and business instead.

This passage states one of the Jains' principles—nonviolence. It also explains how this principle affects the Jains' way of life. Not only are the Jains vegetarians, but they do not kill even insects. In what other ways are Jains influenced by their principle of nonviolence? *(They refuse to farm so they won't kill living things.)* Do you think driving a car would be consistent or inconsistent with Jain philosophy? *(Driving may be consistent if drivers can avoid hitting people or animals; however, it is often difficult to avoid killing flying insects in a car.)*

PRACTICE

Read the following passage and answer the questions that follow:

[Hindu] myths and scriptures ascribe a high status to women: learning is symbolized by the goddess Saraswati and wealth by the goddess Laxmi. . . . [But] a woman must be in a state of perpetual subordination . . . an unmarried woman is dependent on her father, after marriage on her husband, and, when widowed, on her son. . . . Indian women . . . are expected to cook and serve the men of the family first and then the boys. By the time these have finished, the women may be left to subsist on rice that has stuck to the bottom of the pot. . . .

1. According to Hindu myths and scriptures, what is the status of women?
2. In practice, what is the status of many women in Indian society?
3. According to this passage, is the status of women consistent or inconsistent with Hindu principles? Explain your answer.

Source: From AVERTING THE APOCALYPSE: SOCIAL MOVEMENTS IN INDIA TODAY, Arthur Bonner. Copyright 1990 Duke University Press. Reprinted with permission of the publisher.

381

CHAPTER OUTLINE

1 Early India
2 Muslim India
3 British India
4 Independent India

People and Places to Know
Indus River Valley, Aryans, Dravidians, Maurya Empire, Gupta Empire, the Moguls, the British, Mohandas Gandhi, Pakistan, Jawaharlal Nehru, Indira Gandhi, Rajiv Gandhi

Key Terms to Define
rajah, *sepoys*, viceroy, civil disobedience

Objectives to Learn
1. **Identify** contributions early peoples made to India's civilization.
2. **Evaluate** the British presence in India.
3. **Trace** India's independence movement.
4. **Analyze** the political situation in India since 1947.

Peacock Gate in Jaipur, India

An Old and New Land

> Ever since I was a boy I've been interested in the culture and people of my land. India is a vast country with many different kinds of people, religions, customs and even weather conditions. . . .
>
> I'm happy to find that once again our educated young are turning to their own Indian culture. It's very rich and varied.
>
> Our Indus Valley civilization, which dates back to the year 3000 B.C., is one of the oldest civilizations in the world. Scholars and archaeologists from all over the world still come to study the mystery of its ruins.
>
> Soon after the Indus Valley civilization, the fair-skinned Aryan race invaded India. They settled in the north and drove the old inhabitants of India, the dark-skinned Dravidians, to the south. Much later, both the races mingled together, but the Aryans remained the dominating group.
>
> It was the Aryans who divided our society into four groups. The Brahmans were considered to be the élite. Then came the warrior class; then the merchants and traders. Butchers, sweepers, and the menial workers were placed in the lowest class and were supposed to be impure and, therefore, untouchable. . . .
>
> Centuries after the Aryans settled in India, the [Muslims] began invading. In the sixteenth century, the [Muslims] founded a great dynasty and ruled over us for a few hundred years. Then the British arrived and became the masters. So India is a mixture of many cultures rolled into one: Hindu culture of the Aryans, [Muslim] culture, and some British habits.

As indicated above by a present-day Indian scholar, a variety of foreigners have come to India over many centuries. Attracted by its important location and abundance of natural resources, different groups arrived, settled, and ruled all or parts of the country. Each group brought with it a different set of beliefs, customs, and institutions that contributed to the making of Indian civilization, one of the oldest and richest civilizations in the world.

Over the centuries, many Indians have been at the mercy of the power of their rulers and have known hunger, disease, and poverty. Despite this, the Indian people take pride in their past and in the glory of their long-gone kingdoms. Today, India is a democracy that pledges equality for all under the law. Although differences still exist, the Indian people are hopeful that they can reduce their conflicts and achieve social harmony.

Source: Veenu Sandal. "Our civilisation dates back to 3000 B.C." in *We Live in India.* The Bookwright Press, 1984, pp. 26–27.

SECTION 1

Early India

The earliest people came to India more than 400,000 years ago. By 2500 BC, there were villages all along the Indus River. Villagers grew wheat and rice, herded cattle, and built well-planned cities such as Mohenjo Daro and Harappa. Their civilization—the Indus River Valley civilization—soon stretched over 1000 miles (1600 kilometers).

Then, beginning about 1500 BC, invaders known as Aryans entered through mountain passes in the northwest and spread over northern India. They brought an Indo-European language known as Sanskrit, horses, and iron and copper tools. Over time, their religion of Brahmanism, which honored nature deities, took root and developed into Hinduism.

At first, the Aryans were divided into family groups, each led by the oldest male. Later, kingdoms emerged. The most important kingdom was Magadha, where the founders of Buddhism and Jainism preached and spread their religions. The Aryans looked down on the non-Aryans, most of whom were dark-skinned Dravidians. The Aryans were the ruling military class and had the most power. A class of priests dealt with religious rituals and rules. Soon, people with the same kinds of jobs began to group together, and the ideas underlying the caste system began to develop.

MAURYA EMPIRE

About 300 BC, a new empire—the Maurya (MOU·ehr·yeh)—was founded by Chandragupta Maurya. It spread over much of northern and central India and, in the view of some, represents the first great flowering of native Indian civilization.

Maurya rulers developed a strong government administration and encouraged the growth of cities and trade. One of the most famous Maurya rulers was Chandragupta's grandson Asoka. After fighting many wars of conquest, he turned against war and devoted himself to the welfare of the people. Under the influence of Buddhism, he issued new laws, which he ordered carved on stone pillars throughout the empire. The laws reflected Asoka's desire to "exchange good for evil and to forsake violence." Declaring that he wanted to establish a reign of "justice, security, peace, and mercy for all," he decreed the following:

Commendable is the service of the father and mother and so is liberality to friends, neighbors, Brahmans, and sramanas [those who practice self-denial].

It is commendable not to hoard too much gold; to borrow little and to refrain from exploiting [taking advantage of] others.

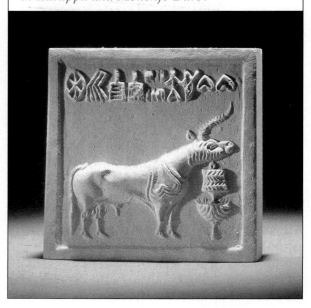

EXAMINING PHOTOGRAPHS *Small Harappan seals like this one are thought to have been good luck charms or labels for merchandise.* *What features of modern cities were present in Harappa and Mohenjo Daro?*

INDIAN EMPIRES

ca. 2500 BC Growth of Indus Valley cities

ca. 1500 BC Aryans migrate into India from Central Asia

ca. 1500–100 BC Early Vedic Period

ca. 540–430 BC Rise of Magadha

563–483 BC Gautama Buddha

322–185 BC Maurya Empire

273–232 BC Rule of Emperor Asoka

320–647 AD Gupta Empire—Golden Age of India

700–1200 The Rajput Period

ca. 1200 Beginning of Turkish Muslim conquests

1206–1526 Delhi Sultanate

1526–1761 Mogul Empire

1556–1605 Rule of Emperor Akbar

EXAMINING CHARTS *For many centuries, India was governed by a series of empires, each of which tried to unite the subcontinent under strong government administration.* *How long did the Moguls rule India?*

Benevolence is difficult and he who performs such acts accomplishes a difficult deed. . . . Reprehensible is he who neglects acts of benevolence, and it is easy, indeed, to sin.

The king desires that all sects [religious groups] may live [freely] everywhere in the land.

Ceremonies should be performed if they promote morality.

You are true to your own beliefs if you accord kindly treatment to adherents of other faiths. You harm your own religion by harassing followers of other creeds.

Observe dharma; be kind to your parents; be generous to kith and kin; be decent to your slaves.

Source: Emil Lengyel. *Asoka the Great.* Franklin Watts, Inc., 1969, pp. 91–97.

GUPTA EMPIRE

The harsh policies of Mauryan rulers that came after Asoka turned the people against the Maurya. About 185 BC, the last Maurya ruler was murdered, and once again India was divided into small kingdoms. Finally, about 320 AD, another empire—the Gupta—came to power in northern India.

Gupta rulers supported learning and the arts, and the period of their rule came to be known as the Golden Age of India. Gupta mathematicians invented the concept of zero and the number symbols 0 through 9, which later reached the West by way of the Middle East. Gupta astronomers studied the heavens, knew that the world was round, and had some knowledge of gravity. Gupta doctors set bones, performed operations, and invented hundreds of medical instruments.

SECTION 1 REVIEW

CHECKING FOR UNDERSTANDING

1. **Chronicle** early Indian civilization before the Mauryan and Gupta empires.

CRITICAL THINKING

2. **Analyzing Information** In what ways did Maurya and Gupta rulers impact Indian society?

SECTION 2

Muslim India

In the late 600's and early 700's, Muslims from the Middle East and Central Asia began moving into India. Some came as scholars to learn about Indian astronomy, medicine, and mathematics. Others came to trade. Still others came seeking riches and converts. By the early 1000's, the entire Indus Valley was under Muslim control.

In the 1200's, Turkish Muslims invaded and conquered northern India. They set up their capital at Delhi. About 300 years later, a Turk named Babur became the new ruler, established a strong central government, and founded the Mogul dynasty. In 1556, Babur's grandson, Akbar, came to power. A skilled warrior and administrator, by 1600 he controlled most of India.

Under the Moguls, the arts thrived. Such local crafts as cotton weaving became important, and luxury goods and precious metals were brought into India. Mogul rulers surrounded themselves with the beautiful and

EXAMINING ART *Under the rule of Akbar, shown here receiving visiting princes to his court, Hinduism was tolerated by the Moguls.* Who founded the Mogul dynasty in India? From where did he come?

the luxurious. The court of Akbar's grandson, the Great Mogul Shah Jahan, is an example:

The court of the Great Mogul was situated in three locations; Delhi, Lahore, and Agra. Of his three principal residences, the Red Fort in Agra was the most impressive. Started by Akbar and completed by Shah Jahan, this walled complex of mosques . . . , gardens, and palaces was the pride of the Moguls. . . . The royal apartments were ornamented with ruby-encrusted arabesques [patterns] and crowned with ceilings of solid gold. Musicians were kept performing continuously even in empty rooms. . . . In the imperial kitchens, fifteen complete meals were always ready to be served at a moment's notice by a unit of richly dressed kitchen slaves. Embroidered tapestries and choice Persian paintings, enamel lamps that burned scented oil, gold decanters filled with lemonade, a box of pearls, trays of guavas or mangoes, or grapes from Kashmir, pillows, carpets, mirrors, melons, silver goblets filled with night wine or lilacs, seven slender pillars wrapped in satin drapery—all were here. . . . Meanwhile, the emperor, the creator . . . of this garden of earthly delights, bathed . . . in his underground pool, where the light of a thousand candles danced in the reflection of ten thousand mirrors and countless gems encrusted on the walls.

Each day of the week Shah Jahan ruled from a different throne. The greatest of these was the Takht-i-Taus, the Peacock Throne, which was built in 1628 to commemorate his coronation. . . . It took seven years to complete and cost a million rupees. . . . The throne itself . . . consisted of an elevated rectangular platform on which twelve emerald-studded pillars were placed, the capitals of each composed of two jeweled peacocks standing on either side of a diamond-leafed tree. These pillars supported a canopy . . . which was covered with [designs] of pearls, emeralds, sapphires, and gold. In order to mount the throne one climbed a staircase of solid silver.

Under the Moguls, social and trade networks tied together villages, towns, and cities, and a culture that was a blend of Muslim and Hindu ways developed. The caste system was followed by Hindus and even influenced Muslim social relationships.

Some Hindu beliefs, however, were in opposition to those of Islam. For example, Hindus had many deities and believed that one's status was fixed at birth. Muslims had only one deity and believed that one's status could change. Muslim leaders after Akbar did not tolerate Hinduism and forced Hindus to convert to Islam. Soon conflict broke out between Hindus and Muslims, and the Mogul empire was broken into small kingdoms led by local **rajahs**, or princes.

SECTION 2 REVIEW

CHECKING FOR UNDERSTANDING
1. **Define** rajah.
2. **Give reasons** why Muslims came to India.

CRITICAL THINKING
3. **Determining Cause and Effect** How were Indian civilization and society affected by the Moguls?

SECTION 3
British India

During the 1400's and 1500's, while the Moguls were still in power, Europeans became interested in India. At the time, India was a source of the spices that Europeans used to cook their food and as perfumes. In the 1400's, Portuguese seafarers reached India. They were followed by the Dutch,

Source: David Carroll and the Editors of the Newsweek Book Division. *The Taj Mahal. Newsweek,* 1972, pp. 67–68.

French, and British. In time, the British proved to be the most powerful and came to dominate India for nearly 200 years.

THE EAST INDIA COMPANY

In 1600, England's Queen Elizabeth I gave a group of English traders called the East India Company exclusive trading rights with India. At first, the Company was interested only in securing control of the Indian spice trade and owned no Indian land. Soon, however, it had its own army, which won enough territory in battles with Indian Muslim leaders to make the Company a real power in India.

The Company's policies and the enormous profits it made by taxing the Indians soon led to unrest. By the late 1700's, the situation had become so bad that the British Parliament stepped in. It passed a series of laws that at first gave the British government more control over the Company's actions in India and ultimately made the government responsible for the administration of India.

By the mid-1800's, many Indians found conditions under the British intolerable. In their effort to encourage the spread of Western culture, the British had banned Indian customs that conflicted with Western values. In addition, some local Indian princes and landowners had lost both their authority and their property. Matters came to a head in 1857, when *sepoys*, Indian soldiers who served as officers in the East India Company's army, revolted against British officers.

The revolt, called the Sepoy Mutiny by the British, came to be regarded by Indians as their first war of independence against British rule. The action came about after a new model rifle was issued to the *sepoys*. The cartridges used in the rifles had to be bitten before they were fired. The *sepoys* believed that the cartridges were greased with cow or pig fat. Putting them in their mouths would violate their religious beliefs, so they refused to accept the rifles. When the British responded by imprisoning *sepoys*, they revolted. In the passage that follows, an Indian officer explains:

EXAMINING ART *The Sepoy Mutiny actually began in the city of Meerut, north of Delhi, when* sepoys *who had been jailed for refusing to accept the new, greased rifle cartridges were forcibly freed by their comrades. The* sepoys *then seized Delhi and held it for more than three months before the British finally recaptured it. It took nearly two years to bring the revolt to an end. Why did the* sepoys *refuse to use the new rifle cartridges provided by the British?*

I have little to say. All you who hear me know why five hundred Brahmins like myself, three hundred Rajpoots of high caste, have been deprived of their daily bread and turned adrift on the world after they had served the English government for many years. . . . Why? Because they would not pollute themselves, because they would not lose their caste—their religion. . . .

All that I have to say to you is this. I have journeyed from Calcutta to here. I have been to every station where sepoy regiments are quartered, been in the lines of thirty or forty regiments. They are all of the same mind. They will not let themselves be the victims. . . . They will not let their caste be [stolen] from them; they will not let their religion be stolen from them. They are firmly of one mind. I have seen many kings and princes and noblemen. . . . They are all of one mind. The reign of the English must cease. I have seen the people in the country and in the towns and cities. They are all of one mind. The reign of the English must cease. . . .

Yes, the whole intention of the English government is to take away our religion and caste, to make us Christians. The new governor-general has come out with . . . orders from the queen to do this.

A NEW REGIME

The British, however, were stronger than the Indians thought, and in 1859 the *sepoy* revolt was put down. The British government ended the rule of the British East India Company and assumed direct control of Indian affairs. India was divided into provinces, each under a governor. A governor-general, known as a **viceroy**, was sent to India to represent the British monarch. British officers took charge of the Indian army.

Under British rule, all of India was united for the first time under one political system

EXAMINING ART *The first locomotive entered Indore, in central India, by means of elephant power. By 1900, India's main railway system was completed.* **How did the railway system affect India's economy?**

and set of laws. British writers, educators, and missionaries encouraged Indians to adopt the English language, Christianity, and British-style education. Schools and hospitals were set up in villages, and universities were opened in major cities.

Many British public officials, remembering the Sepoy Mutiny, however, avoided getting involved in Indian cultural and social life. This led to an almost complete separation between Indians and the British living in India. Many of the British thought Indians were culturally and morally inferior. Many Indians thought the British were interested only in power and did not care about India's welfare.

These attitudes, however, did not diminish British influence in some areas. Roads, seaports, and irrigation systems were improved. An extensive railway system was established that opened the country's interior to the world's markets. Fares on the railroads were so low that even poor Indians could travel or send goods. By bringing together people from all over India for the first time, the railroads contributed to a sense of national unity.

These changes, however, largely benefited the British and not the Indians. Improved irrigation, for example, made more land available to grow food. But the British reaped the profits from the land. The British owned the plantations, or large farms, and the mines and factories. The Indians provided the labor. They worked long hours under poor conditions and received low wages. In addition, British policies blocked the growth of Indian industries that competed with their own. Below, an Indian leader describes the long-term effect of such British actions:

The chief business of the East India Company in its early period was to carry Indian manufactured goods, textiles as well as spices, from the East to Europe, where there was a great demand for these articles. With the developments in industrial techniques in England a new class rose there demanding a change in this policy. The British market was to be closed to Indian products. The Indian market was to be opened to British manufactures. To begin with, Indian goods were kept out of Britain by laws. This was followed by attempts to restrict and crush Indian manufactures. At the same time, British goods could enter duty free. The Indian textile industry collapsed, affecting large numbers of weavers and artisans. The process went on during the 1800's, breaking up other old industries also—shipbuilding, metalwork, glass, paper, and many crafts.

The economic development of India was arrested, and the growth of new industry was prevented. Machinery could not be brought into India. A vacuum was created in India which could be filled only by British goods. This led to rapidly growing unemployment and poverty. India became a farming colony of industrial England. It supplied raw materials and provided markets for England's industrial goods.

The destruction of the skilled working class led to unemployment on a huge scale. What were all these scores of millions, who had so far been in industry and manufacturing, to do now?

All these people had no jobs, no work, and all their ancient skill was useless. They drifted to the land. . . . But the land was

EXAMINING ART
Cotton had been grown on the Deccan Plateau long before the British came to India, and nearly every village had weavers like this one who turned cotton into cloth on their looms. What are some factors that led to the collapse of the Indian textile industry in the 1800's?

EXAMINING PHOTOGRAPHS *Members of the Indian National Congress posed for this group photo, taken in the 1920's. Twenty months after the shootings at Amritsar on April 13, 1919, the Congress, meeting in Nagpur, voted to adopt Mohandas Gandhi's policy of nonviolence and noncooperation with India's British government. What was the goal of the Indian National Congress by the early 1900's?*

fully occupied and could not possibly absorb them profitably. So they became a burden on the land and the burden grew, and with it grew the poverty of the country.

Source: From *THE DISCOVERY OF INDIA* by Jawaharlal Nehru. Copyright 1946, © 1960 by Harper & Row Publishers, Inc. Copyright renewed 1973 by Indira Gandhi. Reprinted by permission of Harper Collins Publishers.

SECTION 3 REVIEW

CHECKING FOR UNDERSTANDING
1. **Define** *sepoys*, viceroy.
2. **Explain** why Europeans became interested in India.

CRITICAL THINKING
3. **Drawing Conclusions** Why did Indians resent British colonialism?

SECTION 4

Independent India

By the late 1800's, anti-British feelings were widespread in India. In 1885, to improve relations with the British and bring unity among diverse groups, the Indian National Congress was formed. Its members wanted to change by peaceful means the government policies that were causing unrest. In the early 1900's, in an effort to please the Congress, the British Parliament allowed more Indians to participate in the Indian government. By then, however, many Indians in the Congress wanted complete freedom for India.

TOWARD FREEDOM

Tensions continued to rise, and the British took strong measures to keep control. They censored Indian newspapers and ordered punishment of Indians suspected of treason. When British soldiers attacked a crowd of unarmed demonstrators in the city of Amritsar and killed and wounded hundreds of Indians, Indian anger reached a new high.

At this time, a new leader named Mohandas K. Gandhi appeared in the Indian National Congress. Gandhi appealed to the masses, especially villagers and the poor. They called him *Mahatma*, "Great Soul," and

India

MOHANDAS K. GANDHI

He seemed terribly frail, all skin and bones, though I knew that this appearance was deceptive, for he kept to a frugal but carefully planned diet that kept him fit, and for exercise he walked four or five miles [6.4 or 8 kilometers] each morning. . . . Over his skin and bones was a loosely wrapped dhoti [traditional male garment], and in the chilliness of a north Indian winter he draped a coarsely spun white shawl over his bony shoulders. His . . . legs were bare, his feet in wooden sandals.

With these words, an American author described Indian leader Mohandas K. Gandhi at age 61. Gandhi, whom Indians revere as the father of their country, was born in southern India in 1869 to a middle-class merchant family. Educated in Great Britain, he later went to British-ruled South Africa, where he practiced law. At the time, Indians living in South Africa faced racial discrimination. Gandhi began a campaign for Indian rights, using non-violent methods based on **civil**

Source: William L. Shirer. Gandhi: A Memoir. Simon & Schuster, 1979, pp. 28–29.

disobedience, the refusal to obey unjust laws.

In 1915, Gandhi returned to India, where he became a leader in the independence movement. With these words, he explained his viewpoint:

We believe that it is the inalienable right of the Indian people to have freedom and to enjoy the fruits of their toil and have the necessities of life so that they may have full opportunities of growth. We believe also that if any government keeps a people from having these rights, the people have a further right to change or do away with that government.

We know that the best way of gaining our freedom is not through violence. We will prepare ourselves by withdrawing, so far as we can, all voluntary association from the British Government, and will prepare for civil disobedience. We believe that if we can but withdraw our voluntary help and stop payment of taxes without doing violence, the end

of this rule is assured.

In 1930, to protest British control of the salt trade, Gandhi led a march to the sea to make salt from seawater. A supporter of the local textile industry, Gandhi convinced Indians not to buy or use British cotton goods. He also revived the arts of spinning and weaving as a symbol of national unity.

After independence, Gandhi worked for tolerance among Hindus and Muslims. In an effort to end the bloodshed, he began a fast. Hindu and Muslim leaders, fearing he would die, agreed to stop fighting. A few days later, however, Gandhi was killed by a Hindu who opposed his peace efforts.

TAKING ANOTHER LOOK

1. How did Gandhi seek to end British rule in India?
2. What movements in your country have used the same methods to bring about change?

Source: D.G. Tendulkar. Adapted from Life of Mohandas Karamchand Gandhi, Vol. III. The Publications Division, Ministry of Information and Broadcasting, Government of India, 1961, pp. 8–9. Reprinted by permission of Navajivan Trust.

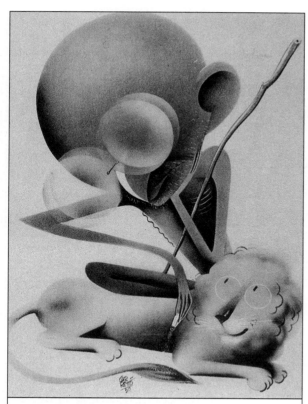

EXAMINING ART *In this cartoon, which represents the success of Gandhi's salt march, the now peaceful lion [British rule] has been tamed by one frail Indian, Mohandas Gandhi.* *What policy was begun under Gandhi?*

he called the untouchables *harijans*, "children of God." Under Gandhi, the Congress began a policy of nonviolent resistance to British rule.

In 1935, the British responded and granted India limited self-government. But, for most Indians, this was not enough. When World War II started four years later, the Indian National Congress said that unless India received independence, it would not aid the British war effort. When the British refused, Congress leaders in the Indian government resigned their posts. The British arrested them and had them jailed.

After the war ended, the British agreed to give India its freedom. But, while independence was being planned, bitterness developed between Indian Hindus and Muslims. This led to the creation of two countries out of British India—Pakistan for the Muslims and India for the Hindus. At midnight on August 14, 1947, Pakistan was founded. The following day, India became independent, and Jawaharlal Nehru, the leader of the Indian Congress Party, became India's first prime minister. Three years before, Nehru had made the following prediction:

India will find herself again when freedom opens out new horizons. The future will then fascinate her far more than the immediate past. . . . She will go forward with confidence, rooted in herself and yet eager to learn from others and co-operate with them. Today she swings between a blind faith in her old customs and a slavish imitation of foreign ways. In neither of these can she find relief or life or growth. She has to come out of her shell and take full part in the life and activities of the modern age. There can be no real cultural or spiritual growth based on imitation. True culture gets its inspiration from every corner of the world, but it is homegrown and has to be based on the wide mass of the people. Art and literature remain lifeless if they are always thinking of foreign models. We have to think in terms of the people. Their culture must be a development of past trends. It must also represent their new urges and creative tendencies.

We are citizens of no mean country. We are proud of the land of our birth, of our people, our culture and traditions. That pride should not be for a past to which we cling. Nor should it allow us to forget our many weaknesses. We have a long way to go before we can take our proper station with others. And we have to hurry for the time is limited and the pace of the world grows ever faster. It was India's way in the past to welcome and absorb other cultures. That is much more necessary today.

EXAMINING PHOTOGRAPHS
Indian prime minister Jawaharlal Nehru, on the left, and Chinese prime minister Zhou Enlai share a light moment during a state visit. Ties between India and the Republic of China were strong during the Nehru years. What predictions did Nehru make in 1944 about India's future?

We march to the One World of tomorrow where national cultures will be mixed with the international culture of the human race. We shall therefore seek wisdom and knowledge and friendship and comradeship wherever we can find them, and co-operate with others in common tasks. We shall remain true Indians and Asiatics, and become good world citizens.

INDIA SINCE 1947

After independence, India faced many problems. The division of British India led to a great migration. Hindus from Pakistan flocked to India, while Muslims from India flocked to Pakistan. This led to violence that resulted in the deaths of about 200,000 people. Yet, despite the problems, India enjoyed political stability and economic progress and became a leader among the nonaligned nations, those countries that refused to side with Western or communist nations.

Source: From *THE DISCOVERY OF INDIA* by Jawaharlal Nehru. Copyright 1946, © 1960 by Harper & Row Publishers, Inc. Copyright renewed by Indira Gandhi. Reprinted by permission of Harper Collins Publishers.

In 1964, Nehru died. Two years after his death, his daughter, Indira Gandhi, became prime minister. She increased the government's role in the economy, strengthened the hold of the Congress Party on local governments, and continued her father's policy of nonalignment. Relations with Pakistan, however, remained tense. In 1971, India intervened in a civil war between East and West Pakistan, two provinces of Pakistan separated by 1000 miles (1600 kilometers) of Indian territory. The result was the formation of the independent Republic of Bangladesh in East Pakistan.

Meanwhile, unrest mounted, and new political groups formed to oppose Gandhi's policies. In 1975, a state of emergency was declared, Gandhi's political opponents were arrested, and limits were put on personal freedoms. In 1977, elections were held, and Gandhi and her party lost to the Janata Party, which was made up of groups who opposed Gandhi's policies. The new leadership, however, lost the support of the people, and in 1981, Gandhi and her supporters were returned to power.

India

INDIRA GANDHI

Indira Gandhi was India's first female prime minister. As the daughter of Jawaharlal Nehru, she became involved in national politics at an early age. In 1942, after completing university studies in India and Great Britain, she married Feroze Gandhi. Both she and her husband took an active part in the movement for Indian independence.

In 1947, after her father became prime minister, Gandhi became known as "the nation's daughter." In addition to serving as her father's adviser and accompanying him on official trips overseas, she held posts in the country's ruling Congress Party. In a letter written to a friend in 1955, she talked about her busy life:

It's certainly true that I have grown enormously since you saw me last. I am confident of myself but still humble enough to feel acutely embarrassed when all kinds of VIPs come for advice and even help in their projects. . . . I still haven't gotten used to being on the Working Committee of the A.I.C.C. (All India Congress Committee)! . . . Can you imagine me being an "elder statesman"?

My duties and responsibilities have also grown enormously. I have my fingers in so many pies that it would take too long even to list them. And if you remember me and what a perfect tyrant of a conscience I have got, you will understand that this does not mean merely lending my name to some association or attendance at committee meetings. It means hard work, planning, organizing, directing, scouting for new helpers, humoring the old and so on, in several fields—political, social welfare and cultural.

Gandhi's experience in the party gave her administrative skills that proved helpful when she became prime minister, a post she held for nearly two decades. In a 1982 interview she talked about some of the problems that were facing India and that, as prime minister, she would have to resolve. As she saw it, the biggest problem was "backwardness,"

Source: Dorothy Norman. *Indira Gandhi: Letters to an American Friend 1950–1984.* Harcourt Brace & Co., 1984.

which she described as the differences "between the haves and the have-nots." She denied, however, that the rich were getting richer, while the poor were getting poorer. She pointed out that, while poverty still existed, the general standard of living had risen and more Indians now belonged to the middle class. Gandhi also acknowledged some other problems with which she had to deal, including urban growth, pollution, environmental and wildlife conservation, and industrial and agricultural development.

Although Gandhi's policies often were controversial, most Indians regarded her as a heroine for her efforts. A few days before her death, she stated, "If I were to die today, every drop of my blood will invigorate the nation."

TAKING ANOTHER LOOK

1. How did Indira Gandhi acquire her political skills?
2. What did Gandhi see as India's greatest problem? Based on what you know about India, do you agree with her? Explain.

This time, Gandhi faced opposition from regional religious and ethnic groups that wanted more freedom. The most violent opposition came from Sikhs in the Punjab. Sikh militants seized the Golden Temple of Amritsar, the holiest Sikh shrine, and used it as a base for terrorist raids. When, on Gandhi's orders, the Indian army stormed the temple and defeated the militants, many Sikhs were angered. Threats were made against Gandhi's life. On October 31, 1984, she was assassinated by two of her bodyguards who were Sikhs. The assassination touched off four days of anti-Sikh riots all over India.

Indira Gandhi's son, Rajiv, succeeded his mother as prime minister. To bolster his power, he called for new elections, which he and his Congress supporters won by a landslide. Gandhi was concerned about Indian unity and was highly critical of the anti-Sikh and Sikh violence in the Punjab and the violence between Hindus and Muslims. Immediately after the election, he appealed for cooperation in his efforts to forge unity.

By 1989, Gandhi's popularity had waned. Violence still raged in the Punjab, and there were charges of corruption in his government. In elections held that year, the Congress party was defeated. A new prime minister—V.P. Singh—took office. When, less than a year later, his government fell from power, Chandra Shekkar took over as prime minister with Congress party support.

On May 20, 1991, India again held general elections. The election campaign was marred by over 200 deaths, street fights between Muslims and Hindus, and charges of election irregularities. On May 21, Rajiv Gandhi, seeking a return to office, was greeting a crowd in Tamil Nadu in southern India when he was killed by a bomb hidden in a bouquet of flowers. In the view of one reporter, Rajiv Gandhi's death "turned India's politics upside down as it ended the 40-year domination of the country's ruling elite by

one family." The reporter went on to point out that the assassination "marked an abrupt end to the family's control over the nation."

P.V. Narasimha Rao, a Congress veteran, was elected prime minister. Below, Indian author Ved Mehta offers his view of some of the problems facing the Rao government:

More than at any other time since Independence, there is political turmoil in India, and it is aggravated by the fact that politicians of every stripe are exploiting religious differences. . . . Secessionist fires, which have been raging for the last decade in Punjab, Kashmir, and Assam, are now out of control. . . .

At the same time, India's civil service, its judiciary, and its other once stable, autonomous governing institutions have been compromised to the point where they are now mere handmaidens of politicians. Corruption and intimidation at every level of society have brought into being a new moneyed class, which exercises ruthless power. Examples of corruption abound. . . .

There is confusion and uncertainty even in the conduct of external affairs—an area in which there was formerly a consensus. . . . In addition, the end of the Cold War means that India can no longer . . . play the Soviet Union against the United States . . . and get, for instance, arms from one, and food and technology from the other. . . .

The abandonment of Communism in Eastern Europe means that India can no longer look to the Soviet Union as an economic model for the country's development. In fact, India is much like the present-day Soviet Union in being economically at sea, and the financial condition of the country is grimmer than it has ever been. Among other things, weak governments . . . have taken their economic toll. . . . The budgetary process is out of kilter. Foreign reserves are exhausted. . . . India is the third-largest debtor nation in the developing world. . . .

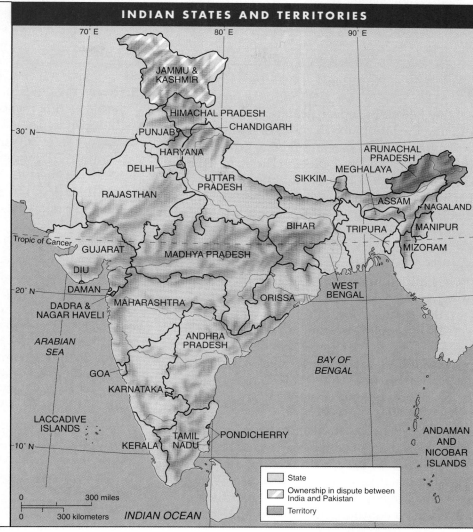

INDIAN STATES AND TERRITORIES

⬤**EXAMINING**
⬤**MAPS** *India is a
federal republic consisting
of a central government
and the governments of 25
states and 7 territories.
The central government
has considerable power
over the states and
territories. The president
of India appoints the state
governors and leading
territorial officials. In an
emergency, the Indian
president also has the
right to dissolve the
government of a state or
territory. The states and
territories often depend on
the central government
for financial assistance.*
**Which state is disputed
by India and its
neighbor, Pakistan?**

In political and official circles here—and
also among people generally—there is a
sense of dread about the economic, political, and religious direction of the country
which I don't remember encountering in
any of my other visits over the past twenty-five years.

While the Rao government has made
some headway since taking office, many
problems remain to be solved. Among
these remains the task of uniting India's
close to 850 million people.

Source: Ved Mehta. "Letter from New Delhi." Reprinted by
permission; © 1991 Ved Mehta. Originally in *The New Yorker.*

SECTION 4 REVIEW

CHECKING FOR UNDERSTANDING

1. **Summarize** the events that led to Indian
   independence.
2. **Identify** problems faced by India since
   becoming independent.

CRITICAL THINKING

3. **Predicting Consequences** How do you think
   democracy in India might be affected if the
   nation's diverse ethnic and religious groups
   cannot be united?

Chapter 24 Review

SUMMARY

Long before European seafarers reached India in the late 1400's, a series of peoples and empires had risen and fallen—from the Indus River Valley people and the Aryans to the Mauryas, the Guptas, and the Moguls. Each contributed a set of beliefs, customs, and institutions and enriched Indian civilization.

In 1600, the East India Company received exclusive English trading rights with India. By the mid-1800's, abuses by the Company and the resulting Indian unrest had led the British government to take control of Indian affairs.

In the late 1800's, a time of widespread anti-British feeling in India, the Indian National Congress was formed. In time, its goal became complete freedom for India. Under the leadership of Mohandas K. Gandhi, the policy of nonviolent resistance was established to achieve this goal.

In 1947, British India was divided into the separate and independent nations of Pakistan and India. Since independence, India has been faced with a wide variety of problems—economic, social, and political. The Indian government continues to work to solve those problems and to cement national unity.

USING VOCABULARY

Use each term below in a sentence that provides an interesting fact about India.

rajah   *sepoys*   **viceroy**
civil disobedience

REVIEWING FACTS

1. **Account** for Asoka's decision to turn against war and devote himself to the welfare of the people.
2. **Discuss** the series of events that led to the British government's control of India.
3. **Name** the political party that has ruled India during most of the period since independence.
4. **Report** on events in India during Indira Gandhi's terms as prime minister.
5. **Give reasons** why Rajiv Gandhi lost the confidence of the Indian people as prime minister in the late 1980's.

CRITICAL THINKING

1. **Determining Cause and Effect** How might India be different today if the Aryan invaders had been prevented from entering the country?
2. **Evaluating Information** What do you think were some of the positive effects of British rule in India? Some of the negative effects?
3. **Identifying Alternatives** Since independence, Indian leaders have sought to preserve unity among their nation's diverse ethnic and religious groups. If you were prime minister of India, what steps would you take to achieve this goal? State the advantages and disadvantages of each.

ANALYZING CONCEPTS

1. **Change** What groups have influenced the development of Indian civilization over the centuries?
2. **Diversity** What effect has India's religious and ethnic diversity had on national unity?

GEOGRAPHIC THEMES

1. **Location** Where in India did early civilizations develop? Why?
2. **Region** Why were two separate countries created out of British India?
3. **Movement** How did Hinduism and Islam become religions of India?

Recognizing Ideologies

In all cultures, *ideologies* play an important role in determining human events and shaping the course of history. An ideology is a set of beliefs or values that guides the actions of individuals and groups. For example, Indians who believed in achieving independence from Great Britain shared a *nationalist ideology*. They participated in demonstrations, marches, and hunger strikes to achieve their goal of freedom. Often, civil organizations, religious bodies, and political parties form to support particular ideologies. The Indian National Congress, for example, promoted Indian nationalism.

Sometimes, opposing ideologies create social conflict. For example, many people in Great Britain supported an *imperialist ideology* that favored the growth of the British Empire. They believed that they were intellectually and morally superior to Indians and, therefore, had the right to rule them. Conflict between British imperialists and nationalists in India lasted for many years.

Most ideologies are rooted in religious, political, or economic philosophies. Differences in religious beliefs often lead to political differences. For example, ideological differences between Indian Hindus and Muslims forced the division of British India and the creation of two separate nations— India and Pakistan.

Recognizing ideologies enables you to understand the motives underlying statements and actions and the sources of conflict among various groups. Here are some steps to follow in recognizing ideologies:

- Learn the values or beliefs associated with ideologies that you consider relevant to your area of study.
- Determine whether the actions or statements of individuals or groups express the views of a particular ideology.
- If statements do express ideological values or beliefs, identify any facts in the statements that can be checked for accuracy.

EXAMPLE

Read the excerpt from Mohandas Gandhi's speech on page 392. In the first paragraph, Gandhi expresses the ideologies of nationalism and democracy. These ideologies developed in eighteenth-century America and France and, since then, have influenced people in many nations throughout the world. Which of Gandhi's beliefs reflect the ideologies of nationalism and democracy? *(People have the inalienable right to freedom and to necessities of life; people can change governments to achieve their rights.)*

The next paragraph expresses the ideology of nonviolent social change. What actions are based on this ideology? *(withdrawal from the British government, civil disobedience, refusal to pay taxes)*

PRACTICE

Read the following paragraph and answer the questions that appear after it.

I am one of the 500 Brahmins who have been deprived of their daily bread. This happened because we refused to use the cartridges for the new rifles the British gave us. The cartridges, which we had to bite before they would fire, were greased with cow and pig fat. Our religion teaches us that animal fat will pollute us. If we bit the cartridges, we would lose our caste. We will not let the British steal our caste from us. On this, every single sepoy is in agreement. The British want to take away our religion. They want us to become Christians. That is why they sent us the new rifles in the first place. The British queen and her government do not care about us.

1. What religious ideology is expressed by the speaker of the paragraph?
2. What statements express this ideology?
3. What actions did the *sepoys* take as a result of their ideology?
4. Which statements about the British are influenced by the Brahmins' ideology?
5. Could the accuracy of these statements be checked? If so, how?

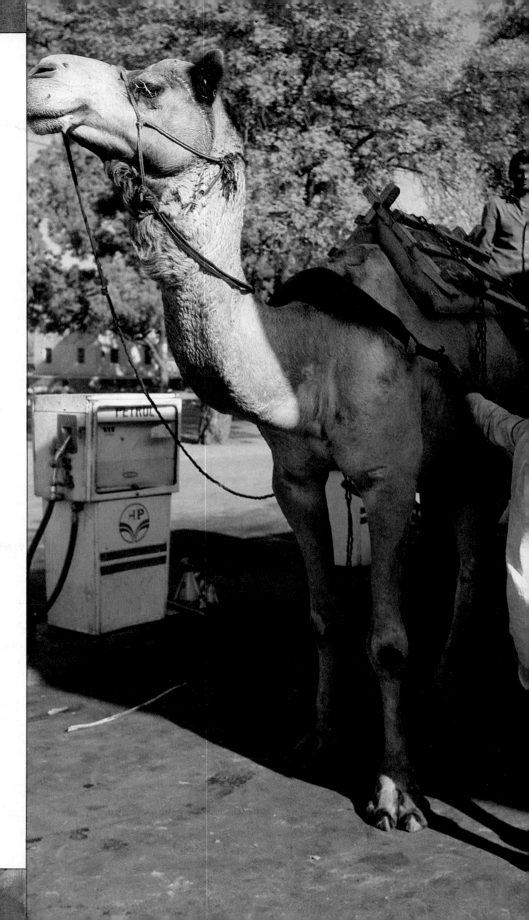

People and Places to Know
Five-Year Plans, Green Revolution, Bhakra Nangal Dam

Key Terms to Define
cooperative, cottage industry

Objectives to Learn

1. **Describe** India's efforts to improve agricultural production.
2. **Characterize** industrial organization in India.
3. **Explain** the role played by natural resources in India's development.
4. **Analyze** the quality of life in India.

Symbols of the old and new in modern India

Developing India

"

India has come a long way since it gained independence. . . .

- India now has the world's third largest pool of scientific manpower. . . . It is producing scientists, engineers, and doctors at a rate that by far outstrips its economy's capacity to absorb them. . . .
- India has the world's fourth largest military machine. . . .
- India has achieved not only agricultural self-sufficiency, but also, at the moment, a glut.

The land of the holy Ganges is industrializing rapidly. As an Indian living in the United States, I sometimes forget this myself. But the change strikes you instantly when you revisit your country. . . . In 1988, when I returned home to New Delhi, I could not believe how the city's road traffic and pollution had grown. . . . The Indian-made cars, motorcycles, and scooters that clog the traffic are only one example of the industrialization. A drive into the countryside shows that the entire society is being transformed. Television antennas perch atop many village homes, small diesel generators at wayside shops beat the perennial power outages, and modern agricultural machinery operates on farms. . . .

New factories producing computers, electronics, and telecommunications equipment have mushroomed across the nation in the past five years. . . .

India's society already is undergoing a major social transformation. . . . Two of the most significant developments have been the emergence of a large and burgeoning urban middle class and, in the countryside, the growth of a politically powerful "kulak" class. . . . A big class of wealthy farmers has emerged from caste groups that traditionally have had a low ranking in the social hierarchy. "

With these words, an Indian journalist describes the India of today, a newly emerging India unlike the one pictured by most Westerners. However, he goes on to say that although India has made great strides, it "remains a country of sharp contrasts. Tradition coexists with modernity. Mud-and-thatch hovels stand beside elegant high-rise buildings and luxury hotels. Farmers produce bumper harvests, but many Indians still starve."

Clearly, Indian leaders are faced with economic and social challenges. In 1991, to help meet these challenges, the national government instituted major economic reforms, including transforming the largely state-controlled economy to a free market economy.

Source: Brahma Chellaney. "Passage to Power" in *World Monitor*, Vol. 3, No. 2, February 1990, pp. 24, 26, 29, 30.

SECTION 1

Agriculture

The Indian government has worked hard to raise the standard of living of its people. To this end, it set up Five-Year Plans, programs designed to develop the nation over five-year periods in the areas of agriculture, industry, and social welfare.

Agriculture has long been the traditional occupation for most Indians. Today 70 percent of the Indian people are farmers. While some still use bullock-drawn plows and traditional tools and methods, others use tractors and other modern farm equipment, pesticides, and chemical fertilizers. Wells operated by diesel pumps or electricity often provide irrigation. The amount of land under irrigation has doubled in the last 40 years.

The government has been working since 1947 to increase farm production. In the past, most farmers expected to do little more than feed their own families and animals. Today India is largely self-sufficient in food. Poor transportation, however, hampers distribution of agricultural products.

The change came about largely because of the Green Revolution, a series of farming improvements introduced in the 1960's. During that time, scientists in different parts of the world developed new types of wheat, rice, and other cereal grain seeds that produced faster-growing crops. To further boost food production, they also developed new kinds of fertilizers.

With the aid of private agencies and foreign governments, the Indian government brought the Green Revolution to India. It provided farmers with the credit they needed to buy the new seeds and to plant such protein-rich crops as soybeans and corn. It promoted increased irrigation and fertilizer use and encouraged farmers to band together to form **cooperatives**, enterprises operated for mutual benefit. The government believed that by working together, farmers could learn better farming methods and be able to use more modern equipment, such as tractors and reapers. In addition, even today most farms are too small for machines to be economically beneficial unless they are shared among farmers. In the following passage, an

EXAMINING PHOTOGRAPHS *In addition to its use for irrigating crops, water from this Indian family's new well also is used for such household tasks as washing laundry, shown here. Financial assistance for wells and other farm projects are offered by the government to help farmers modernize. What did the government expect to accomplish by having farmers form cooperatives?*

anthropologist describes the impact the Green Revolution had in a village where he used to live:

Along the . . . two-lane, tree-shaded, black-top road toward the village, everything looked the same, yet slightly different. This late in the hot season the fields should all have been cleared, plowed, and leveled to preserve moisture. Some crops would have been sown; others would await the rains that were due to begin shortly. Yet many of the fields appeared to have been only recently cleared and were yet unbroken by the first summer plowing. Other fields were full of what appeared to be young rice, a crop almost never grown in this area during my first stay. What had been open sky . . . was now laced with electrical wires on concrete poles. Along the road village after village had small sawmills, machine shops, and new retail shops of all kinds. The towns were noticeably larger and busier. The roadside walls, formerly blank and faded, were now often brightly decorated with advertisements for fertilizers, insecticides, and electric fans. On the road itself the confusing assortment of pedestrians, camels, buffaloes, and goats was still there, but it included many more taxis, scooters, motorcycles, and bicycles than I remembered. Everywhere there was activity and animation. Formerly the period between the onset of the hot season and the beginning of the rains had been a time of cautious waiting, a time when the countryside seemed to hold its breath to conserve its strength. . . .

As we passed through the fields each new thing was pointed out and its origin explained. We rode past cylindrical haystacks . . . of a type I had never seen. They contained wheat straw and the technique for making them had been introduced by Punjab Agricultural University. My impression of the changed agricultural cycle was correct. It was due in part to the fact that the old varieties of wheat, the main winter crop, were no longer grown.

They had been entirely replaced by new high-yielding varieties which were harvested later. The . . . Persian wheels [a form of water wheel] that would have been constantly in use at this season, driven by slowing plodding camels or pairs of bullocks, were now almost gone. . . . Replacing them were mechanized pumping sets in small brick buildings. Small scattered plots of bright green were rice seedlings waiting to be transplanted when the fields were ready—in a few weeks. Overall, it seemed clear that the pattern and rhythm of village agriculture had changed. . . .

We left the paved road and . . . , followed a small dirt path. . . . The last few dozen yards passed through some work areas to the village houses, grouped within what had once been an almost-continuous rampart of adjoining outer walls. Here again was the familiar and new. The approach route was the same: by a line of trees and some tethered buffaloes, we entered the village center through a farmer's courtyard gate, turned to walk past the old Hindu temple and thence into the bricked lanes within the compact mass of houses and barns. The cool, narrow lanes themselves, between high . . . brick walls, were the same. But there had been new houses near the path on the way in, there were electric lines overhead, and the familiar silence was broken by the chugging of a diesel pump somewhere nearby.

SECTION 1 REVIEW

CHECKING FOR UNDERSTANDING
1. **Define** cooperative.
2. **Explain** what Five-Year Plans are and why the Indian government set them up.

CRITICAL THINKING
3. **Determining Cause and Effect** What effect did the Green Revolution have on Indian farmers and agriculture?

Source: From SONG OF HOPE: THE GREEN REVOLUTION IN A PUNJAB VILLAGE by Murray J. Leaf. Copyright © 1984 by Rutgers, The State University.

SECTION 2

Industry

During its early years as an independent nation, India had to import most of its manufactured goods. Over time, however, that has changed. Today, as in the distant past, textile manufacturing is the most important industry. The handicraft industry also is important. But India produces a great variety of other products as well, including sewing machines, bicycles, tractors, automobiles, ships, locomotives, and airplanes. In the high-tech area, India has developed and manufactured electronics, radios, televisions, computers, computer software, and satellites.

ORGANIZATION

There are three major forms of industrial organization—cottage industries, privately owned small industries, and large-scale industries. **Cottage industries**, a system under which family members use their own equipment to produce goods in their homes, are found mostly in villages. There, generally in an effort to add to their farm income, Indians weave fabrics of cotton, rayon, and silk by hand and produce pottery, brassware, jewelry, leather goods, and woodcarvings. Because these industries provide jobs for villagers, the government has always encouraged them. Today, many of the products made in these industries are sold in different parts of the world.

EXAMINING PHOTOGRAPHS *Below left, two Indian women spin yarn in front of their home. Weavers make this yarn into fabrics, which are sold in textile shops like the one shown below right. What cottage industries flourish in India besides spinning and weaving?*

EXAMINING PHOTOGRAPHS
Because of India's large, low-cost labor force, most work is still accomplished by human labor rather than by machine. At this gravel pit near Jaipur in northwestern India, workers are collecting rocks to be crushed into gravel for road repairs. Women, as well as men, commonly perform this kind of work. How does India rank among the industrial nations of the world?

The privately owned small industries generally are plants that employ fewer than 100 workers and use simple machinery. They make such goods as bicycle parts, shoes, and carpets. The large-scale industries include mining, electric power, and iron and steel manufacturing. Until the early 1990's, when India moved to a free market economy, more than 200 of these industries were owned solely by the government. Others were owned jointly by the government and private investors. Still others were owned solely by private investors like the Indian who speaks below:

I started this factory six years ago, producing hand tools such as bench vises. Today, I also make brassware such as door-knobs and nameplates. And there's scope to do much more.

. . . My factory is small compared with the giant industrial complexes at Rourkela and Bhilai. I export my products to the United States, Canada, Germany, Sweden, Australia and the Middle East.

In the last twenty years, our country has advanced tremendously. We are among the top ten industrial nations of the world and we're well on the way to being self-sufficient in making sophisticated machines and gadgets.

We've got our own car factories; and we're making our own aircraft, trains, ships, teleprinters, watches, scooters, motorcycles, drugs, engineering and steel goods. Of course, the cotton textile industry is still the largest single industry in India. There are over 15 million industrial workers in the country.

Under the old economy, India did not welcome foreign investments. All foreign-brand products sold in India had to have Indianized brand names, such as "Lehar Pepsi." Since 1992, however, foreign investment has been encouraged, and products may be sold under their own brand names.

Source: Veenu Sandal. "We have a plentiful supply of cheap labor" in *We Live in India*. The Bookwright Press, 1984, p. 28.

CONSUMER GOODS

Another change that has taken place in recent years is the growth of the consumer goods industry. This is due in great part to the growth of the middle class. As the following article indicates, Indians eager to buy have more to choose from than ever before:

A growing number of Indians go shopping less out of necessity and more out of compulsion. So enormous has been the consumer boom that in six years a virtual no-option situation has transformed into an embarrassing array of choices.

From designer children's clothes to television sets to mouth-fresheners to motorcycles to sportswear to milk shakes to toilet soaps to cooking ranges, a market for an astonishingly wide range of consumer goods and durables of mostly indigenous make has exploded nationwide.

Gone are the days of gawking at pictures of exclusive, western-style stores. Such retail outlets are coming up across the country and increasingly match their western inspirations in service and range of goods. Bangalore, for instance, has reputedly the world's largest children's wear store built over 20,000 square feet. "It is big enough to shelter 200 shanty town families of Bombay," comments an architect.

Jayendra Thakkar, who is in the paper business in Ahmedabad, declares: "All that was thought to be available only in the west until five years ago is now available in India. There is no need for a craze for foreign goods. You can buy Indian video, Indian washing machine, Indian quartz watch, Indian luxury car, Indian everything."

The consumer boom runs through shopping malls, restaurants, fast food chains, video libraries, automobile showrooms, credit card counters, air-conditioned supermarkets and roadside kiosks. . . .

Despite the broad definition of the consumer class, in a general economic sense,

it makes India potentially the world's largest consumer society which gobbles up everything from luxury cars to trendy sportswear.

Source: Mayank Chhaya and Milind Palnitkar. "The Great Lifestyle Revolution" in *India Abroad*, September 13, 1991, p. 21.

SECTION 2 REVIEW

CHECKING FOR UNDERSTANDING
1. **Define** cottage industry.
2. **Characterize** the three types of industrial organization in India.

CRITICAL THINKING
3. **Drawing Conclusions** How has India's consumer goods industry changed in recent years?

SECTION 3
Natural Resources

Another area in which there has been development is natural resources. India is richer than many other countries in resources suitable for industrial development. These resources include iron ore, manganese, and mica, a mineral used in insulation. India also is rich in such energy resources as waterpower, coal, and oil. The country's great river systems supply about 40 percent of the electric power, and several large dams provide electricity to many villages and factories. Below, an Indian engineer explains why he became an engineer and how some of India's resources are being developed:

I've wanted to be an engineer ever since I was in school. Partly because the pay . . . seemed good, as I belonged to a poor family. Partly because, even then, engineers were in great demand in the country.

Today I have no money problems and

EXAMINING PHOTOGRAPHS *An engineer keeps a watchful eye on the control panel of the Tarapur nuclear power plant, India's first such facility. Although the plant, built between 1963 and 1969, is aging and is not run at full capacity, it continues to provide electric power. Recently, the government has built new nuclear power plants at Kota, Bombay, and Madras.* What role does India's rivers play in supplying the country's energy?

. . . can keep my family in comfort. . . . Besides, my job, which is concerned with making power available . . . , keeps me on my toes.

What do I mean by power? I'm talking of electric power, thermal power, nuclear power and so on. As a country, I feel we're very fortunate to have more than twenty large rivers. As you know, the Ganga, or Ganges, is not only the holiest river in the land, it's also the most useful.

On these rivers we've set up twenty-eight large dams and we're planning many more. The dams supply water for irrigation, control floods and also provide power. The Bhakra Nangal Dam is India's biggest . . . river valley project so far.

When I look back over the years, I feel good. We've come a long way since the country's first hydroelectric power station was set up in 1900. In addition to so many hydroelectric projects, thermal stations now supply almost 60 per cent of electricity to the country. And since 1969, the nuclear power station at Tarapur has also been functioning.

Our industries alone use almost 65 per cent of the electricity. But it saddens me to think that only about 35 per cent of our villages possess electricity. It takes time in a vast country like ours.

Source: Veenu Sandal. *We Live in India.* The Bookwright Press, 1984.

SECTION 3 REVIEW

CHECKING FOR UNDERSTANDING
1. **Identify** resources in which India is rich.

CRITICAL THINKING
2. **Evaluating Information** Explain why you agree or disagree with this statement: India is poor in power.

SECTION 4

The Quality of Life

Prosperity and poverty exist side by side in India. There is, in effect, the India of the upper and middle urban classes and the India of the urban and rural poor. The middle class has grown greatly. It numbers somewhere between 100 and 300 million, depending on the statistics used to decide the definition of *middle class*. But, in spite of this and of government efforts and programs to help the poor, the disadvantaged, and minorities, about 40 percent of the Indian population lived below the poverty line in the early 1990's.

Among the poorest are women and children. This is especially true in households headed by widows. Below, a female farm worker expresses her frustrations and poses questions about the plight of the poor:

All our life is on fire, all our prices rising,
  Give us an answer, O rulers of the
  country!

. . . .

We have forgotten the color of milk
Coconuts and dried fruits have gone
  underground
Our children have only jaggery
  [unrefined] tea for nourishment
Sweet oil for cooking is the price of gold
Coconut oil for our hair is not to be had

Without rock oil for lamps we are
  familiar with darkness
We burn in the summer, we are drenched
  in the rains
We bear the rigor of winter without any
  clothes
Why don't we yet have any shelter?

We toil night and day and sleep
  half-starved
While the parasites fill their bellies
  with butter
Why does the thief get food while the
  owner is cheated?

There are pastures for the cattle of the
  rich
For forest development land is preserved
Why is there no land to support living
  people?
Tall buildings rise before our eyes

The roads cannot contain these
  motorcycles and cars
On whose labor has such development
  been built?

Today, unjust treatment of untouchables is illegal, and all professions and trades have been opened to them. Since their living conditions were worse than those of many other Indians, the government has given them financial aid to raise their standard of living. But, although their condition has improved somewhat because of these efforts, the acceptance of such change by many Indians has not been easy to achieve.

HEALTH AND EDUCATION

Two major areas of concern in India are health and education. Although good health care still is not readily available for about half of all Indians, overall health care has improved since independence. Progress has been made in eliminating or controlling such diseases as smallpox, malaria, typhoid, leprosy, cholera, and tuberculosis. The average life expectancy has risen from 32 years to 57 years. Infant mortality has been greatly reduced. Much of the progress is due to government efforts. Among the many government programs are those to immunize children, to test village wells, and to educate villagers about hygiene, sanitation, and nutrition. The government also has built hospitals and supported medical research and the education of doctors and nurses.

In the area of education, the problems are great. The present educational system is based mostly on British models and often favors the rich and males. Many children drop out of school at an early age to find some kind of work or help out at home or in the

---

Source: Bhaskar Jadhav. Isis-wicce (Women's International Cross-Cultural Exchange). 3 Chemin des Campanules, CH-1219, Aire, Switzerland.

fields. More than one-third of all Indians cannot read or write.

In 1986, the government set up a national system of education. The goal is to provide free and compulsory education by the year 2000 for all children up to the age of 14. In villages all over India, the government has built schools. Other groups are helping as well. Below, a reporter discusses a project designed to give computer training to students in the state of Tamil Nadu:

Under the project, initially 25 students will be trained in popular packages in each of the six villages. The learners will collect data about family income, cropping patterns, cattle population and feed them into computers.

The Tamil Nadu Foundation has donated $20,000 for the project and promised to help in other ways as well, Anna University Vice-Chancellor Annandakrishnan told *India Abroad.*

He said multinational computer giants like IBM have shown interest in the computer-on-wheels project. It has also attracted the fancy of Global Harmony Foundation of Switzerland. . . .

Although computer education has begun in India for more than a decade now, students from rural areas have hardly benefited since most of the computer institutes are located in urban and semi-urban areas.

But if the computer-on-wheels project . . . succeeds, this imbalance could be gradually corrected. Annandakrishnan said rural schools in all the 22 districts of Tamil Nadu will be brought under the scheme in the future. He said the project was being started from the most economically backward rural areas to help children compete with their urban counterparts for further education and employment more effectively.

Source: "Taking Computers to Villages" in *India Abroad,* vol. 22, no. 9, November 29, 1991, p. 6.

POPULATION GROWTH AND CONTROL

Another major challenge is the continuing increase in population. India already has some of the densest populated areas in the world. In the early 1990's, the population was growing by 2 percent per year. If it continues to grow at this rate, India will overtake China as the world's most populous nation. As a result, it is hard for the government to fulfill the basic needs of its people and provide ample job opportunities. Thus, it is interested in population control and has taken active steps to limit population growth.

India was the first country in the world to set up a national family planning program. The program encourages young couples to limit their families to two children. Social workers show the people how to use modern birth control methods, and loans and housing are made available to those who agree to family planning. An Indian villager discusses population control:

EXAMINING PHOTOGRAPHS *The sign draped over this elephant promotes the idea of family planning. How does India's national family planning program work?*

As time passes . . . you can't say that the Indian nation will remain the same. There might not be room for people even to stand. There mightn't be space to sit down. There mightn't be land to cultivate. So in my opinion it's better to keep the family as small as possible. I give this advice to everybody. If they listen, well and good, otherwise they'll regret it later. See, I can stop, being an educated man. But because my brothers are uneducated, they want boys. Boys will in future—according to Indian custom, somehow according to Indian custom, if we have sons, they can help with the work. If there are girls, they can't do any ploughing—they might do housework or they might tend the cattle. But if there are boys, they can plough the field. What can a girl do? If there's a son, he'll at least plough the field—provided he's not educated. Old age parents—the sons can help.

So many people are born, . . . so many people die. We should leave someone behind to continue the family. And if there are two sons, one can study and the other work in the fields. Even if there are three, they can all work on the land. They can work and get more land. They can do anything.

Because India is a democracy, government efforts to limit population can be successful only if the people are willing to cooperate. In India many still prefer large families. There are several reasons for this. One has its base in religion. Hindus often feel that it is a sign of virtue to be blessed with children. And, a son is needed to light parents' funeral pyres.

A second reason is economic. In rural areas, many children help a poor family get along. In farming families, children earn much more than their keep by caring for the animals, delivering meals to the field workers, collecting manure, and helping with odd

Source: Sarah Hobson. *Family Web. A Story of India.* Academy Chicago Publishers, 1982, pp. 174–175.

jobs. Even those sent to the city contribute. They send home the money they earn, where it may be used to buy fertilizer or farm machinery or to hire farm laborers.

A third reason is social. Parents with many children—especially many sons—know that someone will be there to care for them when they get old. Even though the government has offered social security plans to give income to retired people, many Indian families think it wiser to rely on their own children than to trust the government's word about their future.

Some experts believe that many of the reasons Indians give for having children will change in the future and that Indians will limit their families voluntarily. They say that economic factors will play an important role. Many people are moving from their villages to the cities, where dwellings are crowded and there are fewer jobs for children. In addition, as farming methods become more modern, machines will do a lot of the small jobs now being done by children. Farms are getting smaller, so having many children will mean that when the head of the family dies, the farm will have to be divided among more people. The changing role of Indian women also might mean fewer children in the future.

SECTION 4 REVIEW

CHECKING FOR UNDERSTANDING
1. **Differentiate** between the "two Indias."
2. **Point out** what the government has done since independence to bring better health and health care to the Indian people.
3. **Restate** the goal of the Indian government in regard to education.

CRITICAL THINKING
4. **Drawing Conclusions** For what reasons have the Indian government's efforts to limit population met with only limited success?

Global Concerns

GROWTH AND DEVELOPMENT

In India, as elsewhere, development and change go hand in hand. This can be seen very clearly in the countryside. Irrigation, for example, has had a major impact on production.

FOCUSING ON THE ISSUE Read the following comments by a farmer from northern India. Then list major changes that have taken place in India since independence; list problems that still face India today; and offer five suggestions to help India continue to develop.

This has been a fine season for me. Look, there in the distance you can see my sugarcane fields ready for harvesting.

My fields weren't always green and smiling like this. Today, our farm has an ample supply of water from wells, so I can expect good crops. But there was a time not very long ago when I had to rely completely on the rains. . . . Of course, a lot still depends on the weather.

The weather gods have been kind to me, but the other day a farmer friend of mine had come from down south and he had a lot of complaints.

"Something or other is always happening," he said. "Sometimes it's too little rain and everything dries up. Other times there are floods and all my labor is washed away. Some years it's a cyclone; other years it's a tornado. Sometimes there are locusts. Nature seems always to be at war with us."

What he said is right to a large extent. But then I say: look at the brighter side. In spite of so many hardships, production has increased remarkably. . . .

You'll find this increase in all the crops—wheat, rice, corn, lentils, cotton, potatoes, vegetables, fruits,—as well as poultry products, tea, coffee, and dairy products, too. Then how is it that almost seventy per cent of my countrymen are poor and don't even get two good meals a day?

Ah, that's the sad part. Our population seems to grow much faster than our production. . . .

Still, I say hats off to our government and agricultural scientists. Now we have high-yielding varieties of seeds, better fertilizers, special TV programs for farmers. And the government is trying to persuade each family to have only two or three children. . . .

Quite honestly, my wife and I feel that family planning is the answer to all our country's problems. We ourselves have only three children and we're a very happy family. . . .

Our children stay in an apartment in town. It makes it easier for them to attend college. You see, they don't want to farm. . . . My wife and I encourage them, as it would be nice to see somebody in the family breaking away from the tradition of full-time farming.

Sundays we all get together either at the farm or in town. We exchange news and views over a good meal. . . .

My earnings vary. Last year, I made a profit of about 25,000 rupees ($2,500). It's more than enough for our family. But, as I said, the gods have been kind to me.

Source: Veenu Sandal. "The weather gods have been kind to me" in *We Live in India*. The Bookwright Press, 1984, pp. 36–37. Reprinted with permission of Franklin Watts, Inc., New York.

Chapter 25 Review

SUMMARY

Since independence, Indian leaders have been faced with economic and social challenges. To develop the nation and better the quality of life of its people, the Indian government established Five-Year Plans.

In agriculture, government efforts and the Green Revolution have brought progress. Once unable to feed its people, India is now largely self-sufficient in food. Due to major advances in industry, India now produces a wide variety of goods and products. The consumer goods industry in particular has boomed in recent years, largely because of the growth of the middle class.

Development and industrialization, however, have not eliminated the gap between rich and poor. Despite government efforts and programs, much remains to be accomplished in the areas of poverty, health care, education, and population growth and control.

USING VOCABULARY

Imagine that you are a government official. Write a speech explaining to the Indian people why the two institutions below are important to India's development and economy.

cooperative   cottage industry

REVIEWING FACTS

1. **Discuss** how Indian farmers today practice agriculture.
2. **State** the government's chief agricultural goal since independence.
3. **Give examples** of major changes that have taken place under India's new economy.
4. **Explain** what has been done to raise the standard of living of untouchables.
5. **Indicate** some of the problems India faces in education.

CRITICAL THINKING

1. **Analyzing Information** Some people believe that "Indian development will not be the same as western development." What do you think they mean by this statement? Do you think Indian and Western development should be the same? Explain.
2. **Drawing Conclusions** Many Indians continue to cling to tradition. How has this affected development in India?
3. **Identifying Assumptions** Although India is a democracy, the government has used strong measures to bring about development. Do you think a government should have such control in a democracy? Explain.
4. **Demonstrating Reasoned Judgment** In planning development, decisions must be made on which aspects of development efforts and resources should be concentrated. On which aspects has the Indian government been concentrating? On which would you concentrate? Explain.

ANALYZING CONCEPTS

1. **Technology** How have India's economy and society developed since India became independent?
2. **Scarcity** How has development affected the standard of living of many Indians?
3. **Culture** What economic and social problems does India face today?

GEOGRAPHIC THEMES

1. **Human/Environment Interaction** For what do Indians use their river systems?
2. **Location** What resources does India have that aid its development?

Interpreting Statistics

A great deal of information in textbooks, magazines, and news reports is expressed as *statistics*. Statistics are collections of numerical information called *data*. In order to interpret statistics, you must understand how they are produced. Here is a short glossary of common statistical terms:

Average: An average (or mean) is the sum of the values in a group, divided by the number of values.

Median: A median is the value in the middle of a group of numbers.

Percentage: A percentage is a fraction of a whole with 100 as the denominator.

Per capita: This term literally means "per head" or per person. It represents an average value for each person in a group.

Birth and mortality rates: The number of births or deaths per year in a group of people. Often, these rates are expressed as percentages. A birth rate of 15 percent means 15 births per hundred people.

Population growth rates: The percentage of population increase, including both births and deaths in a given population.

Because statistics are only as accurate as the source that compiled them, you should always check the reliability of that source. The following steps will help you interpret statistics:

- Identify the type of statistic presented.
- Look up unfamiliar terms in a dictionary or statistics book.
- Express the meaning of the statistic in your own words.

EXAMPLE

Here are some examples of statistics:

Average (or Mean): If your class has twenty students, figure out the average age of your classmates by adding the ages of all 20 students, and then dividing by 20.

Median: To determine the median age of the teachers in your school, collect all of their ages and find the number in the middle. Half the teachers should be older than the median and half should be younger.

Percentage: Suppose 5 out of 20 people have black hair. To find out what percentage has black hair, divide 5 by 20 to get .25, or 25 percent.

Per capita: To determine the number of television sets per capita in the United States, divide the total number of television sets by the number of people in the United States.

PRACTICE

For each statistic given below, write the letter of the best interpretation.

1. Agriculture accounts for ⅖ of India's GNP.
   a. Agriculture accounts for 25 percent of GNP.
   b. Agriculture accounts for 40 percent of GNP.
   c. Agriculture accounts for 50 percent of GNP.

2. In the early 1990's, India's population was growing by two percent per year.
   a. Each year India's total population was two percent larger than the year before.
   b. Each year the total number of births increased by two percent.
   c. Each year the total number of deaths decreased by two percent.

3. Annual per capita income in India is $300.
   a. Everyone in India makes $300 each year.
   b. The average Indian makes $300 each year.
   c. The poorest Indians make $300 each year.

4. In the last twenty years, economic growth in India has averaged 3.5 percent a year.
   a. India's GNP has risen 3.5 percent each year for 20 years.
   b. India's GNP has risen 3.5 percent in 20 years.
   c. Although India's rate of economic growth has gone up and down, the average over 20 years has been 3.5 percent a year.

5. Adult literacy in rural areas, where 85 percent of the poor live, is 36 percent.
   a. About ⅓ of the rural poor can read.
   b. About 85 percent of the rural poor can read.
   c. About 36 percent of the poor live in rural areas.

People and Places to Know
Ajanta, Ellora, Taj Mahal, the *Rig Veda*, the *Mahabharata*, the *Panchatantra*, Rabindranath Tagore, Ravi Shankar

Key Terms to Define
stupa, minaret, epic, *raga*, sitar

Objectives to Learn
1. **Identify** the influences on the development of Indian art.
2. **Characterize** early and modern Indian literature.
3. **Describe** the roles the performing arts play in Indian society.

Indian dancer and musician

The Arts

> ". . . Three days into [my] journey, something showed me that, in India, art and life are one. Sometimes Indian art is in a museum. . . . Sometimes it is a great monument that has been preserved and guarded. . . . But most often it is just there, in the air, on the ground, all over the place, for the taking, and no name is attached to it.
>
> That is what I learned—that art is everywhere in India, if we know how to look, and not only in famous places. It is in the costume . . . of a woman working on the road. It is in the fragments of lapis-lazuli mosaic that lie on the ground beside a temple long left for dead. It is in the bracelets (canary yellow, it may be, or emerald green) that we see on the horns of white oxen by the roadside. It is in the ferocious color of the spices in every small-town bazaar, and it is in the celestial spacing of one building after another in the abandoned city of Fatehpur Sikri, near Agra. . . .
>
> . . . [Indians] identify with Indian works of art with an intensity that is almost unknown in the West. To them, they are not works of art at all, . . . but objects of worship that happen to be in a museum and not in a temple. To see them lay gifts and offerings at the feet of a figure of dancing Siva [a god] is an experience that has nothing to do with "art appreciation". . . . Siva for the Hindu is right there, in person, dancing the universe into being, sustaining it with his perfected rhythms, and finally dancing it out of existence. . . .
>
> In India, the art of the past is always relevant. It will tell you how to distinguish the good people from the bad people among the divinities. . . . It will tell you what goes on in those tiny, many-storied town houses where everyone knows everyone else's business. It will tell you about gardening, and about hunting, and about how to deal with people great and small. . . . "

The above statements by a Western art expert reveal the importance of the arts in Indian life. The arts and crafts of India are among the oldest and richest in the world. And, although they differ from region to region and include a variety of forms and styles, they all express a unity in diversity that is typically Indian.

As in other cultures, the traditional arts of India were influenced by religion. Buddhism, Hinduism, and Islam all helped shape the Indian sense and expression of beauty. The rulers who governed India over the centuries also had a major influence. After the 1700's, much of the influence was Western. In recent years, however, Indian artists have rediscovered their country's rich cultural heritage and are blending it with Western forms to create their own styles.

Source: John Russell. "Art and the Life of India," in *The New York Times Magazine,* June 2, 1985, pp. 26, 30, 32. Copyright © 1985 by The New York Times Company. Reprinted by permission.

SECTION 1

Architecture, Painting, and Sculpture

Until modern times, many Indian artists were not individually recognized. Expected to use their talents to glorify deities and rulers, they built and decorated places of worship and public buildings.

ART AND RELIGION

Some of the oldest examples of Indian art still remaining today are temples, monasteries, and shrines built in caves. The earliest of these, built between 200 BC and 600 AD at Ajanta in the Deccan Plateau, was the work of Buddhist sculptors. Out of a 70-foot (21-meter) granite cliff, they cut large chambers in which Buddhist monks set up shrines. Colorful paintings of the Buddha lined the walls and ceilings.

Another group of cave temples, which date from the 500's to 700's AD, was created by Buddhists, Hindus, and Jains at Ellora and Elephanta, near the Deccan Plateau. In the large complex at Ellora, carved out of solid rock, is a temple that is over 100 feet (30.5 meters) in height.

In addition to cave temples, early artists also built freestanding religious structures. These included *stupas*, large stone mounds that house Buddhist holy objects, and Hindu temples that were viewed as the homes of specific deities. Each temple had a sanctuary that housed a statue or relic, and a large square hall where worshippers gathered. Outside the temple there generally was a porch decorated with carvings. In the north of India, the temples usually had tall towers with curved sides that met at the top, while in the south most had pyramid-shaped gateway towers with many layers of carved images. Below, a journalist describes what she saw and heard when she visited one of the temples of southern India:

EXAMINING ARCHITECTURE *This Hindu temple at Ellora in western India was created by generations of artisans, who carved it in place out of solid cliff walls. What did the early temples of India contain?*

A bell was ringing through the temple, and Sanskrit mantras [chants] echoed the chant of the priest who moved round the inner sanctum, round the idol of Bhadreswami, an incarnation of Shiva. It was dark inside and the flickering light from two small oil lamps shadowed the walls with muted images. The god was barely visible, a blackened statue in a black womb. The chant was constant and repetitious. . . .

The temple was damp and cave-like with its low roof supported by close-set lines of granite [pillars]: there was not the refinement of arches and domes, for this was a temple which came from the earth and gave itself back to the earth, existing for gods not men. . . .

The priest drew down a white curtain in front of the god to hide it while he washed the image with milk, ghee [clarified butter], curds, and coconut water as offering and purification. He also presented food, saying, "Oh God, eat this rice, Oh God, eat this coconut," ringing a bell as he did so. Then he pulled aside the curtain: pink flowers [adorned] the dark stone statue of Bhadreswami, single petals vividly simple against ornate carving. Flames burned, softening the shadows to one complete image, warm and glowing as though caught by the evening sun. The priest swayed beside it, encircling the god with smoke from a wick of camphor. He had washed the god, fed the god, dressed the god in private, and now was the time to show the god and give him light to see.

The statues found in the temples and other places of worship served as images and helped many Hindus who could not read or write to visualize the gods and goddesses of their religion. This remains true today, making sculpting a widespread artistic activity in India. In the view of many, the best sculptures come from southern India. One of the most common subjects is the god Shiva, who is represented as Nataraja, "the Lord of the Dance," who creates and destroys through his dancing. The stage he dances on is the cosmos. In dancing, he connects heaven and earth and time and space.

THE MUSLIM INFLUENCE

During the rule of the Moguls, the arts of India were influenced by Islam. Muslim styles of architecture were introduced as Mogul rulers built mosques and other buildings of marble that had domes and towers called **minarets.** Since the Muslims were forbidden by their religion to carve the human figure, they decorated their buildings with elaborate designs often inlaid in white marble with semiprecious stones.

One of the leading examples of Muslim art and architecture in India is the Taj Mahal in Agra, built in the mid-1600's by Shah Jahan as a mausoleum, or tomb, for his wife. The Taj Mahal has been called "a poet's delight." A nineteenth-century English novelist and artist, after seeing the Taj Mahal, proclaimed, "Henceforth, let the inhabitants of the world be divided into two classes—them as has seen the Taj Mahal; and them as hasn't." In 1953, Eleanor Roosevelt, a delegate to the United Nations and the wife of an American President visited the Taj Mahal. Below, she relates how it affected her:

I must own that by the time we got to Agra I was beginning to feel we had seen a great many forts and palaces and mosques. I realized that I was no longer viewing them with the same freshness of interest and appreciation that I had felt during the early part of my visit. I think the others felt much the same way. . . . Therefore when we got back to Government House after our visit to Akbar's fort, though we knew we should leave immediately to get our first glimpse of the Taj Mahal at sunset, we all pounced on the letters we found waiting for us, and could not tear ourselves away until the last one had been read. Then, to our dismay, we found we had delayed too long; by the time we got to the Taj—about six-thirty—the light was beginning to fade.

. . . As we came through the entrance gallery into the walled garden and looked down the long series of oblong pools in which the Taj and the dark cypresses are reflected, I held my breath, unable to speak in the face of so much beauty. The white marble walls, inlaid with semiprecious stones, seemed to take on a mauve tinge with the coming night, and about halfway along I asked to be allowed to sit down on one of the stone benches and

Source: Sarah Hobson. *Family Web: A Story of India.* John Murray, 1978, pp. 83–84.

EXAMINING ARCHITECTURE *The white marbled Taj Mahal, built between 1632 and 1653, is considered one of the most beautiful buildings in the world. The skill of its artisans is evident both inside and outside the mausoleum.* ***In what art forms did Mogul artists excel?***

just look at it. The others walked on around, but I felt that this first time I wanted to drink in its beauty from a distance. One does not want to talk and one cannot glibly say this is a beautiful thing, but one's silence, I think, says this is a beauty that enters the soul. With its minarets rising at each corner, its dome and tapering spire, it creates a sense of airy, almost floating lightness; looking at it, I decided I had never known what perfect proportions were before. . . .

We returned in the evening to see it in the full moonlight, . . . and though each time I saw it it was breath-taking, perhaps it was most beautiful by moonlight. We could hardly force ourselves to leave, and looked at it from every side, unable to make up our minds which was the most beautiful. . . .

Early the next morning . . . we visited the Taj again to see it in the clear daylight. It was still impressive and overwhelmingly lovely, but in a different way; and the marble looked slightly pinkish, as though it was being warmed by the sun.

As long as I live I shall carry in my mind the beauty of the Taj.

Muslim artists of the Mogul period also excelled in other art forms. They created detailed miniature paintings of brilliantly colored flowers, animals, and scenes of daily life in a style adopted later by Hindu artists. They also made elaborately designed carpets, painted fabrics, carved jade, and produced works of metal, wood, and ivory.

Source: From *INDIA AND THE AWAKENING EAST* by Eleanor Roosevelt. Copyright © 1953 by Anna Eleanor Roosevelt. Reprinted by permission of Harper Collins Publishers.

THE ARTS TODAY

By the 1800's, European influences could be seen in the arts of India, and soon architects, painters, and sculptors were adopting Western styles and techniques. Today, Indian arts reflect a blend of both East and West and old and new. Below, a journalist who visited with a modern Indian artisan relates what he learned:

In his plain home in the Agra neighborhood called Taj Ganj, Mohammad Husain folded himself into a crouch before a grinding wheel on the floor. As his right hand moved a stick, an attached thong spun the wheel's axle. The fingers of his left hand—long, artistic fingers—applied a sliver of malachite [a bright green stone] to the grinding surface.

Mohammad is certain that his craft has not changed since the 1600s, when Taj Ganj was the home of artisans building the Taj Mahal. He is equally certain that his forebears helped decorate that magnif-

icent mausoleum with bits of turquoise, lapis lazuli, jasper, malachite, coral, and carnelian. These became petals, leaves, and trailing tendrils. Inlaid in marble, the floral displays added delicacy and grace.

. . . The morning I met Mohammad he was inlaying a rose in a platter.

He has a craftman's pride in his work, but the pay is meager—five to ten dollars a day. "There is no time for art," he said. "This has become too commercialized."

EXAMINING ART *This Muslim artisan holding a large goblet, displays the fine wares he and his family make in Jaipur.* **What do today's Indian arts reflect?**

Source: Mike Edwards. "When the Moguls Ruled India," in *National Geographic,* April 1985, p. 486.

SECTION 1 REVIEW

CHECKING FOR UNDERSTANDING
1. **Define** *stupa*, minaret.

CRITICAL THINKING
2. **Determining Cause and Effect** How have traditional Indian art forms been affected by modern trends?

SECTION 2

Literature

Like architecture, painting, and sculpture, Indian literature has a long and rich heritage. Today, Indian prose and poetry is written in a variety of languages, including Hindi, Bengali, and Tamil, and is translated into many others as well. But, in the past, most major works of Indian literature were written in the classical languages of Sanskrit and Tami.

THE EARLY YEARS

One of the earliest works of Indian literature is the *Vedas*, a collection of hymns, poems, legends, and religious rituals. The earliest Hindu scriptures, they were repeated for hundreds of years before being written down in 1000 BC. One section of the work, known as the *Rig Veda,* is the world's oldest religious text still in use.

Another major work, the *Mahabharata* (muh·hah·BAH·rah·tuh), is the oldest Indian **epic**, or tale about gods and heroes. It is considered the world's longest poem. If printed in its original form today, it would fill eight large volumes. The *Mahabharata,* which tells the story of a series of battles fought by two warrior families with the help of the gods, includes moral principles and social rules.

Included in the *Mahabharata* is the *Bhagavad Gita* (buh·guh·vud GEE·tuh), the most important text of Hinduism. It tells how the god Krishna appeared before the warrior Arjuna just before a battle, assured him that all souls survive death, and urged him to fulfill his caste duty as a warrior.

Another popular epic poem, the *Ramayana,* relates the adventures of a heroic king named Ram. It tells how Ram searched for his kidnapped wife Sita and rescued her. For centuries, Indians have regarded Ram and Sita as the model of a devoted married couple.

Still another classical work is the *Panchatantra* (pahn·chah·TAHN·trah), a series of short tales that present moral lessons through animals who act like humans. Many of these stories eventually spread to the Middle East and to the West. Some of the stories, like the fable that follows, end with a word of advice:

> In the olden days, in Benaras, lived many carpenters. One day a carpenter was planing some wood. His bald head shone like copper. A certain mosquito came and sat on his head and began to bite him again and again.
>
> Becoming vexed, the carpenter said to his son, "A mosquito is biting and biting my head. Get rid of him for me."
>
> The son was sitting behind his father. He said, "I'll do it. . . !"
>
> He picked up a sharp hatchet and with all his strength, drew back and struck his father on the head. The carpenter's head split in two and he immediately died.
>
> At this time, the Bodhisattva [Buddhist religious teacher] was sitting in the carpenter's shop. He spoke: "Verily, a sensible enemy is better than a stupid friend."

THE TWENTIETH CENTURY

Over the years, Indian literature continued to grow and flourish. During the twentieth century, a number of writers emerged who have received worldwide attention. One of these was Rabindranath Tagore, a Bengali

EXAMINING ART *In this painting, based on the* Ramayana, *Ram and Sita are being attended by three gods. Ram is himself a god, being one of the countless forms taken by the god Vishnu. What story is told in the* Ramayana?

Source: "Assassination of the Mosquito," one of the *Jataka Tales* stories of the Buddha, from *INDIA: A TEACHER AND STUDENT MANUAL,* compiled, edited, and written by Hansen, Mueller and Turkovich, March 1978. Reprinted by permission.

The Arts of India

A succession of invasions throughout India's history has enriched both the culture and the arts of the Indian subcontinent.

? **What cultural influences have shaped the arts of India?**

CLOTH DECORATION
Sikh artisan stamping a traditional pattern onto cloth using a hand block and vegetable dyes.

MODERN ARCHITECTURE
Lakeside memorial at the Punjab University in Chandigarh dedicated to Mohandas Gandhi.

ACTORS
Actors performing the Kathakali, a classical dance drama.

PAINTING
Miniature painting, developed to a high degree of perfection under Mogul rule.

HINDU TEMPLE
Tower atop a gate to an ancient Hindu temple in Madras, with statues representing Shiva and events in his life.

IVORY CARVING
Carving of a rajah riding in a canopied howdah on the back of a royally adorned elephant.

poet who won the Nobel Prize for Literature in 1913. Tagore, who wrote in Bengali, Hindi, and English, produced more than 1000 poems, 2000 songs, and a number of novels, short stories, plays, and essays.

Tagore lived at a time when India was awakening from a long period of British rule, and his works expressed the cultural and patriotic ferment that was sweeping the country. At the same time, he believed that India could reconcile the best of its traditions with modern cultures. In the two excerpts that follow, Tagore reveals how he feels:

Let the earth and the water, the air and
   the fruits of my country be sweet,
   my God.
Let the homes and marts, the forests and
   fields of my country be full,
   my God.
Let the promises and hopes, the deeds
   and words of my country be true,
   my God.
Let the lives and hearts of the sons and
   daughters of my country be one,
   my God.[1]

Where the mind is without fear and the
head is held high;
   Where knowledge is free;
   Where the world has not been broken
up into fragments by narrow domestic
walls;
   Where words come out from the depth
of truth;
   Where tireless striving stretches its arms
towards perfection;
   Where the clear stream of reason has
not lost its way into the dreary desert
sand of dead habit;
   Where the mind is led forward by thee
into ever-widening thought and action—
   Into that heaven of freedom, my Father,
let my country awake.[2]

[1]*Source:* Rabindranath Tagore. "Love's Gift" in *A Tagore Reader.* Amiya Chakravaty (ed.). The Macmillan Company, 1961, p. 348

[2]*Source:* Rabindranath Tagore. *Gitanjali.* Macmillan, 1913.

Two other contemporary Indian authors who have won international notice are Ved Mehta (vehd MAY·tah) and R. K. Narayan. In a book called *Daddyji*, Mehta gives a moving portrait of his father, a noted public health officer. Narayan is known for a number of works that deal with present-day village life in southern India. In the following passage from his short story "A Horse and Two Goats," he describes the life and thoughts of an elderly Indian villager:

Unleashing the goats from the drumstick tree, Muni started out, driving them ahead and uttering weird cries from time to time in order to urge them on. He passed through the village with his head bowed in thought. He did not want to look at anyone or be accosted. A couple of cronies lounging in the temple corridor hailed him, but he ignored their call. They had known him in the days of [plenty] when he lorded over a flock of fleecy sheep, not the miserable gawky goats that he had today. Of course he also used to have a few goats for those who fancied them, but real wealth lay in sheep; they bred fast and people came and bought the fleece in the shearing season; and then that famous butcher from the town came over on the weekly market days. . . . But all this seemed like the memories of a previous birth. Some pestilence afflicted his cattle . . . , and even the friendly butcher would not touch one at half the price . . . and now here he was left with the two scraggy creatures. He wished someone would rid him of their company too. The shopman had said that he was seventy. At seventy, one only waited to be summoned by God. When he was dead what would his wife do? They had lived in each other's company since they were children. He was told on their day of wedding that he was ten years old and she was eight. During the wedding ceremony they had had to recite their respective ages and names.

He had thrashed her only a few times in their career, and later she had the upper hand. [Children], none. Perhaps a large [family] would have brought him the blessing of the gods. . . . He avoided looking at anyone; they all professed to be so high up, and everyone else in the village had more money than he. "I am the poorest fellow in our caste and no wonder that they spurn me, but I won't look at them either," and so he passed on with his eyes downcast along the edge of the street. . . . Only on the outskirts did he lift his head and look up. He urged and bullied the goats until they meandered along to the foot of the horse statue on the edge of the village. He sat on its pedestal for the rest of the day. The advantage of this was that he could watch the highway and see the lorries and buses pass through to the hills, and it gave him a sense of belonging to a larger world.

EXAMINING PHOTOGRAPHS *A glimpse of village life is seen in this photo of a family compound in a village in northwestern India. Which Indian author is known for his works about village life in southern India?*

SECTION 2 REVIEW

CHECKING FOR UNDERSTANDING
1. **Define** epic.
2. **Name** some early Indian writings.

CRITICAL THINKING
3. **Making Generalizations** What are some popular themes of modern Indian writers?

SECTION 3

The Performing Arts

Like the other arts of India, the performing arts have a long and rich history. At their heart are music and dance. Indian musicians play instruments and sing without using chords or other harmonies. A group of musicians starts out with a basic melody called a *raga*, which each player then develops with his or her own improvisations, or musical arrangements performed without preparation. The musicians perform on a number of different instruments, including drums, flutes, and a stringed instrument known as a **sitar.** Their performances often go on for several hours at a time.

A more structured art is dance, which is considered a form of Hindu worship. With the movements of their hands and bodies and the expressions of their faces, dancers act out stories of Hindu gods and goddesses. Because each step and gesture is important and must be precise, many dances require years of training. One, the Kathakali, is performed only by men who are dressed in

India

RAVI SHANKAR

Probably the best-known Indian musician in the world today is Ravi Shankar, often called India's "sitar king." Shankar, almost as well known in the West as in India, has brought an appreciation of Indian music to Western audiences. Below, an Indian journalist discusses Shankar and his career:

Ravi Shankar was clad in a somber off-white kurta and pajama with a touch of embroidered color at the throat. His large, expressive eyes were concealed behind brown-rimmed spectacles. . . .

"Music has been the driving force of my life," he says. "What I search for in music is . . . the nerve-center of my being." Shankar has been in the news for four decades. He has been hailed as a "sitar wizard," "musical genius," and "fabulous musician". . . .

In India, while none doubted his wizardry on the sitar, few appreciated his attempts at bridging the gap between the music of East and West. During the days of the sitar explosion in Britain and the U.S., Pakistani critic Masood Hasan suggested confiscation of all sitars in the two countries and proposed that Shankar be banished to Alaska with a banjo and a mug of coffee. But this piece of unwarranted criticism was overshadowed by violinist Yehudi Menuhin's oft-quoted indebtedness to the maestro "for some of the most inspiring moments I have lived in music."

Born in Varanasi in 1920—the dingy room is now a dilapidated grocer's shop—he received just three years of schooling. His father was the diwan [minister] of the tiny state of Jhalawar. At age ten Shankar joined the dance troupe headed by his famous brother.

He recalls that a trip to Paris "was like going to the moon." He stayed there for eight years. Under his brother's tutelage he was exposed to Western art and culture. . . .

Then in 1935 a chance encounter with Ustad Allauddin Khan . . . transformed his life. . . . Choosing between dance and music was difficult, but Shankar left dance behind and went to Maihar [in India] to become Khan's student. . . .

After practicing the sitar at least fourteen hours daily in Maihar, he spent three years in Bombay, writing music for two ballets and two films, and performing all over India. In 1949 he joined All India Radio as a conductor and director.

In 1956 he embarked on his first major tour abroad and since then has undertaken with passionate sincerity the task of popularizing Indian music in the West. Today Shankar gives about sixty concerts abroad annually. His largest following is in the U.S. . . .

"I have had fame and success," he says, "but I have paid the price. I would like to be like any normal person—have a home, have someone to look after me. But on the whole it has been an extremely lucky, fruitful life."

TAKING ANOTHER LOOK

1. What contribution has Ravi Shankar made to Indian music?
2. How does Ravi Shankar view his career?

Source: Lakshmi Mohan. "India's Sitar King," excerpted from "Indian Express" of New Delhi, as cited in World Press Review, November, 1984, p. 61.

brightly colored costumes and wear heavy makeup. Another dance, the Bharata Natyam, is performed by women. The beauty of the dancing is heightened by the swishing sound of the costumes and the tinkling of small ankle bells.

THEATER

Dance and music, along with literature, play an important role in Indian theater. While a variety of plays are produced today, traditional drama remains very popular. Below, an Indian actor and director talks about the theater and its history:

I direct dramas, all sorts of plays. And I find it a great experience. You know, till some years ago, very few people came to see our plays. Without an audience, naturally, our plays didn't last for more than two or three shows.

Now we have an audience of about 300 for each show and there is actually a demand for good plays. There was a play which ran for 100 days. But I'm speaking of urban theater which is professional and has all the modern aids like lighting and sound effects, specially trained actors and good sets. Professional companies, though still few, exist mainly in our large cities.

Theater in India is more than 2,000 years old. In the olden days, groups of actors used to move around the countryside, giving performances in village streets and courtyards. For centuries, most of our rajahs and nabobs [wealthy men] were great patrons of drama. Of course, the themes were mainly religious and dealt with the deeds of our gods.

Even today, if you happen to be in northern India during October or November, you'll find the *Ram Lila* being acted out in every city, town and village. The *Ram Lila* runs continuously for a month. A different scene from the *Ramayana* is enacted every night.

The actors perform on a temporary

EXAMINING PHOTOGRAPHS *Brightly costumed, a dancer poses in front of a palm tree. Dancers must learn 140 different poses in order to perform the Bharata Natyam. Who performs the Bharata Natyam?*

stage in some open space, with oil lamps providing the light. Entry is free, with everyone sitting in the open on the ground.

At sunset on the last day of the performance, a huge effigy of the many-headed evil God Ravana is burned. This is known as *Dussehra*; thousands come to watch the burning of Ravana.

Like the *Mahabharata*, the *Ramayana* is a great epic and contains the story of Ram and Sita and their fight against the bad Ravana. In every part of the country, people have their own religious dramas in addition to the *Ramayana* and the *Mahabharata*. But in the north, village plays and dance dramas all take their themes

EXAMINING PHOTOGRAPHS *A costumed actor in colorful, grotesque makeup prepares for his role in a traditional drama performance. What is the status of traditional drama in India today?*

from the *Ramayana* and the *Mahabharata.* There are so many, many interesting incidents in them, in which the good always win over the bad.

I don't have time to go see the *Ram Lila* now. *Ram Lila* performances last till around midnight. But many evenings in October and November, when I drive back from my own rehearsals, I'm tempted to step in. Folk theater is really doing very well in India.

FILMS

Although more Indians than ever before are watching television and listening to the radio, movies are probably the most popular

Source: "Theater in India is more than 2000 years old" in *We Live in India.* Veenu Sandal. The Bookwright Press, 1984, pp. 44–45.

form of entertainment in India today. India's motion picture industry is the largest in the world, with the government supporting training for many filmmakers.

One of the best-known filmmakers was Satyajit Ray, who came from a distinguished Calcutta family of writers, teachers, and singers. He was especially known for his film *Pather Panchali,* which tells the story of a young Hindu who moves from the village to the city. Ray's films appeal most to intellectuals and film critics, while the general public prefers films filled with action, adventure, and romance. Below, a young Indian actor talks about Indian films:

Here in India the public simply idolizes movie stars. You know, only about 36 percent of us Indians can read and write, and turn to books and magazines for knowledge and relaxation. For most people, movies are the only form of relaxation and source of information about fashion, sports, history and the world in general.

In the cities, movies are advertised on huge colorful posters and in the daily papers. But in towns and villages, just to make sure that everybody knows, three or four men go around beating drums and announcing a new movie through loudspeakers. . . .

Most of our movies deal with social problems like untouchability, intercaste marriages, family planning, becoming good mothers-in-law and so on. Then there are religious movies, movies for children, and, in recent years, a number of thrillers. In our movies the good guys always win over the bad guys. I prefer to be a good guy in pictures with a social theme.

But I must tell you that, by and large, most movies are made to a set pattern. The theme has to be set in a love story—but no kissing is allowed. Then there have to be lots of songs—at least five or six per picture, along with a few dance numbers. And a gun- or fist-fight between the hero and the villain. . . .

EXAMINING PHOTOGRAPHS *The movie title—"The Companion of the Heart Is the Heart Itself"—on this billboard in New Delhi typifies the love stories told in many Indian films.* *What kinds of movies do Indian filmmakers make?*

An actor can earn between 10,000 and 2,000,000 rupees ($1,000–200,000) per picture. I also own a record shop, so I can afford to live a very luxurious life. But my wife and I have simple tastes. Like thousands of others, we still like nothing better than to spend the evenings watching a movie with our kids.

A Hindi film runs for about two and a half hours, but every movie theater in the country has to run a newsreel and a short documentary film before the main film begins. As a form of entertainment, movies are cheap. Tickets range from 2 to 10 rupees (20 cents to $1.00).

Right now, I'm planning to produce a picture myself. It will require a lot of money, certainly, particularly as more and more movies are being made in color. But then look at the export possibilities. Not only does India lead the world in the production of feature films, it also exports them to nearly ninety countries of the world. So if I'm lucky it should turn out to be a worthwhile investment.

SECTION 3 REVIEW

CHECKING FOR UNDERSTANDING
1. **Define** *raga*, sitar.
2. **Name** some characteristics of the Indian performing arts: music, dance, and films.

CRITICAL THINKING
3. **Synthesizing Information** How do you think religion and Indian dance are linked?

Source: "In our movies the good guys always beat the bad guys" in *We Live in India.* Veenu Sandal. The Bookwright Press, 1984, pp. 48–49.

Chapter 26 Review

SUMMARY

The earliest examples of Indian art remaining today are temples, monasteries, and shrines created by Buddhist, Hindu, and Jain sculptors. Under the Moguls, the arts of India were influenced by Islam. Today, Indian arts reflect a blend of East and West, and Indian artisans carry on many traditional art forms.

The early works of Indian literature, written in Sanskrit, were based on religious teachings. Modern literature, written in various Indian languages, is recognized worldwide and deals with themes of daily life.

Performing arts, such as music and dance, have a long and rich history in India. The Indian theater blends dance, music, and literature to present popular traditional themes and stories. Movies, filled with action, adventure, and romance, are the most popular form of entertainment in India today.

USING VOCABULARY

Explain why each of these terms is used in a chapter about the arts of India.

stupa	*epic*	*sitar*
minaret	*raga*	

REVIEWING FACTS

1. **Discuss** the major contributions of early Indian artists and some of the characteristics of their work.
2. **Name** the places where early Indian monks built cave temples filled with paintings and carvings.
3. **Describe** the general layout and features of a Hindu temple.
4. **Specify** how temples in northern India differed from those in southern India.
5. **Detail** the art forms in which the Muslim artists of the Mogul period excelled.
6. **Identify** some of the earliest Indian writings, their characters, and their major themes.
7. **Name** the modern Indian writer who won the Nobel Prize for Literature in 1913.

CRITICAL THINKING

1. **Demonstrating Reasoned Judgment** An Indian author once stated, "In India, all art is for pleasure." Do you agree or disagree with this statement? Explain.
2. **Drawing Conclusions** In what ways do you think the arts of India have been affected by traditional values? By modern trends?
3. **Identifying Assumptions** What do Indian arts tell you about the beliefs, values, and interests of the Indian people?
4. **Making Comparisons** Compare and contrast public attitudes toward movies in Indian society with those in the United States.

ANALYZING CONCEPTS

1. **Diversity** In what ways, if any, do the arts help promote Indian unity? In what ways, if any, do they reflect Indian diversity?
2. **Interdependence** What impact did early Indian literature have on the Middle East and the West?
3. **Culture** Why did Shah Jahan build the Taj Mahal?

GEOGRAPHIC THEMES

1. **Place** How did early sculptors in southern India make use of the environment in their works?
2. **Movement** In what ways did Islam influence the Indian arts?

Recognizing Bias

Almost everyone has certain opinions or beliefs about particular topics or subjects. For this reason, written material is not always free from the influence of a writer's or speaker's personal views or emotions. Sometimes, even if a writer or speaker does not intend it to happen, what he or she writes or says shows *bias,* a set idea or opinion about something or someone. Bias may be in favor of or against an idea or person. Look, for example, at these three statements:

1. The elegant cat reclined proudly and calmly on the shelf above the girl's head.
2. The sneaky feline crouched on the shelf above the unsuspecting girl's head.
3. The cat sat on the shelf.

Statement 1 expresses a positive bias toward the cat by using such descriptive words as "elegant," and "calmly." In statement 2, however, the cat is "a sneaky feline" and the girl is "unsuspecting." This implies that the cat is about to pounce on an innocent victim, and reflects a negative bias. Statement 3 is a statement that shows no bias, because it presents a straightforward fact.

There are many ways to express bias in written material—by using emotional words; by using italics, underlining, or punctuation for emphasis; or by including *rhetorical questions,* or questions that imply only one answer. Learning to recognize bias allows you to separate facts from the writer's opinions. The following steps will help you recognize bias:

- Identify statements of fact.
- Look for emotional words, opinions, and other signs of bias.
- Research the writer's background and beliefs to determine what biases he or she may bring to the topic.
- Determine the author's point of view.
- If there is bias, determine if it is positive or negative.

EXAMPLE

Read the following passage:
Rabindranath Tagore was one of India's most brilliant writers. He wrote in three languages and produced thousands of poems, songs, novels, short stories, plays, and essays! Tagore wrote his magnificent works during the time that long-suffering India was freeing itself from British rule. His works reflect the patriotic ferment sweeping his beloved country. Can one doubt his genius?

Notice that Tagore's writing is described as "brilliant" and "magnificent." These words indicate a positive bias toward Tagore. In what other ways does the passage reflect this bias? *(emphasizing the number of languages and number of works written, exclamation marks, rhetorical question at the end).* What bias is expressed about India? *(positive bias)* How is this bias expressed? *(India is described as "long-suffering" under British rule and "beloved.")*

PRACTICE

Read the excerpt below and answer the questions that follow:

The few remaining Western diplomats, journalists, executives . . . and volunteer workers . . . now live and work mostly in isolation [from Indians]. . . . [They] are often decent people, but they don't know India. They seem always to be taken by surprise by the twists and turns of the Indian mind and by caste prejudices. . . . They seek to counteract their ignorance by cultivating indifference, which can mean ceasing to trust their most ordinary human impulses—for instance, hesitating to offer a glass of water to their driver for fear of offending some caste convention. A recent remark made by a high-ranking American diplomat suggests the extent of the Westerners' ignorance: "If the average Indian had to choose between going hungry and his country's not having nuclear bombs he would choose nuclear bombs."

1. What facts are given in the passage?
2. What opinions does the writer express about Westerners in India?
3. What incidents are given to support these opinions?
4. Is the author speaking as a Westerner or an Indian?
5. Are the author's biases expressed directly or indirectly?

Source: Ved Mehta, The New India. Viking Press, 1978, p. 11. Copyright © by Ved Mehta.

India's Traveling Tales

India has produced a wealth of literature in the last 3000 years, most of which has survived. A little more than 200 years ago, Europeans began to decode the mysteries of the Sanskrit language and for the first time were able to read these great works. When they did, they discovered that many literary works of Europe and the Middle East had themes and plots similar to those of Indian myths and fables.

Stories from India began to spread as early as the 500's AD. The *Panchatantra*, a collection of Indian fables, traveled as far as Persia by the first half of the 500's. Its fame was so widespread that by the 1400's it had been translated into Arabic, Turkish, Hebrew, German, Spanish, and Latin. Stories from this great work, such as the tale of clever plotting known as "The Monkey and the Crocodile" were the basis of many European fables. The well-known animal fables of the French writer La Fontaine in the late 1600's were based on tales from the *Panchatantra*.

Indian tales also are known in the Middle East and Europe through *The Thousand and One Nights*. In this Arabic classic, written in the 1500's, the beautiful and crafty Scheherazade saves her life by entertaining a brutal king with stories about genies, flying carpets, and fantastic journeys. Although most of the stories are Middle Eastern, *The Thousand and One Nights* contains several Indian tales.

In the 1800's, the Grimm brothers of Germany gathered together and recorded the oral folktales of Europe. *Grimm's Fairy Tales*, as the collection is called, includes many stories of Indian origin. "Faithful John" in the Grimm collection, for example, had a previous life in the old Indian fable, "The Tales' Revenge." The connections between these stories and their European counterparts has led master Indian storyteller and well-known scholar A.K. Ramanujan to comment that Indian tales "have relatives all over the world." He adds, however, that although tales may have similar plots and themes they usually have different meanings depending on the culture from which they come.

Making the Connection

1. Describe how Indian literature has influenced literature in the Middle East and Europe.

2. Why do you think tales from different countries have different meanings?

Unit 4 Review

SUMMARY

India is the largest of the nations that make up the subcontinent of South Asia. One of the most populous nations of the world today, its geography and history are as diverse as its peoples.

Hinduism is the major religion of India. Unlike Buddhism, Islam, Christianity, and other religions of India, it was not based primarily on the teaching of a single individual. Hinduism has been one of the chief influences on India and on Indian life.

When India came under British rule, a great many changes took place. Many of these changes were unpopular with the Indian people. In time, strong Indian leaders emerged to unite the people and press for independence, which was finally gained in 1947.

Since independence, the Indian government has worked to modernize and develop the nation and improve the standard of living of its people. At the same time, it has sought to instill and preserve unity among the nation's great diversity of peoples.

REVIEWING THE MAIN IDEAS

1. **Explain** how geography and climate have influenced the way of life in India.
2. **Discuss** the ways in which religion has influenced the growth and development of India over the centuries.
3. **Evaluate** the quality of life in major Indian cities.
4. **Examine** the role played by the Nehru-Gandhi family in India.
5. **Speculate** about the ways in which the arts reflect the Indian culture.

CRITICAL THINKING

1. **Predicting Consequences** What impact did British rule have on India? Do you think India would be the same today if it had never been a British colony? Explain.
2. **Making Comparisons** Some Indians believe that the middle class in India "has really become the promoter of new ideas and reform." Do you think this is true of the middle class in your country? Give examples to support your answer.
3. **Demonstrating Reasoned Judgment** India possesses within itself numerous contradictions. What do you consider some of those contradictions? How do you think that each affects the nation's future?
4. **Analyzing Information** Explain why you think Indian leaders would agree or disagree with this statement: *Development does not mean changing the values of a group of people.*

PRACTICING SKILLS

Recognizing Bias This statement was made by Mohandas K. Gandhi: *We seek not to destroy English life. We do desire to destroy the system that has weakened our country in body, mind, and soul.* What bias, if any, is reflected? Is it negative or positive?

DEVELOPING A GLOBAL VIEWPOINT

The Indian population has tripled in this century. Approximately 250 people live in each square half mile. If the population continues to grow at its present rate, it will reach 1 billion by the year 2000. What other parts of the world are concerned about population growth? What is India doing to combat population growth? What are the other nations doing? Population growth is a major global issue. Why do you think this is the case?

Latin America

In the 1500's, Spanish and Portuguese explorers encountered new lands rich in gold and other resources. They conquered the peoples living in the lands and built huge colonial empires. In effect, they created a "Latin" America. Today, Latin America encompasses 20 different nations and embraces political systems ranging from democracy to communism. While each nation has its own government and way of life, all have a common heritage that unifies them. Politically, the Latin American nations play a significant role in world affairs. For this reason alone, it is important to gain an understanding of Latin America and its people.

AT A GLANCE

LAND AREA: 7,885,082 sq. mi. (20,422,283 sq. km.)

LAND RESOURCES:
cropland: 8.7%
pasture: 27.9%
forest/woodland: 46.8%
other land: 16.5%

WILDERNESS AREA: 29.1%

MAJOR MOUNTAIN RANGES: Andes, Sierra Madre

MAJOR RIVERS: Amazon, Paraná, Orinoco, Magdalena, Río de la Plata, Uruguay

MAJOR LAKES: Nicaragua, Titicaca

POPULATION: (1992 est.) 453,000,000

POPULATION UNDER 15/OVER 65: 36%/5%

LIFE EXPECTANCY: 67 yrs.

POPULATION PROJECTION: 729,000,000 (by 2025)

POPULATION DENSITY: 58/sq. mi. (22/sq. km.)

URBAN POPULATION: 70%

LARGEST CITIES: (millions)
Mexico City, Mexico (11.1)
São Paulo, Brazil (10.1)
Rio de Janeiro, Brazil (5.6)
Bogotá, Colombia (4.3)

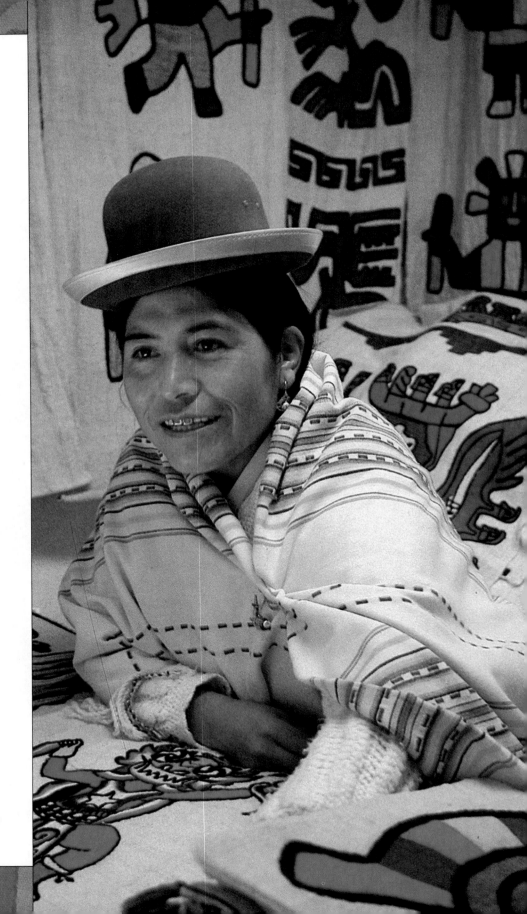

People and Places

the Andes, Chile,
Argentina, Magdalena
River, Orinoco River, Río
de la Plata, São
Francisco River, Amazon
River, the Equator,
Amazon basin, Atacama
Desert

Key Terms to Define
*pampas, llanos, gaucho,
mesa*

Objectives to Learn

1. **Describe** the major
   physical
   characteristics of Latin
   America.
2. **Analyze** the ways that
   Latin America's
   environment affects its
   culture.

*Peruvian merchant
in Andes mountain
village*

Vast and Varied Environment

"Clickety-clacking its way down the track . . . , the train chugs off due east toward Ochomogo, the continental divide. Soon thereafter, mighty Irazú Volcano, a barely sleeping 11,262-foot [3432.6-meter] giant looms off to the left as the train glides into Cartago, the country's former colonial capital. . . .

Winding around lush farmlands and stately forests, small, rounded hills and gently sloping valleys, the train snakes its way through the mountains, leaving the Central Plateau behind. Evergreen farms and forests form a patchwork quilt of varying hues. . . .

This is prime coffee-growing country. . . . Along the tracks the ripening red beans, framed by shiny emerald leaves, seem to beckon the riders to reach out and pluck them. . . .

After the second stop at the small lively town of Paraíso, the spectacular Orosí Valley . . . slips into view. Farmhouses dot the landscape while a hundred shades of green carpeting the valley floor compete for the viewer's attention. The train creeps over an aged, open-slatted bridge spanning a deep gorge. . . .

As the train gently rocks on, it begins its love affair with the Reventazón River. . . . Swirling and thundering toward the sea, the white ribbon of water slices through the fertile valley below. . . . As the train continues its descent, coffee plants are replaced by sugar cane and bananas, and the Cachí Lake and dam come into view. . . .

From Siquirres to Limón the countryside is completely flat and tropical, and the climate hot and steamy.

Toward dusk, giant palms fill the sky and the sparkling Caribbean finally bursts into view. . . . The air is filled with ocean smells. . . . "

The seven-hour, 101-mile (161.6-kilometer) trip on Costa Rica's narrow gauge railroad takes a person through a varied landscape. Such variety is characteristic of Latin America, the name given to a vast region that spans more than one continent.

Source: Veronica Gould Stoddart. "Costa Rica's Jungle Express." AMERICAS, Volume 34, 11/12, 1982, pp. 42–47. Reprinted from AMERICAS, a bimonthly magazine published by the General Secretariat of the Organization of American States in English and Spanish.

Latin America stretches from the Rio Grande in North America to the southern tips of Argentina and Chile in South America. It covers some 7,900,000 square miles (20,400,000 square kilometers), 16 percent of the earth's surface. It includes Mexico and most countries of Central America and South America. It takes in some of the island-nations of the Caribbean. It is a complex area in which the environment influences the way people live and what they expect out of life.

Mountains

Huge mountain ranges dominate much of Latin America. In Mexico, for example, the Sierra Madre Occidental, which runs along the west coast, and the Sierra Madre Oriental, which runs along the east coast, join around Mexico City to form the Sierra Madre del Sur. From Mexico, mountains run south through much of Central America. Still more mountains are found throughout the Caribbean islands. The largest mountain range, however, is found in South America. There, the Andes, the longest continuous mountain chain in the world, forms the backbone of the continent.

The Andes stretch almost 4000 miles (6400 kilometers) from northern Colombia and Venezuela to the southern tip of South America. Below, their grandeur is described by a traveler flying over them in Chile:

Five, six, seven thousand feet [2134 meters] and we turned eastward over the broad valley of the Juncal River and toward the mountains. We gained on them. At first they looked like colossal gobs of sponge cake sprinkled with a thin coating of powered sugar. In another moment they were beneath us, or I thought so. . . . The great gobs of sponge cake were not the Andes at all. They were only the foothills of the Andes. We hadn't started to climb. . . .

The poppies and hayfields gave way to jagged, contorted cliffs and rocks, around and over which wound and twisted the Aconcagua River. . . . All the time we were climbing up—eight thousand feet, nine, ten [3048 meters]—two miles [3.2 kilometers]. The sponge cake became a coconut cake. It was all solid white, completely iced over. This, I thought, is the Andes proper. But as I looked ahead a wall loomed still higher, so high that it seemed to have no top. . . .

Up and up, nineteen, twenty thousand feet, twenty-one thousand, twenty-one thousand five hundred feet [6553 meters]. What an altitude!. . . .

. . . It was like going to heaven in an airplane. We were just above the cordillera, the central range of the mighty mountains. Beneath us, jagged peaks . . . seemed to reach up threateningly. All around were countless slender snowy peaks. To the north, the granddaddy of them all . . . Aconcagua, 28,083 feet [8560 meters] high, looked calmly and silently down upon the whole continent. To the south, Aconcagua's companion, Tupungato, only a hundred feet [30.48 meters] lower. Two giant sentinels of this fantastic garden of the gods.

As we cleared the western edge of the central range and hung . . . between these two magnificent peaks, the morning sun splashed its first yellow rays over the mountains and the great white world became a solid mass of glittering gold. Then it changed. It became a mass of shimmering silver. The rearing peaks looked like great foaming bubbles. . . .

The mountains, however, have created problems. One problem is that they block communications. Most people who live in the mountains are in scattered, isolated villages. Travel is difficult, and many villagers have limited contact with other areas. For this reason, their loyalties and ties often are to their region rather than to their nation. There has been talk about developing more and better transportation systems, but construction work in the mountains is hard, costly, and time-consuming.

Another problem is that the mountains are young geologically. Volcanic eruptions, ava-

EXAMINING PHOTOGRAPHS *The Andes run parallel to the Pacific shoreline and dominate the landscape of western South America. Like these in Peru, most of the peaks are covered by snow year-round, and in their shadow are vast snowfields and glaciers. The melted snow feeds rivers that water the arid coastal plains.* What is the largest mountain range in Latin America?

lanches, and earthquakes are not uncommon. Neither are seaquakes, or underwater earthquakes. In the past, seaquakes have caused tidal waves that have damaged and even leveled coastal towns.

All these acts of nature can take a heavy toll. In 1982, for example, a series of eruptions mingled with earthquakes blew away the dome of El Chichón, a volcano in the Mexican state of Chiapas. Below, a visitor to the area describes the scene two months after the incident:

The signs of destruction were chilling. Four of us . . . rode muleback for six grueling hours . . . to survey the desolation.

Ten kilometers [6 miles] from the summit, as we entered the restricted zone . . . , we saw a stone marker: a skull and crossbones and the words, *"peligro: volcán— danger: volcano."*

Abandoned clothing lay strewn on barbed wire, mute signs of the desperation felt by the Zoque Indians as they fled along the mountainous path to the relative safety of the highway.

Along our route: crushed roofs, trees turned to charcoal, rocks that had fallen from the sky, and the daytime quiet, so devoid of life that the whinny of an abandoned mule was startling. What had been a fertile valley was now a dead, gray, barren desert.

Even worse were the two massive earthquakes that hit Mexico City and its surrounding area in 1985. The result was a disaster that the president of Mexico called "one of the gravest Mexico has suffered in history." Ten thousand people died, 20,000 suffered injuries, and 150,000 were left homeless. One national magazine offered this report of the tragic event:

During the first few moments there was remarkably little alarm. Earth tremors were common enough in Mexico City; the previous weekend most capitalinos [people who live in Mexico City] had endured a moderate earthquake without bothering to leave their beds. But the upheaval last week

Source: Boris Weintraub. "The Disaster of El Chichón." *National Geographic*, Vol. 162, No. 5, November 1982, p. 661.

was different; downtown buildings began to vibrate wildly, their walls and girders groaning from the stress. Metal lampposts swayed and bent like rubber in their sockets in the shuddering streets. Telephone and electrical wires snapped, windows shattered and huge chunks of concrete smashed murderously onto the pavement below. Underground gas lines ruptured in large areas of the city, some erupting in geyserlike flames.

Like thousands of other residents, Teresa Mendoza raced from her home in a panic. "It was absolutely dark from the dust and the smoke," she later recalled. "Everybody was crying—men, women and children. They were saying it's the end of the world." Jorge Herrera had just left his apartment complex when the quake started. "It just came down like a pack of cards," he said. His wife and two sons were still inside. American visitor William Moore fled from the restaurant of his hotel: "Buildings were collapsing, concrete falling and everybody was running. I've never prayed so hard in all my life."

EXAMINING PHOTOGRAPHS *Overlooking the Valley of Mexico, rising 17,887 feet (5452 meters), is the steaming volcano Popocatépetl, "Smoking Mountain." Why have Latin America's mountains been so important?*

EXAMINING PHOTOGRAPHS *Clinging to the side of an Andean mountain in Chile are the town and operations plant of El Teniente, the world's largest underground copper mine. What else is mined in the Andes?*

John M. Pidcock, a tourist from Newark, Del., was particularly struck by the motion of the ground. "It was like a rippling effect, up and down," he said. "If you make a fist and run it under a blanket, the earth looked like the rippling on the blanket." Then three minutes later it was over. The ground felt oddly still. . . .

At first the casualties seemed light. . . . Although about 250 buildings were destroyed by the Thursday-morning quake, authorities privately spoke only of hundreds of deaths. By Friday evening, the official toll reached 2,000, and then, even as 50,000 rescuers were combing the ruins, a second tremor struck, less intense . . . but deadly nonetheless. Several dozen buildings damaged by the first quake collapsed completely. . . .

Still, people are drawn to the mountains. Some come to mine the rich deposits of copper, iron, silver, tin, lead, and other

Source: "Disaster in Mexico." *Newsweek*, November 30, 1985, pp. 16–17.

minerals. Others come to raise livestock or to grow grain and coffee in the rich soil of the valleys and plateaus. It was in such mountains that the great Indian civilizations of Mexico and Peru rose. Today, these areas are among the most important and most heavily populated in Latin America.

SECTION 1 REVIEW

CHECKING FOR UNDERSTANDING
1. **List** some of the major mountain ranges of Latin America.
2. **Cite** the problems the mountains create.

CRITICAL THINKING
3. **Determining Cause and Effect** Why would mineral deposits and rich soil draw people to the mountains?

SECTION 2

Plains

Another feature of the Latin American landscape is plains areas. Coastal plains, seldom more than 50 miles (80 kilometers) wide, extend along the coast of Mexico, through the Yucatán Peninsula, and into Guatemala, Honduras, and Nicaragua. In addition to these, broad inland plains spread over southern Brazil, Paraguay, Uruguay, Argentina, Venezuela, and Colombia. Two of the most interesting of these are the *pampas* of Argentina and Uruguay and the *llanos* of Colombia and Venezuela.

The Argentine *pampas* spread almost 500 miles (800 kilometers) north to the Salado del Norte River and south to the Colorado River. Only a few trees dot the flat surface of the area. It is broken only by a few low mountains in the southeast and northwest. In the east, the *pampas* are hot; in the west, they are dry.

Until the 1800's, the *pampas* were the domain of the **gaucho**, a person who worked the cattle that roamed the vast area. By the late 1800's, the gauchos and their way of life had begun to disappear, pushed out by railroads, immigrants, and farming. This fact is lamented in the following epic Argentine poem about the life of a *gaucho* named Martin Fierro:

A son am I of the rolling plain,
A gaucho born and bred;
For me the whole great world is small,
Believe me, my heart can hold it all;
The snake strikes not at my passing foot,
The sun burns not my head.
. . . .
And this is my pride: to live as free
As the bird that cleaves the sky;
I build no nest on this careworn earth,
Where sorrow is long, and short is mirth,
And when I am gone none will grieve for me,
And none care where I lie.
. . . .
There was a time when I knew this land
As the gaucho's own domain;
With children and wife, he had joy in life,
And law was kept by the ready knife
For better than now; alas, no more
That time shall come again.
. . . .
Ah, my mind goes back and I see again
The gaucho I knew of old;
He picked his mount, and was ready aye,
To sing or fight, and for work or play,
And even the poorest one was rich
In the things not bought with gold.

The neediest gaucho in the land,
That had least of goods and gear,
Could show a troop of a single strain,
And rode with a silver-studded rein,

EXAMINING PHOTOGRAPHS *To many Latin Americans, the* gaucho *is a living symbol of freedom. Though not a frequent sight today, some* gauchos, *like this one riding across the* pampas, *continue to follow tradition and live and work on the small number of large* estancias, *or ranches, still found in the Argentine interior. Of what economic importance are the* pampas *today?*

The plains were brown with the grazing herds,
  And everywhere was cheer.

. . . .

There was work for all—or rather play,
  For a goodly game was yon;
    The plain below, and the sky above,
    A horse and a thatch and a bit o'love,
And a nap in the shade in the heat of day,
  And a dram from the demijohn [large bottle in a wicker holder].

. . . .

There was porridge of corn in steaming pots,
  And fresh-baked bread galore,
    And broth and stew, and a barbecue,
    And caña [drink made from sugar-cane]
      or wine as it suited you,
No wonder I sigh for the days gone by,
  The times that shall come no more,

When by favour of none the gaucho rode
  O'er the rolling pampas wide;
    But now alas, he grows sour and grim,
      For the law and the police they harry him,
And either the Army would rope him in,
  Or the Sheriff have his hide.

Today the *pampas* are the economic heart of Argentina and one of the breadbaskets of the world. Although they make up less than one-fifth of Argentina's territory, almost 40 percent of all Argentines live on them. The rich soil makes the area one of the best in the world for farming. Over 80 percent of Argentina's cereals, 65 percent of its cattle, and 75 percent of its pigs come from the *pampas.*

The other great plains area of Latin America, the *llanos,* stretches from the delta of the Orinoco River in Venezuela westward into southern Colombia. The areas along the rivers are level, but the rest is rolling plains and low **mesas,** broad and flat elevated areas. Here cattle-raising has been the major economic activity since the 1500's. In the past, the climate kept the cattle industry from

Source: From THE GAUCHO MARTIN FIERRO by José Hernández. Translated by Walter Owen. Copyright 1936, © 1964 by Holt, Rinehart and Winston. Reprinted by permission of Henry Holt and Company, Inc.

developing as it should have. A Venezuelan describes the effects of the weather:

It rained, and rained, and rained. For days nothing else happened. The cattlemen who had been outside their houses had returned to them, for the creeks and streams would flow over into the prairie and there would soon be no path. . . .

The marsh was full to overflowing. . . . One day the black snout of a crocodile rose to the surface, and soon there would be alligators too, for the creeks were filling fast and they could travel all over the prairie.

Rain, rain, rain! The creeks had flowed over and the pools were full. The people began to fall ill, . . . They became pale, and then green, and crosses began to spring up in the Altamira cemetery.

But the rivers began to go down at last, and the ponds on the river banks to dry up; the alligators began to abandon the creeks, to gorge themselves on the Altamira cattle. The fever was dying out.

The drought had begun to hold sway. It was now the time for driving to the water holes the cattle who had never known them, or had forgotten them in the agony of thirst. The rutted beds of creeks long dried up ran here and there through the brownish weeds. In some marshes there still remained a little oozy, warm water in which rotting steers, who, crazy with thirst, had leaped into the deepest part of the holes and there, swollen with too much drinking, had been trapped and had died. Great bands of buzzards wheeled above the pools. Death is a pendulum swinging over the Plain, from flood to drought and from drought to flood.

In recent years, things have changed. A dam built across the Guárico River protects the *llanos* against floods and provides

irrigation. Thousands of acres once wasteland during the dry season now are well watered, fertile pasture.

SECTION 2 REVIEW

CHECKING FOR UNDERSTANDING
1. **Define** *pampas, llanos, gaucho,* mesa.
2. **Describe** economic activity and conditions in the plains areas today.

CRITICAL THINKING
3. **Making Inferences** Why would railroads, immigrants, and farming bring an end to *gauchos* and their way of life?

SECTION 3

Rivers

In addition to soaring mountains and flat plains, Latin America has a number of river systems. In South America, for example, there are five major river systems. They are

EXAMINING PHOTOGRAPHS *A seaplane nears Iquitos on the Amazon River in Peru. Once a port for exporting raw rubber, today Iquitos thrives on the export of oil. In what countries do the major rivers flow?*

Source: Gallegos, Romulo, *DOÑA BÁRBARA*, Peter Smith Publisher, Inc., 1948 Gloucester, MA.

the Magdalena in Colombia; the Orinoco in Venezuela; the Río de la Plata, formed by the Paraná and Uruguay rivers and flowing through Argentina, Uruguay, and Paraguay; and the São Francisco and the Amazon in Brazil.

The Amazon is one of the most important systems. It is the longest river in the Western Hemisphere. It stretches for about 4000 miles (6400 kilometers) across South America—from the Peruvian Andes eastward across Brazil to the Atlantic Ocean. About 2300 miles (3680 kilometers) of the river—from the east coast of Brazil to Iquitos, Peru—is navigable. Two journalists described their reaction to the river in this way:

EXAMINING PHOTOGRAPHS *Modern Belém, Brazil, is a gateway to the Atlantic and is the largest port city on the Amazon River. At Belém, what does the Amazon look like? Why is it brown in color?*

We awoke early the next morning still tired yet like schoolchildren on their first day back. We had an appointment that we had been looking forward to for a long time. It was with the Amazon River. That we had spent so long in the Amazon jungle without seeing the lifeline itself was testimony to the river system's breadth and influence.

Walking through the quiet, littered streets of Belém we felt the heat begin to rise. . . .

The main avenue of the town spills out into a dock area, and it was there that we first saw the river, brown and wide. "River Sea" is its common nickname and it is deserved. The water is colored with silt it has carried nearly 4,000 miles [6400 kilometers] in its journey from the Andes. Its brownness is not a sign of pollution, but strength, proof that the river can still alter the topography [features] of the continent. For the next 150 miles [240 kilometers] far out into the Atlantic, the ocean itself is stained brown because of the power of this river.

At Belém the Amazon looks like an ocean. We were unable to follow the shoreline on the other side. From some angles it appeared there was no shoreline; no doubt, it had once been there until it gave way to the incessant flow of the river. *The Mighty, Mighty Amazon* is the title of a book about the river, and it was easy to appreciate that homage to the river's power. . . .

We watched the tide surge in, jostling the 40,000-ton [36,000-metric ton] *Benedict* visiting from Liverpool as easily as it rocked the two-man *Esperança* carrying fish to market. The port for the Esperança and the other fishing boats of the area is upriver from the large commercial docks, a sprawling fish market whose very name, *Ver-o-Peso,* is a warning to consumers: "Watch the weight." To get there we had

to slink through a ribbonwide opening between lines of rickety wooden stalls. . . .

Into the small slip at the Ver-o-Peso
came boats providentially named, like the
Esperanca which means Hope, *Sonhos*
(Dreams) and *Life Is Tough For Him Who Is
Soft*. From these ships tumbled a potpour-
ri of the remarkably varied fish life of the
river . . .

This place which sells crazy ornaments
and exotic fish was, for that morning at
least, the real Belém to us. The highway
from Brasilia, the airplanes flying overhead, and the apartment houses we had
walked by could not distract this town
from the real source of its life. The Amazon River did not disappoint us.

SECTION 3 REVIEW

CHECKING FOR UNDERSTANDING
1. **List** the major river systems of South America.

CRITICAL THINKING
2. **Evaluating Information** What evidence can
you find to support the statement that the
Amazon is one of South America's most
important river systems?

SECTION 4
Rain Forests and Deserts

Still another feature common to Latin
America is the tropical rain forest, the heavily wooded area found in warm, humid regions mostly near the Equator. These forests,
which stay green year-round, are rainy and
hot all the time and may have thunder-
storms several hundred days out of the year.
They have more kinds of trees and animals
than any other area of the world.

Source: Excerpt from AMAZON, copyright © 1983 by Brian Kelly
and Mark London, reprinted by permission of Harcourt Brace
Jovanovich, Inc.

EXAMINING PHOTOGRAPHS *A climber
ascends into the interlocking treetops, or canopy,
of a tropical rain forest above the Sarapiquí River
gorge in Costa Rica. Where are the tropical
rain forests of Latin America found?*

The largest, and probably the oldest,
tropical rain forest is in the Amazon basin. It
covers about one-third of South America. It
is not, however, the only such forest in Latin
America. There are rain forests along the
eastern coast of Central America and in
some islands of the Caribbean as well. One
of these is El Yunque, "the anvil," a mountain in Puerto Rico with a rain forest on its
slopes. Below, a visitor to El Yunque describes what she saw there and how she felt
about it:

There are nearly 200 species of trees
shading the mountains. The palms and
tree ferns give it an airy feeling in sharp
contrast to the montana thickets of
gnarled and twisted trunks. Some such
trees are a thousand years old. When you
see the pink and white begonias coloring

the forest floor, you believe the saying, "Toss a seed into the ground and overnight a garden springs up." Air plants abound, dozens of varieties of tiny orchids snuggling against the trees. . . . If you take one of the side roads or one of the 29 miles [46.4 kilometers] of trails that wind through the forest, you will be in a bamboo forest and you will have the feeling of being in a private cathedral. . . .

There is another song in the air. I hear it again and again, tremulous and piercing sweet. It must be a species of bird. But I am wrong. What I see, after careful inspection, is the coqui—a tree toad—tiny as the fingernail on your smallest finger.

The flowers at El Yunque are particularly rich in color protected as they are with shade. The heliconias are everywhere. You will know them immediately with their orange lobster-claw flowers. Moss hangs from the trees like an old man's beard. Everywhere are varieties of bromeliads (the pineapple plant is one) with pointed leaves beautiful and shiny, almost artificial looking in their severe perfection. The fruit trees are repeated over and over. . . . That brilliant streak of color is a Puerto Rican parrot, green, blue, and red, a full foot tall. He is at home in the forest along with the tanager, the owl, the pigeon, the quail-dove. There is a thrush flying overhead and somewhere a woodpecker is in the distance with its familiar rat-tat-tat. There are no poisonous snakes to mar this paradise, but lizards are common.

Is there any place in the world more beautiful than El Yunque? I would have to be convinced. If you find it, bring me to it!

In direct contrast to the green and moisture-laden rain forests are the drylands of northern Mexico and northeastern Brazil and the Patagonian and Monte deserts of southern and northwestern Argentina. Drier still is Peru's narrow coastal region. A desert

Source: Princine Calitri. *Come Along to Puerto Rico*. T.S. Denison & Company, Inc., 1971, pp. 144–146.

of stone and sand dotted by irrigated farmlands, it stretches for close to 1400 miles [2240 kilometers]. This region is the northern extension of Chile's Atacama Desert, one of the driest areas of the world.

The Atacama runs south from Chile's northern border with Peru for more than 600 miles (960 kilometers). Almost no vegetation grows on the Atacama, and some of its towns never have recorded rainfall. Below, a passenger traveling through the Atacama by train gives her impression of it:

The scenery looks as though one is on some bizarre planet where centuries ago life was sucked off into a black hole, leaving only dusty specters and eidolic [phantom-like] mountains. In spite of, or perhaps because of, the starkness a hypnotic beauty emanates from this windswept land. Strange hues wreathe the mountains and swirl the sands. The nuances of color—the rose, turquoise, gold—are disconcerting and eerie.

For the entire day the train presses across the desert. Borax lakes, resembling late spring snow patches, dot the vast land. Volcanoes creep up the horizon, livid lake beds spring into sight then disappear. Foothills of the Andes form a forlorn backdrop for the desert, slowly fading into the night.

SECTION 4 REVIEW

CHECKING FOR UNDERSTANDING
1. **Identify** the major characteristics of rain forests.
2. **Describe** the drylands.

CRITICAL THINKING
3. **Making Inferences** What does the fact that Latin America is home to both rain forests and drylands tell you about the region's climate?

Source: Sally Wyche. "The Andes by Train." AMERICAS, Volume 31, February 1979, p. 30. Reprinted from *AMERICAS*, a bimonthly magazine published by the General Secretariat of the Organization of American States in English and Spanish.

Latin America

THE DIMINISHING RAIN FORESTS

Nearly two-thirds of Central America's primary forests have been cleared to make room for cattle ranches. Mexico's one remaining rain forest has been encroached on by farmers, timber companies, and ranchers. On most Caribbean islands only small tracts of the forests remain. Even in South America, where large portions of rain forest remain, there is cause for concern.

Industrialists want to tap the forests for organic compounds. Governments look to the forests for mineral wealth. Scientists, however, fear that large-scale burning of the forests will result in changes of climate worldwide. Caught in the middle are the indigenous peoples, those who first settled the land long before the arrival of Europeans. Below, the Coordinating Body for Indigenous People's Organizations of the Amazon, which represents more than 1 million Indian people in Peru, Bolivia, Ecuador, Colombia, and Brazil, has its say:

We, the indigenous peoples, have been an integral part of the Amazon biosphere for mil-

lennia. We use and care for the resources . . . with respect, because it is our home, and because we know that our survival and that of our future generations depend on it. Our accumulated knowledge about the ecology of our forest home, our models for living within the Amazon biosphere, our reverence and respect for the tropical forest and its inhabitants, both plant and animal, are the keys to guaranteeing the future of the Amazon Basin. . . .

We are pleased . . . to see the interest and concern expressed by the environmentalist community for the future of our homeland. . . .

We are concerned, however, that you have left us . . . out of your vision of the Amazonian biosphere. The focus of concern . . . has typically been the preservation of the tropical forests and their plant and animal inhabitants. . . .

We want you . . . to recognize that the most effective defense of the Amazonian

biosphere is the recognition of our ownership rights over our territories and the promotion of our models for living within that biosphere. . . .

We want to represent ourselves and our interests directly in all negotiations concerning the future of our Amazonian homeland. . . .

We propose establishing a permanent dialogue with you to develop and implement new models for using the rain forest. . . .

We propose joining hands with those members of the worldwide environmentalist community who recognize our historical role as caretakers of the Amazon Basin; support our efforts to reclaim and defend our traditional territories; accept our organizations as legitimate and equal partners.

We propose reaching out to other Amazonian peoples, such as the rubber tappers, the Brazil-nut gatherers, and others whose livelihoods depend on nondestructive extractive activities.

DRAWING CONCLUSIONS

Do you think indigenous peoples should have a say in what happens to the rain forests? Explain.

Source: Members of COICA. "It's Our Rain Forest." *Mother Jones*. April/May 1990, p. 47.

Geography

THE LANDSCAPE, CLIMATE, AND RESOURCES OF LATIN AMERICA

The geographic environment of Latin America differs from country to country and from area to area. So do climate, resources, land use, and population density. The four maps that follow illustrate this.

FOCUSING ON THE ISSUE Study the maps. Then, based on the information in them and in the chapter, answer the following questions:

1. What are the seven major landforms of Latin America?

2. What are the major climates of Latin America? Which areas are the warmest? The coolest? The most moderate temperatures? Identify the most pleasant climate in which to live and tell why. What effect, if any, do you think altitude has on temperature?

3. What are some of the major resources of Mexico? Of Central America? Of South America? Of the Caribbean? For the most part, how is the land used in each area?

4. In what areas is the population the most heavily concentrated? The least heavily concentrated? What features of the most heavily populated areas might have led people to settle there?

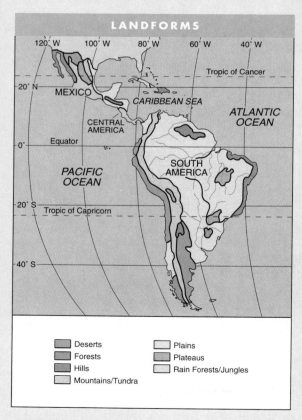

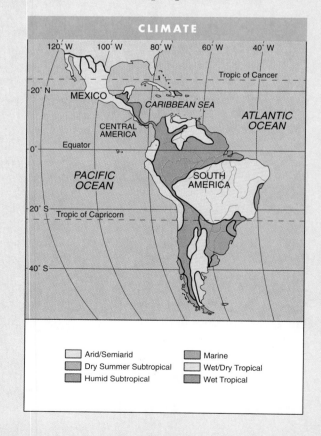

Below, a writer paints a poetic picture of South America by portraying the continent as a woman, using geographic facts as a basis for description. After reading the excerpt, identify facts the writer may have used. Then, using the information in the chapter and in the maps on these two pages as a basis, paint your own written picture for Central America or the island nations of the Caribbean.

She was less than the hemisphere of the west of which she herself formed a large part, and yet she was more. For she was a whole world, infinite in her changing vastness. . . .

She was the southern Americas, half-waking where she lay:

Her long hair of grass and thicket buckled and braided over the 32nd parallel. Left arm stretching to the sea of the Caribs, thumb dipping to the Mexican Gulf. Other arm extended, from her shoulder in the west, down the Sierra Madre, past her delicate Isthmus waist, to the Andes where thighs of silver and gold lift to the world's own ceiling—and her warm, verdant belly, the Amazon! The bulge of Brazil? Her left knee—the leg drawn back, away from Antarctica (but the toes of her feet blanket-warmed in the dazzling snow of Fuegia, Land of Fire).

And so, back through the ages in snow that would be called fire, and on freezing heights in tropic latitudes, . . . the southern lands of half a sphere half-awoke to many sounds.

Source: Abel Plenn. *The Southern Americas: A New Chronicle.* Creative Age Press, 1948, p. 4.

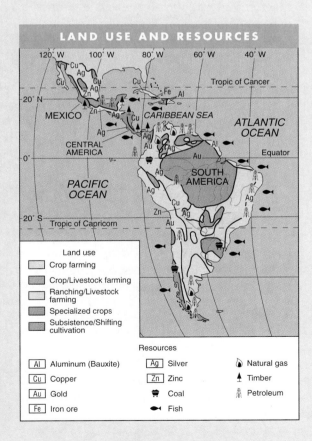

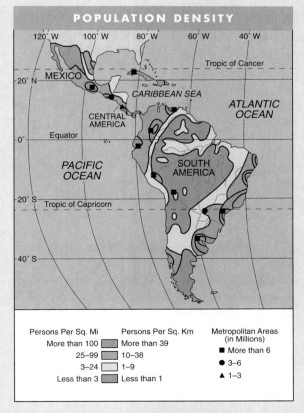

Chapter 27 Review

SUMMARY

The name *Latin America* refers to Mexico, the countries of Central and South America, and some of the Caribbean island-nations.

Latin America boasts an environment that is rich and varied. Huge mountain ranges, like the mighty Andes, can block communications and have been the source of such natural disasters as volcanic eruptions, avalanches, seaquakes, and earthquakes. Coastal plains and broad inland plains, like the *pampas* of Argentina and the *llanos* of Venezuela and Colombia are agricultural and ranching areas. Major river systems, like the Amazon, serve as lifelines. Steamy tropical rain forests, like the one in the Amazon basin, today are endangered and are the subject of controversy. Lastly, there are desolate drylands, like the Atacama Desert of Peru and Chile.

USING VOCABULARY

Use each of the terms below in a brief caption to accompany photographs you have been asked to include in a report about Latin America. Describe each photograph.

pampas	*gaucho*
llanos	**mesa**

REVIEWING FACTS

1. **Describe** the different kinds of environments in Latin America.
2. **Identify** where plains areas are located in Latin America.
3. **List** the produce that comes from the *pampas* of Argentina.
4. **Contrast** rain forests and drylands.
5. **Specify** where the major mountain ranges and river systems of Latin America are located.
6. **State** where the Amazon River begins and where it ends.
7. **Name** the desert area in Chile that is considered one of the driest regions in the world.

CRITICAL THINKING

1. **Demonstrating Reasoned Judgment** Latin America often is referred to as a land of geographic vastness and great environmental variety. Do you agree with this assessment? Explain.
2. **Determining Cause and Effect** Explain how the size and geographical diversity of Latin America might influence the lifestyles and expectations of the people who live there.
3. **Drawing Conclusions** Why are the *pampas* and the *llanos* important to the well-being of Latin America?
4. **Making Comparisons** Compare the size and geography of Latin America and the effect they have on the people's lifestyles with the size and geography of your country and the effect they have on the people's lifestyles.

ANALYZING CONCEPTS

1. **Environment** Why is Latin America's great diversity of geographical environment both an advantage and a disadvantage?
2. **Empathy** Explain why the rain forests of Latin America are a subject of controversy.

GEOGRAPHIC THEMES

1. **Location** Where are the nations that make up Latin America located in relation to the United States?
2. **Place** What physical and human characteristics make the mountain systems dominant in Latin America?

Reading a Plate Tectonics Map

Most maps illustrate features of the earth's surface—continents, oceans, and other bodies of water. Although these maps produce the illusion that the earth's features are fixed and stable, in fact, the continents are moving.

According to the theory of *plate tectonics*, the earth's crust is composed of large plates upon which the continents ride. Hot streams of molten lava which push up from the depths of the earth cause volcanoes and earthquakes, and move the plates carrying the continents. When two plates converge, the land pushes upward to form mountains. When plates move apart, deep trenches form in the ocean floor.

A map of plate tectonics shows both the tectonic plates and surface features. These maps explain how the earth's features were formed and where earthquakes and volcanic activity are likely to occur. Use the following steps to read a map of plate tectonics:
- Identify the continents and oceans.
- Identify the tectonic plates and their direction of movement.
- Find relationships between the plates and surface features.

EXAMPLE

On the map of plate tectonics below, continents are outlined in blue and tectonic plates in black. Because the continents are not labeled, you must identify them by shape and relative position. North America and South America ap-

pear in the center. What plate underlies most of these continents? *(American Plate)* Find the Indo-Australian Plate. According to the arrows, is it moving north or south? *(north)*

PRACTICE

Use the map below to answer the following questions:
1. Are the Cocos and Nazca plates moving toward or away from the American Plate?
2. What geographic features have been formed by the movement of these plates?
3. Which events in Chapter 27 are related to the movement of these plates?
4. What plates are responsible for earthquakes in the Pacific area?

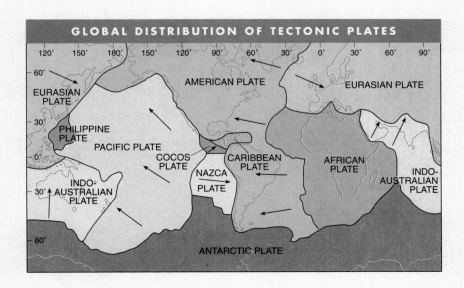

GLOBAL DISTRIBUTION OF TECTONIC PLATES

CHAPTER OUTLINE

People and Places to Know
the Mayas, the Incas, the Aztecs, Mexico, Guatemala, Ladinos, Bolivia, Ecuador, Peru, Uruguay, Caribbean, Brazil, Cuba, Panama

Key Terms to Define
mestizo, mulatto, *conquistador*

Objectives to Learn
1. **Identify** the major ethnic groups of Latin America.
2. **Describe** the heritage and contributions of Latin America's ethnic groups.
3. **Outline** the decline of the Indian way of life in Latin America.

Brazilians at a sports event

The Human Diversity

> Harbor cities are never provincial, and Salvador, one of Brazil's great ports, is no exception. Under constant siege from the foreign, its horizon bustles with the coming and going of ships. Each day's breeze brings exotic shipments, strange customs and foreign garb. The docks throng with humanity, the air is pierced with a gibberish of tongues.
>
> In Salvador—once called São Salvador or Bahia—these ingredients have simmered for hundreds of years. . . .
>
> Salvador is located a thousand miles [1700 kilometers] northeast of Rio de Janeiro. The first Portuguese settlement in the New World, Salvador is perched on a high bluff overlooking the Atlantic Ocean and the . . . Todos os Santos Bay. . . .
>
> History remains alive in Salvador. A city of over a million inhabitants, Salvador maintains a face as colorful as its past. Between the 16th and 19th centuries four million slaves were brought to . . . work the large-scale sugar plantations of Bahia. . . . While the plantation owners grew wealthy and built magnificent churches and mansions, the influx of Africans was forever changing the character of Bahia. Today, . . . [Salvador's] culture is a colorful hybrid of Indian, Portuguese and African traditions.
>
> The Indian influence remains in the decorative arts and some architecture, in the burnished skin tones and high cheekbones of the people, and in the words the Tupi language has given the world. "Cashew" and "tapioca" are only two words from this musical language to be incorporated into dozens of tongues.
>
> The African influence is widespread and fascinating. The depth of its penetration into Bahian life makes the area different from any other in Brazil.

As stated above, the culture of Salvador "is a colorful hybrid of Indian, Portuguese and African traditions." In this sense, Salvador is typical of all Latin America, where the more than 400 million people are of a variety of ancestries. There are Indians, Europeans, Asians, Africans, and mixtures of all these. Over one-half are of mixed heritage.

Source: Carrie Topliffe. "Saucy Salvador." AMERICAS, Volume 36, 1/2, 1984, pp. 15–16. Reprinted from *AMERICAS*, a bimonthly magazine published by the General Secretariat of the Organization of American States in English and Spanish.

Mestizos, persons of European and Indian ancestry, form the largest single group. There are also about 20 million **mulattoes**, persons with one black and one white parent.

The same is true of the language of Latin America, which most people think is Spanish. But the people of Brazil speak Portuguese, not Spanish. In addition, each nation has its own dialects and Indian languages. For these reasons, Latin America can be considered a region of human diversity.

SECTION 1

Indians

The first Americans were the Indians, who, according to many historians, are thought to have come to the Western Hemisphere across the Bering Strait thousands of years ago. It is believed that, at that time, the Bering Strait was a land bridge that connected Asia and present-day Alaska. By the time Christopher Columbus arrived in the Americas in 1492, Indians called Mayas, Incas, and Aztecs already had had their own great civilizations for many years. The Mayan Empire extended through Central America and Mexico's Yucatán Peninsula. The Incan Empire took in Ecuador, Peru, Bolivia, and most of Chile. The Aztec Empire enveloped Mexico. In fact, present-day Mexico City is built on the site of the ancient Aztec capital.

EXAMINING PHOTOGRAPHS *The Great Temple at Tenochtitlán, shown in this model, was a monument to the Aztec gods of rain and war. What happened to much of what the Indian civilizations built?*

THE AZTECS

In 1520, the Spanish *conquistador*, or conqueror, Hernán Cortés, described the Aztec capital city of Tenochtitlán (tay·NOHK·tee·LAHN) to King Charles I of Spain. The following is part of that description:

The great city of Tenochtitlán is built in the midst of this salt lake, and it is two leagues [about six miles or ten kilometers] from the heart of the city to any point on the mainland. Four causeways lead to it, all made by hand and some twelve feet [3.6 meters] wide. . . . The principal streets are very broad and straight, the majority of them being of beaten earth, but a few and at least half the smaller thoroughfares are waterways along which they pass in their canoes. . . .

The city has many open squares in which markets are continuously held and the general business of buying and selling proceeds. One square . . . is . . . completely surrounded by arcades where there are daily more than sixty thousand folk buying and selling. Every kind of merchandise such as may be met with in every land is for sale there. . . .

There are a very large number of mosques [temples] or dwelling places for their idols . . . in the chief of which their priests live continuously, so that in addition to the actual temples containing idols there are sumptuous lodgings. . . . Among these temples there is one chief one . . . whose size and magnificence no human tongue could describe. For it is so big that within the lofty wall which entirely circles it one could set a town of fifteen thousand inhabitants. . . .

Much of what the Aztecs and the other Indian civilizations had built was destroyed by the European conquerors, who needed—and used—the Indians. The Europeans relied on the Indians to do manual labor. In the

Source: Hernándo Cortéz. *Hernándo Cortéz, Five Letters, 1519-1526.* Routledge & Kegan Paul, 1969, pp. 86–93.

Latin America

MOCTEZUMA

When Hernán Cortés invaded the Aztec Empire of Mexico, it was a highly developed civilization ruled by a mighty emperor called Moctezuma. Below, Cortés describes the power and grandeur of Moctezuma and his court:

His service was organized as follows: at dawn every day, six hundred lords, and men of rank, came to his palace. Some of these sat down, and others walked about in the halls and corridors of the palace, talking and passing the time, but without entering the room where he was; the servants and retainers who accompanied them filled two or three great courts, and the street, which was very large. They remained in attendance until night. . . . The larder and the wine cellar were open daily to all who wished to eat or drink. The way they served the meals is this: three or four hundred youths carried in countless dishes, for, every time he wished to dine or sup, they brought him all the different dishes, not only meats, but also fish, and fruits, and herbs . . . ; and as the climate is cold they brought, under each plate and dish, a brazier of coals,

so that the food should not get cold. They placed all the dishes together in a great room where he dined . . . ; its floors were all very well covered and very clean, and he sat on a small cushion of leather. . . . Whilst he was eating, there were five or six elder lords standing a short distance from him, to whom he offered from the dishes he was eating. One of the servants waited to bring and remove the dishes for him, which were passed by others, who stood further off. . . . At the beginning and end of each meal, they always brought him water for his hands, and the towel once used, he never used again; nor were the plates and service in which a dish was served ever brought again. . . .

He dressed himself four times every day, in four different kinds of clothing, all new, and never would he be

dressed with the same again. All the lords who entered his palace came barefooted, and when those whom he had summoned appeared before him, it was with their heads bent, and their eyes on the ground, in humble posture; and, when they spoke to him, they did not look him in the face, because of respect and reverence. . . . When Moctezuma went out, . . . all those who accompanied him and those whom he met in the street, turned their faces aside, and in no wise looked at him, and all the rest prostrated themselves until he had passed. One of the lords, who carried three long thin rods, always went before him. . . . When he descended from his litter, he took one of those rods in his hand, and carried it as far as he went. The ceremonies which this sovereign used in his service were so many, and of such different kinds, that more space than I have at present would be required to relate them.

TAKING ANOTHER LOOK

Cortés was awed and astounded by Moctezuma's way of life and his court. How would you have reacted and why?

Source: Francis Augustus MacNutt (tr.). *The Five Letters of Relation from Hernando Cortés to the Emperor Charles V.* Vol. 1. G.P. Putnam's Sons, 1908, pp. 267–268.

process, many Indians were mistreated or killed. Over the years, millions died of diseases brought to their land for the first time by the Europeans.

THE PLIGHT OF THE INDIAN

In time, many Indian words became part of the Spanish and Portuguese languages, and many European men married Indian women. Out of the mixed marriages came a new ethnic group—the *mestizo*.

Over the years, marriage between Indians and Europeans became so extensive that in many areas of Latin America, the distinction between ethnic groups now rests upon cultural rather than physical distinctions. This, however, has not prevented discrimination against Indians in some areas. Below, a journalist discusses the situation in Guatemala, where more than half of the population is Indian:

Indians can be seen all over the country, though most of them live in the . . . barely arable midsection. There, most of them eke out a living farming tiny, mountainside plots.

The Ladinos [anyone who wears Western-style clothes and follows Spanish-American customs], in contrast, live in the larger towns, hold higher-paying jobs, wear Western attire and speak only Spanish. They usually stay in school longer than Indians. . . .

. . . Centuries of intermarriage among Indians, Europeans, and mixed-blood *mestizos* have blurred physical distinctions; all of them tend to have dark eyes and swarthy complexions. In fact, many who pass for Ladinos are full-blooded Indians who have discarded their Indian language, clothing, and customs. But physical similarity hasn't wiped out discrimination by Ladinos. . . .

"Racism is expressed in subtle ways here . . . ," says an Indian schoolteacher. . . . He adds: "It is still humiliating. Ladinos laugh at our names, they refuse to call us 'sir,' and they won't hire us or rent us a home if we wear our traditional clothes. . . . "

Language probably is the biggest obstacle. . . . [Although] most Indians know enough Spanish to conduct simple business transactions, most can't read or write it or hold much of a conversation.

Moreover, Indians often resist attempts to teach them Spanish. "They realize that to lose their language is to lose their culture," says a Roman Catholic priest who has worked in Guatemala for 30 years. . . .

For the Indians of Guatemala, . . . the path to social acceptance and self-respect

ETHNIC DIVERSITY IN LATIN AMERICA (in percentages)

Argentina		97	21
Bolivia	14	55	31
Brazil	8	54	36 (2)
Chile	25	70	5
Cuba	12 (1)	50	37
Guyana	30	51	14 / 5
Mexico	9	30	60 (1)
Peru	15	45	37 / 3

Legend:
- African
- Asian
- European
- Indian
- Mestizo
- Mulatto
- Other

EXAMINING GRAPHS *Latin America's population consists of many ethnic groups. Which Latin American nation shown on the chart has the highest percentage of Africans? Indians? Mestizos? Mulattos? Europeans? Asians?*

EXAMINING PHOTOGRAPHS *This crowd of Peruvians lining a parade route represent various Latin American ethnic groups.* **What have the Indians of Latin America done to preserve their own cultures?**

seems to . . . involve . . . forsaking, at least for a while, their own culture. In fact, many Indians who have "made it" in the Ladino world have had to leave their homelands before they could become proud of their heritage.

"It wasn't until I went to medical school in Mexico that I stopped being ashamed of being an Indian," says a 39-year-old doctor from Quetzaltenango, Guatemala. "It is a depressing thought, but now that I'm back, I can see that going abroad was the only thing that cured me."

A DYING WAY OF LIFE

Today, the Indian may be a farmer high in the Andes or a hunter in the Amazon. Wherever Indians survive in large numbers, they have tried to preserve their own culture. In Bolivia, Ecuador, Mexico, Peru, and Guatemala, Indians have kept their own dress, language, and social structure. Often they prefer to keep apart from the rest of the

nation. They use their own ways of farming, live in small villages, and, according to tradition, divide their work among their people. They may even use tools like the ones their ancestors used.

Even when their religion and dress show a western influence, the Indians try to keep enough of their own culture to make them a little different from the rest of the country. Yet, despite their efforts, the Indian way of life is slowly declining in many parts of Latin America. As discussed below, this is especially true in the case of the Indians of the Amazon basin:

The great dying has been a quiet affair for the Amazon's [Indian] cultures. No Indian wars, no historic treaties—just a steady attrition [reduction in numbers] from exploitation, disease and occasional small slaughters.

The million Indians who peopled the Amazon in 1900 now number around 100,000. As many as 80 distinct cultures may have been lost.

No Indian wars could have been a more potent killer than disease. A single cold could turn to pneumonia, even death, for

CASE STUDY

Latin America

THE INDIAN TODAY

The Diaguita Indians have for centuries lived in the Andes Mountains in Argentina. Today, they have learned to adapt their lives to modern times. Below, a Diaguita woman talks about her people and their life today:

Diaguita Indians have lived in this region for generations. Life has never been easy for us at this altitude—3,000 meters (9,800 feet). There is less oxygen up here than at sea level, and the variations in temperature are more extreme. It can get very hot during the day, and yet be very cold at night. Also, the soil is of very poor quality. . . .

We are mainly a farming community. We grow beans, corn and potatoes on the mountain slopes. To irrigate these crops, we still use the channels built centuries ago by our ancestors. We also breed llamas. The llama is a very useful animal which provides us with wool, meat, and a means of transportation. Animals like sheep and cattle cannot survive at this altitude. In our community, the more llamas you own, the

richer you are.

Our life styles have altered a little since tourists started coming here. The looms in our homes used to be used only for weaving clothes for the family, using wool from llamas. Nowadays, many of the clothes are for selling to tourists. We always go down to the station to meet the Tren a las Nubes (Train to the Clouds). . . . Many tourists travel on it and we sell them things like blankets, socks, scarves and sweaters. The income we get from this trade is used to buy things we cannot produce ourselves—everything from radios to a small truck.

Our homes are houses made with stones, held together with a mixture of straw and clay. We live in small, independent communities. Each community has its

own leader, . . . usually one of the respected elder members. You can tell to which community someone belongs by the way they dress, the color of their clothes, and the hairstyle of the women.

We consider ourselves Argentines, although we have kept many of our ancestral customs. Religion for us is a mixture of Christianity and our own beliefs. Inti (the Sun), Mama Hilla (the Moon) and Pacha Mama (the Earth) are our main gods. We also have minor gods for thunder, rain and lightning. There are festivals throughout the year which are dedicated to our gods. During them, our community organizes huge parties with music, singing and dancing, and lots of food! The most important festival is the one for Inti.

DRAWING CONCLUSIONS

The Diaguita have had to adapt their lives to survive. Do you think that in the future they can continue to adhere to their traditions yet still contribute to their country? Explain.

Source: Alex Huber. "The Sun, the Moon and the Earth are our main gods." We Live in Argentina. The Bookwright Press, 1984, pp. 16–17. Reprinted with permission of Franklin Watts, Inc., New York.

the Indian, whose long evolution in isolation afforded little or no resistance.

In modern times, the risks to Indians of total contamination have been increased by the building of new roads for development and massive colonization. In some instances, Indians even die from the immunizations. . . .

The other major factor in the Indian's decline has been the loss of his traditional lands. . . .

[An] . . . Amazon Indian tribe without the proper amount of jungle is a culture as good as doomed, anthropologists say.

There always were a few places where the Indian could live best—principally along the rivers, with their cooler, drier climates, access to fish and annually renewed fertile floodplain soils.

Forced [today] into areas less favorable for hunting, gathering of forest foods and shifting agriculture, the Amazon's Indians have lost a nutritional base that, along with lack of disease, was the envy of early explorers.

EXAMINING PHOTOGRAPHS *The exotic costumes worn at this festival in Oaxaca reflect Mexico's largely Indian and European heritage. Where did most European immigrants settle in Latin America?*

SECTION 1 REVIEW

CHECKING FOR UNDERSTANDING
1. **Define** *conquistador*.
2. **Explain** why the Indian way of life is in decline.

CRITICAL THINKING
3. **Evaluating Information** What evidence can you find of the level of development of the Aztec Empire?

SECTION 2

The Europeans

Until the early 1800's, when the Latin American colonies won their independence,

Source: Tom Horton. "The Great Dying Comes Quietly to Amazon Indian Cultures." *The Baltimore Sun.*

about 2000 Spanish and Portuguese immigrants landed in Latin America each year. Later, even more than ever arrived. From the middle of the 1800's until World War I, 12 million Europeans flocked to Latin America. Although most were Spanish and Portuguese, a great many others were Italian, British, and German. Most of the immigrants settled in Argentina, Chile, Uruguay, and the extreme southern part of Brazil.

The European settlers did a great deal to shape the vast area south of the Rio Grande. The Portuguese in Brazil and the Spaniards in other regions tried to pattern life in their new land after the life they had known in Europe. They introduced new grains and fruits, horses, and livestock. They also brought many kinds of technology, and took advantage of the mineral wealth they found in their new land. Over the years, they contributed greatly to the economies of the areas in which they settled.

Today, European immigrants and their descendants make up a large part of the population of Argentina and Uruguay. Below, an Argentinian of Welsh descent talks about why his ancestors came to Argentina:

I'm a direct descendant of one of the 153 Welsh people who landed in Port Madryn in 1865. They were poor people who were escaping from the crowded mining valleys and from an English Parliament which had banned Welsh from being taught in schools and opposed a Welsh independence movement. They chose Patagonia because it was far away from English people! The Argentine government gave the settlers some land along the River Chubut, 64 km (40 miles) across the desert from Port Madryn. The immigrants were very friendly with the Indians and opposed the so-called "War of the Desert," during which the Indians were almost exterminated by the Argentine Army from Buenos Aires. My ancestors began farms and were soon growing good-quality wheat. They also started breeding sheep in the sheltered valleys. Patagonia's *estancias* [ranches] now have the majority of the country's 46 million sheep and help to make Argentina the world's fourth largest wool-producing nation. In the warmer, northern parts of Patagonia, apples, pears and grapes are grown with the help of irrigation projects.

This cafe was opened by my wife's aunt, who thought that the farmers visiting Gaiman for their shopping would like somewhere to have a drink and a bite to eat. It was a great success and other people soon copied her. We serve tea and homemade biscuits, bread and jam. We're very busy on weekends when whole families come to Gaiman to do their shopping.

In 1981, my wife and I went to Wales for the first time. The countryside was beautiful and everyone was very friendly, but

EXAMINING PHOTOGRAPHS *A shepherd takes a break from herding a large flock of sheep across a broad valley in the Patagonian region of Argentina. Why did Welsh immigrants leave their homeland and settle in Argentina in 1865?*

we would never leave here. This is our home. We're Argentine, not Welsh.

| SECTION 3 |

The Africans

In the 1500's, European settlers began to bring black enslaved people from Africa to the Americas. Large numbers ended up in Latin America working on plantations. Of the millions of enslaved Africans brought to the Americas by the 1800's, more than 12 million were imported into Brazil.

As slaves, and later as free people, Africans, most from West Africa, played an important part in the development of Latin America. Their labor made possible the raising of sugar in the West Indies, cocoa in Venezuela, and sugar, cotton, and coffee in Brazil. Their hand labor produced much of the farming wealth of the islands of the Caribbean and parts of Brazil. Africans have served Latin America as skilled craftspeople, fishers, miners, writers, artists, and musicians.

The Africans infused their heritage into many aspects of the Latin American way of life. As the following article shows, this is especially true in Brazil, where more than half the people have African ancestors:

Source: Alex Huber. "Patagonia is a cool desert." *We Live in Argentina.* The Bookwright Press, 1984, pp. 14–15. Reprinted with permission of Franklin Watts, Inc., New York.

EXAMINING PHOTOGRAPHS *In the city of Salvador in Brazil, an African-descended member of the national police force stands guard. What are other occupations of Latin Americans of African descent?*

African-style art flourishes in the galleries and shops of Pelourinno, Salvador's historic central neighborhood. Women in turbans and white dresses with lacy full skirts sell Afro-Bahian snacks on the sidewalks. Books on Afro-Brazilian religions fill the shelves of popular bookstores, and religious shops sell images and supplies for the worship of orishas, the gods of African-origin religions.

While Salvador is Brazil's "most African" city, African influence is also strong throughout the country. Afro-Bahian food is a mainstay of restaurants in all the states. Orishas are important in Afro-Brazilian religions that have become increasingly popular. . . .

Samba music and dancing are the heart of Brazil's pre-Lenten carnival. "It is not African in origin," [Abdias] Do Nascimento said, "but . . . it has become a great manifestation of African culture."

Salvador's annual celebration is a mass outpouring in which neighborhood blocos, or carnival groups, dance through crowded streets. In the 1970s, a Salvador carnival group began calling itself Ile Aiye. . . .

"It was the first 'bloco Afro' in Bahia," said Ile Aiye member Ana Celia Santos, 40. Other groups copied Ile Aiye, and now there are dozens of blocos Afros. . . .

African influence in Brazilian art has been strong since Aleijadinho, often called the country's greatest architect and sculptor, developed a unique Afro-Brazilian baroque style in the 18th century.

Today, African influence is clearly visible in the work of such well-known Brazilian painters as Emanoel Araujo. . . .

Said Yeda de Castro, director of the Center for African and Oriental Studies at the Federal University of Bahia, . . . "Culture is the basis for the formation of nationality, of the mental structure of a people. The African element in this cultural formation in Brazil is the most important.

Today some Latin Americans of African descent are in trade and commerce, while others are prominent military and political figures. Many own their own businesses or are artists or musicians. Yet, despite their rich heritage and many contributions, in some areas of Latin America the opportunities open to many Africans remain limited.

SECTION 3 REVIEW

CHECKING FOR UNDERSTANDING
1. **Explain** why so many Africans settled in Latin America.
2. **Describe** the role Africans played in the development of the Latin American economy.

CRITICAL THINKING
3. **Predicting Consequences** How do you think Latin America might be different today if Africans had not been brought there as slaves?

Source: William R. Long. "Brazil and Africa: Ties that Bind." *Los Angeles Times*, April 10, 1990, p. A1.

SECTION 4

The Asians

In recent years, Asians have added a new dimension to the varied ethnic composition of Latin America. The Chinese, for example, have made their homes in large numbers in Peru, Cuba, and Panama and in smaller numbers in almost every other Latin American country. First brought to Peru, Cuba, and Panama as laborers, today most are merchants and restaurant owners.

The Japanese have settled mostly in Brazil. The Japanese living there today are descendants of the 250,000 Japanese who immigrated to Brazil originally to work on the coffee plantations. Today, the Japanese citizens of Latin America are engaged in such activities as farming, fishing, trade and commerce, and manufacturing. One, Alberto Fujimori, rose to become president of Peru. Below, a Japanese woman who settled in Brazil discusses her life there and her feelings:

My husband and I came to Brazil after World War II. . . . It was difficult to make a living in Japan and when we heard that Brazil was a land of opportunity, we decided to move. . . .

We settled in the town of Atibaia about 66 kilometers (40 miles) from the big industrial city of São Paulo. Atibaia is famous for growing fruit and flowers. As we are experienced gardeners, we were able to find work quite easily.

It wasn't difficult to get used to Brazil, apart from learning the language. I found Portuguese was very hard to learn, especially because we lived among Japanese people. . . .

The cold weather in Japan meant we could only plant for six months in each year, but here we can work all year round. In Atibaia, we have a garden full of

EXAMINING PHOTOGRAPHS *Like other Brazilian teenagers, these young Japanese wear jeans and are avid fans of popular rock singers and movie stars. Proud of its cultural heritage, the local Japanese community of almost every city in Brazil offers young people instruction in the Japanese language.* **Why did Japanese immigrants come to Brazil originally?**

plants, pine trees and *bonsai*, a traditional Japanese art of growing dwarf trees. On Sundays, we load up our van with plants and go to the Oriental Fair held in the district called Liberdade in the center of São Paulo. We set up a stall on the main street and sell our plants. Liberdade is full of people like ourselves from the Far East. . . .

Selling plants is a good business so long as we do not get caught in a downpour! Last year ferns were very popular. This year we sell more climbing-type plants, called *trepadeiras* in Portuguese. . . .

My husband is one of the few gardeners at the fair who practice *bonsai.* . . . We only have a few of these trees for sale. They are expensive and cost about U.S. $500. Besides gardening, I work during the week at the Ceasa market-place in São Paulo, selling fruit and vegetables.

When my husband and I were settled in Brazil, we started a family. We now have five children. The oldest daughter is a dentist, the second-oldest girl won a scholarship to study in Tokyo in Japan and our two younger daughters and son are students in Brazil.

I like my life here. Brazilians are good people and we are seldom made to feel like strangers. The Japanese living in Brazil make up the largest community of Japanese outside Japan. There are 750,000 Japanese in Brazil, with 125,000 of us living in the state of São Paulo. Even after visiting Japan two years ago, . . . I don't want to return there to live. Brazil is my home.

SECTION 4 REVIEW

CHECKING FOR UNDERSTANDING

1. **Name** the Latin American countries in which most Asians have made their homes.

CRITICAL THINKING

2. **Demonstrating Reasoned Judgment** Imagine you are an Asian who has been offered an opportunity to emigrate to Latin America. List reasons for accepting or refusing the opportunity.

Source: Patricia Robb. "We heard that Brazil was a land of opportunity." *We Live in Brazil.* The Bookwright Press, 1985, pp. 48–49. Reprinted with permission of Franklin Watts, Inc., New York.

Chapter 28 Review

SUMMARY

Because of the blending of the diverse groups and languages found within its borders, Latin America is a very diverse region. Its first settlers were Indians. Mayas, Incas, and Aztecs all had advanced civilizations long before Europeans arrived in the Americas.

The Europeans came as conquerors and destroyed many of the Indians and the civilizations the Indians had built. Over the years, many more Europeans came. Out of the intermarriage of Europeans and Indians came a new group—the *mestizo*.

The early Europeans brought enslaved Africans to work their plantations. Later, more Africans came. Marriages between whites and Africans led to yet another group—mulattoes.

More recently, large numbers of Asians have settled in Latin America. Like the other groups, they have brought with them their traditions and ways of life. Also like the others, they have contributed to the progress and development of Latin America.

USING VOCABULARY

Use the three terms below in a paragraph titled "The Human Diversity of Latin America."

mestizo　　**mulatto**　　*conquistador*

REVIEWING FACTS

1. **Specify** where in the Americas the empires of the Mayas, Incas, and Aztecs were located.
2. **Explain** why so many Indians died after the Europeans arrived on the shores of the Americas.

3. **Discuss** the economic and cultural contributions of Africans to Latin American civilization.
4. **Describe** the immigration patterns of Europeans to Latin America from the 1500's until World War I.
5. **Compare** the circumstances under which Africans and Asians first immigrated to Latin America.

CRITICAL THINKING

1. **Identifying Alternatives** What are some ways in which the various groups of Latin Americans can continue to perpetuate their heritage without endangering national unity?
2. **Making Comparisons** Compare the present-day situation and attitudes of the Indian in Latin America with that of the African in Latin America.

ANALYZING CONCEPTS

1. **Culture** How do you define the term "human diversity"? Based on your definition, do you consider Latin America a truly diverse region?
2. **Diversity** What benefits do you think are derived from having different groups living together in the same country or region?
3. **Choice** If you were an Aztec, Inca, or Maya during the time of the conquistadors, would you have adapted to or resisted your conquerors? Explain.

GEOGRAPHIC THEMES

1. **Movement** How was movement important to the development of Latin America?
2. **Place** What features and/or characteristics give Latin America its own identity?

Reading a Circle Graph

Graphs present numerical information in a visual format. They can condense large amounts of information into simple diagrams. Different kinds of graphs serve different purposes. *Circle graphs* show the relationship of parts to a whole. Also called *pie graphs*, they resemble pies cut into slices. Each slice represents a fraction of the whole pie. The following steps will help you read circle graphs:

- Read the graph title to determine the subject.
- Study the labels and key to understand what each part of the graph represents.
- Compare the sizes of the parts to draw conclusions about the subject.

EXAMPLE

The circle graph below illustrates the distribution of different age groups in Mexico. The whole circle represents the entire population, or 100 percent. Each colored section represents an age group. The key to the right of the graph explains which color represents each age group. For example, green stands for people who are 0-14 years old. What color represents people over 60? *(red)* What percentage of Mexico's population is 0-14 years old? *(36.5%)* Does Mexico have more people over 60 or under 15? *(under 15)*

PRACTICE

Study the circle graphs below and then answer these questions.

1. What is the subject of this graph?
2. What color represents agricultural workers?
3. What does the color blue stand for?
4. In which country does a greater portion of the population work in agriculture?
5. Which sectors account for about the same percentage of workers in Mexico and Chile?
6. What are the biggest differences in the distribution of labor in these countries?
7. What does this imply about their economies?

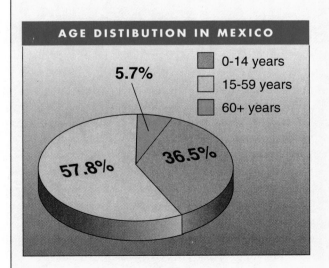

AGE DISTIBUTION IN MEXICO

Key:
- 0-14 years
- 15-59 years
- 60+ years

5.7%
57.8%
36.5%

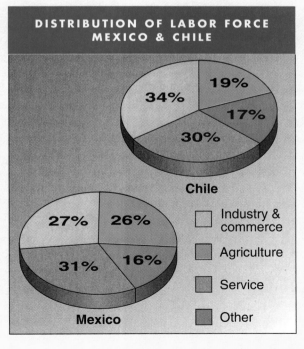

DISTRIBUTION OF LABOR FORCE MEXICO & CHILE

Chile: 19%, 17%, 30%, 34%

Mexico: 26%, 16%, 31%, 27%

Key:
- Industry & commerce
- Agriculture
- Service
- Other

People and Places to Know
El Salvador, Carnival, Pelé

Key Terms to Define
aristocracy, *nouveaux riches*, *hacienda*, godparent, *fiesta*, *fútbol*, *personalismo*, *hombre de confianza*

Objectives to Learn

1. **Characterize** Latin America's three social classes.
2. **Discuss** the role of the family in Latin America.
3. **Explain** common Latin American philosophies of life.

Latin American weavers

464

The Social Fabric

> "There are two worlds of San Salvador, the one of the middle class and rich and the far larger one of the poor. The chasm between those worlds was riveted in my mind each morning as I jogged on the south edge of the capital along the Autopista Sur. . . . Just before the junction of the *autopista* and the Pan American Highway, an entrepreneur put in a go-cart track. . . . Adjacent to it a towering billboard advertises imported golf shirts. Under the billboard . . . are the dirt-floor shacks—sticks, mud, and cardboard somehow kept together under rusting corrugated tin held in place by rocks.
>
> Running on, I would come to the posh residential districts. On one side of the street are the expensive, modern houses, with swimming pools and well-tended gardens. On the other side are the ravines. . . . Into them are plunged shanties and shacks, where extended families share the dirt. From their porches or glassed-in dining rooms, the wealthy can gaze out across the city's expanse, across the top of the ravines. The misery beneath them is not visible. The capital is ringed by a belt of squalid, grimy neighborhoods . . . where merchants peddle their wares from ramshackle clapboard shops and women spread fruits and vegetables on the ground in open-air markets.
>
> But the most glaring contrasts are outside the capital. A paved road leading south from the capital is for the convenience of those who can afford to go to the Pacific coast beaches, where the wealthy have their private clubs or second homes. . . .
>
> But get off the paved roads . . . and you enter a semifeudal society. . . .
>
> Rural Salvadoran villages are built around a central square. The whitewashed Catholic church dominates one side. The other three sides are continuous rows of dull brown mud walls, with veneers of thin plaster. . . . Weeds grow out of the tiles over eaves that angle down over wooden walkways. Outside these villages are clusters of mud hovels, bisected by rutted dirt paths. . . . In the dry season, the dirt, ground to a fine dust, is suffocating."

The two worlds of San Salvador, the capital city of the Central American republic of El Salvador, are not unique to that city or even to that nation. In Latin America

Source: From *WEAKNESS AND DECEIT* by Raymond Bonner. Copyright © 1984 by Raymond Bonner. Reprinted by permission of Time Books, a division of Random House, Inc.

as a whole, wealth and poverty often exist side by side. Here, social class and lifestyle generally hinge on wealth. Here, also, a deep chasm separates the lower class from the upper and middle classes. The wealthy tend to be very wealthy and the poor to be very poor.

SECTION 1

Social Class

In most Latin American nations, there are three social classes—the upper class, the middle class, and the lower class. The upper class is made up of the **aristocracy** and the *nouveaux riches*. The aristocracy are, for the most part, those people descended from the wealthy landowners of the past. The *nouveaux riches* are those people who have made their fortunes in this century through their own efforts and hard work.

The middle class is largely a product of the twentieth century and is growing rapidly. The growth is due to changes that have been taking place in Latin America in recent years. As industry and government have grown, more white-collar and professional jobs have opened up.

The lower class is made up of the rural poor and the urban poor. In most of Latin America, the lower class far outnumbers the middle and upper classes.

HARD WORK, LITTLE REWARD

Within the rural lower class, the biggest group is composed of peasants. Some peasants own and work their own small plots of land. Others work on **haciendas**, large estates owned by the wealthy. In return for tilling the fields, they receive a small plot of land for themselves and their families. Often this is the same land their fathers and grandfathers worked during colonial times.

Another group of the rural lower class is made up of wage hands who generally work on large commercial farms that raise such

EXAMINING PHOTOGRAPHS *North along the coast from São Paulo live most of Brazil's aristocracy, like this Brazilian who owns a large family estate. In what ways do the upper and middle classes differ?*

EXAMINING PHOTOGRAPHS *A middle-class family in Quito, the capital of Ecuador, stands proudly in front of their modern home. Why is Latin America's middle class growing so rapidly?*

EXAMINING PHOTOGRAPHS *High in an Andean village in Ecuador, an Indian mother walks with her children in front of the family home, which is made of adobe bricks for protection from the cold. What groups make up the rural lower class? How do they support themselves?*

export crops as sugarcane, cotton, coffee, and bananas. Their wages are low, and more often than not their work is seasonal.

Of those peasants who work their own land, some can barely eke out enough to provide for themselves and their families. The kind of life described below by a Guatemalan Indian woman is typical of that experienced by the rural poor:

I remember from the age of nine going off to the fields with my hoe to help my father. . . . When the fields were full of plants and we had a bit of maize and a few *tortillas*, we were very happy. . . .

We only use wood fires to cook our *tortillas*. First we get up at three in the morning and start grinding and washing the *nixtamal*, turning it into dough by using the grinding stone. . . . The men get up at that time too because they have to sharpen their hoes, machetes, and axes before going off to work. . . . There are no lights in our village so at night we see by the light of *ocotes*. An *ocote* is a piece cut from a pine tree. . . . You can light it with matches. . . .

Our men usually leave around five or half past every morning. They go and tend the maize or cultivate the ground. Some of the women go with them. . . .

Our maize fields aren't in the village itself. They're a short distance away, . . . so we call all our neighbors and we all go together. . . . We usually go home again at six in the evening. Six o'clock is when our men come home, hungry and thirsty, and the woman who stays at home has to make food again. That's when we do all the extra chores in the house. The men tie up the dogs . . . and the women fetch water . . . , chop wood, and prepare the torches. . . . We usually go to bed at ten or half past . . . and since our house is very small, when one person gets up, we all have to get up.

Our house . . . is . . . made of . . . cane; straight sticks of it we find in the fields and fasten together with *agave* fibres. . . . The houses are not very high, because if there's a lot of wind, it can lift the house and carry it away. . . . There are no nails in our houses. . . . Even the roof props, the corners, or anything supporting the house, comes from trees.

We all sleep in there together. The house has two floors; one above, where the corn cobs are stored . . . and another below where we all live. . . . We don't usually-have beds with mattresses or anything like that. We just have our own few clothes and we're used to being cold. . . . We sleep in our clothes, we get up next day, we tidy ourselves up a bit and off to work. . . .

Although there still are more poor people in the country than in the city, the number of urban poor is on the increase. This is due mostly to the millions of people who have migrated from the country to the cities in search of jobs and a better life. Jobs in the city, however, are hard to find, especially for those who are illiterate or have limited skills. Some never find regular work and have to depend on part-time jobs as laborers or as firewood or water carriers. Those who fail to find work may become beggars.

The poverty of the people of the lower class has a strong influence on their way of life. Many marriages, for example, are what is known by some as common-law unions, or unofficial marriages without legal or religious ceremony. These marriages are accepted for several reasons. One is that the cost of a formal wedding and the celebration that follows it could force a bride's family into debt for many years. Another is the problem of divorce. If a common-law marriage fails, the couple can break up without being concerned about legal or religious problems.

Because there is so little money, young children often are expected to forget about school and go to work. In the country, most boys probably will be working in the fields before they are in their teens. In the city, many boys are expected to have a part-time or full-time job by the time they are eight years old. In both the country and the city, girls must begin at a very early age to do household chores and take care of the younger children. These are the luckier ones.

Source: Ann Wright. I, Rigoberta Menchú: An Indian Woman in Guatemala. Verso Editions, (London and New York) 1984, pp. 43–48.

Two years ago, 15-year-old Ramiro Avila López, his parents, and his brothers and sisters left their small village hoping to find a better life in Mexico City. Poor as they are, they have fared better than many:

Colonia Zapata is a neighborhood of many small houses that cling to the side of a steep hill. On the lower slopes of the hill, the houses are made of concrete blocks, but the ones higher up are little more than rough shacks.

The Avilas live . . . in a one-room house with rock walls and a roof of tin sheeting. They have no running water or plumbing, and they get electricity by tapping in (illegally) to a nearby power line.

Like many of their neighbors, the Avilas are squatters on land that they do not own. . . .

During the two years that the Avilas have been in Mexico City, Señor Avila has gone each spring to the United States to look for work. . . . Each month he sends his family a money order, which is just enough to pay for their basic food and clothing.

While his father is gone, 15-year-old Ramiro is the . . . father of the family. . . . He is in charge of his younger brothers and sisters. . . .

Both Ramiro and his 13-year-old brother, Rafael, go to school . . . , but they also have jobs. Rafael attends day school and works afternoons as a clerk in . . . a neighborhood grocery store.

Ramiro himself works during the day as a cook in a *lonchería*, a tiny restaurant with a carry-out counter and a few tables. His day starts at 7 A.M. . . . By 2 P.M., the *lonchería* is closed, and Ramiro has finished. . . . He has earned . . . about $3 for his hard work, which is below the legal minimum wage. . . .

After work, Ramiro attends the . . . Night School for Young Workers. His classes begin at 5 P.M. and end at 9:30. . . . Eventually, he would like to study engineering, but he isn't sure he will be able

EXAMINING PHOTOGRAPHS *This young child sitting outside her makeshift home in El Salvador is not unlike many of the children of the urban poor, who know only a life of extreme poverty.* What happens to many Latin Americans who migrate from the country to the cities in search of a better life?

to stay in school much longer. His books, notepads, and bus fare already cost more than the family can really afford. . . .

Ramiro's 17-year-old sister, Carmela, left school years ago, after she finished the third grade. Her mother needed her help at home caring for the younger members of the family. . . .

AN EASIER LIFE

Things are very different for those of the upper class. The aristocracy is, for the most part, well-educated and cultured. While in the past most of its prestige and wealth was based on old family names and the ownership of large rural landholdings, today many aristocrats make most of their money from business holdings. The *nouveaux riches* do

Source: From *FOCUS ON MEXICO: MODERN LIFE IN AN ANCIENT LAND*, by Louis B. Casagrande and Sylvia A. Johnson. Copyright 1986 by Lerner Publications Company, Minneapolis, MN. Used with permission.

not have the background and, in some cases, the culture of the aristocracy. Both groups, however, live extremely well. One of the most wealthy is the Argentine discussed below:

At the gold-and-white portals of the opulent high-rise at 2095 Libertador Avenue in Buenos Aires, men with pistols bulging under their open vests flank the doorway. Before anyone is allowed into the building, the guards check via walkie-talkie with the building's most prominent resident: Argentina's new Ambassador-at-Large, Amalia Lacroze de Fortabat. She is the country's richest woman, with an estimated net worth of more than $1 billion. "I hate bodyguards," she apologizes, as she escorts a visitor into the elegance of her Louis XVI salon in a duplex apartment on the uppermost floors. "I hired them only after some people

EXAMINING PHOTOGRAPHS *The designs of Venezuelan socialite Carolina Herrera have made her well known in the world of high fashion. How do aristocrats and the* **nouveaux riches** *differ in Latin America?*

tried to kidnap my teenage grandson two years ago." The physical risks of being rich keep rising in Argentina, as they do in any of the debt-strapped, inflation-ridden countries of Latin America. But the rich keep getting richer. . . .

Every country has its rich and poor, but in Latin America the gap between them is especially vast and is growing worse. . . .

The economic forces at work in Latin America can be seen graphically in the lives of the two societies. Argentina's Fortabat fortune—based on a cement monopoly, a chain of radio stations, oil companies and real estate—keeps growing. . . . In the 13 years since her husband died, boasts Ambassador Fortabat, "I've doubled the value of what I've inherited." After a decade of inflation, families that converted their wealth into U.S. dollars have increased their buying power. "Cattle now costs only $15 a head," she explains. "That's no more than a pair of shoes. I'm buying more." Her new purchases will join a herd of steers and cows

on 17 ranches covering an area twice the size of New York City in Argentina's lush Pampas farmlands. Unlike most of her rich compatriots, Fortabat is a philanthropist. After last June's food riots, she quickly responded to a call from the Roman Catholic Church to help three middle-class Buenos Aires neighborhoods establish temporary soup kitchens.[1]

Although other Latin Americans are not as wealthy as Amalia Lacroze de Fortabat, they still live comfortably, as seen below:

Maria Valdez is thirteen and lives in a section of Mexico City called *Las Lomas de Chapultepec* (the Hills of Chapultepec). It is an area of sturdy single-family homes near Mexico City's famous Chapultepec Park. Maria's father is a dentist. Her mother runs a small shop downtown that caters to American tourists. Maria works part-time in the shop. She enjoys her work because it gives her a chance to practice English. English is her favorite subject at school. Maria attends a private school for which her parents pay about fifty dollars a month. . . .

In Maria's house there is a color television, a stereo, and a piano. The Valdez family also owns a car and uses it to escape Mexico City's smog for weekends in the country. When Maria was a little girl, her family visited her uncle in the United States. Maria still has exciting memories of her one and only trip to *Disneylandia [Disneyland]*. . . .

Maria's family has both a maid and a gardener. All of her neighbors have servants too. Domestic help is still cheap for well-to-do Mexicans. Both of Maria's parents come from prominent Mexico City families. Her oldest brother is now attending medical school. Despite the collapse of the peso, Maria's family and her neighbors continue to prosper.[2]

[1]*Source*: Frederick Ungeheuer. "A Chasm of Misery," *Time*, November 6, 1989, pp. 64–65. Copyright 1989 Time Inc. Reprinted by permission.

[2]*Source*: R. Conrad Stein. *Mexico*. Children's Press, 1984, pp. 103–104.

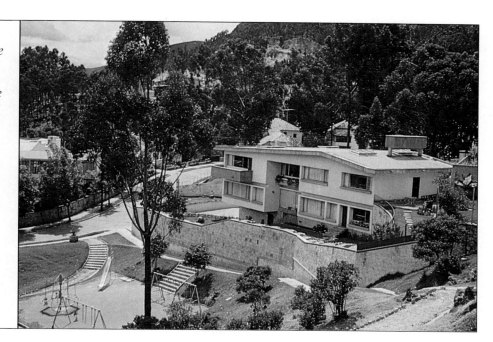

EXAMINING PHOTOGRAPHS *There is little contact between the social classes in Latin America. This comfortable middle-class home in the capital city of Bogotá, Colombia, contrasts sharply with those in which most of the city's residents live. What are some of the modern conveniences of a middle-class home in Nicaragua?*

A NEW GENERATION

In Latin America, it is difficult to determine at times exactly who is a member of the middle class. Incomes range from those of well-to-do bankers to those of poorly paid civil servants or clerks. Housing ranges from high-priced homes in the "better" parts of town to lower-cost ones in less desirable areas. What is considered middle class in one country may well be considered upper class in another. Below, a Nicaraguan talks about the "typical" middle-class family and its lifestyle in his country:

In Nicaragua, a middle class family generally consists of parents with three to six children. Most often they live in the suburbs just outside cities. Their home usually has many family rooms, including three or four bathrooms, a living room, dining room, kitchen, and terrace as well as one or two rooms with baths for servants. Outside are gardens and patios, enclosed by a high hedge or fence made of blocks or bricks.

The houses are of adobe brick or cement block with roofs of zinc sheeting. The ceilings are wood and the floors cement or ceramic brick. Because of the heat, there are a lot of large glass windows. Most of the houses of the neighborhood are of approximately the same value. Apartments are not very popular because people prefer to live in family groups and do not want to live alone or independently.

Each home generally has a refrigerator, washing machine, stereo, radios, toaster, blender, and oven. There generally are two televisions—one color and one black and white. Most people do not have central air conditioning because power is very expensive, but they do have window air conditioners imported from the United States or Japan. Freezers are not very common, because most people prefer to eat fresh food. The same is true of dishwashers. It is cheaper to hire a servant.

Most middle-class families have two or three cars, generally four-cylinder, including a family car and a jeep or pick-up truck to use in their businesses. Big American cars are not popular. Not many families can buy a car every year.

About 90 percent of the young people of middle-class families are full-time students.

When they work, it is in the family business, so they can learn early to administer what will later become theirs. Most of the women do not work outside the home but dedicate themselves to taking care of their families. The few who do work have their own business or profession. They never work for someone else.

EXAMINING PHOTOGRAPHS *This family in Managua, Nicaragua, enjoys a midday meal of rice, fried beans, cheese, and bananas. To Latin Americans, what are some advantages of a close-knit family?*

SECTION 1 REVIEW

CHECKING FOR UNDERSTANDING

1. **Define** aristocracy, *nouveaux riches*, *hacienda*.
2. **Identify** the groups that make up the lower class and the upper class.

CRITICAL THINKING

3. **Making Comparisons** Compare the middle class of Latin America with that of the United States.

SECTION 2

The Family

Latin Americans of all classes have a strong sense of family. For them, "family" includes mother, father, children, grandparents and great-grandparents, uncles and aunts, nieces and nephews, and distant cousins. It also includes **godparents**, people chosen by a mother and father to sponsor their new baby. Godparents are concerned with the child's religious and moral training and help take care of the child if something happens to the parents.

For the most part, the Latin American family is large and closely knit. Even if family members cannot live near one another, they try to keep in constant contact. The family is the center for most social activities, and everyone gathers together to celebrate

birthdays, weddings, and other events. As indicated in this newspaper article, the importance of family remains strong even for those Latin Americans who have emigrated:

A 40-year-old Colombian salesman, who has lived in New York City 10 years, said: "As a father, I see my children as a work of art which I have to present to society. Just as the sculptor shapes the marble until he perfects his work, I have to correct my children and teach them good ways. . . ."

Persons of all ages among the Hispanics interviewed described the family as a major source of personal fulfillment, a precious aspect of Hispanic life. . . .

The words "family unity" were employed by four out of 10 respondents when they were asked to describe traditions that are especially important. . . .

Also mentioned were the "extended family," "fiestas and reunions for unity" and "family meetings. . . ."

Source: Plutarco Pasos. Interview, April 1985.

Source: "U.S. Influence Is Seen as Erosive to Cherished Family," *The Omaha World-Herald*, May 30, 1980, p. 13. Copyright 1980 by *The New York Times*.

CASE STUDY

Latin America

WOMEN

Traditionally, Latin American women were under the control of their husbands, fathers, or brothers and had few legal rights in society. Today, they have the vote in every nation of Latin America. Each year, more attend universities and hold jobs in all the professions. Many have been elected to national legislatures and as mayors of large cities. In Argentina, Bolivia, and Nicaragua, women have served as president.

But progress has been slow and uneven, and in practice, women's legal rights are often not observed. This is especially true when it comes to equal pay for equal work. Progress tends to be limited to urban areas. As indicated by women from the small Peruvian village of Mayobamba, in the countryside change comes slowly:

*On the coast, both spouses express opinions about life in their home. Men begin to leave behind the authoritarian practices of Mayobamba, where women are not allowed to offer opinions. In Lima, the man is still dominant, but less so because of the change in the so-*cial atmosphere. *Also on the coast, women's work is less demanding and women can improve themselves through education. Women have jobs and they still do the work in the home. Women don't have to go to the fields; they don't have to do all the spinning and make all the clothes.*

It is still the case that here a woman is calculated to be an inferior being, a less competent thing that cannot participate. She is only fit to help at home, not publicly.

Some women get accustomed to the fact that their husbands are the heads of everything; others want to participate. But the majority give up leadership to their husbands.[1]

[1]*Source*: Susan C. Bourque and Kay Barbara Warren. *Women of the Andes: Patriarchy and Social Change in Two Peruvian Towns.* University of Michigan Press, 1981, pp. 35, 163, 195.

In Brazil, more than 35 percent of the women were in the work force in 1991. In the following excerpt, a Brazilian newsmagazine reports on some major changes to which this has led:

. . . Women both in and outside of the work force are limiting the size of their families. . . . Thus, the traditional Brazilian family of five or more children has shrunk to have an average of 3.4 children. . . .

With more than one earner in many households, Brazil's standard of living has risen slightly, as shown by the facts that most houses now have electricity and running water and television sales in the past decade increased 1,000 percent.[2]

DRAWING CONCLUSIONS

1. In what ways have women's roles changed in Latin America in recent years?
2. How might you account for the fact that women have made more progress in urban areas than in rural ones?

[2]*Source*: "Women in Brazil." *World Press Review,* March 1991, p. 42.

473

While family ties continue to remain especially important among the wealthy and the poor, many members of the growing urban middle class are finding it harder to maintain them. Most young people of all classes used to remain in their parents' homes even after they married, so it was easy to keep close contact with relatives. Now, many young people move away from home, making it especially hard for those who are illiterate or too poor to use the telephone to keep in touch.

The changed attitude of business and the expansion of government also have had an effect. At one time, Latin Americans could count on family ties to help get them a job. Today, ability is considered to be more important. Also the family used to be responsible for welfare and education. Now it generally is the state.

SECTION 2 REVIEW

CHECKING FOR UNDERSTANDING
1. **Define** godparents.
2. **Discuss** the Latin American sense of family.

CRITICAL THINKING
3. **Drawing Conclusions** Why is the influence of the traditional family beginning to lessen in Latin America?

SECTION 3

Living Life to the Fullest

Most Latin Americans, regardless of background or class, also agree that in order to live life fully, one must feel deeply and strongly about an idea or a person. They have, however, managed to combine with this belief the idea that one should enjoy life today and think about tomorrow when it comes.

There are several reasons for this philosophy. One has to do with physical conditions. Many poor people, for example, believing that they will never escape poverty, see no reason to save for a rainy day. For them, every day is a rainy one. Another reason has to do with geographic location. Much of Latin America is in the tropics, where food must be bought daily and eaten right away or it will spoil. Still another reason relates to the economy. Many Latin American nations are not yet stable economically. When inflation increases, money is worth less. So, it is wiser to spend it while it is worth more.

FIESTAS

Perhaps because of these attitudes, Latin America often is thought of as a land of continuous *fiestas*, or parties. The *fiestas*, however, do not occur very often, and when they do, they serve a purpose. They are a day of relief from the toils and cares of everyday life, a time when a person can forget problems and have a good time.

There are many kinds of *fiestas*. Some last a day and are held in small villages, while others go on for several days and draw tourists from all over the world. One of the most famous *fiestas* is Carnival, which marks the beginning of the Christian Lenten season. Below, two Brazilian writers describe the activities and excitement of the samba schools in the moments before the Carnival celebration begins:

The *abre-alas*, the leading float that symbolizes the [samba] school, is in position. Between it and the allegorical floats that follow come the dancers. The carnival committee is busily at work. The leading figures slowly take up their positions. The musicians tune their instruments. When the command is given, the leading singer, high up on his float, intones the *sambaenredo*, the theme of the samba. In

Arts of Latin America

Many peoples—Indians, Europeans, Africans, and Asians—have contributed to the arts of Latin America. European styles, however, dominated the region's arts for hundreds of years. Today, Latin Americans have developed their own unique styles based on the full richness of their artistic heritage.

? What themes predominate in the arts of Latin America?

ARCHITECTURE
Government buildings in Brasília, Brazil's capital city

SCULPTURE
Wooden figurine from Ecuador

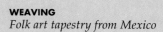

WEAVING
Folk art tapestry from Mexico

DANCING
Festival dancers in Peru

accordance with custom, the entire school listens as he sings it through once and then the musicians take up the melody and everyone starts to sing, repeating the samba two or three times without moving as they await the arrival of any latecomers. Then suddenly, as if by magic, the whole school moves off. This is the beginning of the most beautiful spectacle of popular art in the world. As though out for a stroll, forming a procession, dancing and singing the samba, diffusing joy and rapture, the school parades before us.

SPORTS

At one time, bullfighting was considered the most popular sport of Latin America. In recent years, however, its popularity has dwindled while that of *fútbol,* or soccer, has taken its place. There are both amateur and professional soccer leagues, and children play in leagues while still in grade school.

Source: Amaury Jorio and Hiram Araujo, as quoted by Sergio Alves Teixeira. "Samba Time!" Reprinted from *The Unesco Courier,* December 1989, p. 40.

In Brazil especially, *fútbol* is the national passion and a common ground for most Brazilians. In 1970, Brazil became the first country to win the world soccer championship three times. Every village has some kind of soccer field, and the larger cities have stadiums. In Rio de Janeiro, the stadium can seat 220,000 fans. As with all popular sports, soccer has produced many stars. First among them is the Brazilian known as Pelé, whose story is told below:

As a professional soccer player for 18 years, Pelé made more goals than any other player—1,284—and accumulated titles that included highest scoring player for all the São Paulo area championships between 1957 and 1965, two-time world club champion for the Santos team, three-time world champion, and athlete of the century. Embraced by kings and presidents, applauded in stadiums the world over and received by Pope Paul VI, he was even responsible for a temporary halt in the Biafran War in 1969 when the opposing troops stopped fighting to watch him play. . . .

His story began on October 23, 1940. The son of a soccer forward . . . and his wife . . . , Pelé moved with his family to Belo Horizonte when he was barely two. Later they returned to Tres Coraçoes because his father had injured himself seriously . . . ; the injury ruined his playing career. The family moved to Bauru where Dico (the nickname Pelé comes from his soccer days . . .), the oldest son, took up his father's career. . . .

Pelé's rise in the soccer world happened almost overnight. His mother had him turn down an invitation to play in Rio de Janeiro when he was 15. . . . Later on he was able to accept an invitation from the city of Santos, where he began to train among the best on the first team. . . . His mother and grandmother didn't want him to go, but his father and brothers favored the move. Pelé resisted, cried and ended up signing the contract. . . . In 1956 he

won the first of a seemingly endless series of city championship titles for Santos. The next year, in June, he was visiting Bauru when he heard over the radio that he had been chosen for the national team.

Pelé played 91 games and scored 76 goals for the Brazilian national team. . . . He stopped playing for the team in 1971 and refused to play in the 1974 World Cup in Germany. That same year . . . he retired and left Santos, but he returned to the game to play in the United States for the New York-based Cosmos from 1975 to 1977.

Pelé is the only soccer player to have won three world championship games. In addition, he won two world club championships for Santos. . . . Pelé won international matches all over the world. . . . In total, in Santos and on the national team, he earned 52 titles. His entire star-studded career was a great show that continues today off the playing field. . . .

Pelé, back on the playing field in 1980 for the Beckenbauer farewell game at Giant Stadium, soon became such a focus of general attention that the French newspaper *L'Equipe* declared him the athlete of the century.

Other sports attract supporters as well. Latin Americans have gained world renown as tennis, golf, and baseball players. Baseball is especially popular in the islands of the Caribbean and in the nations that touch upon the Caribbean. In the Andean areas of Chile and Argentina, skiing is enjoyed by many. In Brazil, the beaches of Rio de Janeiro draw people from all over the world.

FUN AND GAMES

Like other young people all over the world, those of Latin America find many different activities to fill their leisure time.

Source: Rodolfo Konder. "Pelé." AMERICAS, Volume 35, 9/10, 1983, pp. 9–11. Reprinted from *AMERICAS*, a bimonthly magazine published by the General Secretariat of the Organization of American States in English and Spanish.

EXAMINING PHOTOGRAPHS *These children are netting crabs in the sparkling, clear waters of the Caribbean Sea. What other recreational sport, besides fishing, is popular in the Caribbean region?*

EXAMINING PHOTOGRAPHS *In Hernández, Mexico, these young adults occupy some of their leisure time by gathering on the stairs of a public building to listen to a friend play songs on his guitar. What other activities do many of the young people of Latin America, such as María Catalina Paz, enjoy?*

Below, a Colombian high school student talks about what she and her friends do:

My name is María Catalina Paz. I am 18 years old and was born in Popayán, a very small city where everyone knows everyone else.

The young Popayanese is very fun-loving, very studious, and very conservative. I say conservative because for generations they have done what their ancestors did. They are fun-loving because they are always looking for something to amuse themselves, and Popayan, being a small city, does not have a lot of diversions for *cocacolos,* young people.

Generally there are groups made up of high school girls and university boys, who are four or five years older. Each weekend we meet to do something. We go to parties, which we have often. They begin between 9 or 10 P.M. and end about 2 or 3 A.M. We dance *cumbia* or *salsa.* When there are no parties, we meet at someone's house and sing, talk, play roulette, or tell scary stories.

During the day, we walk to different places. We enjoy this a lot because during these walks we talk with each other and see everyone. Other times we go to the farms of some of our friends, where there is a lot to do. We can go horseback riding, walk, have water fights, or go swimming

in the river or a swimming pool with our shoes and all our clothes on. When it begins to get dark, we almost always have hot chocolate with cheese and sit around a bonfire. We play the guitar and sing.

I have four best friends. We have been together since first grade and are very close. We always study together, talk to one another on the telephone, and exercise, shop, and go to the movies together. As we all go to the same girls' school, we are together a lot.

At times, when I am alone, I read or study because I am interested in learning more about cultures in general. Sometimes, I like to do things with my hands, like knit, cook, or sew. But what I always try to do is be active and be sure that I am very happy.

SECTION 3 REVIEW

CHECKING FOR UNDERSTANDING
1. **Define** *fiesta, fútbol.*
2. **Name** some common forms of recreation in Latin America.

CRITICAL THINKING
3. **Analyzing Information** Why do Latin Americans think that life should be enjoyed today?

Source: María Catalina Paz, Interview, April 1985.

Cultural Values

PERSONALISMO

FOCUSING ON THE ISSUE Read the discussion of *personalismo* that follows. Based on it, the accompanying photographs, and the information in the chapter, answer the following questions:

1. How do you interpret the concept of personalism? In what ways is your interpretation different from the Latin American one? In what ways is it the same?

2. In what ways do you think *personalismo* is reflected in Latin American class structure? Family life? Leisure activities? Attitudes about the role of women?

One of the principal themes the Latin Americans inherited from their Iberian ancestors is *personalismo*, or personalism. They believe strongly that each individual is unique and has an inner dignity and personality. A strong sense of personal honor and sensitivity to praise, insult, and slight is just part of *personalismo*.

Personalismo is not concerned with outward signs of equality, such as equality before the law, but with a person's inner qualities. Social standing has no influence on *personalismo*. Every person has inner qualities that he or she can fulfill. A boss, for example, is expected to respect the personalism of each employee and show an active concern for him or her. The boss, therefore, may treat an employee as an employee, but never as a nonentity.

At times, personalism discourages involvement with large numbers of people. The individual is somewhat reluctant to form close associations with persons who are not relatives or close friends. Among family and friends, one can just relax and be the way he or she wants to be. Thus, a friend is an *hombre de confianza*, a person with whom one has a close and well-defined friendship, a person in whom one has complete confidence.

Chapter 29 Review

SUMMARY

In Latin America, social class and lifestyle hinge on wealth. There are three social classes—upper class, middle class, and lower class. Members of the upper class—the aristocracy and the *nouveaux riches*—lead comfortable lives because of their wealth. The income of the middle class varies greatly, making it hard to determine who its members are. Most, however, can afford to live relatively well. On the other hand, members of the lower class, both urban and rural, all have one thing in common—they are poor.

Latin Americans of all classes have a strong sense of family. Most also agree that in order to live life fully, one must feel deeply and strongly about an idea or person. Enjoy today, they say, and think about tomorrow when it comes. Enjoyment during leisure time often takes the form of *fiestas*, sports, and other types of recreation.

USING VOCABULARY

Imagine that you are an exchange student in a Latin American country. Use the terms below in a letter home about what you have observed and experienced.

aristocracy	*fiesta*
nouveaux riches	*fútbol*
hacienda	*personalismo*
godparent	*hombre de confianza*

REVIEWING FACTS

1. **Characterize** the three social classes of Latin America.
2. **Explain** the relationship in Latin America between social class, wealth, and lifestyle.
3. **State** what twentieth-century developments have affected the growth of Latin America's middle class.

4. **Compare** the Latin American concept of family with your concept of family.
5. **Explain** why Latin Americans celebrate *fiestas* such as Carnival.

CRITICAL THINKING

1. **Predicting Consequences** What do you think might happen to the distinctions between the classes if the middle class continues to grow? How do you think this will affect the development of the region?
2. **Making Comparisons** Explain how the Latin American philosophy of enjoying life today and not worrying about tomorrow compares with the one prevalent in the United States. Give possible reasons for any differences between the two.
3. **Predicting Consequences** Many Latin American children never go to school and begin working at age eight or younger. How might your life be different today if you were one of those children?

ANALYZING CONCEPTS

1. **Culture** How do Latin Americans view life?
2. **Political Systems** In what ways does the class system of Latin America impact the lifestyles of the people?
3. **Identity** How might you describe the role played in Latin American society by each of the three social classes?

GEOGRAPHIC THEMES

1. **Human-Environment Interaction** Explain how physical environment has affected the Latin American philosophy of life.
2. **Regions** Discuss the features that unite the diverse countries and peoples of Latin America as a cultural region.

Conducting Interviews

People often prefer to hear or read about events directly from people who have actually witnessed them. Often, this information is obtained through an *interview* or a conversation between a person seeking information (interviewer) and another who can provide it (interview subject).

A good interview depends largely upon the preparation and skill of the interviewer. An effective interview has three parts: preparation, the interview itself, and the report. Steps for performing each part are given below:

Preparing for an Interview

- Identify the topic of the interview and decide who could provide information.
- Research the topic and write questions that explore the topic.
- In requesting an interview with the subject, describe the topic and purpose of the interview. Make an appointment and ask permission to record the discussion.

Conducting the Interview

- Bring a notebook, pencils, and, if available, a cassette recorder, batteries, and tapes.
- Ask questions slowly and clearly. Listen carefully, taking notes if necessary. Ask the subject to clarify confusing responses. Record direct quotations exactly.
- At the end, record the subject's name, occupation, and place of business. Request permission to use direct quotations and thank the subject for the interview.

Reporting the Interview

- Using the information in your notes and/or on your recorder, write a report of the interview. Omit repetitious and irrelevant material.
- If necessary, call the subject to clarify points and revise the report.

EXAMPLE

The sample interview below is based on the interview with María Paz on page 478 about leisure activities for young Colombians. Questions have been added to suggest how the interview may have been conducted. In this sample, "IN" stands for interviewer, and "MP" stands for María Paz.

IN: What is your full name?
MP: My name is María Catalina Paz.
IN: How old are you, María? And where were you born?
MP: I am 18 years old and was born in Popayan, a very small city where everyone knows everyone else.
IN: How would you describe the young people in Popayan?
MP: The young Popayanese is very fun-loving, very studious, and very conservative.
IN: Why do you call them conservative?

MP: I say conservative because for generations they have done what their ancestors did.
IN: And what do you mean by fun-loving?
MP: They are fun-loving because they are always looking for something to amuse themselves, and Popayan, being a small city, does not have a lot of diversions for *cocacolos,* young people.

The first three questions focus on basic facts about the subject—name, age, place of birth. The next question, "How would you describe the young people in Popayan?" begins to address the main topic—lifestyles of young Colombians. Why did the interviewer ask the next two questions? *(to clarify the statement that young Popayanese are fun-loving and conservative)* What should be the interviewer's next question? *(Possible answers include: What do they do to amuse themselves? What do they do on weekends? After school?)*

PRACTICE

Imagine that you are a journalist writing an interview for a Latin American magazine. Your topic is the ambitions and goals of American teenagers. Request an interview with one of your friends or classmates, write at least 10 interview questions, conduct the interview, and then write a report.

People and Places to Know
Bartolomé de Las Casas, Protestantism

Key Terms to Define
anticlerical, agrarian reform

Objectives to Learn
1. **Discuss** the establishment of Roman Catholicism in Latin America.
2. **Explain** the anticlerical movement during the national period in Latin America.
3. **Analyze** religious trends in present-day Latin America.

A 200-year-old Catholic Church in Bolivia

Prayer and Politics

> *"* The pilgrimage had been described as a "purely pastoral" visit. But as Pope John Paul II's eight-day trip to Central America and Haiti drew to a close . . . , the dividing line between religion and politics seemed to have all but disappeared. . . . Said a Vatican official traveling with the Pope: "Even when he says Mass it seems to have political implications. . . ."
>
> John Paul's visits to Guatemala, Honduras, Belize and Haiti drew enthusiastic crowds in the hundreds of thousands. Laboring well into the night, Guatemalans laid an 8½-mile [13.6-kilometer] carpet of colored sawdust and grass, decorated with pictures of doves and brilliant floral designs for the papal motorcade. . . .
>
> John Paul traveled by helicopter to Quezaltenango, some 100 miles [160 kilometers] northwest of the capital, for a meeting with Guatemala's Indians. . . . Demanding legislation to protect the Indians, John Paul told a crowd dressed in bright colored handwoven outfits that "the church is aware of the discrimination you suffer and the injustices you must put up with, the serious difficulties you have in defending your lands and your rights, the frequent lack of respect for your culture and customs."
>
> [In neighboring Honduras] . . . the Pope used every opportunity to preach his message of justice. . . . In San Pedro Sula, the country's second largest city, he urged workers in newly industrialized areas to form trade unions and called for a wage system that took account of each laborer's needs. *"*

Pope John Paul II's visit to Central America, discussed above by a North American journalist, demonstrates the influence of the Roman Catholic Church in Latin America. Here, Catholicism is more than a religion. It is a way of life. Crosses and small chapels dot the countryside, and each village has a patron saint whose name it often bears. Each family and family member also has a patron saint. So do such groups as truck drivers, labor unions, and childless women.

Source: John Kohan. "Things Must Change Here." *Time,* March 21, 1983, pp. 38–39. Copyright 1983 Time Inc. Reprinted by permission.

The influence of the Church, however, has its limits. In Latin America, where today political and social turmoil affect more than one country, the Church has found that while it can have a strong influence on political life, it cannot decree the path political life will follow.

In recent years, the Church has been faced with a new challenge as well—the rapid growth of Protestantism. Each year millions of Latin Americans convert to some form of Protestant Christianity. It is estimated that at least 10 percent of Latin Americans are now Protestant.

The Church in the Colonial Era

The influence of Roman Catholicism in Latin America dates back to the Spanish conquest of the Americas in the 1500's, for with the sword came the cross. The priests who came to the New World with the *conquistadores* (kōn·kēs·tah·DOR·āhz) soon took charge of the spiritual needs of the Spanish and Portuguese settlers and tended to the needs of the enslaved Africans. They also worked to convert the Indians to Christianity.

THE RIGHT TO RULE

The Spanish conquest led to a great controversy over the legality of the conquest itself and the right of the Spaniards to convert the Indians living in the conquered lands. Many Spaniards agreed with the Spanish writer and court historian, Juan Ginés de Sepúlveda. He argued that Indians were ignorant barbarians filled with vices, unable to take charge of their own lives. For this reason, the Indians had to accept rule by their superiors—the Spanish—who would civilize them and bring them religion. If they did not accept willingly, the Spanish had the right to conquer and rule them. In this way, the superior civilization and the Catholic faith of the Spaniards could be imposed on the Indians.

Some Spaniards, however, favored the point of view of Father Bartolomé de Las Casas, who maintained that the Spaniards had no right to convert the Indians by force. De Las Casas' ardent defense of the Indians made him unpopular with many Spaniards. Below, he explains why the Indians should not be forced to accept Spanish rule or the Catholic religion:

> [The Indians] . . . have a lawful, just, and natural government. Even though they lack the art and use of writing, they are not wanting in the capacity and skill to rule and govern themselves, both publicly and privately. Thus they have kingdoms, communities, and cities that they govern

EXAMINING ART *In this painting of Spanish* conquistadores, *Hernán Cortés, the bearded figure third from right, is leading the 1519 Spanish expedition to the Aztec Empire, 400 miles (640 kilometers) inland from the Atlantic Ocean. Cortés is accompanied by soldiers, Indian porters, and the young Indian woman Malinche, who served as one of his interpreters. What role did Catholic priests play in the European conquest of the Americas?*

wisely according to their laws and customs. Thus their government is legitimate and natural. . . . From these statements we have no choice but to conclude that the rulers of such nations enjoy the use of reason and that their people and the inhabitants of their provinces do not lack peace and justice. Otherwise they would not be established or preserved as political entities for long. . . . Therefore not all barbarians are irrational or natural slaves or unfit for government. . . . Now if we shall have shown that among our Indians . . . there are important kingdoms, large numbers of people who live settled lives in a society, great cities, kings, judges, and laws, persons who engage in commerce, buying, selling, lending, and the other contracts of the law of nations, will it not stand proved that the Reverend Doctor Sepúlveda has spoken wrongly and viciously against peoples like these. . . . From the fact that the Indians are barbarians it does not necessarily follow that they are incapable of government and have to be ruled by others, except to be taught about the Catholic faith. . . . They are not ignorant, inhuman, or bestial. Rather, long before they had heard the word Spaniard they had properly organized states, wisely ordered by excellent laws, religion, and custom. They cultivated friendship and, bound together in common fellowship, lived in populous cities in which they wisely administered the affairs of both peace and war justly and equitably, truly governed by laws that at very many points surpass ours. . . .

The second argument is that since the Church . . . never forces unbelievers who are its subjects in law and fact . . . to hear the word of God, the conclusion is inescapable that unbelievers who are not subject either in law or fact must not be forced to hear the word of God.

The third argument is the fact that Christ commanded only that the gospel be preached throughout the world. So wherever the gospel is preached, Christ's command is considered to have been carried out. . . .

Note that Christ did not teach that those who refuse to hear the gospel must be forced or punished. Rather, he will reserve their punishment to himself on the day of judgment. . . .

Now since Christ's words and actions should be examples for us, I do not know if anything more express or certain can be discovered than the fact that, in instructing his disciples, he taught them that men must not be forced to listen to the gospel. . . .

. . . Let us represent our teacher and savior by our deeds, and then those who have been ordained to go from paganism to eternal life will hasten of their own free will to the sheepfold of Christ. . . . The most effective solution is for them to see the Christian life shine in our conduct. But to advance the power of arms is not Christian example but a pretext for stealing the property of others and subjugating their provinces. . . .

From the foregoing it is evident that war must not be waged against the Indians under the pretext that they should hear the preaching of Christ's teaching, even if they may have killed preachers, since they do not kill the preachers as preachers or Christians as Christians, but as their most cruel public enemies, in order that they may not be oppressed or murdered by them.

WEALTH AND POWER

In time, the Church grew in wealth and power. In order to serve the needs of everyone in the colonies, priests had to carry their religion outside their churches and missions. Religion quickly became a part of all aspects of community life. An unsafe passage across a mountain was marked by a cross or a small chapel. Each ranch had its own chapel and

Source: Quoted from Bartolomé de las Casas. *In Defense of the Indians,* ed. Stafford Poole, C.M. (DeKalb: Northern Illinois University Press, 1974), pp. 9–11, 12, 13, 14. Used with permission of the publisher.

EXAMINING PHOTOGRAPHS *Some of the finest buildings in colonial Latin America were huge stone churches constructed in elaborate styles. The churches contained exquisitely carved columns and ornate sculptures, and made extensive use of gold and silver.* *What role did church leaders have in colonial Latin America?*

each village and individual family had its own patron saint. The Church alone provided schools, hospitals, orphanages, and welfare services.

Much of the Church's power and wealth came from its close ties with the government. Spanish and Portuguese rulers delegated a great deal of authority to Church leaders. As a result, Church leaders played an important part in almost everything that happened.

SECTION 1 REVIEW

CHECKING FOR UNDERSTANDING
1. **Specify** when Catholicism came to Latin America.
2. **Explain** how the Church became so wealthy and powerful in Latin America.

CRITICAL THINKING
3. **Analyzing Information** Father Bartolomé de Las Casas did not think that the Spaniards had a right to conquer the Indians and force them to convert to Christianity. What arguments did he offer to support this view?

SECTION 2
The National Period

In time, many of the colonists, discontent with foreign rule, sought independence. Some clergy, like Father Miguel Hidalgo in Mexico in 1810, backed the independence movements. Most Church leaders, however, were content with life as it was and backed the European rulers. When independence came, the new political leaders began to question the Church's power. They were joined by **anticlericals**, people who felt that the Church had too much social, economic, and political power. The anticlericals, most of whom were Catholics, were not anti-Catholic. They simply believed that the Church should be less worldly and more spiritual and should be put under State control and its involvement limited to religious matters.

The anticlericals did not like that Church-owned lands and businesses were not sub-

EXAMINING PHOTOGRAPHS *In Latin America, many churches built during the colonial period are still used as places of worship and attract visitors interested in their history. This church in Puerto Rico was built during the 1600's and is one of the oldest in the Caribbean area.* What was the attitude of the anticlericals toward church property?

ject to taxation. They felt that this gave the Church an unfair advantage and deprived the government of badly needed funds. They also objected to the Church's large landholdings, which, according to Church law, could not be sold. In Mexico, for example, before land reform became law, the Church owned one-half of the country's most valuable land. This greatly reduced the amount of land available to the people.

One of the most outspoken and determined anticlericals was Benito Juárez, who, in the mid-1800's, served as deputy in the national legislature, governor of the state of Oaxaca, and president of Mexico. With these words, Juárez explained why he believed the Church's power had to be curbed:

I returned to Oaxaca and dedicated myself to the exercise of my profession. The clergy still found themselves in full possession of their exemptions and prerogatives, and their close alliance with the civil power gave them an influence that was almost omnipotent [all powerful]. The exemption that removed them from the jurisdiction of the common courts served them as a shield against the law of safe-conduct so that they could indulge . . . in every excess and every injustice. The taxes that were the rights of the parishes were a dead letter, and the payment of the perquisites [special fees] was determined in accordance with the greedy wills of the parish priests. There were . . . some honorable and upright priests who limited themselves to charging what was just, and who did not rob the faithful, but these . . . were very rare, and their example, far from deterring the evil ones from their abuses, resulted in their own censure. . . . Meanwhile, the citizens groaned in their oppression and misery, because the fruit of their work, their time, and their personal services was entirely devoted to the satisfaction of the insatiable greed of their so-called shepherds. Justice, if they took steps to seek it, was usually

EXAMINING PHOTOGRAPHS
Many Catholic holidays, festivals, and saint's days are celebrated with processions like this one in Nicaragua, in which men are carrying a statue of Christ and the cross through their rural village. Some worshipers join the procession, while others show their respect by kneeling in prayer as the procession passes. **How has the separation of Church and State affected the traditional role of the Catholic Church in Latin America?**

deaf to them, and commonly they received as their own answer scorn or imprisonment.

Bit by bit, the anticlericals made their reforms. The Church lost many of its property holdings and had to give up many business activities. This led the Church to lose much of its wealth and be short of money.

SECTION 2 REVIEW

CHECKING FOR UNDERSTANDING
1. **Define** anticlerical.
2. **Enumerate** the anticlericals' main objections to the Church.

CRITICAL THINKING
3. **Expressing Problems Clearly** What problems did the anticlericals hope to remedy with their reforms?

Source: Charles Allen Smart. *Viva Juárez!: A Biography.* J.B. Lippincott Co., 1963, pp. 64–65, 67.

SECTION 3
The Church Today

In some areas of Latin America the influence of Catholicism is not as strong as it was. About one-half of the countries of Latin America have ordered the separation of Church and State. In the countries where this separation has taken place, religious marriage ceremonies no longer are considered legal and must be accompanied by a civil ceremony. Religious instruction no longer is allowed in public schools, and the State has taken over most educational, health, and welfare services.

There are several other reasons for the decline of the Church's influence. Two major ones are the lack of priests and the lack of funds. Although there are more than 100 million more people in Latin America today than there were 15 years ago, there are only about 12,000 more priests. The lack of funds is just as serious. Most of the ornate churches, pieces of art, and elaborate altars date back to the times before the Church lost its wealth, and they cannot be sold to raise funds.

Despite its problems, however, the Church is not completely removed from politics and continues to have influence. Members of the clergy continue to take public stands when issues involve matters of faith and reform.

One of the clergy's main concerns is **agrarian reform**, the more equal division of land among the people. In recent years, priests have organized cooperatives that buy and sell at fair prices for members. They also have helped Church lay people form labor unions and political parties that point out

the need for social justice and democratic principles. The article below discusses efforts in Haiti in the 1980's. Later, in the early 1990's, a Roman Catholic priest, Jean-Bertrand Aristide, briefly served as president.

He is a young Roman Catholic priest ministering in the eastern hills. . . . His parish lies in a dry coffee-growing region a half-day's walk from the nearest road passable by bus or car. . . .

"I help them to ask questions," the priest says of his work with the peasants. "We are still in discussion. We don't know where we are going. . . . "

Traditionally as quiescent as the peasants themselves, the Catholic Church of Haiti has emerged . . . as the first broad-based group to mount sustained criticism of the quarter-century-old Duvalier regime. . . .

Most foreign priests fought voodoo, the native folk religion. The new priests are trying to assimilate it into Catholicism. And . . . "the liturgy went into the vernacular, Creole, which is what 90% of the people speak," says the Rev. Thomas Wenski. . . . "The drum was brought in, and Haitian songs." These innovations, Father Wenski says, "brought about a renewal of the church."

With these changes, priests here say, the newly nationalistic church of Haiti gained in confidence and closeness to the people. Many priests feel the church is strongest—perhaps even more influential than the government—in the back country, where once it was remote and weak. "The church has been doing a lot of work at the base, in little groups," says a priest familiar with the peasant education programs.

All of the Church's political efforts are not as effective as it would like. In some countries, divorce laws have been passed and

EXAMINING PHOTOGRAPHS *In Bolivia, a Catholic priest leads Indian children to a Mass held in a courtyard outside the church. What is one of the main concerns of the clergy in Latin America today?*

Source: Thomas E. Ricks. "Defying Duvalier, The Pope Visits Haiti Just as Church There Is Challenging Regime." Reprinted by permission of *The Wall Street Journal.* Copyright 1983, Dow Jones & Company, Inc. All Rights Reserved Worldwide.

family planning programs established in spite of Church resistance. In several countries, a fear of eventual socialism and communism has undermined the Church's efforts to bring about agrarian reform.

But even with such setbacks, the Church continues in its efforts to bring about change and reform. Many of the clergy have begun to live and work directly with the most needy. Padre Jaime Hilgeman, an American Maryknoll missionary priest, is one of those clergy. Below, he talks about his life and his work in Jardim Veronica, a community on the outskirts of São Paulo, Brazil:

I chose Brazil because Maryknoll missionaries were already doing exciting work there and also I wanted to learn a new language. Brazilians speak Portuguese whereas . . . other Latin Americans speak Spanish. . . .

When I arrived in Brazil, I spent four months in Rio de Janeiro learning Portuguese. After that, I visited the slum districts of São Paulo, which is the biggest city in Brazil. It looks like a rich and prosperous city, but there is great poverty in many areas. . . .

I particularly liked one of our communities in São Paulo called Jardim Veronica . . . I rented a simple three-room stucco house close to the *favela* (shanty town) that comes within the boundary of our community. For three years I've been sharing the house with Lucas, a twenty-year-old Brazilian friend.

In Jardim Veronica, I spend my days working with needy people to build a small Christian community which the Maryknolls call a "base" community. By living with the poor, I can understand their problems better and work toward solving them. The community needs paved streets, running water, regular waste disposal, schools, and medical services. . . .

Most of the neighbors work at the nearby glass and chemical factories. In some plants, working conditions are bad and

wages low. . . . In the evenings, we hold neighborhood meetings at the homes of the workers to discuss what we can do to improve the working situation. . . .

SECTION 3 REVIEW

CHECKING FOR UNDERSTANDING
1. **Define** agrarian reform.
2. **Give examples** of the circumstances under which the Catholic clergy takes a public stand in Latin America today.

CRITICAL THINKING
3. **Determining Cause and Effect** Discuss the effects the separation of religion and government has had on Catholicism.

SECTION 4

A New Force

Traditionally, Latin America has been overwhelmingly Catholic. Since the 1960's a new force—Protestantism—has grown at an incredible rate. If Protestantism keeps growing at the rate it has been, by the year 2000 most Brazilians, Guatemalans, Salvadorans, and Hondurans will be Protestants, as will 40 percent of Chileans and about one-third of Costa Ricans and Bolivians.

One journalist summed up the appeal of Protestantism in this way: "The Protestant Gospel offers Latin Americans new hope and spiritual solace . . . amid the dispiriting realities of everyday life." In the following excerpt, a British sociologist offers his thoughts on the "explosion of Protestantism":

In Guatemala City you can hardly fail to notice the number of public buses decorated with evangelical texts. Close to the

Source: Patricia Robb. "The largest Catholic population in the world." *We Live in Brazil.* The Bookwright Press, 1985, pp. 50–51. Reprinted with permission of Franklin Watts, Inc., New York.

tall iron tower commemorating the 1871 liberal revolution are a converted cinema with *"Jesus salva"* [Jesus saves] on its marquee and the tent-like structure of an independent church. . . . As you trundle and bump through the barrios there is a storefront church every two or three hundred yards. . . .

When I visited Merida . . . I was immediately asked, "Whose side are you on?" . . . A hospitable Mexican anthropologist kindly took me . . . to the . . . Protestant village of Xochenpiche. . . . The first thing we saw . . . was the Catholic church, with doors locked and roof fallen in. . . . In the center of the village a Presbyterian bible school stood quietly in the shimmering heat and most amazing of all, a chapel painted in pastel colors which had strayed straight out of the landscape of Presbyterian/Methodist Wales. . . . However, the distaste of my friendly anthropologist was very evident. "I do not like to see it," he confessed. I was given to understand that the souls in the village had been bought . . . by American money, agricultural knowhow, and facilities.

There is . . . much more to it than money and clinics, as I found out when I visited the Girls' Bible School in Merida. Sixteen-year-olds tumbled across the threshold to sing spiritual songs to me in Mayan and Spanish. . . . Clearly the message is spread by popular music. And it also offers roles and opportunities to young women. I was told that next day the girls would be out together in the villages singing—and preaching. . . .

The pastor then handed me his most potent weapon: his translation of the psalms into the Mayan tongue. Everywhere in Latin America there is a connection between saving souls and salvaging languages. . . .

When I went to Rio de Janeiro I encountered more controversies. . . . One young scholar referred to the remarkable courage and stamina of evangelical missionaries

EXAMINING PHOTOGRAPHS *These Guatemalan Indians are participating in a Protestant worship service. If present trends continue, what position will Protestantism hold in Guatemala by the year 2000?*

going to work under appalling conditions among remote tribes. But another scholar . . . plainly saw the followers of the new faith as deluded defaulters from the duty of political revolution. . . .

My last research trip took me to Mexico City. . . . I met a young Chicano, who . . . had gone to Mexico to renew his roots in his father's native land. . . . He had intended to carry out research on healers among Totonac Indians. But when he actually went to live with them he found the healers had turned into pastors and preachers. . . . Where the old spirits of Christo-paganism had once reigned was now a new and all-powerful Holy Spirit.

Source: David Martin. "Speaking in Latin Tongues," *National Review,* September 29, 1989, pp. 31–32.

SECTION 4 REVIEW

CHECKING FOR UNDERSTANDING

1. **Examine** the reasons Protestantism appeals to many Latin Americans.

CRITICAL THINKING

2. **Predicting Consequences** What changes might Protestantism bring to Latin America?

Religion

RITE AND RITUAL IN PERU AND BRAZIL

Although many Latin American Indians and Africans are Catholics, their Catholicism often is blended with their own age-old religious beliefs.

FOCUSING ON THE ISSUE The first article that follows describes a religious pilgrimage made by Peruvian Indians. The second article discusses the religion of *Candomblé*. While almost all those who practice these beliefs feel they are true Catholics, others believe that the Christian elements of the pilgrimage and of *Candomblé* are "merely a thin veneer of Catholicism pasted over ancient Indian and African beliefs." After reading the articles, express your viewpoint.

Pilgrimage to the Sky

I climbed one last rise and then stopped, stunned by an explosion of color and reverberating music. In an isolated valley beneath glistening glaciers, costumed figures danced among thousands of pilgrims. They would spend the night here, at the concrete-

block sanctuary of this sacred place called Qoyllur Riti (Star of the Snow). This days-long Peruvian pilgrimage, held . . . after Easter . . . commemorates a miraculous appearance of Christ in 1780. . . .

To arrive at this spot . . . , I had accompanied Indians on a frigid moonlight trek through the rugged Andes. As I watched the pageant, my companions put on the feathered costumes of the chunchos . . . , representing jungle Indians. They believe that the creation of the sun drove the precursors of these jungle people—who lived in a world illumined only by the moon—into the rain forests, where light could not penetrate. . . .

A wooden cross was set into the snow . . . , as an Indian friend scooped a hollow in the ice, lit candles and prayed. . . . by climbing up the sacred mountain, he links the people of his community with the gods.

After prayers [they] began their descent. At the base of the glacier they stopped, cut chunks of ice, and slung them on their backs. . . . The Indians believe that ice from the mountain has healing powers. As they snaked down the mountain . . . , morning sunlight glinted blindingly off their frozen burdens.

[They] returned to the sanctuary and distributed the ice to the people of their villages, who melted it. Some of the liquid was mixed with barley to make a warm drink; the rest would be carried home in bottles. . . .

At the sanctuary the dancing and praying continued. The sanctuary contains a rock bearing the image of Christ. It commemorates the miraculous appearance of the Christ child to a young herdsman named Mariano in these mountains two centuries ago.

I joined the crush of pilgrims inside. The light from hundreds of candles burnished the faces of those who cried and prayed in front of the sacred rock.

"They cry," I was told, "for the sufferings of El Señor, The Lord."

"Give me your blessing, Señor de Qoyllur Riti, so that I can return to my home." I heard the final Mass said at the sanctuary after the . . . return.

Then the crowds dispersed, except for a group of a thousand or so who headed out for the trek to the village of Tayankani. . . . Many dancers . . . were going, and I joined them. Near the sanctuary we saw a tiny stone house and corrals . . . built by pilgrims who were asking the mountain god for the fertility of their livestock. We walked all day to arrive at a small hamlet where we rested until moonrise. Then we continued—a long single-file line serpentining over the moonlit mountain trails. Along the way stops were made for prayers at various shrines. With the light of dawn the image of Christ was placed at one last chapel . . . before being carried down to Tayankani.[1]

Candomblé

My father came from Africa and set up a terreiro (temple), where he practiced Candomblé. He was a Pai de Santo—father of the gods. Because of his influence, I became an active participant in Candomblé and after fulfilling the necessary obligations, became a Mãe de Santo [mother of the gods]. I practice my religion at a terreiro run by a Pai de

[1]Source: Robert Randall. "Peru's Pilgrimage to the Sky." National Geographic, Vol. 162, No. 1, July 1982, pp. 60, 65, 67, 69.

Santo. He is the most important person and oversees the ceremonies.

According to our religion, each person is under the protection of an orixa or god. Ogum, who is represented as Saint Anthony, is one of my gods and acts as a father symbol. Yansã, who is Saint Barbara, is the goddess who assumes the role of mother to me. Some of our other gods are Yemanjá (the Blessed Virgin Mary), Oxalá (Jesus Christ), Omolú (Saint Lazarus), and Exu, who is the devil.

When we hold a ceremony, we call on the gods and spirits of Africa to descend into the bodies of their children. We beat drums, chant, dance and meditate as our ancestors did so that the gods will come. Certain privileged members called Filho de Santo (son of the gods) are mediums who are

prepared . . . to receive the gods. During a ceremony, a Filho de Santo will go into a trance as a god takes possession of his body. As a Mãe de Santo, I must watch over the mediums until the god leaves, calm the god if he becomes too violent and see that he receives his favorite food. Each god has his own personality. For example, Ogum likes to eat beans, yams and the bull's liver, heart and lungs. He is the divine blacksmith and the war god. He dwells in the forest, and when he dances he triumphantly waves a sword and has a ferocious look on his face.

During the ceremony, I wear white clothes in honor of Oxalá. My beaded necklace is blue because that's the color of my orixa, Ogum. I wear a turban before the gods descend. Once they are amongst us, I exchange it for a festive headdress symbolic of the orixa whose day we are commemorating.

I've been a Mãe de Santo for fourteen years. My religion is very important to me: it's a source of personal strength through union with natural forces and psychic energies. But, besides being a Mãe, I'm an ordinary Brazilian.[2]

[2]Source: Patricia Robb. "We call on the gods and spirits of Africa." We Live in Brazil. The Bookwright Press, 1985, pp. 44–45. Reprinted with permission of Franklin Watts, Inc., New York.

Chapter 30 Review

SUMMARY

In Latin America, where most of the people are Catholic, Catholicism is not just a religion but a way of life. The influence of the Church dates back to the Spanish and Portuguese conquests of the 1500's. In those early years, there was controversy not only over the legality of the conquest, but over the right of the Spaniards to convert the Indians living in the conquered lands.

By the national period, the Church was so powerful and wealthy that some Latin Americans—mostly new political leaders and anticlericals—sought reforms to reduce its social, economic, and political power.

The influence of the Church has declined in some areas in recent years. But it still remains active in issues that involve matters of faith and reform, such as agrarian reform and aid for the needy. One of the greatest challenges the Church faces in Latin America today is the rapid growth of Protestantism.

USING VOCABULARY

For each of the two words below, write three or four sentences explaining what it has to do with the Catholic Church in Latin America.

anticlerical   agrarian reform

REVIEWING FACTS

1. **Examine** the role of the Roman Catholic Church in Latin America during the period of Spanish and Portuguese rule.
2. **Compare** the views of Juan Ginés de Sepúlveda and Father Bartolomé de Las Casas concerning the legality of the Spanish conquest and the right of the Spaniards to convert the Indians living in the conquered lands.

3. **Discuss** the impact of the anticlericals on the standing of the Roman Catholic Church in Latin American society.
4. **State** three reasons why the influence of the Roman Catholic Church has declined in Latin America.

CRITICAL THINKING

1. **Demonstrating Reasoned Judgment** Do you think that the Spanish had the right to convert the Indians? Give reasons for your answer.
2. **Predicting Consequences** Some priests in Latin America believe that native folk religion should be assimilated into Catholicism. What effect do you think this would have on other Latin American Catholics?
3. **Drawing Conclusions** How might the role and influence of the Catholic Church have differed over the years if early priests had remained inside their missions and churches?

ANALYZING CONCEPTS

1. **Change** In what ways has the Catholic Church in Latin America changed over the years?
2. **Culture** In what ways might the rise of Protestantism affect the ways of life in Latin America?

GEOGRAPHIC THEMES

1. **Movement** Why might an increase in the number of people migrating from the countryside to the cities contribute to the "explosion of Protestantism" in Latin America?
2. **Regions** According to sociologist David Martin, "Everywhere in Latin America there is a connection between saving souls and salvaging languages." How do you interpret his statement?

Identifying Central Issues

Are you familiar with the saying, "He or she can't see the forest through the trees"? It describes a person so overwhelmed by details that he or she cannot see the bigger picture. To avoid this situation, you must learn to *identify central issues,* or the main ideas, in any material that you study. Identifying central issues helps you to understand and remember important points and the details which support them.

There are several ways to find and to identify central issues. First, try to determine the purpose of the written material that you are studying. Is it written to persuade, inform, inspire, or perhaps even anger the reader? Second, look for the most forceful statements. Third, identify the main idea of each paragraph and restate it in your own words. Finally, look for details which support a larger issue or idea.

Use the following steps to identify central issues:
- Determine the nature and purpose of the material that you are investigating.
- Identify the most forceful and outstanding statements in the material.
- Find the main idea of each paragraph and paraphrase them. In other words, express them in your own way.
- Identify details which support and reinforce a larger idea or issue.
- Summarize the central issues that you have found.

EXAMPLE

Read the opening passage of Chapter 30 on page 483. According to the footnote at the bottom of the page, it is from an article in *Time* magazine. Therefore, its purpose is to inform the reading public about Pope John Paul II's visit to Latin America in 1983. Notice the more forceful statements in the piece, such as, " 'Even when he says Mass it seems to have political implications . . . ' " What other forceful statements appear? *("the dividing line between religion and politics seemed to have all but disappeared"; "the Pope told a crowd . . . that 'the church is aware of the discrimination you suffer and the injustices you must put up with, the serious difficulties you have in defending your lands and your rights. . . .'")*

Look for the main idea of the first paragraph and restate it in your own words. *(The Pope's visit had both religious and political purposes.)* What is the main idea of the last two paragraphs? *(The Pope urged economic and political justice for the poor people of these countries.)* What details are provided to support these main ideas? *(the Church is aware of hardships and discrimination faced by Indians; the Pope demanded legislation to protect them; he urged workers to form labor unions)* Putting all this together, how would you summarize the central issues of this piece? *(During the Pope's visit to Latin America, he urged economic and political justice, especially for poor people.)*

PRACTICE

Read the following passage and answer the questions below.

During colonial times, the Roman Catholic Church in Latin America grew in wealth and power. One major reason was the Church's close ties with the government. The religious and political life of the colonies was controlled by the rulers of Spain and Portugal. These rulers delegated a great deal of authority to Church leaders. As a result, Church leaders played an important part in almost everything that happened in the colonies.

Favors from the State and gifts from faithful worshipers yielded great wealth for the Church. In addition, the Church had many business interests, including ranching, farming, commerce, mining, and banking. Profits from these added to the Church's wealth.

1. What is the purpose of this passage?
2. What is the main idea of the first paragraph?
3. What details support this idea?
4. What is the main idea of the second paragraph?
5. What details support this idea?
6. Summarize the central issue(s) of this passage.

495

People and Places to Know

Mexico City, São Paulo, Buenos Aires, Rio de Janeiro, Caracas, Bogotá, the Altiplano

Key Terms to Define

favela, villa miseria, barrio, barriada, campesino, hacendado, ejido, minifundio

Objectives to Learn

1. **Analyze** the causes and effects of overpopulation in Latin America.
2. **Discuss** agriculture in Latin America.
3. **Characterize** Latin America's industrial development.
4. **Summarize** the problems facing education in Latin America.

Itaipú Dam, Brazil

Change Takes Many Forms

> It's a few days before the traditional summer break, and just about every Chilean with a savings account is packing for a long holiday on the Pacific beaches. Hyperinflation and recession, self-doubt and pessimism are worries for the rest of Latin America. In Chile, opinion polls register confidence, optimism, even a touch of smugness.
>
> An economic miracle has been under way here for some time. In five of the last six years, the gross national product surged by at least 5 percent. . . . There is no debt crisis. Foreign investment is pouring in . . . , and middle-class income is rising. Salaries have lagged among the poor, but unemployment rates are near historic lows.
>
> And while the miracle has been tarnished by its association with Gen. Augusto Pinochet's harsh dictatorship, the country's image has soared over the last year, thanks to a new, elected president. . . . With democratic stability and the promise of prosperity, Chile has become a model for the third world. . . .
>
> In the northern desert, farmers are using Israeli drip-irrigation techniques to produce bumper harvests of grapes that are sold in North America and Europe during the winter. High in the Andes, a consortium of Australian, British and Japanese investors has opened the world's largest privately owned copper mine. Renewable pine forests in southern Chile are exporting almost $1 billion annually in lumber, wood chips and pulp. Still further south, rain-drenched archipelagos and fjords have hatched a salmon industry with revenues that rival those of traditional fishmongers like Ireland and Scotland. Tourism also has become a billion-dollar business, as hordes of visitors discover the beaches, ski slopes, Swiss-style lakes and primeval forests of a country that embraces every ecosphere except a tropical zone.

Chile is not the only Latin American nation that has experienced change in recent years. The winds of change are sweeping across the region. Much of the change is the result of economic development.

Each year millions of Latin Americans desert the countryside for the city. This flood of people has impacted the cities. Jobs often are hard to find; for many, educational opportunities are limited; and such public services as sanitation are seriously deficient.

Even so, there are reasons for optimism. Shantytowns gradually are evolving into settled communities with better schools and improved sanitary conditions. The population explosion has slowed. And, above all, some nations have created stronger economies.

Source: Jonathan Kandell. "Prosperity Born of Pain," *The New York Times Magazine,* July 7, 1991, Copyright © 1991 by the New York Times Company. Reprinted by permission.

498 UNIT 5 LATIN AMERICA

The People Explosion

Until a short time ago, population growth was thought to be an important part of a country's economic and political strength. More people meant more workers to help raise the standard of living. This, in turn, meant more prestige for the country. But in recent years, some people have begun to question this line of thinking. They believe that the world is reaching the point where there are too many people in it.

In Latin America, the population is expected to double in the next 25 years or so. Traditionally, Latin America had both a high birthrate and a high death rate, and the one offset the other. But, by the 1900's, the death rate had begun to decrease because of immunization against certain diseases and improved sanitary conditions.

While the death rate decreased substantially, the birthrate did not. Most Latin Americans continued to have large families. One reason for this is the stand against birth control taken by the Catholic Church. Another reason is tradition. It has long been the belief of many Latin American men that one way to demonstrate how masculine they are is to father many children. A third reason is a lack of information about family planning.

Many people believe that conditions will not improve in Latin America until the birth-

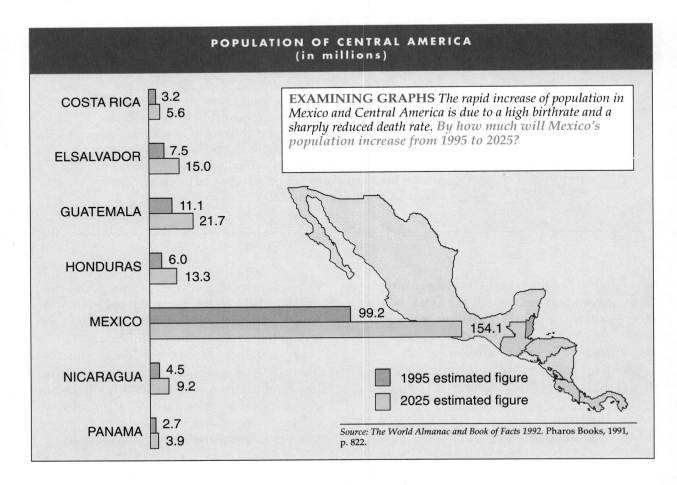

POPULATION OF CENTRAL AMERICA (in millions)

COSTA RICA 3.2 / 5.6
ELSALVADOR 7.5 / 15.0
GUATEMALA 11.1 / 21.7
HONDURAS 6.0 / 13.3
MEXICO 99.2 / 154.1
NICARAGUA 4.5 / 9.2
PANAMA 2.7 / 3.9

EXAMINING GRAPHS *The rapid increase of population in Mexico and Central America is due to a high birthrate and a sharply reduced death rate. By how much will Mexico's population increase from 1995 to 2025?*

1995 estimated figure
2025 estimated figure

Source: The World Almanac and Book of Facts 1992. Pharos Books, 1991, p. 822.

rate decreases and that the population will continue to grow at a rapid rate. Others believe that by the end of the century, as Latin America becomes more urban and industrialized, the birthrate will slow down.

URBANIZATION

Some experts also believe that the problem in Latin America is how people are distributed. Although there is a great deal of land, most of it is forest, mountain, or desert. As a result, most people have settled in the coastal regions.

The never-ending flow of people from the countryside to the cities adds to the problem. Each year, thousands flock to the cities in hope of finding a better education, higher-

paying jobs, broader markets, and decent medical care. Whether they do well or not, almost all the migrants tend to stay in the city, making urban populations soar. This has placed heavy demands on the people and the government. Public services must be expanded continuously.

This one-way migration has led to over-population, more people than resources available to fill their needs. Four of the 10 largest urban areas of the world are in Latin America. Greater Mexico City, Mexico, with 20.2 million people, is the second largest urban area in the world; São Paulo, Brazil, with 18.1 million, is the third; Buenos Aires, Argentina, with 11.5 million, is the ninth; and Rio de Janeiro, Brazil, with 11.4 million, is the tenth. In the following article, a North

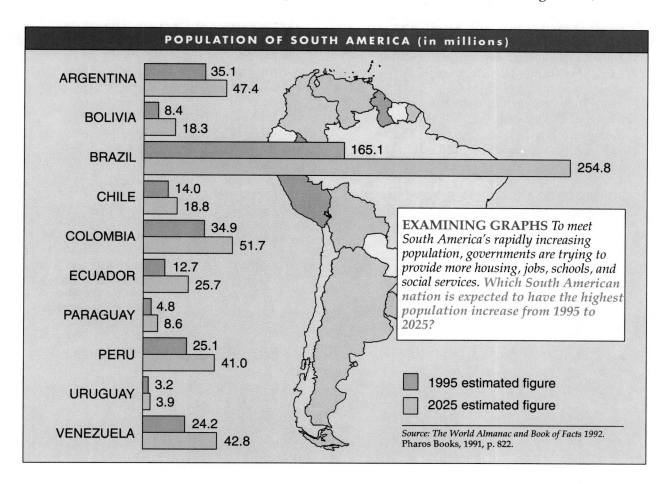

POPULATION OF SOUTH AMERICA (in millions)

Country	1995 estimated figure	2025 estimated figure
ARGENTINA	35.1	47.4
BOLIVIA	8.4	18.3
BRAZIL	165.1	254.8
CHILE	14.0	18.8
COLOMBIA	34.9	51.7
ECUADOR	12.7	25.7
PARAGUAY	4.8	8.6
PERU	25.1	41.0
URUGUAY	3.2	3.9
VENEZUELA	24.2	42.8

EXAMINING GRAPHS *To meet South America's rapidly increasing population, governments are trying to provide more housing, jobs, schools, and social services. Which South American nation is expected to have the highest population increase from 1995 to 2025?*

■ 1995 estimated figure
□ 2025 estimated figure

Source: The World Almanac and Book of Facts 1992. Pharos Books, 1991, p. 822.

American journalist visiting Mexico City gives his impressions:

Stewing, steaming, sinking, straining, striving, smoking and choking, Mexico City is the ultimate city of too much and too little.

There is no other place quite like this runaway colossus. Here is future shock jammed atop centuries of past shock.

. . . The population of greater Mexico City may be 16 million, 17 million, or 18 million, depending on who is counting or when.

The figures "are out of date by the time they are collected," said . . . the city's beleaguered planning director.

Population has increased sixfold in the last 35 years and has doubled in the last decade. . . .

Mexican land reform has fizzled, and many peasants are hungry. Thousands of them squeeze in here every week, quitting the land for slums that stretch for miles and embrace millions of people.

More than one-fifth of the entire country lives in this metropolis.

Squatter towns and shantyvilles—"lost cities," as they are called—huddle in garbage dumps, virtually next door to mansions and leafy upper-class neighborhoods. . . .

Squatters and beggars are a common . . . sight. But for every beggar, there are a thousand street vendors. . . .

The country has no welfare or food stamps, and the streets consequently are full of people hustling anything—gum, candy, tortillas, bracelets, dolls, shawls, toys. . . .

At traffic stops, youngsters rush up and wipe windshields for a penny tip. Others try to sell motorists a puppy, a blanket, a newspaper with giant headlines. . . .

In this airy center of outdoor selling, the air is blinding and choking, possibly the worst of any great city.

Every morning, motorized Mexico City awakens under a hood of gray smog that hides its once-familiar crest of mountains and clogs its once-clear air. Sometimes nothing can be seen 100 yards [90 meters] ahead. . . .

And yet a surprising number of neighborhoods retain a colonial charm. Some streets even remain free of the hideously noisy, choking traffic.

Parks are generally clean, and workmen weed superhighway strips. Corner bakeries sell crusty . . . rolls. . . .

EXAMINING PHOTOGRAPHS *The layer of smog that hangs over Mexico City is clearly visible in this photograph. At least 70 percent of the smog comes from the city's more than 3 million automobiles. Much of the rest is due to smoke from the city's 30,000 factories. The poor air quality harms the health of many of the people who live and work in the city. What are some other characteristics of Mexico City?*

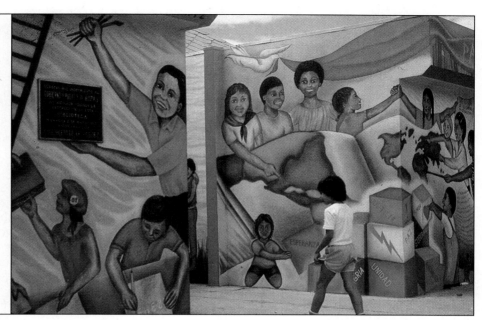

EXAMINING ART *The front walls of the Children's Library of Managua, Nicaragua, are decorated with this bright mural that shows students using the library's resources to learn about the world in which they live. Murals are a common sight in many Latin American cities, including those of Mexico.* *What are some other artistic features of Mexico City?*

Markets brim with fruits and vegetables, although stores may be short of toothpaste or milk. . . .

And museums, shops, historic ruins and architecture, murals and the lavishly decorated university are facets of a vivid supercity.

Business growth has brought with it an expanding middle class and clouds of skyscrapers that defy earthquakes and the city's steady slippage into the muck that it is built on. Everyone complains about crowding, noise, and dirty air, but for people earning, say, the equivalent of $30,000 a year, the city offers the sweet life, or at least the bittersweet.

SHANTYTOWNS AND SLUMS

Most of the people who migrate from the countryside to the cities do not find what they seek. The majority cannot read or write and do not have the skills for the kinds of work available. As a result, they end up trading their huts in the countryside for old

Source: M.W. Newman. "Mexico City's Population May Top 30 Million by Year 2000," *Chicago Sun-Times*, September 11, 1983.

houses or shantytowns at the outskirts of the city.

All major Latin American cities today have their slums and shantytowns. In Rio de Janeiro and São Paulo, Brazil, shantytowns are called *favelas*. In Buenos Aires, Argentina, they are known as *villas miserias*. In Caracas, Venezuela, they are *barrios*, and in Bogotá, Colombia, they are *barriadas*.

Although conditions in the shantytowns are far from good, some experts argue that the settlements provide the poor with free or inexpensive housing. For some Latin Americans, like the Mexicans discussed in the following article, the shantytowns represent hope for a better future:

Late on a cool summer evening, against a faint glow from the city lights below, 18 Mexicans struggled up the side of a towering hill in the Mexican state of Sonora. . . . Most were new arrivals at the northern edge of Mexico. Pushed from the south by rural poverty and vast unemployment, pulled to the north by the promise of jobs in American-owned factories, they had joined the productive work force of a new industrial revolution on the border. Now, their arms laden with clothes, blankets, and flattened cardboard boxes, they move slowly up the darkened hillside to claim a place to live.

At the top they moved quickly across the rocky terrain, and yet another invasion of the Nogales hills was essentially complete. "It was such a great feeling," remembers Norma, who works on an assembly line making hospital gowns. . . . "We built a bonfire and sat up all night talking. We were all united, aiming for a common goal. We didn't have homes. The hill was there. We simply took it over."

. . . On the steep hill that towers above Nogales, Norma has carved into the rocky incline with pick and shovel, leveling the land where she plans to build her home. Soon after she and the others arrived, the owner of the land came by, demanding payment. The 18 residents agreed to pay 1.25 million pesos ($400) each for their lots, in installments of about $9 a week, or about a quarter of Norma's salary. Then

Norma will begin saving for materials to build a home of plywood and cement block.

"I want to be my own provider and not be a burden on others," says Norma, who lives in a cardboard home down below while she pays off her lot. "I want something that is mine. Something that no one can take away, not with laws or anything. I need to discipline myself. I have been here for three years now. I don't even go to parties. . . ."

Today, Norma's land, cleared and smoothed, awaits the first pieces of wood and block. . . . "I would have to make one week's food money last for two weeks so that I could start saving money just for the plywood sheets," she says. "Then there are nails, plus the roof. It's a lot. But I know that my dreams will be accomplished, and that in itself is the best reward."

EXAMINING PHOTOGRAPHS *This hillside shantytown on the outskirts of Lima, Peru, is typical of the* pueblos jovenes *that surround Lima and other Peruvian cities. What are some positive features of shantytowns?*

SECTION 1 REVIEW

CHECKING FOR UNDERSTANDING
1. **Define** *favela, villa miseria, barrio, barriada.*
2. **Give reasons** Latin America has experienced rapid population growth.

CRITICAL THINKING
3. **Expressing Problems Clearly** Why have so many Latin Americans migrated from the countryside to the city? What problems has this migration caused?

SECTION 2

In the Countryside

Although about one-third of the people of Latin America live in the countryside and are farmers, Latin America does not produce enough food to feed its people. Nor are enough earnings brought in through exports to pay for the imported food and industrial goods that are needed. With the expansion of farm products slow, the need for imported foods has been rising rapidly, and nearly 75 percent of all manufactured goods must be imported.

In the past, *campesinos*, people who live and work in the countryside, stayed close to home. But in recent years, improved roads and bus service have allowed them to travel to large urban areas. These trips, along with radio, television, and movies, have given the *campesinos* a glimpse of a different life, better than their own. They hope to gain this life through agrarian reform. To this end, *campesinos* in many parts of Latin America have taken part in strikes and have taken over large estates.

HACIENDAS AND COMMERCIAL FARMS

In most Latin American countries, a few people—some 10 percent—own 90 percent of the land, and even today *haciendas* still account for a large part of the big landholdings. Most of the work is done by peasant sharecroppers, who generally keep one-third or one-half of the crop and give the rest to the **hacendado**, or *hacienda* owner. The *hacendado* provides the sharecroppers with a hut, a small piece of land, seeds, simple tools, and at times, work animals and a small wage. A store and religious and social activities also may be provided.

Most work on the *hacienda* is done by hand, and the amount produced per acre is quite low. Most *hacendados* plant only about 10 to 15 percent of their land at one time, and much is not farmed at all. With taxes on the land low and labor cheap, most *hacendados* feel no need to provide up-to-date machinery or training, to push to produce more, or to sell some of the land to a tenant farmer.

The *hacienda* system allows the *hacendado* to dominate the local area and discourages peasants from trying to improve their lot. In

EXAMINING PHOTOGRAPHS *On this Honduran* hacienda, *workers are cutting tobacco leaves that will be stored and cured in the drying barns in the background.* How does the hacienda system work?

the end, it holds back economic progress. Because the peasants get little or nothing for all their work, most do not have enough money to buy many manufactured goods. This means that there is a lack of consumers, which, in turn, keeps new industry from growing and new jobs from opening up.

Some peasants continue to work on the *hacienda* because of tradition. They believe that leaving the land that their ancestors tilled would be desertion. Others are held by the debts they owe the *hacendado*. Still others stay because they feel that they have no other choice. They cannot expect to acquire their own land, and moving to another *hacienda* will not improve their lives. Their only hope for a better life lies in the city. But that would mean adapting to urban life, and many are afraid or unwilling to do so.

Today, many of the large landholdings are commercial farms that produce bananas, sugar, coffee, meat, cereals, and wool for sale on the world market. A great deal of money is spent on machines, fertilizer, and insecticides to help the farmer use the land to the fullest. While most workers labor only during the four-month harvest season, they receive fixed wages and, in some cases, medical and educational services.

Commercial farms are important to Latin America because their products are needed for both export and domestic use. Such farms produce more than half the export earnings of Argentina, Brazil, Colombia, the Dominican Republic, Ecuador, Guatemala, Honduras, Nicaragua, and Uruguay.

EJIDOS AND MINIFUNDIOS

Not all landholdings in Latin America are large. In Mexico, for example, there are many *ejidos*, small farms owned by a community of people. There are two types of *ejidos*. One is the individual *ejido*, which is a piece of land the community gives a farmer for personal use. The farmer must agree not to sell or mortgage the land and to cultivate it for two years. Failure to meet the terms of the agreement means loss of the land. The other is the collective *ejido*, a farm on which the members work together. Each member's share of the harvest depends on how much labor he or she has contributed.

The most common type of Latin American landholding, however, is the **minifundio**, a 2- to 15-acre [.8–6 hectare] farm. Most *minifundios* are too small and their soil too poor to provide a decent living. This often forces people to find other ways to earn additional income. Some sell produce or run small stores. Others make handicrafts. Still others work for larger landowners. Even when they do this, though, they often do not earn enough for more than the barest essentials.

The life of these peasants is hard. Below, a Chilean woman tells her story. Like that of many others, hers is really not a story of a woman or of family life, but of work:

I was born and grew up in Reinoso, and I came to San Felipe when my father died. My birth had never been registered, so when I applied, the Civil Registrar asked me, "Do you want to be registered as born in 1915?" I said yes. . . . My mother left me with my grandmother and some aunts when I was seven months old; when my grandmother died, I was eight years old, and I had to go to live with my stepmother. That is when I went to work.

My father was given a small piece of land, and I worked it with him planting garlic, peppers, and tobacco for sale in town. At home we also had a garden, where we planted beans, potatoes, and other things to be kept for winter use. Sometimes the house got real crowded in the winter as we kept three or four sacks of wheat to make flour or *harina tostada* [toasted wheat]. Then we had boxes of things like tallow to be stored there also.

I worked all year round, in the winter because that's when garlic was planted. What I earned, I had to give to my stepmother. She was in charge of the money. I didn't know what shoes were until I was ten years old. . . .

EXAMINING PHOTOGRAPHS *Fresh produce is brought to towns from commercial farms by the truckload. Because refrigeration is not common, the produce must be sold quickly. Why are these farms important?*

EXAMINING PHOTOGRAPHS *High in the Andes is the bleak plateau known as the Altiplano, which extends from Peru through Bolivia and Argentina into Chile. In this photo, a woman watches her sheep grazing on the sparse vegetation of the Bolivian Altiplano.* *What role does work play in the life of the Chilean woman from San Felipe?*

I also had to help in the house; I came in from the field, got washed, and then I had to clean, scrub, or do other things. By the time I was nineteen, I began to work as a cook in a house in town. But I always went out to pick beans and do field work in season.

When I was twenty-six, I got married, but that didn't work out. My husband ran off with someone else, and I was left alone with three children. Two died; the oldest, Carlitos, went into the hospital when he was twelve. He had heart trouble and died after five years. Then I had a daughter, Carmen. She died, too. That left me with one child, Juan.

When I was young, I never wanted to work at daily wages but always worked on contract because I worked hard. I worked as hard as two men. It was never too cold or too wet for me to work. I could always put food on the table for my family.

In this area, women usually work in the fields. I couldn't get used to being in the house, I had to go out to work. I never had the chance to go to school. I learned to read by myself. I can read anything, but I don't know how to write. I learned to sign my name when I was already a woman. I found out then how to take care of my own money, that I earned by the sweat of my brow.

Then, when I was 38 years old, I got together with Abel. After that I worked in the stables; in the summer cutting beans; and then picking and taking apart nuts; in the winter I picked onions. I always worked, whether it was raining or not. Abel didn't work if it was raining.

Well, I'm old now. It's been eight years since I have gone into the fields. There is not enough work for everyone, and they say, "Let the young ones work to feed their families." Work is all I have ever done. Now, I have to wait for someone to take care of me.

SECTION 2 REVIEW

CHECKING FOR UNDERSTANDING

1. **Define** campesino, hacendado, ejido, minifundio.
2. **Explain** why some Latin American peasants continue to work on the *hacienda.*

CRITICAL THINKING

3. **Making Comparisons** Identify and compare the different kinds of landholdings in Latin America today.

Source: María Elena Cruz and Rigoberto Rivera. *Y los campos eran nuestros,* Vol. II *La Realidad.* Study by el Grupo de Investigaciones Agrarias de la Academia de Humanismo Cristiano, Special adaptation and translation by Donald W. Waddell, pp. 29–32.

CUBA—AN ECONOMY IN TROUBLE

During the 30-plus years that Fidel Castro has ruled Cuba, its economy has seen much change. As a journalist notes in the following excerpt, Cubans now are faced with hard times and a deeply troubled economy:

Crippled by the demise of socialism in the east and the end of generous Soviet trade subsidies, the Cuban economy has shrunk by at least 25 percent . . . since 1989. . . . Factories all across the island have closed, energy is strictly rationed, gasoline is scarce, and public transportation has been slashed to a bare minimum, playing havoc with the distribution of food and other goods.

. . . even such basic items as newspapers and magazines are hard to find because of a shortage of paper occasioned by cuts in trade with Moscow. On a recent Sunday morning, for example, a news kiosk in downtown Havana was mobbed by 100 Cubans, jostling and elbowing for a place in line despite the efforts of three police officers to keep order. . . .

Because of shortages of grain feed, domestically produced meat and eggs are scarce. Within the state-sponsored rationing system, most Cubans are receiving less than a pound and a half of meat a month. . . . They can buy about five eggs each week per person. . . . Milk is for young children and senior citizens almost exclusively.

Most Cubans report having plenty of money in their pockets . . . but nothing to spend it on. . . . "I could be a millionaire here, but look for yourself: What can you buy with all your pesos?" says a laid-off linguistics instructor. "I spend half my day waiting in lines for shoes or for vegetables. There's nothing else to do. . . ."

Seeking to trim state spending as well as absorb the glut of pesos in the economy, the government has ended subsidies and increased prices for a number of basic items. . . .

With so many factories closed and construction projects mothballed, the Cuban government is admitting for the first time to a certain level of unemployment—about 6 percent of the work force in Havana. . . .

. . . The streets of Havana are clogged with people, young and old, who have nothing to do. They survive with the help of friends and family, and with food provided by the state rationing system.

DRAWING CONCLUSIONS

What factors do you think might have contributed to the present state of the Cuban economy? Explain.

Source: Lee Hockstader. "Castro Out? Not by the Hair on His Chinny Chin" in *The Washington Post*, May 18–24, 1992, p. 14, © 1992 *The Washington Post*. Reprinted with permission.

The State of Development

Many Latin Americans believe that industrial development will take care of most of their problems, make them self-sufficient, and provide them with a higher standard of living. Recent increases in the production of electrical energy, steel, automobiles, oil, cement, and other products, have not met the needs of the growing population.

There are many reasons why industry has not grown rapidly. Included are lack of money and of skilled labor and too few transportation systems. Most Latin Americans just do not have enough purchasing power to support rapid industrial expansion. Still, some countries are making headway. Plan 936, for example, is a program conceived in 1985 by the governor of Puerto Rico to provide low-interest loans to members of the Caribbean Basin Initiative (CBI). A journalist discusses some of the results:

In addition to preserving jobs at home, Puerto Rico has promoted 92 production-sharing or "twin-plant" projects in 12 CBI countries which have created more than 20,000 jobs and generated $800 million in investment. . . .

Projects already utilizing 936 funds range from the tiny to the immense. One of the smallest projects . . . is a $2.1 million cardboard box plant on the island of Dominica. The factory, a production-sharing venture between the Dominica Banana Growers Association and Puerto Rico Container Corporation, will provide 35 jobs in Dominica and up to six million corrugated boxes annually for Dominica's . . . banana industry. Roberto Valentin, president of Puerto Rico Container, said his company is saving $100,000 a year by using 936 funds . . . rather than borrowing the money from a commercial bank. . . .

The same concept, but on a much larger scale, was recently used to finance $17 million of the . . . cost of AT&T's TCS-1 fiberoptic telephone cable linking Florida, Puerto Rico, Jamaica, the Dominican Republic and Colombia. Section 936 funds have also been used to . . . finance the construction of a . . . floating power plant to

EXAMINING PHOTOGRAPHS *In many Latin American countries, more and more emphasis is being put on development. In recent years, workers like these, who are pouring and spreading wet cement at a large construction site in Puerto Rico, are becoming a common sight. How do many Latin Americans expect industrial development to help them?*

supply electricity to . . . the Dominican Republic. . . .

Costa Rica . . . currently has 11 twin-plant operations with Puerto Rico. . . .

Most importantly, through the CBI-936 link, Puerto Rico hopes to maintain its hard-won prosperity and at the same time improve the standard of living for all of its Caribbean basin neighbors.

One of Latin America's leading industrial nations is Brazil. Yet, despite the progress it has made, Brazil suffers from economic problems that are impacting its industries. As pointed out in the article below Brazilian industries need investment:

A nationwide study coordinated by Brazil's University of Campinas . . . has discovered that in the modernization of its machinery and products, Brazilian industry is between 15 and 20 years behind the major economies in the Northern Hemisphere. . . .

The study suggests that the country is losing so much ground in some sectors that it is not worth the trouble to stay in the race. For instance, it says that Brazil has lost its chance in genetic engineering and that it cannot provide medicines. It is not that medicines are not produced in Brazil: They are, but the formulas come from research laboratories overseas. When Brazilian firms develop new products, they are copying processes that were known abroad 20, 30, or even 50 years ago, the study says.

In the 1980s, the majority of Brazil's industries went into hibernation and stopped investing in themselves. One result of this is that Brazilian industry began the 1990s with virtually the same productive capacity it had a decade earlier. . . .

The steel industry, once an object of pride for Brazilians, has become lazy and

Source: Larry Luxner. "High Hopes for Low-Interest Loans." AMERICAS, Volume 43, 5/6, 1991, pp. 23–25. Reprinted from *AMERICAS*, a bimonthly magazine published by the General Secretariat of the Organization of American States in English and Spanish.

rusty. According to the study of the 35 steel companies in Brazil, only eight possess a research lab, and only one invests in research and development at an international standard. The mills have improved their production methods and even bring out new products, but they do not invent anything. . . .

The performance of the textile industry, with the exception of a few companies, varies from fair to terrible. "About 80 percent of the nation's textile machinery is more than 10 years old," says the study. Worse, it says, most of the industry's business people know nothing about common business practices.

The Brazilian automotive industry is the least productive in the world, the report says, and it ranks among the world's most backward for the quality of the vehicles it produces. . . .

The report misses some areas in which there is room for pride about the Brazilian economy—for example, its scope. Brazil is probably the only nation of its size that produces virtually everything—from aircraft

EXAMINING PHOTOGRAPHS *Dams, such as the Itaipú Dam, owned jointly by Brazil and Paraguay, are converting Latin America's water power into electricity. In what other industrial projects is Brazil involved?*

EXAMINING PHOTOGRAPHS *In a bamboo schoolroom in rural Nicaragua, which is not unlike rural classrooms in other Latin American countries, a student reads a lesson aloud to his classmates.* Who controls public school education in most Latin American countries?

and computers to silk ties—and all of it reasonably well. The study cites two industries—paper and aluminum—in which Brazil is still competitive internationally.

Source: "Way Behind in Brazil," Veja *and* World Press Review.

SECTION 3 REVIEW

CHECKING FOR UNDERSTANDING
1. **Indicate** why some of Brazil's industries are losing ground.
2. **Detail** the problems Latin Americans face in striving for industrialization.

CRITICAL THINKING
3. **Analyzing Information** What are the authors trying to get across about the state of development in Latin America?

SECTION 4

The State of Education

For many years, large numbers of Latin Americans could not afford to go to school, and many were illiterate. Today, education is free in most of Latin America. This, however, has not solved all the problems. The literacy rate remains low in many countries, and there are too few schools and teachers. More than half the teachers, especially in rural areas, do not have teaching degrees. All have little prestige and are paid very poorly.

In most countries, public schools are controlled by the government, which decides when and where to build schools, what teachers to hire, what courses to teach, and what books students will use. Often, the officials responsible for these decisions have had little or no experience as educators. As a result, education remains an important issue in Latin America today.

PUBLIC AND PRIVATE SCHOOLS

In Latin America, children generally start school at the age of six or seven and spend about six years in grade school and six in secondary school. Some go on to college. Below, a teacher discusses the system in her home—Puerto Rico:

In Puerto Rico, there are elementary, intermediate, and high schools. There also are colleges and universities. Everyone has

EXAMINING PHOTOGRAPHS *Uniformed private school students on a field trip listen to their teacher explain the day's lesson. At about what age do children in Latin America begin school?*

the right to a public school education, and elementary and intermediate schooling are obligatory. High school and college are not.

In addition to public schools, we have two kinds of private schools—secular and parochial. Although most of the parochial schools are Catholic, there are some Lutheran, Baptist, and Episcopalian ones as well. The private schools generally are called *colegios,* a term also used at times to refer to universities. Entrance requirements and fees for the private schools depend on the school and where it is located.

Parents pay for their children's schooling. In both the public and the private schools, the students wear uniforms, for which parents also pay. In the public schools, the books are free, but in the private schools, parents have to pay for them.

Source: Wanda I. Feliciano. Interview, April 1985.

Most of the countries of Latin America have both public schools and private schools. In most cases, those people who can afford it prefer to send their children to private school. As a Brazilian journalist indicates below, in her country, private school vs. public school education is a major issue:

During the 1970s, the "economic miracle" fed the illusion that the sons and daughters of the middle class could go to private schools, and they virtually abandoned the public school system. Now that it is clear that the "miracle" was but a farce, the situation is being reversed at an alarming rate.

Without the means to pay tuition at private schools, these families now are looking for refuge in the public school system, an institution that shows the classic symptoms of underdevelopment: low salaries for the teachers, inadequate classrooms and insufficient teaching materials.

In the past three years, the public school system in São Paulo . . . grew by between 2 and 3 percent a year. At the same time, the private school network began to shrink. One pessimistic estimate put its loss of students at around 10 percent.

This means that as many as 50,000 students will be descending on the public schools which . . . are unable to provide the quality and variety of education that the middle class is accustomed to receiving in private schools.

In a 1982 survey of 400 housewives in five large Brazilian state capitals, 25 percent said they had been forced to put their children in public schools. For the middle-class family that traditionally considers "a good education as our most important legacy to our children," such a move carries with it connotations of social decay.

Only one of the housewives whose children had transferred to public school said that "it was wonderful." All the others admitted to being worried and apprehensive. . . .

Distant from . . . ideological, political and philosophical discussions, Brazilian children deal with the situation the best they can. Such is the case of the Ribeiro do Valle family. The father, Jaime, is a 45-year-old architect. . . . The mother, Cecilia, 35, is a fashion designer for a São Paulo boutique. . . . The couple has two children: Luciana, 5, and Marcos, 12. Until last year, the children attended a private school. . . .

"It was too much for our budget," says Jaime Ribeiro do Valle. . . . Adds Cecilia: "I know its risky, but there is no other way. If they had stayed at private school we would have had to cut our food expenditures."

VOCATIONAL AND AGRICULTURAL SCHOOLS

The aim of vocational schools is to train students to be skilled and technical workers, which are in short supply in Latin America. Although some Latin American countries actively promote this type of education, there is not always enough financial support to maintain the schools.

Less than 40 percent of Latin American students take such courses as industrial arts, home economics, and agriculture. One reason for this is that by the time they are 12 or 13 years old, the age required to take part in vocational training, many of them no longer are in school. In addition, vocational training and many of the jobs to which it leads are associated with manual labor, which traditionally has been looked down upon by Latin Americans.

At an adult level, however, vocational and agricultural training has met with success in some countries. As the following article indicates, this has been the case in Honduras:

Nearer to Tegucigalpa on the route from Las Manos, I met . . . men uniformly dressed—students in denim. They planted bananas, sacked seed corn, and sprayed insecticide. The Pan-American Agricultural School at El Zamorano believes in getting dirt under the fingernails.

"The trouble with most agricultural schools in Latin America is that they produce *agrónomos* who don't know what to do when they hit reality," said Dr. Simon E. Malo, the school's director. "You don't learn farming just by reading books."

At the urging of Samuel Zemurray [a U.S. planter], . . . the United Fruit Company founded this school in 1942; it is independent of the government.

No agricultural school in Latin America enjoys a better reputation. Students work hundreds of hours on its 12,000-acre [4800-hectare] farm, besides going to classes. This labor helps the school earn half a million dollars a year from vegetables and seed. Some 15 nations . . . are represented among this year's 425 students. . . .

Food production lags in Honduras and other Latin American nations, which import much of what they eat. "There aren't nearly enough trained men to take information to the farmer," Dr. Malo said. He hopes the school can find funds to quadruple enrollment.

SECTION 4 REVIEW

CHECKING FOR UNDERSTANDING
1. **List** the problems facing education in Latin America today.
2. **Give reasons** why there is not more vocational education in Latin America.

CRITICAL THINKING
3. **Making Comparisons** Compare public and private schools in Latin America.

Source: Regina Echeverría. "Brazil's recession forces parents to pull their children from private schools." *WorldPaper,* January 1984, p. 12.

Source: Mike Edwards. "Honduras: Eye of the Storm." *National Geographic,* Vol. 164, No. 5, November 1983, pp. 631–632.

Global Concerns

ECONOMIC PROSPERITY

Most, if not all, Latin Americans would agree with the research analyst who claimed that the 1980's brought economic woes to Latin American nations. The 1990's, however, promised a brighter future for Latin America. This led the same researcher to make the following prediction:

. . . Latin America's long-term outlook is neither bleak nor discouraging. Abundant natural resources, relatively cheap labor and large, youthful internal markets could attract significant foreign investment. Democracy has taken new root throughout the continent, marking the beginning, perhaps, of an era of greater stability following years of political chaos. . . .

Not too many years ago Latin America was a thriving place. . . . If Latin America stays the course, the 1990s will not duplicate the lost decade of the 1980s.[1]

FOCUSING ON THE ISSUE Read the following excerpts from an

interview with Mexico's President Carlos Salinas de Gotari that appeared in the August 1992 *Reader's Digest*.[2] Based on the information in the interview and in the chapter, write a paper giving reasons why you agree or disagree with the researcher's prediction.

Q. Your presidency has been characterized by a bold willingness to break with traditional Mexican politics. Why did you decide to denationalize the banks and other state enterprises?

A. We live in a world that is changing very rapidly. For many years in Mexico, it was thought that increased nationalization would improve the standard of living. Then in the late 1970s and early 1980s we entered a deep recession. We found that the more property

the state had, the less well-being the population had. So I applied a simple Mexican proverb: Los bienes se hicieron para remediar los males. *(Our assets can be used to right many wrongs.)*

We have been using the proceeds of privatization, in which state enterprises are sold at public bidding, to reduce domestic debt. Today Mexico's domestic debt is 15 percent of its gross domestic product. In the United States it's over 40 percent. This means that with fiscal discipline, we have room in our budget for social programs.

Also, by privatizing many state-owned enterprises, we have made it possible for Mexican investors to bring back their money from abroad. In

---

[1]*Source:* Steven E. Cerier. "Latin America: The long road back" in *D & B Reports*, January/ February 1991, p. 21.

[2]*Source:* Excerpted with permission from "Behind Mexico's 'Economic Miracle'" *Reader's Digest* August 1992. Copyright © 1992 by the Reader's Digest Assn., Inc.

buying denationalized businesses, they can generate employment opportunities here at home. Last, and not least, we've encouraged workers to participate in privatization.

Q. How have you involved the average Mexican?

A. When the telephone company was government-owned, its employees asked for a wage increase. I went to the union hall and explained that higher wages required increased productivity—something that could be done only through additional investment in the plant, which the government could not afford.

The union put my proposition to a vote and 45,000 workers unanimously approved the privatization of their company. We didn't give them shares in the new company. We provided them with loans to acquire 4.4 percent of the company. The stock has done so well that they have repaid the loans, and now the workers have assets worth more than $700 million.

The success of privatization has reversed the traditional way of thinking in Mexico— that more nationalization could provide a better standard of living. Today privatization is providing improved living standards and opening new market opportunities for those who will risk their money and their efforts.

Q. What are the toughest decisions you have made in office?

A. One was related to debt renegotiation and our relationship with the banks. Another was deciding to propose to my country a free-trade agreement with the United States and Canada. For years, for good historical reasons, Mexicans tried to live as far away as possible from the United States. But I explained to the people that in this world of economic interrelationships, the only way for the Mexican economy to grow at the rate we need is to get closer to our neighbor, which happens to have the biggest economy in the world.

Another difficult decision to implement was the modification of Article 27 of the constitution, which traditionally guaranteed land to any farmer who demanded it. When we were 15 million people, when we were 30 million, even when we were 50 million, this was a wise concept. But at 85 million and growing by two million a year, this meant creating plots too small to sustain a family. A measure that brought justice in the past now spelled total inefficiency and inequality.

Q. Mexico has halted hyperinflation and modernized its economy when such countries as Brazil and Argentina have had less success. Are there lessons here for others?

A. I can tell you what's been good for us, but I couldn't tell you if it would be good for others. What was essential for us was to bring fiscal discipline first to the public sector. We used to run annual budget deficits of about 13 percent of gross domestic product. Last year the deficit was 1.3 percent, and this year we will have the first surplus in our history. Fiscal discipline has been the main tool against inflation. But labor and management have also contributed by finding common purpose in reaching wage agreements. This helped to bring inflation down from more than 150 percent in 1987 to less than 19 percent last year, and we are going toward ten percent this year

Q. What are the lessons to be learned from Mexico's Solidarity Program to fight extreme poverty?

A. Trust the people. In the past, we relied on the central government to determine what the poorest people needed. Now we have reversed this process. No longer will officials in Mexico City decide the needs of people in rural areas. Local, democratically elected committees decide how to use some of the proceeds of privatization and savings from debt renegotiation to have running water and electricity, to build schools and clinics, and to pave roads. All of these are decisions that people, not bureaucrats, are making today.

Chapter 31 Review

SUMMARY

Over recent decades, Latin America has been experiencing population growth. Some experts believe that the issue is not so much the number of people but how those people are distributed. The migration of millions of people from the countryside to the city has resulted in overpopulation of urban areas. This, in turn, has led to inadequate city services and unsanitary and overcrowded living conditions. At the same time, *campesinos* working on *haciendas*, commercial farms, *ejidos*, and *minifundios* find it almost impossible to make a decent living. As a result, many *campesinos* are pressing for agrarian reform.

Many Latin Americans believe that the challenge of the future lies in industrial development. But, even in those countries that have met with some success, development has not reached a point where it meets the needs of the growing population.

Education, too, has its problems. Although public education generally is free, the quality of education is not as high as many Latin Americans would like it to be.

USING VOCABULARY

Imagine that you are a member of the Peace Corps in Latin America. Using the terms below in sentences, write a report to your supervisor describing what you have observed.

favela	*barriada*	*ejido*
villa miseria	*campesino*	*minifundio*
barrio	*hacendado*	

REVIEWING FACTS

1. **Discuss** the relationship in Latin America between rapid population growth, slum conditions, and poverty.

2. **Point out** the negative and positive aspects of Latin America's shantytowns.
3. **Indicate** the agricultural challenges faced by Latin American nations today.
4. **State** what Latin Americans hope to gain by agrarian reform.
5. **Explain** the role of government in Latin America's educational systems.

CRITICAL THINKING

1. **Making Generalizations** Make two generalizations about the changes currently taking place in Latin America.
2. **Formulating Questions** What three questions might you ask to help determine if industrialization can solve most of Latin America's problems?
3. **Identifying Alternatives** Pollution is a major problem for many Latin American cities. Suggest four alternatives to help solve the problem. For each suggestion, identify the advantages and disadvantages.

ANALYZING CONCEPTS

1. **Change** Most of Latin America is trying to evolve from an agricultural to an industrial society. If reforms are not made in education, do you think this is possible? Explain.
2. **Culture** In what ways might overpopulation affect Latin America's social structure and economic system?

GEOGRAPHIC THEMES

1. **Movement** What happens to most of the Latin Americans who migrate from the countryside to the city?
2. **Human-Environment Interaction** Discuss the effect urbanization has had on the environment.

Reading a Bar Graph

Graphs are drawings that present statistics in a clear, visual format. One common form of graph is the *bar graph*. Quantities are represented by bars of various lengths which are drawn horizontally or vertically. Some bar graphs illustrate changes over time. For example, the first bar graph shows the percentage of graduates from one high school who went to college between 1988 and 1992.

Bar graphs can also compare quantities that occur at the same time, but in different places. For example, the next graph compares the percentages of college-bound graduates from five different schools in a single year.

The steps below will help you in reading bar graphs:

- Read the graph title to learn the subject. Study the information presented on the horizontal and vertical axes, and in the use of different colors on the bars.

- Compare the lengths of the bars and draw conclusions.

EXAMPLE

Look at the graph on page 498. According to the title, this graph shows the population of Central America. Estimated population figures are given for 2 different years. What year is represented by each color? *(yellow=1995, green=2025)* Each nation is represented by bars along the vertical axis on the left side of the graph. This graph, however, has no horizontal axis. Instead, the population figures are written at the end of each bar. What do these numbers stand for? *(millions of people)*

Mexico is expected to have the largest population in 1995 and 2025. Which country is expected to have the smallest population in both years? *(Panama)* Compare the yellow bars to find the countries which will have more than 10 million people in 1995. *(Cuba, Guatemala, Mexico)* In 2025? *(Cuba, Dominican Republic, El Salvador, Guatemala, Haiti, Honduras, Mexico)*

PRACTICE

Use the graph on page 499 to answer the questions below.

1. What is the subject of this graph?
2. What is listed on the vertical axis? The horizontal axis?
3. What do yellow bars represent? Green bars?
4. What will Chile's population be in 1995?
5. Which country is expected to have the largest population in each year shown?
6. Which countries are expected to double their populations from 1995 to 2025?

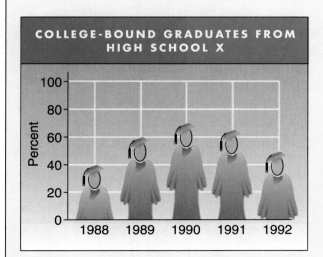

COLLEGE-BOUND GRADUATES FROM HIGH SCHOOL X

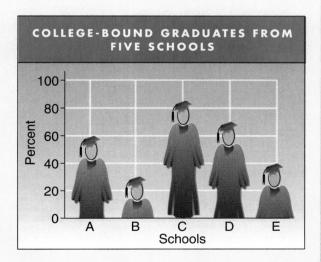

COLLEGE-BOUND GRADUATES FROM FIVE SCHOOLS

CHAPTER OUTLINE

People and Places to Know
Alberto Fujimori, Benito Juárez, Nicaragua, Sandinistas, *contras*, Violeta Barrios de Chamorro, Fidel Castro, Havana, Colombia, M-19

Key Terms to Define
conservative, liberal

Objectives to Learn
1. **Identify** the groups involved in traditional Latin American politics.
2. **Summarize** changes in Latin American politics since the end of the 1800's.
3. **Compare** political change in Nicaragua, Cuba, and Colombia.

Diego Rivera mural in Mexico City

516

Dictatorships and Democracies

> With civilian governments now the rule rather than the exception, Latin America's armies have to find new things to do. . . . Border disputes . . . are increasingly papered over in the name of regional economic integration. And the idea of ruling the country seems to have lost its appeal.
>
> In the new civilian systems, the military has become just one more lobbying group, competing with political parties, unions and businesses to influence government budgets and policies. In this environment, military men are scrambling to find useful work to defend their budgets.
>
> "Army engineers are building roads, schools and bridges in remote places," Anibal Rejis Romero, a Paraguayan general, said. "We are preparing the infrastructure for agrarian reform settlements."
>
> To strengthen the foundations of civilian rule, several speakers cited the need to break down the barriers between the military and civilian worlds. "We cannot ignore that the distance between the civilian world and the military world in Chile dates back more than half a century," said Arturo Frei, a . . . Chilean senator.
>
> Civilian politicians see military issues as a political dead end, said Julio Maria Sanguinetti, who was president of Uruguay in the late 1980's. "'If you get a group of Latin American politicians together in a room and ask, "'Who wants to be foreign minister?' everyone will wave his or her hand in the air," said Mr. Sanguinetti, whose presidency ended a long period of military rule in Uruguay. "But if you ask 'Who wants to be defense minister?' everyone stares at the floor."

The newspaper article above discusses some of the challenges that are facing the military in Latin America today. The changing status of the military is just one result of a trend that began in Latin America during the 1980's—the move from military rule to civilian rule, from dictatorship toward democracy.

The transition to democracy has not been easy. Most Latin American nations are still trying to recover from the economic depression that set in during the early 1980's. In 1990, two out of every five Latin Americans were living in poverty. The economic situation has impacted the progress of democracy and led many experts to conclude that "democracy in the Americas is still on trial."

Source: James Brooke. "Latin Armies Are Looking For Work" in *The New York Times*, March 24, 1991, p. E2. Copyright © 1992 by *The New York Times* Company. Reprinted by permisssion.

SECTION 1

The Old Tradition

In the 1800's, political affairs in most of Latin America were controlled by a small group made up of rich landowners, army officers, clergy, merchants, intellectuals, and professionals. Most of the rest of the people failed to vote, were denied the vote, or voted as they were told to by those in power. For the most part, the Latin American minority who were involved in politics were divided into two separate groups—**conservatives** and **liberals**. The conservatives consisted mostly of the upper class and the clergy. The liberals consisted mostly of merchants and professionals. Both groups were satisfied with life as it was and had little or no interest in helping the lower class. Their major concerns were form of government and Church-State relations.

The conservatives, who wanted to keep the social system as it was, favored a strong central government, a powerful president, and a weak legislature. The liberals, who wanted changes that would bring them greater wealth and political power, sought local self-rule, a weak president, and a strong legislature. The liberals especially wanted to curb the influence of the Church and the army. Their attacks on the Church met with a fair amount of success. Their attacks on the army, however, had little effect, and it was not uncommon for the military to step in and take over a government. Most of the soldiers who gained control were more interested in personal power than in helping the people. An example, described below, was Mariano Melgarejo, who ruled Bolivia from 1864 to 1870:

Melgarejo . . . was a man without the most basic notion of government. He did not even represent any political belief. He was not supported by anyone who, on his own, could have raised a banner that would have captured the sympathies of the masses. For the moment there was

EXAMINING ART *Military officers of the 1800's, known as* caudillos, *included (left to right) Mexican presidents General Antonio López de Santa Anna and General Porfirio Diaz, and Argentinian ruler General Manuel de Rosas. What role did the military play in politics in the 1800's?*

only one sure fact. Melgarejo had engineered a revolution. But for whom?

A man of humblest origin, his education was the training he had in the barracks. Melgarejo's whole life was made up of treason and crimes.

Before it had been in power a month, the new government issued two decrees. By a stroke of the pen, they did away with the Constitution of 1861.

The country began to show alarm. It plainly saw that this soldier would trample underfoot all its institutions. Armed protests broke out, in the name of upholding the Constitution.

After Melgarejo put down the revolts, the whole country gave up. And the same men who in secret talked against using force yielded too and forsook their principles. They even went further. Many rushed to offer their services to the victor, who found himself surrounded, through fear, by the best elements in the country.

At this time, it was very fashionable to drink many toasts at the palace banquets. Each of the guests was eager to show his allegiance.

When his turn came, one of the guests spoke in words of praise of the new charter which would surely govern the acts of Melgarejo.

Melgarejo's instant response was brutal.

"I want the gentleman who has just spoken and all the deputies gathered here to know that I have put the Constitution of 1861, which was very good, in this pocket" (pointing to his left trouser pocket) "and that of 1868, which is even better in the opinion of these gentlemen, in this one" (pointing to his right pocket). "Nobody is going to rule Bolivia but me."

Not all political leaders of the era, however, were in the military or like Melgarejo. Some, like liberal Benito Juárez, who served as president of Mexico from 1858 to 1872,

Source: From THE GREEN CONTINENT by German Arciniegas, trans. Harriet De Onis et al. Copyright 1944 and renewed 1972 by Alfred A. Knopf, Inc. Reprinted by permission of the publisher.

EXAMINING PHOTOGRAPHS *Visitors to the birthplace of Mexican president Benito Juárez view a large mural depicting important events in his life.* **Why did many Mexicans think Juárez was a good governor?**

cared about the people and wanted reforms. Below, an author provides some insights into the life and goals of Juárez:

Benito Juárez . . . was the first Indian ruler since Cuauhtemoc [the Aztec ruler]. Benito grew up in the . . . southern town of Oaxaca, where he lived in the streets most of the time, more often hungry than not. . . .

As Benito grew older, a priest noticed the thoughtful black eyes under shaggy hair and offered to teach him. The boy learned quickly. He went to school and later studied law. And then, while still a young man, he became Governor of Oaxaca.

Benito Juárez was a good governor. People talked to him with respect because he was honest, and he saw that those who worked under him were honest. Where so many officials accepted bribes and made fortunes one way or another while in office, Juárez was never known to have taken a centavo beyond his salary. . . . He said little, but when he spoke, people listened.

Years before, . . . Juárez was imprisoned for opposing [the dictator Santa Anna]. He soon escaped to New Orleans, however, where he made cigars for a living. He returned to Mexico . . . and was named Minister of Justice. His new laws provided for the sale of church property not used for worship and restricted the political power of the Catholic Church. Soon the church sympathizers revolted and civil war broke out. Juárez and his companions were hunted from town to town and many people were killed. . . .

For several years, Juárez lived near the northern border of Mexico, going from place to place in his black carriage. . . . In the resistance to the French, it was he who held out and finally defeated Maximilian. . . .

After the war with the French, Juárez undertook many reforms. He started schools to educate Indian children and reduced the size of the army. This angered the officers who tried to start revolts. Juárez also met resistance from the church. He was so opposed by powerful landowners that he was unable to give out much land to the people who needed it.

SECTION 1 REVIEW

CHECKING FOR UNDERSTANDING
1. **Identify** the groups that controlled Latin American politics in the 1800's.
2. **Distinguish** between conservatives and liberals during the 1800's.

CRITICAL THINKING
3. **Making Comparisons** Compare the ideals and actions of Melgarejo and Juárez.

SECTION 2
The New Tradition

By the end of the 1800's, some Latin Americans felt there was a need to modernize. They believed that to accomplish the needed social and economic changes, the traditional style of politics had to be destroyed. In some countries, labor began to organize, and the middle class began to voice its political opinions. The workers supported the middle class in its efforts to gain free elections. In return, the middle class worked to pass social welfare laws.

Today, the desire for social change dominates Latin American politics, and the few conservative parties that remain active are not strong. In recent years, pressure groups have become common. Among these are the Catholic Church, wealthy landowners, organized labor, and college students. But by far the most powerful pressure group is the army. It has the deciding voice in almost

EXAMINING PHOTOGRAPHS *Armed Nicaraguan soldiers search a man at a checkpoint during a civil war in 1979. How have the goals and attitudes of the military in Latin America been changing in recent years?*

EXAMINING PHOTOGRAPHS
College students, carrying a banner calling for "Democracy for the University," stage an anti-government demonstration in Santiago, Chile, to protest government control of university life. Besides students, what other pressure groups exist in Latin American politics? Which is by far the most important?

every Latin American country and has seized power on a regular basis in the region. At any one time, one-half of the Latin American nations may be ruled by the military.

Although in most cases today's military shows little concern for democracy, it does not have the same goals or attitudes of the military of the past. The strongest branch of the military remains the army. Most of its officers favor economic development, and many support social reform. There are several reasons for this change of attitude. One is that today most Latin American military officers come from the middle or lower class. Therefore, they tend to be favorable to the middle-class desire for modernization. Another reason is that today a professional outlook dominates in the military, and great stress is placed on producing a well-trained officer corps. Officers must receive the equivalent of a college degree at a military academy and receive their promotions on the basis of examinations.

The new professionalism of the military has not lessened greatly its intervention in politics. In most cases, as part of their training, members of the military are taught that economic modernization is important, and many believe that the government should make extensive use of its power to stimulate this modernization. Often, this means starting government-owned industries.

As in the past, the military still may intervene in and even overthrow governments that pursue policies of which it does not approve. In some cases, this action may be brought on by a concern for economic development. In others, it may be the result of dissatisfaction with the ineffectiveness, unconstitutionality, corruptness, or weakness of a civilian government. In still others, it may be seen as a solution to unresolvable power struggles between civilian powers.

In most cases, military interventions have at least some civilian support. Some civilian groups believe they will profit from a military intervention, while others believe that the military is the only group strong enough to maintain internal order or keep unprincipled politicians in line. Whatever the reason, once in power, most military governments rarely establish a better record than civilian governments when it comes to solving economic problems or battling corruption.

SECTION 3

Reaction to Change

Since the 1800's, almost every nation of Latin America has experienced some form or degree of change. Power struggles, war, dictatorships, severe violations of human rights, and poverty have been an all too common theme for many Latin Americans.

For some nations, the change has been radical. For others, it has been more conservative. How government has reacted to change has varied from nation to nation. Nicaragua, Cuba, and Colombia are just three of the Latin American nations that have experienced change in recent decades. While the government of each has faced many of the same problems, the reaction by each government has differed in certain aspects.

NICARAGUA

In 1979, after 40 years of rule by his family, Nicaraguan dictator Anastasio Somoza Debayle was overthrown and replaced by the Sandinista National Liberation Front. The Sandinistas promised to put an end to the civil war that was raging, revive the economy, and hold free elections. Instead, they restricted civil liberties, censored the press, took control of television, and used the police, the military, and Defense Committees to

EXAMINING PHOTOGRAPHS *Many Nicaraguan youths, like this 14-year-old soldier, were rounded up by the Sandinistas to fight the* contras. *How did the Sandinistas come to power?*

maintain their political control.

By 1984, a rebel group known as *contras* was waging a guerrilla war against the Sandinistas. The war took 50,000 lives, cost tens of millions of dollars, and led to the widespread destruction of property.

In 1990, bowing to pressure from nations whose economic aid was vital to Nicaragua, the Sandinistas held free elections. Much to their surprise, Sandinista Daniel Ortega won only 41 percent of the popular vote. Fifty-five percent went to Violeta Barrios de Chamorro, who promised to end the war and the military draft, to restore democracy, and to revive the economy. In the article that follows, a reporter discusses Chamorro, and the steps her administration has taken to combat her country's problems:

Wen Doña Violeta Chamorro, all dressed in white, swept into the Nicaraguan presidency last spring, she embodied the hopes of her people for national rebirth. . . .

The overwhelming victory was not so much an endorsement of Chamorro's National Opposition Union (UNO) party . . . but a popular plea to end both the civil war and the stifling, U.S.-led sanctions against the Sandinista government. . . .

Despite Chamorro's victory, all is not well in Nicaragua. True, the government has mustered a fragile peace. On her inauguration . . . , Chamorro abolished the military draft. She has aggressively downsized the army from 86,000 to 27,000 soldiers and cut its budget by two-thirds. Critically, she has disarmed many civilians in the countryside, confiscating more than 40,000 weapons. . . .

"We can't rest on our laurels because we won an election. But building democracy takes a while," [Ernest] Palazio [ex-contra who is Nicaragua's ambassador to Washington] said. To Chamorro's credit, some institution-building is taking place to better promote democracy. Freedom of the press and freedom of association are

standard, in contrast to the Sandinista decade. The National Assembly is functioning. . . . School curriculum is no longer decided by Sandinista ideologies, and steps have been taken toward market reform.

Nevertheless, the fundamental challenge, lying at the heart of the vote for Chamorro, is the battered economy. . . . Prices went up 13,000 percent last year. Downsizing the army upped unemployment, now 40 percent and climbing. While some contras returning from the countryside have been given land, they have neither the tools nor the capital to work it. . . .

Even today, the banking and credit systems are reportedly controlled by Sandinistas. . . . And, as Palazio pointed out, aid to jumpstart the economy has not materialized from the traditional sources: "The World Bank says no loans until we pay our arrears. We are paying the World Bank $360 million in Sandinista debt. Our total foreign debt is $11 billion, the highest per capita in the world. Tell me, where did all that money go?"

To combat these problems, the government has instituted a program . . . which includes price control as well as the

EXAMINING PHOTOGRAPHS *Since her inauguration as president of Nicaragua, Violeta Chamorro has actively sought Sandinista support for her policies. What is the most basic challenge that Chamorro's government faces?*

devaluation of the new currency, the "gold cordoba," by 500 percent. . . .

While peace has been delivered, much of the nation still lies in rubble. While democratic institutions have been established, wheeling and dealing between elite decision-makers sometimes circumvents them. Importantly, promises of economic deliverance have not been fulfilled.

. . . Chamorro has shown some courage and vision in consolidating peace, but with almost half the work force out of jobs, that peace is tentative at best. For many Nicaraguans suffering poverty, homelessness, joblessness and disease, the long-awaited economic recovery may be too late, if ever.

CUBA

Cuba, like Nicaragua, suffered under the rule of a dictator—Fulgencio Batista—who ruled for more than 20 years. Then in 1959 Fidel Castro took power and made Cuba the first Marxist nation in the Western Hemisphere. He promised the Cuban people reforms and a better standard of living.

Castro's are the only efforts at radical change in Latin America that have survived into the 1990's. Below, a visitor to Cuba gives his impressions of Cuba and of its leader:

From the commandante [Fidel Castro] on down, officials never tire of pointing out now, 32 years after "the triumph of the revolution," there are proportionately more doctors—some 40,000!—and universities—35—for Cuba's ten and a half million people than anywhere else in Latin America. . . .

On the other hand, one soon discovers that here is an economy so pinched, so beset by shortages, that people think themselves lucky if they can find a jar of mayonnaise to buy, or a plastic comb, or a tin of shoe polish. . . .

Source: April Oliver. "Nicaragua: peace with more problems than plans," *National Catholic Reporter,* April 19, 1991, p. 8.

EXAMINING PHOTOGRAPHS *A jubilant crowd in Havana, the capital of Cuba, carries aloft a larger-than-life poster of Fidel Castro during a celebration to honor Cuba's war dead. When did Castro come to power?*

For nearly three decades communist Cuba has depended primarily on trade with the Soviet Union and its . . . East European allies. Now, Castro says, such commerce with countries of the "former socialist community" has virtually ceased. . . . "We have swept away the capitalist system," [Castro] says, "and it will never return as long as there is a communist, a patriot, a revolutionary in Cuba. . . ."

One symbol of scarcity is *la cola.* The word means . . . a line, standing and waiting. Getting to work in Havana, by bus, and home again, may take hours; the old Hungarian buses keep breaking down. You plan a birthday party with a dozen guests, and you want to serve pork? Your ration book won't get you enough, so you'll stand in line today, hour after hour, and tomorrow too, at a special Havana market where unrationed meat *may* be available at higher prices. . . .

On the terrace of a hotel full of Canadians, a middle-aged Cuban who plays in the band tells guests that life here is hell. "On the surface all is nice and relaxed," he says, "underneath it's tightly controlled. People who have to talk to tourists are carefully selected." As he talks, he smiles in case he's being watched. . . ." He's had trouble because he doesn't like the band he's assigned to. . . . He's said so, and that's bad. No, he doesn't want to leave Cuba; he loves his country. . . .

On a Sunday morning in Santiago de Cuba . . . first graders race go-carts with deafening noise. A dozen nine-year-old boys and girls in made-to-measure army uniforms display a torn-down gasoline engine; they're from the Fuel and Lubricants Club of Tania the Guerrilla Primary School. Their teacher explains they don't have rifles yet, but they're learning about the history and importance of oil. "We want our children to know our weapons," an army major tells me while high school girls shove a blank shell into a 57-mm antitank gun. . . .

CASTRO, CLOSE UP. It's the 26th of July, the anniversary of the Monacada assault—Commander in Chief Fidel Castro, First Secretary of the Communist Party of Cuba and President of the Councils of State and of Ministers, is about to speak in Havana's Revolutionary Square. Balloons rise, leaflets float down, tens of thousands cheer the massive figure in olive green fatigues.

He puts on his glasses. A little wave of his outstretched left hand and there is silence. He begins slowly, clearly, with expansive gestures to right, to left; by turns he is outgoing, sarcastic, impassioned—his craggy face and silvery beard reminiscent now of Michelangelo's Moses. His theme is struggle, struggle, resist and resist. "The imperialists think we won't be able to resist—how little they understand

EXAMINING PHOTOGRAPHS *Cuban soldiers and students often perform volunteer work on farms and in factories. What was the condition of the Cuban economy in the early 1990's?*

our people. . . . We are millions of men and women, armed to the teeth, willing to win or die!"

However, as a journalist reports below, although most Cuban youth remain loyal to Castro and the Cuban Revolution, they are not completely satisfied:

It is 2 a.m. Sunday in the Havana Club, but Juan Antonio isn't dancing. Madonna's disco beat befuddles his salsa-savvy feet. It's just as well. A young woman in a white micro-mini has claimed his attention. . . . Juan Antonio, 19, has gone to heaven in Fidel Castro's Cuba. He may never be unhappy again.

Source: Peter T. White. "Cuba at a Crossroads," *National Geographic,* Vol. 180, No. 2, August 1991, pp. 94–95, 98–99, 102, 110, 114, 115–116.

He may also never be inside the Havana Club again: tickets can be bought only with dollars, and by law he is allowed to hold no more than $5 in U.S. currency, half the price of admission. A visiting tourist pays Juan Antonio's way, but he is worried . . . that the police will arrest him for consorting with foreigners, so he asks that his real name not be used. . . .

Cuba is a nation of young people. Nearly 60% of the island's 10.7 million people were born after Castro came to power in 1959. They have known only socialism. They are the healthiest and best-educated younger class in Latin America, but they are greedy for more. . . . They have had their fill of rhetoric and bureaucracy, of long lines for buses and *hamburguesas,* the Cuban version of an American favorite, made with pork. The most visible rebels . . . hang out in the park . . . , flaunting long hair and T shirts splashed with logos of heavy-metal bands. But even government-approved bands like Carlos Varela sing openly of Cuba's woes. "The inequities in society frustrate the young. I couldn't make a popular song about how great things are here now," admits American-born Cuban rock singer Pablo Menendez, a Castro supporter. "The young have

created pressure for change."

The dissatisfaction is particularly acute today. Last August Cuba tightened its rationing measures. . . . Every Cuban is entitled to only two rolls a day and less than a pound of meat every nine days. Particularly painful to the fashion-conscious young is rationing that limits them to just one new dress, a pair of pants and a pair of dress shoes a year. Grandmothers hand over their yearly ration of textile coupons to the young; mothers sell their gold jewelry for consumer goods like TVs and radios. . . .

Fed up with the economic hardships and the restrictions on personal liberties, hundreds of young have set out for Florida in flimsy rubber tubes or rafts. . . . After months of leniency, malcontents are again being hauled off to jails or rounded up for warnings. Local block groups, with 4 million members, have formed "rapid reaction brigades" to nip any protests in the bud. . . .

Around Havana the youthful influence has spiced up revolutionary slogans, which are now splashed in neon colors on the walls. *Súmate!* (Get involved!) says one.

Yet university teachers say it is increasingly hard to get students to believe socialism will ever provide them with the standard of living they want. "They complain about a lack of stylish clothes," says Blanca Munster Infante, 30, a professor of Marxism at one of Havana's advance polytechnic institutes. "They don't reject socialism, but they are pessimistic about making it work. They are disillusioned."

It would be wrong, however, to assume this discontent will translate into demise of Castro and Cuba's brand of socialism. While some 175 million live in poverty in Latin America, there are no beggars on the streets of Havana. The infant mortality rate is 10.7 per 1,000 births, in contrast to 60 before the revolution. "We see socialism is difficult to achieve, but capitalism isn't the answer either," says Sierra Wald, 17. "Nobody wants Fidel to step down. People worry about what might happen without him." Young Cubans increasingly see themselves as the last idealists in a world that cares only about money. . . . Says a 25-year-old teacher: "Everybody's really worried about the future, but my students don't talk about politics. They want something fresh, but they don't want to change the whole system. They just want to enjoy life."

COLOMBIA

Unlike Cuba and Nicaragua, Colombia has had a long tradition of democratic government. The military has seized power only once during this century, in 1953. And that takeover was supported by the nation's two political parties. At the same time, however, Colombia has been plagued by political violence that has caused the deaths of hundreds of thousands of Colombians over the last 45 or 50 years.

In 1989, the voters of Colombia elected a new president—César Gaviria Trujillo. His main political objective has been to restruc-

Source: Cathy Booth. "Dancing the Socialist Line," *Time,* August 12, 1991. Copyright 1991 Time Inc. Reprinted by permission.

ture the Colombian state. In the following article, a Latin American reporter talks about developments in Colombia:

Colombia has been one of the nations of Latin America least affected by the economic crisis. However, Gaviria has had to confront serious economic problems, including the renegotiation of the nation's $18-billion foreign debt. Another serious problem is unemployment. . . .

Over the past 58 years, 95 percent of elections in Colombia have been held under a state of siege. In Medellín, the seat of the most powerful drug cartel, more people have died since 1988 than died in the war in Lebanon.

The first major cause of violence in Colombia is drug trafficking. Money and power have turned the production and sale of drugs . . . into one of the fundamental elements of the destabilization of the nation. The drug czars have created a state within a state. The bribes, death threats against, and killings of more than 200 judges in Colombia are evidence of the traffickers' power. . . . However, during Gaviria's first year in office, the Medellín cartel suffered severe losses. . . .

The other major source of the violence that afflicts Colombia is the guerrilla movements. Last year, in a historic act, the M-19 guerrilla group decided to join the nation's political process and participated as a party in the presidential elections. After the assassination of M-19 leader Carlos Pizarro, Antonio Navarro Wolff ran as the party's candidate. . . . Navarro . . . is a member of the Constituent Assembly and is a key player in the current transformation of Colombian politics. The Gaviria administration has also been negotiating a ceasefire with other guerrilla organizations.

At the same time, the Constituent Assembly has been busy revising Colombia's constitution, which dates to 1886. . . .

The Constituent Assembly has already made a number of important decisions. . . .

EXAMINING PHOTOGRAPHS *In 1990, many guerrilla forces in Colombia decided to end armed resistance. Here a young guerrilla fighter lays down his weapon. How has the M-19 guerrilla movement transformed itself in order to participate in Colombian political life?*

EXAMINING PHOTOGRAPHS *On March 1, 1991, Colombia formally adopted a new constitution that further extended civil rights guarantees to Colombians. Here, an Indian delegate places his signature on the document. What group might soon benefit from the constitution's support for civil rights?*

A unicameral Congress will be set up, consisting of 210 deputies. And the old constitutional article that permitted government by decree and the suspension of normal laws has been revoked. This may free thousands of people imprisoned for political crimes.

The events of the past year are signs of a transformation more important than any that has taken place in Colombia in 100 years. None of Colombia's problems has been entirely resolved. . . . But one thing cannot be denied: Colombian society is ready to renew itself.

Source: Gloria Abella. "Colombia Emerges from the Siege," *El Nacional, World Press Review,* September 1991, pp. 36–37.

SECTION 3 REVIEW

CHECKING FOR UNDERSTANDING

1. **List** the accomplishments of the Chamorro administration in Nicaragua.
2. **Identify** the major causes of violence in Colombia.

CRITICAL THINKING

3. **Synthesizing Information** In the chapter, two writers discuss Cuba and Castro in the 1990's. Discuss what you have learned about Castro, about Cubans, and about present-day conditions in Cuba from their commentaries.

GLOBAL FOCUS

Government

A NEW OUTLOOK FOR CHILE

Not all Latin American nations have been ruled by strong-arm governments. Chile, for example, had an almost unblemished record of democratic governments until 1973 when a military junta headed by General Augusto Pinochet Ugarte took control. Finally, in 1988, Pinochet allowed elections, and under Patricio Aylwin, Chile's democratic tradition was restored. Below, a noted Peruvian writer offers his views on Chile.

FOCUSING ON THE ISSUE Based on the information in the article and in the chapter, compare Chile with the other nations discussed in the chapter. Explain in your own words the writer's views about government and the economy. Give reasons why you agree or disagree.

I spent a week in Chile, in Santiago and in the south, listening to politicians . . . and to journalists, writers, business people, professionals, students and artists. I heard nothing but phrases expressing confidence in Chile and its future. . . .

The optimism is justified. The Chilean economy grew in 1990 for the seventh year in a row. . . . Inflation has been maintained at 0.4 percent per month over the past year. . . . Last year, exports grew to a record level of $8.5 billion. . . . Unemployment has fallen to 5 percent, the lowest level in the region. . . .

This does not mean that Chile is a paradise, but it does indicate a stability and an economic dynamism that are without parallel in Latin America. . . .

It is not the numbers . . . that indicate that Chile is the first Latin American country to emerge from underdevelopment and reach the standard of living of a modern nation. It is the change in political culture that Chilean society has experienced that makes such a claim possible. The ideas of economic liberty, a free market open to the world, and private initiative as the motor of progress have become imbedded in the people of Chile. Those ideas have penetrated into the lives of the unions, the political parties, the media, and even . . . into the minds of many of Chile's intellectuals. . . .

The economic reforms that have brought prosperity . . . do not justify Pinochet's crimes. . . . But the fact that these reforms were carried out under this dictatorship does not invalidate them, either. . . . Above all, we should remember that liberty is indivisible. If it holds only in the economic sphere, and not in politics as well, the progress that may result will always be crippled and founded on feet of clay. . . . It is only now, under the democratic Aylwin government, that these reforms have attained permanence and solidity. . . .

The lesson of Chile is very simple. It is not that political liberty does not work but that economic liberty is an indispensable complement to it for any people who want tolerance, pluralism, respect for human rights—and jobs, economic growth, opportunities, development, and modernity. For this, it is necessary for the popular mandate to precede the adoption of these policies, a mandate that comes from persuasion and elections.

Source: Mario Vargas Llosa. "The Chilean Exception" in "A Region Moving Toward Democracy" in *World Press Review,* July 1991, pp. 24–25.

Chapter 32 Review

SUMMARY

The Latin American political tradition has been marked by revolutions, dictatorships, and military takeovers. Throughout the 1800's, political affairs were controlled by a small group made up of rich landowners, army officers, clergy, merchants, intellectuals, and professionals whose chief concerns were form of government and Church-State relations. By the end of the 1800's, in an effort to bring about reforms and modernize, some Latin Americans sought to destroy the traditional style of politics.

More recently, the desire for change has dominated Latin American politics. Pressure groups, such as the military, have gained importance. In the late 1980's, a new trend toward democracy emerged, bringing new voices into the political arena.

USING VOCABULARY

Imagine that it is the mid-1800's and that you are a Latin American. Write two profiles of yourself, each of which includes your political beliefs and goals. Write one from the perspective of a **liberal** and the other from the perspective of a **conservative**.

REVIEWING FACTS

1. **Characterize** politics in most of Latin America during the 1800's.
2. **Speculate** why civilians in Latin America might support military intervention in government.
3. **Summarize** what took place in Nicaragua between 1979 and 1991.
4. **Contrast** Colombia's tradition of politics and government with those of Cuba and Nicaragua.

5. **Cite** the change that came to Chile's government in the late 1980's.

CRITICAL THINKING

1. **Making Generalizations** Bolivian dictator Mariano Melgarejo was typical of most of the *caudillos*, military leaders, who have ruled Latin American countries. Based on what you know about Melgarejo, write two generalizations about military rulers of Latin America.
2. **Drawing Conclusions** Despite the hard times they are experiencing, many Cubans remain strong supporters of Fidel Castro and of his political philosophies. What reasons can you give for this?
3. **Demonstrating Reasoned Judgment** Even the least democratic governments of Latin America often have been supported by the poor. Give reasons why you would or would not support such a government if you were a poor Latin American.

ANALYZING CONCEPTS

1. **Change** In what ways have Latin American politics changed since the 1800's?
2. **Power** What factors do you think have contributed to the instability that has been an integral part of the Latin American political tradition?
3. **Interdependence** Many governments of Latin American nations have been short-lived. If your nation was one of these, what effect do you think this political instability might have on its role in the global community?

GEOGRAPHIC THEMES

Regions Do you think Latin America can be considered a region politically? Give reasons for your answer.

Distinguishing Fact from Opinion

At one time or another, everyone is faced with the need to make a decision based on the facts and opinions he or she hears or reads. These decisions may have to do with all sorts of things, ranging from what outfit to wear to a party to what kind of car to buy to which candidate to vote for in an election.

Suppose you hear someone say, "This is definitely the best movie I've ever seen!" Although this statement may be true for the speaker, it is not a statement of *fact* because there is no way to check its accuracy. Instead, this statement explains how the speaker feels about the movie. It is a statement of *opinion*. If the person had said, "This movie made more money than any other movie this year," *that* statement would be a fact because its accuracy could be checked against box office statistics.

To get a clear picture of events, it is important to know both facts and opinions. Facts explain what happened, who was involved, where and when an event occurred, and so on. Facts can be verified by evidence. Opinions, on the other hand, express people's beliefs, feelings, or conclusions about events. They cannot be proved or disproved. Opinions often begin with words such as *I believe, probably, it seems,* or *in my view.* Opinions often contain qualifying words such as *may, might, could, should, ought,* and superlatives such as *best, worst,*

greatest, outstanding, and *extraordinary.*

It is important to distinguish between facts and opinions. If you accept opinions as facts without checking their accuracy, you may develop an inaccurate understanding of events. Distinguishing facts from opinions enables you to form your own conclusions about events. The steps below will help you distinguish facts from opinions:

- Identify facts by looking for statements which can be checked for accuracy such as names, dates, places, numbers, and specific actions. Often, facts answer the questions *who? what? where? and when.*
- Identify opinions by looking for statements expressing beliefs or feelings. Often, they contain phrases such as *I believe* or *In my view* or qualifiers and superlatives.

EXAMPLE

Read the following statements:

1. Violeta Chamorro promised to end the war and the military draft, to restore democracy, and to revive the economy.
2. The outcome of Chamorro's campaign was astonishing.
3. I believe the Cuban Revolution has been a striking success.
4. While 175 million Latin Americans live in poverty, there are no beggars on the streets of Havana.

Sentence 1 is a fact because it can be verified by reading accounts of Chamorro's campaign promises. However, sentence 2 is an opinion because it expresses one person's reaction to the election results. Are statements 3 and 4 facts or opinions? How can you tell? *(Sentence 3 is an opinion; it begins with "I believe" and expresses a personal feeling; sentence 4 is a fact because it makes a statement that could be verified by statistics and observations.)*

PRACTICE

For each statement, write **F** if it is a fact, or write **O** if it is an opinion. Explain each answer.

1. Benito Juárez was the first Indian ruler of Mexico since the Aztec Cuauhtemoc.
2. In most Latin American countries, it seems that the military have little concern for democracy.
3. Most military officers in Latin America come from the lower or middle classes.
4. In the late 1980's, leaders in Peru, Argentina, and Brazil were swept into power by a magical aura that they projected to their people.
5. In 1959, Fidel Castro took power in Cuba.
6. In my view, U.S. support for the Nicaraguan *contras* destroyed the economy of that country.
7. Costa Rica is the best place to live in Latin America.
8. The major cause of violence in Colombia is drug trafficking.

Latin American Music Moves North

Latin American music, with its blend of Indian, Spanish, and African rhythms and sounds, has enlivened American music since the end of the 1800's. From ragtime to the pop music of the 1990's, American musicians have found inspiration, new beats and melodies, and even new musical instruments south of the border.

Cuban music was the first Latin influence on American musicians. As early as the late 1800's, ragtime pianists borrowed musical rhythms from Cuba. It was, however, the 1920's in Harlem, New York City, the new capital of jazz, when Cuban music became a real force. Latin American musicians like the Cuban flautist Alberto Socarras and the Puerto Rican Juan Tizol joined America's big jazz bands. They brought with them the exotic rhythms of the conga and the bongo, the bolero and the guaracha. American bandleaders like Duke Ellington and Cab Calloway were charmed by these new rhythms and introduced them into their musical pieces.

In the late 1930's, Cuban trumpeter Mario Bauza formed a band called the Afro-Cubans that blended Cuban rhythms with jazz. Bauza introduced Americans to the conga drums and drumming, which fascinated people. The fusion of Cuban music with American jazz produced a daring new sound called "cubop" (from Cuba and bebop), then later, Latin jazz.

Brazilian music became a popular part of the Latin sound in the 1950's. American musicians and their audiences were entranced by the energetic beat of the samba and the swaying rhythms of the bossa nova. One listener described the music of the bossa nova as "floating, suspended between beats." More recently, Brazilian musicians like Milton Nacimento, with his dream-like music full of strange harmonies, have influenced American jazz musicians, such as Sarah Vaughan and Herbie Hancock.

Latin American music continues to play a big part in the American music scene. It is popular among American rock musicians like Paul Simon and Talking Heads star David Byrne, who have made recordings based on Latin rhythms. In addition, stars such as Gloria Estefan have brought Latin-based pop right into America's heartland—during one concert it was reported that she had 11,000 people dancing the conga on the banks of the Mississippi River.

Making the Connection

1. How has music from Latin America influenced music in the United States?

2. Why do you think Latin American music has had such a strong influence in the United States?

Unit 5 Review

SUMMARY

Latin America is a diverse area in terms of people and geography. As a region, it has benefited from the rich cultural heritage of each of the groups that make up its population. Over the centuries, social class has continued to be of importance. Despite reforms and the emergence of a middle class, the gap between the rich and the poor and between urban dwellers and rural dwellers still tends to be great.

During this century, Latin America has experienced continuing change. Even the Catholic Church, which for centuries influenced almost every aspect of life, has had to deal with a decline in influence. Although in some countries the political life remains tense, the overall trend is toward more democratic government.

REVIEWING THE MAIN IDEAS

1. **Describe** some of the ways in which life in modern Latin America reflects the area's diversity of cultures.
2. **Examine** the role of the Catholic Church in Latin America over the centuries.
3. **Identify** the factors that have contributed to the changes that have taken place in Latin America in recent decades.
4. **Discuss** the ways in which the changes taking place in Latin America have affected the way of life of most Latin Americans.

CRITICAL THINKING

1. **Analyzing Information** In the 1800's, an Argentine said: "The age of heroes has passed; we enter today the age of common sense." Do you think this was true in Latin America in the 1800's? Do you think it is true today? Explain.

2. **Identifying Central Issues** According to a journalist, "During the . . . 1980's, Latin America, with the exception of Cuba, became free of dictators. But, at the same time, the region's per-capita gross domestic product fell nearly 10 percent, and the number of poor people increased by 71 million. Slightly more than 41 percent of the population of Latin America is now living in poverty." What point was the journalist trying to make?

PRACTICING SKILLS

Identifying Central Issues Read the following passage about democracy in Central America. How would you summarize the central issues of the passage? *Democracy in Latin America could be more than it is at the present moment. There is a deep lack of confidence in democracy among the people. For example, in one nation, people did not defend democracy when it was threatened by a military coup. People do not believe in democracy strongly enough to take risks for it. They are coming to believe that democratic government is an empty form without any real substance.*

DEVELOPING A GLOBAL VIEWPOINT

The Overseas Development Council says that true development is "improving the well-being of men, women, and children around the world, and sustaining the environment on which the rich and poor depend." What other parts of the world have been seeking development in recent decades? What have they been doing to help achieve their goal? What success have they had? Do you think Latin American nations will be considered "developed" in the near future?

Middle East

As the birthplace of three great religions, the crossroads for trade between Europe and Asia, and now a major supplier of vital oil supplies, the Middle East has long been one of the most important regions of the world. Today, outside nations seek to protect or advance their interests in the region. Numerous internal conflicts also threaten to have wider consequences. Thus, understanding this volatile and vital region is important for economic and political reasons. It also is important because learning about the Middle East helps one appreciate some of his or her own cultural roots and other people's ways of life.

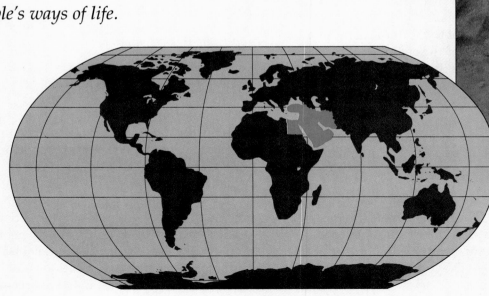

AT A GLANCE

LAND AREA: 2,681,404 sq. mi. (6,944,809 sq. km.)

LAND RESOURCES:
cropland: 8.4%
pasture: 23.5%
forest/woodland: 6.3%
other land: 61.7%

WILDERNESS AREA: 21.1%

MAJOR MOUNTAIN RANGES: Elburz, Pontus, Tuwayq, Zagros

MAJOR RIVERS: Nile, Tigris, Euphrates

MAJOR DESERTS: An Nafud, Arabian, Great Salt, Libyan, Syrian

POPULATION: (1992 est.) 253,700,000

POPULATION UNDER 15/OVER 65: 42%/4%

LIFE EXPECTANCY: 63 yrs.

POPULATION PROJECTION: 574,400,000 (by 2025)

POPULATION DENSITY: 95/sq. mi. (37/sq. km.)

URBAN POPULATION: 56%

LARGEST CITIES: (millions)
Cairo, Egypt (6.2)
Tehran, Iran (5.7)
Istanbul, Turkey (5.5)
Alexandria, Egypt (2.8)

CHAPTER OUTLINE

People and Places to Know

Nile River, Tigris River, Fertile Crescent, the Empty Quarter, the Negev, the Nile Delta, Cairo, Baghdad, Istanbul, Black Sea

Key Terms to Define

nomad, desalination, fallahīn, *kibbutzim, moshavim, sūq*

Objectives to Learn

1. **List** the nations of the Middle East and describe its geography.
2. **Discuss** how the Middle East's geography has influenced lifestyles.
3. **Explain** how water is a factor in the lives of Middle Eastern peoples.
4. **Describe** urban life in the Middle East.

Egyptians sailing on the Nile River

Environment and People

> " The Nile is one of the great wonders of the world. It is the longest river flowing from south to north. . . . It flows through every natural formation from towering mountains and well-watered highlands of the most barren of deserts. Within this vast area [people] in Egypt and the Sudan [have] watched the rich, brown waters of the Nile flow northward to the Mediterranean Sea anxiously awaiting for the life which came with them, for without the river there would be only sand and rock and wind. [Humans] cannot survive where there is no water and cannot multiply where there is no fertile soil. The Nile provides both these necessities of human existence. . . .
>
> . . . Throughout the northern reaches of the Nile [human civilizations] have been dependent upon the river for . . . survival. . . . At times the river has given too much, resulting in disastrous floods which swept away . . . habitations huddled by the Nile. In other years, the waters did not come, and there was drought and famine in the land. "

The worst famine of the kind discussed above took place in Cairo, the capital of Egypt, in the year 1200. The famine came about because the Nile River had not risen enough to water the farmers' fields. For the same reason, there were 11 more famines within 50 years throughout the region.

Water has always been a key factor in people's lives not only in Egypt but in all of the Middle East. Today, this region at the eastern end of the Mediterranean Sea—where Europe, Asia, and Africa meet—includes large countries with many people—such as Egypt, Turkey, Iran, and Iraq. It includes countries with some of the richest oil fields in the world—such as Iran, Iraq, Saudi Arabia, and the tiny states of Kuwait, Bahrain, Qatar, and

the United Arab Emirates. It includes the small but politically significant nations of Israel and Lebanon. It also includes the countries of Syria, Jordan, the Republic of Yemen, and Oman.

About two-thirds of the Middle East receives less than eight inches (20 centimeters) of rain each year, the least amount needed to grow most food crops. Most of the rain comes during the winter months when the growing season is over. During the growing months of the summer, the skies are clear and temperatures soar over 100° Fahrenheit (38° Celsius).

Water, then, means life. For centuries, it has determined where people settle and how long they stay there. It also has determined how many people can live in one spot. Because of water, people have fought wars, have moved long distances, and have suffered or prospered.

Source: R.O. Collins. "Historical View of the Development of Nile Water" in The Nile Resource Evaluation, Resource Management, Hydropolitics and Legal Issues. P.P. Howell and J.A. Allan. Royal Geographical Society and the School of Oriental and African Studies. p. 154.

The Region

One hundred fifty million years ago, much of the Middle East was covered with dense tropical forests and swamps. Marshes were thick with grasses and ferns, which rotted in slow waters. Today these same areas contain valuable oil fields, and the land and the climate have changed. Coastlines, rugged mountains, rocky hills, deserts, and areas of watered fertile lands now make up much of the landscape.

Running through almost every country are mountains. Among others, there are the Taurus Mountains, which run east and west through the southern edge of Turkey. There is Mount Ararat, in northeastern Turkey. There is the Zagros range which, stretching northwest to southeast, divides Iran and Iraq. Then there are the Elburz Mountains of Iran, the Asir Mountains of Saudi Arabia, and the Red Sea Mountains of Egypt.

The many mountains of the Middle East block the flow of rain clouds to the inland side of the region. Thus, even though the Middle East is bounded on the west by the Mediterranean Sea, to the north by the Black and Caspian seas, and on the south by the Persian Gulf and the Arabian Sea, fresh water inland is scarce and unpredictable. Only Turkey, northwest Iran, and a narrow rim of land along the seas in Yemen, Saudi Arabia, Israel, Syria, and Lebanon flourish with regular and adequate rainfall.

Growing and living conditions differ in areas with little water and in those where there are rivers, springs, and oases, green spots in dry lands where groundwater comes to the surface. In the watered areas, more crops can grow, and more people tend to settle. The Nile River, more than 4000 miles (6400 kilometers) long, flows north from east Africa through Egypt to the Mediterranean Sea. Today the Nile Valley and its delta support almost 55 million Egyptians. Two other major rivers, the Tigris and Euphrates, flow through southeastern Turkey, Syria, and Iraq and empty into the Persian Gulf. In the following passage, a visitor tells what he and his friends found as they rafted down the Euphrates:

EXAMINING PHOTOGRAPHS *These travelers, whose trip down the Euphrates River is described on the next page, appear small in size compared to the steep cliffs that line the river. Today, the Euphrates meets with the Tigris before emptying into the Gulf, but, in ancient times, this was not the case. How have the rivers of the Middle East influenced the development of civilization in the region?*

[In] Ankara we link up, . . . hop a plane to Elazig and take a minibus west to the Keban Dam, which backs up the largest reservoir in Turkey. . . .

By 12:30 we're on the great, green, cold expanse called the Euphrates. It's beautiful, but somehow anticlimactic. It feels no different from the Colorado, the Blue Nile or a dozen other big rivers. I somehow expected a deeper sense of ancient history, ruins at every bend, caravans crossing the shallows. The yellow canyon, illustrated with folding whorls [circular ridges] and faults, is still, save for the sounds of birds. It feels as though we're floating through an empty coliseum . . . punctured with caves and rimmed with winding paths.

At dusk, as we camp, we see two other inflatable rafts drifting toward us. . . . We thought we were the only inflatable for 1,000 miles [1600 kilometers] and at least as many years. The vessels gradually wave into focus as though emerging from a desert mirage. They're jerryrigged rafts, tractor-tire innertubes lashed to planks, piloted by farmers. . . . I remember that farmers and herders along the Euphrates have been using inflatables for millenia. . . .

The next morning I poke my head from my fiberfill sleeping bag and witness, in the flat dawn light, a tractor in the middle of the Euphrates. . . . The river is gone. A tiny trickle remains. . . . They've turned off the dam! . . . The mighty Euphrates, river of antiquity, . . . reduced to a rivulet, the victim of the flick of a switch at the Keban Dam. . . .

[The] river's still not there the next day. We break the wait by hiking across the ridge behind us, where we discover the real Euphrates rushing by in sizeable volume. We're on an island, . . . and have parked in a channel. . . . We wrestle the boat down to the trickle and proceed to drag it over the rocks downstream. . . . Within hours we've floated . . . to Kale, at the head of the Kermer Khan Canyon. . . .

Through this Grand Canyon of the Euphrates, the river cuts its most imposing course, scything around a lava mass erupted from the Karajali volcano, and stabbing across the . . . Taurus Mountains. Here, too, are the river's biggest rapids. Lulled by days of flat water, we're taken by surprise when we plummet into the first cataract [waterfall]. . . . This is not a complacent river after all. . . .

. . . Beyond the oblique canyon we can sometimes see snow-capped mountains and, at tributary mouths, we occasionally spot Kurdish women fetching water in long-necked clay jugs.

Late on the sixth day we enter a . . . gorge pocked with shallow caves. High on the west bank, fitted into a limestone alcove, sits a remarkable sight—a masterfully constructed, ancient, abandoned Byzantine monastery. . . . Honeycombed with dank passages, festooned with swallow nests, graced with Roman-arched doors, filled with bats and with no easy access to the world beyond the river gorge, the place is a hidden wonder. . . .

On Sunday, after the river has broken from the canyon, dropped off the Adiyaman Plateau and started its long, sluggish journey across the flatlands, we round a bend and see a glint of steel . . . : the Akinjilar Bridge, our takeout. As we pull in under the abutment, some teenagers manning an open-air soda fountain for bus travelers scramble down to meet us.

The history of the Middle East began in the areas near the Nile River and in the Fertile Crescent. In the Tigris and Euphrates Valley lies the biggest part of the Fertile Crescent. The Crescent is an arc-shaped area of land that arches from the Persian Gulf north into Turkey and then south along the Mediterranean coast. Here began one of the earliest Western civilizations. Here and along the Nile were the "cradles of civilization."

Source: Richard Bangs. "Down the Gorge" in *ARAMCO WORLD Magazine,* January-February 1981, p. 32.

SECTION 1 REVIEW

CHECKING FOR UNDERSTANDING

1. **Describe** the physical features of the Middle East.

CRITICAL THINKING

2. **Analyzing Information** How do you think mountains have affected the way Middle Eastern peoples live?

SECTION 2

Deserts

Mountains and prevailing winds have created vast deserts in many parts of the Middle East. Not all of the desert lands, however, are the same. One, the Empty Quarter of Saudi Arabia, consists of shifting sand dunes on which almost nothing grows. Another, the Negev, is mostly barren rock with eroded hills. In northern Saudi Arabia, the desert is covered with scrubby bushes. When there is rain, colorful wildflowers burst into bloom and dense grasses grow.

One group of people, the Bedouins, has made their homes on the edges and around the oases of such deserts for centuries. Because food and water for their herds are too scarce to allow them to settle permanently in one spot, the Bedouins are **nomads**, people who move from place to place. They do not just wander aimlessly, however. They know exactly where they are going and when. A Bedouin clan usually ranges over the same area each year. Some raise herds of camels, while others tend flocks of sheep and goats. Their lives and their travels are carefully planned to catch fleeting rainstorms and to survive in the harshest settings.

In recent years, however, life has changed for the Bedouins, and few remain nomadic. Today, under 3 percent of the Middle Eastern population is nomadic. Bedouins are settling and living in houses instead of tents. Jeeps and pickup trucks are putting markets within easy reach for Bedouin livestock herders who want to sell their dairy products, wool, hides, and live animals to customers in the cities. Some young Bedouins are going into the army, while others are taking jobs in the oil fields and in other businesses. Even those Bedouins who prefer not to abandon their way of life have had to make some changes. Below, an anthropologist who studied the Āl'Azab, a clan of Bedouins in the Empty Quarter, describes their life today:

To the Āl'Azab, fall pasturing deep inside the [Empty Quarter] is a time of happiness and contentment. They always say it is the best season. There is the excitement of game to be hunted; there is the absence of the influences of the city, of the oasis, of the central government; there is bound to be relatively good grazing. But by November, the herders begin to scan the northern skies at night in hope of seeing flashes of lightning in the distant skies. *Insh'allah*, if Allah [God] wills, the rains will come.

Throughout the late fall, the herdsmen are keenly interested in news about the rains. Word is brought about once a month by the members of the Reserve National Guard, who travel by truck to . . . the headquarters of the amir [leader]. While [there], they obtain as much precise information as possible from other members . . . who have been in the north or who have been in touch with others . . . in the north. Each person who reports rains is carefully questioned about how he obtained his information, whether it is first-hand or based on the reports of others. If there is any doubt about the reports . . . , they ask the amir for his opinion. He is in a position to hear the reports of a wide range of [Bedouins], and he considers it part of his business to provide information as reliable as possible for the herdsmen. . . .

Any time after the first of December and when reliable news establishes that rains have fallen in the north, each Āl'Azab household changes the rhythm of its movements. Instead of short moves every few days within a given area, the camels are herded . . . in marches that last from about two hours after sunrise until around sunset, with the camels grazing for a few hours near the camp after sunset.

Depending on how cold the weather is, either tents or enclosure walls are set up about an hour before sunset. The herds graze for a couple of hours and arrive just after dark, at which time they are milked. Camp fires glow in the men's sections of the tents or in front of the enclosures, and one hears the ringing beat of coffee beans being pounded into powder. . . .

. . . The men eat a communal meal of rice about three hours after sunset. They drink milk later on, and most of the youths sit up until well past midnight talking about camels and the state of the grazing, reciting poems, and listening to the Bedouin Hour on Radio Kuwait. All too soon, the morning call to prayer comes, just before sunrise, and a new day begins as the march goes on toward the north.

Source: Donald Powell Cole. *Nomads of the Nomads: The Al Murrah Bedouin of the Empty Quarter.* Aldine Publishing Company, 1975, pp. 43–45.

EXAMINING PHOTOGRAPHS *This Bedouin family has pitched its tent near the grassy northern edge of the desert. What is fall grazing like among the Bedouin herders of the Āl'Azab clan?*

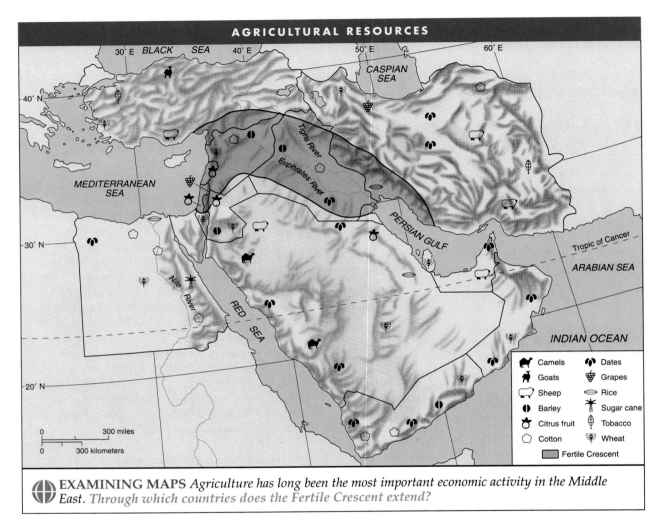

AGRICULTURAL RESOURCES

Legend:
- Camels
- Goats
- Sheep
- Barley
- Citrus fruit
- Cotton
- Dates
- Grapes
- Rice
- Sugar cane
- Tobacco
- Wheat
- Fertile Crescent

EXAMINING MAPS *Agriculture has long been the most important economic activity in the Middle East. Through which countries does the Fertile Crescent extend?*

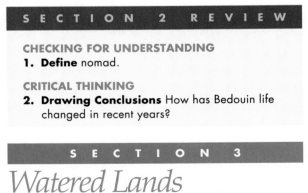

SECTION 2 REVIEW

CHECKING FOR UNDERSTANDING
1. **Define** nomad.

CRITICAL THINKING
2. **Drawing Conclusions** How has Bedouin life changed in recent years?

SECTION 3

Watered Lands

All of the Middle East is not desert. The region also contains some of the most fertile soil in the world. There is the Nile Valley, made fertile by silt left over thousands of years by the annual floods of the Nile River. There is the Fertile Crescent, described in the Bible as "a land of brooks and water, of fountains . . . ; a land of wheat and barley, and vines, and fig trees, and pomegranates; a land of olive oil and honey." In western Iran, in Turkey, and in Yemen, there is good farmland.

But even fertile land needs water, and this has always been a challenge in the Middle East. Long ago, when the earliest settlers began to spread beyond the fertile areas near the rivers, they found that they had to irrigate the land before crops would grow. Isolated families alone could not build irrigation systems, but groups of families, forming villages, could. Today about 50 percent of all Middle Easterners are farming peasants who live in villages. Until the 1950's, most of the best farmland was owned by wealthy landlords or by royal families. Now, most of the land is owned by villagers.

All over the Middle East, modern technology and human determination are reclaiming land to support more people. In a process called **desalination**, seawater is made fresh and usable for drinking and irrigation. Huge dams, such as the Aswan in Egypt and the Tabaqa in Syria, harness the great rivers and bring water to millions of acres of soil.

THE NILE DELTA

In areas with water and fertile land, Middle Easterners have been able to produce rich harvests. One such area is the Nile Delta. Over the past 100 years, a series of dams and canals have been built in the delta region. These improvements have enabled the **fallahīn,** or Egyptian farmers, to raise

three crops a year instead of one. Now the Delta's yields of rice, cotton, sugar, wheat and corn are among the highest in the world.

The Delta is one of the most densely populated areas of the world with 2500 people per square mile (2.6 square kilometers) living there. Human labor and hard work are responsible for the achievements made in the region. Other factors in the Delta's agricultural transformation are mechanization and the Aswan High Dam. The Dam traps the Nile's waters for irrigation and protects crops from seasonal flooding. Although benefiting agriculture, the dam has seriously affected the environment. Because floodwaters no longer deposit fertile silt, farmers must now add chemical fertilizers to their fields. Also, the absence of silt has increased land erosion in many areas. Below, a North American journalist describes life in the Delta:

"This is the best place on earth," said Ahmed, an Egyptian. . . farmer, I encountered in the Nile Delta, that incredibly fertile 8,500-square-mile [22,015-square-kilometer] triangle between Cairo and the Mediterranean coast. . . .

EXAMINING PHOTOGRAPHS *This Egyptian farmer is harvesting wheat by hand with a sickle. This method of cutting grain dates back to the ancient Egyptians and the time when, because of its huge exports of grain, Egypt was known as the granary of the world. What are some other crops grown in the fertile soil of the Nile Delta today?*

"Truly Allah [God] has blessed us," Ahmed exclaimed piously. "Soil, water, sun—we can grow anything!"

In the gathering dusk Ahmed and his five companions had invited me to join them. Their *galabias* [long tunics] and turbans stained by the sweat and dirt of a long day's work, they sat in front of a wayside shop. . . . At the edge of a nearby canal, donkeys laden with fresh harvested alfalfa waited for their masters to lead them home, braying a fretful counterpoint to the steady thud of an irrigation pump. . . .

From the nearby town of Rashid, . . . I drove south through the delta, through villages where veiled women passed among walls on which the name of God had been written over and over by the pious. I stopped often to watch the [farmers] at work in their fields. Modern equipment driven by diesel or electric motors is a common sight. But so are ancient irrigation devices. . . .

ISRAEL

Much also has been done in Israel. Here, part of the Negev Desert has been reclaimed, and farming settlements called *kibbutzim* (KEE·boo·TSEEM) have been established. In theory, *kibbutzim* are collective communities in which all members are equal. No one is paid a wage. Instead, everyone shares in the land, labor, and produce. In practice, however, many Israeli farms are tending to operate on free enterprise principles. The *kibbutzim* are small in number. There are only about 250, which represents about 3 percent of the Israeli population. Below, a 61-year-old Israeli describes the beginning of his *kibbutz* and his pride in its early accomplishments:

At first, we lived in tents. . . . I didn't even get a bed for myself—I had to share

Source: Robert Caputo. "Journey Up the Nile" in *National Geographic*, May 1985, pp. 579–581, 584.

one with another guy for a while after I arrived. Then, during the summer, we built little tree houses in the trees, which was fun. When we moved to our present location, we, as a married couple, had a tent first and a little hut later. The hut was 4-by-6 meters [13.2-by-19.8 feet] and shared by three couples; . . . No restrooms, no showers—nothing. . . .

We had a malaria epidemic at the kibbutz, which was awful. . . . Only about one or two of the men were spared this disease. I caught it, too. We all suffered—malaria is a disease that completely drains you. So we started sleeping under mosquito nets—imagine, in this heat! To sleep under a net was a nightmare. At night I felt as if I would suffocate, and I couldn't escape.

To complete the picture: the food. I can't even start to describe it for you. . . . We had lots of bread, oil, and sugar. Half an egg sometimes. We used to get jam in a tablespoon, smoothed out by a knife so that you wouldn't get too much. Butter appeared rarely. A piece of cake or an egg was a whole day's ration for a working man, a man doing hard physical work outside. . . .

Women, too, had it hard then. . . . They had neither warm water nor heating in the homes. And, worst of all, there were no roads or paved paths within the kibbutz. If you have never experienced rain here, you cannot imagine it. . . . You really cannot walk—and we had just one pair of shoes. Our children grew up on our shoulders. . . . Now, there is no problem. You can wear sandals in the winter and walk on the paved path, and it's fine.

What kept us going (those of us who did) during that period? I really cannot tell you . . .

Maybe I kept going because of the conviction that we were building something out of nothing. And this is, apparently, something of great significance. The constant planning of what is to come, the ecstasy of the beginning! I remember

EXAMINING PHOTOGRAPHS *These workers are picking grapefruit at an Israeli* kibbutz *in the Negev Desert. Experience on these farms has made Israel a world leader in such desert-farming technology as trickle irrigation, a system by which plastic pipes carry exact amounts of water and nutrients to each individual plant.* What have kibbutzim and moshavim added to their economic activities in recent years?

when the first buildings, such as our first barn, were erected here. We dug the ground, which is all basalt rocks and heavy soil, with our bare hands. Now we have all the necessary equipment. Yet all of us competed with great enthusiasm to see who would be the first one to reach the basalt, to get deep down to the foundation. This gave all of us tremendous satisfaction.

This stubborn will to build the kibbutz, to settle the area, is what inspired us. And for me, my work kept me going, too. I always loved working in the fields; to this very day I derive a great deal of satisfaction from it.

More recently, in addition to growing crops, these *kibbutzim*, and another type of cooperative of small individual farms called **moshavim** (MOH·sha·VEEM), have begun to add industries and fish-breeding ponds to their other economic activities.

Source: From KIBBUTZ MAKOM by Amia Lieblich. Copyright © 1981 by Amia Lieblich. Reprinted by permission of Pantheon Books, a division of Random House, Inc., pp. 19–21.

SECTION 3 REVIEW

CHECKING FOR UNDERSTANDING
1. **Define** desalination *fallahin, kibbutzim, moshavim.*

CRITICAL THINKING
2. **Identifying Central Issues** How do you think modern technology has affected Middle Eastern agriculture?

SECTION 4

Cities

Where water was available, cities grew. Cairo on the Nile River, Baghdad on the Tigris River, and Istanbul on the Bosphorus Strait all flourished because of location. Some cities have been trade and population centers for centuries.

The early cities were laid out to fit the environment. Narrow streets, for example, were a defense against invaders and against

EXAMINING PHOTOGRAPHS *This scene in an old section of Cairo, above left, contrasts markedly with the modern buildings in the newer section of the city, above right.* What was Cairo architecture like in the late 1800's?

the intense rays of the sun. Below, a traveler to Cairo in the late 1800's explains how architecture was adapted to the environment:

The inner court of the home is almost as silent and deserted as the guarded windows which overlook the street. We shall see nothing of the domestic life of the people who live there. After the bustle of the street this quiet and ample space is very refreshing. One feels that the Egyptian architects have happily realized the needs of eastern life. They make the streets narrow and overshadow them with projecting meshrebiyas (carved wooden screens), because the sun beats down so fiercely. But they make the houses large and surround them with courts and gardens, because without air one could not

bear the heat of the rooms in summer. The Eastern architect's art lies in so building your house that you cannot look into your neighbor's windows, nor he into yours. The obvious way is to build the rooms round a high open court, and to closely veil the windows with lattice blinds. This lets in some light and air, and allows an outlook without allowing the passing stranger to see through.

THE *SŪQ*

At the heart of every Middle Eastern city then—and now—is its *sūq* (sook), or marketplace. Covering the *sūq* are high-ceiling tentlike arrangements. Windows in the sides allow the air to flow through, while the "roof"

Source: Stanley Lane-Poole. *Cairo.* Virtue, 1898, p. 10

provides people with shelter from the hot sun and the rain. In many modern-day cities, the mall-like *sūq* provides a marked contrast to other areas, some of which may be only a block or two away. This contrast and how one might react to it is described below by a visitor to Bahrain:

> I drifted into a maze of streets on which mine was the only Western face in sight. One narrow alley was full of carpenters and the smell of freshly sawn pine; another was a dazzling canal of brilliant Hong Kong cottons; another, the car-repair zone, was loud with lines of men banging shapeless bits of metal with hammers. . . . The protective labyrinth, in which every trade has its own allocated quarter fixed by use and tradition, is Arabia's strongest bastion [stronghold] against monoculture. Things are kept separate—gold and meat, vegetables and clothing, spices and hi-fi sets . . . every category has at least one street to itself. This separation of objects keeps people apart too; at each turn in the maze one notices a distinct difference in skin color and style of dress. You cannot go more than a hundred yards [90 meters] without trespassing across a clearly defined boundary. A blind man could find his way through the labyrinth by smell alone: machine oil gives way to turmeric and coriander, sweet sawdust to the acrid barnyard odor of live chickens, roast coffee to the oddly musky scent of cheap plastic.

EXAMINING PHOTOGRAPHS *This colorful scene of a mall-like* sūq *in modern Cairo is bustling with shoppers stopping here and there to look at merchandise or to make a purchase. What are some of the characteristics of* sūqs *in the Persian Gulf state of Bahrain?*

In one step at the end of a street I crossed from a world of mud and wood to one of marble, glass and concrete. I had been threading my way through a long, rustling procession of black veils; suddenly there were only business suits and sharkskin document cases. The line of banks on Government Road was taller and wider than the lines of spice sellers and carpenters; but it had the same air of being a single specialized component in a labyrinthine system. . . . When I crossed the street and walked behind the back of a great glass investment-company building, money gave way to wood shavings and resin, and two men on a makeshift platform caulking the hull of a dhow [boat used for trade in the Persian Gulf].

ISTANBUL

The lifeblood of many early Middle Eastern cities was trade. This has remained true for Istanbul, formerly known as Constantinople. Located at the neck of the Bosphorus, it could control the flow of trade from Russia and the Black Sea to the Mediterranean world. In the mid-1500's, a French visitor to the city wrote, "It seems to me that while other cities are mortal, this one will remain as long as there are men on earth."

Istanbul is the only city that occupies land on two continents. For over 2000 years, it has been a bridge for overland and sea traffic between the East and the West. Below, a visitor to Istanbul paints a picture of the city:

Istanbul is a child of the sea. Few cities are invested so totally, so intimately, by water. It laps the twin shores of the Stamboul peninsula, defines the blunt head of Beyoğlu across the Golden Horn [a wide inlet], washes the long front of Asian Üsküdar. The sea, perilous and rich with the flux of trade and war, has always been the city's chief highway. As for anchorage, the water is so deep around the city that ocean-going liners berth cheek-by-jowl with streets and markets; and huge freighters, when they need repair, back their sterns without trouble on to shore. . . .

EXAMINING PHOTOGRAPHS *On most days, the ancient and modern bridges of Istanbul are hubs of activity with a steady flow of motor and pedestrian traffic. What three waterways meet in Istanbul?*

. . . Istanbul's three waterways—the Bosphorus, the Golden Horn and the Sea of Marmara—collide with an eccentric glamour. The sea is ploughed and churned by an embroglio [confused mass] of ships. Hooting, belching, whistling, whooping, groaning, they slide and bump in disorder between one another, miming the insane turmoil of streets not far away. At some moments, in morning or early evening, the whole sea seems to convert itself into a maritime Place de la Concorde or Piazza Venezia, where crashes are avoided only by hardwon expertise and perpetual hornblowing—while overlooking all, as from the tiers of an amphitheatre, the steep shores are thronged with mosques, palaces, banks, offices, bazaars.

A lover of ships can dawdle here for days. They range through a hundred types and ages . . . [T]he deep-water anchorage of the Karaköy district is filled with the liners of the world . . . [Across from it] . . . snout-nosed car ferries oscillate between Europe and Asia, and the wharves are crowded with passenger-boats of the nationalized Turkish State Line that journey along the Bosphorus and among the villages of the Marmara and the Princes' Isles. Even these boats are dissimilar. The diesel-powered modern ones, their yellow funnels blazoned with red anchors, are mimicked by sluggish ancestors—coal-burning warriors that steam in of a morning with their bows almost under water, listing under hordes of commuters.

SECTION 4 REVIEW

CHECKING FOR UNDERSTANDING
1. **Define** *sūq*.
2. **Explain** how location has influenced Istanbul.

CRITICAL THINKING
3. **Demonstrating Reasoned Judgment** How are shopping districts arranged in Middle Eastern cities? Why are they arranged this way?

Source: From THE GREAT CITIES: *Istanbul.* By Colin Thubron and the Editors of Time-Life Books © 1978 Time-Life International B.V.

Geography

LAND AND PEOPLE PATTERNS

In the photographs on the next page, taken from National Aeronautics and Space Administration (NASA) satellites, each color represents a distinct feature: Healthy trees and plants are bright red. Subur- ban areas with little vegetation are bright pink, and barren lands, light gray. Cities and in- dustrial areas are green or dark gray. Clear water is dark blue or black. Look at the pho- tographs and the maps that precede them, and answer the questions:

1. What geographic features of the Middle East can be seen?
2. Where is water scarce? Plentiful?
3. Where are the areas of the Middle East in which the greatest number of people live? Where are the areas that have permanent settlements?
4. What is the relationship be- tween the red areas on the photographs and the areas of high population on the maps? Between the red areas and the population patterns' map?
5. Based on information in the chapter, photographs, and maps, how has the environ- ment shaped ways of life in the Middle East?

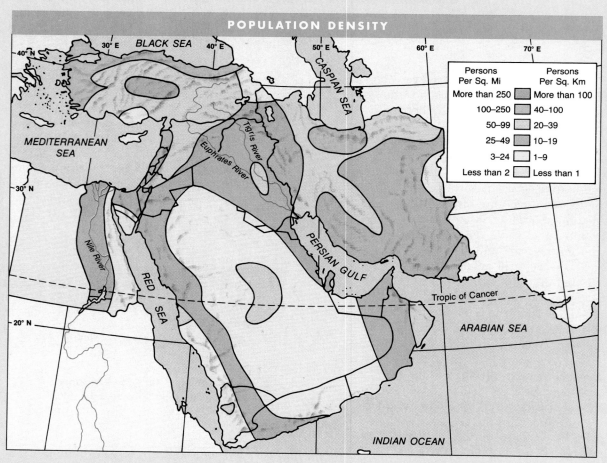

POPULATION DENSITY

Persons Per Sq. Mi	Persons Per Sq. Km
More than 250	More than 100
100–250	40–100
50–99	20–39
25–49	10–19
3–24	1–9
Less than 2	Less than 1

POPULATION PATTERNS

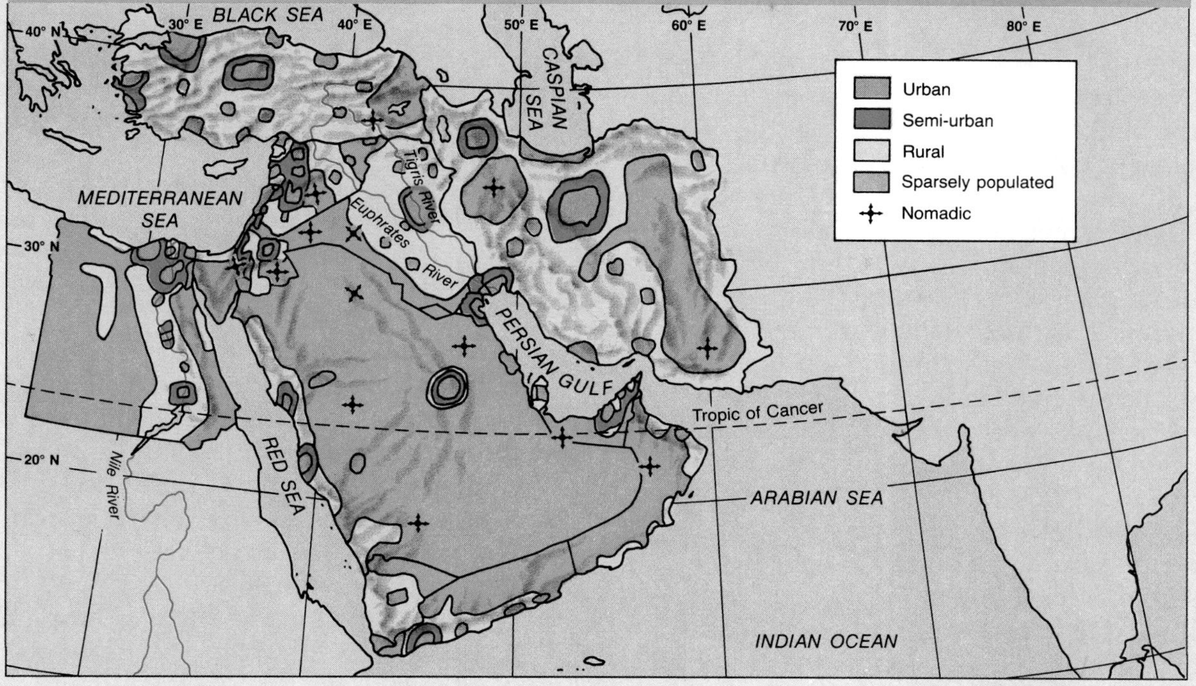
BLACK SEA
CASPIAN SEA
MEDITERRANEAN SEA
Tigris River
Euphrates River
PERSIAN GULF
RED SEA
Nile River
ARABIAN SEA
INDIAN OCEAN
Tropic of Cancer
40° N
30° N
20° N
30° E
40° E
50° E
60° E
70° E
80° E
Urban
Semi-urban
Rural
Sparsely populated
Nomadic

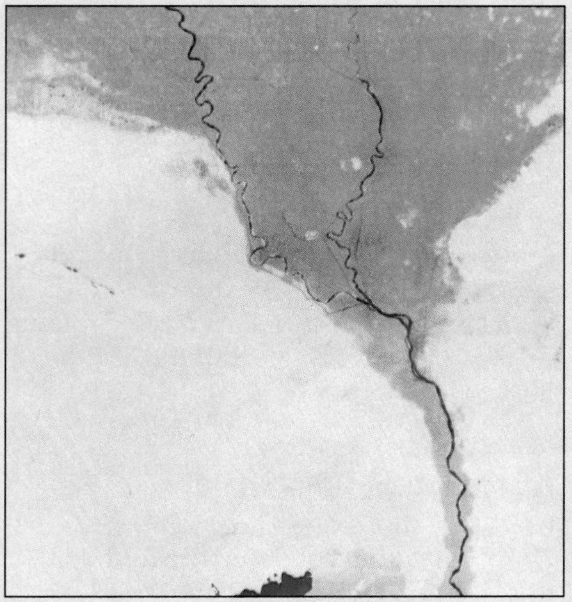

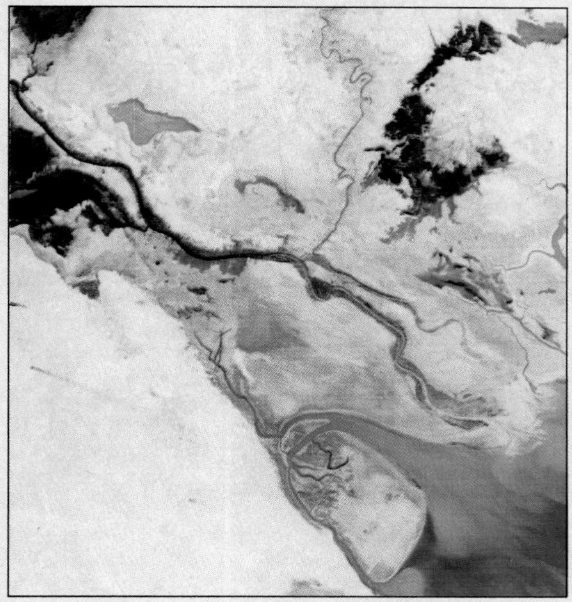

Chapter 33 Review

SUMMARY

The Middle East, located at the eastern end of the Mediterranean Sea, includes the nations of Egypt, Turkey, Iran, Iraq, Saudi Arabia, Kuwait, Bahrain, Qatar, the United Arab Emirates, Israel, Lebanon, Syria, Jordan, Yemen, and Oman.

Water plays a key role in the Middle East. Mountains prevent adequate rainfall from reaching many areas, limiting the availability of fertile watered land. With hard labor and irrigation, however, fertile lands produce abundantly and support most of the region's people.

The Middle East contains many types of desert. Bedouins make their homes on the desert, moving their herds to take advantage of limited food and water supplies. In recent years, the number of Bedouins has decreased, and their way of life has changed.

Middle Eastern cities arose in locations where water was plentiful. The layout and architecture of the cities were developed to advance trade and to fit the environment.

USING VOCABULARY

Use the following terms to explain how people in the Middle East have adapted to their environment.

nomad fallahīn *moshavim*
desalination *kibbutzim* *sūq*

REVIEWING FACTS

1. **Name** the countries of the Middle East that have some of the richest oil fields in the world.
2. **Locate** the fertile lands found in the Middle East.

3. **Indicate** the major characteristics of farming in the Nile Delta.
4. **Describe** the conditions that affected early *kibbutzim* life.
5. **Name** the Middle Eastern city that occupies land on the continents of Europe and Asia.

CRITICAL THINKING

1. **Making Comparisons** What areas of your country have a geography and climate comparable to the Middle East? How does the natural water supply of those areas compare to that of the Middle East?
2. **Synthesizing Information** What factors do you think have led to changes in the Bedouin way of life?
3. **Determining Cause and Effect** Today dams on Middle Eastern rivers keep floodplains dry. Electric fans and air conditioning are utilized in urban areas. How do you think these changes have altered city architecture and growth in the Middle East?
4. **Predicting Consequences** What effects do you think Middle Eastern development projects, such as the Aswan Dam in Egypt, have had on the environment?

ANALYZING CONCEPTS

1. **Environment** How were Middle Eastern cities built to fit their environment?
2. **Scarcity** In what ways does water continue to affect the development of the Middle East?

GEOGRAPHIC THEMES

1. **Location** Where is the Middle East located? Of what nations does it consist?
2. **Place** What kinds of desert are found in the Middle East?

Reading a Population Density Map

Maps can give information about many cultural features of an area, such as language groups, ethnic diversity, and religious differences. A *population density map* is a cultural map that illustrates the distribution of people in a given area. It shows which areas have the greatest and smallest numbers of people. Population density is connected to many aspects of people's lifestyles. In densely populated regions, competition for basic resources such as food, water, and shelter often drives up prices for these commodities. In sparsely populated areas, more people earn their living directly from the land. Large population centers, however, lead to the development of cultural institutions such as schools, universities, libraries, and the arts. Population density

also yields information about natural resources and climate. Fewer people live in places that have extreme climates or few natural resources because it is more difficult to sustain life. A population density map can reveal much information about human adaptation to their environment.

Use the following steps to read a population density map:

- Determine what geographic region is covered by the map.
- Study the map key to learn what the colors and symbols on the map represent.
- Determine which areas have the largest and smallest population densities.
- Draw conclusions to explain the differences in population density shown on the map.

EXAMPLE

Look at the population density map of China on page 137. In this map, the country is shown in one color. How is population density shown? *(Each dot represents one million people.)* Which areas have the least population? *(west and far north)* Where are the heaviest concentrations of people? *(east, especially near the ocean)* Look at the other maps on these two pages and explain why there is so little population in western China. *(Western China has mountains and deserts while there is little or no agriculture to support large populations.)*

PRACTICE

Use the map on this page to answer the questions below:

1. What region is shown in this map?
2. What does the color purple represent?
3. What color represents areas having 1 to 9 people per square kilometer?
4. Which area has the densest population?
5. What do all the areas with 100 to 250 people per square mile have in common?
6. What accounts for the sparse population of the landmass between the Red Sea and the Persian Gulf?
7. What accounts for the extreme differences in the population density of Egypt?

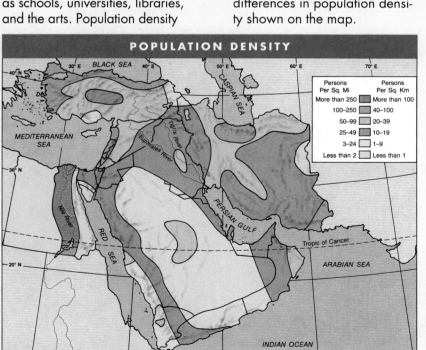

POPULATION DENSITY

Persons Per Sq. Mi		Persons Per Sq. Km
More than 250		More than 100
100–250		40–100
50–99		20–39
25–49		10–19
3–24		1–9
Less than 2		Less than 1

People and Places to Know

Arabian Peninsula, Aryans, Firdausi, Seljuk Turks, Ottoman Turks, the *Gadna,* Palestine, West Bank, Gaza, Republic of Armenia, Kurdistan, Iraq

Key Terms to Define

subjugation, *sabra*

Objectives to Learn

1. **Identify** the major ethnic groups of the Middle East.

2. **Analyze** the roles of language, religion, nationality, and history in creating group identity in the Middle East.

Peoples of the Middle East

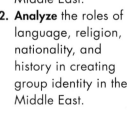

A Mosaic of Peoples

> "By using . . . service-taxis it was possible to explore most quarters of the town. This was like moving between different countries: from Armenia, to Arabia, to the Maronite people, and then on to the Anglo-Saxons. Seventy to eighty percent of each community lived within its own main quarter, mingling in the Burj, the downtown square, with adjacent sūqs . . . and banking, and in Ras Beirut, the most westernized quarter. . . .
>
> And [there] were the separate schools, separate hospitals, separate churches—the separately formed hearing and seeing. . . . The principal loyalty, the means of self-identification, rested within the primary community.
>
> "What are you, then? Are you Lebanese?"
>
> "You see, my family is Armenian. We live here. My brother is in America. My other brother has returned to . . . Armenia. We stay inside our history. . . . "
>
> "Yes, yes, I follow your question. In England, of course, I would answer to people that I am Lebanese, but in myself, you know, I am still a Syrian. We are Sunni Muslims; we came from Damascus; we have lived in Beirut for a hundred years."
>
> "Lebanese? Why yes. What else? I am a Christian—that is, I am a Catholic Christian. An Orthodox might answer you differently!"
>
> "Lebanese? You put a difficult question. I am a Druze. We lived here first on the Mountain. I am a Druze. Hah, I am a Druze. *C'est tout!*"

The above conversation took place in a crowded taxicab in Beirut, Lebanon, in which all but one of the passengers were from Lebanon. Similar conversations, however, could take place in other parts of the Middle East, for the region is not a melting pot. It is a mosaic of many diverse groups.

What sets one group apart from another may vary. The difference may be language, religion, nationality, history, or something else. Each of these will give some clues to a person's background.

Throughout its long history, the Middle East has been home to many peoples. Some vanished long ago—defeated in wars, wiped out by famines, or absorbed by more powerful groups. Some have survived for hundreds of years and dominate the region today. The Arabs make up the majority in several countries, while groups such as the Iranians, Turks, and Israelis each have their own country. Other groups—such as the Palestinians and the Kurds—continue to dream of and struggle for a homeland.

Source: John Sykes. *The Mountain Arabs: A Window on the Middle East.* Chilton Book Company, 1968, p. 54.

SECTION 1

The Arabs

More than half the people of the Middle East are Arabs. Their religion of Islam and their culture have had a profound impact on the entire region. Before the spread of Islam in the 600's, Arabic-speaking people lived in the Arabian Peninsula and some areas north of the peninsula. Today, they live in 20 countries in the Middle East and Africa.

Not all Arabic-speaking people, however, trace their roots to the Arabian Peninsula. Many are descendants of such groups as the Philistines and Egyptians, all of whom became Arabs by learning Arabic. Ninety percent of the Arabs are Muslim. Most of the others are Christian.

Three forces—a belief in Islam, the Arabic language, and Arabic culture—govern the attitudes and actions of Arabs. Despite this, it is hard to answer the question, "Who are the Arab people?" As one author explains, being an Arab is being part of history:

If you asked one of the world's [190] million Arabs just why he considers himself an Arab, he would answer you immediately that he speaks the Arabic language—a language for which every Arab has great affection and admiration.

Then he would tell you of the more than two thousand years of history shared by the Arab people, and of the Arab Empire which carried the torch of learning and scholarship for six hundred years while Europe was shrouded in the darkness of the Middle Ages.

He would tell you of the two predominant religions of Arab worshipers—Islam, the majority religion; Christianity, the minority—both cradled in Arab lands, both acting as unifying forces.

He would mention some of the great names of the Arab world: the physicians Rhazes [Razi] and Avicenna [ibn Sina]; the great historical philosopher, ibn-Khaldun; the map maker and geographer, al-Idrisi; the philosophers, al-Kindi, al-Farabi, and Averroës, and scores of other scientists, astronomers, mathematicians, musicians, translators, and physicians who made a lasting contribution to world science and scholarship.

EXAMINING PHOTOGRAPHS *Arabs include people from many different lands, such as this Syrian woman dressed in traditional clothes, far left, and this Saudi Arabian man wearing a construction hard hat, left.* In the view of Arabs, who is an Arab?

EXAMINING PHOTOGRAPHS *Above left, musicians in Turkey entertain their audience with traditional music. Above right, two children from Iran pose for their photograph. What do Iranians and Turks have in common?*

He would recall some of the outstanding Arab monuments: the Alhambra, the Giralda Tower, and the Mosque of Cordova in Spain; the Dome of the Rock Mosque in Jerusalem; the Umayyad Mosque in Damascus; . . . and the Citadel in Cairo.

He would remind you of the Arab wood carving, ceramics, inlaid metalwork, weaving, glass, illuminated manuscripts, tiles, and ivory caskets, which are now . . . priceless treasures. . . .

It is this heritage of knowledge, history, language, and religion that makes an Arab feel truly an Arab and proud to be one, wherever he may live in the Arab countries.

Source: Ruth Warren. *The First Book of the Arab World*. 1963, pp. 1, 4. Reprinted with permission of Franklin Watts, Inc., New York.

SECTION 1 REVIEW

CHECKING FOR UNDERSTANDING
1. **Discuss** the origins of the Arabs.

CRITICAL THINKING
2. **Making Generalizations** What two generalizations might you make about the Arabs?

SECTION 2
Iranians and Turks

Two groups of Middle Easterners who have had their own lands for many years are the Iranians and the Turks. Neither the Iranians nor the Turks are Arab, but, like the Arabs, most are Muslim. Each group, however, has its own language and history.

HERITAGE OF THE PERSIANS

Today more than 50 million people live in Iran, which was once called Persia. The term "Iran" means "land of the Aryans," and many Iranians believe that they are descendants of the Aryans, Indo-Europeans who migrated into the region from southern Russia about 1000 BC. Iranians today speak Persian, or *Farsi*, an Indo-European language that is distantly related to English.

Iranians take pride in their long past, which they trace back 2500 years to the

Persian Empire and the rule of Cyrus the Great. As one author explains below, they also take pride in the fact that their culture has continued to flourish despite periods of **subjugation**, or control, by foreign peoples:

In the days of Cyrus . . . , nothing, it seemed, could stop the powerful and confident Persians. In most of the centuries since Alexander, the Iranians have had to accept military defeat and try to turn it into cultural victory, usually with remarkable success. A few years after [the Mongol ruler] Genghis Khan conquered and razed [Persia] for example, his descendants had been converted into thoroughly Persian poets and calligraphers. "We were invaded by Greeks, Arabs, Mongols, and Turks, but we did not lose our originality," [a] former Prime Minister . . . pointed out to me. . . . "In Persia, the Bedouins found a richer culture than their own, and the Persians recognized that this more powerful enemy could not be [destroyed]. So we [absorbed him into our culture]." A wry Persian proverb says: "Defeat makes us invincible."

The early history of Iran is told in the country's national epic poem, the *Shah Namah*, or *Chronicles of the Kings*, written around 1000 AD by the Persian poet Firdausi (fihr·DOW·see). In the poem's 40,000 lines, mythological heroes and historical figures show the rise of the Persians and their triumph against evil. Portions of the epic are still memorized by Iranians today and recited in private homes and coffeehouses. As one writer explains, for many Iranians history and myth are still linked closely:

European archaeologists focus on the cliffside tombs of Darius, Xerxes, Artaxerxes I, and Darius II, six miles [9.6 kilometers] from Persepolis, but the Iranians still refer to this place as Naqsh-i-Rustam, or Picture

of Rustam [a mythical hero in the *Shah Namah*], simply because they see no objection to confusing history and mythology. Persian parents name their children Kiyumars and Jamshid after the mythical kings as readily as Ardashir and Khosrow after historical kings. Fact and fiction, for the Iranian imagination, seem forms that fit familiarly into the same Persian miniature. This characteristic has moved Sir Roger Stevens to write, . . . "There can be no proper understanding of what underlies modern Iran unless we recognize the significance of this triumph of legend over history, or art over reality, this preference for embellishment as against unvarnished fact, for ancient folk beliefs as against new-fangled creeds."

A BLENDING OF PEOPLES

The close to 56 million people of Turkey are a blend of the many peoples who have lived for centuries in the area of the Middle East once known as the peninsula of Asia Minor. The original inhabitants, Hittites and Greeks, were absorbed by the Seljuk Turks, who migrated from Central Asia in the 1000's. The Seljuks, who converted to Islam and became some of its fiercest fighters and defenders, were followed by other Turkish groups. The most important of these were the Ottoman Turks, whose empire ruled much of the Middle East, North Africa, and southeastern Europe for more than 600 years.

The Turks speak Turkish, which comes from their Central Asian roots but now is written in the Latin alphabet. After World War I, when Mustapha Kemal Ataturk (MOO·stah·fah keh·MAHL ah·tah·TURK) came to power, he called for changes in Turkish customs and traditions. Since then, the Turks have become more and more westernized until their culture today is a blend of Turkish, Islamic, and Western elements.

Source: William H. Forbis. *Fall of the Peacock Throne*. Harper & Row Publishers, Inc., 1980, p. 25.

Source: William H. Forbis. *Fall of the Peacock Throne*. Harper & Row Publishers, Inc., 1980, p. 26.

Despite their modernization, the Turks continue to treasure traditional tales like the one that follows about Nasrudin Hodja, a Muslim official:

Nasrudin heard that there was a banquet being held in the near-by town, and that everyone was invited. He made his way there as quickly as he could. When the Master of Ceremonies saw him in his ragged cloak, he seated him in the most inconspicuous place. . . .

Nasrudin saw that it would be an hour at least before the waiters reached the place where he was sitting. So he got up and went home.

He dressed himself in a magnificent sable cloak and turban and returned to the feast. As soon as the heralds of the Emir, his host, saw this splendid sight they started to beat the drum of welcome and sound the trumpets in a manner consonant with a visitor of high rank.

The Chamberlain came out of the palace himself, and conducted the magnificent Nasrudin to a place almost next to the Emir. A dish of wonderful food was immediately placed before him. Without a pause, Nasrudin began to rub handfuls of it into his turban and cloak.

'Your Eminence,' said the prince, 'I am curious as to your eating habits, which are new to me.'

'Nothing special,' said Nasrudin, 'the cloak got me in here, got me the food. Surely it deserves its portion?'

SECTION 2 REVIEW

CHECKING FOR UNDERSTANDING
1. **Define** subjugation.
2. **Identify** the peoples from whom Persians and Turks are descended.

CRITICAL THINKING
3. **Making Comparisons** Compare Persian and Turkish cultures.

Source: Reprinted by permission from THE EXPLOITS OF THE INCOMPARABLE MULLA NASRUDIN by Idries Shah (Octagon Press, London) page 20.

SECTION 3

The Israelis

About 5 million of the people in the Middle East are Israelis, citizens of the country of Israel. Of these, about .9 million are Arab, and most of the rest are Jewish.

The Israeli Jews have come from such places as Europe, the Middle East, North Africa, Asia, and the Americas. They trace their ancestral roots, however, to the Hebrews. According to the Bible, the ancient Hebrew leader Abraham led his people to the land of Canaan, where God had promised them a permanent home. The Hebrews later built a nation in the area, but it fell to a series of invasions. By 200 A.D., most Jews, as the descendants of the Hebrews were called, had settled in other countries. A small number, however, continued to live in their ancestral homeland.

Over the centuries, the Jews were bound together by their religion and by a long struggle to keep their religion and identity in spite of persecution. Many of them dreamed of returning to the land they believed was promised by God to Abraham. In the late 1800's, many Jewish thinkers called for the restoration of a Jewish nation in the Middle East as the only means of preserving a Jewish identity. In 1948, Israel was founded to provide a secure homeland for the world's Jews.

Today, Israeli Jews are held together by the Hebrew language, their religious heritage, and their devotion to their country. Although many of them are immigrants, the majority were born in Israel. Jews born in Israel are called **sabras**. This nickname comes from the Hebrew word for cactus fruit, which is hard and prickly on the outside but sweet and tender inside. The sabras are known for being energetic, strong, and independent. They are proud of their country, and take great pride in Jewish culture and

traditions. The following excerpt discusses how archaeology helps Israelis to understand their past:

An archaeologist begins to tingle when he or she sees a smoothly rounded mound or hill rising out of a flat plain. It is likely to be made of layers of ancient towns built on top of each other. This kind of hill is called a tell (*tel* in Hebrew), and Israel is dotted with them. Tel Hatzor in northern Israel has twenty-one layers of towns and fortresses that have been built one on top of the other over a period of 4,000 years. The tell beside the town of Jericho on the Jordan river is even older. Its bottom layer is made of houses that were built when lions, bears, and leopards hunted in the jungles of the Jordan valley.

Why are there so many tells and so many more ancient buried things in Israel than, for example, in New Jersey? One of the reasons is that Israel is part of a land bridge between Asia and Africa. Many more soldiers and merchants and herdsmen have traveled through or settled down in Israel over the centuries than in New Jersey. And each group of people has left a layer of things behind.

With such treasures underfoot and tucked into odd corners, any Israeli might be lucky enough to make a fantastic discovery. For example, early one morning in Jerusalem a man followed his sniffing dog through a crack in a stony hillside. He found himself inside a huge, echoing, chilly cave, a cave he had never known about. He snatched up the dog and rushed home to get a torch and a ball of string. Then he tied one end of the string to a rock near the entrance and slowly unraveled it as he explored a chain of great, dark caves. The dog walker had accidently discovered King Solomon's quarries. They are a group of giant caves under the city from which King Solomon's builders had cut stone blocks to build Jerusalem. . . .

In Jerusalem you can walk along a street that people used 1,800 years ago.

You can even go shopping in the same stores in which they shopped. The street is called the Cardo. Built by the Romans, it was a wide street that went from one side of Jerusalem to the other. . . .

The ever-curious archaeologists dug below the Cardo and found two stone city walls that had been built long before the Romans came. King Hezekiah built one of them about 750 B.C.E. [B.C.], and the Hasmonean Kings . . . built the other. . . .

On top of a steep, lonely hill near the Dead Sea stands the ruined fortress of Masada. It wasn't accidentally discovered. People always knew about Masada because its tragic story was told by the historian Josephus many years ago. But it's a grim, hot, forbidding place, and nobody explored it carefully until in 1963 a team of young Israelis climbed up the hill.

The bloodthirsty King Herod built Masada as a hideout from his enemies. Two hundred years later, in 70 C.E. [A.D.], Jewish men, women, and children escaped from the burning city of Jerusalem. They climbed the steep, rocky hill and fought for freedom against the Roman army for two years. . . .

Israeli archaeologists found scrolls of law, synagogues, ritual baths, storehouses for grain, and giant cisterns for water at Masada. . . .

Why do [the Israelis] care about ancient cisterns and jugs and gravestones when there are exciting new things to play with like video games and computers? Well, they enjoy the new things, too, but, as a sunburned volunteer at a dig explained, archaeology is special. "I like to dig," she said, "because it shows how deep are my roots in this place. My grandfather comes from Boston and my great grandmother from Russia. But my ancestors were here. See?" And she pointed to the stone she was carefully cleaning. Hebrew letters were carved deep into the gray surface. "It's my language. It proves to me that my people were here many centuries ago and wrote these words."[1]

SECTION 3 REVIEW

CHECKING FOR UNDERSTANDING
1. **Define** *sabra*.
2. **Identify** the Israelis.

CRITICAL THINKING
3. **Making Generalizations** What do you think united Israeli Jews in the past? What unites them today?

SECTION 4

The Palestinians

The area of Middle Eastern land surrounded by Egypt, Saudi Arabia, Jordan, Syria, and Lebanon used to be called Palestine; and Muslims, Jews, and Christians lived there. Then, in 1948, the Jewish state of Israel was created in part of Palestine. Arabs throughout the Middle East, however, did not want a Jewish state on land that they claimed as their own. As a result, conflict broke out between Arabs and Israelis. It brought severe hardships to all the people, including the Palestinians, or the Arabs of Palestine. Below, a Palestinian discusses the conflict:

> We were a big family. . . . We were living on a big street. . . . They were shelling. We couldn't leave the house. . . . Our neighbors told us to leave for one week and then come back, for the sake of the children. So we left my father and my two elder brothers, and we came to the south of Lebanon. We couldn't go back.[2]

The Palestinian woman was one of many who lost their homes, farms, and businesses. Many Palestinians became refugees, scattered in the countries bordering Israel, with

[1]*Source*: Chaya M. Burstein. *A Kid's Catalog of Israel.* The Jewish Publication Society, 5748/1988, pp. 194, 195, 197, 198.
[2]*Source*: Frank H. Epp. *The Palestinians.* Herald Press, 1976, p. 57.

more than 2 million living in refugee camps. Some others, such as the ones discussed below, created new lives. Because of an emphasis on education, they held posts throughout the Persian Gulf region:

> Many of the Palestinians I had met on the Gulf, . . . who were largely responsible for running [the cities of] Doha and Abu Dhabi, had started out in refugee camps. The doctors and teachers at Marqa Camp were refugees themselves, and the camp schools had a high record of getting students into technical colleges and universities. It was not too improbable that a hungry-looking child with his bowl of slop and paper cup of skim milk might wind up at the Massachusetts Institute of Technology or the London School of Economics. The pressure to succeed was intense.[1]

Today, nearly 1 million Palestinians live in Israel, while another 1.8 million live in the Israeli-controlled West Bank and Gaza areas. Some of these Palestinians are torn by divided loyalties such as the ones described below by a Palestinian living in Israel:

> I feel that I'm an integral part of the country, and I think that I should be loyal to the state of Israel, but still I feel that no power in the world whatsoever can cause me or force me to carry arms and kill my Arab brothers even if I wasn't a pacifist, which I am. And the only thing that I can do is work for peace because my own people, my own nation, is fighting my own state. We Arabs in Israel have quite a dilemma when our own government is fighting against our own people. At the same time our compatriots don't consider us a part of them. Our own people see us as agents and traitors.[2]

Many Palestinians feel that their hopes can be fulfilled only by rebuilding their land and by creating a fully independent Palestinian state. Some Israelis, however, fear that such a state would threaten Israel. They argue that Jews from all over the world have already come and settled in Israel and that Israel should not have to hand over territory that is vital to its security.

On the other hand, other Israelis fear the outcome of continuing Israeli rule over a large Palestinian population. They claim that Arab restlessness and discontent under Israeli rule would only threaten the "Jewishness" of the Israeli state. In their opinion, it would be better if the Palestinians had some form of self-rule apart from Israel.

In the early 1990's, certain Palestinian leaders stated that they would not use violence against Israel and expressed a willingness to talk peace. Leaders from the Arab world and Israel later entered into negotiations to determine the future status of the West Bank and Gaza areas. The talks, however, have not produced a quick settlement.

Despite all the difficulties, the Palestinians are sure of one thing—above all else, they are Palestinians. A student summed it up this way: "I am an Arab from the West side but not from Israel. I'm not Egyptian and not Jordanian. I'm a Palestinian."

---

[1]*Source*: Jonathan Rabin. *Arabia: A Journey Through the Labyrinth.* Copyright © 1979 by Jonathan Rabin. Reprinted by permission of Simon & Schuster, Inc.

[2]*Source*: Frank H. Epp. *The Palestinians.* Herald Press, 1976, p. 76.

SECTION 4 REVIEW

CHECKING FOR UNDERSTANDING
1. **Identify** the Palestinians.
2. **Explain** why many Palestinians left their land in 1948.
3. **Indicate** where many of the Palestinians live today.

CRITICAL THINKING
4. **Analyzing Information** What do you think is the basis of the disagreement that exists between Palestinians and Israelis?

SECTION 5
Armenians and Kurds

Among the many groups living in the Middle East are two large ethnic groups— the Armenians and the Kurds. In recent years, both groups have struggled to form their own countries.

A STRUGGLE TO SURVIVE

There are 5 million Armenians in the world. About 1.5 million live in the Middle East. Another 3.5 million are in the former Soviet Union, most of them living in the Republic of Armenia.

Most of the Armenians once lived in Turkey, the center of the Ottoman Empire. Christians living in a country of Muslims, they had their own culture and language. Then, in the late 1800's, Armenians wanted to form a separate state. Fearing rebellion, the Turkish sultan, Abdul-Hamid II, ordered the Armenians massacred. As a result, between 1894 and 1896, about 300,000 Armenians were killed.

During World War I, the Armenians, like the Arabs, sought European support for independence. Some Armenians began to sympathize with the armies opposing Turkey. Once again, Turkish anger focused on the Armenians, and in 1915 and 1916, an estimated 1 million were massacred, deported, or died of illness. This was more than half of the Armenian people living in Turkey. Many of those who survived fled to other lands. Most who remained in the Middle East settled in cities, where today they work in business. But for many Armenians, there remain feelings of emptiness and of bitterness. In the poem that follows, an Armenian poet laments the loss of his people:

EXAMINING PHOTOGRAPHS *Armenian priests worship in a church in Jerusalem. Where do most Armenians live today?*

And I stood up, so that
In keeping with our ancestral laws,
I may read a last prayer
On the hapless victims of my nation,
Who in city and mart,
On hill and plain,
From sea to sea,
Extinguished are,
Dead, strewn, scattered
In their thousands. . . .

I stood there sullen and alone,
Solid like Mount Massis;
I called upon those miserable spirits,
Strewn forever as far as Mesopotamia,
As far as Assyria, the Sea of Armenia,
As far as the Hellespont,
As far as the stony shores of Pontus.

"Rest in peace, my orphans,
In vain are the bitter tears,
In vain and useless,
Man the man-eating beast
Shall remain thus
For a long, long time."

Source: Hovhaness Tourmanian. "Rest in Peace" from *Armenian Folk Festival at the New York World's Fair: 1964–65.* Translated by Zabelle Boyadijan.

EXAMINING PHOTOGRAPHS *This Kurdish woman is spinning yarn in the shade of a reed enclosure. What restrictions have been placed on the Kurds?*

A STRUGGLE FOR SELF-RULE

The Kurds are the fourth largest ethnic group in the Middle East. About 20 million live in the border region separating Turkey, Iraq, Iran, Syria, and the former Soviet Union. They call their land Kurdistan, but their efforts to win self-rule have been repeatedly crushed.

In Turkey, for example, Kurds do not officially exist. Turkish laws ban Kurdish publications, forbid the teaching of the Kurdish language, and, until recently, barred Kurds from speaking Kurdish or singing Kurdish songs in public. This has led to the twofold lifestyle described below:

I once met a Kurd from Turkey who had been named Mewan—"Guest." . . . In Kurdish, "guest" is *mewan;* in Turkish, *misafir.* From the time that this Kurd set foot in a Turkish schoolroom, he was Misafir. Only at home and around his hometown among Kurdish friends did he remain Mewan. The Kurds of Turkey are used to such duality. The town where Mewan was born also had two different names—one imposed by Ankara [the Turkish capital] and one that had been used as long as anyone could remember. In informal conversations out of government and secret police hearing, people always use the old name, even though it has been erased from the official map for years.[1]

Kurds renew their struggle for self-rule whenever a central government weakens. They have suffered terribly for their efforts. When Kurds fled from Iraq after their brief rebellion at the end of the Persian Gulf War in 1991, it was fear of Iraq and the memory of earlier attacks that motivated them. A journalist tells of the refugees' panic:

[An] English-speaking Kurd . . . offered the common explanation: "We suffered a lot, the Iraqis used terror weapons, even gas, and we know our enemy." . . .

Their terror is almost unimaginable. This came home during a visit to a Turkish refugee camp in Silopi, not far from the Iraqi border. . . . An aging Kurd in a hospital ward sought out journalists with this plea in English:

"I cannot live in this place. I have cancer, I am dying. I want to die with my family. We live in Erbil, very near Turkish border. But the Turks won't let me go. I don't know why. Can you help me?"

Notebooks out, the journalists asked his name. Panic overwhelmed him. "No names, please no names." A lifetime in Iraq had turned him mute, expressing better than words the plight of an entire people.[2]

SECTION 5 REVIEW

CHECKING FOR UNDERSTANDING
1. **Identify** the Armenians and the Kurds.
2. **Discuss** why the Armenians suffered at the hands of the Turks.

CRITICAL THINKING
3. **Identifying Central Issues** Why do you think the Kurds want self-rule?

[1]*Source*: Margaret Kahn. *Children of the Jinn: In Search of the Kurds and Their Country.* Seaview Books, 1980, p. 33.

[2]*Source*: Karl E. Meyer. "Why the Kurds Fled" in *The New York Times,* May 2, 1991, p. A24.

Multicultural View

DIVERSITY IN THE MIDDLE EAST

On the map, locate the major groups of people who live in the Middle East. Explain the similarities and the differences between each.

FOCUSING ON THE ISSUE Read the quote and then answer the following questions:

1. What is meant by "Syria is typical"?
2. Do you think that many other Middle Eastern countries have the cultural differences that Syria has? Explain your answer.

Syria is typical. Mostly of Arab-Semitic stock, Syrians speak Arabic. The Muslim ma-jority in Syria is made up of five major sects, and the Christians are split into eight sects. Jews practice their religion as they have done for hundreds of years under Arab rule. The Syrian radio broadcasts in Arabic, French, and English with "foreign" programs in Hebrew, Spanish, and Portuguese.

Source: "The Arabs: People and Power." Bantam Britannica Books, 1978, p. 16.

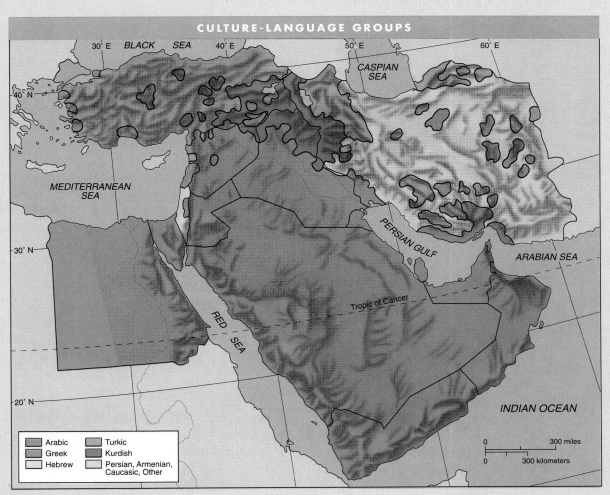

CULTURE-LANGUAGE GROUPS

BLACK SEA
CASPIAN SEA
MEDITERRANEAN SEA
PERSIAN GULF
ARABIAN SEA
RED SEA
Tropic of Cancer
INDIAN OCEAN

Legend:
- Arabic
- Greek
- Hebrew
- Turkic
- Kurdish
- Persian, Armenian, Caucasic, Other

0   300 miles
0   300 kilometers

565

Chapter 34 Review

SUMMARY

Throughout its long history, the Middle East has been home to many peoples. More than half of the region's people are Arabs. Ninety percent of the Arabs are Muslim and all speak Arabic and are influenced by Arabic culture. Iranians claim an Aryan past and are proud of having survived long periods of foreign rule. Turks, who descend from the Hittites, Greeks, and Seljuk and Ottoman Turks, have a culture that is a blend of Turkish, Islamic, and Western elements.

Israeli Jews are bound together by their past, the Hebrew language, and their will to survive as a nation. After Israel was founded in 1948, many Palestinians were displaced. Many continue to live in refugee camps and to seek creation of a nonreligious state in Palestine.

Armenians and Kurds each have their own language and culture. An independent Armenian republic has emerged in the former Soviet Union; the Kurds, however, have not been able to establish a nation of their own.

USING VOCABULARY

Write sentences about the peoples of the Middle East using these vocabulary words.
subjugation *sabra*

REVIEWING FACTS

1. **State** how many people in the Middle East are Arab.
2. **List** some of the contributions the Arabs have made to world civilization.
3. **Discuss** the origins of the Persians.
4. **Name** the epic historical poem that traces the early history of the Persians.
5. **Tell** how Mustapha Kemal Ataturk affected Turkish culture after World War I.
6. **Discuss** the relationship between religion and the founding of Israel.

CRITICAL THINKING

1. **Identifying Alternatives** The Middle East is a mosaic of many diverse groups of peoples. Based on the information provided in the chapter and your knowledge of the Middle East, what advantages do you see in having such a diverse population? What disadvantages do you see?
2. **Demonstrating Reasoned Judgment** If you were a member of a United Nations committee trying to come up with a solution for the dispute between Palestine and Israel, what plan would you submit to establish trust between the two peoples?
3. **Evaluating Information** Most of the groups mentioned in the chapter have their own languages. Do you think minority groups should be forced or required to adopt the majority's tongue and customs? Explain.

ANALYZING CONCEPTS

1. **Identity** What elements have created group identities among each of the different peoples of the Middle East? Give examples.
2. **Culture** What are some major themes in the literature of the Middle East?

GEOGRAPHIC THEMES

1. **Location** Where did Arabic-speaking people live before the spread of Islam? Where do most live today?
2. **Movement** What impact have Armenians had on the Middle East?

Demonstrating Reasoned Judgment

We often must make judgments about events. Suppose you are the head of a committee that is planning a big school dance. You must choose other students for the committee. You may be tempted to make this judgment based on emotion and choose only your best friends. You will probably end up with a stronger committee, however, if you use facts and reasoning to choose committee members.

Which facts will form the basis of your judgment? When making reasoned judgments, you must set criteria, or standards, on which a judgment can be based. Criteria are like yardsticks against which you can measure particular examples. In the case of the dance committee, you could use the following criteria to choose members: Does the person work well with others? Does the person complete tasks on time? Can the person devote two hours a week to the committee? Evaluate each prospective member according to these criteria and eliminate those who fall short of these standards. By using reasoned judgment, you will form a committee that can work effectively. Here are some steps to follow in demonstrating reasoned judgment:

- Identify the criteria for making a judgment.
- For each criterion, decide what facts are needed and gather the information.
- Evaluate the event according to the criteria to arrive at a judgment based on reason and fact.

EXAMPLE

The following paragraph contains two conflicting viewpoints:

Many Palestinians believe that their hopes can be fulfilled only by the creation of an independent Palestinian state. Many Israelis, however, do not agree. They argue that an independent Palestinian state would be a threat to Israel.

What is the Palestinian viewpoint? *(that Palestinian hopes can be fulfilled only by the creation of an independent Palestinian state)* To judge the validity of this viewpoint, first we must set criteria to measure its validity. For example, what exactly are the Palestinians' goals? Are they primarily economic, political, religious? This information could be provided by public statements made by Palestinian leaders and by public opinion polls reflecting the views of ordinary Palestinians. When more specific information is available, then we could judge whether an independent state in Palestine would, in fact, meet these goals.

Why do many Israelis oppose the creation of an independent Palestinian state? *(They believe that it will be a threat to Israel.)* What criteria could be used to judge the validity of this claim? *(the public statements of Palestinian leaders, the actions of individual Palestinian military and political groups, the overall economic and military position of both sides)* What kinds of sources could provide information on

these criteria? *(the press, public opinion polls, economic and military statistics, etc.)* When this information has been gathered, we could form a reasoned judgment on the Israeli viewpoint.

PRACTICE

1. Suppose you are a delegate to the United Nations. The Kurdish people want to establish their own nation in northern Iraq, western Iran, and southern Turkey. List three criteria you would use to form a judgment on the Kurdish situation.
2. What sources of information could provide facts on the Kurds and their desire for a homeland?

CHAPTER OUTLINE

1 The Family
2 Social Life
3 Breaking With
   Tradition

Objectives to Learn

1. **Discuss** the Middle
   Eastern concept of
   family and the roles of
   men and women in a
   traditional family unit.
2. **Understand** the process
   of social interaction in
   Middle Eastern
   societies.
3. **Discuss** changes in
   traditional roles and
   ideas and reaction to
   those changes.

*Urban Middle
Eastern couple*

The Way of Life

> " . . . coming home one evening you hear the high warbling of the neighborhood women at a distance. Rounding the corner, you see a house draped with lights, strings of them running across the street. There out in front in a large square of light a crowd of men stands in a circle singing choruses to the songs called out from one side by a professional singer and his drummer. The men take their turns, leaping into the center to dance with their knives. Someone is marrying.
>
> The marriage contract was devised, signed, and registered at court days earlier, after months of negotiations between the families. No simple certificate, this. The properties of two families are involved, carefully accumulated over the generations. Too many others are affected by a mismatched marriage; the choice and contract must be sound. . . .
>
> The men dance before the family house of the groom, where the couple will live. The bride was moved there with great ceremony earlier; now she sits upstairs on a home-made throne in the main reception hall at her own party. She must be a model of demureness and innocence, with little talk and only rare, shy smiles. All of the ladies in the room are watching, thinking of their own weddings with nostalgic tenderness or anticipation. It's a solemn moment; only the occasional laughing glance of the bride's eyes betrays her excitement.
>
> After half an hour has passed, the women usher the bride down from the throne and out to her new rooms. The signal is given; the rhythm of the dance changes. Men on both sides crowd forward; the oval becomes a corridor. The groom, led by the dancers, moves slowly towards the door, encouraged onward by a rapidly chanted cheerful song with the chorus half sung, half shouted; "God bless the Prophet and all of his kin; God bless this house and all within . . . welcome! "

The wedding described above is a traditional ceremony in Yemen. Most likely, the bride and groom met only a few times and barely know each other. The marriage is the carefully matched joining of their families. All wedding ceremonies in the Middle East are not like this one. All, however, mark the beginning of a new life for the bride and groom and concern entire families. The family is at the very core of Middle Eastern life. Most socializing centers around it. The roles men and women play in it more often than not mirror their traditions and values.

Source: Jon Mandaville. "Impressions from a writer's notebook—At Home in Yemen" in *Aramco World,* Vol. 32, No. 3, May-June 1981, p. 30.

SECTION 1
The Family

Love, obedience, mutual help, and respect are the cornerstones of the traditional Middle Eastern family which, for most Middle Easterners, is an extended family that includes grandparents, aunts, uncles, and cousins as well as parents and brothers and sisters. Individuals find their identity through membership in the family. If one family member does well, the entire family shows pride. If one family member does not behave properly, the entire family shares the shame.

In the Middle East, then, the proper marriage partner is very important for marriage generally is a relationship, in which each partner contributes what the other partner may lack or need. Below, Ommohamed, a woman from a village in Egypt, explains to her son Shahhat what marriage and family mean to her and why:

"**M**arriage means you are establishing a household. You must become a real man who looks to the needs of the house and the land, a man who fathers many children and raises them. It means to prosper and lead a decent life so that everyone must respect you." Ommohamed described the kind of marriage she had expected—expected as by right—as a small girl: a husband who would give her love and comfort and an expected place. She knew from hard-earned experience that a villager's freedom and dignity depended upon observing the time-honored codes. The ideal of every *fellah* [farmer] was to own land and a buffalo, marry, father children—especially sons—and prosper. Ommohamed knew young men like Shahhat were ardent, sensual, and romantic, but that the heat of such passion cooled all too soon; after thirty or so it was the chil-

dren, the household, the needs of the land, and the family's social position within the village that bound a husband and wife together. In her eyes men were kept in place less by their own virtue than by Islamic law and village social pressure.

To Ommohamed, family, property, and social position were everything; the family's task was to uphold such values and work the land, producing children as helpers and eventual replacements in a task that would go on forever. The institutions of family and property had been strengthened by time and tradition, and anyone who lightly violated the customs that supported them would be severely punished and ostracized [excluded].

Religion and traditional customs have influenced the roles of men and women in marriage and family. By taking on the responsibilities of their roles, men and women act to ensure the welfare of their families.

THE MEN
Traditionally, men have held the superior role and have been responsible for the care and protection of their families. Within the family, their word has been law, and it is a shock when something threatens that role. Below, a young Israeli remembers what happened when his father had to resort to doing labor considered beneath him:

My father believed, he honestly believed, that with Israel's establishment the Messiah was coming. So when Arabs in Tripoli [Libya] burnt our synagogue, we came to Israel with all the rest. I'll never forget that first winter in a tent—mud and cold and meager rations; it was sheer misery. My father and two older brothers finally got jobs, road building. That first evening they came home their backs were breaking. My mother cried, my brothers and sisters cried, we all cried. We wouldn't let

Source: Richard Critchfield. *Shahhat, an Egyptian.* Reprinted by permission of Sterling Lord Literistic, Inc. Copyright © 1978 by Richard Critchfield.

EXAMINING PHOTOGRAPHS
These Saudi Arabian men are meeting for tea, cards, dominoes, and conversation. What is the benefit to Middle Eastern families when men and women fulfill their complementary roles?

our father go back to that job, not for anything. You have to understand. Where we came from a Jewish father is a patriarch; he is king of the family. He commanded our absolute obedience and God help us if we ever disobeyed. Our father used to have a small leather shop in the *mellah*, the ghetto. He didn't earn much but he was his own master. Now, here in Israel, he was made into a common laborer—a common laborer! . . . But my father did go back to that job. He had no choice—we had to eat. In my eyes, as a youngster, he was never the same again. He was no longer family king, not to me.

Young boys learn how to be men by imitating their fathers and by taking over their responsibilities when they are absent. In villages, they help in the fields. They learn how to drive the oxen or the tractor and help

Source: Yehuda Avner. *The Young Inheritors.* Doubleday & Company, Inc., 1982.

EXAMINING PHOTOGRAPHS *Led by the head of the family, who wears a small black cap called a* yarmulke, *this Jewish family celebrates* Sukkot, *the Jewish festival of thanksgiving. How do young boys learn the role of an adult male?*

maintain wells and canals. In towns and cities, they help in the family shops. In the evenings, boys often sit in on the men's family councils. There they learn such skills as mediation, or the settling of disputes. Below, a writer visiting the Republic of Yemen comments on this process:

> **S**even- or eight-year-old boys sit silently with the men in the family council while business decisions are made. They sit through negotiated land and water disputes with other families, assimilating bargaining postures, the diplomacy of negotiations, preparing for their turn. They learn the usefulness of mediation.
>
> Mediation is critical. In this land, family honor and personal pride can easily drive one and one's family into a struggle which reason knows is foolish. . . . Many a town has been founded in Yemen as a *hujra*, a place where the mediator, called in from outside, first settled then stayed to guarantee the peace. Watching their fathers, the boys learn this duty early. It is not uncommon to see a passing boy place himself between two angry children, talk their anger down and turn them away from fighting. It's no more than adults do; an argument out of hand demands mediation from the first passerby. Every member of the community must help keep the peace; peace is too fragile to have it otherwise.

THE WOMEN

In the past, women were considered subordinate, or secondary, to men. They were expected to obey and please their husbands and to stay at home and raise their children. *Purdah*, the seclusion or separation of women from men, was practiced by many women.

Some extended the concept by wearing veils to hide their faces from men who were

Source: Jon Mandaville. "Impressions from a writer's notebook—At Home in Yemen" in *Aramco World,* Vol. 32, No. 3, May-June 1981, pp. 30–31.

not members of their families. In some Muslim homes, women had their own entrances separate from those of the men and ate their meals only in the company of other women.

The ideal Muslim wife and mother was expected to be obedient, quiet, patient, affectionate, self-sacrificing, and devoted to her husband and children. Girls learned these qualities and their roles by imitating their mothers, by helping with household chores, and by listening to what their mothers told them. Girls who had been allowed to attend school as youngsters often were made to stay home once they became teenagers. Their marriages were arranged for them at an early age so that the family honor would not be endangered by a mismatched marriage or the birth of a child out of wedlock.

For most Middle Eastern women, the "proper behavior" has become so ingrained that trying to break the pattern is hard and, at times, embarrassing. An American discovered this when she brought her husband to lunch with Iranian Kurdish friends:

EXAMINING ART *These Yemeni women and girls mix the modern and the traditional in their clothing. Why is it hard for some Middle Eastern women to break old patterns?*

"**W**ould you like to eat with your husband or upstairs with me?" Aisha asked me when Jared arrived.

We were down in the sheikh's sitting room, because the kitchen was also downstairs and Aisha was alternating in her roles as chef and hostess. Sheikh Avdila was leaning back in one of the enormous easy chairs which lined the walls of his sitting room, making small talk. . . .

When Jared came to the doorway of the room I looked from him to Sheikh Avdila and back to Aisha. Here was Jared, getting to meet Sheikh Avdila on his first visit to this house, a chance I had waited weeks for. But if I chose to stay with the men, what would Aisha do? She would have to eat alone. Craftily, I appealed to Sheikh Avdila's Western sensibilities.

"Can't we all eat together?" I asked.

"Of course," he said genially, and he instructed Aisha to eat with us. For Sheikh Avdila it was simple. But for Aisha, I saw it was not so easy. She barely touched her food, and I felt badly that my curiosity had outweighed my feelings of consideration for her.

Source: **Margaret Kahn.** *Children of the Jinn.* Seaview Books, 1980, p. 140.

SECTION 1 REVIEW

CHECKING FOR UNDERSTANDING
1. **Identify** the basic values of the traditional Middle Eastern family.

CRITICAL THINKING
2. **Synthesizing Information** Discuss male and female roles in the Middle East.

SECTION 2
Social Life

Socializing is an important part of daily life for most Middle Easterners. They enjoy interacting with other people and, as can be seen in this description of a crowded working-class Cairo neighborhood, there is constant activity and interchange:

The household brigade is everywhere— women bring water; women running errands; women baking bread in ovens beneath the stairways; women washing clothes and hanging them from balconies to drip on the passerby below; women preparing vegetables or picking through rice with keen-eyed inspection; women protecting chickens set free from their coops under the bed to scratch for a few minutes of freedom in the street below; women rocking babies and chatting with their neighbors between tasks. They shout across the alley addressing each other in the traditional way. . . . Other women, usually older ones, take up accustomed spots on street corners, sitting crosslegged to sell the products of their morning efforts: stuffed squash and cabbage, aromatic soups, fried fish, or eggplant. The hours pass in this way, shifting from time to time as quarrels break out, as accidents occur, as sewer pipes burst, as a child needs reprimanding. When women hear news of the death of someone, or a birth, or a marriage in trouble they flock to the scene dropping everything to offer condolence, to give help, and to dispense advice.

As the sun creeps higher in the sky the *muezzin* [Muslim crier who calls the people to prayer] calls the midday prayer, one of the five calls of the day, and mosques fill up with men emerging from workshops, behind counters, and from the ranks of the hard-core coffee shop habituées. Despite their numbers there is no diminution of the bustle outside. The women retire about this time to fill the alleyways with the delicious smells of garlic and frying onions, the poor man's "caviar." Again the [errand runners] emerge with their enamelled bowls bringing back dishes to supplement the family fare or to provide

EXAMINING PHOTOGRAPHS *The members of this Egyptian family read, write, and spend time together in their "family circle." What are several characteristics of some middle-class Egyptian social gatherings?*

the main dish for families too poor to cook. Their scurryings and the penetrating aromas build anticipation until two or three o'clock when the men return and the family consumes its biggest meal of the day. From then until late afternoon, the pace relaxes as dishes are slowly washed and several of the family members drift off to sleep. . . .

By late afternoon and evening activity picks up again for the mostly male coffee shop crowd. Women chat quietly in doorways and from the slower pace of their conversations and movements it is clear that the important events of their day are over. They slowly withdraw their children and their attention from the streets to the shuttered interiors of their homes. By ten or eleven the streets are again empty and grown wider as shopkeepers draw in their displays and close up for the night.

Source: Andrea B. Rugh. *Family in Contemporary Egypt.* Syracuse University Press, 1984, pp. 18–19.

THE FAMILY CIRCLE

A good deal of the socializing takes place within the family. It is especially important that families and friends exchange visits at times of births, deaths, weddings, and holidays. Social events on these occasions serve to strengthen the bonds of family and friendship. Below, a visitor describes one such event, a seven-day party in celebration of the birth of a son in an Egyptian middle-class family:

Each person (relatives of the mother and father and some work colleagues of the mother) who came was greeted with kisses and individual attention, even down to the tiniest baby. If anyone was quiet for a while, he or she was drawn into conversation again, regardless of age. The conversations included comments about events that took place on the way to the visit, about events of importance to those assembled, news about persons who were not present. The remarks were normally personal, and the topics rarely touched upon . . . matters beyond the immediate experience of the people present. The host and hostess were active in directing the conversation, asking the critical questions that would bring out each person in turn. There were no long soliloquies [talking by one person] except when a story was told about a sequence of events that everyone could enjoy; more common was rapid-fire comment around the group. The time passed quickly, and the conversation was light and full of jokes. Meanwhile, there was the constant movement of people going and coming, bringing drinks and taking the empty glasses away. It was not easy to distinguish the hosts from the guests; everyone helped out. Age groups were not segregated in different locations nor did they assume special functions at the party. Everyone was included in all aspects of the activity.

Source: Andrea B. Rugh. *Family in Contemporary Egypt.* Syracuse University Press, 1984, p. 150.

PROPER SOCIAL BEHAVIOR

"Give the guest food to eat even though you yourself are starving." This is but one of many Middle Eastern "rules" about social behavior. When visiting or entertaining in the Middle East, certain rules set down over time by religion and customs must be followed. As explained below, hospitality must be extended and certain rules followed:

The ultimate aim of civility and good manners is to please: to please one's guest or to please one's host. To this end one uses the rules strictly laid down by tradition: of welcome, generosity, affability, cheerfulness, and consideration for others. . . .

. . . To persuade a friend to stay for lunch is a triumph and a precious honor. To entertain many together is to honor them all mutually.

It is equally an honor to be a guest. Besides the customary obligations of cordiality and welcome, there is the need for the warmth of personal contact and cheerful company, the desire to congregate in groups, and the wish to please. It is common when preparing food to allow for an extra helping in case an unexpected guest should arrive. . . . When a meal is over there should always be a good portion of food left, otherwise one might think that someone has not been fully satisfied and could have eaten more.

The host should set before his guest all the food he has in the house, and apologize for its meagerness, uttering excuses such as: "This is all the grocer had," or "For the past two weeks I have been preparing for my niece's wedding and have not had time to make anything else."

If a guest comes unexpectedly, the host must never ask why he has come, but receive him with a smiling face and a look of intense pleasure. After a ceremony of greetings, he should remark on the pleasure of seeing him and the honor of such a visit. The guest should never say right away why he has come . . . but first inquire about the family, friends, and affairs of his host. The latter must treat his guests as though he were their servant; to quarrel with them would be a disgrace. He must never argue with them about politics or religion. . . .

EXAMINING PHOTOGRAPHS
Although the table at which these two Kuwaitis are seated has been set with eating utensils, they prefer to follow the age-old Arab custom of eating with bread and fingers. Traditionally, only the right hand was used for eating. **What is the aim of proper social behavior in the Middle East?**

He must never ask his guests if they would like food or drink, but provide these automatically, insisting that they have them. . . .

A guest, in turn, must also play his role correctly. He should "guard his voice, shorten his sight, and beautify (praise) the food." That is, although he must commend everything, exclaim in admiration, and congratulate, he should not look about too much, nor inspect too closely. The Quran advises him to talk nicely and politely: "Sow wheat, do not sow thorns; all the people will like you and love you." "Don't enter other people's houses, except with permission and good manners." "Beautify your tongue and you will obtain what you desire."

SECTION 2 REVIEW

CHECKING FOR UNDERSTANDING
1. **List** Middle Eastern rules of social behavior.

CRITICAL THINKING
2. **Making Comparisons** What is the same about socializing in the Middle East and in your country? What is different?

SECTION 3

Breaking With Tradition

Over the past 30 years, broad changes have taken place in the Middle East, upsetting many traditional ideas about the family and the roles of men and women. Increased access to education has led some young men and women to broaden their horizons and, in some cases, to question their traditional roles. Imported television programs and movies have spread Western ideas and values. Hard economic times in some countries

Source: From *A BOOK OF MIDDLE EASTERN FOOD* by Claudia Roden. Copyright © 1968, 1972 by Claudia Roden. Reprinted by permission of Alfred A. Knopf, Inc.

and new job opportunities in others have brought more women into the job market.

FAMILY BONDS

Throughout the Middle East, family bonds have been strained as young people seek less traditional ways of life. The "generation gap" discussed below by Maysa is not unusual. A Palestinian, Maysa is a social worker who graduated from Hebrew University in Israel, where her parents live:

The person I do occasionally get into battles with is my mother. She's real proud of me and glad to see me working as a professional person. . . . In a way, I think that I . . . fulfilled some of her own wishes. We did what she couldn't do in her time. *But* she's sixty-four and I'm twenty-four, and she has many thoughts of the old generation. That generation was brainwashed in a way, particularly about the role of women. And on these things we do disagree and we have some arguments.

What kind of arguments? Well, take the example of children, boys versus girls. My mother would not have minded having ten boys, even if she never had a girl. . . . Me, I want girls and boys. Both. To me, one is not more valuable than the other. But in my mother's eyes, girls can cause problems, or they can bring shame on the family. . . . And girls don't protect the parents in their old age. Boys do, supposedly. That's what she argues. I tell her, "Mother, that's really nonsense. In our family, who causes more troubles, boys or girls? And who helps the family now?" She knows I'm right. She'll even admit it herself, that my brothers don't help them much financially. It's me who helps them now. The new washing machine and oven, they came from my salary. I make good money . . . , and I help them. Much more than my brothers. My mother knows this, but if you ask her it's better to have girls or boys, she'll tell you straight—boys.

EXAMINING PHOTOGRAPHS *This Omani policewoman, a radio dispatcher for a large metropolitan police force, reflects the changing role of women in the Middle East. Before 1970, for example, few Omani girls attended school, but in recent years, the government has encouraged education for girls as well as boys.* How do some Middle Eastern parents view their children's moves away from the traditional?

Another area of disagreement, sort of, is in the whole business of getting married. . . . My mother is better than many mothers in the village. She'll stand up for us with my father and help us to marry a man that we want—not just someone that my father thinks is right for us because he comes from the right family. But she has this thing about getting married *soon*, before you get too old. To her, at twenty-four I'm already an old woman! "Nobody is going to want you anymore," she tells me. . . .

The reaction of a family in Yemen to their son's decisions illustrates that family bonds are equally affected when young men break with tradition:

Taha is the result of the new style schools and knowledge. Bright and ambitious, he began as a farmer's son. He knows animals and crops; he knows the land. He also knows literature, and teaches as an instructor at the new University of Sanaa.

Source: From DAYS OF HONEY by Michael Gorkin. Copyright © 1991 by Michael Gorkin. Reprinted by permission of Beacon Press.

Back on the farm, his older brother is managing the operation. Taha's father wanted him to come home, but the call of language [studies] and literature led him to refuse. He wants to learn more, research, teach.

It's not that his love for his parents, the land and the village is less. He visits when he can. . . . Recently he spent three weeks away from the library contracting with a drilling crew to put in a well at the farm. He sits when he can with the family, helping in land dispute matters. I visited the farm with him once, and could see the love shared between him and his parents. I could also see . . . the small signs of growing estrangement.

Two years ago his father in desperation played his last card; he arranged a marriage for Taha with a local village girl.

"My mother says that she's pretty and bright," said Taha. "I'm sure she is. But the point is, she'll never agree to leave the village and father knows this."

The real point was, Taha had already chosen his wife-to-be. This girl, 'Aisha, grew up in the same area as Taha. But like him, she worked her way through the new school system and is in the process of

EXAMINING PHOTOGRAPHS *Iranian women dressed in the* chador, *a traditional covering, shop in an outdoor market in Tehran, the capital of Iran.* *How would you describe the role of women in the Middle East today?*

finishing her B.A. in biology at the university. Over this past year Taha has, on his own, negotiated the marriage with her family, negotiations complete with long, serious talks with her father about his future plans. They will be married in June, after she graduates. The house will be finished by then, and waiting.

CHANGING ROLE OF WOMEN

Some Middle Eastern countries take a conservative view of the role of women, while others are more liberal. Saudi Arabia, Iran, and the Gulf states take a conservative view. For example, Saudi women may enroll at universities; but men and women attend separate classes. Kuwaiti women do not have the same right to vote as men. But, as a female assistant professor of library and information science at Kuwait University explains, the situation is "full of conflicting images":

Though Kuwait is situated in the most conservative part of the Muslim world, Kuwaiti women drive, are allowed to travel alone, and enjoy a central role in their own families. Yet this does not seem to be new or controversial to the conservative Kuwaiti society.

Before the discovery of petroleum, many men were away for much of the year fishing, pearl diving, or trading. Women were left behind to take care of the family and business at home. After the discovery of oil, their skills were enhanced by the introduction of modern, state-supported education.

Presently, 41 percent of Kuwait University degree holders are female. As a result, Kuwait women hold positions in government, business, academia and the professions. . . .

One of the several small political newspapers that appeared in the country after the Iraqi occupation, *Al Kuwaitia* (the Kuwaiti woman), was written and distributed by women and published by "the movement for the women and children of Kuwait. . . . "

One of the basic challenges to a woman's movement is the ability to utilize the information and experience gained to aid women. . . . Issues to be tackled relate to marriage and divorce laws, day care and work laws and regulations.

In the Middle East, where the family is still considered a strong and central institution, Kuwaiti women have much to offer and much to learn in creating foundations for new thinking and behavior that will support their role in the family and in society.

Source: Jon Mandaville. "Impressions from a writer's notebook—At Home in Yemen" in *Aramco World,* Vol. 32, No. 3, May-June 1981, p. 33.

Source: Dr. Taghreed Alqudsi-Ghabra. "Women in Kuwait: Educated, Modern and Middle Eastern" in "As a Middle Eastern Woman, What I Would Change in My Country: Three Views" in *The Washington Report on Middle East Affairs,* July 1991, p. 29.

In Jordan, Egypt, Iraq, Syria, Turkey, Lebanon, and Israel, women began entering public life in the 1940's, and a more liberal view is taken. The governments have encouraged women to enter the work force, especially when there has been a shortage of male workers. In Egypt, for example, about 25 percent of the male labor force was working in other countries in the 1980's. Below, a journalist discusses the impact this has had on the role of Egyptian women:

> As husbands and older sons went off to work in Iraq or the Gulf states, the independence of village women grew enormously. In the Nile Delta and Upper Egypt some villages now have no adult males. Suddenly women have had to learn about buying and selling to get the best prices for their eggs and cows and to make all the decisions about the education of their children.
>
> Responsibility for their children's schooling has made it much more important for women to learn to read and write. . . .
>
> In the cities women who once would not have thought of entering a furniture store or calling a plumber have been forced into the world. . . .
>
> Another significant change is the increasing representation of women in professional life. Now that the best-trained male teachers, professors, engineers, scientists, and doctors have gone abroad, their places must be filled by women. Women today hold almost half of the jobs in radio, television, and the press, and most of the teaching positions in elementary education.
>
> Not all Middle Easterners have accepted the changes in women's roles. Even in more liberal Egypt, Muslim religious leaders believe that God has ordained that a woman's role is in the home, and some of the more traditional members of the parliament want to pass laws that would ban women from all jobs.

Source: Harm Botje. "Egyptian Women Advance," translated from "NRC Handelshlad," Rotterdam in *World Press Review,* December 1983.

Resistance to a broader role for women is not confined to Islamic countries. In the largely Jewish state of Israel, religious fundamentalists have been calling for laws that would return women to the home and establish separate schools for girls and boys. The greatest acceptance of a broader role for women is found among educated upper- and middle-class people in Istanbul, Beirut, and Cairo. But, even for these groups, when there is a conflict between job and family, obligation to family is expected to come first.

SECTION 3 REVIEW

CHECKING FOR UNDERSTANDING

1. **Discuss** ways in which the role of women has changed in the Middle East.

CRITICAL THINKING

2. **Drawing Conclusions** What factors have contributed to changing roles for men and women in the Middle East?

EXAMINING PHOTOGRAPHS *This Israeli is training for army duty. Unmarried Jewish women must serve two years in Israel's armed forces. Who opposes a broader role for women in Israel?*

Cultural Values

THE FAMILY AND THE ROLES OF MEN AND WOMEN

FOCUSING ON THE ISSUE Read the following statements about the Middle Eastern attitude toward family life. Then answer these questions:

1. Which statements do you think reflect traditional Middle Eastern views of family and the roles of men and women? Identify the traditional view reflected in each.

2. Which statements do you think show change? Identify each change.

I work all day. Must I fight every night? [My wife] says I don't talk to her. When am I supposed to talk to her? It's part of our way of life to have an open house with friends walking in at any time. I can't lock our door to make time to talk to her. And I don't want to—what else is there that matters in life but your friends and your family?

I don't believe in her covering her face but I

wouldn't bring shame on my family by letting her be seen unveiled in daylight. But at night, if we're going by car to friends, I don't even ask that of her. I just ask her to put on her cloak and a thin chiffon scarf. Don't women wear head-scarves in Europe? Is that a terrible sacrifice? Ten years ago I couldn't have driven with her sitting beside me in the car, let alone without a veil. I couldn't have let her go to Europe for the summer to get away from the heat. Why won't she see how things have changed for the better?[1]

[1]*Source:* Linda Blanford. *Oil Sheikhs.* George Weidenfeld and Nicolson Limited/Arthur Barker Limited, 1976, p. 53.

I met a teacher who had returned to Syria after a ten-year absence: "I couldn't believe what I found," he said. "Ten years ago the great majority of women went veiled. Now, even in the villages, few do. Most girls wear blue jeans and are really indistinguishable from Europeans or Americans."[2]

I am no longer just a house-wife. No, I'm part of the work force which is creating the direct change in my society. I have spent my life raising children and I am proud of that because this role—raising the future generation—is very important. But this role does not exclude me from others. By being productive, I can also be a full partner in establishing the structure of our society.[3]

. . . Divorce laws aim to make it difficult for partners to divorce in an effort to avoid the breakup of families. But it is more difficult for women to divorce than it is for men. . . .

Most homes are owned by men and therefore divorce means that the woman goes

[2]*Source:* Howard La Fey. "Syria" in *National Geographic,* Vol. 154, No. 3, September 1978, p. 333.

[3]*Source:* Um Khalid as quoted by Dr. Suka Sabbagh. "Women Must Change the Arab Male's Attitude Toward Female Employment" in "As a Middle Eastern Woman, What I would Change in My Country" in *The Washington Report on Middle East Affairs,* July 1991, p. 28.

back to her family home or out in the street. How could a woman who has nowhere to go throw her children away and decide to be homeless? Any woman is ready to bear a good deal of hardship before deciding to face an even graver one.[4]

My wife must be a [Muslim] bedouin. My mother will see her first and report back to me—whether she is good-looking; whether the economic situation of her family is good; whether she has gold—and then I decide if I want to marry her. I see her for the first time on our wedding day. . . . Some bedouins still buy their brides with camels. Seven is considered a fair price.[5]

We live in a large Arab home with a garden full of orange and pomegranate trees. . . . It's normal for a working woman to help her husband pay for the upkeep of the home. The Arabs are very family-minded and since my husband is the only son in the family, he takes care of both his family and me. I find it a bit difficult to live with them; naturally, I'd like complete privacy with my husband. . . .

I work in a pharmacy every day in Afulla until one o'clock. My television job as a news announcer is only twice a week from six o'clock until eight o'clock. My husband drives me down to Jerusalem; we usually have a meal or see some friends before returning home. It does make a break for us. So it isn't difficult for me to combine both my jobs.[6]

[4]*Source:* Dr. Bouthaina Shaaban. "Apply the Equality Women Are Attaining in Professional and Education Life to Family Law" in "As a Middle Eastern Woman, What I would Change in My Country" in *The Washington Report on Middle East Affairs,* July 1991, p. 28.

[5]*Source:* Gemma Levine. "Our Life is with the sheep and goats" in We Live in Israel. The Bookwright Press, 1983, p. 15. Reprinted with permission of Franklin Watts, Inc., New York.

[6]*Source:* Gemma Levine. "The Arabs are very family-minded" in *We Live in Israel.* The Bookwright Press, 1983, p. 47. Reprinted with permission of Franklin Watts, Inc., New York.

Chapter 35 Review

SUMMARY

In the Middle East, the most important institution is the family. It is through membership in the traditional extended family that most individuals find their identity. In the family—and in marriage—religious teachings, traditional customs, class, and region have influenced the role of men and of women.

In a traditional marriage relationship, men hold the superior position and are responsible for the care and protection of their families. Women, considered subordinate, are expected to obey, please their husbands, and stay at home and raise children. Children learn these roles by imitating their parents.

Visiting, entertaining, and socializing are a part of daily life and serve to strengthen the bonds of family and friendship. These activities are governed by certain rules of etiquette set down over time by religious teachings, customs, and proverbs.

In recent years, broad economic and social changes have impacted many traditional values and expectations. This is especially true in regard to the role of women.

REVIEWING FACTS

1. **Name** the most important social unit in Middle Eastern society.
2. **Indicate** what factors have influenced male and female roles in the Middle East.
3. **Tell** how Middle Eastern boys and girls learn the roles they will play in the family as an adult.
4. **Explain** why socializing is important to Middle Easterners.
5. **Discuss** how the family may be affected by the resistance of some young people to traditional ways of life.

CRITICAL THINKING

1. **Making Comparisons** In the Middle East, individuals find their identity through their membership in the family group. Is this true in your society? Give examples to support your answer.
2. **Demonstrating Reasoned Judgment** If you were a Middle Easterner of marriageable age, what reasons would you give your family for wanting to select your own husband or wife? What arguments might your parents give you against taking such a step?
3. **Drawing Conclusions** During the Egyptian party discussed in the chapter, "age groups were not segregated in different locations nor did they assume special functions at the party." What conclusions can you draw from this statement as to how Egyptians treat their children and their elderly? What does this indicate to you about Middle Eastern society as compared to your own?
4. **Evaluating Information** "The first task in the Arab world is to change the consciousness of Arab men." What relevance does this statement have to the way of life in the Middle East?

ANALYZING CONCEPTS

1. **Identity/Social Roles** What is the role of the family in the Middle East?
2. **Justice** How are traditional roles and patterns changing in the Middle East today?

GEOGRAPHIC THEMES

Place What features and characteristics of the way of life of Middle Easterners give the Middle East an identity of its own?

Building Skills

Connecting Ideas in Paragraphs

Just as a tailor stitches together pieces of cloth, so ideas in a paragraph must be connected in order to express a single main idea. But instead of using thread, zippers, and buttons, writers "stitch" ideas together by putting them in a logical sequence and by using transitional words, phrases, and punctuation.

In each paragraph, ideas should be presented in a logical order. Sometimes that order is chronological—listing events in the sequence in which they occurred. Sometimes a paragraph begins with a large idea, followed by details or specific examples. Whatever order is used, the reader should be able to follow the ideas easily.

Transitional words and phrases help readers identify relationships between ideas. The words *first, second, next, then,* and *finally* indicate ideas arranged chronologically. The words *but, in contrast, in comparison, however, on the other hand,* and *although* show opposition or contrast between ideas, or list a series of similar ideas. *In addition to, also, for example, in this way,* and *furthermore* introduce examples of an idea in action. *Because, therefore, so, as a consequence, thus,* and *led to* show cause-effect relationships between ideas.

Finally, punctuation marks clarify connections between thoughts. A question is often followed by a sentence that answers it. Commas connect series of ideas, whereas periods end complete thoughts. By mastering these tools, you too can become a "stitcher" of ideas. Use the following steps to connect ideas in paragraphs:

- Identify the main idea of the paragraph.
- Arrange the sentences in a logical order.
- Clarify relationships between sentences with transitional words, phrases, and punctuation marks.

EXAMPLE

Read the first paragraph under the heading "Changing Role of Women" on page 578. The paragraph begins with a topic sentence: "Some Middle Eastern countries take a conservative view of the role of women, while others are more liberal. The other sentences explain what the topic sentence means, including details and examples.

The second sentence states "For example, Saudi women may enroll at universities; but men and women attend separate classes." Which transitional phrase is used in this sentence *(for example)* What relationship does this phrase express? *(It introduces an example of an idea in action)* How does the last sentence in the paragraph relate to the topic sentence? *(It is a specific example of uneven change.)* What transitional word is used in this sentence? *(but)*

PRACTICE

Read the following paragraph and answer the questions below:

One cannot understand the history of the peoples of the Middle East without realizing that essentially we are desert peoples. In the desert there is nothing you can claim or own as your own. There may be large rock formations, but what attracts your attention is the sky and the earth. And so in a very natural way you come within reach of perceiving the divine. You begin to grasp the mystery that is beyond what you can see, touch, and taste. In this way, it seems so clear how we—the people in this region—hold strongly to the belief in one God.

1. What is the main idea of the paragraph?
2. How are the sentences of the paragraph arranged?
3. What transitional word is used in the third sentence of this paragraph?
4. What relationship does this word express?
5. In the next sentence, what relationship does the phrase "and so" express?
6. Why are dashes used in the last sentence?

583

CHAPTER OUTLINE

1 Three Religions

2 A Divine Chain

3 Islamic State

People and Places to Know

Abraham, Moses, Jesus, Muhammad, Makkah, Medina, Ishmael, Isaac, the Quran, the Hajj, Al-Idrīsī, Maimonides

Key Terms to Define

patriarch, monotheism, covenant, exodus, messiah, *shahāda, zakāt, khalīfa, ulema, muftīs, imāms, ayatollahs,* millets, *waqf, ahl al-dhimma*

Objectives to Learn

1. **Compare** the major beliefs of Judaism, Christianity, and Islam.
2. **Outline** the establishment of Islam.
3. **Trace** the development of the Islamic state.

Religions of the Middle East

Religion and State

> And We said: O Adam! Dwell thou and thy wife in the Garden, and eat ye freely (of the fruits) thereof where ye will; but come not nigh this tree lest ye become wrongdoers.
>
> O Children of Israel! Remember My favour wherewith I favoured you and how I preferred you to (all) creatures.
>
> And (remember) when We did deliver you from Pharaoh's folk, who were afflicting you with dreadful torment, slaying your sons and sparing your women: That was a tremendous trial from your Lord. And when We gave unto Moses the Scripture and the Criterion (of right and wrong), that ye might be led aright.
>
> (And remember) when the angels said: O Mary! Lo! (God) giveth thee glad tidings of a word from Him, whose name is the Messiah, Jesus, son of Mary, illustrious in the world and the Hereafter, and one of those brought near (unto [God]).
>
> [Muhammad] is but a messenger, messengers (the like of whom) have passed away before him. Will it be that, when he dieth or is slain, ye will turn back on your heels?
>
> Know that [God] is severe in punishment, but that [God] (also) is Forgiving, Merciful.

Many of these statements may seem familiar. They parallel Jewish and Christian beliefs, and similar ideas can be found in the Bible. Yet they are not from the Bible but from the Quran, the holy book of Islam. The third great religion that began in the Middle East—Islam—has much in common with Judaism and Christianity. All three of these religions share the same roots.

Within 20 years after the death of Muham-

Source: The Meaning of the Glorious Koran. Mohammed Marmaduke Pickthall (tr.), George Allen & Unwin Ltd., pp. 36–37, 66, 73, 105.

mad, the prophet of Islam, in 632 AD, the Muslim Arabs had conquered Syria, Egypt, and Persia. By the early 700's, they had created an empire that extended from the Atlantic Ocean to India and that covered an area greater than any empire that had come before it. The empire was the home of golden ages of achievements. At different times, it was divided into kingdoms and smaller empires. The last of these—the Ottoman Empire—survived until World War I.

Three Religions

In ancient times in the Middle East, there were many religions. People prayed to numerous gods and offered sacrifices to idols.

JUDAISM

Then, among the Hebrews, a new and different religion began to emerge. Genesis, the first book of the Bible, tells the Hebrews' story. Abraham, the first in a line of **patriarchs**, or male leaders, urged Hebrews to believe in only one god, an idea known as **monotheism**. When Abraham was willing to sacrifice his son to demonstrate his faith, God made a **covenant**, or agreement, with him. It called for Abraham and his descendants to worship and obey only God. In turn, God would keep the following promise:

I will indeed bless you, and I will multiply your descendants as the stars of heaven and as the sand which is on the seashore. And your descendants shall possess the gate of their enemies, and by your descendants shall all the nations of the earth bless themselves, because you have obeyed my voice.

Around 1900 BC, Abraham led the Hebrews to Canaan, where they stayed for about 100 years. Abraham's idea of one god did not take hold at once. Old beliefs were hard to give up, but repeated disasters —periods of war, famine, plague, and enslavement—helped convince the Hebrews to accept God as the only true God.

The Hebrews were forced to leave Canaan by a drought. They went to Egypt where, several hundred years later, they were forced into slavery. They were led out of Egypt by a leader named Moses. During their **exodus**, or escape, Moses made a covenant with God, in which God promised:

If you will obey my voice and keep my covenant, you shall be my own possession among all peoples; for all the earth is mine, and you shall be to me a kingdom of priests and a holy nation. These are the words which you shall speak to the children of Israel.

God then repeated His promise to the Hebrews to give them "a land flowing with milk and honey."

Over hundreds of years, the Hebrews' beliefs slowly changed. Through a series of revelations, or disclosures, they came to believe that God was not theirs alone but of all humanity. But they continued to believe they were "the chosen people." The religion of the Hebrews was called Judaism, and the Hebrews came to be known as Jews.

CHRISTIANITY

A second religion to come out of the Middle East was Christianity, which is based on the life and teachings of Jesus. When Jesus was born, Palestine was ruled by the Romans. According to the Bible, when Jesus was about 30 years old, he began to travel throughout Palestine preaching. He told the people, "Think not that I have come to destroy the law or the prophets; I have come not to destroy but to fulfill them."

Jesus had been born a Jew and had received a Jewish education. The Jews believed that some day a **messiah**, or savior, would come from among them and save them. When Jesus arrived in Jerusalem, many Jews thought he was the messiah. They believed he would defeat the Romans and Jews once

Source: Genesis 22:17–18 (RSV)

Source: Exodus 19:5–6 (RSV)

EXAMINING PHOTOGRAPHS *This Jewish boy is reading from the Torah, the first five books of the Bible, on the day of his bar mitzvah, the celebration of a boy's thirteenth birthday, marking his entry into adulthood in the eyes of the Jewish community. After his bar mitzvah, a boy is morally responsible for keeping all the commandments of his faith.* **What covenants did God make with Abraham and Moses?**

more would rule themselves. Jesus, however, was interested only in creating a spiritual kingdom, not in challenging the Romans. He said, "Render therefore to Caesar the things that are Caesar's, and to God the things that are God's."

Jesus taught that God was merciful, loving, and forgiving, and that anyone who was faithful and who lived by His teachings could be saved, or rewarded with everlasting happiness after death. He also believed in a final judgment, a time when the faithful would be saved while sinners would face eternal suffering and torment. Many people accepted what Jesus taught and became Christians. Most Jews, however, did not view Jesus as their messiah or accept his teachings. Their belief that a messiah was yet to come remains a major difference between Jewish and Christian belief today.

ISLAM

The third religion to come out of the Middle East was Islam, preached by an Arab named Muhammad, who was born in the city of Makkah (Mecca). Not much is known about Muhammad's early life. An orphan reared by his uncle Abū Tālib, at the age of 25 he married a well-to-do widow named Khadījah (kuh·DEE·juh).

Makkah was an important trading center in the Arabian Peninsula. It had grown up at the crossroads of two caravan routes, one from the east and the other running north to the Mediterranean. Because there was a constant supply of well water at this spot, Makkah became a regular stopping place for caravans. Some residents had become wealthy from serving and helping travelers.

Makkah was also a center of pagan worship. Pilgrims came from far away to pray there, giving Makkah its second largest source of income. Trade fairs, poetry contests, and festivals also attracted many people to the city.

In time, Muhammad became troubled by conditions in Makkah and wanted to change them. Members of one wealthy family controlled the city, while most of the townspeople were poor. Drinking, gambling, and corruption were widespread, and the people worshiped idols. Muhammad began to spend time alone, praying and fasting in a cave outside the city. At the time, Muhammad's actions were considered a normal step toward solving problems. Both Moses and Jesus had done the same thing.

According to Islamic tradition, an angel appeared to Muhammad one day while he was fasting. The angel said that God wanted Muhammad to be His messenger and had chosen him to carry His final revelations to the people. At first, Muhammad was hesitant, but with the support of his wife Khadījah, he decided to try to do what God wished. Over a period of years, the angel Gabriel spoke God's words, in Arabic, to Muhammad. Muhammad memorized the words and then repeated them to anyone who would listen. Later, the words were written down and became the Quran.

Muhammad urged the citizens of Makkah to give up their idols and submit to God. He stressed that submission—the word "Islam" in Arabic—should be made to no other god but "Allah"—the word for God in Arabic. Allah, he said, was the same god as the God of the Jews and the Christians.

Muhammad's message was not a popular one with Makkah's business and religious leaders, who feared that their personal prosperity would be ruined. At first, they laughed at Muhammad; later, they became worried and started to threaten him and his followers. Although Muhammad refused to stop spreading the words of God, opposition grew. In 622, he and his followers went to Yathrib, a city 250 miles (400 kilometers) to the north. Earlier, pilgrim leaders from Yathrib had been impressed by Muhammad and had invited him to come and settle a dispute in their city. The year of the emigration from Makkah was later chosen to mark the beginning of the Muslim calendar.

The emigration was a turning point in Muhammad's life. Shortly after his arrival in Yathrib, the people accepted him as God's

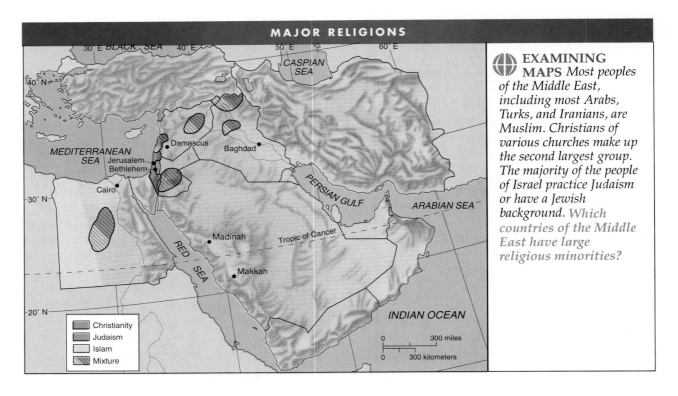

MAJOR RELIGIONS

EXAMINING MAPS *Most peoples of the Middle East, including most Arabs, Turks, and Iranians, are Muslim. Christians of various churches make up the second largest group. The majority of the people of Israel practice Judaism or have a Jewish background.* Which countries of the Middle East have large religious minorities?

Legend:
- Christianity
- Judaism
- Islam
- Mixture

300 miles
300 kilometers

EXAMINING ART
Calligraphy is one of the highest art forms of the Islamic world. To this panel, a master calligrapher has written an important article of the Islamic faith using 15 different styles of calligraphy. To what were many Islamic beliefs and practices parallel?

messenger and as the ruler of their city. Yathrib was given the new name of al-Medina al-Munawara, "the enlightened city," and became known as Madinah (Medina). There, Muhammad continued to teach and to gain many converts. Within ten years, he had defeated the old leaders of Makkah and returned to that city in triumph.

SECTION 1 REVIEW

CHECKING FOR UNDERSTANDING
1. **Define** patriarch, monotheism, covenant, exodus, messiah.

CRITICAL THINKING
2. **Making Generalizations** What two generalizations can you make about the rise of religion in the Middle East?

SECTION 2

A Divine Chain

Islam was not an entirely new religion. Many of its beliefs and practices were parallel to Judaism and Christianity. Muslims believe that the process of divine revelations started with Adam, the first human, and that Muhammad was the last in a divinely in-

spired chain of prophets, or religious leaders or teachers claiming to have messages from God. According to the Quran, God gave revelation to Muhammad just as He did to Adam, Abraham, David, and Jesus. At no time were humans without knowledge of God's will.

As a result, Muslims have great respect for all the prophets as well as for the Bible, Judaism, and Christianity. They call Jews and Christians "People of the Book" and hold Abraham in special esteem. They believe that Arabs are descendants of Abraham through his son Ishmael and Jews descendants of Abraham through his son Isaac. Abraham's act of taking his son Ishmael to the top of a hill and preparing to sacrifice him is thought to be the first example of submission to God's will. Because of this, Muslims consider Abraham to have been a Muslim and a major Muslim prophet.

The Quran also repeats many of the events surrounding the birth and life of Jesus. Muslims believe that Jesus was born of the spirit of God and that he transmitted the Lord's message and performed many miracles. As the Quran states:

And [God] will make him [Jesus] a messenger unto the children of Israel, (saying): Lo! I come unto you with a sign from your Lord. . . .

Taking their lead from Muhammad, devout Muslims see their lives as a preparation for the Day of Judgment, when people will rise from death and be judged according to their actions. If they were faithful, they will be rewarded with eternal happiness in paradise. If they were not faithful, they will be damned forever in hell. These and other beliefs are set down in the Quran, which Muslims believe is the direct word of God.

THE QURAN

In addition to containing the basic beliefs of Islam, the Quran tells Muslims in a specific manner how they are to lead their daily lives.

EXAMINING ART *Jesus preached the Sermon on the Mount, in which he provided a model for Christian behavior.* *How do Muslims believe Jesus served God?*

And (I come) confirming that which was before me of the Torah [Jewish law], and to make lawful some of that which was forbidden unto you. I come unto you with a sign from your Lord, so keep your duty to [God] and obey me.

MUHAMMAD AND GOD

To Muslims, God has no equal and there is no god but God. For this reason, they do not worship Muhammad, and object to being called Muhammadans. When Muhammad died, many Muslims were grief-stricken. One of his closest followers comforted them, saying ". . . if anyone worships Muhammad, let him know that Muhammad is dead. But he who worships God, let him know that God is living and does not die."

Source: The Meaning of the Glorious Koran. Mohammed Marmaduke Pickthall (tr.), George Allen & Unwin, Ltd., p. 66.

EXAMINING ART *Muslims use calligraphy to present passages from the Quran.* *What role does the Quran play in the life of a Muslim?*

But God is the best Protector
And He is the most Merciful
of those who show mercy.
Sura 12:64.

■ – But God (is)
■ – (the) best
■ – Protector
■ – And He
■ – (is the) most Merciful
■ – (of) those-who-show mercy

It forbids the eating of pork, the drinking of liquor, and gambling and provides guidelines for marriage and divorce. It also spells out the Five Pillars of faith, the essential religious practices Muslims must fulfill.

The first of the Five Pillars is the confession of faith, or *shahāda.* This requires Muslims to believe and say that there is no god but God and that Muhammad is the messenger of God.

The second pillar involves prayer. Muslims must pray five times a day—at dawn, noon, afternoon, sunset, and evening. Prayers can be offered anywhere—at a mosque, in the fields, in a home, or in an office. To offer a prayer, a worshiper must kneel, bow, and touch his or her forehead to the ground. This is important as a symbol of submitting to the will of God. On Fridays, Muslims usually perform their noon prayers at a mosque. In keeping with a long-standing Islamic practice, Muslims when they pray face in the direction of the holy city of Makkah.

The third pillar concerns care for the poor and needy. Any Muslim with an income must give some money, or *zakāt*, to charity each year. For some time, the *zakāt* was set at 2.5 percent of one's assets. Muslims who can afford to give more are asked to do so. Government and religious leaders spend some of the money on schooling.

The fourth pillar requires fasting. Once a year, during Ramadān (RAH·muh·dahn), the month in which the Quran was revealed to Muhammad, Muslims must show their obedience to God by fasting every day from dawn to dusk. Pregnant women, children, travelers, and those who are ill, however, are excused. Those people who do fast generally have light meals before sunrise to help them through the day.

The fifth pillar is the Hajj, or pilgrimage to Makkah. All Muslims who are able and can afford it are expected to make the pilgrimage

EXAMINING PHOTOGRAPHS *This Saudi Arabian child reads from the Quran. When do Muslims believe the Quran was revealed to Muhammad? How is this event observed?*

at least once in their lifetimes. To be able to do so is the high point in Muslims' lives.

Today, more than 1 million people from all over the world come to Makkah each year to fulfill this duty. The trip has to be made during the Feast of Sacrifice, which commemorates Abraham's offering of his son to God. The pilgrims pray facing the Ka°bah, a large cubicle that sits at the center of the courtyard of Makkah's Sacred Mosque. Below, a young American woman who became a Muslim gives an account of the Hajj as she experienced it:

❚ put on the *Ihram* (white robe) and drove along on the road from Jiddah to Mecca [Makkah]. The road was crowded with cars, buses and trucks. They were all packed with pilgrims chanting the Hajj refrain, the *Talbiyah.* . . .

As we drove along I had joined in, *"Labbayk . . . Labbayk!"*. . . . a tunnel of sound from Jiddah to Mecca. . . .

At the end of the tunnel the car plunged into busy city streets, crept down the steep side of the bowl that holds the Holy City and stopped at the Mecca Hotel, directly across the street from the Masjid al-Haram, the Sacred Mosque.

Like most pilgrims, I could barely resist the desire to pay my formal respects at the Kaʿbah at once, but the crowds were so thick that I thought it smarter to wait. I stood in the arched cloisters and looked out at the wonderful scene taking place.

The center of it, of course, was the Kaʿbah, draped in black silk, with a wide band of golden calligraphy two-thirds of the way to the top. Just that morning the Kaʿbah had received its ceremonial washing, and the corners of the covering had been raised for the Pilgrimage, showing the dark-gray blocks of Mecca stone of which it is built. . . .

The next day at ʿArafāt I set out at once for Jabal al-Rahmah, the Mount of Mercy. There, at the foot of a dark granite hill on the edge of the plain, the Prophet had stood to deliver the sermon during his Farewell Pilgrimage. . . .

As I began to climb the Mount a tall African generously shared the shade of his green silk umbrella with me and I remembered the Prophet's word: ". . . Above all else, never forget that each Muslim is the brother of all others: for all Muslims in this world form one race of brothers."

As the sun dropped toward the horizon, the multitude at ʿArafāt began to put their things on top of the buses, to strike their tents and pull up poles and stakes. I took my place again on top of my bus.

To complete the rituals of the Hajj I had to perform a sacrifice. . . . I had balked at the idea of the Sacrifice long before being faced with it—and now the time had come to do it. What was I to do? A com-

panion had insisted. "You must do the Sacrifice. There is no question of your not being able to afford it."

Back at our building . . . I turned to the Koran (Quran). I found that the Sacrifice has many meanings: it celebrates Abraham's giving in to God's will; it marks the end of idolatry among the Arabs; it is an offering of thanksgiving to the God of Creation.

As I thought about what I had read, a great weight was lifted from my conscience. I saw that the Sacrifice *upholds* the sacredness of life, that it is a pledge by the pilgrim that he will kill for food only. And where I had felt reluctance before I now felt eagerness.

I explained to my friend that I would perform the Sacrifice only if I could arrange to have the animal cooked, eat a part of the meat and give the remainder to

EXAMINING ART *This group of pilgrims, who fulfilled the Hajj about 1236, is just one of many that traveled to Makkah bearing palm leaves to show that they were on a pilgrimage. What does the Hajj Sacrifice mean?*

واخصصي بأبنك ومنزل ومولى اخيارك ومنزل ولاكلى انك لك عزل
وهب لحا فيك فيئر عاصم واندفعى كامنيع عبروأهيم والذى مانى الأزار

EXAMINING PHOTOGRAPHS

Considered by Muslims to be the most sacred spot on earth, the Kaʿbah, surrounded in this photo by pilgrims, serves as a visible link between all Muslims and God. Set in a corner of the Kaʿbah is the holy Black Stone, believed to be a piece of the original Kaʿbah built by Abraham. One goal of the Hajj is to touch or kiss the Black Stone. **Why did Abraham build the Kaʿbah?**

someone who was less fortunate than I. We went ahead, therefore, to the Place of Sacrifice, bought a sheep, sacrificed it and took it, cleaned and ready for cooking, to [a shop where the owner] had agreed to cook it for me. . . .

Before I had begun the Pilgrimage its rituals seemed to me just so many curious exercises. But as I took part in the events of the Pilgrimage, the meaning of these rites became clear, my understanding of Islam was deepened and I learned more fully what it meant to be a Muslim. . . .

The courtyard was not crowded as it had been the first day. From the minarets above us the call to prayer pierced the silence of the Sacred Mosque and my guide led us to the edge of the oval floor where we prepared for the congregational devotions of the evening *Salah* (prayer). All of us stood and knelt together round the House built by Abraham to proclaim the oneness of God and the unity of mankind. At that moment I understood why Muslims turn toward this great black cube in prayer.

Source: Adapted from "An American Girl on the Hajj" by Michael E. Jansen. *ARAMCO WORLD*, Vol. 25, No. 6, November-December, 1974.

CHECKING FOR UNDERSTANDING
1. **Define** prophets, *shahāda*, *zakāt*.
2. **Tell** why Muslims object to being called Muhammadans.

CRITICAL THINKING
3. **Recognizing Ideologies** What are the Five Pillars of Islam and what does each involve?

SECTION 3

Islamic State

While Muhammad was in Medina, he established an Islamic state. He organized the Muslim community and was its religious as well as its political leader. After taking Makkah, he urged all Arabs to accept Islam and required them to swear allegiance to him as their ruler. The Muslim community emerged as a well-organized, religious state.

By the time of Muhammad's death in 632, the Islamic state included nearly all of Arabia. Less than two decades later, after Mus-

FOCUS ON PEOPLE

Middle East

AL-IDRĪSĪ

Al-Idrīsī, a descendant of Muhammad, was born in Morocco and studied at the university in Cordoba, Spain. He settled in the Mediterranean island of Sicily under the circumstances described below:

In the year 1138, the royal palace at Palermo, Sicily was the scene of a long-awaited meeting between a Christian king and a Muslim scholar. As his visitor entered the hall, the king rose, took his hand and led him across the carpeted marble to a place of honor beside the throne. Almost at once the two men began to discuss the project for which the scholar had been asked to come: the creation of the first accurate—and scientific—map of the entire known world.

The monarch was Roger II, King of Sicily; his guest the Arab geographer Al-Idrisi.

To carry out the project, Roger set up an academy of geographers, with himself as director and Al-Idrisi as secretary, to gather and sort information. The king wanted to know the exact conditions of every area under his rule, and of the world outside. He wanted to know its boundaries, climate, roads, the rivers that watered its lands, the seas that

bathed its coasts.

The academy began by studying and comparing the works of earlier geographers. After studying at length the works they had, the king and the geographer saw that they were full of errors. They decided to begin original research.

Finally, the long study was finished and the task of map making began. First, under Al-Idrisi's direction, a working copy was produced on a drawing board, with places sited on the map with compasses. Then a great disk almost 80 inches (200 centimeters) in diameter and weighing over 300 pounds (135 kilograms) was made out of silver.

Al-Idrisi explained that the disk merely symbolized the shape of the world: "The earth is round like a sphere, and the waters adhere to it and are maintained on it through natural equilibrium." It remained "stable in space like the yolk in

an egg. Air surrounds it on all sides."

On the disk, lines were cut to mark the limits of the seven climates of the habitable world, from the Arctic to the Equator. Following the rough drawing prepared by Al-Idrisi, the silversmiths transferred the outlines of countries, oceans, rivers, gulfs, peninsulas and islands to the globe.

To go along with the silver map, Al-Idrisi prepared for Roger a book that gave the information gathered by the geographers. Al-Idrisi presented the globe, a silver celestial sphere and the book to his patron in 1154, just a few weeks before Roger died.

The book was *The Excursion of the Eager to Travel Beyond the Horizons.* It described both geographical features and ways of life. An important feature of the work were the 70 maps that covered the known world at the time. Translated into several languages, Al-Idrīsī's work is considered one of the great achievements in early geography.

TAKING ANOTHER LOOK

1. Who was Al-Idrīsī?
2. What were Al-Idrīsī's achievements?

Source: Adapted from "Al-Idrisi and Roger's Book" by Frances Gies in *ARAMCO WORLD,* Vol. 28, No. 4, July-August, 1977, pp. 15–19.

lim armies conquered the Persian and Byzantine empires, the Islamic state became a powerful empire in its own right.

Before he died, Muhammad left these words of advice for his followers and the caliph, the leader who would become his successor:

I charge the Caliph after me to fear God, and I commend the community of the Muslims to him, to respect the great among them and have pity on the small, to honor the learned among them, not to strike them and humiliate them, not to oppress them and drive them to unbelief, not to close his doors to them and allow the strong to devour the weak. . . .

Hear and obey, even if a . . . slave is appointed over you. . . .

He who sees in his ruler something he disapproves should be patient, for if anyone separates himself from the community, even by a span, and dies, he dies the death of a pagan.

Obey your rulers, whatever happens. If their commands accord with the revelation I brought you, they will be rewarded for it, and you will be rewarded for obeying them; if their commands are not in accord with what I brought you, they are responsible and you are absolved. . . .

Do not revile [legitimate authority], for it is God's shadow on God's earth.

Obedience is the duty of the Muslim man, whether he like it or not, as long as he is not ordered to commit a sin. If he is ordered to commit a sin, he does not have to obey. . . .

He who commends a [ruler] in what God condemns has left the religion of God.

GOVERNMENT

When Muhammad died, his followers chose as their leader Abū Bakr, a highly

Source: From ISLAM FROM THE PROPHET MUHAMMAD TO THE CAPTURE OF CONSTANTINOPLE by Bernard Lewis. Copyright © 1974 by Bernard Lewis. Reprinted by permission of Harper Collins Publishers.

respected member of the community and Muhammad's father-in-law. They called him **khalīfa** (ku·LEE·fuh), or caliph. When he took his place as caliph, he made the following speech:

O people, I have been appointed to rule over you, though I am not the best among you. If I do well, help me, and if I do ill, correct me. Truth is loyalty and falsehood is treachery; the weak among you is strong in my eyes until I get justice for him, and the strong among you is weak in my eyes until I exact justice from him, if God is willing. Do not refrain from fighting in the name and for the sake of God. God strikes with degradation those who refrain. Obey me as long as I obey God and His Prophet. And if I do not obey God and His Prophet, you do not have to obey me. . . .

The caliph, like Muhammad, was both the religious and the political leader of the state. He chose his own troop commanders and ministers. His power, however, was limited by the Quran and the Hadīth, a record of the tradition and teachings of Muhammad. It also was limited by regional commanders and governors. Nevertheless, he had nearly full power over the management of government affairs.

Caliphs ruled the Islamic Empire in the East until the 900's. With the growth of the empire, however, their duties became so numerous and complex that they began to depend on specialists for important decisions. One group of specialists was the *ulema,* Muslim jurists who explained Islamic laws. The *ulema,* who had to study and train for many years, became very important and had a good deal of power. In later years, some of them were made *muftīs,* officials who made sure the government laws and actions did not violate Islamic teachings.

Source: Ibn al-Athīr, al-Kāmil fi Tārīkh, Vol. II. Mounir A. Farah (tr.). Dār al-Kitāb al-ʿArabī, 1967, pp. 224–225.

MAIMONIDES

Moses ben Maimon, known in the West as Maimonides (my·MAHN· ih·deez), was a rabbi, philosopher, physician, and prolific writer. Born in Cordoba, Spain, in 1135, his family left Spain when he was a young man to escape anti-Jewish persecution. After wandering for several years in North Africa and Palestine, the family departed for Egypt, where Maimonides spent the rest of his life.

During those unsettled years of travel and uprooting, Maimonides pursued his study of medicine, ancient Greek and medieval Islamic philosophies, and Jewish law and tradition. In Egypt, he and his family took up residence in Fustāt, near Cairo. Before long, he became the recognized leader of the Jewish community in Egypt and a court physician for Saladin, the Muslim ruler of Egypt and Syria. His fame as a doctor reached England, whose ruler, King Richard the Lionheart, is said to have invited him to become his personal physician.

Maimonides refused Richard's offer. As seen below, in a letter written to a friend, Maimonides' days were full:

I dwell at Misr (Fustāt) and the sultan resides at al-Qahira (Cairo); . . . I am obliged to visit him every day, early in the morning; and when he or any of his children, or any of the inmates of his harem, are indisposed, I dare not quit al-Qahira, but must stay during the greater part of the day in the palace. . . . I do not return to Misr until the afternoon. . . . [Then] I find the antechambers filled with people, both Jews and gentiles [non-Jews] . . . who await the time of my return. . . .

. . . I partake of some slight refreshment, the only meal I take in the twenty-four hours. Then I go forth to attend to my patients (who) go in and out until nightfall. . . . On [the Sabbath] the whole congregation [of Jews], or at least the majority of the members, come to me after the morning service, when I *instruct them as to their proceedings during the whole week; . . .*

Although Maimonides wrote in both Arabic and Hebrew, most of his medical works after 1190 were written in Arabic. Among these were treatises on asthma, drugs, poisons and their antidotes, and symptoms of depression as well as commentaries on the writings of Galen and Hippocrates. His most distinguished achievements, however, were in the field of Jewish thought. He wrote many volumes, explaining in a systematic way the Jewish tradition. According to the *Encyclopedia Judaica,* no Jewish leader of the period has exercised as great an influence.

When Maimonides died in 1204, Jews and gentiles alike mourned. His remains were taken to Palestine for burial. His grave remains an object of pilgrimage.

50 CENTS

GRENADA
INTERNATIONAL EDUCATIONAL YEAR 1970

MAIMONIDES 1135-1204

TAKING ANOTHER LOOK

1. Who was Maimonides?
2. What were some of Maimonides' major achievements?

Source: A letter to Samuel ben Judah ibn Tibbon, quoted in the *Encyclopedia Judaica, Vol. II.* Keter Publishing House Jerusalem Ltd., 1972, col. 757.

During Ottoman rule, the highest of the *muftīs* was the *Sheikh al-Islam*. Even today, most Middle Eastern countries have Grand Muftīs. Other high religious leaders, especially in Iraq, Yemen, and Iran, are called *imāms*. In Iran, the highest are called *ayatollahs* (eye·ah·TOHL·luhs).

AHL AL-DHIMMA

Non-Muslims who lived under Islamic rule, known as *ahl al-dhimma*, were protected and permitted to govern their own internal affairs. Many of them prospered, and some held responsible positions in the government. Many of the famous court physicians, for example, were Christians or Jews.

EXAMINING ART *These are examples of clothing styles worn by people living in the Ottoman Empire. How did Islamic law require non-Muslim women to dress in the mid-1300's?*

Because *ahl al-dhimma* did not have to serve in the army, they were required to pay a special poll tax.

Under Ottoman rule, non-Muslims lived in communities called **millets**. Each millet had its own schools and *waqf*, funds used for charity and to run religious houses. Each also took charge of its own civil affairs, such as marriage and divorce contracts.

During certain periods of Islamic rule, non-Muslims in some areas were restricted in their activities and in the way they dressed. This generally happened when there was an invasion by foreigners toward whom local non-Muslims were sympathetic. Below are some of the restrictions detailed in a decree issued in 1354:

> They shall not build any new church in the lands of Islam, nor rebuild any such building which is destroyed. They shall not harbor spies nor any who are suspect to the Muslims, nor shall they plot against the Muslims. They shall not obstruct any of their relatives who wish to accept Islam. They shall not dress like the Muslims, but shall wear blue and yellow distinguishing dress. They shall not ride on a horse or mule but only on donkeys. They shall not sell intoxicating drinks. They shall keep to their special dress wherever they are. The Christian woman who appears in public shall wear a cotton veil, dyed blue, and the Jewess a yellow veil. . . . They shall not work in the service of our exalted state, nor shall any of them hold a position which would give him authority over any of the Muslims.

The millet system and poll tax were abolished in the 1900's. Today, in the constitutions of the modern states of the Middle East, all citizens are considered equal. In the majority of the states, however, Islam remains the

Source: From *ISLAM FROM THE PROPHET MUHAMMAD TO THE CAPTURE OF CONSTANTINOPLE* by Bernard Lewis. Copyright © 1974 by Bernard Lewis. Reprinted by permission of Harper Collins Publishers.

ENGLISH WORDS OF ARABIC ORIGIN		
Arabic	**Arabic Meaning**	**English**
dar-es-sina'a	place of industry	arsenal
ka'ba	cube	cube
ta'rifa	fee	tariff
sherab	drink	syrup
githar	guitar	guitar
mosul	city of Mosul	muslin
al-jabr	algebra	algebra
taftah	taffeta	taffeta
ameer-al-bahr	commander of the sea	admiral
e'sar	tornado	hazard
kutn	cotton	cotton
al-kuhul	alcohol	alcohol
sukkar	sugar	sugar
dimashq	city of Damascus	damask
al-'ud	lute	lute

EXAMINING CHARTS *Arabic belongs to the Semitic language group, which also includes Hebrew. The Arabic alphabet is written from right to left or from the top of the page to the bottom. Arabic became one of the dominant languages of the Mediterranean area during the Islamic Empire. Through trading contacts, Arabic words entered the vocabularies of Europe's languages. As this chart shows, many English words have come from Arabic. What European country was profoundly influenced by Islamic civilization?*

state religion and both Muslims and non-Muslims serve in the armed forces.

IMPACT AND ACHIEVEMENTS

The impact of Islamic civilization has been great. Even in a country such as Spain, where the Muslims have not been in power since 1492, Islamic influence abounds in the language, architecture, and music.

The study of sciences, as well as arts, flourished under Islamic rule. In mathematics, the system of Arabic numerals, the zero, and logarithms were developed. In medicine, Muslim doctors such as al-Rāzī and Ibn Sīnā advanced the understanding of the human body and the ways to treat sickness. Al-Rāzī was the first to identify the medical differences between measles and smallpox. Ibn Sīnā was the first to recognize that tuberculosis could be transmitted from person to person. His encyclopedia of medicine, the

Canon of Medicine, was used in European medical schools for 500 years.

Nor were philosophy and sociology neglected. Not only were the works of such Greek scholars as Socrates and Aristotle studied by Muslims, but the works of such Muslim thinkers as Averröes (uh·VEHR·oh·eez), and Ibn-Khaldūn (ihb·uhn khahl·DOON) were discussed by scholars in Europe. Ibn-Khaldūn, thought by many to be the founder of the philosophy of history, became the forerunner of today's sociologists.

SECTION 3 REVIEW

CHECKING FOR UNDERSTANDING
1. **Define** khalīfa, ulema, muftīs, imāms, ayatollahs, ahl al-dhimma, millets, waqf.

CRITICAL THINKING
2. **Synthesizing Information** How would you describe the relationship between government and religion in the Islamic Empire?

GLOBAL FOCUS

History

CULTURE AND ACHIEVEMENT IN THE ISLAMIC STATE

FOCUSING ON THE ISSUE The three photographs in this Global Focus feature reflect different aspects of culture and achievement in the Islamic state from about 700 to 1500. Based on the photographs, discuss in a brief paragraph the Islamic state's level of culture and achievement.

The five statements that accompany the photographs reflect some philosophical and political views widely held by people in the Islamic state.

Based on the statements and on the information in the chapter, give your impressions of the way of life in the Islamic state.

The hearts of the subjects are the treasure houses of their kings. Whatever they deposit in them, they know it is there.

Fight against those who do not believe in God nor in the Last Day, who do not hold forbidden what God and His Apostle have forbidden, until they pay the poll tax from their hand, they being humbled.

Islam assigns four things to government: a system of justice, booty, the Friday prayer, and the Holy War.

Government and religion are two brothers; neither can stand without the other.

Do not stay in a country which lacks these five things: a strong rule, a just judge, a fixed market, a wise physician, and a flowing river.

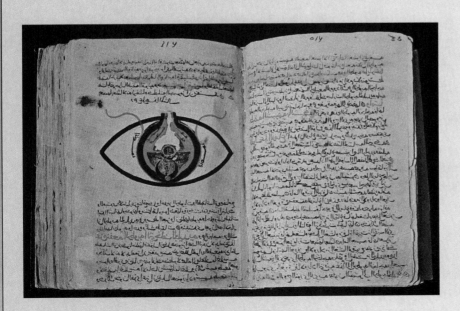

Chapter 36 Review

SUMMARY

Three great religions—Judaism, Christianity, and Islam—began in the Middle East, and all share the same belief in one god. Judaism emerged among the Hebrews when Abraham urged his people to accept a covenant with God. In time, the Hebrews became known as Jews. Christianity developed out of the teachings of Jesus, who believed that God was merciful and forgiving. Jesus' followers became known as Christians. Muhammad, who believed in submission to no other god but Allah (God), won converts to Islam. According to the Quran, God gave revelation to Muhammad, who was the last in a chain of prophets that included Abraham and Jesus.

Muhammad established the idea of an Islamic state, which, by the mid-600's, became a powerful empire. The impact of Islamic civilization has been great throughout the world. Islamic influence abounds in the arts and sciences.

USING VOCABULARY

Use the following terms in sentences or short paragraphs. Relate them by using two or more of the terms in each sentence or paragraph.

patriarch	shahāda	imāms
monotheism	zakāt	ayatollahs
covenant	khalīfa	ahl al-dhimma
exodus	ulema	millets
messiah	muftīs	waqf

REVIEWING FACTS

1. **Indicate** the major difference between Hebrew beliefs and earlier ones.
2. **Detail** some of Jesus' teachings.
3. **Examine** the role of the Quran in the religion of Islam.
4. **Name** the person who was chosen by Muhammad's followers to lead the Islamic community after Muhammad's death.
5. **Discuss** the relationship between religion and government in the Muslim nations of the Middle East today.

CRITICAL THINKING

1. **Making Comparisons** In what ways are Jewish, Christian, and Islamic beliefs alike? Different?
2. **Recognizing Ideologies** Why do Muslims have great respect for the prophets, the Bible, Judaism, and Christianity?
3. **Drawing Conclusions** What traits do you think a caliph was supposed to have had in the Islamic state? Give examples from the chapter to support your answer.
4. **Recognizing Bias** If you were a non-Muslim living in the Islamic state, how would you have reacted to the restrictions placed upon you? Why would you have reacted this way?

ANALYZING CONCEPTS

1. **Political Systems** How was the government of the Islamic state organized?
2. **Interdependence** In what ways did Islamic civilization influence western Europe?
3. **Diversity** What ethnic groups lived in the Islamic state at the height of its development?

GEOGRAPHIC THEMES

1. **Movement** How did military expansion affect the Islamic community?
2. **Place** What physical and human characteristics of Makkah do you think helped promote the growth of Islam?

Narrowing a Topic

Suppose you must write a research report about the Middle East. At the library, you look up *Middle East* as a subject in the card catalog or library's computer. But there are so many books on this topic that you don't know where or how to begin your research.

Sound familiar? Almost every researcher has faced the problem of "information overload," or too much information. The solution to this dilemma is to *narrow the topic,* or identify a more specific question to explore that fits within a larger topic. Narrowing the topic allows you to focus your research time on finding answers to a specific research question or set of related questions.

To begin narrowing a topic, write the main subject on a piece of paper. Then list as many smaller subtopics as possible. For example, if the Middle East is the main topic, subtopics might include religion, politics, history, geography, oil, family life, and culture. Then choose the subtopic that interests you most. Write three to five questions about that subtopic. For example, if you chose the subtopic "Oil in the Middle East," you might ask: "Where is oil produced in the region? How has oil changed the way of life in the Middle East? What political problems are caused by oil in the region?" Choose the most interesting question as your topic and look for answers in your research. In the process, you may discover an-swers to some of the other questions too, but try to keep your research and report focused on a single question. The following steps will help you narrow a research topic:

- Write the main topic on a piece of paper.
- List several subtopics of the main topic.
- Choose the most interesting subtopic and write three to five questions about it.
- Choose the most interesting question as your research topic. Include information about related questions if you have time to do so.

EXAMPLE

Suppose you must write a report on one of the three major religions of the Middle East—Judaism. First, identify several subtopics of this main topic. They might include: the early history of Judaism, the global impact of Judaism, fundamental Jewish beliefs, how Judaism is practiced today. What are some other subtopics? *(Answers will vary, but should relate to the main topic, Judaism.)*

Then choose the subtopic that most interests you. Suppose, for example, you want to learn more about Jewish beliefs. Questions about this subtopic could include: What are the most fundamental beliefs in Judaism? How do these beliefs differ from Christianity and Islam? What are the major Jewish holidays? What other questions might relate to this subtopic? *(Questions will vary, but should relate to the subtopic, Judaism—for example, what is the Torah, or what are bar mitzvahs? How do Jews celebrate weddings and funerals? What are important Jewish rituals?)* Once you have chosen the question that interests you most, begin your research. If you were writing this report, what question would you choose to begin your research? *(Answers will vary.)* If time allows, research other questions from the list as well.

PRACTICE

1. Suppose you must write a report on the following main topic: *Islam.* From the list below, write the letter of each subtopic that relates to this main topic.
   a. main beliefs of Islam
   b. geography of the Middle East
   c. history of Islam
   d. life of Muhammad
   e. Muslim family life
   f. shipping and trade in the Middle East
   g. Muslim women today
   h. economies of the Middle East
   i. conflict between Arabs and Israelis
   j. Muslim contributions to the arts and sciences
2. From the subtopics on your list, choose the one that most interests you and write three to five questions about it.

CHAPTER OUTLINE

People and Places to Know
Sykes-Picot Agreement, United Arab Republic, Gamal Abdel Nasser, Mohammed Mosaddeq, Mohammed Reza Pahlevi

Key Terms to Define
colonialism, mandate, nationalize

Objectives to Learn
1. **Trace** colonialism in the Middle East.
2. **Summarize** the history and significance of the Suez Canal.
3. **Discuss** the background of the Arab-Israeli conflict.
4. **Describe** Britain's role in the Persian Gulf and Middle Eastern reactions to its presence.

European travelers in Egypt—1890's

The Great Bitterness

> " . . . The position that we occupy in Egypt may be said to be the result of accident. But it has more than accidental justification. Alike by the nature of our interests, by the nature of our power, and by certain special qualities in our national character, we seem marked out for the discharge of this particular duty. Our interests in Egypt are absolutely identical with those of the Egyptian people. We are their principal customers, and they also are very important customers of Great Britain. With the deficiency of outlets which threatens our vast foreign trade, the great and growing market of Egypt is evidently not a thing which we can afford to despise. And if Egyptian prosperity is a British interest, so is Egyptian independence. We have no desire to possess ourselves of Egypt, but we have every reason to prevent any rival power from so possessing itself. . . .
>
> . . . The circumstances must decide. As native governing capacity develops, as natives come forward who are fit for responsible posts now held by Englishmen, these posts should be resigned to them. Perhaps some element in the Government would always be necessary. Perhaps the British Minister would always need to exercise some control on the most important questions of policy. But that control might in the end be very light. . . .
>
> Such would be the natural, the wholesome development of British policy in Egypt. "

*I*n this way, the British Under-Secretary for Finance in Egypt justified the 1882 British takeover of the Egyptian government. The British action was prompted by a crisis that threatened to topple Egypt's government, which was controlled by France and Great Britain.

In the Middle East, **colonialism**, foreign occupation of a land with intent to exploit its resources, began in the 1800's when Great Britain, France, and Russia were actively seeking economic concessions, or special privileges. The British wanted new markets,

Source: Alfred Milner. *England in Egypt.* Edward Arnold, 1892, pp. 435–436, 440, 442.

raw materials for industry, and control of strategic routes, especially to Asia and the British colony in India. The French wanted control of trade in the Levant, the east coast regions of the Mediterranean Sea.

By 1920, Great Britain and France had gained control of northern Africa and most of the Arab lands of the Middle East. European rule caused frustration and humiliation among Middle Easterners. The colonial territories underwent a great deal of struggle and sacrifice, and many Middle Easterners fought and died for independence. Among the areas affected were Syria and Lebanon, Egypt, Palestine, and the Persian Gulf.

Syria and Lebanon

When World War I broke out in 1914, Syria was part of the declining Ottoman Empire. Arabs in Syria and other Middle Eastern countries saw the war as an opportunity to free themselves from Turkish rule. So when the Turks allied themselves with Germany, the Syrian Arabs asked the British to help them gain their independence.

In the Husayn-McMahon correspondence, an exchange of letters between British diplomat Sir Henry McMahon and Arab leader Sherif Husayn, the British pledged their support for an independent Arab state. Below, in an excerpt from an October 24, 1915 letter, McMahon wrote:

It is with great pleasure that I communicate to you on . . . behalf [of the government of Great Britain] the following statement. . . .

The two districts of Mersina and Alexandretta and portions of Syria lying to the west of the districts of Damascus, Homs, Hama and Aleppo cannot be said to be purely Arab, and should be excluded from the limits demanded.

With the above modification, and without prejudice to our existing treaties with Arab chiefs, we accept those limits.

As for those regions lying within those frontiers wherein Great Britain is free to act without detriment to the interests of her ally, France, I am empowered in the name of the Government of Great Britain to give the following assurances and make the following reply to your letter:—

(1) Subject to the above modifications Great Britain is prepared to recognise and support the independence of the Arabs in all the regions within the limits demanded by the sherif of Mecca [Makkah].

(2) Great Britain will guarantee the

Holy Places against all external aggression and will recognise their inviolability.

(3) When the situation admits, Great Britain will give to the Arabs her advice and will assist them to establish what may appear to be the most suitable forms of government in those various territories.[1]

A year after this letter was written, the British and the French signed the Sykes-Picot Agreement. It stated that if the Germans lost the war, the Arab territories of the Ottoman Empire would be divided between France and Great Britain. When the Arabs found out about the agreement, they sent Husayn's son, Prince Faisal, to London to ask the British prime minister how the agreement would affect the independent Arab state the British had promised his people.

In spite of Faisal's efforts, the Arab claims for independence were ignored in the World War I peace treaties. Syria was made a French **mandate**, or territory administered by another country. The French established headquarters in Beirut, which at the time was part of Syria. They divided the country into districts, based in part on religious groupings. They added four areas to the district known as Mount of Lebanon and made them the separate country of Lebanon.

For the next 20 years, there were revolts to protest French rule. The following story tells about one Syrian's fight for freedom:

"Milk, milk." It was six o'clock in the morning, and I could hear the voice of Abū Hāmid, the milkman. I went down the stairs, picked up the milk jug from the kitchen, opened the door and was greeted with a wide, warm smile from Abū Hāmid. While he poured three cups of milk into the jug, my ten-year-old eyes watched his big gnarled hand with its bent fingers.

While pouring the milk at breakfast, my mother said, "Abū Hāmid is a splendid

[1]Source: Fred J. Khouri. *The Arab-Israeli Dilemma.* Syracuse University Press, 1968, p. 359.

EXAMINING PHOTOGRAPHS *In this photo taken in 1919, troops are shown leaving France to occupy the territory France was given in Syria and Lebanon as part of the peace treaties ending World War I. How was the country of Lebanon created?*

milkman. God bless him. He never dilutes the milk. He is a man of righteousness."

One day my father left his bed and came down with me when he heard the milkman's voice. In low voices, he and Abū Hāmid discussed the affairs of the revolt in Ghūta, the orchard villages that form a ring on the three sides of Damascus. I could hear references made to battle, to patriots being killed, and to fights against the French.

Abū Hāmid whispered, "But they killed many, many French soldiers before they were killed. They are all young and heading for heaven. I wish I were one of them. But this hand will not permit me. I just can't use a rifle with it."

One wintry day, I heard Abū Hāmid tell my father, "It is getting very cold, sir. Most of the patriots have no ʿabāʾ at [heavy robes which can be used as blankets]. Sleeping outdoors without ʿabāʾ at is brutal. God help them."

That evening I overheard my mother telling father, "I checked with all the houses on our street and not a single family refused to help. I was able to collect enough to purchase fifty ʿabāʾ at."

"It's better that you buy the ʿabāʾ at, but buy no more than two from any store. You don't want to draw attention to yourself, the French have traitors and spies everywhere," father cautioned.

The following morning, and every morning thereafter, Abū Hāmid would wear one ʿabāʾ at that my mother had bought until the stacks of ʿabāʾ at were gone.

One dreary morning, our old clock struck six, but I heard no call for milk. I wondered why Abū Hāmid did not come this morning.

Later, after school, some of the students were gathering at the corner. They were repeating the news that some patriots were killed and their bodies were displayed at Marje Square. I joined them, and in a few minutes we were heading there.

We stood frightened, staring at the dreadful sight. There were bodies twisted and broken in torn clothes covered with blood and dirt.

A French officer laughed and pointed at them saying, "Patriots! Patriots!"

I almost screamed when I recognized one of the bodies. It was Abū Hāmid. I knew his clothes and his gnarled hand.

We retreated in silence. One boy said, "Those bodies are not of patriots. Those bodies are of poor peasants. The French shot them to scare us."

All of the boys agreed. Each one left for his home wearing a pale face and with a fast-beating heart. I hurried home and went straight to the courtyard. There, my mother was seated and sad-looking, with eyes filled with tears. I rushed to her and asked the whereabouts of my father.

She answered with a trembling voice, "Your father went to the village. He will be back in a few days."

I looked straight into her eyes and replied, "You are not telling me the truth. Father joined the revolt and left us in the care of God."

She hugged me and said, "How did you know that? Don't dare mention anything about it. If the French find out, they will demolish our home immediately."

I slept little that night. As morning drew near, I heard a voice calling "milk, milk." It was my friend Hāmid, the milkman's older son. Hāmid, one of the best students, will have to quit school and forget his sweet dreams so that he can support a big family. Instead of a book bag in his hand, he will be carrying the big milk can and peddling milk for the rest of his life. Two tears wet my cheeks, and deep inside me I felt a great bitterness.

The fight for freedom did not end until 1946, when Syria and Lebanon became fully

Source: Ilfat al-Idulbi. *Farewell Damascus* (adaptation). Mounir Farah (tr.) Atlas Publishing and Distribution, 1963, pp. 13–22.

independent. Independence brought democratic governments, and for the next few years, each country experienced rapid social and economic growth.

In Lebanon, democratic governments continued to rule under stable and peaceful conditions until 1958. That year, a civil war broke out between mainly Christian, pro-Western forces and anti-Western forces that favored stronger ties with Egypt and Syria. After a few weeks of fighting, order was restored, and a new president was elected.

In Syria, the peace did not last as long. In 1949, dissatisfaction over a military defeat at the hands of Israel led to a military coup that set up a dictatorship. Other coups followed until 1958, when the country voted to unite with Egypt and form the United Arab Republic. That union lasted three years.

SECTION 1 REVIEW

CHECKING FOR UNDERSTANDING
1. **Define** mandate.
2. **Discuss** how the Syrians reacted to French rule.

CRITICAL THINKING
3. **Analyzing Information** Why do you think the French created Lebanon? Explain.

SECTION 2

The Suez Canal

In 1854, Ferdinand de Lesseps, a French engineer, set out to build the Suez Canal, a 100-mile [160-kilometer] waterway that would link the Mediterranean and Red seas. Said Pasha, the Viceroy who ruled Egypt for the Ottoman sultan, approved de Lesseps' plans. The canal was to be built and run by an international company headed by de Lesseps. At the end of 99 years, however, the canal was to come under Egyptian control.

EXAMINING ART
This old engraving shows some of the laborers who built the Suez Canal digging earth and loading it onto the backs of camels. Most of the canal's excavation was done this way. Earth-moving machinery was not used until the last few years of the project. How did the building of the Suez Canal affect many Egyptian fallahīn and their families?

Work began on the canal in 1859. Ten years later, it was completed—at a cost of $287 million and the lives of a great many Egyptian laborers. The Viceroy had agreed in the concession that Egypt would supply laborers to work on the canal. As a result, thousands of Egyptian *fallahīn* were forced to leave their families and work on the project. In 1863 a new Viceroy came to power, which complicated the already controversial issue of the forced labor. Below, a reporter for *The Times of London* comments on the situation:

The present Viceroy has not yet announced his final views upon the subject [of forced labor]; but it is very generally believed that he has already arrived at the conclusion that the [Egyptian] Government is bound by the engagements entered into towards the Company by his predecessor. Both labour and money must accordingly continue to be supplied. About 20,000 men are at this moment ei-

ther engaged upon the works or on their way . . . collected . . . from all parts of Egypt. To each party, as it arrives, a certain portion of the excavations is allotted. . . . The task is usually completed in about a month, when the men are allowed to return to their villages, generally carrying with them the trifling balance of their earnings after paying the cost of the simple food upon which the Egyptian [*fallahīn*] are content to live.

By 1875, six years after the canal was completed, the Egyptian ruler was deeply in debt. To solve his financial problems, he sold the major portion of stock in the canal company to the British government. In 1876, the British, along with the French, took over the financial management of the canal. Six years later, Egyptian nationalists demanded an end to all foreign control.

Source: The Times of London (1863) in *Suez: De Lesseps' Canal.* John Pudney. J.M. Dent and Sons, Ltd., 1968, p. 100.

By this time, the British had become the major user of the canal and relied on it heavily for both strategic and economic purposes. Fearful that they would lose control of the canal, they landed troops in Egypt. In the battle that followed, they defeated the national army led by Egyptian Colonel Ahmad ᶜUrābī and occupied Egypt.

Although the British claimed that their occupation would be temporary, the last British troops did not leave Egypt until 1956. By that time, Arab nationalism, stirred by Egyptian president Gamal Abdel Nasser, had taken root firmly. Nasser believed that foreigners had no right to control his country or its people. On July 26, 1956, he announced that the canal would be **nationalized**, made the property of the government. He also announced that the money Egypt earned from the canal would go toward building the Aswan High Dam on the Nile River at Aswan. Below, Nasser explains why he nationalized the Canal:

The Suez Canal Company was formed, and Egypt got 44% of the shares. Egypt undertook to supply labour to dig the Canal . . . , of whom 120,000 died without getting paid. We also paid De Lesseps in order that he might give up some concession. We gave up the 15% of the profits which we were supposed to get over and above the profits of our 44% of the shares. Thus, contrary to the statements made by De Lesseps . . . in which he said that the Canal was dug for Egypt, Egypt has become the property of the Canal. . . .

The result of the words of De Lesseps in 1856, the result of friendship and loans, was the occupation of Egypt in 1882. Egypt then borrowed money. What happened? Egypt was obliged . . . to sell its 44% of the shares in the company. Immediately, England sent out to purchase the shares. It bought them for 4 million pounds. Then, [the Viceroy] gave up his 5% of the company's profits against the ceding of some concessions by the Company which were granted to it.

Then the [Viceroy] was obliged to pay to Britain the 5% profit which he had relinquished. This amounted to over 4 million pounds. In other words, Britain got Egypt's 44% of the Company's shares free. This was the history which took place a century ago. . . .

Today, the Suez Canal, where 120,000 of our sons had lost their lives . . . and for the foundation of which we paid 8 million

EXAMINING PHOTOGRAPHS
Egyptian President Gamal Abdel Nasser waves to crowds in Cairo in 1956 after formally taking control of the Suez Canal. After nationalizing the canal, Nasser became a worldwide symbol of the Arab people, and many Arab nations looked to Egypt for leadership. What did Nasser want to do with the money earned from operating the Suez Canal?

pounds, has become a state within the state. It has humiliated ministers and cabinets.

This Canal is an Egyptian canal. It is an Egyptian Joint Stock Company. Britain had forcibly grabbed our rights, our 44% of its shares. Britain still collects the profits of these shares. . . .

The income of the Suez Canal Company in 1955 reached . . . 35 million [English pounds], or 100 million dollars. Of this sum, we, who have lost 120,000 persons, who have died in digging the Canal, take only . . . 1 million (English pounds) or 3 million dollars! This is the Suez Canal Company, which . . . dug for the sake of Egypt and its benefit! . . .

We shall not repeat the past. We shall eradicate it by restoring our rights in the Suez Canal. This money is ours. This Canal is the property of Egypt because it is an Egyptian Joint Stock Company.

SECTION 2 REVIEW

CHECKING FOR UNDERSTANDING
1. **Define** nationalize.
2. **State** the result of Ferdinand de Lesseps' efforts in Egypt during the mid-1800's.

CRITICAL THINKING
3. **Predicting Consequences** What effect do you think Nasser's takeover of the Suez Canal had on the Egyptian people?

SECTION 3

The Arab-Israeli Conflict

The conflict between Israel and its Arab neighbors has been going on for many years. At the base of the dispute is a disagreement

Source: Speech by Gamal Abdel Nasser (1956) in "The Suez Canal Problem," publication 6392, October 1956, U.S. Department of State, pp. 26–27.

between the Arabs and the Israelis as to who owns the land of Israel, once called Palestine. Both Palestinian Arabs and Israelis claim ownership.

Toward the end of World War I, Palestine, which was inhabited by 500,000 Arabs and 50,000 Jews, came under British control after nearly 400 years of Ottoman rule. During the war, the British had made conflicting promises to the Arabs and the Jews regarding the area. In the Husayn-McMahon correspondence of 1915, they promised the Arabs an independent state. The Arabs believed that this state would include all of Palestine. Then, in the Balfour Declaration of 1917, the British promised the Jews a home in Palestine. In the words of Lord Balfour:

I have much pleasure in giving you, on behalf of his Majesty's Government, the following declaration of sympathy with Jewish Zionist [those who want an independent Jewish country] aspirations. . . .

His Majesty's Government view with favour the establishment in Palestine of a national home for the Jewish people, and will use their best endeavors to facilitate the achievement of this object, it being clearly understood that nothing shall be done which may prejudice the civil and religious rights of existing non-Jewish communities in Palestine, or the rights and political status enjoyed by Jews in any other country. . . .

After World War I, however, the British broke their promise to the Arabs for an independent state and occupied and ruled Palestine. Meanwhile, the flow of Jewish immigrants into Palestine continued and grew until by the late 1930's, Jews accounted for nearly one-third of Palestine's population. The number of Jews continued growing during World War II and after as Jews fled to Palestine to escape Nazi persecution.

Source: Fred J. Khouri. The Arab-Israeli Dilemma. Syracuse University Press, 1968, p. 360.

EXAMINING ART *In this cartoon, a dove with an olive branch, a symbol of peace, is shown emerging from a bomb, a symbol of the Middle East embroiled in conflict.* **What was the Arab reaction when Israel became a state in 1948?**

So too grew the bitterness between the Arabs and the Jews. Before long, riots and armed conflict broke out. Although the British tried to work out a compromise between the two groups over the future of Palestine, the dissent continued. In 1947, the British referred the matter to the United Nations, which voted to partition, or divide, Palestine into two states—one Arab and one Jewish. In 1948, the British withdrew from Palestine, and the Jews set up the new state of Israel. The Arabs, however, refused to accept the partition or to recognize Israel and demanded an election for a government for all of Palestine.

In the spring of 1948, the forces of Egypt, Syria, Lebanon, Trans-Jordan, and Iraq invaded Israel, where they were defeated by the Israeli army. By the following year, a cease-fire was in effect. As a result of the war, Israel occupied Arab territory, and nearly three-quarters of a million Palestinian Arabs fled or were forced to leave their homeland to become refugees in neighboring Arab countries. By 1956, the conflict erupted into war once more.

SECTION 3 REVIEW

CHECKING FOR UNDERSTANDING
1. **Specify** the promises Britain made to Arabs and Jews in the early 1900's.

CRITICAL THINKING
2. **Identifying Central Issues** What issue is at the heart of the Arab-Israeli conflict?

SECTION 4

The Persian Gulf

As early as the 1500's, Europeans had established strategic and commercial bases in the area of the Persian Gulf. By the 1800's, Great Britain had become the dominant power in the area. India was Great Britain's most important colony, and the Gulf states, located between the Mediterranean region and India, were India's link to Europe.

At first, the British limited their interests in the Gulf to trade and foreign affairs. To protect their interests, they made treaties with the Gulf states. Most of the treaties were written to favor the British. When other European countries became interested in the area, the British became concerned and concluded many treaties with the Gulf states, often resorting to pressure and force. The 1899 secret bond between Great Britain and Kuwait, part of which appears below, was not uncommon:

The object of writing this lawful and honorable bond is that . . . Sheikh Mubarak-bin-Sheikh Subah, Sheik of Koweit [Kuwait] . . . of his own free will and desire does hereby pledge and bind himself, his heirs and successors not to receive the Agent or Representative of any Power or Government at Koweit [Kuwait], or at any other place within the limits of his territory, without the previous sanction of the British Government; and he further binds himself, his heirs and successors not to cede, sell, lease, mortgage, or give for occupation or for any other purpose any portion of his territory to the Government or subjects of any other Power without the previous consent of Her Majesty's Government.

When oil was discovered in the Persian Gulf in the early 1900's, the area took on new importance. British companies were quick to gain concessions for exploration and production, and as the world's dependence on oil rose, they made large profits and became even more established in the Gulf. This foreign presence aroused considerable resentment and opposition among many Arabs and Iranians. The Middle Easterners particularly resented the fact that while their oil was making other countries more prosperous, it was bringing very little income to them. They wanted a greater financial return for their oil so they could develop their own resources.

Iran took the lead in the move for change. In 1950, the Iranian parliament responded to the widespread anti-British feeling by naming as prime minister nationalist leader Mohammed Mosaddeq. Mosaddeq opposed Iran's ruler, Shah Mohammed Reza Pahlevi, accusing him of dealing too easily with the Western powers. On June 21, 1951, with the following statement, Mosaddeq justified the nationalization of Iran's oil industry:

Our long years of negotiations with foreign countries . . . have yielded no results this far. With the oil revenues we could meet our entire budget and combat poverty, disease, and backwardness among our people. Another important consideration is that by the elimination of the power of the British company, we would also eliminate corruption and intrigue, by means of which the internal affairs of our country have been influenced. Once this tutelage has ceased, Iran will have achieved its economic and political independence.

The Iranian state prefers to take over the production of petroleum itself. The company should do nothing else but return its property to the rightful owners. The nationalization law provides that 25 percent of the net profits on oil be set aside to meet all the legitimate claims of the company for compensation. . . .

Source: "Exclusive Agreement: The Kuwayti Saykh and Britain" in C.U. Aitchison, Collection of Treaties (1933, 5th ed.), Vol. II, p. 262.

Source: Amin Saikal. *The Rise and Fall of the Shah*. Bipin Shah Associates, Inc., 1980, p. 39.

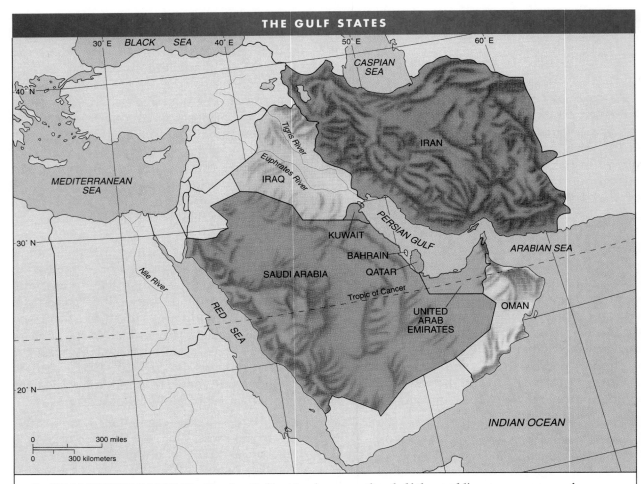

THE GULF STATES

EXAMINING MAPS *The Persian Gulf region has more than half the world's proven reserves of petroleum and natural gas. Oil and gas from the Persian Gulf provide power to much of the world's industry and have brought prosperity to Gulf nations.* *What nations border the Persian Gulf?*

Fearing the spread of nationalization, Western nations responded by boycotting, or refusing to buy or sell, Iranian oil. Because Iran had no way to market its oil, the Iranian economy began to suffer. Within two years, the country's oil revenues dropped to almost nothing. As the Iranian people suffered economic hardship, they became discontent.

In 1953, the Shah, supported by Western governments, dissolved Mosaddeq's government. Nationalization was repealed and the British company restored. A few years later, using diplomacy, the Shah gained a larger share of the oil profits for Iran.

SECTION 4 REVIEW

CHECKING FOR UNDERSTANDING

1. **Cite** the steps taken by the British to gain control of the Persian Gulf area.

2. **Discuss** how Iran rid itself of foreign control.

CRITICAL THINKING

3. **Determining Cause and Effect** Why do you think the Arabs and the Iranians resented the presence of foreigners in their countries?

History

THE BRITISH AND THE FRENCH IN THE MIDDLE EAST

FOCUSING ON THE ISSUE The two maps that follow show the Sykes-Picot Agreement of 1916 and the British and French mandates in the Middle East. After reading the chapter and studying the maps, answer these questions:

1. Based on the information in the maps and in the chapter, how do you think the British and the French felt about the Middle East? How do you think the Arabs felt about the Sykes-Picot Agreement and colonialism? Why do you think they felt this way?
2. Which Middle Eastern countries were included in the British mandate? In the French mandate?
3. According to the Sykes-Picot Agreement, which countries were to be under British influence? Under French influence?

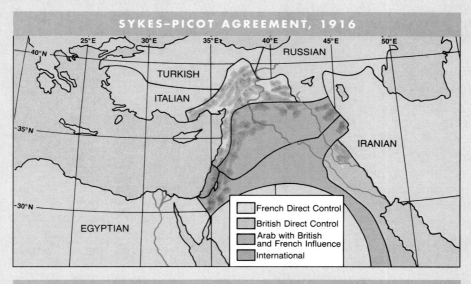

SYKES–PICOT AGREEMENT, 1916

French Direct Control
British Direct Control
Arab with British and French Influence
International

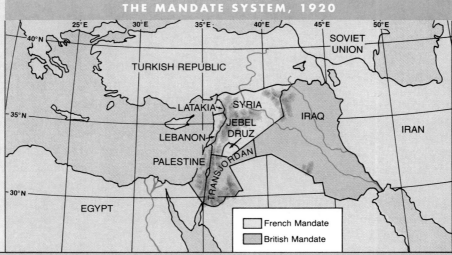

THE MANDATE SYSTEM, 1920

French Mandate
British Mandate

Chapter 37 Review

SUMMARY

Colonialism began in the Middle East in the 1800's when the Europeans wanted new markets, raw materials for industry, and control of strategic trade routes. Despite promises to support Arab independence, the British and the French dominated the Arabs until the mid-1900's. At that time, Arab nations, such as Syria and Lebanon, gained their freedom.

An important European asset was the Suez Canal in Egypt. To bolster European control, the British occupied Egypt, where they stayed until 1956. At that time, the Egyptian government nationalized the canal.

During the early 1900's, conflict developed between Arabs and Jews over the ownership of Palestine. In the late 1940's, the UN vote to partition Palestine led to the creation of Israel, which most Arabs refused to recognize.

The discovery of oil in the early 1900's tightened the European grip over the Persian Gulf area. Middle Easterners, however, demanded and won a larger share of oil profits in the mid-1900's.

USING VOCABULARY

Use the terms below in a paragraph that explains key events in the Middle East from 1800 to 1960.

colonialism   mandate   nationalize

REVIEWING FACTS

1. **Summarize** the Sykes-Picot Agreement and its impact on the Middle East.
2. **Examine** how Syria and Lebanon were governed after World War I.
3. **State** Nasser's reasons for nationalizing the Suez Canal.
4. **Discuss** the Balfour Declaration and its impact on relations between the Jews and Arabs of Palestine.
5. **Explain** why the British during the 1800's considered the Persian Gulf area an important region.
6. **Name** the Iranian monarch who dissolved Premier Mosaddeq's government in 1953.

CRITICAL THINKING

1. **Determining Cause and Effect** Some people believe that the present Arab-Israeli conflict is a direct result of British actions. Do you agree or disagree? On what basis?
2. **Identifying Central Issues** In 1951, Premier Mosaddeq called for the nationalization of Iran's oil industry, and in 1956 Egypt's President Nasser nationalized the Suez Canal. Do you think government has the right to nationalize industry? Give reasons to support your answer.
3. **Drawing Conclusions** Some people claim that colonial rule was beneficial to the Middle East. Others believe that it was harmful. Based on the information in the chapter, what do you think? Give examples to support your opinion.

ANALYZING CONCEPTS

1. **Power** Why did the British land troops in Egypt in the 1880's? How long did they stay there?
2. **Change** How did the growth of Arab nationalism affect European control of the Middle East?

GEOGRAPHIC THEMES

1. **Location** Why is the Suez Canal considered a valuable geographic asset?
2. **Region** How did the discovery of oil affect the Persian Gulf region's place in world affairs?

Expressing Problems Clearly

When studying past and current events, it is often difficult to understand the actions of individuals and groups. Most actions are taken to resolve problems. By accurately identifying these problems, the actions of individuals and groups will make more sense.

Problems—especially problems among groups of people—are usually complex and have many layers. When analyzing an action, first you must recognize the surface problem, or the most obvious cause for the action. For example, suppose your best friend decides suddenly that she no longer wants to be your friend because her after-school job takes up too much of her time. In this case, the action was that your friend cut off your friendship. The explanation, or surface problem, is that she hasn't got time to be your friend anymore.

But what, if any, are the root problems? To find out, you must ask, "What caused this problem?" Perhaps your friend really is too busy; perhaps you have quarreled with her recently; perhaps she has made new friends at her job. By searching for underlying causes, you will discover the root problems of any situation. The following steps will help you express problems clearly:

- Identify an action of an individual or group.
- To discover the surface problem, ask "Why was this action taken?"
- To analyze root problems, ask

"What caused the surface problem?"
- State the root problems in a clear sentence.

EXAMPLE

Reread the section under the heading "Syria and Lebanon" on pages 604–606. According to this section, after a decade of peace, civil war broke out in Lebanon in 1958. To understand what problems led to this action, first ask, "What surface problem sparked armed conflict in Lebanon?" The conflict erupted between mainly Christian pro-Western groups and various anti-Western groups who wanted closer ties with Egypt and Syria. So the war developed from a power struggle between these groups for control of Lebanon's future.

To discover the root problems, ask, "What ultimately caused the conflict between these groups?" Remember that Lebanon, which came under French rule after World War I, was divided into separate districts based partly on the area's many religious groups. Although Lebanon was a nation on paper, differences among these groups prevented the achievement of any lasting form of national unity. Also, because of the colonial history of the region, hatred of the West continued even after Lebanon became an independent nation. Can you state the root problems of the civil war in

Lebanon in a single sentence? *(The civil war in Lebanon was caused by a lack of national unity aggravated by continued hostility between groups and based on a heritage of colonial rule.)*

PRACTICE

Answer the following questions based on your knowledge of this chapter's content.

1. In 1882, British troops occupied Egypt. What surface problem was this British military action intended to resolve?
2. What were the root problems underlying the British occupation of Egypt?
3. In 1956, Egypt's President Nasser nationalized the Suez Canal. What surface problem was this action intended to resolve?
4. What were the root problems underlying the Suez crisis of 1956?
5. In 1947, the United Nations voted to partition Palestine. What surface problem was the partition of Palestine intended to resolve?
6. What were the root problems underlying the partition of Palestine?
7. In the early 1950's, the Western nations boycotted Iranian oil. What surface problem was this action intended to resolve?
8. What were the root problems underlying the Western boycott of Iranian oil?

CHAPTER OUTLINE

People and Places to Know

Camp David Accords, Anwar el-Sadat, Golda Meir, West Bank, Gaza Strip, the *Intifada*, Palestine Liberation Organization (PLO), Beirut, Ruhollah Khomeini, Shi'ites, Saddam Hussein

Objectives to Learn

1. **Recognize** the underlying issues in Arab-Israeli relations.
2. **Summarize** the causes and effects of the civil war in Lebanon.
3. **Identify** the causes and consequences of the war between Iran and Iraq.

A newstand in the Middle East

The Middle East Today

> " In my dream, O mother mine,
> I saw an angel with wings pure white
> Breaking the rifles one by one,
> Shattering into pieces each gun,
> Which then into the fire he dashes
> And turns into smouldering ashes.
>
> In my dream, O mother mine,
> I saw an angel with wings pure white
> Scattering the ashes clean
> Over the glittering scene.
> And the ashes turning into a white dove,
> Hovering over the East, jubilant above.
>
> In my dream, O mother mine,
> I saw an angel with wings pure white
> Lifting [Jews] and [Arabs] up to the skies
> And demanding they shake hands and be wise.
> I heard his voice thunder and echo after them:
> Quick, make haste, O sons of Shem—
> Behold he is coming, the herald of Peace,
> Singing a song of praise to Peace. "

As reflected in the poem above, the greatest challenge facing the people of the Middle East is to bring about a lasting peace. Many factors have contributed to the unrest that has plagued the region for decades. One of these is conflicts—three local wars, a civil war, and an international operation in the past 20 years. They have caused much suffering and the loss of hundreds of thousands of lives and precious resources.

Interwoven with these conflicts—contributing to them and resulting from them—are other problems. In the Middle East as elsewhere, ways must be found to improve economies, provide for rapidly growing populations, and share fairly in natural resources. Resolving conflicts will go a long way toward resolving these problems.

Source: Gassoub Serhan. "O, Mother Mine" in *My shalom, my peace.* Sabra Books, 1975, p. 69.

Arab-Israeli Relations

During the three decades before 1977, wars and conflicts dominated the relationship between the Arabs and the Israelis. At the core of these was disagreement over who owns the land of Israel, once called Palestine. After the war of 1948, three other wars broke out between the two groups—in 1956, 1967, and 1973. Instead of solving existing problems, these wars created new ones. During these wars, the Israelis occupied new territories, which the Arabs want back. The Arabs also want the several million Palestinians who fled or were displaced during the fighting to have their homes and land returned to them.

A SEPARATE PEACE

Over the years, many efforts have been made to bring about peace between the Arabs and the Israelis. One of the boldest and most controversial moves took place in 1977, when, at the invitation of the Israeli government, President Anwar el-Sadat of Egypt arrived in Jerusalem to make a speech before the *Knesset,* the Israeli parliament. Sadat was the first Arab head of state to make an official visit to Israel.

About two years later, on March 27, 1979, President Sadat and Israeli Prime Minister Menachem Begin signed the Camp David Accords, the first formal peace treaty between Israel and an Arab country. The Israelis agreed to withdraw over a three-year period from the Sinai Peninsula, which they had occupied after the 1967 war. Egypt agreed to end the state of war and establish normal and peaceful relations with Israel. Also, elections for local governments were to be held in the West Bank and Gaza, two other territories won by the Israelis in the 1967 war, and their future was to be decided at a later date.

Reactions to the peace treaty were mixed. Many Arabs felt that Egypt, once the leader of the Arab world, had deserted the "Arab and Muslim family" and should have held out until all outstanding problems had been solved. Most Egyptians and Israelis, however, took a "wait-and-see" attitude. Said one Egyptian, "Egyptians are not sure of

EXAMINING PHOTOGRAPHS
Israeli Prime Minister Menachem Begin, left, and Egyptian President Anwar el-Sadat, right, are shown at the 1977 session of the Knesset *in which Sadat called for an end to the state of war, a just solution for the Palestinians, and Arab acceptance of Israel as a state. To what did Israel and Egypt each agree under the terms of the 1979 peace treaty?*

Middle East

GOLDA MEIR AND ANWAR EL-SADAT

Golda Meir served as prime minister of Israel from 1969 to 1974. Anwar el-Sadat was president of Egypt from 1970 until his death in 1981. Both had served their countries well for many years before attaining their respective offices.

Both Meir and Sadat achieved great success in their efforts to make life better for their people and their country. But, as the two excerpts that follow indicate, their philosophies of life and their reactions to election to high government office were very different.

I had never planned to be prime minister; I had never planned any position, in fact. I had planned to come to Palestine, to go to Merhavia, to be active in the labor movement. But the position I would occupy? That never. I only knew that now I would have to make decisions every day that would affect the lives of millions of people. . . . I became prime minister because that was how it was, in the same way my milkman became an officer in command of an outpost on Mount Hermon. Neither of us

had any particular relish for the job, but we both did it as well as we could.[1]

Golda Meir

I knew that this . . . meant I should have to challenge many conditions and ethical codes in existence at the time; but I believed I had the capacity for this. Indeed, due to the inner power I always felt, I had never been afraid to challenge existing conditions. And now that I was President, I felt I wielded a tremendous real power, which had to be used in doing good. This was my forte, and I proceeded from the ideals I had always adopted, inspired by my love of Egypt and my desire to make the country a happy one.

[1]Source: Golda Meir. *My Life*. Putnam Publishing Group, 1975, pp. 364–365.

Never had I had a better chance of putting my principles into practice than when the people elected me President.[2]

Anwar el-Sadat

TAKING ANOTHER LOOK

How did Golda Meir feel about becoming Israel's prime minister? Anwar el-Sadat about becoming Egypt's elected president?

[2]Source: From *In Search of Identity* by Anwar el-Sadat. Copyright © 1977, 1978 by the Village of Mit Abul-Kum. English translation copyright © 1977, 1978 by Harper & Row Publishers, Inc. Reprinted by permission of Harper Collins Publishers.

The Arts of the Middle East

The arts of the Middle East developed over time. Ancient civilizations produced temples, palaces, and monuments. Later, Judaism, Christianity, and Islam provided inspiration for architects, writers, and artists. Today, the arts of the Middle East reflect the influence of East and West as well as the old and the new.

? **In what ways do you think Middle Eastern art forms have changed or remained the same over the centuries?**

ARCHITECTURE
Ancient Egyptian temple and sculpted head in the Valley of the Kings, Egypt

MUSIC
Traditional orchestra performs in a television studio in Jeddah, Saudi Arabia

DECORATIVE TILES
Ceramic tile decoration with geometric patterns and verses from the Quran on the wall of a mosque in Baghdad, Iraq

SCULPTURE
Holocaust Memorial at Yad Vashem (Holocaust Museum) in Jerusalem, Israel

EXAMINING PHOTOGRAPHS *This Jewish settlement on the West Bank is one of 200 that have been established since 1967, when Israel captured the region from Jordan. More than 100,000 Jewish settlers now live on the West Bank, many attracted by low rents and the area's historical significance to Jewish history.* Why do the Israelis want to keep the occupied territories?

anything—they are still suspicious. The land is not back yet." Similar sentiments were voiced by an Israeli: "I would very much like to believe we've fought the last war, at least with Egypt. But I want to see. Sadat may not be around tomorrow. Or he may change his mind."

Some Israelis were willing to meet some of the Arab demands in return for an end to the conflict. Others opposed returning any of the territories. Many of those opposed felt that the occupied land was needed as a security belt around Israel, while some wanted to keep the land because it was once a part of ancient Israel.

UNRESOLVED ISSUES

Three major issues were not resolved in the Egyptian-Israeli peace treaty. One was control of East Jerusalem, which the Israelis had occupied in 1967, and the Arabs wanted returned. Another was the fate of the 1.8 million Palestinians living on the West Bank of the Jordan River and in the Gaza Strip. A third was control of the Golan Heights. The Arabs wanted return of all these territories.

The failure to resolve these issues weakened Sadat's position in Egypt. Boycotts by other Arab countries hurt the Egyptian economy as did the halt of economic aid from oil-exporting Arab states. At the same time, rumors of corruption and mismanagement circulated throughout Egypt, and Muslim religious extremists accused Sadat of betraying his religion. In 1981 Muslim extremists assassinated Sadat, and Vice President Husni Mubarak assumed the presidency of Egypt. Mubarak assured the world community that Egypt would honor its peace with Israel and worked to restore good relations with other Arab countries.

THE OCCUPIED TERRITORIES

From 1967 to the early 1990's, the discontent of the Palestinians living under Israeli occupation in the West Bank and Gaza grew. Their schools were subject to Israeli censorship. The Israelis took over areas of public land surrounding their villages to build settlements for Jewish immigrants. Those who spoke out against the occupation risked being deported.

EXAMINING PHOTOGRAPHS *Palestinians in the West Bank display a portrait of PLO leader Yasir Arafat during a demonstration against Israeli policies. What steps have been taken to secure peace between Israel and the Palestinians?*

In December of 1987, the situation exploded in an uprising the Palestinians called the *Intifada*. It started in Gaza and spread quickly to the West Bank. All through the occupied territories, Palestinian workers went on strike. Young Palestinians flooded the streets, erecting barricades and throwing stones at Israeli soldiers. Attempts by the Israeli army to put down the uprising failed.

The *Intifada* focused world attention on the plight of the Palestinians and brought international pressure to deal with their conditions. A new leadership for the Palestinians emerged in the occupied territories, leading the Palestine Liberation Organization (PLO), a group dedicated to regaining Palestinian territory, to publicly change its attitude to-

ward Israel. In 1988 PLO chairman Yasir Arafat stated that he would give up armed struggle and accept Israel's right to exist. He also called for the establishment of a Palestinian state side-by-side with the Israeli. The *Intifada* also forced many Israelis to rethink their relationship with the Palestinians and to search for a solution.

In 1991 representatives of Israel, of its neighboring Arab countries, and of the Palestinians met face-to-face officially for the first time in Madrid, Spain, for what became the first of a series of peace talks. As one journalist discovered, in the occupied territories feelings ran strong and reactions were mixed:

Like every farmer in the world, Sayed Salayiyeh is proud to talk about his crops. Here in Jericho . . . his Arab ancestors have converted "the sun, the fresh water, and the soil" into juicy fruits and nutritious vegetables for more than 10 centuries. Salayiyeh intends to pass his fields to his five children. "This is my country," he says. "I was born in Jerusalem, and I have lived in Jericho for many years." At noon, while he sips scented tea at a shabby cafe near the Israeli police headquarters, he adds, with a stony expression: "Can we live together, Jews and Arabs, in Palestine? Yes, unless the Jews come in waves."

Along with many others in the West Bank . . . Salayiyeh has serious doubts about the real intentions of the Israelis in the Middle East peace talks. "When will there be a Palestinian state?" he asks. "I don't know. . . . We have waited a century already. We are very patient." But not all of the Palestinians in the occupied territories are willing to wait as long as Salayiyeh. A quarter of the West Bank's 850,000 Palestinians are crammed into refugee camps run by the United Nations. . . .

To the north of Jericho . . . is Mochan Patsahel, one of the first Jewish settlements to have been founded. . . .

Pierre Hammel, a 44-year-old settler who was born in France, is one of Mochan Patsahel's pioneers. . . . "I came here because I am Jewish, and Jews should live in Israel," he says. . . .

Hammel gets angry when he speaks of returning these lands in exchange for peace. . . .

Not all the Jewish settlers are as hard-line as Hammel. One of his neighbors, Rafi Ovadia, is much more flexible. . . .

Ovadia, who was born in Turkey, moved to the settlement 21 years ago and expects that his three children will continue living there. . . . "I am in favor of granting autonomy to the Arabs living in Judaea and Samaria and in Gaza," says Ovadia. "With [Palestinian] autonomy, I could continue to live here. . . . If a Palestinian state is created, I will leave. I wouldn't have any other choice."

In June of 1992, a national election in Israel brought a new government willing to exchange some land for peace with the Arabs and to grant self-government to the Palestinians. Since then, steps have been taken to bring about an ultimate solution to the conflict, but much remains to be done.

SECTION 1 REVIEW

CHECKING FOR UNDERSTANDING
1. **Identify** the underlying issues affecting Arab-Israeli relations.
2. **Discuss** the issues not resolved in the 1979 peace treaty and the effect on Egypt and Sadat.

CRITICAL THINKING
3. **Determining Cause and Effect** What were the consequences of the *Intifada*?

Source: Juan Altable. "Settlers on Sacred Land" in *Cambio 16* as cited in *World Press Review,* April 1992, p. 49.

SECTION 2
Civil War in Lebanon

At the same time the Arab-Israeli conflict was brewing, the seeds of a new civil war were growing in Lebanon. Since independence, power in the government had been divided among Christians and Muslims proportionately to their numbers. As Christians were the majority, for many years they had more political power. But by the 1970's, the population had changed, and Muslims were in the majority. When their request for an even sharing of power was refused, their discontent grew.

Meanwhile, economic problems also were surfacing. Since the increase in oil prices in the early 1970's, a great deal of Middle Eastern oil money had been invested and used in Lebanon. The resulting sudden increase in spending caused prices to rise sharply. The wealthy and the upper-middle class had benefited from the oil money and were able to keep ahead of the rising prices. The poor, who included more than 400,000 Palestinian refugees, could not.

By 1975, the situation had become very tense. As the number of poor Lebanese and Palestinians rose, so did discontent. Many of the Palestinians were members of the PLO which was using Lebanon as a base to launch attacks on Israel. While many Lebanese Muslims supported the Palestinians and the PLO, the majority of Lebanese Christians did not. Afraid that a revolution would upset the religious balance of power, political and sectarian parties formed and trained their own armies. Before long, civil war broke out. Some viewed the conflict as basically religious; others saw it as a struggle between "haves" and "have-nots."

In 1976, at the request of the Lebanese government and other Arab states, Syrian

EXAMINING PHOTOGRAPHS *This Lebanese family is hiding in fear behind a car during a battle between two rival Muslim factions.* **What role did Syria play in Lebanon in 1976?**

agreed to a more even sharing of government positions between Christians and Muslims and elected a new president.

In 1990, Elias Hrawi was elected president of Lebanon, and barricades that for 15 years had separated the east and west sides of Beirut were removed. As a writer who lives in Beirut reports, since then the country has been moving closer to normalcy:

The air-conditioned coaches are filled with camera-toting types looking very much "the tourist." They point, stare and chat with their seatmates as the bus bounces along the old Green Line crossing near Beirut port. Rutted by 15 years of war and neglect, flooded with leaking waste water and crammed with port-bound trucks, this half-mile stretch leads to the city's hottest "tourist" attraction, the ruined remains of Martyr's Square, the old city center.

The happy bouncing tourists are the latest phenomenon of peace. Although they are, in fact, Lebanese, even the ever-present soft drink vendors jokingly call them tourists. . . .

They leave the bus and climb up the base of the bronze statue that gave the square its name. . . . The statue was riddled by bullets over the 15 years of recent conflict. . . .

. . . The pictures are taken. Then the group wanders around the devastated square guessing and arguing about what was what 16 years ago. Those under 30 can't play the game. They are too young to remember.

Once the city's business center, the "Bourj," as Martyrs' Square is called locally, is again showing signs of commercial life. At first it was only Pepsi, Seven-Up and bottled water displayed on carton boxes. Then beer was added. Old-fashioned ice boxes now assure the drinks are served cold. . . .

In the villages, balconies have sprouted

troops arrived to help restore peace. Although order was restored for a time, the conditions that led to the war still existed. Clashes with the Israelis continued. An Israeli invasion took place in 1982, directed at driving the PLO out of southern Lebanon and securing peace for northern Israel.

International attempts made during the 1980's to restore peace did not stop the violence. In 1989, representatives of the United States and Lebanese, Syrian, and other Arab diplomats met in Taif, Saudi Arabia. Out of this meeting came a peace agreement that ended the civil war. Syria pledged to gradually withdraw its troops as a series of reforms were put in place. The parliament

colorful mattresses put out in the sun for airing. Houses have been given a double spring cleaning. . . .

Village girls of marriageable age thumb through fashion magazines for eye-catching haircuts and the latest styles. Village matchmakers . . . find themselves busy for the first time in years. . . .

But the real test of peace for many Lebanese is the hoped-for return of the Western community. . . .

. . . water and electricity cuts are as predictable as the setting of the summer sun. Even if there is enough water for a shower, the question is, "Has there been enough electricity today to heat it up?" . . .

Another chronic problem in both cities and villages is garbage disposal. . . . Not long ago [the mayor of Beirut] claimed that Beirut was the dirtiest city in the world.

The militias are off the stage. . . . But the cast still has to clean up the act, repair the roads and enforce law and order before those-dreamed of foreigners start booking passage for Beirut.

EXAMINING PHOTOGRAPHS *This rubble in Beirut used to be an apartment building before the city was shattered by invasion and civil war. What are some problems still facing Beirut?*

SECTION 2 REVIEW

CHECKING FOR UNDERSTANDING
1. **Discuss** the underlying causes of the civil war in Lebanon.
2. **Summarize** events and conditions in Lebanon since 1976.

CRITICAL THINKING
3. **Drawing Conclusions** Do you think the situation in Lebanon might have been different if the PLO had not set up a base there? Explain.

SECTION 3
Revolution and War

Another area of the Middle East that has seen major conflict and change since the 1970's is the Persian Gulf. In Iran, Iraq, and Kuwait, events took place that have impacted the entire global community.

UPHEAVAL IN IRAN
Iran had grown wealthy over the years through the sale of oil. By the 1970's, however, many Iranians were discontented with

---

Source: Marilyn Raschka. "With Militias Offstage, Beirut No Longer a Theater of War" in *The Washington Report on Middle East Affairs,* July 1991, p. 17.

conditions in their country. They did not approve of the ways in which their ruler, Shah Mohammed Reza Pahlevi (RAY·zuh pah·LAH·vee), spent the nation's money. They also thought that the Shah had disregarded traditional Iranian and Islamic values in his efforts to modernize and westernize. In 1978, opposition to the Shah erupted into revolution.

In 1979, the Shah fled and a new government was set up under Ayatollah Ruhollah Khomeini (eye·ah·tohl·LAH ROOH·huhl·LAH koh·MAY·nee), a Muslim leader who had been living in exile in France. Anger against the Shah soon was directed against the United States, which for many years had supported the Shah. In November 1979, Iranian demonstrators in Tehran took 52 American diplomats as hostages. They remained in captivity until 1981.

Under Khomeini, who remained in power until his death in 1989, Iran became an Islamic Republic run according to strict Islamic principles. Below, an Iranian diplomat discusses Khomeini's impact on Iran:

> **H**is followers did not follow him just for religious reasons but for national reasons. He made it possible for the Iranians to find their original roots, to get out from foreign influence, to be real masters of their own country's destiny. . . . He is the great man who gave them back their religion, their identity and their self-determination, and did away with all these foreign powers moving around here in Iran.

After Khomeini's death, Hashemi Rafsanjani became president of Iran. Below, a journalist discusses Rafsanjani and his goals:

> "**I** believe he is the ideal, the model President . . . ," said Mohammed Hashemi, the

Source: Caryle Murphy. "Iran's Islamic Evolution" in *The Washington Post National Weekly Edition,* June 1–7, 1992, p. 11. © *The Washington Post.*

EXAMINING PHOTOGRAPHS *Ayatollah Ruhollah Khomeini greets supporters in Tehran a few days after the Shah was overthrown. What was Khomeini's goal when he took over Iran's government?*

President's younger brother, who runs the country's official radio and television. "His ideal is to bring Iran to the highest level of its economic, industrial and cultural potential. He's in for the struggle."

If the late Ayatollah Ruhollah Khomeini was the austere revolutionary determined to smash the old regime, Mr. Rafsanjani is the state builder, just as determined to create institutions that will restore the country to a position of power in the region.

WAR IN THE GULF

When Khomeini came to power in Iran, neighboring Iraq had a secular, or nonreligious, government that believed in separating state and religion. About half of Iraq's Muslims were Shi'ites, belonging to the same sect as Khomeini's followers. Khomeini appealed to Muslim leaders in Iraq to spread the Islamic revolution to their country.

Source: Elaine Sciolino. "Rafsanjani Drives for Goal: New Iranian Image and Clout" in *The New York Times,* April 19, 1992, p. 1.

Tension mounted between the two nations. In 1980, determined to keep revolution from sweeping his country, Iraqi president Saddam Hussein (sah·DAHM huh·SANE) invaded Iran. The result was a bloody and costly war that raged until 1988, when international pressure and exhaustion finally forced the two governments to accept a United Nations-sponsored cease-fire.

Iraq emerged from the war strong militarily but shattered economically. To solve his country's problems, Saddam Hussein turned to aggression. Stating that neighboring oil-rich Kuwait was a historic part of Iraq and had unfairly drilled Iraqi oil, he massed his troops along the Kuwaiti borders. On August 2, 1990, Iraq invaded Kuwait. The conquest was swift and complete, leaving many Kuwaitis in shock. George and Suad Araj were two of those Kuwaitis:

EXAMINING PHOTOGRAPHS *In February 1991, young Kuwaitis celebrated the liberation of their country by Allied coalition forces. What country had invaded Kuwait in August 1990?*

Suad Araj: "The invasion of Saddam Hussein came as a surprise in every way. In fact, July 17 is Revolution Day in Iraq. I remember very well, for my husband was away at a conference . . . in Canada. I followed the newspapers very carefully. On the 17th there were at least six pages about Saddam; a Kuwaiti newspaper with pictures of Saddam, a very fine issue in praise of him."

. . . Shortly after this her husband returned from Canada and insisted they go on a vacation. . . . She was reluctant but agreed. Kuwaiti military headquarters were nearby and there was no sign of increased activity the evening before they left, just three days before the Iraqi invasion. Everything looked normal. . . .

Suad Araj: "I left all my jewelry at home. I left everything, even my notebook with addresses and telephone numbers. . . .

"On July 31 we arrived in Limassol, Cyprus. We unpacked in our rented apartment. . . . On August 1 my husband told the renting office that he would pay the rent in advance the following morning."

At seven the next morning there was an impatient ringing of the doorbell. When Suad went to the door, . . . there was a woman from the renting office asking them to . . . pay the rent immediately. Suad was furious. . . . The woman from the office was surprised and asked whether they hadn't heard the news about the invasion.

Suad's first thought was that this meant clashes at the border, but the woman reported that Kuwait City and the Amir Palace were occupied. . . .

Suad Araj: "They wouldn't accept Kuwaiti currency. They called two banks. They would not accept it either.". . . There were many Arabs . . . who could not change their currency and were out on the streets. No one would accept credit cards from Kuwait and the airlines stopped functioning. . . .

"We were stunned. It was a real shock . . . to wake up with virtually nothing: no money, no clothes, no documents. . . . We had worked so hard for so many years and we ended up with nothing. A lot of people had heart attacks. . . . What could we do? We did not have telephone numbers, addresses, bank account numbers. Nothing, nothing, nothing at all!"[1]

The United Nations called for Iraq to withdraw from Kuwait unconditionally by January 15, 1991. When Iraq refused, troops from an American-led coalition of 35 countries, including several Arab nations, launched Desert Storm—a massive air and land attack on Iraq. Hussein responded by launching Scud missiles on Israel. He hoped the bombing would drag Israel into the war. That, he reasoned, would lead the Arab nations to support him. But his strategy failed. In a letter to his family in the United States, a young Israeli social worker gives his views on what Hussein had done for Israel:

First Saddam Hussein has solved our problem of divisiveness. Before this conflict began . . . every other minister was under investigation, the government was always on the verge of collapse, and demonstrations against the government were the place to be on a Saturday night. Now the country is unified, nobody opposes anything, and everyone supports the government. . . .

Second, Saddam has solved our image problem. After the Israeli government invested years of cultivating the world's disgust and outrage towards us . . . , Saddam has turned us into the "good guys". . . .

Third, Saddam Hussein has solved this country's tourism problem. . . . Two weeks ago hotels in Israel were virtually empty. . . . Now, with the exception of Tel Aviv, you can't find a room anywhere in the country. Tel Avivians (who haven't visited Jerusalem for three years because of their fear of the Intifada) are now flocking to Jerusalem to get a safe night's rest before commuting back to Tel Aviv the following morning.[2]

In February 1991, the coalition forces moved into Kuwait and defeated the Iraqi army. Before they withdrew, Iraqi troops destroyed buildings and set oil wells on fire. As one reporter observes below, the impact of the war on the environment has been enormous:

A few miles to the south, where the Persian Gulf washes the sands of the Arabian Peninsula, . . . probably the largest oil spill ever known, covering some 600 square miles of sea surface, blackens 300 miles of coastline and much of the wildlife it nurtured. Blasting pipelines and storage facilities and emptying loaded tankers, the Iraqis deliberately spilled

EXAMINING PHOTOGRAPHS *During the Persian Gulf War, Iraqi oil spills brought danger to the wildlife and vegetation of the region. What other effects did the conflict have on the environment?*

[1]*Source:* Patrick White. "Two Stories from the West Bank" in *Commonwealth*, January 31, 1992, pp. 22–23.

[2]*Source:* Danny Ballin. Letter, February 7, 1991.

as much as six million barrels of crude. . . .

Each day relentless flames devoured about five million barrels of oil, generating more than half a million tons of aerial pollutants, including sulfur dioxide, the key component of acid rain. Billowing two miles high, the sooty pall rode the winds to smudge far beyond Kuwait: Black rains fell in Saudi Arabia and Iran; black snow greeted skiers in Kashmir more than 1,500 miles eastward.

SECTION 3 REVIEW

CHECKING FOR UNDERSTANDING
1. **Chronicle** events in Iran since the 1970's.
2. **Give reasons** for the Iran-Iraq war.

CRITICAL THINKING
3. **Determining Cause and Effect** What have been the effects of Saddam Hussein's decision to invade Kuwait?

SECTION 4

A Land in Transition

Until recently, much of the Middle East was poor by Western standards. Today, however, Middle Eastern countries that export oil do not have to worry as much about money. With their added wealth, the people of these countries have been able to buy more food and other goods. This, however, has led to higher prices all over the Middle East and has created problems in those countries that do not export oil.

Aggravating the problem of rising prices is the rapid increase in urban population. Improved health care has reduced infant deaths and enabled people to live longer. At the same time, however, the birthrate has stayed

Source: Thomas Y. Canby. "After the Storm" in *National Geographic,* Vol. 180, No. 2, August 1991, p. 10.

about the same. As a result, the population of the region has more than doubled in the last 40 years.

In addition, the rate of rural to urban migration is very high. The population of the large cities has been doubling every 15 years or so. Many people migrate because the land near their villages can no longer support them. When the population of a village increases but the area of cultivated land does not, some villagers must go elsewhere. And that elsewhere is the city.

The migration has made it hard for governments to maintain—let alone improve—living conditions. Public services often are inadequate or nonexistent; there are not enough jobs to go around; and in some areas, housing has become a major problem. In Egypt, for example, one person in three has adequate living accommodations. In Cairo, entire families often live crowded together in one or two tiny rooms. With too few dwellings and the high cost of living, the poor often are forced to make their homes on rooftops, in cemeteries, or in makeshift wood or metal huts in wastelands or fields.

Israel, especially, has experienced a rise in population. Between mid-1989 and the end of 1991, 350,000 Jews from the former Soviet Union immigrated to Israel. The excerpt that follows discusses the new immigration and its impact:

"**Y**ou start with a family just arrived in Israel," says Dan Biron, an Israeli . . . who works for . . . an organization that assists immigrants, "and you see that they don't know the language. They don't know how to get health insurance, they don't know the banking system, they never wrote a check in their lives. They never had a credit card. They never used so many appliances, they never bought so many goods. So they have to be helped by someone. . . . "

. . . some 40 percent of the olim (new immigrants) are highly educated, having

EXAMINING PHOTOGRAPHS *In the late 1980's and early 1990's, a large number of Soviet Jews emigrated to Israel in hopes of finding a better way of life. Some, such as this child and grandmother, were able to make a relatively smooth adjustment to their new homeland. Many more, however, have faced hardships as Israeli society tried to cope with mass arrival of new citizens. What difficulties did Soviet Jewish immigrants experience in Israel?*

university degrees in medicine, pure science, architecture, mathematics, classical music, and the arts. . . . Much of this talent will be sacrificed. Israel already has an unemployment rate above 11 percent, and 38 percent of the immigrants are unemployed. . . .

Despite Israel's heroic effort to make newcomers feel welcome, the country found itself unprepared for the sudden influx. This strikes me in Karmiel, a town in northern Galilee, where Soviet families have set up a tent city in a park. . . . The city provides the tents with electricity, and the neighborhood uses the bathrooms of a government building nearby. . . .

In the larger cities the olim are trying to make do by moving into apartments with one another. One Saturday morning in Jerusalem I call on 12 people—all living in one four-room apartment. . . .

To get more elbow room, many of the olim are bypassing the overcrowded cities for the empty deserts of the south and north. And to the anger and consternation of Palestinians, some immigrants are moving into the occupied territories. . . . Other immigrants are moving into apartments abandoned years ago by young Israelis who fled the pioneer towns in Galilee and the Negev desert for the excitement of Tel Aviv and Haifa.

Source: Tad Szulc. "The Great Soviet Exodus" in *National Geographic,* Vol. 181, No. 2, February 1992, pp. 45–46, 48–49, 55–56.

Throughout the Middle East, the rise in population, combined with such other factors as economic development and changing weather conditions, have resulted in a growing shortage of fresh water. Below, a journalist discusses the extent of the problem:

Last winter's rainy season in Israel and Jordan was the driest in 70 years. A decade of drought has depleted the vast Nile watershed in East Africa. Even the Euphrates Valley faces a crisis as Turkey draws more of the river's water for a giant irrigation project in Anatolia. Iraq and Syria, which depend heavily on the Euphrates, consequently face increasingly severe cuts over the next 10 years. In Saudi Arabia's al-Hasa province, where enormous sums of money have effected an agricultural miracle in the desert, the deep-drill wells have lowered the water table by seven or eight feet.

Israel made the desert bloom. . . . Irrigation has been expanded sixfold since 1948. Now reality is asserting itself. There is no longer enough water. In normal years, Israel averages less than five inches of rainfall. . . . But the past three years have been subnormal. To be sure, Israel does not depend on rainwater. One major source, roughly 40 percent, is the Jordan River. . . . The Sea of Galilee . . . is the Jordan's greatest reserve. Today the level of the lake is the lowest it has been in 60 years, down to the "red line" level at which it can no longer be pumped without becoming saline.

The other major source of water is two aquifers. . . . Experts say they have both been overdrawn by a year's supply and continue to be overpumped by 15 to 20 percent annually. The water in the tiny Gaza Strip . . . is becoming brackish and unfit for agriculture and for human consumption.

Source: Richard C. Hottelet. "The Drain on Middle East Water Reserves" in *The Christian Science Monitor,* August 19, 1991, p. 19.

EXAMINING PHOTOGRAPHS *Proposals have been made to build a pipeline that would supply water from Turkey to the six Gulf states, Syria, Jordan, and perhaps Israel. What factors have contributed to water shortages?*

SECTION 4 REVIEW

CHECKING FOR UNDERSTANDING

1. **Give reasons** urban population has increased in the Middle East in recent years.
2. **Identify** the problems created by increased population and rising prices.

CRITICAL THINKING

3. **Predicting Consequences** How do you think a continued rise in population will impact the water shortage in the Middle East? Explain.

Chapter 38 Review

SUMMARY

Bringing about a lasting peace is the greatest challenge facing the people of the Middle East. Relations between the Arabs and the Israelis have been tense and marked with conflict since the 1940's. At the heart of the issue has been disagreement over who owns the land of Israel, formerly Palestine. Other issues—religious, political, and economic—also have contributed, making peace elusive in other areas as well. Lebanon and the Persian Gulf countries of Iran, Iraq, and Kuwait all have suffered revolution and war.

While new governments and peace talks have brought the region closer to peace and normalcy, other challenges must be dealt with. These include rising prices and the high cost of living, the high rate of rural to urban migration, the rise in population, and the growing shortage of water.

REVIEWING FACTS

1. **Explain** why Anwar el-Sadat's visit to Israel was important.
2. **Enumerate** the results of the 1989 Taif conference.
3. **Give reasons** Iranians were discontent with the rule of the Shah.
4. **Specify** Hashemi Rafsanjani's goals for Iran.
5. **Relate** the reasons Saddam Hussein gave for invading Kuwait.
6. **Tell** why Israel has had a major increase in population in recent years.
7. **Identify** the areas of the Middle East that are faced with a drain on water reserves and growing shortages of fresh water.

CRITICAL THINKING

1. **Demonstrating Reasoned Judgment** In 1991, General H. Norman Schwarzkopf, commander of the United States Persian Gulf forces during Desert Storm, stated: "The single greatest contribution to peace in this area is going to be a just settlement of the Palestinian question. So long as the Palestinian question is around, it's going to be a cause that divides the Middle East and causes people to side on one side or another, and it's going to be a constant source of conflict." Explain why you agree or disagree.
2. **Drawing Conclusions** Because of the flood of new immigrants, by the end of 1992 the population of Israel had grown by more than 10 percent. In what ways do you think this mass arrival might affect Israel and the Israelis and Palestinians who live there?
3. **Synthesizing Information** What steps have been taken by governments and world organizations in recent years to ease problems in the Middle East?

ANALYZING CONCEPTS

1. **Empathy** What conflicting attitudes do Arabs and Israelis hold in regard to the occupied territories, such as the West Bank and the Gaza Strip?
2. **Change** What factors have contributed to revolution and war in the Middle East in the past 20 years or so?

GEOGRAPHIC THEMES

Human-Environment Interaction What is one of the major reasons for the shortage of fresh water in the nations of the Middle East?

Evaluating Oral History

An *oral history* is a spoken first-hand account of past or current events, usually recorded on audiotape or videotape and later transcribed into writing. Although oral histories can provide valuable information, they must be evaluated very carefully. Each subject has a particular point of view, or bias, which will affect his or her account of events as they took place. Therefore, you must know the speaker's identity, experiences, and group affiliations in order to recognize this bias. A collection of oral histories should include people representing a wide range of experiences to reflect many viewpoints.

Use the following steps to evaluate oral history:

- Identify who the subject is, and when and where the events described took place.
- Determine what kind of bias the subject may bring to the history of the subject.
- Identify the central issues in the account and the subject's point of view.
- In a collection of oral histories, determine whether or not a variety of viewpoints is presented and explained.

EXAMPLE

Reread the excerpt from an oral history about Iraq's invasion of Kuwait in August, 1990 on pages 627–628. Suad Araj's name is placed before the first quotation, followed by a colon. This identifies Suad Araj as the subject, or person relating the oral history. Paragraphs between her statements summarize what developments happened between the events that she describes.

The first two paragraphs in the excerpt describe the political and military climate in Kuwait shortly before the Iraqi invasion. What details are given in the account? *(Kuwaiti newspapers ran favorable stories about Saddam Hussein in mid-July; no sign of increased military activity three days before the invasion)* Why does Araj give these details? *(to show that relations between Iraq and Kuwait seemed normal)* Where were George and Suad Araj when Iraq invaded Kuwait? *(on vacation in Limassol, Cyprus)* They learned of the invasion from the woman at the rental office of their vacation apartment in Cyprus. What were the immediate effects of the Iraqi invasion on George and Suad Araj? *(Suddenly they had no valid money, credit, or passports; their property was in Kuwait and could be confiscated or destroyed.)* What viewpoint does Suad Araj express in the last paragraph? *(stunned, angry at losing what they had)*

PRACTICE

Read the following excerpt from an oral history by a female Western journalist who lived in hiding during the 1990 Iraqi occupation of Kuwait. Then answer the questions that follow.

The longest two minutes of anticipation in my life occurred that Friday September 14. Our waiting was about to end. It took that long from the moment George spotted the Red Berets scramble down from their jeeps until they broke down the door of our apartment and poured in. The game was up. The relief did not come right away, but by the time I had dealt with the practical aspects of being arrested—packing, answering their questions and changing clothes—I had forgotten about fear. I was no longer afraid. The soldiers said they would be taking us to Baghdad. We were to follow in the footsteps of the other hostages. We more or less knew what to expect; we would be taken to Iraqi military installations and kept as human shields against allied air attacks.

1. When and where did these events take place?
2. Who is telling the story? What kind of bias might the subject bring to the account?
3. What event is described in this excerpt?
4. How did the Iraqi soldiers treat the subject and her companions?
5. How did the subject feel about these events? What details indicate these feelings?

Source: From UNDER SIEGE IN KUWAIT by Jadranka Porter. Copyright © 1991 by Jadranka Porter. Reprinted by permission of Houghton Mifflin Company. All rights reserved.

633

Cultural Connections

Middle Eastern Science

The Middle East made great progress in science from the second half of the 700's AD to the end of the 1000's AD. Under Islamic rule, Arabic became, as one historian of science wrote, "the scientific, the progressive language of mankind. . . ." The achievements of the Middle East laid the foundation for the development of science in the West.

The first contribution of the Middle Eastern science was the transmission of Greek knowledge. Middle Eastern scholars, including Jews, Christians, and Muslims, translated and studied important Greek writings in the physical sciences, philosophy, and mathematics. In many instances, they expanded on the original works. The famed Muslim philosopher Averröes, for example, translated and commented upon Aristotle. The Europeans translated Averröes' work from Arabic to Latin. Today he is credited with bringing the logic of Aristotle, an important tool in the development of science, to the West.

Mathematical achievements under Islamic rule also helped to advance Western science. Arab numbers, the concept of zero, algebra, and trigonometry were all passed on to Europe from the Middle East. For Europeans, these developments simplified mathematical problems and made easy computations that would have been impossible with Roman numerals.

The Middle East also made remarkable progress in the physical sciences, especially in medicine. In addition to the contributions of doctors, such as Maimonides, al-Rāzī, and Ibn Sīnā, there were other significant discoveries. Ibn Khatib and Ibn Khatima were the first to discover that germs were a

first to discover that germs were a factor in the spreading of disease. Al Majusi had a good idea of the circulatory system. Up to the end of the 1500's, Arabic translations of Greek medical books, along with new discoveries from the Middle East, served as the basis of European medicine.

Making the Connection

1. How did the Middle East affect the development of science in the West?

2. What do you think was the most important scientific achievement to come out of the Middle East? Explain your answer.

Unit 6 Review

SUMMARY

The Middle East was home to the early civilizations of the Nile and the Fertile Crescent and birthplace of three major religions. Oil has brought great wealth to some nations of the region and created problems for others. Traditional beliefs and values, including the importance of family, however, remain strong for most Middle Easterners.

In the past, the scarcity of fresh water led most of the people to settle along the fertile river valleys and the seacoasts. Modern technology changed that pattern, making it possible to farm and build cities in even the most arid areas. Today, however, there is major concern about the rapidly dwindling supplies of fresh water.

For a period of time, much of the Middle East was under colonial rule. Even though ultimately freedom and independence was won, some of the decisions made by the colonial powers have continued to impact the region. Having lived with unrest and conflict for many years, today more than ever before Middle Easterners seek a lasting peace.

REVIEWING THE MAIN IDEAS

1. **Give examples** of ways in which traditional Middle Eastern family values have been shaped by Islamic teachings.
2. **Detail** the major components and features of the Islamic state.
3. **Explain** what led to colonialism in the Middle East.
4. **Discuss** the *Intifada* and the factors that led to it.
5. **Discuss** the choices that Israel and the Palestinians faced in resolving their differences.

CRITICAL THINKING

1. **Synthesizing Information** How has physical environment affected the course of Middle Eastern history?
2. **Analyzing Information** "To Westerners, Middle Easterners are what the media has always chosen to reflect." What do you think is meant by this statement? Give examples of impressions you have had of Middle Easterners as a result of media coverage.
3. **Demonstrating Reasoned Judgment** Why do people describe the Middle East as a "mosaic of peoples" rather than as a "melting pot"?

PRACTICING SKILLS

Writing a Paragraph Select one of two topics—"People of the Middle East" or "Environment of the Middle East"—about which to write a paragraph. The paragraph must be written in class using references available in the classroom. Identify two criteria for making a judgment about which topic to select. Identify at least three subtopics for the topic you have chosen. Write three questions about the subtopic that interests you most. Then, using the guidelines for connecting ideas in a paragraph, write a brief paragraph about one of the questions.

DEVELOPING A GLOBAL VIEWPOINT

In recent years, events in the Middle East have had a major impact on the global community, including the United States. What examples can you give of this? Explain why you think the United States should or should not get involved in the affairs of the Middle East.

The Commonwealth of Independent States

In early 1991, the Soviet Union was the largest country in the world and a global superpower. By year's end, both the Soviet Union and its communist system no longer existed. The individual Soviet republics had declared their freedom, and most of them had formed the Commonwealth of Independent States.

Beset by many problems, the Commonwealth today faces an uncertain future. Whatever direction the Commonwealth republics take, however, their peoples will still play an important role in world affairs.

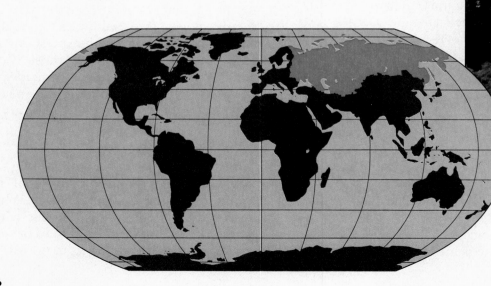

CHAPTERS

AT A GLANCE

LAND AREA:
8,521,670 sq. mi.
(22,070,642 sq. km.)

LAND RESOURCES:
cropland: 10.4%
pasture: 16.7%
forest/woodland: 42.4%
other land: 30.5%

WILDERNESS AREA: 34%

MAJOR MOUNTAIN RANGES:
Carpathian, Caucasus, Kolyma, Pamirs, Sayan, Stanovoy, Verkhoyansk, Ural

MAJOR RIVERS:
Amur, Dnieper, Dniester, Don, Kama, Lena, Ob, Volga, Yenisey

POPULATION: (1992 est.)
221,400,000

**POPULATION UNDER
15/OVER 65:**
26%/9%

LIFE EXPECTANCY: 70 yrs.

POPULATION PROJECTION:
344,100,000 (by 2025)

POPULATION DENSITY:
33/sq. mi. (13/sq. km.)

URBAN POPULATION: 66%

LARGEST CITIES: (millions)
Moscow, Russia (8.6)
St. Petersburg, Russia (4.4)
Kiev, Ukraine (2.5)
Tashkent, Uzbekistan (2.1)

People and Places to Know
Black Sea, Siberia, the steppe, Caspian Sea, Lake Baikal, Volga River, Kama River

Key Terms to Define
continental climate, permafrost, tundra, taiga

Objectives to Learn
1. **Cite** examples that illustrate the vastness of the Commonwealth.
2. **Describe** the effect the Commonwealth's global position and climate have on the way of life.
3. **Identify** and characterize the vegetation zones and bodies of water in the Commonwealth.

Siberian forest

Giant Among the Gigantics

> I love my country, but my love is strange
> And rare, a love that reason cannot change.
> It is not my country's victories, nor fame
> So dearly bought with blood, nor ancient claim
> Of rich tradition, glory, and command
> That stir sweet reveries about my native land.
>
> Not these bring quiet joy. I love—I know
> Not why—her rivers at the flood like seas,
> The voices of her boundless forest trees,
> The frozen silence of her plains in snow.
> I love to ride for days inside a jolting cart
> On dusty lanes, and, searching slow the evening shadows,
> To dream of lodgings near and hail with thankful heart
> A blur of trembling village light among the meadows.
>
> I love the smell of stubble burning,
> The wagons huddled on the plain
> At night, a pair of silver birches
> Above a field of yellow grain.
> With gladness few can share, I see
> The grain upon the threshing floor,
> The lowly cottage with its trim
> Above the window and the door.
> I'm glad to watch on holidays
> The stamp of dancers on the ground,
> And hear until the morning's near
> The talk of tipsy peasants round.

This poem was written by a noted Russian poet almost 150 years ago. Russia, the country to which the poet refers, is now part of the Commonwealth of Independent States. In spite of many changes, the peoples of the Commonwealth still hold a deep love for their land.

Source: Mikhail Lermontov. "My Native Land" in MIKHAIL LERMONTOV *The Demon and Other Poems.* Eugene M. Kayden (tr.). Kent State University Press, 1965, p. 87.

Factor of Size

The Commonwealth of Independent States (C.I.S.), with its 8,521,670 square miles (22,070,642 square kilometers) of territory, is one of the world's largest political units. It covers about one-sixth of the earth's land surface, and is more than the size of Canada, China, and the United States combined.

The size of the Commonwealth has affected its history and economic development. As discussed below, it also has made the land one of mystery and fascination:

To the ancients, [today's C.I.S.] was the end of the known world, a land inhabited by Hyperboreans [legendary people of the Far North] and cannibals, by fantastic creatures, half man and half monster. Marco Polo called it the coldest part of the world and the land north of it a region of darkness, with neither the sun, the moon, nor the stars to give it light. Still later, the Europe of the Enlightenment looked with interest and concern on the autocratic treasure-laden Russian empire, trying to guess the intentions of the "Russian bear."

Even the rulers of the land did not know how big it was. In January 1725, Peter the Great sent forth an expedition under Vitus Bering to find the place where Asia and America "meet." It took Bering and his crew three and a half years to reach Kamchatka, from where they sailed on the *St. Gabriel* to reach the straits separating the Chukchi Peninsula and Alaska.

The world has changed much since then. [The C.I.S.] is an industrial power with close ties to other countries. . . . Today, Bering's journey could be made in less than ten hours. The cloak of mystery that at one time had covered this vast country has been lifted, even if not removed altogether.[1]

CHECKING FOR UNDERSTANDING
1. **Specify** the size of the C.I.S.

CRITICAL THINKING
2. **Making Generalizations** How have people viewed the C.I.S.?

Global Position and Climate

The C.I.S. spans the two continents of Europe and Asia, or Eurasia. The dividing line between the two is the Urals, a long, low range of mountains running north to south. Below, a Russian author describes what he sees and feels as he stands along the border:

Europe and Asia meet on this forest clearing. One fir tree grows in Europe, the other, within sight of it, in Asia. A flock of waxwings rises from an ashberry tree, circles over the clearing and settles on a mountain ash in Asia. The people in the clearing, feeling chilled, run back and forth between Europe and Asia. A bus stops. The passengers read the words "Europe-Asia" on the stone marker, draw a line on the pavement and jump across it into Asia. . . .

. . . In some places the border passes between neighboring villages. When visiting the city of Magnitogorsk you spend the day on the right bank of the Ural River and then take a streetcar to your hotel in Asia. Though the border is of no actual

---

[1]*Source:* Reprinted from "The USSR" by Natalya Shemiatenkova in RUSSIA: THE LAND AND PEOPLE OF THE SOVIET UNION by Dieter Blum. Published in 1980 by Harry N. Abrams, Inc., New York. All rights reserved.

EXAMINING PHOTOGRAPHS *The Ural Mountains, composed of rounded peaks like these, contain rich mineral deposits. What two geographic areas do the Urals divide?*

significance in everyday life, there is something solemn about crossing the line the first time. Thousands of kilometers lie behind you. Ahead are the frost-tinted crests of the dark forest, yet more thousands of kilometers of your native land stretching endlessly before you. At a moment like this you have a physical sensation of your country's vastness.

The C.I.S. is one of the northernmost territories on earth. This location influences its climate, which has been the most fundamental element in shaping the natural environment. For the most part, the Commonwealth has a **continental climate**. This means short hot summers and long cold winters separated by a very short spring and fall. Global location, distance from great bodies of water, and lack of mountains near lowland areas are three major factors that account for the climate being what it is.

The C.I.S. is not the land of constant cold many people believe it to be. From the Caspian Sea eastward are desert areas with a

Source: Vasili Peskov. "Europe-Asia" in *This Is My Native Land.* Progress Publishers, 1976, pp. 124–125.

hot, dry climate that makes much of the area barren. In the Kara Kum, or "black sand," desert, the temperature has been known to rise above 120° Fahrenheit (48.9° Celsius) in the shade. In the area along the coast of the Black Sea, a favorite vacation spot of the Commonwealth's people, the winters are short and rainy, while the summers are hot and dry.

Much of the country, however, does experience very cold winters, which last for many months. This is especially true in the north of Siberia, a Russian region in northern Asia. Below, a visitor to the Siberian city of Yakutsk (yah·KOOTSK) describes how the cold feels and what effects it can have:

The day I arrived in Yakutsk . . . , it was 46 (-43.3° Celsius) below. When our plane landed, the door was frozen solidly shut, and it took about half an hour for a powerful hot-air blower—standard equipment at Siberian airports—to break the icy seal. Stepping outside was like stepping onto another planet, for at those low temperatures nothing seems quite normal. The air burns. Sounds are brittle. Every breath

EXAMINING PHOTOGRAPHS *Parts of the Kara Kum provide enough vegetation to support herd animals, like this camel, who seems undisturbed by the gas well. Where are the desert areas of the C.I.S. located?*

hovers in a strange slow-motion cloud, adding to the mist of ice that pervades the city and blurs the sun. When the breath freezes into ice dust and falls almost silently to the ground, Siberians call it the whisper of stars. Frost as fine as sand shifts into crevices, clings to power lines, coats the scrubby trees along the main avenues until they look like misshapen sculptures. Every few minutes people on the streets put gloved hands over their mouths and noses to keep the flesh from freezing. The smallest children are wrapped in layer after layer so that little more than their eyes are exposed. Buildings have triple windows and triple doors. Private cars are put away for the winter. Taxis are kept in heated garages and are fitted with thick double panes of glass that look like portholes peering into a sea of frost. Trucks for lumbering and other work are kept running constantly through the six months of winter, for to let their engines cool would be to lose the ability to start them again until spring. In this climate, where the low that year was 72 degrees below zero Fahrenheit (-57.8° Celsius), steel cranes can snap, photographic film can shatter like glass, rubber soles on boots can break cleanly in half.

Siberia is one of the areas of the C.I.S. where a condition known as **permafrost**, permanently frozen ground, occurs. This is because much of the C.I.S. is too far away from the Atlantic Ocean to be influenced by its mild westerly winds.

Permafrost is a problem, especially in Siberia, where soil freezes to a great depth. It makes building roads very difficult and causes buildings not constructed on piles to sink and tilt in the summer. It also makes extra heat insulation necessary for water mains and sewers and forces steam-heat

EXAMINING PHOTOGRAPHS *These warmly dressed passengers are boarding a bus to go to work on a typical morning in Siberia. Why does the condition of permafrost occur in Siberia? What problems can it cause?*

pipelines to be built aboveground. Above all, it can be ruinous for agriculture.

In addition to permafrost, areas north of the Arctic Circle also experience polar night, darkness which lasts for more than 24 hours. This occurs during the winter when the northern part of the earth is tipped away from the sun. Below, a reporter describes what happens in the port city of Murmansk when the sun finally appears:

[After] seven weeks of darkness, the city turned out for a holiday on the last Sunday of January. Signs reading "Zdravstvui sointse" (Hello, sun) went up around town, stalls were raised for amateur skits, and women in folk garb went out with baskets full of oranges, apples and candies. No matter that the sun was still limited to an orange glow through the hazy horizon.

Technically the polar night had ended a week earlier, but because of the rolling hills surrounding Murmansk, it took the sun some time to gain elevation to become visible. The temperature was around zero Fahrenheit (-17.8° Celsius). . . .

Hazy or cold, it was a day to be out in the streets, to affirm despite evidence to the contrary, that days would get longer and warmer now that the long darkness was at an end. . . .

In Semyonovskioye Lake, . . . a cluster of diehard "morzhi" (walruses) . . . were cavorting in the icy water.

Nearby a stage dominated by a huge smiling sun was set up alongside a bus bursting with children. Groups of these took turns dashing out to perform a skit or a song. . . .

. . . In . . . a winter sports complex . . . , several hundred young people massed for a cross-country ski race. Downtown, . . . sailors joined in an impromptu weight-lifting contest. . . .

The sun is an obsession at these latitudes. Old-timers describe the depressing effect the gloomy polar night has on newcomers, and speak of a drowsiness that afflicts even longtime residents.

"It is an effort to get out of bed in the morning," said a taxi driver. "One feels like a lazy fly, the kind that wanders dazedly into your soup."

To counter the adverse effect of the polar night, powerful sodium lamps bathe thoroughfares in dazzling light, and shops offer more oranges, apples and green onions than those in Moscow. In school, children are given sun-lamp treatment, and school cafeterias have carrots and milk available at all times.

But it is the real sun that people crave. . . .

The climate of the C.I.S. makes it one of the driest territories in the world. This is a major problem in terms of agriculture. Some areas are too cold for productive agriculture. Others do not know how much rainfall they will get during the year. Some years there is a drought, which causes some farm products to be in short supply. As a result, often there is not enough grain and other farm products to feed all the people. Then, the Commonwealth must import these goods.

EXAMINING PHOTOGRAPHS *The kernels this woman is looking at are from grain growing in this experimental Arctic greenhouse at a Moscow research center.* *In what ways does climate affect agriculture in the C.I.S.?*

SECTION 2 REVIEW

CHECKING FOR UNDERSTANDING
1. **Define** continental climate, permafrost.
2. **Discuss** the kind of climate found in most of the C.I.S.

CRITICAL THINKING
3. **Determining Cause and Effect** Why do you think the C.I.S. has to depend on foreign nations for some farm produce?

Source: Serge Schmemann. "In Soviet North, a Party Greets the Sun" in *The New York Times,* February 19, 1984. Copyright © 1984 by The New York Times Company. Reprinted by permission.

SECTION 3

The Lay of the Land

Like the rest of the land surface of the world, the territory of the C.I.S. has clearly defined climate and vegetation zones. These include expanses of treeless plains called **tundra**, several kinds of forest, steppe, semi-desert and desert areas, and humid subtropical zones. Sprinkled among these are mountains and bodies of water.

TUNDRA

Commonwealth territory in the far north, along the Arctic shore, consists of hundreds of thousands of square miles of tundra. Here, the low hills and level marshy plains are covered with snow and ice for most of the year, and the ground is almost always frozen. There are no tall trees, only moss, small shrubs, and low grasses.

Not many people live on the tundra. The people who do live there make their living by fishing, hunting, or herding reindeer. Below, a writer who grew up on the tundra talks about the area and its people:

My birthplace, the settlement of Uelen on the Chukchi Peninsula, is situated on a narrow pebble spit. To the north lies the Arctic Ocean, which came up to our *yaranga,* or family dwelling. During autumn storms, waves often beat against the walrus-skin walls of the hut, while in winter masses of broken ice reached the hole where we kept our winter supplies. . . .

Our whole life was bound up with the sea. Early on summer mornings, the hunters set off from land in their *baydars,* or kayaks, paddling out into the sparkling patches of sunlight among the drifting ice floes to chase the herds of walruses and whales. In winter the men hunted seals on foot, hiding in the light blue twilight among the masses of broken sea ice. . . .

The Chukchi Peninsula, where I was born, is gripped by gale-force winds and severe cold. For all practical purposes there is no summer here, if one excludes the one and a half or two months of relatively warm weather when the temperature rises as high as 21° C (70° F). This is the time when the tundra vegetation blossoms and the midnight sun hardly disappears below the horizon. . . .

Today, . . . many inhabitants of the . . . Arctic have not only absorbed the ancient heritage that was passed on by their forefathers but also have adopted much of the contemporary outside world. They have shifted from yarangas to modern-style houses furnished with arrays of modern conveniences. . . . Some have exchanged reindeer or dogsleds for snow mobiles or all-terrain vehicles, and they fly from village to nomad camp by helicopter.

But for all their ability to adapt, the native inhabitants of the . . . Arctic remain inexorably bound to their homeland. They may change, but they will never leave their beloved seacoast or tundra; they will remain hunters and reindeer herders, dwellers amid lands covered for most of the year by ice and snow. . . .

. . . Flying by helicopter from my village of Uelen, I paid a visit to the Chukchi reindeer herders at the state farm known in Russian as Mayak Severa, or "beacon of the north."

Arakamchechen [the island on which the farm is located] is well suited for reindeer farming; in summer the winds blowing across the island sweep the swarms of mosquitoes out to sea, and the pastureland is rich. . . .

Vladimir Tukkay [leader of the farm's reindeer workers] has his own reindeer. . . . His spacious yaranga is packed with recent newspapers and magazines. A powerful all-terrain vehicle with a transceiver stands by his home.

Surveying these comforts, I asked Tukkay if he would live in any other place.

"Any other place?" he pondered. "Most likely not. I was born in the tundra, my parents and forefathers were always reindeer herders. I studied at school, I lived in the dormitory, then served in the army. Could I live in any other place but Arakamchechen? To do that, I would be deprived of a certain part of my very self. Here in the tundra, among the reindeer, . . . I feel the life I was created for."

FOREST

South of the tundra is forest, which covers more than 40 percent of the C.I.S. It constitutes one-fifth of the forest area of the world and contains about one-fourth of the world's supply of timber. Cold climate, poor soil, and a short growing season make most of the eastern forest lands unsuitable for farming. In parts of the western zone, however, trees have been cut down to make room for cities and farms. The soil is good, and rye, barley, and oats grow well.

Most of the forest region is **taiga**, or evergreen forest. The Siberian taiga has so many trees that it is called a "green ocean." Below, a journalist describes his first encounter with the Siberian taiga:

The taiga is the wellspring of legend and adventure. [The Siberians] go off to hunt, or fish through the open ice, or build a campfire and cook a sumptuous meal in the open, surrounded by the cleanest snow you ever saw. So Yuri and our other guide, Yelena Pankova, . . . were delighted by our interest. And when one day the weather showed the first sign of spring and the temperature rose to minus 20 [-29° Celsius], five of us . . . piled into a four-wheel-drive Gazik, a [Russian] version of the Jeep, and headed along a narrow, unpaved road west from Yakutsk. We were going on a picnic.

About twenty-five miles [40 kilometers]

Source: Yuri Rytkheu. "People of the Long Spring" in *National Geographic,* Vol. 163, No. 2., February 1983, pp. 206, 209, 212, 214–215.

EXAMINING PHOTOGRAPHS *Largest of the Commonwealth's vegetation zones, the thick taiga consists mostly of spruce, larch, and pine trees.* **Why is the eastern part of the taiga unsuitable for farming?**

out of town we turned onto a little-used track that led into the forest. The Gazik scrambled through axle-deep snow, wound for miles among the trees, and came to a stop at a flat expanse of pristine woods. The engine was left idling, but we walked up to our knees in snow, back, back into the deep forest where we could hear neither engine nor any other whisper of distant civilization. Within minutes the fluffy snow had been shoveled away from a chosen spot, dry wood had been gathered from dead branches, and a fire was going. A blackened teapot had been filled with snow and was hanging over the flames. A . . . bucket, also brimming with light snow, sat on the logs, the snow melting and sizzling and hurling steam into the icy air. . . .

The first course was then spread out . . . : the *stroganina* [fish], some sliced salami, smoked *omul* [fish] and *ryapushka* [fish], black and brown bread cut into thick slices, and chunks of lightly smoked colt's meat. . . . There were cups of steaming tea. The bread froze, and the apples turned to stone until they were brought close to the fire. Yuri had to keep waving his jackknife through the flames so he could pry it open. The vodka, poured into metal cups, had to be kept close to the heat; otherwise the metal cup would stick to your lips.

After the first course Yelena and Uri turned to making a soup called *ukha*. . . . The soup was done when the fish floated to the surface and the eyes turned white, Yelena said. And she spooned it out. It had a thick, wonderful flavor. And in the woods around the fire, dusk came slowly, turning the snow blue and moving the darkness closer until it pressed against the tight glow of the flames.

STEPPE

South of the forest is the steppe, the main agricultural area of the C.I.S. This great plain stretches more than 3000 miles (4800 kilometers) from eastern Europe to Asia. For centuries, it served as an invasion route for foreign armies. Today it is an important industrial area, and its soil is considered among the best in the world for farming. Below, a Russian author discusses the challenges of life on the steppe:

The sun is unrestrained and pitiless. It burns you up, it sets the body on fire, making it impossible to think of anything but the heat. "The sun of the steppelands is like a boiling kettle, pouring yellow boiling water over your back," wrote the poet Yuri Pankratov. In this quiet, cozy little town on the steppes, about half the

Source: From RUSSIA: BROKEN IDOLS, SOLEMN DREAMS by David K. Shipler. Copyright © 1983 by David K. Shipler. Reprinted by permission of Times Books, a division of Random House, Inc.

EXAMINING PHOTOGRAPHS *This farmer uses a modern multi-disc tractor to plow the rich soil of this farm and prepare it for a new growing season. Where is the main agricultural area of the C.I.S. found?*

people are Kazakhs, and they have their own way of dealing with the sun.

It is almost unbearable to look at one of them during the hottest time of the day. You will see a man walking in the heat wearing a long, heavy robe and a fur hat. Not a drop of perspiration shows on his bronzed face, and not much more than that of real expression, either. He looks alert but untroubled, in sharp contrast to those who are strange to the area, and who begin to suffer visibly when the thermometer rises menacingly.

The people here assure the visitor that there are two main rules for fighting off the scorching heat: Do not drink, and keep yourself well covered. They always observe these rules, and they never take an afternoon siesta, not even when the temperature is so high that an egg buried in the sand is hard-boiled in a minute. They just go on working their allotted seven hours a day, as they do in any other weather.

Source: Leonid V. Finkelstein (Vladimirov). *The Russians.* Frederick A. Praeger, 1968, pp. 11–12.

BODIES OF WATER

The C.I.S. also has a great many bodies of water. Two of the world's largest lakes are found here. One is the Caspian Sea, which is really a salt lake. The other is Lake Baikal (by·KAHL), which is the deepest continental lake in the world. Both are important as sources of fish.

Then there are the rivers, which have played an important part in the country's trade and development. They are, to a great extent, a product of the climate. The direction in which the rivers flow is determined by the locations of the mountains and the higher elevations. Climate, however, determines how much water each river bears and for how many months of the year each river is frozen.

Most Siberian rivers flow from south to north into the Arctic Ocean and are frozen for most of the year. Because of this, they are not very effective links to the outside world. Most of the rivers in the European part of the Commonwealth, however, are connected to one another and to the seas by a system of canals. This makes possible a flow of river traffic that has helped unify the country.

One of the most important rivers is the Volga, Europe's longest river. Although it is frozen for almost four months of the year, it handles almost half of the country's river-freight traffic. One of the rivers flowing with the Volga is the Kama. Below, a Russian author explains why the Kama often is described as a "hardworking river":

Just thirty kilometers [18 miles] from its source the little Kama shoulders its first load: lumber. This load keeps increasing constantly, with lumber, lumber and more lumber from its countless tributaries, down its entire length to the Volga. The Kama has for centuries been a lumber-carrier from the moment the ice breaks up in spring till the river freezes over again. Its small tributaries carry the logs before they are made up into rafts. As seen from above, the logs look like matchsticks some-one has dropped on the surface. They are so closely packed that raftsmen can easily run back and forth across them. Sometimes a jam packs the small river bed with logs and then a tractor can roll along the surface. Navigation stops in the upper reaches of the Kama in spring, for then

EXAMINING PHOTOGRAPHS *Some parts of the steppe can be very cold. This is reflected in the warm clothing worn by this family enjoying a meal in their home on the Central Asian steppe. Why is the steppe so important to the people of the Commonwealth?*

EXAMINING PHOTOGRAPHS *This structure stretched across the Kama River is used to catch logs so they can be sorted and lashed into rafts. The lumberjacks who do this work often live with their families in huts aboard the rafts when they are riding their harvested logs to sawmills farther down the river. Besides logs, what other products are transported down the Kama River?*

lumber is king. Farther downstream the logs are knocked into rafts. . . . Barriers are set up in the river, and the place where the lumber accumulates makes you think the river is paved with logs. . . .

From above I was now looking at a river covered with an endless string of rafts. . . .

These giant rafts follow each other in close succession. No sooner does one disappear from view than another appears. There is always a steamer at the head of a raft. Sometimes these are old water-wheel river boats. The rafts once used to float downstream unaided, but the Kama has now overflown its banks like a sea before the dam at the city of Perm, and the current has practically disappeared. This means the rafts have to be towed: six hundred of them each season. . . . The Kama is fondly called the lumber carrier. However, the river carries much more than lumber on its back. Oil from the Kama oil fields is transported by water, as are paper, machinery and chemicals. Salt

barges have always gone down the Kama to the Volga. . . . The river demanded that all who traversed it be skilled pilots, which meant one generation handed its knowledge down to the next. There is still an old custom of presenting a bridegroom with an oar in one of the Kama settlements.

SECTION 3 REVIEW

CHECKING FOR UNDERSTANDING
1. **Define** tundra, taiga.
2. **Examine** how climate influences the rivers of the C.I.S.

CRITICAL THINKING
3. **Making Comparisons** Compare the ways in which people make a living in the tundra, taiga, and steppe.

Source: Vasili Peskov. "Sister to the Volga" in *This Is My Native Land.* Progress Publishers, 1976, pp. 20–21.

The Commonwealth of Independent States

THE DYING SEA

The former Soviet Union often promoted economic goals at the expense of the environment. As a result, the Commonwealth inherited a number of environmental disasters.

One such catastrophe is the Aral Sea, an inland body of water in Central Asia. In the 1950's, to boost the number of irrigated fields in Central Asia's steppes and deserts, the Soviets ordered waters drained from two large rivers feeding into the Aral. The following article discusses the impact their decision has had:

On the bitter desert that used to be the Aral Sea. [Muynak, Uzbekistan's] fishing fleet fulfills its tragic final mission.

The rusted, hollow hulls beached on salty dunes once sailed high above, on the surface of a teeming lake that was Central Asia's foundation of life. Thirty years ago, the Aral Sea was the size of West Virginia and men hauled 160 tons of fish from it each day. . . . The lake has shriveled into a lifeless lagoon, its shore now more than 20 miles from here.

The Aral's destruction has marooned Muynak, its boats and its giant fish cannery in a desert. . . .

. . . officials for years allowed aerial spraying of pesticides and defoliants while workers were in the fields. . . .

Much of the chemicals is washed back into the rivers.

The poisoning of Central Asia's land, economy and people is seen most clearly . . . in the Amu River delta. . . .

People here drink whatever the Amu River brings. Increasingly, it brings toxic chemicals. . . .

"The ecological situation affects . . . illness, and what is happening to us is literally an epidemic," says [Amet] Madreyimov. . . . As chlorides, sulfates and salts in the

water—and in locally grown produce—have risen, so have hepatitis, other liver illnesses, cancer and anemia. . . .

The Karakalpak Academy of Sciences confirms . . . that the loss of the Aral, whose huge volume of water moderated the weather, has cut two month's off the region's growing season.

DRAWING CONCLUSIONS

How has the "death" of the Aral Sea affected the area's environment?

Source: James Rupert. "Death of a Desert Sea" in *The National Post Weekly Edition,* July 6–12, 1992, p. 10. © 1992, *The Washington Post.* Reprinted with permission.

GLOBAL FOCUS

Geography

LAND AND RESOURCES

The natural resources of the Commonwealth are as vast and diversified as the lands its members encompass. When the territory was all one nation—the Soviet Union—a writer penned this statement about what he called the "im-mense and rich land":

A popular patriotic song likens the Soviet citizen to a landlord proudly striding across his domain. And indeed he has reason for his pride. That land contains an un-equaled plentitude of the sub-stances people covet: an estimated one fourth of the earth's energy reserves, a prospector's bonanza of miner-als, seemingly endless forests, and great tracts of fertile soil.

FOCUSING ON THE ISSUE Study the maps, and use the infor-mation provided in them to defend or negate each of the 10 statements that follow. Then determine if the writer's comments are accurate and reliable. Give information

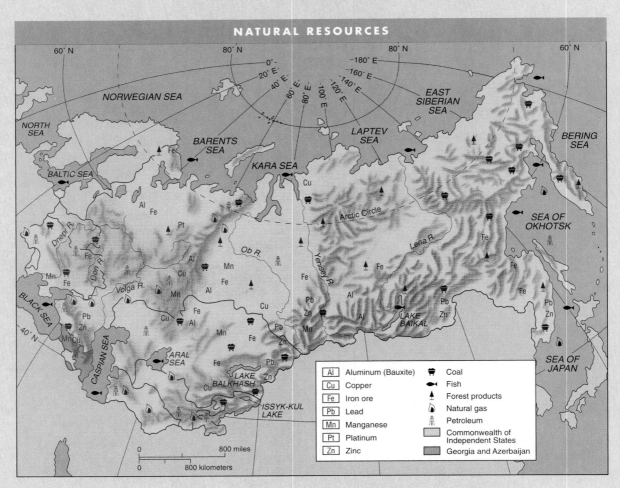

NATURAL RESOURCES

Al	Aluminum (Bauxite)	⛏	Coal
Cu	Copper	🐟	Fish
Fe	Iron ore	🌲	Forest products
Pb	Lead	💧	Natural gas
Mn	Manganese	🛢	Petroleum
Pt	Platinum		Commonwealth of Independent States
Zn	Zinc		Georgia and Azerbaijan

presented in the maps to support your conclusion.

1. The territory of the Commonwealth includes few tracts of fertile soil that, when irrigated, are excellent for farming.

2. Very few natural resources are found in the desert areas and mountain areas of the Commonwealth republics.

3. At least one-third of the territory of the republics of the Commonwealth of Independent States is forest.

4. Timber is one of the major natural resources of the Commonwealth republics.

5. Almost every major mineral can be found in Commonwealth territory.

6. There are very few deposits of coal, oil, and natural gas in the Commonwealth republics.

7. One resource that the Commonwealth lacks is fish.

8. The greatest portion of Commonwealth territory is taiga.

9. The Commonwealth lacks waterpower, which is used to produce electricity.

10. In Commonwealth territory, almost all the deposits of oil are in desert areas.

Source: From LIBRARY OF NATIONS: The Soviet Union. By the Editors of Time-Life Books © 1985 Time-Life Books, Inc.

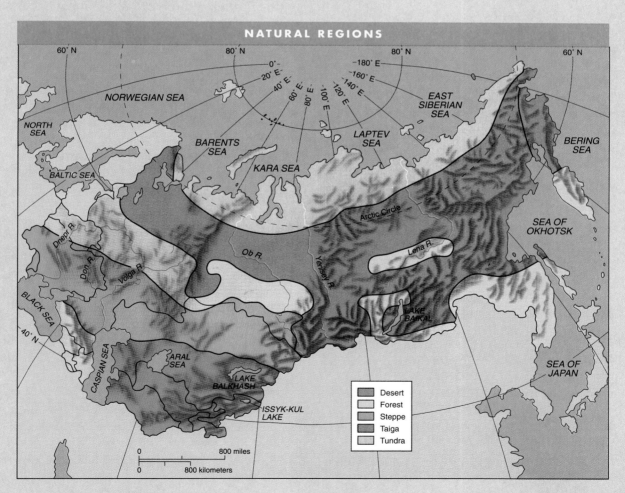

NATURAL REGIONS

Legend:
- Desert
- Forest
- Steppe
- Taiga
- Tundra

0   800 miles
0   800 kilometers

Chapter 39 Review

SUMMARY

The Commonwealth of Independent States is one of the largest territories in the world, spanning the continents of Europe and Asia. Its size has affected its history, economic development, and conduct in world affairs.

Climate has been the most basic element in shaping the Commonwealth's natural environment. Three factors—global location, distance from great bodies of water, and lack of mountains near lowland areas—have influenced climatic conditions. Extremes of climate and inadequate rainfall have had a major impact on the Commonwealth's agricultural production.

The Commonwealth has clearly defined climate and vegetation zones. These include tundra, forest, steppe, desert areas, and humid subtropical zones. The rivers of the Commonwealth have played an important part in the area's trade and development.

USING VOCABULARY

Imagine that you are traveling in the Commonwealth of Independent States. Using the terms below, write a paragraph describing the types of environment you are encountering on your journey.

continental climate	tundra
permafrost	taiga

REVIEWING FACTS

1. **Name** the two continents that the C.I.S. spans.
2. **Identify** the three factors that influence the climate of the C.I.S.
3. **Discuss** the effect of permafrost on the people of Siberia.
4. **Describe** the kind of physical environment found in the tundra region of the C.I.S.
5. **Name** the grains that are grown in the western area of the taiga region.
6. **Explain** the kind of economy that thrives in the steppe.

CRITICAL THINKING

1. **Identifying Alternatives** In what ways has the C.I.S.'s vast size been both an advantage and a disadvantage?
2. **Demonstrating Reasoned Judgment** Because of the C.I.S.'s icebound seaports in the north and high mountain ranges in the south, historically it has been thought of as a "landlocked" country. In what ways do you think this may have affected development and national character?
3. **Identifying Central Issues** In what ways do you think climate has been the most basic element in developing the natural environment of the C.I.S.?
4. **Analyzing Information** Three-fourths of the C.I.S.'s people live in the steppe. Why is the C.I.S.'s population so unevenly distributed?

ANALYZING CONCEPTS

1. **Environment** What are the major characteristics of rivers in the C.I.S.? What role have they played in the Commonwealth's development?
2. **Diversity** Where are each of the Commonwealth's climate and vegetation zones located?

GEOGRAPHIC THEMES

1. **Human-Environment Interaction** How do people live in the Black Sea coastal areas of the C.I.S.?
2. **Place** Why is the taiga called a "green ocean"?

Understanding Latitude and Longitude

To accurately describe locations, maps and globes are divided into an imaginary grid called *lines of latitude and longitude.* Latitude lines, or *parallels,* circle the earth east and west. Longitude lines, or *meridians,* run north and south through the poles. Both latitude and longitude lines are measured in *degrees* (°).

Latitude lines are measured from the *Equator,* which is 0°; the numbers increase both north and south to the poles which are at 90°. Longitude lines are measured from the *prime meridian,* which is 0° and runs from pole to pole through western Europe and the western part of Africa. Longitude lines increase in number both east and west of the prime meridian to the 180th meridian that runs through the Pacific Ocean. You can find any location on earth if you know its *coordinates*—its latitude and longitude. Just find the point where the two lines meet. For example, the coordinates for Moscow are 56°N (north) and 37°E (east). These steps will help you use latitude and longitude:

- If you have the coordinates of a place and want to locate it on a map or globe, find the right latitude and longitude lines and follow them to their meeting point.

- To identify the coordinates of a place, use a map or globe to find the nearest latitude and longitude lines.

EXAMPLE

Look at the map of Eurasia in the atlas on pages 894–895. Notice that the Equator crosses Africa, the Indian Ocean, and Indonesia. Now find the prime meridian. Through which European nations does it pass? *(Great Britain, France, Spain)* Through which Russian peninsula does the 180th meridian pass? *(Chukotsk Peninsula)* The Commonwealth of Independent States actually spreads almost halfway around the globe from 30°E to about 160°W. Find a dotted line marking the Arctic Circle at 67°N. Much of Russia lies north of this parallel. How far north are the New Siberian Islands? *(about 75°N)* At about what longitude is Odessa? *(30°E)*

PRACTICE

Use the map below to answer the following questions:
1. Between which longitudes is the Black Sea located?
2. What cities of the C.I.S. lie near the 40th parallel?
3. What body of water lies north of the Arctic Circle?
4. What are the approximate coordinates for Kiev?
5. Moscow is 56°N, 37°E. Minsk is 54°N, 27°E. Tashkent is 41°N, 69°E. Which city is farthest south? Which city is farthest east?
6. What city is closest to the Arctic Circle?

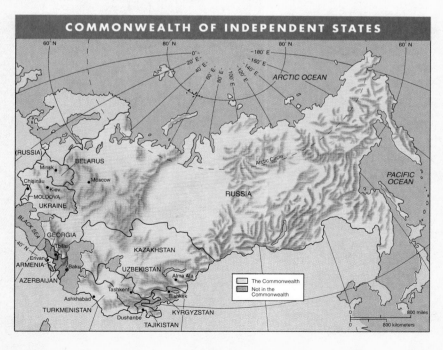

COMMONWEALTH OF INDEPENDENT STATES

People and Places to Know

the Slavs, Ukraine, Kiev, Eastern Orthodoxy, Bulgaria, the Mongols, Poland, Ivan III, Moscow, the Kremlin, Ivan IV, Peter I, Baltic Sea, Catherine II, Nicholas I, Alexander II, Alexander III

Key Terms to Define

boyar, icon, *khan*, czar, autocratic, serf intelligentsia, *mir*, socialism

Objectives to Learn

1. **Trace** the development of early Russia.

2. **Identify** Russia's major czars and their roles in Russia's development.

3. **Discuss** the effect of political, social, and economic changes on the Russian people.

Throne of the czars in St. Petersburg

The Russian Past

> We find ourselves in the depths of a thick forest. . . . In a clearing on a steep river bank is a small village. . . . Outside the village is a field. It was no easy matter to work this field. At first all the villagers worked many months to chop down a large patch of forest. . . . Then everything that had been chopped down was burned in big bonfires. With hoes and spades the villagers loosened the earth and mixed it with the ashes. When the time for sowing came, an old man walked into the field and scattered the grain on the loosened earth. . . .
>
> The ancient Slavs were not only farmers. The dense forests were full of birds and animals. . . . [A group of hunters] are carrying a rich trophy, a bear that they have killed. The villagers will now have meat, while the bear skin will make warm winter clothing. Towards evening the shepherd returns with his small herd of cows and flock of sheep and goats. The fishermen also have come back with their catch.
>
> The houses in which the villagers live have been put together with logs and roofed with planks of wood or straw. The tiny windows, which are right down by the ground, hardly let in any light at all. The floor inside is of earth. In one corner a hearth has been built of stones. The smoke from the fire escapes through the doorway, as there is no chimney. Along the walls stand wooden benches. Shelves hold clay and wooden utensils.
>
> Dusk will have fallen when the villagers, tired out after their long day of work, will sit down to eat. Their food is plain and it is almost the same for everyone. There are no poor or rich villagers. They work together and the land and cattle belong to them all.

This passage from a modern history book describes the life of the early Slavs. Today, the Russians, Ukrainians, and Belarussians are the leading Slavic groups in the C.I.S. They can trace their origins to groups of Slavs who settled in the forests and steppes of Ukraine and Russia around the year 500.

At first, these Slavs were peaceful farmers who lived an isolated life in scattered villages. But, in time, they began to use the rivers in their area for transportation and trade. Before long, they set up trading towns that had contact with the Mediterranean, western Europe, and Scandinavia. In the 800's, they came under the rule of the Varangians, a group of warrior-traders from Scandinavia. A Varangian leader, Oleg, is believed to have set up the first state in the region at Kiev, a trading town on the Dnieper (NEE·pur) River. Within 100 years, the Varangians had adopted the Slavic language and customs, and Kiev had emerged as a center of civilization.

Source: T. Golubeva and L. Gellerstein. *Early Russia—the USSR.* 1976, pp. 7, 10, 11.

SECTION 1

Beginnings

By the year 900, the Slavs living in the area that is now Ukraine and Russia had organized into a loose union of city-states and territories ruled mostly by princes. Although each region enjoyed self-government, all paid special respect to the ruler of Kiev, known as the Grand Prince. To support his court and army, the Grand Prince collected tribute from the local princes. The local princes administered justice and defended frontiers. They were aided by councils of wealthy merchants and landed nobles called **boyars**. Together, the upper classes ruled over the vast majority of people—peasants who farmed the land.

The interests of both the peasants and the ruling classes were represented in the assemblies. Made up of all free, adult male citizens, the assemblies handled daily affairs.

CHRISTIANITY

Until 987, the Slavs worshiped many deities representing the forces of nature. That year, Vladimir, the Grand Prince of Kiev, converted to Eastern Orthodox Christianity. Vladimir made Eastern Orthodoxy the official religion and required all of his subjects to become Christians. The *Russian Chronicles,* an early collection of Slavic history and legends, records Vladimir's actions as follows:

When the prince arrived at his capital, he directed that the idols should be overthrown and that some should be cut to pieces and others burned with fire. . . .
   Thereafter Vladimir sent heralds throughout the whole city to proclaim that if any inhabitant, rich or poor, did not betake himself to the river [to be bap-

tized], he would risk the prince's displeasure. . . .
   . . . Having spoken thus, [Vladimir] ordained that churches should be built and established where pagan idols had previously stood. He thus founded the Church of St. Basil on the hill where the idol of Perun [the god of thunder] and the other images had been set, and where the prince and the people had offered their sacrifices. He began to found churches and to assign priests throughout the cities, and to invite people to accept baptism in all the cities and towns.
   He took the children of the best families, and sent them to schools for instruc-

EXAMINING ART *The early Slavs' skill in wood construction is evident in this church. What ruler made Eastern Orthodox Christianity the official religion of Kiev?*

EXAMINING ART
This panel from a fifteenth-century icon tells of a struggle in 1169 between two rival Slavic cities. Carrying a cross and an icon of the Virgin Mary, nobles and priests of Novgorod, right, force the prince of Vladimir-Suzdal to retreat. What factors other than internal conflict led to Kiev's decline and fall?

tion in book learning. The mothers of these children wept bitterly over them, for they were not yet strong in faith, but mourned as for the dead. When these children were assigned for study, there was thus fulfilled in the Russian land the prophecy which says: "In those days, the deaf shall hear the word of Scripture, and the voice of the stammerers shall be made plain" (Isaiah, 29:18, 32:4).

Vladimir's acceptance of Eastern Orthodoxy gave the Slavs a sense of belonging to the Christian world and strengthened their region's ties with the Byzantine Empire and the kingdom of Bulgaria. Soon, the Byzantine and Bulgarian influence could be seen in many areas. Byzantine priests introduced the Slavs to colorful religious rituals and taught them the art of painting **icons**, or sacred pictures. Byzantine architects helped build stone cathedrals and churches with onion-shaped domes. The Bulgarians gave the Slavs a Slavic alphabet on which to base a written language. Known as the Cyrillic (suh·RIL·lik) alphabet in honor of Cyril, a Byzantine missionary to the Slavs, the alphabet is still in use today.

Source: Reprinted by permission of the publishers from HARVARD STUDIES AND NOTES IN PHILOLOGY AND LITERATURE, Volume 12, "The Russian Primary Chronicle," by Samuel Cross, Cambridge, Mass.: Harvard University Press, Copyright © 1930 by the President and Fellows of Harvard College.

MONGOL RULE

During the 1100's, the Grand Princes of Kiev expanded their territory, increased trade, and advanced Slavic culture. Then other princes began to challenge the power of Kiev. Weakened by conflict and interruptions of trade, Kiev began to decline and lose much of its influence. In 1240, Mongol invaders from central Asia destroyed the city. For the next 200 years, all Slavic lands were part of a vast Mongol domain that stretched from eastern Europe to China. Although the Mongols allowed the Slavs self-rule, they made the princes pay tribute to the *khan*, the Mongol leader. During this time, Moscow, a city north of Kiev, became the center of a new Slavic state known as Russia.

Opposition to Mongol rule gave the Russians a sense of unity. At the same time, however, the Russians became largely isolated from the outside world, especially from western Europe, which was entering a period of great scientific and artistic achievements. As a result, Russia developed its own unique civilization based largely on the values of Eastern Orthodoxy. This civilization stressed obedience to authority and placed the community's rights ahead of those of the individual. In this way, it was believed, Russia's unity would be preserved against outside threats.

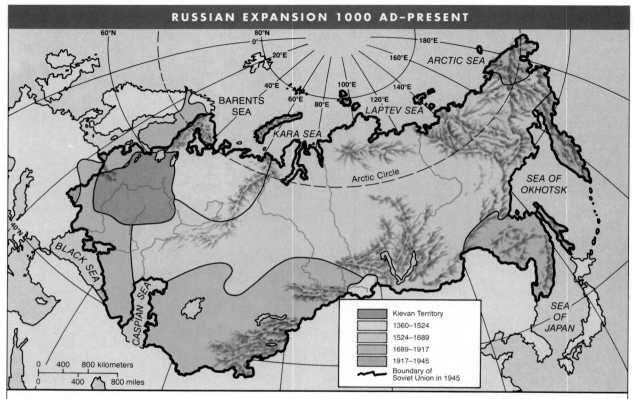

RUSSIAN EXPANSION 1000 AD–PRESENT

Kievan Territory
1360–1524
1524–1689
1689–1917
1917–1945
Boundary of Soviet Union in 1945

EXAMINING MAPS *From the 1300's to the present century, Russian rulers expanded the country's territory in all directions. Their goals were to increase Russian power, protect the Russian heartland from foreign invasion, and acquire warm water seaports.* What group of Russian rulers were the first to expand Russian territory?

SECTION 2

The First Czars

By the mid-1400's, Kiev and its surroundings—most of what is present-day Ukraine—

had been conquered by neighboring Poland. Farther north, Russia had come under the rule of powerful monarchs known as **czars**. Over time, the czars became **autocratic**, or all-powerful, rulers who crushed their opponents. The Church, the nobles, and the townspeople were effectively blocked from challenging the czars' authority.

IVAN III

The first czar of Russia was Ivan III. When he was Grand Prince of Moscow, Ivan centralized the Russian state by conquering other Russian princes. Then he challenged Mongol rule by refusing to pay taxes. In

1462, after defeating the Mongols, Ivan took the title of czar. Later, he became known as Ivan the Great.

The Russian Orthodox Church gave its full support to a strong Russian monarchy. Under Ivan's rule, Moscow became the center of Russian Orthodoxy and was known as the "Third Rome." The "First Rome" was the capital of the long vanished Roman Empire. The "Second Rome" was Constantinople, the capital of the recently fallen Byzantine Empire.

To emphasize the heritage of the empire, Ivan introduced Byzantine rituals into the court. He also encouraged a national style of architecture and icon painting. He had Moscow's Kremlin, or fortress, rebuilt and filled it with churches and palaces.

IVAN IV

Ivan III's grandson, Ivan IV, became the most powerful of the early czars. Known as "the Terrible" or "the Awesome," he ruled from 1533 to 1584. Ivan IV was learned, pious, and cruel. Because he suspected the *boyars* of disloyalty, he seized their lands and placed them under his direct control. At the same time, he set up the *Oprichniki* (oh·preech·NEE·kee), a secret police force that terrorized the common people into submission.

Under Ivan IV, Russia expanded its territory and increased contacts and trade with western Europe. One western nation that traded with Russia was England. In 1583, the English ambassador visited Ivan's court. The following is an account of that visit:

EXAMINING ART *Ivan the Great (below left), who ruled until 1505, established a new class of nobles who received land in return for service to the czar. His grandson, Ivan IV (below right), took land away from the* boyars. *What did the two Ivans do for the development of Russia?*

EXAMINING ART *The family life of the peasants shown here revolved around the large fireplace of their one-room home. The infant in the family sleeps in a suspended cradle near the fireplace, while the older children make their beds on a ledge atop the warm fireplace oven.* How did the lives of many Russian peasants change during the 1600's?

When the ambassador had been in Moscow for some days . . . he was sent for to go to court. He was accompanied there by about forty gentlemen, richly dressed and well mounted. . . . At the entry into the court he was met by four noblemen dressed in cloth of gold and rich furs, their caps embroidered with pearls and precious stones. They took him toward the emperor until he was met by four others of a higher rank who led him still further on his way. In the corridor there stood along the walls, or sat on benches and forms in rows, seven or eight hundred noblemen and gentlemen. . . .

These four noblemen accompanied him to the Emperor's [czar's] chamber door, where the Emperor's herald met him. With him were all the great officers of the chamber and they all led him to the place where the emperor sat in state. He had three crowns by him, . . . and he was attended by four young noblemen. . . . When the ambassador had been brought to the Emperor in this way to kiss his hand . . . the Emperor commanded him to sit down in a place provided for him,

some ten paces away. From here the Emperor wanted him to hand over the Queen [of England's] letters and present, but the ambassador thought this unreasonable and stepped forward toward the Emperor. The chancellor then came to meet him and wanted to take the letters, but the ambassador told him that the Queen had not sent any letters to him, and went on to give them to the Emperor himself.

TIME OF TROUBLES

After Ivan IV's death in 1584, the country was torn apart by foreign invasions, famine, plague, and peasant revolts. Finally, in 1613, Michael Romanov was chosen as czar, and order was restored. This was the beginning of the Romanov dynasty, which ruled Russia until 1917.

Accompanying the political changes taking place after Ivan's death were social and

Source: From THE MAKING OF RUSSIA by Joan Hasler. Copyright © 1969 by Longman Group Ltd. Used by permission of Delacorte Press, a division of Bantam Doubleday Dell Publishing, Inc.

economic changes. Until the late 1500's, *boyars* and peasants both owned their own land. There was a small but prosperous middle class of townspeople, primarily merchants. Then, over the next century, the freedoms enjoyed by these groups gradually were destroyed by the czar's government. The *boyars* were replaced by a new group of landowning nobles who were tied to the czar and served as officials in the growing state bureaucracy and in the army. The influence of the townspeople declined, and many peasants became **serfs**, laborers owned by landowners and bound to the land. The serfs, who worked in the palaces and on the estates of the czars and nobles, had to pay taxes to the government and serve in the army.

As government controls tightened, many Russian peasants escaped to the borderlands south of Moscow. There, they formed into groups of pioneers known as Cossacks. The Cossacks set up self-governing communities and became skilled fighters. At the same time, other Russian pioneers moved eastward into Siberia, some of them reaching as far as the coast of the Pacific Ocean.

SECTION 2 REVIEW

CHECKING FOR UNDERSTANDING
1. **Define** czar, autocratic, serf.

CRITICAL THINKING
2. **Making Generalizations** What significant changes took place in Russia under the early czars?

SECTION 3
Early Romanovs

During the late 1600's and early 1700's, the Romanov czars tried to make Russia into a European nation. In the process, they placed more burdens on the Russian people.

PETER THE GREAT
In 1689, a Romanov became Czar Peter I. A towering, muscular figure, nearly seven feet (2.1 meters) tall, Peter had large ambitions, boundless energy, and strong emotions. Early in his reign, realizing that Russia was

EXAMINING ART *The luxury enjoyed by Russian nobles is reflected in this etching of a Russian gentleman's carriage sleigh, being pulled by a team of horses, ridden and tended by servants. Standing at the rear of the sleigh are regally attired footmen. What roles did nobles play in the court of the czars?*

far behind western Europe in learning and technology, he decided to end Russia's isolation and bring it into the mainstream of European civilization. To this end, he and a group of assistants visited western Europe. There they toured shipyards, factories, mills, and laboratories, learning firsthand how to handle ships and machines.

When Peter returned home, he forced a series of changes on his people in an effort to adapt them to western ways. He reorganized the government along the lines of the Swedish one and created a regular army and navy like those of the Germans and the Dutch. He founded the first modern industries and tried to introduce western-style forms of education. He also brought the

Church under his direct authority. The most controversial change came when he demanded that members of his court wear western European clothing and that men entering Moscow shave their beards. He also ordered women, who had always been excluded from social gatherings, to attend parties.

Peter wanted to secure land along the Baltic Sea so that Russia could have access to major sea routes. To this end, he fought a series of wars. In 1703, on land won in a war with Sweden, he founded St. Petersburg, his new capital and "window to the West." As noted below, his "window" was carved out of the wilderness at a high price:

EXAMINING ART *Peter the Great ordered members of his court to wear western European clothing.* *Why did Peter want Russia to adopt western ways?*

Peter's first exploration of the site of Petersburg would have discouraged most men. Soundings taken down the channel of the Neva [River] showed only eight feet [2.44 meters] of water—not enough to float full-size frigates. Digging along the marshy shores struck water at two feet [.61 meters]. Still Peter insisted. Stones gathered into massive crates were sunk into the marshes, and piles driven, to serve as foundations for buildings. Building stone was transported by water from the Volga, and good timber from Kazan.

For in this undertaking Peter followed the advice of no one. Here was a port free from ice six months in the year, opening into the Baltic—the sea upon which, at whatever hazard, his fleet-to-be could sail.

Winds from the west drove the gulf waters into the Neva's mouth, flooding and destroying the works around Petersburg. There was no stopping such floods. Peter ordered the shore works rebuilt and town dwellings reinforced. . . .

Work upon [Peter's] paradise was carried on "by a vast number of hands." Actually it was done by human hands. Tools lacked. Dirt was carried in coats or kaftans [traditional robes worn by Russian males].

Finns of the countryside, peasant soldiers and prisoners, slaved. Their bodies strained against ice and wind and water.

RUSSIAN PROVERBS

EXAMINING CHARTS *The Russians often expressed their views about life in the form of proverbs. From reading the proverbs in this chart, what generalizations can you make about Russian attitudes toward life?*

• Pray to God, but keep rowing to the shore.

• Don't be so smart; smarter ones than you are in jail.

• A bad peace is better than a good war.

• Life is unbearable, but death is not so pleasant either.

• Marriage is like sneezing: even when you feel it coming on, you can't stop.

• Happiness is not a horse; you cannot harness it.

• Be friends with the wolf, but keep one hand on your axe.

• Make peace with men and quarrel with your faults.

They died from typhus and from starvation, and their bodies were shoved into the swamps. No one kept count of the bodies.

When a flood came the survivors grieved more for the cattle that had been lost than for the humans, because the cattle had meant food. . . .

Peter talked only of roads to be opened, iron to be found, stones to be cut for the new council house to be called the Admiralty.

Petersburg meant to him not merely access to the sea but the building of a city for the future. This was to be the ground on which he would stand. It was to be in fact the ground of conflict between Peter and the majority of his own people.

For no nation until then had tried to thrust its capital city out into foreign territory.

Source: Harold Lamb. *The City and the Tsar.* Doubleday & Company, Inc., 1948.

CATHERINE THE GREAT

After Peter's death, one weak czar after another came to the throne until 1762, when Catherine II took control. During her reign, Russia expanded into areas of Ukraine and Poland and became a leading country in European affairs. Because of this successful foreign policy, Catherine became known as Catherine the Great.

To strengthen Russia, Catherine built up the army and navy, both of which had declined following Peter's death. Like Peter, she favored western culture and wanted to westernize Russia. She bought huge collections of French, English, and Dutch paintings and followed French fads and fashions.

Under Catherine's influence, wealthy Russians imitated French ways. Some of them even went to France as part of their education. As a result, the ruling classes drew apart from the masses of ordinary Russians, who remained loyal to traditional Russian culture. This growing split between the rulers and the ruled led to a heightening of tensions in Russian society.

Catherine studied the works of the leading western European thinkers of the time and corresponded with some of them. While visiting Catherine, the French philosopher Denis Diderot (dee·DROH) encouraged her to make reforms to help her people. But Catherine did not listen. When peasant rebellions threatened her rule, she turned to the nobles for support. She allowed nobles to treat serfs as they pleased. More peasants were forced to become serfs than ever before, and their conditions worsened. By 1800, the common people of Russia had fewer rights than those in any other part of Europe.

EXAMINING ART *To gain support from the nobles, Catherine the Great allowed them to draw up a constitution, which, however, was never implemented.* **What was Catherine's attitude toward reform?**

SECTION 3 REVIEW

CHECKING FOR UNDERSTANDING
1. **State** the goals of Peter the Great and Catherine the Great.

CRITICAL THINKING
2. **Predicting Consequences** How do you think Peter and Catherine's actions affected the Russian people?

SECTION 4

Later Romanovs

The Romanovs remained in power for 121 years after the death of Catherine the Great. During that time, there were six different Romanov czars, each of whom faced opposition to the power of the Russian throne.

ALEXANDER I

The reign of Alexander I, from 1801 to 1825, was marked by wars that brought both land and international respect to Russia. Internally, however, the country was in a state of unrest. The serfs were no better off than they had been under earlier czars, and educated Russians wanted more personal freedoms. Alexander was a weak ruler who called for reforms but failed to honor his word.

In 1812, Russia was invaded by the army of the French Emperor Napoleon I. Although the Russians won the struggle with the French, they paid a high price for victory. They lost a great part of their population. In addition, to halt the French advance, they had set fire to Moscow. Despite their losses, however, most Russians were proud of their part in Napoleon's defeat. The war had made Russia a great power. Educated Russians, however, were disappointed because the reforms they expected after the war did

EXAMINING ART *St. Petersburg, pictured in this etching, remained an important city during the time of the reign of Alexander I. For three centuries after its founding, Russian rulers continued to enhance the city's beauty by adding palaces, cathedrals, parks, and public squares.* **What other Russian city played an important role during Alexander's rule? What happened to it?**

not come. In the following passage, a Russian soldier explains how many Russians felt:

The war was still on when the soldiers, upon their return home, for the first time [broke up] grumbling among the masses. "We shed blood," they would say, "and we are forced to sweat under feudal obligations. We freed the Fatherland from the tyrant, and now we ourselves are tyrannized over by the ruling classes." The army, from generals to privates, upon its return did nothing but discuss how good it is in foreign lands. A comparison with our own country naturally brought up the question, "Why should it not be so in our own lands?"

DISCONTENT AND REFORM

Throughout the 1800's, as Russia grew in size and strength, the feelings of discontent increased. As Russia slowly industrialized, new classes of business people and factory workers developed in the cities. Many of

Source: Michael Bestuzhev-Ryumin as quoted in *Russia in War and Peace* by Alan Palmer. Weidenfeld & Nicolson Ltd., 1972, p. 199.

these people felt uncomfortable with the traditional social order and wanted Russia to modernize more quickly. At the same time, a movement for revolution arose among the **intelligentsia**, or the educated people. Made up chiefly of students, writers, and artists, the intelligentsia soon became the leading opponent of the government.

In spite of the pressures for change, Nicholas I, who had become czar in 1825, opposed any limits on his power by either a constitution or a parliament. Even though free workers were needed in the country's small but growing industries, he refused to free the serfs. To eliminate opposition to his government, he set up a secret police force.

In 1854, the Russians went to war against Britain and France. Two years later, Russia lost the war. That same year, Nicholas died, and his son became Czar Alexander II. Alexander recognized Russian weaknesses and wanted to make Russia into a major industrial power. To this end, he and his advisers began a series of reforms that eased restrictions on the people, improved government services, and promoted education. In 1861, Alexander freed the serfs.

For the serfs, freedom was a mixed blessing. By law, they were personally free and had the right to obtain land the government had purchased from the nobles. In reality, however, the great majority of the newly freed serfs became dependents of the government that had freed them. In return for land, the peasants were expected to make payments to the government. To insure that this debt was paid, the government bound individual peasants to *mirs* (meerz), or local village organizations. Officials in each *mir* made sure the peasants worked the land and paid the government from their earnings.

One peasant explained why, even after receiving his freedom, his life was hard:

> My grandfather, my father, and I have paid so many taxes for our five desiatinas [13.7 acres] here, that the land could be quite covered with the money that we gave for it. My father and I were made to pay thirty-six roubles [Russian unit of currency] every year, and to get that money in the old days cost us plenty of sweat and blood.
>
> There was scarcely a week in all the year that we were not working hard. All through the summer we worked on the farm. From October until May, we fished and logged on the river. And when there was no other work to do, we used to drag

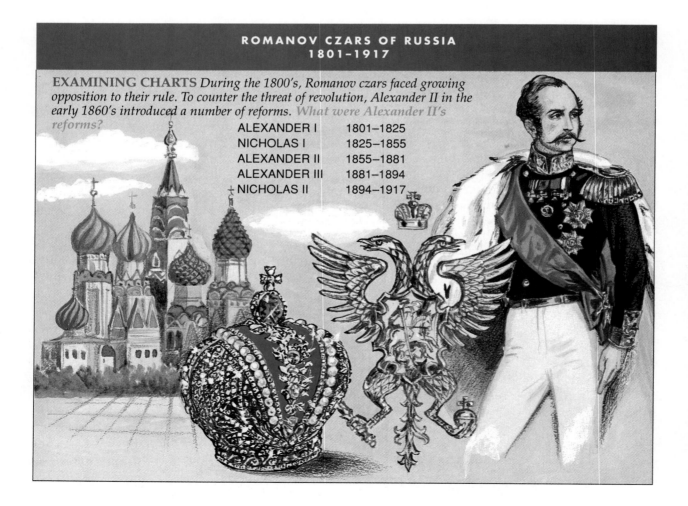

ROMANOV CZARS OF RUSSIA
1801–1917

EXAMINING CHARTS *During the 1800's, Romanov czars faced growing opposition to their rule. To counter the threat of revolution, Alexander II in the early 1860's introduced a number of reforms. What were Alexander II's reforms?*

ALEXANDER I	1801–1825
NICHOLAS I	1825–1855
ALEXANDER II	1855–1881
ALEXANDER III	1881–1894
NICHOLAS II	1894–1917

EXAMINING ART
Alexander III encouraged gangs, like this one beating an elderly Jew, to attack Jews and to destroy their shops and homes. Any person who did not speak Russian or who followed a religion other than Eastern Orthodoxy was considered disloyal to the state. **Why did Alexander III rule harshly?**

sunken logs from the river bottom. That was a slow, hard job. On a freezing winter morning we would take two boats out on the ice. With our axes we would chop through the ice and make a space as big as this hut. Into the space we would shove the two boats and fill them with water. Then with spiked poles we would feel for the logs on the bottom twenty feet [6.1 meters] below. We would drive four poles into a log and fasten the poles by chains to the boats. Then we would bail the water out, and the boats would rise because they must—as you might say, by the will of God. And as they rose, with the spiked poles they would pull the log loose from the mud below. It took nearly a day to get one log; and for this we received between one and two roubles.

TOWARD REVOLUTION

The peasants were not alone in their disappointment with Alexander II's reforms. Growing numbers of urban factory workers complained about long hours and poor

Source: Ernest Poole. *The Village: Russian Impressions.* The Macmillan Company, 1918, pp. 93–94.

working conditions. Meanwhile, many of the intelligentsia favored **socialism,** a philosophy that called for ownership of all land and factories by peasants and workers. They wanted to overthrow the czar and form a new society based on social equality.

In 1881, Alexander II was killed by young revolutionaries, and his son, Alexander III, became czar. Believing that reforms had ruined Russia, Alexander III ruled harshly. He limited freedom of speech, placed restrictions on the peasants, and persecuted the Jews and non-Russian nationalities. Alexander's government silenced its critics but could not crush them. By the time Alexander's son, Nicholas II, came to the throne in 1894, Russia was ripe for revolution.

SECTION 4 REVIEW

CHECKING FOR UNDERSTANDING
1. **Define** intelligentsia, *mir,* socialism.

CRITICAL THINKING
2. **Recognizing Ideologies** How did czars and the intelligentsia differ in their views about Russia's future?

History

THE POOR AND THE RICH

During the 1800's, Russian writers reached a level of achievement that won them and their country an esteemed place in Western culture. In their works, they presented in vivid detail aspects of daily life that often depicted the gap in living standards between the classes. The two accounts that follow, the first by Ivan Turgenev and the second by Leo Tolstoy, are examples of this literature.

FOCUSING ON THE ISSUE Read the accounts, and tell what impressions they give you of peasants, the upper class, and their lives. Explain how these impressions compare with those you got reading the chapter.

The Orlov muzhik [peasant] is of no great stature, is squat, glum; he eyes you from under his brows, lives in wretched little huts of aspen wood, does compulsory labor for his masters, doesn't go in for trading, eats poorly, wears bast [tree bark] sandals. The Kaluzhsk muzhik pays quitrent to his masters, dwells in roomy huts of pine, is tall of stature, eyes you boldly and cheerfully, is clean-shaven and white of face,

trades in butter and birch tar and, of Sundays, goes about in boots.

The Orlov village . . . is usually situated amid plowed fields, near some gully which has been haphazardly turned into a muddy pond. Outside of a few willows, which are always ready to oblige by growing almost anywhere, and two or three scraggly birches, you won't see as much as a sapling for miles around; hut clings to hut, their roofs strewn, rather than thatched, with fusty straw. The Kaluzhsk village, on the contrary, is in most cases surrounded by woods; the huts have more space around them and stand more uprightly; they are roofed with hewn timbers. . . .

. . . I met in the field and became acquainted with a certain

small Kaluzhsk landowner, Polutykin. . . .

We rode off at a walk; beyond the village a man of about forty . . . caught up with us. This was Kalinych. His good-natured, swarthy face, pock-marked in spots, proved to my liking at first sight. Kalinych . . . went out hunting with his master every day, carrying the latter's gamebag and, at times, his gun as well, noting where the birds alighted, procuring water, gathering strawberries, putting up tepeelike shelters of branches, trotting after the droshky [sleigh]—Polutykin could not take a step without him. Kalinych was a man of the merriest, the meekest nature. . . .

During the course of the day he got into talk with me more than once, waiting on me with servility; when it came to his master, however, he kept an eye on him as if the latter were a baby. [1]

Natasha had not had a moment to herself since early morning, and had not once had time to think of what lay before her.

In the damp, chill air, and the confined semi-darkness of the swaying carriage, for the first time she vividly pictured what was in store for her there at the ball, in those brightly lighted halls—the music, the flowers, the dancing, the Tsar, all the dazzling young people of Petersburg. The prospect was so splendid, and so incongruous with the chill darkness of the cramped carriage, that she could hardly believe it would come true. She only realized what was before her when, after walking over the red baize at the entrance, she had entered the hall, taken off her fur cloak, and, with Sonya at her side, preceded her mother up the lighted staircase between the flowers. Only then did she remember how she would behave at a ball, and tried to assume the stately air she considered indispensable for a girl on such an occasion. . . . Before and behind them other guests were entering, also in ball gowns, and talking in low tones. The mirrors along the staircase reflected ladies in white, pale blue, and

pink gowns, with diamonds and pearls on their bare arms and necks.

Natasha looked in the mirrors and could not distinguish herself from the others. All blended into a shimmering procession. On entering the ballroom the steady hum of voices, footsteps, and greetings deafened Natasha; the light and glitter blinded her. The host and hostess, who had already been standing at the door for half an hour repeating the same words to each arriving guest, "Charmé de vous voir," [So nice to see you], greeted the Rostovs and Peronskaya in the same manner. . . .

There was a sudden stir; a murmur ran through the crowd as they surged forward then fell back, leaving a passage down the middle of which walked the Tsar to the strains of the orchestra that struck up as he entered. Behind him came the host and hostess. He walked in rapidly, bowing to right and left, as if anxious to get through the first formalities as quickly as possible. The orchestra played a polonaise in vogue at the time. . . . The Tsar passed on to the drawing room and the crowds made a rush for the doors, several persons dashing forward and then back again, their faces transformed. The wave receded from the doors of the drawing room, at which the Tsar reappeared in conversation with the hostess. A young man, looking distraught, bore down on the ladies and begged them to move aside. Several of the ladies, with expressions that betrayed a total obliviousness to the rules of decorum, pressed forward to the detriment of their attire. The men began to choose partners and take their places. [2]

[1]Source: From THE HUNTING SKETCHES by Ivan Turgenev, translated by Bernard Guilbert Guerney. Translation copyright © 1962, 1990 by Bernard Guilbert Guerney. Used by permission of New American Library, a division of Penguin Books USA Inc.

[2]Source: From WAR AND PEACE by Leo Tolstoy, translated by Ann Dunnigan. Translation copyright © 1968 by Ann Dunnigan. Introduction copyright © 1968 by New American Library. Used by permission of New American Library, a division of Penguin Books USA Inc.

Chapter 40 Review

SUMMARY

Early Slavs in what is now Ukraine and Russia accepted Eastern Orthodoxy and gained a sense of belonging to the civilized world. In the mid-1400's, Russia emerged as a separate Slavic state under the rule of powerful czars, such as Ivan III and Ivan IV. After Ivan IV's death, Russia suffered a period of decline during the late 1500's and early 1600's.

The Romanov czars, whose dynasty came to power in 1613, restored order to Russia. Peter I carried out reforms designed to westernize the country. Later, Catherine the Great made Russia a leading country in European affairs.

As Russia became a large and powerful empire during the 1700's and 1800's, the discontent of the people increased under the Romanov czars. Even the reforms of Alexander II did not improve the situation. By the time Nicholas II came to the throne, Russia was about to enter an era of revolutionary change.

USING VOCABULARY

Explain why each of these terms is used in a chapter about the Russian past.

boyar	czar	intelligentsia
icon	autocratic	*mir*
khan	serf	socialism

REVIEWING FACTS

1. **Discuss** how the early Slavs of Ukraine and Russia were ruled.
2. **State** the cultural contributions of the Byzantines and Bulgarians to early Russian civilization.
3. **Evaluate** the impact of Mongol rule on the Slavic lands.
4. **Name** the dynasty that was established in Russia in 1613.
5. **Indicate** Peter the Great's reasons for building the city of St. Petersburg.
6. **Examine** why people in the Russian Empire became discontent with czarist rule during the 1800's.

CRITICAL THINKING

1. **Drawing Conclusions** The early Slavs in Ukraine and Russia were isolated. Yet they developed rich and unique heritages. What explanation can you give for this?
2. **Evaluating Information** Do you think the czarist system aided or hurt the development of Russia? The development of the peoples of the Russian Empire?
3. **Identifying Central Issues** All reform in Russia came from the top, brought into being by the czars. Why do you think this was so?
4. **Demonstrating Reasoned Judgment** What reasons can you give for the great gap between the peasants and the other classes in the Russian Empire? Do you think the educated elite of a country have any responsibility to those less fortunate? Explain.

ANALYZING CONCEPTS

1. **Justice** Why did Alexander II's reforms fail to satisfy the peasants?
2. **Culture** How did Russian culture differ from that of western Europe? Why?

GEOGRAPHIC THEMES

1. **Location** Why was Kiev's location an important factor in the city's growth?
2. **Movement** What role did the Cossacks and other pioneers play in the development of the Russian Empire?

Conducting Research

Many times during your life, you will have to find answers to particular questions. Learning to *conduct research* efficiently and effectively can help you write research papers, find a used car, plan a vacation, or obtain college loans. The best place to start your research is at your local library. Even small libraries have many good sources of information that you can utilize. It is important to know what kind of information each source provides.

1. General Reference Works. Dictionaries, encyclopedias, atlases, and almanacs all provide a great deal of general information of a particular type.
   - *Dictionaries* give definitions and spellings of words arranged in alphabetical order.
   - *Encyclopedias* contain short articles on a wide variety of topics, also arranged alphabetically.
   - *Atlases* contain various kinds of maps, both physical and historical.
   - *Almanacs* give facts and statistics about different places or topics for a particular year or time period.
2. *Books, Magazines, and Pamphlets.* Libraries also have books, magazines, pamphlets, and other sources of information. Find books which relate to your research question either in the card catalog or the computerized directory. Both list every book in the library by subject, author, and title. To find maga-

zine articles about your topic, consult the *Readers' Guide to Periodical Literature.*

Once you have found a source of information, look specifically for the answer to your question. Use the table of contents at the beginning, or the index at the end of a book to find the pages that discuss your topic. Here are some steps to follow in conducting research:
- Narrow your research topic to a particular question to which you can find answers.
- Identify several possible sources of information, including general reference works and other books, magazines, and pamphlets.
- Read the information provided in the general works.
- Use the tables of contents and indexes to find information about your topic in books.

EXAMPLE

Suppose you are writing a report on the following question: "How did Peter the Great change the Russian Empire?" Which of the sources listed below is likely to contain information on this question?
1. World Almanac, 1993
2. Encyclopedia article: "Russia—History"
3. World Atlas, 1990
4. *Modernization of Russia Under Peter I and Catherine II,* by Basil Dmytryshyn

5. *Voices of Glastnost, Interviews with Gorbachev's Reformers,* by Stephen F. Cohen and Katrina vanden Heuvel
6. Historical Atlas of Europe, 1400 to present
7. *Peter the Great, Reformer or Revolutionary?* by Marc Raeff
8. Textbook: European history, 1815 to present

The 1993 Almanac and 1990 Atlas are far too current to be useful. However, the historical atlas of Europe may show how the boundaries of Russia changed during the reign of Peter the Great. Which other sources would you eliminate and why? (Voices of Glasnost *and* textbook on European history, 1815 to present; both discuss more recent historical events.)

PRACTICE

Using the library, write a list of 10 sources of information about one of the research questions below. Include both general reference works and other books or magazines. Also, write the page numbers where answers to your questions can be found in these sources.
1. What were the strengths and weaknesses of Catherine the Great's rule over Russia?
2. What was life like for Russian peasants in the 1800's?
3. Who were the greatest artists and writers in Russia during the late 1800's and what were they known for?

671

CHAPTER OUTLINE

People and Places to Know

Nicholas II, Bolsheviks, Vladimir Lenin, Karl Marx, the Whites, USSR, Joseph Stalin, Siberia, Adolf Hitler, Stalingrad, Nikita Khrushchev, Mikhail Gorbachev, Afghanistan

Key Terms to Define

soviets, proletariat, capitalism, communism, war communism, *kulaks*, dissident, détente, *glasnost, perestroika*

Objectives to Learn

1. **Explain** the causes and effects of the Russian revolutions of 1917.
2. **Discuss** social, economic, and political changes under Vladimir Lenin and Joseph Stalin.
3. **Trace** changes in the USSR since the death of Joseph Stalin.

Vladimir Lenin

The Soviet Era

> " It has been Russia's lot to see most clearly, and experience most keenly and painfully the sharpest of sharp turning-points in history as it swings round from imperialism [the control of foreign lands] towards the communist revolution. In the space of a few days we destroyed one of the oldest, most powerful, barbarous and brutal of monarchies. In the space of a few months we passed through a stage of collaboration [cooperation] with the bourgeoisie [the middle class] and of shaking off petty-bourgeoisie illusions, for which other countries have required decades. In the course of a few weeks, having overthrown the bourgeoisie, we crushed its open resistance in civil war. We passed in a victorious triumphal march of Bolshevism [the early Communist movement] from one end of a vast country to the other. We raised the lowest strata of the working people oppressed by czarism and the bourgeoisie to liberty and independent life. We established and consolidated a Soviet Republic, a new type of state, which is infinitely superior to, and more democratic than, the best of the bourgeois-parliamentary republics. We established the dictatorship of the proletariat [working class] supported by the poor peasantry, and began a broadly conceived system of socialist reforms. We awakened the faith of millions upon millions of workers of all countries in their own strength and kindled the fires of enthusiasm in them. Everywhere we issued the call for a world workers' revolution. We flung a challenge to the imperialist plunderers of all countries. . . .
>
> Russia will become mighty and abundant if she abandons all dejection and all phrase-making, if, with clenched teeth, she masters all her forces and strains every nerve and muscle, if she realizes that salvation lies *only* along that road of world socialist revolution upon which we have set out. "

These words were spoken in 1918 by Vladimir Ilyich Ulyanov (ool·YAH·nahf), founder of the Union of Soviet Socialist Republics, commonly known as the Soviet Union. Ulyanov, better known to the world as Lenin, and his followers were part of a revolutionary movement that began in Russia during the 1800's. They blended a Russian sense of outrage against czarism with the thinking of a nineteenth-century German named Karl Marx.

Karl Marx had predicted that a workers' revolution would begin in industrialized Europe and spread socialism throughout the world. Lenin believed that, even though Russia was backward economically, it could become the starting point of the revolution. In 1917, Lenin's goal was achieved, and the world's first socialist state was established in Russia.

Source: V.I. Lenin. "The Chief Task of Our Day" in *The Lenin Anthology*. Robert C. Tucker (ed.). W.W. Norton and Co., Inc., pp. 434, 435.

SECTION 1

The Double Revolution

In the early 1900's, revolution was a dominant feature of Russian life. In 1905, peasants, workers, and the small middle class forced reforms on the czar, Nicholas II. But Nicholas ignored the changes and continued to act as an absolute ruler, carrying out harsh measures against anyone who criticized the government.

Nicholas's efforts to silence the opposition were fairly successful for a time. Then, in 1914, World War I broke out. When the conflict began, the Russians were confident of a rapid victory over the Germans. But they were ill-prepared for war, and their poorly trained and equipped army suffered heavy losses in eastern Europe. In 1915, they were pushed back by a German-Austrian attack, and Russian land was conquered and occupied. The Russian economy could not meet the needs of soldiers and civilians, both of whom needed food, clothing, and fuel.

THE FIRST REVOLUTION

Most of the Russian people were against the war and wanted to withdraw. Nicholas, however, refused to do so. Meanwhile, the people grew more discontent. The educated classes had been unhappy for a long time. The peasants wanted land still held by the wealthy. The people in the cities resented being without food and fuel because of the broken-down transportation system. The situation continued to worsen until finally, as described below, dissatisfaction grew into revolution:

On the eighth of March, 1917, a hundred thousand striking factory workers, men and women, jammed the streets of Petrograd [St. Petersburg] demanding bread and freedom. It was International Women's Day, February 23, in the old calendar. This was the day that marked the beginning of the February Revolution and the downfall of the Russian Emperor. The next day and the day after, despite the absence of plan or leaders, the demonstrations snowballed. Crowds of workers

EXAMINING PHOTOGRAPHS
Nationwide strikes and demonstrations protesting Russia's poor domestic conditions, like this women's march held in 1905, were sparked by "Bloody Sunday," a Sunday in January 1905 when striking workers were killed in a confrontation outside the czar's palace in St. Petersburg. What did the factory workers who took part in the March 1917 strike demand?

surged across the ice on the Neva and into the center of the city. The Czar's police could not contain the demonstrators, and the soldiers had to be called out as the workers offered themselves to be shot at.

It was Saturday, February 25, when Czar [Nicholas II] decided that the situation had gotten out of hand and wired the Petrograd commander General Khabalov, "I command you to put an end as of tomorrow to all disorders in the streets of the capital."

The next day, Sunday the 26th, several units opened fire on the crowds, and scores of demonstrators were killed, but at this point the troops rebelled at the further prospect of cutting down their own compatriots. In a matter of hours almost all the soldiers had joined in with the mobs, and the people went wild. Jails, courts, police stations—all the physical symbols of the old rule—were broken into and burned. In the twenty-third year of his reign, the authority of [Nicholas] Romanov, [Czar] of All the Russias, ceased to be.

Nicholas's government fell because it could not govern the country. The troops most loyal to the czar were still at the front. Except for a small group of conservative nobles, there was no one willing to defend the monarchy. War and revolution destroyed the czarist system.

THE SECOND REVOLUTION

After Nicholas gave up power, liberal nobles and middle-class politicians set up a provisional, or temporary, government under Alexander Kerensky. The new government wanted to continue the war with Germany and to wait to distribute land to the peasants. The government, however, did not

really rule Russia. Instead, it was ruled by **soviets**, councils formed by Russian revolutionaries to represent workers, soldiers, and peasants. Closely linked all over the country, the soviets spoke for the people and were the only ones who could sway the disorganized soldiers and the unruly crowds in the streets. At the heart of the soviets was the Petrograd Soviet in the capital city.

Revolutionaries known as Bolsheviks (BOHL·shuh·viks) knew that the soviets were the key to power in Russia and set out to control them. They wanted to make peace with Germany at once and encouraged the peasants to seize landed estates and the workers to manage factories. Within nine months, under the leadership of Vladimir Lenin, they were in the majority in the Petrograd Soviet.

In November 1917, the Bolsheviks took over the city of Petrograd and proclaimed a socialist revolution. Once they seized power, they made Lenin the head of a new revolutionary government. Lenin had a long record as a revolutionary. In 1887, when he was 17, his older brother had been put to death for trying to kill the czar. His brother's death led him to join the revolutionary movement to overthrow the monarchy.

While in exile because of his revolutionary activities, Lenin developed political ideas based on Marxism, or the teachings of Karl Marx. Like Marx, he believed that the **proletariat**, or working class, would end **capitalism**, the system in which the means of production are privately owned and operated for profit. The workers would overthrow the rule of the factory owners and the members of the government, and set up their own system under which they would own the factories and produce the goods. There would be no upper or lower classes. All the people would be workers in a classless society. A well-known journalist describes Lenin and the impact he had on his followers:

EXAMINING ART
This painting shows Vladimir Lenin, the head of Russia's new Bolshevik government, captivating his audience in a 1920 meeting of a group of his youthful followers. In what ways did Lenin want Russian society to change?

It was just 8:40 when a thundering wave of cheers announced the entrance of the presidium, or executive committee, with Lenin—great Lenin—among them. A short, stocky figure, with a big head set down on his shoulders, bald and bulging. Little eyes, a snubbish nose, wide, generous mouth, and heavy chin; clean-shaven now, but already beginning to bristle with the well-known beard of his past and future. Dressed in shabby clothes, his trousers much too long for him. Not impressive, to be the idol of a mob. A strange popular leader—a leader purely because of intellect; without color, without humor, uncompromising and detached—but with the power of explaining deep ideas in simple terms.

Gripping the edge of the reading stand, letting his little winking eyes travel over the crowd as he stood there waiting, not seeming to pay any attention to the long-rolling ovation, which lasted several minutes. When it finished, he said simply, "We shall now proceed to construct the Socialist order!" Again that overwhelming roar.

"The first thing is the adoption of practical measures to realize peace. . . . We shall offer peace to the peoples of all war-ring countries upon the basis of Soviet terms. . . ."

His great mouth seeming to smile, opened wide as he spoke; his voice was hoarse—not unpleasantly so, but as if it had hardened that way after years and years of speaking—and went on monotonously, with the effect of being able to go on forever. . . . For emphasis he bent forward slightly. No gestures. And before him, a thousand simple faces looking up in intent adoration.

SECTION 1 REVIEW

CHECKING FOR UNDERSTANDING
1. **Define** soviets, proletariat, capitalism.
2. **Discuss** Lenin's major political ideas.
3. **Explain** how the Bolsheviks gained power in Russia.

CRITICAL THINKING
4. **Determining Cause and Effect** What factors led to the revolutions of 1917? How did the two revolutions affect Russia and its people?

Source: John Reed. *Ten Days That Shook the World.* Random House, 1960, pp. 170–172.

SECTION 2
The Communist State

Lenin became known as the "Father of the Revolution" and the Bolsheviks as Communists. Together, they worked to bring **communism**, the teachings of Marx and Lenin, to Russia.

THE EARLY YEARS

Not all Russians agreed with the policies of Lenin and his followers. Anticommunist groups called Whites, made up of people ranging from monarchists to moderate socialists, were strong enough to start a civil war. But even with their strength and the military support they received from Western governments that feared the spread of communism, the communist government was able to hold power. There were several reasons for this. For one, while the Whites found it hard to cooperate with each other, a close associate of Lenin named Leon Trotsky had organized communist forces into an efficient Red Army. For another, most Russians preferred the Communists because many of the Whites wanted to bring back the old ways.

By 1921, the Red Army had defeated the Whites, and all of Russia was under communist rule. In December of the following year, the government established the Union of Soviet Socialist Republics (U.S.S.R.), a new Soviet state made up of the four republics of Russia, Ukraine, Byelorussia, and the Transcaucasus. The capital was Moscow.

During the civil war, the communist government had worked to restore the declining economy. Because peasants were paid so little for grain, they hoarded it, and little food was available in the cities. Factory production had slumped, and there were few manufactured goods for sale. The money system had broken down, and trade was carried on through a barter system of exchanging goods.

To cope with this crisis, the government instituted **war communism**, a policy under which all factories and land were taken over by the government and workers and peasants had to follow government decrees regarding production, wages, and prices. The

EXAMINING PHOTOGRAPHS *As seen in this early photograph, during the civil war, many people were forced to leave their homes and search for food. What did the government do after the civil war to cope with Russia's economic crisis?*

policy, however, only added to the chaos. Dissatisfaction among workers, peasants, and soldiers led to revolts and strikes. Hunger and suffering gripped the nation, and it seemed that the government was about to collapse.

Finally, in 1921, Lenin announced the New Economic Policy (NEP), which departed from Marxist theory by encouraging a limited amount of capitalism. Large-scale industries still remained under government control, but small private businesses were allowed to operate and peasants could own land and sell their produce for a profit. Under the NEP, industrial and farm production gradually improved and reached prewar levels.

Meanwhile, Lenin tightened political controls throughout the country. All opposition to the communist leadership was banned, and anyone suspected of being an "enemy of the Revolution" was imprisoned, shot, or forced into exile. By the end of the 1920's, the Communist party was the only legal political organization in the Soviet Union.

STALIN

Lenin died in 1924, and a power struggle developed within the communist leadership between Leon Trotsky and Joseph Stalin. Trotsky, who came from a cultured middle-class background, was the Communist party's leading thinker. Stalin, who was the son of artisans from a territory south of Russia called Georgia, was a dedicated administrator who controlled appointments to top party posts. Each had a different outlook regarding the Soviet Union's future. Trotsky wanted to promote a world socialist revolution, while Stalin wanted to postpone world revolution and concentrate instead on building up the Soviet Union.

THE FIVE-YEAR PLANS By 1928, Stalin was able to outmaneuver Trotsky, who fled into exile.

Once in power, Stalin's primary goal was to industrialize the Soviet Union as quickly as possible. To this end, he replaced the NEP with the first of a series of Five-Year Plans under which the government controlled all aspects of industrial and farm production. Goals were set over a five-year period to boost production.

Under the plan, primary attention was given to heavy industry. Little importance was paid to the manufacture of consumer goods, such as radios and refrigerators. As a result, many power plants, dams, and factories were built throughout the country, while the average Soviet citizen faced housing, appliance, and food shortages. As the account that follows reveals, great sacrifices were demanded of the Soviet people to fulfill Stalin's first Five-Year Plan:

As the Arctic winter broke suddenly into spring, Magnitogorsk [a new city which rose in the wilderness] changed beyond recognition. In early April it was still bitter cold; we had had hardly a single thaw; everything was still frozen solid. By May 1 the ground had thawed and the city was swimming in mud. Leaving our barrack we had to wade. Welding became next to impossible, as our ragged cables short-circuited at every step. At about this time I saw that my friend the doctor was very busy. He told me later what it was all about. Bubonic plague had broken out in three places not far from Magnitogorsk. The three villages had been surrounded by soldiers and isolated. All of the medical staff of Magnitogorsk was getting prepared for a possible outbreak in the city. The resistance of the people was very low because of not enough food during the winter and too much overwork. Sanitary conditions, particularly during the thaw, were frightening.

This was Magnitogorsk in 1933. A quarter of a million people—Communists, foreigners, Tartars (Mongols), and a mass of blue-eyed Russian peasants—building the

EXAMINING PHOTOGRAPHS *This old photograph shows mothers on a collective farm going to work in the fields while their children stay behind in a government-run nursery. Which groups opposed the government's policy of collective farms? What was Stalin's response to the opposition?*

biggest steel mill in the middle of the barren Ural steppe. Money was spent like water, men froze, hungered, and suffered, but the building went on.

OPPOSITION AND PURGES Although Stalin's plans were turning the Soviet Union into a leading industrial power, his forceful methods carried a high price and led to much opposition. Under the Five-Year Plans, farmland was to be owned collectively, or jointly, by the peasants. When *kulaks,* or prosperous farmers, refused to give up their land to the collective farm, fighting broke out in the countryside. Thousands of *kulaks* were killed or arrested and sent to labor camps in Siberia. By 1929, the *kulaks* as a group were completely wiped out. Despite the resistance of many peasants, the collective farms—on which the government controlled output—became a permanent feature of Soviet agriculture.

Opposition also mounted among such other groups as writers, scientists, and engi-

Source: John Scott. *Behind the Urals* (adaptation). Houghton Mifflin Co., 1942, pp. 65, 67.

neers. This led Stalin to increase the powers of the secret police who used terror to enforce obedience. A climate of fear spread through Soviet society. Soviet citizens accused of disloyalty were shot or sent to labor camps in Siberia. Even members of the Communist party were not safe. In the late 1930's, Stalin removed many of Lenin's old associates from their positions and had them tried and executed.

WORLD WAR II During the 1930's, fearing the rise of Nazi Germany and its eastward expansion, Stalin looked for an alliance with the democracies of the West. When they did not give him a direct or immediate response, Stalin turned to the German leader, Adolf Hitler. In late August 1939, they pledged that the Soviet Union and Nazi Germany would not attack each other. They also made plans to carve up Poland and other areas of eastern Europe between them. A week later, German troops rolled into Poland, beginning World War II, and shortly after, Stalin seized his portion of eastern European territory.

The Commonwealth of Independent States

EUGENIA GINZBURG

One of the 20 million victims of Stalin's terror was Eugenia Ginzburg, a teacher, journalist, and Communist party member. Arrested in 1937, she spent 18 years in prisons and labor camps and in exile in Siberia. After her release, Ginzburg wrote about her experiences in *Journey into the Whirlwind*. Below, she describes her transfer from prison in Kazan to trial in Moscow:

> "Bring your things!"
>
> What a lot of meaning was contained in these few words! Once again you are bound to the wheel, spinning and dragging you away at your master's will from everything that's near and dear. . . .
>
> A fairly large number of people were being sent to Moscow for the session of the military tribunal. Our sharpened hearing told us that they were being collected from several cells. . . .
>
> The idea that membership in the Communist Party was bound to aggravate the defendant's case had by now taken firm root in everyone's mind. How indeed could the situation be explained except as Stalin's death blow to the Party. . . .
>
> The door opened. We were taken out into the corridor and down the stairs. . . .
>
> All four of us were to appear before a military tribunal on a charge of political terrorism. Rimma assured us that we were the only women sent on this grim journey. . . .
>
> The gates of the ancient prison clanged behind us. . . . Coughs and sighs came from inside the cells. . . . The Black Maria [transport truck] had already been filled up. . . . We could see a little through the crack in the rear door. . . .
>
> We stopped. . . .
>
> "Everybody out!"
>
> . . . [There] was no one on the platform but a large covey of interrogators and guards. . . .
>
> "This way! This way!"
>
> It was an ordinary third-class coach divided into compartments. . . . There was a guard at the door of each compartment. . . .
>
> A jolt as the engine was coupled on . . . and we were off. . . . I knew what I was leaving behind—my children . . . , my mother, my university, my books, a clean and happy life full of the consciousness of having chosen the right way. As for our destination—only those who were taking us there could tell.

TAKING ANOTHER LOOK

What effect do you think arbitrary arrests, like that of Ginzburg, might have had on others under Stalin's rule?

Source: Eugenia Semyonova Ginzburg. Journey into the Whirlwind. Arnoldo Mondadori Editore-Milano, 1967. English translation by Harcourt, Brace Jovanovich, Inc. 1967.

EXAMINING PHOTOGRAPHS *During the German siege of Leningrad (formerly Petrograd), residents had to dig into snowpacked streets to obtain drinking water. Where did the Soviet army succeed in stopping the German advance?*

A year and a half later, on June 22, 1941, Hitler launched a surprise attack on the Soviet Union, and German forces drove deep into Soviet territory. They reached the outskirts of Moscow and besieged the city of Leningrad. Below, a Soviet army major describes the ordeal faced by the people of Leningrad during the 900-day siege:

In those days there *was* something in a man's face which told you that he would die within the next twenty-four hours. . . . I have lived in Leningrad all my life, and I also have my parents here. They are old people, and during those famine months I had to give them half my soldier's ration, or they would certainly have died. As a staff officer I was naturally, and quite rightly, getting considerably less than the people at the front: 250 grams [8.8 ounces] a day instead of 350 [13.3 ounces]. I shall always remember how I'd walk every day from my house near the Tauris Garden to my work in the center of the city, a matter of two or three kilometres [1 or 2 miles]. I'd walk for a while, and then sit down for a rest. Many a time I saw a man suddenly collapse on the snow. There was nothing one could do. One just walked on. . . . And on the way back, I would see a vague human form covered with snow on the spot where, in the morning, I had seen a man fall down. One didn't worry; what was the good? People didn't wash for weeks; there were no bath houses and no fuel. But at least people were urged to shave. And during that winter I don't think I ever saw a person smile. It was frightful. And yet, there was a kind of inner discipline that made people carry on. A new code of manners was evolved by hungry people. They carefully avoided talking about food. . . . Yet we never lost heart.

In spite of the German pressure, the Soviets refused to surrender, and in early 1943, the tide of battle finally turned in their favor at Stalingrad, a port city on the Volga River. There, the Soviets stopped the German advance and destroyed the German army.

After the war in Europe ended, the Soviets joined in the war against Japan, and Soviet armies entered Manchuria, a Japanese-held province in northern China. The war had a profound impact on the Soviet people. The Soviets suffered more casualties than any other country in the war. At least 20 million people lost their lives. In addition, there was widespread destruction throughout the European part of the Soviet Union.

Source: From RUSSIA AT WAR: 1941–1945 by Alexander Werth. Copyright © 1964 by Alexander Werth. Used by permission of the publisher, Dutton, an imprint of the New American Library, a division of Penguin Books USA Inc.

SECTION 3

A New Superpower

After World War II, the Soviet Union emerged as a superpower in rivalry with the United States. In what became known as the cold war, each sought world influence by means short of total war. In Europe, Stalin set up communist governments in eastern Europe. At home, he continued the drive for industrialization under Five-Year Plans.

Stalin died in 1953. Several years later, Nikita Khrushchev (kroosh·CHOF) became the new Soviet leader. He denounced Stalin as a murderer of innocent people, put an end to Stalin's methods of terror, and allowed writers and artists more freedom. Soviet society became more relaxed, but criticism of the party was still forbidden. Although Khrushchev sought better relations with the West, he boasted about the superiority of communism over capitalism and vowed that the Soviet Union would surpass the United States as a world power.

Many of Khrushchev's policies, however, failed. During his rule, agricultural and industrial production slowed. In foreign policy, the Soviet Union lost prestige when the United States forced the removal of Soviet missiles from Cuba in 1962. Two years later, Khrushchev was removed from office.

By the early 1970's, Leonid Brezhnev (BREZH·nef) had become the most powerful Soviet leader. During his rule, the government cracked down on **dissidents**, Soviet citizens who opposed government policies. Although the country's military power increased, the nonmilitary areas of the economy continued to grow very slowly. Realizing that Western technology was needed to improve their industries, the Soviets turned to **détente**, a relaxation of global tensions.

Détente brought about cultural and scientific exchanges between the Soviet Union and Western nations as well as treaties that placed limits on the production of nuclear weapons. During the late 1970's, however, relations again grew tense as the two superpowers began a renewed arms buildup and increased their rivalry for influence in various parts of the world.

In 1985, three years after Brezhnev's death, Mikhail Gorbachev (GOHR·buh·chof) became the leader of the Soviet Union and set the country on a new course. He supported a policy of *glasnost*, or openness, to find solutions to the problems of Soviet society. Newspapers began commenting on once forbidden topics, such as government corruption, inefficient industries, crime, and alcoholism. Meanwhile, the Soviet government released political prisoners and held elections in which challengers often defeated Communist party candidates. It also allowed freer emigration for Soviet Jews, who had suffered discrimination in the past. The greatest test to glasnost came in 1986 when a reactor at the Chernobyl nuclear plant caught fire, sending a radioactive cloud into the air, killing scores of people and threatening thousands more with the risk of cancer. After some early hesitation, the Soviet government finally admitted the catastrophe to the Soviet people and the rest of the world.

Gorbachev pushed for a rebuilding of the Soviet economy, a policy called *perestroika*

EXAMINING PHOTOGRAPHS *Soviet leader Mikhail Gorbachev, left, greets workers at a new Soviet manufacturing plant. What changes did Gorbachev want to make when he came to power?*

(pehr·ehs·TROY·kah), or "restructuring." He began reducing the central government's rigid economic controls and allowed more decisions to be made at the local level. Gorbachev's economic reforms permitted Soviet citizens to start small businesses and encouraged investment from the West.

Gorbachev realized that the success of his reforms at home depended on an easing of tensions abroad. In the following speech before an international gathering in Moscow, the Soviet leader reassured the global community about the purpose of his policies:

These changes are of immense significance for our society, for socialism as a whole, and for the entire world. . . . Before my people, before those present and before the whole world, I state with full responsibility that our foreign policy is today a greater extent than ever before determined by domestic policy, by our interest in concentrating our efforts on constructive activities aimed at improving our country. And that is why we need a lasting peace, predictability, and constructiveness in international relations. . . .

I must note that the restructuring, which we have launched on such a large scale and which is irreversible, shows to everyone: this is where we want to direct our resources, this is what our thoughts are concentrated on, these are our actual programs and intentions and this is what we intend to spend the intellectual energy of our society on.

Our main idea is to bring out the full potential of socialism by activating all the people's energy. To do this it is necessary that all our public and state agencies, all our production collectives and creative unions, function fully and freely. We need to create new forms of civic activity and to restore those which have been unfairly forgotten. In brief, we seek the broad democratization of our entire society. . . .

As part of a strategy to improve Soviet relations with the West, Gorbachev entered into new arms-reduction agreements with the United States. The Soviet Union also withdrew its troops from Afghanistan, admitting that their invasion of that country in 1979 was "morally wrong." The Soviets also sought more trade with Western nations and allowed the nations of eastern Europe to pursue their own policies free of Soviet controls. At last the cold war was ending.

SECTION 3 REVIEW

CHECKING FOR UNDERSTANDING
1. **Define** dissident, détente, *glasnost, perestroika.*
2. **Summarize** the changes that took place in Soviet foreign and domestic policies after the death of Stalin.

CRITICAL THINKING
3. **Recognizing Ideologies** In what ways do you think Mikhail Gorbachev broke with the Soviet past? In what ways did he continue its policies?

Source: Mikhail Gorbachev. At the Summit. Richardson, Steirman & Black, 1988, p. 7.

Government

PUBLIC OPINION

In 1990, at the request of *Reader's Digest*, the Institute of Sociology at the Soviet Academy of Sciences polled 1050 Russians between the ages of 18 and 25 from six regions of the Soviet Union about their country and its leaders.

FOCUSING ON THE ISSUE Read the following excerpts from the report that appeared in the March 1991 *Reader's Digest*. Then write your own report. In it, summarize in chart form the results of the poll and give your personal reactions to them:

The poll . . . found that:

- *By a substantial margin, young Russians believe 70 years of communism have been bad for the Soviet Union. They favor private ownership of land, unlimited freedom of the press and even private ownership of industry.*
- *They express an astonishing lack of confidence in Soviet President Mikhail Gorbachev, with only six percent of those surveyed citing him as the most admired political figure. By contrast, 39 percent prefer his chief rival, Boris Yeltsin. . . .*
- *An overwhelming majority express positive attitudes toward the United States and would like to see an independent Rus-*

sia become a more integral part of Europe. . . .

After the poll was conducted, I interviewed 30 respondents separately in Moscow, Tyumen in Siberia and Ufa near the Ural Mountains. . . .

Asked if 70 years of socialism have been good or bad for the Soviet Union, a striking 74 percent reply in the negative. To the question of whether socialism in the Soviet Union has a future, almost 50 percent answer no, whereas only 22 percent say yes. . . .

Asked whether there should be private ownership of land, almost 85 percent say yes. A mere 10 percent disagree and five percent are undecided. The margin in favor is still over-

whelming when the question applies to industry and commercial firms, with 70 percent positive, 19 percent opposed and 11 percent undecided. . . .

Fifty-four percent . . . say the state, rather than the individual, should be responsible for finding and preserving jobs for the people. Thirty-two percent say the individual should have primary responsibility, and 14 percent are undecided. . . .

Young Russians fault the current political leadership for the failures of communism and the inability or unwillingness to make a break with the past. Is Gorbachev helping or hindering political change in the country? A

stunning 51 percent declare he is an obstacle and 20 percent are not sure. . . .

From a list of ten Soviet political figures, a bare six percent cite Gorbachev as the leader they most prefer compared with 39 percent for Boris Yeltsin. Significantly, eight percent say they don't like anybody on the current political scene, and 29 percent don't answer. . . .

The young believe, by a large margin, that improvements at home should receive priority over international commitments. When asked to select from a list of potential concerns, 52 percent say they are most worried about economic

collapse. Civil strife is the primary concern of 38 percent. Fewer than three percent are worried about "external threats." . . .

. . . Should Soviet republics be allowed to secede from the Union if they so desire? Seventy percent . . . say yes. Only 19 percent disagree, and 11 percent are undecided. . . .

Fifty-eight percent favor freedom of the press. But only 31 percent say they favor unlimited freedom of political activity. . . . Many of those surveyed express mistrust of politics generally. . . .

When asked if they would publicly protest government

policies that they dislike, 37 percent say they would; 24 percent say they would not. A large group, 39 percent, are unsure. . . .

The huge majority of those surveyed are friendly to America, with 86 percent saying they have positive attitudes toward the United States. Only three percent report a negative view; 11 percent are neutral. In addition, 72 percent say if the Russian Republic becomes independent, it should seek to join the European Community.

Source: Excerpted with permission from "What Young Russians Really Think" by David Satter, *Reader's Digest,* March 1991. Copyright © 1991 by The Reader's Digest Assn., Inc.

Chapter 41 Review

SUMMARY

In early 1917, a revolution in Russia toppled the czar and established a provisional government and a system of soviets. Later in the year, the Bolsheviks under Vladimir Lenin carried out a socialist revolution. After the Bolsheviks defeated their opponents in a civil war, they established the Soviet Union.

In 1928, Joseph Stalin came to power and used force and terror to extend his power and to achieve the rapid industrialization of the Soviet Union. During World War II, German forces invaded Soviet territory but were eventually defeated by Soviet armies.

After World War II, the Soviet Union emerged as a superpower to rival the United States. After several decades of cold war with the West, the Soviets in the 1980's sought a reduction of global tensions and an expansion of domestic reforms under the leadership of Mikhail Gorbachev.

USING VOCABULARY

Each of these terms below has significance for the Soviet period. Use these terms in a paragraph that explains high points in Soviet history.

soviets	war communism	détente
proletariat	*kulaks*	*glasnost*
capitalism	dissident	*perestroika*
communism		

REVIEWING FACTS

1. **Examine** the role of Leon Trotsky in the rise of the Soviet state.
2. **Compare** the New Economic Policy and the Five-Year Plans.
3. **Discuss** how the Soviet Union entered World War II.
4. **Describe** the changes Khrushchev's rule brought to the Soviet Union.
5. **Name** the event that was the greatest test to Gorbachev's *glasnost* policy. Explain.

CRITICAL THINKING

1. **Predicting Consequences** What do you think might have happened to the czarist system if Nicholas II had carried out reforms? Explain.
2. **Demonstrating Reasoned Judgment** What reasons can you give for the success of Lenin and the Bolsheviks in establishing a socialist state?
3. **Identifying Alternatives** Stalin achieved his goal of industrializing the Soviet Union rapidly. Do you think he would have been as successful as rapidly had he used different methods? Explain your answer.
4. **Identifying Central Issues** What points do you think Mikhail Gorbachev was trying to make in his speech about Soviet reforms and foreign policy? How did his address reflect a change in Soviet attitudes?

ANALYZING CONCEPTS

1. **Power** What was the role of the Communist party in the Soviet Union?
2. **Human Rights** How did the Soviet government treat its opponents from 1917 to the 1980's?

GEOGRAPHIC THEMES

1. **Human-Environment Interaction** What were some of the environmental obstacles that workers faced in carrying out the first Five-Year Plan?
2. **Place** What geographic feature made Stalingrad an important strategic site during World War II?

Evaluating Information

Evaluating information involves many skills, such as analyzing sources, recognizing bias, and drawing conclusions. Use the following steps to evaluate information:

- Analyze the purpose and nature of the information: Is it a primary or secondary source? Who wrote it? Why was it written?
- Identify the central issue.
- Determine whether the author is qualified to write about this subject. What bias does the author bring to the subject?
- Check the accuracy of factual statements against other sources.
- Draw conclusions about the reliability of the information.

"
a) [My sisters and I] would sometimes complain, 'This thing isn't right, and that thing isn't right.' My mother would say. . . , 'Do you know what it used to be like [before the revolution]? Do you know I had nothing to wear? That we had only enough to eat until March?. . . That I had to work from sunrise to sunset? But . . . you've become fat and lazy.' . . . So there was real popular enthusiasm during the Stalin years. The Soviet people put out an enormous effort. Yes, all sorts of terrible things happened. Yes, the humane aims of socialism were not realized. But we sincerely believed in it all.[1]
"

"
b) Most people my age grew up with a great many illusions about Stalin and his policies, and I shared those illusions. On the other hand, I never worshiped the Stalin cult, as many did. Though I never admitted it to others, and hardly to myself, I couldn't accept the idea of a living god. Also, quite a few of my school friends were arrested. . . . I knew that all those arrested could not have been guilty. Still, Stalin's death was a very emotional event for me, as it was for most people . . .[2]
"

EXAMPLE

Read the excerpt from V.I. Lenin's speech on page 673. Written in 1918, this speech describes the sweeping changes brought by the revolution. What is the purpose of this speech? (to promote socialism) As a leader of the revolution, Lenin is qualified to discuss these events. However, his bias may affect the factual accuracy of his statements. The speech contains statements such as, "we destroyed one of the oldest, most . . . brutal of monarchies." What kind of statement is this? (opinion or unsupported generalization) Try to identify other assumptions and generalizations.

PRACTICE

The statements above describe Soviet attitudes during the Stalin period. Both speakers were Communist party members who supported Gorbachev's reforms in the 1980's. Read the statements and answer the questions below.

1. Are these primary or secondary sources?
2. Are the speakers qualified on this subject? Why or why not?
3. What biases does each speaker have?
4. Which statements could be checked for accuracy? How would you check them?
5. How do these two views of Stalin's rule differ? How are they the same?
6. Are these statements reliable sources of information about the Stalin period? Why or why not?

[1]Source: "Interview with Aleksandr Yakovlev," from Stephen F. Cohen and Katrina vanden Heuvel, Voices of Glasnost: Interviews with Gorbachev's Reformers. W.W. Norton & Company, 1989, pp. 36–37.

[2]Source: "Interview with Georgi Arbatov," from Stephen F. Cohen and Katrina vanden Heuvel, Voices of Glasnost: Interviews with Gorbachev's Reformers. W.W. Norton & Company, 1989, p. 308.

CHAPTER OUTLINE

1 Gorbachev's Dilemma
2 The Failed Coup
3 End of Soviet Communism
4 The Emerging Commonwealth

People and Places to Know

Boris Yeltsin, the KGB, St. Petersburg, the Baltic republics, the Slavic republics

Key Terms to Define

nationalities, coup

Objectives to Learn

1. **Analyze** how the reforms in the Soviet Union contributed to unrest.
2. **Summarize** the events that brought an end to Soviet communism.
3. **Describe** problems faced by the Commonwealth of Independent States.

Moscow citizens celebrate collapse of the coup— August 22, 1991

688

A New Revolution

> Emma Bruk, a cardiologist in her 50s, lived next to the U.S. embassy [in Moscow] and had lately been wakened by the sounds of workmen hammering and drilling, repairing the damage of a recent fire. But this morning there was complete silence.
>
> Then came the curt statement on television. Gorbachev's reforms had led the Soviet Union toward a national catastrophe, said the announcer. "A mortal danger hangs over our great homeland." All power has been transferred to an eight-member emergency committee.
>
> Emma watched, paralyzed with shock. Could her country really be going back to the time before *perestroika*, when she spent nights in her room reading forbidden literature, fearful that every unexpected sound meant the police were coming for her?
>
> Emma had been close to dissident circles, but had not become active herself. After the death of her husband in 1975, she feared for her daughter: who would look after the child if she was sent to the labor camps?
>
> Remarried now, Emma had a stepson and stepdaughter to worry about too. For them, for her, the Gorbachev era was a failing revolution. The economy had fallen further into ruin; corruption ran rampant. And there were still closed sections at hospitals that served only the party elite—two or three patients to a room compared with as many as 12 in the general wards, with the best food and special nurses.
>
> Yet at the same time, the release of political prisoners and the liberation of the media were like a miracle to Emma. . . . At last people could say what they felt in the Soviet Union.
>
> But now. . . .

*L*ike Emma Bruk, people in the Soviet Union and throughout the world were stunned by the announcement on August 19, 1991, that a group of communist hardliners had ousted Soviet President Mikhail Gorbachev. For a short time, it seemed that the hardliners would succeed. Soviet citizens, however, defiantly resisted the takeover. As a result of their stand, the 74-year-old communist system came to an end; and by year's end, the Soviet Union itself had passed from the scene. In rapid succession, the 15 Soviet republics declared or affirmed their independence from Moscow. Despite their many differences, many of the republics joined to form a new international community—the Commonwealth of Independent States (C.I.S.).

Source: Excerpted with permission from "Three Days That Shook the World" by Lawrence Elliott and David Satter, *Reader's Digest* January 1992. Copyright © 1992 by The Reader's Digest Assn., Inc.

Gorbachev's Dilemma

As the 1990's began, Mikhail Gorbachev was hailed abroad as a statesman. At home, however, he was increasingly viewed as an ineffectual leader. Hardline Communists accused Gorbachev of undermining the communist system with his reforms. Democratic reformers, on the other hand, expressed concern that *perestroika* was moving too slowly. Gorbachev tried to move carefully between these two groups, often zigzagging between liberal and conservative positions. Instead of building confidence, Gorbachev's actions only created more uncertainty.

Another serious problem for Gorbachev was the wave of nationalist feeling sweeping the country. In the early 1990's, the Soviet Union consisted of 15 republics, each based on one of the major **nationalities**, or ethnic groups, in the country. The republics had the right to run their local affairs, but they were actually controlled by the Russian-dominated central government in Moscow, the capital of both the Soviet Union and Russia, the largest of the 15 republics.

The peoples of the non-Russian republics had long resented Russian rule. In addition, the Soviet Union's nationalities and many smaller ethnic groups had cultural and political differences among themselves. Before the time of Gorbachev, strict communist rule had kept these rivalries under control. In the relaxed atmosphere of *glasnost*, old hatreds quickly resurfaced. By early 1991, many of the republics were demanding independence, and ethnic violence had become widespread.

As the Soviet Union's internal problems worsened, Gorbachev soon faced new challengers to his leadership. His most outspoken rival was a former ally, Boris Yeltsin. Believing that *perestroika* was moving too slowly, Yeltsin took his case directly to the Russian people and was elected president of Russia. In the excerpt below, an American writer visiting Moscow in 1990 describes the mood in the Soviet capital as Gorbachev and Yeltsin tried to deal with the country's growing crisis:

EXAMINING PHOTOGRAPHS *Soviet President Mikhail Gorbachev, shown here with United States President George Bush, was praised abroad for his policies.* How was Gorbachev viewed in the Soviet Union?

> [**O**]n May Day [the international workers' holiday] . . . , I was beside the Kremlin—it means "fortress"—in Moscow with throngs that shook the walls. "Down with the Communist party!" they cried. For people with scant experience at uninhibited protest, they showed surprising flair. "Gorbachev to Chernobyl!" some cried. Declared the . . . sign of one protestor: "We have *partkomy* but no *portki*—We have communist committees but not even peasant's pants."

EXAMINING PHOTOGRAPHS
During the 1990 May Day demonstration in Moscow's Red Square, Soviet citizens used their newly gained freedom of speech to voice opposition to the communist system. What problem did Gorbachev face as a result of glasnost?

Yet again on Revolution Day, November 7, when the birth of the communist regime is massively celebrated, anger filled Red Square. Among communist marchers were workers who hurled obscenities as they passed Gorbachev. Then came a truculent [fiercely angry] anti-party mob, bearing a hugh funeral wreath that proclaimed the anniversary a day of mourning and signs equating communism with fascism [political philosophy associated with Hitler].

Gorbachev's Nobel Peace Prize—however well deserved for reducing superpower tension—cut little ice with hungry and frustrated Muscovites [citizens of Moscow]. As he loosed the reins on speech and permitted multiparty elections, the long-stagnant economy was collapsing. The list of vanishing commodities grew to include not only sausage and vodka, long rationed, but also potatoes, eggs, bread, and cigarettes.

What to do? Torrents of rhetoric rose from halls where convened the Soviet legislature, the Russian congress, and the Communist Party. Television carried their fulminations [denunciations] to all the union—mercifully interrupting to present the regular 8 p.m. puppet show, *Goodnight Kids,* featuring a hare, a dog, a bird, and a pig. All over the U.S.S.R. these creatures tuck children into bed.

Then back stormed the politicians. Though many Communists were defiant, they surrendered their right of ultimate control. Boris Yeltsin . . . , the popular president of the Russian Republic, proposed a crash program of staggering change. In a 500-day transition period state industries worth billions would be sold, and citizens would regain the right to own land.

Gorbachev seemed to buy in, but then, probably pressed by standpat Communists, opted for more gradual change. The threat of collapse—political and/or economic—was so great that the Soviet legislature granted his request for emergency powers with which to hold the wheezing machinery together. Moscow was awash with rumors of a coup. And life got worse. . . .

Source: Mike Edwards. "Mother Russia on a New Course" in *National Geographic,* February 1991, pp. 12, 14.

CHECKING FOR UNDERSTANDING
1. **Define** nationalities.
2. **State** the problems that the Soviets faced in the early 1990's.

CRITICAL THINKING
3. **Drawing Conclusions** Do you believe Gorbachev was an effective leader? Why or why not?

S E C T I O N   2

The Failed Coup

In the summer of 1991, Mikhail Gorbachev agreed to give the republics more control over their local economies. Communist hardliners, however, feared this move would permanently weaken the central government's hold over the republics. In August, they tried to force Gorbachev to declare a state of emergency. When Gorbachev refused, the hardliners ousted the Soviet President from power and formed a ruling committee.

Russian President Boris Yeltsin rallied public support against the **coup,** or swift seizure of power, and for democracy. Appearing before a throng in front of the Russian parliament building, Yeltsin called for nonviolent resistance and urged military officials to refuse to carry out committee orders. Tens of thousands of unarmed Moscow citizens defied a ban on demonstrations and stood guard to protect Yeltsin and his aides, who remained holed up in the Russian parliament building. The resistance soon spread beyond Moscow to other parts of the country. In the following excerpt, Anatoli Sobchak, the reform-minded mayor of Leningrad, describes the actions he took to preserve democracy in his city:

I headed to the TV studios, just a few minutes before I was scheduled to appear on a live telecast. With me were Shcherbakov and Yarov, the regional council chief, both of whom the junta members had included on their committee without permission. We got there five minutes before airtime. The head of Leningrad TV, Boris Petrov, had even arranged a satellite hook-up, so we were seen far beyond the borders of Leningrad.

While on the air, it occurred to me to refer to the Moscow junta members as the "former" this (vice president, minister of defense, etc.) and "former" that, and then just plain "citizen," as though they were already sitting in the dock. . . .

Following the broadcast, we kept the OMON [security] forces busy. . . . An endless stream of people kept on coming up to me with new details of the plot. . . .

Meanwhile, [General] Samsonov [commander of the Leningrad military district] was under fire in Moscow. The members of the junta were screaming hysterically over the phone that he had sold out to the democrats. At the same time, we learned that two columns of military equipment were moving towards the city from the south. Barricades were needed, but it was clear that we would not have time to build them. The tanks would be here within the hour. . . . Samsonov gave me his word as an officer that he would not allow them to enter the city. The column turned at Gatchina. For three days, the tanks would stand motionless at the military airfield there. . . .

The tension was dissipated a bit when we linked up with Yeltsin. Then I grabbed an hour's catnap on the sofa in my office. At 6:00 o'clock in the morning, I went to Putilovsky (now the Kirov factory) before the start of the new shift. A car with a loudspeaker was parked and waiting in front of the factory. We held a small rally, after which the manager's office distributed passes to the workers so anyone who wanted to could attend the rally we were

EXAMINING PHOTOGRAPHS
Moscow residents responded to the coup by building barricades to block tanks from passing through the streets. In an afternoon of heated exchanges with civilians who climbed aboard their tanks, many soldiers said that they did not want to shed Russian blood. How was Gorbachev affected by the coup's collapse?

calling for the whole city. As I left, a column of three or four thousand people was already turning onto Strachet Boulevard. I wanted to lead the people to the rally in Palace Square, but my security guards advised me not to.

At 10 A.M., the whole city was in Palace Square. We had to divert entire columns of people onto distant approaches. The square is wide, but nothing so wide as this ocean of people. We had decided to ask everyone to return to their workplaces by 6 P.M., and that's what happened. No one skipped work. I was told later that even the convicts in the prisons asked to be allowed out into the barricades, promising to return afterwards to their cells. . . .

In the face of public resistance, widespread international condemnation, and growing splits within its ranks, the coup crumbled two days after it was announced. As troops and tanks withdrew from Moscow,

Source: Reprinted with the permission of The Free Press, a Division of Macmillan, Inc. from FOR A NEW RUSSIA: *The Mayor of St. Petersburg's Own Story of the Struggle for Justice and Democracy* by Anatoly Sobchak. Copyright © 1992 by Anatoly Sobchak.

the Soviet Parliament announced that it had formally reinstated Gorbachev as president.

Although Gorbachev was back in power, the coup and its failure had made him lose face. It was now widely recognized that the coup stemmed from Gorbachev's inability to solve the Soviet Union's many problems and his unwillingness to break with the communist old guard. The failed coup, on the other hand, had boosted the standing of Boris Yeltsin. Having rallied his people to resistance, Yeltsin was acclaimed as a world-respected leader.

SECTION 2 REVIEW

CHECKING FOR UNDERSTANDING
1. **Define** coup.
2. **Discuss** why the communist hardliners staged the coup against Mikhail Gorbachev.
3. **Detail** the steps taken by Yeltsin, Sobchak, and other Soviets to resist the takeover.

CRITICAL THINKING
4. **Determining Cause and Effect** Why do you think the coup failed? How did it affect the Soviet Union?

End of Soviet Communism

Within a few days of the coup's collapse, Gorbachev and Yeltsin began forging a new relationship, one in which Yeltsin had the upper hand. Gorbachev removed from government posts the people who had tried to oust him and promised a renewed push for democratic reforms. He also announced the appointment of committed reformers to government posts. These people were chosen with the consent of Yeltsin and other leaders.

Meanwhile, anticommunist riots and demonstrations swept cities, towns, and villages throughout the Soviet Union. The excerpt below tells what happened in Moscow:

The crowd, heady with victory and relief, streamed out of the barricaded square and marched to the Kremlin, Red Square, and the KGB, waving new Russian flags. Other Muscovites abandoned their offices, apartments, and jobs to join the celebration. "What would have been my son's fate if this had not happened," said fifty-year-old historian Larisa Yakovleva, panting as she hurried from the Museum of the History of Moscow toward the chanting crowds on Dzerzhinsky Square, site of the notorious Lubyanka, the KGB [secret police] headquarters. "We are all so happy!"

On that square, hundreds of people whistled and chanted, "Down with the Communist Party." A young man in a tank driver's uniform climbed the statue of Felix Dzerzhinsky to install a Ukrainian independence flag, desecrating the monument to the founder of the Soviet secret police [KGB] and defying the KGB with the symbol of freedom.

Around KGB headquarters, thousands of citizens stabbed their fists in the air in

EXAMINING PHOTOGRAPHS *After the coup's collapse, the statue of Felix Dzerzhinsky, the founder of the Soviet secret police, was removed from a public square in Moscow. What political changes came as an immediate result of the coup's failure?*

anger, shouting, "Executioners!" at the shadowy figures behind curtained windows and exorcising [casting out] the dark spirit of decades of terror that had come from the building. With the KGB chairman himself under arrest, the agency had suddenly lost its immunity from public complaints and criminal prosecution. . . .

By midnight, construction cranes were lifting the . . . statue of "Iron Felix" off his pedestal in Dzerzhinsky Square. They had him by the neck. A crowd of 3,000 cheered and set off flares in joy. When he was down, demonstrators kicked at his face. . . .

"We are all sick of the Communists. They have been strangling us for seventy years," Alexander Filippova, a pensioner [said]. . . . Mayor [Gavril] Popov [of

Commonwealth of Independent States

BORIS YELTSIN

In 1991, Boris Yeltsin emerged as the most popular and most powerful leader in the former Soviet Union. A member of the Communist party since the 1960's, he had risen quickly through the ranks and by 1985 was party leader in Moscow. In this excerpt from his autobiography, *Against the Grain*, Yeltsin tells what happened when he decided to find out firsthand just how overloaded Moscow's transportation system was:

. . . I made a point of traveling by subway and bus, particularly at rush hours, in order to get a physical feel for how Muscovites were transported to work and back home. . . .

En route, those tired, tense, wound-up workers told me a great deal about the way we, the leaders, had ruined the country. I resolved to change things for the better. Certain measures were instituted. For instance, the Moscow enterprises were put on a flexible system, so that the starting times of the working day were staggered. We created new bus routes and made several other innovations.

The Politburo's [leading Soviet government committee] reaction to these trips of mine

was somewhat odd. They didn't disapprove openly, but echoes of their annoyance reached me. When they began to criticize me, all their pent-up feelings came pouring out. My journeys by subway and bus, they said, were an attempt to gain cheap popularity.

This was untrue. My chief aim had been to discover what was actually happening in the transportation system and what was needed to ease the burden on ordinary people of traveling at rush hour.

As for the smear about cheap

popularity, no one but myself seemed to want to earn it! If it was so easy to achieve with just a hop on a bus, why didn't all politicians do it?

TAKING ANOTHER LOOK

What kind of party leader was Boris Yeltsin? What do his comments reveal to you about Soviet life under communism?

EXAMINING PHOTOGRAPHS *In late 1991, the Kremlin became the headquarters of the government of Russia. Who was the leader of Russia?*

Moscow] was the first to sense the mood of the people and realize the time had come to kill off communism. He moved quickly to suspend the Party's activities in the capital—and set off a firestorm of similar moves over the next two days.

In other areas of the Soviet nation, statues of communist leaders were removed from public squares. In the weeks that followed, many cities began adopting their pre-1917 names. One such city was Leningrad, which had given birth to the 1917 Bolshevik Revolution. It took back its historic name—St. Petersburg.

On August 24, responding to the rising wave of anticommunism, Gorbachev resigned as Communist party leader. Keeping his position as Soviet president, he urged the Central Committee—the Communist party's decision-making body—to disband. This signaled the political collapse of the institution

Source: Stuart Loory and Ann Imse. *CNN Reports Seven Days That Shook the World.* Turner Publishing, Inc., 1991, pp. 156–157.

that had ruled the Soviet Union with an iron hand for more than seven decades.

Gorbachev's authority eroded even further when a number of Soviet republics declared their independence from the central government. Acting on earlier independence declarations, Armenia, Georgia, Moldova, and the Baltic republics of Lithuania, Latvia, and Estonia declared their full separation from the Soviet Union. At about the same time, Ukraine and Belarus took the first steps toward independence. Before long, the Baltic republics and many of the other republics received diplomatic recognition from the Soviet Union, the United States, and the European Community.

SECTION 3 REVIEW

CHECKING FOR UNDERSTANDING

1. **Give examples** of the anticommunist movement that swept the Soviet Union after the coup's failure.
2. **Identify** the republics that either completely broke away from the Soviet Union or took the first steps toward independence.

CRITICAL THINKING

3. **Demonstrating Reasoned Judgment** Why do you think Gorbachev's power as Soviet president continued to decline even after he renounced his post as Communist party leader?

SECTION 4

The Emerging Commonwealth

By late 1991, political power had shifted completely from the Soviet central government to the individual republics. In December, the leaders of the three Slavic republics of Russia, Ukraine, and Belarus declared that the Soviet Union had ceased to exist and announced the formation of a new Commonwealth of Independent States. They named themselves the first three members of the new union, and opened membership to all republics of the former Soviet Union.

In a few weeks, eight other former Soviet republics—Kazakhstan, Uzbekistan, Kyrgzstan, Tajikistan, Turkmenistan, Armenia, Azerbaijan, and Moldova—joined the Commonwealth. Only the Baltic republics and Georgia did not join the new union. The republics of the Commonwealth agreed that the hammer and sickle flag would be lowered from the towers of the Kremlin. Mikhail Gorbachev, now a man without a country to govern, resigned the Soviet presidency.

The loosely structured Commonwealth was intended to replace the highly centralized Soviet Union. Under the new arrangement, each member republic was independent. A central administration, however, was established in the Belarussian city of Minsk to coordinate economic and monetary policies. In matters of defense, the Commonwealth agreed to set up a permanent unified command over the nuclear weapons held by Russia, Ukraine, and Kazakhstan. Each republic, however, asserted the right to maintain its own non-nuclear military forces.

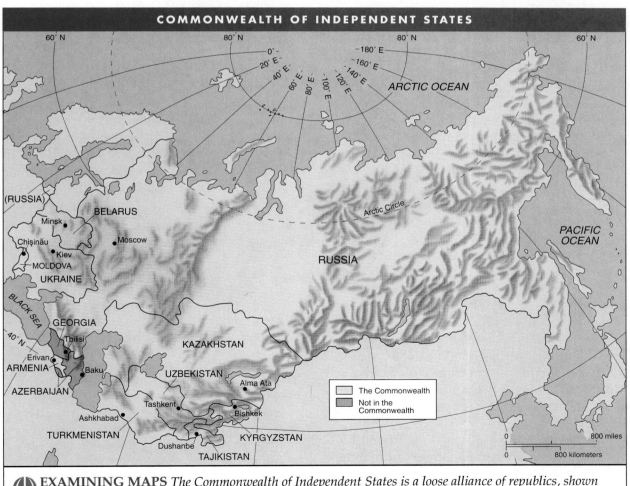

COMMONWEALTH OF INDEPENDENT STATES

The Commonwealth
Not in the Commonwealth

EXAMINING MAPS *The Commonwealth of Independent States is a loose alliance of republics, shown above with their capitals. What political formation did the Commonwealth replace?*

EXAMINING PHOTOGRAPHS
Belarussian shoppers purchase higher-priced clothing items in a department store in Minsk, the capital of Belarus. What primary factor accounted for the problems faced by Commonwealth republics?

Although the new Commonwealth broke decisively with the Soviet past, its member republics faced a host of economic problems, including rising prices, stagnant trade, a decaying transportation system, and a declining standard of living. Many of these problems stemmed from policies of the former Communist government. Under the communist system, the government had owned the land, industries, banks, and communication and transportation systems. Through Five-Year Plans, a large centralized bureaucracy had set production targets, fixed prices and wages, and distributed labor and raw materials. Because of widespread corruption and inefficiency in the bureaucracy, goods had not been delivered to their intended destinations and state stores had faced continual shortages of produce. Adding to this were machine shortages, outdated farming practices, and inadequate transportation.

These problems were now heightened by months of political turmoil and governmental neglect. Now no central agency was in control of the flow of food and supplies between the republics. By December 1991, there were serious food shortages in many cities.

In January 1992, to try to bring more food to store shelves, Yeltsin and leaders of other republics lifted long-standing price controls. Although this caused the prices of goods to climb, they felt that it had to be done in order to move their economies toward capitalism. By August 1992, some Russians were having second thoughts about the events of the past year—and about Yeltsin:

In the street outside the quaintly named Sailors' Rest prison, everyone had a different opinion about the hard-line Communists who tried and failed to change the course of Russian history a year ago.

"They should be put on trial," said Rosa Evliyeva, a biologist in her late 40s, as she looked at the fortress-like building where leaders of the August 1991 coup were incarcerated. "They wanted to create a dictatorship. Of course, life has gotten more difficult for most of us, but some positive things have happened, too. We feel freer now."

Anatoly Ivanov, a pensioner, said his views have been modified by the performance of President Boris Yeltsin. "I was against the coup," he said, "but I am beginning to think that the putschists had a point. They wanted to prevent the disintegration of our country and the economy. Yeltsin has not fulfilled his promises."

. . . It is now clear that the road to a free-market economy will be long and hard. . . .

In the euphoria that followed defeat of the coup, between 80 percent and 90 percent of the Russian population expressed support for Yeltsin's actions in supporting Gorbachev. But declining living standards and rapidly rising prices have eroded the president's popularity.

"We can't buy toys or clothes for our kids," said Vassily Shpak, a veteran of the Afghan war struggling to raise three children on a monthly income of 4,500 rubles ($30). "Meat is so expensive that we have become vegetarians. I used to believe in Yeltsin, but I don't anymore. Last August I went to the White House (the Russian parliament building) to defend it from the tanks, but I would not go there again."

But although public support for Yeltsin has dropped significantly, he retains a solid political base. Polls indicate that roughly a third of the people trust the president. . . .

The polls suggest that during the past year, Russia has become more pluralistic politically, economically, and socially. The number of people living below the poverty line have increased substantially but at the same time, the reforms have given many people an interest in seeing them continued. . . .

A recent study sponsored by the parliament showed that one in three Russians was taking advantage of new economic possibilities. Many families have been given small private plots where they can grow vegetables to see them through the winter. Others supplement their . . . incomes by buying and selling foodstuffs and consumer goods in the flea markets that have sprung up in Moscow and other major cities.

PRICE INCREASES IN RUSSIA, EARLY 1992

EXAMINING CHARTS *The Russian government relaxed many price controls, and prices rose during the next few months.* Why did the Russian government end price controls?

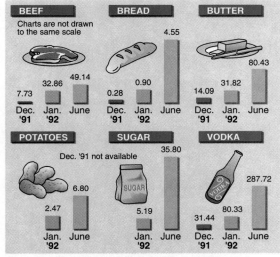

BEEF
Charts are not drawn to the same scale
7.73 — Dec. '91
32.86 — Jan. '92
49.14 — June

BREAD
0.28 — Dec. '91
0.90 — Jan. '92
4.55 — June

BUTTER
14.09 — Dec. '91
31.82 — Jan. '92
80.43 — June

POTATOES
Dec. '91 not available
2.47 — Jan. '92
6.80 — June

SUGAR
5.19 — Jan. '92
35.80 — June

VODKA
31.44 — Dec. '91
80.33 — Jan. '92
287.72 — June

* All figures show cost of items in rubles per pound except for vodka, which is in rubles per quart.

Source: Department of Social Economic Development of the Russian Supreme Soviet

SECTION 4 REVIEW

CHECKING FOR UNDERSTANDING
1. **Discuss** how the Commonwealth of Independent States was formed.
2. **Specify** the economic problems faced by the Commonwealth republics as well as the steps taken by Commonwealth leaders to create free-enterprise markets.

CRITICAL THINKING
3. **Making Comparisons** Compare the political principles and organization of the Commonwealth of Independent States with those of the Soviet Union.

Source: Michael Dobbs. "Year after coup try, Russians debate the turn lives have taken" in *The Washington Post,* August 17, 1992.

The Arts of C.I.S.

The arts of the Commonwealth republics range from architecture and painting to folk music and dancing. Each republic has its own rich heritage of religious architecture, decorative arts, folk music, dance, and literature. With the end of communism, modern artists now enjoy freedom to develop their own individual styles.

? What traditional influences do you think have impacted the arts of the Commonwealth?

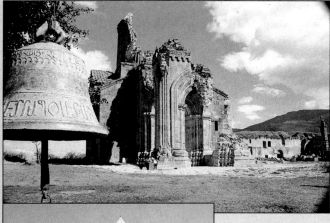

METALWORK
Armenian church bell

DESIGN
Mosaic from Uzbekistan

PAINTING
Russian icon

ARCHITECTURE
Georgian fortress

ARTIFACTS
Decorated wooden Easter egg

Government

THE FALL OF COMMUNISM

In the view of one journalist, "the most surprising feature of the communist experiment is not that it collapsed so quickly, but that it lasted so long."

FOCUSING ON THE ISSUE Read the following comments by four former Soviet citizens. What reasons does each give for the power and the fall of communism? Do you think any of the four would agree with the journalist? Explain.

The Communists pursued the same geopolitical goals as the czars. That's why they were able to remain in power for so long. . . . The communist idea was an imperialist idea, based on a system of unprecedented repression. . . .

Soviet power was based on lies and violence. The whip had to be used continuously and it had to be backed with lies. As soon as our leaders stopped using the whip, the system began to fall apart. After Gorbachev introduced glasnost, and the lies diminished, communism was doomed. The Soviet state never received the loyalty and support of its citizens.

Lev Rozgon, writer
and prison camp survivor

The collapse of communism is the result of a long process of its own internal erosion—erosion of ideology, of the economy, of political power itself. The erosion started after Stalin's death in 1953. By the time (Mikhail S.) Gorbachev came to power, we had simply ceased to believe in communism. The entire post-Stalin era was a preparation for the destruction of the system. It was not efficient, it was cruel, and it could not compete with modern, Western civilization.

Fydor Burlatsky, former
aide to Nikita Khrushchev

Communism was a very powerful ideology because it rested on illusions that had accumulated over the centuries. The Bolsheviks talked about the happiness of mankind, the building of God's kingdom on our planet. It was an ideology that made fanatics out of politicians and warriors out of common people.

Lev Timofeyev,
human rights activist

Communism was a system for mobilizing the masses. When confronted with a single task, it was able to achieve fantastic results. The Great Patriotic War (World War II) was the ultimate test of the system—and it passed with flying colors. But after the war, and particularly after Stalin's death, the system began to exhaust itself.

Alexander Galkin,
sociologist

Source: Lev Rozgon, Fydor Burlatsky, and Alexander Galkin, as quoted in "Soviet Union died of lies" by Michael Dobbs © 1992 *The Washington Post.* Reprinted with permission.

Chapter 42 Review

SUMMARY

As the 1990's began, President Mikhail Gorbachev's reforms failed to halt economic decline and ethnic unrest throughout the Soviet Union. In the summer of 1991, communist hardliners overthrew Gorbachev in an effort to return the country to traditional communist ways. Public resistance led by Boris Yeltsin and other reformers thwarted this attempt.

After the coup's failure, an anticommunist movement swept the country, ending 74 years of rule by the Communist party. By late December, the continued spread of nationalism had led to the breakup of the Soviet Union, Gorbachev's resignation, and the formation of a loosely tied Commonwealth of Independent States. Boris Yeltsin and other Commonwealth republic leaders faced continuing problems in trying to move their economies from communism to capitalism.

USING VOCABULARY

Imagine that you are a Soviet citizen who has experienced the upheaval in your country during the early 1990's. Explain the changes that have occurred with sentences that use each of the terms below.

nationalities   coup

REVIEWING FACTS

1. **Explain** how *glasnost* heightened nationalist feeling in the Soviet Union.
2. **Point out** how the coup and its failure affected both Gorbachev and Yeltsin.
3. **Name** the three republics that led the movement toward the creation of the Commonwealth of Independent States.

4. **Summarize** the defense agreement reached by Commonwealth leaders.

CRITICAL THINKING

1. **Identifying Alternatives** While in power, Mikhail Gorbachev followed a middle course between communist hardliners and democratic reformers. If early on Gorbachev had broken all ties to the Communists and had pushed strongly for his reforms, could he have avoided the breakup of the Soviet Union and his political decline? Give reasons for your answer.
2. **Recognizing Ideologies** Boris Yeltsin and the other Commonwealth leaders are moving ahead to build their economies on capitalist principles. Do you think their reforms will be successful? Why or why not?
3. **Predicting Consequences** The Commonwealth of Independent States is a loose alliance of independent, sovereign, and equal republics. Russia, however, is by far the largest republic in land area, population, and natural resources. Do you believe that Russia's strong position will put strains on Commonwealth of Independent States unity? Explain.

ANALYZING CONCEPTS

1. **Power** How did coup leaders try to seize power from Gorbachev?
2. **Choice** How have Commonwealth of Independent States citizens coped with economic crisis?

GEOGRAPHIC THEMES

1. **Movement** Why were reformers able to organize resistance to the coup?
2. **Place** How did the coup's collapse affect many Soviet towns and cities?

Predicting Consequences

Every action or decision produces logical outcomes, or consequences. To *predict consequences*, first imagine all the possible outcomes of a decision or action. Then evaluate which consequences are most likely to occur. Projecting possible outcomes in advance allows you to make better decisions.

But how do you actually accomplish this? After all, no one can really see into the future. Instead, you must gather information about the situation and use your knowledge of past events to predict future ones. For example, after years of studying storms, weather forecasters now know that they occur when low and high pressure areas collide. Past experience enables them to predict future storms. The more information you have about a situation, the better your predictions will be.

The following steps will help you to predict consequences:
- Gather information about the decision or action.
- Use your knowledge of history and human behavior to identify possible consequences.
- Analyze each possible consequence by asking: How likely is it that this will occur? Predict consequences for different groups of people involved in the decision or action.

EXAMPLE

Think about the political situation in the Soviet Union in the summer of 1991. Although Gorbachev was president and head of the Communist party, there were pressures on him from all sides. Democratic reformers wanted change to happen more quickly. Some republics wanted independence. Meanwhile, communist hardliners predicted that Gorbachev's reforms would cause the collapse of the Soviet Union and communism. To avoid this, they took a drastic action; they ousted Gorbachev from power by a military coup. They predicted that this action would keep the Soviet Union together and maintain communist control.

Unfortunately for the hardliners, their predictions were wrong. Instead of accepting the rule of force as they had in the past, the Soviet people staged mass demonstrations. Eventually, the coup leaders were arrested and Gorbachev was returned to power. What other consequences followed the unsuccessful coup? *(Yeltsin became the reform leader, the Soviet people rejected the Communist party's leadership, and the Soviet Union broke up.)* In this case, the coup leaders' action had exactly the opposite consequences from those they had predicted.

PRACTICE

Read each passage below and then answer the questions that follow:

1. *Under the Communist party's leadership, the Soviet Union had a planned economy. The central government decided what was produced, where it was produced and distributed, and how much it cost. Basic necessities such as food, clothing, housing, health care, and education were provided at low cost to most citizens. In the new Commonwealth of Independent States (CIS), under a free-market economy, private owners can charge whatever people will pay for these goods and services.*

   a. What information would help you make predictions about this situation?

   b. Predict three or more consequences of these economic changes on average consumers.

   c. Which of these consequences is most likely to occur?

2. *Before 1991, there were two nuclear superpowers: the United States and the Soviet Union. When wars erupted in smaller countries, the superpowers often supported and supplied arms to opposing sides and, thus, maintained a balance of power in the world. Now that the Soviet Union has dissolved, the United States is the only nuclear superpower.*

   a. Predict three or more consequences of these changes on international relations.

   b. Which of these consequences is most likely to occur?

People and Places to Know
Russia, Ukraine, Belarus, Moldova, Moscow, Kiev, Minsk, Chişinău

Key Terms to Define
sovkhozes, kolkhozes

Objectives to Learn

1. **Identify** and distinguish the European republics.
2. **Explain** the status of religion and culture in the European republics.
3. **Characterize** urban lifestyle in the European republics.
4. **Describe** the condition of agriculture in the European republics.

Russian dacha, *or summer cottage*

The European Republics

> "Mikhail I. Stepanov and his wife, Natasha, are a particularly striking example of the intermingling of old patterns of Russian life with the new.
>
> Mikhail . . . has what at first seems to be a typical worker's existence under the old regime: regular hours at an institute cafeteria, access to certain bargains and small privileges, a taste for vodka and television and a hectic, crowded home life . . . in a small, three-room apartment in which his in-laws and his wife and their two young children all live.
>
> But the substructure of his life has changed fundamentally, in ways he does not always understand.
>
> The cafeteria in which he works . . . used to be Cafeteria No. 20 of the Kirovsky District.
>
> Now it is Cafeteria No. 20—Avangard, a fancy new name for the newly privatized business, which issued shares to its workers last September. . . .
>
> Pushed by Natasha, Mikhail bought 8,000 rubles' worth of shares in the cafeteria, all they felt they could afford. . . .
>
> Previously, Mikhail said, unless they lived with Natasha's parents, they could not get by. . . . But forced by circumstances, and suddenly finding a talent within herself, Natasha began to make clothes for her friends. . . .
>
> In the last three months, she said proudly as she pulled out examples of her own designs, she has made a profit of 26,000 rubles, over six times her husband's take-home pay. . . .
>
> In September, in fulfillment of a long dream, they expect to move into an apartment of their own, in a cooperative now being built."

M any changes have been taking place in the lives of Mikhail and Natasha Stepanov. The Stepanovs, who are in their twenties, live in Moscow in Russia, the largest of the four European republics. The changes and challenges experienced by this couple have been echoed all over Russia as well as the other three European republics—Ukraine, Belarus, and Moldova.

In these republics, as elsewhere in the former Soviet Union, the breakup of the Soviet Union impacted almost every facet of life. It led to a reemergence of religion and made necessary new strategies for the arts. Equally important, it led to change in lifestyle and in the workplace and on the farm.

Source: Steven Erlanger. "In Choppy Russian Economy, A Family Jury-Rigs a Budget" in *The New York Times,* July 20, 1992, pp. A1, A7. Copyright © 1992 by The New York Times Company. Reprinted by permission.

The Republics

Spreading from the Baltic Sea to the shores of the Pacific Ocean is Russia, the largest and richest of the European republics. More than half of all the peoples of the Commonwealth live in Russia. Making up its population of nearly 150 million people are over 100 nationalities, or ethnic groups, that together speak 80 different languages.

Most of the people—83 percent—are Russians, however. The Russians are a complex people with a deep sense of spirituality. Some Russians see themselves as "long on debating, arguing, philosophizing, or reciting poetry" and "good at feasting, drinking, toasting, and talking deep into the night."

Below, a noted writer gives his impressions of the Russian character:

I have found Russians generally to be a warm and sentimental people. One reason many Russians don't especially like the Baltic peoples—Estonians, Lithuanians, and Latvians—is that they find them too cool and reserved, too self-contained. . . . Russians are more emotional, more likely to strike deep friendships. . . . They make great sacrifices for those within their trusted circle, and they expect real sacrifices in return. Their willingness, indeed their eagerness, to engage at a personal level makes private life in Russia both enormously rich and incredibly entangling.

Source: Hedrick Smith. *The New Russians.* Random House, 1990, pp. 181–182.

THE EUROPEAN REPUBLICS					
Republic (Date Independence Declared)	Capital	Population Estimates	Ethnic Groups	Major Products	Before U.S.S.R. Breakup
Russia (6/12/90)	Moscow	149,386,000	83% Russian more than 100 ethnic groups	chemicals, building materials, machine steel, cars, trucks, wheat, barley, rye, potatoes, sugar beets	76.6 % land 51.4 % pop. 61.1% GNP
Ukraine (8/24/91)	Kiev	51,704,000	74% Ukrainian 21% Russian 1% Jewish	wheat, sugar beets, iron, oil, chemicals, machinery	2.7% land 18.0% pop. 16.2% GNP
Belarus (8/25/91)	Minsk	10,200,000	79% Byelorussian 12% Russian 4% Polish 2% Ukrainian 1% Jewish	chemicals, agricultural machinery, paper, building materials, potatoes, livestock	1.0% land 3.5% pop. 4.2% GNP
Moldova (8/27/91)	Chişinău	4,521,000	65% Moldovan 14% Ukrainian 13% Russian	wines, tobacco, grain, vegetables	0.2% land 1.5% pop. 1.2% GNP

EXAMINING CHARTS *The people of the European republics make up most of the population of the C.I.S.* **What are the three largest ethnic groups in the European republics?**

EXAMINING PHOTOGRAPHS *The ethnic Russians are the largest Slavic group in the Commonwealth of Independent States. These young Russian girls are standing outside their home in the city of Ufa.* *What percentage of the people of the Russian Republic are ethnic Russians?*

Just south and west of Russia lie two other European republics—Ukraine and Belarus. Ukraine, with its fertile, black soil, has the Commonwealth's richest land. For centuries, it has been known as the "breadbasket of Europe." Nearly 52 million people live in Ukraine. Of these, the greatest number—74 percent—are Ukrainian, while another 21 percent are Russian. Despite intense Russian influence over the years, the Ukrainians have remained fiercely proud of their own unique heritage. They have their own language. Their cultural heritage includes music, literature, especially poetry, and art. Faith also plays a large role in the Ukrainian heritage. A visiting journalist once remarked that, "The number who attend services is only a small fraction. But behind them is a thousand years of tradition."

Ukrainians proudly point out that Kiev was a capital when Moscow was "a wheel track in the forest." The leading center of traditional Ukrainian culture is the countryside, with its white-washed mud-brick and stone houses with thatched roofs hung with elaborate embroidery.

Smaller in size than Ukraine, Belarus was formerly Byelorussia. With a population of a little more than 10 million people, it is home to about 3.5 percent of the total Commonwealth population. Close to 80 percent of the people are Byelorussians. Like the Russians and the Ukrainians, the Byelorussians are descendants of Slavic groups who settled northern central Europe in prehistoric times. Once ruled by Poland, the people have a strong Polish influence in their culture.

The fourth and smallest European republic is Moldova, formerly Moldavia. The 4.5 million people who live in the primarily rural republic are 65 percent Moldovan, 14 percent Ukrainian, and 13 percent Russian. The majority of Moldovans are Romanians, originally from the Bessarabia region of Romania, and speak Romanian. According to one British writer, despite Soviet efforts to "convert" the Moldovans, "they will never be anything but Romanian."

SECTION 1 REVIEW

CHECKING FOR UNDERSTANDING

1. **Name** the four European republics.
2. **Characterize** each of the European republics.

CRITICAL THINKING

3. **Making Comparisons** In what ways are the populations of the European republics the same? In what ways are they different?

SECTION 2

A Religious Awakening

Although the Soviet constitution granted people freedom of religion, officially the Soviet Union was atheistic, disbelieving in the existence of God. Religious beliefs were ridiculed in the press, believers were denied good jobs, religious activities were forbidden outside of places of worship, and many religious buildings were closed. In spite of this, many Soviet citizens clung to their religious beliefs, and with the collapse of communism they looked to religion for spiritual renewal. As one reporter notes below, the religious awakening was especially evident in Moscow:

The great bells of the soaring towers of Ivan the Great burst into life at midnight today, ringing in Easter for the first time in seven decades. . . .

Today, the search for spiritual content is everywhere evident. Huge banners declaring "Christ is Risen!" rise across Moscow, and in Red Square a giant icon depicts the Resurrection. . . .

All through the many church services of Holy Week . . . Russians from all walks of life have packed the churches. Some were believers, familiar with the rites and chants. Others had no inkling of the complex Byzantine rite. . . .

More than 6,000 churches have reopened over the last three years, and millions of Russians have come to be baptized, many as a first step in the search for a missing identity. Monasteries long used for factories or museums have returned to the life for which they were built; monks serve again at the great Novospassky Monastery. . . .

The search has hardly been limited to the Russian Church. Western evangelizers regularly draw large crowds for their crusades, young Jews gathered last week for Passover seders all across Moscow. . . .

On television, for every rare program on economic reform on television, there are at least 10 evocative documentaries on the church, the village or some other cultural heritage, in which the invariable theme is Russia's urgent need to recover its "dukhovnost," its spirituality. Even at the noisy Congress of Peoples' Deputies, the highest elected body in Russia, a debate over the state's proper name draws lengthy speeches on Russia's spiritual heritage.

SECTION 2 REVIEW

CHECKING FOR UNDERSTANDING
1. **Discuss** how the Soviet government viewed and dealt with religion.

CRITICAL THINKING
2. **Recognizing Ideologies** What is the current attitude toward religion in Russia?

SECTION 3

A New Cultural Landscape

Because the Soviet government believed that culture was an important tool in advancing the goals of communism, it actively-controlled cultural activities. At the same time, it promoted and supported a wide variety of cultural activities.

Today the citizens of the European republics remain devoted to all forms of the arts. But, when the Soviet Union ceased to exist, so did the cultural policy that provided extensive financial support for the arts. As can be seen in the article that follows, this has changed the cultural landscape in Russia:

The U.S.S.R.'s culture budget not only supported such institutions as . . . the Hermitage museum . . . but also subsidized festivals, exhibitions, foreign tours, and art classes in school, as well as publishing and theater in the languages of various minorities. . . . Such events are threatened now, and they may even disappear.

EXAMINING PHOTOGRAPHS *These Jewish men are reading Torah, or the sacred law, at Moscow's largest synagogue. What was the former Soviet Union's official policy toward religion?*

Source: Serge Schmemann. "An Awakened Church Finds Russia Searching for Its Soul" in *The New York Times*, April 26, 1992, p. 3. Copyright © 1992 by The New York Times Company. Reprinted by permission.

EXAMINING PHOTOGRAPHS
Russia's former Communist leaders discouraged free artistic expression. Today, Russian artists can freely paint and exhibit. Here, art students are painting at an open air museum in the city of Nizhni Novgorod. How have the arts become part of the ongoing disputes involving Russia and the other republics of the Commonwealth?

Another concern . . . is the demands from other former Soviet republics for the return of their heritage. Ukraine, for example, says that Russia is unjustly keeping some of its artistic treasures in Russian museums.

"The worse thing is the general demoralization (among artists)," says Vadim Gayevsky, a well-known writer on cultural issues. "But, on the other hand, a general housecleaning in our cultural life would be a good thing. Much of what is disappearing is nothing to cry about."

In artistic circles, what has created the most unrest is the government's list of cultural treasures—pieces of the national heritage—that must be preserved. These will receive special funding. On this list are the Kremlin, the Bolshoi Theater, the Hermitage, and the Moscow Conservatory. But critics question why the Moscow Art Theater and the Mariinsky Theater (the former Kirov Opera) and the Russian Museum in St. Petersburg were not included and why no signal has been given regard-

ing the preservation of a single symphony orchestra, or a folk-dance troupe, or even a monastery.

The name of the game in the new Russian cultural landscape is sponsorship. It is now obligatory to thank donors. . . . "We are glad not to be controlled by the ministry," says Vladimir Kokonin, director of the Bolshoi Theater. "But now we have to seek our own sources of financing, and, in part, that is already under way." A "Friends of the Bolshoi" group has been organized, he says. "Tapes and records will be sold commercially. We used to sell tickets to Intourist (the state travel bureau) for hard currency. Now we may set up a ticket kiosk for foreigners. We must take the money where we can find it."

A few blocks away from the Bolshoi is the Moscow Art Theater. . . . Its artistic director, Oleg Yefremov, just chuckles when I ask him about the Ministry of Culture's list. . . . "We will get by," he says.

Source: Dagens Nyheter. "Russia's New Cultural Landscape" in *World Press Review*, May 1992, p. 33.

Writers, editors, and publishers, too, faced major change. Many wrote and published for the state, receiving high government salaries and other benefits for producing works that glorified Soviet society and communist goals and accomplishments. Now they are not government-subsidized, and the people want a different kind of literature, such as detective stories and science fiction. According to one Russian writer, Lev Novogrudsky, the subject of the newspaper article that follows, "Times have never been as difficult for writers as they are now":

Lev Novogrudsky used to spend three months a year in various retreats belonging to the Union of Soviet Writers.

In these places, called Houses of Cre-

ativity, . . . he wrote plays for children, far from the annoying realities of Soviet life, living out a writer's dream courtesy of Litfund, the union's literary aid society.

"I spent one third of my life in those places," Mr. Novogrudsky said, "I had my own room. No one bothered me. I didn't have the responsibilities that consume most people—all in comfortable surroundings, in the company of other writers. It made life beautiful."

Now those days are gone. . . . The Union of Soviet Writers, now the Commonwealth of Writers' Unions, is in disarray. Litfund is on the verge of bankruptcy, and the old privileges . . . have become unaffordable luxuries for ordinary writers like Mr. Novogrudsky. . . .

There are a few hopeful voices. At Text, a private publishing house, Vitaly T. Babenko is too busy working to lament the passing of the trappings of the old regime.

"It is difficult for everyone now, so why should it be any different for writers," he said. "Life is difficult for doctors, teachers, and yes, writers. But there is no blow to literature or culture. Real writers are writing, and they don't feel any blows. If we are really moving toward a market, then culture too will benefit. What we have now is a temporary situation."

EXAMINING PHOTOGRAPHS *Today, some of the world's leading ballet schools are found in the cities of Russia, especially in St. Petersburg.* *How have recent political changes affected the arts in Russia?*

SECTION 3 REVIEW

CHECKING FOR UNDERSTANDING
1. **State** the concerns Russians have regarding culture.
2. **Explain** why many Russian writers, editors, and publishers are experiencing difficulties.

CRITICAL THINKING
3. **Drawing Conclusions** Why do you think some people feel that "The market [economy] threatens to become the grave of culture."?

Source: Celestine Bohlen. "Once-Privileged Writers Share the Russian Pain Now" in *The New York Times,* March 22, 1992, p. 6. Copyright © 1992 by The New York Times Company. Reprinted by permission.

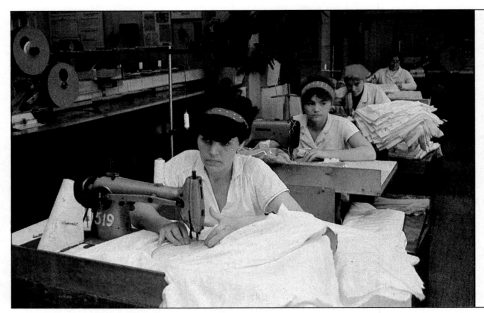

SECTION 4

In the Cities

During much of their history, the European republics of Russia, Ukraine, Belarus, and Moldova—as well as the rest of the former Soviet Union—were largely rural. Industrial development, however, changed the appearance of the landscape. City populations swelled and new cities were built as workers swarmed from villages to cities and from farms to factories. Today, of the capitals of the four European republics—Moscow, Kiev, Minsk, and Chisinău—only the Moldovan capital of Chișinău has fewer than 1 million people.

Industry brought many people to the cities and determined their lifestyles. But, because of the economic restructuring that has been taking place in the republics, some industries no longer exist, and those that do are not the same as they were before. An American journalist who toured the Commonwealth with an Ohio farm delegation reports on what she discovered during a visit to a tractor factory in Minsk:

Officials at the Belarus tractor factory . . . weren't sure they wanted Ohio farmers touring their plant. . . .

Jaroslaw Romanchuk, manager-in-chief of the Department of Foreign Affairs for the Union of Entrepreneurs of the Republic of Belarus, explained the officials' reticence.

About 70 percent of the plant's production was used for tanks and military components. Now there are no orders from the military, Romanchuk said, and at least part of the plant faces closure. Some 3,000 of the 30,000 workers could lose their jobs, and the three-shift, 24-hour-a-day production line is likely to drop to a four-day workweek.

Visitors saw the main tractor assembly line humming, however. Lines of reddish-orange and blue parts moved through the noisy, cavernous plant, with one tractor rolling off the line every 3 ½ minutes. Each tractor takes 1 ½ hours to complete, Michael Meleshko, deputy managing designer, said. . . .

Many factories in the former Soviet

Union have been hurt by the breakup into individual countries, because suppliers of components and parts were scattered across the country.

Meleshko said nearly all of the factory's 300 suppliers are located in Belarus, and that finding components was not a problem. . . .

Before *perestroika,* factories were required to turn over 90 percent of profits to the state. Now Belarus can keep 50 percent of its profits.

Some of that money is used to purchase Western goods, such as clothing, VCRs and refrigerators, which are then made available for the workers to purchase. . . .

Safety did not seem to be a concern at the plant. Workers did not wear hard hats or safety glasses, although heavy machinery moved about them. Water puddled on the floor.

EXAMINING PHOTOGRAPHS *Kiev, the capital of Ukraine, is today a crowded urban center. What factors encouraged people to move to cities?*

Source: Suzanne Steel. "Tractors plow field of capitalist dreams." Reprinted, with permission, from *The Columbus* (Ohio) *Dispatch.*

Among the industries affected is the building industry. Housing had long been a problem in most cities. Not only was there a serious shortage of housing, but the typical apartment had been designed to allow each person a living space of only 10 feet (3.04 meters) by 10 feet (3.04 meters). Now, with governmental changes and shortages of building supplies, the problem is even greater. As the article that follows points out, finding an apartment in Moscow can be a frustrating experience:

The only thing two-and-a-half-year-old Mitya lacks is space: His desire to move around is great, but his quarters are cramped. Mitya lives with his parents, Lena and Sasha Sorokin, in a one-room, 180-square-foot apartment. . . . Sasha has been looking for a larger apartment for some time now. Last year alone, he spent 15 weeks looking. Nothing turned up.

The Sorokins first placed their hopes on an apartment swap. They both have Ph.D. degrees in sociology and earn a good living. They had stashed away a few thousand rubles to be used in an exchange. They issued announcements, hired a broker, and negotiated with would-be takers, but it was all in vain. . . .

With a little luck . . . , Sasha found an in. A broker . . . made him a "good offer"—a two-bedroom apartment for $30,000, in hard currency. The offer did not seem entirely out of the question. But where could he get the money quickly? The banks, which cannot pay their own debts on time, could not be expected to extend him any credit in dollars.

In his despair, Sasha thought of an acquaintance. . . . This man had made a fortune. . . . But . . . the former comrade turned down Sasha's plea for a loan. . . .

Despite efforts by Moscow Mayor Gavril Popov to privatize the housing market, corruption and control remain the weapons of the housing bureaucracy. . . . Sasha explains how this bureaucracy functions as we stand before a huge bulletin

EXAMINING PHOTOGRAPHS *New houses, like these in central Russia, reflect the greater concern given by government officials to meeting the needs of ordinary citizens. Many Russians, however, still have to cope with housing shortages, inadequate housing space, and other substandard living conditions. What is the average living space for the typical apartment dweller?*

board covered with forms bearing the names of every citizen who has been granted an apartment in 1991. Just who comes to this board and when is decided by the city authorities alone. In 1991, the 10-15 families granted apartments had waited only two or three years. Single mothers, families with many children, and mentally ill people have to wait significantly longer. . . . Bringing up the rear are families with "normal requirements"—that is, no special characteristics. They must wait the longest—10 years or more. . . .

. . . Sasha even tried . . . to cut the waiting time by offering gifts and money, but he was sent packing. . . .

One last way to get an apartment is through large enterprises that build rental housing for their employees. But those who have chosen the "wrong occupations"—including teachers, doctors, artists, and sociologists—seldom find fi-

nancially sound employers who build and rent apartments. That is why, at the end of last year, the Sorokins finally gave up their apartment hunt.

SECTION 4 REVIEW

CHECKING FOR UNDERSTANDING

1. **Give examples** of changes in the tractor factory in Minsk and in the lives of the people who work there.
2. **Describe** how people are chosen to get apartments in Moscow.

CRITICAL THINKING

3. **Determining Cause and Effect** In what ways have governmental changes and economic restructuring affected urban industry and housing?

Source: Mária Huber. "A Desperate Search for Apartments" from "Die Zeit" of Hamburg in *World Press Review,* April 1992, p. 21.

SECTION 5

In the Countryside

Under the Soviets, most people who lived in rural areas worked on government-controlled farms—*sovkhozes*, huge state farms, or *kolkhozes*, large collective farms. The government allowed some workers from these farms to tend small private gardens and sell the produce in city markets.

With the end of the communist system, the farms and the workers themselves became responsible for their futures. A journalist tells what happened at a state farm in Russia:

Soft shoots of green have begun to emerge from the brown fields of Volochanova State Farm, but that is little cause for optimism among the workers who for years have tended the plots.

"Today we are on the verge of bankruptcy," Volochanova's director, Sergei Filipov, says glumly, as he surveys the early results of the spring planting season. . . .

Prices are so high now that the farm cannot replace broken equipment or do major repairs. Old, ailing tractors will be left to rust when they fail for lack of repairs. The milking equipment's woeful state has hampered production. . . .

Spring planting is on schedule, but the farm has fuel for only another month or so. . . .

Volochanova's stock of feed for cattle and pigs is also low. . . . Animal feed on the free market is priced out of reach for Volochanova. . . .

Two families from the farm have already opted out. . . .

This is a policy that many in Volochanova do not understand or sympathize with. "People have to eat. The country needs my produce," Filipov says. . . .

"I'm sure we will be able to survive until the end of this year," he says. "But if

EXAMINING PHOTOGRAPHS *This former collective farm in the Novosibirsk region of Siberia is now run by private shareholders. How was farming practiced under the old Soviet system?*

there are no more subsidies from the state, we will be ruined."[1]

Like many farmers in the republics, the two families that "opted out" started their own farms. Below, a journalist reports on a Ukrainian farmer who made the same decision:

[Vladimir] Kravchenko is one of a tiny, but growing breed of farmers working to possess and farm their own land.

It hasn't been easy. The frustration shows on his face and in his voice; at other times his optimism shines through. . . .

It took him two months of meetings with collective farm chairmen and governmental officials near Teplik, Ukraine, to get permission to own and rent land that had already been promised.

Finally, two weeks ago, he got word that he would be permitted to buy 100 acres

---

[1]*Source:* Margaret Shapiro. "In Russia, The End of the Row For Collective Farming" in *The Washington Post National Weekly Edition,* June 1–7, 1992, p. 16, © 1992, *The Washington Post.* Reprinted with permission.

EXAMINING PHOTOGRAPHS *A farmer and his grandson are stacking hay in the Penza region of Russia. Under the government's recent privatization measures, Russian farmers are able to own, sell, rent, or inherit land. What difficulties has private ownership brought to farmers?*

and rent 800 acres from a nearby collective farm, and began working it this fall after the harvest.

While Kravchenko now has the support of the county president . . . most bureaucrats are threatened by the loss of power that privatization brings.

Vladimir Krut, vice president of the Ukrainian Academy of Agricultural Sciences, said the government had to be careful of who is allowed to privatize, because farmers would only ruin the land. . . .

Kravchenko said officials at the collective farm that finally granted him land were resistant and angry. . . .

Often private farmers are given small bits of acreage located here and there, miles apart from each other.

Kravchenko, however, is happy with the productivity and location of the land he was granted—all 900 acres are located in one rectangle. . . .

This land will belong to him, in the true sense of the word. He will be able to sell it, rent it to another farmer, or pass it on. . . .

He believes that his profits will be 10 times those of the collective's. . . .

His costs, especially for labor, . . . will be lower. Kravchenko believes at least 25 percent of collective farm workers don't really work.

Now he must jump the next hurdle: financing.

He estimated he will need about $50,000 for land, machinery and labor the first year . . . a fortune when you consider the average salary in the former Soviet Union ranges between 1,500 to 4,000 rubles per month, $11 to $30.

The two banks Kravchenko has contacted so far said he can have all the money he wants, but he's not celebrating. One wants 45 percent interest with repayment in two years. The other offered financing at 11 percent—but only if he agrees to give up a full 25 percent of his profits for the rest of his life.

SECTION 5 REVIEW

CHECKING FOR UNDERSTANDING

1. **Define** *sovkhozes, kolkhozes.*
2. **Speculate** about why farms like Volochanova are failing.

CRITICAL THINKING

3. **Demonstrating Reasoned Judgment** As a farmer in Ukraine or Russia, would you start your own farm? Why or why not?

Source: Suzanne Steel. "Privatizing tests mettle of Russians." Reprinted with permission, from *The Columbus* (Ohio) *Dispatch.*

Cultural Values

A SENSE OF IDENTITY

The breakup of the Soviet Union turned out to be more painful than many of its citizens expected. As a Moscow University graduate points out below, the confusion and frustration is not just a question of borders.

FOCUSING ON THE ISSUE Based on the article and on the information in the chapter, write an editorial explaining what you would do to help people regain a sense of place, of purpose, and of identity.

I have reached the end of my tether. It is a terrible feeling: the sense of a dead end. A sense of helplessness in the face of what is happening. . . . I am trying to analyze where it comes from. On the first level is the everyday routine: waiting in line, prices and "STP" (streetcar-trolleybus psychosis). I have the sense . . . of being homeless. I do not own my own apartment, and now I evidently never will have one. . . . The second level is emotional hunger. The rupture of friendships that once seemed strong, the incredible embitterment of the crowds in the street, the alienation among people, even the closest rela-tives. . . . The third level is about the meaning of existence. I am not sure that anything I have done up to now has had meaning. . . .

Some political events (for example, the creation of some kind of community of former Soviet republics) bring a glimmer of hope. Perhaps people will realize that even though everything has been eaten, consumed, divided, and despoiled, we must rebuild our house at any cost, without looking back at either Lenin or Stalin. . . . The issue is really survival, both spiritual and physical. . . .

A very painful blow has been dealt to people who are used to living in the "Soviet" manner. The state has abandoned them, leaving them on their own to resolve problems not only of personal happiness but also of housing and sustenance. Our people were not prepared. . . .

The time has come when life is no longer explained from on high. People have to find meanings for themselves.

Source: Vasily Golovanov. "A Deep Despair in Yeltsin's Russia" from "Literaturnaya Gazeta" in *World Press Review,* April 1992, pp. 18, 20, 21.

Chapter 43 Review

SUMMARY

With the collapse of the Soviet Union, four independent European republics emerged—Russia, Ukraine, Belarus, and Moldova. With the exception of Moldova, these republics have predominantly Slavic populations.

Like the people who populate them, the republics differ in size, appearance, and personality. All, however, have been challenged by governmental changes and the restructuring of the economy. The result of the upheaval has been a religious awakening, new outlooks and tactics for ensuring preservation and continued growth of the arts, new priorities in the workplace, and privatization of both industries and farms.

USING VOCABULARY

Use the terms below in a short paragraph that tells how life has changed in the European republics since the Soviet collapse.

sovkhozes   kolkhozes

REVIEWING FACTS

1. **Name** the largest and richest European republic.
2. **Name** the European republic that is known as the "breadbasket of Europe."
3. **Identify** the nationality of the people of the Moldovan republic.
4. **Indicate** what was the policy of the former Communist government toward religion.
5. **Speculate** about why there is an awakening of religion in the republics.
6. **Specify** the major reason for the changing cultural landscape in the republics.
7. **Explain** why there is an urban housing shortage, especially in Moscow.

8. **Identify** who is responsible for the futures of the republics' farms and farm workers.

CRITICAL THINKING

1. **Drawing Conclusions** Russia is the most powerful of all the republics. What reasons can you give for this?
2. **Demonstrating Reasoned Judgment** Some state farms and collectives have tried to find foreign investors to subsidize them. Explain why, if you were the head of a foreign corporation, you would or would not consider such an investment.
3. **Predicting Consequences** Since they became independent republics, there has been a struggle for dominance between Russia and Ukraine. If the rivalry continues and grows, what might it mean for the future of the Commonwealth?
4. **Making Generalizations** Based on the information in the chapter, make two generalizations about religion and culture in the European republics.

ANALYZING CONCEPTS

1. **Change** What two major factors contributed most to the many changes that have been taking place in the European republics?
2. **Choice** What option do industrial workers and farmers have now that they did not have under the Soviet system?

GEOGRAPHIC THEMES

1. **Place** Which republic has the Commonwealth's richest land?
2. **Location** Where are Ukraine and Belarus located in relation to Russia?

Analyzing Newspaper Articles

Newspaper articles provide information about both current and past events. The purpose of a news article is to present facts *objectively*. To do this, news writers must check the accuracy and reliability of their information. Instead of giving their own opinions, news writers quote the opinions of other people, who are called *sources*. A balanced news story includes two or more conflicting opinions.

News articles begin with a *headline*—an attention-getting phrase that captures the main point of the story. Many news stories also have *bylines*, giving the writer's name or the news service that furnished the story. Sometimes they contain *datelines* telling when and where the story was written.

The *lead*, or first, paragraph of a news story summarizes the essential facts. It usually contains answers to the "five W" questions—who, what, where, when, and why. The other paragraphs provide supporting details, explanation, and comments. Here are some steps to follow in analyzing newspaper articles:

- Read the headline to find the main idea.
- Using the byline and dateline, identify the writer's name and origin of the article.
- Find answers to the "five W" questions in the first and second paragraphs.
- Determine what conflicting opinions are given about the subject.

EXAMPLE

Read the newspaper article beginning on page 712. The author, headline, newspaper, and publication date are given in a footnote on page 713. What is the headline of this article? (*"Tractors plow field of capitalist dreams"*) Which of the "five W" questions are answered in the first paragraph? (*who—factory officials, Ohio farmers; what—touring a tractor factory; where—Belarus*) What is the main point of this article? (*to show how independence has affected factories in Belarus*) What sources provided information? (*Jaroslaw Romanchuk, Union of Entrepreneurs, Republic of Belarus; Michael Meleshko, deputy managing designer*)

PRACTICE

Read the following newspaper article and answer the questions that follow.

United Nations Observers Arrive in War-torn Moldova
Associated Press

CHIŞINĂU, Moldova—UN observers arrived yesterday as clashes between Slavic separatists and Moldovan forces in the Trans-Dniester region of Moldova left seven people dead and more than 20 wounded, officials said. . . .

Both sides in the escalating conflict between Moldovans and ethnic Russians welcomed the three-member UN delegation and pledged cooperation to end the fighting.

According to reports, up to 300 people have been killed and hundreds more wounded in the past week in Trans-Dniester. . . . Gilberto Schittler, head of the UN delegation, said that during a three-day stay the group 'hopes to get in touch with all the parties concerned and listen to their views on all the aspects of the problem.'

Moldovans have accused the Russian troops of aiding the separatists, but the Russian government said the soldiers were acting on their own.

Trans-Dniester's 600,000 ethnic Russians and Ukrainians have declared independence from Moldova for fear the republic will reunite with Romania. Moldova has refused to relinquish Trans-Dniester.

1. According to the headline, what is the main point of this article?
2. Where does this story come from?
3. Which of the "five W" questions are answered in the lead paragraph?
4. What conflicting views are presented?
5. What sources are quoted in the story?

Source: Boston Sunday Globe, Boston, Massachusetts, June 28, 1992, p. 15.

CHAPTER OUTLINE

1 Armenia

2 Azerbaijan

3 Georgia

People and Places to Know

Caucasus Mountains, the Caucasus, Yerevan, Baku, the Azeris, Nagorno-Karabakh, Black Sea, Tbilisi, the Ossetians

Objectives to Learn

1. **Compare** the religious and ethnic composition of the republics of the Caucasus.
2. **Describe** the people of the Caucasus.
3. **Summarize** the political situation in the Caucasus.

Traditional mountain village in Georgia

Republics of the Caucasus

> " The Caucasus lay spread before our gaze,
> An unmade bed, it seemed, with tousled sheets. . . .
> Massed in the mist and out of sorts, it reared
> The steady malice of its icy crests. . . .

Those words were written in 1931 by (Russian author and poet) Boris Pasternak. If the poet seems ambivalent in his imagery—the comfort of a tousled bed, the malice of ice—he reacts like history itself: The Caucasus Mountains have alternately protected and punished the peoples who live in the three constituent republics of the Transcaucasus—Georgia, Azerbaijan, and Armenia. There is no wonder that these folk should differ in attitude, custom, and even chemistry from people of the northern steppes. For one thing, they are Asian.

"Not true! We are not Asian," insisted a pretty Georgian girl named Nana. But wasn't Georgia south of the Caucasus? "Who said that's the boundary? Everyone says Mount Elbrus is the highest point in Europe. And look in this book: 'Georgians . . . belong to the Europoid race'."

I backed away from that argument. The people of each Transcaucasian republic have their own ethnic specialties: Through history, Georgians have been Christian and defensively European; Armenians defensively Christian but vividly Asian; and Azerbaijanians contentedly Asian and Muslim. With all their differences, the three peoples still provide a kind of colorful, clashing unity. "

Nearly 2 decades have passed and much has changed since the writer who penned the words above took his journey across Russia. Then, Georgia, Armenia, and Azerbaijan accounted for 3 of the 15 republics that made up the Soviet Union. Now, all 3 are independent states, and one of them—Armenia—is a member of the Common-

Source: Bart McDowell. *Journey Across Russia*, © 1977, National Geographic Society, p. 219.

wealth of Independent States. Georgia decided not to become a member when the Commonwealth was formed. Azerbaijan at first was a member but later withdrew.

What has not changed, however, is the makeup and character of each of the three republics. Each has been strongly influenced by the history, culture, and religion of the ethnic groups that populate it. In each, this ethnic diversity has created strife.

Armenia

Armenia, which is home to a little more than 3.6 million people, is the smallest republic of the Commonwealth. Along with Azerbaijan and Georgia, it lies south of the Caucasus (KAW· kuh·suhs) Mountains, between the Black and Caspian seas, in a wide neck of land called the Caucasus. The present-day capital of Yerevan (yehr·UH·vuhn) is located on the bank of the Razdan River in the Ararat valley. Founded in 782 BC, it is one of the most ancient cities in the world.

LINKS TO THE PAST

Armenia is a land with a long and violent history punctuated by a seemingly endless series of invasions and massacres. Romans, Persians, Byzantines, Turks, Mongols, and Russians—all have left their mark. History—and heritage—is very important to the ethnic Armenians who make up about 90 percent of the nation's population. In the words of one Armenian, "We never forget the good done us. Nor the bad, for we have merciless enemies. Our character is like our climate: sharply continental. We love or hate strongly." Below, a noted journalist shares what he discovered about Armenian ties to the past and the Armenian character:

The Armenians I met . . . saw their history as an open wound, an injustice awaiting redress. The most important monument in modern Armenia sits on top of a hill called Tsitsernakaberd, or the Castle of the Sparrows, a mile or two from the center of Yerevan. On clear days, the site affords a view of Mr. Ararat. The monument itself is simple and impressive. It consists of a steep, bifurcated [forked] gray pyramid rising abruptly from the ground at the end of a long concrete plaza. Next to it are twelve stone slabs, arranged in a circle and tilted to form an open dome around a gas flame. All the stone surfaces are blank; no words are etched anywhere.

EXAMINING PHOTOGRAPHS
Armenians by the thousands gather at the monument of Tsiternakaberd outside of Yerevan, the capital of the Republic of Armenia. The monument commemorates the Genocide of 1915, in which millions of Armenians perished as a result of Ottoman Turkish policies. What theme has been prominent in Armenian history?

The government of Armenia permitted the construction of the monument after thousands of Armenians dared to march and protest to commemorate the fiftieth anniversary of the Genocide of 1915, and to demand some sort of official recognition of the massacres. . . . The monument is entirely abstract. Nevertheless, Armenians know exactly what it is about. The pyramid, a young woman named Hasmik Khurshudyan told me, represents the bifurcated peak of Ararat. The twelve stone slabs represent the twelve Armenian provinces lost in Turkey. The slabs tilt over the flame as if bent in grief, and represent the sorrow of the nation. The flame, of course, is the memory of those who have perished.

At Yerevan State University, I dropped in one day on the chairman of the Psychology Department, Ruben Aguzumtsyan. . . . When I asked him about the Armenian national character, he replied that he was not a specialist in that subject but he did have a few general opinions. The exigencies of climate and terrain, he said, had forced Armenians to become smart and hardworking. "Just to live, a man has to expend enormous energy, because the territory is steep and mountainous, and the plains where it's possible to live and grow things are very small. People have had to carry dirt on their backs up mountainsides, spread it out, then plant something. It's hellish work." The long history of strife and suffering had further tempered them, he added.

I asked how Armenians conveyed that history—particularly the history of 1915.

"It's hard for me even to remember how I learned about it," he replied. . . . "We have a fine tradition of education by parents on national themes. Even the littlest kid must know in general terms the history of the nation. It reflects a self-defense mechanism, self-preservation."

Source: Robert Cullen. "A Reporter at Large: Roots". Reprinted by permission; © 1991 Robert Cullen. Originally in *The New Yorker.*

THE CHURCH

In the 300's AD, Armenia became one of the first nations to adopt Christianity as a state religion. Today, as then, most Armenians are members of the Armenian Apostolic Church. As the theologian who wrote the following article discovered, in Armenia religious faith and nationalist sentiment are intertwined:

The bishop of Yerevan in Armenia, Karekin Nersissian, is a young and enormously energetic man. He has responded to the revival of faith among Armenian youth by almost literally turning over to them his diocesan building and the parish church of St. Sarkis. They come to sing and dance, learn the ancient hymns and study Scripture. The parents complain that the children are neglecting their school work. The young people hurry to the church in the afternoons and evenings to attend meetings and practices. An inspired group of high school and college students edit the journal. . . . The bishop spends several hours a day with those youth in Bible studies and discussions of their projects.

During my visit this past spring Bishop Karekin organized a pilgrimage for the youth and their families. Three hundred people piled into buses and cars and made an hour-and-a-half trip some 7,000 feet up into the foothills of snow-capped Mt. Aragats. . . . Our destination was the church of the medieval fortress of Amberd, which dates from the 11th to the 13th centuries. . . .

I arranged two lengthy afternoon Bible discussions with the cadre of young church activists at St. Sarkis to talk about what it means to be a Christian and Armenian. I asked the students if they might begin with a scriptural passage that was important to them. Psalm 68:11 was selected at the first meeting. "The Lord gives the command;/great is the company of those who/bore the tidings." What did

THE REPUBLICS OF THE CAUCASUS					
Republic (Date Independence Declared)	Capital	Population Estimates	Ethnic Groups	Major Products	Before U.S.S.R. Breakup
Armenia (9/23/91)	Yerevan	3,605,000	90% Armenian 5% Azeri 5% Russian	chemicals, machinery, textiles, grapes	0.2 % land 1.2 % pop. .9% GNP
Azerbaijan (8/30/91)	Baku	7,145,600	78% Azeri 9% Russian 9% Armenian 4% Daghestani	oil, copper, chemicals, cotton, rice, grapes, tobacco, silk	0.3% land 2.4% pop. 1.7% GNP
Georgia (8/23/91)	Tbilisi	5,588,000	70% Georgian 9% Armenian 10% Russian	tea, citrus fruits, grapes, silk, tobacco, manganese, coal	0.3% land 1.9% pop. 1.6% GNP

EXAMINING CHARTS *A variety of ethnic groups live in the republics of the Caucasus—Armenia, Azerbaijan, and Georgia. What are the major products of the Caucasus republics?*

this say to them? Armen spoke first. "This verse is about spreading the gospel. God commands it. . . . But the Armenian church is failing. The Armenian Church doesn't know how." There were nods of approval throughout the room.

Several of these young people had for a long time been drawn away from the Armenian church by Baptists and Pentecostals. They had a certain admiration for these churches which through the preached word were able to convey hope to ordinary people. They had returned to the Armenian church because it was the church of the Armenian people.

SECTION 1 REVIEW

CHECKING FOR UNDERSTANDING

1. **Identify** two things that are important to ethnic Armenians.
2. **Explain** the significance of the monument on Tsiternakaberd hill in Armenia.

CRITICAL THINKING

3. **Making Inferences** What does the revival of faith suggest about nationalist sentiment in Armenia?

Source: Vigen Guroian. "The Ferment of Faith in Post-Soviet Armenia." Copyright 1992 Christian Century Foundation. Reprinted by permission from the January 22, 1992 issue of *The Christian Century.*

SECTION 2

Azerbaijan

Bordering Armenia is the Republic of Azerbaijan. Ruled by Mongols and Persians in ancient times, it has been invaded by Arabs, Turks, and Russians. About 1.5 million people live in Baku. Founded more than 1000 years ago, the capital city got its name from Persian words meaning "windy town."

THE AZERIS

Ethnic Azeris speak a language very much like Turkish. Most are Shi'ite Muslims, with historical ties to Iran. A visitor to Baku observes Azeri lifestyles in the following article:

On a clear, calm evening, Baku is a stroller's city, as residents promenade and take a glass of cool sweet sherbet with friends. Swarthy old men wear the *papakh*, a kind of fur fez long part of the Azerbaijanian costume. Women seem a bit more

Western, though the veil was not abolished in this Muslim land until 1921.

We visited two of the city's . . . mosques during prayers. Most of those present were old, though a young man told me, "I believe, though I rarely go to prayers. . . ."

Our driver was contemptuous of the attendance at big city mosques. "In my town, Sheki, . . . in front of the mosque you cannot enter the street for the crowd!"

Azerbaijanians also remain Oriental in secular ways. Their language resembles modern Turkish so much that they can easily converse with visitors from Istanbul. . . .

Azerbaijan calls up a touch of *A Thousand and One Nights*. In Moscow we had seen the Bolshoi Ballet dance the . . . *Legend of Love*, a highly romantic Azerbaijanian story with music composed by Arif Melikov. Now, sampling the verse of the 12th-century poet Nizami, I could appreciate the local tradition of imagery. For example, Nizami describes a princess this way: "Graceful was she as the willow tree and stately as the cypress; bracelets of jade adorned her slender wrists, and her eyes were greener than emeralds. . . ."

EXAMINING PHOTOGRAPHS *An artist sells his paintings in an Azeri market. How do the paintings contrast with the scene in the picture below?*

We saw a performance one evening by a new national folk-dance ensemble. The dancing girls were as willow-graceful as Nizami's. Afterwards the troupe's manager . . . talked with us.". . . Here all our music is song, and every song is dance. During any festival, whenever music sounds, people get up and dance. Always. We are people of movement."

WAR WITH ARMENIA

About 8 percent of the more than 7 million people who live in Azerbaijan are Christian Armenians. In mountainous Nagorno-Karabakh (nah·ghor·NOH KHUR·uh·back), an autonomous region administered by Azerbaijan, they make up between 80 or 90 percent of the population of about 200,000. The rest of the people who live there are Muslim Azeris. Nagorno-Karabakh has been

EXAMINING PHOTOGRAPHS *Azeri men in traditional dress drink tea and discuss local events. What language is similar to the Azeri language?*

Source: Bart McDowell. *Journey Across Russia,* © 1977, National Geographic Society p. 226.

EXAMINING PHOTOGRAPHS *An Armenian woman mourns her soldier son who was killed in Nagorno-Karabakh. What religious differences separate Armenians and Azeris?*

ruled by Azerbaijan, whose territory surrounds it, since 1923.

In the winter of 1987, thousands of Armenians rallied in Nagorno-Karabakh, demanding union with Armenia. The desire of the Christian Armenians to separate from predominantly Muslim Azerbaijan ultimately resulted in armed conflict between Azerbaijan and Armenia. By 1992, several thousand lives had been lost in the fighting. In the following account, a journalist chronicles the effects of life in Stepanakert (step·uh·NUH·kert), the capital city of Nagorno-Karabakh:

After six months of daily bombardments by Azerbaijani missiles, the damage that is visible in this isolated city of 70,000 Armenians is frightening enough. There are jagged, blackened holes in nearly every building. There is no water, electricity, food or fuel.

But it's the unseen destruction . . . that is even more terrifying. Four years of fighting . . . has utterly twisted life here. . . .

Thus, it is that in the basement of Stepanakert's bombed-out city hall, a handful of doctors and nurses have set up what they ruefully describe as a maternity ward to replace the women's hospital that was destroyed by the rockets. . . .

The doctors have no electrical generator, so all procedures are performed by candlelight in a frigid, stone-walled room. . . .

Next door . . . , another group of doctors has started up a jerry-built casualty hospital, in the bombed-out office block of the former ruling Communist Party. . . .

"This war is about our battle to be human," said Emma Avanisian, 41, a nurse struggling with few medicines and fewer bandages to treat wounded residents and soldiers. "We've been beat on, and they keep hitting us. Ours is a just struggle and a just cause.". . .

Up is down. Black is white. . . . And the rudiments of civilization in Stepanakert have grown badly frayed.

Strangers bark at each other in the streets at the slightest provocation. Neighbors quarrel over petty things, like whose turn it is to fetch scraps of firewood for the communal stove.

The young muscle the elderly out of the way in urgent scrambles for a few drops of gasoline from a leaking tanker truck. . . .

Life in Stepanakert grew desperate last November when the Azeris . . . began raining missiles onto the city. . . . Stepanakert's residents were driven into basements and bomb shelters. . . .

Commerce and industry ground to a halt. All utilities stopped functioning. Supplies dried up. People unlucky enough to need hospitalization had to bring their own linens, food, bandages and firewood—to heat the stove used for sterilizing instruments.

Three weeks ago, the siege of Stepanakert was finally broken. . . .

Now the rockets have stopped, and people here are emerging into the sunlight, venturing back onto the streets, climbing the rubble-strewn stairs of their fractured apartment buildings to begin patching up crumbling walls. . . .

"We're happy now, but we don't want to get too happy. Our hope has been battered so many times," said Sveta Ishania, 45, as she surveyed the balcony of her apartment, shattered by a rocket.

In the view of the journalist who wrote the magazine article that follows, the war with Armenia "is the catalyst for Azeri nationalism":

My host in Baku, once the oil boomtown of the East and now the capital of . . . Azerbaijan, is a short and comical man called Ishshat. . . .

Ishshat is the architect rebuilding many of the disused mosques in the city of Baku. . . .

Ishshat tells me that Azerbaijan should be allied with Turkey against Armenia: "We are truly Turks. We speak a Turkic language; we are Musulmen; our only hope is to be true Musulmen, independent of Moscow, closer to Turkey. . . ."

Despite Ishshat's reopening of mosques, Baku is a Western city populated by Oriental people. Its avenues boast the vast ornate mansions of Baku's oil tycoons . . . from the turn of the century, when half the world's oil was pumped from here. Ishshat is renovating some of these palaces. He takes me to one thoroughly European mansion. . . .

Thus Ishshat's palace is now rented out for weddings; among intricate murals, gilded staircases, engraved ceilings, Corinthian pillars, and Gothic facades . . . an Azeri wedding goes on, complete with Turkish clothes, fezes, kebabs, and

coffee. We are greeted by a band of musicians, dressed in flowery blouses and baggy pantaloons . . . , playing Turkish music. . . .

Finally, we are in a Turkish bath, luxuriously outfitted by Ishshat. . . . All conversation concerns the war with Armenia; the hatred for their Christian neighbor rises with each new tale of barbaric atrocity, even though the brutality is on both sides. . . . Ishshat is determined to convince me that Baku is the Turkic capital of a triumphant culture that has dominated the history of the human race. . . .

. . . I sink into the bath, realizing that fanatical Azeri nationalism is clearly capable of moving mountains.

Source: Simon Serag-Montefiore. "Baku Postcard: Turkish Bath" in *The New Republic,* June 8, 1992, pp. 13–14.

EXAMINING PHOTOGRAPHS *The major source of wealth for the economy of Azerbaijan is oil. The Caspian Sea shoreline near Baku has many oil refineries. What is the major characteristic of Baku?*

SECTION 3

Georgia

Georgia lies on the eastern shore of the Black Sea, sandwiched between two mountain ranges. It is a rugged land said to have been named for St. George. Because the country is mountainous, most of the people of Georgia live in valleys where they grow flowers and fruits and raise sheep and livestock. More than 1 million people live in the capital of Tbilisi (tih·BLEE·see) on the banks of the Kura River. The city got its name, which means "warm," from a warm spring discovered there 1500 years ago.

THE GEORGIANS

Almost 70 percent of the 5.6 million people who make Georgia their home are ethnic Georgians who speak a Caucasian language and are passionately individualistic. The ethnic Georgians also have their own alphabet and Christian Church. They are known for their business skills, love of festivals, and friendliness to foreign visitors. Known for their hospitality, they believe that guests come from God and judge a person's worth by how many friends the person has. A recent magazine article offered the following insights on Georgians:

Georgians are a proud and fiery people. Nothing offends them more than to be called Russians. And rightly so, for the only thing they have in common is the frontier that straddles the massive Caucasian mountain chain. . . . In every other respect they are different.

. . . I could sense the Georgian temperament by just strolling down Rustaveli Avenue, the grand main street in Tbilisi. Here, in the warm evening, the women, dressed predominantly in black, parade arm in arm, while the young men swagger with a typically southern mix of raw aggressiveness and breezy good humor. This is the Middle East, not Siberia.

These days, to address a Georgian in Russian . . . is likely to evoke . . . a rude reply. Yet their own language is a nightmare for any foreigner to learn. It is unrelated to Russian or any other tongue beyond Caucasia. . . .

The language is even written in a kind of "secret code"—a beautiful alphabet, elegant curving characters that bear no relation to Latin or Cyrillic. . . .

. . . Two things in particular seemed to embody the resilience and optimism of Georgians: the land and the vine. . . .

In rural Georgia, time is measured not by clocks but by sunrises and solstices, history not by revolutions . . . but by the birth of sons and the burial of fathers, seasons not by calendars but by the planting and harvesting of the vine.

"Wine is the lifeblood of Georgia, for it is made of the sap of the earth and the sun," said Konstantin Cholokashvili, an old Georgian nobleman. . . .

. . . "Wine has helped us preserve our national psychology in the face of constant invasions. It is an integral part of our life. . . . With wine we say farewell to the dead and welcome to the newborn. With wine we make declarations of love."

Source: Angus Roxburgh. "Georgia Fights for Nationhood" in *National Geographic,* Vol. 181, No. 5, May 1992, pp. 94–95, 107–108, 110.

LANGUAGE, HOMELAND, AND FAITH

Georgians take great pride in the fact that theirs is one of the world's oldest Christian countries. A Georgian poet once said, "Three divine gifts have been bestowed on us by our ancestors: language, homeland, faith." In the excerpt that follows, a writer explains how the three "gifts" are intertwined:

The memorial that stands at the main government building on Rustaveli Avenue in Tbilisi to honor the Georgians killed by Soviet Army soldiers on April 9, 1989, has three words on it: "language, homeland, faith." . . . These concepts are . . . intertwined with Georgians' Christian identity. . . . The faith was declared the state religion in the fourth century when St. Nino baptized the ruler Mirian. . . . The Georgian language took visible form when its alphabet was created to transmit the Christian faith. The Georgian homeland has been defined as that territory in which the liturgy [system of public worship in the Christian church] is sung in Georgian. . . .

How does religious piety fit into the reawakening of Georgian national identity? . . . the number of working [Georgian Orthodox] churches has grown from 40 five years ago to 300 as of last summer. A new spiritual and a revitalized seminary flourish in Tbilisi. Many people, especially the young, wear crosses, the churches are centers of much activity.[1]

Not all the people of Georgia are Christian. In Tbilisi, for example, within walking distance of each other are a cathedral, a mosque, and a synagogue. In the article that follows, a writer discusses the Georgian attitude toward the Jewish population:

A Jewish community continues to flourish, even though depleted in its numbers

EXAMINING PHOTOGRAPHS *Candlelight illuminates the main synagogue in Tbilisi, the capital of Georgia.* **How have Jews and Christians related to each other in Georgia?**

by emigration to Israel. Once there were 800 families; now there are 350. . . . The relationship between Jewish and Christian Georgians appears to be wholly relaxed and without tension, and the Georgians take pride in insisting on their own record of tolerance of minorities. As one Georgian told me, "We treated the Jews as equals, like everyone else. So much so that, in the nineteenth century, Jews were serfs, just like the others—no discrimination at all. Now where else in Europe did you have Jewish serfs? Just tell me that." . . . Georgians are eager to have an Israeli consulate in Tbilisi and to establish a regular flight to Lod. A delegation from the Georgian Academy of Sciences has been to Israel, and altogether, there is a tendency to think of the two countries as being natural allies, sharing the same predicament of very nearly being islands in a Muslim sea.[2]

---

[1]*Source:* Paul Crego. "Georgia on Their Mind." Copyright 1991 Christian Century Foundation. Reprinted by permission from the June 12–19, 1991 issue of *The Christian Century.*

[2]*Source:* "Ethnicity and Faith in Eastern Europe." Ernest Gellner, reprinted by permission of *Daedalus,* Journal of the American Academy of Arts and Sciences, Winter 1990, Vol. 119, No. 1.

DISSENSION AND CIVIL WAR

Not all minorities have been content to co-exist with Georgians. Some have sought to break away entirely. One such group is the Ossetians of South Ossetia, an autonomous region on the southern Georgian slopes of the Caucasus. In the newspaper article that follows, a journalist discusses the results of the Ossetians' efforts to secede from Georgia and unite with North Ossetia, an autonomous region in Russia:

Cradling his Kalashnikov automatic rifle, Nevgzar Dezagoiyev stared across the deserted main square of this besieged city [Tskhinvali] . . . and fixed his glance on the idle train station.

"It's been at least a year and a half since a train stopped here," said the weary-looking Mr. Dezagoiyev, a member of the militia force defending the city.

EXAMINING PHOTOGRAPHS *Guards stand behind a stone barricade marking the border between South Ossetia and the rest of Georgia. What is the goal of the South Ossetians?*

A feeling of isolation is weighing heavily on the few remaining residents of Tskhinvali, the capital of the South Ossetia. . . . Georgian militants have besieged the city for most of the last 18 months, pounding buildings with artillery and automatic weapons from surrounding hills. The constant shelling has forced many people off the debris-strewn streets and into basements.

"Everyone is suffering terribly and there is very little food," says Galya Antasevich, one of the cellar-dwellers. "This life isn't fit for a dog.". . .

South Ossetians charge the Georgians with conducting a "genocide" as part of a "Georgia-for-the Georgians" government policy. Georgians, meanwhile, say they are fighting to maintain their territorial integrity. . . .

"The only way out now is to reunite North and South Ossetia under Russian jurisdiction," said Alan Chechiyev, deputy chairman of the South Ossetian parliament. . . .

[Talk] of continued fighting only heightens the gloomy feeling at refugee camps near the North Ossetian capital of Ordzhonikidze. "All I want is peace, I don't care anymore about independence," says Marina, a refugee who declines to give her last name.

SECTION 3 REVIEW

CHECKING FOR UNDERSTANDING

1. **Examine** the Georgian attitude regarding hospitality and a person's worth.
2. **Name** the three "divine gifts" bestowed on Georgians by their ancestors.

CRITICAL THINKING

3. **Identifying Central Issues** What reasons do Ossetians give for wanting South Ossetia to secede from Georgia? What reason do Georgians give for not allowing South Ossetia to secede?

Source: Justin Burke. "Ossetians Are Weary of War, Wary of Peace" in *The Christian Science Monitor,* June 26, 1992, p. 6.

GLOBAL FOCUS

Cultural Values

NATIONAL CHARACTER

FOCUSING ON THE ISSUE Each of the three photographs on this page symbolizes the national character of a republic of the Caucasus. Study the photographs and the descriptions that accompany them. Then, based on what the photographs and descriptions have told you, write a paragraph about the national character of each republic.

Traditional Azeri Gathering

Armenian Religious Ceremony

Georgian Shepherds

Chapter 44 Review

SUMMARY

Armenia, Azerbaijan, and Georgia are independent republics nestled in the Caucasus between the Black and Caspian seas. Of the three, only Armenia is a member of the Commonwealth of Independent States. Georgia refused to join the Commonwealth when it was formed, and Azerbaijan later withdrew.

All three of the republics of the Caucasus are ancient lands with long, and often violent, histories in which their people take great pride. The culture of each republic stems from and reflects its unique history and heritage. The majority of the people of Armenia and Georgia are Christian, for example, while most Azeris are followers of Islam.

For Armenians, Azeris, and Georgians alike, religious faith and ethnic and nationalist sentiment are very much entwined. Since becoming independent, all three have been faced with conflict stemming from decisions made by ethnic minorities both within and outside of their borders.

REVIEWING FACTS

1. **Name** the republics of the Caucasus that are not members of the Commonwealth of Independent States.
2. **Identify** the republic of the Caucasus that is the smallest member-republic of the Commonwealth of Independent States.
3. **Distinguish** between Yerevan, Baku, and Tbilisi.
4. **Tell** how Armenians view their history.
5. **Contrast** the major languages spoken by Azeris and Georgians.
6. **Specify** the major religion of each of the republics of the Caucasus.
7. **Identify** the region that has been disputed between Armenia and Azerbaijan.
8. **State** which republic of the Caucasus is a major producer of oil.
9. **Name** some national characteristics associated with the Georgians.

CRITICAL THINKING

1. **Making Generalizations** What generalization might be made about the Armenians of Nagorno-Karabakh and the Ossetians of South Ossetia?
2. **Analyzing Information** When discussing Tbilisi, the author of the magazine article about Georgians stated, "This is the Middle East, not Siberia." What point do you think he was attempting to make?
3. **Making Comparisons** In what ways are Armenia, Azerbaijan, and Georgia similar? In what ways are they different?
4. **Demonstrating Reasoned Judgment** Why might Georgia want to foster good relations with Israel?

ANALYZING CONCEPTS

1. **Interdependence** How did the desire of the Armenian Christians of Nagorno-Karabakh to separate from Azerbaijan impact the relationship between Azerbaijan and Armenia?
2. **Choice** What decision did South Ossetians make that led to conflict with the Georgian government?

GEOGRAPHIC THEMES

1. **Location** Where are Armenia, Azerbaijan, and Georgia located in relation to the Caucasus Mountains and the Black and Caspian seas?
2. **Human-Environment Interaction** What affect has the physical environment had on the people of Armenia?

Synthesizing Information

When doing research, it is often necessary to *synthesize*, or combine, information from more than one source. Synthesizing information allows you to see relationships between sources and to check the reliability of each one. The following steps will help you in synthesizing information.

- Analyze each source separately to understand its meaning.
- Determine what information each source adds to the subject.
- Identify points of agreement and disagreement.

EXAMPLE

Review the excerpts describing the national character of Azeris (pages 724–725) and Georgians (pages 728). Both excerpts are taken from magazine articles, and reflect the views of outsiders. According to the first article, how do Azeris exhibit their cultural heritage? *(dress, Islamic religion and mosques)* According to the second article, what is distinctive about the Georgian national character? *(strong rural roots and customs based on hospitality)* Notice that, taken together, the two articles show regional similarities—environment and Middle Eastern cultural roots. What differences between the two cultures are evident? *(language and alphabet, religion)*

PRACTICE

Source A discusses recent conflict in Nagorno-Karabakh. Source B is a survivor's account of the Armenian genocide of 1915. Read

> A)[Conflict over the] Karabakh [region] had roots deep in Armenian history; it was a long suppressed territorial grievance that electrified the masses, and that instantly made it a cause celebre for the entire nation of Armenians. And Karabakh was much more: It was an aching wound, a symbol of the injustice done to the Armenian nation by Soviet rulers and, before them, by the Turks; it was a holy cause for the Christian Armenians . . . ; it was an icon of Armenian suffering through the centuries. In a very real sense, Karabakh is a microcosm of Armenia.[1]

> B) Finally, our caravan reached a little town or village. . . . We stayed there that night and crying, looked toward the bridge, to see if our beloved father would return; but we had no hope. . . . The next morning there was new agitation in the caravan. Everyone had to abandon their wagons. . . . In addition to making us march quite a long time in the heat, we were denied water. During that march people became thirsty. . . . A lot of people dropped from exhaustion. It was a nightmare: all of us were exhausted and suffering from the sun and thirst. . . . Finally, we approached a village where there was a very lush pasture. . . . we tried to rest our caravan there. . . .[2]

both sources and answer the questions below:

1. Are these primary or secondary sources?
2. What is the main point of each source?
3. What information does Source A offer about the roots of the struggle in the region of Nagorno Karabakh?
4. What information does Source B add to this topic?
5. Does Source B explain or contradict Source A? Explain.

[1]*Source:* Hedrick Smith. The New Russians, Random House, 1990, p. 332.

[2]*Source:* John Yervant. *Needle, Thread and Button,* Zoryan Institute for Contemporary Armenian Research and Documentation, Inc., Cambridge, Mass., 1988, pp. 18–19. The Zoryan Institute is an international center for contemporary Armenian research and documentation based in Cambridge (USA) with affiliates in Toronto and Paris.

People and Places to Know

Kazakhstan, Kyrgyzstan, Turkmenistan, Uzbekistan, Tajikistan, Caspian Sea, Muslims, Nursultan Nazarbayev

Objectives to Learn

1. **Locate** the Central Asian republics and identify their major ethnic groups.
2. **Discuss** the importance of Islam in the Central Asian republics.
3. **Describe** the economies of the Central Asian republics.

Carpet sellers in Central Asia

Central Asian Republics

> In Central Asia, 55 million former Soviet citizens are adrift. This huge territory, which is far from being homogeneous, stretches from the Caspian sea to Xinjiang in China and includes the Pamirs and the Kazakh desert. . . .
>
> The one battle that is under way right now is over which alphabet will replace the Cyrillic letters that Soviet leader Joseph Stalin imposed on these countries. . . . The Kazakhs, Turkmens, and Kyrgyz are expected [to switch to the Roman alphabet]. But Uzbekistan is hesitating between the "European" formula and reverting to the old Uzbek, . . . which uses Arabic-Persian characters. The Tajiks tend toward the Arabic-Persian alphabet.
>
> In appearance, at least, nothing has changed in these new "independent" countries. At the Hotel Tajikistan in Dushanbe, all signs are in Russian and English. There is not a word in Tajik. . . .
>
> Small businesses are picking up, and the bazaars are gradually becoming more animated. Stalls with cases of beer are being set up along the cotton fields, and customers are openly invited to sample *plov* (rice pilaf) in the stall owner's *chaikhana* (teahouse)—that is, in his courtyard.
>
> After being swept up in events that they neither wanted nor controlled, the republics for the most part were content merely to change labels in October, 1991. With the exception of a few . . . victims, they have kept their leaders and political structures. . . .
>
> An earthquake has nevertheless struck the whole of Central Asia—particularly Uzbekistan and Tajikistan. It is the return to Islam, and it is both a religious resurgence and a compelling political factor.

*I*n mid-1992, all five Central Asian republics—Kazakhstan, Kyrgyzstan, Turkmenistan, Uzbekistan, and Tajikistan—were members of the Commonwealth of Independent States. But, as a French journalist noted in the article above, change was slower to come to these republics than to the other former Soviet republics.

Source: Bernard Lecomte. "Communism Confronts Islam: A 'Strange Revolution'." Copyright © 1992, *L'Express.* Distributed by *The New York Times* Special Features.

Since then, varying degrees of change have taken place and will continue to do so as new freedoms and influences take hold. With these freedoms has come a major resurgence of Islam, which remained the religion of most Central Asians despite the Soviet policy of atheism. In most instances, Islam and efforts to generate nationalism and turn a long-passive people into a politically active society have become intertwined.

SECTION 1

Land and People

In the view of many, the Central Asian republics are "the bridge" between Europe and Asia. Reaching from the Caspian Sea to China, they embrace an immense area, one as large as all of western Europe. Below, a noted author offers his impressions of this vast territory:

What is not steppe in Central Asia is often semidesert or desert. . . . In some places dunes rise 300 feet high. And when these variously sandy or grassy, mostly flat lands finally expire, it is because they have run up against range after range of mountains. . . .

It is and always has been a struggle to wrest sustenance from this territory. . . .

It is hard to think of the Turkmenian capital as an oasis, though technically that is what Ashkhabad is, in the midst of all that arid land. Like the other Central Asian capitals, this is a considerable city and a mostly modern one. . . . In appearance it is not so different from Kazakhstan's Alma Ata, Kirghizia's Frunze, or Tajikistan's Dushanbe. In each case there are buildings which date back to the 19th century, when the Russian influence was first felt in Central Asia. The roads leading out of each city are often bordered with traditional Russian cottages . . . but these are soon overtaken by sometimes depressing varieties of 20th-century architecture, ranging from mass-produced high-rise homes to often grandiose buildings. . . . There is much space between

THE CENTRAL ASIAN REPUBLICS

Republic (Date Independence Declared)	Capital	Population Estimates	Ethnic Groups	Major Products	Before U.S.S.R. Breakup
Uzbekistan (8/31/91)	Tashkent	19,906,000	69% Uzbek 11% Russian 4% Tatar	cotton	2.0% land 6.9% pop. 3.3% GNP
Kazakhstan (10/26/90)	Alma-Ata	16,538,000	36% Kazakh 41% Russian 6% Ukrainian	cotton, millet, coal, oil, lead, zinc, copper	12.1% land 5.7% pop. 4.3% GNP
Tajikistan (9/9/91)	Dushanbe	5,112,000	59% Tajik 23% Uzbek 10% Russian	cattle, sheep, fruit, hydroelectric power	0.7% land 1.8% pop. 0.8% GNP
Kyrgyzstan (8/31/91)	Bishkek	4,372,000	52% Kirghiz 22% Russian 13% Uzbek 4% Ukrainian 2% Tatar	wool, livestock, machine and instrument production	0.9% land 1.5% pop. 0.8% GNP
Turkmenistan (8/22/90)	Ashkhabad	3,621,000	68% Turkmeni 13% Russian 9% Uzbek	oil, sulphur, cotton, dates, olives, figs	2.2% land 1.3% pop. 0.7% GNP

EXAMINING CHARTS *The people of the Central Asian republics are ethnically diverse, but share a common Islamic heritage.* **Which of the republics is the largest in population?**

EXAMINING PHOTOGRAPHS *These women at a factory in Ashkhabad, the capital of Turkmenistan, are making carpets, one of the Central Asian republic's noted products.* **In what kind of environment is Ashkhabad located?**

these and it is usually well planted with trees and shrubbery, except in Tashkent, the capital of Uzbekistan . . . where there is often space so empty that it becomes oppressive.

One tends, therefore, to distinguish Central Asian cities from each other less by their appearance than by their surroundings or by some local habit. . . .

The traffic along the Silk Road played its part in forming the rich cultural complexity of Central Asia; as, too, did the long history of warfare here, with freebooting armies from every direction forever roaming the steppe and the mountain passes, sometimes settling for winter quarters. . . .

On any street, in any marketplace, one can see a medley of people whose ancestors settled in at almost any time across a dozen centuries. . . .

Beyond the cities, after the last farm village has been left behind in the urban hinterland, the indigenous population dom-

inates the wide open spaces. Almost everywhere except in Tajikistan, whose people have traditionally been cultivators, this means that many spend part of the year on the move with their flocks in search of good grazing across the desert, the steppe, and the mountain pastures. . . .

SECTION 1 REVIEW

CHECKING FOR UNDERSTANDING
1. **Describe** the capital cities of the Central Asian republics.
2. **Account** for the "rich cultural complexity" of Central Asia.

CRITICAL THINKING
3. **Drawing Conclusions** Why do Central Asians tend to be more Eastern than Western in their outlook and ways of life?

SECTION 2

The Islamic Awakening

Almost all the non-Russians in the Central Asian republics were—and are—Muslims. Fearful that Islam would unite the diverse peoples of the region and foster nationalism, the Soviets closed down, converted, or destroyed thousands of mosques. This action, however, was not as successful as was hoped. Central Asians continued to honor Islamic customs and rituals. Instead of praying at mosques, many prayed at home.

Since the collapse of the Soviet Union, Russian culture, language, and influence have been receding throughout the Central Asian republics. At the same time, the influence and popular strength of Islam have been growing. In spite of the long period of Rus-

Source: Geoffrey Moorhouse. "Kazakhstan & Central Asia" in *The Soviet Union Today.* Copyright © 1990, National Geographic Society, pp. 156–162.

EXAMINING PHOTOGRAPHS
Devout Muslims in Tajikistan are now free to practice their faith openly, without fear of government oppression. Why is Islam growing in importance in Tajikistan and other Central Asian republics?

sian influence, many of the Central Asian peoples still live in rural areas and have retained their traditional beliefs and customs. Those Central Asians living in the cities are turning to Islam as the basis of a new-found sense of national identity and pride. In the following article, a journalist describes the situation in Tajikistan, where Islam had been suppressed or controlled by the Soviets:

The growing influence and popular strength of Islam is striking here in Tajikistan. Seven weeks of street demonstrations aimed at the overthrow of the old Communist leadership and apparatus took an increasingly Islamic character. . . .

During those weeks, many thousands of Tajikistan's Muslims, who had been prevented from open worship and religious instruction during their entire lives, learned how to pray. . . .

Khodzhi Mansur Jalilzodekh is the head of the madresseh, the religious school of Dushanbe's main mosque, which is filled all day, these days, with men in the traditional four-cornered cap designed to ward off evil, and women with their hair, legs and arms covered. "We feared the Communists the way the people fear a wild dog," he said. Now that religious education may be freely undertaken, the school already has 150 students and is doubling in size. . . .

Asked to speak more about his goals, he said: "We ultimately want an Islamic republic here, but we must go through democratic government first, because for 74 years people did not know their rights, and they are not ready. People became distant from Islam and we do not want them to fear it.". . .

The party does not want to impose Islam on anyone, he said. . . . "Tajiks don't like to go fast, and we're not ready."

"People don't have a clear understanding of Islam or politics," he continued. "They repeat what they hear like parrots. So we must rely on current leaders to decide, and then in time have a referendum."

Asked about his model for Tajikistan, Mr. Jalilzodekh said the country would find its own way, at its own pace.

"But you must understand one thing," he continued. "We'll never accept a modern Islam, a Western-style Islam of the kind encouraged by the Russians."[1]

In the view of another journalist, "For the 55 million Muslims in the former Soviet Union, Islam is rapidly filling the ideological void left by the fall of communism." As proof, he points to Uzbekistan:

In the crooked alleys outside the Hodzha Zudmurod mosque, the buzz of commerce mingles with the Muezzin's call to prayer.

Booksellers hawk leather-bound copies of the Koran in Arabic, Uzbek and Russian, while customers thumb through religious pamphlets containing the latest wisdom from the great Islamic sages. . . .

A few years ago, such scenes would have been unthinkable. . . . Samarkand, an ancient center of Islamic learning, had only three functioning mosques . . . in 1985.

Today there are 105 mosques in Samarkand, with new ones opening every week. . . .

Before entering the mosque for Friday prayers, Mukhtar Achmedov, a 32-year-old mathematics teacher, and Abdulrauf Mrazyav, a 27-year-old agricultural worker take a moment to leaf through some of the Islamic literature offered at one of the bookstalls.

"We have always been Muslims," Achmedov tells a visitor. "We didn't show it because it was prohibited, but the roots are still there."

Mrazyav nods. "The people believe what is written in the Koran. It is like our constitution. What we want now is a real constitution based on the Koran."

Achmedov is not so certain. Tucked under his arm is a newspaper published by an Uzbek opposition party led by intellectuals, strongly opposed to Islam as a political vehicle. The party's name is Erk—"free will" in Uzbek.

When asked about this, Achmedov offers a primer on the marketing of political ideas:

"We are interested in a good life, and we think Islam can give us this. But if Erk can give us a good life, we will support them."[2]

Popular Turkmen writer Akh-Muhammed Velsapar agrees that Central Asians are "seeking to acquire another ideology to fill the void" and believes that they count on Islam to do this. The following excerpt focuses on Velsapar's homeland—Turkmenistan:

Though Islam has always been taken for granted as the recognized way of life here, the Turkmens were never overzealous about their religion, unlike some of their neighbors—perhaps, because of their nomadic ways. "When could they pray five times a day, if they are constantly on the move?", shrugs a local journalist. "Traditions are another thing, though. Everyone here, including Communist party members always took part in Muslim rituals. Even if the top brass punished them for that." The journalist smiles. . . .

But now [President] Niyazov is building new mosques and always has a mullah in his entourage, wherever he travels in his country or whenever there is a public ceremony. "A lot of people I know since my university days," says the journalist, "have grown beards, and turned into mullahs, though they don't know a single Sura of the Koran."[3]

[1]*Source:* Steven Erlanger. "An Islamic Awakening in Central Asian Lands" in *The New York Times,* June 9, 1992, pp. A1, A16. Copyright © 1992 by the New York Times Company. Reprinted by permission.

[2]*Source:* Tom Hundley. "Soviet downfall sparks an upsurge for Islam" in *The Chicago Tribune,* © Copyright 1992, Chicago Tribune Company, all rights reserved, used with permission.

[3]*Source:* John Kohan. Letter, February 20, 1992.

SECTION 3

Czar Cotton

According to one journalist, "nowhere is the 'post-colonial' crisis more acute than in Uzbekistan," where the collapse of Soviet power left behind a host of unsolved ecological, pollution, and economic problems.

Uzbekistan produced 62 percent of all the cotton grown in the former Soviet Union. Its entire economy was oriented toward the production of that one resource, which Russians called "the white gold of Uzbekistan." Freed from Soviet rule, Uzbeks determined to free themselves as well from "Czar Cotton." Below, a reporter discusses the changes that have been taking place:

The changes are obvious here, on a cotton-growing collective farm along the fabled Silk Road to Samarkand. The farm's director, Dzumobay Sayibnazarov, is nobody's fool. "I'm a peasant," he says cheerfully, his eyes careful and shrewd.

As an independent country, Uzbekistan is switching to a system in which land can finally be bought and sold, and Mr. Sayibnazarov, 49 years old, is raring to go. "Piece by piece," he said, he intends to get 370 acres for himself and his family— 54 percent of the entire collective farm that now includes 270 families.

Maybe he will. Mr. Sayibnazarov has good connections in the People's Democratic Party of Uzbekistan, the new name for the Communist Party, which still runs the country. . . .

EXAMINING PHOTOGRAPHS
Uzbekistan's agriculture is based on irrigation. The republic was the chief cotton-growing area in the former Soviet Union. How did the era of Soviet rule affect Uzbekistan?

With his sons, he walks a visitor around the pear and cherry orchards, shows off the cows and goats, points out the two large, plastic-covered flower beds. . . .

Last year, the farm could sell 5 percent of the cotton fiber privately, with the rest going to the state. This year, the figure is 15 percent, and farmers can do what they like with half their vegetables, fruits and grains.

Even after paying a 30-percent tax to the Government on the private sale, Mr. Sayibnazarov said, the farmers still make more than twice as much money on cotton sold privately. . . .

Farmers are also now taking better care of their land, said Renat S. Nazarov, an agronomist and director of cotton for the Uzbekistan Ministry of Agriculture. . . .

The use of pesticides is way down now, Mr. Nazarov said, with biological methods being used instead. Irrigation is being made more efficient, with more ditches being lined with concrete, to prevent waste. . . .

Still, he said, the saltiness of the land is getting worse, and the Aral Sea . . . may never recover. . . .

The hope now is to reduce the percentage of land devoted to cotton to 55 percent by the year 2000, but Mr. Nazarov says any notion that Uzbekistan can stop depending on cotton is a pipe dream.

Gafur S. Abdurakhmanov, head of Foreign Relations at the Agriculture Ministry, said that . . . between 400,000 and 600,000 tons [of cotton fiber] are now being sold outside the old Soviet Union. Among the republics, barter relations are common, with cotton being traded for Kazakh meat or Ukrainian sugar. . . .

On his collective farm, Mr. Sayibnazarov is worried about the rain, but otherwise has the incessant optimism of a newly hatched capitalist.

"Private land and more competition, that's the way," he said. . . . "I'll try to produce the best cotton, and then I'll build some factories and work the cotton

EXAMINING PHOTOGRAPHS *Stock and sheep raising are important economic activities in Uzbekistan, which also produces cotton, almonds, and raisins.* Why did the Russians call cotton "the white gold of Uzbekistan"?

and make shirts, and then pass it on to my children and grandchildren."

SECTION 3 REVIEW

CHECKING FOR UNDERSTANDING

1. **Tell** toward what the entire economy of Uzbekistan was oriented.

CRITICAL THINKING

2. **Analyzing Information** What points is the reporter who wrote the excerpt in this section trying to get across?

SECTION 4

The Market Economy

In recent years, political feuding, ethnic turmoil, and religious militancy have dominated the agenda of most leaders on the southern rim of the old Soviet empire. This, however, has not been the case for one Central Asian republic—Kazakhstan, which is bigger than any republic but Russia. For Kazakh president Nursultan Nazarbayev, the major issues have been primarily economic and geopolitical. Under his government, Kazakhstan has been conducting what the reporter who wrote the following article calls "the biggest laboratory experiment in the entire ex-Soviet Union for economic ex-perimentation in a transition from Communism to capitalism":

Kazakhstan is Central Asia's "Wild East," where business men from Houston to Seoul are doing everything . . . to get dibs on the newly free republic's milk and honey—read, "oil and gold.". . .

. . . above all stands the incredible cast of characters: business men of fortune, swaggering adventurers, frontier oilmen and even a few serious scholars and politicians.

In the elegant conference room of the presidency, the star of the Kazakh show is President Nursultan Nazarbayev, who is holding court with the visiting French foreign minister's delegation. . . .

"Where do you want to see Kazakhstan five years from now?" I ask.

Commonwealth of Independent States

A NOMADIC LIFE

Before modern times, many Central Asians were nomads who roamed the steppe in search of pasture for their flocks of sheep and herds of horses. From April through November, they were on the move, making their homes in a type of tent known as a *yurt*.

In recent years, this way of life has become less common. But, as a traveler observes below, for some native Kazakhs and Kirghiz the old traditions and way of life remain alive:

I saw but one yurt during my own journey. . . . There was a wooden door so small that I had to crawl to get inside. . . . From the slatted framework of the circular wall, clothes had been hung, and so had decorated woolen pouches which contained utensils and other tackle, and a couple of paraffin lamps to provide the only light. There was a carpet covering the floor and a rectangle of tiles on which stood a cast-iron stove, throwing out much heat. The lattice wall-frame and the strips of willow that rose above it to the apex of the dome, were covered with dark felt. . . . The inside of the yurt was warm and comforting, though the felt outside had

been covered with plastic sheeting for greater protection. It was home for a young man, his heavily pregnant wife and their tiny child. . . .

Many of the old traditions persisted as they had always done. The horsemen still hunted saiga, a kind of gazelle, with especially trained eagles. . . . They still played the game, common throughout Central Asia . . . and said to have originated in Mongol training for cavalry warfare, in which the decapitated body of a sheep or goat is struggled for by a score or more of competing riders, who gallop and jostle until a winner manages to deposit the carcass in some appointed

place, which may be miles across rough terrain. . . .

It was nomad peoples such as these who first introduced the utterly different cultures of East and West to each other.

DRAWING CONCLUSIONS

Why do you think some people of Central Asia continue to cling to the old traditions and the nomadic way of life?

Source: Adapted from ON THE OTHER SIDE: A JOURNEY THROUGH SOVIET CENTRAL ASIA by Geoffrey Moorhouse. Copyright © 1991 by Geoffrey Moorhouse. Reprinted by permission of Henry Holt and Co., Inc.

EXAMINING PHOTOGRAPHS *Kazakhstan has taken the first steps toward a free market economy. This woman operates her own small-scale business at a market in Alma-Ata, Kazakhstan's capital. What kind of government rules in Kazakhstan?*

"I will answer the lady," Nazarbayev says gallantly. "Kazakhstan has many possibilities. I hope that in five years Kazakhstan will have entered the market economy. In those five years, we will lay the foundation from the old philosophy to new varieties of property . . . and then finally create a developed democratic state that is recognized by the world as a sovereign country."

Nazarbayev has studied the economic records of South Korea, China and Singapore. He has concluded that for rapid development, Kazakhstan must have a period of authoritarian yet representative rule that develops the economy and leads to democracy later.

In a lovely old mansion of the former Communist Party, the . . . economist who is Nazarbayev's leading adviser paces up and down trying to figure out how to

carry Kazakhstan, with all of its contradictory energies, ahead to a healthier privatized economy. Chan Young Bang is a Korean-American professor from San Francisco. . . .

"To be fair," he told me, "Kazakhstan is way ahead of the other republics—but changing people's attitudes is a tremendously difficult task."

As the scene described below illustrates, private enterprise abounds in Kazakhstan's capital city:

Two fresh-faced young Russian girls in dark blue jackets, ties and jaunty red caps open the doors of the modernistic, bright mauve portal and politely bow to customers entering Shaggie's café in downtown Alma-Ata, capital of Kazakhstan. The illuminated plastic menu in cyrillic lettering above the take-out counter advertises decidedly Western fare like hamburgers and fried chicken. But

Source: "Profit hunters seek fortunes in Kazakhstan." Taken from the Georgie Anne Geyer column by Georgie Anne Geyer. Copyright 1992 UNIVERSAL PRESS SYNDICATE. Reprinted with permission. All rights reserved.

EXAMINING PHOTOGRAPHS *Kazakhstan has made great strides in moving toward a capitalist economy. What is one major challenge that Kazakhstan may face?*

EXAMINING PHOTOGRAPHS
Kazakhstan's quick embrace of the free market has resulted in greater trade opportunities and an increased standard of living. What are some of the items bid for at the auctions?

the proof is in the eating. The hamburger paddy has the consistency of Soviet-style kielbasa, drowned in horseradish sauce, and the chicken has a coating reminiscent of egg-roll pastry. Still, for Alma-Ata residents willing to pay the relatively steep price of 35 rubles (roughly 35 cents) for a piece of fried chicken or a hamburger, a visit to the South Korean fast-food outlet—which, as numerous signs on the plate glass windows point out, is run by "the Teolbo family"—offers a tantalizing taste of the outside world and the free enterprise system.

Along the tree-lined avenues of Alma-Ata, signs and banners promoting commodity markets, advertising agencies, and computer-telecommunication firms have supplanted . . . Communist Party propaganda posters. Other placards for new commercial ventures hang from the balcony of a more traditional venue for private enterprise: Alma-Ata's thriving free market, where counters groan with piles of the juicy, reddish green fruit that has given the city its name—"Father of Apples"—as well as spicy Korean cabbage salads, jars of sour cream and honey, and

cuts of beef and pork, selling for about half of the price in Moscow. In a hanger-like pavilion on the grounds of Alma Ata's Exhibition of Economic Achievements, some 700 "brokers" from the Alma Commodities Exchange, the largest of 18 in the city, now bid in daily auctions for goods ranging from helicopters and refrigerators to newsprint and bricks. Since the exchange first opened last July, business has been so brisk that the volume of trade in a single day has topped 50 million rubles.

SECTION 4 REVIEW

CHECKING FOR UNDERSTANDING

1. **Relate** President Nazarbayev's goals for Kazakhstan.
2. **Indicate** what President Nazarbayev thinks Kazakhstan needs for rapid development.

CRITICAL THINKING

3. **Synthesizing Information** What evidence can you give of efforts to foster and establish a market economy in Kazakhstan?

Source: John Kohan. Letter, February 17, 1992.

Chapter 45 Review

SUMMARY

The five Central Asian republics—Kazakhstan, Kyrgyzstan, Turkmenistan, Uzbekistan, and Tajikistan—cover an area that stretches from the Caspian Sea to the borders of China. The geography of the area is as diverse as the nationalities who populate it.

The majority of the people of the Central Asian republics are followers of Islam. Suppressed under the rule of the Soviets, Islam has seen a major resurgence in the independent republics. In most of the republics, it is closely linked with political thought and government.

In Uzbekistan and Kazakhstan especially, there is a strong focus on the economy. Uzbeks have taken steps to reduce the production of cotton, the one resource toward which its entire economy was oriented under the Soviets. Kazakhstan is actively pursing entrance into the market economy.

REVIEWING FACTS

1. **Enumerate** about how many nationalities live in the Central Asian republics.
2. **Identify** the major ethnic group of each of the Central Asian republics.
3. **Speculate** about why the best criteria to distinguish among Central Asian cities is by their surroundings or by some local habit.
4. **Tell** what divides most sharply the indigenous peoples of Central Asia from the Russians and other Slavs.
5. **Contrast** the influence of Russian and Islam in the Central Asian republics.
6. **Give examples** of ways in which farmers already have benefited or may benefit in the future from changes taking place in Uzbekistan.

7. **Name** the Central Asian republic that is the largest in size.

CRITICAL THINKING

1. **Making Comparisons** In what way(s) is the ethnic makeup of the various Central Asian republics similar? In what way(s) is it different?
2. **Evaluating Information** In this chapter, the statement was made that many people saw the Central Asian republics as "the bridge" between Europe and Asia. Explain why you agree or disagree with this view.
3. **Drawing Conclusions** In Uzbekistan, cotton is referred to as "Czar Cotton." Why, do you think, it is called this?
4. **Analyzing Information** The author of the article about Alma-Ata concluded that a visit to Shaggie's café "offers a tantalizing taste of the outside world and the free enterprise system." Provide evidence to support his conclusion.

ANALYZING CONCEPTS

1. **Power** Why did the Soviet government control and suppress the religion of Islam and close down and destroy thousands of mosques?
2. **Political Systems** What economic system are the governments of Uzbekistan and Kazakhstan trying to establish?

GEOGRAPHIC THEMES

1. **Location** Where are the Central Asian republics located in relation to the Caspian Sea?
2. **Regions** What do the vast majority of the ethnic groups of all the Central Asian republics have in common?

How to Use the Readers' Guide to Periodical Literature

Suppose you want to buy a new CD player. How can you determine which model is the best value? You could read magazine articles comparing CD players. However, would you have to thumb through every magazine to find these articles?

Absolutely not! Instead, look up CD players in the *Readers' Guide to Periodical Literature,* an index of articles in hundreds of magazines. Each annual edition lists articles published in that year. Monthly updates provide listings of the most recent magazine articles. Subjects are arranged alphabetically. Under "CD players," you will find a list of all the magazine articles on CD players which were published that year. Also, you may find a *cross-reference* to a related heading, such as "compact discs." The *Guide* lists the title and author of each article, and the magazine and issue in which it appears. The librarian will find the magazines you want.

Here are some steps to follow in using the *Readers' Guide:*

- Select editions of the *Readers' Guide* for the exact time period.
- Find headings for your topic.
- List articles relevant to your topic, by title, periodical, and date of issue.

EXAMPLE

Look at the above labelled diagram of a *Readers' Guide* entry.

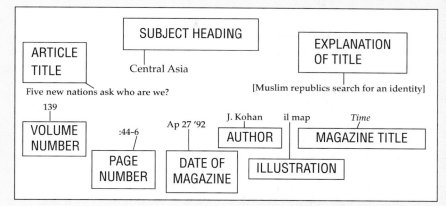

The subject heading shown here is "CENTRAL ASIA." What is the title of the article? *("Five new nations ask who are we?")* The short explanation in brackets says that this article is about the Muslim republics searching for a new identity. Who wrote this article? *(J. Kohan)* In which magazine does this article appear? *(Time)* What illustration appears in the article? *(a map)* Magazine issues are organized by volume number; this article appears in Volume 139. On what pages does the article appear? *(pages 44–46)* When was the article published? *(April 27, 1992)*

PRACTICE

A) Study the following excerpt from the February 1992 *Readers' Guide* and answer the questions that follow:
1. Under what subject are these articles listed?
2. Under what other heading can you find information on this topic?

CENTRAL ASIA
See also
Afghanistan

Another Islamic revolution. V. Pope. il *U.S. News & World Report* 111:65-7 D 16 '91
Choosing sides in the Asian republics. A. Zein. *World Press Review* 38: 21 N '91
Shedding the past. M. Gray. il *Maclean's* 104:34-5 N 25 '91

3. How many articles are listed?
4. What article appears in a December 1991 issue of *U.S. News and World Report?*
5. Who wrote "Shedding the past"?
6. In what magazine, volume, page number, and issue does the article "Choosing sides in the Asian republics" appear?
7. How long is the article "Another Islamic revolution"?
B) Choose a topic related to the Central Asian republics. Using the *Readers' Guide*, make a list of five magazine articles about your topic, including the magazine, volume, and date.

Ballet: A Russian Gift to the World

Ballet began in Italy and France in the late 1400's as a pastime of the nobility. Almost 300 years later, ballet came to Russia, where it took on a new character. Today Russia is recognized as the birthplace of modern ballet and the greatest influence on this form of art throughout the world.

Marius Petipa was the first ballet creator and arranger to make a dramatic change in the way classical, or traditional, ballet was danced. Trained as a dancer in Paris, Petipa left France to join the Russian Imperial Ballet—now called the Kirov Ballet—in St. Petersburg. Petipa had a genius for choreography, or composing dances for the ballet. He introduced the graceful arm movements that are so much a part of ballet today. "The dance of the arms" is featured in Petipa's most famous ballets—*Sleeping Beauty* and *Swan Lake*. These ballets, created in the 1890's, are still among the most popular ballets.

Another important influence on ballet was the Russian ballet producer Sergei Diaghilev (sehr·GAY DYAH·gih·lehf) and the company that he established in 1909—the Ballets Russes. Diaghilev, who is sometimes called "the father of modern ballet," rejected many of the principles of classical ballet. He believed that ballet should express the real conditions of human experience and not portray the "calm hinterland of fairy tale." Diaghilev looked to the folk dances

of the Russian peasants to give ballet new expressiveness and depth. In Diaghilev's opinion, these rural dances of the common people were never empty or formal, but were true expressions of the human spirit.

Diaghilev joined forces with many noted musicians and painters to transform the ballet, and his Ballets Russes produced some of the greatest ballet dancers of all time. Among the most famous were Vaslav Nijinsky (vahts-LAHF nih-ZHIHN-skee) and Anna Pavlova. Diaghilev also staged the twentieth century's first great ballets. Masterpieces, such as *Firebird* and *Petrouchka*, still leave audiences stunned by their great emotional power and beauty.

When Diaghilev's company

split up after his death in 1929, many of his Russian dancers and choreographers traveled abroad to dance, teach, and to start companies of their own. Among these was the choreographer George Balanchine, who directed the New York City Ballet until his death in 1983.

Russia continues to be known for its great ballet. In the past few decades, a number of the best dancers in Europe and the United States have been Russians who fled communist rule in their homeland. The contribution of dancers, such as Mikhail Baryshnikov (bah·RIHSH·nih·kahf) and Natalia Makarova (mah·KAH·rah·vah), has continued to enliven and change the direction of ballet throughout the world.

Making the Connection

1. How has Russia influenced ballet throughout the world?

2. Why is Diaghilev called "the father of modern ballet?"

Unit 7 Review

SUMMARY

The vast territory occupied by the republics of the Commonwealth spans two continents. The broad geographic diversity of this territory has played a major role in its development. At the same time the open land served as an avenue for foreign invaders, the natural environment helped isolate it from other parts of the world.

The territory's early history centered around the Slavs and what is now Russia and Ukraine. What began as a loose union of city-states and territories expanded and evolved into an empire ruled until the early 1900's by czars. A turbulent period of revolution marked the end of czarist rule and the beginnings of an era of communism and Soviet rule.

After Soviet rule came to an abrupt end in the 1990's, the Soviet republics became independent states. The people of the newly independent republics have been striving to deal with the social, economic, and political changes brought on by the fall of communism and the breakup of the Soviet Union.

REVIEWING THE MAIN IDEAS

1. **Specify** the years Romanov rule of Russia began and ended.
2. **Explain** why World War I was a contributing factor to the downfall of czarist rule of Russia.
3. **Compare** life in the Soviet Union under the Communists and life in Russia under the czars.
4. **Differentiate** between the hardline Communists' and democratic reformers' view of Mikhail Gorbachev as the 1990's began.
5. **Compare** the former Soviet republics in terms of the challenges that they faced after the collapse of the Soviet Union.

CRITICAL THINKING

1. **Identifying Alternatives** The Central Asian republics are at a crossroads. They can develop a new concept of statehood by trying to imitate western, secular societies; by following the path of Islamic fundamentalism; or by finding their own middle way. What advantages and disadvantages do you see in each of these?
2. **Demonstrating Reasoned Judgment** The peoples of the republics have found it hard to adjust to their new-found freedoms and to many of the changes taking place. What reasons can you give for this?

PRACTICING SKILLS

Synthesizing Information Analyze the newspaper articles on pages 715 and 716 of this text. Then conduct research by using the *Readers Guide to Periodical Literature* to find a recent article on the privatization of farms in the European republics. Evaluate the article you selected and the two in the text. Synthesize the information and use this to predict three or more possible consequences of the privatization of farms in the European republics. Indicate which consequence you think is most likely to occur and explain why.

DEVELOPING A GLOBAL VIEWPOINT

The effects of the fall of communism and the breakup of the Soviet Union were more than regional. How might these events affect other Communist countries? Developing countries? The United States?

Europe

The diverse lands of Europe are peopled by many different ethnic groups, each with its own language, culture, beliefs, and values. In ancient times, Greeks and Romans set standards of excellence that dominated the Mediterranean region of the continent. In later centuries, western and eastern Europe followed different paths. In western Europe a vigorous civilization emerged whose powerful political, economic, social, and religious ideas enabled it to explore and dominate much of the globe. In eastern Europe, invasion and conflict led to constantly changing boundaries and a persistent mixture of glory and tragedy.

CHAPTERS

AT A GLANCE

LAND AREA: 1,986,000 sq. mi. (5,142,000 sq. km.)

LAND RESOURCES:
cropland: 29.7%
pasture: 17.6%
forest/woodland: 33.2%
other land: 19.6%

WILDERNESS AREA: 3%

MAJOR MOUNTAIN RANGES:
Alps, Apennines, Carpathian, Dinaric Alps, Pyrenees, Sierra Nevada

MAJOR RIVERS:
Danube, Elbe, Marne, Oder, Po, Rhine, Rhône, Seine, Thames

POPULATION: (1992 est.) 511,000,000

POPULATION UNDER 15/OVER 65:
20%/14%

LIFE EXPECTANCY: 75 yrs.

POPULATION PROJECTION:
516,000,000 (by 2025)

POPULATION DENSITY:
257/sq. mi. (99/sq. km.)

URBAN POPULATION: 75%

LARGEST CITIES: (millions)
London, Great Britain (6.9)
Madrid, Spain (3.1)
Berlin, Germany (3.1)
Rome, Italy (2.8)

CHAPTER OUTLINE

1 The Continent

2 Mountain Areas

3 Plains and Rivers

4 City and Countryside

People and Places to Know

North Atlantic Drift, Central Uplands, the Alps, the Carpathians, North European Plain, the Ruhr, the Danube, the Rhine, London, Slovakia

Key Terms to Define

estuary, maritime

Objectives to Learn

1. **Define** Europe and identify its geographic features.
2. **Recognize** the relationship between Europe's diverse geography and its peoples.
3. **Compare** city and country life in Europe.

The town of Agios Nikolaos on the Greek island of Crete

Varied Lands and Peoples

> Ruschuk, on the lower Danube, where I came into the world, was a marvelous city for a child, and if I say that Ruschuk is in Bulgaria, then I am giving an inadequate picture of it. For people of the most varied backgrounds lived there, on any one day you could hear seven or eight languages. Aside from the Bulgarians, who often came from the countryside, there were many Turks, who lived in their own neighborhood, and next to it was the neighborhood of the Sephardim, the Spanish Jews—our neighborhood. There were Greeks, Albanians, Armenians, Gypsies. From the opposite side of the Danube came Rumanians; my wetnurse, whom I no longer remember, was Rumanian. There were also Russians here and there.
>
> As a child, I had no real grasp of this variety, but I never stopped feeling its effects. Some people have stuck in my memory only because they belonged to a particular ethnic group and wore a different costume from the others. . . . My mother's best friend was Olga, a Russian woman. Once every week, Gypsies came into our courtyard, so many that they seemed like an entire nation. . . .
>
> Ruschuk was an old port on the Danube. . . . As a port, it had attracted people from all over, and the Danube was a constant topic of discussion. There were stories about the extraordinary years when the Danube froze over; about sleigh rides all the way across the ice to Rumania; about starving wolves at the heels of the sleigh horses. . . .
>
> It would be hard to give a full picture of the colorful time of those early years in Ruschuk, the passions and the terrors. Anything I subsequently experienced had already happened in Ruschuk. There, the rest of the world was known as "Europe," and if someone sailed up the Danube to Vienna, people said he was going to Europe. Europe began where the Turkish Empire had once ended.

With these words, Elias Canetti, a Nobel Prize winner for Literature, shares his memories of his growing-up years in the southeastern corner of Europe. His memories raise important questions—What is Europe? Is it a place? Is it a state of mind?

There are no simple answers to these questions. In its geography, history, and peoples,

Europe embodies diversity. Excluding the European parts of Turkey and the former Soviet Union, it occupies only about 3 percent of Earth's landmass. Yet it is home to more than 30 countries, whose peoples speak some 50 different languages. In recent years, Europeans have been working toward unity. But for centuries tremendous variety, conflict, and competition have been far more characteristic.

Source: Elias Canetti. The Tongue Set Free. Continuum Publishing Corporation, 1979, pp. 4–5.

SECTION 1

The Continent

The continent of Europe is a huge peninsula that extends westward from the landmass of Asia. It covers about 1.9 million square miles (5.1 million square kilometers) and is smaller than any other continent except Australia. The Arctic Ocean, the Mediterranean Sea, the Baltic Sea, and various extensions of the Atlantic Ocean, however, provide Europe with a long, irregular coastline and

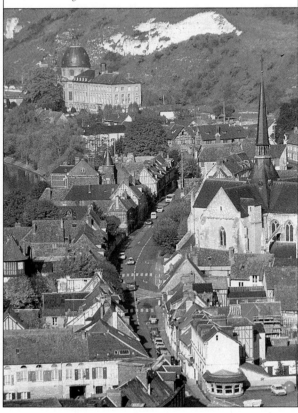

EXAMINING PHOTOGRAPHS *These homes, typical of those found in France's northwest province of Normandy, house the many sailors and farmers who live in the area. What do the roofs indicate about the weather in Normandy?*

many offshore islands. Deep bays, narrow seas, and well-protected **estuaries,** or inlets, shelter many fine harbors. This has encouraged trade with foreign lands and made some European countries great **maritime,** or seafaring, nations.

Closeness to the sea also has had a favorable impact on Europe's climate. Most of the continent is within 300 miles (400 kilometers) of the Atlantic Ocean. A current known as the North Atlantic Drift brings warm water from the tropical South Atlantic to the western coast of Europe. The water warms the winds that blow across the continent from the Atlantic Ocean. These winds affect most of the continent because no mountain barriers are large enough to block them. The result is that, despite Europe's northern latitude, many areas of the continent enjoy relatively mild year-round temperatures. In general, however, northern Europe has longer, colder winters and shorter, cooler summers than southern Europe. Also, winters are longer and colder, and summers are shorter and hotter, in the east than in the west.

Europe also has great environmental diversity. For example, its landscapes vary from mountainous to flat. Environmental factors have an important impact on the way Europeans live. An author who traveled across the continent talks about some aspects of Europe's environmental diversity:

The roofs of Europe, the old roofs at least, . . . have some interesting things to say. . . . They offer a record of how [people] have come to terms with rain and wind and heat and cold and, of course, other people. . . .

In Normandy [a French province] we saw rooflines of moderate pitch—no need there, evidently, for steep slopes to get rid of heavy rains or snows. Their eaves showed only a moderate overhang—no need for them to be extended to offer shelter, and no need for them to be retracted to avoid ripping winds. . . . The tiles of the roofs looked tightly fitted, and window shutters were closed against the night air. . . . Bent working backs were a part of the landscape. The climate seemed to prevent inhibitions from thawing: we heard no one sing aloud out-of-doors in the daylight, and no Normandy child would return our waves. But the wheat with its company of red poppies and cornflowers waved. . . .

Southward from Paris we watched the roofs flatten and broaden, displaying wide eaves that shaded the windows. . . .

Bent working backs were no longer part of the landscape; they were replaced by backs bent to conform to the curve of the chaise lounge. Here a French child might return a friendly wave, people might sing outdoors. . . .

As we continued south into Provence [a French province], we observed one change. . . . Something had happened to the roofs. They had pulled in their eaves. Windows . . . were absent from the north walls of houses, and some roofs had rocks on them.

We were in the area of the mistral, that fearful northwest wind that comes off the Alps each winter and spring, blowing bitter cold for days on end. . . .

As we traveled west into Italy's watery Po Valley, we saw that the tiled roofs of the two-storied farmhouses had extended themselves into L shapes and taken on added responsibilities. One wing of each house . . . accommodated cattle downstairs and the family upstairs. . . . The other wing was open except for its roof and one side, which was built up with openwork brick lattice. . . .

From the productive farmlands spread flat under the sun, we soon turned south. The hill towns and long slopes of olive trees and grape vines beckoned. . . .

The roof lines of Italian cities displayed records of human conflict, pride, and hope. . . . Spires and domes raised bells, and columns raised soldiers and statesmen and wolves and horses and gods.

And mingled with these against the sky we enjoyed the lighter note of many dovecotes and decorative chimney pots, and lines of laundry flapping from high balconies.

In southern Italy the roofs became completely flat, and remained that way across Greece and the Mediterranean countries. In these warm lands, now shorn of all but the most sparse covering of drought-resistant and goat-resistant plants, the flat roofs have long been popular places in the night breeze, places offering unbroken views of the stars over the sea and the treeless hills. . . .

From the flat Mediterranean roofs we turned northward again, and westward, and skyward into the Swiss Alps. The roofs sloped there but shallowly. Thick slabs of slate were used for shingles, and boulders anchored them against the wind. During the winter thick featherbeds of snow provide additional warmth. The eaves were wide and spread like the wings of brooding hens. . . .

For us in our wet raincoats and rainhats it was easy to understand why the roofs had been built so wide, and why porches and balconies were tucked under the eaves.

SECTION 1 REVIEW

CHECKING FOR UNDERSTANDING
1. **Define** estuary, maritime.
2. **Describe** Europe's location and its relationship to the sea.
3. **Classify** the European houses described in the reading according to location, climate, building materials, and design.

CRITICAL THINKING
4. **Determining Cause and Effect** What impact do you think geography and environment have had on the building of homes in Europe?

Source: May Theilgaard Watts. *Reading the Landscape of Europe.* Harper & Row, Publishers, Inc., 1971, pp. 1–4, 6–9.

Europe

LAND FROM THE SEA

According to an old Dutch saying, "God made Heaven and Earth, but the Dutch made Holland." The Dutch, the people of the land known today as the Netherlands, have struggled against the sea for centuries. Their country is a small densely populated nation in northwestern Europe whose flat terrain borders the North Sea. To relieve overcrowding, they have used their skills to obtain new land from the sea. No other people, in fact, have been more successful in increasing their territory at the expense of the ocean.

The Dutch first started to gain land from the sea during the Middle Ages. Around 1000 AD, they began building dunes and dikes, or seawalls, to hold back the seawaters. Four hundred years later, they erected windmills. They used the windmills to convert sea winds into energy to pump water from polders, land below sea level surrounded by dikes and drained artificially.

Today a large portion of the Dutch countryside consists of polders, and the picturesque, but inefficient, windmills have been replaced largely by electric pumps and other modern equipment. With new technology, Dutch engineers have developed large drainage and flood-control systems. Two projects, in particular, have attracted worldwide attention—the Zuider Zee Project and the Delta Plan.

The Zuider Zee Project was begun in 1920. Its aim was to seal off the Zuider Zee, a large shallow bay stretching deep into the Netherlands, from the North Sea. In 1932, Dutch engineers completed the building of a 19-mile (30-kilometer) barrier dam that succeeded in separating the Zuider Zee from the ocean. In time, the Zuider Zee became a freshwater lake known as the Ijsselmmer.

Over time, parts of the Ijsselmmer were pumped dry and converted into polders. Today, most of the new land that has been created consists of farmland or recreation areas. Although even more sections of the Ijsselmmer are planned for drainage, high costs and disagreements about the use of new land have delayed final completion of the project.

The Delta Plan, a flood-control project, got underway in 1958 as a reaction to a flood five years earlier that killed nearly 2000 people in the southwestern part of the country. To prevent future flood disasters in the region, Dutch engineers began the Delta Plan. It involves a series of dams, barriers, and artificial islands that will prevent the sea from flooding into rivers and inland waterways. It will shorten the coastline by 450 miles (720 kilometers) and reduce the amount of salt in the soil. It also will enable the Dutch to gain 25,000 more acres (10,000 hectares) of land from the North Sea.

DRAWING CONCLUSIONS

What methods have the Dutch used to gain land from the sea? What plans might you devise to gain land from the sea?

Mountain Areas

The mountains that cover much of Europe vary considerably in age, height, and composition. Some mountainous areas are rich in minerals and provide good opportunities for mining and industry. They often have good soil, sufficient water, and a climate favorable to economic prosperity. Others, however, lack valuable minerals and are so dry and badly eroded that little can grow and only a few people can earn a worthwhile living.

HIGHLANDS AND UPLANDS

Two old and relatively low mountainous areas mark the landscape of Europe. One is the Northwestern Highlands of Iceland, Scandinavia, and the British Isles. The other is the Central Uplands, which stretch from Portugal and Spain through central France and Germany to western Czechoslovakia. France's portion of the Central Uplands is called the *Massif Central.* It is an area of high plateau and eroded mountains. In the fol-

lowing excerpt, a French historian describes a journey through part of the *Massif Central:*

I recently made the journey from Beaune to Vezelay by Autun, then took a leisurely route across the national park of the Morvan. The hillsides around Beaune are the most beautiful series of vineyards I know in the world—the pleasure of the eye can be combined with certain other pleasures. Before you reach Nolay (with its old market-hall, church and sixteenth-century houses) you are in the Massif Central, and it is like entering another world: here vines are few and in the broad meadows divided by hedges or lines of trees, herds of creamy white Charollais cattle are grazing. It feels as if one is going back into the past, an impression even stronger in Autun, in the quiet and lovely streets of the old town. But the countryside round Autun still has an air of openness and easy living, which one leaves behind as one approaches the Settons reservoir, built by damming the bed of the Cure. Not so long ago this was a way-station for logs floating down river to Paris. Even on a sunny day in October, entering the Morvan national park means travelling through a dense and dark forest of deciduous

EXAMINING PHOTOGRAPHS *A small town nestles among the hills of the Massif Central in France. What two geographic features are characteristic of this region?*

trees, punctuated here and there by compact regiments of conifers. Can it be that these silent woods, with roads almost empty and edged with golden bracken [large ferns] in autumn, are no longer being forested? Alongside some impressively high piles of logs by the roadside, I saw no workmen and only one logging machine, which was not working. From time to time there are clearings, valley beds with a few acres of cultivable soil. . . . In each of these one finds a hamlet of three or four houses. The further north one goes, slates gradually begin to replace tiles on their roofs. There are a few sparse villages too, and some fields of wheat, rye, or potatoes, but mostly there are meadows and yet more meadows, with hedgerows or lines of trees.

Source: From THE IDENTITY OF FRANCE, Volume I by Fernand Braudel, translated by Sian Reynolds. Reprinted by permission of HarperCollins Publishers.

SOUTHERN MOUNTAIN RANGES

The mountains of the Southern Mountain Ranges are younger and less eroded than those of the highlands and uplands areas. They are made up of several mountain chains—the Sierra Nevada in southern Spain, the Pyrenees along the Spanish-French border, and the Apennines in Italy. They also include the Alps, which cover part of southeastern France and northern Italy, most of Switzerland, and part of southern Germany and Austria.

Because of their many openings, or passes, the Alps have aided communication and trade. Merchants with teams of mules laden with goods made their way through Alpine passes more than 2000 years ago. Today, rail traffic through the Alps is so heavy and environmentally damaging that 2 train tunnels through the Alps are being considered.

Although much of the Alps are forested, dairy farming and cheese making have also flourished there—and, more recently, tourism and winter sports. The dazzling beauty of the Alps attracts 100 million visitors a year. Construction of ski runs and resorts now endangers the ecology of the region. The following story of a Swiss farmer highlights some of the region's complexities:

George Roth, a farmer who looks out over three stunning Swiss valleys on the heights above Leysin, says he does not mind skiers. Even in winter, Mr. Roth and his wife, Josianne, get up early and milk the cows. Then they take the cable car up to 6,000 feet [1,829 meters], where they have converted a summer stable into a skiers' cafe.

They like the extra income and mingling with the visitors. But they hate "all those machines."

"Everyone wants bigger and better ski runs," said Mr. Roth, so machines flatten the runs and harden the snow, which turns to ice. The ice melts later than snow, "so we get less grass." Mrs. Roth added, "There must be a way to ski and not destroy so much.". . .

Experts say that good ski-runs need not be an ecological hazard if properly shaped and lined with vegetation. But such rules are often overlooked.

"Ski-runs generally create more run-off," said Mr. Nielson, the watershed specialist. "Water comes down faster and in bigger quantities. You need bigger culverts [drains] and check dams. With excess run-off, ravines quickly become deeper and slopes become more unsteady and slide or collapse."

The Roth family owns one of the last four farms around Leysin. Twenty years ago, there were 25. The story of the vanishing farmers is repeated throughout the Alps, although many governments subsidize farmers to keep them on the land, to take care of trees and guard the landscape.

"If you take away the farmers, the landscape degrades even faster," said Mr. Berghold, the adviser in Zurich. "Many chalet owners are outsiders and they don't know or care."

Furthermore, Government officials and environmentalists worry about the dwindling number of cows, seeing cattle as useful, rather than the environmental burden they are viewed as elsewhere: The cows crop grass, and short grass holds snow, while long grass bends and lets the snow slip off, leading to snowslides in these steep slopes.

EASTERN EUROPEAN RANGES

Farther east lie a number of other high mountain ranges—the Dinarics of the Yugoslav republics and Greece, the Balkans of Bulgaria, and the Carpathians. The Carpathians, the longest mountain chain in eastern Europe, run in an 800-mile (1280-kilometer) arc through Slovakia, Poland, Hungary,

Source: Marlise Simons. "Alps Caught in Vise Between Tourism and Trucks," in *The New York Times,* April 6, 1992, p. A12. Copyright © 1992 by The New York Times Company. Reprinted by permission.

and Romania. Fertile soil in their numerous valleys makes farming, animal herding, and fruit growing possible. Below, an eastern European journalist talks about the Carpathian way of life:

Near the medieval city of Sibiu, in Transylvania [a Romanian province] . . . , softly contoured mountains form a backdrop for plains dotted with village communities. Other villages, concealed by pine and oak forests, are scattered in the foothills. One of these is Poiana Sibiului . . . , whose approach is a steep climb through the high plateau, past cornfields and patches of sunflowers. The hilly terrain suddenly gives way to apple orchards and lush, green, velvety pastures. On this landscape, the shepherd, his sheep, and his dog . . . have left their imprint for millennia. . . .

Of the 800 families in Poiana Sibiului, four-fifths own sheep herds, ranging from 200 to more than 3,000 animals. . . . Many Poianar shepherds travel three to four hundred miles [4.8 to 6.4 hundred kilometers] each year. . . .

A shepherd starts his journey to his winter grazing area toward the end of September, when the mountain pastures are depleted. Traveling on foot, shepherds go across mountains and through valleys, following watercourses to the warmer plains. Aaron Banu and his uncle have traveled the same route for the past ten years. They walk 250 miles, [400 kilometers] passing through forty-seven villages.

Shepherds with small herds often travel together. Donkeys and horses transport their blankets, food, and other necessities. While the trip can take anywhere from three weeks to two months, the shepherds are never in a hurry, as long as they are able to feed their herd en route. The winter shelters are, at best, makeshift lean-tos of wood and tar paper, used to store food and clothing and for sleeping. The shepherds build them themselves and return to them each year. Life is generally lived out-

EXAMINING PHOTOGRAPHS *The Chiele Bicazului Cliffs in Transylvania, Romania, are part of the Carpathian mountain chain.* *How long is the Carpathian chain?*

doors; at night, near a roaring fire, the shepherds enjoy a few moments of refreshment with a pot of soup and *mamaliga* (cornmeal mush).

In the winter months, finding sufficient food for the herds becomes difficult. If they can, shepherds prefer to stay near a collective farm, where the animals can graze on beet stubs and cornstalks. The sheep even eat overripe pumpkins left in the fields. In the middle of winter, when the fields are devoid of any food, shepherds feed the sheep corn, bought from the state at high market prices. The shepherd's isolation from his home and family, the struggle for food, and the vigil for the birth of the lambs are hardships lightened by hope for the spring.

Source: Ayşe Gürsan-Salzmann. "Shepherds of Transylvania" in *Natural History*, July 1984, Vol. 93, No. 7, The American Museum of Natural History, 1984, pp. 42, 44.

SECTION 3
Plains and Rivers

In addition to mountains, Europe has broad fertile plains. In southern Europe, plains areas are found in Italy and the Iberian Peninsula. Nestled among eastern Europe's mountain ranges are the Danube plains of Romania and the Plain of Thrace in Bulgaria. Farther west is the Great Hungarian Plain, a treeless stretch of land that covers about half of Hungary and extends into the Balkan Peninsula. Before World War II, Hungarian nobles raised horses and crops, such as corn, potatoes, sugar beets, wheat, and wine grapes on vast estates that covered the plain. Today, the region is still known for its agriculture and horse-raising.

NORTH EUROPEAN PLAIN

The largest and most important plains region is the North European Plain. It extends from southern Britain in the west, across northern France, Belgium, the Netherlands, and central Germany, to Poland and Ukraine more than 1800 miles (2880 kilometers) to the east. It is made up of flat land, broken occasionally by rivers, rolling farmland, and low hills. For centuries, ease of movement and the fertility of the land have drawn invaders to this area.

The North European Plain is the most heavily populated area of Europe. Once heavily forested, the land was long ago cleared for farming. In the past 200 years, it has also become a major industrial area with large cities and busy factories.

Coal mining contributed to the industrial growth of the Plain. Although Europe had coal deposits in Britain, Belgium, and Poland, the largest concentration of high quality coal needed to produce steel was found in the Ruhr, a small area of western Germany around the city of Essen. In the 1800's, giant steel mills were built to take advantage of the coal found in nearby mines. Below, an author describes the continuing importance of coal and steel in the life of Essen today:

Looking across the mill yard, you watch processions of trains arriving, freighted with iron ore. Their cargo comes from all over the world. . . . Most of the ore has been shipped from Africa, Asia, and the Western Hemisphere. . . . [A]s the trains dump their cascades of glinting rock into bins, chains of buckets brimming with coal appear from holes in the earth and are shuttled upward, on moving ropes, toward the factory. Good coke [coal by-produce used to make steel] is more precious than ore; the plant is here because the coal is just below.

Like the mine, the mill is uncomfortably hot. . . . Unlike the tunnel, however, the plant provides spectacles of blinding beauty. A major steel tap, with hundreds of tons of liquid metal streaming from several open-hearth furnaces simultaneously, throwing off great clouds of sparks as they race through the earthen forms provided for them, is breathtaking. Crusts of iron oxide flaking off hot ingots [bars of cast metal], the cherry-red glow of metal moving through blooming mills, the way monster forgings repeatedly burst into gouts [fluid masses] of flame as automatic presses five stories high shape and trim them—the whole pageant is exciting, even glorious. . . .

. . . Striking out across the centers of heavy industry, one acquires a feeling for the setting. The peculiar, introverted society that has grown up in the shadow of the towering chimneys is a milieu [setting] all its own. It becomes evident in little ways. You are struck by the angular, topheavy silhouettes of the terra-cotta houses; by the dark, smoke-colored patina [covering] that gives even the newest buildings an aura of age. . . .

. . . Ruhr workers really work. Indeed, one's most enduring impression of the region is of activity. Each of its industrial complexes seethes, and every artery in and out of the arena is crowded with trucks, trains, barges, and planes, bringing fodder for the plants and departing with finished products. It is noisy, it is incredibly busy.

EXAMINING PHOTOGRAPHS *Steel remains a key industry in Germany.* **What natural resource fuels the steel industry?**

Source: From THE ARMS OF KRUPP, *1587–1968* by William Manchester, Copyright © 1964, 1965, 1968 by William Manchester. By permission of Little, Brown and Company.

RIVERS

Many of Europe's rivers flow through the plains regions. Until the development of the railroad and automobiles, these rivers were the easiest means of transportation from one place to another. Even today, rivers and canals play an important role as transportation routes linking the interior of the continent with coastal seaports. They also provide water to irrigate farmland and to produce electricity. In France, the Loire, Seine, Rhône, and Garonne rivers are used extensively for irrigation and navigation. Much of Poland's shipping depends on the Vistula River. Then there is the Danube, the longest river in eastern Europe. It flows for 1770 miles (2832 kilometers) from Germany's Black Forest to the Black Sea. Each year, ships traveling on the Danube carry about 77 million tons (70 million metric tons) of cargo. The Danube is also used for irrigation, fishing, and hydroelectric power.

One of the most important and busiest rivers in western Europe is the Rhine. A major part of the inland waterway system that links many industrial cities, it flows for 700 miles (1120 kilometers) from the Swiss Alps through Germany to Rotterdam in the Netherlands, one of the busiest seaports of the world. To some, the Rhine is more than just a river. Below, a famous French writer named Victor Hugo described the feelings the river brought out in him when he visited it early in the 1800's:

Yes, the Rhine is a noble river,—feudal, republican, imperial; worthy at the same time of France and of Germany. The whole history of Europe is combined within its two great aspects,—in this flood of the warrior and of the philosopher; in this proud stream, which causes France to bound with joy, and by whose profound murmurings Germany is bewildered in dreams.

The Rhine is unique; it combines the qualities of every river. Like the Rhône, it is rapid; broad, like the Loire; encased, like the Meuse; serpentine, like the Seine; limpid and green, like the Somme; histori-

EXAMINING PHOTOGRAPHS *The Rhine, long a river of historical, economic, and cultural influence, flows through one of Europe's most heavily populated and industrialized regions. The longest section of the Rhine lies in Germany, whose people view it as a national symbol.* **What are some of the other major rivers in Europe?**

cal, like the Tiber; royal, like the Danube; mysterious, like the Nile; spangled with gold, like an American river; and like a river of Asia, abounding with phantoms and fables. . . .

The Rhine . . . is the great moat which divides the north from the south. The Rhine for thirty ages has seen the forms and reflected the shadows of almost all the warriors who tilled the old continent with that [plow] share which they call sword. . . .

The Rhine—that noble flood, . . . bore at one time upon its surface bridges of boats, over which the armies of Italy, Spain, and France poured into Germany, and, which . . . were made use of by the hordes of barbarians when rushing into the ancient Roman world; at another, on its surface floated peaceably the fir-trees of Murg and of Saint Gall, . . . the marble of Bale, the salt of Karlshall, the leather of Stromberg, . . . the wine of Johannisburg, the slates of Coab, the cloth and earthen-ware of Wallendar, the silks and linens of Cologne. It majestically performs its double function of flood of war and flood of peace, having . . . upon the ranges of hills which embank the most notable portion of its course, oak-trees on one side and vine-trees on the other,—signifying strength and joy. . . .

The Rhine . . . seems to be a symbolical stream. In its windings, in its course, in the midst of all that it traverses, it is . . . the image of civilization to which it has been so useful, and which it will still serve. It flows from Constance to Rotterdam; from the country of eagles to the village of herrings; from the city of popes, of councils, and of emperors, to the counter of the merchant and of the citizen; from the great Alps themselves to that immense body of water which we term *ocean*.

Source: Victor Hugo. *The Rhine*, Volume I, Estes and Lauriat, pp. 130–131, 144–145, 148–149.

CHECKING FOR UNDERSTANDING
1. **List** some of the major plains areas of Europe and their locations.
2. **Examine** the role that rivers play in Europe's economy.

CRITICAL THINKING
3. **Demonstrating Reasoned Judgment** What do you think are the advantages and disadvantages of living on the North European Plain? If you were European, would you prefer to live on the Plain or would you prefer to live elsewhere? Explain.

SECTION 4

City and Countryside

Excluding the European area of the Commonwealth of Independent States, Europe has 511 million people—a large number for a small space. It is one of the world's most densely populated areas. Yet, it is not all equally crowded. Most Europeans live in major cities or their suburbs, while large stretches of countryside have few people. Southern Europe remains more rural than northern Europe, but even here change is occurring.

CITIES

Europe's cities have distinct characters that reflect years of historical development. Some are world famous, such as London, Paris, Amsterdam, Madrid, Rome, Berlin, Vienna, Budapest, Prague, and Warsaw. Their palaces, churches, open spaces, parks, and monuments recall great moments in their histories. Rivers and waterfronts add unique vistas.

Modern times have blurred some of the differences among Europe's cities. Some cities were heavily damaged during World War II. While special buildings—and even a few districts—were restored to their original look, most were rebuilt in modern style.

Urban renewal projects have also contributed to the changing face of the cities. Skyscrapers have transformed their skylines and modern office buildings, apartment blocks, and shopping complexes have replaced neighborhoods and their variety of small shops. Heavy traffic and noise have become part of life. These changes have not happened without controversy. The following excerpt discusses the impact of modernization on London's traditional working-class neighborhoods along the Thames River:

East of the Tower of London, another London begins. Seen from the air, it appears to be more water than land, a Thames-side archipelago formed by a series of huge [human]-made lakes: the docks. Scarcely four miles from Buckingham Palace, it has echoed through the

EXAMINING PHOTOGRAPHS *Stockholm, Sweden has blended traditional and modern styles of architecture. How have urban renewal projects changed many cities?*

ages with the greatest names of maritime and commercial history, from Nelson to Cook to Captain Kidd, the *Mayflower* crew, Frobisher, and Drake. It has always been a world apart, and happy—no, proud—to remain so. But with a tidal wave of money and promises, all that is changing.

Between 1967 and 1981 commercial pressures forced the docks to close, and shipping moved downstream to Tilbury, where it could be more competitive. In the ten years since, new commercial forces have been at work in a redevelopment effort of stupendous proportions . . . under one resounding name: Docklands.

New housing, new offices, new people have sprung up virtually overnight; real estate speculators and foreign investors have plunged in . . . ; new roads are being gouged out, old roads redrawn or renamed, and whole blocks of longtime residents uprooted, with crowds of newcomers—so-called yuppies with phones in their BMW's—moving in.

Not surprisingly, nobody is neutral. Everyone from reporters to real estate analysts to the average bloke in the pub has an opinion, usually several. One thing is clear: The old riverside communities that struggled to stick together through the Blitz [the World War II German bombing of London], rising unemployment, and floods of immigrants are now receiving the final blow. To hear the old working-class families talk, you'd think somebody had died. . . .

"It's all changed," says cab driver Billy Collins. "It's changed so much it's unbelievable. The people were close, and they're not close now."

"It used to be nice, didn't it?" says Lil Bannister, as she pulls on her pint of stout during a break in the Monday night meet of the Mile End and District Ladies Dart Leagues. "But today people are greedy and they're nasty. We worked hard, but anybody would say they'd rather have the old days back. We have more life then than we do now. We was united."

"Maybe their intentions were right, but they've gone over the top," says Renee Hames, the fourth generation of her docker family. "They've ripped the guts out of the place, they've taken its soul."

"They" are commonly understood to be the London Docklands Development Corporation. Approved by then Prime Minister Margaret Thatcher in 1981, LDDC's primary function was to attract an unorthodox mix of public and private money to revitalize the area. "We think we're building a new center for London that will allow it to remain the capital of Europe," declared former chief executive Michael Honey. "We'll enable London to expand while preserving the historic area.". . .

Virtually every event and personage that made England great was connected with these shores. After all, "London is one of those rare capitals that is also a port," explains librarian Bob Aspinall at the Museum in Docklands. "It's impossible to separate the history and capital from the docks; the city was built on trade. . . ."

The Romans made London an important port, and the following centuries saw trade increase. In medieval days Geoffrey Chaucer served as commissioner of maintenance of the river between Woolwich and Greenwich. Captain James Cook organized his voyages from the village of Deptford. The *Mayflower* crew boarded their ship in Rotherhithe. John Newton, who forswore his career as a slave captain and wrote "Amazing Grace," was a native of Wapping. And generations of Britons have taken pride in the riches of empire that poured through the docks. . . .

Living in Docklands . . . is about as comfortable as living in a house on moving day, with the resident large and noisy family refusing to vacate while the new large and noisy family begins unpacking. The turmoil of this regeneration is difficult to overstate. The workday air shudders with the thunder of pile drivers and

EXAMINING PHOTOGRAPHS *Modern sculpture contrasts sharply with the traditions of Canary Wharf in Docklands, London. What changes have occurred recently in Docklands?*

jackhammers as concrete mixers and Esso tanker trucks vie with Rolls-Royces and Daimlers; motorcycle messengers swoop in between struggling city buses; parking is nonexistent; traffic is paralyzed. . . .

But some locals are ready for improvements. There is even optimism. "Nah, the neighborhood hasn't changed," said young "Noddy" Goodman at the wheel of his mini-cab. "If people are getting something by hard work, let them enjoy it. Good luck to 'em. They've never done me no harm."

"I think it's for the better," chirps bus driver Peter Tilden. "We need something down in the East End. All the old 'uns—they'll complain about anything, won't they? But the young ones are 'Yeh, let's go for it.' It's giving jobs, innit?"

Source: Erla Zwingle. "Docklands, London's New Frontier" in *National Geographic,* July 1991, pp. 36, 39–41, 44, 47.

THE COUNTRYSIDE

Most rural dwellers are farmers who raise livestock, grow fruits and vegetables, or produce such grain crops as barely, oats, rye, and wheat. Most of the farms in northwestern Europe use modern equipment and chemical fertilizers and are known for their high productivity, while in the Mediterranean lands farmers are just starting to use modern machinery and methods, so crop yields are not as high. In the former communist nations of eastern Europe, government-owned farms are being transformed into privately owned farms in the hope that farmers will produce more if they own the land.

In rural areas of Europe, the village often is the center of life. There, the pace of living is slower and quieter than in the cities. Villages are adjusting to modern ways, but many villagers still hold on to many traditional customs. For example, on special occasions, weddings and national holidays, villagers dress in the traditional clothing of their ancestors. Below, a young American journalist describes a visit to relatives in Slovakia:

Just as the train approached the station of Poprad, I caught a glimpse of the High Tatras. Despite the "rough and tumble" landscape I had just crossed, the jagged-edged, snow-capped peaks took me by surprise. . . .

After stepping from the train, I received an emotional welcome from aunts, uncles, and cousins. We packed ourselves into several cars for the trip to the village. On the ride farther up into the mountains, we rounded sharp turns that revealed striking views of distant valleys in blues, greens, and golds, and mountain meadows ablaze with wild poppies. A horse-driven hay wagon passed, with several women in tightly tied head scarfs and bright dresses sitting in the back holding wooden rakes. One of many roadside shrines, a painted cross decorated with freshly cut wild flowers, zipped by. We also passed a crowded blue and white bus—the local from the nearby town of Levoča. Still we had farther to go, into the remote highland areas.

Suddenly, like a mirage, Olšavica appeared in the distance nestled in a sheltered valley. Clouds of steam rose from the moisture-laden green hills around the village. A brief hint of sun glistened from the metal roofs of a cluster of houses. Ranging from white and light pastels to richly dark browns and ambers, they seemed to grow from the earth like the lush meadow grass that covered the neighboring hills or the tall stately pines that pushed up in groves from wilder stretches of countryside. Soon we were heading down a stretch of straight road, and I spied quickly a blue marker with Olšavica printed in yellow letters.

As we drove into Olšavica, the road divided in two. The upper, more traveled route was a stop for daily buses on their way to the towns. The lower road was almost a dirt path favored by the village cows as they headed out in a long, orderly row to pasture. Both roads joined near a community center, a plain building used for village social and political activities. A tiny stream shadowed by hanging willows veered sharply to the right. It led to the centuries-old church of Saints Peter and Paul with its bulb-shaped tower. Beyond the church was the village dairy works and the pasture.

We finally stopped in front of a gray plastered house. Amidst tears, kisses, and hugs, I walked arm-in-arm with my relatives into the house and up to a second-floor room that had been spread for a feast. The house itself was a puzzle. Although the section facing the street was recently built, I had only to walk farther into the backyard to see that it was attached to a wooden cabin of indefinite age. The cabin, in turn, was linked to an even more ancient, wooden, cattle barn.

EXAMINING PHOTOGRAPHS *Small villages and towns like this one dot the rolling countryside of Slovakia. There, fertile soil drained by the Danube River and its tributaries provides rich agricultural growing regions.* **What traditional customs are practiced in rural Slovakia?**

Much to my surprise, I noticed that Olšavica had not rushed into the twentieth century in one leap, but in measured steps. Then, there was the matter of dress. Though my teenaged-cousin Maria was fashionably dressed, the rest of the women displayed a traditional uniformity of style. Each had a scarf tied at the neck, a blouse worn over a dark skirt with vertical pleats down the center of the front and back, and laced boots. In fact, it required a careful eye to distinguish at first among the numerous women. For the most part, they smiled shyly and remained silent as they placed heaping plates of roast pork, dumplings, and pickled cabbage flavored with caraway seeds on the table before us. Shortly afterward, a large bottle of vodka appeared, and toasting began. The celebration became lively and continued into the early hours of the morning!

SECTION 4 REVIEW

CHECKING FOR UNDERSTANDING
1. **Name** some European cities and their characteristics.
2. **Describe** the impact of modernization on European cities.

CRITICAL THINKING
3. **Making Comparisons** How does life in Europe's cities compare with life in its countryside?

Source: John Kohan. Personal observations, July 1977. Reprinted by permission.

Geography

EUROPE'S DIVERSITY

FOCUSING ON THE ISSUE

What is true for one area of Europe may not be true for another. Based on the information in the maps that follow, determine whether each of the following statements is true or false. If a statement is false, give the correct answer.

1. Most of Europe has a humid continental climate.
2. There are very few mountain ranges in Europe.
3. Western Europe is more densely populated than eastern Europe.
4. The Danube River flows only through Germany.
5. Two major plains dominate the landscape of Europe.

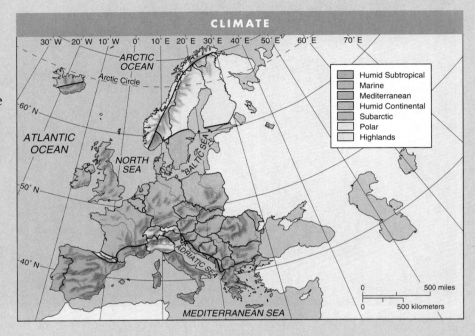

CLIMATE

Humid Subtropical
Marine
Mediterranean
Humid Continental
Subarctic
Polar
Highlands

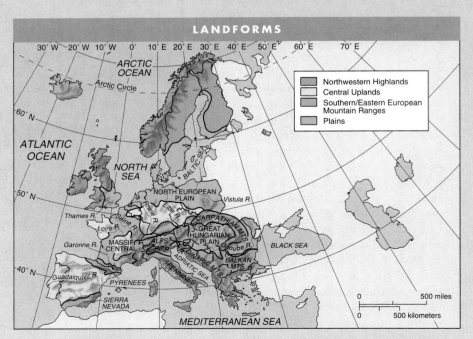

LANDFORMS

Northwestern Highlands
Central Uplands
Southern/Eastern European Mountain Ranges
Plains

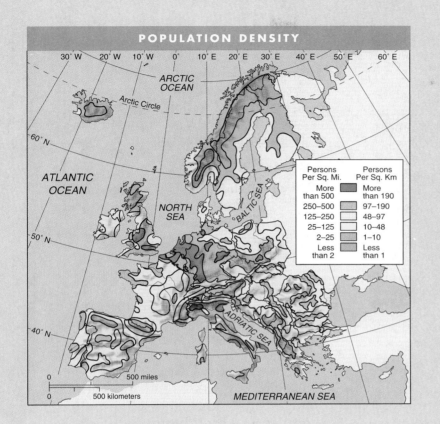

POPULATION DENSITY

ARCTIC OCEAN

Arctic Circle

ATLANTIC OCEAN

NORTH SEA

BALTIC SEA

ADRIATIC SEA

MEDITERRANEAN SEA

Persons Per Sq. Mi.	Persons Per Sq. Km
More than 500	More than 190
250–500	97–190
125–250	48–97
25–125	10–48
2–25	1–10
Less than 2	Less than 1

0 500 miles

0 500 kilometers

Chapter 46 Review

SUMMARY

Europe is a large peninsula that extends westward from Asia. Closeness to the sea has given Europe a relatively mild climate and has encouraged European trade with foreign lands. Major rivers, especially the Rhine and the Danube, provide trade links between the interior of Europe and coastal ports.

Although it is a small part of the world's landmass, Europe has geographic diversity. It has a long, irregular coastline with many islands. Among the continent's variety of landforms are mountains and plains. The heavily populated plains areas contain most of Europe's cities, industries, and agriculture. Europe also has great cultural diversity. It includes more than 30 nations, and its peoples speak some 50 languages.

Europe has many large cities, all of which blend the modern and the traditional. In the countryside, although modern ways are advancing, life is slower and more traditional.

USING VOCABULARY

Use these vocabulary words in a statement about Europe's coastline and its impact on the continent's economic development.

estuary   **maritime**

REVIEWING FACTS

1. **Name** the bodies of water that provide Europe with a long, irregular coastline and many offshore islands.
2. **List** the major landforms of Europe and their characteristics.
3. **Compare** the climate of northern Europe with that of southern Europe.
4. **Examine** how mountains have helped and hindered Europe's economy.

5. **Discuss** the challenges facing many modern European cities.
6. **Compare** the practice of agriculture in northwestern Europe with that in the Mediterranean areas of the continent.

CRITICAL THINKING

1. **Analyzing Information** The Alps are more heavily developed than the Northwestern Highlands and the Carpathians. Explain why this is so.
2. **Demonstrating Reasoned Judgment** Water is one of the most significant factors in the development of Europe. Give reasons why you agree or disagree with the statement.
3. **Making Comparisons** If you lived in Europe, would you rather live in the city or in the countryside? Explain your answer.
4. **Predicting Consequences** The Rhine and Danube rivers are considered central Europe's important lifelines. If they were to dry up, in what ways might the area be affected?

ANALYZING CONCEPTS

1. **Culture** How is Europe's cultural diversity affected by its geography? Consider such aspects of culture as architecture, food, and clothing.
2. **Interdependence** Success can have dangerous and unforeseen results. Explain how the statement applies to environmental damage in the Alps.

GEOGRAPHIC THEMES

1. **Place** What do Europe's major cities have in common?
2. **Movement** How have oceans, seas, and rivers contributed to the spread of European ideas and trade?

Formulating Questions

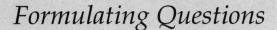

Engraved over the door of a university library is this motto: "Half of knowledge is knowing where to find it." If there had been more space above the door, the stone carver might have added, "And knowing which questions to ask." One essential key to acquiring information is knowing how to ask effective questions—questions that produce the desired information.

Suppose you want to find out what students think of the school cafeteria's food, so you ask students: "Do you do homework while you eat? Do you have enough time to eat lunch without rushing?" While these questions may be interesting, you won't get the information you need. Instead, you might ask: "What cafeteria foods do you like best and least? What foods should be kept on the menu? What should be added or eliminated?"

Effective questions are straightforward, specific, and directly related to your research topic. Broad or vague questions—such as, "Do you like the cafeteria food?"—should be rewritten as narrower questions. Also, questions that reflect personal bias often produce inaccurate or misleading results. For example, which question is likely to yield the most reliable answers: "Do you like the pizza?" or "Do you like that tasteless, cardboardy pizza?" Use the following steps to help you in formulating questions:

- Identify exactly what you want to know.

- Write questions related to this topic.
- Determine whether each question is directly related to the topic.
- Rewrite any vague, broad, or biased questions.

EXAMPLE

Which of the questions below would help you to write a report about the location and physical characteristics of Europe's mountains?

1. How many mountain areas does Europe have?
2. Where are the mountains located?
3. What is the name of each mountain range?
4. What kinds of houses are built in these mountain areas?
5. What are the main economic activities in each mountain area?
6. How high are the mountains in each area?
7. How old is each mountain range?
8. How have the mountains of Europe affected its political history?
9. What kind of vegetation is found in each?
10. Where are the lowest regions of Europe?

Questions 1 and 3 are useful because they identify the European mountain ranges. Question 2 is written too broadly. How

could you make the question more specific? *(In what countries are the mountain areas located?)* Why are Questions 6, 7, and 9 effective? *(They relate to physical characteristics—elevation, age, and vegetation.)* Because Questions 4 and 5 refer to human culture, not physical characteristics, they are not effective questions for this topic. What is wrong with Question 10? *(The question is not about the mountains.)*

PRACTICE

A) Suppose you are writing a research paper on the economic importance of rivers in Europe. Decide which questions below would be useful in researching this topic and explain why.

1. Which European rivers carry the most cargo?
2. Which are the two longest rivers in Europe?
3. What is the most scenic river in Europe?
4. What major cities are located on the banks of the Danube River?
5. What are the busiest seaports in Europe?
6. Are major industries located on the Rhine River? If so, which ones?

B) Write ten questions that would help you research the following topic: How do geography and climate affect the way people live in different parts of the European continent?

CHAPTER OUTLINE

1 The Greeks

2 The Romans

3 The Middle Ages

People and Places to Know

Athens, Sparta, Alexander, Pax Romana, the Christians, the Germans, Byzantine Empire, Charlemagne, Roman Catholic Church, the Crusades

Key Terms to Define

tragedy, comedy, scientific method, republic, plebian, patrician, feudalism, vassal, manor, knight, monastery

Objectives to Learn

1. **Identify** Greek and Roman contributions to Western civilization.
2. **Discuss** the effect of feudalism on European development.
3. **Analyze** the role of religion in Europe during the Middle Ages.

Temple of Poseidon, Sounion Cape, Greece

Roots of European Civilization

"Echoing the warlike lyrics of their national anthem, French traditionalists are girding for battle against reformers who want to transform *The Marseillaise* into a gentle hymn of brotherhood.

"Don't touch *The Marseillaise*—it belongs to our history," newspaper editorialist Georges Suffert wrote in yesterday's *Le Figaro.*

Criticism of the anthem's bloodthirsty lyrics has surfaced intermittently over the years. . . .

The anthem was written the night of April 24, 1792, by Claude Rouget de Lisle, an army captain, whose garrison at Strasbourg, in eastern France, was besieged by Prussian forces. He called it a war hymn. . . .

It became the official national anthem in 1795.

A survey by the polling firm Sofres indicated that 40 percent of French adults consider the anthem's lyrics too bloody, yet 75 percent don't want them changed.

On Monday, worried by calls for change, former Security Minister Robert Pandraud announced formation of a defense committee for *The Marseillaise.*

"All patriots should unite to be sure no one touches our national anthem," he said. "We must preserve our collective memory."

"*The Marseillaise* is ridiculous, but we should leave it alone," writer Michael Tournier told *Le Figaro.* "It's like those horrible buildings that nobody wants that become precious 100 years later."

The reluctance of the majority of the French people to change even a few of the lyrics of *The Marseillaise,* their 200-year-old national anthem, would not come as a surprise to most Europeans. Throughout Europe, history was—and still is—important. In fact, in most European nations, history is a part of everyday life.

All across the European continent, ancient and medieval structures still dot much of the countryside, serving as potent reminders of the distant and the not-so-distant past. These structures represent the common cultural heritage that continues to bind Europeans today. That heritage, in which European peoples take great pride, can be traced in part to the Mediterranean world of ancient Greece and ancient Rome. Another factor in Europe's heritage is the influence of Christianity, a religion that began in the ancient Middle East but reached its full flowering in Europe during the Middle Ages.

Source: Associated Press. "Traditionalists tell reformers: Hands off 'The Marseillaise'" in *The Columbus Dispatch,* March 4, 1992, p. 5A.

The Greeks

One of the first advanced civilizations on the European continent was developed by the ancient Greeks, who by the 500's BC had many colonies throughout the Mediterranean. To a large extent, the intellectual and artistic achievements of these early Greeks shaped European civilization.

THE CITY-STATES

At the heart of Greek civilization were several city-states that traded among themselves, worshiped the same gods and goddesses, and shared a common language and customs. Chief among these city-states were Athens and Sparta.

ATHENS Athens led Greece into a "golden age" of art and learning. Its government was one of the first democracies in history and its society the freest yet known to the world. Below, an Athenian leader named Pericles explains why, in his view, Athens was unique:

Our government is not copied from those of our neighbours: we are an example to them rather than they to us. Our constitution is named a democracy, because it is in the hands not of the few but of the many. But our laws secure equal justice for all in their private disputes, and our public opinion welcomes and honours talent in every branch of achievement. . . . And as we give free play to all in our public life, so we carry the same spirit into our daily relations with one another. . . . Open and friendly in our private intercourse, in our public acts we keep strictly within the control of law. We acknowledge the restraint of reverence; we are obedient to whomsoever is set in authority, and to the laws. . . .

Yet ours is no work-a-day city only. No other provides so many recreations for the spirit. . . . Moreover, the city is so large and powerful that all the wealth of all the world flows in to her. . . .

We are lovers of beauty without extravagance, and lovers of wisdom without unmanliness. Wealth to us is . . . an opportunity for achievement. . . . Our citizens attend both to public and private duties. . . . We differ from other states in regarding the man who holds aloof from public life not as "quiet" but as useless; we decide or debate . . . all matters of policy. . . . We secure our friends not by accepting favours but by doing them.

SPARTA In Sparta, athletic and military feats were glorified, while the arts and intellectual accomplishments were ignored. Many of Sparta's laws were the work of a legislator named Lycurgus. Below, an Athenian comments on the laws of Sparta and their effect:

Throughout the rest of the world the young girl, who will one day become a mother . . . , is nurtured on the plainest food . . . , with the scantiest addition of meat or other condiments. . . . [We], the rest of the Hellenes, are content that our girls should sit quietly and work wools. That is all we demand of them. . . .

Lycurgus pursued a different path. Clothes were things . . . the furnishing of which might well enough be left to female slaves. And, believing that the highest function of a free woman was the bearing of children, . . . he insisted on the training of the body as incumbent no less on the female than on the male; and in pursuit of the same idea instituted rival contests in running and feats of strength for women as for men. . . .

. . . Throughout the rest of Hellas . . . as soon as the children are of an age to understand what is said to them they are

Source: Thucydides. *The History of the Peloponnesian Wars.* Sir Richard Livingstone (tr.). Oxford University Press, 1956, pp. 111–114. By permission of Oxford University Press.

immediately placed under the charge of . . . (tutors), . . . and sent off to . . . school. . . . Besides this they are given shoes to wear which tend to make their feet tender, and their bodies are enervated by various changes of clothing. And as for food, the only measure recognized is that which is fixed by appetite.

. . . Lycurgus, instead of leaving it to each member of the state privately to appoint a slave to be his son's tutor, he set over young Spartans a public guardian . . . with complete authority over them. . . .

Instead of softening their feet with shoe or sandal, the rule was to make them hardy through going barefoot. . . .

Instead of making them effeminate with a variety of clothes, his rule was to habituate them to a single garment the whole year through. . . .

Again, as regards food, according to his regulation the . . . head of the flock, must see that his messmates gathered to the club meal, with . . . moderate food. . . .

His belief was that by such training in boyhood they would be better able when occasion demanded to continue toiling on an empty stomach. . . .

Furthermore, . . . he gave to any citizen who chanced to be present authority to lay upon [the boys] injunctions for their good, and to chastise them for any trespass committed. . . .

Furthermore, in his desire firmly to implant modesty in them he imposed a special rule. In the streets they were to keep their hands within the folds of the cloak; they were to walk in silence and without turning their heads to gaze, but rather to keep their eyes fixed upon the ground before them. . . . The plainest answer to the question asked, that is all you need expect to hear from their lips. . . .

There are yet other customs . . . which Lycurgus instituted in opposition to the rest of Hellas. . . . We all know that in the generality of states every one devotes his full energy to the business of making

EXAMINING ART *A goal of the Spartans was to become the strongest people in Greece. To achieve this goal and build physical strength, endurance, discipline, and fighting skills, they promoted physical conditioning, shown here in the form of wrestling.* **What characteristics did the Spartans scorn?**

money. . . . But at Sparta Lycurgus forbade his freeborn citizens to have anything whatsoever to do with the concerns of moneymaking. . . .

. . . We are all aware that there is no state in the world in which greater obedience is shown to magistrates, and to the laws themselves, than Sparta. . . . In Sparta, . . . the stronger a man is the more readily does he bow before constituted authority. . . .

Moreover, he laid upon them . . . the obligation to cultivate the whole virtue of a citizen. Provided they duly performed the injunctions of the law, the city belonged to them, each and all, in absolute possession and on an equal footing. . . . But as for him who . . . shrank from the performance of the law's injunction, the legislator pointed him out as disqualified to be regarded longer as a member of the brotherhood of peers.

THE ARTS AND SCIENCES

Government was not the only area in which the Greeks made lasting contributions. In the physical arts, for example, they introduced the Olympic Games, a sporting event that drew male athletes from Greece and all its colonies. In the fine arts, they created sculptures, architecture, and other works that incorporated the basic ideals of simplicity, dignity, and proportion. In theater, they developed two types of drama—**tragedies**, plays about human suffering, and **comedies**, plays with humorous themes.

At the same time, the Greeks made history an important part of literature. The first Greek historian, Herodotus, is known today as the "Father of History." Another important historian was Thucydides. In his work on the Peloponnesian Wars, a series of wars between Athens and Sparta, he offered ex-

Source: Xenophon. "The Constitution of the Spartans." From _The Greek Historians_ by Francis R.B. Godolphin. Copyright 1942 and renewed 1970 by Random House, Inc. Reprinted by permission of Random House, Inc.

EXAMINING PHOTOGRAPHS _In one of the great naval battles of history, the Greeks defeated the Persians at the Battle of Salamis in 490_ BC. _The Greek city-states later fought each other in the Peloponnesian Wars._ What Greek historian wrote about the Peloponnesian Wars?

planations as to why events took place and what motivated political leaders. The Greeks also made many advances in science and laid the foundations for modern Western philosophy and thought. The scientist Thales of Miletus, for example, developed the first two steps of what is known today as the **scientific method**, systematic ways to seek knowledge. Another scientist, Hippocrates, concluded that diseases came from natural, rather than supernatural, causes. The code he wrote for doctors, known as the Hippocratic Oath, is still sworn by new physicians today. A philosopher named Socrates developed the Socratic method, a method of teaching by asking questions. Another philosopher, Plato, carried out early studies in political science, the study of political systems. One of his students, Aristotle, created the system of reasoning known as logic.

END OF EMPIRE

In 338 BC, the Greek city-states were defeated by King Philip II of Macedonia, who wanted to unify the city-states and spread Greek culture. Two years later, Philip was murdered. His 20-year-old son, Alexander, became king, and, over time, created a vast empire. Below, the Greek biographer Plutarch explains Alexander's motives:

Alexander . . . did not . . . rule the Grecians like a moderate prince and insult over the barbarians like an absolute tyrant; nor did he take particular care of the first as his friends and domestics, and scorn the latter as mere brutes and vegetables. . . . But believing himself sent from Heaven as the common moderator . . . of all nations, . . . he labored . . . that he might bring all regions, far and near, under the same dominion. And then, as in a festival goblet, mixing lives, manners, customs, wedlock, all together, he ordained that every one should take the whole habitable world for his country. . . .

Alexander died at the age of 33, but his Hellenistic civilization, which was a blend of Greek and eastern cultures and customs, flourished long after his death. His idea of a universal state, a state that brings all peoples under one government, found new life in later kingdoms and empires.

SECTION 1 REVIEW

CHECKING FOR UNDERSTANDING

1. **Define** tragedy, comedy, scientific method.
2. **Identify** some of the major contributions of the Greeks.

CRITICAL THINKING

3. **Making Comparisons** In what ways were Athens and Sparta different?

Source: Plutarch's Morals. Vol. I, corrected and revised by William W. Goodwin. Little, Brown, and Company, 1883, pp. 481, 484.

SECTION 2

The Romans

Rome began as a small farming settlement on the banks of the Tiber River in central Italy. In 509 BC, the Romans set up a **republic**, a form of government in which people elect leaders to represent them. By 130 BC, they had brought much of the known Western world under their rule.

THE REPUBLIC

In the early years, the government of the Roman Republic was headed by two consuls, elected officials who ran the city, and a Senate and an Assembly. Although **plebians**, or common people, could vote, only **patricians**, or aristocrats, could hold public office.

By 451 BC, plebians had forced the patricians to give them more rights, and, for the first time, the laws were put down in written form. Known as the Twelve Tables, they provided the basic legal code of Rome for almost 1000 years. As seen below, they dealt chiefly with rules that apply to the rights and duties of the individual citizen:

If anyone commits a theft during the day, and is caught in the act, he shall be [whipped], and given up as a slave to the person against whom the theft was committed. . . .

A father shall have the right of life and death over his son born in lawful marriage. . . .

No matter in what way the head of a household may dispose of his estate, and appoint heirs to the same, or guardians; it shall have the force and effect of law. . . .

If a husband desires to divorce his wife, and dissolve his marriage, he must give a reason for doing so. . . .

If you cause any unlawful damage . . . accidentally and unintentionally, you must

EXAMINING ART
Rome, capital and largest city of the Roman Empire, achieved a size and splendor unequaled in its time. At its center was the forum, the large open space shown in this photo. Surrounded by government buildings, temples, and markets, the forum was open to all Romans, rich and poor alike. **When did Roman civilization reach its peak?**

make good the loss, either by tendering what has caused it, or by payment. . . .

If anyone who has arrived at puberty, secretly, and by night, destroys or cuts and appropriates to his own use, the crop of another, . . . he shall be . . . hung. . . .

When one publicly abuses another in a loud voice, or writes a poem for the purpose of insulting him, or rendering him infamous, he shall be beaten with a rod until he dies. . . .

Anyone who kills a [superior], shall have his head wrapped in a cloth, and after having been sewed up in a sock, shall be thrown into the water. . . .

When a judge, or an arbiter appointed to hear a case, accepts money, or other gifts, for the purpose of influencing his decision, he shall suffer the penalty of death. . . .

THE EMPIRE

In 27 BC, the Roman Republic came to an end. The Roman Empire came into being, and a Roman named Octavian was declared

Source: "The Laws of the Twelve Tables" in *The Civil Law,* Vol. I. S.P. Scott. The Central Trust Company, Cincinnati, pp. 57, 60, 64, 66, 69–73, 76.

emperor. Known as Caesar Augustus, he was the first of a long line of emperors who ruled for the next 500 years.

During the first 200 years of the Empire, known as the Pax Romana, Roman civilization reached its peak. Rome, with a population of about 1 million people, became the largest city in the Western world. Below, a modern historian relates what Rome was like at the time:

Ships from all over the known world fed and clothed and beautified her. Her corn came from Africa, Egypt, Sicily, and Sardinia; her pepper from as far away as India. Her marble came from Africa, Egypt, and Asia Minor; her tin from Britain and Northern Spain. Silk came from China, cotton from India. Linen, embroidery, papyrus, came from Egypt. Her citizens ate meat, poultry and game, and fish imported often at great cost. They ate bread and cakes, olives and fruit of many varieties, and drank various kinds of wine. All classes wore simple gowns and tunics, those of the rich being of fine linen and wool, sometimes of silk, and richer women began to wear fine jewels.

In appearance Rome became proud and beautiful. . . . The Roman emperors built themselves mighty triumphal arches and victory columns. . . . They built fine temples to the Roman gods, warehouses and offices and shops, often within beautifully constructed arcades. There were government buildings . . . and magnificent palaces for their emperors. . . .

Though the Romans had on the whole little interest in Greek athletics, they were enthusiastic about chariot-racing and built large circuses for the sport. While the charioteers raced around the oval arena spectators watched from tiered seats, as in a theatre.

The theatre itself also developed from the Greek pattern, and the Romans popularized a form of entertainment which had never flourished in Greece—gladiatorial combats between men, and man and animal. Great amphitheatres modeled on the pattern of a theatre were built for these spectacles. . . .

Far more enlightened was the Roman's pleasure in the public bath. This was more than merely bathing or swimming; it constituted a complete social entertainment. The baths were large, and elaborately and beautifully constructed, with mosaic floors . . . and a liberal display of statues. From the ante-room, where he undressed, the

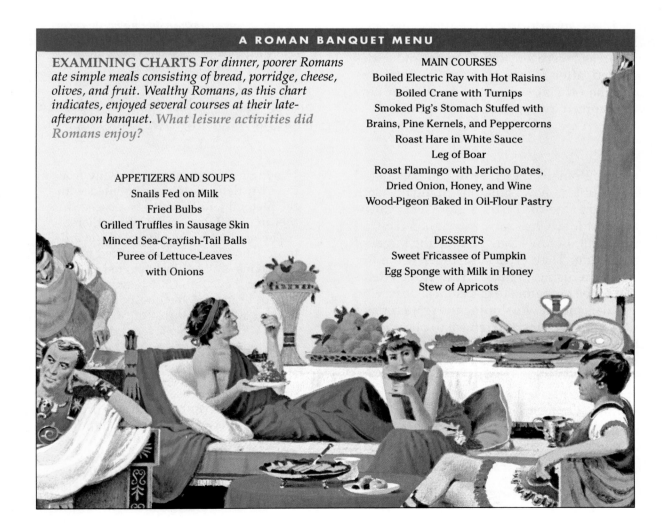

A ROMAN BANQUET MENU

EXAMINING CHARTS *For dinner, poorer Romans ate simple meals consisting of bread, porridge, cheese, olives, and fruit. Wealthy Romans, as this chart indicates, enjoyed several courses at their late-afternoon banquet.* *What leisure activities did Romans enjoy?*

APPETIZERS AND SOUPS
Snails Fed on Milk
Fried Bulbs
Grilled Truffles in Sausage Skin
Minced Sea-Crayfish-Tail Balls
Puree of Lettuce-Leaves
with Onions

MAIN COURSES
Boiled Electric Ray with Hot Raisins
Boiled Crane with Turnips
Smoked Pig's Stomach Stuffed with
Brains, Pine Kernels, and Peppercorns
Roast Hare in White Sauce
Leg of Boar
Roast Flamingo with Jericho Dates,
Dried Onion, Honey, and Wine
Wood-Pigeon Baked in Oil-Flour Pastry

DESSERTS
Sweet Fricassee of Pumpkin
Egg Sponge with Milk in Honey
Stew of Apricots

bather went first to the frigidarium for his cold bath. . . . Then he passed through a series of heated rooms and finally relaxed in the caldarium, the hot bath, after which he was massaged with sweet-smelling oils. But the actual bath was only a small part of the entertainment. In all the large public baths was a large open court where he would wrestle, play ball-games, or exchange the gossip of the day.

At first, the people of the various provinces of the Empire were allowed to keep their own languages, laws, and customs. In time, however, the Empire was made Roman in character and style. Roads and bridges were built, making it easier for people to travel and ideas to spread. Aqueducts, elevated structures that transported water from distant areas, were erected. Towns and cities modeled after Rome were built. Latin became the official language, and Roman law was enforced throughout the Empire.

THE RISE OF CHRISTIANITY

As the Romans traded with and conquered new peoples, new religions mingled with their own. One of these religions was Christianity. At first, Christians were ignored or tolerated. But, in time, they became the target of persecution. They especially angered the Romans by refusing to take part in rituals dedicated to the emperor. To Christians, observing the rituals meant worshiping the emperor as a god. To the Romans, the refusal to observe the rituals was political disobedience.

Christians began to be blamed for all kinds of disasters. When a fire burned much of Rome in 64 AD, the emperor accused Christians and began to put them to death. Although persecution lasted for many years, the religion continued to grow. About 112 AD, a Roman governor named Pliny, con-

Source: Pauline Gregg. *The Chain of History.* Harrap & Co., Ltd., © 1958, pp. 78–83.

EXAMINING ART *Roman guards have discovered Christians worshiping in catacombs, underground passages dug by early Christians hoping to escape persecution. Why did the Romans persecute Christians?*

cerned about the spread of Christianity, wrote the following letter to the emperor:

Having never been present at any trials of the Christians, I am unacquainted with the method and limits to be observed either in examining or punishing them. . . .

The method I have observed towards those who have been denounced to me as Christians is this: I interrogated them whether they were Christians; if they confessed, I repeated the question twice again, adding the threat of capital punishment; if they still persevered, I ordered them to be executed. . . .

. . . A placard was put up, without any signature, accusing a large number of persons by name. Those who denied they were, or had ever been, Christians, who repeated after me an invocation to the Gods, and offered adoration . . . to your image, . . . and who finally cursed Christ —none of which acts, it is said, those who are really Christians can be forced into performing—these I thought it proper to discharge. Others who were named . . . at first confessed themselves Christians, and then denied it; true, they had been of that persuasion but they had quitted it. . . . They all worshipped your statue and the images of the Gods, and cursed Christ.

They affirmed, however, the whole of their guilt, or their error was, that they were in the habit of meeting on a certain fixed day . . . , when they sang . . . a hymn to Christ, as to a god, and bound themselves by a solemn oath . . . never to commit any fraud, theft, or adultery, never to falsify their word, nor deny a trust. . . . Even this practice, however, they had abandoned. . . .

. . . Persons of all ranks and ages, and of both sexes are, and will be, involved in the prosecution. For this contagious superstition is not confined to the cities only, but has spread through the villages and rural districts.

By early 300 AD, Christianity was well organized and strong, but the persecution was worse than ever. Then, a new emperor named Constantine came to power in part of the Empire and granted the people in his domain the right to worship as they pleased. In 324 AD, he became the first Christian emperor of the Roman Empire.

Source: Reprinted by permission of the publishers and the Loeb Classical Library from Pliny, LETTERS, VOLUME II, translated by William Melmoth and revised by W.M.L. Hutchinson, Cambridge, Mass: Harvard University Press, 1963.

SECTION 2 REVIEW

CHECKING FOR UNDERSTANDING
1. **Define** republic, plebian, patrician.
2. **Describe** the changes that took place in the Roman Empire during the Pax Romana.

CRITICAL THINKING
3. **Identifying Central Issues** Why do you think Christianity was able to survive Roman persecution?

SECTION 3
The Middle Ages

In the late 300's AD, the Roman Empire divided into eastern and western parts. In time, Christianity reflected this division—the Roman Catholic Church in the west and the Eastern Orthodox Church in the east.

During the 400's AD, the western Roman Empire fell to Germanic invaders. They set up kingdoms in western Europe and spread Germanic-Roman culture to the Slavs in the northern part of eastern Europe. Meanwhile, in the southern part of eastern Europe, the eastern Roman Empire survived and became the Byzantine Empire. From about 500 to 1500 AD, the Byzantines passed on their Greco-Roman culture to the Slavs of the Balkan Peninsula.

This era of decline and growth in Europe is called the Middle Ages, the period between ancient and modern times. During this time, new ideas of trade, government, and society began to develop.

FEUDALISM

During the early Middle Ages, a new system took root. Known as **feudalism**, it was based on the ownership of land and on ties of loyalty among nobles. Landholders, known as lords, granted protection and land to other nobles, known as **vassals**, in return for loyalty and service. Below, a young man asks a lord to make him a vassal:

Inasmuch as it is known to all and sundry that I lack the wherewithal to feed and clothe myself, I have asked of your pity, and your goodwill has granted to me permission to deliver and commend myself into your authority and protection . . . in return you have undertaken to aid and sustain me in food and clothing, while I

Europe

CHARLEMAGNE

During the early Middle Ages, a Germanic people known as Franks built a new empire in western Europe that reached its height in the late 700's and early 800's under Charles the Great—Charlemagne. He united western Europe under a common set of ideas and laws. Below, a follower of Charlemagne talks about the leader he called Karl:

The person of Karl was large and robust. . . . His walk was firm, and the whole of his carriage was manly. . . .

He took constant exercise in riding and hunting which was natural for a Frank, since scarcely any nation can be found to equal them in these pursuits. . . .

In his eating and drinking he was temperate; more particularly so in his drinking, since he had the greatest abhorrence of drunkenness in anybody. . . .

While he was dining he listened to music or reading. . . .

While he was dressing and binding on his sandals, he would receive his friends; and also, if the Court of the palace announced that there was any cause which could only be settled by his decree, the suitors were immediately ordered into

his presence, and, as if sitting in court, he heard the case and gave judgement. . . .

He was ready and fluent in speaking. . . . He did not confine himself to his native tongue, but took great pains to learn foreign languages. . . . He was an ardent admirer of the liberal arts, and greatly revered their professors. . . .

The Christian religion, in which he had been brought up . . . was held . . . as most sacred, and he worshipped in it with the greatest piety. . . .

To the Pope he made many and rich presents; and nothing lay nearer his heart . . . than that the city of Rome should attain to its ancient importance . . . and that the church of St. Peter should . . . not only be in safe keeping and protection, but should also by his wealth be ennobled and enriched. . . .

Karl . . . went to Rome . . . to reform and quiet the Church. . . . It was at this time that he received the title of Emperor

and Augustus. . . .

After he had taken the Imperial title, he turned his attention to the laws of his people. . . .

He also wrote out and committed to memory the . . . very ancient songs which told . . . of the kings of old. He also began a grammar of the speech of his country. He also gave names in the national tongue to the months of the year. . . .

. . . Above his tomb was erected a gilded monument. . . . His dignity was thus described—

. . . Under this tomb is placed the body of Karl, The Great and Orthodox Emperor, who gloriously enlarged the realm of the Franks, and successfully reigned during forty-seven years.

TAKING ANOTHER LOOK

What were some of Charlemagne's accomplishments? What did he contribute to the development of Europe?

Source: Eginhard. *Life of the Emperor Karl the Great.* William Glaister (tr.). George Bell & Sons, 1877, pp. 73–88.

have undertaken to serve you and deserve well of you as far as lies in my power. And for as long as I shall live, I am bound to serve you and respect you as a free man ought, and during my lifetime I have not the right to withdraw from your authority and protection, but must, on the contrary, for the remainder of my days remain under it.

During this period, much of the land was organized into **manors**, self-supporting estates belonging to one or more lords. Each manor generally consisted of a large house or castle where a noble or a **knight**, or mounted warrior, lived; a home farm; and the surrounding fields, woods, and pasture. The estates of some nobles were made up of as many as 20 or 30 manors. Although life for the lords and their families varied according to custom and wealth, most followed the pattern here described:

As lord of the manor, Robert Fitzralph . . . must see that his estate is kept in good

Source: Marjorie Rowling. *Everyday Life in Medieval Times.* B.T. Batsford Ltd., 1968, pp. 31–32.

order, that his tenants work hard and pay their rents and that every tenant is treated fairly. He has a large home farm that is managed for him by a bailiff. It is Lord Robert's duty to maintain law and order in the village and to deal with minor crimes and disturbances. . . .

Most of Lord Robert's time is taken up with the day-to-day running of the estate, but sometimes he has to do service directly for the king. Although he no longer has to serve as a knight for so many days a year, he still has certain obligations to the crown. For example, he must give evidence for tax and other financial enquiries. . . . Sometimes he will have to serve as one of the king's tax collectors. . . .

For amusement, Lord Robert enjoys hunting. . . . Hawking is a favourite sport, too, and the ladies can join in. The hawks are very carefully trained to fly after ducks and small animals. . . . One of his tenants looks after them and it is almost a fulltime job. . . . Other amusements are chess, checkers, singing, dancing, and storytelling. Lord Robert also enjoys riding and fencing, which keep him in condition for fighting. . . .

EXAMINING PHOTOGRAPHS *During the Middle Ages, lords often allowed traveling merchants to find protection within castle walls. In many cases, merchants set up permanent shops in or near castles that eventually developed into towns.* *How was the countryside organized in much of Europe during the Middle Ages?*

Lord Robert's wife is the daughter of . . . a rich man. . . . When she married, the Lady Mathilda brought a 'dowry' of land . . . with her, and, in return, Lord Robert promised her a small house and piece of land on his other estate to support her in her widowhood, should he die first. . . .

Lady Mathilda supervises the household and servants and sees to the running of the manor house. She is in charge of all the stores, including the wine-cellar, and oversees all the baking and brewing for her family. . . . In the little spare time she has, she enjoys embroidery and makes fine belts and ribbons. . . . She also makes vestments for the parish church. . . .

Though their life is easier than the peasants', it is not luxurious and they would

be looked down on by the richer nobles, and even some of the wealthier townfolks.

The land that made up the fields of the manor generally was divided among peasants, most of whom were serfs bound to the land. They could not leave the manor, marry, or inherit land without the lord's permission. Serfs were expected to work three days a week in the lord's fields, perform certain services for and make certain payments to the lord, and carry the manor's produce to fairs whenever the lord ordered. All of their flour had to be ground in the lord's mill and all of their bread baked in the lord's ovens, services for which they were

Source: Gwyneth Morgan. *Life in a Medieval Village.* Cambridge University Press, 1975, pp. 36, 38.

expected to pay. As can be seen in the excerpt that follows, taken from a school text written about the year 1000, the life of a serf was hard:

Now Ploughman, what work do you do?

I work very hard. I go out at dawn driving oxen a-field and yoke them to the plough. For fear of my lord I dare not stay at home even when the winter is very cold. Every day I must plough a full acre or more.

Have you any companions?

I have a boy to threaten the oxen with a goad. He is quite hoarse with the cold and shouting.

What else do you do?

I have to get hay for the oxen, water them and clean out the sheds.

Great is your labor!

Verily, it is because I am not free!

THE CHURCH

Life in the Middle Ages revolved around feudalism and the Roman Catholic Church. According to one writer of the time, society could be compared to the human body. Peasants were the feet and legs, because they were the source of the labor on which society depended. Nobles were the hands and arms, because they were the protectors and defenders. Priests and clerks were the head and eyes, because they were the spiritual guides of all the people.

Since the fall of the Roman Empire, the Church had become western Europe's largest landholder, making it both rich and powerful. All Christians, from the poorest serf to the most powerful noble, belonged to it and were influenced by it. Enemies of the Church were viewed as enemies of God. As seen in this passage, almost every village had a church and a priest:

All the land in Christendom was divided up into parishes, which usually consisted of a village, and the farms in neighboring fields. The village . . . boasted two stone buildings. One was the mill to which everyone brought his corn to be ground. The other was the parish church. . . . To one side of the church was the churchyard, . . . and close by was a two-roomed house, which served as a second home to everyone in the parish, for here lived the village priest.

The village priest did not pretend to be a clever man, but he knew more than his neighbors, because he could read and write. . . . He could decline a Latin noun, conjugate a Latin verb, and knew many Psalms by heart. But best of all he knew the hearts of his people, for he had grown up among them, and was a peasant like themselves. Therefore, they trusted him and came to him with their sins and difficulties, certain that he would help them. . . .

In every little hamlet and village the priest was the leader of the people. He christened, married, and buried them. He served them in church on Sundays and holidays. In his sermons . . . , he comforted the heartsore and wretched, and taught all . . . to hold fast to right living. He also taught the children in the shade of the little church porch. . . .

. . . in most things the people obeyed their priest; for to them he stood for the majesty of Rome. Each man set aside a tenth of his goods each year for the Church, and at harvest time one sack of corn found its way to the priest's spare room, or into his barn. Each woman brought the first basket of berries she gathered, a fat spring chicken, a dozen eggs, a honeycomb, or a round yellow cheese. One third of these good things had to go to the bishop of the diocese, and another third to the lord of the village, but the rest belonged to the priest.

Source: Aelfric's Colloquies, as quoted in *The Middle Ages* by Dorothy Mills. G.P. Putnam's Sons, 1935, p. 174.

Source: Olive Beaupré Miller. *A Picturesque Tale of Progress.* Part I. United Educators, Inc., 1935, pp. 191–194.

Europe

THE CRUSADES

In the 1000's AD, Europeans took part in the Crusades, a series of holy wars against Muslims who lived in Palestine. Within Muslim territory were the Christian shrines associated with the life of Jesus and the early Christians. The Europeans wanted to gain control of Jerusalem and the Holy Land for the Christian nations of Europe.

The Crusades continued for over 200 years and brought significant changes in Europe. A modern-day author, in the foreward to his work on the Crusades, offered the following insights:

It was a migration, and a journey, and war. All kinds of people joined the marchers, lords and vagabonds, weapon men and peasants, proud ladies and tavern drabs. "A thing unheard of," said a chronicler of the day, "that such diverse people and so many distinguished princes, leaving their splendid possessions, their wives and their children, set forth with one accord and in scorn of death to seek the most unknown regions."

They were marching out of the familiar, known world into Asia to set free with their own hands the Sepulcher of Christ.

They wanted to live there, in the promised land, ruled by no king but by the will of God. On the shoulders of their jackets they wore a cross, sewn out of cloth, and because of this they were called the cruciati, *or cross bearers. So we, today, call them the crusaders.*

Most of them died on the way. But they went on, and after three years some of them reached their destination. . . . For the first time all the peoples of Christendom, speaking different languages and separated from each other until now, were united in a common enterprise. Christendom had taken up the sword against Islam, and the war went on for more than three centuries and some two million human beings perished in it.

The Crusades failed to achieve their goal. They did, however, have a lasting impact on Europe and its people. They united Europeans under the banner of Christianity and inspired idealism, sacrifice, and chivalry. At the same time, they brought the West and the East into contact with each other and gave each an awareness and knowledge of civilizations and religions different from their own.

The Crusades also renewed European interest in art, learning, and knowledge. Trade increased and expanded, and money became more important in the European economy. Economic growth, in turn, led to the rise of towns and the beginnings of a new middle class. These changes, along with others, helped to bring much of Europe out of the Middle Ages and into modern times.

DRAWING CONCLUSIONS

Why did Europeans carry out the Crusades? What effect did the Crusades have on Europe and Europeans?

Source: Harold Lamb. *The Crusades.* Doubleday & Company, 1930.

EXAMINING ART *Monasteries, such as this one, considered model centers of Christian living, housed communities of monks who lived under common rules and took vows of celibacy, poverty, and obedience. What duties did the monks perform?*

The Church also established **monasteries**, places where men called monks withdrew from everyday life to devote their lives to worship and to serving God. The monks worked as farmers, cared for the sick and poor, and copied ancient manuscripts. Women also took part in religious life and formed their own separate communities. Known as nuns, they combined prayer with spinning and weaving and taught needlework and the medicinal use of herbs to the daughters of nobles. Without the efforts of monks and nuns, much land would not have been cultivated, more people would have died of disease or of hunger, and many classics of literature would have been lost.

SECTION 3 REVIEW

CHECKING FOR UNDERSTANDING
1. **Define** feudalism, vassal, manor, knight, monastery.
2. **Discuss** the type of economy that supported feudalism.

CRITICAL THINKING
3. **Analyzing Information** How would you describe the role of the Church during the Middle Ages?

Chapter 47 Review

SUMMARY

The ancient Greeks developed one of the first advanced civilizations in Europe. They made major contributions in government, the arts, literature, theater, science, and philosophy.

The Romans later built a powerful empire that united much of Europe under a common system of law. In western Europe, the Roman Empire was eventually replaced by Germanic kingdoms; in eastern Europe, the Roman Empire survived and developed into the Byzantine Empire.

During the Middle Ages, the era between ancient and modern times, the ideas of Christianity blended with those of ancient Greece and Rome to form a new European civilization.

USING VOCABULARY

Write three headings: *Greeks, Romans,* and *Middle Ages.* Classify each of the following terms under the headings to which they are related.

tragedy	plebian	manor
comedy	patrician	knight
scientific method	feudalism	republic
vassal	monastery	

RECALLING FACTS

1. **Describe** the form of government that developed in ancient Athens.
2. **State** some of the major contributions of the Greeks.
3. **Point out** the changes that Alexander brought to early European civilization.
4. **State** the importance of the Twelve Tables in the Roman Republic.
5. **Name** the first Roman official who took the title of emperor.
6. **Indicate** the change that the emperor Constantine brought to the Roman Empire.
7. **Specify** the roles of nobles and peasants in Europe during the Middle Ages.
8. **Summarize** the contributions of monks and nuns to European civilization during the Middle Ages.

CRITICAL THINKING

1. **Expressing Problems Clearly** Alexander wanted to spread Greek culture while creating a state that united many different peoples. Do you think these two goals conflicted? Explain.
2. **Identifying Assumptions** Like Pliny, most Roman officials were concerned about the growth and spread of Christianity. For what reasons do you think they feared the expansion of the new religion?
3. **Evaluating Information** Do you think feudalism helped or hindered progress and development in Europe? Provide reasons for your answer.

ANALYZING CONCEPTS

1. **Structures and Systems** How was the government of the Roman Republic organized?
2. **Technology** What technology was developed by the Romans?

GEOGRAPHIC THEMES

1. **Movement** To what European people did the Byzantines spread their Greco-Roman culture?
2. **Human-Environment Interaction** What products did Rome obtain from its empire?

Finding Information in a Library

A library's *card catalog* is a good way to find books on a particular subject. The card catalog contains three separate listings for each nonfiction book in the library—by author, title, and subject. Index cards beginning with either the author, title, or subject heading are arranged alphabetically. Each card also has a *call number*, which classifies the book by subject. Books on the same subject have similar call numbers and are shelved in the same area.

Many libraries now use *online, or automated, catalogs*, which list the library's holdings on computer. To use an online catalog, just type in a title, author, or subject heading and the computer will display all the items that meet your request. For example, if you type in a subject heading, the computer will list items related to that heading. To find out more about a particular title, type the code number of that item. The computer will display its call number and tell whether or not it is available. Many libraries have formed networks to share information and resources. In library networks, the online catalog lists the holdings of all the libraries in the network. Follow these steps in using a card or online catalog:

- Search for subject headings related to your topic in a card or online catalog.
- List relevant titles and call numbers.
- Find these books on the library shelves.

EXAMPLE

Study the sample catalog card below.

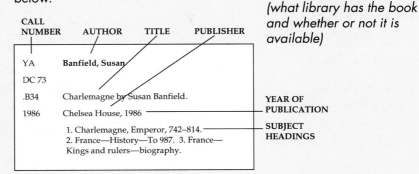

This card is an author card because the author's name appears on the first line. What is the title of the book? *(Charlemagne)* The card also tells the publisher's name, date of publication, and call number. It also lists subject headings under which this book would be classified. Now look at a listing for the same book on an automated library network:

AUTHOR:	Banfield, Susan			
TITLE:	Charlemagne			
PUBLISHER:	Chelsea House 1986			
SUBJECTS:	Charlemagne, Emperor, 742–814. France—History—To 987. France—Kings and History—To 987, France—Kings and rulers—Biography.			

##	Call number	Material	Location	Status
1	JBCHARLEMAGNE	Juv Book	Watertn	Available
2	YA DC 73 .B34 1986	Book	Watertn	out

It also lists the author, title, publisher, publication date, call number, and relevant subject headings for this book. The computer catalog, however, also shows that the library has two copies of this book, one shelved under juvenile biography, the other in a nonfiction section. What other information is found in the online catalog? *(what library has the book and whether or not it is available)*

PRACTICE

Use the card or online catalog at your local or school library to identify six to ten books on one of the following subjects:
a) Contributions of ancient Greece
b) History of the Roman Empire
c) Society in the Byzantine Empire
d) Life in the Middle Ages
For each book, list the title, author, subject heading, and call number.

People and Places to Know
Martin Luther, Christopher Columbus, Napoleon Bonaparte, Adolf Hitler

Key Terms to Define
indulgences, absolutism, popular sovereignty, mass production, Holocaust

Objectives to Learn
1. **Summarize** changes in Europe during the Renaissance and the Reformation.
2. **Discuss** the impact of the Enlightenment.
3. **Cite** the changes of the Industrial Revolution.
4. **State** causes and effects of World Wars I and II.

European warfare in the 1500's

Conflict and Change

"   In the Middle Ages, when knights fought wars in Europe's fields, robbers roamed the roads, and the dark forests seemed filled with unknown dangers, men put their trust in walls. Around each little town rose ramparts of massive stonework, a strong defense against the evils outside. . . .

In such a town a man knew his place. He was a nobleman or a knight, a churchman, a craftsman, or a farmer, and there were ancient invisible walls that marked off the little world in which each kind of person belonged. . . .

The world of Europe also had its walls. . . . To the east and south, along the edge of Asia and the top of Africa, Europe was hemmed in by a chain of towns and fortresses. . . . On the north and west there was the Ocean Sea, a vast body of water that some men said was endless. . . .

And, for centuries, . . . life in the walled towns and the shape of the world men knew went unchanged. . . .

Then, at the turn of the fifteenth century, there was a restless stirring in Europe. Men began to peer beyond the walls. . . .

It was a time of change, a time for adventurous men, . . . men who dared to think for themselves and to act on their thoughts. . . .

It was a time of revolution, and afterward nothing seemed to be as it had been. . . .

Men of faith seeking peace with God had little in common with adventurers seeking fortunes and empires. Yet both shared the courage of an age that dared to look beyond the boundaries of the old. . . . And, as they searched for new lands and new ideas, the thick walls . . . came tumbling down. "

During the early Middle Ages, Europeans lived within "walls," bound by an orderly system that seemed as if it would never change. But it did change. By the early 1500's, Europeans had survived plague and conflict and had begun to prosper. Monarchs had established strong governments, trade had flourished, and towns and cities had begun to grow. Merchants had grown more powerful, and banking families had established networks across Europe.

The outburst of learning, scientific advances, and discoveries that took place spurred European growth and expansion and marked the dawn of modern times. By the late 1800's, the great powers of Europe had control of much of the globe. In the next century, these same powers nearly destroyed themselves in two terrible world wars.

Source: From THE UNIVERSAL HISTORY OF THE WORLD, VOL. VIII, Reformation and Exploration. © 1966, Western Publishing Company, Inc. Used by permission.

SECTION 1

Rebirth and Reform

Beginning in the 1300's, important changes began to take place in Europe in the form of intellectual and religious developments. These developments, which came to be known as the Renaissance and the Reformation, had far-reaching consequences.

THE RENAISSANCE

The Renaissance was a rebirth of learning that began around 1350 in the city-states of Italy. It started with a new interest in classical Greek and Roman writings and soon led to a flowering of the arts and sciences. Once again, the classical beliefs of intellectual inquiry and the dignity and worth of the individual became important. Careful inquiry and experimentation came to be admired, and many old beliefs were challenged.

During this time, the Italian city-states competed with one another for superiority in trade and for artistic and intellectual leadership. The city-state of Florence soon led the others. Florence was ruled by Lorenzo de' Medici, who many modern historians have come to regard as the idealization of Renaissance values. In the following excerpt,

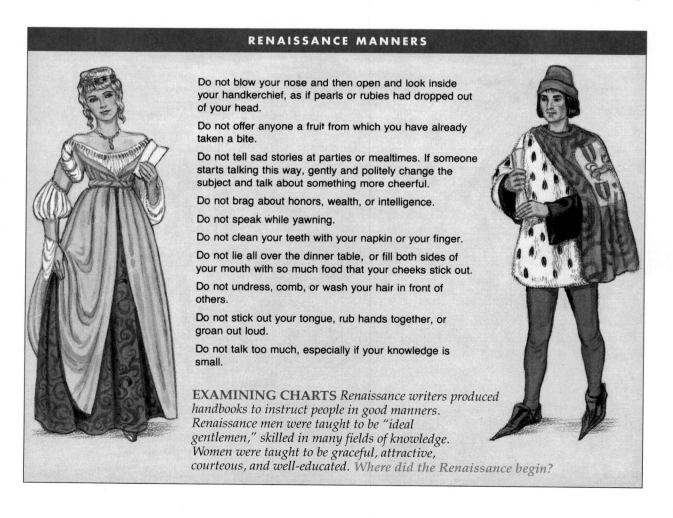

RENAISSANCE MANNERS

Do not blow your nose and then open and look inside your handkerchief, as if pearls or rubies had dropped out of your head.

Do not offer anyone a fruit from which you have already taken a bite.

Do not tell sad stories at parties or mealtimes. If someone starts talking this way, gently and politely change the subject and talk about something more cheerful.

Do not brag about honors, wealth, or intelligence.

Do not speak while yawning.

Do not clean your teeth with your napkin or your finger.

Do not lie all over the dinner table, or fill both sides of your mouth with so much food that your cheeks stick out.

Do not undress, comb, or wash your hair in front of others.

Do not stick out your tongue, rub hands together, or groan out loud.

Do not talk too much, especially if your knowledge is small.

EXAMINING CHARTS *Renaissance writers produced handbooks to instruct people in good manners. Renaissance men were taught to be "ideal gentlemen," skilled in many fields of knowledge. Women were taught to be graceful, attractive, courteous, and well-educated. Where did the Renaissance begin?*

an Italian historian of that time provides some insights into the personality of the Florentine ruler:

Lorenzo was a man of many outstanding virtues. He also had several vices, some of them natural, some the products of necessity. . . . His accomplishments do not shine with the splendor of arms. But we will indeed find in him all those signs and evidence of virtue that are connected with civic life. No one, not even his enemies . . . , can deny that his was a great and singular mind. . . .

His judgment was sound and wise, but not of a quality comparable to his intellect. . . .

He desired glory and excellence more than any man. . . . He wanted to equal and compete with all the princes of Italy in everything. . . . On the whole, . . . his ambition was praiseworthy and brought him glory and fame everywhere, even outside Italy, for it caused him to strive to make the Florence of his time stand out above all other Italian cities in all arts and skills. He had a university founded in Pisa, principally for the study of letters. . . . In his time, all the most excellent and most famous men in Italy taught there and received very high salaries, for he avoided neither expense nor labor to get them. . . . Lorenzo showed the same favor to . . . all the arts of mind and hand, so that the city overflowed with all these exquisite things. And these arts flourished all the more because Lorenzo, a universal man, could pass judgment and distinguish among men, so that they competed with one another to please him. Furthermore, there was his infinite liberality, which provided all talented men with livelihoods and with all the instruments necessary for their work. To give an example: when he decided to establish a Greek library, he sent the very learned Lascaris all the way to Greece to look for good ancient books. . . .

. . . His death deeply grieved all those in Italy who excelled in letters, painting,

sculpture, and similar arts, for they had either received highly paid commissions from him, or else they were held in all the greater esteem by other princes, who feared that if they stopped treating them well they would go to Lorenzo.

THE REFORMATION

The Reformation began as an effort to reform the Catholic Church, which had gained great power in Europe. Along with the power had come much corruption. Not only did the Church hold a great deal of land, but it allowed Church positions to be bought and many church officials to live in luxury. For more than 100 years, Europeans who had dared to speak out against the Church were silenced. Then, in the 1500's, a German monk and university professor named Martin Luther denounced certain Church practices. Luther was particularly troubled by the sale of **indulgences**, pardons that freed their owners from time in purgatory, a place of suffering after death.

The Church viewed the payments as a sign of repentance for wrong deeds. But Luther believed that salvation, forgiveness for sin, could be received only by faith. Because Luther's beliefs directly challenged the authority of the Pope, he was brought before the emperor and asked to take back his teachings. He agreed to retract any passages in his books that proved contrary to the Bible. As can be seen below, this did not satisfy the archbishop questioning him:

Martin, . . . your plea to be heard from Scripture [the Bible] is the one always made by heretics. . . . Martin, how can you assume that you are the only one to understand the sense of Scripture? Would you put your judgment above that of so

Source: Excerpt from THE HISTORY OF FLORENCE by Francesco Guicciardini, translated by Mario Domandi. Copyright © 1970 by Mario Domandi. Reprinted by permission of HarperCollins Publishers.

EXAMINING ART
While a group of nobles looks on, Martin Luther defends his beliefs before the emperor and Church leaders. Many of Luther's doctrines found support among the German nobility, while his forceful preaching and writing helped spread his ideas throughout the Western world. **Why did Luther translate the Bible into German?**

many famous men and claim that you know more than they all? You have no right to call into question the most holy orthodox faith, instituted by Christ the perfect lawgiver, proclaimed throughout the world by the Apostles, sealed by the red blood of the martyrs, confirmed by the sacred councils, defined by the Church in which all our fathers believed, . . . and which now we are forbidden by the pope and the emperor to discuss lest there be no end of debate. I ask you, Martin—answer candidly . . . —do you or do you not repudiate [reject] your books and the errors which they contain?

Thus, the archbishop expressed the view of the Church. Luther, however, stood firm. Believing that the Scripture should be open to everyone, he translated the Bible into German. In time, Luther's efforts to reform the Church resulted in a new form of Christianity known as Protestantism.

Source: Roland H. Bainton. *Here I Stand: A Life of Martin Luther.* Copyright © 1950, Abingdon Press, Copyright renewal © 1978 by Roland H. Bainton. Used by permission.

SECTION 1 REVIEW

CHECKING FOR UNDERSTANDING
1. **Define** indulgences.
2. **Name** some ideas that became important during the Renaissance.

CRITICAL THINKING
3. **Predicting Consequences** Do you think the Reformation could have occurred without Luther? Explain.

SECTION 2

Age of Expansion

During the late Middle Ages, Europeans entered an era of overseas discovery and expansion. This new period of European history was spurred by two important developments—the desire to obtain the riches of distant Asian lands and the development of new technology that enabled Europeans to sail great distances beyond their shores.

TRADE NETWORKS

During the 1300's, coastal cities in Italy and Spain dominated European trade in the Mediterranean area. Their ships sailed to the Middle East and North Africa, where they bought from Muslim traders spices, silks, gold, and other precious goods that they resold throughout Europe. Italian merchant and banking families established business and financial branches across the continent. In the following excerpt, a modern historian discusses the career of an Italian merchant, whose influence was far-reaching in European trading centers:

A mere glimpse at his vast correspondence shows how wide his net was flung, and how very frequently, in spite of war, plague, robbers, and bad roads, even the smaller trading-houses of the fourteenth century managed to communicate with each other across the whole of Europe. The files of Barcelona and Valencia, for instance, show not only an almost daily exchange with the Majorcan branches and with other Spanish cities, and frequent letters home, but dealings with Paris and London and Bruges, Nice, Arles, Perpignan and Aiguesmortes, Lisbon, Rhodes, Alexandria, Tunis, and Fez. There are letters in Latin, French, and Italian, in English and Flemish, in Catalonian, Provencal, and Greek, and even a few in Arabic and Hebrew. Moreover, all these letters have one thing in common: every event they report—a battle or a truce, a rumour of pestilence, famine or flood, a Pope's election or a prince's marriage—is noted only with a view to its effect upon trade. When Visconti [the ruler of the Italian city-state of Milan] descended upon the fields of Tuscany just before the harvest and it was plain that a famine might ensue, Tuscan merchants were not concerned with the defence of their territory, but with swiftly buying up Genoese wheat. When peace was at last signed, the merchant who sent the good news did not

so much rejoice at the deliverance of his city from Gian Galeazzo's ruthless rule, as at the thought that "God be thanked, journeying will be safe again." When, further afield, the Hundred Years' War [between France and England] was interrupted in 1408 by a three years' truce between England and Flanders [a French ally], Datini's Florentine correspondents in Bruges lost no time in sending him the good news: "Now many English merchants will tarry [stop] here, and we shall trade much more with them." But when, two years later, hostilities broke out again, the repercussion on trade was immediate. "The fair here took place on the seventh, but never was there so sad a one; and all for default of the English, who ever spend most at this fair and who may not journey here, because of their war with the French."

GLOBAL EXPLORATIONS

Beginning in the late 1400's, the rulers of Spain and Portugal, jealous of the wealth of the Italian city-states, became interested in exploration. They saw exploration as a way to put more money in their treasuries and to spread Christianity to new lands.

To these ends, first Portugal, and then Spain, supported a series of voyages to find an alternate route to the East Indies, which were the distant source of the spices Europeans needed to preserve and flavor their meats. Apart from the Mediterranean-Middle East route, no other trade route was known, nor was the size of the oceans. Portuguese explorers, however, using new navigational instruments and improved ships, gradually worked their way down the west coast of Africa. Vasco da Gama capped these voyages in 1497 when he reached India and the islands of the East Indies by sailing around the tip of Africa. Within a few years, Portugal had gained control of the East Indian trade.

Source: From THE MERCHANT OF PRATO: FRANCESCO DI MARCO DATINI by Iris Origo. Copyright © 1957 by Iris Origo. Reprinted by permission of Alfred A. Knopf, Inc.

In an effort to compete with Portugal, Spain sought a westward route to the Indies. In the late 1400's and early 1500's, an Italian navigator named Christopher Columbus made four westward voyages for Spain, discovering the islands of the Caribbean. Shortly afterward, other explorers flying the Spanish flag found the continents of North and South America.

All the voyages of discovery involved a great deal of risk, but none more so than the one made by Ferdinand Magellan, who set out with 5 ships and 270 men to accomplish what Columbus had failed to do—reach Asia by sailing west. In the account that follows, a member of the expedition recalls some of the hardships endured by Magellan's crew on the journey home:

They sailed . . . into the Pacific Sea on the 28th of November in the year 1520, and they were three months and twenty days without eating anything (*i.e.*, fresh food), and they ate biscuit, and when there was no more of that they ate the crumbs which were full of maggots. . . . They drank yel-

EUROPEAN EXPLORERS

EXAMINING CHARTS *Portugal, Spain, the Netherlands, France, and England were the leading European nations that sponsored voyages of exploration. What nation conquered civilizations and created the largest empire in the Americas?*

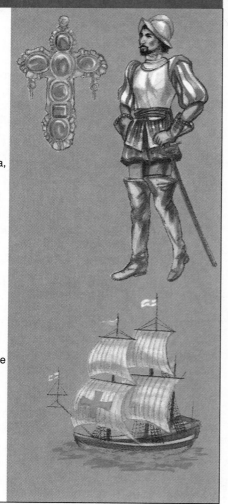

Name	Country	Achievements
CHRISTOPHER COLUMBUS	Spain	reached the Americas, 1492-1493
JOHN CABOT	England	led the first English expedition to North America and explored the coasts of Newfoundland, Nova Scotia, and New England, 1497
VASCO DA GAMA	Portugal	led the first European fleet to reach India and opened first all-water trade route between Europe and Asia, 1497–1499
AMERIGO VESPUCCI	Portugal	explored Atlantic coast of South America; one of the first to believe he had reached a new continent, 1501–1502
FERDINAND MAGELLEN	Spain	led the first expedition to sail around the world; proved the earth is round, and discovered the Strait of Magellan, 1519–1522
SIR FRANCIS DRAKE	England	first English explorer to sail around the world, 1577–1580
JACQUES CARTIER	France	first European to sail up the St. Lawrence River, 1535–1536
HENRY HUDSON	Netherlands	sailed farther north than any earlier explorer and explored the Hudson River to Albany (New York), 1609
ROBERT DE LA SALLE	France	tracked the Mississippi River to the Gulf of Mexico and claimed the Mississippi Valley for France, 1682

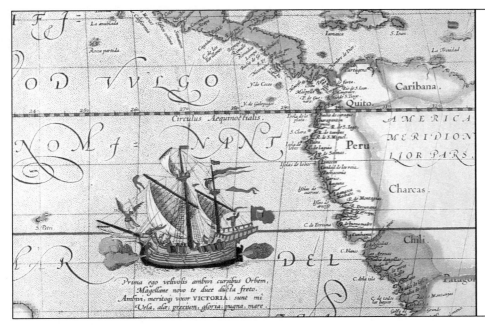

low water, already several days putrid. And they ate some of the hides that were on the largest shroud [a line that supports the mast] to keep it from breaking and that were very much toughened by the sun, rain and winds. And they softened them in the sea for four or five days, and then they put them in a pot over the fire and ate them and also much sawdust. A mouse would bring a half a ducat [gold coin] or a ducat. The gums of some of the men swelled over their upper and lower teeth, so that they could not eat and so died. . . . And if God had not given them fine weather, they would all have perished of hunger. . . . And they were certain that such a voyage would never again be made. . . .

. . . And on September seventh [1522] only eighteen men and the most of them sick, all that was left of the sixty that left from the Moluccas [islands in the East Indies], entered the bay of San Lúcar [on the Spanish coast]. Some were dead of hunger, the others killed on the island of Timor for their misdeeds. . . . On the eighth of September they dropped anchor in the port of Seville. And they shot off all the artillery, gave thanks to God in their shirts, barefooted, and with torches in their hands.

The Spanish conquered the civilizations of the Americas they found, spread Christianity, established colonies, and brought great wealth to Spain. Soon, France, England, and the Netherlands were drawn into the competition for overseas trade. The success of their voyages had a powerful impact on Europe. The fact that humans could triumph over the dangers of the unknown created optimism in Europe. New plants and animals brought back by the explorers improved the diet of Europeans. The wealth obtained from the voyages spurred the economic growth of northern Europe.

On a global scale, the age of European exploration brought the peoples of Europe, Asia, the Americas, and Africa into direct

Source: From the book: THE VOYAGE OF MAGELLAN: The Journal of Antonio Pigafetta. Translated by Paula Spurlin Paige © 1969 by The William L. Clements Library. Used by permission of the publisher, Prentice Hall/A division of Simon & Schuster, Englewood Cliffs, N.J.

EXAMINING ART
During the late 1500's, the English began to take a greater interest in the Americas. By the early 1600's, they had established colonies there. One of these was Jamestown, Virginia, founded in 1607. This was the home of Pocahontas. The daughter of the Indian chief, Powhatan, she is shown here in 1616 being presented at the English court. What countries besides England competed for colonies and trade in the Americas?

contact for the first time. Through exploration, the size and dimensions of the world and of the world's oceans became known. Europeans established control over other parts of the world and left a permanent—and often negative—effect on the cultures they conquered. In extending trade and in establishing overseas settlements, Europeans often destroyed many of the valuable contributions of these cultures and enslaved or treated as inferior many of the conquered peoples. It was not until the twentieth century that the dignity and freedom of the peoples brought under European colonial rule were once again fully realized.

SECTION 2 REVIEW

CHECKING FOR UNDERSTANDING
1. **Describe** European trade during the late Middle Ages.
2. **Explain** why Europeans became interested in voyages of exploration.

CRITICAL THINKING
3. **Determining Cause and Effect** What effect do you think the discovery of new lands had on Europe and Europeans?

SECTION 3

The Nation-State

Before 1500, Europe was made up of many independent political units whose rulers had little power beyond their own local areas. Gradually, through such means as marriage, flattery, conspiracy, and force, some rulers managed to bring more territory under their control. Their efforts were supported by wealthy merchants and banking families. Finally, between 1500 and 1700, England and France emerged as powerful nations in western Europe.

ABSOLUTE MONARCHY

The rulers of France and England believed in **absolutism**, the concept that monarchs have absolute power by the will of God. In 1609, James I of England explained the belief in this way:

The state of monarchy is the supremest thing upon earth; for kings are not only

EXAMINING ART *This seventeenth-century cartoonist used his art to speak out against the way the nobility treated peasants. How did Louis XIV treat the nobles in his court?*

The Noble is the Spider and the Peasant the Fly

The more the devil has, the more he wants

Absolutism in Europe reached its peak in France under Louis XIV, who ruled from 1643 to 1715. Louis, known as the Sun King because the government and the nobility revolved around him and he lived in grand style, proudly boasted, *"L'etat, c'est moi"*—"I am the state." He had many different ways of keeping his nobles under his control and making his power known to all. Some of these are detailed below by a French aristocrat named Saint-Simon:

The frequent entertainments, the private drives to Versailles [a palace in the country], and the royal journeys, provided the King with a means of distinguishing or mortifying his courtiers [followers at court] by naming those who were or were not to accompany him, and thus keeping everyone eager and anxious to please him. He fully realized that the substantial gifts which he had to offer were too few to have any continuous effect, and he substituted imaginary favours that appealed to men's jealous natures, small distinctions which he was able . . . to grant or withhold every day and almost every hour. The hopes that courtiers built upon such flimsy favours and the importance which they attached to them were really unbelievable, and no one was ever more artful than the King in devising fresh occasions for them. . . .

[One] device was the granting of the *justaucorps a brevet*, blue [jackets], lined with scarlet, with scarlet facings and waistcoat, embroidered with gold thread and a little silver in a particular pattern. Only a certain number of these jackets were made. . . . The greatest persons at the Court used to beg one for themselves or another. . . .

He not only required the constant attendance of the great, but was also aware of those of lower rank. . . . He saw and noticed every one of them, marked very well the absences of those usually at Court and even of those who attended more

God's lieutenants upon earth, and sit upon God's throne, but even by God himself they are called gods. . . .

Kings are justly called gods, for that they exercise a manner or resemblance of divine power upon earth: for if you will consider the attributes to God, you shall see how they agree in the person of a king. God hath power to create or destroy, make or unmake at his pleasure, to give life or send death, to judge all and to be judged nor accountable to none; to raise low things and to make high things low at his pleasure, and to God are both soul and body due. And the like power have kings: they make and unmake their subjects, they have power of raising and casting down, of life and of death, judges over all their subjects and in all causes and yet accountable to none but God only.

Source: Speech by King James I in *Pageants of Europe* by Raymond Phineas Stearns. Harcourt, Brace, and World, Inc. 1961, p. 216.

rarely, and took care to discover the reason, drawing his own conclusions and losing no opportunity of acting upon them. He took it as an offense if distinguished people did not make the Court their home, or if others came but seldom. And to come never, or scarcely ever, meant certain disgrace. When a favour was asked for such a one, the King would answer haughtily, 'I do not know him at all,' or, 'That is a man whom I never see,' and in such cases his word was irrevocable [unchangeable].

The absolute monarchies provided a certain degree of peace and order—enough to allow the economic, artistic, and intellectual life of Europe to expand and become great. It was from these monarchies that, in time, many of the modern nations of Europe emerged.

POLITICAL REVOLUTION

In the 1600's, some western Europeans, unhappy with absolutism, began to stress the importance of reason in solving human problems. Using the Renaissance ideals of individual worth and freedom, they developed many new ideas about government and social life, bringing about what came to be known as the Enlightenment.

Many Enlightenment thinkers argued in support of **popular sovereignty**, the idea that governments should be based on the consent or agreement of the people. Some, like England's John Locke, believed that people were equal; had natural rights to life, liberty, and property; and had the right to form a new government if the old one was not protecting their rights. In time, some western European nations began to act on

Source: From *Saint-Simon At Versailles,* selected and translated from the memoirs of M. Le Duc De Saint-Simon by Lucy Norton. (Hamish Hamilton, 1958), copyright © Hamish Norton Ltd. and Harper Brothers, 1958. Reprinted by permission of Penguin Books Ltd.

these ideas. In the late 1600's, for example, the English limited the power of their monarchs.

In France, the largest and most advanced nation of western Europe in the late 1700's, reason turned to revolution. The country was in serious economic trouble, and the government was nearly bankrupt. In 1789, needing approval for new taxes he wanted to impose, the king called into session the Estates-General, the French legislative body. It had been almost 200 years since the last Estates-General had met.

But, the Estates-General and the king could not come to terms. In the end, the Estates-General, full of Enlightenment arguments, dissolved itself and declared itself a new body called the National Assembly. On August 26, 1789, it stated its goals in the Declaration of the Rights of Man and of Citizens, part of which follows:

The representatives of the people of France . . . considering that ignorance, neglect, or contempt of human rights are the sole causes of public misfortunes and corruptions of Government, have resolved to set forth, in a solemn declaration, these natural and unalienable rights. . . .

I. Men are born, and always continue, free, and equal in respect of their rights. . . .

II. All governments should try to protect man's natural rights. These rights are liberty, property, security, and resistance to oppression.

III. The nation is essentially the source of all Sovereignty; nor can any INDIVIDUAL or ANY BODY OF MEN, be entitled to any authority which is not expressly derived from it.

IV. Political liberty consists in the power of doing whatever does not injure another. . . .

VI. The law is an expression of the will of the community. All citizens have

EXAMINING ART *On July 14, 1789, an angry French mob, fearing that the National Assembly would be dissolved, stormed the Bastille, a prison in Paris.* **What did the National Assembly do the following month?**

a right to concur, either personally, or by their representatives, in its formation. It should be the same to all. . . .

IX. Every man [is] presumed innocent till he has been convicted. . . .

X. No man ought to be molested on account of his opinions, not even on account of his *religious* opinions, provided his avowal of them does not disturb the public order. . . .

XI. The unrestrained communication of thoughts and opinions being one of the most precious rights of man, every citizen may speak, write and publish freely, provided he is responsible for the abuse of this liberty in cases determined by the law. . . .

XIII. A common contribution [tax] being necessary . . . , it ought to be divided equally among the members of the community, according to their abilities [to pay].

XIV. Every citizen has a right . . . to a free voice in determining the neces-

sity of public contributions, the appropriation of them, and their amount, mode of assessment, and duration. . . .

XVII. The right to property being inviolable and sacred, no one ought to be deprived of it. . . .

The result was the French Revolution. Using as their slogan, "Liberty, Equality, Fraternity," the people overthrew the monarchy and took over the country. Their actions inspired peoples of other nations who sought freedom and basic rights. In the view of some historians, the French Revolution had a far greater impact than any other revolution that came before or after it.

SECTION 3 REVIEW

CHECKING FOR UNDERSTANDING

1. **Define** absolutism, popular sovereignty.
2. **Examine** the impact of the Enlightenment on the governments of western Europe.

CRITICAL THINKING

3. **Identifying Central Issues** Why do you think the French Revolution was a key event in Europe's political development?

SECTION 4

The Industrial Revolution

Meanwhile, in England, a different sort of revolution was taking place. In this case, events happened so gradually that it was 100 years before its developments were given the name Industrial Revolution.

Before this time, goods had always been made by hand. Now, these handcrafted,

Source: Thomas Paine. *Rights of Man: Being an Answer to Mr. Burke's Attack on the French Revolution.* J.S. Jordan, 1791, pp. 116–119.

Europe

NAPOLEON BONAPARTE

In 1796, the young general Napoleon Bonaparte was given command of the French army in Italy, where he defeated the Austrian and Sardinian armies. By 1804, he was Emperor of the French. Within a few years, he ruled much of Europe. Below is a chronicle of Napoleon's coronation:

Never before has a pope been summoned in this way. When the Emperor meets the pope at the gate of the city, the Holy Father does not fail to note that Napoleon neither kneels . . . nor kisses hands. . . .

On December 2, 1804, in Notre Dame, an abundance of precious stones reflects the light of a myriad candles. . . . Everything has been prepared for weeks beforehand. A skillful museum director has even produced a colourful imitation of Charlemagne's sceptre. . . .

. . . The great procession drives to the cathedral. Napoleon, robed in an antique imperial mantle, strides to the altar leading the empress by the hand. . . . Surrounded by attendant cardinals, the pope is seated, waiting. The organ peals forth.

Then, when the appointed instant has come . . . to kneel before the Holy Father, Napoleon, to the amazement of the congregation, seizes the crown, turns his back on the pope and the altar, and standing upright as always, crowns himself in the sight of France. Then he crowns his kneeling wife. . . .

Moreover, the crown on the Emperor's head is not a Christian crown at all, but a small pagan circlet of golden laurel leaves. . . .

Thus, in this symbolical hour, Napoleon reduces to mockery the legitimate formalities he is affecting to copy. . . .

As soon as all is over, and, alone with [the Empress] Josephine, he . . . says with a sigh of relief: "Thank goodness we're through with it! A day on the battle-field would have pleased me better!"

TAKING ANOTHER LOOK

What do Napoleon's actions before and after his coronation indicate about his personality?

individually produced items were replaced by machine-made ones. Workers became specialized, with each person making part of an item and then passing it along in a process known today as **mass production**. Workers who had produced goods in their homes were employed in factories.

New towns and cities grew up near the factories, and people left their homes in the countryside to seek work in the factories. New, time-saving inventions bloomed in almost every area—from the textiles industry to transportation to mining to the refining of coal, iron, and steel. With the support of entrepreneurs, people who risk their resources for potential profits, new industries were built around the new inventions.

In the 1800's, the pace of change quickened. The development of steam locomotives and railroads opened new possibilities for growth. Poets and writers sang hymns of praise such as the one that follows to the progress brought by machines and to the future they would bring:

Gather, ye Nations, gather! From forge,
  and mine, and mill!
Come, Science and Invention; Come, Industry and Skill!
Come with your woven wonders, the blossoms of the loom,
That rival Nature's fairest flowers in all but
  their perfume.
Come with your brass and iron, your silver and your gold
And arts that change the face of earth,
  unknown to men of old.
Gather, ye Nations, gather! From ev'ry
  clime and soil,
The New Confederation, the Jubilee of
  toil.

But, as the Industrial Revolution spread, some people became less sure about its promise. Many had become dismayed by the

Source: Francois Bedarida. *A Social History of England 1851–1975.* A.S. Forster (tr.). Methuen, 1979, p. 7.

rapid growth of cities with polluted skies and by the shocking working and living conditions of the new class of factory workers. In 1832, a member of Parliament conducted an inquiry into conditions of textile workers in Great Britain. Part of what he discovered is revealed in this excerpt:

What age are you?—Twenty-two.
  What is your occupation?—A blanket manufacturer.
  Have you ever been employed in a factory?—Yes.
  At what age did you first go to work in one?—Eight.
  How long did you continue in that occupation?—Four years.
  Will you state the hours of labour at the period when you first went to the factory, in ordinary times?—From 6 in the morning to 8 at night.
  Fourteen hours?—Yes.
  With what intervals for refreshment and rest?—An hour at noon.
  When trade was brisk what were your hours?—From 5 in the morning to 9 in the evening. . . .
  During those long hours of labour could you be punctual; how did you awake?—I seldom did awake spontaneously; I was most generally awoke or lifted out of bed, sometimes asleep, by my parents.
  Were you always in time?—No.
  What was the consequence if you had been too late?—I was most commonly beaten. . . .
  In those mills is [punishment] towards the latter part of the day going on perpetually?—Perpetually. . . .
  . . . the machine turns off a regular quantity of cardings [combed-out sections of wool], and of course [the children] must keep as regularly to their work the whole of the day: . . . [the overlooker] must keep up with the machine or be found fault with, [so] he spurs the children to keep up also by various means but that which he commonly resorts to

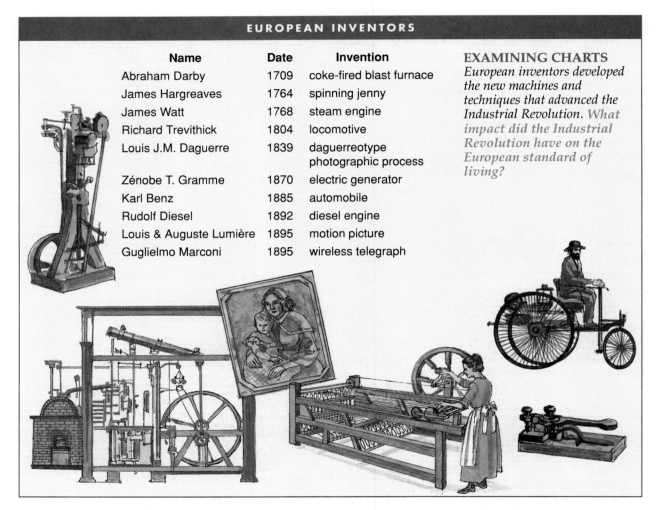

EUROPEAN INVENTORS

Name	Date	Invention
Abraham Darby	1709	coke-fired blast furnace
James Hargreaves	1764	spinning jenny
James Watt	1768	steam engine
Richard Trevithick	1804	locomotive
Louis J.M. Daguerre	1839	daguerreotype photographic process
Zénobe T. Gramme	1870	electric generator
Karl Benz	1885	automobile
Rudolf Diesel	1892	diesel engine
Louis & Auguste Lumière	1895	motion picture
Guglielmo Marconi	1895	wireless telegraph

EXAMINING CHARTS
European inventors developed the new machines and techniques that advanced the Industrial Revolution. What impact did the Industrial Revolution have on the European standard of living?

is to strap them when they become drowsy. . . .

When you got home at night after this labour, did you feel much fatigued?—Very much so. . . .

What did you do?—All that we did when we got home was to get the little bit of supper . . . and go to bed immediately. . . .

Were the rest of the children similarly circumstanced?—Yes, all of them; but they were not all of them so far from their work as I was.

Source: "Report of Committee on Factory Children's Labour" in *Parliamentary Papers, 1831–32,* as quoted in *Pageants of Europe* by Raymond Phineas Stearns. Harcourt, Brace & World, Inc., 1961, pp. 493–494.

The Industrial Revolution greatly increased western European power over other parts of the world. With more accurate and efficient weapons and gunboats, European nations overwhelmed nations that in the past had resisted domination. In time, it became clear that the Revolution raised the standard of living of western Europeans. Before long, the Revolution had spread to the world beyond Europe, bringing with it social, political, intellectual, and economic change. According to one historian, the Industrial Revolution "was transforming the world. Nothing could stand in its way. The . . . kings of the past were powerless before the businessmen . . . of the present."

CHECKING FOR UNDERSTANDING
1. **Define** mass production.
2. **Give examples of** how ways of production were changed by the Industrial Revolution.

CRITICAL THINKING
3. **Evaluating Information** What were the positive and negative effects of the Industrial Revolution on Europe and other parts of the world?

SECTION 5

Empires and Nationalism

From the 1400's to the early 1900's, eastern Europe's development differed greatly from that of western Europe. Unlike France and England, which had long–established national borders, the borders of eastern European lands were constantly changing. Nations like Poland and Hungary enjoyed periods of greatness, then declined and were conquered by powerful neighbors. Continual warfare and migrations of people left eastern Europe with a diverse population. Each nationality had memories of glory and tragedy, and each resented its latest master. In addition, eastern Europe missed the full impact of the Industrial Revolution and remained largely agricultural.

The Russian, Austrian, and Ottoman, or Turkish, empires ruled much of eastern Europe until the 1800's, when news of revolutions in France and other western European countries stirred a spirit of nationalism throughout eastern Europe. Among those eastern Europeans who became actively involved in the struggles for independence were artists, writers, and musicians. Using the religion, history, legends, and folk music

of their nationalities for inspiration, they created original art that voiced the hopes, joys, and sorrows of their peoples. One of those writers was the Polish poet Adam Mickiewicz (meh·kee·YEH·vehtz), who wrote the following poem in response to an 1831 Polish national uprising. In the poem, Mickiewicz, through the dream of a Polish soldier, urges the Poles to win back their freedom:

I find no rest or slumber here;
  Give me another room, my host!
These chamber windows are too near
  The road along which rides the post
  [guard].

And when by night he sounds his horn,
  My sad heart gives a mighty leap;
I think he wakes our steeds at morn,
  And then till break of day I weep.

I close my weary eyes and dream!
  A vision brings our banner's steed,
The sentries' cries, the campfire's gleam,
  Our soldiers' songs of doughty deed.

I wake, before my wondering eyes
  To find my corporal at my side:
He claps me on the shoulder: "Rise!
  Against the Muscovites [Russians] we
  ride!"

I rise, can this be Prussian soil!
  Far better that I rest or toil
In cold and hunger, mud and rain,
  If in my native land again!

Then would I fall asleep no more,
  But wait to hear, throughout the night
My corporal calling as before!
  "Arise! We seek the Muscovite!"

Source: Adam Mickiewicz. "The Soldier's Song, 1831." George Rapall Noyes and Marjorie Beatrice Peacock, in *Adam Mickiewicz, 1798–1855, Selected Poetry and Prose, Centenary Commemorative Edition,* Stanislaw Helsztynski (ed.). Polonia Publishing House, 1955, p. 87.

SECTION 6

The World Wars

By 1900, Europe was at the height of its power. In the arts and quality of life, it seemed to have reached a "golden age" in which it controlled or influenced the rest of the world. Yet, below the surface, there were troubles. The nations of the continent were divided by rivalry and fears. Kings no longer could make foreign policy by themselves. National pride and public opinion had become important factors in international affairs, forcing officials to consider the views of the people when making decisions.

WORLD WAR I

By 1914, the major European powers had grouped themselves into two military alliances with Germany, Italy, and Austria-Hungary on one side and Great Britain, France, and Russia on the other. When, in June of that year, the heir to the throne of Austria-Hungary was assassinated by Slavic nationalists who opposed Austrian rule, the result was war between the two alliances. Before long, more nations were drawn into a conflict that lasted four years and was known first as the Great War and later as World War I. This war was different from all those that had gone before it. New techniques of warfare and new weapons increased the terror and the number of casualties. By war's end, more than 8 million soldiers were dead and more than 20 million were maimed or wounded. Germany and its allies were defeated, but Europe was exhausted and nearly bankrupt. The old values of national honor and sacrifice suddenly seemed hollow, and the old way of life was discredited. Below, a British poet who fought in the war speaks out about the horrors of the battlefield and the disillusionment that followed:

Bent double, like old beggars under sacks, Knock-kneed, coughing like hags, we cursed through sludge,
Till on the haunting flares we turned our backs
And towards our distant rest began to trudge.
Men marched asleep. Many had lost their boots,
But limped on, blood-shod. All went lame, all blind;
Drunk with fatigue; deaf even to the hoots
Of tired, out-stripped Five-Nines [gas-shells] that dropped behind.
Gas! Gas! Quick, boys! An ecstasy of fumbling,
Fitting the clumsy helmets just in time;
But someone still was yelling out and stumbling
And flound'ring like a man in fire or lime . . .
Dim, through the misty panes and thick green light,
As under a green sea, I saw him drowning.
In all my dreams, before my helpless sight
He plunges at me, guttering, choking, drowning.
If in some smothering dreams you too could pace

EXAMINING PHOTOGRAPHS *One of the new techniques of warfare was* trench warfare, *shown here, in which ditches protected by barbed wire formed defensive lines to slow down the enemy. One of the new weapons was mustard gas, a colorless, oily liquid. Mustard gas bombs caused permanent damage to the eyes and lungs of soldiers not wearing gas masks.* Why was World War I different from all previous wars?

Behind the wagon that we flung him in,
    And watch the white eyes writhing in his face,
    His hanging face, like a devil's sick of sin;
    If you could hear, at every jolt, the blood
    Come gargling from the froth-corrupted lungs,
    Obscene as cancer, bitter as the cud
    Of vile, incurable sores on innocent tongues,—
    My friend, you would not tell with such high zest
    To children ardent for some desperate glory,
    The old Lie: *Dulce et decorum est Pro patria mori.* [It is sweet and dignified to die for the fatherland.]

WORLD WAR II

Because of World War I, the old empires of eastern Europe had been replaced by newly independent states, such as Poland, Czechoslovakia, and Yugoslavia. Most people thought that the war was "the war to end all

Source: "Dulce et Decorum Est" in *The Poems of Wilfred Owen.* Jon Stallworthy (ed.). Chatto & Windus: The Hogarth Press, 1985, p. 117.

wars." But, within slightly more than 20 years, a second world war had broken out in Europe, a war even longer and more devastating than World War I.

Germany, humiliated by the treaty that had ended World War I and in grave economic trouble, in 1933 accepted the leadership of Adolf Hitler, who promised to lead the country to a new age of greatness. Taking one bold step after another, Hitler gained territory and power. At first, in the hope of avoiding another war, Great Britain and France did not oppose him. But, in 1939, when Hitler overran Poland, they realized that the only way to stop him was by force. The British were spurred on by their prime minister, Winston Churchill. Below, in a speech he made in 1940 just after France fell to the Germans, Churchill explains why the British must fight:

What General Weygand called the Battle of France is over. I expect that the Battle of Britain is about to begin. Upon this battle depends the survival of Christian civilization. Upon it depends our own British life, and the long continuity of our institutions and our Empire. The whole fury and

Europe

THE HOLOCAUST

Adolf Hitler made the Jews scapegoats for Germany's ills and set out to eliminate them. The result was the **Holocaust**, in which 12 million people—6 million of them European Jews—perished.

The truth about the Holocaust became known when the concentration camps, prison camps set up by Hitler for Jews and other groups, were liberated at the end of the war. The condition of the survivors shocked the liberators. In the words of one medical officer, "They [the survivors] have not yet overcome their fear of authority. It will take them time to become human beings again."

Below, Doctor Franz Blaha, a survivor of four years in the concentration camp, or prison camp, of Dachau, talks about the experience:

In 1941 and 1942 we had in the camp [Dachau] what we called invalid transports. These were made up of people who were sick or for some reason incapable of working. We called them Himmelfahrt Kommandos (suicide squads.) About one hundred or so were ordered each week to go to the showers. There, four people gave injections . . . which soon caused death. After 1943 these invalids were sent to other camps for liquidation. I know they were killed because I saw that their records were marked with a cross and the date of departure. . . . One thousand to two thousand went away every three months, so there were about five thousand sent to their death in 1943, and the same in 1944. In April 1945 a Jewish transport was loaded at Dachau and was left standing on the railroad siding. The station had been destroyed by bombing, and they could not leave. So they were left there to die of starvation. . . .

Many executions by gas or shooting or injection took place right in the camp. . . .

. . . Sometimes prisoners were killed only because they vomited or had dysentery or gave the nurses too much trouble. . . . Prisoners could be shot just outside the crematorium and carried in. I have seen people pushed into the ovens while they were still breathing and making sounds, although if they were too much alive they were usually hit on the head first.

DRAWING CONCLUSIONS

What was the impact of the Holocaust? Do you think it could have been prevented? Explain your answer.

Source: Dr. Franz Blaha. Reprinted by permission of The Putnam Publishing Group from *Many Kinds of Courage: An Oral History of World War II* by Richard Lidz. Copyright © 1980 by Visual Education Corporation.

EXAMINING PHOTOGRAPHS *In the shadow of war-damaged buildings, these Berliners are planting vegetable gardens to provide themselves and their families with food.* According to Winston Churchill, what would have been the result if Germany had won World War II?

might of the enemy must very soon be turned on us. Hitler knows that he will have to break us in this island or lose the war. If we can stand up to him, all Europe may be free and the life of the world may move forward into broad, sunlit uplands. But if we fail, then the whole world, including the United States, and all that we have known and cared for, will sink into the abyss [pit] of a new Dark Age, made more sinister, and perhaps more protracted, by the lights of perverted science. Let us therefore brace ourselves to our duties, and so bear ourselves that, if the British Empire and its Commonwealth last for a thousand years, men will still say, "This was their finest hour."

Source: Winston S. Churchill, as cited in *The World's Greatest Speeches.* Lewis Copeland (ed.) Dover Publications, 1958, p. 446.

Not until 1945 was Germany finally defeated. By this time, between 15 and 17 million soldiers and 12 million civilians had died. Of the civilians, 6 million were Jews. The war ended Europe's dominance in world affairs, and the United States and the Soviet Union emerged as the two most powerful nations in the world.

SECTION 6 REVIEW

CHECKING FOR UNDERSTANDING
1. **Summarize** Europe's global role by 1900.
2. **Discuss** the effects of the two world wars.

CRITICAL THINKING
3. **Demonstrating Reasoned Judgment** Was World War I a war worth fighting? World War II? Give reasons for your conclusions.

Geography

CHANGING BOUNDARIES

Many changes took place in Europe in the early and mid-1900's. Some of these are reflected in the following three maps that show Europe during 1915, 1919, and 1939.

FOCUSING ON THE ISSUE After reading the chapter and studying the maps, answer these questions:

1. How did the map of Europe change from 1915 to 1919? Where did the most change take place?

2. How did the map of Europe change from 1919 to 1939? Where did it change most?

3. What nations came into being from 1915 to 1919? From 1919 to 1939?

4. Which nations lost territory between 1919 and 1939? Gained territory?

5. What reasons can you give for the changes that took place in the map of Europe?

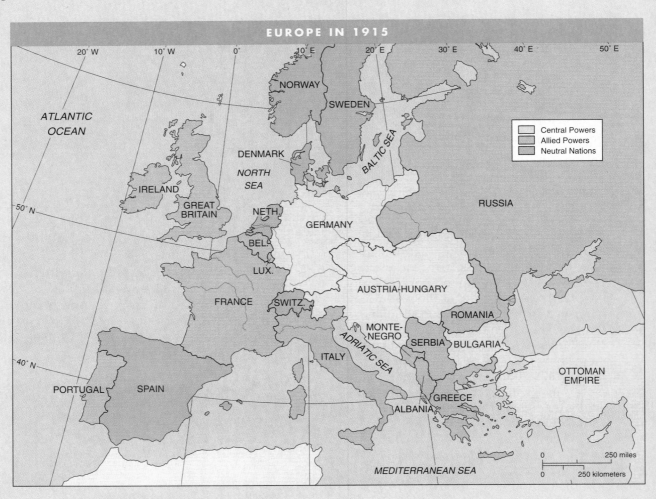

EUROPE IN 1915

Central Powers
Allied Powers
Neutral Nations

EUROPE IN 1919

ATLANTIC OCEAN

NORWAY

SWEDEN

FINLAND

NORTH SEA

DENMARK

ESTONIA

LATVIA

LITHUANIA

BALTIC SEA

IRELAND

GREAT BRITAIN

NETH.

BEL.

LUX.

GERMANY

EAST PRUSSIA (GER.)

POLAND

RUSSIA

FRANCE

SWITZ.

AUSTRIA

CZECHOSLOVAKIA

HUNGARY

ROMANIA

BLACK SEA

YUGOSLAVIA

BULGARIA

ADRIATIC SEA

ITALY

TURKEY

SPAIN

PORTUGAL

ALBANIA

GREECE

MEDITERRANEAN SEA

Territories Lost
- by Russia
- by Austria-Hungary
- by Bulgaria
- by Germany

500 miles

500 kilometers

EUROPE IN 1939

ATLANTIC OCEAN

NORWAY

SWEDEN

FINLAND

NO. IRELAND

IRELAND

GREAT BRITAIN

DENMARK

NORTH SEA

BALTIC SEA

ESTONIA

LATVIA

LITHUANIA

Danzig

POLISH CORRIDOR

USSR

NETH.

BEL.

LUX.

GERMANY

POLAND

RHINELAND March 1936

March 1939

CZECHOSLOVAKIA

SUDETENLAND September 1938

AUSTRIA March 1938

HUNGARY

ROMANIA

FRANCE

SWITZ.

YUGOSLAVIA

BULGARIA

BLACK SEA

ADRIATIC SEA

ITALY

TURKEY

SPAIN

PORTUGAL

CORSICA

SARDINIA

ALBANIA April 1939

GREECE

SICILY

MEDITERRANEAN SEA

- Germany
- Areas controlled by Germany, September 1, 1939
- Italy
- Areas controlled by Italy, September 1, 1939

500 miles

500 kilometers

811

Chapter 48 Review

SUMMARY

From the 1300's to the 1600's, important changes transformed Europe. The Renaissance promoted learning and the idea of individual self-worth, while the Reformation led to a new form of Christianity known as Protestantism. During this period, western Europeans expanded overseas, conquered civilizations, and promoted trade and colonization.

From 1600 to 1900, political revolutions in western Europe increased freedom for the common people. Meanwhile, the Industrial Revolution transformed western Europe's economy and in the long run improved its people's standard of living. In eastern Europe during this period, traditional empires faced growing challenges from nationalist movements.

Competition among Europe's nations and empires contributed to World Wars I and II. These global conflicts put an end to western Europe's global dominance.

USING VOCABULARY

Use each of these terms below in a paragraph that explains the key developments in Europe's political and economic history.

indulgences   mass production
absolutism   Holocaust
popular sovereignty

REVIEWING FACTS

1. **Summarize** how the Renaissance and Reformation changed European society and culture.
2. **Describe** the impact of Martin Luther on the religious life of Europe.
3. **Name** the French ruler who represented the ideal of absolute monarchy in Europe.
4. **Explain** why Europeans became interested in overseas exploration.
5. **List** some of the rights proclaimed in the Declaration of the Rights of Man and of Citizens.
6. **Tell** how the Industrial Revolution altered Europe's economic production.
7. **Indicate** the general causes of both World War I and World War II.

CRITICAL THINKING

1. **Synthesizing Information** What relationship do you see between the Renaissance and Reformation and the Age of Reason? Explain.
2. **Recognizing Ideologies** How did the emphasis on human freedom and popular sovereignty contribute to Europe's global influence?
3. **Demonstrating Reasoned Judgment** Historian Hans Kohn stated that "a dynamic self-centered nationalism [is] the gravest menace to peace." Give reasons why you agree or disagree with this view.

ANALYZING CONCEPTS

1. **Change** What part did competition and conflict play in the development of Europe?
2. **Technology** How was warfare affected by the Industrial Revolution?

GEOGRAPHIC THEMES

1. **Movement** How did the European discovery of the Americas affect Europe? The people of the Americas?
2. **Location** How might eastern Europe's location have been a factor in its separate development from western Europe?

Interpreting Political Cartoons

There are many ways to express political opinions, such as editorials, letters, and speeches. One form of political expression that has been popular for hundreds of years is the *political cartoon*. Political cartoons use both drawings and words to convey a message about current issues, events, or problems. Political cartoons inform and influence public opinion in an entertaining, and often humorous, way. Often, they poke fun at public figures, programs, or ideas.

To understand a political cartoon, examine both the drawing and the written labels or messages that accompany the drawing. Often political cartoonists use symbols that the audience will readily understand; a dove, for example, may represent peace. Also, cartoonists often exaggerate drawings to make their point clear. A very poor nation might be represented by a thin, shabbily-dressed person.

Political cartoons from the past can provide excellent sources of information about people's attitudes about problems and issues of their own time period. The following steps will help you in interpreting political cartoons:

- Read the titles and labels of the cartoon to identify the general topic that is presented.
- Identify the main characters in the cartoon and determine whether their features are exaggerated and why this is done.
- Analyze symbols used in the cartoon.
- Draw conclusions about the message the cartoonist is trying to convey.

EXAMPLE

Look at the cartoon in the third column, which is reproduced from page 799. Notice the action that is taking place in the drawing; one man is about to give another man a sack and a basket of fruit and vegetables. How are the two men presented? *(One man is elegantly dressed, sits on a throne-like chair next to a dog wearing a jeweled collar; the other man is simply dressed with no hat, and stands slightly bowed.)* What do these characters represent? *(The seated man represents the nobility; the other man, the peasants.)* What written messages are included in the cartoon? *("The noble is the Spider and the Peasant the Fly." "The more the devil has, the more he wants.")* Notice that the cartoonist also drew a spider web above the noble's head. What is the cartoonist's message about nobles and peasants? *(Nobles are like spiders who take advantage of, or devour, poor peasants; peasants are caught in their trap*

The Noble is the Spider and the Peasant the Fly

The more the devil has, the more he wants.

with little hope of escape. The more they give, the more the nobles demand.)*

PRACTICE

Find a political cartoon on the editorial page of a current newspaper or magazine, and answer the following questions about it:
1. What is the general subject of the cartoon?
2. What titles or written messages are included?
3. Who are the main characters and what do they represent?
4. What other symbols are used?
5. What is the cartoonist's message?

CHAPTER OUTLINE

1 From Out of the Ashes

2 A House Divided

3 Toward Unity

People and Places to Know

Berlin, NATO, Winston Churchill, Hungary, Poland, Solidarity, the European Community, Yugoslavia

Objectives to Learn

1. **Summarize** political conditions in Europe after World War II.
2. **Compare** conditions in Eastern and Western Europe during the cold war.
3. **Describe** recent trends in European politics.

Celebration at the Brandenburg Gate in Berlin, New Year's Eve 1990

The New Europe

> "Americans are often surprised and irritated by the slowness with which Europeans are making the new Europe. They do not understand our hesitations. . . .
>
> It is impossible to forget or to underestimate the fact that for centuries Europeans have continually made war on each other. Sometimes victors, sometimes vanquished, they have all of them, brought to their neighbor's territory all the fury and cruelty of battles and occupation. They have done each other much harm and this harm naturally left terrible memories, deep resentment and profound, mutual suspicion.
>
> The peoples of Western Europe speak about fifteen different languages. This is more significant than is generally considered. These differences constitute very real barriers between the peoples. . . . The mass of people remains isolated, real strangers to each other. . . .
>
> Finally, the economic interests which are to be coordinated have existed for a long time. . . .
>
> . . . In spite of everything Europe can still be rich and powerful, if abandoning her outmoded habits, she reassembles and organizes her forces. . . .
>
> There are 151 million Americans. There are 180 million Russians. There are, let us not forget, in this mutilated Western Europe which stretches from Stockholm to Ankara, 290 million Europeans. . . .
>
> Salvation is in our hands. With adaptations based on current necessities, we need only do today what Americans did in the eighteenth century; we must create the United States of Europe."

These words were written in 1952 by Paul-Henri Spaak, a Belgian. Spaak envisioned a Europe in which western European countries would be unified into a great federation that would be one of the superpowers of the modern world.

At the time Spaak voiced his hopes, many western European nations were still trying to

Source: Paul-Henri Spaak. "Creating a New Europe—'It Must be Done'" in *The New York Times,* April 20, 1952. Copyright © 1952 by The New York Times Company. Reprinted by permission.

recuperate from the physical, political, and financial devastation of World War II while many eastern European nations were under Soviet control. The superpowers were in the throes of the **cold war**—the peace-time rivalry between the Soviet Union and the United States. Decades were to pass before unity became a reality, and then it was not only for nations of western Europe but for those of eastern Europe as well.

815

SECTION 1

From Out of the Ashes

In April of 1945, not long before he killed himself, German leader Adolf Hitler made this prediction:

> **W**ith the defeat of the Reich [Nazi Germany], there will remain in the world only two great powers capable of confronting each other—the United States and Soviet Russia. The laws of both history and geography will compel these two powers to a trial of strength, either military or in the fields of economics or ideology. And it is equally certain that both these powers will sooner or later find it desirable to seek the support of the sole surviving great nation in Europe, the German people.

Source: From WORLD WAR II: *Victory in Europe.* By Gerald Simmons and the Editors of Time-Life Books © 1982 Time-Life Books Inc.

Over time, Hitler's prophecy proved true. After the war, the world was a different place. No longer were the nations of western Europe the powers they had been. No longer did Europe lead the world economy. Instead, the United States and the Soviet Union dominated world affairs.

A NEW ORDER

World War II had raged across Europe, leaving destruction in its wake, maiming people and nations alike. In the article that follows, a journalist recounts his family's ordeal and tells how the war changed the map of the world:

> **W**hen the Allied invasion of Europe reached Beilngries, a modest town in Bavaria, I was very young. But I remember American tanks rumbling down the cobbled main street, as I peered from the second-floor window of the Gasthof Wagner Bräu, an inn where my family had sought shelter.
> We had reached Beilngries from the lost nation of Estonia—four among the hundreds

EXAMINING PHOTOGRAPHS
Londoners browse in a library, despite being surrounded by the massive destruction caused by Nazi bombing. Similar devastation plagued most of Europe. Which two nations replaced Europe as the leader of the world economy?

of thousands of refugees wandering a charred and rotting German landscape. . . . Forty million Europeans were dead, and a sickness of spirit numbed the living.

Weeks before, as my father pushed a wheel-barrow of our belongings along a railroad line near the town of Landshut, Allied bombers had descended to systematically destroy the rails. He shoved the three of us into a bomb crater that had not been there ten seconds earlier, and with his broad back he sheltered us for hours from the hurtling stones and stinging earth. For eight days we hid in the hayloft of a kind German farmer, along with 20 Hungarians. . . .

While we struggled with our personal losses that summer, the nation-states of Europe lay exhausted to the marrow. The winners redrew the map. Czechoslovakia, Austria, Poland, and Yugoslavia reappeared as whole nations. Estonia, Latvia, and Lithuania disappeared, absorbed into the Soviet Union.

Occupied Germany was divided into four zones—United States, British, French, and Soviet. By 1949 the three Western zones had joined to form the Federal Re-

public of Germany. But the Soviets refused to relinquish their gains and created the German Democratic Republic (GDR), or East Germany, splitting Germany as they had split all Europe.

Once proud Berlin . . . lay deep within the Soviet zone. . . . It also was divided into four sectors. But the Soviets made East Berlin the capital of the GDR. So the three other sectors combined as West Berlin, a remnant capitalist island in a Marxist sea.

. . . In the displaced-persons camp in Geislingen, West Germany, where 4,000 Estonian refugees huddled, no one believed this would last. . . .

West Berlin, dangling in the East, became a magnet for new refugees. On August 13, 1961, a tight-lipped, hemorrhaging GDR put the final ugly touch on the division of Europe. They walled off West Berlin.

The Allies—France, Great Britain, the Soviet Union, and the United States—had agreed that war was no excuse for crimes

Source: Prit J. Vesilind. "Berlin's Ode to Joy" in *National Geographic,*
Vol. 177, No. 4, April 1990, pp. 116, 118.

like those committed by the Nazis. In 1945 and 1946, trials were held in Nuremberg, Germany, to bring justice to the guilty and to rid Germany of Nazi influence. Three of the 21 high-ranking Nazi officials accused of pursuing "aggressive war" and of "crimes against humanity" were acquitted. The rest were sentenced to death or sent to prison.

The same year the trials got underway—1945—a new permanent international organization was established. Known as the United Nations (UN), its goal was to maintain peace and to help solve economic and social problems.

THE COLD WAR

Meanwhile, Europe—and its people—were weak and exhausted. Large sectors of major cities, bridges, highways, warehouses, stores, factories, and electric-generation plants had been reduced to rubble. Millions of homes had been demolished, and millions upon millions of families were homeless and displaced. Food was in short supply.

By 1947, it had become clear that the ravaged European countries needed help to restore their prosperity and rebuild their economies. In the view of the United States, collapse of Europe's economy would open Europe to the Soviets and communism. So, when Greece and Turkey asked for financial and economic assistance, the United States provided it under what came to be known as the Truman Doctrine.

Later that year, the United States proposed an aid program—the Marshall Plan—designed "to place Europe on its feet economically." The plan was open to all European countries. But only those of western Europe accepted the loans the plan offered. The Soviet Union countered the U.S. offer with one of its own, the Council of Mutual Assistance (COMECON), which provided aid for the countries of eastern Europe.

With the year 1948 came the first real confrontation in the cold war between the two superpowers. Practically no food or essential materials were produced in Berlin. Almost all the goods the city's 2.5 million inhabitants needed for survival were transported by land into West Berlin. A Soviet blockade of the land routes into West Berlin brought an almost immediate response—the Berlin Airlift, described in the excerpt that follows:

Operation Vittles was begun by the US Air Force on June 26. . . . Operation Plain Fare was begun by the RAF [Royal Air Force] two days later. . . . Nothing like it had ever been attempted. The Allied commanders conferred hastily, discussed the use of bombers to augment the lift, of bringing in forces from the USA and British Dominions, of using gliders, parachuted supplies and civil aircraft. . . .

By the end of June the US Air Force was operating a shuttle service. . . . The British forces had organised a huge augmented ground organization, and the Royal Army Service Corps were loading and unloading aircraft at top speed. Thousands of men and women found themselves doing unfamiliar duties, thousands of reservists were recalled, RAF scheduled services to the Middle and Far East were taken over by airlines, and the Berlin Airlift grew daily. The aircraft flew from four airfields in the Western Zones along the corridors, each 20 miles wide. . . . They converged on the vital airfield of Gatow in West Berlin. Here the air traffic controllers worked around the clock, the hardstanding was quadrupled in size by German contractors who used rubble from the city . . . and the main runway was lengthened day-by-day. . . .

The Russians had hoped the West's nerve would break, and that the Allies would back down. But all that happened was that the lift grew day-by-day. . . .

. . . In terms of weight the most important loads were flour, coal and petrol [oil]. Tudors, built to carry passengers in luxury,

EXAMINING PHOTOGRAPHS

During the Soviet blockade of Berlin, American and British Commonwealth planes airlifted tons of medicine and food into the western half of the city for 11 months. How did the Berlin Blockade affect the nations of western Europe in their foreign policies?

acquired a reek of petrol and a black and white lining from the other two commodities.

There was never a respite. Captain C. Treen, of Bond's Air Service, made six round trips . . . in one 26-hour period, without a minute's sleep. An RAF Dakota flew 11,000 miles from the Far East, checked in with the controllers and was airborne with a load within three hours. . . . Meanwhile, tired pilots sketched on scraps of paper methods of wiping the bodies and blood of millions of insects from their windscreens, and of avoiding each other—and the hostile red-starred fighters—in the crowded corridors. . . .

And there is no doubt that the flyers got the job done and well. Day and night the piston-engined transports thundered along the disputed corridors, lurching . . . through the rough air, braving electrical storms, torrential rain and blizzards, finally to . . . alight heavily on the runway at Gatow or at Tegel. . . . Scores of willing hands would heave out the tons of vital food or fuel. . . . Officials would screen the queues [lines] of hopeful passengers and the aircrew, having just had time for a quick cigarette and a cup of coffee, were back in the cockpit. Queuing up for take off they would soon climb back into the gloom and murk. . . .

By 1949 crews from the air forces of Australia, New Zealand and South Africa were at work . . . , and there were eight all-weather dispatch airfields. An 8,000 ton day was not uncommon, and on April 16, 1949 a record 12,840 tons were flown in. Every day many hundreds of pilots would bring succor to the city. . . . Not only the Allies but the Germans toiled mightily to keep Berlin free. It was clear they could go on doing it indefinitely. So at midnight on Wednesday May 11, 1949, the Soviet troops suddenly raised all the barriers.

The Berlin Blockade had intensified western concerns about the dangers of communism and about military defense. In April 1949, the majority of the western European nations, the United States, and Canada formed a new military defensive alliance— the North Atlantic Treaty Organization (NATO). An attack on one member of NATO

Source: The Encyclopedia of Air Warfare. Thomas Y. Crowell Company, 1975, pp. 162, 165.

would be regarded as an attack on all members. In 1955, the Soviets responded. They and the eastern European nations under their control formed their own military alliance—the Warsaw Pact.

SECTION 2

A House Divided

While the Allies had liberated, or freed, the countries of western Europe from Nazi rule, the Soviets had liberated the countries of eastern Europe. Even before the war was over, they had succeeded in having these countries placed in their sphere of influence. This meant that while the Soviet Union would respect the countries' independence, it would play an important part in their affairs.

In 1946, Winston Churchill in a speech at Fulton, Missouri, gave this appraisal of the situation in Europe:

A shadow has fallen upon the scenes so lately lightened. . . . Nobody knows what Soviet Russia and its Communist international organization intends to do in the immediate future, or what are the limits, if any, to their expansive . . . tendencies. . . .

From Stettin in the Baltic to Trieste in the Adriatic, an iron curtain has descended across the Continent. Behind that line

EXAMINING PHOTOGRAPHS *Rugged mountains tower over the village of Mostar in the Republic of Bosnia-Herzegovina. Bosnia-Herzegovina was once part of the nation of Yugoslavia. What action did Yugoslavia take after World War II?*

lie all the capitals of the ancient states and central and eastern Europe. Warsaw, Berlin, Prague, Vienna, Budapest, Belgrade, Bucharest and Sofia, all these famous cities and the populations around them lie in what I might call the Soviet sphere, and all are subject, in one form or another, not only to Soviet influence but to a very high and in some cases increasing measure of control from Moscow.

With these words, Churchill gave voice to a bitter truth. Europe was now divided into two distinct parts—non-Communist western Europe and Communist eastern Europe.

Source: Winston Churchill, as cited in The World's Great Speeches. Lewis Copeland (ed.). Dover Publications, 1958, p. 615.

BEHIND THE IRON CURTAIN

By 1947, the countries of eastern Europe were Soviet satellites, tightly controlled by the Soviet Union and ruled by pro-Soviet communist governments. The Soviets tried to regulate almost every aspect of life, from the economy to religion. Only Yugoslavia succeeded in freeing itself from the Soviets' tight grip.

The people of eastern Europe resented Soviet domination. As time passed and communist promises of a bright future went unfulfilled, resentment turned into resistance and revolt in some countries. In 1953, for example, bricklayers in East Berlin walked off the job in protest against the higher productivity quotas set by Moscow. The next day, the whole country went on strike.

In 1956, in Hungary, what began as a demonstration by students and workers evolved into a full-scale uprising. A freedom fighter tells what happened in Budapest:

It was just after 5 A.M. when we saw flickering lights and shadows that could only mean hundreds upon hundreds of people gathering at the foot of Gellert Hill on the other side of the Danube. When we passed by the bridge and got closer to the huge assembly, we saw that they were the women of Budapest. While their husbands and sons fought, they stood in long queues, candles in hand. . . .

They were offering their prayers to the Almighty that our revolution would succeed.

On Bela Bartok Street we were passed by dozens of trucks loaded with armed workers, heading . . . to join the insurrection.

The workers carried flags with our national red, white, and green colors and a large hole in the center of each, where the Red Star had been. They had cut out the star with pocket knives—and this was more or less the flag of the revolution, the Hungarian flag with the dread Communist symbol missing. . . .

There wasn't a single Russian soldier to be seen in the street. We heard later . . . that the Soviet commanding officer had ordered Soviet troops . . . not to interfere in the revolution at this point.

I waved good-by to my two friends at the door of the house we had come to know as home, and ran upstairs to see [my wife] Eva. . . .

Cars with loudspeakers passed under our window, calling on all Budapest citizens to join the freedom battle in any way they could. "Fight if you can fight! Help the wounded. Bring supplies. But for the love of God, help Hungary!"

Neither the East German nor the Hungarian rebellion was successful. Soviet troops crushed them both. The result was the same in 1968, when Czech Communist party leader Alexander Dubçek introduced reforms designed to "democratize" his country. Troops from the Soviet Union and its eastern European allies invaded, seized the capital city of Prague, and ended the reforms.

Over time, some eastern European countries succeeded in loosening the Soviet grip and gaining some freedoms. One of those countries was Poland, whose people had demanded greater personal freedom from the very beginning. In 1980, Polish workers, tired of high prices and shortages of consumer goods and food, banded together to form a non-Communist union—Solidarity. As explained in the following excerpt, Solidarity became a symbol of freedom for all Poles:

The Polish trade union Solidarity was born in August 1980 amid the waving of workers' banners and religious icons. For almost a year and a half its posters blanketed walls, kiosks [newsstands] and factory fences. Calls for "Strike!" and "On your knees!" were aimed at government offi-

Source: From A STUDENT'S DIARY by Lazlo Beke. Copyright © 1957 by Lazlo Beke. Used by permission of Viking Penguin, a division of Penguin Books USA, Inc.

EXAMINING PHOTOGRAPHS *The banner carried by these Polish union supporters symbolized the Solidarity movement.* What was the aim of the artist who created the symbol?

cials, who watched and waited for the right time to strike back. In the process the white poster with the blood-red letters *Solidarnosc* (Solidarity) smeared across it became famous in its own right. It carried a new message, and a political one. . . .

The unassuming artist behind the now famous *Solidarnosc* logo [symbol] is a young Gdansk designer, Jerzy Janiszewski. He rearranged the white and red of Poland's flag in a symbolic gesture aimed at unifying a society of workers, intellectuals and farmers. It was a large idea conveyed with striking simplicity. Although a trained artist and an established poster maker, he dashed off his best-known work while caught up in the fervor of events surrounding him.

Under pressure, the government finally recognized both Solidarity and its leader, Lech Walęsa. Under Walęsa's leadership,

Source: Susan Hornik. "In Poland a poster is a fiery art and a way to speak out" in *Smithsonian,* January 1983, p. 88.

Solidarity led workers in demonstrations and strikes and called for free elections.

A FREE EUROPE

While eastern European countries churned under the iron grip of Soviet rule, most western European countries continued under or adopted democratic forms of government. Nations like Great Britain, France, Belgium, Spain, and Portugal shed their colonial empires in response to the growth of nationalism in Asia and Africa after World War II. They began devoting their energies to internal economic and social development. Governments took an active role in their national economies, and the people prospered. As explained in the following excerpt, almost no one prospered more than the French:

In some ways France began to stir and change deeply after 1945, and this led to the major economic and social transformations of the postwar decades. One important factor was the rise in the birthrate. In the 1930s the population was gently falling, but in 1945–46 the birthrate leapt from 93 to 126 percent and then stayed for many years at well above the European average. For this reason and because of immigration and longer life-expectancy France's population has risen from 40 to 56 million since 1945. The post war bébé-boom, as it was called, was spurred by the generous new family allowances, though sociologists believe that its cause was also partly psychological—a survival instinct and reaction against prewar decadence [decline]. Certainly, the 1940 defeat [at the hands of the Germans] and the Nazi occupation shocked a number of French people outside politics into reconsidering the future. In the civil service, the innovating technocrat emerged alongside the conservative bureaucrat, while, in the country, young farmers began to challenge the attitudes of older peasants. At first,

Europe

A CHANGE OF GOVERNMENT

Spain, Portugal and, for a time, Greece, were the only western European nations that did not adopt democracy after World War II. Spain and Portugal were ruled by dictators; Greece was at first a democracy, but political instability eventually led to military rule. By the mid-1970's, democracy had triumphed in all three countries. As reported below, 48 years of dictatorship ended in Portugal in 1974:

Shortly after midnight on April 25, 1974, Lisbon's Radio Renascensa played "Grandola vila morena," an old ballad that was an anthem of the Portuguese Left. For a few listeners, most of them middle-ranking Army officers waiting in barracks up and down the country, the spirited lyrics had special meaning. . . .

The ballad was a signal for rebel units to take up positions in six cities. As people were going to work in Lisbon that Thursday morning, Army vehicles were rolling to the waterfront Praca do Comercio and other key points in the capital. Radio announcements by a group called the Armed Forces Movement (MFA) explained that a coup was under

way "to put an end to the regime which had oppressed the country for so long."

The collapse of the late António de Oliveira Salazar's New State was swift. Almost no one would fight for the dictatorship. When a squadron of "loyalist" tanks entered Lisbon, its men declined to fire on the rebels: A young sublieutenant who clearly approved of the coup happily said to an MFA officer, "I am here to attack you, but all I want to do is laugh." Students took to the streets chanting "Down with fascism," and the censorship office . . . was ransacked. When a joyous mob of 15,000 gathered at Caxias prison, near the capital, guards freed all 200-odd political prisoners.

Prime Minister Marcello Caetano surrendered to the MFA's representative, General António de Spínola. . . . "You must maintain control," Salazar's successor told the general. "I am frightened by the idea of power loose in the streets."

DRAWING CONCLUSIONS

What group carried out the coup in Portugal? How do you think the Portuguese people felt about the coup? Explain.

Source: Thomas C. Bruneau. "Portugal: Discovering Democracy." From *THE WILSON QUARTERLY*, Summer 1985. Copyright © 1985 by The Woodrow Wilson International Center for Scholars.

this new ethos of renewal and progress was confined to a few pioneers, but gradually it spread to infect public opinion more widely. . . .

A key figure in France's postwar reconstruction was Jean Monnet, a brandy-merchant from Cognac. A pro-European idealist and visionary, in 1945 he won [provisional President Charles] de Gaulle's support for a central state Plan and then became its first Commissioner-General [director]. Monnet cut through the usual barriers in France between different interest groups and succeeded in bringing civil servants, business representatives and trade-union leaders around the same table and persuading them to work together. The Plan was not the only force behind postwar renewal, but it made a major contribution and created its own mystique, which bred widespread optimism. Helped by Marshall Aid funds from the United States, the Plan became the prime motor of early French postwar

recovery in austere times when much infrastructure still lay shattered and poverty was severe in many areas. Industry soon regained its pre-war peak, and annual growth in the 1950's exceeded 5 percent. Meanwhile, mechanization of farming produced a rural exodus that provided labor for the booming new industries, as towns swelled in size and France finally shifted from an agricultural-based to an industrial economy.

After the war, the people of western Europe sought financial and physical security. As a result, many governments made social welfare policy. Among these was the government of Norway. In the following excerpt, a journalist discusses Norwegians and some of their government benefits:

Norway boasts a combination of material security and "quality of life" found nowhere else in Scandinavia—or, perhaps in the rest of the Western democracies. . . .

The macadam streets in Oslo are as close to spotless as streets can be. Citizens stride purposefully along the sidewalks. They are not generous with smiles and greetings, perhaps, but their eyes are not burning with tension, or vacant with alienation, either. In winter, children . . . —rosy cheeked, bright eyed, wearing wool scarves and mittens—frolic in the parks. But, in school or at home, they accede to the requests of teachers and parents without undue resistance. They will live to be older than citizens of almost any other nation. . . .

Citizens partake of one of the richest smorgasbords of social entitlements found anywhere. Hospital care costs them nothing (except in high taxes). By law, workers get four weeks of paid vacation per year. One-fourth of them own vacation homes. Those few who wind up unemployed receive more than half of their previous salaries while they seek new work.

EXAMINING PHOTOGRAPHS *Paris, France, is now a modern city, after being rebuilt since the late 1940's.* *What program initiated the rebuilding of France?*

Source: THE CULTURAL ATLAS OF FRANCE by John Ardagh and Colin Johns. Copyright © 1991 by Andromeda (Oxford) Ltd. Reprinted with permission of Facts On File, Inc., New York.

A college education is free to all who can pass the stiff entrance examination. Norway is a world leader in books published per capita, thanks partly to government subsidies. Newspapers, too, receive support from Oslo—both directly and through a ban on TV advertising. . . .

The government also subsidizes the past. While all nations pay homage to tradition, few have taken such pains to preserve old ways of living as has Norway. . . .

In spite of the government's generosity, Norway's solvency is not in doubt. And it never was. . . . By the fall of 1983, Norway had the lowest unemployment rate . . . in Scandinavia. . . .

Moreover, Norway seems to have resisted the side affects of postwar affluence and urban growth. . . . Its divorce rate is . . . one of the lowest in the West. . . . In many small Norwegian towns, front doors are never locked. . . .

The oil discovered in the Norwegian sector of the North Sea during the 1960s has helped keep . . . the economy close to full employment, even in the worst of times.

A major factor in western Europe's economic prosperity was the decision to unite and coordinate economic activities. In 1950, the French foreign minister proposed a plan for "lifting Europe out of the rubble of World War II"—pooling European coal and steel industries. In response, France, Italy, West Germany, Belgium, the Netherlands, and Luxembourg agreed in 1951 to end trade barriers and develop uniform standards in the coal and steel industries.

Their success led to the creation of another economic union in 1957—the European Economic Community (EEC), also known as the Common Market. The six member nations—France, Italy, Belgium, Luxembourg, the

Source: Robert Wright. "Norway: Paradise Retained." From *THE WILSON QUARTERLY,* Summer 1984. Copyright © 1984 by The Woodrow Wilson International Center for Scholars.

EXAMINING PHOTOGRAPHS *European charm and economic prosperity have grown out of the rubble of war-torn Munich, Germany. How did the EEC contribute to prosperity?*

Netherlands, and West Germany—agreed that manufacturers could sell their goods in other member nations without paying tariffs and that workers from one member nation could take jobs in any other member nation. By 1992, EEC membership had doubled from 6 to 12, with more nations eager to join.

SECTION 2 REVIEW

CHECKING FOR UNDERSTANDING

1. **Examine** the causes of the rebellions in eastern European countries after the war.
2. **Speculate** about the reasons for France's economic prosperity in the post-war years.
3. **List** the social entitlements afforded the people of Norway during the post-war years.

CRITICAL THINKING

4. **Predicting Consequences** What might have happened if the British, French, or Americans had liberated eastern Europe?

Toward Unity

When the French foreign minister suggested pooling European coal and steel industries in 1950, he saw the move as a first step toward a united Europe. Over the years, more steps were taken toward that goal. But not until the 1990's did the majority of Europeans agree that the goal could become reality.

THE COLLAPSE OF COMMUNISM

All through the 1980's, discontent and dissension grew among the peoples of eastern Europe. Beset by problems at home, Soviet leader Mikhail Gorbachev decided that it would be in the best interest of the Soviet Union to loosen its grip on its eastern European satellite nations. In March 1989, he announced that his government would not interfere if eastern European countries moved toward democracy. One by one, the Communist governments of eastern Europe fell.

The most dramatic symbol of the Communist collapse in eastern Europe was the fall of the Berlin Wall, which for more than 40 years had stood as a powerful physical reminder of the "iron curtain" that divided Europe. At midnight on November 9, 1989, the East German government opened the Brandenburg Gate at the wall that separated East Germany and West Germany. One writer described the scene this way:

In East Berlin, people began to go to the Wall to see if what they had heard was true. It was. Within two hours of the announcement, the trickle of people had turned into jubilant crowds. By midnight, thousands of East Berliners were walking, biking, or driving to crossing points in the Wall and entering the western half of the city—something that, just a few hours earlier, they could only dream of.

At Checkpoint Charlie, the place where U.S. and Soviet tanks had faced off while the infamous Wall was being erected, long

EXAMINING PHOTOGRAPHS
Crowds gather at the Berlin Wall, long a symbol of the division of eastern Europe and western Europe, shortly before its fall on November 9, 1989. Why did the crowds become jubilant after the wall fell?

lines of cars and people moved into West Berlin unimpeded. Berliners were shouting, "Gates open! Gates open!" and "The Wall is gone!" Some exuberant Germans even scampered to the top of the Wall, now that all fear of being shot was gone.

As East Berliners drove their cars down the splendid [boulevard] Kürfurstendamm, . . . their enthusiasm grew. They had dreamed of entering the western zone for years. . . . One woman exclaimed, as she viewed the shop windows of West Berlin, "There is so much color, so much light." "It's incredible," "The eighth wonder of the world!" "I never believed I would be able to do this!" were other remarks. Of the West Berliners, one East German student said, "It's amazing how warmly we were greeted. We were applauded. They cried. They were just as happy as we were." A blind man, guided by a seeing-eye dog, remarked, "I just wanted to smell the air of a free Berlin."

East German guards, who hours before would have shot anyone trying to escape, now posed happily as people snapped pictures of the scene. "The East German soldiers don't know what to do now," said one West Berliner. "They behave a bit crazy tonight, so calm and so quiet." One man rushed across the border carrying a newspaper that proclaimed, in an enormous headline, "Berlin is Berlin Again!" The guards, who previously would have confiscated such material, merely reached out eagerly to see the newspaper.

The celebrations continued all through the night and into the morning. People began to dance on top of the Wall. Others blew trumpets, embraced, and laughed while tears streamed down their faces. The ringing of chisels and hammers could be heard as people began to chip away at the once-impregnable barrier.

Source: Doris M. Epler. *The Berlin Wall.* The Millbrook Press, 1992, pp. 96, 98, 100.

EXAMINING PHOTOGRAPHS *The fruits of democracy are evident on this Austrian street. What European countries embraced democracy and free markets in the late 1980's and early 1990's?*

A NEW ERA

From 1989 into the early 1990's, the hallmark of Europe was change. France and Great Britain came under new leadership. The two Germanies were finally unified. Democracy flourished in Spain and other Mediterranean countries. New governments came into being in the once-Communist nations of eastern Europe, governments that for the most part embraced free elections, the free-market economy, and closer ties with the West.

While the western European countries were not without problems during this time, the difficulties faced by the eastern European nations loomed larger. In many of these countries, hopes for democracy and prosperity were impacted by economic woes and rising nationalism. Some countries, such as Czechoslovakia and Yugoslavia, became fragmented, with ethnic rivalries breaking up existing boundaries into separate smaller states based on language, religion, or culture. Complicating the situation has been the effects on the people of eastern Europe of decades of forced obedience to the Soviet state and communism. In the excerpt that follows, a journalist focuses on the concern this has caused in the Baltics:

[It] is not the economy, nor the politics, nor the eroded culture that concerns Baltic leaders most—it is the widespread degradation of the human being after 50 years of communism. They worry about the kind of people they have become.

Listen to one of Lithuania's parliamentarians, Emanuelis Zingeris. . . :

"Ours is the struggle of 3.7 million people who have, since early childhood, been injected with fear and submission. We have lived in a system where no one could be different. Tens of thousands of our intellectuals were exiled to Siberia in the 1940s. We have a few capable leaders, but we are not used to speaking out, as other people are. . . ."

Listen to physician Leopold Ozolinsh in Latvia. . . : "We are in a state of ruin, and no one is left to protest. Most of our people who had brains were bought out by the government. Our scientists were simply bribed—with coffee, vacation homes, apartments. We have very few honest people left."

Listen to Estonia's new foreign minister, Lennart Meri . . . : "When you shut people's mouths so they cannot talk, when you close their eyes by forbidding them to travel, when you plug their ears by jamming air waves, the population becomes very passive. In this condition, when people don't care, it seems as if nature herself reacts: Fields produce less wheat, forests die of pollution, fouled rivers catch fire. The entire society degrades. This catastrophe is so far unrecognized in the West, but it has been obvious here. Life expectancy has fallen, and the infant mortality rate has risen to its highest level.

"Even the ability of students to learn has deteriorated. Today's technology is so exact and refined that only a person who

EXAMINING PHOTOGRAPHS *The typical eastern European factory includes out-dated and unsafe machinery, which generally results in an inefficient and less-productive economy. According to one journalist, what is the problem that most concerns eastern European leaders?*

thinks freely and critically can use it well—a person who has been taught since age four that he has individual worth, who has been taught by age eight that he has rights and responsibilities.

"In our society this new person has been weeded out; people with capabilities, with intelligence, practically the entire educated class, went to jail. Farmers who did better work had their heads mowed off like grass.

"The rest of the world has evolved, but we have gone backward."

A UNITED EUROPE

In spite of their individual problems, the nations of Europe continued to work toward a united Europe. In 1991, members of the European Community (EC) laid out a blueprint for future political and economic unity—the Maastricht Treaty. To make the people of the 12 EC member nations aware of what it would mean to them if the treaty were enacted, a French newspaper offered this "primer":

Automobiles: A European Community (EC) resident will be able to buy a car anywhere in the community without additional paperwork or taxes. . . . There will be a Europe-wide driver's license. Technical inspection of automobiles, with the obligation to repair problems, which now applies only to car brakes, may be extended to 53 other items.

• Consumer protection: Stricter safety standards will apply to certain products, such as toys, and stricter health standards will be applied, such as a maximum tar content for cigarettes.

• Currency: The single European currency will take effect January 1, 1999, in all countries that meet the economic and financial conditions spelled out by the Maastricht Treaty. The European Currency Unit (ECU) will then replace national currencies. . . .

EXAMINING PHOTOGRAPHS *The flag of the EC (left), a symbol of a united Europe, flies next to the French flag. When will the EC begin a single currency?*

• Customs: Barriers among the 12 countries will be abolished as of 1993. Community citizens will be able to go from one country to another without any border checks except for "measures of public order."

• Elections: A national of any community country will have the right to vote and be elected to office in municipal elections in a country of which he is not a national.

• Immigration: Here, there will be a general transfer of sovereignty. The granting of visas, border checks on the external borders, asylum policy, and the system of work and residence permits will gradually become a community matter.

• Taxes: Every citizen will continue to pay taxes to the country where he receives his income.

• Television: A uniform system will be introduced. Called HD Mac (high-

EXAMINING PHOTOGRAPHS *In a united Europe, students will be able to complete their education in any of the member nations. How will unity affect workers?*

definition Mac), it should bring about a gradual revolution without rendering present TV sets useless.

- Universities: If the universities allow it, students will be able to complete part of their curriculum in one community country and the rest in another. Degrees and professional qualifications will be recognized everywhere. But many universities are filled to capacity. Consequently, the selection of students by universities will become the general rule.
- Work: A residence card will no longer be needed to reside or work outside one's own country.

As the following newspaper report reveals, many Europeans had reservations about the treaty—and about the type of unity it proposed:

This is 1992, a year that was supposed to take its place in history next to 1776, 1492 and 1989.

It would be the year that the borders of Western Europe would fall just as the Berlin Wall fell three years before. Europe would begin its inexorable [unstoppable] march toward becoming a united superpower.

Why, then, is everyone so grumpy?

"We don't want to be part of some new United States of Europe," said Torben Gross, spokesman for a new anti-European organization in Denmark. "It's all very undemocratic. I want to be a good neighbor to Germany but not part of some European Union. I don't want to be like some state in the United States, like California."

Asked a 40-year-old woman from eastern Germany: "How can you unify all these countries that are so different? Take us and the French and Poles. What do we have in common? What is there to be unified?"

From Denmark in the north to Germany and France in the heart of Europe, Europeans are having second thoughts about their march toward unity. . . .

In Denmark, opponents are gearing up for a referendum . . . on joining a single, European currency and forming closer political cooperation. Polls predict a close vote. Defeat could signal the unraveling of the treaty . . . that laid out plans to bring Europe closer together by the end of the century.

In France, an unlikely coalition of conservatives, communists and far-right extremists say they, too, oppose the Maastricht Treaty and the quick march to a united Europe.

And here in Germany, the percentage of people who say they oppose giving up the

Source: Hubert Preux. "A Maastricht Primer" in *Le Figaro,* as cited in *World Press Review,* August 1992, p. 11.

deutsche mark [German currency] for a common European currency has grown from 49 percent in December to 68 percent in February to 72 percent. . . .

The issues that are stirring concerns are . . . fundamental ones, involving loss of national currencies, control over foreign policy and the military and growing power of Germany even within a united Europe.

The treaty commits the European Community to abandon the lira [Italian currency] the franc [French currency], the deutsche mark and all other European currencies by the end of the century and replace them with a single European currency administered by a single European bank, although Britain has reserved the right to opt out of this part of the treaty.

The treaty also lays out plans for greater cooperation in foreign and defense policy.

The parliaments of all 12 European Community members are scheduled to vote on the treaty. . . .

The treaty is "madness," Marie-Garaud, president of the International Geopolitical Institute, a Paris-based think tank, wrote recently. "We have overestimated the benefits of unity and underestimated the costs."

Economically, a slowdown across Europe has sapped enthusiasm for new ventures and turned people inward. A poll at the end of last year indicated that half of Europeans felt their economic situation was getting worse. Only 20 percent said it was getter better.

Within many national governments, there is growing concern that the stronger Europe becomes, the weaker their own role will be.

In June, 1992, Danish voters rejected the treaty. In September, shortly after the French endorsed the treaty, Danish officials announced that Denmark no longer wanted to be part of a single-currency system. At about

Source: "The Cold Feet are Legion as Europe's Union Nears," by Jonathan Kaufman, April 27, 1992. Reprinted by permission of *The Boston Globe.*

EXAMINING PHOTOGRAPHS *A single European currency is a goal of the European Community, as is symbolized by the 12 currencies in the center of the EC flag.* ***What nation rejected the single-currency system in 1992?***

the same time, the British prime minister expressed his doubts about the present plan, saying that European leaders "must take a profound look at where Europe is going" and set "a course which can command majority support."

SECTION 3 REVIEW

CHECKING FOR UNDERSTANDING

1. **Explain** why the fall of the Berlin Wall was important.
2. **Give examples** of the changes that took place in Europe from 1989 into the early 1990's.

CRITICAL THINKING

3. **Drawing Conclusions** Why do some Europeans want to reject the Maastricht Treaty?

Geography

FROM DIVISION TO UNITY

Significant political changes shaped and reshaped Europe during the last half of the twentieth century. This impact is reflected in the two maps that follow. The maps show Europe during two periods of time—1955 and 1992.

FOCUSING ON THE ISSUE After reading the chapter and studying the maps and the photos below them, answer these questions:

1. How did Europe change from 1955 to 1992? Where did the most change take place?

2. What reasons can you give for the changes that took place in Europe?

3. How do you think the map of Europe will look in the year 2050?

EUROPE, 1955

- Warsaw Pact Member
- Communist Nation Outside Soviet Bloc
- Neutral
- NATO Member

EUROPE, 1992

30° W   20° W   10° W   0°   10° E   20° E   30° E   40° E   50° E

ARCTIC OCEAN

Arctic Circle

ICELAND

60° N

☐ European Community

ATLANTIC OCEAN

FINLAND

NORWAY

SWEDEN

ESTONIA

DENMARK

BALTIC SEA

LATVIA

LITHUANIA

NORTH SEA

REP. OF IRELAND

50° N

GREAT BRITAIN

NETH.

BEL.

GERMANY

POLAND

COMMONWEALTH OF INDEPENDENT STATES

LUXEMBOURG

CZECH. REP.

SLOVAKIA

FRANCE

SWITZ.

AUSTRIA

HUNGARY

ROMANIA

SLOVENIA

CROATIA

BOSNIA & HERZEGOVINA

40° N

CORSICA

ITALY

ADRIATIC SEA

SERBIA

BULGARIA

MACEDONIA

PORTUGAL

SPAIN

SARDINIA

GREECE

ALBANIA

0   500 miles

0   500 kilometers

SICILY

MEDITERRANEAN SEA

Chapter 49 Review

SUMMARY

World War II changed the map of Europe. It also changed the lives of the Europeans. While the two superpowers—the United States and the Soviet Union—engaged in a cold war, Europeans strove to rebuild their lives, their nations, and their economies.

Europe was now divided into non-Communist western Europe and Communist eastern Europe. Most eastern Europeans resented Soviet rule, and in some countries they revolted. The Soviet Union, however, would not loosen its grip on the eastern European nations. At the same time, most western European nations adopted democracy. In some, social welfare became policy. In most, the people prospered.

The breakup of the Soviet Union and the fall of communism ushered in a new era for Europeans. While change has been a constant since that time and many European nations are faced with a variety of problems individually, they have continued to work toward a new and united Europe.

REVIEWING FACTS

1. **Compare** the Truman Doctrine and the Marshall Plan.
2. **Distinguish** between NATO and the Warsaw Pact.
3. **Examine** the efforts made toward European economic unity in the 1950's by western Europeans.
4. **Discuss** the impact of Mikhail Gorbachev on the development of events in eastern Europe during the 1980's.
5. **Account** for the fragmentation of some eastern European countries in the 1990's.
6. **Specify** what the Maastricht Treaty is, who created it, and when.

CRITICAL THINKING

1. **Making Comparisons** Compare developments in the countries of eastern Europe with those in western Europe from the 1940's to the early 1980's.
2. **Determining Cause and Effect** What has been the effect on the people of eastern Europe of decades of forced obedience to the Soviet state and communism?
3. **Demonstrating Reasoned Judgment** The Maastricht Treaty has been a subject of great debate among Europeans. If you were a citizen of one of the European nations, would you be in favor of the treaty or would you oppose it? Give reasons to support your answer.
4. **Analyzing Information** In 1992, an American journalist made these comments about European unity: "With the Soviets gone and the Americans looking homeward, the countries of Western Europe are free to go back to acting like independent nations with separate identities and sometimes conflicting ambitions. They will all have to look out for their own interests because they can't be sure anyone else will do it for them. Lacking outside forces to hold them together, they will most likely drift apart." Give reasons why you agree or disagree with the journalist's comments.

ANALYZING CONCEPTS

1. **Power** What was the role of the Soviet Union in Europe after World War II?
2. **Change** In what way was Europe transformed as a result of World War II?

GEOGRAPHIC THEMES

Regions In what ways did World War II change the map of Europe?

Analyzing Editorials

Editorials express opinions about current events and issues. While an unsigned editorial reflects the opinion of the publication's editorial staff, a signed editorial (called an "op-ed piece") expresses the views of an individual writer. Editorials try to educate and to influence public opinion. By focusing and sparking debate about issues, they encourage a free flow of ideas. They are excellent sources of information about public attitudes, both past and present.

To analyze editorials, first read the headline and opening paragraphs to identify the topic. Then, determine the author's viewpoint on this topic. Finally, look for factual statements and arguments supporting this viewpoint. Try to determine whether the facts are accurate and the arguments are logical. Use the following steps in analyzing newspaper editorials:

- Determine the subject of the editorial.
- Identify the writer's opinion on the subject.
- Look for supporting facts and arguments.
- Determine whether the supporting facts and arguments are logical.

EXAMPLE

Read the following editorial about the 1992 conflict in the former nation of Yugoslavia.

If the besieged corner of northwestern Bosnia between Bihac and Velika Kladusa falls to the 'ethnic cleansing' [the attempt, mainly by Serbs, to use military force to clear Serb-held areas of Croats and Slavic Muslims] being inflicted elsewhere in that dying republic, it will be unforgivable.

And the unforgiven will include more than the Serb paramilitary gangs aiming to drive the region's largely Muslim population into flight. The international community, which has been sluggish to respond, will deserve much of the blame. . . .

Bihac . . . is one of four towns in a . . . Muslim enclave, . . . south of the Croatian capital of Zagreb. . . . The Serbs want this area because it abuts land they occupy in Croatia and sits on a strategic rail line. But although the four towns are being shelled, they are mostly still intact. . . . The third of a million people here have not yet joined the flood of refugees. This enclave can be saved. . . .

UN officials are distracted by the endless crises in Sarajevo and other cities in the south. They understandably seek a comprehensive plan for Bosnia, of which the Bihac area is only one part. . . . But the Bihac enclave is one of the few remaining bases on which a viable UN protectorate for Bosnia could be based. It can anchor what remains of the republic when the ethnic cleansing is stopped. That is why the United Nations must move at once to break the siege and snatch this building block for the future of Bosnia out of the fire.

For the European Community and for the sake of a 'new world order,' the Bihac enclave is vital. Unlike much of Bosnia, with a modicum of effort it can still be saved.

This editorial discusses the northwestern corner of Bosnia, where Serbs were trying force Muslims out of their homes. What viewpoint does this editorial express? *(Inaction by the international community may allow Serbs to succeed.)* What arguments are given to support strong UN action in this area? *(create a base for a Bosnian protectorate, vital to preserving European Community and 'new world order')* What facts are given to support this position? *(third of a million Muslims still live there, towns intact)* Why has the UN ignored this area? *(attention focused on Sarajevo)*

PRACTICE

Complete one of the following activities.

1. Find an editorial about Europe, and answer these questions:
   a) What is the topic of the editorial?
   b) What opinion is expressed on the topic?
   c) What supporting facts are given?
   d) What other arguments support the opinion? Do they make sense?
2. Write an editorial about a local or school issue. State your opinion clearly and support your position with facts.

Source: Boston Globe, August 20, 1992. p. 20.

835

CHAPTER OUTLINE

1 Family

2 Social Class

3 Place

4 Language

5 Religion

6 History and Tradition

People and Places to Know
the Catalans, Lithuania, the Balkans

Objectives to Learn

1. **Describe** the roles played by family in European cultures.
2. **Discuss** national, regional, and local loyalties in Europe.
3. **Evaluate** the importance of language to identity in Europe.
4. **Explain** the role of religion in shaping identity for Europeans.

The grandeur of Paris, France

A Sense of Themselves

> " . . . Hour after hour I can think of Ireland, I can imagine without going far wrong what is happening in any one of the little towns by day or by night, can see the tillage and the walled garden, see the split porter [beer] foam along the counters, I can hear argument and ballads, hear the . . . prayers for the dead. I can almost tell what any one of my friends might be doing at any hour so steadfast is the rhythm of life there. I open a book, and I have only to see the names of Ballyhooly or Raheen to be plunged into that world from which I have derived such a richness and an unquenchable grief. The tinkers [traveling repairpersons] at Rathkeale will be driving back to their settlement by now I say, and the woman who tells fortunes in her caravan will be sending her child down for the tenth loaf of sliced bread, while a mile or two away in her domain Lady so-and-so will tell the groomsman how yet again she got her horse into a lather, and on some door in a town a little black crêpe scarf dangling from a knocker will have on it a handwritten black-edged card stating at what time the remains will be removed. . . .
>
> It is true that a country encapsulates our childhood and those lanes, byres [barns], fields, flowers, insects, suns, moons and stars are forever reoccurring and tantalising me with a possibility of a golden key which would lead beyond birth to the roots of one's lineage. Irish? In truth I would not want to be anything else. It is a state of mind as well as an actual country. It is being at odds with other nationalities, having [a] quite different philosophy about pleasure, about punishment, about life, and about death. "

The Irish woman who wrote these words is like most other Europeans in that she has strong feelings of identity with her surroundings. She is—and always will be—Irish, and the feelings she shares with her Irish kinspeople and her intimate sense of the Irish landscape set her apart from people of other European countries.

Source: Edna O'Brien. *Mother Ireland.* Wylie, Aitken, & Stone, 1976, pp. 143–144.

Each European people has some distinctive qualities that unite them—and, at the same time, set them apart from other Europeans. Their particular feelings about family and class, their interaction with their terrain or place, their languages and religious practices, and their historical traditions and contemporary experience combine to give each of these peoples an identity, a sense of themselves.

SECTION 1
Family

All Europeans value family. In some countries, however, family has traditionally been more important than in others. This is especially true in Mediterranean countries, where the family is often the main focus of a person's life. Links with grandparents, aunts, uncles, and cousins provide both emotional and financial security. A Greek writer explains:

To most Greeks, family is the most important thing in the world. Parents, children, grandparents, aunts, uncles, cousins, godparents, and even close friends are all considered to be family. Members of a

EXAMINING PHOTOGRAPHS *To the Greeks, a wedding is a special celebration to which the entire family is invited. What other celebrations are important to Greek families?*

family feel a deep loyalty and sense of responsibility toward each other. When most Greeks have a problem, they can count on their family for support and advice.

Greek families are usually very open about expressing emotions. They also take great pride in each other's accomplishments, and enjoy sharing these feelings of pride with others. In fact, there is an old Greek proverb which says, "If you don't sing the praises of your house, it will fall down on you"

. . . Grandparents in Greece are honored by their families, and children are taught to respect them from a very young age. A Greek child may spend a lot of time with his or her grandparents, listening to stories, getting advice, and learning different skills. This respect for elders is a part of the Greek philotemo [self-respect].

In the past, the father made most of the important decisions about the family. In modern Greece, however, this is changing. Many young people feel that marriage should be an equal partnership, where men and women share in decision-making and chores. . . .

Raising the children, however, has always been a shared responsibility. Greek fathers are known for being very strict. This does not mean, though, that Greek fathers are responsible only for discipline. . . .

Mothers, too, are treated with great respect . . . Even today, while many women have careers outside their home, almost all put their families first. . . .

Children are usually at the center of their parents' lives. Many are raised to feel that they are special and important people. They are raised to be responsible, too. . . .

Greek children are expected to devote much of their time to their families. From an early age, Greek children take part in family gatherings, such as baptisms, weddings, name days, and other celebrations. In this way, they learn to behave well with people of all ages. . . .

In addition to special celebrations, families share many activities together. . . . In the past, this togetherness was common even when children got married. After marriage, couples usually lived with the husband's family. Today, however, this is beginning to change. Fewer young people are choosing to stay at home.[1]

As the following excerpt shows, Italy is another country in which family is considered a source of strength and support:

Italy as a nation has often been described as a mosaic of millions of families who survive rather by instinct than moral imperatives and written laws. "No Italian who has a family is ever alone. He finds in it a refuge in which to lick his wounds after defeat, or an arsenal and a staff for his victorious drives," wrote Luigi Barzini in his book *The Italians*."

This family loyalty is the core of political alliances, business associations, matrimonial matches and employment. It is also at the heart of centuries-old and bloody feuds. The family is also a social institution which cares for the aged who continue to be respected and useful until the day they die. No decent Italian would send a parent into an old people's home, a fact well-illustrated by the scarcity of these institutions.

At the top of the family hierarchy is the controversial father figure, the stern custodian of rigid family law and morals. . . . He is responsible for the family prestige and deals with the hostile world outside. . . .

Next to the *pater familias* [father], on a pedestal all her own, is the kindly figure of the *Mamma*, always merciful, always forgiving, always on the side of her children. Italians dote on their mothers. It is often said that Italian men are forever under maternal wings, first those of their mothers, then those of their wives.[2]

[1]*Source:* Reprinted with the permission of Dillon Press, an Imprint of Macmillan Publishing Company from GREECE: *A Spirited Independence* by Diana Spyropulos. Copyright © 1990 by Dillon Press.

[2]*Source:* Uli Schmetzer. "A Mediterranean Mosaic," *Insight Guide: Continental Europe.* APA Publications (HK) Ltd., 1989, pp. 182–183.

For many Europeans, the importance of family and family ties remain strong in spite of such obstacles as distance and time. Such is the case of one Romanian-American. Below, she describes what happened when she, her sister, and their parents returned to Romania, the country from which her father had fled 47 years earlier:

The scene at the Bucharest airport plays back to me now like slow-motion film footage. I remember soldiers standing guard at the gates. . . . Beyond them a thick crowd pressed together impatiently, waving arms, handkerchiefs and flowers. Individual faces from photographs sent to us over the years: Aunt Silvia and Uncle Virgil, Uncle Octavian, my cousins Corina and Liviu—plus all the husbands, wives, children . . . my family.

Sixteen people piled into Aunt Silvia's tiny Bucharest apartment for our welcome dinner. The dining table stretched from one end of the room to the other; I thought it would collapse from the weight of the feast spread across it. . . .

Uncle Virgil filled little glasses with Romania's national drink, the clear, potent, double-distilled plum brandy called *tuica*. . . . Between the toasts and the tears and the clinking and the laughter, I felt the linking of our generations and of our worlds. We ate. We talked. We argued over who looked like whom, asked a hundred questions, translated a thousand answers, and settled into one another's company as if we had gathered daily around that table. Perhaps we had. I looked across the room to the bookcase and a photograph of my mother, father, sister and myself smiling on the happy scene. . . .

Eight months have passed, and images of that journey are still finding their way into my dreams. . . .

Connecting us are the telephone and the mailbox. Yes, there is still the uncertainty of distance. But now that we have made

EXAMINING PHOTOGRAPHS *The way of life of these upper-class Britons enjoying horse racing at Ascot (above left) is very different from that of the working-class Briton selling flowers.* *Who made up the second class in Europe in early times?*

the first journey together, I can find my way home—by heart.

Source: Rodica Iliescu. "Return to Romania" in *New Choices,* December 1990, pp. 19–21.

SECTION 1 REVIEW

CHECKING FOR UNDERSTANDING

1. **Explain** how families are regarded in Greece and Italy.

CRITICAL THINKING

2. **Making Comparisons** In what ways are European attitudes about family the same as yours? In what ways are they different?

SECTION 2

Social Class

In Europe, class divisions have existed since early times. Classes were organized into ranks, each giving obedience and respect to the one above it. At the top of society was royalty. Below it were nobles, who had titles and owned large tracts of land. Together, royalty and nobles made up the highest class. Next came church officials, such as bishops and priests. And, lastly, came everyone else—peasants, small landowners, artisans, merchants, lawyers. These divisions remained rigid for centuries, with class a matter of birth. Children learned the same skills as their parents and were expected to marry within their class.

In time, however, the classes changed, and the barriers broke down. No longer were church officials a separate class. A new middle class emerged—one made up of successful lawyers, doctors, merchants, and industrialists. The lower class, in turn, was made up of peasants, day laborers, and factory workers. Movement between classes became possible through marriage, educational achievement, or financial success.

During the 1900's, the class structure has changed even further. Nobles still exist in many European countries, but they do not have the power they once had. Even so, class divisions and class identity still exist in some areas. As evidenced in the following newspaper article, Great Britain is one of those areas:

"Open-plan offices, that sort of thing," Michael Cookson says in the library of the house built for his great-great-great-grandfather in 1832. . . .

Mr. Cookson stands and puts on his shooting coat, his sharp features backlit against a Regency window [window dating from the period between 1811 and 1820] looking onto his . . . estate. . . .

Beyond the rose garden, a man on a ladder is training a plum tree to grow against a brick wall. . . .

By the [rules] of Britain's bureaucracy, the gardener on the ladder . . . belongs to social class "D." Mr. Cookson, "gentleman farmer," belongs in class "A." The gardener may be as poor as his father was; Mr. Cookson is definitely less rich than his.

Mr. Cookson's son might well end up working on that ladder; the gardener's son . . . could end up living in [an elegant] house. But all the cars and open-plan-offices in the kingdom wouldn't allow them to trade classes.

. . . the British use clues to spot their classes. The working class plays soccer;

the middle class rugby. The working class takes its holidays on the Costa del Sol [Spanish coastal region on the Mediterranean]; the middle class tours France. The working class likes aluminum door handles; the middle class buys brass.

The classes dress differently, comb their hair differently, eat different food at different times of the day. But accent and [dialect] remain the strongest status signals. The middle classes speak alike wherever they live. The working classes speak west country, cockney, geordie, scouse. When they miss a word in conversation, the lower classes say, "I beg your pardon." The upper classes don't beg; they just say, "What?"

Since rising to the top in Britain means playing by the rules, the working classes hug bottom; its members rarely get to find out what the rules are. Working-class youths might succeed in advertising or the media, if they find jobs, but can pretty much forget about big business . . . and the elite civil service. They grow up in separate neighborhoods, go to separate and often unequal schools. . . .

On a back street in Morpeth, one of Northumberland's market towns, the Comrades Club occupies an old house. . . .

"We provide cheap beer for the working class," says the young man behind the long bar inside. "The middle class go to the Conservative Club. It's jazzier." He draws a pint of strong draught ale and serves it to a long-haul driver in from Manchester.

"It's birds of a feather, isn't it?" the driver says. . . .

"It's a way of life," says Ian Moore, coming up to the bar for a beer with Tommy Hindhaugh. "Some men enjoy a Jaguar. I enjoy a pint and the art of conversation. It's your upbringing." "Class doesn't matter much," Mr. Hindhaugh puts in. "We have a millionaire in town. Self-made. He can come in here anytime."

But would the Duke of Northumberland invite him to tea?

EXAMINING PHOTOGRAPHS *The people of Catalonia, a region in northeastern Spain, are proud of their unique language and traditions.* **About how many people speak Catalan, the native tongue?**

Mr. Hindhaugh's eyebrows shoot up. "Now that's going a bit too far."

SECTION 2 REVIEW

CHECKING FOR UNDERSTANDING
1. **Detail** the characteristics of the classes that existed in pre-twentieth-century Europe.
2. **Specify** ways in which a person could move from one class to another.

CRITICAL THINKING
3. **Analyzing Information** What determines class membership in present-day Great Britain?

SECTION 3

Place

Before nations were formed in Europe, people identified themselves by the locality or region in which they lived. Each region

Source: Barry Newman. "A Briton Needn't Pay Much Heed to Class; He Knows His Place," *The Wall Street Journal,* May 6, 1985. Reprint by permission of *The Wall Street Journal* © 1985 Dow Jones & Company, Inc. All Rights Reserved Worldwide.

developed its own character with its own style of architecture, art, and music, its own customs and traditions, and, at times, its own language or dialect.

In many of the smaller and more isolated towns and villages, Europeans today continue to identify themselves in the same way. Spain, for example, has been unified for hundreds of years, but many of its people identify more with their region than with the nation as a whole. In the words of one Spanish writer and thinker, "Spain is not a country, but a country of countries." As a visiting journalist discovered, Spain's northeastern region of Catalonia is one of those "countries":

Tell a Catalan [native of Catalonia] that you are doing an article on Spain, and he will likely reply, with only a hint of irony, "Then what brings you to Catalonia?"

Millions of Spaniards do not speak Spanish as a first language, and a significant few do not speak it at all. . . . In Catalonia the lingua franca is Catalan. . . .

One day I asked José María Carandell, an open and [talkative] Catalan writer and playwright, the difference between Barcelonans and Madrileños. "The people of Madrid are more ambitious, more eager to make money, but also more generous," he told me. I had by this time learned that most people in Spain have emphatic, and often engagingly [insulting], opinions about the people of every other region, so I was surprised to hear Carandell praising the denizens of Barcelona's historic rival.

"Oh, yes, Madrileños are very generous, I admit it. We Catalans on the other hand are stingy—not just with our money but even with our words. The only thing we are not stingy with is our architecture. We spend *fortunes* on buildings, which is why we have so many beautiful ones," he told me.

He reflected a moment and added: "We are also, I think, more cosmopolitan. Catalonia has always looked toward Europe. We are physically nearer to Europe and we belonged to Charlemagne, not to the Moors. It has always made us more European than the rest of Spain."

So do Catalans feel un-Spanish? "It is Spanish not to want to be part of Spain. In that sense, Catalonia is very Spanish." Carandell smiled at the paradox [contradiction]. . . .

One very visible divide between Catalonia and the rest of Spain is language. Menus, signs, billboards, and other printed [matter] of daily life are now given almost exclusively in this curious language that seems strikingly more akin to French than to Spanish. In Catalan, for example, "please" is *si us plau*, closer to the French *s'il vous plaît* than to Spanish *por favor*.

Catalan is spoken by seven million people, but its survival has only recently been assured. Since 1716, when King Philip V's Decree of the New Plan imposed Castilian [language spoken in Madrid] as the official language, Catalan, along with other minority languages in Spain, has suffered long periods in which it was not allowed to be taught in schools, used in courts, or even, sometimes, spoken in public. The 16

EXAMINING PHOTOGRAPHS *Europeans attach special significance to their capital cities. For example, Hungarians are especially proud of their capital, Budapest. Located on the banks of the Danube River, Budapest is known for its churches, palaces, outdoor cafes, and steep wooded hills.* ***What factors in modern life have strengthened European national identities?***

years since [Francisco] Franco's [Spain's former ruler] death have marked the longest period of linguistic peace in Catalonia in almost 300 years.

"The freedom to write in one's own language is refreshing . . . ," says Carandell.

In other parts of Europe, many local and regional differences have faded. Central governments have required that the national languages be taught in school. Modern transportation and communication systems and work opportunities have broadened people's horizons. As a result, for most people, regional loyalties have been replaced by strong national identities.

Source: Bill Bryson. "The New World of Spain" in *National Geographic*, Vol. 181, No. 4, April 1992, pp. 13–14, 18.

Hungarians, for example, may remind others of a very old Latin saying, *Non est vita extra Hungaria*—"There is no life outside Hungary." In the words of one Hungarian, "Hungarians believe that the whole world is Hungarian, that Hungary is truly the Garden of Eden."

Scots are another people who identify strongly with their nation. One writer, when asked to describe the Scottish character, began this way: "A native of Scotland, it has been said, considers himself a Scot before he thinks of himself as a human being, thus establishing a clear order of excellence."

A French president, François Mitterand, summed up the feelings of many Europeans for their own nations in this comment about his feelings for his nation—France:

I live France. I have a deep instinctive awareness of France, of physical France, and a passion for her geography, her living body. For it is there that my roots have grown. There is no need for me to seek the soul of France—it lives in me.

CHECKING FOR UNDERSTANDING
1. **Name** the features that, before nations were formed, gave European localities and regions their distinctive characters.
2. **Examine** how Catalans perceive Catalonia and the characteristics and features that differentiate them and Catalonia from other peoples and regions of Spain.

CRITICAL THINKING
3. **Demonstrating Reasoned Judgment** Local and regional differences continue to persist in Europe in spite of efforts to create strong national identities. What reasons can you give for this?

Source: François Mitterand. *The Wheat and the Chaff.* Seaver Books/Lattes, 1982.

SECTION 4
Language

Language is another important part of people's identity. This high regard for the written and spoken word is seen in the efforts of people to protect their languages and to have them recognized by others.

Europeans speak some 50 languages and 100 dialects. Each country has a national language. Some countries, like Switzerland, have more than one. A teacher in the bilingual community of Biel, Switzerland, talks about language in her country and in her community:

Switzerland has four national languages: German, French, Italian and Romansh. The majority speak German, while French is spoken mainly in the southwest and west. Italian in the south and Romansh (by a very small minority) in the east. In fact the situation is more complicated than this because a great many dialects of each language are also spoken in different places. The German-speaking Swiss, in particular, have many variations of Schweizerdeutsch, which is itself a dialect and quite different from the written Hochdeutsche, which is taught in schools. Hochdeutsche is used mainly for official and business purposes.

Biel is on the border between the French- and German-speaking regions and is the only officially bilingual community in Switzerland. This means that everything is written in both languages, including official documents and such things as street signs and advertisements. We even have a bilingual newspaper, where all the articles and even the cartoons are written in both languages.

Language isn't just a matter of communication—it's also an expression of cultural background. We try to teach people about their own cultural heritage, while

LLANFAIRPWLLGWYNGYLLGOGERYCHWYRNDROBWLLLLANTYSILIOGOGOGOCH

ST MARYS CHURCH IN THE HOLLOW OF THE WHITE HAZEL NEAR TO THE RAPID WHIRLPOOL OF LLANTYSILIO OF THE RED CAVE

MAES PARCIO   CAR PARK

EXAMINING PHOTOGRAPHS
Many areas of Europe carefully preserve their heritages, including their regional languages. European governments who have tried to unify their countries by suppressing these languages have faced strong opposition. This exceptionally long one-word sign in Welsh over the entrance to a parking area identifies the name of this town in Wales. What are some other regional languages in Europe?

appreciating that of others. Thus parents have the right to decide whether to send their children to a French- or German-speaking school. The classes will be taught in one language and will have a cultural bias, but in the fourth year the other language will be taught very intensively, so all the inhabitants here are bilingual. I could ask someone a question in German and be answered in French and I probably wouldn't even notice.

As there are more German- than French-speaking people, all foreign children are sent to the French schools. This is also because most of the foreigners are Italian and find French easier than German. There is a great cultural mix here and because everyone has friends speaking another language, they make more of an effort to understand each other.

That isn't to say that there aren't any problems. For one thing, it's more difficult for the French, because they get used to hearing and speaking Schweizerdeutsch, but then have to learn Hochdeutsche, which they have no opportunity to prac-

tice. For another, the mentalities of the different groups are different, but this is a problem that concerns the country as a whole. As the majority of Swiss speak German, they are in a position to pass laws that aren't necessarily to the liking of those speaking French. The Germans tend to prefer to regulate things more than the French, who prefer to leave things alone.

As the teacher pointed out, language gives a person a sense of belonging. In the words of one European writer, the language a person speaks "is a veritable world in which he [or she] lives and acts. . . ." Speaking a language well often has more emotional meaning than identifying with a particular nation-state. This is especially true of those who speak regional languages like Catalan or Welsh. In the article that follows, the director of a European Community-funded project concerned with regional lan-

Source: Inge Margot. "Everything is written in two languages" in *We Live in Switzerland* by Fiona Cameron and Preben Kristensen. The Bookwright Press, 1987, pp. 14–15. Reprinted with permission of Franklin Watts, Inc., New York.

CASE STUDY

Europe

THE RESILIENCE OF NATIONALITY

According to a British journalist, "It is the small things that make the interesting differences between countries, and there are far more of them than ever come under discussion at diplomatic meetings." Below, she gives examples:

I had a friend who never knew what to do with her hands during meals. Brought up half in England ("Hands in your lap, dear") and half in France (. . . "Hands on the table"), she was thoroughly confused. A couple I know built a little house in Greece and joyfully completed it. The Greeks thought they were mad, because once a house is finished, the owner must pay taxes on it. That is why so many Greek houses have iron rods sticking out of the top—to show there is more concrete to come. . . .

We think of ubiquitous pizzas and hamburgers, but we forget the foods you buy in the streets—chestnuts in London, tapas in Spain, liahapiirakka (meat patties) in Finland. . . .

The Dutch hardly ever use their ovens; they prefer to wallow in margarine on top of the stove. The French seldom grill, except inside the oven. . . . And the Spanish do not go in for kettles. . . .

Computers, compact discs, and cameras may be the same everywhere, but in Britain you go to a pharmacy to buy film, because the British used to get their developing fluid there. Continental pharmacies may . . . sell nothing but drugs. Few of them will sell hair products or stockings or hot water bottles. . . .

. . . It is no good telling a Turk to celebrate his birthday and not his name day, or trying to make an Italian child, all agog on Christmas Eve, wait until Christmas Day to open his gifts. . . .

Or take Sundays. The Anglo-Saxon Sunday of church-going and inertia has just about had it, but many remember when people spoke with horror of the wicked "continental Sunday." It conjured up visions of the . . . French singing in the streets. Plainly, no one cares to think about German Sundays, when you not only cannot shop—you also may not wash your car, lest the swooshing of your hose disturb your neighbors.

DRAWING CONCLUSIONS

Do you agree with the writer that fear of losing differences makes Europeans scared of the unified Europe? Explain.

Source: Katharine Whitehorn. "In the United Europe, 'Vive les Différences'" . OBSERVER NEWS SERVICE, reprinted by permission of UFS, Inc.

guages provides insights on the role, impact, and future of such languages:

There can be no simple equation of language with region, or language with nation-state. Catalan, with more speakers than Danish, is still a minority language within Spain. Less than a quarter of a million people speak Icelandic, but it is not a minority language—as Welsh, with twice as many speakers, undoubtedly is.

Over the old nation-state map you must now place the map of regions, and over that, the changing mosaic of linguistic and cultural realities. Then . . . , you have to plot the new lines of influence and patronage linking the regions directly with European Community [EC] institutions . . . and also the alliances between particular regions, or particular interest groups.

The Bureau for Lesser-Used Languages of the EC, which has its office in Dublin, claims there are 50 million speakers of non-official languages in the EC. . . .

According to the Bureau, there are 35 territorial linguistic groups in the EC speaking languages that are not the official language of their nation-state. . . .

Linguistic minorities with democratic political institutions of their own at regional level do better than those without them. . . .

But there are groups that not only have no regional governments but cannot realistically aspire to have them. Whether or not Scotland becomes independent, 80,000 Gaelic-speakers will find it difficult to live in Gaelic jurisdictions that are more than local government units. The Sorbs, a . . . group of about the same size, living in what used to be East Germany and divided between two areas of mixed Sorb and German population, face the same problem, as do the 90,000 Albanians of southern Italy who again, do not occupy one solid territory. . . .

Then there are the trans-frontier minorities that in the past have been the cause of wars designed to redraw the map. . . .

With the globalisation of communications and the economic integration of Europe, it seems that some of the smaller official EC languages, such as Dutch, Danish, Greek and Portuguese are being pushed towards minority status. The sense of threat to secure official cultures may result in more repression of the unofficial minorities. Or it may build new alliances between the smaller nation-states and the larger cultural regions.

SECTION 4   REVIEW

CHECKING FOR UNDERSTANDING
1. **Explain** what being an "officially bilingual community" means in Biel.
2. **Speculate** about the advantages and disadvantages of being a bilingual community.

CRITICAL THINKING
3. **Predicting Consequences** Which do you think will result from "the sense of threat to secure official cultures"—"more repressions of the unofficial minorities" or "new alliances between the smaller nation-states and the larger cultural regions"? Explain.

SECTION 5

Religion

Religion has long been a powerful factor in European life. Even where personal faith may not have been strong, the cultural aspects of religion have been learned as naturally and unconsciously as learning how to speak. Believers of the same faith developed close bonds and a sense of community that separated them from believers of other faiths. Sometimes, to build solidarity, fear of other beliefs was heightened. Periods of religious persecution and religious wars have left permanent marks on Europe.

Source: Ned Thomas. "Unofficial Babel" in *New Statesman,* June 19, 1992, p. S5.

EXAMINING PHOTOGRAPHS *St. Peter's Basilica, in Vatican City in Rome, is of special importance to Catholics because it is the "church of the popes." Which four European nations are almost totally Roman Catholic?*

Today, most Europeans are members of the Christian, Jewish, or Muslim faiths. Christianity, however, dominates. Some countries are almost totally Christian—Roman Catholic, Protestant, or Eastern Orthodox—while others have a diversity of Christian and non-Christian faiths.

Most of Europe's Christians are Roman Catholics. The Catholics live chiefly in the southern areas of western Europe and the northern areas of eastern Europe. Ireland, Poland, Spain, and Italy are almost totally Roman Catholic. Catholicism is also very strong in the Baltic nation of Lithuania. As one journalist discovered, even Communist rule could not extinguish the faith of the Lithuanians:

Lithuania is a deeply religious nation, imbued with Roman Catholic traditions. Long ago a once mighty Lithuanian State had merged with Poland, and cultural ties remain strong. . . .

. . . faith has served Lithuania well. We arrived on Easter Sunday morning in a forest glade in rural Lithuania, at the church in Paberže, where the crests of tall maples were still leafless but thick with crows' nests. The bells pealed, the procession of villagers wound around the wooden church, the crows exulted on the highest branches, for a Lithuania free to worship fully.

The priest of Paberže, a Capuchin monk named Father Stanislovas, greeted us with a gentle smile, sweet bread, and colored eggs dyed in the old way—by wrapping them in the skins of yellow onions and boiling them until the color transferred. Nine years in prison camp had only strengthened the priest. "They didn't like my sermons," he laughed.

"When the Bolsheviks were in power, religion was the cement that held us together. They repressed us, they jailed us, harassed, yelled, and scolded us, all these things. But we held it together here. The Lutherans in Latvia and Estonia—when their pastors died and the sermons stopped, there was nothing left. Here we had the rituals and the processions, the lanterns, the incense.

"And now, I baptize a hundred adults a year. Our atheists were like snow in the spring; they melted away. . . . [Here,] if you don't believe, what kind of Lithuanian are you?"

In southeastern Europe, some nations, such as Bulgaria, Romania, and Greece, are mostly Eastern Orthodox. Others, such as Bosnia-Herzegovina and Albania, are Muslim. In northern Europe, lands such as Great Britain, the Netherlands, Denmark, and Sweden are largely Protestant. In the excerpt that follows, a Lutheran clergyman in

Source: Prit J. Vesilind. "The Baltic Nations" in *National Geographic,* Vol. 178, No. 5, November 1990, p. 35.

Sweden talks about the part the church and religion play in his country:

About 50,000 people live in [my] parish, but unfortunately only a small proportion attend church regularly. My salary is paid by those who live in the parish. Part of their annual taxes are paid to the State Church which then distributes the money to clergymen as a monthly salary. If anyone objects to their taxes being used for such purposes . . . they can apply to have their annual tax contributions reduced.

Religious education is the only subject on the school curriculum in Sweden which is compulsory. Although our state Church is Lutheran, religious education in our schools is not only about the Lutheran Church but about all major world religions. At my parish church we have special children's groups during the week for those especially interested in the Lutheran faith. . . . We teach them about Christianity, sing songs . . . and spend a lot of time outdoors during the summer months, including a summer camp. There's a lot more to being a vicar than working on Sundays. . . .

There are school visits, hospital visits, and a whole range of church social events. . . . I have fifteen assistants, so I'm also a boss![1]

Almost all European nations have a Jewish population. On the eve of the Holocaust, about 400,000 Jews lived in Hungary. Today, Hungary is home to about 100,000 Jews—one of the largest Jewish communities in eastern Europe. Below, a young Hungarian shares her thoughts about growing up Jewish in Hungary:

We just moved here last year from Szolnok, which is a small town south of Budapest. I wanted to be with Jews my age and live as a Jew, and it was difficult in Szolnok. There are only about seventy Jews there, and some of them do not even know they are Jews. I was the only Jew in my high school. When I was in primary school, some kids began bothering me because I was Jewish. My mother said be proud of your Judaism. And from then on I have a strong Jewish identity. My grandfather is a Jew, and so is my mother, but I don't have any other living relatives because of the Second World War. Many Jews today didn't know they were Jewish until they were young adults. . . .

Now many parents don't have any idea about religion, and it is their children who teach them. It wasn't like this for me. After my grandmother died, I went to live with my grandfather for ten years. He was . . . my teacher. We need more knowledgeable Jews who can teach us in high school, especially about the Holocaust. It's not the same when a non-Jew teaches us. You must feel it to be able to teach it. . . .

I . . . believe in my Judaism. I'm a Jew and I'm proud of this.[2]

Although for the most part religion is a unifying force in European daily life, it has also in some cases contributed to division between peoples and regions. In the Balkans, Eastern Orthodox Serbs are trying to assert their power over Roman Catholic Croats and Muslim Bosnians. Bitterness between Roman Catholics and Protestants also exists in parts of Europe today. In Northern Ireland, disputes between Roman Catholics and Protestants have led to much violence in that country since the 1960's. No end to the discord is in sight. For the young Irish newlyweds discussed in the following excerpt, the conflict is a constant source of pressure:

---

[1]*Source:* "Vicars work all week, not just on Sundays" in *We Live in Sweden* by Stephen Keeler and Chris Fairclough, 1985, The Bookwright Press, pp. 30–31. Reprinted with permission of Franklin Watts, Inc., New York.

[2]*Source:* From Szilvia Dotsch interview in A TREE STANDS STILL by Yale Strom, copyright © 1990 by Yale Strom. Reprinted by permission of Philomel Books.

Ian is Protestant and Maureen is Catholic in a country where Protestants and Catholics have hated each other for hundreds of years. . . .

. . . Maureen . . . grew up in Ardoyne, a working-class Catholic section of Belfast; Ian's home was in Dunmarry, exclusively Protestant. Maureen is a teacher and Ian a member of the Community Relations Branch of the Royal Ulster Constabulary (RUC), the police of Northern Ireland. They now live in one of the "mixed" areas of Belfast. . . .

On Sunday mornings Ian drives out to Dunmarry to attend services at the Church of Ireland with his mother. . . . Maureen would like to go to mass in Ardoyne with her mother and . . . brothers and sisters . . . , but she's afraid to go to a Catholic area known to be dominated by the IRA, the Irish Republican Army. So she attends church near home. . . .

"Why are you afraid to go home to Ardoyne?" I asked Maureen. . . .

"I'm afraid somebody will shoot me."

"Why would somebody shoot you?"

"Because I married a Prod [Protestant]. And even worse than that, because I married a policeman."

"I can't go there *ever,*" Ian said. "I used to be assigned to that neighborhood, and all the kids recognize me."

There's a blue minibus parked outside their house, they said, used to transport mixed groups of Catholic and Protestant children to swimming pools, to weekend camps, to specially organized discos and quiz competitions. Ian described how he drives through Catholic neighborhoods, collecting Catholic kids, and then waits at the edge of the Protestant area for Protestant kids to come out to him. It would not be safe to drive though a Protestant area with a busload of Catholics; the Protestants would be enraged, and the Catholics would be scared to death. And the same holds true for Protestants in a Catholic area.

Ian and Maureen met when they were both involved in working with young people. . . . The Catholic school in which she taught had given her a year off for special community projects, but when she became engaged to Ian, her old teaching position was made "redundant"—meaning that they didn't need her any more. . . .

Maureen went to the principal of the school, a nun, and demanded an explanation. "It's because of your personal situation," the nun told her. Hurt and angry, Maureen took legal action . . . and although she knew she was entitled to compensation, she stopped short of pressing for that. . . .

The Community Relations Branch of the RUC where Ian has worked since he first joined the force has been eliminated in many areas. . . . The police have become a hated organization, the target of violence from both Protestants and Catholics. Ian had already been transferred from an earlier post because he was "too good," too successful in getting mixed groups of Protestant and Catholic children together. He was the target of anger from both sides; the transfer was for his own safety. . . .

. . . "It makes me sad," Maureen said, "that I can't share my faith with Ian, something that's so important to me." Ian said the same thing was true from his side.

SECTION 5 REVIEW

CHECKING FOR UNDERSTANDING

1. **Identify** the religions practiced in Europe and nations in which each predominates.
2. **Speculate** about ways in which religious conflict within a nation might affect people who live there.

CRITICAL THINKING

3. **Synthesizing Information** What role does religion play in the nations of Europe?

Source: Carolyn Meyer. *Voices of Northern Ireland.* Gulliver Books, 1987, pp. 1–4, 6.

EXAMINING PHOTOGRAPHS *This parade through the streets of London by the Queen's Household Cavalry, which accompanies and protects members of the royal family as they make the rounds of their official duties, is one of the age-old traditions revered by the British and enjoyed by visitors.* In what other way do Europeans celebrate history and traditions?

History and Tradition

Europeans live with their past. It is an inescapable part of their identity. Ancient ruins, stone bridges that have survived countless earthquakes, houses that have sheltered generations of families, monuments to great victories or tragic losses, and old cathedrals, mosques, and synagogues dot the landscape. Stories, songs, and tales reinforce shared memories. All across Europe, history and tradition are celebrated in festivals. Below, a journalist describes Scottish festivals celebrating the New Year:

> Fiery New Year processions which will drive out and ward off evil spirits have been held for centuries at Comrie, Burghead and Stonehaven. At the Comrie Flambeaux procession, locals walk through the town carrying burning torches; at Stonehaven, participants swing fireballs attached to a long wire and handle. Some suggest that the swinging of fireballs is a[n] . . . attempt to lure back the sun from the heavens during the dark winter months.

> The Burning of the Clavie at Burghead is held on the evening of January 11. (This is when Hogmanay [the eve of the New Year] falls according to the old-style calendar which was abandoned in 1752 but which still holds sway when deciding the date of many celebrations.) The ceremony begins with the Clavie King lighting a tar-filled barrel which is then carried in procession through the town and from which firebrands are distributed. Finally, the Clavie is placed on the summit of Doorie Hill and allowed to burn for a time before being rolled down the hill. Fragments of the Clavie are treasured because they offer protection from the evil eye.

A major element of European history is conflict and suffering. World War II, for example, remains a living part of the heritage of several generations of Europeans. This is particularly true in Germany. Some Germans want to forget that part of the past. Others believe it must be remembered so that there are no more tragedies like the Holocaust. In 1985, Richard von Weizsäcker, president of what was then West Germany, declared that

Source: Marcus Brooke. "A Fondness for Festivals," *Insight Guide: Scotland,* APA Publications (HK) Ltd., 1991, p. 281.

EXAMINING PHOTOGRAPHS
Young Jewish students attend Hebrew school in Germany. In the early 1990's, however, anti-Semitic hostility increased in some areas of Germany. What was the German chancellor's response to the hostility?

although younger generations of Germans "cannot profess a guilt of their own for crimes they did not commit," they had been left "a grave legacy." He went on to say the following:

> . . . It is not a case of coming to terms with the past. . . . It cannot be . . . modified or made undone. However, anyone who closes his eyes to the past is blind to the present. Whoever refuses to remember the inhumanity is prone to new risks of infection. The Jewish nation remembers and will always remember. We seek reconciliation. Precisely for this reason we must understand that there can be no reconciliation without remembrance. . . . If we for our part sought to forget what had occurred . . . , this would not only be inhuman, we would also impinge upon the faith of the Jews who survived and destroy the basis of reconciliation.

Source: Richard von Weizsäcker, as quoted in "Facing Up to Germany's Past" by James M. Markham in *The New York Times Magazine*, June 23, 1985, pp. 25, 30. Copyright © 1991 by The New York Times Company. Reprinted by permission.

In the early 1990's, government leaders of the united Germany spoke out against neo-Nazi groups violently promoting their philosophy of a "Germany for the Germans." In a nationally televised address, German chancellor Helmut Kohl, calling hostility against foreigners and anti-Semitism "a disgrace for our land," stated that "Such perpetrators of violence must feel the full force of the law like any other criminal." President von Weizsäcker echoed Kohl's sentiments. "Racist anti-Semitic attacks," he proclaimed, "outrage us. Whoever claims to use such violence in the interest of Germany abuses the name of our nation."

SECTION 6 REVIEW

CHECKING FOR UNDERSTANDING
1. **Give examples** of ways in which history and tradition continue to live in Europe.

CRITICAL THINKING
2. **Drawing Conclusions** Why might concern with the past be especially strong in Germany?

Multicultural View

FOREIGNER OR FRENCH?

During the late 1980's and early 1990's, a large number of immigrants arrived in western Europe. Some came from former colonies; others came from less prosperous areas of the continent.

FOCUSING ON THE ISSUE The article that follows focuses on immigrants in France. Jean-Paul, the French journalist quoted in the article, believes that "the foreigners" are "a menace." Explain why he might react that way. What argument can you offer to help change his view?

Pick any dozen Frenchmen and one will be a foreigner. Pick any twenty and one will be a Muslim. Go to the great Mediterranean port of Marseille and pick any six. One will be Arabe.

Those numbers, especially the last, have in recent years tested France's long tradition of accommodating foreigners. . . .

After the 1789 Revolution the young French republic became known as a "land of asylum." Today it shelters 140,000 political refugees: Vietnamese, Chileans, Irani- *ans, Poles, Palestinians.*

After both World Wars, workers flowed in from Italy and Spain and Portugal. . . . They blended in; perhaps 750,000 Portuguese remain.

Then came the revolts in Indochina and Algeria and the ending of France's empire. French colonials came home, many of them bitter. After them came thousands upon thousands of former colonial subjects in search of work— perhaps a million and a half from Algeria, Morocco, and Tunisia alone.

They were welcomed at first, since France had a labor shortage. The labor shortage evaporated, but the population of Muslims in France continued *to grow. . . .*

. . . Marseille is the gateway for the Arab influx. Some of the immigrants entered illegally. Many more were legal but have remained strangers to almost all aspects of French society. Yet others have become fully acclimated. . . .

"Each of those ferryboats [that come into Marseilles] brings another 800 problems into the country," complained a journalist acquaintance. . . . Jean-Paul was an educated man, well traveled. . . . "Their birthrate is twice as high as ours. They'll change our way of life. They'll take over."

Source: Thomas J. Abercrombie. "Unsettled Immigrants" in *National Geographic,* Vol. 176, No. 1, July 1989, pp. 121, 124, 126.

Chapter 50 Review

SUMMARY

Each European people has distinctive qualities that unite them and, at the same time, set them apart from other European peoples. The value peoples place on family, what class or classes they belong to, how they interact with their region and nation, what language they speak, what religion they practice, their history, and their traditions constitute their identity—their sense of themselves.

History, tradition, and conflict have all left their marks on Europeans' identities. Yet, in spite of this—and, at times, because of it—the sources of European identity have seen much change over the years. Class structure has been modified more than once, and movement between classes has become possible. For many Europeans, regional loyalties are being replaced by national loyalties. Minority languages are being studied. In most areas, religious differences have lessened.

REVIEWING FACTS

1. **List** the different elements that contribute to Europeans' sense of themselves.
2. **Evaluate** the importance of respect in Italian and Greek families.
3. **Explain** why it is difficult for members of the working class in Great Britain to "rise to the top."
4. **Tell** how the people of Europe identified themselves before nations were formed throughout the continent.
5. **Account** for the fact that most Europeans have exchanged regional loyalties for strong national identities.
6. **Examine** Europeans' attitudes about the languages they speak.

7. **Identify** the religious groups that are found in Europe today.

CRITICAL THINKING

1. **Identifying Assumptions** If you met some Europeans who ate and dressed much as you do, would it be reasonable to believe that they also think the way you do? Why or why not?
2. **Demonstrating Reasoned Judgment** To whom do you think a Greek person would be more likely to feel a close personal relationship—a Swede, an Italian, or a Pole? Explain.
3. **Recognizing Ideologies** The Catalan poet Joan Brossa believes that language is "the basic characteristic" of the personality of his province and its people and that without his language he has no culture. Do you think the same is true of your language? Explain.
4. **Making Comparisons** Europeans place a great deal of importance on history and tradition. Do you think they are as important to most Americans? Explain why or why not.

ANALYZING CONCEPTS

1. **Identity** What are the sources of Europeans' identities?
2. **Diversity** In what ways is Europe's cultural diversity a source of its strength and its weakness?

GEOGRAPHIC THEMES

Movement What effect might efforts to unite Europe into a single economic unit have on regional and national loyalties?

Making Comparisons

You may have heard people say: "You can't compare apples and oranges!" In other words, you can't compare two totally different things. But this is not necessarily true.

Making comparisons means to identify similarities and differences between two or more things. You can compare things that are very different, so long as they share at least one common quality. For example, although apples and oranges are different kinds of fruit, they are both fruits. Also, both are round and about the same size and weight. However, they are different in color, taste, growing area, growing season, and often price.

Making comparisons is a good way to organize information about different groups, events, and situations. The following steps will help you to make comparisons:
- Decide what items will be compared.
- Determine which qualities or characteristics will be used to compare them.
- Identify similarities and differences in these qualities.

EXAMPLE

Read the passage on pages 841-842 about social class in Great Britain. Mr. Cookson is compared to his gardener; the two are in different social classes. However, each man is also compared to his own father. The passage says that Mr. Cookson is probably poorer than his father and the gardener is probably richer. What qualities or characteristics are used to compare working-class and middle-class people in Great Britain? *(sports, holiday spots, door handles, accents and dialects, educational and employment opportunities, clubs)* What are some differences between the two classes? *(Accept any comparison mentioned in the text.)*

PRACTICE

Study the following chart comparing four European nations. Then, answer the questions below:
1. Which four countries are compared in the chart?
2. What characteristics are used to compare the countries?
3. Which two countries are most similar in size?
4. Are these countries also similar in population density?
5. In what ways is Norway different from the other countries?
6. How are Hungary, Norway, and Poland similar in ethnic composition?
7. What category shows the greatest differences among the countries?

	POPULATION	POPULATION DENSITY	SIZE (in sq. miles)	ETHNIC GROUPS	LANGUAGES	RELIGIONS
FRANCE	56,184,000	252/sq. mi.	220,663	French, Arab	French, Basque, Breton, Alsatian, Flemish, Italian, Catalan	Roman Catholic, Muslim
HUNGARY	10,546,000	293/sq. mi.	35,919	Magyar, German, Gypsy	Hungarian	Roman Catholic, Protestant
NORWAY	4,214,000	33/sq. mi.	125,181	Norwegian, Lapp	Norwegian Lappish	Protestant
POLAND	38,363,000	317/sq. mi.	120,727	Polish, German, Ukrainian	Polish	Roman Catholic

CHAPTER OUTLINE

1 The Early Years

2 Artistic Trends

3 Scientific and Political Thought

People and Places to Know

Michelangelo Buonarroti, Charles Dickens, Johann Sebastian Bach, Ludwig van Beethoven, Frédéric Chopin, Franz Liszt, Béla Bartók, Giuseppe Verdi, the Impressionists, Pablo Picasso, Franz Kafka, Dylan Thomas, Albert Einstein

Key Terms to Define

classicism, romanticism, absolute monarchy, liberal, nationalist, socialist, capitalism, nationalism

Objectives to Learn

1. **Trace** the development of European painting, music, and literature.
2. **Identify** trends in European scientific and political thought.

Artist painting at the Louvre Museum in Paris, France

Arts and Thought

" . . . I was very lucky to be offered a contract with the Royal Shakespeare Company (R.S.C.). . . .

Shakespeare is Britain's best-known playwright. He . . . wrote thirty-seven plays as well as many poems. Visitors come from all over the world to see his birthplace here at Stratford-upon-Avon in Warwickshire. . . .

The Royal Shakespeare Company itself was formed in 1960, although its history dates back to 1769. In that year a man called David Garrick presented a festival of acting, music and revelry to the local inhabitants of Stratford. Now it is one of the largest and most famous theater companies in the world and plays to an audience of over a million people every year. . . .

Although the R.S.C. probably attracts larger audiences than any other theater company in the world, it is impossible to finance the vastly expensive productions that we put on from ticket sales alone. So, like so many of the 270 professional theater companies in Britain, we rely on the Arts Council of Great Britain to provide for a third of our costs. Like other theater companies, too, we receive a certain amount of help through sponsorship from industry and TV coverage of our plays.

I love working as an actress but it is very hard work indeed. I spend a lot of my time learning my lines or rehearsing on the stage. I don't only act in plays by Shakespeare though. . . . I'll be appearing in *Peer Gynt* by [the Norwegian playwright] Henrik Ibsen and *Lear* by [the English playwright] Edward Bond, as well. . . . Most of the parts are quite small at the moment, but . . . I hope to tackle some of the bigger and more ambitious parts. "

In the above excerpt, a young British actress talks about her career and about theater in Great Britain. Through her artistry, she, like many others, carries on a European cultural tradition—the theater. Theater is just one of the many shapes and forms assumed by European art. Others include music, painting, literature, and film.

The arts of Europe have evolved over many centuries and have served diverse purposes. Their origins can be traced to a variety of different sources. All of the arts, however, express basic European attitudes about truth and beauty. At the same time, all reflect and are shaped by such other aspects of European culture as religious faith; scientific inquiry; and social, economic, and political thought.

Source: "Shakespeare is Britain's best-known playwright" in *We Live in Britain* by Chris Fairclough. The Bookwright Press, 1984, pp. 28–29. Reprinted with permission of Franklin Watts, Inc., New York.

SECTION 1
The Early Years

Like the site of an archaeological dig, Europe's culture includes many layers. These layers came about as the contributions of early peoples were enriched and extended by others who came later.

AN ANCIENT LEGACY

The ancient Greeks made one of the first important contributions to European culture with their ideas about gods and human beings. In the excerpt that follows, a scholar of Greek mythology explains:

In the earliest Greek poets a new point of view dawned, never dreamed of in the world before them, but never to leave the world after them. With the coming forward of Greece, [human beings] became the center of the universe, the most important thing in it. This was a revolution in thought. Human beings had counted for little heretofore. . . .

The Greeks made their gods in their own image. That had not entered the [human mind] . . . before. . . . Until then, gods had had no semblance of reality. They were unlike all living things. . . . In Egypt, a

EXAMINING PHOTOGRAPHS *The Parthenon is an ancient Greek temple that stands on the Acropolis, a hill overlooking Athens, Greece. Built between 447 and 432 BC to honor the city's patron goddess Athena, the rectangular-shaped temple was constructed of white marble. The Parthenon is considered to be the best example of ancient Greek architecture.* How did the ancient Greeks view the relationship between humans and gods?

towering colossus. . . . Or a rigid figure, a woman with a cat's head. . . . Or a . . . mysterious sphinx, aloof from all that lives. . . .

. . . In Greece alone in the ancient world people were preoccupied with the visible; they were finding the satisfaction of their desires in what was actually in the world around them. The sculptor watched the athletes contending in the [Olympic] games and he felt that nothing he could imagine would be as beautiful as those strong young bodies. So he made his statue of Apollo [god of the sun]. The storyteller found Hermes [god of orators, writers, and commerce] among the people he passed in the street. . . . Greek artists and poets realized how splendid a man could be. . . . He was the fulfillment of their search for beauty. They had no wish to create some fantasy shaped in their own minds. All the art and all the thought of Greece centered in human beings.

THE MIDDLE YEARS

The ideas set forth by the Greeks were adopted by the Romans, who brought them to Europe. After Rome fell, a new layer of culture emerged, one based not only on Greek and Roman ideas but on those of Christianity as well.

In western Europe, from about 500 to 1700, members of the wealthy upper classes acted as patrons, or financial backers, using their riches to support learning and the arts. In some cases, this dampened the artist's creativity. In others, the results were magnificent. In the 1500's, for example, with constant prodding from his patron, Pope Julius II, Italian artist Michelangelo Buonarroti painted the Sistine Chapel in the Vatican. One incident in their often stormy relationship is recounted in the following excerpt by one of Michelangelo's pupils:

Source: Edith Hamilton. *Mythology.* Little, Brown and Company, 1942.

It is true that I have heard [Michelangelo] say that it is not finished as he would have wanted it, as he was hampered by the urgency of the pope, who asked him one day when he would finish that chapel, and when Michelangelo answered, "When I can," the pope, enraged, retorted, "You want me to have you thrown off the scaffolding." Hearing this, Michelangelo said to himself, "You shall not have me thrown off," and he removed himself and had the scaffolding taken down, and on All Saints' Day he revealed the work, which the pope . . . saw with immense satisfaction, and all Rome admired it. . . . What was lacking was the retouching of the work . . . with ultramarine and in a few places with gold, to give it a richer appearance. Julius . . . really wanted Michelangelo to furnish these touches; but when Michelangelo thought about the trouble it would give him to reassemble the scaffolding, he answered that what was lacking was nothing of importance. "It really ought to be retouched with gold," answered the pope, to whom Michelangelo responded . . . , "I do not see that men wear gold." The pope said, "It will look poor." Michelangelo rejoined, "Those who are depicted there, they were poor too." So he remarked in jest, and so the work has remained.

In what is today Poland, Czechoslovakia, Germany, and Hungary, wealthy monarchs and nobles built ornate castles, palaces, and churches in Gothic and classical styles. In Romania, Bulgaria, and Yugoslavia, religious art emerged that was influenced in form and style by the Byzantines. There were mosaics—colorful pictures formed with inlaid pieces of stone, glass, or enamel; frescoes—wall paintings made on moist plaster; and icons—symbolic religious images painted on wood.

Source: Ascanio Condivi. *The Life of Michelangelo.* Alice Sedgwick Wohl (tr.). Louisiana State University Press, 1976, pp. 57–58.

The subjects of this art generally were Jesus, the Virgin Mary, angels, saints, and apostles, all rendered in a formal style and giving a timeless, otherworldly appearance. Churches and monasteries were built in the Byzantine style as well, with interior walls and ceilings covered with richly hued mosaics and masterpieces in fresco. Many of the outside walls were covered over with frescoes as well.

MASS APPEAL

From the late 1700's to the 1900's, another layer of European culture was formed as middle- and lower-class Europeans became

EXAMINING PHOTOGRAPHS *The religious theme of this fresco in Yugoslavia is typical of Byzantine art.* *What is one effect of this formal style of the art?*

better educated, experienced a rise in their standard of living, and began to take an interest in the arts. For the first time, great numbers of people of the middle and lower classes began attending concerts; visiting museums; and buying books, sheet music, and paintings. To appeal to this new mass audience, artists developed new styles and themes. The daily lives and personal struggles of common people became acceptable subject matter for the arts. What was known as **mass culture** had emerged.

One of the earliest writers to capitalize on this new market was a nineteenth-century British author named Charles Dickens. According to a modern British novelist, Dickens' fame "came earlier and more completely than that of any other of the great novelists." Below, the novelist explains why:

By twenty-five [Dickens] was a national figure and from then on he never ceased to be one. This began because of *The Pickwick Papers.* No first novel in any language has made such a stir. . . .

The story was issued in monthly parts. . . . The first numbers didn't sell. [Then] Dickens introduced a comic, clever, witty servant. . . . From that number he was home. The country went mad on *Pickwick.* It was something like the reception today of a supreme hit record. The publishers were made, and so was he. . . .

While *Pickwick* was still in progress, and Dickens having to meet the monthly deadline, he was already building on the success. . . . Plans for new novels! *Oliver Twist, Nicholas Nickleby, Barnaby Rudge* beginning to take shape in his imagination! Contracts for new novels! . . . Work, riches, fame! As for the books themselves, he wasn't yet the conscious artist that he was to become. . . . None of his [early] novels . . . has a coherent theme. They started off with the random eye-flash of a brilliant journalist—the workhouses, juvenile crime in London,

The Arts of Europe

From the time of the ancient Greeks to the present day, Europeans have created art forms in a variety of styles. Major influences on the European arts have been the classical heritage, Christianity, and modern individualism. Before the 1700's, the European arts focused mainly on religious and classical themes; since then, they have focused more on humanity's place in the modern world.

? **What key social change led to the transformation of the European arts after the 1700's?**

Oil painting, The Hay Harvest, *by Flemish artist, Pieter Brueghel, 1565.*

Illuminated manuscript, from The Book of Kells, *Ireland.*

Facade of Casa Batllo in Barcelona, Spain, designed by Spanish architect, Antoni Gaudí.

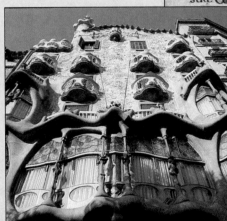

The Thinker, *bronze by French sculptor, Rodin.*

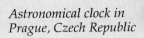

Astronomical clock in Prague, Czech Republic

the schools in the north for [illegitimate children] whom no one wanted. Everyone knew about these miseries; Dickens knew he could light them up with his spectacular vision.

SECTION 1 REVIEW

CHECKING FOR UNDERSTANDING
1. **Identify** what the ancient Greeks contributed to European culture.
2. **Indicate** the role the upper classes played in the development of European culture.

CRITICAL THINKING
3. **Determining Cause and Effect** What effect did the emergence of mass culture have on European arts?

SECTION 2

Artistic Trends

Traditionally, European music, art, and literature have been based on certain rules. But, over the centuries, as tastes and ideas changed, so did the rules. Often, what was considered beautiful or important during one period was rejected later, only to be rediscovered and appreciated still later.

During certain periods, for example, Europeans, believing that the arts should appeal to the mind's sense of order and balance, followed strict artistic rules. This was known as **classicism**. During other periods, believing that the arts should appeal to the heart, they turned away from the rules. This was known as **romanticism**. These changes in attitude, which reflected a conflict between intellect and emotion, can be seen in all forms of European arts, including music, painting, and literature.

Source: Reprinted with the permission of Charles Scribner's Sons, an Imprint of Macmillan Publishing Company from THE REALISTS: *Portraits of Eight Novelists* by C.P. Snow. Copyright © 1978 C.P. Snow.

Classical artists strove to achieve the ideals of ancient Greece and Rome, which to them represented order, harmony, and simplicity. Romantic artists instead looked to the Middle Ages and to foreign cultures, which they thought were unique and mysterious.

MUSIC

Traditional European music, which began during the Renaissance, was made up of a single melody or tune. In time, however, composers found that music could be made more interesting if they used two or more melodic lines at once. This led to what is known as counterpoint, or polyphonic music, a style of music developed to its highest level by an eighteenth-century composer named Johann Sebastian Bach.

Later, another direction was taken by musicians who began to stress harmony. They created their music around a basic melody and chords, or several notes played at the same time. Then, to enrich the music further, other voices and instruments accompanied the solo voice or instrument carrying the melody. This type of music was known as homophonic. It became standard during the 1800's, when composers like Ludwig van Beethoven, Felix Mendelssohn, Hector Berlioz, and Johannes Brahms composed symphonies for larger orchestras with newly developed, stronger pianos and more brass instruments.

Some composers drew on their homeland's rich cultural heritage for their compositions. Polish composer Frédéric Chopin, for example, spent most of his life in exile in France. But many of the piano compositions he created use the music of two Polish dances—the polonaise, a dance from the Polish royal court, and the mazurka, the Polish national dance popular among the peasants of rural Poland. Hungarian composer Franz Liszt, who wrote many concertos, sonatas, and ballads, incorporated the haunting live-

FOCUS ON PEOPLE

Europe

WOLFGANG AMADEUS MOZART

One of the most creative geniuses of European music was an Austrian named Wolfgang Amadeus Mozart. Mozart, whose musical talent was discovered at an early age, toured Europe, performing before the pope, monarchs, and nobles, and amazing audiences wherever he went. In 1793, Mozart visited Paris, France. Below, a journalist of the time offers his reactions:

. . . A [church musician] of Salzburg named Mozart has just arrived here with two children. . . . His daughter . . . plays the clavier. . . . Her brother . . . is so extraordinary . . . that we can scarcely credit what we see with our own eyes and hear with our own ears. Easily and with utmost accuracy, the child performs the most difficult pieces with hands that are scarcely large enough to span a sixth. . . . The finest conductor has not so deep a knowledge of harmony. . . . Such is his adeptness on the keyboard that if it is covered with a napkin he continues to play . . . with the same speed and precision. He has not the slightest difficulty deci-phering anything that is put before him; he writes and composes with wonderful ease. . . .

. . . A lady asked him . . . whether he would accompany her by ear. . . . She began to sing; the child tried a bass that was formally correct. . . . But as soon as the song was over he asked the lady to begin again . . . , and this time he not only played the entire melody with the right hand, but at the same time added the bass with his left. . . . Then he requested her ten times in succession to begin again, and with each repetition he changed the character of his accompaniment. He would have gone through it twenty times more had he not been asked to stop.

Mozart continued to amaze audiences as he grew older. He produced an enormous amount of music, including the operas *Don Giovanni* and *The Marriage of Figaro*, and wrote symphonies, chamber music, and piano concertos as well. Yet, he could not get a position as composer for a royal court and had many financial difficulties. He died in poverty at age 35 and was buried in an unmarked grave set aside for the poor. Only after his death was his genius rediscovered, and he was ranked among the greatest of Europe's composers.

TAKING ANOTHER LOOK

Why might some people consider Mozart one of the most creative geniuses of European music?

Source: Excerpt from MOZART by Peggy Woodford is reproduced by permission of Omnibus Press, a division of Book Sales Limited.

liness of gypsy music in his works. He created the symphonic poem, a form of music based on a literary or philosophical theme. Twentieth-century composers like Béla Bartók have continued the tradition. Bartók, known worldwide for his instrumental works, often uses Hungarian folk music in his compositions.

Other composers, such as Richard Wagner, Giuseppe Verdi, and Bedřich Smetana, composed operas, plays in which all or most of the dialogue is set to music and sung by elaborately costumed performers to orchestral accompaniment. Many people consider opera one of Europe's greatest musical achievements. In Italy, for example, operatic performances are as popular as sports. Italians view opera with passion, as a Russian-born opera star discovered when a famous conductor made some changes in the production of a Verdi opera opening at Milan's La Scala opera house:

EXAMINING PHOTOGRAPHS *Milan's La Scala (shown to the right) is one of the leading opera houses in Europe. Opera, as it is known today, developed in Italy in the 1500's. By the end of the next century, opera had spread from Italy to other European countries.* *How do modern Italians regard the opera?*

Coming into the hotel restaurant on the day of the premiere . . . I could already detect all the signs of the approaching storm. The level of noise and excitement in the room was extraordinary. Waiters with a warlike air were gathering in groups, shouting something and [gesturing] vigorously. Our waiter came up to us at once . . . and inquired, "The signora [lady] plans, of course, to be at the opera this evening?". . .

"The signora absolutely must come! There'll be a scandal the likes of which we've never seen at La Scala. We're all going to be there," he explained. . . .

Before we had a chance to look around, several people had gathered at our table and were . . . trying to explain to me . . . just what was going on.

"We'll teach him to respect our Verdi! We already know what he's been up to. The tempos are all wrong!"

"What do you mean, 'wrong'?" I asked. . . . [He] is a great conductor, and it wouldn't hurt you to hear his interpretation. . . ."

"O Madonna!" howled our waiter. . . .

"Do you know what you're saying, Signora? He's strangled all the singers. He doesn't let them hold the high notes! . . . He wants to kill our Verdi!"

Unable to go on, he fell silent . . . and wept. . . .

. . . But around my table the shouting continued. Someone, waving his arms, was singing an aria, trying to prove to me that some note or other must not be cut short, while someone else was explaining how the orchestra should play this or that phrase. . . .

That night the audience came to the theater . . . determined to wreck the performance. . . .

. . . Everyone was . . . busy concentrating on the singing and on the conductor, who, in not permitting the singers to hold the high notes until they were blue in the face, deprived the audience of its usual pleasure. [Fiercely] expressing their opinions, shouting back and forth . . . , reacting stormily to each imperfect note, the audience grew more and more inflamed. . . . When the curtain finally went down on the first act, people hissed, booed, and swore. Fights even broke out in the gallery. And so on throughout the performance, and then late into the night on the public square.

PAINTING

Traditionally, European paintings have been concerned with representing scenes, stories, or individuals. Even though styles changed over time, the meanings of the art were easily understood by anyone.

During the Middle Ages, artists devoted themselves chiefly to religious subjects painted in a flat, two-dimensional way. They were not concerned with being realistic. Then, during the Renaissance, ancient Greek and Roman statues were unearthed, and artists acquired a new interest in the human form for its own sake. In an effort to show their subjects realistically, they created rounded, seemingly three-dimensional figures and developed rules for perspective, or depth relationships. They began to paint more nonreligious subjects and to pay attention to the sources of light and the way shadows fell.

In the mid-1800's, another change took place when a group of French painters known as Impressionists rebelled against the concern for realism. Rather than portray a scene that was fixed and timeless, they tried to capture the fleeting moment. To this end, they painted outdoors, portraying scenes of nature and human activities in change.

In the 1900's, European artists developed new styles—styles not concerned with realism but with imparting a feeling, mood, or idea.

Source: Galina Vishnevskaya. Galina: A Russian Story. Harcourt Brace Jovanovich, 1984.

One of these artists was Spanish painter Pablo Picasso. He believed that nature and art were two different things. "In art," he said, "we express our conception of what is not visible to nature." For him, color was a way of expressing emotion rather than of describing reality. Picasso developed a style of art known as Cubism in which objects are reduced into geometrical, unrealistic planes and shapes rearranged into new forms.

Painting and other forms of visual art remain important in Europe today. As in the past, contemporary European artists are creating new styles and forms, not only in paintings but in other areas as well. As the following newspaper article shows, nowhere is innovation in art and design more appreciated than in the Spanish province of Catalonia:

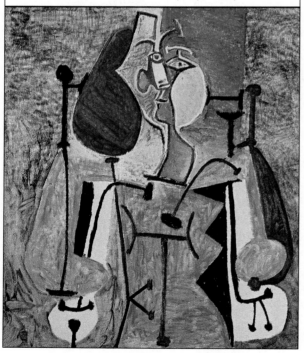

EXAMINING PHOTOGRAPHS *This painting by Pablo Picasso,* Woman in an Armchair, *features the geometrical forms and multiple views of the subject typical of Cubism. For Picasso, what was the purpose of color?*

If *seny* (good sense) is one side of the Catalan character—then *rauxa* (eccentric passion) is the other. This comes to the forefront in the Catalan love of outlandish architecture, art, and design.

Eyebrows were raised around the world when the (1992) Olympic mascot Cobi was unveiled; a sort of twisted dog, it is a far cry from the usual Disney-like designs. And the minimalist Olympic logo itself, a dot and two lines in primary colors designed by Josep M. Trias, is almost as unusual, yet [distinctively] Mediterranean and unstuffy.

The Catalan interest in art and design is not new. Some of Spain's greatest artists, such as [Joan] Miró and [Salvador] Dali were Catalans and young architects, such as Ricardo Bofill and Fernando Arribas, are building on a playful tradition exemplified by Antonia Gaudi, whose twisted buildings defy logic and some would say, good taste. After all, why shouldn't you stick a 20 foot lobster on top of a bar?

The lobster, and Cobi, are the work of Javier Mariscal, a Catalan by adoption and probably the best known of the new crop of Barcelona designers. From his trendy workshop in a former tannery, he and a small young team create comic strips, posters, paintings and furniture as well as collaborating on animated cartoons, interior design projects and architecture.

Although Cobi has raised his profile even further, it is not directly making him rich—he charged his normal fee and gave the copyright to the Olympic Committee, which is making handsome profits on all the marketing spin-offs.

Any visitor to Barcelona will be impressed by the city's design-consciousness; bars, restaurants, offices, and even the palm-filled airport demonstrate the Catalan urge to be different, and not to care what more conservative tastes might think of it.

Source: "Design Drawing Ahead" in *The Washington Post National Weekly Edition,* May 25–31, 1992, p. S1.

LITERATURE

As with other arts, European literature evolved over the centuries. While the ancient Greeks and Romans wrote histories, biographies, speeches, epic poetry, tragedies, and philosophical works, Renaissance writers focused mostly on drama and poetry. Later, in the 1800's, novelists created fictional worlds with realistic people, and the novel emerged as the favored form of literature.

As literary forms changed, so did the use of language. Until after the Middle Ages, educated people used Latin and Greek. Then, in the 1300's, writers began using the vernacular, the everyday speech of the common people, which later developed into the modern languages of much of Europe. Until the 1900's, writers tended to express themselves in formal and elaborate ways. In recent times, more direct forms have become typical. This excerpt from Czech author Franz Kafka's *The Metamorphosis*, a short story about a man who turns into a giant insect, is an example:

> Gregor had a shock as he heard his own voice answering [his mother's], unmistakenly his own voice, it was true, but with a persistent horrible twittering squeak behind it like an undertone, that left the words in their clear shape only for the first moment and then rose up reverberating round them to destroy their sense, so that one could not be sure one had heard them rightly. Gregor wanted to answer at length and explain everything, but in the circumstances he confined himself to saying: "Yes, yes, thank you, Mother, I'm getting up now."

Contemporary European writers, who comment on current issues, have had a decided impact on modern world literature.

EXAMINING PHOTOGRAPHS *European literature remains an important aspect of the continent's culture. Under what restrictions did eastern European writers work until the late 1980's?*

Until the late 1980's, writers in eastern Europe had limits placed on their freedom of expression. In spite of restrictions, many were still able to comment on the state of affairs in their lands. Most western European writers also feel a strong sense of responsibility—to their society, to their readers, and to themselves. In a 1946 radio program, Dylan Thomas—considered by many the most important Welsh poet of this century—offered these sentiments about the responsibilities of a poet:

> I think there's an inverted snobbery—and a suggestion of bad logic—in being proud of the fact that one's poems sell very badly. *Of course,* nearly *every* poet wants his poems to be read by as many people as possible. Craftsmen don't put their products in the attic. And contempt for the public, which is composed of potential

readers, is contempt for the profound use-fulness of your own craft. Go on thinking that you don't *need* to be read, and you'll find that it may become quite true: no one *will* feel the need to read it, because it is written for yourself alone; and the public won't feel any impulse to gate-crash such a private party. . . . What's more, a poet is a poet for such a very tiny bit of his life; for the rest, he is a human being, one of whose responsibilities is to know and feel, as much as he can, all that is moving around and within him, so that his poetry . . . can be his attempt at an expression of the summit of man's experience on this very particular . . . earth.[1]

Not all modern writers adhere to the traditional. Nobel Prize-winning French author Claude Simon, for example, has written 18 books. Of these, 15 are novels—all of which break with the traditional form of the novel and its emphasis on a story. Below, a journalist discusses Simon and his philosophy:

> [**S**imon] believes that the *raison d'être* [purpose] of literature is not to represent reality. His motivation to work, he says has "changed greatly over the years." He writes "1) because of a need to do something; 2) in order to represent; 3) in order to communicate; 4) to discover." He continues, "Starting with the order 1, 2, 3, 4 thirty years ago, I have little by little arrived at the order 1, 4, 3—No. 2 appearing more and more dubious to me."
>
> In each work Simon tried a new technique. He used musical forms. . . . He used stream of consciousness. . . . He used sentences five or six pages long, without punctuation.[2]

---

[1]*Source:* Dylan Thomas, as quoted in *The New York Times Book Review,* April 26, 1992, p. 35.

[2]*Source:* Marie-Claudette Kirpalani. "France's New Nobelist," *The Statesman* of New Delhi as excerpted in *World Press Review,* December 1985, p. 60.

SECTION 3

Scientific and Political Thought

Another major feature of European culture is the development of science and political thought. Both have played a major role in the rise and expansion of Europe and have had a major impact worldwide.

SCIENCE

Until the 1500's, European thinkers believed that philosophy and theology, the study of the nature of God and religious truth, were more important than the natural sciences. As a result, their views of the universe remained very much the same as those of the ancient Greeks. For example, most Europeans believed that the earth was at the center of the universe with the sun and other heavenly bodies moving around it.

Then, about the 1600's, a number of thinkers began to challenge and disprove the traditional views. Through observation, experimentation, and applied mathematics, they sought to improve knowledge of the

Europe

NICOLAUS COPERNICUS

In a period of relative peace in Poland in the 1500's, the Poles experienced a "golden age" during which art, architecture, and the sciences flourished. Polish scholars became renowned throughout Europe. One of the best-known Polish scientists was Nicolaus Copernicus, who was born in Torun, Poland, in 1473. Educated at the university at Krakow, Copernicus continued his studies at universities in Italy, returning to Poland in 1503.

Considered by many to be the founder of modern astronomy, Copernicus proposed that the sun was the center of the universe and that the earth revolved around it. This was in direct opposition to the scientific view of the time that the earth was the center of the universe. Below, in the preface to his book, *On the Revolutions of the Heavenly Orbs*, published in 1543, Copernicus explains to Pope Paul III how he arrived at his theories:

> . . . when I thought about the lack of certainty in traditional mathematics concerning the movements of the spheres of the world, I began to be annoyed that . . . philosophers . . . had discovered no sure explanation for the movements of the machinery of a world built for us by the Best and Most Orderly Workman of all. I, therefore, took the trouble to reread all the books by philosophers that I could get hold of, to see if any of them even made a guess that the movements of the spheres of the world were different from those taught by the professors of mathematics. . . . I did find . . . that some ancient writers thought the earth moved. . . .
>
> This discovery moved me to think about the mobility of the Earth. And, although it seemed at first absurd, . . . I thought that I . . . had the right to test whether or not, by assuming that the Earth had some movement, I could not find proofs for the revolutions of the heavenly bodies. . . .
>
> And so, after much long observation I discovered that if the movements of the other wandering stars are correlated with the circular movement of the Earth, and if the movements are computed in accordance with the revolution of each planet, not only do all the other facts about them follow from this but this correlation binds the order and magnitudes of the planets, the spheres in which they orbit, and the heavens themselves so closely together that nothing can be shifted around in any part of them without disrupting the remaining parts and the universe as a whole.

TAKING ANOTHER LOOK

What was Copernicus' theory about the sun and earth? What led him to arrive at this theory?

Source: Nicolaus Copernicus. Preface to *On the Revolutions of the Heavenly Orbs*, as cited in *The Shaping of Western Civilization, Volume Two,* Ludwig F. Schaefer, Daniel P. Resnick, and George L. Netterville (eds.). Holt, Rinehart, and Winston, Inc., 1970, p. 6.

universe. Their discoveries seemed to reveal a natural order in the universe that scientific inquiry could describe and explain.

In the 1800's and early 1900's, the explosion of new ideas advanced understanding of the sciences. A number of important discoveries were made; such new disciplines as bacteriology, psychology, chemistry, and physics were created; and the first truly comprehensive theories of science were developed and combined. Science became an important part of the university courses of study, and research laboratories were founded. In the field of medicine, breakthroughs based on research led to the elimination of many diseases. For the first time, scientists and inventors realized that science and technology were of use to one another. This realization led to many new inventions and discoveries. It also increased Western status in the eyes of many non-Westerners. Below, an Arab born in Sudan and educated in the West describes the reaction of some Easterners to Western "mechanical inventions":

The telegraph and the railway had been there [the Near East] for some time. . . . Now new wonders were appearing. The electric tram, electric light, motor-cars, and gramophones. Miracle after miracle, and all invented by Europeans. . . . There were, too, rumours of stranger, more incredible miracles, of motor-cars that could fly, ships that went under sea, and telegraphy without wire; and all, all invented by the extremely clever Europeans. . . .

I was eleven when I saw the first aeroplane. It was in 1914. . . . Early in the winter rumors began to go round that a French aviator was coming to Khartoum. No aeroplane had yet visited the Sudan, so everybody was tremendously excited about it. . . . Then the rumours became more and more definite. . . . At last the day and hour were announced; and the whole population of Khartoum . . . assembled to see the miracle. The landing-place

was in a stretch of sand some way outside the town, and we went there by cab. I was consumed with excitement. . . . Impossible that a man, a real man, should come in a machine flying like a bird. Impossible.

2 o'clock . . . 2:15 . . . 2:30 . . . And then a distant drone, and a black speck in the sky. . . . A hush for a second . . . exclamations, jabberings, strained necks, stretched arms. There he is. . . ! The noise is louder, the speck is bigger. "What? that thing," said a doubting Sudanese standing next to us. "Why it is a vulture, and the noise is coming from the Power Station." But soon all doubt, all argument ceased. The vulture was above our heads, huge as ten eagles, filling the air with its deafening drone, and as it circled down, a human arm stretched out of it and waved to the crowd. . . .

Before the machine reached the ground, the seething crowd, beyond itself with excitement, had broken through the police cordon, and rushed towards the landing spot. The Governor-General . . . had to forget his dignity and advance with hurried steps . . . , while the crowd pushed and jostled in its mad eagerness to see this huge artificial bird, and especially the man in it. Was it really a man, this weird-looking creature with its leather head and huge protruding oval eyes, stepping down on to the ground? See, see he's waving his arm again, he is shaking hands with the Governor-General. *Wallahi zol, zol sahih.* (By God, it's a man, a real man!) But even after this, our old Sudanese woman-servant had still some lingering doubts. "Really, Ya Sitt," she asked my mother . . . , "is it a real man, a *zol* like us, who eats and drinks and gets married?"

As the 1900's progressed, so did the number of advances. Foremost among these was the theory of relativity proposed by German physicist Albert Einstein. The theory

Source: Edward Atiyah. *An Arab Tells His Story.* John Murray (Publishers) Ltd., 1946, pp. 29–32.

EXAMINING PHOTOGRAPHS *European scientists had a profound impact on the growth of the sciences in other parts of the world, especially in North America. The detail of the mural by American artist Ben Shahn (left) symbolically shows Albert Einstein and other European immigrants arriving in New York. Einstein later became a United States citizen and researched physics at a scientific institute in Princeton, New Jersey. How did Einstein's theory of relativity change the view of the universe that had been held for centuries?*

shattered the view of the universe that had been held for centuries. It proposed that there were no absolutes in measuring time and space and that time and space depended on the relative motion of bodies in space.

After World War II, although scientific leadership passed from Europe to the United States and the former Soviet Union, Europeans continued to play an important part in scientific research. In the field of medicine, for example, an artificial heart developed by a French surgeon currently is being tested by surgeons associated with a research laboratory in the United States:

Today there is reason to hope that before the turn of the century, Aérospatiale of France will market a permanent artificial heart whose recipients could lead nearly

normal lives. They wouldn't be plugged into machines, nor would they take potentially harmful blood-thinning drugs. Most importantly, no one would have to die waiting for a heart transplant. . . .

For more than a year, surgeons of the Texas Heart Institute's Cullen Cardiovascular Research Laboratory in Houston have been conducting trials of the LATAH, or Lapeyre-Aérospatiale Total Artificial Heart. The device named for its inventor, French surgeon Didier Lapeyre and the firm spearing the development effort, is passing many tests with flying colors.

The LATAH has "important potential," according to Dr. O.H. Frazier, director of the Texas surgical team . . . , who has worked with Lapeyre for 20 years. . . .

Lapeyre . . . became convinced that if an artificial heart were to work, it would have to duplicate the anatomy and physiology of the natural heart. "Form and function must be closely related," he said. . . .

The whole point is to return heart patients to quality lives, and the LATAH can do this. Although it has been powered by an air-driven console in animal studies, Aérospatiale engineers are working to miniaturize an actuator that will be placed just under a patient's diaphragm. The actuator has been designed by the French company SAGEM. . . . The actuator will be connected to a battery pack small enough to be worn on a belt. The technology to build these small batteries has come from Aérospatiale's work with satellites.

Aérospatiale funded the $2-million preliminary development phase for the LATAH with some support from the French Ministry of Research and Technology.

POLITICAL IDEAS AND PRACTICE

During the 1600's and 1700's, revolutions in some European lands led to the end of **absolute monarchy**, a government in which a king or queen claims total power. At the same time, new ideas about government emerged. Such thinkers as Britain's John Locke and France's Jean-Jacques Rousseau stressed that government must be based on the consent of the people and must protect individual rights.

Later, during the 1800's, what remained of Europe's traditional political system was challenged by three powerful groups—**liberals**, **nationalists**, and **socialists**. The liberals, most of whom came from the middle class, wanted democratic reforms. They favored voting rights for citizens, protection of private property, freedom of speech, and **capitalism**, or private ownership of industry.

Source: "French Artificial Heart Aces Tests in Texas" in *The Washington Post National Weekly Edition*, June 22–28, 1992, pp. S1, S4. Reprinted with permission of The Texas Heart Institute.

The nationalists supported **nationalism**, the idea that all national groups that share the same language, customs, and history should have the right to form their own independent states. The nationalists supported the liberals until they failed to realize certain nationalist goals.

The socialists believed that the people as a whole should own all land, factories, and means of production, as well as have the right to vote. Most socialist ideas came from middle-class thinkers. But the movement itself received most of its support from the working class. Many socialists, like the German Karl Marx, believed that a just society could come about only through a revolution led by workers.

In the 1900's, the governments and politics of Europe underwent further change. World Wars I and II lessened Europe's role in world affairs and forced European leaders to settle their differences and work together for greater economic and political unity. A major goal was more social justice and equality at home. In time, full political democracy was achieved in the countries of western Europe. At the same time, communism took hold in most eastern European countries.

Today all European countries share a common commitment to democracy and free enterprise. Even though all the governments share common political goals, all are not the same in form or practice. Some, such as Great Britain and Belgium, are headed by monarchs, while others are republics. There is also great diversity in the way Europeans apply their democracy. Sweden, for example, is a constitutional monarchy with a government headed by a prime minister. But, until the early 1990's, it was a model of socialism, with a "welfare state" philosophy. Swedes counted on the state to provide for them. In the following article, a journalist relates what happened:

EXAMINING PHOTOGRAPHS *Nobel Prize ceremonies are held in Sweden, a nation that was for many years a model of the welfare state. What changes are likely to be made in the 1990's?*

Maria Jilken's new Octopus alternative day care center in a suburb of Sweden's capital city requires parents to do maintenance work, closes entirely for weeks at a time, pays some teachers less than do regular schools, meets for fewer hours a day and provides the children with less supervision.

Still, the school's waiting list is so long that Jilken has had to cut it off. . . .

Jilken's Octopus school is based on the view that Sweden's welfare system has produced a people who believe government will do everything for them, whose initiative and responsibility have been sapped by life in a society where everything from low rents to good jobs is guaranteed and served up by the [all-knowing] state.

"In the regular schools, everybody does the same thing at the same time . . . ," Jilken says. "Our children choose what they want to and learn to be responsible for themselves. We Swedes never had to do that. . . ."

In a country where more than 40 per-

cent of workers toil either directly for government or for the 60-odd corporations and banks that the government owns, a move to reduce the state's role has most business people cheering.

"I hope they [the government] will be able to stay the course," says Peter Wallenberg, vice chairman of Skandinaviska Enskilda Banken and [heir] of one of the country's wealthiest families. "This is a revolution, and people do see it as a threat. In the past 50 years, we created in this country about the biggest welfare state ever seen. But it was done at the expense of the economic awareness of every citizen. People really had no idea of the cost of everything."

Government subsidies paid 60 percent of housing costs, leaving Swedes used to artificially low rents. The . . . government is gradually reducing housing subsidies, which are to be halted by 1999. A tax code that routinely claimed half of people's income . . . made it pointless for entrepreneurs to expand businesses. . . .

"Okay, people wanted change," says Christina Ingre, an airline flight attendant. "But we're afraid of what's happening in our private lives now. Jobs are being cut. For the last five years, we all knew that the system had gone too far. But now people are scared. I could see a return to the socialists."

SECTION 3 REVIEW

CHECKING FOR UNDERSTANDING
1. **Define** absolute monarchy, liberals, nationalists, socialists, capitalism, nationalism.
2. **List** the breakthroughs that were made in the 1800's and 1900's in the field of science and in scientific thinking.

CRITICAL THINKING
3. **Making Comparisons** In what ways are the three groups that challenged Europe's political system in the 1800's different?

Source: Marc Fisher. "Sweden's Reagan Revolution" in *The Washington Post,* June 8–14, 1992, p. 18. © 1992 *The Washington Post.* Reprinted with permission.

Chapter 51 Review

SUMMARY

European culture has evolved over the centuries and is made up of many layers. First, Greek and then Roman ideas prevailed. After the fall of Rome, a new layer emerged, which included the ideas of Christianity. From the late 1700's to the 1900's, mass culture emerged, forming yet another layer. Over the centuries, as ideas and tastes changed, so did the rules that governed artists of all kinds, including composers, painters, and writers. Like culture, scientific and political thought developed and changed over the centuries as new thinkers challenged and disproved traditional views.

USING VOCABULARY

Use each of the terms below in a sentence about the culture or political thought of Europe.

classicism	nationalists
romanticism	socialists
absolute monarchy	capitalism
liberals	nationalism

REVIEWING FACTS

1. **Name** the social groups that supported the work of artists and thinkers in Europe from about 1500 to 1700.
2. **Point out** a major influence on the arts of eastern Europe from about 500 to 1700.
3. **Name** the eighteenth-century European composer who developed polyphonic music to its highest level.
4. **Discuss** the changes in European painting that were introduced by the Impressionists.
5. **Examine** the ways in which European literature has changed since ancient times.
6. **Explain** why Europeans' view of the universe did not change until the 1500's.

7. **Describe** the ideas about government that emerged in Europe during the 1600's and 1700's.
8. **Indicate** what all European countries share today.

CRITICAL THINKING

1. **Drawing Conclusions** To what extent is present-day European culture a product of the past? Explain your answer.
2. **Demonstrating Reasoned Judgment** Many people believe that culture is the mainstay of civilization. Do you agree or disagree? Present an argument to support your position.
3. **Predicting Consequences** In what ways might today's world be different if scientists and inventors had not realized that science and technology were of use to one another?
4. **Determining Cause and Effect** What effect did World War I and World War II have on the governments and politics of Europe?
5. **Demonstrating Reasoned Judgment** Do you think that there is a link between the arts, science, and political thought? Explain.

ANALYZING CONCEPTS

1. **Culture** What are some of the major features and characteristics of European arts and thought?
2. **Change** What are the factors that have shaped the development of European culture?

GEOGRAPHIC THEMES

Movement Which groups of peoples influenced the development of European culture and political and scientific thought?

Identifying Alternatives

How many questions like these have you asked yourself this week? "What should I wear today?" "What do I want for lunch?" "Who should I go to the school dance with?" Each question requires that you make a decision. But in order to make an informed decision, you must *identify the alternatives,* or the possible options in each situation. Once you have identified alternatives, you must try to predict both the positive and negative consequences of each alternative. Then you will be able to make the best possible decision. Use the following steps to identify alternatives:

- State the problem or decision to be made.
- List all the possible alternatives for solving this problem or making this decision.
- Gather information to evaluate each alternative.
- Predict both positive and negative consequences of each alternative.

EXAMPLE

Suppose you have to select an elective course in school this year. In order to make this decision, you must identify the alternatives. In the time period you have free, the only courses available are art history, German, or advanced mathematics. These are the alternatives.

To evaluate these alternatives, you must find out more about them. You could ask the teachers what each course covers. Also,

you could talk to students who have taken these courses to find out which was most interesting, how much and what kind of work was required, and what preparatory courses are needed.

Once you have this information, you can predict the consequences of each alternative. For example, taking German might be useful if you plan to travel in German-speaking countries or study medicine. But other German students say that it is a difficult language, and you have had trouble even with easy foreign language courses. Art history would be interesting, but not very useful in preparing to study science in college. Advanced math would be useful in college entrance exams and as background for a science major; but this particular math course requires a great deal of outside preparation and you are taking many other hard courses this year too.

One way to organize this information would be to put it in a chart like the one below:

Once you can clearly see your alternatives, it will be easier to make an informed decision.

PRACTICE

Read the following passage. Then make a chart identifying Mario's alternatives and evaluating the consequences of each one.

Mario, a young Spaniard from Valencia, must help his family financially. His elderly parents can no longer work on the family farm and face poverty. His mother is very ill. Life on the farm and in the nearby village is the only one Mario knows and enjoys. He could go to France or Germany to find factory work at a high wage in a big city. But he might be away a long time, and his sick mother may not live to see him return. He could take a job in the provincial capital, Valencia. It would not pay as well as jobs abroad, but he could come home more frequently, and help out on the farm when needed. Or he could find several jobs in the village and live there. That way he could see his family every day. But all these jobs together might still not pay enough to provide for his family.

ALTERNATIVES	PROS	CONS
German	travel medicine	difficult
Art History	interesting	not related to college major
Advanced Math	college prep	lots of outside work

Democracy's European Roots

The beginnings of modern democracy can be traced to Europe. The word *democracy* comes from the Greek word *demokratia,* which means "rule by the people." In the 500's BC, the Athenians formed the first government in recorded history that placed political power in the hands of a large number of people. All male citizens were required to serve in an assembly that passed laws and decided government policy. In the early period of their history, the Romans also experimented with forms of democracy. The Roman statesman Cicero asserted that people have natural rights, which every government must respect.

Over many centuries, the idea that all people have basic rights, including the rights to freedom and self-rule, slowly took hold in Europe. People began to challenge the powerful rule of monarchs. In England in 1215, the nobles forced King John to sign the Magna Carta. This document, which placed the monarch under the law and granted rights to the nobles, was one of the first steps in England's long road to democracy.

Over time, England's Parliament, or legislative assembly of nobles, clergy, and upper middle-class citizens, gained more and more power. By the late 1600's, Parliament, rather than the monarch, was the country's supreme authority. In 1689, Parliament passed the Bill of Rights, which guaranteed the people fundamental civil rights.

Voltaire, Montesquieu (MAHN·tuhs·kyoo), and Rousseau (roo·SOH) promoted the ideas of liberty and equality that eventually led to the French Revolution.

The rise of democracy in Europe shaped the political future of the world. By the late 1700's, the ideas of the Enlightenment had spread to the Americas and helped inspire the American revolution. In the 1800's, the example of the American and French revolutions encouraged other countries in Europe and the Americas to work toward independence and democratic government.

Repressive governments and the hunger of people everywhere for equality and freedom have led to even more democratic upheavals in the late twentieth century. In a wave of political change, nations throughout the world—including many in the former communist world—have been experimenting with democracy. Today, over one-third of the world's countries have democratic forms of government.

Making the Connection

1. What developments in Europe contributed to the growth of democracy?

2. Why do you think democracy has spread throughout the world in the twentieth century?

Unit 8 Review

SUMMARY

Stretching westward from Asia is the geographically diverse peninsula of Europe. Here the ancient Greeks and Romans developed advanced civilizations that forged the foundations of most of Europe. In the Middle Ages, a new era began for Europe as the ideas of Christianity merged with those of the Greeks and Romans. Later, with the Renaissance, the Reformation, and then the Industrial Revolution, came more change.

Western and eastern Europe did not develop at the same rate or in the same ways. Both, however, felt the effects of World Wars I and II. Following World War II, eastern Europe came under the control of the Soviet Union and communism, while most of western Europe prospered under democratic governments. In the 1990's, with the nations of eastern Europe freed from Soviet control, European efforts to forge a united Europe were increased. Complicating this is the strong sense of identity of each European people, an identity based in great part on a culture that has evolved over many centuries.

REVIEWING THE MAIN IDEAS

1. **Specify** how the population of Europe is distributed.
2. **Identify** the two groups to which Europeans can trace their early heritage.
3. **Examine** the role played by Martin Luther in the Reformation.
4. **Indicate** what made World War I different from all previous wars.
5. **Tell** how the global balance of power changed as a result of World War II.
6. **Explain** how Germany has been affected by the changes that have taken place in Europe since the end of World War II.

7. **Discuss** the kinds of styles that European artists developed in their work during the twentieth century.

CRITICAL THINKING

1. **Drawing Conclusions** In what ways might geography and climate have influenced European history and ways of life?
2. **Determining Cause and Effect** How has Europe's ethnic and religious diversity influenced its development and unity?
3. **Synthesizing Information** Do you think the political and social change in Europe over the centuries has affected European thought, arts, and literature? Explain.

PRACTICING SKILLS

Suppose you are the leader of a European nation who has to decide whether or not to become a member of the European Community (EC). What five questions might you ask about the Community to help you make an informed decision? What alternatives do you have in regard to membership? What are the positive and negative consequences of each alternative? Once you have made your decision, write an editorial expressing your viewpoint about your nation's membership in the EC.

DEVELOPING A GLOBAL VIEWPOINT

Experts agree that true European unity must include both western and eastern Europe. Given the history of the past 50 years, do you think eastern and western Europe can achieve true unity in this decade? Why or why not? How might true European unity affect other nations, especially the United States?

Objectives to Learn

1. **Identify** the challenges presented by global population growth.
2. **Discuss** ways in which the world's economies have become interdependent.
3. **Recognize** the effects of political change on the global community.
4. **Describe** how recent technological advances have affected the world.

Laser technology

The World Today

> I was in the small London sales office of a *Kansas City* company that turns mountains of paper into sophisticated computer databases. These range from *American* hospital records to *British* voter rolls to electronic "archives" of *international* newspaper and magazine articles. . . . In previous weeks I had watched the company's data-entry operators working at terminals in *Manila's* sweltering business district, on the *Scottish* shore of the gray Irish Sea, and in a plain industrial park in *Dayton, Ohio.*
>
> "What are you doing here?" a worker in the London office asked.
>
> I told her I was writing a book on global interdependence.
>
> "What," she said with dead seriousness, "does that have to do with us?"
>
> It was one of those offhand comments that say a lot. In a casual conversation we marvel, "It's a small world." We've made "interdependence" a watchword of the times. Yet we have difficulty comprehending the welter of social, culture, economic, and political ties that have come to bind geographically distant peoples together. The most straightforward global relationships often elude us—as they evidently eluded that office worker in London—even when they directly shape our lives.
>
> The problem, to begin with, is that interdependence is not an event, something that *has happened.* It is *happening.* . . .
>
> Perhaps we are on the verge of a period of creative, constructive change, with people joining together to solve common problems. . . .
>
> One thing, though, is certain. Ask "What does interdependence have to do with me?" and the same answer will keep coming up: "Everything."

As the writer points out, interdependence "is happening." No longer do most people live in self-sufficient communities free from outside influences. Technology has helped forge a new world with ever-broadening horizons.

In recent decades, a global culture has emerged. Distinct national and ethnic cultures still exist but boundaries between them are not as sharp as they were, and features they share are growing.

Today people live and work with others from different lands, of different cultures and beliefs. They can phone and fax anywhere in the world. They wear clothes manufactured on another continent, made of fibers produced on yet another continent. Effects of hurricanes, wars, and famines are felt across the globe. And such issues as population growth, economic and political development, trade, and the environment have become the concern—and the responsibility—of an entire global community.

Source: John Maxwell Hamilton. "The Globe and You" on *World Monitor: The Christian Science Monitor Monthly,* August 1990, pp. 70, 72.

SECTION 1

Global Population Pressures

A simple fact of life governs day-to-day existence. Each and every human being has certain basic needs—food, shelter, and clothing. Until the Industrial Revolution, most people lived in an agricultural environment and produced most of what they needed. A family's wealth was not only its material possessions but its children. The more children in a family, the more there were to work in the fields. Infant mortality was high, and life spans were short.

In more modern times, the situation

EXAMINING PHOTOGRAPHS *During the early 1990's, foreign aid agencies distributed grain in Somalia to relieve that country's severe famine.* **What were the causes of the famine in Somalia?**

changed drastically. People became more mobile. They left the farms to find work in the cities. They traveled to other cities—and to other nations. In much of the world, technology and medical advances lowered infant mortality rates, eradicated many life-threatening diseases, and lengthened average life spans. People began to seek a better life, a higher standard of living.

But, as population grows, so does the drain on resources, both natural and otherwise. And this has created major pressures and concerns, especially in urban areas and in the developing nations of the world. In the year 1500, the world's population was estimated at 500 million people. Today, China alone has an estimated population of about 1.2 billion—double the number of people in the entire world in 1500. It is predicted that the world population will continue to increase at the rate of 95 million to 100 million a year during the next three decades. To quote one expert, "That's more than an additional Mexico every year." Some 97 percent of the increase in the world population is expected to occur in the developing nations of Asia, Africa, and Latin America. In the words of one journalist, "Such a population explosion could set off great migrations as the poor seek better lives in richer lands. And it would test anew the human race's ability to achieve a balance among its drive to produce, its ability to grow food, and nature's own capacity to trim back populations when they grow too large."

Even if the world's rate of population growth slows, which many experts claim it is doing, a major challenge still remains—matching resources to needs. More people and a higher standard of living invariably means a greater demand on scarce resources—and, more often than not, poses a severe threat to the environment. To provide food, forests are leveled for farmland, oceans are overfished, and pastures are overgrazed.

In the developing world, without a huge increase in food production, millions of Africans, Latin Americans, and Asians will face poverty and starvation in the next century. According to a geography professor who directs a world hunger project, research has shown that "the proportion of the hungry is being cut while the number of hungry stays the same or rises. That number is around 500 million people." He goes on to point out that while famine has ended in India and China, in nations suffering from drought and armed conflict—like Somalia—famine continues to occur.

EXAMINING PHOTOGRAPHS *Japanese-made cars ready for export sit on a dock in Japan. What impact does the existence of a global economy have on the world's nations?*

SECTION 2

Economic Development and World Trade

In the past, nations produced what they needed, and trade among them was limited—by distance and by lack, or nonexistence, of adequate transportation and communication systems. In the 1800's, a pattern was set up that continues to this day. Colonies shipped raw materials to the nations that ruled them. Those nations used them in the manufacture of goods. To complete the circle, the colonies bought the manufactured goods. Cotton, for example, had been grown in India long before it became a British colony, and weaving was an important part of the Indian economy. The British outlawed weaving in colonial India and shipped Indian cotton to England to be made into cloth—which was sent to India for Indians to buy.

Today, no nation by itself can control its own economic health. There is a global economy, and nations must cooperate with each other. A sharp decline in the U.S. or Japanese stock market, for example, is registered—and felt—all around the world within a matter of minutes. An increase in Germany's interest rate has an immediate impact on the bond markets of other nations. A strike in an American automobile factory affects manufacturers in Mexico, Canada, and other nations of the world.

International trade has become a way of life for most nations. The greatest volume of trade, however, is between the industrial nations, partly because these nations have the technical knowledge needed to produce today's goods and consumers with money to buy them. There is much concern about the economies and economic well-being of developing nations. Many are struggling to meet the basic needs of their citizens. They lack the technology and skilled labor to industrialize and are deeply in debt. The gap between rich nations and poor nations—the "haves" and the "have-nots"—has continued to grow and has become a pressing issue. It also has become a controversial one. Some believe that the wealthier nations have an obligation to help the poorer ones. Others say that "teaching how to catch fish is better than giving fish." In other words, it would be better to help the poorer nations achieve the ability for self-help than to merely provide charity.

According to the trade and industry minister of France, the list of challenges facing the world economy in the 1990's is "daunting." He thinks the most important issues in the years ahead will be technological progress, protection of the environment, the changing face of labor relations, work-sharing in the rich countries and wealth-sharing between rich and poor countries, the safety of nuclear power stations, and the flow of investment into the countries of eastern Europe. In his view, the only possible approach to these problems is to extend international economic cooperation "to cover all these areas."

SECTION 3

Changing Political Power Structures

With the end of World War II came major changes in the world map and in the political power structure. European dominance in global affairs came to an end, and some nations lost their empires. Some countries ceased to be, and others came into being. Most of the countries of Europe were in ruins, and some fell under the shadow of the Soviet Union. Germany and Japan were occupied by the armies that had defeated them. There were two new superpowers—the United States and the Soviet Union. A cold war set in between the two, distinguished, among other things, by a deadly arms race.

At first, only the United States had a nuclear bomb. Over the years, the number of nations possessing nuclear weapons grew to include the former Soviet Union, Great Britain, France, the People's Republic of China, and India. And the number has continued to grow. In 1983, it appeared that China had sold Pakistan the plans for a nuclear bomb, plus enough weapons-grade uranium to make two warheads. It was, as far as the West knew, the first time that one developing country had given the complete design of a tested nuclear weapon to another. Today, the list of those with nuclear weapons includes nations of the Middle East, Africa, and Latin America. The spread of nuclear weapons, known as nuclear proliferation, greatly increases the chance of yet another world war, one that could devastate the global ecological system.

With the breakup of the Soviet Union, its arsenal of nuclear weapons was scattered among the diverse republics, almost all of which have been challenged by major economic, ethnic, and environmental problems. Today, the strategic weapons are under the political control of the presidents of four of the republics.

Nuclear experts have been concerned for decades about the spread of nuclear weapons. In an effort to maintain some controls, the International Atomic Energy Agency (IAEA) created a policy of using special inspections to prevent countries from secretly developing nuclear arms. But execution of the policy has been limited in its practice because a country has to agree to allow its nuclear facilities to be inspected. Libya and Iraq, for example, refused to allow international inspection.

The arms trade—which includes laser-guided and television-guided bombs, computerized radar systems, and Patriot missiles—is big business. In the last decade nearly $1 trillion dollars a year—about $2 million a minute—was spent on arms globally. Between 1983 and 1990, the Middle East accounted for more than 50 percent of the arms traffic. According to one British publication, in 1992, when the rest of the world was scaling down on arms-buying, Asia was "on an arms-buying spree."

There is global concern about arms and armies in general, given the rapidly changing political scene of the 1990's. The collapse of communism in the Soviet Union and eastern Europe created civil unrest and political and economic instability and inspired anxiety in other areas of the world. In many areas, there has been ethnic and religious conflict. In addition, nationalism has been on the rise in many parts of the world. Europeans have been having second thoughts about some of the features of the proposed plan for European unity. In many of the developing nations of Africa and Latin America, governments have not been stable, and coups have become common. And, in the Middle East, despite the many efforts made over the years, peace remains elusive.

Environmental Concerns

In June 1992, representatives from over 180 nations and international organizations met in Rio de Janeiro, Brazil, to discuss ways to protect the environment. The conference, known as the Earth Summit, was history's largest gathering of world leaders. Shortly before it began, the head of the UN World Commission on Environment and Development warned that one could not save the environment without "profoundly changing basic human activities: the way people govern themselves . . . the way people do business; the ways in which energy and food are produced; and the rates at which our species reproduces."

EXAMINING PHOTOGRAPHS
During the Communist era in the former Soviet Union, the government pushed industrialization projects, such as the building of this large Siberian steel works. Often the projects were carried out at the expense of the environment. What environmental problems have been reported in Russia?

The list of major ecological problems caused by industrialization and human misuse of the environment is long—bad air, dirty water, the loss of trees, soil deterioration, ozone depletion, endangered species, and global warming. Sewage, soil erosion, pesticides, and toxic waste have polluted the waterways, destroyed coastal habitats, and killed much of the marine life. Deforestation has contributed to erosion, flooding, desertification, global warming, and acid rain. Each day, a billion people breathe smog, sulfur dioxide, carbon monoxide, and other toxic pollutants. In Africa, water, wind erosion from overgrazing, and deforesting are creating deserts. By the year 2000, depletion of the ozone layer is expected to lead to drought, change in agricultural patterns, and higher rates of skin cancer. In 20 to 30 years, one-fourth of earth's current species of plants and animals may be extinct.

One-fourth of the world's population lives in the industrialized countries—the North. They consume 75 percent of energy supplies, 85 percent of commercially used wood, and 75 percent of all steel production. Most of the industrial nations believe that all nations have the same duty to protect endangered environmental resources. Developing nations—the South—believe that they have a "right to development." Conservation measures can be very costly. Many of these nations of the South suffer from extreme poverty, which they cannot escape unless they develop. At the Summit, the developing nations called upon industrial nations for financial help.

One of the nations battling overwhelming environmental and related health problems is Russia. In a report published in October 1992, the Russian government released statistics that the Communist government had kept secret. A quarter of Russia's drinking water is unsafe. All major rivers are polluted. The death rate is higher than the birth-

EXAMINING PHOTOGRAPHS *Excessive logging is seriously threatening the Amazon rain forest in South America. What dangers does deforestation pose to the planet?*

rate. The infant mortality rate is more than twice that of other industrialized countries. More than one-third of the people live in cities where air pollution exceeds the levels Russia itself permits. In Russia alone, more than 2.5 million people lived in areas contaminated by the 1986 nuclear disaster at Chernobyl.

Because the earth's environment affects all people, there must be global cooperation for there to be constructive change. The Earth Summit made this point clear.

SECTION 5

Technology and the Global Community

In recent decades, technological development has been advancing at an unrivaled rate. Estimates indicate that because of the tools that technology has produced, the rate of human knowledge can be expected to double every 10 years. Because of the technological revolution, global connections intensify every day. Technology has improved and expanded communication and transportation systems, forging new relationships and linking the peoples of the world.

New technologies have invaded homes and the workplace. Businesspeople may breakfast in New York and jet to Zurich in time to attend a dinner meeting. Cable and satellite networks have made television a global venture. International transactions are dealt with on the telephone, through computer terminals, with the added aid of videos and fax machines. People work at home and transmit the results of their labor over a modem directly into a corporation's computer network. Robots assemble parts in factories. Doctors perform intricate eye surgery with a laser and successfully transplant body organs.

Computers have made it possible to store huge amounts of information. In the 1950's, most experts predicted that each nation would have one computer. Today, computers are an integral part of almost every business organization, and the number of schools and homes that have computers continues to grow. It has been predicted that "the manufacture of computer hardware, software, telecommunications gear, and other information technology will be the largest industry worldwide by the mid-1990's."

But not all that has resulted from technological advances and change has proved beneficial. Many new technologies are raising serious ethical issues. What are the limits—if any—of the application of technology? Should we, as global citizens, be permitted to do anything we are capable of doing?

Ethical concerns are not merely abstract questions. While new technologies may lead us to uncharted regions, they also remind us

that we as humans must assume responsibility for our actions and for the well-being of our world.

Technology can be steered in any direction that humans desire. As more industries become automated, many jobs once performed by unskilled workers have been eliminated. Often these workers find that without training to acquire new skills, they cannot find employment. The decision of some large manufacturers in industrial nations to operate in other countries where labor costs are lower has demoralized many workers and increased the rolls of the unemployed. In the poorer nations, there are not sufficient funds to educate workers and help them gain the new knowledge and skills they need in the modern, technological age.

Great advances have been made in the medical field. With the aid of new technologies, diseases can be diagnosed more easily and with greater speed. Many diseases have been arrested or eliminated. But, with travel and trade carrying people and goods to all corners of the world, promoting greater contact, there has been an increase in the spread of some diseases. In some cases, the diseases can be diagnosed and treated—but only if the technology and adequate health care are available. Others—including AIDS—are still being researched, and there is no readily available cure.

Often, Western ideas transmitted through the media and through commerce have led to the rejection of traditional values and ways of life. This has created conflict in some societies. Sometimes, it is a matter of people discovering that the quality of their life is not adequate, and they want—or demand—improvements or services that governments cannot provide. Other times, Western values are in direct opposition to a society's traditional religious beliefs and values. Iran is an example. Many people believe that a contributing factor to the return to an

Islamic state in that country was the westernization that had surfaced there.

Steps taken in the name of progress endangered the world environment and inflicted economic hardship. Emissions from factory smokestacks, cars, trucks, and other vehicles have polluted the air and stained and rotted buildings and other structures, especially in large urban areas like Mexico City. Air pollution in the form of acid rain is destroying earth's forests and lakes. Toxic waste dumped into landfills and waterways has poisoned soil and water supplies, killed marine life, and created major health problems among humans.

A prime concern, especially of the developing nations, is that technology has also enlarged the gap between industrial and developing nations. With one-fourth of the world's population living in the industrialized nations and accounting for 85 percent of the global personal income, the governments of the developing countries must apportion the remaining small percent of global income and resource use among their vast populations. Most developing nations today are struggling to feed and house their people and provide them with resources to meet their most basic needs. To develop and modernize, nations need capital and a labor force of skilled workers. Many developing nations, lacking sufficient capital, have gone deeply in debt in their effort to obtain the funding they need.

Most experts and governments agree that these and the other problems confronting the world today can be solved. The key is global cooperation. One government official explained it in this way: "We are nearing a rare test that will determine the capacity of international society to respond adequately to the problems that jeopardize the future of the human species and life forms upon the earth. It is a choice between the generous path of cooperation, through which we will

EXAMINING PHOTOGRAPHS *Traditional agricultural methods are still used in most developing nations. What are some major concerns that confront many developing nations?*

attain development, and egocentric [self-centered] retreat that will condemn us to a worsening of environmental risks and the deepening of inequalities among nations."

The Earth Summit in Rio focused worldwide attention on the environment. Twenty-seven principles on environmentally acceptable development were named at the Summit in the Rio Declaration. The declaration, which strives to incorporate the world's poorest nations into the international community, ties production, consumption, and population-control policies to the new goal of environment-compatible industrial development. Principle 25 best sums up the central theme of the paper—"Peace, development, and environmental protection are interdependent and indivisible."

While environmentalists and other experts agree that progress has been slow, they acknowledge that progress has been made in recent years. For example, almost 2 billion people—a little less than one-third of Earth's population—still cook their meals on open fires. In developing nations, billions of cubic feet of wood are burned each year, most of it for cooking. Not only has this had a major impact on the supply of firewood but, according to development experts, the effects on the world's forests and on the health of the women and children who stand over the fires in smoke-filled huts is devastating. To address this problem, about a dozen European institutions have formed a research council whose goal is to produce solar cooking techniques as a "realistic assistance at an affordable cost."

In Amsterdam, cars are now banned in the city center, eliminating about 60 percent of all parking and traffic. And a French railway company is planning high-speed railroads from Ankara to Oslo to combat pollution and ease highway and airport congestion. In Mexico, in an attempt to stop the environmental decay of Mexico City, the government and private industry are investing $5 billion over the next 3 years to meet minimum standards of pollution control. In addition, 25 factories will leave the Mexico City area. All of the jobs lost as a result of the move will be replaced by jobs in "clean" industries, industries that use nonpolluting technology to acquire and process their products.

Many environmentalists claim that more needs to be done more quickly. According to environmental activist David Brower, "What we really need to be strong is to take a very different course. We must put all our energies into undoing the damage we have done to our planet." One group of developing nations has intentions of doing just that. It is planning to set up a gene bank to preserve medicinal plants and herbs that have been threatened with extinction by environmental destruction.

Many strides are being made in the medical field as well. Researchers at a medical institute in Bogotá, Colombia, believe they have perfected the first synthetic vaccine against malaria, which kills some 2.3 million people each year. And, according to Luc Montagnier, the French doctor who discovered HIV, an effective solution to AIDS could be discovered by the year 2000.

EPILOGUE REVIEW

CHECKING FOR UNDERSTANDING
1. **Specify** where the greatest increase in the world population is expected to occur in the near future.
2. **Explain** why the greatest volume of international trade is between the industrial nations.
3. **Speculate** about the consequences to the global community of nuclear proliferation.
4. **List** major ecological problems caused by industrialization and human misuse of the environment.
5. **Differentiate** between the environmental views of industrial nations and those of developing nations.
6. **Discuss** the benefits and drawbacks resulting from recent technological advances and change.
7. **State** the central idea of the Rio Declaration that followed the Earth Summit.

CRITICAL THINKING
8. **Analyzing Information** With which statement do you agree? A. Wealthier nations have an obligation to help poorer nations. B. It is better to help poorer nations achieve the ability for self-help than to provide charity. Explain.
9. **Identifying Alternatives** What can you personally do to help undo the damage that has been done to our planet?

Atlas

ATLAS KEY

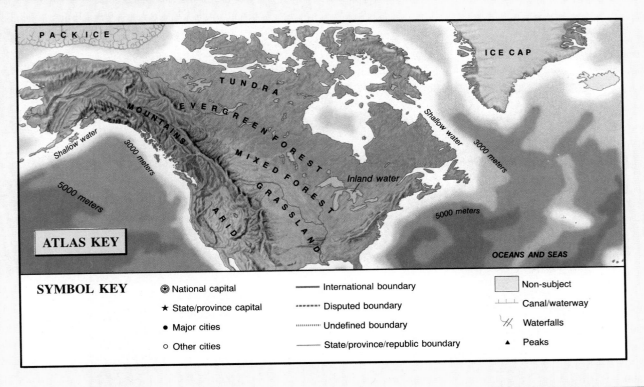

PACK ICE

ICE CAP

TUNDRA

EVERGREEN FOREST

MOUNTAINS

Shallow water

3000 meters

5000 meters

MIXED FOREST

GRASSLAND

ARID

Inland water

Shallow water

3000 meters

5000 meters

ATLAS KEY

OCEANS AND SEAS

SYMBOL KEY

⊛ National capital

★ State/province capital

● Major cities

○ Other cities

———— International boundary

------- Disputed boundary

·········· Undefined boundary

———— State/province/republic boundary

☐ Non-subject

⊥⊥⊥ Canal/waterway

✕ Waterfalls

▲ Peaks

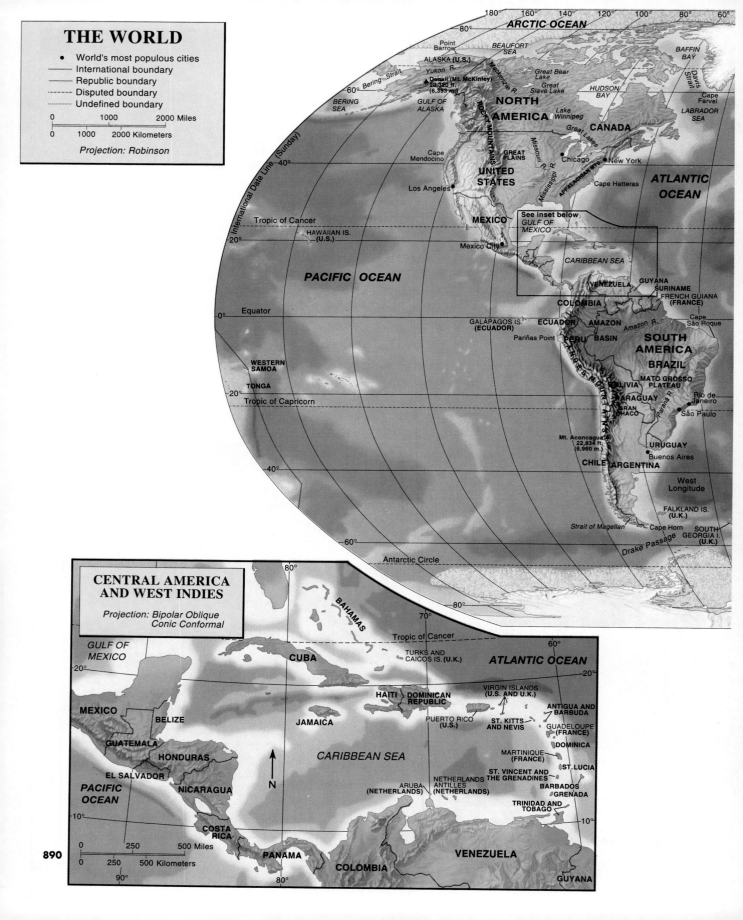

THE WORLD

- World's most populous cities
- —— International boundary
- —— Republic boundary
- --- Disputed boundary
- ···· Undefined boundary

0 — 1000 — 2000 Miles
0 — 1000 — 2000 Kilometers

Projection: Robinson

ARCTIC OCEAN

BEAUFORT SEA
Point Barrow
BAFFIN BAY
Bering Strait
Yukon R.
Denali (Mt. McKinley) 20,320 ft. (6,193 m)
GULF OF ALASKA
ALASKA (U.S.)
Mackenzie R.
Great Bear Lake
Great Slave Lake
HUDSON BAY
Cape Farvel
LABRADOR SEA
Davis Strait

NORTH AMERICA
CANADA
ROCKY MOUNTAINS
Lake Winnipeg
Great Lakes

Cape Mendocino
GREAT PLAINS
Missouri R.
Mississippi R.
Chicago
New York
APPALACHIAN Mts.
ATLANTIC OCEAN

UNITED STATES
Los Angeles
Cape Hatteras

Tropic of Cancer
MEXICO
See inset below
GULF OF MEXICO

HAWAIIAN IS. (U.S.)
Mexico City
CARIBBEAN SEA

PACIFIC OCEAN
VENEZUELA
GUYANA
SURINAME
FRENCH GUIANA (FRANCE)
COLOMBIA

Equator
GALÁPAGOS IS. (ECUADOR)
ECUADOR
AMAZON
Amazon R.
Cape São Roque

Pariñas Point
PERU
BASIN
SOUTH AMERICA
BRAZIL

WESTERN SAMOA
MATO GROSSO PLATEAU
Rio de Janeiro
Paraná R.
São Paulo

TONGA
BOLIVIA
Tropic of Capricorn
PARAGUAY
GRAN CHACO

Mt. Aconcagua 22,834 ft. (6,960 m.)
URUGUAY
Buenos Aires

CHILE
ARGENTINA
West Longitude

40°
FALKLAND IS. (U.K.)

Strait of Magellan
Cape Horn
SOUTH GEORGIA I. (U.K.)
Drake Passage

Antarctic Circle

International Date Line (Sunday)

CENTRAL AMERICA AND WEST INDIES

Projection: Bipolar Oblique Conic Conformal

GULF OF MEXICO
BAHAMAS
Tropic of Cancer
TURKS AND CAICOS IS. (U.K.)
ATLANTIC OCEAN

CUBA
VIRGIN ISLANDS (U.S. AND U.K.)
ANTIGUA AND BARBUDA

MEXICO
HAITI
DOMINICAN REPUBLIC
ST. KITTS AND NEVIS
GUADELOUPE (FRANCE)

BELIZE
JAMAICA
PUERTO RICO (U.S.)
DOMINICA

GUATEMALA
MARTINIQUE (FRANCE)
ST. LUCIA

HONDURAS
CARIBBEAN SEA
ST. VINCENT AND THE GRENADINES

EL SALVADOR
BARBADOS
GRENADA

PACIFIC OCEAN
NICARAGUA
N
NETHERLANDS ANTILLES (NETHERLANDS)
ARUBA (NETHERLANDS)
TRINIDAD AND TOBAGO

COSTA RICA
0 — 250 — 500 Miles
0 — 250 — 500 Kilometers

PANAMA
VENEZUELA

COLOMBIA
GUYANA

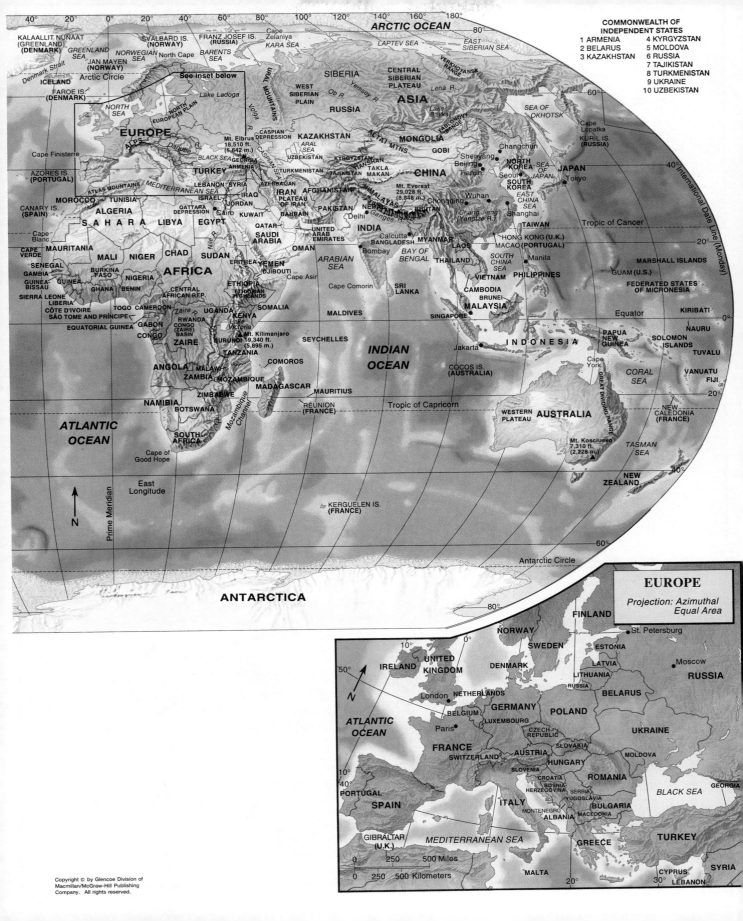

ARCTIC OCEAN

KALAALLIT NUNAAT
(GREENLAND)
(DENMARK)

GREENLAND
SEA

SVALBARD IS.
(NORWAY)

FRANZ JOSEF IS.
(RUSSIA)

Cape
Zelaniya

EAST
SIBERIAN SEA

NORWEGIAN
SEA

North Cape

BARENTS
SEA

KARA SEA

LAPTEV SEA

JAN MAYEN
(NORWAY)

ICELAND

Arctic Circle

See inset below

SIBERIA

VERKHOYANSK
RANGE

FAROE IS.
(DENMARK)

NORTH
SEA

Lake Ladoga

URAL
MOUNTAINS

WEST
SIBERIAN
PLAIN

Ob R.

Yenisey R.

CENTRAL
SIBERIAN
PLATEAU

Lena R.

Cape
Lopatka

Cape Finisterre

EUROPE

NORTH
EUROPEAN
PLAIN

Volga

CASPIAN
DEPRESSION

ALPS

Danube

RUSSIA

Lake
Baykal

ASIA

KURIL IS.
(RUSSIA)

ALTAI
MTNS.

SEA OF
OKHOTSK

AZORES IS.
(PORTUGAL)

BLACK SEA
GEORGIA
ARMENIA

TURKEY

CASPIAN SEA

KAZAKHSTAN

MONGOLIA

YABLONOVY
RANGE

MEDITERRANEAN SEA

LEBANON SYRIA

ARAL
SEA

UZBEKISTAN

KYRGYZSTAN

TIANSHAN

Mt. Elbrus
18,510 ft.
(5,642 m.)

AZERBAIJAN

TURKMENISTAN

TAJIKISTAN

TAKLA
MAKAN

GOBI

Changchun

Shenyang

Beijing

NORTH
KOREA

CANARY IS.
(SPAIN)

MOROCCO

ATLAS MOUNTAINS

TUNISIA

ALGERIA

ISRAEL
JORDAN

IRAQ

IRAN
PLATEAU
OF IRAN

AFGHANISTAN

HIMALAYAS

Mt. Everest
29,028 ft.
(8,848 m.)

CHINA

Tianjin

Seoul

SOUTH
KOREA

SEA OF
JAPAN

JAPAN

Tokyo

LIBYA

EGYPT

KUWAIT

BAHRAIN

PAKISTAN

NEPAL

BHUTAN

Chongqing

Wuhan

Chang Jiang
(Yangtze R.)

Shanghai

EAST
CHINA
SEA

SAHARA

Cape
Blanc

MAURITANIA

MALI

NIGER

CHAD

SUDAN

Cairo

Nile R.

QATTARA
DEPRESSION

SAUDI
ARABIA

QATAR

OMAN

UNITED
ARAB
EMIRATES

Delhi

Ganges

INDIA

Calcutta

BANGLADESH

MYANMAR

LAOS

HONG KONG (U.K.)
MACAO (PORTUGAL)

TAIWAN

Tropic of Cancer

International Date Line (Monday)

CAPE
VERDE

SENEGAL

GAMBIA

GUINEA-
BISSAU

BURKINA
FASO

GUINEA

NIGERIA

BENIN

AFRICA

CENTRAL
AFRICAN REP.

ERITREA

YEMEN

DJIBOUTI

ETHIOPIA

ETHIOPIAN
HIGHLANDS

Bombay

ARABIAN
SEA

Cape Asir

BAY OF
BENGAL

THAILAND

SOUTH
CHINA
SEA

Manila

VIETNAM

PHILIPPINES

GUAM (U.S.)

MARSHALL ISLANDS

FEDERATED STATES
OF MICRONESIA

SIERRA LEONE

LIBERIA

GHANA

CÔTE D'IVOIRE

TOGO CAMEROON

SÃO TOME AND PRÍNCIPE

EQUATORIAL GUINEA

GABON

CONGO

Zaire R.

CONGO
(ZAIRE)
BASIN

RWANDA

UGANDA

BURUNDI

Lake
Victoria

KENYA

SOMALIA

MALDIVES

Cape Comorin

SRI LANKA

CAMBODIA

BRUNEI

MALAYSIA

SINGAPORE

SEYCHELLES

INDONESIA

Jakarta

PAPUA
NEW
GUINEA

Equator

KIRIBATI

NAURU

SOLOMON
ISLANDS

TUVALU

ZAIRE

Mt. Kilimanjaro
19,340 ft.
(5,895 m.)

TANZANIA

COMOROS

INDIAN
OCEAN

COCOS IS.
(AUSTRALIA)

Cape
York

CORAL
SEA

VANUATU

FIJI

ANGOLA

MALAWI

ZAMBIA

MOZAMBIQUE

MADAGASCAR

MAURITIUS

GREAT DIVIDING RANGE

NEW
CALEDONIA
(FRANCE)

NAMIBIA

ZIMBABWE

BOTSWANA

Mozambique Channel

RÉUNION
(FRANCE)

Tropic of Capricorn

WESTERN
PLATEAU

AUSTRALIA

ATLANTIC
OCEAN

SOUTH
AFRICA

Cape of
Good Hope

Mt. Kosciusko
7,310 ft.
(2,228 m.)

TASMAN
SEA

N

East
Longitude

Prime Meridian

KERGUELEN IS.
(FRANCE)

NEW
ZEALAND

Antarctic Circle

ANTARCTICA

EUROPE

Projection: Azimuthal
Equal Area

FINLAND

NORWAY

SWEDEN

St. Petersburg

ESTONIA

LATVIA

Moscow

RUSSIA

IRELAND

UNITED
KINGDOM

DENMARK

LITHUANIA

RUSSIA

BELARUS

London

NETHERLANDS

GERMANY

POLAND

N

ATLANTIC
OCEAN

BELGIUM

LUXEMBOURG

UKRAINE

Paris

CZECH
REPUBLIC

FRANCE

SWITZERLAND

AUSTRIA

SLOVAKIA

HUNGARY

MOLDOVA

SLOVENIA

CROATIA

ROMANIA

PORTUGAL

SPAIN

ITALY

BOSNIA-
HERZEGOVINA

SERBIA

YUGOSLAVIA

MONTENEGRO

ALBANIA

MACEDONIA

BULGARIA

BLACK SEA

GEORGIA

TURKEY

GIBRALTAR
(U.K.)

MEDITERRANEAN SEA

GREECE

0   250   500 Miles

0   250   500 Kilometers

MALTA

CYPRUS

LEBANON

SYRIA

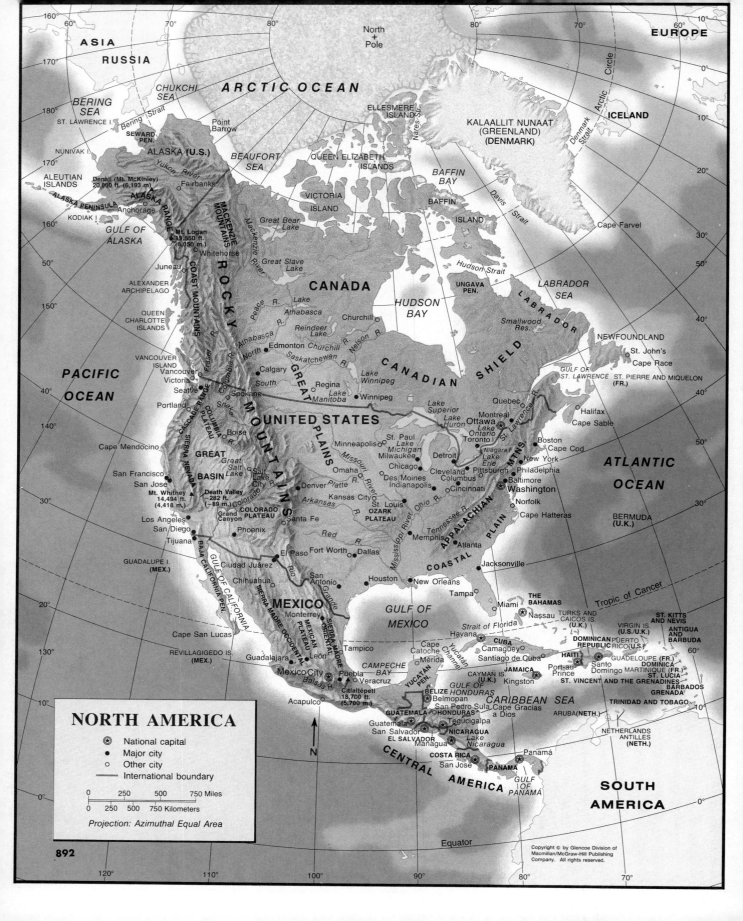

NORTH AMERICA

- ⊛ National capital
- • Major city
- ○ Other city
- —— International boundary

0   250   500   750 Miles
0   250   500   750 Kilometers

Projection: Azimuthal Equal Area

892

ASIA

RUSSIA

North
+
Pole

EUROPE

ARCTIC OCEAN

BERING
SEA

CHUKCHI
SEA

ST. LAWRENCE I.

Bering Strait

Point
Barrow

SEWARD
PEN.

ELLESMERE
ISLAND

Nares Str.

KALAALLIT NUNAAT
(GREENLAND)
(DENMARK)

ICELAND

Arctic Circle

Denmark Strait

NUNIVAK I.

ALASKA (U.S.)

BEAUFORT
SEA

QUEEN ELIZABETH
ISLANDS

BAFFIN
BAY

ALEUTIAN
ISLANDS

Denali (Mt. McKinley)
20,000 ft. (6,193 m)

Yukon River

Fairbanks

VICTORIA
ISLAND

BAFFIN

Davis Strait

Cape Farvel

ALASKA PENINSULA

ALASKA RANGE

Anchorage

KODIAK I.

GULF OF
ALASKA

Mt. Logan
19,850 ft.
(6,050 m.)

Whitehorse

MACKENZIE MOUNTAINS

Great Bear
Lake

Mackenzie River

ISLAND

Juneau

COAST MOUNTAINS

Great Slave
Lake

HUDSON
STRAIT

UNGAVA
PEN.

LABRADOR
SEA

ALEXANDER
ARCHIPELAGO

R O C K Y

CANADA

NEWFOUNDLAND

Peace R.

Lake
Athabasca

Churchill

HUDSON
BAY

LABRADOR

Smallwood
Res.

St. John's
Cape Race

QUEEN
CHARLOTTE
ISLANDS

Athabasca R.

Reindeer
Lake

Churchill R.

Nelson R.

CANADIAN SHIELD

ST. PIERRE AND MIQUELON
(FR.)

VANCOUVER
ISLAND

Fraser R.

North

Edmonton

Churchill

GULF OF
ST. LAWRENCE

Vancouver
Victoria

Columbia R.

Saskatchewan R.

GREAT

Calgary

South

Lake
Winnipeg

Quebec

Halifax

Seattle

Spokane

Regina

Lake
Manitoba

Winnipeg

Montreal
Ottawa

St. Lawrence R.

Cape Sable

Portland

Snake R.

CASCADE RANGE

COLUMBIA PLATEAU

MOUNTAINS

PLAINS

UNITED STATES

Lake
Superior

Lake
Huron

Toronto

Lake
Ontario

Boston

Cape Cod

Cape Mendocino

Boise

Minneapolis

St. Paul
Lake
Michigan

Detroit

Lake
Erie

Niagara F.

New York

ATLANTIC
OCEAN

GREAT
BASIN

Great
Salt
Lake

Milwaukee

Chicago

Cleveland

Pittsburgh

APPALACHIAN MTNS.

Philadelphia

San Francisco

SIERRA NEVADA

Salt Lake
City

R.

Omaha

Des Moines

Columbus

Cincinnati

Baltimore

San Jose

Mt. Whitney
14,494 ft.
(4,418 m.)

Death Valley
–282 ft.
(–89 m.)

Denver

Platte R.

Kansas City

Indianapolis

Missouri River

St. Louis

Ohio R.

Washington

Norfolk

BERMUDA
(U.K.)

Los Angeles

COLORADO
PLATEAU

Colorado R.

Arkansas R.

OZARK
PLATEAU

Tennessee R.

COASTAL

Cape Hatteras

San Diego

Grand
Canyon

Santa Fe

Red R.

Memphis

Atlanta

PLAIN

Tijuana

Phoenix

El Paso

Fort Worth

Dallas

Mississippi River

BAJA CALIFORNIA PEN.

GUADALUPE I.
(MEX.)

Ciudad Juárez

Rio Grande

San
Antonio

Houston

New Orleans

Jacksonville

REVILLAGIGEDO IS.
(MEX.)

GULF OF
CALIFORNIA

Chihuahua

MEXICO

Tampa

Miami

THE
BAHAMAS

Tropic of Cancer

Cape San Lucas

Monterrey

SIERRA MADRE ORIENTAL

MEXICAN
PLATEAU

Tampico

GULF OF
MEXICO

Nassau

TURKS AND
CAICOS IS.
(U.K.)

VIRGIN IS.
(U.S./U.K.)

ST. KITTS
AND NEVIS

ANTIGUA
AND
BARBUDA

Guadalajara

León

SIERRA MADRE OCCIDENTAL

Cape
Catoche

Mérida

Havana

CUBA

Strait of Florida

DOMINICAN
REPUBLIC

PUERTO
RICO
(U.S.)

GUADELOUPE (FR.)

DOMINICA

Mexico City

Puebla

Veracruz

Balsas R.

Citlaltépetl
18,700 ft.
(5,700 m.)

CAMPECHE
BAY

YUCATÁN
PEN.

Yucatán
Channel

Santiago de Cuba

CAYMAN IS.
(U.K.)

JAMAICA

Kingston

HAITI

Port-au-
Prince

Santo
Domingo

MARTINIQUE (FR.)

ST. LUCIA

ST. VINCENT AND THE GRENADINES

BARBADOS

GRENADA

Acapulco

BELIZE

Belmopan

GULF OF
HONDURAS

San Pedro Sula

Cape Gracias
a Dios

CARIBBEAN SEA

ARUBA(NETH.)

TRINIDAD AND TOBAGO

GUATEMALA

HONDURAS

Tegucigalpa

Guatemala

San Salvador

EL SALVADOR

Managua

NICARAGUA

Lake
Nicaragua

NETHERLANDS
ANTILLES
(NETH.)

CENTRAL

COSTA RICA

San Jose

PANAMA

Panamá

GULF
OF
PANAMÁ

SOUTH
AMERICA

AMERICA

N

Equator

PACIFIC
OCEAN

LATIN AMERICA

⊛ National capitals
• Major cities
○ Other cities
━━ International boundary

0   500   1000 Miles

0   500   1000 Kilometers

Projection: Miller Cylindrical

UNITED STATES

ATLANTIC OCEAN

PACIFIC OCEAN

ATLANTIC OCEAN

Tropic of Cancer

Equator

Tropic of Capricorn

MEXICO

MEXICAN PLATEAU

GULF OF CALIFORNIA

SIERRA MADRE OCCIDENTAL

SIERRA MADRE ORIENTAL

GULF OF MEXICO

Tijuana
Ciudad Juárez
Rio Grande
Monterrey
GUADALUPE I. (MEX.)
Cape San Lucas
Guadalajara
León
Mexico City
REVILLAGIGEDO IS. (MEX.)
CAMPECHE BAY
▲ Citlalépetl 18,700 ft. (5,700 m.)
Mt. Tajumulco 13,845 ft. (4,220 m.) ▲
YUCATÁN PENINSULA
Cape Catoche
Yucatán Channel
THE BAHAMAS
Havana
CUBA
GREATER
CAYMAN IS. (U.K.)
Windward Passage
Belmopan
BELIZE
GULF OF HONDURAS
JAMAICA
Kingston
GUATEMALA
HONDURAS
Guatemala
San Salvador
EL SALVADOR
Tegucigalpa
NICARAGUA
Managua
Lake Nicaragua
COSTA RICA
San José
ISTH. OF PANAMÁ
Panamá
PANAMÁ
GULF OF PANAMÁ
HAITI
Port-au-Prince
DOMINICAN REPUBLIC
Santo Domingo
San Juan
PUERTO RICO (U.S.)
TURKS AND CAICOS IS. (U.K.)
VIRGIN IS. (U.S. & U.K.)
ST. KITTS AND NEVIS
ANTIGUA AND BARBUDA
GUADELOUPE (FR.)
DOMINICA
MARTINIQUE (FR.)
ST. LUCIA
BARBADOS
ST. VINCENT AND THE GRENADINES
GRENADA
Port-of-Spain
TRINIDAD AND TOBAGO
LESSER ANTILLES
ANTILLES
CARIBBEAN SEA
ARUBA (NETH.)
NETHERLANDS ANTILLES (NETH.)
Point Gallinas
Barranquilla
Cartagena
Valencia
Maracaibo
Lake Maracaibo
Caracas
Ciudad Bolívar
Orinoco R.
Ciudad Bolívar
VENEZUELA
Georgetown
Paramaribo
GUYANA
SURINAME
Cayenne
FRENCH GUIANA (FR.)
GUIANA HIGHLANDS
Medellín
Cali
Bogotá
COLOMBIA
CORDILLERA OCCIDENTAL
CORDILLERA ORIENTAL
LLANOS
ECUADOR
Quito
▲ Cotopaxi 19,347 ft. (5,897 m.)
Guayaquil
GULF OF GUAYAQUIL
▲ Mt. Chimborazo 20,561 ft. (6,267 m.)
Pariñas Point
Marañón R.
Iquitos
Negro R.
AMAZON BASIN
Manaus
Amazon R.
Delta of the Amazon
Belém
São Luís
Fortaleza
Teresina
Cape São Roque
Natal
Recife
PERU
Chiclayo
Trujillo
Chimbote
▲ Huascarán Peak 22,204 ft. (6,768 m.)
Callao
Lima
SELVAS
Purus R.
Rio Branco
Madeira R.
Tapajós R.
Xingu R.
Tocantins R.
São Francisco R.
Sobradinho Reservoir
Salvador
BRAZILIAN HIGHLANDS
ANDES
MOUNTAINS
Cuzco
Lake Titicaca
La Paz
Cochabamba
BOLIVIA
Santa Cruz
Sucre
BOLIVIAN PLATEAU
Lake Poopó
Potosí
Arequipa
GALÁPAGOS IS. (ECUA.)
MATO GROSSO PLATEAU
Brasília
BRAZIL
Belo Horizonte
Rio de Janeiro
Cape São Tomé
São Paulo
Santos
Curitiba
Guaporé R.
Paraguay R.
Salta
GRAN CHACO
Asunción
PARAGUAY
Iguazú Falls
Pôrto Alegre
Antofagasta
SAN FÉLIX I. (CHILE)
SAN AMBROSIO I. (CHILE)
ATACAMA DESERT
Tucumán
Corrientes
Paraná R.
Salado R.
Mar Chiquita Lake
Córdoba
Santa Fé
Rosario
Uruguay R.
Mirim Lake
URUGUAY
Montevideo
JUAN FERNÁNDEZ IS. (CHILE)
▲ Mt. Aconcagua 22,834 ft. (6,960 m.)
Valparaíso
Santiago
Mendoza
Buenos Aires
La Plata
Río de la Plata
PAMPAS
CHILE
ARGENTINA
Concepción
Negro R.
Bahía Blanca
BLANCA BAY
GULF OF SAN MATÍAS
VALDÉS PEN.
Chiloé I.
PATAGONIA
Chubut R.
Comodoro Rivadavia
GULF OF SAN JORGE
Cape Tres Puntas
L. Buenos Aires
L. San Martín
Argentina
GRANDE BAY
Stanley
FALKLAND IS. (U.K.)
Punta Arenas
TIERRA DEL FUEGO
Strait of Magellan
Cape Horn
Drake Passage
SOUTH GEORGIA I. (U.K.)

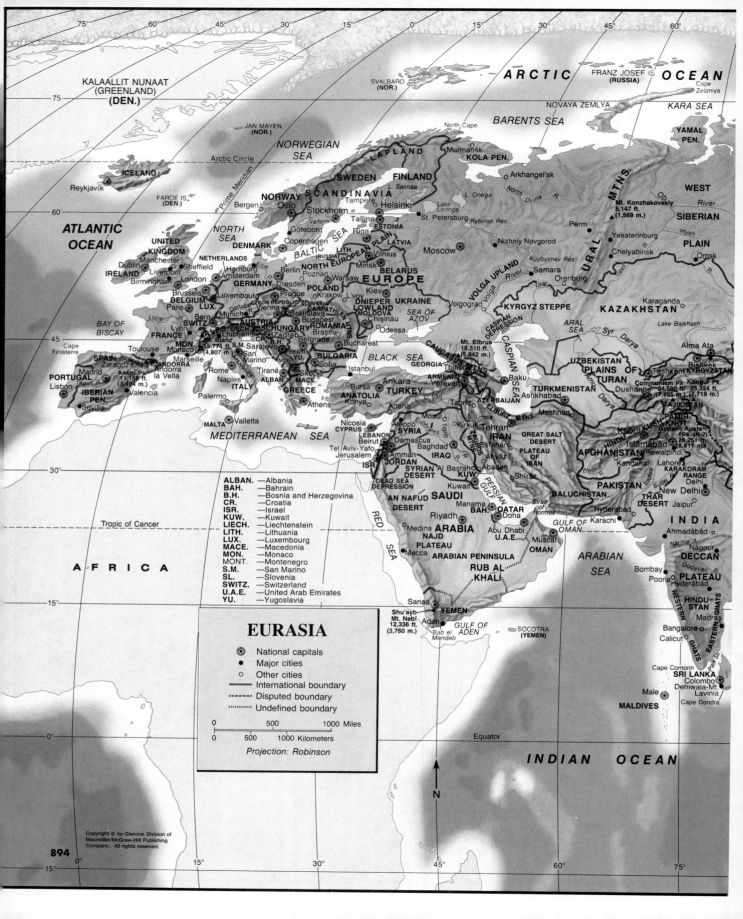

ARCTIC OCEAN

FRANZ JOSEF IS (RUSSIA)

Cape Zelaniya

NOVAYA ZEMLYA

KARA SEA

KALAALLIT NUNAAT (GREENLAND) (DEN.)

SVALBARD (NOR.)

BARENTS SEA

YAMAL PEN.

JAN MAYEN (NOR.)

NORWEGIAN SEA

Arctic Circle

North Cape

Murmansk

KOLA PEN.

Arkhangel'sk

Mt. Konzhakovskiy 5,147 ft. (1,569 m.)

WEST SIBERIAN PLAIN

Ob River

ICELAND

Reykjavík

FAROE IS. (DEN.)

ATLANTIC OCEAN

North Dvina R.

LAPLAND

SWEDEN FINLAND

L. Saimaa

Tampere

L. Onega

Lake Ladoga

Rybinsk Res.

URAL MTNS.

Irtysh

Perm

Yekaterinburg

Chelyabinsk

Omsk

NORTH SEA

SCANDINAVIA

NORWAY

Bergen

Oslo

Stockholm

Helsinki

St. Petersburg

Nizhniy Novgorod

Göteborg

Tallinn

ESTONIA

Moscow

UNITED KINGDOM

Manchester

Sheffield

Liverpool

DENMARK

Copenhagen

BALTIC SEA

Riga

LATVIA

NORTH EUROPEAN PLAIN

Volgograd

Samara

Orenburg

Ural R.

Kuybyshev Res.

KAZAKHSTAN

Karaganda

Dublin

IRELAND

Birmingham

London

NETHERLANDS

Hamburg

Amsterdam

Berlin

Elbe

Poznań

LITH.

Vilnius

Minsk

BELARUS

Kiev

Warsaw

EUROPE

Lake Balkhash

Brussels

BELGIUM

LUX.

Luxembourg

Paris

Dresden

Prague

GERMANY

POLAND

CZECH REPUBLIC

L'vov

UKRAINE

DNIEPER LOWLAND

VOLGA UPLAND

ARAL SEA

Syr Darya

Alma Ata

SLOVAKIA

Kraków

CARPATHIANS

MOLDOVA

Chişinău

CASPIAN DEPRESSION

KYRGYZ STEPPE

Bishkek

SWITZ.

Bern

Munich

AUSTRIA

LIECH.

Bratislava

HUNGARY

Budapest

Odessa

SEA OF AZOV

UZBEKISTAN

PLAINS OF TURAN

KYRGYZSTAN

Tashkent

LYON

Mt. Blanc

15,771 ft. (4,807 m.)

SLOVENIA

Ljubljana

Zagreb

CR.

ROMANIA

Braşov

Belgrade

Bucharest

Mt. Elbrus

18,510 ft.

(5,642 m.)

CAUCASUS MTNS.

CASPIAN SEA

Baku

TURKMENISTAN

Ashkhabad

Dushanbe

Communism Pk.

24,590 ft.

(7,495 m.)

Kongur Pk.

25,324 ft.

(7,719 m.)

TAJIKISTAN

FRANCE

Loire R.

Toulouse

MON.

Monaco

Marseille

ITALY

ANDORRA

Andorra la Vella

SPAIN

Zaragoza

Madrid

Aneto

11,168 ft.

(3,404 m.)

PYRENEES

S.M.

San Marino

Sarajevo

B.H.

MONT.

YU.

SERBIA

Sofia

BULGARIA

Skopje

MACE.

Tiranë

ALBAN.

GREECE

BLACK SEA

Istanbul

Ankara

GEORGIA

Tbilisi

ARMENIA

Yerevan

AZERBAIJAN

ELBURZ MTNS.

Mashhad

KARAKORAM RANGE

Godwin Austen

Pk. (K-2)

28,251 ft.

(8,611 m.)

PAMIR KNOT

HINDU KUSH

Kabul

Islamābād

Rawalpindi

Lahore

PORTUGAL

Lisbon

Valencia

Seville

IBERIAN PEN.

BAY OF BISCAY

Cape Finisterre

Rome

Naples

Palermo

Tiranë

Athens

ANATOLIA

Konya

Adana

Bursa

TURKEY

Aleppo

Mosul

Kirkuk

L. Urmia

Tabriz

L. Van

Tehran

Eṣfahān

IRAN

GREAT SALT DESERT

PLATEAU OF IRAN

Mashhad

AFGHANISTAN

Kandahar

Helmand

BALUCHISTAN

PAKISTAN

Indus

Delhi

New Delhi

Jaipur

THAR DESERT

MALTA

Valletta

MEDITERRANEAN SEA

NICOSIA

CYPRUS

LEBANON

Beirut

Damascus

SYRIA

Euphrates

Tigris

Baghdad

Ahvāz

Abadan

Shiraz

Sutlej

Hyderabad

Karachi

INDIA

Tel Aviv-Yafo

Jerusalem

ISR.

Amman

JORDAN

SYRIAN DESERT

Al Basrah

IRAQ

KUW.

Kuwait

PERSIAN GULF

Strait of Hormuz

Ahmadābād

Narmada

Nagpur

DEAD SEA DEPRESSION

AN NAFUD DESERT

SAUDI

Riyadh

Manama

BAH.

QATAR

Doha

Abu Dhabi

U.A.E.

Muscat

GULF OF OMAN

ARABIAN SEA

DECCAN PLATEAU

Bombay

Poona

Hyderabad

Godavari

Tropic of Cancer

AFRICA

RED SEA

Medina

Mecca

ARABIA

NAJD PLATEAU

ARABIAN PENINSULA

RUB AL KHALI

OMAN

WESTERN GHATS

HINDU-STAN

Bangalore

Calicut

Madras

EASTERN GHATS

Sanaa

Shu'ayb

Mt. Nabi

12,336 ft.

(3,760 m.)

YEMEN

Aden

GULF OF ADEN

Bab el Mandeb

SOCOTRA (YEMEN)

Cape Comorin

SRI LANKA

Colombo

Dehiwala-Mt. Lavinia

Cape Dondra

Male

MALDIVES

EURASIA

ALBAN. —Albania
BAH. —Bahrain
B.H. —Bosnia and Herzegovina
CR. —Croatia
ISR. —Israel
KUW. —Kuwait
LIECH. —Liechtenstein
LITH. —Lithuania
LUX. —Luxembourg
MACE. —Macedonia
MON. —Monaco
MONT. —Montenegro
S.M. —San Marino
SL. —Slovenia
SWITZ. —Switzerland
U.A.E. —United Arab Emirates
YU. —Yugoslavia

⊛ National capitals
● Major cities
○ Other cities
— International boundary
---- Disputed boundary
···· Undefined boundary

0   500   1000 Miles
0   500   1000 Kilometers

Projection: Robinson

Equator

INDIAN OCEAN

N

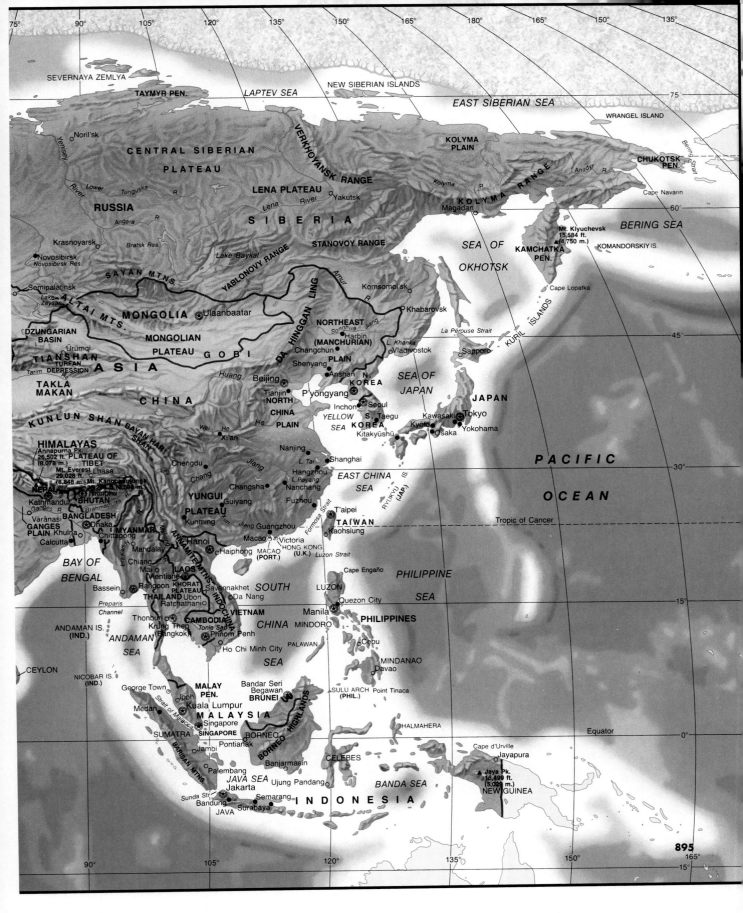

75°   90°   105°   120°   135°   150°   165°   180°   165°   150°   135°

SEVERNAYA ZEMLYA

TAYMYR PEN.   *LAPTEV SEA*   NEW SIBERIAN ISLANDS   *EAST SIBERIAN SEA*   75

WRANGEL ISLAND

Noril'sk   KOLYMA   CHUKOTSK

CENTRAL SIBERIAN   PLAIN   PEN.

PLATEAU   Kolyma   R.   Bering Strait

RUSSIA   Lower   Tunguska   R.   Cape Navarin

Yenisey   LENA PLATEAU   Anadyr   R.

River   60

Angara   Lena   River   Yakutsk   Magadan   Mt. Klyuchevsk   BERING SEA

Krasnoyarsk   SIBERIA   15,584 ft.

Bratsk Res.   KAMCHATKA   (4,750 m.)   KOMANDORSKIY IS.

Novosibirsk   STANOVOY RANGE   PEN.

Novosibirsk Res.   Lake Baykal   Komsomol'sk   SEA OF   Cape Lopatka

Semipalatinsk   SAYAN MTNS.   Amur   Jiang   Khabarovsk   OKHOTSK

Lake   YABLONOVY RANGE   KURIL

Zaysan   ALTAI MTS.   NORTHEAST   L. Khanka   La Pérouse Strait   ISLANDS

DZUNGARIAN   MONGOLIA   Ulaanbaatar   (MANCHURIAN)   Harbin   Vladivostok   Sapporo   45

BASIN   MONGOLIAN   Changchun   PLAIN

TIANSHAN   PLATEAU   GOBI   Shenyang   N.   SEA OF

Ürümqi   TURFAN   ASIA   Beijing   Anshan   KOREA   JAPAN   JAPAN

Tarim   DEPRESSION   Huang   Tianjin   P'yongyang   Kawasaki   Tokyo

TAKLA   CHINA   NORTH   Inchon   Seoul   Kyoto   Yokohama

MAKAN   He   CHINA   S.   Taegu   Osaka   30

KUNLUN SHAN   BAYAN HAR   Wei   He   PLAIN   YELLOW   KOREA   Kitakyūshū

SHAN   Xi'an   SEA

HIMALAYAS   PLATEAU OF   Nanjing

Annapurna Pk.   TIBET   L. Tai   Shanghai   PACIFIC

26,502 ft.   Lhasa   Chengdu   Chang   Hangzhou

(8,078 m.)   Mt. Everest   Jiang   L. Poyang   Nanchang   EAST CHINA

29,028 ft.   Changsha   Fuzhou   SEA   OCEAN

(8,848 m.)   NEPAL   Guiyang   SEA

Kathmandu   BHUTAN   Thimphu   YUNGUI   Kunming   RYUKYU   30

Ganges R.   Brahmaputra   PLATEAU   Jiang   Guangzhou   T'aipei   (JAP.)

Vārānasi   Kunming   Macao   Kaohsiung   TAIWAN   Tropic of Cancer

BANGLADESH   Dhaka   Hanoi   Victoria   Formosa Strait

GANGES   Khulna   Chittagong   MYANMAR   MACAO   HONG KONG   Luzon Strait

PLAIN   Calcutta   Mandalay   (PORT.)   (U.K.)

Chiang   ANNAMITE MTNS.   Cape Engaño   PHILIPPINE

BAY OF   Mai   LAOS   LUZON   SEA   15

BENGAL   Vientiane   SOUTH   SEA

Bassein   Rangoon   KHORAT   Savannakhet   CHINA   Quezon City

THAILAND   PLATEAU   Ubon   LUZON

Preparis   Ratchathani   Da Nang   Manila

Channel   Thonburi   Krung Thep   CAMBODIA   SEA   MINDORO   PHILIPPINES

ANDAMAN IS.   (Bangkok)   Tonle Sap   VIETNAM   CHINA   MINDORO

(IND.)   Phnom Penh   PALAWAN   Cebu

ANDAMAN   INDOCHINA   Ho Chi Minh City   SEA

CEYLON   SEA   MINDANAO

NICOBAR IS.   Davao   Point Tinaca

(IND.)   MALAY   Bandar Seri   SULU ARCH.

George Town   PEN.   Begawan   (PHIL.)

Ipoh   BRUNEI

Medan   Kuala Lumpur   BORNEO   HALMAHERA

MALAYSIA   HIGHLANDS   Equator   0°

Singapore   Cape d'Urville

SUMATRA   SINGAPORE   BORNEO   CELEBES   Jayapura

Jambi   Pontianak   Jaya Pk.

Palembang   Banjarmasin   18,499 ft.

BARISAN MTNS.   JAVA SEA   Ujung Pandang   BANDA SEA   (5,029 m.)

Jakarta   NEW GUINEA

Sunda Str.   Bandung   Semarang   INDONESIA   15

Surabaya   150°   165°

JAVA

895

90°   105°   120°   135°

EUROPE

- ★ National capital
- ● Major city
- ○ Other city
- ⌇⌇⌇ International boundary
- ── Republic boundary
- ┴┴┴ Canal

0 100 200 300 Miles
0 100 200 300 Kilometers

Projection: Azimuthal Equal Area

ICELAND
Reykjavik

NORWEGIAN SEA

Arctic Circle

FAROE IS.
(DEN.)

SHETLAND IS.
(U.K.)

OUTER HEBRIDES IS.
Cape Wrath
ORKNEY ISLANDS

NORWAY
Trondheim
Bergen
Goldhöpiggen
8,097 ft.
(2,468 m.)
Oslo
SWEDEN
Uppsala
Stockholm
Lake Vänern
Lake Vättern
ÅLAND I.
GULF OF BOTHNIA
HIIUMAA
SAAREMAA I.
GOTLAND I.

SCOTLAND
Glasgow
Edinburgh

NORTHERN IRELAND
(U.K.)
Belfast
PENNINE RANGE

UNITED KINGDOM

NORTH SEA

Skagerrak
Göteborg
Kattegat
JUTLAND
Copenhagen
DENMARK
Odense
Malmö
BORNHOLM I.
ÖLAND I.
BALTIC SEA
RUSSIA

IRELAND
Dublin
ISLE OF MAN
IRISH SEA
Cork
Liverpool
Manchester
Leeds
Sheffield
ENGLAND
WALES
Birmingham
Cardiff
Bristol
London

Cape Clear
St. George's Channel

English Channel
Strait of Dover

NETHERLANDS
Amsterdam
The Hague
Rotterdam
Kiel Canal
Hamburg
Elbe R.
Bremen
Rostock
Hannover
Mittelland Canal
Magdeburg
Berlin
Gdańsk
Szczecin
NORTH
POLAND
Poznań
Warsaw
Vistula R.
Oder River
Łódź

GUERNSEY I. (U.K.)
JERSEY I. (U.K.)
BRETON PEN.
Le Havre
Seine River
BELGIUM
Brussels
Liège
LUXEMBOURG
Luxembourg
Antwerp
Essen
Dortmund
Cologne
Bonn
Frankfurt
GERMANY
Leipzig
Dresden
Chemnitz
Wrocław
Katowice
Kraków
Prague
CZECH REPUBLIC
Ostrava
Brno
SLOVAKIA

ATLANTIC OCEAN

Nantes
Loire River
Paris
Marne R.
Marne-Rhine Canal

FRANCE

Strasbourg
Danube
Rhine
Stuttgart
Munich
Bodensee
LIECHTENSTEIN
Zurich
Vaduz
Linz
Salzburg
Innsbruck
AUSTRIA
Vienna
Bratislava
Miskolc
Graz
Budapest
HUNGARY
L. Balaton
Pécs
Tisza R.

Cape Finisterre
BAY OF BISCAY

Bordeaux
Garonne R.
CENTRAL MASSIF
Lyon
Lausanne
Geneva
Bern
SWITZERLAND
Mt. Blanc
15,771 ft.
(4,807 m.)
St. Gotthard
(4,634 m.)
ALPS
Ljubljana
SLOVENIA
Zagreb
CROATIA
Novi Sad
Belgrade

CANTABRIAN MTNS.
Bilbao
Ebro River
PYRENEES
Aneto Peak
11,168
(3,404 m.)
Toulouse
Midi Canal
Montpellier
Marseille
Nice
Monaco
MONACO
Turin
PO VALLEY
Milan
Po R.
Venice
Genoa
Bologna
SAN MARINO
San Marino
DINARIC ALPS
Sava R.
ADRIATIC SEA
BOSNIA-HERZEGOVINA
Sarajevo
Split
MONTENEGRO

Porto
Valladolid
IBERIAN
Duero River
Madrid
Zaragoza
ANDORRA
Andorra la Vella
GULF OF LION
Barcelona
CORSICA (FR.)
VATICAN CITY
Rome
APENNINES
ITALY
MACEDONIA
Tirane
ALBANIA

PORTUGAL
Lisbon
Setúbal
Tagus
PENINSULA
SPAIN
Guadiana
River
SIERRA MORENA
Valencia
Murcia
Palma
BALEARIC IS. (SP.)
SARDINIA (IT.)
Cagliari
TYRRHENIAN SEA
Naples
Bari
G. OF TARANTO

Cape St. Vincent
Seville
Granada
Málaga
Strait of Gibraltar
GIBRALTAR (U.K.)

MEDITERRANEAN

Strait of Sicily
Palermo
SICILY
Catania
IONIAN SEA
KEFALLINIA I.

PANTELLERIA (IT.)
MALTA
Valletta

AFRICA

896

SEA

North Cape
30°
40°
70°
50°
60°
70°
60°
80°
80°

BARENTS SEA

Murmansk

KOLA PENINSULA

TIMAN RIDGE

Pechora R.

URAL MOUNTAINS

RUSSIA

WHITE SEA

Arkhangel'sk

White Sea-Baltic Waterway

N. Dvina River

Vychegda River

Mt. Konzhakovskiy 5,147 ft. (1,569 m.)

Kama R.

ASIA

70°

FINLAND

Lake Onega

60°

Perm

50°

Tampere

Lake Saimaa

Lake Ladoga

Volga-Baltic Waterway

Sukhona River

Kama River

Turku
Helsinki
Espoo

St. Petersburg

Rybinsk Reservoir

Kazan

Ufa

GULF OF FINLAND

Tallinn

Yaroslavl

Kuybyshev Reservoir

ESTONIA

Chudskoye Lake

Nizhniy Novgorod

GULF OF RIGA

Volga River

Volga-Baltic Waterway

Samara

Orenburg

LATVIA

Riga

Moscow

Ural River

50°

BALTIC PLAIN

W. Dvina R.

VOLGA UPLAND

LITHUANIA

Kaunas

Smolensk

Oka R.

Tula

RUSSIA

Volga River

Vilnius

Saratov

KAZAKHSTAN

BELARUS

CENTRAL RUSSIAN UPLAND

Don R.

Volgograd Reservoir

Minsk

Kursk

Voronezh

ARAL SEA

Pripet River

Desna River

Kiev

Kremenchug Reservoir

Khar'kov

Volgograd

Tsimlyansk Reservoir

Volga River

DEPRESSION

L'vov

DNIEPER UPLAND

Lugansk

Don River

Astrakhan

CARPATHIAN MTNS.

Dniester R.

UKRAINE

Dnepropetrovsk

Donetsk

Rostov

CASPIAN

Delta of the Volga

Debrecen

MOLDOVA

Krivoy Rog

Zaporozhye

60°

Cluj-Napoca

Chisinău

Dnieper River

Kakhovka Res.

CASPIAN SEA

Prut River

ROMANIA

Odessa

SEA OF AZOV

Krasnodar

Groznyy

Timișoara

Brașov

CRIMEA

Mt. Elbrus 18,510 ft. (5,642 m.)

CAUCASUS MTNS.

WALLACHIA PLAIN

Bucharest

Constanța

SERBIA

Danube River

BLACK SEA

YUGOSLAVIA

Ruse

Niš

Varna

BULGARIA

Sofia

Plovdiv

Burgas

Skopje

Musala Peak 9,596 ft. (2,926 m.)

Bosporus

TURKEY

PENINSULA

SEA OF MARMARA

Salonika

BALKAN

Dardanelles

Larissa

AEGEAN SEA

ASIA

GREECE

Patras

Athens

Piraeus

PELOPONESE PEN.

30°

RHODES

CRETE (GR.)

Iráklion

40°

30°

50°

40°

897

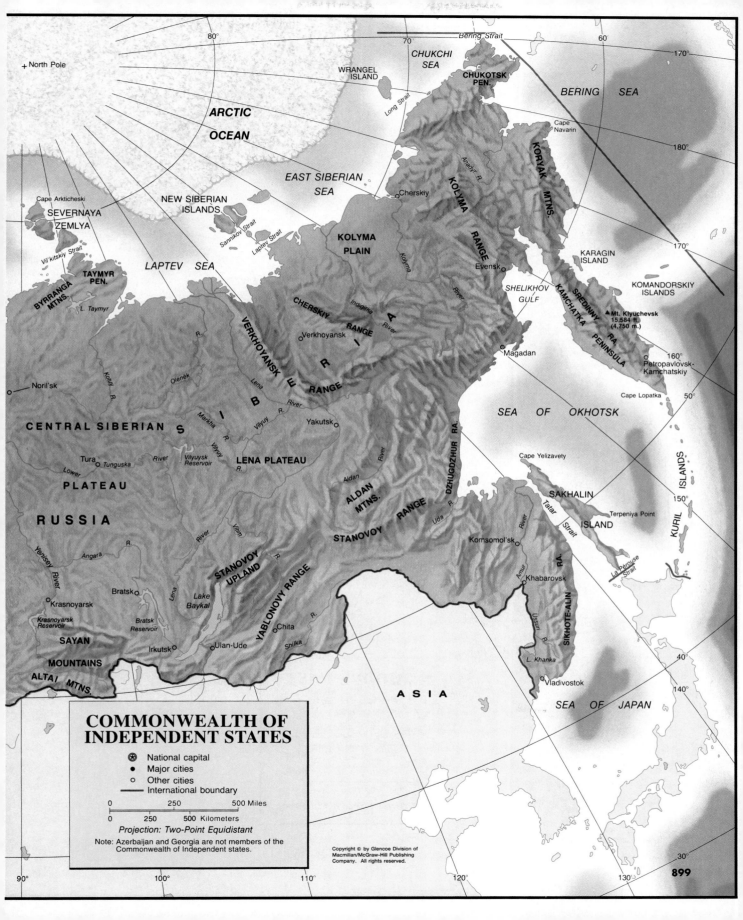

+ North Pole

80°   70°   Bering Strait   60°   170°

ARCTIC

OCEAN

WRANGEL
ISLAND

CHUKCHI
SEA

CHUKOTSK
PEN.

BERING   SEA

180°

Cape
Navarin

Long Strait

EAST SIBERIAN
SEA

Cherskiy

KORYAK MTS.

Cape Arkticheski

SEVERNAYA
ZEMLYA

NEW SIBERIAN
ISLANDS

170°

KARAGIN
ISLAND

KOMANDORSKIY
ISLANDS

Sannikov Strait

Laptev Strait

KOLYMA
PLAIN

KOLYMA RANGE

Evensk

SHELIKHOV
GULF

KAMCHATKA
PENINSULA

SREDINNY RA.

▲ Mt. Klyuchevsk
15,584 ft.
(4,750 m.)

BYRRANGA
MTS.

TAYMYR
PEN.

Vil'kitskiy Strait

LAPTEV   SEA

L. Taymyr

CHERSKIY
RANGE

Indigirka
River

Kolyma

River

Magadan

160°

Petropavlovsk-
Kamchatskiy

VERKHOYANSK RANGE

Verkhoyansk

SIBERIA

R.

Olenek

Lena

Vilyuy

R.

Yakutsk

Cape Lopatka

50°

SEA   OF   OKHOTSK

Noril'sk

Kotuy
R.

CENTRAL SIBERIAN

S

Markha

Vilyuy

Vilyuysk
Reservoir

R.

LENA PLATEAU

River

Aldan

ALDAN
MTNS.

STANOVOY RANGE

DZHUGDZHUR RA.

Cape Yelizavety

SAKHALIN

Terpeniya Point

KURIL   ISLANDS

150°

Tura

Tunguska

PLATEAU

Lower

RUSSIA

River

Vilim

R.

Uda

ISLAND

Tatar

Strait

Yenisey River

Angara

R.

River

Lena

STANOVOY
UPLAND

R.

Komsomol'sk

River

Amur

Khabarovsk

La Perouse
Strait

40°

Bratsk

Lake
Baykal

YABLONOVY RANGE

Chita

R.

Ussuri

R.

SIKHOTE-ALIN RA.

Krasnoyarsk

Bratsk
Reservoir

L. Khanka

Krasnoyarsk
Reservoir

Ulan-Ude

Shilka

SAYAN

Irkutsk

MOUNTAINS

ALTAI MTS.

ASIA

Vladivostok

SEA   OF   JAPAN

140°

30°

COMMONWEALTH OF
INDEPENDENT STATES

⊛ National capital
● Major cities
○ Other cities
— International boundary

0   250   500 Miles
0   250   500 Kilometers

Projection: Two-Point Equidistant

Note: Azerbaijan and Georgia are not members of the
Commonwealth of Independent states.

90°   100°   110°   120°   130°

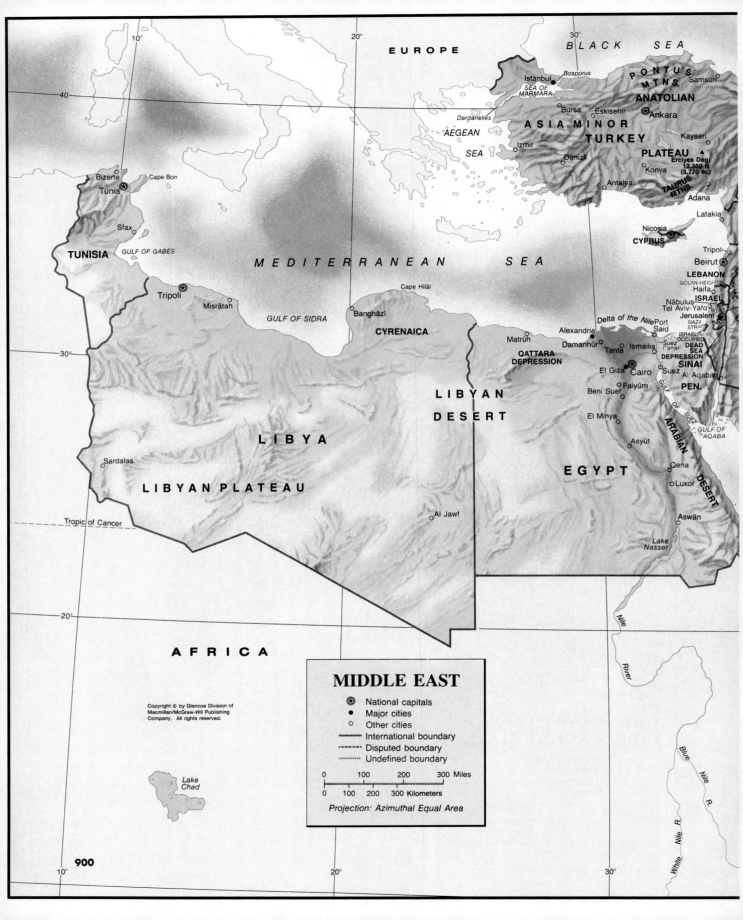

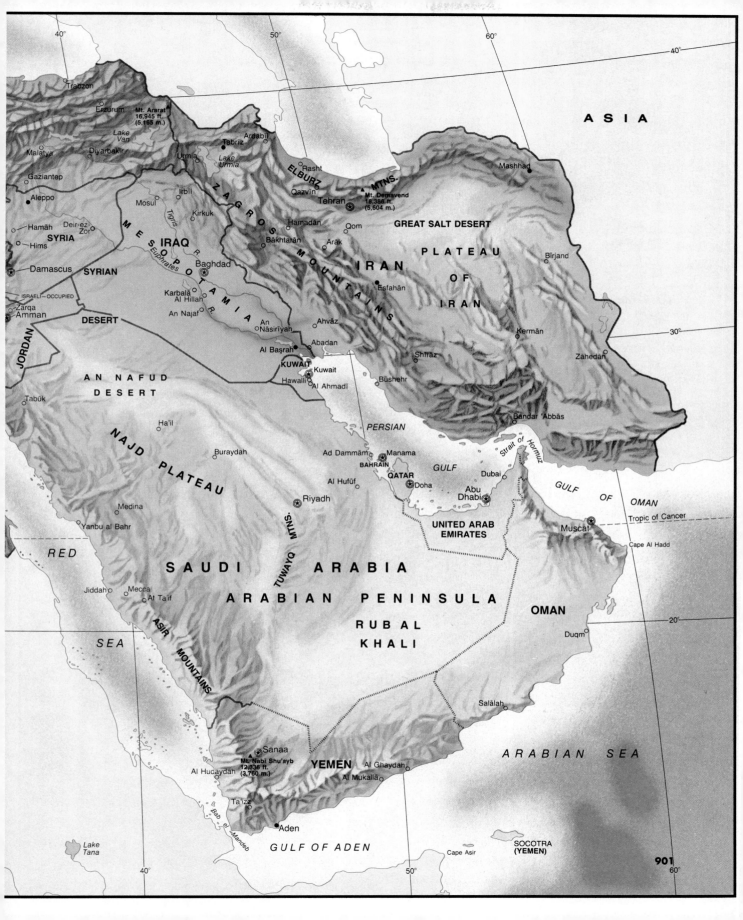

40°

50°

60°

40°

ASIA

Trabzon

Erzurum

Mt. Ararat 16,945 ft. (5,165 m.)

Ardabīl

Tabrīz

Lake Van

Urmia

Lake Urmia

Rasht

ELBURZ MTNS.

Mashhad

Malatya

Diyarbakir

Qazvīn

Tehran

Mt. Demavend 18,386 ft. (5,604 m.)

Gaziantep

Irbīl

Mosul

Kirkuk

Aleppo

Hamadān

GREAT SALT DESERT

Bīrjand

Hamāh

Deir-ez-Zor

Bākhtarān

Arāk

Qom

PLATEAU

SYRIA

IRAQ

ZAGROS MOUNTAINS

IRAN

OF

Hims

MESOPOTAMIA

Baghdad

IRAN

Damascus

SYRIAN

Euphrates R.

Tigris R.

Esfahān

Karbalā

Al Hillah

ISRAELI—OCCUPIED

An Najaf

An Nāsirīyah

Ahvāz

Kermān

Zāhedān

Zarqa

Amman

JORDAN

DESERT

Abadan

Shīrāz

Al Başrah

Abadan

KUWAIT

Kuwait

Hawalli

Al Ahmadī

Būshehr

Bandar 'Abbās

Tabūk

AN NAFUD DESERT

Ha'il

PERSIAN

Strait of Hormuz

NAJD PLATEAU

Buraydah

Ad Dammām

Manama

BAHRAIN

GULF

Dubai

GULF

OF

OMAN

Tropic of Cancer

Medina

Al Hufūf

QATAR

Doha

Abu Dhabi

Muscat

Yanbu al Bahr

Riyadh

UNITED ARAB EMIRATES

Cape Al Hadd

RED

SAUDI   ARABIA

TUWAYQ MTNS.

OMAN

Jiddah

Mecca

At Ta'if

ARABIAN   PENINSULA

Duqm

SEA

ASIR MOUNTAINS

RUB AL KHALI

Salālah

Sanaa

Mt. Nabi Shu'ayb 12,336 ft. (3,760 m.)

YEMEN

Al Ghaydah

ARABIAN   SEA

Al Hudaydah

Al Mukallā

Ta'izz

Bab el Mandeb

Aden

Lake Tana

GULF OF ADEN

Cape Asir

SOCOTRA (YEMEN)

30°

20°

40°

50°

60°

901

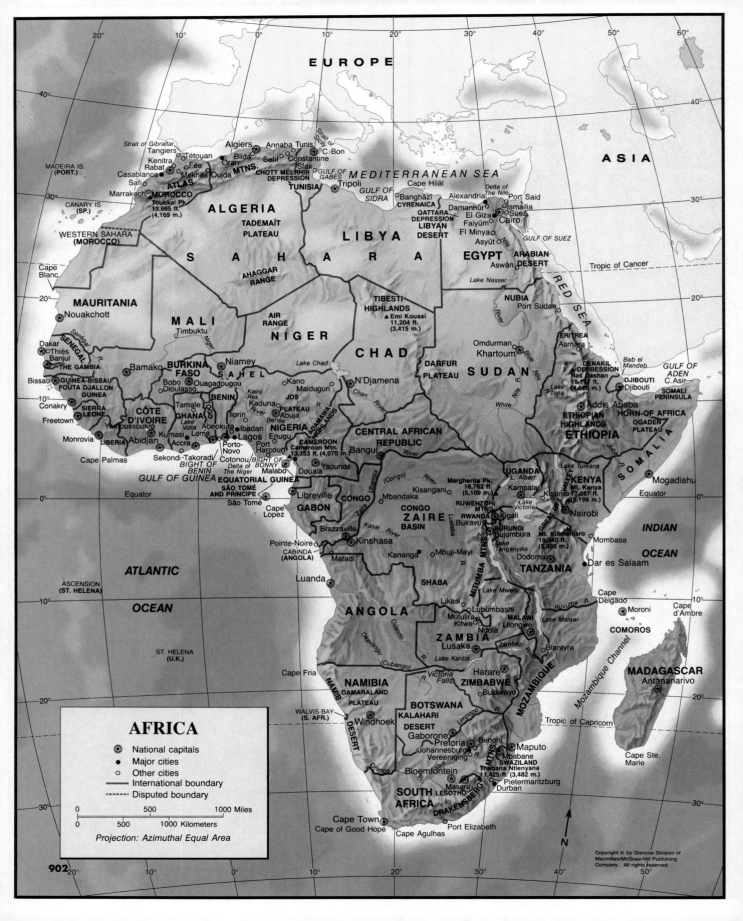

AFRICA

⊛ National capitals
● Major cities
○ Other cities
─── International boundary
‑‑‑‑ Disputed boundary

| 0 | 500 | 1000 Miles |
| 0 | 500 | 1000 Kilometers |

Projection: Azimuthal Equal Area

EUROPE

ASIA

MEDITERRANEAN SEA

Strait of Gibraltar
Tangiers
MADEIRA IS. (PORT.)
Tétouan
Kenitra
Rabat
Casablanca
Safio
Marrakech
Toubkal Pk.
13,665 ft.
(4,165 m.)
MOROCCO
Algiers
Annaba Tunis
Blida
Oran
Fès
Setif
Constantine
Meknes
Oujda
ATLAS MTNS.
C. Bon
Sfax
CHOTT MELRHIR DEPRESSION
TUNISIA
GULF OF GABES
Tripoli
GULF OF SIDRA
Cape Hilâl
Banghazi
CYRENAICA
Alexandria
Damanhûr
El Giza
Faiyûm
El Minya
Asyût
Port Said
Ismailia
Suez
Cairo

CANARY IS. (SP.)
Cape Blanc
WESTERN SAHARA (MOROCCO)

ALGERIA
TADEMAÏT PLATEAU
AHAGGAR RANGE
SAHARA
LIBYA
LIBYAN DESERT
QATTARA DEPRESSION
EGYPT
Aswân
Lake Nasser
ARABIAN DESERT
Tropic of Cancer
RED SEA
GULF OF SUEZ

MAURITANIA
Nouakchott
MALI
Timbuktu
AIR RANGE
NIGER
CHAD
TIBESTI HIGHLANDS
▲ Emi Koussi 11,204 ft. (3,415 m.)
DARFUR PLATEAU
SUDAN
NUBIA
Port Sudan
ERITREA
Asmara
DENAKIL DEPRESSION
Ras Dashan 15,157 ft. (4,620 m.)
Bab el Mandeb
GULF OF ADEN
C.Asir

Dakar
Thiès
Banjul
SENEGAL
THE GAMBIA
Bissau
GUINEA-BISSAU
FOUTA DJALLON
GUINEA
Conakry
SIERRA LEONE
Freetown
Monrovia
LIBERIA
Cape Palmas
Senegal R.
Bamako
BURKINA FASO
Niamey
SAHEL
Bobo Dioulasso
Ouagadougou
Kano
Maiduguri
Lake Chad
N'Djamena
CENTRAL AFRICAN REPUBLIC
Omdurman
Khartoum
Lake Tana
Addis Ababa
ETHIOPIAN HIGHLANDS
ETHIOPIA
HORN OF AFRICA
OGADEN PLATEAU
SOMALI PENINSULA
DJIBOUTI
DJIBOUTI

Niger R.
BENIN
Tamale
GHANA
Kaduna
JOS PLATEAU
Abuja
Ilorin
Ibadan
NIGERIA
Enugu
ADAMAWA HIGHLANDS
Chari River
Bangui
Congo River
White Nile
Blue Nile
SOMALIA
Mogadishu

CÔTE D'IVOIRE
Yamoussoukro
Kumasi
Abidjan
Lake Volta
Lomé
Abeokuta
Lagos
Porto-Novo
Port Harcourt
Cotonou
BIGHT OF BENIN
Delta of The Niger
Malabo
Douala
CAMEROON
Cameroon Mtn. 13,353 ft. (4,070 m.)
Yaoundé
EQUATORIAL GUINEA
SÃO TOMÉ AND PRINCIPE
São Tomé
Cape Lopez
Sekondi-Takoradi
BIGHT OF BONNY
GULF OF GUINEA
Equator
Libreville
CONGO
GABON
Brazzaville
Pointe-Noire
CABINDA (ANGOLA)
Kinshasa
Matadi
Kananga
Mbuji-Mayi
Mbandaka
Kisangani
Zaire R.
CONGO BASIN
ZAIRE
Kasai River
Lualaba
Bukavu
RWANDA
Kigali
BURUNDI
Bujumbura
UGANDA
L. Albert
Kampala
Lake Victoria
RUWENZORI MTNS.
Margherita Pk. 16,762 ft. (5,109 m.)
Lake Turkana
KENYA
Kisumu
Mt. Kenya 17,057 ft. (5,199 m.)
Nairobi
GREAT RIFT VALLEY
Mombasa
Equator
INDIAN OCEAN

ATLANTIC OCEAN
ASCENSION (ST. HELENA)
ST. HELENA (U.K.)
Luanda
ANGOLA
SHABA
Likasi
Lubumbashi
Mufulira
Kitwe
Ndola
Cuanza
Cuango
Okavango
(Cubango)
Kasai
Lake Mweru
MITUMBA MTNS.
Lake Tanganyika
Dodoma
TANZANIA
Mt. Kilimanjaro 19,340 ft. (5,895 m.)
Dar es Salaam
Cape Delgado
Cape d'Ambre
COMOROS
Moroni

ZAMBIA
Lusaka
Lake Kariba
MALAWI
Lilongwe
Lake Malawi
Ruvuma R.
Zambezi R.
Blantyre
MOZAMBIQUE
MADAGASCAR
Antananarivo

Cape Fria
NAMIBIA
DAMARALAND PLATEAU
NAMIB DESERT
WALVIS BAY (S. AFR.)
Windhoek
KALAHARI DESERT
BOTSWANA
Gaborone
Victoria Falls
ZIMBABWE
Harare
Bulawayo
Limpopo R.
Tropic of Capricorn
Mozambique Channel

Orange R.
Vaal R.
Pretoria
Johannesburg
Vereeniging
Benoni
Maputo
Mbabane
SWAZILAND
Thabana Ntlenyana 11,425 ft. (3,482 m.)
Pietermaritzburg
Durban
Bloemfontein
SOUTH AFRICA
LESOTHO
Maseru
DRAKENSBERG
Cape Town
Cape of Good Hope
Port Elizabeth
Cape Agulhas
Cape Ste. Marie

N

902

Copyright © by Glencoe Division of Macmillan/McGraw-Hill Publishing Company. All rights reserved.

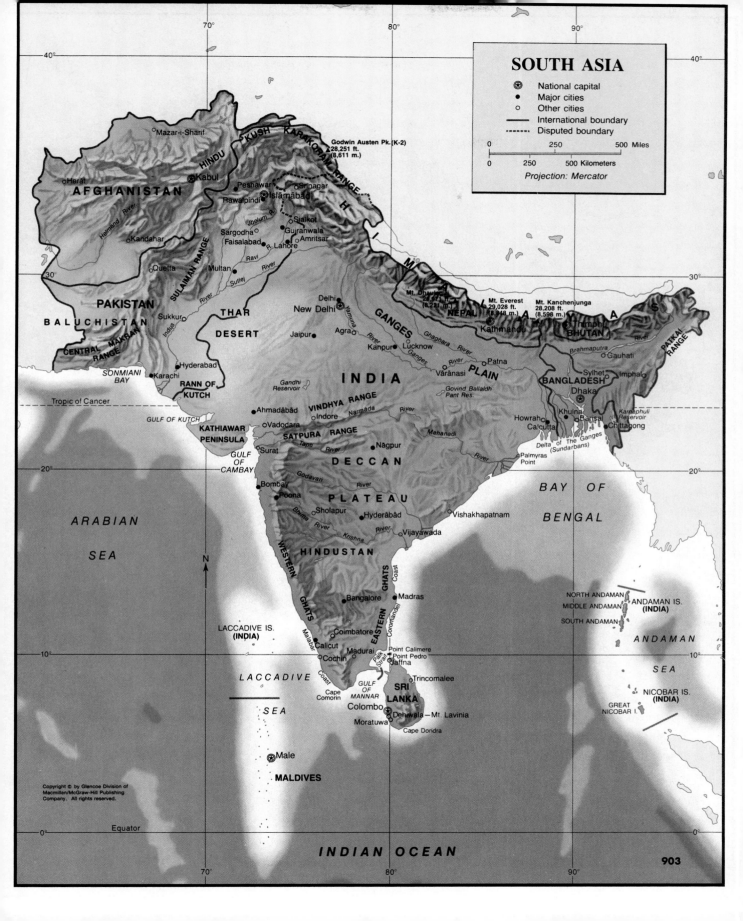

SOUTH ASIA

⊛ National capital
● Major cities
○ Other cities
— International boundary
---- Disputed boundary

0   250   500 Miles
0   250   500 Kilometers
Projection: Mercator

AFGHANISTAN

○ Mazar-i-Sharif

HINDU KUSH

KARAKORAM RANGE

Godwin Austen Pk. (K-2)
▲ 28,251 ft.
(8,611 m.)

○ Herat
⊛ Kabul
Peshawar ○
Rawalpindi ○ Srinagar ○
⊛ Islāmābād

○ Sialkot
Jhelum R.
Gujranwala ○
Sargodha ○
Faisalabad ○ ○ Amritsar
R. Lahore ●
Ravi
River

○ Kandahar

SULAIMAN RANGE

Quetta ○
Multan ●
Sutlej
River

PAKISTAN

BALUCHISTAN

Sukkur ○
Indus

CENTRAL MAKRAN RANGE

THAR

DESERT

Delhi ●
New Delhi ⊛

Jaipur ●

Agra ●
Yamuna
River

Mt. Dhaulagiri
26,811 ft.
(8,221 m.)

NEPAL

Mt. Everest
29,028 ft.
(8,848 m.)

Mt. Kanchenjunga
28,208 ft.
(8,598 m.)

Kathmandu ⊛
⊛ Thimphu

BHUTAN

PATKAI RANGE

Kanpur ●
Lucknow ●
GANGES
Ghaghara River

○ River
Patna ●
Varanasi ●
Ganges

PLAIN

Brahmaputra
River

Gauhati ○

Sylhet ○
Imphal ○

Hyderabad ●

Karachi ●
SONMIANI
BAY

RANN OF KUTCH

INDIA

Govind Ballabh
Pant Res.

BANGLADESH
Dhaka ⊛

Gandhi
Reservoir

Khulna ●
Karnephuli
Reservoir

Tropic of Cancer

KATHIAWAR PENINSULA

GULF OF KUTCH

Ahmadābād ●
○ Vadodara

VINDHYA RANGE
Indore ○
Narmada
River

Howrah ●
Calcutta ●

Barisal ○
Chittagong ●

GULF OF CAMBAY

○ Surat

SATPURA RANGE
Tapti
River

Godavari

Delta of The Ganges
(Sundarbans)

Mahanadi

Nāgpur ●

DECCAN

River

Palmyras
Point

Bombay ●
Poona ●

PLATEAU

Sholapur ○
Hyderābād ●

Bhima
River

Krishna
River

Vishakhapatnam ●

Vijayawada ●

BAY OF

BENGAL

ARABIAN

SEA

N
↑

HINDUSTAN

WESTERN

GHATS

Bangalore ●
Madras ●

Coast

EASTERN

GHATS

Coromandel

NORTH ANDAMAN

ANDAMAN IS.
(INDIA)

MIDDLE ANDAMAN

SOUTH ANDAMAN

ANDAMAN

LACCADIVE IS.
(INDIA)

Coimbatore ○

Calicut ○
Cochin ○
Madurai ○

Malabar

Coast

Point Calimere
Point Pedro
Jaffna ○

Palk Strait

SEA

LACCADIVE

Cape
Comorin

GULF
OF
MANNAR

Trincomalee ○

SRI
LANKA

NICOBAR IS.
(INDIA)

GREAT
NICOBAR I.

SEA

Colombo ⊛
Dehiwala—Mt. Lavinia
Moratuwa ○
Cape Dondra

⊛ Male

MALDIVES

Equator

INDIAN OCEAN

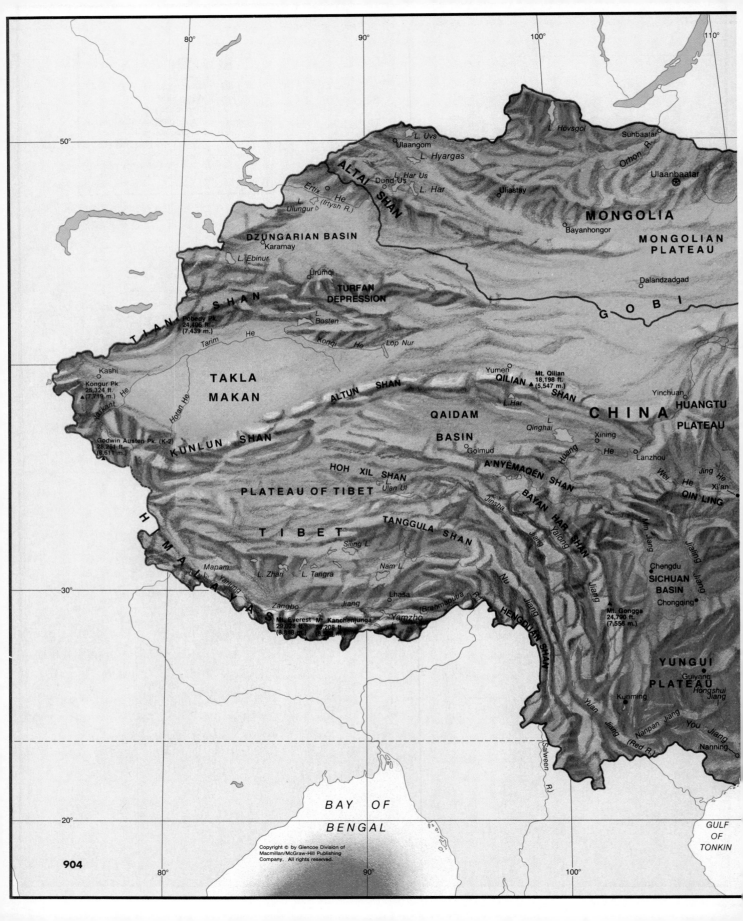

80°

90°

100°

110°

50°

L. Uvs

Ulaangom

L. Hyargas

SÜhbaatar

L. Höysgol

ALTAI SHAN

Orhon R.

Dund-Us

L. Har Us

Ertix   He

(Irtysh R.)

Uliastay

Ulaanbaatar

Ulungur

L. Har

DZUNGARIAN BASIN

MONGOLIA

Karamay

Bayanhongor

MONGOLIAN

L. Ebinur

PLATEAU

Ürümqi

Dalandzadgad

TURFAN

TIAN   SHAN

DEPRESSION

G O B I

Pobedy Pk.
24,406 ft.
(7,439 m.)

L. Bosten

He

Konqi   He

Lop Nur

Kashi

Tarim

He

Yumen

Mt. Qilian
18,198 ft.
(5,547 m.)

Yinchuan

HUANGTU

QILIAN   SHAN

Kongur Pk.
25,324 ft.
(7,719 m.)

TAKLA

ALTUN   SHAN

C H I N A

PLATEAU

He

L. Har

MAKAN

QAIDAM

L.

Hotan He

BASIN

Qinghai

Xining

Godwin Austen Pk. (K-2)
28,251 ft.
(8,611 m.)

KUNLUN   SHAN

Golmud

Huang

He

Lanzhou

HOH XIL SHAN

A'NYÊMAQÊN SHAN

Wei

Jing He

Yarkant

Xi'an

L.

BAYAN HAR SHAN

Min Jiang

QIN LING

PLATEAU OF TIBET

Ulan Ul

Jinsha

He

Jialing Jiang

HIMALAYAS

T I B E T

TANGGULA SHAN

Jiang

Yalong

Chengdu

SICHUAN

Siling L.

BASIN

Mapam

Nam L.

Jiang

Chongqing

L. Zhari

L. Tangra

Yarlung

Nu

Jiang

Mt. Gongga
24,790 ft.
(7,556 m.)

30°

Zangbo

Jiang

Lhasa

Brahmaputra

HENGDUAN SHAN

Mt. Everest
29,028 ft.
(8,848 m.)

Mt. Kanchenjunga
28,208 ft.
(8,598 m.)

Yamzho

YUNGUI

PLATEAU

Guiyang

Hongshui
Jiang

Kunming

Yuan

Nanpan Jiang

You Jiang

Jiang

(Red R.)

Nanning

20°

BAY   OF

BENGAL

GULF
OF
TONKIN

80°

90°

100°

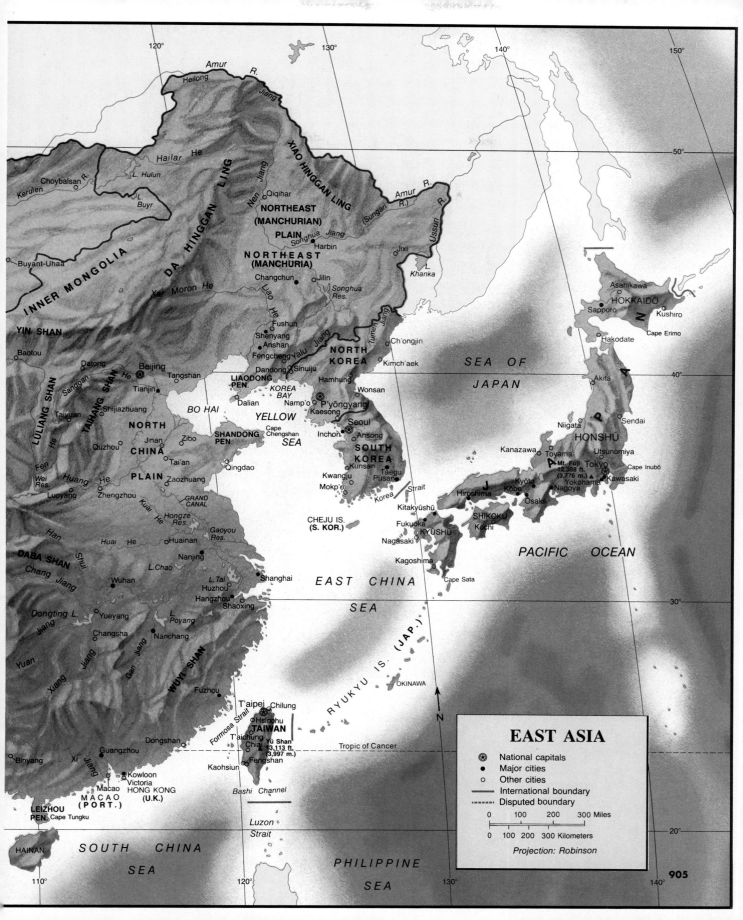

EAST ASIA

- ⊛ National capitals
- ● Major cities
- ○ Other cities
- —— International boundary
- --- Disputed boundary

| 0 | 100 | 200 | 300 Miles |

| 0 | 100 | 200 | 300 Kilometers |

Projection: Robinson

905

Labels on map

Amur R.
Heilong
Hailar He
Choybalsan
Kerulen R.
L. Hulun
L. Buyr
Buyant-Uhaa
INNER MONGOLIA
YIN SHAN
Baotou
Datong
LULIANG SHAN
Taiyuan
Fen He
Wei Res.
Luoyang
Huang He
Zhengzhou
DABA SHAN
Chang Jiang
Dongting L.
Yuan Jiang
Xiang Jiang
Changsha
Yueyang
Wuhan
Huai He
Huainan
Nanjing
L. Chao
L. Tai
Huzhou
Hangzhou
Shaoxing
Shanghai
L. Poyang
Nanchang
WUYI SHAN
Fuzhou
Gan Jiang
Xi Jiang
Binyang
Guangzhou
Dongshan
Kowloon
Victoria
HONG KONG
(U.K.)
MACAO
(PORT.)
LEIZHOU
PEN.
Cape Tungku
HAINAN
SOUTH CHINA SEA

Qiqihar
Nen Jiang
Songhua Jiang
NORTHEAST
(MANCHURIAN)
PLAIN
Harbin
NORTHEAST
(MANCHURIA)
Changchun
Jilin
Songhua Res.
Jixi
L. Khanka
Amur R.
(Sungari R.)
Ussuri R.
XIAO HINGGAN LING
DA HINGGAN LING
Xar Moron He
Liao He
Fushun
Shenyang
Anshan
Fengcheng
Dandong
Sinuiju
Yalu Jiang
Tumen Jiang
Ch'ongjin
Kimch'aek
NORTH KOREA
Hamhung
Wonsan
P'yongyang
Kaesong
Namp'o
Seoul
Inchon
Ansong
SOUTH KOREA
Kunsan
Kwangju
Taegu
Pusan
Mokp'o
Korea Strait
CHEJU IS.
(S. KOR.)

Beijing
Tangshan
Tianjin
TAIHANG SHAN
Sanggan He
Shijiazhuang
NORTH CHINA PLAIN
Jinan
Zibo
Tai'an
Quzhou
Zaozhuang
Hongze Res.
Gaoyou Res.
Kuai He
GRAND CANAL
Han Shui
Huang He
LIAODONG PEN.
BO HAI
Dalian
KOREA BAY
SHANDONG PEN.
Cape Chengshan
YELLOW SEA
Qingdao

SEA OF JAPAN
Asahikawa
HOKKAIDO
Sapporo
Kushiro
Cape Erimo
Hakodate
Akita
Sendai
HONSHU
Niigata
Utsunomiya
Kanazawa
Toyama
Mt. Fuji
12,388 ft.
(3,776 m.)
Tokyo
Cape Inubo
Yokohama
Kawasaki
Kyoto
Kobe
Nagoya
Osaka
Hiroshima
SHIKOKU
Kochi
Kitakyushu
Fukuoka
KYUSHU
Nagasaki
Kagoshima
Cape Sata
PACIFIC OCEAN

EAST CHINA SEA
RYUKYU IS. (JAP.)
OKINAWA
N
Tropic of Cancer

T'aipei
Chilung
Hsinchu
TAIWAN
T'aichung
Chiai
Yu Shan
13,113 ft.
(3,997 m.)
Fengshan
Kaohsiun
Formosa Strait
Bashi Channel
Luzon Strait
PHILIPPINE SEA

905

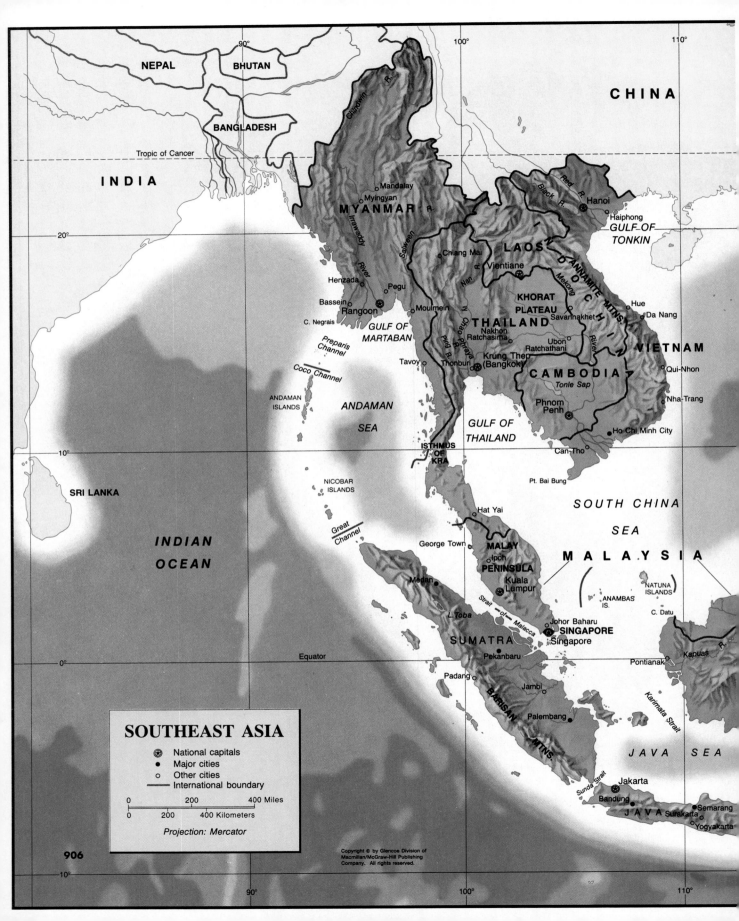

SOUTHEAST ASIA

- ⊛ National capitals
- ● Major cities
- ○ Other cities
- — International boundary

0   200   400 Miles

0   200   400 Kilometers

Projection: Mercator

906

Copyright © by Glencoe Division of
Macmillan/McGraw-Hill Publishing
Company. All rights reserved.

NEPAL

BHUTAN

BANGLADESH

CHINA

Tropic of Cancer

INDIA

MYANMAR

○ Mandalay
○ Myingyan

Irrawaddy River

Salween

Chindwin R.

LAOS

○ Chiang Mai
○ Vientiane

Red R.
Black R.
⊛ Hanoi
Haiphong

GULF OF TONKIN

D'ANNAMITE MTNS.

○ Henzada
○ Pegu

Nan

Mekong River

KHORAT PLATEAU

○ Bassein
Rangoon ●
C. Negrais

○ Moulmein

THAILAND

Ping R.
Chao Praya
Nan

Nakhon
Ratchasima ○

Savannakhet ○

Ubon
Ratchathani ○

Hue ○
Da Nang ○

VIETNAM

GULF OF MARTABAN

Tavoy ○

Thonburi ○
Krung Thep
(Bangkok) ⊛

CAMBODIA

Tonle Sap

Phnom
Penh ⊛

○ Qui-Nhon

○ Nha-Trang

Preparis Channel

Coco Channel

ANDAMAN ISLANDS

ANDAMAN SEA

GULF OF THAILAND

Ho Chi Minh City ●

Can-Tho ○

SRI LANKA

NICOBAR ISLANDS

ISTHMUS OF KRA

Pt. Bai Bung

SOUTH CHINA SEA

Great Channel

○ Hat Yai

INDIAN OCEAN

George Town ○

MALAY PENINSULA
○ Ipoh

MALAYSIA

Medan ●

Kuala
Lumpur ⊛

NATUNA ISLANDS

C. Datu

L. Toba

Strait of Malacca

ANAMBAS IS.

Johor Baharu ○
⊛ SINGAPORE
● Singapore

SUMATRA

Pekanbaru ○

Padang ○

Equator

Pontianak ○

Kapuas

Karimata Strait

Jambi ○

BARISAN MTNS.

Palembang ●

JAVA SEA

Sunda Strait

Jakarta ⊛

Bandung ●

JAVA

Surakarta ○
Semarang ●
Yogyakarta ○

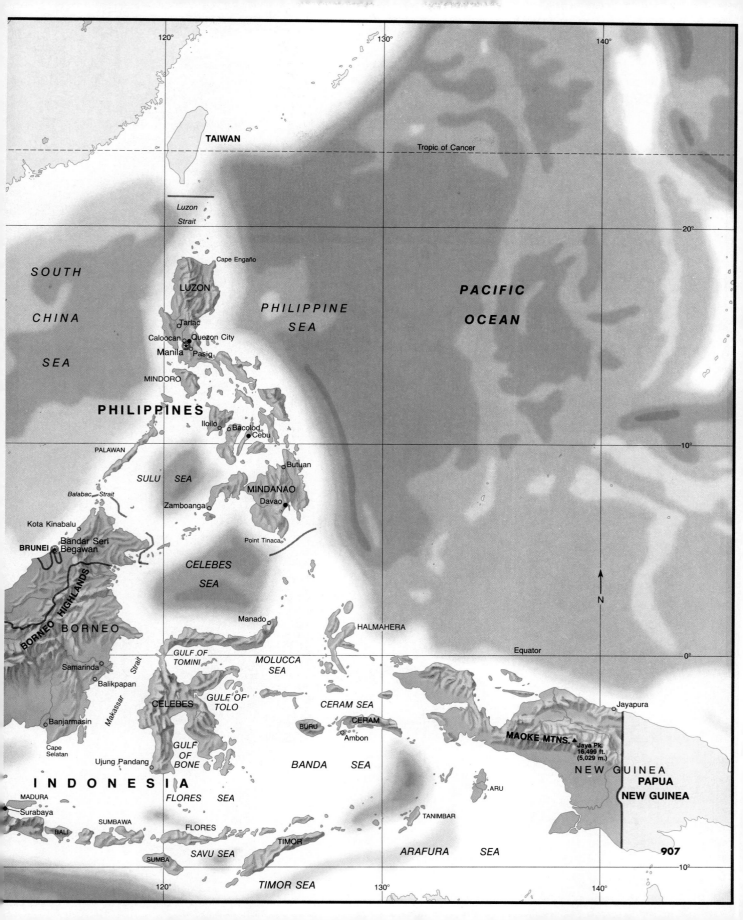

120°

130°

140°

TAIWAN

Tropic of Cancer

20°

Luzon
Strait

SOUTH

Cape Engaño

CHINA

LUZON

PHILIPPINE

PACIFIC

SEA

Tarlac
Caloocan Quezon City
Manila Pasig

SEA

OCEAN

MINDORO

PHILIPPINES

Iloilo Bacolod
Cebu

PALAWAN

Butuan

10°

SULU SEA

MINDANAO
Davao

Balabac Strait

Zamboanga

Kota Kinabalu

Point Tinaca

Bandar Seri
BRUNEI Begawan

CELEBES

SEA

BORNEO HIGHLANDS

Manado

HALMAHERA

BORNEO

Samarinda

GULF OF
TOMINI

MOLUCCA
SEA

Equator

0°

Balikpapan

Makassar Strait

CELEBES

GULF OF
TOLO

CERAM SEA

CERAM

Jayapura

Banjarmasin

BURU

Ambon

MAOKE MTNS.

Cape
Selatan

GULF
OF
BONE

BANDA SEA

Jaya Pk.
16,499 ft.
(5,029 m.)

NEW GUINEA

Ujung Pandang

PAPUA
NEW GUINEA

MADURA

I N D O N E S I A

FLORES SEA

ARU

Surabaya

SUMBAWA

FLORES

TANIMBAR

BALI

SAVU SEA

TIMOR

ARAFURA SEA

907

SUMBA

10°

TIMOR SEA

120°

130°

140°

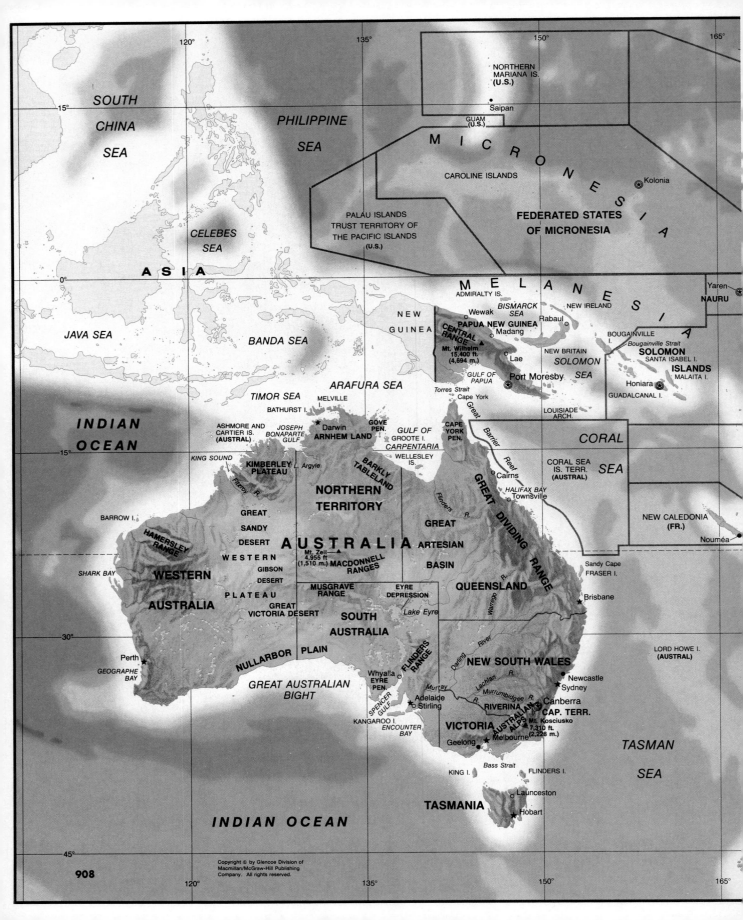

SOUTH
CHINA
SEA

PHILIPPINE
SEA

NORTHERN
MARIANA IS.
(U.S.)

• Saipan

GUAM (U.S.)

M I C R O N E S I A

CAROLINE ISLANDS

◉ Kolonia

FEDERATED STATES
OF MICRONESIA

Yaren ◉
NAURU

CELEBES
SEA

PALAU ISLANDS
TRUST TERRITORY OF
THE PACIFIC ISLANDS
(U.S.)

ASIA

M E L A N E S I A

ADMIRALTY IS.

JAVA SEA

BANDA SEA

NEW
GUINEA

Wewak •
BISMARCK
SEA

NEW IRELAND

PAPUA NEW GUINEA
CENTRAL
RANGE
Mt. Wilhelm
15,400 ft.
(4,694 m.)

Madang •
• Lae

Rabaul •
NEW BRITAIN

BOUGAINVILLE
I.
Bougainville Strait

SOLOMON
SANTA ISABEL I.

SOLOMON
SEA

ISLANDS
MALAITA I.

INDIAN
OCEAN

TIMOR SEA

ARAFURA SEA

GULF OF
PAPUA

Port Moresby ◉

Honiara ◉

GUADALCANAL I.

Torres Strait
Cape York

LOUISIADE
ARCH.

CORAL

MELVILLE I.

BATHURST I.

★ Darwin

GOVE
PEN.

CAPE
YORK
PEN.

Great

CORAL SEA
IS. TERR.
(AUSTRAL)

SEA

ASHMORE AND
CARTIER IS.
(AUSTRAL)

JOSEPH
BONAPARTE
GULF

ARNHEM LAND

GULF OF
GROOTE I.
CARPENTARIA
WELLESLEY
IS

Barrier

Cairns •

KING SOUND

KIMBERLEY
PLATEAU

Argyle

BARKLY
TABLELAND

HALIFAX BAY
Townsville •

Reef

NEW CALEDONIA
(FR.)

Fitzroy R.

NORTHERN

GREAT

Flinders

GREAT

Nouméa •

BARROW I. •

GREAT
SANDY
DESERT

TERRITORY

R.

ARTESIAN

DIVIDING

Sandy Cape
FRASER I.

HAMERSLEY
RANGE

AUSTRALIA

Mt. Zeil
4,955 ft
(1,510 m.)

MACDONNELL
RANGES

BASIN

RANGE

WESTERN

GIBSON

QUEENSLAND

R.

LORD HOWE I.
(AUSTRAL)

SHARK BAY

WESTERN

DESERT

PLATEAU

MUSGRAVE
RANGE

EYRE
DEPRESSION

Warrego

Brisbane •

AUSTRALIA

GREAT
VICTORIA DESERT

SOUTH

Lake Eyre

River

AUSTRALIA

NEW SOUTH WALES

Darling

Perth ★

NULLARBOR

PLAIN

FLINDERS
RANGE

Newcastle •

GEOGRAPHE
BAY

Whyalla
EYRE
PEN.

R.

Lachlan

Murrumbidgee R.

★ Sydney

GREAT AUSTRALIAN
BIGHT

SPENCER
GULF

Murray

Adelaide ◉
Stirling •

R.

RIVERINA

Canberra ★
CAP. TERR.

KANGAROO I.

ENCOUNTER
BAY

VICTORIA

AUSTRALIAN
ALPS

Mt. Kosciusko
7,310 ft.
(2,228 m.)

TASMAN

Geelong •

★ Melbourne

SEA

KING I.

Bass Strait

FLINDERS I.

INDIAN   OCEAN

TASMANIA

Launceston ○

Hobart ★

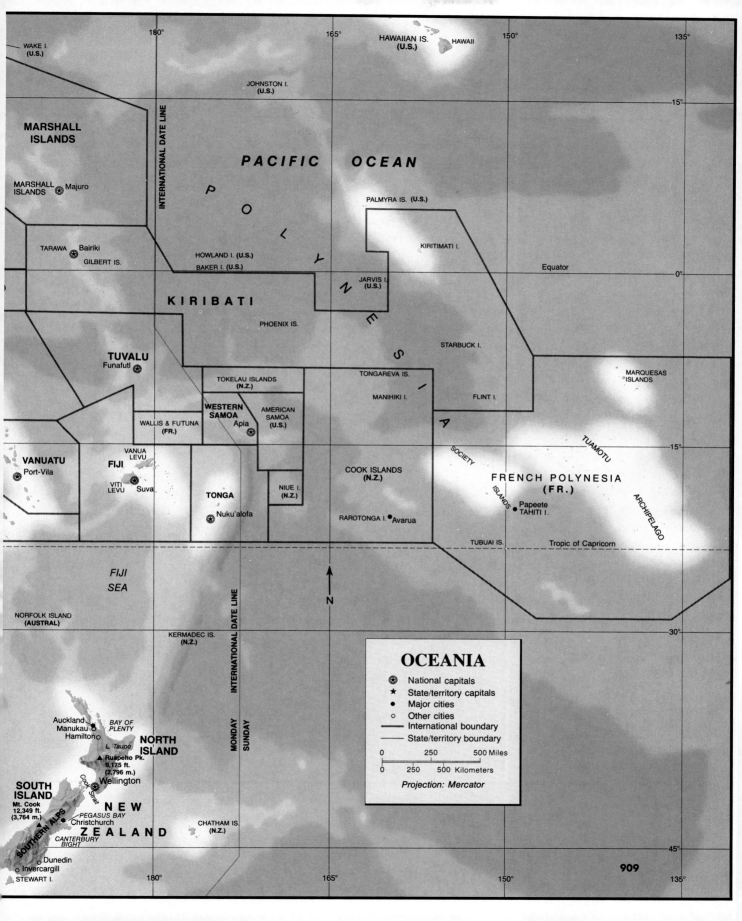

WAKE I.
(U.S.)

180°

165°

HAWAIIAN IS.
(U.S.)

HAWAII

150°

135°

JOHNSTON I.
(U.S.)

15°

**MARSHALL
ISLANDS**

PACIFIC   OCEAN

P
O
L
Y
N
E
S
I
A

MARSHALL
ISLANDS

Majuro

PALMYRA IS. (U.S.)

KIRITIMATI I.

Equator

0°

TARAWA   Bairiki
GILBERT IS.

HOWLAND I. (U.S.)

BAKER I. (U.S.)

JARVIS I.
(U.S.)

K I R I B A T I

PHOENIX IS.

STARBUCK I.

MARQUESAS
ISLANDS

TUVALU
Funafuti

TOKELAU ISLANDS
(N.Z.)

TONGAREVA IS.

MANIHIKI I.

FLINT I.

15°

**WESTERN
SAMOA**
Apia

AMERICAN
SAMOA
(U.S.)

SOCIETY

TUAMOTU

VANUATU
Port-Vila

WALLIS & FUTUNA
(FR.)

VANUA
LEVU

FIJI

VITI
LEVU   Suva

COOK ISLANDS
(N.Z.)

NIUE I.
(N.Z.)

**FRENCH POLYNESIA
(FR.)**

ISLANDS

Papeete
TAHITI I.

ARCHIPELAGO

TONGA

Nuku'alofa

RAROTONGA I.   Avarua

TUBUAI IS.

Tropic of Capricorn

*FIJI
SEA*

INTERNATIONAL DATE LINE

N

NORFOLK ISLAND
(AUSTRAL)

KERMADEC IS.
(N.Z.)

INTERNATIONAL DATE LINE

MONDAY   SUNDAY

30°

Auckland
Manukau
Hamilton

BAY OF
PLENTY

**NORTH
ISLAND**

L. Taupo

Ruapeho Pk.
9,175 ft.
(2,796 m.)

Wellington

Cook
Strait

**SOUTH
ISLAND**

Mt. Cook
12,349 ft.
(3,764 m.)

SOUTHERN ALPS

PEGASUS BAY

Christchurch

N E W

Z E A L A N D

CHATHAM IS.
(N.Z.)

CANTERBURY
BIGHT

Dunedin

Invercargill

STEWART I.

180°

165°

150°

OCEANIA

National capitals

State/territory capitals

Major cities

Other cities

International boundary

State/territory boundary

0   250   500 Miles

0   250   500 Kilometers

Projection: Mercator

45°

135°

909

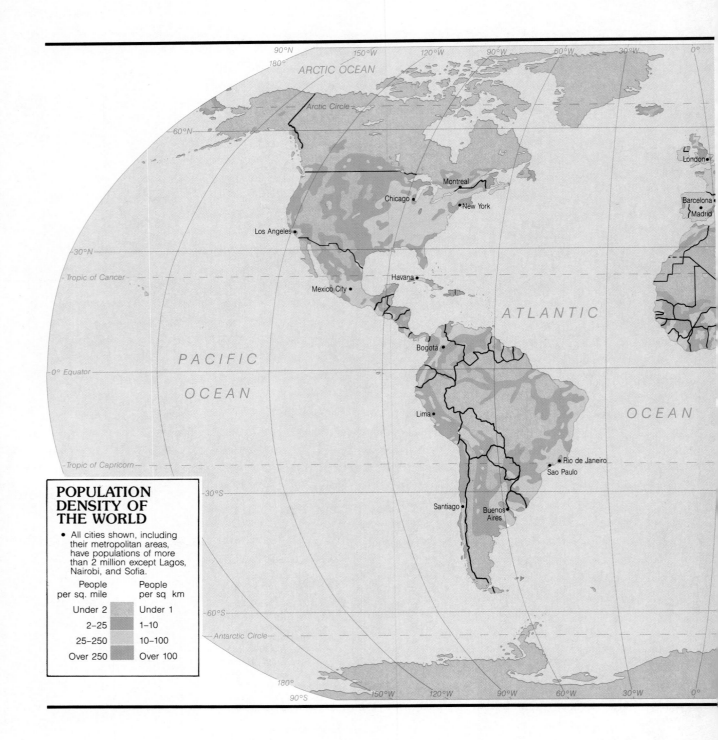

POPULATION DENSITY OF THE WORLD

- All cities shown, including their metropolitan areas, have populations of more than 2 million except Lagos, Nairobi, and Sofia.

People per sq. mile		People per sq km
Under 2		Under 1
2–25		1–10
25–250		10–100
Over 250		Over 100

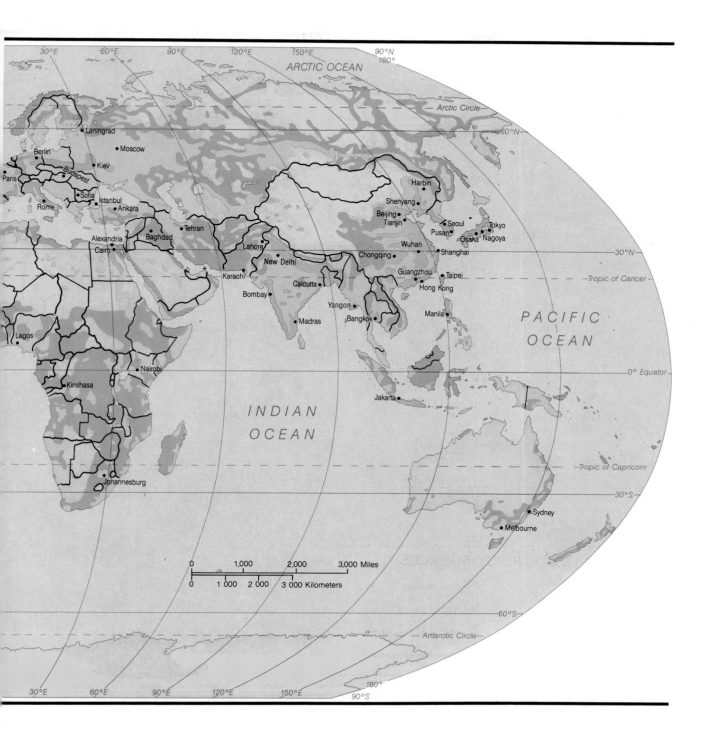

ARCTIC OCEAN

Arctic Circle

60°N

Leningrad
Moscow
Berlin
Kiev
Paris
Budapest
Sofia
Rome
Istanbul
Ankara

Harbin
Shenyang
Beijing
Tianjin
Seoul
Pusan
Tokyo
Osaka Nagoya

Alexandria
Cairo
Baghdad
Tehran
Lahore
New Delhi
Karachi
Bombay

Wuhan
Chongqing
Shanghai
30°N
Guangzhou Taipei
Hong Kong
Tropic of Cancer

Calcutta

Madras
Yangon
Bangkok
Manila

PACIFIC
OCEAN

Lagos

Nairobi

Kinshasa

Jakarta

0° Equator

INDIAN
OCEAN

Tropic of Capricorn

Johannesburg

30°S

Sydney
Melbourne

0   1,000   2,000   3,000 Miles
0   1 000   2 000   3 000 Kilometers

60°S

Antarctic Circle

30°E   60°E   90°E   120°E   150°E   180°
90°S

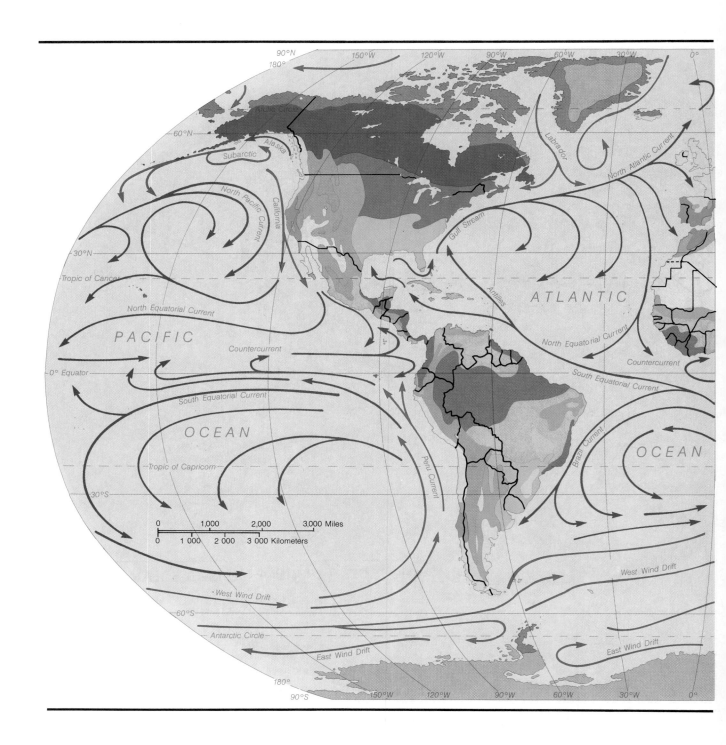

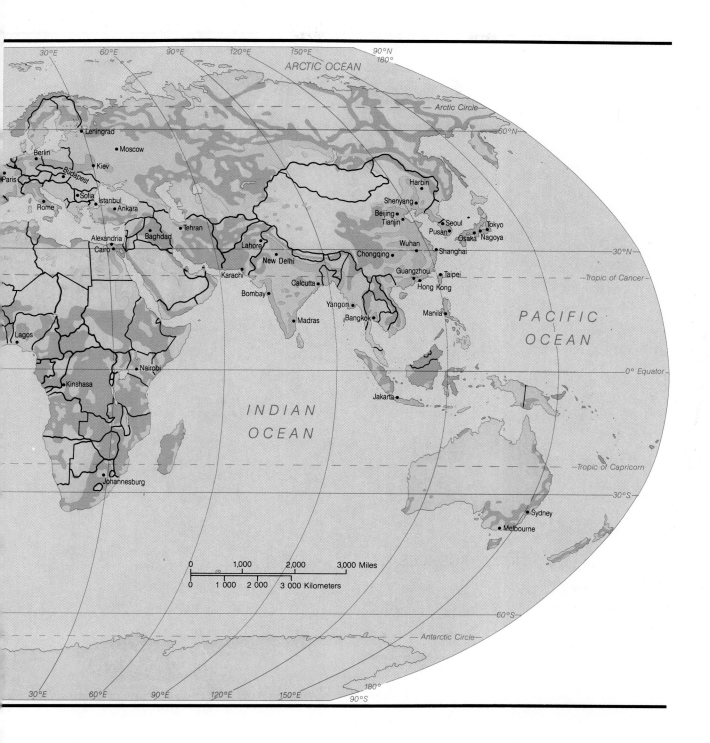

30°E   60°E   90°E   120°E   150°E   90°N
180°
ARCTIC OCEAN

Arctic Circle

• Leningrad   60°N

• Moscow
Berlin
•   • Kiev
Budapest
Paris•
•Sofia
Rome• •Istanbul
•Ankara   Harbin•
                                          Shenyang•
•Tehran   Beijing•
Alexandria• Baghdad•   Tianjin•   •Seoul   •Tokyo
Cairo•   Lahore•   Pusan• •Osaka •Nagoya
                 •New Delhi   Wuhan•
                          Chongqing•   •Shanghai   30°N
Karachi•   Tropic of Cancer
            •Calcutta   Guangzhou• •Taipei
Bombay•   •Hong Kong
                  Yangon•   •Manila   PACIFIC
              •Madras Bangkok•   OCEAN
Lagos•

•Nairobi
•Kinshasa   Jakarta•   0° Equator

INDIAN
OCEAN

Tropic of Capricorn
Johannesburg•
                                          •Sydney   30°S
                                      •Melbourne

0   1,000   2,000   3,000 Miles

0   1 000 2 000   3 000 Kilometers

60°S

Antarctic Circle

30°E   60°E   90°E   120°E   150°E   180°
90°S

911

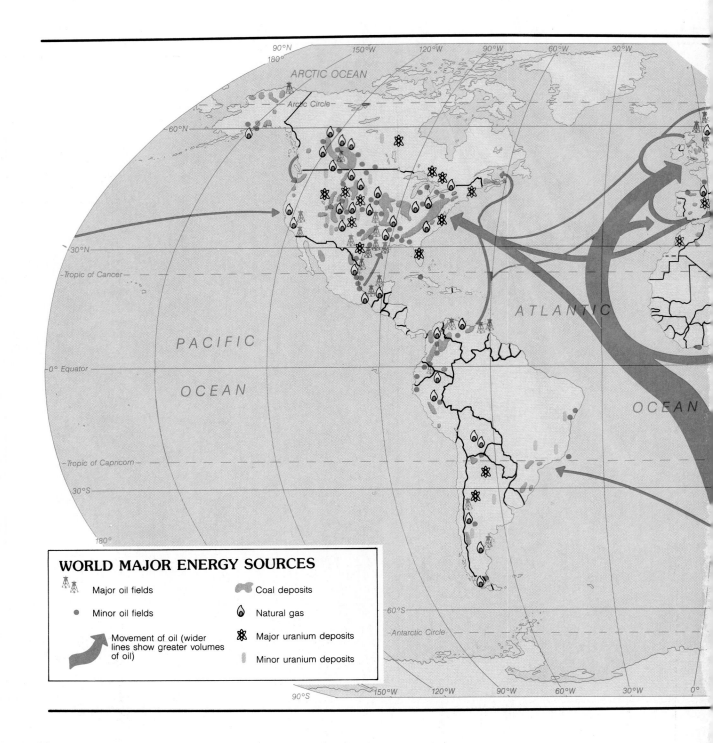

WORLD MAJOR ENERGY SOURCES

⛏ Major oil fields

● Minor oil fields

➡ Movement of oil (wider lines show greater volumes of oil)

🪨 Coal deposits

🔥 Natural gas

✳ Major uranium deposits

▮ Minor uranium deposits

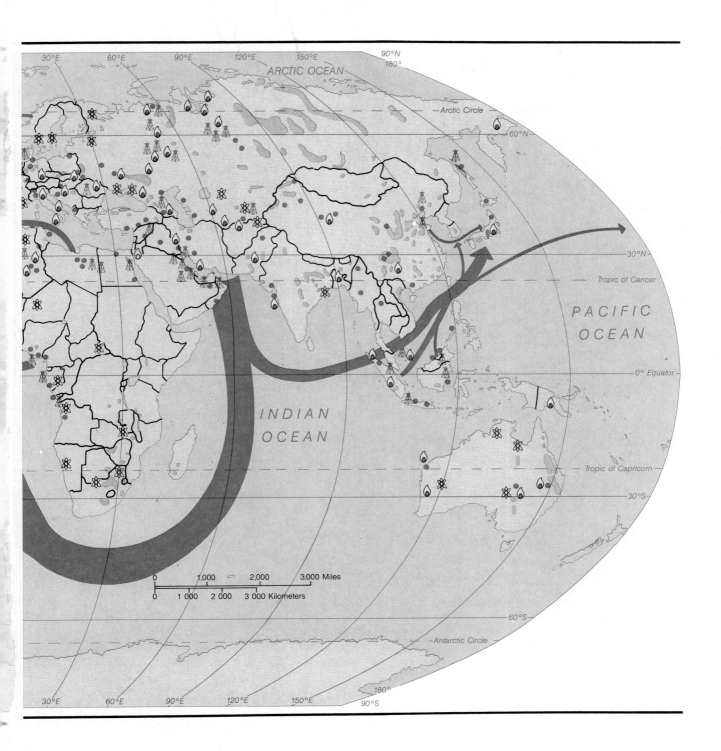

ARCTIC OCEAN

Arctic Circle
60°N

90°N
180°

PACIFIC
OCEAN

30°N

Tropic of Cancer

0° Equator

INDIAN
OCEAN

Tropic of Capricorn

30°S

30°E   60°E   90°E   120°E   150°E

| 0 | 1,000 | 2,000 | 3,000 Miles |
| 0 | 1 000 | 2 000 | 3 000 Kilometers |

60°S

Antarctic Circle

180°

90°S

30°E   60°E   90°E   120°E   150°E

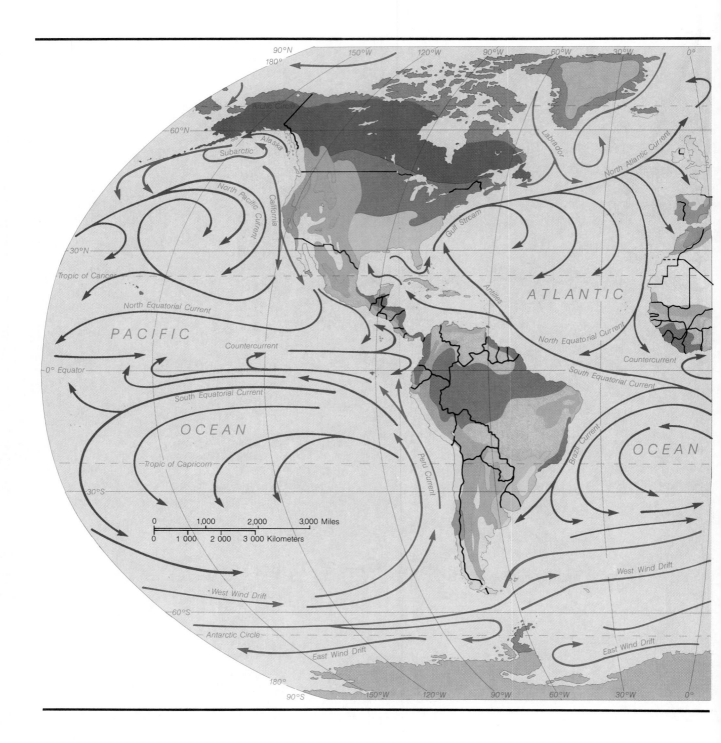

90°N
180°
150°W
120°W
90°W
60°W
30°W
0°

Arctic Circle

60°N

Alaska

Subarctic

North Pacific Current

California

Labrador

North Atlantic Current

Gulf Stream

30°N

Tropic of Cancer

ATLANTIC

North Equatorial Current

Antilles

PACIFIC

Counter current

North Equatorial Current

0° Equator

Counter current

South Equatorial Current

South Equatorial Current

OCEAN

OCEAN

Tropic of Capricorn

Brazil Current

Peru Current

30°S

| 0 | 1,000 | 2,000 | 3,000 Miles |

| 0 | 1 000 | 2 000 | 3 000 Kilometers |

West Wind Drift

West Wind Drift

60°S

Antarctic Circle

East Wind Drift

East Wind Drift

180°

90°S

150°W

120°W

90°W

60°W

30°W

0°

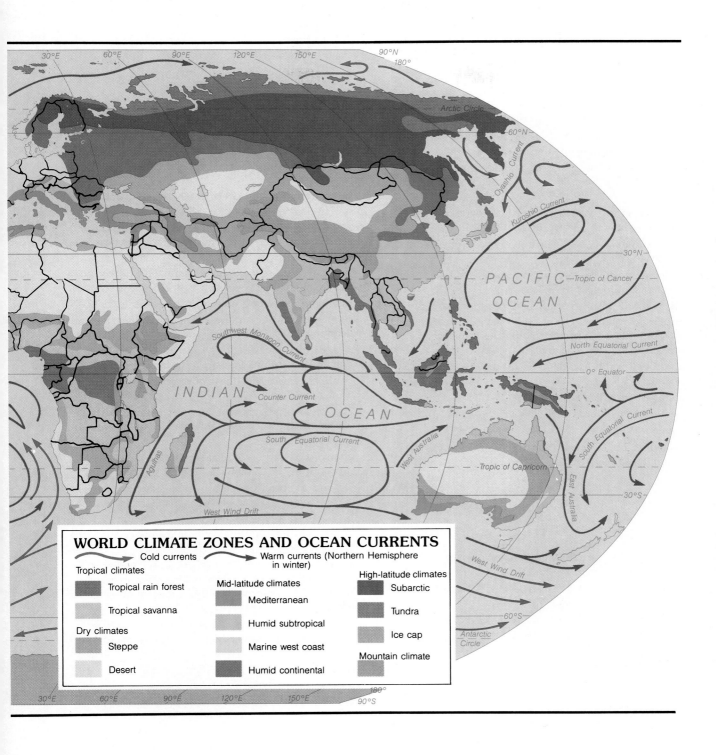

WORLD CLIMATE ZONES AND OCEAN CURRENTS

⟶ Cold currents ⟶ Warm currents (Northern Hemisphere in winter)

Tropical climates
- Tropical rain forest
- Tropical savanna

Dry climates
- Steppe
- Desert

Mid-latitude climates
- Mediterranean
- Humid subtropical
- Marine west coast
- Humid continental

High-latitude climates
- Subarctic
- Tundra
- Ice cap

Mountain climate

Map labels: PACIFIC OCEAN, INDIAN OCEAN, Arctic Circle, Oyashio Current, Kuroshio Current, Southwest Monsoon Current, Counter Current, South Equatorial Current, North Equatorial Current, Aguihas, West Australia, East Australia, West Wind Drift, Tropic of Cancer, Tropic of Capricorn, Equator, Antarctic Circle

Coordinate labels: 30°E, 60°E, 90°E, 120°E, 150°E, 180°, 90°N, 60°N, 30°N, 0° Equator, 30°S, 60°S, 90°S

A

absolute monarchy form of government in which the ruler has total sovereignty (p. 872)

absolutism belief that monarchs hold supreme power and are responsible only to God (p. 798)

acupuncture Chinese practice of relieving pain and treating disease by inserting needles into the body (p. 162)

agrarian reform system of land division for a more equal distribution among the people (p. 489)

ahl al-dhimma non-Muslims who lived in the Islamic empire (p. 597)

alchemy practice of attempting to change lesser substances into gold (p. 177)

alluvial soil soil deposited by floodwaters (p. 335)

anticlerical person who opposed the influence of the Roman Catholic Church in Latin American social, economic, and political matters (p. 486)

apartheid South African policy of the separation of races (p. 55)

archipelago group of islands (p. 237)

aristocracy noble class (p. 466)

autocratic having unlimited power (p. 658)

ayatollah one of the highest Muslim religious leaders of Iran (p. 597)

B

bakufu Japanese military government during the Kamakura shogunate (p. 258)

bantustan black South African territory having limited self-government (p. 60)

barbarian person lacking an advanced civilization; term used by the ancient Chinese for a foreigner (p. 147)

barriada Spanish term for a poor area of Bogota, Colombia (p. 501)

barrio Spanish term for a poor area of Caracas, Venezuela (p. 501)

bonsai potted plant or tree kept very small through special cultivation techniques (p. 242)

boyar member of an aristocratic Russian order (p. 656)

bureaucrat any official who serves in a government's administrative structure (p. 143)

C

cadre trained group or individual that serves as the core of an organization, as in the People's Republic of China (p. 220)

calligraphy Chinese art of brush-and-ink handwriting (p. 166)

campesino Spanish term for a member of the lower class who lives in the country and performs farm labor (p. 503)

capitalism economic system characterized by private ownership of business (pp. 676, 872)

cash crop produce grown primarily for sale (p. 12)

cha-no-yu ancient Japanese ceremony of serving and drinking tea (p. 295)

civil disobedience refusal to obey governmental demands or commands seen as unfair (p. 392)

civilian person who does not belong to the police or armed forces (p. 274)

civil service government system, created in early China, under which officials are hired on the basis of exams (p. 158)

clan one of a group of related families believed to be descended from a common ancestor (p. 253)

classicism attitudes and principles based on the culture, literature, and arts of ancient Greece and Rome (p. 862)

classic any historically memorable work of literature (p. 176)

collective any business or other enterprise owned by the workers; agricultural collectives were an early reform in the Chinese economic program under communism (p. 196)

colonialism system under which one nation rules or extends its control over another for its own economic benefit (p. 603)

comedy drama that is intended to amuse and whose plot ends happily (p. 776)

commune rural cooperative farm, as those controlled by the government in China (p. 196)

communism economic and political system characterized by the common ownership of the means of production and the absence of social classes (p. 677)

compound in Africa, enclosed area containing a home residence (p. 46); in old China, walled urban residence of a member of the gentry (p. 158)

conquistador Spanish term for leader of an expedition of conquest, especially in the New World (p. 452)

conservative person who tends to favor the existing order (p. 518)

continental climate hot, moist summer and cold, dry winter separated by a brief spring and fall (p. 641)

cooperative consumer-owned business or enterprise (p. 402)

cottage industry small business consisting of family members working at home (p. 404)

coup sudden action, especially the sudden overthrow of a government or its leaders (p. 692)

covenant solemn, binding agreement (p. 586)

cremate to dispose of by burning (p. 336)

czar one of the rulers of the Russian empire (p. 658)

D

daimyo Japanese feudal baron (p. 260)

desalination process by which salt is removed from seawater (p. 543)

détente easing of conflicts, especially those between the Soviet Union and the West (p. 682)

dharma in Hinduism, a person's moral obligation (p. 368)

dictatorship form of government in which absolute power is concentrated in one person (p. 191)

diet body of persons who make laws (p. 270)

dissident person who disagrees with government regulations or policies (p. 682)

divination practice of attempting to predict the future (p. 175)

dowry money, goods, or property that a woman brings to her husband in marriage (p. 350)

dynasty series of rulers from the same family (p. 141)

E

ejido Spanish term for piece of land owned and shared by a community (p. 504)

entrepreneur any person who assumes financial risk for a business venture (pp. 205–206)

epic long poem that narrates the deeds of deities or heroes (p. 420)

estuary arm of the sea that extends inland to meet the mouth of a river (p. 754)

ethics branch of philosophy in which right and wrong conduct and thought are studied (p. 173)

exodus mass departure (p. 586)

extended family family group that includes parents, children, and other relatives (p. 352)

extraterritoriality exemption from local legal jurisdiction (p. 188)

F

fallahín Egyptian peasant or farmer (p. 543)

favela Portuguese term for a poor area of Rio de Janeiro or São Paulo, Brazil (p. 501)

feudalism medieval political and economic system based on the relation of lords and vassals (p. 781)

fiesta Spanish term for party; also, a holiday or festival (p. 475)

filial piety deep respect for parents and ancestors (p. 174)

fútbol Spanish term for soccer (p. 476)

G

gaucho person who tends cattle on the plains of Argentina and Uruguay (p. 439)

gentry wealthy landholders, as in old China (p. 158)

glasnost Soviet policy allowing greater freedom of discussion, a broader range of political and artistic choices, and a relaxation of restrictions on some groups who had faced discrimination (p. 682)

godparent person chosen by a baby's parents to undertake certain responsibilities for the child (p. 472)

guru in Hinduism, a personal religious teacher (p. 369)

H

hacendado Spanish term for owner of a large plantation (p. 503)

hacienda Spanish term for large plantation owned by a member of the upper class (p. 466)

haiku short unrhymed verse form developed by the Japanese (p. 291)

harambee Kiswahili term for community cooperation (p. 71)

Holocaust the mass extermination of 12 million people, especially Jews, during World War II (p. 808)

hombre de confianza Spanish term for close friend and confidant (p. 479)

homeland any black South African territory (p. 60)

I

icon sacred image or picture (p. 657)

ideology body of political or social belief (p. 141)

ikebana Japanese art of displaying flowers (p. 295)

imām high Muslim religious leader (p. 597)

imperialism the policy of establishing a politically and economically strong empire (p. 30)

indulgence document of the Catholic Church that freed its owner from time in purgatory (p. 793)

intelligentsia intellectuals who form an artistic, social, or political élite (p. 665)

Islamic empire Muslim nation-state (p. 25)

J

jati any grouping within the Hindu caste system (p. 374)

joint family family group in India that includes parents, children, and adult sons with their spouses and children (p. 352)

K

kabuki traditional Japanese pantomime theater with singing and dancing (p. 292)

kami in Shintoism, anything with superior power or that is awe-inspiring (p. 286)

kana written characters that represent basic sounds in Japanese (p. 291)

kanji Chinese picture words incorporated into written Japanese (p. 291)

karma in Hinduism, the total of a person's conduct in past lives, which determines his or her destiny (p. 368)

karoshi death resulting from overwork, one characteristic of traditional insistence upon company loyalty in Japan (p. 319)

kendo highly stylized form of swordplay, featuring bamboo swords, popular in Japan (p. 320)

khalifah religious and political leader of a Muslim state (p. 595)

khan Mongol ruler (p. 657)

kibbutzim Israeli farm communities in which the land is held in common (p. 544)

kimono traditional Japanese loose-fitting outer garment (p. 285)

knight medieval soldier (p. 783)

kolkhoz Soviet cooperative farm whose profits are shared by the families who work it (p. 715)

kowtow action of kneeling and touching the forehead to the ground to show respect (p. 147)

kulak wealthy Soviet peasant farmer (p. 679)

kyudo traditional Japanese sport of archery (p. 320)

L

lama monk or priest of the form of Buddhism known as Lamaism (p. 209)

legend traditional folk tale or myth (p. 342)

liberal person who believes strongly in individual freedoms and favors political reforms (pp. 518, 872)

lingua franca any mixed language used as a means of communication between peoples who speak different languages (p. 72)

llanos grassy, treeless plains of Colombia and Venezuela (p. 439)

loess fine-grained silt or clay deposits resulting from wind-blown dust (p. 127)

M

mandate authority to govern (p. 141); region under the administration of another nation (p. 604)

manor any area over which a lord had domain during the Middle Ages in Europe; also, the lord's residences (p. 783)

maritime relating to navigation or commerce on the sea (p. 754)

mass production manufacture of goods in large quantities using machines and division of labor (p. 801)

mesa broad, flat-topped hill (p. 440)

messiah promised savior or liberator (p. 586)

mestizo in Latin America, person with one European and one Indian parent (p. 451)

militarism policy of aggressive military preparation (p. 274)

millet non-Muslim community within the Islamic empire (p. 597)

minaret slender tower of a mosque, from which Muslims are called to prayer (p. 417)

minifundio small non-commercial farm in Latin America (p. 504)

mir one of the Russian peasant villages set up during czarist rule (p. 666)

monastery residence for those who wish to live in seclusion and devote themselves to religious pursuits (p. 787)

monotheism belief that there is only one god (p. 586)

monsoon wind that reverses direction seasonally, producing South Asia's dry and wet seasons (p. 240)

moshavim Israeli cooperative farm communities in which farms are individually owned (p. 545)

mosque building used for public worship by Muslims (p. 25)

muftī Muslim official who reconciled civil law with Islamic teaching (p. 595)

mulatto in Latin America, person with one black and one white parent (p. 451)

myth story that embodies the cultural ideals of a people (p. 257)

N

nationalism loyalty to a national group or nation and belief in its right to self-determination (pp. 32, 872)

nationalist person devoted to a national group or nation (p. 872)

nationality group of people who share a common cultural heritage and, in many cases, the same territory (pp. 690, 754)

nationalize to transfer from private control to control by the national government (p. 608)

Noh **play** traditional form of Japanese dance-drama (p. 292)

nomad person who moves seasonally within a defined territory to secure a food supply (p. 540)

nouveaux riches people who have recently become wealthy (p. 466)

nuclear family family group consisting of a father, mother, and their children (p. 352)

O

opium narcotic, addictive drug made from poppy plants (p. 188)

oral traditions stories and history of a group passed by word of mouth from generation to generation (p. 23)

origami Japanese art of folding paper to represent objects (p. 295)

orographic lifting process by which moisture-filled clouds are forced upward and release rain (p. 339)

P

pachinko game played in Japan on a pinball machine (p. 320)

pampas grassy plains of Argentina and Uruguay (p. 439)

panchayat group of elders elected to govern an Indian community (p. 356)

pass law any of the former regulations of the South African government that placed travel and labor restrictions upon black South Africans (p. 60)

patriarch male religious leader or founder; also, male head of families (p. 586)

patrician rich and powerful upper-class citizen of ancient Rome (p. 777)

peninsula long projection of land into water (p. 333)

perestroika Soviet program of widespread economic reform, including encouragement of private enterprise and western investment (pp. 682-683)

permafrost permanently frozen upper layer of earth (p. 642)

personalismo Spanish term for an individual's personality and sense of personal identity and honor (p. 479)

plebian poor and lower-class citizen of ancient Rome (p. 777)

polyrhythm combination of two or more simultaneous beat patterns (p. 88)

popular sovereignty belief that a nation's government needs the consent of and must be responsible to its people (p. 800)

population density average number of individuals per square unit of area (p. 131)

proletariat laboring class; especially, industrial laborers (p. 676)

prophet religious orator who claims to speak for God, under divine inspiration (p. 589)

proverb any brief, popular saying that expresses common, practical wisdom (p. 91)

provisional serving for the time being (p. 190)

purdah seclusion of women from public view (pp. 355, 572)

R

raga in Indian music, any of the traditional patterns of notes upon which a composition is built (p. 423)

rain forest tropical woodland with heavy annual rainfall (p. 8)

rajah traditional local Indian ruler (p. 387)

reincarnation Hindu belief of rebirth of a soul in a new body or form of life (p. 368)

republic form of government in which citizens elect their leaders (p. 777)

reserve portion of land set aside in South Africa for ownership by blacks (p. 60)

romanticism European artistic and literary movement that began in the 1700's, emphasizing imagination and the emotions (p. 862)

S

sabra Jewish person born in Israel (p. 559)

sadhu Hindu holy man who denies himself the comforts of life (p. 370)

sage any person recognized for great wisdom and judgment (p. 173)

samurai member of the noble and military class of medieval Japan (p. 260)

savanna tropical or subtropical grassland containing scattered trees (p. 8)

scientific method way of seeking knowledge in an orderly fashion (p. 776)

sect group of people who follow a variation of a major religion's doctrine (p. 287)

sepoy Indian officer in the British army during the colonial period (p. 388)

serf member of the lowest class, bound to the land and its noble owner (p. 661)

service industry business that sells services rather than products (p. 318)

shahādah Muslim pillar of faith that requires a statement of belief in one God and in Muhammad as God's messenger (p. 591)

shinjinrui younger Japanese who reject traditional loyalties, especially regarding career development (p. 319)

shogun military governor in feudal Japan (p. 258)

shogunate government of a military ruler in feudal Japan (p. 258)

sitar Indian long-necked lute (p. 423)

socialism doctrine that calls for the collective ownership of all means of production (p. 667)

socialist person who favors collective ownership of land and industry (p. 872)

soviet committee or council formed by Russian revolutionaries to represent the people after the fall of the czar (p. 675)

sovkhoz farm in the Soviet Union owned and run by the state (p. 715)

special economic zone region in which foreign businesses are allowed to operate with relative freedom from government interference (p. 212)

steppe semiarid grassy plains (p. 126)

stupa dome-shaped Buddhist shrine (p. 416)

subcontinent landmass of great size but not considered a continent (p. 333)

subjugation act of being brought under another's authority, as through conquest (p. 558)

subsistence farming growing food solely for one's own use (p. 12)

sumo Japanese form of wrestling (p. 320)

sūq mall-like area of shops and vendors found in Middle Eastern cities (p. 546)

T

taiga subarctic forests, mostly of spruce and fir (p. 645)

talking drum West African drum used for communication (p. 88)

tonal in a language, having different tones for the same syllable, resulting in different words (pp. 88-89)

totalitarian relating to government under which the individual is subordinate to the state (p. 220)

township suburban tract of land set aside for black South Africans expelled from a city (p. 60)

tragedy drama that focuses on human sorrow, especially that involved in the downfall of a hero (p. 776)

tsunami Japanese term for tidal waves (p. 243)

tundra cold, treeless flatlands (p. 644)

typhoon tropical cyclone that occurs in the western Pacific (p. 240)

U

uhuru Swahili term for freedom or emancipation (p. 71)

ulema Muslim judges (p. 595)

unequal treaties nineteenth-century agreements that opened China to unwanted western trade and influence (p. 188)

untouchable low-ranked Hindu who performs the dirtiest jobs and is looked upon as impure (p. 374)

urban migration movement of rural people to cities (p. 47)

V

varna any of Hinduism's four categories of society (p. 373)

vassal in medieval Europe, person who owed allegiance to a lord (p. 781)

viceroy ruling representative of a sovereign (p. 389)

villa miseria Spanish term for a poor area of Buenos Aires, Argentina (p. 501)

visual arts visible art, such as paintings, sculpture, and woven and dyed cloth (p. 93)

W

waqf funds and properties earmarked for charity by non-Muslims in the Islamic empire (p. 597)

war communism postcivil war Soviet economic policy in which the government controlled production, wages, and prices (p. 677)

warlord any Chinese military commander who ruled a local area by force in the early 1900's (p. 191)

Y

yang and yin in Chinese philosophy, opposite forces that must be balanced to achieve a perfect life (p. 123)

yoga form of Hindu exercise and worship designed to produce complete physical and mental well-being (p. 369)

yokozuna superstars of Japanese wrestling, idolized nationwide (p. 322)

Z

zaibatsu industries run by leading families of Japan during Meiji rule (p. 270)

zakāt money given to charity in accordance with Muslim religious law (p. 591)

INDEX

A

Abdul-Hamid II, 563
Abraham, 559, 586, 589
absolutism, 798–800, 872
Abū Bakr, 595
Abuja, 40
Aconcagua, Mount, 436
acupuncture, 162
Adire **cloth,** 93–94
Adiyaman Plateau, 539
Adulis, Axum, 24
Afghanistan, 333
　Soviets in, 683
Africa. *See also individual countries*
　adoption of national language, 114–115
　agriculture in, 10–16, 24, 45–46, 73, 103, 105–106, 108
　AIDS problem in, 66, 112–113
　animals of, 14–15, 80
　arts and architecture of, 28, 41, 87–99
　celebrations and ceremonies in, 87, 94–96
　challenges to development in, 103–115
　Christianity in, 23, 35, 40
　cities of, 16–17, 24, 26–27, 28, 42, 47–48
　climate in, 8–9, 12–16, 77, 107–108
　colonialism in, 8, 9, 30–35, 104
　dance in, 42, 87
　deserts in, 8, 15
　development of, 109–115
　drought in, 15–16, 106–107
　early societies in, 24–28
　economy of, 18–19, 46, 103, 105–106, 109
　education in, 111–112
　empires in, 25–27
　environmental awareness in, 11, 15, 110
　ethnic groups in, 13, 104, 114–115
　Europeans in, 29, 30–35, 43, 56–57, 62, 82
　filmmaking in, 96–97
　game preserves in, 80
　geography of, 8–9, 77
　gold in, 57–58
　governments in, 103, 105
　health in, 66, 108, 112–113
　heritage of, 23, 87, 103
　history of, 7, 23–33
　hunger in, 15–16, 18–19, 107
　imperialism in, 30
　industrial development in, 109
　Islamic empire in, 25, 42
　Islam in, 40, 72
　island states of, 8
　languages of, 63, 72, 90, 114–115
　literature of, 44–45, 51, 71, 91–93
　mining in, 9
　music in, 7, 88–89, 90
　nationalism in, 31–33, 73–74
　nations in, 4, 8
　oil in, 106
　oral literature of, 23, 91–93
　population growth in, 16, 19, 39, 105, 108–109
　problems in, 103
　rain forests of, 8, 12–13
　religions of, 23, 25, 40, 72, 75, 94–96, 103
　savanna in, 13–15
　slave trade in, 29, 42
　trade in, 10, 24–25, 28, 43
　urbanization in, 16–17
　wars in, 15–16, 107
　women in, 110
African National Congress (ANC), 58, 62, 64, 65
Africans
　in Brazil, 451
　in Latin America, 459–460
Africanus, Leo, 27
Afrikaans language, 63
Afrikaner Nationalist Party, 60
Afrikaners (Boers), 56–60
Against the Grain, 695
Age of Expansion, 794–798
Age of Reason, 800–801
agrarian reform, in Latin America, 489–490, 517
agricultural schools, 511
agriculture. *See also* farming methods
　in Africa, 10–16, 24, 45–46, 73, 103, 105–106, 108
　in China, 124, 127, 205, 221–222
　in C.I.S., 643, 649, 655, 715–716, 740–741
　in Europe, 766
　in India, 336, 341, 357, 390, 402–403, 411
　in Japan, 246, 247
　in Latin America, 440, 459, 466–467, 503–504
　in Middle East, 537, 542–545, 544–545, 622, 631
ahl al-dhimma, 597–598
AIDS, in Africa, 66, 112–113
Ainu, 242
Ajanta, India, 416
Akbar, 387
Akihabara, 315
Akihito, Prince, 279, 290, 325

Āl'Azab, 541
Albania, 848
Alexander I, 664–665
Alexander II, czar, 665–667
Alexander III, czar, 667
Alexander the Great, 558, 777
Al-Idrīsī, 594
Al Kuwaitia, 578
Allah, 588
Allahabad, India, 359
alluvial soil, 335
Alma-Ata, Kazakhstan, 744, 745
al Majusi, 634
alphabets. *See also* language; writing
　Arabic-Persian, 735
　Cyrillic, 657, 735
Alps, 758–759
al-Rāzī, 598, 634
Amadi, Elechi, 44
Amaterasu, 253
Amazon basin, 443, 455, 457
Amazon River, 442–443
amusement parks, 318
Analects **(Confucius),** 178, 182
ancestors, reverence for, 174–175
Andes Mountains, 436, 456
animals
　of Africa, 14–15, 80
　sacred, in China, 130
Ankara, Turkey, 539, 564
anticlericals, 486–487
anti-Semitism, 852
apartheid, in South Africa, 55, 58–64
　end of, 65, 67
Apennines, 758
aqueducts, 780
Arabia, 556, 593
Arabian Peninsula, 556
Arabian Sea, 333
Arabic language, 556, 596
'Arābī, Ahmad, 608
Arab-Israeli conflict, 609–610, 618–619, 621–623
Arabs
　in Africa, 23, 24, 72
　conflict with Israelis, 561, 609–610, 617–623
　in France, 853
　in Middle East, 555–557, 560, 604
　Palestinian, 609
Arafāt, 592, 622
Aral Sea, 649
Ararat, Mount, 538, 722, 723
archipelago, 237, 239

207, 219
trade in, 149, 150, 164
traditional beliefs in, 133–134, 174–175
and the U.S., 150, 195, 197
villages in, 131–135
warfare in, 164–165
warlords in, 191
and the West, 147–151, 153, 188
women in, 157, 165–166, 193, 223–224
in World War II, 194
writing in, 291
Xia (SYAH) dynasty in, 142
yang and yin, 123, 133
youth in, 225–226
Yuan dynasty in, 145
Zhou (JOH) dynasty in, 142
China, Republic of. See Taiwan
Chinese, in Latin America, 460
Chopin, Frédéric, 862
Christianity. See also Catholicism;
Protestantism
in Africa, 23, 35, 40
in ancient Rome, 780–781
in China, 181, 189
in C.I.S., 656, 725–727
in Europe, 848
in India, 377
in Japan, 262
in Latin America, 484–485
in Middle East, 586–587, 589
and Reformation, 794
Chukchi Peninsula, 644–645
chullahs, 350
Churchill, Winston, 807–809, 820
Cicero, 876
C.I.S. See Commonwealth of
Independent States
Cissé, Souleymane, 96
city-states
Greek, 774–777
in Italy, 792
civil disobedience, 392
civilian, 274
civilization, cradle of, 539
civil service, 158
Cixi, Empress, 152, 166
classicism, 862
climate. See also environmental
awareness; geography
in Africa, 8–9, 12–16, 106–107
in China, 126, 136
in C.I.S., 640–648, 736
in Europe, 754–756, 768
in India, 338, 339, 342, 344
in Japan, 239, 240, 243, 248
in Latin America, 435, 445, 446–447
in Middle East, 537–541
coal, 127
cold war, 815, 818–820

collective farms, 196, 715–716
Collor de Mello, Fernando, 517
Colombia
government in, 527–528
leisure time in, 478
llanos of, 439–441
mountains in, 436
rivers in, 441
colonialism
in Africa, 30–35, 104
in Middle East, 603
opposing views of, 34–35
coloreds, in South Africa, 60, 65
Columbus, Christopher, 452, 796–797
comedies, 776
commerce. See trade
commercial farms, 503–504
Commonwealth of Independent States.
See also Russia; Soviet Union; *names of
republics*
agriculture in, 643, 649, 655, 715–716,
740–741
arts in, 657, 749
ballet in, 749
bodies of water in, 647–648
Central Asian republics in, 735–749
cities in, 712–714
climate in, 640–648, 736
cultural activities in, 709–711
dance in, 709, 710
deserts in, 641, 649, 736
economy in, 698–700, 742–745
ethnic groups in, 655, 721
European republics in, 705–717
fishing in, 647, 649
foods of, 646
forests in, 645–646
formation of, 689, 696–699
geography of, 640–643
housing in, 713–714
industrialization in, 712–714
Islam in, 735, 737–739
languages in, 728
literature of, 639, 655, 668, 680, 711,
721, 722
military in, 697
mountains in, 640, 721, 722, 728
Muslims in, 725–726
natural resources of, 650–651
nomads in, 743
religions in, 708–709, 723–724, 725, 729,
737–739
republics joining, 697
republics of the Caucasus, 721–731
rivers in, 647, 648
rural life in, 715–716
Russian heritage, 639, 640, 655–669
sense of identity in, 715–716
Slavs in, 655

Soviet era, 673–685
steppe in, 646
trade in, 655
tundra in, 644–645
communes, 196, 205, 222
communism
in China, 187, 191, 204, 207, 219–221
in Eastern Europe, 682, 820–825,
826–827, 832
in Soviet Union, 677–681, 682, 684–685,
690, 694–696, 698
compounds, 46, 158
computers, 409
concentration camps, 808
Conference of Ministers, Africa, 106
Confucianism, 143–144
in China, 157, 177–180, 182–183, 192,
233
in Japan, 233, 254
Confucius, 143–144, 173, 177–180
Congo Free State, 32
conquistadores, 452–454, 484
conservatives, 518–521
Constantine, Emperor, 781
Constantinople, 659
consumer goods industry, 406
continental climate, 641
contras, 522
cooperatives. See also collective farms;
communes
in India, 402–403
**Coordinating Body for Indigenous
People's Organizations of the
Amazon,** 445
Copernicus, Nicolaus, 869
Cortés, Hernán, 452–454, 453
Cossacks, 661
Costa Rica, 435
cottage industries, 404
cotton, in Uzbekistan, 740
**Council of Mutual Assistance
(COMECON),** 818
coup, 692
covenant, 586
cremated, 336
Croats, 849
Crusades, 786
Côte d'Ivoire, 94–96
Cuba
Asians in, 460
economy in, 506
government in, 524–527
music in, 533
Soviet missiles in, 682
Cubism, 866
Cyril, 657
Cyrillic alphabet, 657, 735
Cyrus the Great, 558
czars, 658

Unit One: Africa

Africa: Portrait of a Continent. Teaching Resources Films. Sound filmstrips, color: Dispels common stereotypes as it examines the terrain, peoples, and cultures of Africa.

Cry, the Beloved Country. Media Basics. Sound filmstrips (3), color. Filmstrip version of the motion picture starring Sidney Poitier. Deals with apartheid in South Africa.

Soyinka, Wole. *Ake: The Years of Childhood*. New York: Vintage Books, 1983. Autobiography by Nigerian Nobel-Prize-winner.

Unit Two: China

Behind the Wall: A Journey Through China by Colin Thubron, 1987, Atlantic Monthly Press. Written before the Tiananmen Square protests, this book makes it clear that the bloodshed was inevitable.

China in Perspective: Roots of Civilization. Guidance Associates. Sound filmstrips (2), color. Explores the achievements of ancient Chinese civilization as background to modern China.

China in Revolution: A Sleeping Giant Awakes. The New York Times. Sound filmstrip, color. Depicts China from the late 1800's to the communist victory in 1949.

The Last Emperor. 1987 film, color, 164 min. Epic drama of China's last emperor; won nine Oscars.

Life and Death in Shanghai, by Nien Cheng, 1986, Grove Press. A Chinese woman's personal account of her experiences during the period of the Cultural Revolution.

Unit Three: Japan

Black Ships and Rising Sun by John G. Roberts, 1971, Julian Messner. Tells how Japan was opened to the West and how it industrialized and modernized.

The Human Face of Japan. Learning Corporation of America. Films (6), color, 28 minutes each. Profiles individuals from diverse socio-economic backgrounds in modern Japan.

Japan: A Historical Overview. Coronet Films. Film, color, 17 minutes. Recounts major events in Japan's history from 800 BC to the early 1960's.

Japan: Of Tradition and Change. National Geographic Society. Film, color, 23 minutes. Focuses on the life of a young woman in modern Tokyo whose life demonstrates a harmony of tradition and change.

Unit Four: India

The Indian Subcontinent. Educational Design. Sound filmstrips (4), color. Examines current social and economic issues in the major geographic areas of the Indian subcontinent.

Through Indian Eyes, Vol. 1: The Wheel of Life, edited by Donald and Jean Johnson, 1981, Center for International Training and Education (CITE), revised edition. Twenty-eight selections describe childhood, education, and other aspects of life in traditional India.

Through Indian Eyes, Vol. 2: Forging a New Nation, edited by Donald and Jean Johnson, 1981, Center for International Training and Education (CITE), revised edition. Examines contemporary issues. Selections from fiction, news media, and memoirs.

Unit Five: Latin America

Christopher *Columbus and the Great Adventure*. Video Knowledge. Videocassette, color, 28 minutes. Traces the voyages of Columbus to the Americas and examines the impact of European exploration on the first peoples of North and South America.

Latin America: Its History, Economy, and Politics. McGraw Hill. Film, b/w, 33 minutes. A survey of Latin American history from early American civilizations until recent times. Focus on struggles for independence and subsequent problems.

Portrait of Castro's Cuba. TBS. Videocassette, color and b/w, 92 minutes. A revealing look at Cuba since Fidel Castro took power in 1959. Includes an up-to-date look at how Cuba is coping since the collapse of the Soviet Union.

Unit Six: Middle East

Essence of Israel. Kevin Donovan Films and I.S. Associates. Sound filmstrips (4), color. The history of the Jews from ancient times to the post-World War II period.

In the Holy Land. ABC News Interactive. Optical Data Corporation. Analysis by Ted Koppel. With lesson guide, hypercard application, Spanish audio, closed captioning.

Islam: The Faith and the People. United Learning. Videocassette, color, 20 minutes. The program focuses on the religion's history, its faith, and its arts.

The Shifting Sands: A History of the Middle East. NBC News. Videocassette, color and b/w, 48 minutes. An overview of 5,000 years of Middle Eastern history, from the Tigris-Euphrates civilizations through the Persian Gulf War.

Unit Seven: Commonwealth of Independent States

Against the Grain by Boris Yeltsin, 1990, Summit Books. Autobiography of the Russian president, written before the events of 1991.

October. Image Entertainment. 1927 Film, b/w. Soviet filmmaker Sergei Eisenstein recreates events leading to the 1917 Bolshevik Revolution.

Red Empire. Yorkshire Television. Videocassettes (7), color and b/w, 54 minutes each. Traces the history of the Soviet Union from the 1917 revolutions to the rise of Mikhail Gorbachev.

The Week That Shook the World. Videocassette, color, 65 minutes. News footage and commentary on the attempted Soviet coup of August 1991.

Unit Eight: Europe

Europe on the Brink. CNN, Turner. Videocassette, color, 106 minutes. Examines European developments in light of the collapse of the Soviet Union and the rise of a united Germany.

The Berlin Wall: How It Rose and Why It Fell by Doris M. Epler. Photographs and text highlight the causes and effects of the division of Berlin and the events of the Cold War.

Epilogue The World Today

Spaceship Earth: Our Global Environment. WORLDLINK. Videocassette, color, 25 minutes. Explores three global issues: deforestation, global warming, and ozone depletion.

The United Nations: It's More Than You Think. Cambridge Research Group. Videocassette, color, 30 minutes. Provides an inside look at the history and structure of the United Nations and how it functions on the global stage.

Cover:

DECODE, INC./Linc Cornell.

Geographic Themes:

.. By permission of The Folger Shakespeare Library; .. Maptec International Ltd, Science Photo Library/Photo Researchers; .. Anne van der Vaeren/The Image Bank; .. Pagnotta/REA/SABA; .. Bernard P. Wolff/Photo Researchers; .. Wolfgang Kaehler; .. David L. Perry; .. Shepard Sherbell/SABA; .. Elaine Shay; .. Mary Evans Picture Library.

Africa:

4–5, Dwight Cendrowski; 6, Ric Ergenbright Photography; 8, Syndication International, Ltd; 10, Andy Bonczyk; 11, Geoslides (London); 12, Hewett/UNICEF; 14, P. Morris Photographics; 15, Georg Gerster/Photo Researchers; 17, David Northrop; 22, Dave G. Houser; 25, E. Steichen/Shostal Associates; 26, Eliot Elisofon/Elisofon Archives/Smithsonian Institution/Museum of African Art; 27, The British Library; 29, Peabody Museum, Salem; 31, Photri; 32 (t) Jak Kilby, (b) Vivienne Silver/Art Resource; 33, UPI/Bettmann Newsphoto; 34, file photo; 35, Shostal Associates; 38, Eliot Elisofon/National Museum of African Art/Eliot Elisofon Archives/Smithsonian Institution; 40, Bruno Barbey/Magnum Photos; 41, Burt Leidmann/Shostal Associates; 42 (tr) Brian Brake/Photo Researchers, (c) G. Ricatto/Superstock, Inc, (l) (br) John Elk III; 43 (l) Bruno Barbey/Magnum Photos, (r) Ken Heyman; 44, D. McCullin/Magnum Photos; 45, Robert Harding Picture Library; 46, Marc and Evelyne Bernheim/Woodfin Camp & Assoc; 48, Shostal Associates; 49, Leo de Wys, Inc; 50, Ian Steele/International Stock Photo; 51 (t) Courtesy Professor Flora Nwapa, (b) The Nobel Foundation; 54, J. Kyle Keener/Philadelphia Inquirer/Matrix; 56, IDAF Publications; 57, BBC Hulton/Bettmann Archive; 58, Historical Pictures Service/Division Stock Montage; 59, Ian Berry/Magnum Photos; 60, Mark B. Peters/Black Star; 63, David Turnley/Detroit Free Press/Black Star; 64, Mark B. Peters/Black Star; 66, AP/Wide World Photos; 67, Balic/Sygma; 70, Ric Ergenbright Photography; 72, file photo; 74, AP/Wide World Photo; 75, H. Armstrong Roberts; 76, Anne Martens/The Image Bank; 77, Shostal Associates; 79, Peter Tenzer/International Stock Photo; 80, David Bartruff/FPG; 81, W. Shostal/Shostal Associates; 82, Roger K. Burnard; 86, Dave G. Houser; 88 (l) Lois Greenfield/Bruce Coleman, Inc, (r) Jean M. Borgatti; 90, Courtesy Shanachie Recording Artists; 91, Marc Bernheim/Woodfin Camp & Associates; 92 (tl) Edward S. Ross, (tr) Tim Courlas, (bl) Frank Willett, (bc) Lee Boltin, (br) Jak Kilby; 93, Michigan State University/African Cultural Heritage Program; 95 (l) Jean M. Borgatti, (r) Robert Shay; 96, The Christian Science Monitor/Fotografie Pieter Vandermeer; 97, The Christian Science Monitor; 98, Bryant Cherry Alexander; 99 (l) Lee Boltin, (r) Dave DeRoche; 102, Michele Burgess; 105 (l) Peter Marlow/Magnum Photos, (r)Steele-Perkins/Magnum Photos; 107, Ron Lutz; 108, Maggie Murray/Format Photographers Ltd; 109, A. C. Hinton/Art Resource; 110, Margaret Courtney-Clarke; 112, Mike Goldwater-Network/Matrix; 119 (t) Sassoonian/Art Resource, (b) © 1992 ARS, New York/SPADEM, Paris.

China:

120–121, Ric Ergenbright Photography; 122, Allen Russell/ProFiles West; 125, S. Vidler/Leo de Wys, Inc; 126, EROS Data Center; 127 (l) Robert Harding Picture Library, (r) Galen Rowell/High & Wild Photography; 129, Sovfoto/Eastfoto; 131, Shashinka Photo Library; 132, EROS Data Center; 133, Wellcome Institute Library, London; 134, Robert Harding Picture Library; 139, Eugene Gilliom; 140, Robert Lee II; 144, Stock Concepts/Nadine Orabona; 148, The Granger Collection; 149, Scala/Art Resource; 151, Bettmann Archive; 152, Historical Pictures Service/Division Stock Montage; 156, Wan-Go H. C. Weng/Photo Researchers; 158, China Pictorial; 159, Bettmann Archive; 160, The Granger Collection; 161, Brown Brothers; 163, file photo; 164, National Palace Museum, Taipei; 165, The British Museum; 167 (tl) Shashinka Photo Library; (tr) Curtis C. Cook; (c) Ronald Sheridan/Ancient Art & Architecture Collection, (bl) Allen Russell/ProFiles West, (bc) Ronald Sheridan/Ancient Art & Architecture Collection, (br) Cameramann International; 168, Shashinka Photo Library; 169, Keren Su; 172, Carl Purcell/Words & Pictures; 174, The British Museum; 177, Museum of Fine Arts, Boston; 178, ZEFA; 179, Freer Gallery of Art; 181, Giraudon/Art Resource; 185, Freer Gallery of Art; 186, Henri Cartier-Bresson/Magnum Photos; 188, New China Photo Service/Historical Pictures Service/Division Stock Montage; 190, Bettmann Archive; 193, Bettmann Archive; 195, Rene Burri/Magnum Photos; 196, Historical Pictures Service/Division Stock Montage; 198, Kinhua News Agency/UN Bureau; 199, Gwendolyn Stewart; 202, Robin Moyer/TIME Magazine; 204, Mark Averyll/AP/Wide World Photos; 205, Ric Ergenbright Photography; 206, D. E. Cox; 208, Robin Moyer/TIME Magazine; 209, Galen Rowell/Mountain Light; 210, Cameramann International; 212, D. E. Cox; 217, Eugene Gilliom; 218, Gerald Lim/Unicorn Stock Photos; 222, Sovfoto/Eastfoto; 224, Forrest Anderson/TIME Magazine; 225, Gavin Hellier/Robert Harding Picture Library; 226, Focus On Sports; 227, Cameramann International; 233, Robert McLeod/Robert Harding Picture Library.

Japan:

234–235, TSW; 236, Miwako Ikeda/International Stock Photo; 238, J. P. Nacivet/Leo de Wys, Inc; 239, Michael S. Yamashita/Woodfin Camp & Associates; 241, J. P. Nacivet/Leo de Wys, Inc; 243, Topham Picture Library; 245, Alexander M. Chabe/Worldwide Photo; 246, J. P. Nacivet/Leo de Wys, Inc; 252, Robert Harding Picture Library; 256, Gemini Smith/Bradley Smith; 257, Shashinka Photo Library; 258, Gemini Smith/Bradley Smith; 259, Shashinka Photo Library; 261, Suzanne J. Engelmann/Shostal Associates; 262, Gemini Smith/Bradley Smith; 263, Gemini Smith/Bradley Smith; 264, Eiji Miyazawa/Black Star; 265, Historical Pictures Service/Division Stock Montage; 267, Freer Gallery of Art; 268, Chad Ehlers/International Stock Photo; 270, Gemini Smith/Bradley Smith; 273, H. Armstrong Roberts; 274, Photoworld/FPG; 277, USAF/DAVA; 278, Navy Department; 280 (l) (c) The Granger Collection, (r) Shashinka Photo Library; 281 (l) file photo, (c) UPI/Bettmann Archive, (r) Richard Kalvar/Magnum Photos; 284, Norma Morrison/Hillstrom Stock Photo; 286, Dave Wade/Lightwave; 288, Frank Lambrecht/Berg & Associates; 290, R. A. Reaz/Shostal Associates; 292, Bruno Barbey/Magnum Photos; 293, Dirck Halstead/Liaison; 294, TSW; 295, Ralph Gates; 296, Robert Harding Picture Library; 297 (tl) Courtesy of the Trustees of the Victoria and Albert Museum, (tr) Far Eastern Collection/Royal Ontario Museum, (bl) The Metropolitan Museum of Art, gift of Elizabeth Gordon, 1967, (bc) Steve Brown/Leo de Wys, Inc, (br) Freer Gallery of Art, Washington DC; 299, The British Museum; 300, Tadanori Saito/PPS/Photo Researchers; 302, file photo; 304, Norma Morrison; 306, Suzanne J. Engelmann/Shostal Associates; 307, Norma Morrison; 308, Richard Kalvar/Magnum Photos; 309, Michal Heron/Woodfin Camp & Associates; 310, Burt Glinn/Magnum Photos; 311 (tl) (tr) Norma Morrison, (bl) Messerschmidt/Bruce Coleman, Inc, (br) Dirck Halstead/Liaison, 314, Mark S. Wexler; 316, Richard Kalvar/Magnum Photos; 317, David Bartruff/FPG; 318, Gil & Ann Loescher/Shostal

Associates; 320, Nicholas Maraventano; 321, Norma Morrison; 322, Nicholas Maraventano; 323, Nik Wheeler/Black Star; 324, Stephanie Maze/Maze Productions; 325, Norma Morrison; 328, Chad Ehlers/International Stock Photo.

India:

330–331, Albert J. Gordon/ProFiles West; 332, Lindsay Hebberd/Woodfin Camp & Assoc; 334, Vincent Rakestraw; 336, M. Epp/FPG; 338, Jacques Jangoux/Peter Arnold, Inc; 339, Vincent Rakestraw; 340, Val Mezzenga/Chicago Tribune; 341, Gemini Smith/Bradley Smith; 342, Ric Ergenbright; 348, Dr. B. Desestres/TSW; 350, Tom Hanley; 351, Bennett Coleman & Company Ltd, Bombay; 353, Jane Richardson/FPG; 354, Vincent Rakestraw; 355, B. Bhansali/Shostal Associates; 356, Volker Corell; 357, 360, Ellen Johnson; 361, Jimmy Holmes; 362, Robert Frerck/Odyssey Productions; 363, Adrien Murrell/TSW; 366, Robert Frerck/Odyssey Productions; 368 (l) Ann & Bury Peerless Slide Resources and Picture Library, (c) (r) Bettmann Archive; 370, Roberta Collier/FPG; 371, Albert J. Gordon/ProFiles West; 372, Jehangir Gazdar/Woodfin Camp & Associates; 373, Ann & Bury Peerless Slide Resources and Picture Library; 375, Robert Frerck/Odyssey Productions; 376, Ellen Johnson; 377, Patricia G. Foschi/Art Resource; 378, H. Armstrong Roberts; 381, file photo; 382, Tony Stone Images; 384, Smithsonian Institution; 386, Robert Harding Picture Library; 388, Bettmann Archive; 389, 390, Historical Pictures/Division Stock Montage; 391, Bettmann Archive; 392, 393, Historical Pictures/Division Stock Montage; 394, Mark Riboud/Magnum Photos; 395, Jehangir Gazdar/Woodfin Camp & Associates; 400, Robert Frerck/Odyssey Productions; 402, 404 (l) Marc & Evelyne Bernheim/Woodfin Camp & Associates, (r) Jehangir Gazdar/Woodfin Camp & Associates; 405, Bernard Pierre Wolff/FPG; 407, Jehangir Gazdar/Woodfin Camp & Associates; 409, Indian Consulate; 411, Dinodia; 414, Ben Edwards/TSW; 416, Patricia G. Foschi/Art Resource; 418 (l) A. Palmer/H. Armstrong Roberts, (r) Raghu Rai/Magnum Photos; 419, Tom Hanley; 420, 421 (tl) Ann & Bury Peerless Slide Resources & Picture Library, (tr) Robert Frerck/Odyssey Productions, (c) (bl) Ann & Bury Peerless Slide Resources and Picture Library, (bc) file photo, (br) Ann & Bury Peerless Slide Resources and Picture Library; 423, Robert Frerck/Woodfin Camp & Associates; 424, Geoffrey Hiller/Leo de Wys, Inc; 425, Vince Rakestraw; 426, Dillip Metha/Contact Stock Images; 427, Robert Holmes; 430 (l) The Granger Collection, 430 (r), Giraudon/Art Resource, New York.

Latin America:

432–433, Visum/Michael Lange; 434, Benjamin Porter; 437, Jack Riesland/Berg & Associates; 438 (t) UPI/Bettmann Archive, (b) Flora L. Phelps; 440, Editions Vilo, Inc; 441, Ron Butler; 442, Betty Crowell; 443, James Beach/Donald L. Perry; 445, Loren McIntyre; 450, Rogerio Reis/Black Star; 452, Shostal Associates; 453, The Granger Collection; 455, Elliott Smith; 456, Stock Imagery; 457, Bob Thomason/TSW; 458, Peter Frey/The Image Bank; 459, Dave Bartruff; 461, Delfim Martins/F4; 464, Jeffrey Jay Foxx; 466 (l) Bruno Barbey/Magnum Photos, (r) David Mangurian; 467, Wolfgang Kaehler; 469, Victor Aleman/FPG; 470, Co Rentmeester/PEOPLE WEEKLY, ©1982 Time, Inc; 471, Robert Hatton; 472, David Mangurian; 473, David L. Perry; 475 (t) Lucien Niemeyer, (c) Victor Englebert, (bl) (br) Walter R. Aguiar; 476, Wide World Photos; 477, Rich Brommer; 478, Hernandez/Art Resource; 479 (l) U. Sjostedt/FPG, (r) Eric L. Wheater/The Image Bank; 482, Loren McIntyre; 484, Biblioteque Nationale, Paris, Courtesy NEWSWEEK; 486, Historical Pictures/Division Stock Montage; 487, Robert Frerck/Odyssey; 488, John Hoagland/Gamma Liaison; 489, Marcel Minee/International Stock Photo; 491, Rich Frishman/TIME Magazine; 492, Loren McIntyre; 493, Manchete/Pictorial Parade; 496, Robert Fried/DDB Stock Photo; 500, Chip & Rosa Maria Peterson; 501, Tom McGuire; 502, Victor Engelbert; 503, Brett-Smith/Bruce Coleman, Inc. 504, Rich Brommer; 505, Chip & Rosa Maria Peterson; 506, Leo de Wys, Inc; 507, Doug Martin; 508, Gamma Liaison; 509, Susan Meiselas/Magnum Photos; 510, Doug Martin; 512, Horacio Villalobos/Gamma Liaison Network; 516, Norma Morrison; 518, Historical Pictures/Division Stock Montage; 519, Norma Morrison; 520, Alon Reininger/Woodfin Camp & Associates; 521, 522, D. Goldbert/Sygma; 523, Wesley Boxce/SIPA Press; 524, Claude Urraca/Sygma; 525, Jose Azel/Contact Press Images; 526, Jose Azel/Contact Press Images; 528, Carlos Angel/Gamma Liaison Network; 529, Eduardo Gil/Black Star; 533, J. Belissimo/LGI Photo.

Middle East:

534–535, Dave G. Houser; 536, M. Timothy O'Keefe; 538, Richard Bangs/Sobek Expeditions; 540, Ralph Gates; 541, A. F. Kertsing; 543, Fred J. Maroon; 545, Photo Researchers; 546 (l) H.C.B./Magnum Photos, (r) A. F. Kertsing; 547, Marc Bernheim/Woodfin Camp & Associates; 548, John Elk III/Bruce Coleman, Inc; 549, Don Smetzer/TSW; 551, NASA; 554 (tl) Ric Ergenbright Photography, (tr) (bl) Dave G. Houser, (br) Gard Harbandian/Robert Harding Picture Library; 556, Aramco; 557 (l), Shostal Associates, (r) Roloc Color Slides; 560, Richard C. Nowitz; 563, A. Duncan/MEPhA; 564, Bruce Coleman Inc; 567, William Karel/Sygma; 568, Eric Bouvet/Odyssey/Matrix; 571 (t) James Green/Robert Harding Picture Library; 571 (b) Richard Nowitz/FPG; 572, Aramco; 574, Kurt Scholz/Shostal Associates; 575, Christine Osborne; 577, M. Hoare/MEPhA; 578, Don Smetzer/TSW; 579, Gordon Gahan/Photo Researchers; 580, Jonathan T. Wright/Bruce Coleman Inc; 581 (t) Amedeo Vergani/The Image Bank, (b) John Running; 583, Aramco; 584 (t) Christina Dameyer/Photo 20-20, (c) Israel Talby/Robert Harding Picture Library, (b) Don Smetzer/TSW; 587, Photo Researchers; 590, Aramco; 590 (t) Bettmann Archive, (b) Aramco; 591, Aramco; 592, Historical Pictures Service/Division Stock Montage; 593, Aramco; 594, The Granger Collection; 596, Robert F. White; 597, Historical Pictures Service/Division Stock Montage; 599 (tl) (b) The Granger Collection, (tr) NavaSwan/FPG; 602, The Granger Collection; 605, Bettmann Archive; 607, Historical Pictures Service/Division Stock Montage; 608, AP/Wide World Photos; 610, Atlanta Journal/NEA; 616, Aaron Haupt; 618, Jean Gawmy/Magnum Photos; 619, Sygma; 620 (t) (br) Dave G. Houser, (c) Peter Carmichael/TSW, (bl) Christina Dameyer/Photo 20-20; 621, James Nachtwey/Black Star; 622, Alexander Avakian/Woodfin Camp & Associates; 624, Aral/SIPA; 625, John Running; 626, Woodfin Camp & Associates; 627, Bruno Barbey/Magnum Photos; 628, Steve McCurry/Magnum Photos; 630, James Nachtwey/Magnum Photos; 631, Mark N. Boulton/Photo Researchers; 634 (t) The Granger Collection, (b) file photo.

Commonwealth of Independent States:

636–637, Carla Gilbert/Dave G. Houser; 638, Toma Babovic Fotoarchiv/Black Star; 641, Sovfoto/Eastfoto, 642, Emil Schulthess/Black Star; 643, Magnum Photos; 645, Tass from Sovfoto; 646, Novosti Press Agency; 647, ENTAI/ZEFA/H. Armstrong Roberts; 648, Progress Publishers, Moscow; 649, Pinkhassov/Magnum Photos; 654, John Launois/Black Star; 656, John Kohan; 657, The Granger Collection; 659, Historical Pictures/Division Stock Montage; 660, 661, The Free Library of Philadelphia; 662, 664, Historical Pictures/Division Stock Montage; 665, Hubert Jasse/Editorial Photocolor Archives; 667, Historical Pictures/Division Stock Montage; 668, Henry Miller News Pictures/FPG; 669, file photo; 672, The Granger Collection; 674, Brown Brothers; 676, Photri; 677, 679, Bettmann Archive; 680, Archive Photos/G. D. Hackett; 681, Sovfoto/Eastfoto; 683, Tass/Sovfoto; 684, Earl Young/Robert Harding Picture Library; 685, Novosti/Sovfoto; 688, Peter Turnley/Black Star; 690, Black Star; 691, Christopher Morris/Black Star; 693, Reuters/Bettmann Newsphoto; 694, 695, Peter Turnley/Black Star; 696, David L. Shearer; 698, Nik Wheeler/Westlight; 700 (t) Alon Reininger/Leo de Wys, Inc, (cl) RIA-Novosti/Sovfoto, (cr) Haroldo & Flavia de Faria Castro/FPG, (bl) Novosti/Sovfoto, (br) Daniel Sheehan/Black Star; 701, file photo; 704, Tim Riley/Art Wolfe, Inc; 707, 708, Carla Gilbert/Dave G. Houser; 709, Daniel Zirinsky/Photo Researchers; 710, Carla Gilbert/Dave G. Houser; 711, Bob Krist/Leo de Wys, Inc; 712, Bruno Barbey/Magnum Photos; 713, Mike Goldwater/Network/Matrix; 714, Tass/Sovfoto; 715, Itar-Tass/Sovfoto; 716, Tass/Sovfoto; 717 (tl) (bl) (br) Tom Owen Edmunds/The Image Bank, (tr) Robert Harding Picture Library, (c) Margaret W. Peterson/The